Contemporary
Literary Criticism

Guide to Gale Literary Criticism Series

When you need to review criticism of literary works, these are the Gale series to use:

If the author's death date is:	You should turn to:
After Dec. 31, 1959 (or author is still living)	***CONTEMPORARY LITERARY CRITICISM*** for example: Jorge Luis Borges, Anthony Burgess, William Faulkner, Mary Gordon, Ernest Hemingway, Iris Murdoch
1900 through 1959	***TWENTIETH-CENTURY LITERARY CRITICISM*** for example: Willa Cather, F. Scott Fitzgerald, Henry James, Mark Twain, Virginia Woolf
1800 through 1899	***NINETEENTH-CENTURY LITERATURE CRITICISM*** for example: Fedor Dostoevski, Nathaniel Hawthorne, George Sand, William Wordsworth
1400 through 1799	***LITERATURE CRITICISM FROM 1400 TO 1800*** **(excluding Shakespeare)** for example: Anne Bradstreet, Daniel Defoe, Alexander Pope, François Rabelais, Jonathan Swift, Phillis Wheatley ***SHAKESPEAREAN CRITICISM*** Shakespeare's plays and poetry
Antiquity through 1399	***CLASSICAL AND MEDIEVAL LITERATURE CRITICISM*** for example: Dante, Homer, Plato, Sophocles, Vergil, the Beowulf Poet

---

Gale also publishes related criticism series:

CHILDREN'S LITERATURE REVIEW

This series covers authors of all eras who write for the preschool through high school audience.

SHORT STORY CRITICISM

This series covers the major short fiction writers of all nationalities and periods of literary history.

ISSN 0091-3421

R

Volume 53

Contemporary Literary Criticism

Excerpts from Criticism of the
Works of Today's Novelists, Poets,
Playwrights, Short Story Writers, Scriptwriters,
and Other Creative Writers

Daniel G. Marowski
Roger Matuz
EDITORS

Sean R. Pollock
Thomas J. Votteler
Robyn V. Young
ASSOCIATE EDITORS

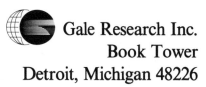 Gale Research Inc.
Book Tower
Detroit, Michigan 48226

STAFF

Daniel G. Marowski, Roger Matuz, *Editors*

Sean R. Pollock, Thomas J. Votteler, Robyn V. Young, *Associate Editors*

David Segal, Anne Sharp, *Senior Assistant Editors*

Cathy Beranek, Mary K. Gillis, Bridget Travers, *Assistant Editors*

Susan Miller Harig, Debra A. Wells, *Contributing Assistant Editors*

Jeanne A. Gough, *Production & Permissions Manager*
Linda M. Pugliese, *Production Supervisor*
Christine A. Galbraith, David G. Oblender, Suzanne Powers, Linda M. Ross,
Lee Ann Welsh, *Editorial Assistants*
Maureen A. Puhl, *Senior Manuscript Assistant*
Donna Craft, Jennifer E. Gale, *Manuscript Assistants*

Victoria B. Cariappa, *Research Supervisor*
Maureen R. Richards, *Research Coordinator*
Mary D. Wise, *Senior Research Assistant*
Rogene M. Fisher, Kevin B. Hillstrom, Karen D. Kaus,
Eric Priehs, Filomena Sgambati, *Research Assistants*

Janice M. Mach, *Text Permissions Supervisor*
Kathy Grell, *Permissions Coordinator*
Josephine M. Keene, *Senior Permissions Assistant*
H. Diane Cooper, Kimberly F. Smilay, *Permissions Assistants*
Melissa A. Brantley, Lisa M. Lantz, Denise M. Singleton, *Permissions Clerks*

Patricia A. Seefelt, *Picture Permissions Supervisor*
Margaret A. Chamberlain, *Picture Permissions Coordinator*
Pamela A. Hayes, Lillian Quickley, *Permissions Clerks*

Mary Beth Trimper, *Production Manager*
Anthony J. Scolaro, *Production Assistant*

Arthur Chartow, *Art Director*
Linda A. Davis, *Production Assistant*

Laura Bryant, *Production Supervisor*
Louise Gagné, *Internal Production Associate*
Shelly Andrews, Sharana Wier, *Internal Production Assistants*

Contents

Preface   vii

Authors Forthcoming in *CLC*   xi

Acknowledgments   433

Literary Criticism Series Cumulative Author Index   445

CLC Cumulative Nationality Index   509

CLC-53 Title Index   519

Preface

Literary criticism is, by definition, "the art of evaluating or analyzing with knowledge and propriety works of literature." The complexity and variety of the themes and forms of contemporary literature make the function of the critic especially important to today's reader. It is the critic who assists the reader in identifying significant new writers, recognizing trends in critical methods, mastering new terminology, and monitoring scholarly and popular sources of critical opinion.

Until the publication of the first volume of *Contemporary Literary Criticism (CLC)* in 1973, there existed no ongoing digest of current literary opinion. *CLC,* therefore, has fulfilled an essential need.

Scope of the Work

CLC presents significant passages from published criticism of works by today's creative writers. Each volume of *CLC* includes excerpted criticism on about thirty-five authors who are now living or who died after December 31, 1959. Nearly 2,000 authors have been included since the series began publication. The majority of authors covered by *CLC* are living writers who continue to publish; therefore, criticism on an author frequently appears in more than one volume. There is, of course, no duplication of reprinted criticism.

Authors are selected for inclusion for a variety of reasons, among them the publication of a critically acclaimed new work, the reception of a major literary award, or the dramatization of a literary work as a film or television screenplay. For example, the present volume includes Robert Penn Warren and Richard Wilbur, the first two Poet Laureates of the United States; William Kennedy, whose Pulitzer Prize-winning novel *Ironweed* was recently adapted for film; and Jerzy Kosinski, whose latest novel, *The Hermit of 69th Street: The Working Papers of Norbert Kosky,* received much attention from critics and reviewers. Perhaps most importantly, authors who appear frequently on the syllabuses of high school and college literature classes are heavily represented in *CLC;* Edward Albee and Anne Sexton are examples of writers of this stature in the present volume. Attention is also given to several other groups of writers—authors of considerable public interest—about whose work criticism is often difficult to locate. These include the genres of mystery and science fiction, as well as the writings of literary and social critics, whose insights are considered valuable and informative. Foreign writers and authors who represent particular ethnic groups in the United States are also featured in each volume.

Format of the Book

Altogether there are about 600 individual excerpts in each volume—with approximately seventeen excerpts per author—taken from hundreds of literary reviews, general magazines, scholarly journals, and monographs. Contemporary criticism is loosely defined as that which is relevant to the evaluation of the author under discussion; this includes criticism written at the beginning of an author's career as well as current commentary. Emphasis has been placed on expanding the sources for criticism by including an increasing number of scholarly and specialized periodicals. Students, teachers, librarians, and researchers frequently find that the generous excerpts and supplementary material provided by *CLC* supply them with vital information needed to write a term paper, analyze a poem, or lead a book discussion group. In addition, complete bibliographical citations facilitate the location of the original source and provide all of the information necessary for a term paper footnote or bibliography.

A *CLC* author entry consists of the following elements:

- The **author heading** cites the author's full name, followed by birth date, and death date when applicable. The portion of the name outside parentheses denotes the form under which the author has most commonly published. If an author has written consistently under a pseudonym, the pseudonym will be listed in the author heading and the real name given on the first line of the biographical and critical introduction. Also located at the beginning of the introduction to the author entry are any important name variations under which an author has written. Uncertainty as to a birth or death date is indicated by question marks.

- A **portrait** of the author is included when available.

• A brief **biographical and critical introduction** to the author and his or her work precedes the excerpted criticism. However, *CLC* is not intended to be a definitive biographical source. Therefore, *cross-references* have been included to direct the reader to these useful sources published by Gale Research: *Contemporary Authors,* which includes detailed biographical and bibliographical sketches of more than 92,000 authors; *Children's Literature Review,* which presents excerpted criticism on the works of authors of children's books; *Something about the Author,* which contains heavily illustrated biographical sketches of writers and illustrators who create books for children and young adults; *Dictionary of Literary Biography,* which provides original evaluations and detailed biographies of authors important to literary history; *Contemporary Authors Autobiography Series,* which offers autobiographical essays by prominent writers; and *Something about the Author Autobiography Series,* which presents autobiographical essays by authors of interest to young readers. Previous volumes of *CLC* in which the author has been featured are also listed in the introduction.

• The **excerpted criticism** represents various kinds of critical writing—a particular essay may be descriptive, interpretive, textual, appreciative, comparative, or generic. It may range in form from the brief review to the scholarly monograph. Essays are selected by the editors to reflect the spectrum of opinion about a specific work or about an author's literary career in general. The excerpts are presented chronologically, adding a useful perspective to the entry. All titles by the author featured in the entry are printed in boldface type, which enables the reader to easily identify the works being discussed. Publication information (such as publisher names and book prices) and parenthetical numerical references (such as footnotes or page and line references to specific editions of a work) have been deleted at the editors' discretion to provide smoother reading of the text.

• A complete **bibliographical citation** designed to help the user find the original essay or book follows each excerpt.

Other Features

• A list of **Authors Forthcoming in *CLC*** previews the authors to be researched for future volumes.

• An **Acknowledgments** section lists the copyright holders who have granted permission to reprint material in this volume of *CLC*. It does not, however, list every book or periodical reprinted or consulted during the preparation of the volume.

• A **Cumulative Author Index** lists all the authors who have appeared in *CLC, Twentieth-Century Literary Criticism, Nineteenth-Century Literature Criticism, Literature Criticism from 1400 to 1800,* and *Classical and Medieval Literature Criticism,* with cross-references to these Gale series: *Short Story Criticism, Children's Literature Review, Authors in the News, Contemporary Authors, Contemporary Authors Autobiography Series, Contemporary Authors Bibliographical Series, Dictionary of Literary Biography, Something about the Author, Something about the Author Autobiography Series,* and *Yesterday's Authors of Books for Children.* Readers will welcome this cumulated author index as a useful tool for locating an author within the various series. The index, which lists birth and death dates when available, will be particularly valuable for those authors who are identified with a certain period but whose death date causes them to be placed in another, or for those authors whose careers span two periods. For example, Ernest Hemingway is found in *CLC,* yet a writer often associated with him, F. Scott Fitzgerald, is found in *Twentieth-Century Literary Criticism.*

• A **Cumulative Nationality Index** alphabetically lists all authors featured in *CLC* by nationality, followed by numbers corresponding to the volumes in which they appear.

• A **Title Index** alphabetically lists all titles reviewed in the current volume of *CLC.* Titles are followed by the corresponding page numbers where they are discussed in the series. In cases where the same title is used by different authors, the authors' surnames are given in parentheses after the title, e.g., *Collected Poems* (Berryman), *Collected Poems* (Eliot). For foreign titles, a cross-reference is given to the translated English title. Titles of novels, novellas, dramas, films, record albums, and poetry, short story, and essay collections are printed in italics, while all individual poems, short stories, essays, and songs are printed in roman type within quotation marks; when published separately (e.g., T.S. Eliot's poem *The Waste Land*), the title will also be printed in italics.

• In response to numerous suggestions from librarians, Gale has also produced a **special paperbound edition** of the *CLC* title index. This annual cumulation, which alphabetically lists all titles reviewed in the series, is available to all customers and will be published with the first volume of *CLC* issued in each calendar year. Additional copies of the index are available upon request. Librarians and patrons will welcome this separate index: it saves shelf space, is easily disposable upon receipt of the following year's cumulation, and is more portable and thus easier to use than was previously possible.

Acknowledgments

No work of this scope can be accomplished without the cooperation of many people. The editors especially wish to thank the copyright holders of the excerpted essays included in this volume, the permissions managers of many book and magazine publishing companies for assisting us in securing reprint rights, and the photographers and other individuals who provided portraits of the authors. We are grateful to the staffs of the Detroit Public Library, the Library of Congress, the University of Detroit Library, the University of Michigan Library, and the Wayne State University Library for making their resources available to us. We also wish to thank Anthony Bogucki for his assistance with copyright research.

Suggestions Are Welcome

The editors welcome the comments and suggestions of readers to expand the coverage and enhance the usefulness of the series.

Authors Forthcoming in *CLC*

Contemporary Literary Criticism, Volumes 54 and 56, will feature critical excerpts on a number of authors not previously listed as well as criticism on newer works by authors included in earlier volumes. Volume 55 will be a yearbook devoted to an examination of the outstanding achievements and trends in literature during 1988.

To Be Included in Volume 54

Gina Berriault (American short story writer and novelist)—An author who first attracted critical attention during the early 1960s for fiction dealing with themes of alienation and frustration, Berriault employs a compact, unsentimental prose style to examine the often disturbing reactions of characters to psychological or moral crises.

André Breton (French poet, novelist, nonfiction writer, and critic)—One of the major figures of the Dada and Surrealist movements, Breton is perhaps best known for his *Surrealist Manifesto,* which espouses artistic tenets that are still held in high regard. Criticism in Breton's entry will focus upon his poetry and such prose works as *Nadja* and *Mad Love.*

Luis Cernuda (Spanish poet and critic)—Among the most controversial members of the "Generation of 1927," a group of Spanish artists that included such acclaimed authors as Federico García Lorca and Jorge Guillén, Cernuda was best known for surrealist poetry in which he often explored the individual's alienation from society.

Michael Crichton (American novelist, scriptwriter, director, and nonfiction writer)—Best known for such novels as *The Andromeda Strain* and *The Terminal Man,* Crichton combines the taut plot and rapid pace of the suspense thriller with the technical emphasis of science fiction to comment on humanity's self-assured attitudes toward scientific crises and the conflict between primitive natural instinct and rational intellect.

Don DeLillo (American novelist, dramatist, and short story writer)—Regarded as an important satirist of modern American culture, DeLillo is acclaimed for his novel *White Noise,* which won the American Book Award for fiction. Commentary in this entry will center on *Libra,* DeLillo's recent novel about the assassination of President John F. Kennedy.

Ralph Ellison (American novelist, essayist, short story writer, and editor)—A prolific nonfiction writer, Ellison is best known for his only novel, *Invisible Man.* Regarded as a formidable contribution to American postwar fiction, this portrait of black repression and the search for identity will serve as the focus of Ellison's entry.

Gert Hofmann (German dramatist, novelist, short story writer, and essayist)—Recipient of Germany's prestigious Alfred Döblin Prize for his novel *The Spectacle at the Tower,* Hofmann is respected for fabulistic fiction that has been compared to the works of Franz Kafka and Günter Grass.

Tadeusz Konwicki (Polish novelist, short story writer, filmmaker, and journalist)—In such novels as *A Dreambook for Our Time* and *The Polish Complex,* Konwicki reflects upon the grim realities of modern Polish life, including the devastating effects and memories of World War II and the subsequent Communist domination of his homeland. Criticism in Konwicki's entry will examine such recent works as *Moonrise, Moonset* and *A Minor Apocalypse.*

Antonine Maillet (Canadian novelist, dramatist, and short story writer)—Regarded as the foremost contemporary chronicler of the Acadians, a French-speaking Canadian ethnic group, Maillet is renowned for her drama *La sagouine* and her novel *Pélagie-la-charrette,* which was the first French-Canadian work to be awarded the Prix Goncourt.

Léopold Sédar Senghor (Senegalese poet, essayist, and editor)—President of Senegal from 1960 to 1980, Senghor is largely responsible for establishing the concept of négritude, a literary aesthetic adopted by French-speaking African authors who uphold tribal traditions and values in their work.

Steven Berkoff (English dramatist)—Berkoff has gained notoriety for his satirical portrayals of British society and his innovative modernizations of classical drama. Among his most recent productions is a controversial adaptation of Shakespeare's *Coriolanus.*

Edmund Blunden (English poet, critic, and biographer)—Greatly influenced by the English Romantic movement of the nineteenth century, Blunden evoked the beauty of nature in his predominantly pastoral poetry. Reflections on his experiences as a military officer during World War I temper the idyllic qualities of such collections as *The Shepherd* and *The Waggoner.*

Bruce Jay Friedman (American novelist, short story writer, dramatist, and scriptwriter)—Friedman's fiction focuses on the serious and comic aspects of Jewish assimilation into American society. In such novels as *Stern* and *A Mother's Kisses,* he examines the guilt and repression felt by his luckless protagonists and their families.

John Clellon Holmes (American novelist, essayist, poet, and short story writer)—Holmes is best remembered for his objective portrayals of the rebellious lifestyles of writers who were involved in the Beat movement of the 1950s. His novel *Go* is generally credited as the first authentic chronicle of the Beat phenomenon.

Ivan Klima (Czechoslovakian short story writer, novelist, dramatist, and essayist)—A dissident writer whose fiction has been banned in his native country since 1970, Klima portrays the lives of ordinary individuals living under communist rule. Among his works to be translated into English are *A Summer Affair* and *My Merry Mornings: Stories from Prague.*

Rhoda Lerman (American novelist)—Best known for such metaphorical novels as *Call Me Ishtar* and *The Book of the Night,* Lerman uses elements of fantasy to comment on contemporary sexual relationships and the role of women in society.

François Mauriac (French novelist, nonfiction writer, critic, dramatist, and poet)—Winner of the 1952 Nobel Prize in Literature, Mauriac is considered one of the most important Roman Catholic authors of the twentieth century. Both his fiction and nonfiction writings reflect his concern with sin, redemption, and other religious issues. Such novels as *Thérèse* and *Vipers' Tangle* also offer vivid depictions of life in the Bordeaux region of southwestern France.

William Saroyan (American dramatist, short story writer, and novelist)—A prolific author of works in several genres, Saroyan was praised for his romantic and nostalgic celebrations of American innocence and idealism. Critical commentary in Saroyan's entry will focus on his Pulitzer Prize-winning drama, *The Time of Your Life.*

Arno Schmidt (German novelist, short story writer, translator, critic, biographer, and essayist)—An important figure in German literature, Schmidt is renowned for bold innovations with prose structure and typography and for satirical novels that present a dystopian vision.

Andrei Voznesensky (Russian poet)—A protégé of Boris Pasternak, Voznesensky is one of the Soviet Union's most prestigious contemporary poets. His complex experimental verse reveals a profound love for his country and often explores the alienation of youth in industrial society.

Kōbō Abé

1924-

Japanese novelist, dramatist, short story writer, and script-writer.

An important figure in contemporary Japanese literature, Abé has attracted an international audience for novels in which he explores the nihilism and loss of identity experienced by many in post-World War II Japanese society. Abé's works are often linked to the writings of Franz Kafka and Samuel Beckett for their surreal settings, shifting perspectives, grotesque images, and themes of alienation. The labyrinthine structures of his novels accommodate both precisely detailed realism and bizarre fantasy, and his use of symbolic and allegorical elements results in various metaphysical implications. Scott L. Montgomery stated: ''Abé's most powerful books . . . displace reality in order to highlight the fragility of an identity we normally take for granted.''

Many critics contend that Abé's recurring themes of social displacement and spiritual rootlessness derive from his childhood in Manchuria, a region in northern China seized by the Japanese Army in the early 1930s, and by his brief association during the late 1940s with a group of avant-garde writers whose works combined elements of existentialism and Marxism. In 1948, the year that he published his first novel, *Owarishi michino shirubeni*, Abé earned a medical degree from Tokyo University. Although Abé never practiced medicine, his background in the sciences figures prominently in his fiction. For example, *Daiyon kampyoki* (1959; *Inter Ice Age Four*) is a science fiction novel set in a futuristic Japan that is threatened by melting polar ice caps. The protagonist of this novel is a scientist who designs a computer capable of predicting human behavior. After the machine foretells that its creator will condemn government experiments on human fetuses that would insure Japan's survival in a subaqueous environment, the scientist's wife gives birth to a child with fish-like fins instead of arms. While a reviewer for the *Times Literary Supplement* deemed the novel's plot ''too phantasmagorical and implausible,'' several critics favorably noted Abé's accurate use of scientific terminology.

Abé garnered international acclaim following the publication of *Suna no onna* (1962; *Woman in the Dunes*). This novel relates the nightmarish experiences of an alienated male teacher and amateur entomologist who is enslaved by a group of people living beneath a huge sand dune. Condemned to a life of shoveling the sand that constantly endangers this community, the man gradually finds meaning in his new existence and rejects an opportunity to escape. William Currie remarked: ''Like Kafka and Beckett . . . , Abé has created an image of alienated man which is disturbing and disquieting. But also like those two writers, Abé has shown a skill and depth in this novel which has made it a universal myth for our time.'' With Hiroshi Teshigahara, Abé wrote the screenplay for a film adaptation of *Woman in the Dunes* which was awarded the Special Jury Prize at the 1964 Cannes Film Festival.

Abé's next three novels further examine human estrangement and loss of identity. *Tanin no kao* (1964; *The Face of Another*) details a scientist's attempts to construct a mask that covers

his disfiguring scars. *Moetsukita chizu* (1967; *The Ruined Map*) follows a private detective who gradually assumes the identity of the person he has been hired to locate. *Hakootoko* (1973; *The Box Man*) focuses upon a man who withdraws from his community to live in a cardboard box in which he invents his own idyllic society. Jerome Charyn commented that *The Box Man* ''is a difficult, troubling book that undermines our secret wishes, our fantasies of becoming box men (and box women), our urge to walk away from a permanent address and manufacture landscapes from a vinyl curtain or some other filtering device.'' In Abé's succeeding novel, *Mikkai* (1977; *Secret Rendezvous*), the wife of a shoe salesman is mysteriously admitted to a cavernous hospital even though she is not ill. While searching for her at the facility, the woman's husband discovers that the hospital is run by an assortment of psychopaths, sexual deviants, and grotesque beasts.

Abé's recent novel, *The Ark Sakura* (1988), is a farcical version of the biblical story of Noah and the Flood. Mole, the protagonist, is an eccentric recluse who converts a huge cave into an ''ark'' equipped with water, food, and elaborate weapons to protect himself from an impending nuclear holocaust. Mole's vision of creating a post-apocalyptic society inside his ark is thwarted by a trio of confidence men whom he enlists as crew members and by the invasion of street gangs and cantankerous elderly people. Edmund White observed: ''*The Ark Sakura* may be a grim novel, but it is also a large, ambitious work about the lives of outcasts in modern Japan.... It is a wildly improbable fable when recalled, but it proceeds with fiendishly detailed verisimilitude when experienced from within.''

Abé's works in other genres include the plays *Tomodachi, enemoto takeaki* (1967; *Friends*), which examines the cruel and predatory nature of members of a family who intrude upon the life of a bachelor, and *Bo ni natta otoko* (1969; *The Man Who Turned into a Stick*). His short stories are collected with other pieces in the fifteen-volume omnibus *Abé Kōbō zensakuhin* (1972-1973).

(See also *CLC*, Vols. 8, 22; *Contemporary Authors*, Vols. 65-68; and *Contemporary Authors New Revision Series*, Vol. 24.)

SCOTT L. MONTGOMERY

[The Japan of today] is to be found in the pages of Abe Kobo and Oe Kenzaburo. These are the two principal authors that have broken out of the classical genres of sentimental storytelling and lyrical obsession. The styles and subjects of their work have moved Japanese literature into the international arena, have transcended the mannerism of their predecessors and examined with acumen and empathy the cultural landscape before their eyes. It is for this reason that they are the most significant fully accessible writers to the West.

Both have been stylistically innovative, not simply for aesthetic reasons, but in order to blend form and content in their work. Abe, certainly the more well-known in the West, uses a type of writing which has been called ''reportage.'' It has the narrative logic, lucidity, and attention to minute detail that Kafka used to enforce alienation between realistic voice and bizarre situation. This is Abe's way also, of exposing disturbingly enigmatic circumstances in a perfectly calm, familiar manner. Thus, through technique, he is able to thoroughly disorient the reader, to place him, as reader, in a position similar to that of his protagonists. Abe's most powerful books, *Woman in the Dunes, The Box Man, The Face of Another,* and *The Ruined Map,* all displace reality in order to highlight the fragility of an identity we normally take for granted. In his work, we are taken into a world of sand in which all inhabitants live like ants fighting back the encroaching dunes; we are shown a man who withdraws from society to live in a cardboard box, or who, severely scarred by a chemical explosion, dons a mask to hide both the gruesome facial scars and the ugliness of his character. Finally, we are introduced to a marvelous irony in the form of a detective who loses his own identity in the depths of Tokyo's pullulating back streets while searching for a man he has never seen. Abe's chosen literary method is satire that underlies the surface brilliance. Situations are continually described that have no solution, much as in Beckett or Ionesco. But more than this, each of his novels reveals the modern Japanese individual as a victim—not of the ''fates'' so often invoked in former literature—but of a battle between the self and a strange, changing environment. All his anti-heroes are oppressed from *within* and thus cannot escape. Abe is literally describing the predicament of each and every adult in contemporary Japan who make themselves victims by continuing to worship a past that they are daily destroying. His alien settings

are each versions of the new, urban Japan, with its unending glitter and centripetal activity.

In a recent interview on Japanese TV, Abe expressed the opinion that ''Except for writers, who have always been cursed in Japan with vision and therefore estrangement, the modern, mass-media-consuming Japanese works blindly and is successful at suffering. The new, westernized society of self can only exist by devouring the old.'' His characters show us a new type of internal man who does not simply follow the strict rules and rituals provided for every action in daily life, but who hopelessly seeks a way to create his own reality, usually through retreat. That there are no opportunities for social release in Japanese, no allowance for real individuality, only for withdrawal and eccentricity, is a fact of Abe's society that he makes clear again and again. (pp. 30-1)

> *Scott L. Montgomery, ''Abe Kobo and Oe Kenzaburo: The Problem of Selfhood in Contemporary Japan,'' in* Book Forum, *Vol. VII, No. 1, 1984, pp. 30-1.*

PUBLISHERS WEEKLY

Abe's first novel in eight years [*The Ark Sakura*]—an allegorical fantasy at once Kafkaesque, funny and apocalpytic—dazzles even when it may confuse. The principal character, nicknamed Mole, has converted a huge underground quarry into an ''ark'' capable of surviving the coming nuclear holocaust and is now in search of his ''crew.'' ... In the surreal drama that ensues, the ark is invaded by a gang of youths and a sinister group of elderly people called the Broom Brigade, led by Mole's odious father, while Mole gets his leg trapped in the ark's central piece of equipment, a giant toilet powerful enough to flush almost anything, including chopped-up humans, out to sea. Abe (*The Woman in the Dunes, The Box Man*), generally considered Japan's leading novelist, is a literary magician with a very special bag of tricks. Among them is a deadpan matter-of-factness that gives his chilling vision of human destiny much of its impact.

> *A review of ''The Ark Sakura,'' in* Publishers Weekly, *Vol. 233, No. 8, February 26, 1988, p. 182.*

MICHIKO KAKUTANI

With such earlier novels as *The Woman in the Dunes* (1964), *The Ruined Map* (1969) and *The Box Man* (1974), Kobo Abe has established himself as one of Japan's preeminent authors, and as an international writer with a distinctive vision of the contemporary world as a menacing, urban labyrinth in which people hunger for freedom but find themselves trapped in alienating rituals and roles. It's a vision of society that clearly reflects Japanese struggles with conformism authority and rapid industrialization, but the setting of the novels is only nominally Japan, and Mr. Abe seems to have less in common with more orthodox Japaneses authors than with science fiction writers and such European innovators as Kafka, Samuel Beckett and Harold Pinter. His latest novel, *The Ark Sakura* ... is no exception. Indeed, the story stands as a kind of recapitulation of many of the ideas and motifs employed in Mr. Abe's previous books.

A hero who, by choice or accident, is abruptly transported from normal society to a brave new world—this is the setup that Mr. Abe has used in novel after novel. In *The Woman in the Dunes,* an amateur biologist stumbles upon a hidden community by the sea, and soon finds himself entombed in a sand-pit house with a lonely widow. In *The Ruined Map,* a private detective's search for a missing husband leads him to an urban underworld, where everyone is sinister and deceptive, where his own identity is challenged and subverted. And in *Secret Rendezvous,* a salesman wanders the terrifying corridors of a huge underground hospital looking for his wife, who appears to have been abducted by an evil doctor.

As for *The Ark Sakura* it involves a fat eccentric named Mole, who's prepared a vast, subterranean "ark" in anticipation of what he sees as an inevitable and imminent nuclear war. Mole has built his ark in the far reaches of an abandoned quarry, and stocked it with water, food and guns. The result is half boys' clubhouse, half survivalist bunker: there are ingenious devices designed to purify the air, generate electricity and collect dust, as well as lots of wicked booby traps, designed to maim and kill unwanted visitors.

Though Mole had planned to invite carefully selected "crew" members to join his paranoid fantasy in an orderly and logical manner, his well laid plans abruptly go awry, when he runs into a group of con artists, who find their way into the ark and set in motion a series of violent and bizarre events. They are Komono, a vendor, who sells Mole a strange insect at a flea market, and his two associates—a smarmy fellow, referred to as "the shill," and a pretty woman, known as "the girl."

Like so many Abe characters, none of these people seem to be on the level, and Mole himself comes across as a fairly untrustworthy narrator. As the four of them nervously circle around one another, we slowly learn more about their unsavory pasts. We learn that the insect dealer is a member of something called the "Self-Defense Forces," that he loves guns and uniforms and has been arrested for selling pistols on the black market. We learn that the shill has worked for loan sharks and has borrowed large sums of money from assorted banks. And we learn that Mole has been illegally disposing of contaminated industrial wastes and dead bodies, using the ark's gigantic toilet as an all-purpose garbage disposal.

As described by Mr. Abe, repeatedly and in grotesque detail, this surreal toilet becomes the presiding image in this novel—a blunt symbol of modern society's disposability and foulness, and it also serves as a pivot around which much of the increasingly manic plot of *The Ark Sakura* can turn. Though relationships between Mole and his three crew members are messy to begin with—the three men are all vying for the girl's attention, while trying to outmaneuver one another—they are complicated further by the arrival of other intruders. . . .

For all these narrative complications, *The Ark Sakura* never becomes terribly suspenseful—or provocative. There's something predictable about putting a group of strangers together in a closed environment, like rats in a lab; and as executed by Mr. Abe, nothing develops to appreciably alter our expectations. Farcical scenes, in which everyone behaves like a vaudeville character cast in an experimental play, supply intermittent moments of levity, but they hardly brighten the novel's sour tone or enliven its banal society commentary. The recurrent analogies drawn between people and insects (especially a kind of bug that feeds on its own excrement), the bathroom humor and Mole's intimations of a coming nuclear apocalypse are no doubt meant to galvanize Mr. Abe's dark view of modern society, but they're tired devices used to make obvious points—points made with considerably more imagination and force by the author's earlier books.

Michiko Kakutani *"Half Boys' Clubhouse and Half Survivalist Bunker,"* in The New York Times, *March 23, 1988, p. C24.*

EDMUND WHITE

A fat hermit fears imminent nuclear disaster and outfits a vast former quarry inside a mountain with everything necessary for the survival of a small community. Then he heads for town and shops for candidates to invite into his bomb shelter.

At a flea market he encounters an unsuccessful merchant who is selling an insect known as the eupcaccia, which has no legs and feeds on its own feces. As the hermit explains, "It begins ingesting at dawn and ceases at sunset, then sleeps till morning. Since its head always points in the direction of the sun, it also functions as a timepiece." The hermit, a creature of regular habits who might be said to feed on his own bile, takes a liking to the self-sufficient eupcaccia and even dreams of starting a country where the national flag would bear an image of the insect.

He also meets the merchant's two shills, a seductive young woman and a hired stooge, who pretend to buy his goods in order to encourage legitimate customers. The hermit (who also narrates the novel) invites the merchant and the two shills to be "crew members" of his survival "ark." They accept, not because they believe in either the holocaust or the ark but because they have nothing better to do. The idea of escape—from bill collectors, tedium, lovelessness—stirs them with tepid enthusiasm. . . .

Kobo Abe, who first became known in the West in the early 1960's through the powerful film based on his novel *The Woman in the Dunes,* has since published many books (notably *The Ruined Map*) and established his own theater company. His theater experience has undoubtedly contributed to his mastery in fiction of sustained dramatic confrontation conveyed through charged, sharply characterized dialogue. Since the death of Yukio Mishima and Yasunari Kawabata, Kobo Abe is the Japanese writer with the broadest international reputation.

The Ark Sakura may be a grim novel, but it is also a large, ambitious work about the lives of outcasts in modern Japan and such troubling themes as ecological destruction, old age, violence and nuclear war. People often use the word "dreamlike" loosely to suggest a floating or unreal quality in fiction ("dreamy" might be a better choice). But in the strictest sense *The Ark Sakura* is dreamlike. It is a wildly improbable fable when recalled, but it proceeds with fiendishly detailed verisimilitude when experienced from within.

For instance, the hollowed-out interior of the mountain is so well described that by the end of the book the reader is capable of drawing a map of its intricate corridors and chambers, its booby traps and depots—and especially its high-suction toilet that has the talismanic force of a coffin in a painting by Max Beckmann and feels like a symbol of shame or a source of fear. When the narrator (who is variously known as Mole or Pig) trips and falls into the toilet, his leg is gripped so tightly that he's unable to extricate it and his companions hint at amputation, or even suggest finishing off the job by flushing his entire body down the drain. This sinister section will seem familiar to anyone who has ever eaten a quart of chocolate ice cream directly before retiring; sweats and liver collapse are the physical correlatives to the inexplicably guilt-edged quality of this book.

Equally nightmarish are the conversations the characters indulge in at startling length. Everyone in the novel is easily persuaded by the most lopsided arguments—or they just chatter on, each riposte spawned by the previous remark. . . .

Behavior is as slippery as speech. X confides that Y has cancer and just six months to live; 50 pages later Y confides that X is similarly terminal. Perceptions waver psychotically. ''When you focus on particulars, things shrink and miniaturize again: the thirty-two storage drums to my right in the corner of the hold were like scales on a carp; the shill, staring open-mouthed at the ceiling, was no bigger than my thumb.'' Pig is so named because of his girth, but also because of his Calibanlike past. His infamous father—drunk, dirty, violent—begot him in rape. When Pig becomes a teenager he, too, is accused of rape although he merely observing a rape. Despite his unsavory past he's quite capable of almost bestial devotion to one of the shills, a seductive young woman. Usually, he prefers to live as the eupcaccia does, self-sufficient and remote. But his desire to know the shill intimately, plus his urge to save some forms of life from the holocaust, tempt him into sociability.

The Ark Sakura is highly cinematic: psychological observation that is suggested through close-ups; lots of punchy dialogue; a convincing sense of place; a building of suspense; and a pervasive atmosphere of sexuality and violence. I find it grim and impressive, sickening and memorable.

Edmund White, ''Round and Round the Eupcaccia Goes,'' in The New York Times Book Review, *April 10, 1988. p. 9.*

JACK D. KIRWAN

Although first-class Japanese fiction goes back to the 11th Century Tales of Genji, the novel is essentially an import from the West. As such, the Japanese novel does not have the rigid standards and traditions of so many other Japanese literary forms; there is no template the Japanese novel must fit. Thus is it probably the most individualistic of all Japanese art.

Kobo Abe is very different from other Japanese novelists known overseas—the subtle and reserved Kawabata or the flamboyant, body-building, right-winger Yukio Mishima. For one thing, Abe switched careers (a very rare thing in Japan) from physician to novelist. And most of the big-name Japanese novelists have been more or less literary conservatives—not so the ex-doctor. Since his first book, *Woman in the Dunes*, Abe's novels have been as traditional as computerized pinball. *The Ark Sakura*, his first in eight years, is a mixture of Beckett and Kafka—with a fair amount of Godzilla, Monty Python and Pink Flamingos added for good measure. As with raw seafood, you're either hooked or nauseated by Abe right from the first bite. (p. 6)

This book is as Japanese as Huck Finn is American, and the more you know about Japanese customs and history, the more you'll appreciate its fine points.

However, even if you can't tell sushi from sashimi, this strange, often scatological novel still has a lot to offer. The book is full of nice turns of phrase (''The watery taste of disappointment grows as familiar as a pair of old shoes . . . as snug as a yolk in its egg'') and has plenty of humor, both satirical and slapstick. The rollercoaster story line and Laurel & Hardy subplots are made for literary speculation. ''What does it all boil down to?'' a character asks. ''I don't know,'' says the author/narrator, ''Haven't any idea. That exactly why I want to get

together with you and talk things over. Maybe *you* can tell *me*.'' (p. 7)

Jack D. Kirwan, ''Casting a Theater of the Absurd Deep Inside a Japanese Cavern,'' in Chicago Tribune—Books, *April 24, 1988, pp. 6-7.*

BRAD LEITHAUSER

''None,'' Kobo Abe replied when an American journalist asked him, not long ago, which of his fellow Japanese novelists had influenced his work. For all its terseness, Abe's answer represented a show of two-pronged defiance. It was a reproach to a West that often regards Japanese literature as exclusively inbred and indrawn. And it was an act of subversion against literary traditions in Japan, where artistic discipleship continues to be viewed as a source not only of creative vigor but of spiritual merit. In his interviews and books alike, Abe aspires to confound, and a reader puzzled by one of his mulling, enigmatic novels—including the newest, *The Ark Sakura*—can take consolation in the notion that puzzlement just might be what the author is after.

Among that loose-knit aristocracy of contemporary writers who could be termed world-class novelists—those elevated men and women whose failures no less than their successes demand translation and international scrutiny—probably none is more vexatious than Abe. Or, at times, more downright irritating. His novels can seem matchlessly uninviting, both for their mysteries of motivation (Abe rarely explains why anyone does anything) and for their grotesqueries of conduct (which include necromancy, human vivisection, incarceration, rape, kidnapping, murder, suicide, and a stubborn refusal to bury the dead). He tends to punctuate long stretches of murky uneventfulness with sharp moments of extraordinary grisliness, in an uneasy stylistic alliance usually subsumed, in dust-jacket copy and critical discourse, under the catchall designation ''psychological thriller.'' But as is true of Poe and Kafka—two writers whose influence does seem apparent—Abe creates on the page an unexpected impulsion. One continues reading, on and on, while an internal voice alternately announces ''This book is ghastly'' and ''This book is good.'' (p. 122)

Abe's elusiveness, his avoidance of generalization and summary, at times may foster—particularly at the typically abrupt close of one of his novels—a sense of incompletion and frustration. His books linger in the mind like obscure reprimands. One recalls an unspoken grief, the author's manifest dismay over the injustice around him, but little sense of where or how he would see it remedied.

Of the seven Abe novels so far translated into English, one can say, with remarkably little stretching of a point, that all concern missing persons. In *The Woman in the Dunes*, which was published in this country in 1964 and which for Western readers remains his first book (some earlier novels have not yet been translated), the hero disappears, like Wonderland-bound Alice, into a hole in the ground—where he is condemned to spend the remainder of his days shoveling and transporting the down-drifting sand that threatens to smother his hellish new home. *The Woman in the Dunes* was followed, in 1966, by *The Face of Another*, in which a scientist whose face has been grievously disfigured (in a laboratory accident, although his keloid scars inevitably evoke Hiroshima and Nagasaki) painstakingly constructs a resinous mask that promises him a new life. Like Dr. Jekyll in Stevenson's novella (a tale that *The Face of Another* echoes in numerous ways), Abe's unnamed scientist "vanishes" in order that an alternate, ascendant self can run amok. The hero of *The Ruined Map* (translated in 1969) is a detective on the trail of a fugitive who may have been murdered. *Inter Ice Age 4* (1970) centers on the shadow—glimpsed fleetingly through a window—of a man or woman who has killed an accountant. In *The Box Man* (1974), the hero retreats into a cardboard container (suggestive of an insect's carapace), which renders him indistinguishable from the "fake Box Man," a similarly outfitted acquaintance, who becomes his rival in what must be one of literature's most bizarre love triangles. The protagonist of *Secret Rendezvous* (1979) spends most of the novel wandering through a hospital in search of his wife, who was spirited away from home early one morning by a mysterious, unrequested ambulance. (He finally locates her inside a secret amphitheatre, where she is a formidable contender in an Orgasm Contest, and promptly abandons her for a teen-age girl suffering from a bone disease that, by the novel's close, reduces her skeleton to putty.)

In the new book, *The Ark Sakura*, the missing eventually come to outnumber the present. Early on, a man disappears by the banks of a subterranean river; later, a party of junior-high-school girls vanishes (hotly pursued by a band of lecherous retirees); finally, in a visionary, sunblasted coda, the world itself seems to shimmer into invisibility. The novel is labyrinthine in both method and setting: its piecemeal revelations are disclosed mostly under the earth, within the echoing vaults of a colossal and only partially mapped abandoned quarry.

Pig is the grossly overweight narrator's nickname, but he yearns to be addressed as Mole. As ambitions go, this drive to be perceived as a cousin to a rodent may seem pathetically modest, but it proves touching as well, since Mole reveals in time a winsome temperament. He calls the quarry an ark and designates himself its captain, although he has no crew; he passes his troglodytic life in solitude, studying aerial maps of Japan. The novel retails his attempts to enlist a suitable crew with whom to "set sail." But it turns out that few are prepared to exchange the pleasures of life aboveground for a dubious Ticket to Survival.

Like Noah's flood, the apocalypse that Mole envisions is a deluge—the radioactive rain of nuclear holocaust. . . . Mole's ark is, of course, immovable, and the voyage he envisions will be temporal rather than geographical; snug in their subterranean chambers, captain and crew will float into the future. Unfortunately for Mole, the crew he winds up with is a supremely unreliable bunch. It includes an aging mountebank, who peddles an insect that "thrives on a peculiar diet—its own feces," a young man who has committed extensive credit-card fraud, and the young man's skittish and manipulative girlfriend. Mole quickly succumbs to the tarty charms of the girl—who, in order to soften his disapproval of her boyfriend, confides that the latter unknowingly suffers from cancer and has only six months to live. Later, the young man informs Mole that the girl does not yet realize that she is a cancer victim; she, too, has only six months left. Meanwhile, it transpires that the ark may be not only infiltrated by stowaways but also riddled with toxic chemical wastes.

Step by sinking step, Mole's pristine passenger ship comes to resemble human intestines. Mole— who in early adolescence was chained for a week to the pipes of a toilet after falsely being accused of rape—spends the last quarter of the novel with one foot wedged inextricably in a toilet bowl. As the leg swells up, the reader begins to sense that the toilet, like some

primitive deity, may exact a dire sacrifice—that amputation alone can win his liberty.

Lest all this sound hopelessly unsavory and contrived, I should hastily add that, as such vessels go, Abe's *Ark* is a buoyant, weathertight construction—clearly his strongest novel since *Inter Ice Age 4*, and perhaps since *The Woman in the Dunes*, which might credibly be judged a masterpiece. Humor isn't something one always associates with Abe, even though he has been called a Japanese Beckett—if he shares the Irishman's flair for rendering metaphysical confrontation in honed, visually dramatic forms, he often lacks the inspired loopiness that repeatedly saves *Waiting for Godot* or *Endgame* from ponderousness. But *The Ark Sakura*, for all its grimness, reveals a droll, slapstick imagination. And one is heartened to discover, deep in the bowels of the earth, where a bickering, misfit crew awaits the world's end, intermittent bursts of belly laughter.

What makes the book's triumph so fascinating is that most of the limitations one identifies with Kobo Abe are on display here. If funnier than its predecessors, *The Ark Sakura* departs very little from the obsessions and occlusions that have shaped his work from the outset. In this novel, too, adult affection and love—as well as all the novelistically fertile dissemblings, tensions, dares, and deliverances that accompany sexual desire—are virtually absent. Mole may be enamored of his one female crew member, but so adolescent are his yearnings. . . . that one views theirs unfulfillment as amusing rather than desolating. And when minimal physical contacts do occur, a clinically detached, physiological exactitude renders them profoundly unromantic. . . . (pp. 122-24)

An even more significant absence is that of history. Japanese literature in this century has, in the main, been suffused by a grandly impersonal, elegiac nostalgia. . . . In Abe's world . . . , people seem to lack both a national and a personal history (a blankness turned absolute in *The Ruined Map*, whose hero ultimately becomes an amnesiac). Abe's singular childhood—as a Japanese boy growing up in Manchuria, where his father was on the staff of a medical school—may explain why his books are so frequently set in an unlocalized Anywhere: the sterile, fortresslike hospital of *Secret Rendezvous*, the city "where every block bears exactly the same number" of *The Ruined Map*, the derelict quarry of *The Ark Sakura*. Abe once described himself as a "man without a home town." Naturally, one can descry traditional themes in his work (his obsession with electronic surveillance, for instance, might be linked to the porous, perilous households of the Kabuki stage, where an eavesdropper is forever poised beneath the floor or behind the shoji screens), but one does so at the risk of distorting the degree to which he has managed to deracinate himself.

Abe's indifference to the past is balanced by, and perhaps largely justified by, an obsession with the future. Each of his books seems to take up anew the task of extrapolation; each freshly investigates emergent aspects of modern life—nuclear proliferation, environmental spoliation, cybernetics, overpopulation, bioengineering, statistical prediction. (pp. 124-25)

Like his Polish contemporary Stanislaw Lem, or his Italian contemporary the late Italo Calvino, Abe is a writer so obsessed with technology and its social impact that these can become a central artistic presence, to which mere characters seem subordinate. Lem is almost always grouped with science-fiction writers, Calvino and Abe are only occasionally so, but the three men evince a kindred impatience with the conventions of literary realism, particularly in regard to social change and technological expansion. The "real" world, each would remind us, is moving with breathtaking speed toward evolutions and upheavals that its inhabitants cannot begin to compass. And, given our velocity, what lies behind us increasingly blurs.

The Japanese reading public that composes Abe's primary audience no doubt has a heightened appreciation of the dislocation that comes from living in proximity to a future that threatens to engorge the past. Anyone familiar with modern Tokyo knows the giddy, befuddling feeling that derives from a gleaming, unweathered architecture. Although the city's mapped outlines may still reflect—as the guidebooks tell us—the careful, concentric encampments by which both shogun and emperor protected themselves from insurrection, what strikes the stroller's eye is the unbroken newness of it all: block after high-tech block of buildings erected in the last few decades.

Abe's latest novel extends the challenge he posed in *Inter Ice Age 4,* where he asked the reader to contemplate "a rapidly evolving future, one which may well destroy, deny the present—a severed future." In *The Ark Sakura* he urges us to ponder a further—a final—dislocation: one brought about by nuclear devastation. He implies that in conceiving a world whose past has been reduced to deadly, glowing rubble we might see ourselves without any distorting overlay of pretension or sentiment. Although he once observed that "it is extremely doubtful whether one has the right to sit in judgment of the values of the future," the truth is that his projections are unrelievedly harrowing. Unlike Lem or Calvino, he seems unwilling to entertain, even occasionally, the possibility of a roseate future.

Abe's books threaten us with loss—of government, of the environment, of those values which sustain the dignity of humankind. One is left, dimly, with a sense of the sweet, vulnerable virtues of the past—and a suspicion that this implicit affirmation of historical values may approach as close to nostalgia as this dour and challenging novelist will permit himself to go. Anguish and loneliness, he suggests, must reside in the national soul that is severed from its past. And must reside, one is tempted to add, in the soul of any novelist who would answer "None" when asked which of his countrymen had influenced him. *The Woman in the Dunes, The Face of Another, The Ruined Map, Inter Ice Age 4, The Box Man, Secret Rendezvous,* and now *The Ark Sakura*—these are not the offspring of a happy man. But what else would one expect, given the vision that obsesses Abe? It's an abyss that lies before us, and a wall behind. (p. 126)

Brad Leithauser, "Severed Futures," in The New Yorker, *Vol. LXIV, No. 12, May 9, 1988, pp. 122-26.*

LOUIS ALLEN

Perhaps to call *The Ark Sakura* science fiction is wrongly to classify it, or at least to raise the wrong expectations, though it has every appearance of setting out to be SF. Many people know the word *sakura,* meaning "cherry". It has another meaning, the accomplice of a confidence trickster who shows interest in the phoney merchandise and draws gullible outsiders into a sale; a "shill", in other words. The shill is marginal to the central figure, a large repulsive creature who calls himself "Mole" and has developed the Ark, a vast, subterranean, Piranesi-like labyrinth of disused quarry workings. Inside, a booby-trapped complex of corridors, tunnels and galleries is ready to house 385 individuals thought worthy to survive a nuclear holocaust.

Mole foolishly admits to his labyrinth a shill and his girlfriend, the partners of a crooked bug-vendor, Komono, from whom Mole buys mythical *tokeimushi* ("clock bugs"), or "eupcaccia". Mole admires these bugs because he believes they have solved the problem of existence. The bug lives on its own excrement and ingests and excretes so slowly that it can move in a circle after its own dung, thus creating a perfect clock-like motion. This theme is developed in great detail, then the metaphor gets lost.

Once installed in the labyrinth, Mole finds many of his booby-traps have been sprung, and suspects that his secret hide-out has been penetrated. The prime suspect is his half-brother Sengoku, who negotiates with Mole on behalf of their father (referred to as "biological" father), a rapist and murderer whom Mole—perhaps not unnaturally—detests. The father, Inototsu, leads a band of rubbish disposers, the Broom Brigade, made up of disciplined and aggressive old people, or, as they prefer to be called "Quintessential Castoffs", who intend to found a Kingdom in Mole's labyrinth. Komono kills Inototsu, and assumes the leadership of the Castoffs. Disturbed by the turn of events, and by the appearance of young interlopers (further proof that the Ark's entrances are known), Mole activates dynamite explosions which seal off the Ark, proclaiming the start of a nuclear war. In the ensuing darkness he makes off with the girl.

Reversing the expectations of the narrative, he still decides to stay in the Ark and keep to himself the knowledge that there has been no nuclear holocaust. . . . Mole's deception of the invaders of his labyrinth has found its accomplice because, as the girl adds, "believing it was true might make us happier in the end".

Whether we are meant to believe that Mole's discovery of the transparency of the town and its people, when he re-emerges into it, is in fact the result of a nuclear explosion . . . is far from clear; and the various currents of symbolism remain opaque throughout. But this is only one source of the disappointment that the book, in the end, inspires. The idea behind the story, to start with, is interesting enough, the development is not. And the relations between the characters are appropriate to a long short story, not a novel. Hence the undoubted *longueurs* and the regrettable impression that Abe, who has created symbolic abysses and labyrinths successfully in the past (*Woman in the Dunes, Secret Rendezvous*), has this time promised more than he delivers.

Louis Allen, "Piranesian Prospects," in The Times Literary Supplement, No. 4454, August 12-18, 1988, p. 892.

JASCHA KESSLER

[Kobo Abe] is very much a post-Modernist fabulist: neo-Surreal, neo-Existential, neo-Black Humorist. *The Ark Sakura,* his seventh work since 1964 is a wild, zany piece of Apocalypticism, which at the same time utters the most serious possible warning about our immanent, imminent end. Such books have appeared since the 1970's, and most of them, like Malamud's last novel, *God's Grace,* have been full of satirical laughter. It is as though most of our tears were wept during World War II, and the rest blown away at Hiroshima and Nagasaki. That it is coming is suggested by Abe when he says, "The leadership may change, but not the strategy. The old men are very keen on their strategy." Or, "the important thing is not really survival *per se,* but the ability to go on hoping, even in one's final moments. And we would certainly be guaranteed a gigantic tomb, at least the size of the pyramids!''

The tomb is the Ark Sakura, residue of a careless, chaotic postwar Japanese construction industry, and outfitted by Abe's nameless narrator, an alienated, obese young man, a rejected bastard who hates his father and has sought refuge from the world in a vast, abandoned, underground quarry. He has supplied it with all sorts of useless, dangerous weapons, archaic and modern, from crossbows to hand grenades, stocked it with food and machinery to light, heat and ventilate it, and booby-trapped all its corridors and entrances. He needs companions on his Ark, which is about to set sail. At a department store rummage fair he finds a con man, and a man and a woman, his two shills, who he invites to be his first passengers. . . . Once ensconced underground with him, they promptly set out to take over the life and property of the dreamer-hero, a sex-starved Candide quite inexperienced in the ruthless ways of the wicked world.

In the course of this quirky, witty, but too-long novel that ends with the attack of an army of volunteer street-sweeping pen-sioners and disaffected gang youths, we are treated to a series of scenes satirizing the private, social, commercial and military modes of Japanese life today. The anarchistic disorderlies underground in the Ark Sakura pit themselves in their fantasy against the dominant culture of order, the group, greedy developers, and blind ambition for wealth and power. The hero, our loser, who has spent most of the last day or so with one foot caught in the Ark's toilet, isn't bitter, reflecting before he is expelled by the usurpers from his Ark into a world of people about to be rendered transparent by the nuclear flash of the end, ''Most people get the death sentence.''

The Ark Sakura is a Swiftian satire by a much-praised novelist from whom we can learn a lot about a Japan few have imagined. It might have been a better book in English had its original been written leaner and paced swifter. A lot of its rumination and by-play seems turgid, over-written, and its effect is one of self-indulgence, a fault not a few highly-touted ''serious'' writers are permitted by their editors.

*Jascha Kessler, in a review of "The Ark Sakura,"
in* Los Angeles Daily News, *August 28, 1988, pp.
22, 25.*

Bella (Akhatovna) Akhmadulina

1937-

Russian poet, translator, scriptwriter, and short story writer.

Considered among the foremost contemporary Russian poets, Akhmadulina writes lyrical, introspective verse on such topics as creative inspiration and conflicts between the individual and society. While traditional in form, Akhmadulina's poetry is distinguished by her wit, emotional intensity, and inventive use of rhyme, syntax, and imagery. Akhmadulina's early verse is characterized by her exuberant use of extended metaphors that impart a sense of wonder to ordinary objects and events. Her later poems often express melancholy or pensive moods and examine such subjects as aging and the loss of creative powers.

Akhmadulina's first two collections, *Struna* (1962) and *Uroki muzyki* (1969), contain what many critics regard as her finest poems. A selection of these early works was translated into English in *Fever and Other New Poems* (1969). ''Oznob'' (''Fever'') and ''Skazka o dozhde'' (''A Tale about Rain''), two of Akhmadulina's most celebrated early poems, convey her contention that creativity has a liberating effect on individuals yet leads to scorn and alienation from society. In ''Fever,'' the narrator's inspiration to compose poetry is likened to a strange illness that makes her a social outcast. In the long poem ''A Tale about Rain,'' the poet's creativity is symbolized by the rain that follows her wherever she goes. The narrator is initially embarrassed by the rain, which sets her apart from the dry world around her. When a group of friends representing the forces of conformism conspire to eliminate the rain, however, the poet defends herself and embraces her identity. Elaine Feinstein stated: ''At her finest, Akhmadulina combines a fierce, comic invention with her most passionate utterance: she turns her wit upon herself (as in 'Fever'), or upon the complacent materialism of the worldly (in ['A Tale about Rain']).'' In other noted poems, Akhmadulina pays tribute to such literary predecessors as Anna Akhmatova, Mariana Tsvetaeva, Mikhail Yuryevich Lermontov, and Alexander Pushkin. In the poem ''I Swear,'' for example, Akhmadulina vows to destroy the social forces that drove Tsvetaeva to commit suicide in 1941. In later collections, including *Stikhi* (1975), *Metel* (1977), and *Taina* (1983), Akhmadulina expands upon the themes of her earlier work and explores such topics as death, eternity, and the transitory nature of existence.

(See also *Contemporary Authors,* Vols. 65-68.)

YEVGENY YEVTUSHENKO

I hate the work ''poetess.'' It brings to mind something vague and nebulous, rustling with its false wings, something with affectionately sheeplike eyes, awkwardly holding in its chubby little hand a pencil tracing out painstakingly touching things in a little album with a golden edge. Let us agree to call only poets' wives poetesses. But let us call women who write gen-

uine poems poets, because a master is a master and in art there is no allowance for weakness of sex.

In Russian poetry there were a great many poetesses. But one has not the heart to call Akhmatova or Tsvetaeva poetesses. They are poets who occupy their own particular yet valued place alongside the best male poets in Russia. Maybe they are on the summit of a different kind of rock formation, but in any case it is a summit of equal height.

And Bella Akhmadulina is one of the few women who write poems and who possess the full right to be called a poet and not a poetess. Just like other poets she has her detractors (rather of the female sort, naturally), but probably none of them would take the risk of expressing any doubt as to whether she has a genuine, God-granted, poetic gift. (pp. 1-2)

Bella Akhmadulina started to publish early; when still a schoolgirl she studied in the literary circle of the Stalin car plant under the guidance of the poet Yevgeny Vinokurov. She was lucky, because Vinokurov, poetically an extraordinarily well-educated man, succeeded in imparting to her the sense and skills of poetic techique. But, although she was noticed right after her first publications and on entering the Literary Institute was immediately recognized as a queen of rhyme, Bella still remained only a poetess. Her poetic world was childishly unstable. This unstableness was felt (when she tried to express it) in the way she expressed that world. Genuine poetry demands two qualities: range, and the confinement of that range in the tight container of form.

Some poets acquire range first and only later master the formal incarnation. Only in some rare cases do both achievements come together. Bella was too young to have any range in her knowledge of the world. She lacked the personal suffering to feel with her own skin "the tragic essence of the world." Of course, she did feel something instinctively, but that did not blend in her with the intimate experiences of a large-eyed girl, with Komsomol badge and schoolgirl's plaits. But instead she began seriously to study form. In the instability of her gifted sentimental lines something concrete and concise started to appear. Endowed with an amazing poetic ear, Bella grasped the inner law of freshness of rhyme, resilience of rhythm, and delicacy of epithet, and that is one of the most important components of real poetry. She managed to master in only one year as much as I did in at least ten. She learned the charm of grammatical incorrectnesses which creates a special air in a poem. She understood that sentimentality and metaphors alone cannot get her very far if there is a lack of tension and compactness in her poems. Out of her sleeves, like an enchantress from a Russian fairy tale, she produced a sparkling shower of epithets, rhymes, intonations, images. Formerly her verses merely rustled. Now they started to ring. However, the compactness of the form, still combined with the poverty of the content, as yet could not command faith in her future in the minds of many serious people, although it did raise some hopes.

Her name became known among readers, but for the sake of honesty one has to admit that this was due not to her poems, but to some kind of promise which was contained in them, as well as to her participation in the general new wave of Soviet poetry and to other accompanying circumstances.

Her first book, *The String* (*Struna*), was sold out immediately, but the content of the book did not come up to the reader's anticipations. It was lacking in range, far too many things happening in life and imperiously demanding to be expressed were left outside the limits of the book. The content was too elegant, and alongside the lack of elegance of the knifelike problems which rip one's chest every day, it seemed criminally frail and infantile. But as far as Bella is concerned, the time was not yet ripe for her to speak about those problems. The oratorical intrusion into life peculiar to me at some periods, or the explosiveness of the monologues of Voznesensky, who also appeared at that time, was alien to her very nature. Bella was looking for her own path to the age, or maybe the age was looking for its own path to her. And this path of connecting her personal pulse to the pulse of the age lay through her inner suffering, which life, despite her apparent well-being, fortunately did not grudge her. She was happily gifted with kindness, and although for a while she did not know enough of personal sufferings and sorrows, nevertheless she was able to take part in other peoples' experiences and they became her own. She was always a faithful friend who shared in her friends' troubles and who was ready to defend them.

It was precisely this ability to share in her friends' sorrows which compelled her to write the poem "**And once more like the lights of the open-hearth furnace,**" in which, which a boyish anger surprising in contrast to her former soft intonations, she mercilessly pilloried the murderers of poetry. She did not become a publicist—this was completely outside her talent, but her own nerves, by now independent of herself, became the nerves of the age, and in her apparently most

intimate poems, behind the snow, the twilight, the lights, and the swaying of the branches, glared the terrible face of our epoch.

Whatever she wrote, whether about a fellow poet:

> Whether you want to praise or damn,
> there is both prophet and clown in him,
> and the hot world like a frying pan
> burns his hands below the skin . . .

or about a boy who as he pedals his bicycle:

> . . . suddenly looks at the wide world
> and feels serene and sad . . .

or about that "cordial" encounter in a café when:

> . . . a murderer in a gray coat came in.
> His victim was sitting not far away . . .
> My friends, what a wonderful reunion! . . .

or about Yelabuga, who once killed Marina Tsvetaeva and is now trying out her red gaze on other victims.

In all this one can see a great feeling of suffering for herself, for others, for history—and great suffering always was and will remain the basic content of great poetry.

The poem about Tsvetaeva in which Akhmadulina swears to kill Yelabuga became some kind of inner Rubicon, which she crossed, and was then overcome with a nervous trembling of responsibility for everything that was, that is, and that will be. The only imperative responsibility for her was the challenge to all kinds of yelabugas and petty-yelabugas hiding their venomous fork-tongued stings behind sweetly smiling lips. The struggle of Akhmadulina does not look like a struggle, because it is not thundering but lyrical; however, a slender silver flute gives us strength just as much as a bugle in the difficult battle of life. One should not forcibly thrust into someone's hand a musical instrument unsuited to him. But the musician chooses his instrument and the instrument the musician.

And the tragic symphony theme of responsibility started to sound through Akhmadulina's flute, which had apparently been created for chamber music only. This was poignantly uncovered in her poem "**Longing for Lermontov.**" For Bella, as for many Russian poets, Georgia meant something eternally beautiful, which offered healing space and genuine hospitality in the most difficult periods of time. And yet in that country, so generously endowed by God, Bella, suffocating with the happiness of the open spaces, tells herself:

> Stand on the mountain! The more the longing for the
>   unknown,
> a foreign country's mysterious novelty,
> the more furious the temptations of your own,
> the more you need her sweet severity.

"The more you need"—what a prosaic phrase compared to the attributes of poetic grace usually served as a fulcrum in Bella's former poems. And suddenly this "need." It's even strange! And yet this shows her spiritual maturity. Only the feelings of sufferings experienced and shared make you understand that not only is the world necessary for yourself, but that you are necessary for the world. And this understanding leads you away from endearments, from tenderness, from beauty, as though you do not deserve them because they are not yet for everyone, it leads you to the temptation of that most sweet severity of unaccomplished reality, it leads you to participate in misfortunes—it does not matter if they are not yours but belong to others, but precisely because of this they are yours and not others'. And the pain spreads through the air and the very air injures yours skin. If, when you feel fine, someone else, who breathes the same air as you do, does not feel fine, then you must feel pain.

This astonishingly strong sensation of the air causing injury is expressed by Bella with the greatest audacity and power in her two startling masterpieces, **"Fever"** and **"A Tale About Rain."**

It is as if nothing happens in the first poem. Even the cause of the fever is not explained, but the very shivering, which lashes, drives in sharp tacks into one's skin, cries out how in this uncomfortable world covered with slush the soul feels feverish.

If you are a poet, you may even try remaining motionless, but you won't escape this fever. (pp. 2-6)

In Bella's poems there appeared the resoluteness to doubt till the end, which it is impossible to compare with her former childish formal resoluteness.

Akhmadulina is acquiring what is not simply a boyish impudence but a refined fury armed with the venom of ruthless irony. She wants to tear away the garments of decorum from everything, to tear away everything from her own soul and place it, fearlessly naked and contemptuous, right before the slippery gaze of other people. (p. 7)

The Rubicon is crossed and she will never betray her vow to Tsvetaeva to kill Yelabuga. She will never betray the Rain who sat on her shoulder with the trustfulness of a monkey. She will never betray her sacred chill, which like a child invisibly beats inside her asking to be let out. On the path chosen by her she still has a lot to suffer, but at the same time a lot to accomplish. But even if she is predestined not to accomplish much more, just the same she will remain in Russian poetry a poet and not a poetess. And if life breaks her, after all she is a woman, so what—just the same she will be able to use Blok's words about herself!

> Let me die in the gutter like a dog,
> Let life trample me down into earth—
> I know it was God who covered me with snow!
> And the blizzard that was kissing me!
>
>   (pp. 7-8)

Yevgeny Yevtushenko, in an introduction to Fever & Other New Poems *by Bella Akhmadulina, translated by Geoffrey Dutton and Igor Mezhakoff-Koriakin, William Morrow and Company, Inc., 1969, pp. 1-8.*

ROSEMARY NEISWENDER

In his introduction [to *Fever and Other New Poems* (see excerpt above)], Yevtushenko places Bella in the company of such heroic figures as Marina Tsvetaeva and Anna Akhmatova, a possibly overgenerous judgment. Nonetheless, of the 21 poems capably translated here at least four are of major importance in both length and technical brilliance. Akhmadulina's preferred métier is the short, intensely feminine, often aphoristic lyric; her frequent subject, the soul in the winter of its discontent. No socialist realist, she is preoccupied with the symbolic ague of our age (**"Fever"**), the spiritual dichotomy between the Russian North and the Georgian South (**"Longing for Lermontov"**), and the martyrdoms of her great predecessors (poems to Tsvetaeva, Pushkin, Pasternak). These new poems (written since her first collection, *Struna,* in 1962) show an increasing maturity and breadth of concern and a more controlled poetic technique.

Rosemary Neiswender, in a review of "Fever and Other New Poems," in Library Journal, *Vol. 94, No. 16, September 15, 1969, p. 3071.*

HELEN MUCHNIC

There is an enormous difference between [Akhmadulina and older Russian poets Anna Akhmatova and Alexander Blok]. She seems to be less sure of herself, uneasy and lost, anxious about her poetic gift, and uncertain of her place in society. She has neither Blok's strength to denounce or transform a hateful reality nor Akhmatova's ability to elicit from it an inherent pity and terror. Her world is grotesque, her experience fantastic.

Yelabuga, the town where Marina Tsvetaeva killed herself, takes the form of a demonic reptile which she vows to crush with her heel—a passage that for loathesomeness is like the hideous nightmare of Dostoevsky's Ippolyt Terentiev in *The Idiot;* her own poetic gift is now a ceaseless rain that, while the city is suffering from drought, dogs her footsteps, soaks her through and through and inundates the house to which she is invited; now it is a dream of little airplanes that are like chicks eating out of her hand and children climbing on her knees; and now it is a fever that frightens her and disgusts her neighbor and breaks the doctor's stethoscope; her nervous system bursts out "like a spring through an old mattress," tears in her "pupils hang over the cliff" of her face. But she does not wish to get well:

> Fever, beat on my drawn skin with your drumstick,
> don't spare me. I'm yours! Without you I am lost!
> I am a ballerina to your music!
> I am the frozen puppy of your frost!

These grotesque hyperboles remind one of Mayakovsky. But unlike him, she is not an orator and propagandist. Nor is she a realist like Akhmatova, nor a symbolist like Blok. . . . [Akhmadulina's] poetry is a deliberate distortion of reality, a form of allegorical writing, in which cleverness counts for a great deal: a speeding motorcyclist typifies the active life by contrast to the snail-like progress of the poet's work; an automatic soda water machine is a magic dispenser of unexpected bliss; building a snowman becomes an emblem of poetry and love.

Fantastic, often amusing, her work [in *Fever and Other Poems*], to my ear at least, is predominantly plaintive, with a kind of yearning tenderness and a somehow baffled capacity to love, great loneliness, helpless dissatisfaction, and a sense of estrangement from both the world and herself. Her excited, nervous poetry is unhappy rather than tragic, restless rather than passionate. She speaks of suffering as wisdom, but hers is the self-induced, self-inflicted suffering of useless sympathy, a pained, perhaps guilt-ridden, identification with the torments that others have endured and that have passed her by. Blok and Akhmatova wrote only of what they had themselves experienced, their work has the intense compactness of actual encounters; Akhmadulina seems haunted by the misery she has not lived, and her poetry is discursive and meditative, not intense, but longing for intensity.

She has not been faced with the difficult choices that her predecessors had to make at the time of the revolution and the civil war; she has spent her adult life in post-Stalin Russia, and her interests are apolitical. But she was born in the year of the great purges, and in one of her poems, **"The Night of St. Bartholomew,"** which, unlike her other work, is imbued with a kind of somber passion, she seems to point to the root of her suffering.

A child born in the vicinity of bloodshed, she says, is mysteriously, and of necessity, corrupted by both the executioner and his victim; his infant's cry is the teething of a werewolf; and when, through branches, one glimpses something that makes one's blood run cold, it's just the faces of little children nurtured in the shadow of crime—while, at the same time, in Heaven, there is another cry, the faint voice of St. Bartholomew, centuries before the awful night that bears his name, weeping for its own defenselessness in strains of horror greater than a line of verse can hold; these are the tears of one between two fires, not yet Huguenot nor Catholic, foreseeing what he cannot help—an image, it may be, of Akhmadulina herself, whose anger, tenderness, and longing are the unavailing voice of the poet between two fires, neither Huguenot nor Catholic, the poet-child of 1937, aware of monsters, victims, hangmen, weeping for its own fragility. (pp. 42-3)

Helen Muchnic, *"Under the Sign of Blok,"* in The New York Review of Books, *Vol. XVI, No. 2, February 11, 1971, pp. 41-3.*

CHRISTINE RYDEL

Akhmadulina's whimsical relationship with her Muse shows through in all of her lyrics on varied themes. Even when she is writing about the construction of a new blast-furnace, she sees it as a circus and the construction worker as an acrobat walking on a tightrope. Akhmadulina's relationship with her own poetic inspiration is the subject of many of her poems. This, together with love lyrics, forms the main portion of her first collection [*Struna*].

Akhmadulina's love and metapoetical poems share a recurrent symbolism. She finds refuge from her alienation from the crowd either in poetry or with her lover. In most cases the man she loves shares her inspiration. Where most poets look to love for inspiration, Akhmadulina looks to inspiration for love. It is ironic that it is inspiration which alienates her from the crowd and also consoles her when she feels this isolation. An excellent illustration of this symbiotic relationship between love and inspiration is the poem **"December."** She and her lover are building a snowman and the people crowd around them to watch their actions. The two lovers answer the questioning glances of the crowd with the words, "We're building a snowman, that's all." The dialogue between the two as they build their snowman clearly shows how love and inspiration are integrally related:

> You say, "Look, how I am sculpting."
> Really, how well you sculpt,
> And how you create form out of formlessness.
> I say, "Look how I love."

In the second half of this poem she describes her beloved. She sees his "child-like face" (*detskoe litso*). Here the snow is a variant of rain, an important symbol of inspiration. In Akhmadulina's symbolic system children also represent poetry, or creative literature in general. She is aware of her calling as a poet and celebrates it in a number of her poems. In **"An Alien Craft"** (**"Chuzhoe remeslo"**) she tells us of the power that writing has over her. But even though it treats her cruelly, she is loyal to it. . . . She further tells us that she is not only jealous of other writers who can create, but greedily covets the right

to produce poetry and is glad that she can also participate in the joy of creation. Akhmadulina combines this greed with an awe for creation and even feels unworthy to soil clean paper with her handwriting. (pp. 327-28)

Children as well as rain, flowers, and dogs are the main symbols of poetry and inspiration in Akhmadulina's symbolic system. When inspiration takes hold of her, she flies, thus escaping from the real into the fantastic. Many poems such as **"With the deep voice of a prophet"**(**"Glubokim golosom proroka"**), **"Flowers"** (**"Tsvety"**), **"There's the sound of rain"** (**"Vot zvuk dozhdia"**), **"In that month of May"** (**"V tot mesiats Mai"**), and **"Your House"** (**"Tvoi dom"**) contain these main symbols and themes—which have their full development in **"A Fairytale about the Rain."** In **"With the deep voice of a prophet"** nature calls her to drink the water meant for the flowers. She lingers behind, and even when the water springs up to meet her longing, she delays, does not drink and therefore does not quench her thirst. This foreshadows the first half of **"A Fairytale"** where the Rain is following the poetess and she chases it away:

> —Shame, you good-for-nothing,
> Kitchen farmers call out to you in tears,
> Go to the flowers!
> What have you found in me?

"Flowers" can be viewed as a lyrical description of flowers and their need for rain. But viewed in total perspective, the flowers can represent poetry—which cannot be stifled in a house where rules and regulations are enforced, but needs the freedom and nourishment of the rain (here clearly poetic inspiration). (p. 329)

In contrast to the themes of inspiration and freedom, the poem **"Your House"** portrays the stifling atmosphere of a house that the poetess visits. When she enters the house she is greeted with a loud kiss (note the parched onomatopoetic quality of *shcheku chmokal* ["smacked my cheek"]). The house is good and delicate, but dry—the tea service looks out of the mirror "as if it were a fish out of water" and only a cactus is growing in the window. When she enters, a dog runs up to her, but unfortunately the people in the house kill him. When she leaves the house, it is with a bitter goodbye: "Don't comfort me with a lie." This poem contains the germ of the scene at the house in **"A Fairytale."** (p. 331)

The various symbols and themes of the lyrics and of **"A Fairytale"** act together to give form to the latter work. **"A Fairytale about the Rain"** is a highly subjective poem in which Akhmadulina describes the process of creation which Rain activates within her. She tells how uncomfortable it is when the Rain follows her wherever she goes and how alienated she feels when people do not accept her with the Rain. Because it is somehow improper to have the Rain as her constant companion when the rest of the land is suffering from drought, she sends it away. It is only after she enters a certain house where the people ask her about her "gift" that she realizes how desperately she wants the Rain to be with her. She calls it, but when it comes the people in the house destroy it. Left without the Rain, Bella avows her love for it and demonstrates this love by kissing a small puddle of water on the dry asphalt. This puddle is the only remnant of her Rain. And no more precipitation is promised.

Rain, together with drought, the house and the children, are the four main symbols which represent Akhmadulina's poetic inspiration, the insensitive, vulgar materialistic world, and poetry. These are included in a tightly constructed network of other symbols which provides the basis for the structure of the poem and for the development of the main theme. On the periphery of this network are many other symbols and images which occur with less frequency, but are striking in their use and pertinently connected with the basic images. (pp. 332-33)

The period following the writing of "**A Fairytale about the Rain**" corresponds to the era of drought which Akhmadulina predicted; it is truly a bleak time. If her poetic world has hitherto been inhabited by flowers, children, puppies, snowmen and rain, it is now composed of sickness, insomnia, shadows, muteness and suffering over inability to write.

The poems of the years following 1965 bear witness to Akhmadulina's inability to function as a poet—to sing songs. She can only be a silent observer, and when she tries to sing: "The sound of muteness, ferrous and rough, demeans my throat . . ." ["**The Word**" ("**Slovo**"), 1965]. The inability to produce verse even permeates the air, which itself takes on a solid state, holding Akhmadulina back and inhibiting her creative processes. . . . She tries to write, objects around her call out to be praised, but she suffers as she looks around "under the torture of muteness" ["**Night**" ("**Noch**"), 1965].

Occasionally Akhmadulina can write a few lines, but she regards them as worthless trifles. She says that it is already habit to put word after word, stanza after stanza. She is concerned with something more meaningful and intense ["**Something Else**" ("**Drugoe**"), 1966]. Akhmadulina says that she has been struggling this way for an entire year, but the only result is muteness. In the poem "**Muteness**" ("**Nemota**," 1966) itself, she expresses her frustration: she looks about the room, hears objects call out to her; but when she tries to answer—she can only produce "muteness."

When Akhmadulina does manage to write, what does she choose as her subjects? In addition to muteness, she is concerned with farewells, fear of loneliness, the pleasures of Georgia and the evocation of the past in the figures of Pushkin, Lermontov, Akhmatova and Tsvetaeva. But the majority of the poems deal frankly with her sufferings as a silent poet.

In the poems written before 1964, Akhmadulina had suffered alienation from the crowd simply because she had been singled out by inspiration—she was different and somehow unacceptable. Ironically, she found refuge in her poetry and in the presence of her lover: both shared her inspiration. She still occasionally finds solace in privacy. The extraordinary "**Adventure in an Antique Shop**" ("**Prikliuchenie v antikvarnom magazine**," 1967) is the direct result of her need to be alone:

> Why?—just as people go into deserted aspen groves
> for the quiet and solitude of strolling,
> I went into an antique shop.

And perhaps it is only in privacy such as "**In a Deserted Rest Home**" ("**V opustevshem dome otdykha**," 1967) that Akhmadulina can dismiss the muteness plaguing her. However, the constant need to be alone with friends is more prevalent in her later poetry. In "**I think: how stupid I have been**" ("**la dumaiu: kak ia byla glupa**," 1967) she is to meet friends at six o'clock in a cafe. Because her watch is fast, she arrives before the others. While she is waiting she enumerates their good qualities and finally comes to the conclusion that she is "afraid to be alone" ("**la poniala: ia byt'odna boius**'"). Akhmadulina also seeks the company of friends when she can no longer endure the futility of trying to write. . . . Akhmadulina's search for solace in the company of friends is a logical result

of her predicament—especially since poetry, ostensibly, and a lover, obliquely, are not there when she needs them. After "**A Fairytale about the Rain**" the absence of a lover is implied (and perhaps erroneously inferred) by the lack of love poetry so prevalent and intricately bound with inspiration in the early verses.

The symbols of poetry and inspiration do appear sometimes, but now Akhmadulina views them from a different perspective. Previously she played in the Rain with her symbols of poetry—children, puppies, little animals and flowers. They appear frequently in the early poems. They meet and combine in "**A Fairytale about the Rain**." Unfortunately, Akhmadulina can no longer play with them, she is either ashamed before them or hides from their view. Thus in the poem "**To live as foolishly as I lived yesterday**" ("**Tak durno zhit', kak ia vchera zhila**," 1969), she recollects the drunken atmosphere of the previous evening's frivolities and says that she must avert her eyes from public gardens and must not dare even to be in the presence of children and animals.

The poem "**Sickness**" ("**Bolezn'**," 1969) combines all of these symbols. Wisdom is pain; genius is a destructive element:

> O, pain, you are wisdom. The essence of decision
> is a trifle before you,
> and dark genius dims
> the eye of the little animal growing ill.

Here the little beast appears again, but now it is slowly dying. Akhmadulina compares herself to this same animal and finds some comfort in the stem of a flower. Later she cries over the children and forgives the condemning eyes of a dog. The eyes are condemning her because she is not writing poetry. (pp. 336-38)

Akhmadulina's latest cycle of poems is entitled "**House of Creation**" ("**Dom tvorchestva**"). It is composed of a series of descriptions of a room, the night, a pain in the solar plexus and a hoopoe. In these poems she still has difficulty writing, but she achieves results—now with the help of shadows. Although she still suffers in this cycle, the atmosphere does not seem to be as hopeless as it was in the poems specifically about muteness.

Consistency of formal device, as well as symbolic system, is evident in Akhmadulina's poetry. The metrics of her poems are not distinguished by any new experimental forms; but rather, she gives freshness and variety to the traditional forms. (p. 339)

Akhmadulina has been influenced by both Akhmatova and Tsvetaeva. She is most often compared to Akhmatova, especially because of her love lyrics. But this is mainly because of matter rather than manner. Recently, in fact, Akhmadulina has been writing in the manner of a latter-day Tsvetaeva. Simon Karlinsky has examined the technical aspect of Tsvetaeva's lyrics, finding that some of her favorite devices are the juxtaposition of archaisms and colloquial diction, a tendency toward "verblessness," and the frequent use of the instrumental case. These same devices have been appearing with more frequency in Akhmadulina's recent poems. She is beginning to pun more often also—as in "**Description of a Pain in the Solar Plexus**" (1970), in which she laments the name of the solar plexus and attributes its unfortunate label to an absent-minded astronomer.

In "**A Fairytale about the Rain**" Akhmadulina ably fulfills the role of a sorceress which she attributes to herself. She predicts the future. Is she now, once again, making a prediction? One hopes so. In the poems of the last two years there is a tendency on her part to be resigned to the present situation and wait for a solution to her problems. Recently she has been reassuring her friends that she will live through the torments. In **"Incantation"** (**"Zaklinanie,"** 1968) she admonishes her friends not to cry for her because she will go on living. And in **"Once, rocking on the edge"** (**"Odnazhdy, pokanuvshis' na kraiu,"** 1970) she says that she has started to live and will live a long time.

Perhaps the most reassuring bit of news is the report of a rain storm hovering over the city [**"Don't write about the storm"** (**"Ne pisat' o groze,"** 1969)]. She tries not to write about it, but eventually she does. She says that she wants the storm to be exactly what it is and not the subject of a poem. Perhaps Akhmadulina does not want to scare away the storm. This is the closest the Rain has been in many years. (p. 340)

> *Christine Rydel, "The Metapoetical World of Bella Akhmadulina," in* Russian Literature Triquarterly, *No. 1, Fall, 1971, pp. 326-41.*

RICHARD GREGG

Few nations in this century have produced finer women poets than Russia. Akhmatova, Tsvetaeva, Inber—these are not effusive lady epigones indulging in *sensiblerie*, but big, professional, and "hard" (to borrow Pound's term) talents with a sound like nobody else's. On the basis of *Struna* (1962) and *Oznob* . . . , Bella Akhmadulina asks admittance to—and comparison with—this élite.

To some, "contrast" may seem the fitter word. For Akhmadulina's is neither the obliquity and restraint of Akhmatova nor the technical daring—and not infrequent obscurity—of Tsvetaeva. Muscular and often hyperbolic (a touch of Mayakovsky here?), with a special gift for strikingly extended metaphors, she follows her own poetic paths.

A certain consanguinity among the "sister poets" nonetheless exists. Like Akhmatova and Tsvetaeva, Akhmadulina manages to be intensely—in a less umbrageous decade one would say *femininely*—subjective without seeming narcissistic. Certain of her favorite themes—*e.g.*, the individual's revolt against conformism (the remarkable **"Tale about Rain in Several Episodes"** has discernible anti-establishment overtones); a strong attachment to Russia's literary past; love for one's birthplace (Georgia)—were dear to them as well. Moreover (to touch on the formal aspect of things), she, like them, is able to extract fresh beauties from the rhymed iambic quatrain—a form which is as alive in modern Russian verse as it is dead in our own. (pp. 88-9)

> *Richard Gregg, in a review of "Fever and Other New Poems," in* The Russian Review, *Vol. 31, No. 1, January, 1972, pp. 88-9.*

EDWIN MORGAN

One of Bella Akhmadulina's most striking poems [in *Fever and Other New Poems*] is addressed to Tsvetayeva, and in a process of identificatory revenge across two generations (she was born in 1937, Tsvetayeva in 1892) she swears to kill the monster that caused the older poet's suicide in a remote provincial town, the horrible Tartar demon yelabuga. . . . It is solidarity with a poet, but also solidarity with pain. In other poems she similarly looks back at Pasternak, at Lermontov, at

Pushkin. "An unknown soul's indistinct gesture/ was appealing to me to come to its defence." Yet the truth is in a sense the opposite: that she is appealing to these earlier poets to come to *her* defence. Her attractive vulnerability shows as an uncertainty about who and what she really is as woman and poet. Living in easier days than those writers, she seems almost to be searching, in their difficulties and sufferings, for a reality she can attach her own more mysterious uneasiness to. She tries to define this unease (which is also, however, a kind of distinction, a kind of power): it is a feverish shivering which makes it hard for the doctor to examine her, it is dreaming about small aircraft that come to peck grain from her palm, it is walking about accompanied by a personal rain "sitting on my shoulder like a monkey" and upsetting the dry rooms of the conventional and the bourgeoisified.

This last fantasy, nicely worked out in a series of episodes, makes **"A Tale about Rain"** one of her best pieces. It, and the **"Adventure in the Antique Shop"** where she evokes the ghost of Pushkin, are poems of tingling accomplishment and convincing atmospheric quality. (pp. 1132-33)

> *Edwin Morgan, "Political Theory and Poetic Licence," in* The Times Literary Supplement, *No. 3788, October 11, 1974, pp. 1132-33.*

EVGENI SIDOROV

People write about Akhmadulina either enthusiastically or grumpily. Her poetry is equally defenceless against criticism and adoration. The virtues and failings of her poetic voice appear so evident that it is difficult, for instance, to resist the temptation of writing a moralising review and proving, like "twice two is four", where play and mannerism prevail over naturalness and depth of feeling, and where poetry triumphs. Very apt here is a word which explains nothing, "crisis," followed by a more or less tactful instruction about the way she should go if she is to overcome it.

In all this people often overlook a small detail—the poet's particular fate, the nature of her talent and the organic quality of her voice. Akhmadulina has evolved her own system of poetry and it can accommodate far from all we would like to see there.

Other good poets write differently. But they will not say what Akhmadulina, and she alone, will say.

Her principal theme is the poet's heart and the act of creation. Indeed all Akhmadulina has written lies within these co-ordinates. The real earthly world enters her poetry in everyday material detail but the detail is instantly transformed by the music of the words. One might say that basically the orientation of her work is towards sonority, and there is a nonformal moral sense in this.

She firmly upholds the merit of harmonious Russian verse. From early youth she has remained loyal to its tradition and in this sense she has every right to say along with Afanasi Fet: "Seeking to recreate harmonious truth, the soul of the artist sets itself in the appropriate musical tonality. . . . there can be no work of art without musical attunement." Direct evidence of this are the titles of Akhmadulina's books—*String* and *Music Lessons*. It is characteristic that the literary critics, too, no matter how different are their views of her poetry, unanimously choose to title their reviews with lines from her poems: "The habit of setting word to word . . ."; "Two nylon wings" "The centrifugal surge of love and grief"; "A reason for writing verse''. What does this signify? Above all that her musical formulae contain a magnetic living truth, often unfavourable to the poetess herself but, as a rule, convincing to others in its selfless and frank significance.

In her quest to harness sense and sound Akhmadulina may, of course, lapse into chill exquisiteness and then, only the symbol, only the outward sign of her poetry, remains on the surface, while the intense ethical content of the poem disappears as an invisible fallout. But mature poets must nevertheless be judged by their highest achievements and by their place in modern Soviet poetry. Our veteran authors Marietta Shaginyan and Pavel Antokolsky sensed the importance of Akhmadulina perhaps better even than we who were her contemporaries. The contradictoriness of her poetic nature was more evident to us than the stubborn integrity of her poetic ideals. At the same time the elegance and grace of her verse should not blind us to the basis of her poetry which Antokolsky described as ''a constantly alert sense of the times, of history and of her duty to serve people.'' Akhmadulina is by nature averse to any ''coterie'' writing (and there were such reproaches), her very poetry continues the classic tradition of a frank confession addressed not to her interlocutor, not to a sole friend, but to people trustfully responding to her appeal for spiritual communion. (pp. 118-20)

This quality undoubtedly gains strength in time. The lessons in music and the lessons of life lead to a sober awareness of her profound personal involvement in the destiny of her own country, its culture and people. Her speech with its virtuoso instrumentation is not ''rejected'', the speech natural to her verse remains, as before, ''a form of conscience'', the form of natural and free existence she has chosen once and forever. The movement is taking place within her poetry, it acquires new meaningful impulses, history enters her verse not as an epic element, but as a feeling experienced. All Akhmadulina's poems are purely lyrical. They are lived through, not just written down. (p. 120)

In Soviet poetry in the sixties there was a turn towards meditation, towards profounder thinking in verse. Lyric poetry sought a firm starting-point for fresh soaring flight. Such a basis was naturally found in re-interpreted tradition. Space and time gained a new depth in poetry, the poet began more clearly to sense his ties with people not only on the horizontal plane but in the vertical plane—with the people of the past and the future. In her poem **"My Genealogy"** Akhmadulina was one of the first to detect with sensitivity these underground stirrings of the time.

In a short poem she boldly attempted to write the history of her vocation, of her entry into life, which she regards as an everlasting and unrivalled blessing.

> It pleases me that Life
> > is always right,
> The everlasting habit
> > there rejoices
> Of spreading roots out,
> > planting trees upright,
> Preparing gifts of fruit
> > among the branches.
> I shall remain in Life
> > right to the end,
> Before the end—
> > my gratitude expressing
> To fleet-foot girls
> > that from the porch descend,
> To everyone
> > creative gifts possessing.

The ''old manner'' and the slightly archaic vocabulary are very appropriate here because stylistically they turn our thoughts to an existence in which we are a link in the chain. In her poem the roar of revolution is akin to the biological current of the birth of a new life. These two melodies, intersecting in the narrator's heart, make this far from a ''drawing-room'' poem. (p. 121)

Evgeni Sidorov, ''Bella Akhmadulina: Life's Always Right,'' in Soviet Literature, *No. 3, 1977, pp. 117-21.*

ELAINE FEINSTEIN

[The essay excerpted below is a condensed version, revised by the critic, of three talks originally delivered on the British Broadcasting Corporation, Radio 3, in 1978.]

Bella Akhmadulina is probably the most gifted of the poets who rose to fame alongside Yevtushenko and Vozhnozhensky. . . . It is, I believe, no accident that it is Bella Akhmadulina who has most boldly taken upon herself the inheritance of her great women predecessors, Anna Akhmatova and Marina Tsvetayeva. Yevtushenko dates her maturity as a poet from the moment she first acknowledged that weight upon her, and singles out particularly her poem **"I Swear"**. In **"I Swear"** Akhmadulina personified the murderous forces of bureaucratic pettiness as a fairy-tale monster, to which she gives the name of Yelabuga, the town where Marina Tsvetayeva took her own life. When she spoke about the poem to me, she was at pains to point out that the inhabitants of that town were of course innocent. What she was vowing to destroy was the vicious small-mindedness which left Marina so alone and friendless in 1941, and still remains an enemy Bella can recognise in her own society. . . . (pp. 147-48)

At her finest, Akhmadulina combines a fierce, comic invention with her most passionate utterance: she turns her wit upon herself (as in **"Fever"**), or upon the complacent materialism of the worldly (in **"A Fairy Tale of Rain"**), with equal ferocity. Her voice often recalls the voice of Tsvetayeva in ''Praise to the Rich''. In many of her poems the figure of the poet is compelled to behave in ways that bring the contempt of more conventional people upon her. I asked Akhmadulina whether she felt that her poetic gift was a kind of curse:

> I am not sure it would be quite accurate to say that. What is more important to me is the state I experience when I write . . . I think whenever a gift is given to a human being it affects her fate, or her gift is affected by her fate. Particularly a poet. Perhaps a poetic gift does sentence whoever has it to some kind of grief or doom. Sometimes I do feel it is a heavy burden. And I say to myself, I don't want to write, I won't write. But I have never been able to stop . . . Sometimes when young people come to me for advice I tell them . . . If you're able *not* to write, then stop. The only valid reason for writing poetry is the total inability to live without doing so.

Nothing could be more like Tsvetayeva's own words, in her essay ''Art in the Light of Conscience'', where she describes poetry at its greatest as a kind of possession 'to which the poet must abandon himself, as Blok did when he wrote *The Twelve* in a single night and got up in complete exhaustion, like one who has been driven upon'. In **"Fever"** the poet experiences her gift as a kind of delirium which isolates her from her neighbours: it is a sharp, witty poem, as much self-mocking as self-explaining, and the central image rises to an absurdity that is elegant as well as surreal. . . . (pp. 149-50)

Akhmadulina often works best within the context of an extended metaphor, and clearly prefers to embody the evils of a materialistic society in surprising and fantastic images. No one can ever be in doubt, however, about the nature of what is under attack. At the centre of **"A Fairy Tale of Rain,"** another heroine who feels herself to belong to a world of values ignored in her society finds herself pursued by Rain, which takes many shapes, but always suggests the playful fertility of the human spirit. Whether Rain is the gift of poetry, or poetry itself, its one determination is to prevent the heroine making a peaceful adjustment to the arid materialism she feels on every side. (p. 154)

[There] must be many who share with me Yevtushenko's belief that she is the best poet of her generation, and very much in the tradition of the two great women poets who stand over her shoulder. (p. 158)

Elaine Feinstein, "Poetry and Conscience: Russian Women Poets of the Twentieth Century," in Women Writing and Writing About Women, *edited by Mary Jacobus, Croom Helm, 1979, pp. 133-58.*

ROCHELLE STONE

[Akhmadulina's] verse collections, from **String** (1962), to **Chills and Other Poems** (1968), through **Candle** (1977) and now **A Secret,** present an admirably concise, insightful, sensitive, at times humorous, romantic yet pragmatic and unmistakably feminine poetry. The latter is evidenced by the consistent use of a heroine whose "lyrical I," the persona, reveals a closeness to the author.

We find [*A Secret*] features characteristic of Akhmadulina's preceding work, such as a rich thematic variety, vivid imagery and a dramatized style in which the persona addresses an interlocutor. Old themes and motifs also figure prominently here: a preoccupation with poetic creation and the requisites associated with it—e.g., the moon, nature, the wax candle, the white page, the seasons, the specific months symbolizing the process of creative gestation and poetic harvest (**"February's Full Moon"**). However, *A Secret* introduces a new dimension in Akhmadulina's oeuvre. Whereas in the poem **"Sluggishness,"** from an earlier collection, the persona admits that her full life lacks only old age, whose wisdom is indispensable for creating great poetry, here the persona is aware of her approaching old age. This awareness generates new themes and images and a new tonality. Even the poet's usual references to her idols (Pushkin, Lermontov and Tsvetaeva) and to her favorite places (the Caucasus, Tarusa, Moscow and Leningrad) appear now in a different context. Her epistles to Okudzhava, Neruda, et alia transmit a wistful mood. Love lyrics have been replaced here by a meditative, philosophical poetry dealing with the temporariness of existence, the elusive moment, the persona's "stroll" through life (**"Progulka"**), eternity, fame and death. The poetic idiom reflects these thematic changes. Although precise, it is more complex, abounding in enjambments, while verse lines and poems are often much longer.

I find the structure of this collection most ingenious. Its title and its leading poems are closely linked with the persona's growing awareness of her aging, which, as stated in the initial verse of the opening poem, is accompanied by a creative upsurge: "I have a secret born of wonderful florescence." The persona's new awareness develops through frequent allusions to Tsvetaeva, whose name symbolizes "florescence." Furthermore, a poem, "Sad (Garden), written by Tsvetaeva when she was of Akhmadulina's present age, is referred to throughout the volume, appears as an epigraph and, moreover, becomes *the* leitmotiv of the entire collection. The puzzling "secret" hinted at in the opening poem is revealed in the closing one, lending the work a ring structure. However, to appreciate fully the 'secret' of this collection, one has to be intimately familiar with the life and works of the poets alluded to.

Rochelle Stone, in a review of "Taĩna: Novye stikhi," in World Literature Today, *Vol. 58, No. 4, Autumn, 1984, p. 624.*

Edward (Franklin) Albee (III)

1928-

American dramatist, poet, short story writer, scriptwriter, and dramatist.

Best known for his first full-length drama, *Who's Afraid of Virginia Woolf?*, Albee is among the United States's most acclaimed and controversial contemporary dramatists. Although initially characterized either as a realist or an absurdist, Albee usually combines elements from the American tradition of social criticism established by such playwrights as Arthur Miller, Tennessee Williams, and Eugene O'Neill with those of the Theater of the Absurd as practiced by Samuel Beckett and Eugène Ionesco. While Albee often portrays alienated individuals who suffer as a result of unjust social, moral, or religious strictures, he usually offers solutions to conflicts rather than conveying an absurdist sense of inescapable determinism. According to Allan Lewis, Albee "writes plays that grip an audience, that hold with their elusiveness, their obscurity, their meaning; and he has functioned in the true role of the playwright—to express the human condition dramatically and metaphorically."

Albee was the adopted child of Reed and Frances Albee, heirs to the multi-million dollar fortune of American theater manager Edward Franklin Albee I. Many critics suggest that the tense family conflicts of Albee's dramas derive from his lonely childhood. After attending several private and military schools and enrolling briefly at Trinity College in Connecticut, Albee achieved limited success as an author of poetry and fiction before turning to drama. Although he remained associated with off-Broadway theater until the production of *Who's Afraid of Virginia Woolf?*, Albee first garnered critical and popular acclaim for his one-act dramas, which prompted comparisons to the works of Tennessee Williams and Eugène Ionesco. His first one-act play, *The Zoo Story* (1959), is a satire set in New York City in which a young homosexual attempts to force conversation on a reticent conservative. After intimidating the man into defending himself with a knife, the homosexual purposely impales himself on its blade. While most reviewers regarded *The Zoo Story* as an absurdist examination of the artificiality of American values and the failure of communication, others described this work as an allegory of Christian redemption in which the young man martyrs himself to demonstrate the value of meaningful communication. Albee's next one-act drama, *The Death of Bessie Smith* (1960), revolves around the demise of black blues singer Bessie Smith, who died after being refused treatment at a Southern hospital that catered exclusively to white patients. Although initially interpreted as an indictment of Southern racism, Albee's ambiguous portrayal of the tensions that Smith's death provokes between a nurse, an intern, and an orderly have led many critics to regard *The Death of Bessie Smith* as an attack on dehumanizing American social values.

Albee's next major one-act plays, *The Sandbox* (1960) and *The American Dream* (1961), are generally viewed as expressionistic or burlesque satires of middle-class family values. In *The Sandbox*, a domineering Mommy and an emasculated Daddy tire of Grandma, the play's only sympathetic character, and abandon her on a beach to be collected by a handsome young

man who symbolizes death. *The American Dream* (1961) focuses on a similar Mommy and Daddy years after they had adopted a son who died as a result of the severe punishments they had inflicted upon him for failing to fulfill their ideal of "the American Dream." Confronted by the vacuous, opportunistic twin brother of their deceased child, the parents ironically believe that they have found their own "American Dream." Although faulted as defeatist and nihilistic, *The American Dream* was commended for its savage parody of traditional American values. Albee commented: "Is the play offensive? I certainly hope so; it was my intention to offend—as well as amuse and entertain."

Albee's most acclaimed drama, *Who's Afraid of Virginia Woolf?* (1962), has generated popular and critical notoriety for its controversial depiction of marital strife. This play depicts the alternately destructive and reconciliatory battle for dominance that ensues between George and Martha, a middle-aged history professor and his wife, following their return home from a faculty party with Nick, George's shallow colleague, and Honey, his spouse. As the evening proceeds, George and Martha alternately attack and patronize their guests before Martha seduces Nick to humiliate her husband and George retaliates by announcing the death of their nonexistent son, whom they had created to sustain their relationship. The play concludes with George emerging as the dominant, concerned spouse and Martha revealing her dependence and uncertainty by admitting that she is ''afraid of Virginia Woolf''—afraid of the reality that their life of artful illusion has obscured. Although faulted as morbid and self-indulgent, *Who's Afraid of Virginia Woolf?* was honored with two Antoinette Perry Awards and a New York Drama Critics Circle Award. Variously interpreted as a problem play in the tradition of August Strindberg, a campus parody, or a latent homosexual critique of conventional relationships, this drama has generated a wide array of critical analyses. When Albee failed to receive the Pulitzer Prize because one trustee objected to the play's sexual subject matter, drama advisors John Gassner and John Mason Brown publicly resigned. *Who's Afraid of Virginia Woolf?* has since been assessed as a classic of American drama for its tight control of form and command of colloquial and abstruse dialogue.

While several of Albee's plays written since 1962 have failed commercially and elicited scathing reviews for their abstract classicism and dialogue, many scholars have commended his commitment to theatrical experimentation and refusal to pander to commercial pressures. *Tiny Alice* (1964) addresses such metaphysical problems as humanity's tendency to question physical reality and to form tangible yet illusory ideas from abstract phenomena. In this morality play, a female philanthropist promises a troubled Catholic lay brother that she will divest him of illusions of faith. She then forces him to confront contrary realities by seducing him, marrying him, and having him shot. As the play concludes, the young man dies amid the ambiguous sound of a heartbeat that may signify either hallucination or the arrival of a malevolent deity. Although many critics considered the drama incomprehensible, Richard Gilman praised *Tiny Alice* as ''far and away the most significant play on Broadway [in 1965],'' commending its ''scenes that break down the walls of reticence and safety that mark the commercial theater.'' In *A Delicate Balance* (1966), a troubled middle-aged couple examine their relationship during a prolonged visit from two close friends. While the husband comes to realize that avoidance of love and compassion can lead to remorse and self-contempt, his wife remains oblivious, and their guests eventually feel compelled to leave. While garnering approval for its synthesis of dramatic elements, this drama was widely faulted for lacking action and cohesive ideas. When *A Delicate Balance* was awarded the Pulitzer Prize, most regarded the decision as a belated attempt by the Pulitzer committee to honor Albee for *Who's Afraid of Virginia Woolf?*.

Albee has stated that in his abstract, interrelated one-act plays *Box* and *Quotations from Chairman Mao Tse-Tung* (1968), he attempted to apply ''musical form to dramatic structure.'' *Box*, which involves no physical action or movement, consists of a monologue on the decline of Western civilization that is delivered by an unseen woman whose voice issues from the back and sides of the theater while a bright light illuminates a large cube that has been interpreted as a cage, a womb, or a coffin. In *Quotations from Chairman Mao Tse-Tung*, the same cube encompasses a steamship deck upon which Chairman Mao reads from a book of aphoristic quotations, while an elderly woman recites doggerel verse written by nineteenth-century poet Will Carleton and another woman relates a personal anecdote. Like *Box*, this play addresses the deterioration of Western culture, but its inherent meaning depends upon random associations resulting from contrapuntal dialogue. In *All Over* (1971), Albee returns to the predominantly realistic mode of his earlier plays to examine the vicious resentments and rivalries that result among the mistress, best friend, and family of an old man near death. Although most critics faulted the

play's characters as lacking dramatic urgency, Richmond Crinkley called *All Over* ''a beautiful and exciting piece of theater,'' and Harold Clurman commented: ''Listening attentively . . . [to] this largely verbal play, one comes to recognize that it contains not only feeling but pathos all the more poignant for its severe repression.''

In *Seascape* (1975), which Brendan Gill described as ''a short, wryly witty, and sometimes touching play about discovery,'' Albee depicts a middle-aged couple who are accosted on a beach by a pair of intelligent lizard-like creatures that have been driven from the sea by the processes of evolution. The four characters discuss topics of mutual understanding, including the purpose of existence, before concurring that human and alien creatures should aid and inspire one another despite life's uncertainty and despair. Although regarded by some critics as banal and pretentious, *Seascape* was commended for its originality and intriguing dialogue and earned Albee a second Pulitzer Prize. In his one-act plays *Listening: A Chamber Play* (1977) and *Counting the Ways: A Vaudeville* (1977), Albee returns to the abstract musical structure and experimental forms of *Box* and *Quotations from Chairman Mao Tse-Tung*. *Listening*, adapted from Albee's radio play of the same title, blends four voices to achieve the effect of a chamber quartet. The protagonists of this drama meet by a fountain pool and exchange observations and insults until one character drives another to commit suicide. *Counting the Ways* is a comic play consisting of twenty-one scenes that reflect the divergent moods of married life. In this work, a couple known as He and She question their love for one another before concluding that their bond depends on simple faith. Thomas P. Adler commented that ''this entertaining 'diversion'—for that seems an apt classification—can delight with its considerable charm and wit and occasional beauties of language.''

In his next play, *The Lady from Dubuque* (1980), Albee posits that reality is a subjective phenomenon capable of multiple interpretations. This drama concerns a woman dying of an unspecified disease who vents her pain and hostility on her friends and husband prior to the arrival of an ambiguous, commanding woman who alternately evokes the images of archetypal mother and angel of death. While this play closed after only twelve performances, Gerald Clarke deemed *The Lady from Dubuque* Albee's ''best work since *Who's Afraid of Virginia Woolf?*,'' and Otis Guernsey included it among *The Best Plays of 1979-1980*. *The Man Who Had Three Arms* (1983) also failed financially. Although Albee denied any autobiographical intent, critics dismissed this play for what they perceived as a self-pitying portrayal of his negative reception since the early 1960s. This play centers on Himself, a man who acquired wealth and fame after growing a third arm that later disappeared. Addressing the audience from a lecture podium, Himself alternately pleads for sympathy and attacks his audience for his loss of prominence. Although most reviewers concurred with the contention of Clive Barnes that this play contains ''a freefall of writing, some of it remarkably good, all of it dangerously unedited, and most of it sadly bitter,'' Gerald Weales deemed *The Man Who Had Three Arms* ''a great deal more substantial than its reception and very brief run suggests.''

Albee described his stylized drama *Finding the Sun* (1983) as ''pointillist in manner.'' This play counterbalances groups of characters, in one example contrasting a young man's forthcoming freedom with an old man's awareness of his impending death. Linda Ben-Zvi commented: ''There is much that is strong and theatrical about the piece. It plays well . . . thanks in large measure to the vivid personalities that Albee has created.'' In his recent *Marriage Play* (1987), which Dana Rufolo-Hörhager praised as ''a resonant, poetical, and cleanly hewn work,'' Albee returns to the themes of his earlier plays to portray the ambivalent relationship between a cynical woman and her detached husband. According to Jeanne Luere, *Marriage Play* ''comes alive onstage and arrests the audience through starkly contrasting visual elements to depict the couple's sometimes warm, sometimes cool reaction to each other's physical presence.''

(See also *CLC*, Vols. 1, 2, 3, 5, 9, 11, 13, 25; *Contemporary Authors*, Vols. 5-8, rev. ed.; *Contemporary Authors New Revision Series*, Vol. 8; *Dictionary of Literary Biography*, Vol. 7; and *Concise Dictionary of American Literary Biography: 1941-1968*.)

THOMAS P. ADLER

Edward Albee's latest offering, *The Man Who Had Three Arms*, [is] a play in the form of a lecture (or, perhaps more accurately, a lecture parading as a play), which is set . . . in an elegant lecture hall. . . .

Albee's new work is a meditation on celebrity in America. The central character, called simply Himself . . . , actually grew, we're to believe, a temporary third arm from the middle of his back, which gave him instant notoriety, put him on the covers of the most popular weeklies, and made him the talk of the nation. But such fame proved transitory. Now that the extra appendage has receded, the man who had once been lionized for his difference as well as exploited for his freakishness is left pretty well drained, his personal life ruined and his usefulness on the circuit at an end.

A lecture hall makes no pretense of having a fourth wall, and so Himself plays directly to us and interacts with us—or at least attempts to, since audiences are notoriously reluctant to join in. He illustrates his hour-and-a-half talk with slides that are sometimes employed wittily and contrapuntally. We're kept continually aware of ourselves as an audience, voyeurs anxious for the promised titillation that never quite materializes, while we are proffered vituperation and castigation in its stead. . . . [Himself is supported by The Woman and The Man], each of whom deftly assumes a succession of minor roles, some coming to life from Himself's memory of the past.

The proceedings have their pleasant moments. . . . Albee can still pen those wonderful verbal arias for which he's always been noted, yet even for an Albee aficionado, this isn't much of a play, even in any nontraditional sense of the term.

Not only are the metaphor and the meaning extremely blatant, but Albee's essay reflects on contemporary America's almost ghoulish need for culture heroes—for someone or something set apart from the commonplace that can help us forget the daily pattern of our lives and reaffirm the ever-diminishing possibility for making it an society. Furthermore, the play's connection with Albee's own playwriting career is all too obvious. For the first time, Albee makes ''himself'' the overt subject of his drama, exposing the love-hate/attraction-repulsion complex between himself and his critics and audiences, who once canonized him as the wonder boy of the American

theatre but have of late, more often than not, rejected him by summarily dismissing his work.

As *The Man Who Had Three Arms* comes to a close, Himself alternately orders us to get out of the theater and begs us to stay; reviles us with his hate and yet just as desperately needs us for the love that only we, his audience, can give him. The burden falls squarely on us for having succumbed to the celebrity promoters and having aided them in turning Albee/ Himself into an institution (''The Last Best Hope for American Drama''). In making him into an object we have refused him the room to grow and change and develop in the direction he chooses for himself rather than along the lines that would suit us.

If *The Man Who Had Three Arms* proves to be only a temporary ''growth'' like the appendage on Himself's back, we can perhaps understand and tolerate this denunciation as a necessary purging of Albee's pent-up rage at audiences and critics who have been so fickle to him over the past decade and a half. But if this latest effort hasn't rid its author of his anger, then we fear that an Albee who has turned in upon himself may cripple himself as a dramatist at a time when the American theatre most needs his voice.

> *Thomas P. Adler, in a review of ''The Man Who Had Three Arms,'' in* Theatre Journal, *Vol. 35, No. 1, March, 1983, p. 124.*

CLIVE BARNES

[*The Man Who Had Three Arms*] is vastly concerned with a *danse macabre* with fame, a fatal brush with the eternity of passing celebrity.

The piece is really a lecture. Or, even more really, it's a sermon in the form of a paradoxical parable. It is also extraordinarily self-indulgent, sometimes oddly touching, and written in prose of the finest purple that for the most part explodes like firecrackers on a winter night. . . .

[The play's protagonist is Himself], the man who once, for some golden, fame-clad moments, had a third arm, but is now a painfully mortal mortal who drinks a little, talks like a self-congratulatory, self-lacerating gush of sound and fury in the form of words, and is giving a lecture. . . .

It is a freefall of writing, some of it remarkably good, all of it dangerously unedited, and most of it sadly bitter. Bitter? Yes, because the fame that Albee is really writing about . . . is his own. And the strange envy of people for it.

Albee is abrasive. Albee is arrogant. Albee also has some rights as one of the major playwrights of our time—and one of the most cheerfully self-destructive. I think I used ''self,'' tactfully hyphenated in that literary fashion that Albee understands so well, four times. Maybe five. This play—as he tells us—is concerned with a ''sense of self.''

Albee's hero, despite his hectoring style, is desperately concerned to distinguish between ''self-disgust and disgust at others.'' But he sees himself not only as ''an exceptional man'' but also a ''freak.'' And a drunken priest at a party once told him: ''You were an accident of nature!''

In one painfully revealing passage—when the hero has told about the way his third arm sprouted, the event ''that changed my life and all my definitions,'' he exclaims with marked poignancy: "You want the climax at the beginning—a life of detumescence."

An ugly image perhaps, but surely a heart-felt one coming from an author who, more than most of his generation, has known the slings and arrows of outrageously fortunate early success.

For here the hero loses his instant fame—his third arm withers, and goes away as mysteriously as it arrived. His entrepreneur, a wily Southern Colonel, disappears at the same time, taking with him most of the money that came from this freak notoriety. The gig was up—our hero became overnight a former celebrity—a man who once happened to have had three arms.

The play is not quite a monologue—but comes close to it. Albee tries to open it up a little; the two representatives of this crazy lecture-cum-picnic society who make the introductions . . . also play out little illustrative cameos. . . .

In the final test—does Albee's play work? Well, I cannot see it being often revived; and it is, if you take my meaning, more theatrical than theater, more dramatic than drama. With that proviso let me stress that it is surprisingly worth seeing—the words sizzle and the ideas sear. Albee may not be writing a play as such—but he is certainly cooking.

> Clive Barnes, "Two Cheers for Albee's 'Man with Three Arms'," in New York Post, April 6, 1983.

FRANK RICH

Edward Albee's **Man Who Had Three Arms,** at the Lyceum, isn't a play—it's a temper tantrum in two acts. A celebrated man known only as Himself—why is it always so hard for Mr. Albee to give people proper names?—stands at a lecture-hall podium, backed by potted plants and flags, and spends nearly two hours alternately insulting the audience and announcing how bitter he is.

This static premise is not, per se, a hopeless idea for theater: if Mr. Albee were inclined to be ruthlessly honest, he might have written a work as excoriating and funny as a Lenny Bruce routine. But the bitterness that pours out of Himself is a mixture of unearned self-pity and abject rancor. **The Man Who Had Three Arms** arouses roughly the same emotions as those *People* magazine cover stories in which movie stars grouse about how hard it is to escape grasping fans while shopping in Beverly Hills. . . .

[Himself] is mad because he was once "the most famous man in the world" and now he isn't so famous anymore. A standard-cut advertising man with a wife and three kids, he had one day awakened to discover that he was growing a third arm on his back. Suddenly Himself was sought after by royalty, cheered by ticker-tape parades and toasted by talk-show hosts. He had become, one might say, a contemporary Elephant Man—complete with trunk.

But when we meet Himself, the parade has passed by. The third arm ultimately withered away, and so did the protagonist's celebrity. . . . Drunk and in debt, he's now just another ordinary-looking man at the end of his rope.

One of the more shocking lapses of Mr. Albee's writing is that he makes almost no attempt even to pretend that Himself is anything other than a maudlin stand-in for himself, with the disappearing arm representing an atrophied talent. Though the speaker tells us about his family and advertising career, we

never believe in these fictional biographical details for a second. They're thrown in without specificity or conviction, and, before long, they're forgotten as Himself lashes out against drama critics, speaks in the same overripe language as past Albee narrators and starts wrapping himself in the cloaks of such literary men as Agee, Melville and Nabokov.

But whoever Himself is—whether a one-time freak or a playwright in mid-career crisis—his beefs with the world are shrill and unmoving, no matter how much the author tries to inflate them into an indictment of "the American dream." It's hard to feel much sympathy for a man who, by his own account, greedily helped himself to the perks of fame—unlimited publicity, power, money and sex—and now complains that the adulation was "idiotic," that the power was short-lived, that the fortune was recklessly squandered, and that the sex was empty. . . .

Thrown into this mix is a virulent and gratuitous misogyny that has little relevance to the character at hand but is totally of a piece with the last Albee play, *Lolita:* "baggage" is easily the nicest term by which Himself refers to women. Indeed, the only person not treated contemptuously during the monologue is the speaker, who frequently likens his martyrdom to Christ's.

Whatever one thinks of the content of **The Man Who Had Three Arms,** the craftsmanship is rudimentary. Act I is all throat-clearing and padding. . . . The jokes include many wordplays on the hero's former appendage—"arm in arm in arm" and so on—and canned wisecracks about the press. . . .

[Only at the play's] end does the anger come to a point. It's then that Mr. Albee at last begins to deal seriously with the issue his play wants to be about—an inability, as Himself puts it, "to distinguish between my self-disgust and my disgust with others." . . .

It's a painful, if embarrassing, spectacle, because it shows us the real and sad confusion that exists somewhere beneath the narcissistic arrogance and bile that the author uses as a dodge to avoid introspection the rest of the time. While **The Man Who Had Three Arms** is mostly an act of self-immolation, its final display of self-revelation holds out at least the slender hope that Mr. Albee might yet pick himself up from the floor.

> Frank Rich, "Drama by Albee, 'Man Who Had Three Arms'," in The New York Times, April 6, 1983, p. C15.

BRENDAN GILL

Edward Albee's **The Man Who Had Three Arms** is a curiosity—not so much a play as a literary exercise that happens to take place in a theatre. . . . An elderly man of evident good breeding stations himself at one of the lecterns, welcomes his audience—us, but not really us—and informs us that we are about to hear still another of a very long series of talks being given under the general heading "Man on Man." He then introduces a chirrupy little woman, some years his junior, who announces that the speaker promised for the occasion is unable to be present, owing to his death; luckily, a substitute has been found, whom we are invited to welcome. The substitute speaker strides in from the wings and begins a harangue that, when it ends, ends the evening. Known in the program only as "Himself," the speaker, who appears to be in his early forties, has an air about him of sour, defiant seediness. It turns out that the subject of his harangue is an account of how he became one of the great celebrities of the age, how his celebrity corrupted him, and how the loss of that celebrity proved a further source of corruption. Nearly every word that he utters is unpleasant, though a few of the words are witty as well as unpleasant; Himself . . . is a repellent figure, whose last words are a cry for pity that is sure to go unanswered.

For reasons inexplicable to me, Albee has chosen to make the basis of Himself's fame an event that is preposterous even as a metaphor. It is nothing less than the emergence between Himself's shoulder blades of a third arm, which grows and then withers; we are supposed to believe that this grotesque affliction suffices to put Himself in a class with such notables as Sinatra, Kissinger, and, almost too obviously, Albee himself. The dry, anguished text of *The Man Who Had Three Arms* is full of echoes: *The Elephant Man*, Lenny Bruce, Nabokov, Mark Twain's ghost story ''The Golden Arm,'' and a dozen others, all of them literary and at a remove from life; they give the text what amounts to a borrowed robustness and at the same time keep us at a distance from it. (pp. 130, 132)

Brendan Gill, ''Bellyacher,'' in The New Yorker, *Vol. LIX, No. 9, April 18, 1983, pp. 130, 132-33.*

JOHN SIMON

What can I say about Edward Albee's *The Man Who Had Three Arms* that I haven't said about some dozen of his preceding offerings? The author of two good plays, Albee has written nothing of merit since *Virginia Woolf*. Here he has concocted a monologue in lecture format for the hero (the two other actors, in a variety of small roles, might as well be part of the unimaginative slide projections meant to juice up this lectern drama), a man who once sprouted a mysterious third arm on his back, and so became famous, rich, and sought after; but now that it has vanished, he ekes out a measly existence from $500 lectures (overpriced, if the play is a fair sample) in the course of which he tells his life story, blames everyone else for his troubles, viciously insults the audience, and indulges in pitiful verbal games that insult the intelligence.

In other words, Himself, as the monologist is called (Albee regularly eschews anything as unsymbolic as a name), is Albee himself, who briefly displayed talent; he acquired fame, wealth, easy sexual conquests, and now berates the world for withdrawing these gifts—whereas it should be blamed for having proffered them prematurely and excessively. Accompanying the invective is an obbligato of whining self-pity: As the audience is being baited and verbally booted out of the theater, it is also begged for compassion and companionship. The play snarls and snivels alternatively or even simultaneously, has no dramatic invention or introspective honesty, and is as abject as it is vile.

In addition, it is humorlessly foul-mouthed, pretentiously would-be-cultured, crammed with every conceivable desperate pun on arms, and, despite protestations of heterosexuality, full of venomous misogyny, campiness, and an acrid degradation of sex that I do not perceive as particularly heterosexual characteristics. The verbal wit is on the level of ''not a situation most people come face to face or crotch to crotch with,'' and the culture scales the heights of a Piaf tag in French and a slight misquotation of two of E. E. Cummings's best-known lines, ''how do you like your blueeyed boy / Mister Death.'' Albee's English is, as usual, poor, though no worse than his ethnic jokes.

John Simon, in a review of ''The Man Who Had Three Arms,'' in New York *Magazine, Vol. 16, No. 17, April 25, 1983, p. 92.*

CATHARINE HUGHES

[Edward Albee, who] once received a Pulitzer for the wrong play, has just had another ''wrong'' play open on Broadway, the lugubrious, self-indulgent *The Man Who Had Three Arms*.

[Hope] springs eternal in the critical heart, especially for playwrights who have produced substantial, provocative and theatrically viable and effective work in the past. With Albee's latest, the patience has begun to wear thin. It is a bad play and never would have been produced on Broadway were it not for the playwright's earlier successes. . . .

The Man Who Had Three Arms is set in a lecture hall, which should be warning enough, for Albee is about to attempt to exorcise his personal demons concerning early success and recognition. His central character is—with justification—called Himself, who once, in the days of his fame, had three arms. Now, he is a mere mortal, possessing only two, perhaps drinking a bit too much, both self-satisfied and self-lacerating, certainly self-indulgent. . . .

Some of the writing is sharp and incisive, a testimony to the fact that Albee's talent has not altogether deserted him. His play is concerned with what the playwright calls a ''sense of self'' and the work ventures between ''self-disgust and disgust at others.''

After the hero's third arm—his source of fame—has withered, he says what Albee himself would very likely say: ''You want the climax in the beginning . . . a life of detumescence.''

The play is not entirely a monologue, though it might as well have been; there are two cameo roles. . . . But Albee, who also directed—probably a mistake, for the play would have profited from substantial scissoring—is concerned only with one character, Himself. . . . For Albee, one can only hope that the demons indeed have been exorcised.

Catharine Hughes, ''The Pulitzer Puzzle,'' in America, *Vol. 148, No. 18, May 7, 1983, p. 361.*

GERALD WEALES

[The protagonist of *The Man Who Had Three Arms*] is a man who, having once sprouted a third man and become an instant celebrity, finds himself forced to work cheaply at the less glamorous end of the lecture circuit after the third arm disappears. The play is his lecture, an exercise in abuse of himself and his audience, a one-man performance . . . that is interrupted by very brief (and quite unnecessary) dramatic scenes in which an actor and an actress, who opened the play with very obvious parody of lecture-club types, perform all the other roles.

The Man Who Had Three Arms was rather viciously attacked by critics as an exercise in self-pity—a reaction that almost certainly confirmed Albee in his belief (apparently endemic among playwrights) that the critics are all out to get him. . . . [In recent years, he] has been roughed up a bit by critics and audiences alike, although his standing in the academy is strong (v. all those books and journal articles on his work). Yet, he has not had a popular success for twenty years (unless *A Delicate Balance* qualifies), and his tendency to whine in public has taken an unpleasant turn. When he brought his one-acters, new and old, to the University of Pennsylvania a few years ago . . . , he conceived his appearance before the audience as a confrontational occasion. He performed with more finesse than his protagonist does, but he was essentially dismissive, treating most of the questions as intrusions on his artistic and personal privacy.

Insofar as *Man* reflects Albee's sense of being at once abandoned (''Abandon-ed!'' as Martha put it) and subjected to pushy inquisitiveness, it is unfortunate, if only because the gossipy elements in the play distracted viewers from what was best about it. *Man,* whatever else it is, is a serious attempt to deal with the concept of celebrity in America, the triviality that sometimes creates it, its rewards and its punishments, the way in which it is packaged (there is a folksy manipulator who suggests Elvis Presley's Colonel Parker). Even the device, the combination of self-flagellation and aggression, is a wedding of those poles of stand-up comedy, Rodney Dangerfield and Don Rickles, men whose success as comedians is surely a comment on the audience. Many of Albee's jokes were obvious, his satire foolish (is there a current need to attack banquet food?), his characters cartoon figures. But behind this façade, which I suspect is deliberately corny, *The Man Who Had Three Arms* is a great deal more substantial than its reception and very brief run suggests. (pp. 605-06)

> *Gerald Weales, in a review of ''The Man Who Had Three Arms,'' in* The Georgia Review, *Vol. XXXVII, No. 3, Fall, 1983, pp. 605-06.*

THOMAS P. ADLER

Although Edward Albee's *The Lady from Dubuque* was neither a critical nor a popular success when it opened on Broadway early in 1980 only to close precipitately after twelve performances, Otis Guernsey, Jr. rightly includes it among *The Best Plays of 1979-1980*, predicting with some justification, I suspect, that ''this distinguished and durable play . . . will surely be heard in time, globally.'' From one point of view, *Lady from Dubuque* is a continuation of several stylistic and thematic and structural themes in Albee's plays. It is related, for example, in its corruscating wit and sometimes bitter exchanges between hosts and guests to *Who's Afraid of Virginia Woolf?* (1962); in its focus on the rights and responsibilities of family and friends to *A Delicate Balance* (1966); and in its form as a death-watch to *All Over* (1971). From yet another perspective, however, it is a culmination of Albee's interest in epistemological and ontological problems, a strand that can be traced back through *Counting the Ways* and *Listening* (1976), the pair of lengthy one-act plays written immediately preceding it, and to *Tiny Alice* (1964). Even a cursory examination of *Dubuque*'s language reveals Albee's interest in—almost obsession with—the problem of knowing. The word ''know'' recurs, in fact, again and again in the text as both the play's characters and audience are asked to consider exactly who and what can actually be known—for within the play we are asked if we can, indeed, know ourselves or others, substances or only surfaces, essences or only their representations. Moreover, the play goes on to challenge its audience with questions concerning not only the content of our knowledge but the very process by which we come to know. *Tiny Alice* forces us to question the dependability of knowledge obtained in the most usual fashion, through the reading of observable phenomena, by asking if our merely thinking something makes it so.

The central metaphysical concern of *Tiny Alice* is clearly the problem of finite man's understandable tendency to question the reality of what cannot be perceived by the senses and, following from that, the almost universal human need to concretize the abstract, to discover or—barring that—to create a manageable representation of the unknown. Brother Julian, the play's central figure, finds upsetting and disorienting man's anthropomorphizing habit through which he simplifies mystery in order to control what cannot be understood. The widespread need to ''represent'' something before it can be worshipped plunges him into a dark night of the soul, for to ''personify,'' to resort to symbolism, is to ''limit it, demean it.'' That anthropomorphizing frame of mind is rendered visually in the stage setting: in the library of the mansion where the action occurs is a model of the mansion, exact in all its details. Perhaps, it is hinted, there is even a miniature model of this model in the library *within* the model! Ultimately, the play moves its audience toward a direct confrontation with the epistemological question of which came first: the model or the mansion? If the mansion, then the model is merely a shadow of a pre-existing form; if the model, then the mansion is only a replica of the model. A similar question can be asked of the characters on stage: are there also miniatures of them in the model? And, if so, is the onstage library simply a room within a larger model, with characters watching these characters watching? (pp. 109-10)

Counting the Ways likewise hinges on the distinction between ''knowing'' as a certainty and only ''thinking'' that something is so as a supposition. What is at question here, though, is not metaphysical truth, but the truth of the emotions. Each desiring from the other an auricular assurance and measurement, the man and the woman (called simply ''He'' and ''She'') ask of each other, ''Do you love me?'' But to quantify what is essentially qualitative, to measure depth of feelings by words is, as Lear learned too late, to reduce. In *The Lady from Dubuque*, it will be the pain of dying and loss that cannot be measured, and because of its futility, such attempts at measuring the unmeasurable inevitably become little more than childish games. Within *Counting the Ways*, such Lear-like attempts to measure love inevitably result in games such as ''She loves me? She loves me not?'' or ''Me loves he? Not me loves he?''—the latter while putting the petals back on. In the end, such games are so obviously incapable of proving that one loves or is loved that the lovers are ultimately left to live on faith. . . . But in this ''Vaudeville,'' the question of knowing extends as well to the actors' and audience's awareness and perception of themselves. When a ''sign descends'' and lights up commanding, ''IDENTIFY YOURSELVES,'' the actors step out of their roles as characters, address the audience now as actors (as they earlier had as characters) and improvise a thumbnail sketch of themselves, sending the audience to consult their programs ''*after* the play'' if they desire more information about the real lives of the actor and actress playing He and She. But to what extent can that sketch or the printed biography consisting of external facts and figures really define the person? And when the sign descends, the members of the audience might have the uneasy feeling at first that *they* are each being required to identify themselves to the others sitting around them.

If *Tiny Alice* asks about knowing religious truth and *Counting the Ways* about ascertaining truths of the heart, *Listening* explores one's ability to know and, thus, to control the psyche of another person. In this Strindbergian ''Chamber Play,'' The Woman, whom we take to be an analyst in a psychiatric hospital, can manipulate and ultimately drive the patient/inmate

Girl to suicide. The Woman is literal-minded, cold, emotionless, rational—so calculating that her extreme rationality becomes a kind of Iago-like rationalism devoid of moral scruple or consideration. By knowing the way in which The Girl's mind works, The Woman is able to prompt The Girl to use the sharp glass in the empty fountain to slit her own wrists. . . . Playing on The Girl's fear of blood (menstruation) by graphically describing the analogous case history of another female patient, The Woman will drive the girl to suicide just as surely as The Woman has already driven The Man to tears by turning away from and rejecting him in a previous encounter since, as The Man points out, "Effect comes *after* act." (pp. 111-12)

This consistent concern on the part of the playwright with what and how people can know—or hope to know—in the metaphysical, emotional, and psychic spheres in all of these works suggests Albee's position about reality as multi-layered and essentially unknowable in any but a relativistic sense—one of the hallmarks of Pirandello's thought as well. Moreover, these brief remarks perhaps disclose other hints of Pirandello's recurrent emphases: on the fragmentation and multiplicity of personality; on the convergence and/or contrast between life and theater, role-playing and reality, the mask and its wearer; and on the audience's self-reflexivity. And in light of these themes, *The Lady from Dubuque*, which insists on the necessity to perceive life as essentially multi-leveled, seems to be Albee's most Pirandellian play to date.

Clearly, the most obviously Pirandellian aspect of *The Lady from Dubuque* is the audience's awareness that they are watching a play—an awareness pursued thematically by Pirandello in such works as *Six Characters in Search of an Author* and *Tonight We Improvise,* which are aesthetic inquiries into the nature of the theatre—[which] extends to *The Lady from Dubuque,* wherein Albee exploits this Modernist convention of making the audience conscious of themselves *as* audience by having the characters address them directly in either brief remarks or longer speeches some eighty or so times. As his "Performance Note" indicates, "this is done without self-consciousness, quite openly, and without interrupting the flow of the play." As with much of *The Lady from Dubuque,* the device does not depart from Albee's earlier practice, extending back through *Counting the Ways* (where, as we have noticed, the technique is employed adroitly and purposefully), *Box* and *Quotations from Chairman Mao Tse-Tung* (1968), *The American Dream* (1961), and even *The Sandbox* (1960). (pp. 112-13)

To be sure, the self-conscious, Pirandellian lines which the characters in *The Lady from Dubuque* speak directly to the audience serve several functions. Sometimes, they simply furnish exposition; at other times, they provide the kind of editorializing to underscore a point that we ordinarily expect from a choral character. Infrequently, they are philosophic or nostalgic or sardonic meditations on some facet of existence. Often, their tone is defensive or mildly conspiratorial, demanding some complicity from the audience in the form of a supportive or empathic response in the face of a challenge issuing from one of the other characters. No matter what their purpose, however, Albee insists emphatically that in every instance these lines be spoken not by the actors as actors (as had been the case in *Counting the Ways*), but instead by the actors *in* character. As his stage directions indicate, "It is of the utmost importance that the actors make it clear that it is not they, but the characters, who are aware of the presence of the audience." Furthermore, these lines are not in the nature of "asides" as traditionally understood in drama, since the other onstage char-

acters hear them and respond to them as they normally would to dialogue exchanges. Indeed, many of these lines are addressed simultaneously to the other characters and across the footlights to the audience. So while this technique is non-illusionistic—deliberately heightening our awareness that we are in a theatre watching a play—this device ultimately requires not so much that we reflect on ourselves as an audience but rather that we regard ourselves as, and associate ourselves with, the onstage characters who represent us. We are among the guests at this party-turned-deathwatch. Instead of being mere observers, we—though silent—are participants in this ritual. Here, then, Albee shifts emphasis from audience as audience to audience as character.

In regard to *The Lady from Dubuque,* the action which the audience is expected both to bear witness to and take a part in might well be termed a "coming of death" play, with Elizabeth, *The Lady from Dubuque,* and her black companion Oscar as the summoners. . . . Jo, dying of an unspecified disease which has all the symptoms of cancer, vents her pain and bitterness on the friends who gather around, "need[ing] a surface to bounce it all off of." Knowing that she must not succumb to self-pity, that if she cries for herself she might fall totally apart, she requires also a husband who possesses the necessary strength to see her through her last agony—as she becomes less and less. . . . Her husband Sam, however, also knows his needs, especially the necessity to "hold on to the object we're losing" and not let go, as Jo diminishes "To bone? To air? To dust?", but these needs threaten to render him impotent in responding to Jo's. He resents, though, any intrusion from others who might try to fulfill some of his role for him. Perhaps understandably, yet surely self-indulgently, he needs to be the only sufferer. . . . Although the Lady from Dubuque assures him, "you don't know what it *is,*" Sam sobs, "I'm dying." For in Albee's dramas, the survivors exist under a peculiar burden not felt by the victims: not only must they live seeing the process of dying, but they must continue on after the death and the finality which means aloneness. They must, in short, suffer *after* the suffering has ceased for the dead. (pp. 113-15)

Yet, the crux of Sam's suffering is not that he will go on alone, though that is surely a part of it, or even that he evidently has no religious belief to sustain him—though in any case religion is most often, in Albee, simply one of the many illusions that man falls back on. Rather, it is Sam's inability to plumb the mystery of "things [he] would not be expected to understand," to know what the moment of death will be like. He desires the certainty that, at the point of her death, Jo have "No time to be afraid"—and by extension that he, too, will not have time for fear either. And although Elizabeth grants him that assurance, he can still not be absolutely certain of that fact. What is proffered in place of that certainty, or of any hope grounded in a religious system, is the fact of a multi-layered reality. Since, in Pirandello-fashion, Sam can know neither his own identity (either in games or in life) nor that of death, all he can hope to know and all he needs to know is that existence moves not just on a literal but, ritualistically, on a symbolic, metaphoric, and archetypal plane as well.

Within *The Lady from Dubuque,* Albee alludes explicitly to Pirandello's *It Is So! (If You Think So!).* When Elizabeth remarks to Sam, "You have a woman upstairs. You *say* she is your wife; I say she is my daughter," we recall the tension between Signor Ponza and his mother-in-law Signora Frola over the identity of Signora Ponza. Ponza claims that his wife is not Signora Frola's daughter, but instead his second wife who simply pretends, for the sake of the older woman, to be her deceased daughter. Signora Frola, on the other hand, insists that Ponza has only been deluded into thinking that her daughter is his second wife in order to assuage the guilt he feels over having treated her so badly that she needed to be sent to a sanatarium. The other characters in Pirandello's play demand to know the absolute truth about Signora Ponza's identity. . . . For Pirandello, however—and herein resides the existential dilemma in his drama—truth is multiple and subjective, as he insists when he has Signora Ponza say at the close of the play that she is both Signora Frola's daughter *and* Ponza's second wife. And it is such hallmarks of Pirandellianism as the multiplicity of personality and the relativity of truth that Albee carries over into his own drama. (pp. 115-16)

That so much of the surface action in *The Lady from Dubuque* revolves around game-playing puts us in mind of the mask/wearer dichotomy and the life/theatre and stage/world metaphors that abound in Pirandello's plays. For instance, Albee structures one of his games as a play-within-the-play in which Sam and Carol gull the other characters who are then cast as an outraged audience to their ruse. Carol returns from the powder room, feigning the violated maiden in exaggerated fashion and claiming that Sam has attempted to seduce her. By playing this role, she manages to elicit a response of threatened manhood from her fiancé Fred, who can see nothing but the surface appearance which he immediately accepts as the truth. Fred's outraged reaction is only a humorous inversion and reduction of the kind of hysteria which everyone experiences when his or her own certainty is shaken. In his already tense condition, Sam, when faced with the unexpected appearance of Elizabeth and Oscar, is especially susceptible to anxiety over the unknown. Verbally, Albee underscores the convergence of his concerns with those of Pirandello. . . . When Elizabeth insists that "Everything is true," she demands the same sort of acquiescence to subjective reality that Signora Ponza does. Yet if, for Pirandello, such assent to the multiplicity of truth renders each person's reality as "real" as that of the next—leaving every person with at least the assurance of his or her own subjective certainty—for Albee the suspicion always remains that if, indeed, "Everything is true," then "nothing is true." All solipsistically perceived realities become just another of the many illusions we depend upon to see us through life. (p. 116)

[Thus, the] Lady from Dubuque and her companion demand to be perceived on something other than just the literal level, as is clearly apparent from the text. . . . Elizabeth's first line "we *are* in time," is ambiguous in the way that many lines in the later Albee are: It may mean that they have arrived before Jo dies, but it might just as well, especially given Albee's own emphasis on the word *"are,"* indicate that they have entered the dimension of time from somewhere out of time. Sam's persistent question when he comes upon them the next morning, "Who are you?"—uttered ten times in four pages—linguistically echoes the line that the other characters addressed to Sam at the beginning of the first act when they were playing the game of Twenty Questions. . . . Sam now asks Elizabeth if she claims to be Jo's mother. Clearly, Elizabeth does not appear to be she; Jo's mother, we are told, is "tiny, thin as a rail, blue eyes—darting furtive blue eyes . . . pale hair, tinted pink, balding a little," whereas the character description tells us Elizabeth is "a stylish, elegant, handsome woman." Furthermore, Elizabeth hails from Dubuque rather than New Jersey. A mythical creation of *New Yorker* editor

Harold Ross, the Lady from Dubuque became an archetype of the kind of reader the magazine was supposedly not appealing to and refused to play down to. She is, thus, an imaginary creature who has entered into the collective imagination and who is talked about as if she really existed. Jo, it is true, does feel that her real mother has deserted her; yet if no reason exists for believing that Elizabeth is Jo's mother, there is, as one of the guests comments, just as little reason for believing that she is not. Like the endless riddle of the model and the mansion in *Tiny Alice,* the Pirandellian drama of Elizabeth's "true" identity can never be resolved and is never intended to be. (p. 117)

At the very end, Sam is still asking Elizabeth, "Who are you? Really?" Of course, not knowing himself, he cannot possibly hope to know the other. The bedrock question remains the Sphinx's "Who am I" since "all of the [other] values [are] relative save" that. But then, to reach any certitude about who one is and who another is in Albee, as in Pirandello, is an impossible dream. What Sam might more profitably have done was to probe the fuller dimensions of existence by confronting the Lady from Dubuque with the question: "Who are you, metaphorically?" That, perhaps, would have been a first step in approaching the ineffable mystery at the very heart of existence—something that Carol, who began as the most bewildered of all the guests, seems able to do. She intuitively senses who and what the Lady from Dubuque and Oscar are, grasps what is happening, and honestly tries to help Sam help Jo. To see anagogically, to perceive existence as multi-leveled, is Albee's only answer to the problem of knowing that he poses in his plays. To remain always on the level of the literal reality (unknowable as even that level is) is, indeed, "too little." To know metaphorically, symbolically, archetypally is, to paraphrase Hemingway, what humankind in Albee has instead of God. (p. 118)

> *Thomas P. Adler, "The Pirandello in Albee: The Problem of Knowing in 'The Lady from Dubuque',"* in Edward Albee: An Interview and Essays, *edited by Julian N. Wasserman with Joy L. Linsley and Jerome A. Kramer, The University of St. Thomas, 1983, pp. 109-19.*

LINDA BEN-ZVI

"Pointillist in manner," is how Edward Albee, in program notes, describes his newest play *Finding the Sun.* . . . Structurally the play resembles Seurat's "Sunday Afternoon on the Island of la Grande Jatte:" highly stylized, frieze-like figures, mainly in groups of two, precisely positioned at sharp angles, poised to take the rays of the sun. It was Seurat's contention that art must balance contraries: "Art is harmony; harmony is the analogy of opposites, the analogy of like things, of tone, of line." A character in *Finding the Sun* makes a similar observation: "Everything proceeds comparatively, it is true—there is no light without dark, rest without acting, and so forth and so on . . . that's the ticket! Everything comparative; everything in season."

In Albee's play the season is summer—"August in a NE clime"—and the setting is a beach. And while there are no umbrellas or shade trees to provide the essential pointillist play between light and dark, Albee attempts to create harmonies out of the numerous relationships among his eight characters. In twenty-two swiftly moving scenes—some as short as a few lines and others running to eight pages of dialogue—he mixes and matches three married couples and a mother and son, systematically introduced in alphabetical order. . . . We quickly learn that the assorted people who have come to find the sun on this particular afternoon in August are related in various ways. Cordelia is the daughter of Gertrude, and Daniel is the son of Hendon, each from previous marriages; Benjamin and Daniel have been lovers in a previous relationship. When Hendon tries to explain the complicated relationships to the young, inquisitive Fergus, he talks of a "complex twine." Rather than unknot it, Albee seems content with displaying the various threads that thicken it.

Albee employs a three-leveled raked stage, the only props beach chairs, placed in isolated groupings of two, demarcating discrete playing areas to which characters move in order to converse or deliver the three monologues interspersed throughout the play. There is almost no action. Albee's characters move only to position themselves for speeches, advancing, retreating, and ever circling around their own complicated stories, reveries, and pains. For example, Benjamin and Daniel move toward each other, and briefly reminisce about their past love affair, Benjamin wishing to return to the comfort of his lost love, Daniel clearly indicating that such a relationship is now impossible because of their marriages. Later, Albee brings Abigal and Cordelia, to the same spot, and they discuss their marriages to homosexuals. . . .

While the relationships between the two men and their wives take up much of the action of the play, the more arresting and strongly written sections concern another pair of contraries: youth and old age. In the scenes between Fergus, a young man seeking experience, and Hendon, an old man about to die, Albee offers his most harmonious and successful analogies. "There's a theory afoot . . . that we young and we old have things in common should bind us together against those in the middle," Fergus observes. It is a theory Albee has played with in *The American Dream,* where the young and old spoke a language that excluded the "middle aged." Unlike the character in the earlier play, the young man here is neither muscle-bound nor brain cramped. . . . (p. 102)

In tone Fergus resembles Albee's Grandma, her old people laments are echoed, in strikingly similar rhythms, by Fergus's adolescent plaints. A naif still open to experience, not prematurely warped by American society as earlier avatars were, he provides, or could provide, a focus to the elaborate canvas Albee offers. In an early prospectus for the play, Albee indicated that the theme would center around "the possession of Fergus"; however, in its present form, *Finding the Sun* relegates the character to a peripheral position, where he is overshadowed by the numerous debates among the older couples. He actually disappears from the action after scene 17, following a long scene in which he attempts to play ball with Benjamin and Daniel and finds that they are unreceptive since they "have their own game," and a scene in which he stands silently behind his mother and Gertrude as the former laments her son's inevitable loss of grandeur, the "tarnish" she sees as a corollary of aging.

Fergus' departure is paralleled by three other events: the death of Hendon, the attempted suicide of Abigal, and the inclusion of Benjamin in the relationship of Daniel and Cordelia. Albee's brief program notes conclude, "The author believes the play examines how we are startled by the inevitable." While the death of an old man and the leave-taking of a youth may be both startling and inevitable, the attempted suicide of Abigal and the new relationship of the three remaining young characters do not convey equal force. Yet Albee seems to want

Benjamin's newfound role as surrogate child and lover to Cordelia and Daniel to be significant. When Cordelia accepts him, the sun suddenly moves behind a cloud as if signaling some important new alignment. However, the focus of the play does not support the dominance of this relationship. Perhaps Albee has attempted too many analogies in his one hour, one-act play. Rather than offering a structured scene, balanced and harmonious as his pointillist imagery would imply, he has created an over-abundant, busy composition, vivid at times but finally too cluttered and in need of refocusing.

Part of both the strength and the weakness of the work comes from Albee's handling of language. In the introductory scene, he is able to deftly sketch his characters with subtle alterations of a simple refrain. Abigal enters first, assertively beginning with the imperative, "Find the sun," and is echoed dutifully by the malleable Benjamin. Cordelia, deferring to Daniel, offers, "Find the sun, you said" and her husband, who continually hedges throughout the play, responds with a series of four questions: "Did I? Find the Sun? Well? So?" Edmee, the instructive mother enters next saying, "Finding the sun should always be your first action, Fergus," shifting the form from the imperative to the progressive, implying an ongoing search from which the title—and presumably Fergus' own continuing education—stems. . . . Unfortunately such quick effective dots of dialogue are balanced by some of Albee's most banal language, particularly in the reparatee between Benjamin and Daniel where Albee even manages to squeeze in a herpes joke. When he does allow one of his characters to attempt a summary of their complicated lives and strike a serious note, he turns to another playwright for the words. Daniel, in response to Benjamin's complaint, "It's hope-less, then," responds, "It's hopeless, then. What did Beckett say?: I can't go on; I'll go on?" Even presented as a question rather than in the original declarative form, the words seem inappropriate for the actions that have preceded them and point to the paucity of the struggle and the language that describes it.

Albee admitted that *Finding the Sun* is a work in progress and hopes to revise it. There is much that is strong and theatrical about the piece. It plays well . . . , thanks in large measure to the vivid personalities that Albee has created. What the play needs is a coherence, a blending of the contraries that now seem to swamp the canvas, not unify it. (pp. 102-03)

> *Linda Ben-Zvi, in a review of "Finding the Sun,"
> in* Theatre Journal, *Vol. 36, No. 1, March, 1984,
> pp. 102-03.*

MATTHEW C. ROUDANÉ

The most conspicuous element in Edward Albee's *The Man Who Had Three Arms* is its blatant assault on the audience. Whereas in *The Zoo Story, Who's Afraid of Virginia Woolf?, A Delicate Balance,* and *Seascape* Albee created a certain objective distance between the actor and the audience, the playwright banishes the fourth wall altogether in *The Man Who Had Three Arms.* "Himself," the protagonist fixed behind the podium, lectures his invisible audience for two acts, presenting his own ethical conflicts directly to both an imagined and real audience. . . . It's a Pirandellian audience, of course, for the audience is both the imaginary group of listeners attending the "Man on Man" lecture series and the actual theatergoer or reader. Except for the Man and the Woman, whose repartee with Himself is minimal, we the audience ineluctably become central participants in the drama.

The largely negative critical reception to the play may be understandable. Between the play's antimimetic texture, its alleged autobiographical nature (which Albee denies), and Himself's adamantine monologue of cruelty, critics found little to praise. Further, within the play's two-act structure, as Beckett scholar Vivian Mercier would say, nothing happens, twice. But what does occur—Himself's hostile account of his sudden rise to the top of fortune's wheel and his pathetic descent to the bottom—invites us to explore Albee's purpose. I would like to suggest that we may gain insight into Albee's dramatic theory and technique by considering the play's relationship with its fictional and actual audience.

Albee's Pirandellianism permeates the play. The stage directions, for instance, signal the multiple roles the Man and the Woman will assume, allowing them to complement or disagree with Himself's narrative when decorous. At one point the Man and the Woman become, respectively, a physician and a nurse, aiding Himself's account of the medical world's reaction to his third appendage. Earlier, when Himself mocks the Catholic Church, the Man suddenly appears in clergy garb and accuses the speaker, "You are a freak of nature." Also, like Pirandello before him, Albee embellishes scenes with a deliberate self-consciousness.... (p. 187)

Albee's Pirandellian technique, one employed in **The Lady From Dubuque,** functions on two important levels. First, such a technique invites the audience to question its willing suspension of disbelief. By calling attention to the very nature of theatricality, Albee experiments with the illusion of dramatic mimesis, challenging traditional responses to the theater. **The Man Who Had Three Arms** testifies to Albee's willingness to examine, in C. W. E. Bigsby's words, "the nature of theatrical experiment..." and his refusal "to accept conventional notions of theatrical propriety" [see *CLC,* Vol. 13].

Second, like [Pirandello's] *Six Characters in Search of an Author,* **The Man Who Had Three Arms** forces the audience to break down its barrier between itself and the actors. In **The Man Who Had Three Arms** Albee minimizes the barrier radically, however, involving the audience directly as participants throughout the action. At one point Himself talks to the audience, with the stage directions and dialogue suggesting the intimacy between the actor and spectator.... Albee does not direct Himself to start fighting with the actual audience, as Julian Beck had members of The Living Theatre do with his audience. Still, Albee creates an overly aggressive text, expanding the boundaries of theater as collective, communal spectacle. Albee discussed this point, observing the relatedness of the actors and audience within his theory of drama:

> In nine or ten of my plays, you'll notice, actors talk directly to the audience. In my mind, this is a way of involving the audience; of embarrassing, if need be, the audience into participation. It may have a reverse effect: some audiences don't like this; they get upset by it quite often; it may alienate them. But I am trying very hard to *involve* them. I don't like the audience as voyeur, the audience as passive spectator. I want the audience as participant. In that sense, I agree with Artaud: that sometimes we should literally draw blood. I am very fond of doing that because voyeurism in the theater lets people off the hook. **The Man Who Had Three Arms** is a specific attempt to do this. It is an act of aggression. It's probably the most violent play I've written.

The play's audience, for better or worse, stands as the recipient of the violence.

Himself puts into concrete voice Albee's Artaudian dramatic theory. By drawing "blood," Himself supports the use of cruelty as a means of purging oneself of demons, of effecting a sense of catharsis, two factors which seem germane to Artaud's theater of cruelty. Moments into the play, Himself chides the audience, but the sarcasm quickly transforms to the opprobrious verbal assault.... (pp. 188-89)

[In his monologue of cruelty], Himself not only chronicles the growth of his third arm and its enervating effect on his world, but implicates the audience throughout for contributing to his present condition. To be sure, his sudden fame had its positive points: he hobnobbed with British royalty; earned $25,000 an hour for public appearances; visited the White House; starred in ticker-tape parades; graced the covers of *People, Newsweek,* and *Times;* in brief, Himself became "the most famous man in the world." But the public, people like the omnipresent journalist he (may have) attacked, the fame, the wealth conspire, according to Himself, to undermine his sense of self-balance. Unable to deal with the decadence of celebrity-hood, Himself loses sight of objective reality: his marriage dissolves, his own agent hornswoggles him, and, after his mysterious arm disappears, the public discards him. That is why he stands as a last minute substitute speaker in this play, his last pathetic connection with a public he both needs and abhors.

On a thematic level, **The Man Who Had Three Arms** thus exposes the monstrous effects of stardom on the individual's spirit. The play addresses, for Thomas P. Adler, "contemporary America's almost ghoulish need for culture heroes [see excerpt above]."... Within this context, the public, the sycophants accentuate Himself's internal as well as external freakishness, canonizing him one moment, abandoning him the next, even though by his own admission he has *no* talent, has done nothing exemplary to achieve social accolades. As the third arm dissipates, so Himself's fame diminishes, reducing him to a pathetic figure consumed with self-pity. Like the unnamed hero in Pirandello's *When One Is Somebody,* Himself becomes a prisoner completely trapped within his (post)celebrity-hood. In Albee's own assessment, the play thematically charts

> the specifically American thing called "hype": the creation of celebrity. The play is about the creation of celebrity and the destruction of celebrity-hood, because his third arm starts going away ... So **The Man Who Had Three Arms** is about that particular kind of hype and celebrity: undeserved, unearned, and how we need it and how we destroy the person once we created him.

Albee explores the corrupting and transitory effect of "celebrity-hood" on the Great, the near-Great, and the pseudo-Great. On top of fortune's wheel one moment, relegated to the bottom the next moment, Himself experiences financial as well as spiritual bankruptcy. This is why near the close of the play he specifically reflects on the loss of his self. Himself's hostility towards the audience measures the intensity of such loss. His anger, his directly involving the audience in his world, is apparently his form of expiation. Disassociated from his self and the other, the hurlyburly of his life now producing a new form of freakishness, Himself closes the play with a loving plea to stay, a hateful cry to leave, a pitiful gesture to understand. Throwing over the podium, Himself thus begs:

> No one leaves until you apologizes to me!! I want an apology for all the years!! For all the humiliation!! *(Sudden change of tone; abrupt realization of futility; a great weariness)* Nah! You don't owe me anything. Get out of here! Leave me alone! Leave me alone!

(Curtain Starts; Himself notices.) (Off) No! Don't do that! Don't leave me alone! *(Out)* Stay with me. Don't . . . leave me alone! Don't leave me! Don't . . . leave me alone. *(Curtain completes itself)*

The ambivalence of Himself's closing lines reflects Albee's larger thematic concerns in the play. Himself does not wish to banish all people and institutions who have exacerbated his freakishness. Rather, he insists, without success, that those people and institutions not dismiss the private individual beneath the public facade. Himself's aggressive assault of the audiences belies his inner need for sympathetic understanding of his humanness. . . . Himself's social devoir seems so irreverent, his angry monody so relentless, of course, that he can never gain the audience's sympathy.

Many of Albee's past heroes protest honestly, what the existentialists would call authentically, against an absurd cosmos. Himself protests against a commercialized universe that divests him of self-freedom, understanding, and love. And Albee implicates the audience for its support of a Madison Avenue mentality promoting Himself's entrapment. As such, he represents the latest Albee hero who has the courage to face life without absurd illusions. As Albee remarked, ''The entire structure of what happens to Himself is based totally on absurdity; and it is precisely the absurdity that he's railing against.''

In theory and structure, in language and theme, *The Man Who Had Three Arms,* boldly attempts to extend the conventions of the contemporary theater. Perhaps Richard Schechner's following observations about contemporary theater will prove helpful in coming to critical terms with Albee's play:

> The poison of the commercial theatre has so soaked into our ways of thinking about theatre that even in experimental work a production is regarded as a success or a failure. . . . This is a stupid way of advancing theatrical thought: for why can't a work in the theatre be neither a success nor a failure but a step along the way, an event that yields some interesting data? . . . [Those] of us devoted to experimentation in the theatre need to be particularly rigorous in separating out from each of our works what is useful, regardless of the overall ''success'' of the project.

Albee exhibits an artistic courage to experiment, without regard to the play's commercial impact. However, I would like to conclude, but cannot, that the play succeeds in shocking the audience into self-awareness, in producing the catharsis we experience at the closure of *The Zoo Story* or *Who's Afraid of Virginia Woolf?. The Man Who Had Three Arms* never matches the multivalency of a Pirandello play, never achieves the cleansing effect of cruelty Artaud envisioned. This play may ''yield some interesting data,'' but it remains to be seen if it stands as ''useful'' material for future experiments. (pp. 189-92)

> *Matthew C. Roudané, ''A Monologue of Cruelty:*
> *Edward Albee's 'The Man Who Had Three Arms','*
> in Critical Essays on Edward Albee, *edited by Philip*
> *C. Kolin and J. Madison Davis, G. K. Hall & Co.,*
> *1986, pp. 187-92.*

DANA RUFOLO-HÖRHAGER

If one is a devotee of Albee's existentialist, anxiously American perspective on social intercourse, then [*Marriage Play*] is an event of distinct importance in the dramatist's thirty-year' career.

After several fuzzily metaphysical plays stretching back to the 1964 *Tiny Alice,* Albee in *Marriage Play* successfully combines his recent explorations into the meaning of life with the study of love and violence of his first play *The Zoo Story* and the marital dynamics of his most widely known play *Who's Afraid of Virginia Woolf?* And yet, *Marriage Play* is purged of the narrational clutter of all these early plays. It is a resonant, poetical, and cleanly hewn work, akin to his *Listening* (1976) and a continuation of his experiment with musical structure in *Box* and *Quotations from Chairman Mao Tse Tung* (1968). . . .

[The play's three] years of gestation have resulted in a carefully written piece. It begins with Jack returning home to reveal to his caring but cynical wife Gillian that his 'life is undergoing the profoundest change.' At work that day all the things around Jack, secretary included, suddenly seemed to be disconnected from him, strange and unknown.

Gillian suggests that Jack is having a 'dalliance' and her refusal to commiserate provokes Jack into making another entrance, and then another, mounting the same or nearly the same words in an effort to convince her of the genuineness of his distress. Gillian's wonderfully clever remark that perhaps they ought to 'put in a revolving door' promotes Jack to hit her. When this physical contact is introduced, his despair and her responses gain authenticity.

And so it goes. Jack announces, 'I am leaving you.' Gillian discloses that the book he so often sees her read is her 23 year long chronicle of their sexual experiences together, 'a record of our touching.' They fight. That means, they touch: a sort of violent orgasm. After the interval, she continues to mock him, they reminisce. The word 'nothing' comes up often. The talk turns to planting a garden, and Jack with T. S. Eliot-like insecurity claims, 'All that stands between the vision and the thing itself is me. Will I do it?' The final lines are uttered: Jack's, 'I'm leaving you,' and Gillian's, 'I know.'

Not unlike Samuel Beckett, Albee has here frozen action and converted the life-force into relentless self-absorption. Marriage in *Marriage Play* has become a wedding in the sense of welding; the male and female are two halves of a perpetual-motion machine which is propelled by a perfect balance between hostility and need. The characters are like two sumo wrestlers deadlocked. Yet, along with its beauty and balance, the excessive abstraction of the play has produced flaws. These two characters' universe seems sterile—significantly, the one reference to children during the play rings false and is likely to have been tacked on. One senses that the characters desire to live more fully than their author has allowed. (p. 34)

> *Dana Rufolo-Hörhager, ''Albee in Austria,'' in* Plays
> & Players, *No. 406, July, 1987, pp. 33-4.*

JEANNE LUERE

Marriage Play, Edward Albee's latest work, is a two-act, two-character play with a disturbing aura akin to that of his earlier *Who's Afraid of Virginia Woolf.* It focuses on a married couple and their belief that even a bad marriage is better than no marriage at all. (p. 108)

The play is structured so that its middle-aged and unhappy pair, Jack and Gillian, swing rhythmically back and forth between episodes of violence and calm, gall and honey. Sheer cacophony rings out in bitter times of jabbing and slapping, followed by harmony in their good times when they recall old love and touch each other. The fully staged marital battles give free reign to violence and reflect a trend in contemporary drama, where terror has reappeared as violence.

Like Voltaire, who advised his hero at the conclusion of *Candide,* "Go and cultivate your garden," Jack, who is distraught over sexual plateaus and other boredoms, is told to "Go plant . . . even if all you do is scatter the seeds." This advice comes from the lips of Gillian and seems to the husband only a placebo as he strives to regain the piquancy of his life.

For twenty-three years, Gillian has kept a record of the couple's "touching." Her journal contains over two thousand entries noting date, position, duration, effect, attendant conversation if any. As the curtain rises she is curled in her chair, alone for the moment, reciting aloud with smug pleasure selected intimate passages from her journal.

Jack and Gillian scratch and claw on the floor at the close of Act I, and the spectacle hits us hard. When the prone and caterwauling couple, bodies entwined and aroused, stop short, pull their upper torsos slightly apart, and look with wide-eyed interest at each other, we are forced to ask ourselves: will Albee make us unwilling voyeurs? But then a hard jab of a knee at a crotch breaks the clinch of the lower regions and we ease back with a twinge of shame at our error. The close of the play makes us squirm, with the pair by now inured to pain, husband and wife are sunk in the lackluster comfort of each one's special chair, relieved at having rounded off one more exercise in futility.

The play is not about why a relationship fails; rather it is a dramatization of why a failed one continues. Jack and Gillian hazard the words "vacuum," "void," and "nothingness," but cling to what they have, accept its anguish, perhaps in terror of facing a life with no relationship at all, a ritual-less vacuum sans birthdays and orchid corsages.

Their dread of nothingness is a personalization of mankind's primal fear of the unknown and uncertain. The play depicts what this fear engenders: a lethargic pseudo-serenity that too frequently follows halfway reconciliations after marital battles and precludes a real effort to resolve deeper issues.

In the play's marital battles, Albee—like playwrights Beckett and Pinter—settles for the impact of physical shock rather than opting for a gradual approach to violence through terror. Jarring blows to the head and hard kicks to the viscera occur to the tune of "you piece of filth" and "you withered woman." Unpremeditated as in life, these onslaughts often flash onstage unanticipated. Hence our imaginations have no time to work and we are deprived of much of the pleasure of terror. It takes time to make our flesh crawl.

Battles aside, the playwright does give its audience time to observe other interactions of the pair and to build up fears for them. Gillian responds to abuses (a blow to her head, a slur at her intellect, a slam of the door) with facetious retorts and smirks that are open invitations to more abuse. Whenever she sees Jack make a solid attempt to leave the marriage (apart from his cry-wolf attempts in Act I), she alerts herself to danger and calls upon her wiles to hold him. The impact of the play springs from the recognition that this wife—any wife—can live day to day more in terror of being left than in dread of being hit.

Albee, as director of his own play, has chosen a partly presentational style. Important passages begin as exchanges between Jack and Gillian but end as downstage or off-center monologues where the actors speak with eyes front. This presentational style appears more frequently in Act II than earlier, and at one point, when Jack relaxes on the rug between the couple's chairs for a second exploration of ". . . it used to mean something, . . ." the effect is static. Notwithstanding, the play comes alive onstage and arrests the audience through starkly contrasting visual elements to depict the couple's sometimes warm, sometimes cool reaction to each other's physical presence. When this "withered woman" wants to draw a show of affection from her mate, she attempts coy glances and sensual gyrations of her thin hips and shoulders to arouse him, but Jack's stolid response is just one delayed and feeble clap of palms that lie in his lap—a stark picture of a man unaroused. (pp. 108-09)

[Jack's weakness] is not the subservience of Albee's "daddies" in plays like ***American Dream*** and ***Sandbox,*** but rather a boring preoccupation with self along with a penchant for spouting philosophical hogwash at us. His efforts are mockingly assessed by Gillian as his "attempts at TROOF" (truth). (p. 109)

[Gillian is] a wise-acre, yet less shrewish and more likable than many earlier Albee women. Gillian emerges as the less dominant of the couple, yet one not to be bested.

The language of the play surges with rhetorical power. A flow of sound and sense comes at us through Albee's frequent use of classic lists. Gillian counts off for us the weaknesses of this man whom she had hoped so foolishly in her youth would fall in love with her. She flows through an extensive list of adjectives in a periodic phrase that paradoxically grows more lovely as it becomes more caustic, to the end that we sit motionless to absorb the full impact.

Language is also used for comic effect, as in Jack's attempts at rhetoric to make his wife take his anxieties seriously. But Gillian interjects an aside to the audience, "As the man said, 'No one talks like that,'" giving the playwright carte blanche to continue, after which Gillian ridicules Jack with the mocking judgment, "Rhetoric—you are not up to it!"

The power of the play's archetypal themes and the impact of its spectacle make it a disturbing evening of theatre. The terrifying undercurrent of Albee's play is the sense that while being human entails more than "being," it is relationships that create our existence, and the quality of those relationships defines the quality of that existence. Too often we may choose to become human corpses, emotional zombies, or worse, spiritual vampires, viciously, violently feeding on the very souls of our acquaintances to maintain our existence. (pp. 109-10)

Jeanne Luere, in a review of "Marriage Play," in Theatre Journal, *Vol. 40, No. 1, March, 1988, pp. 108-10.*

David Bottoms

1949-

American poet, novelist, and short story writer.

A native of Georgia, Bottoms evokes Southern locales and lifestyles in his poetry to explore themes related to domestic existence, the decline of tradition, and humanity's kinship with nature. Employing free verse and informal diction, Bottoms conveys experiences in the lives of ordinary individuals while creating works that are variously humorous, eccentric, poignant, and bleak. His poems detail particulars of the physical world yet are also rich in spiritual imagery due to a subtle use of metaphor that imbues his work with multiple layers of meaning. Although a few critics have faulted Bottoms's verse for self-consciousness, technical contrivance, and repetition of phrases and subjects, most admire his poetic craftsmanship and praise him for thematic continuity and vivid, evocative descriptions. Robert Penn Warren stated: "David Bottoms is a strong poet, and much of his strength emerges from the fact that he is temperamentally a realist. In his vision the actual world is not transformed but illuminated."

Bottoms's first major publication, *Shooting Rats at the Bibb County Dump* (1980), establishes his interest in rural and small-town Southern milieus. Divided into five thematically unified sections of short narrative poems, this volume utilizes such settings as honky-tonks, amusement parks, dumps, and grave-yards while focusing on universal concerns, including death, social and spiritual collapse, ancestral connections between past and present, and the alienation of individuals in the modern world. Populated by a menagerie of Southern characters whose attempts to flee desperate situations meet with varying degrees of success, these pieces often exude moods of disillusionment, despair, and spiritual desolation. Bottoms's next book, *In a U-Haul North of Damascus* (1983), develops ideas initiated in his first collection: ambivalence toward organized religion, the abiding nature of love and suffering, death, and the enduring presence of humanity's repressed primeval instincts. Several of the pieces in this volume center on domestic concerns, emphasizing relationships between responsibility, disillusionment, and maturity, the value of quotidian experience, and the redemptive powers of love. Critics noted Bottoms's use of metaphor and precise, casual language.

In *Under the Vulture-Tree* (1987), Bottoms discovers deeper meaning in the artifacts of everyday life while displaying greater openness and autobiographical focus. He continues his first-person narrative approach and makes use of such devices as montage and flashback to analyze humanity's struggle with its primordial urges and the natural world. Identifying fewer strained expressions and less striving for significance in this volume than in his previous works, reviewers praised Bottoms's unadorned presentations of incidents from daily life. Joel Conarroe observed: "[Bottoms] is clearly a meticulous craftsman whose highest pleasure is not in shooting rats or gigging frogs or killing squirrels . . . but in finding a language, supple and evocative, to communicate the implications of these experiences." Bottoms's novel, *Any Cold Jordan* (1987), focuses on a successful country music guitarist and his wife whose idyllic lifestyle is disrupted by marital problems, financial compli-

cations, and the musician's frustrations over the commercial aspects of popular music.

(See also *Contemporary Authors*, Vol. 105; *Contemporary Authors New Revision Series*, Vol. 22; and *Dictionary of Literary Biography Yearbook: 1983*.)

DAVID CLEWELL

Shooting Rats at the Bibb County Dump relies on strong narrative thrusts. Bottoms has some fine stories to sing. In a time when "imagination" is too often synonymous only with "invention," his narratives are refreshing reaffirmations that imagination is *recognition* as much as anything else. Mere invention, in outsmarting itself, is seldom capable of reaching beyond the moment of its own pyrotechnic brilliance. A keen sense of imagination pervades these poems, but it is significantly rooted in the speakers' immediate world. Rarely posing, they avoid generalized feelings of rhetorical reflection; they are *engaged* as well as *engaging*. As a result, the reader is comfortable participating in these poems. We are more than voyeurs watching a scene unfold. Eerily, we find some part of ourselves unfolding with Bottoms' characters, waiting to see how things will turn out *this* time. (p. 67)

Bottoms' best narratives are entertaining stories about individuals, and the speakers are single, identifiable voices making what they can out of what is happening. The poems are variously humorous, bizarre, pathetic, and grimly bleak. Whatever the tone, beauty lies in the poet's (and, consequently, the personae's) willingness to be modulated by the poem's music—his willingness to give up overt exertion and manipulative control, contributing to a sense that neither we nor the poet can necessarily count on what we *expect* to come next. We are lulled and started in interesting and significant ways that help us to understand what we discover.

Bottoms is a native Georgian, but I hesitate to label him a "regional" poet, even though so many of the poems reflect the South. Because he deals with specific characters and actions (not stereotypes and stereotypical poses) his poems are rooted in the larger region of a diverse imagination. **"Jamming With the Band at the VFW"** and **"Writing on Napkins at the Sunshine Club"** are two examples of the poet's desire and willingness to reach beyond a built-in atmosphere (in this case, a tavern) and to focus on particular people, movements, and human changes. Bottoms' South *is* rich in poetic possibilities, and his imagination recognizes and actualizes that richness. In doing so, Bottoms offers much more than a mere atmospheric tour of Southern back roads and bistros; he offers something more generally human, as in **"Writing on Napkins at the Sunshine Club"**: "All night a platinum blonde has brought beer / to the table, / asked if I'm writing love letters on the folded napkins, / and I've been unable to answer her / or find any true words to set down on the wrinkled paper."

In many of the more meditative and less narrative poems, Bottoms gets to the heart of his own obsessive concerns which underpin several of his longer poems. (pp. 67-8)

In his search for foundations the poet throws us back to primordial driving forces—something more remote from human . . . faith. In the humorous **"Crawling Out At Parties"** the speaker tells us "My old reptile loves the scotch, / the way it drugs the cells that keep him caged / in the ancient swamps of the brain." But the reptilian sensibility can't cut it at the party: "Out of date, he just can't swing / so slides back always to his antique home, / the stagnant, sobering water." In **"The Catfish"** the beached fish is called a "document of evolution," and the speaker goes on to throw it "back to the current of our breathable past." In many of the poems Bottoms looks back, through his characters, to the past—a time construed as somehow less complicated by considerations of faith and systems of belief that inevitably disintegrate.

Bottoms is a poet obsessed with human history, personal loss, and the frailty of systematic faith in the context of everyday life. Most of the time he puts these obsessions to efficient use. But any poet obsessed (and most, if not all, good poets are) is put in the immediate danger of self-imitation. Bottoms is already a good enough poet to have to be concerned about this danger—one that he slips into a few times in this collection. **"A Trucker Drives Through His Lost Youth"** is one of the highlights of the book, but **"A Trucker Breaks Down"** covers the same ground, coming off the worse for wear after we've experienced both. . . . Little is gained by including both poems in the collection. The first is far more riveting, musical, and immediately human. Likewise, **"All Systems Tower and Collapse"** overshadows **"All Systems Break Down."** Taken in-

dividually, they are competent works, but both poems suffer from the inevitable juxtaposition. When images recur in various poems, the effect can be one of continuity, of explorations of obsessions. There is ample evidence of this positive force in *Shooting Rats.* But when repeated images emerge in the context of repetitive strategies and subsequent developments of the poems themselves, the effect is one of diffusion.

Bottoms treads this fine line again in the book's final section. These poems about sick and dying grandparents weave in and out of each other in mostly effective ways, and the final poem, **"Speaking Into Darkness,"** is the standout of the group. Yet the final section of the book squirms like an uncertain appendage, not belonging to the body (diverse as it is) of the book's first fifty pages.

But these few problems are relatively minor in comparison to the exciting accomplishments that make *Shooting Rats at the Bibb County Dump* such an exhilarating book. Bottoms will do well riding his obsessions, discovering the new places they lead him, the new obsessions that are bound to spring from the old. These are human poems, soaked in an accessible and compassionate imagination. They are full of this real world's potential for magic, for rejuvenation through recognition and action. For Bottoms "making do" no longer suffices; survival means *seeing again*, making new. I will follow this much-needed sensibility as long as he remains firm in his conviction that—no matter how fashionable invention has recently become—"we must let the water turn an image back on us, / learn to look inside it and find what magic remains" (from **"Learning to Let Water Heal"**). (pp. 68-9)

David Clewell, "Vital Assurances," in The Chowder Review *No. 14, Spring-Summer, 1980, pp. 64-9.*

DAVID M. CICOTELLO

[*Shooting Rats at the Bibb County Dump*] is divided in five sections: **"Into the Darkness We're Headed For,"** **"Country and Western,"** **"All the Animal Inside Us,"** **"How Death Isolates,"** and **"No Ticket For the Body to Travel On."** These titles then become the distinguishing metaphors of the poetry in each chapter.

Included in the first section is **"Shooting Rats at the Bibb County Dump,"** the title poem which focuses on the recreational violence of a midnight rat hunt. Drunk on beer and whiskey, the revellers paralyze the rats with car headlights and then shoot indiscriminately. Bottoms deftly captures the irony of such behavior: "We drink and load again, let them crawl / for all they're worth into the darkness we're headed for." This chapter also contains the legendary old Jack of **"The Drunk Hunter,"** a man who "would never come back empty handed." In a hauntingly ambiguous conclusion, old Jack does not return but "In two or three days / they will tell what found him in the deeper woods."

Truck drivers, farmers, and country and western musicians populate Chapter 2, **"Country and Western."** But of special merit in this section are the faith healers of both **"The Lame"** and **"The Faith Healer Come to Rabun County."** Bottoms expertly controls the tone of the **"The Lame,"** shifting from a mood of expectation. . . . to one of brutal objectivity, irony, and understatement. . . .

The poems in **"All the Animal Inside Us"** examine the curious biological ties that link the "ancient swamps of the brain" with our strange cousins: animals. **"The Catfish"** is exemplary of this section. After watching a fisherman discard a catfish "too small to keep," the persona is mysteriously compelled to leave his car and walk to the curb where "the catfish swimming on the sidewalk / lay like a document on evolution." The speaker then returns the fish to water, to "the current of our breathable past."

Three poems comprise **"How Death Isolates,"** including the notable **"Learning to Let Water Heal."** A vacation trip to Cumberland Island provides the speaker of this poem with more than momentary escape. The island "looks like an older time / darker men still belong to," where "Gullahs . . . know the healing power of water" and "Indonesians . . . sprinkle the body / with water and spices." The speaker and the reader are urged to contemplate how "we must let the water turn an image back on us, / learn to look inside it and find what magic remains."

The final chapter is devoted to six poems which, collectively, deal with the final rite of passage: the onset, the progression, and the aftermath of death. The grandmother of **"After the Surgery,"** whose "cure / wasn't written in the cards," thrives for two months "on fluids" and finally leaves the hospital, "a white withered bud." The discursive **"Speaking Into Darkness"** and two companion poems, **"The Sun"** and **"The Sun"** (the second a pattern poem), focus on the agonizing death and funeral of a grandfather. (pp. 312-13)

An exceptional volume, *Shooting Rats at the Bibb County Dump* marks a propitious beginning for David Bottoms. The settings are Southern and whether a truck driver, a bar maid, a faith healer, a drunken hunter, or a vandal, these characters consistently reveal traits of purposelessness and ennui: two inescapable and symptomatic features of *all* American life. These are short narrative poems of admirable poetic craft that owe a thematic debt to the rituals of life and to the irreparable losses of life. It is a volume that will repeatedly instruct and delight the reader. (p. 313)

David M. Cicotello, "Loss and Ritual in the South," in Prairie Schooner *Vol. 55, Nos. 1 & 2, Spring & Summer, 1981, pp. 311-13.*

CHARLES BERGER

It shouldn't come as a shock to learn that the author of *Shooting Rats at the Bibb County Dump* teaches writing courses at a university, nor that his volume is carefully constructed to lead the reader from a gutsy opening piece like **"The Drunk Hunter"**—"Spun on a flat rock / his whiskey bottle points out magnetic north"—to a gushy finale addressed to the poet's grandfather: "I am holding nothing in my clenched hands. / Speaking into darkness is the closest I can come to prayer." David Bottoms is yet another American vitalist, friend of truckers and hunters, who turns out to be absorbed primarily in the making of his own poems. In other words, another narcissistic poet. . . .

True words for Bottoms often seem to consist of place or brand names: Pabst or Red Man, Roswell (Georgia), Western Sizzler, Moultrie, Golden Eagle Motor Inn. He has a sharp but somewhat self-conscious eye; and despite the Country and Western settings, I don't hear the inflection of the region in Bottoms's poetry:

> The girl in bluejean shorts
> walks by our table and gives us the once over,
> eyes painted like we used to paint ours before ball games.

This is good description, but only description. It would be nice to hear some of these people talk, if only to disrupt the patness of these poems—or convince us that the poet is listening. Bottoms has a tendency to sentimentalize his subjects, whether writing about others or himself, and he doesn't want any jarring noises. This is true even of the dead rats down at the Bibb County Dump, who die rather too emblematically: "We drink and load again, let them crawl / for all they're worth into the darkness we're headed for." The problem is that when David Bottoms reaches for his gun he hears the word culture. (pp. 41-2)

Charles Berger, "Laurels," in Poetry, *Vol. CXL, No. 1, April, 1982, pp. 35-50.*

KELLY CLASPILL

Any unsuspecting "Fish & Game" patron could be snared into reaching for David Bottoms' *Shooting Rats at the Bibb County Dump,* and subsequently become fascinated with the book's content. Bound between the covers are, yes, poems filled with hunters, truckers, and dope smokers, as well as booze drinking, bar frequenting good-old-boys and their women. I don't mean to suggest the subject matter is limited to these topics alone, nor that any one with any "refinement" will find them prosaic—actually, quite the opposite. With tight, unadorned diction, Bottoms delves beneath the colloquial surface of a TV-oriented stereotype to encapsulate in his one-page poems the frontierless emptiness, the plasticity of a down-home-gone-urban ancestry. **"Jamming With the Band at the VFW"** melds the old with the new to possess a moment, to inhabit an echoing inheritance. . . . (p. 182)

Static sincerity is projected onto a fluid, changing instability and is carefully immortalized in words that leave the sense of motion intact. This tenacious resilience is flexed in **"Writing on Napkins at the Sunshine Club,"** in which a quarter-pocketed "man with a heart/tattoo and [having] a five-dollar thing for Hank and Roy," feeds a jukebox with "nothing recorded since 1950." In the glow of a Big Red Man pinball machine, beer guts flash with purple, yellow, and orange. The frustrated napkin author can't

> find any true words to set down on the wrinkled paper.
> What needs to be written is caught already
> in Hank's lonesome wail,
> the tattooed arm of the man who's all quarters,
> the hollow ring and click of the tilted Red Man,
> even the low belch of the brunette behind the flippers.

Somewhere in this lucid imagery we are convinced that whatever needed to be written was.

A recurrent symbol of darkness is foreshadowed in the book's first section, **"Into the Darkness We're Headed For."** Its affinity with death, nature, and predatory instinct is evident in **"Below Freezing on Pinelog Mountain."** . . . (pp. 182-83)

The title poem, **"Shooting Rats at the Bibb County Dump,"** is set in a dump at night where headlights illuminate drunk yahoos picking off light-transfixed rats. The graphic imagery resolves with an ironically deflated challenge:

> It's the light they believe kills.
> We drink and load again, let them crawl
> for all they're worth into the darkness we're headed for.

Another glaring aspect of the country and western mode is the stereotypical platinum blond beehives, tight skirts, and deep red fingernails that apparently constitute all of womankind. However, the ultimate exploit involves the gang rape of a young woman in **"The Farmers."** Committed in a barn, the bullish act seems, appropriately, animal-like. . . . This subordination and consequent alienation of women intensifies the overwhelming isolation so prevalent throughout the book.

The regression of women, as well as of the masculine speaker, is completed in **"All The Animal Inside Us,"** when the brain is referred to as "An old reptile at the top of my spine." **"Crawling Out at Parties"** is exemplary because of the consistency of its extended metaphor. . . . Earthy analogy engages the primeval with the present—sometimes building, sometimes ebbing, but always sluggish until given the right environment. In **"Hunting on Sweetwater Creek,"** a man enters the woods at dusk and discovers a competency for hunting he never knew he had, a talent that is inversely proportional to the light in the sky. (pp. 183-84)

Slowly we detect a yearning quest for an answer in the impeccable diction, the clever line breaks, and facilitative social tones of David Bottoms—some sort of truth, some sort of frame to embrace the here and now in context with the past and the future, or as Bottoms states in **"Scavengers at the Palm Beach County Landfill,"** "a redemption for all things cast aside." The poems become progressively more hopeless and disillusionment is tangible in the dumps, the graveyards, the waste— be it genetic, religious, or commercial—ultimately, the rubble of "any philosophy that demands the found absolute of any method." . . . (p. 185)

It is in the last two sections, **"How Death Isolates"** and **"No Ticket For the Body to Travel On,"** that an earlier poem's resolution, "It's a strange place where graves go / so much of us already geared for the journey," actually develops maturity. Death looms over every shifting tone—indignation, desperation, acknowledgement, resignation. The reactionary hopefulness carried over from **"All the Animal Inside Us"** is repeated one last time in the poem **"Learning to Let Water Heal."** . . . Yet emptiness is fulfilled in **"Speaking Into Darkness"** as the author laments over his grandfather's corpse:

> It was the failure of needles, tubes, scalpels,
> stethoscopes, electrocardiograms,
> all things that calculate precisely
> probabilities of survival.
> It was all the long days you both spent dying
> while medicine lost magic by degrees.
> It was the loss of magic itself.

Death seems to be the earlier prophesied redemption itself. This idea of rebirth is sometimes tinged with irony, as in **"Rubbing the Faces of Angels"**:

> All over Charleston
> things will move routinely toward one fact.
>
> Yes, after all this time
> we are coming to judge death less critically . . .

or more reverent, as these lines from **"The Sun"** imply. Looking at his casketed grandfather, the author observes:

> seemed no different from the people you gathered
> around you. We were all the same function.
> All were waiting for the same revival.
> All were waiting for the sun to come up
> again on the other edge of the world.

Another poem, also entitled **"The Sun,"** is a metamorphic rendition that follows its parent by a page. Apparently jumbled, but a surprisingly structured version of the first, it seems an architectural manifestation of Bottoms' assertion in his final poem, "My head is a kaleidoscope of crossed images." . . .

In this last poem, the longest one in the book, the similes are poignant, and David Bottoms' imagery is amassed and offered with no excuses. The subject of death, which dominates this section, finally induces a flood of agitated soul searching in **"Speaking Into Darkness."** Ancestral and biblical antiquity is juxtaposed with the present and denounced, the present juxtaposed with tradition and similarly denounced. Only a black continuity is left uncompromised—the sole "system" that never falls. Thus, we finally realize this haunting timelessness which appeared to be the framework of a search, the island of a treasure hunt, has crystallized into the treasure itself. (pp. 185-87)

> *Kelly Claspill, in a review of "Shooting Rats at the*
> *Bibb County Dump," in* Quarterly West, *No. 16,*
> *Spring-Summer, 1983, pp. 182-87.*

JOEL CONARROE

The setting for Bottoms' title poem [in ***In a U-Haul North of Damascus***] is a small Georgia town on Route 45. If the implied juxtaposition of a rental truck and the Biblical Damascus creates a small *frisson*, this is of less importance than the evocation of a specific American locale. The poems, in fact, are filled with place names, especially of the area's rivers—the Wakulla, the Etowah, the Ocmulgee. In this context Damascus is not a remote historical city but a place where 18-wheelers pull off the road.

Bottoms is a solitary observer who takes in and transmutes into lucid English the flora, fauna, sounds, and sights of a landscape he knows intimately. We are made to see "the sea oats wash back and forth in a gold froth," to hear the frogs' "bass-throb belching in the starless night" and the wind "cutting high notes over reeds of broken glass." The play of words on "high notes" and "reeds" is typical of this poet, who likes to discover secondary meanings in ordinary locutions. The speaker of the title poem, for example, after leaving his wife, finds himself moving "from one state / to another," for once "in the driver's seat." In a poem about a father teaching his son to lay down a bunt, we can be sure to find a reference to "sacrifice." Time and again the literal is translated into the figurative, as when the speaker sees a gull catch a bait in midair, and suggests "We've all swallowed a line or two, / a real estate deal, some bad investment of faith. . . ."

The imagery of being hooked, or trapped, is recurrent, suggesting a world in which Faulkner's wilderness has been domesticated to "half-acres of razored grass, / trellised vines, boxwoods manicured by wives." When these wives are not taming suburban yards they are worrying about groceries, throwing dishes in anger, or guarding the Gatorade (and asking foolish questions) while the males play baseball. Women clearly represent a threat in this good-old-boys world in which true satisfaction comes from throwing knives into animals—even if they are merely Magic Marker images on plywood squares— gigging frogs on the Allatoona, or drinking beer on a fishing boat. **"Kinship"** is dedicated to James Dickey, and one finds in several of the poems, with their emphasis on guns and adolescent values, a sensibility that suggests the author of *Deliverance*. The titles of Bottoms' first two books, in fact, reveal something of his muscular posturing: ***Jamming With the Band at the VFW*** (1978), and ***Shooting Rats at the Bibb County Dump*** (1980).

I say posturing because he is clearly a meticulous craftsman whose highest pleasure is not in shooting rats or gigging frogs or killing squirrels (why in the world would anyone want to do these things?) but in finding a language, supple and evocative, to communicate the implications of these experiences. I should stress that one need not be attracted to Bottoms' material (as I obviously am not) to find his poems satisfying. They are sensuous, accessible, and, well, entertaining, a quality not always associated with contemporary poetry.

> *Joel Conarroe, in a review of "In a U-Haul North of Damascus," in* Book World—The Washington Post, *August 7, 1983, p. 4.*

PENELOPE MESIC

David Bottoms has a gift for the deliberately graceless title. His previous volume was called *Shooting Rats at the Bibb County Dump,* from which readers easily deduced that the poet is a Southern outdoorsman. That the poet remains, and [*In a U-Haul North of Damascus*] reflects his pastimes: **"In a Jon Boat During a Florida Dawn"** is immediately followed by **"Drunks in the Bass Boat," "Sounding Harvey Creek,"** and, at a little interval, by **"Sleeping in the Jon Boat."** Unsurprisingly, the poet's mind runs a little in a groove and phrases of description repeat very occasionally from poem to poem. But the reality each poem strives for is present; the avowal "What I love about water is mystery" (**"Sounding Harvey Creek"**) is made less commonplace by a landscape strange enough to force the poet into strong physical reality, upon which Bottoms relies as the one eternal verity. Here is his certainty, deep in the flesh and its quickening to sounds in the greyish dark, or the tremor of surrounding air or water. (p. 296)

A particularly fine poem is **"Under the Boathouse,"** a narrative of true exactness, which, after the poet's sudden fall and entanglement underwater, inventories subaqueous debris and physical sensations and answers the feeling of "shock of all / things caught by the unknown" with the relief of breaking upward into "the loved, suffocating air hovering over the lake." The balance of "loved" and "suffocating" reveals Bottoms's particular, stubborn truthfulness, which will not be shifted even by desperate need and which suggests that gratitude for things as they are requires that their qualities be mercilessly examined. (pp. 296-97)

> *Penelope Mesic, in a review of "In a U-Haul North of Damascus," in* Poetry, *Vol. CXLIII, No. 5, February, 1984, pp. 296-97.*

MICHAEL CASS

The settings in Bottoms' poems are almost always dramatic and unusual. The title poem of his first book, *Shooting Rats at the Bibb County Dump,* illustrates this, as do other poems in that volume. The poems, set in honky-tonks and amusement parks, evoke both the humanity of "good old boys" and semi-outlaws and the strongest connections all of us have with nature. One poem recalls college boys sitting in an open grave, singing gospel music (**"I'll Fly Away"**) and smoking marijuana (**"We bury ourselves to get high"**), unaware, as the poet is, how "high" they are going, all the way to death, "So much of us already geared for the journey." Another poem, chilling and yet inviting, enters the imagination of vandals in a cemetery.

There are similar actions in *In a U-Haul North of Damascus*: drunken hunters vandalize an abandoned church; someone steals or "repossesses" an automobile; in a drunken duel no one is hurt, yet the result is more conclusive than if someone were;

a nervous guard, part of an illegal narcotics operation, hides with his surprisingly meaningful World War II rifle in a pine thicket near a clearing where an airplane is to make a drop. There are, however, poems with more domestic settings: a husband fleeing his marriage after the mutual pain of his wife's miscarriage; nearly middle-aged men playing softball as their wives wonder why they do it; a son's remembering and appreciating his father's way of teaching him baseball; children in a **"Nativity Scene"** shivering on the church lawn; a fisherman fascinated with mystery returning to his split-level suburb "occupied by men / who sleep and and dream of deals and mortgages, / point spreads and golf swings."

A careful eye and tightly controlled language convert dramatic action to dramatically rendered meaning in these poems, and the meanings are often reversals of what the actions seemed first to imply. Bottoms' poems are convincing at the literal level and yet are also successful as metaphorical elevations to the level of suggested meaning—which is to say that they "work."

Many of the poems in this volume are concerned with mystery and very often involve the imagery of water. In **"The Drowned,"** a dead man floating face down in a river, suspended in the limbs of a fallen tree, gazes "into the deepest part of the Etowah / as though fascinated by something I couldn't see." (pp. 743-44)

One of the mysteries which Bottoms pursues seems to be the relationship of beauty and danger. At least a third of the poems record a fascination with danger. The fisherman returned to his sterile suburb (**"Sleeping in the Jon Boat"**) wonders why he dreads "the first wave of sleep" and why he wakes fearing his own hand, which had dangled in the water during his earlier sleep in the boat. That sleep had been "an entrance into water," "a dream of diving," his hand's "white, loose flesh melting together / between the bones." Now he is afraid to go to sleep, because something dangerous may occur under the water's surface, something perhaps like a transformation. . . . (p. 744)

In reading several of these poems together, one senses that the poet recognizes that beauty can be dangerous and danger can be beautiful. If beauty is "another word for reality," as the epigraph from Warren states, and beauty is dangerous, then danger and beauty are both deeply part of reality. The poem **"Sounding Harvey Creek"** reveals a copperhead snake "burdening the reeds / with a beautiful danger." What the poet "sounds" is mystery.

This "sounding" may serve to illuminate the complexities of human love. In one poem, two lovers have come to an abandoned motel in the wilderness "to fill a vacancy," and they do so: among shredded mattresses and "caked layers of leaf-rot" they celebrate "the comfort, the company of ruin." Their love participates in and affirms the resurrective durability of nature. In the title poem [**"In a U-Haul North of Damascus"**], however, a husband is unable to endure the ruin of his wife's miscarriage. Having run away, heading from west Georgia to Florida in a U-Haul containing his few possessions, he stops in a makeshift parking lot for trucks north of Damascus, Georgia, and thinks of the sunlight "falling / through the windows of my half-empty house." Those who have suffered miscarriages are closer to the old knowledge, now diminished by modern obstetrics, that mortal danger is one of the implications of the beauty of erotic love. The speaker of the poem begins to realize that, like Paul, he is "another sinner who needs to be blinded / to see" that suffering as well as love is binding.

"Converted" near Damascus, he will return to make the half-empty house full again. Danger and beauty are imbricated aspects of reality.

There is much more that is rewarding in this book. The poems **"Kinship," "In a Jon Boat During a Florida Dawn," "Wakulla: Chasing the Gator's Eye,"** and **"The Copperhead"** continue from Bottoms' earlier work the theme of connections between animal and human nature. In **"Sign for My Father, Who Stressed the Bunt,"** Bottoms does his part in attempting to revive the serious pun in American poetry. In **"Under the Boathouse"** the dramatic suspense and precision of language is breathtaking: this poem should evoke gasps at a poetry reading. Poems that may initially seem to be expressions of machismo, like **"Local Quarrels,"** eventually reveal not only the poet's awareness of the ludicrous but also an ironic seriousness. David Bottoms is one of our strongest poets. (p. 745)

> *Michael Cass, "Danger and Beauty: David Bottoms'* *'In a U-Haul North of Damascus',"* in The Southern Review, *Louisiana State University, Vol. 20, No. 3, Summer, 1984, pp. 743-45.*

PUBLISHERS WEEKLY

A critically acclaimed poet (his first collection, *Shooting Rats at the Bibb County Dump,* won the 1979 Walt Whitman Award) has written a haunting first novel [*Any Cold Jordan*]. Billy Parker, probably the best flat-pick guitarist anywhere around Tallahassee, Fla., lives with his wife Jean in a pleasant house by a pond outside of town. Billy's performances bring in a steady income, he does a lot of fishing, and the couple seem to have an idyllic, laid-back life. But both the marriage and the music have gone sour. Jean, desperate to have a baby, but prevented by an unspecified ailment of Billy's, conducts affairs with other men. Meanwhile Billy finds it increasingly difficult to reconcile his ideas about what music should be with the restrictions imposed by the pop marketplace and his own abilities. Enter Jack Giddens, a Special Forces Vietnam vet who leads Billy deeper and deeper into danger and the novel to a violent climax. Bottoms has fashioned a meditation on the possibilities for a romantic life in our time. They're not very good, he concludes, yet still worth exploring. This is hardly earth-shattering news, but the precision, force and lyricism of Bottoms's writing make his moral fresh again.

> *A review of "Any Cold Jordan," in* Publishers Weekly, *Vol. 231, No. 8, March 6, 1987, p. 104.*

PETER L. ROBERTSON

[*Any Cold Jordan*] by award-winning poet Bottoms is a tale of frustrated ambitions and hard compromises. When Jack proposes intercepting drug money on a Florida country road, Billy, a struggling country-music guitar player, reluctantly agrees. His alliance with Jack represents an emotional crossroads. Billy is frustrated by the commercial aspects of country music and embittered by his wife's unhappiness and infidelity; he finds release only in drifting about on his "jon boat" and fishing the rural waters of northern Florida. Bottoms' novel develops in a slow, languid manner that mirrors the story's Florida landscape. Although the book's characters are not as fully developed as one might wish, the author brings the countryside to life vividly, and the sudden bursts of violence, as events drive Billy to a crisis point, are effectively understated.

> *Peter L. Robertson, in a review of "Any Cold Jordan," in* Booklist, *Vol. 83, No. 15, April 1, 1987, p. 1176.*

BETTINA DREW

These poems of Georgia country life [in *Under the Vulture-Tree*] by the 1979 Walt Whitman Award winner are highly accessible. The merciful vultures of the title poem [**"Under the Vulture-Tree"**] and a horse caught in a frozen pond, "half a white statue in a fountain of ice," are indeed memorable, and Bottoms grapples effectively with the dead that "stare fish-blind into the lights of hospitals" or, like his father, hauntingly await doom in World War II photographs. But most poems are told in a first-person narrative that becomes wearing, as the poet doesn't quite manage to be the vehicle for universality such a voice demands. The story-telling and the focus on our struggle with nature will appeal to some, but readers hungry for rich language and deep insights may be disappointed.

> *Bettina Drew, in a review of "Under the Vulture-Tree," in* Library Journal, *Vol. 112, No. 9, May 15, 1987, p. 87.*

BILL OTT

In his third collection [*Under the Vulture-Tree*]—following *Shooting Rats at the Bibb County Dump* and *In a U-Haul North of Damascus*—Bottoms more than justifies the many critical accolades that have come his way in the past several years. Although these poems address many of the same subjects treated in the earlier work—southern life, animals, banjo pickers, his father—they reflect an ever-evolving poetic consciousness, an ability to find new levels of meaning in the artifacts of the everyday. As before, violence and beauty are inextricably linked in Bottoms' view of nature, both animal and human; his version of pastoral is never tranquil, teeming instead with images of death—the vulture's "one slow wing beat, the endless dihedral drift"—that somehow serve to vivify the living. Above all, Bottoms is a narrative poet whose stories (whether about touring a fallout shelter, **"Shingling the New Roof,"** or stealing a desk on which his father once carved his initials) move carefully but inevitably from the specific to the general, from the sound of a ball-peen hammer cracking a window pane to a sense of the futility of recapturing the past. A remarkable achievement. (pp. 1712-13)

> *Bill Ott, in a review of "Under the Vulture-Tree," in* Booklist, *Vol. 83, No. 22, August, 1987, pp. 1712-13.*

VERNON SHETLEY

David Bottoms's poems inhabit two contiguous landscapes, one the small-town and rural South, the other a realm of elemental nature often found lurking just beyond the zone of human habitation. In the peopled world are love, loss, and a desperate caring energized by the proximity of nature's ruthless otherness, which continually reminds us of the brute fact of death. Nature hints at transcendence, an order beyond the merely human, in those moments when, Bottoms writes, "I get so entranced by the stars swelling / in the black sky, I believe they're busting / to tell me something." But that promise of revelation goes always unfulfilled, the natural order is forever opaque to the human understanding, and so the only emblem of transfiguration Bottoms offers is the flock of vultures, "who pray over the leaf-graves of the anonymous lost, / with mercy enough to consume us all and give us wings.'' Into the fierce irony of the pun on ''prey'' disappears the sentimentalist's hope for accommodation between man and the earth he inhabits. Bottoms honors the natural world in his attempt to see it clear-sightedly, but it is only in the blind grip of the instinct for survival that human and natural become one.

Under the Vulture-Tree is Bottoms's third collection. His style has undergone a modest evolution toward a greater openness, with a correspondingly increased autobiographical emphasis. Bottoms reaches for the ''deep image'' less frequently in this new volume than in his previous work, and the proportion of poems based on enigmatic or apparently imaginary narrative lines has diminished. Bottoms now stands firmly within the strain, descended from the *Lyrical Ballads* through Frost, of plain-style presentation of incidents of everyday life. This style derives its energy from the juxtaposition of stark simplicity in diction and verse-form (Bottoms writes a loose, conversational *vers libre*) with a great sophistication of narrative device— montage, flashback, jump cut, dissolve. The danger of any plain syle, of course, is poeticism—the poeticism induced by the anxiety that the verse will collapse into mere prose—and Bottoms suffers some occasional lapses: ''At nine below, water expands into rock, the pipes peel / back like ripe fruit'' is probably stronger without the simile. For the most part, however, Bottoms's lines are clean and unadorned, a near-transparent medium for recording the rhythms of incident and reflection that weave these poems.

The technical development of Bottoms's work has gone hand in hand with its increasingly personal focus; the ''deep image'' necessarily belongs to a poetry of nature, but the best work in *Under the Vulture-Tree* seems to me for the most part not Bottoms's confrontations with the elemental world but rather his small-scale dramas of caring and estrangement. **''White Shrouds''** is Bottoms's version of ''Frost at Midnight,'' swerving from that great original in seeing the frost not as an emblem of communion between mind and nature but as an enveloping stasis hostile to the dynamic principle of life. A hard freeze and power failure reduced the poet and a loved one to a primitive shift for survival, and provide the occasion as well for a modest but affecting expansion of sympathy towards a suffering mankind. . . . And in **''The Guitar''** that instrument becomes an uninsistently handled objective correlative for marital misunderstanding. . . . One hopes that this vein of Bottoms's work will deepen and expand in the future. (pp. 100-01)

Vernon Shetley, in a review of ''Under the Vulture-Tree,'' in Poetry, *Vol. CLII, No. 2, May, 1988, pp. 100-01.*

Paul (Frederick) Bowles

1910-

American novelist, short story writer, translator, composer, poet, travel writer, autobiographer, and scriptwriter.

Perhaps best known for his novel *The Sheltering Sky,* which is regarded as a masterpiece of existentialist literature, Bowles is an influential author who explores the fundamental discord between Western and Moslem cultures. An American expatriate who has lived for many years in Tangier, Morocco, Bowles sets most of his fiction amid the exotic communities and harsh climate of Northern Africa. His protagonists are usually rootless Americans or Europeans who travel to primitive lands in hopes of shedding the nihilism and malaise instilled by Western society but instead encounter misunderstanding, hostility, and death. Critics often compare Bowles's work to that of Edgar Allan Poe for its preoccupation with psychic processes, depictions of macabre violence, and detached narrative style.

Bowles's initial artistic ambitions involved poetry and music. The stories of Poe, read to him by his mother when he was a child, profoundly influenced his imagination. Bowles's first published poem, "Spire Song," appeared in the Paris journal *transition* when he was sixteen. He briefly attended the University of Virginia before studying music in New York under composer Aaron Copland. In 1931, Bowles traveled to Paris, where he met Gertrude Stein. She advised him to write fiction instead of poetry and to move to Morocco, a region which she believed would enhance his creativity. Bowles spent much of the 1930s and 1940s traveling between the United States, Europe, and Tangier, composing scores for the theater, and writing music reviews for the *New York Herald Tribune*. His interest in fiction was revived during the early 1940s when his wife Jane, whom he married in 1938, was working on her novel *Two Serious Ladies*. In 1947, Bowles stopped composing music and has since concentrated on literature.

The Sheltering Sky (1949) established Bowles as an important American novelist and set the thematic pattern for most of his subsequent fiction. In this work, three New Yorkers travel to Northern Africa, wander across the Sahara Desert, become separated, and are drawn into a series of bizarre experiences that lead to their loss of identity and sanity. O. B. Hardison, Jr. observed: "[Bowles's] travelers are aliens in their world in the manner explored by Camus in *L'etranger*. The existential sense of rational life as anguish, of consciousness as a thin wire stretched between death and animal instinct, is as powerful in *The Sheltering Sky* as the desolate infinity of the desert." Bowles's second novel, *Let It Come Down* (1952), traces the mental dissolution of a New York bank clerk after he relocates to Tangier and experiments with narcotics in order to erase his dreary past from his memory. In a paranoid, drug-induced state, the protagonist accidently kills an Arab acquaintance, and he spends the rest of the novel alone and hunted yet curiously satisfied with his situation.

The Spider's House (1955), considered by many critics Bowles's most conventional novel, laments the passing of the traditional Moroccan lifestyle by examining the effects of a national revolution on the son of a Moslem prophet. In *Up above the World*

(1966), an American couple vacationing in Latin America are kidnapped, brainwashed, and killed by a madman who thinks they have witnessed a murder that he committed. *Points in Time* (1982) is a fictionalized history of Morocco related through legends, historical anecdotes, and the lyrics of traditional songs. This work is divided into several sections, or "movements," that exhibit Bowles's musical training.

The major themes of Bowles's novels recur throughout his short fiction. In such collections as *The Delicate Prey and Other Stories* (1950), *The Time of Friendship* (1967), *Pages from Cold Point and Other Stories* (1968), and *Midnight Mass* (1981), Bowles investigates the unbridgeable differences between primitive and civilized cultures, the search for meaning in an absurd world, the failure of human relationships, and the destructive forces of nature. In a review of *Collected Stories, 1939-1976* (1979), Michael Krekorian noted that Bowles's short fiction "represents the work of an innovator in American literature who seeks to debunk apparent order residing deep within nature and to dismiss man's reasoning power over the world as irrelevant hallucination."

In his verse, gathered in *Next to Nothing: Collected Poems, 1926-1977* (1981), Bowles employs surrealism and musical language to convey humanity's impotence before the power of nature. As in his fiction, nihilism is a pervasive element of

Bowles's poetry. Bowles has also written several volumes of travel essays, including *Yallah* (1956) and *Their Heads Are Green and Their Hands Are Blue* (1963), and *Without Stopping: An Autobiography* (1972). In addition, he has translated into English numerous works from French, Arabic, and Moghrebi.

(See also *CLC*, Vols. 1, 2, 19; *Contemporary Authors*, Vols. 1-4, rev. ed.; *Contemporary Authors New Revision Series*, Vols. 1, 19; *Contemporary Authors Autobiography Series*, Vol. 1; and *Dictionary of Literary Biography*, Vols. 5, 6.)

MICHAEL KREKORIAN

There is little doubt that Paul Bowles is one of the most important—if largely unrecognized—influences on contemporary American literature. His novels and stories are startling, violent, and disturbing enough not to be easily forgotten. For over thirty years, Bowles has been exploring themes involving the contrasts between the primitive and civilized, the impossibility of love, and of nature that is typified by chaotic violence—breakthrough themes in the non-realistic tradition of contemporary literature. . . . *Collected Stories 1939-1976* covers over thirty years of his writing. Chronologically arranged, it marks the re-appearance of many out-of-print stories.

A strange transformation in character and setting takes place when we enter the world of the Bowles story. A "civilized" outsider finds himself or herself surrounded by the sounds and smells of the rain forests of Latin America or the harsh desert of North Africa. Something takes hold of this character immersed in this foreign setting as he or she moves among the strange sounds and colors of this world. The rattling sound of a jungle insect, the persistent growth of vegetation as it chokes out human activity, puts this character face to face with a violent topography—the booming silent sounds of the abyss. Contact with the primitive world seems to strike a corresponding chaotic chord which easily undermines the identity of the character—and of the reader.

The results are startling. In stories such as **"At Paso Rojo"** or **"Pastor Dowe at Tacate,"** a character becomes suddenly violent or sadistic, erratic and unpredictable as his or her civilized notions are shaken to their very roots. Bowles utterly rejects the traditional notion that nature equals serenity and order but instead sees, as many very recent writers do, nature as a violent exercise in disorder.

Human nobility is absent in these stories. In **"The Delicate Prey"** a young boy is raped and mutilated by a traveling companion, and this man is in turn methodically tortured when found out by neighboring villagers. A reader can never forget the transformation that takes place in a character called the Professor in **"A Distant Episode"** as his curiosity about primitive North American tribes is ended by violent capture and the slitting out of his tongue so that he will better serve his "new" purpose as valuable object and trained animal for the tribe. These pre-Kosinski stories clearly illustrate the disturbing results of an intersection between primitive and civilized mentalities, and most importantly reflect the violent act as central to the natural world.

The chronological arrangement of his collection demonstrates Bowles' development as a writer of stories containing vague undefined characters who are subservient to the horrors of a natural setting that develops a strangely character-like presence. (pp. 288-89)

This Bowles retrospective, **Collected Stories,** represents the work of an innovator in American literature who seeks to debunk apparent order residing deep within nature and to dismiss man's reasoning power over the world as irrelevant hallucination. As with the finest of contemporary works, the thrust of the Bowles story rests in the disjointed ambiguity of human activity rather than the germ of order in a world, as Kosinski put it, where identity cannot exist, only situations. Paul Bowles mixes disharmonious elements of reality, the jungles working within the imaginative framework of human-like impulses and actions, to create a character of chaotic situation, rather than a stable identity. This personification of the setting, in the end, meshes with the violent jungle of human situation—posing as human identity.

Thus, Bowles' **Collected Stories** take the arguable position that rationality and pragmatism, the hallmarks of contemporary Western Civilization—our "rage for order"—appear to be hollow gestures in the face of the jungles that appear before us or within us. (p. 289)

> *Michael Krekorian, in a review of "Collected Stories, 1939-1976," in* fiction international, *No. 12, 1980, pp. 288-89.*

WENDY LESSER

The problem with reviewing Paul Bowles's **Collected Stories** is that any description of their content would be too specific, would belie their hard-won lack of definition by giving them too firm an outline. Plot summary has the same effect on these stories that conversion to film has on good novels: by giving you an image to hold in your mind, the film—however faithful to the novel—forever cuts off imaginative possibilities that the novel made available. The most essential aspect of Bowles's stories—the way in which things *don't* get said explicitly—is inevitably lost in any discussion of their content. Yet these stories must be talked about, because it is rare for any writer's "Collected Works" (and this one spans 47 years of writing) to present the kind of uniform perfection that this book does.

"Uniform" is a misleading word here, in that it suggests lack of variety. Certainly the 39 stories in this collection could not be more various. They range in setting from South American jungles to mountainous villages to African deserts to the subways of Manhattan. They deal with virtually every imaginable intimate human relationship: husband to wife, parent to child, sister to sister and brother to brother, employee to employer, pastor to congregation, killer to victim, human to animal, lover to lover, and stranger to stranger. Even their narrative technique varies widely, from the first-person distorted reality of the mad narrators in **"You Are Not I"** and **"If I Should Open My Mouth,"** to the removed, neutral, folk-myth-like telling of **"The Scorpion"** and **"The Water of Izli."** Yet there *is* something common to all these stories, and I think that sameness has to do with tone, or what Bowles himself . . . calls the "voice" of a story. In all of the stories Bowles has written, that voice is shaped by one particular effort—the strenuous withholding of judgment.

Not that the strain shows in the stories themselves: if anything, their language seems at first glance to be as fluid and straightforward as the language of folk tales and fireside stories. The narrative voice itself never suggests that judgment is in any way called for. Yet a brief look at the kind of stories Bowles *seems* to borrow from—for instance, the [five Moroccan] oral tales he translates in *Five Eyes*—reveals that authorial opinions are pervasive in those stories: the narrators think nothing of saying "This was good" or "She was ugly" whenever they feel like it. Bowles, on the other hand, has consciously excised such narrative judgments from his own stories, leaving a gap that creates strong tension between the seemingly traditional form and the far-from-traditional voice. Moreover, the events in Bowles's stories are the sort that cry out for judgment: enormous cruelty, bizarre and inexplicable behavior, psychological and cultural conflict. Yet judgment is consistently suppressed, and therefore the events never fully take shape as "bizarre" or "cruel"—they are simply events.

If I have given the impression that Bowles is a sort of Robbe-Grillet who writes on action-packed topics, this is a false impression. Whereas Robbe-Grillet and other writers who experimented in that manner were interested in the photographic, "objective" look of things, Bowles is at least as much concerned with internal states. Even the stories which are written from a third-person viewpoint frequently focus on a single character's perceptions, and all of Bowles's landscapes seem tinged by human response to them. But such distinctions—internal/external, subjective/objective, alien/familiar, willed/fated, and even cruel/kind—begin to seem pointless in relation to Bowles's work. His stories, if they are uniformly about anything, are about the annihilation of such barriers—and yet he depends on us to remember these barriers, and thereby to give the stories something solid to work against. Bowles's stories about the loss of distinctions are written for an audience that believes in the necessity of distinctions.

A common theme in these stories is the transformation of a Self into an Other. In **"You Are Not I"** (which explicitly echoes that theme in its title), a madwoman comes to believe that she has turned into her sister: hence the "I" of the beginning and the "I" of the end represent two different characters in the story. In **"A Distant Episode,"** a linguistics professor becomes a tongueless idiot who dances for the amusement of his captors. In **"The Circular Valley,"** a ghost-like spirit, the Atlájala, entertains itself by taking on the perceptions first of animals, then of humans. And in **"Allal,"** a boy enters into the body of a snake and sees his own abandoned body from the outside. . . . In many of these stories, the loss of self is linked with speechlessness (the man who has his tongue cut out in **"A Distant Episode,"** the boy who becomes a silent snake in **"Allal"**), with a journey whose destination is unknown (as in **"Pastor Dowe at Tacate," "Señor Ong and Señor Ha,"** and, again, **"A Distant Episode"**), and with a general sense of cultural disorientation (which pervades the New York of **"If I Should Open My Mouth"** and **"How Many Midnights"** as much as it does the Latin America of **"Call at Corazón"** or the Bangkok of **"You Have Left Your Lotus Pods on the Bus"**).

Themes like speechlessness and journeying reek of allegory, yet Bowles's stories are anything but allegorical in tone. I said at the beginning that to specify was to belie the stories, but there is one kind of specificity that particularly suits them: it is quite possible, and even instructive, to talk about Bowles's language, about the actual words he uses. In accord with his evasion of judgment, Bowles allows the greatest weight to rest on the tiniest and least significant words.

Wendy Lesser, in a review of "Collected Stories 1939-1976," in The American Book Review, *Vol. II, No. 4, May-June, 1980, p. 24.*

TOBIAS WOLFF

[*The Sheltering Sky*] is one of the most original, even visionary, works of fiction to appear in this century and was widely recognized as such when it came out. Edwin Muir perfectly caught the book's pitch when he described it as that rare novel "which does not repeat the pattern of commonplace existence that readers of novels know so well, but makes us realize that our life is extraordinary."

The main actors, Port Moresby and his wife Kit, are refugees of a sort peculiar to our age: affluent drifters dispossessed spiritually rather than materially, severed from the possibility of believing that they can be safe anywhere or, consequently, be anywhere at home. In the course of their wanderings they visit North Africa, and this proves a mistake. In the silent emptiness of desert and sky, the knowledge of their absolute isolation from other people comes upon them so violently that it subverts their belief in their own reality and in the reality of their connection to each other.

Doubting this connection is, of course, prelude to betraying it. And betray it they do, in every way, until betrayal grows instinctual. Kit abandons Port in his dying hour and puts herself in the hands of another man. (p. 221)

The identity of others has ceased to have any meaning for Kit except in their ability to dominate her, because she can define her own identity only in the experience of being dominated. When the French colonial authorities eventually find her, she carries no identification and does not answer to her name.

The Sheltering Sky has been called nightmarish; that description lets us off the hook too easily, because it implies a fear of the unreal. The power of this novel lies precisely in the reality of what it makes us fear—the sweetness of that voice in each of us that sings the delight of not being responsible, of refusing the labor of choice by which we create ourselves. This appetite for the "mindless contentment" of self-surrender is nothing new in our makeup, but we modern folk have devised for ourselves a singularly rich offering of oppressions to satisfy it. We all know the menu: totalitarian ideologies, totalitarian theologies, drugs, guru-worship, mass-market advertising, television addiction, pornography, and, just so we won't feel too bad about any of this, determinist psychologies and sociologies that speak of us as products with only a culturally induced illusion of free will.

Our failing resistance to these attacks on our sense of worth as individuals is the central drama of our time. *The Sheltering Sky* records the struggle with complete fidelity, impassively noting every step in the process of surrender. Like *The Sun Also Rises* and *Under the Volcano*, Bowles's novel enacts a crucial historical moment with such clarity that it has become part of our picture of that moment.

Bowles followed *The Sheltering Sky* with a collection of stories. *The Delicate Prey,* published in 1950, extends the perceptions of the novel into even more exotic and disturbing terrain. Here the characters no longer simply acquiesce in their own destruction; they seem to be in search of it. In **"A Distant Episode,"** a professor of linguistics, presumably an American, travels to a remote Saharan town where he has no connection to anyone—only a vague memory of a café owner with whom he'd become acquainted when he passed through some ten years earlier. He has no real reason for going there; he simply "decides" to. Like the Moresbys' decision to visit the same area, it works out very much to his disadvantage.

The café owner is dead. The Professor strikes up a conversation with the waiter who gives him this news, though the man is openly contemptuous of him. Unwilling to lose the waiter's company, the Professor hires him to broker the purchase from a hostile nomadic tribe of some boxes made from camel udders. This involves accompanying the waiter on a perilous trek by moonlight to the lip of a cliff. They pass a corpse and are attacked by a wild dog, but the Professor keeps on going. He doesn't trust the waiter, he knows that the tribe is dangerous; but in spite of his suspicion and fear, he finds himself powerless to turn back. The waiter abandons him at the cliff's edge, and still the Professor goes on, descending the cliff alone to the desert floor, where the tribesmen seize him and cut out his tongue and dress him in a tinkling suit of flattened tin cans, in which costume he is taught to entertain them by jumping up and down and waving his arms. The curiosity-seeker has himself become a curiosity, comically and ineffectually armored in the detritus of his own culture.

The story is a tour de force, an ominous parable of the weakening of the individual will to survive. The other stories in the book, mostly set in Morocco and Latin America, are equally unsettling. *The Delicate Prey* is in fact one of the most profound, beautifully wrought, and haunting collections in our literature. (pp. 221-22)

[Bowles's] novels and stories come at you from every direction, told from the points of view of men, women, Europeans, Arabs, priests, lunatics, murderers, merchants, beggars, animals, and spirits—occasionally several of these presented in the same story, a virtuoso mingling of perspectives that has become a characteristic flourish in the Bowles signature. His tales are at once austere, witty, violent, and sensuous. They move with the inevitability of myth. His language has a purity of line, a poise and authority entirely its own, capable of instantly modulating from farce to horror without a ruffle and without giving any signal of delight in itself. It never goes on parade. . . .

[*Points in Time*] is a nervy, surprising, completely original performance, so original that it can't be referred to any previous category of fiction or nonfiction. Divided into eleven sections, or movements, the book presents a series of legends, snatches of popular song, incidents from history, writings from ancient explorers, all woven together with invented stories and interludes of pure description. Through these changing forms, each with its own angle of vision, Bowles creates an impression of the actions of man and nature upon the land that is now Morocco. The unpredictable structure of the book gives you no chance for a drowsy, complacent read. Instead, you are kept in a state of uncertainty that leaves you acutely vulnerable to the book's vivid sensory suggestions and shifting moods. Print and page vanish; it plays on you with the directness of music and brands indelible images on the memory.

Points in Time is a brilliant achievement, innovative in form, composed in a language whose every word, every pause feels purposeful and right. "No iron," Isaac Babel wrote, "can pierce the heart with the force of a well-placed period." Of course this isn't true, as Babel knew only too well, but to experience the writing in this book is almost to believe it true. And I am not alone in this response. In England *Points in Time* received enthusiastic notices. But in the year since is publication here, not a single review has appeared anywhere. Not one.

Why is that? How is it possible that a writer of Bowles's stature should not have his work discussed in his own country?

The reasons aren't easy to figure out, but I have a few guesses.

To begin with, most of his stories and all but one of his novels are set in North Africa—the other novel, *Up Above the World,* takes place in Latin America. And we're not much interested in books that have characters named Ahmed or Hassan in them. We think we're being cosmopolitan enough when we read García Márquez. That's one possible reason. Another, related to the first, is that Bowles lives in Morocco. Which means that he hasn't been around to ride the reading circuit, work the floor at literary conferences, get himself on talk shows, sign petitions in the *Times,* contribute his favorite recipes to the Style section, have cutting-edge photographers take pictures of him in his underwear, and generally do the hard time that is required of literary personages. Bowles has instead, in his life as in his writing, been eerily self-effacing. In the world of American letters, where hustle and genuine achievement are apt to get confused, reticence doesn't bring home the bacon.

I suspect another, more troubling reason for this recent neglect of Bowles's work. That is the growing tendency of book reviewers to evaluate writers on the basis of their attitudes rather than their artistry. Writers are supposed to be cheerleaders now. They are supposed to be positive and write uplifting books that demonstrate their faith that The Human Spirit Will Prevail. Bowles would be out of place at this love-fest. He is notoriously not an optimist. He gives no evidence of faith in our culture or in our future. He has tried modern man in the crucible of his art and found him fatally slow on the uptake. He's a party pooper. Forget him.

But his writing has a life of its own; once read, it can't be forgotten. (p. 222)

> *Tobias Wolff, "A Forgotten Master: Rescuing the Works of Paul Bowles," in* Esquire, *Vol. 103, No. 5, May, 1985, pp. 221-22.*

LINDA W. WAGNER

Much of the criticism of Paul Bowles's fiction traces its development as existential or nihilistic statement. Given its appearance in the mid-to-late forties, the starkly outlined plots and purposely sketchy characters were particularly noticeable. The forties saw Pulitzer Prizes for fiction being given to John Hersey, James A. Michener, James Gould Cozzens, Ellen Glasgow, Upton Sinclair, and John Steinbeck. Bowles's vision was most assuredly different from that of many American novelists then living.

His locale seemed to provide some explanation for the difference: exotic places provoked the inexplicable events of his stories and novels. (That critics turned readily to this rationale shows once again the pervasiveness of the threateningly provincial American mind set.) And his parallels with Camus surface repeatedly: *The Sheltering Sky* in 1949 was often compared with *L'Etranger.* Both setting and characterization (especially in the remote psychological distance between narrator and protagonist) remind readers of Camus.

There is no reason to deny these views of Bowles and his fiction. So far as they go, they are accurate and useful. What I would like to suggest in this essay, however, is that to categorize Bowles as *only* a nihilist or an existentialist, as *only* an imitator of Camus, is to diminish the complexity of his work, and to deny it the growth that seems to have been occurring.

Johannes Bertens, in his 1979 study [*The Fiction of Paul Bowles*], describes Bowles as a writer concerned—perhaps obsessively—with relationships, with "attempts to belong, to find meaning in relationships with others. They usually pivot on the tension that arises when an attempt to make serious contact meets with resistance, offered either by those with whom the protagonist wants to belong or, paradoxically, by the protagonist himself. . . . In Bowles's stories the desire for emotional contact with another person—or with a group of persons—as a source of meaning plays a central role." Bertens' view is at odds with the earlier critics who have found Bowles the master of the isolated character, but structural analysis of Bowles's work supports Bertens' argument. I would qualify this present argument only to suggest that in much of Bowles's fiction, the tension results from a possible male-female relationship, not only a male-male or male-group nexus.

In *The Sheltering Sky* and the stories of *The Delicate Prey* (1945-1950), Bowles shows women characters as adversarial. By the fiction of *Midnight Mass,* in 1981, however, Bowles is presenting his female characters in much more positive ways. On the one hand, they are less antagonistic to male characters, although they manage to achieve power for themselves. In presentation, they are often more sexless than sexual and, perhaps compatible with their functions in the fiction, they perform almost ritualistic or mythical roles. Malika, in **"Here to Learn,"** surely shows less malice toward any of her lovers than did the honeymooning wife in **"Call at Corazón"** toward her husband. In the earlier story, we are conscious of *personal* emotion. In the latter, the chief impression is of willed action, fated movement, destiny separate from idiosyncratic fortunes.

In *The Sheltering Sky,* 1949, Bowles's first novel, he achieves effects very much like those of Hemingway in *The Sun Also Rises* and the early stories. In those works, Hemingway stressed the similarities between his female protagonist and his male: Brett Ashley was "one of us" because she understood Jake Barnes's values: Nick Adams, in the process of knowing Marjorie, had taught her everything he knew himself—only to find that she, like Brett, could go beyond his example in matters of moral courage. Bowles, too, models his female protagonist, Kit Moresby, after her husband Port. In fact, because of the obvious likenesses between the two, their personal traits—world-weary cynicism, wide mood swings, reliance on idiosyncratic mores—are presented as positive, even though the traits themselves are hardly that. As the novel progresses, however, Port's nearly complete disaffection—for life as well as for Kit—tends to turn the reader from him. Temporarily, Kit appears as a more complete character, a woman who tried in some way to reach her spouse:

> It made her sad to realize that in spite of their so often having the same reactions, the same feelings, they never would reach the same conclusions, because their respective aims in life were almost diametrically opposed.

Some readers have seen both Kit and Port as Bowles's examples of nihilism, but others have found in this novel the beginning of what appeared to be Bowles's interest in dichotomies—in this case, the difference between men and women, between despair and hope. What Bowles gives us structurally is Port's despair set against the quasi-optimism—or at least energy—of Kit: Port's death balanced against Kit's action and sexuality. The dichotomy is complex, however, for Kit's capacity to act is marred by her need for, her identification with, violence.

As Bertens has suggested, the key to unraveling some of the motivation for both these protagonists is understanding their relationship, but Bowles purposely prevents the reader from doing that. He shows their affinities, their often unspoken rapport ("Recognizing the gesture, but not understanding why she was making it, he paid no attention to it"); but instead of a sympathetic relationship, the Moresbys end up with a blank wall of hostility. This is the ostensible dilemma of the novel: why Port, who vaguely loves his wife after their twelve years of marriage, does not take any action to make peace, does not join with her in any act, either sexual or intellectual. Even for Port, the situation is confused. In Chapter 14, Bowles writes,

> Since the day he and Kit had gone bicycling together he had felt a definite desire to strengthen the sentimental bonds between them. Slowly it was assuming an enormous importance to him . . . much as he desired the rapprochement, he knew that also he dreaded the emotional responsibilities it would entail.

Yet, in Chapter 16, he has relinquished all such motivation: "he would temporarily abandon the idea of getting back together with Kit. In his present state of disquiet, he would be certain to take all wrong turnings, and would perhaps lose her for good. Later, when he least expected it, the thing might come to pass of its own accord."

Port's lack of volition is imaged in that passivity, yet Bowles shows clearly that his whole life is built around Kit's presence in it. Neither identity is separate from the other . . . , yet neither is capable of relinquishing enough to truly merge. Bowles presents this crucial piece of characterization through another of his sharply imaged scenes:

> He abandoned himself to the perverse pleasure he found in continuing mechanically to put one foot in front of the other, even though he was quite clearly aware of his fatigue. . . . A faint vision began to haunt his mind. It was Kit, seated by the open window, filing her nails and looking out over the town. And as he found his fancy returning more often, as the minutes went by, to that scene, unconsciously he felt himself the protagonist, Kit the spectator. The validity of his existence at that moment was predicated on the assumption that she had not moved, but was still sitting there.

The central confrontation scene, between Port and Kit, occurs as they watch the Arab at prayer, and face their own knowledge of "darkness . . . Absolute night"—and their own inability to achieve a happy relationship. It is important to *The Sheltering Sky* that the scene occurs relatively early in the novel. The impasse between his protagonists is, therefore, accepted; it is not likely to change, and the progress of the fiction deals less with the relationship than with the individual characters. That Kit lives on into Part III of the novel, then, causes no problem for the reader who wants to see Port as the primary protagonist. What Bowles achieves in the last section of the novel, of course, is an ironic reversal. Kit should be freed, by Port's death, to find fulfillment. Instead she finds further punishment and shows herself responding to patterns she had learned during her earlier life. (pp. 15-18)

In 1982, Peter Owen published Bowles's short montage fiction, *Points in Time.* Extending the dialogue begun in *The Sheltering Sky* about timelessness and time, memory and impermanence, this work moves further from the pervasive theme of male-female relations and closer to considerations of nature and its effect on human beings. The opening vignettes are of rivers, lakes, and—once intruded upon—lands once fertile that now were only dust. A more contemporary, and less Western, version of Eliot's *The Waste Land*, *Points in Time* chronicles despairing episodes of religious intolerance, political persecution, piracy, murder, and hypocrisy. As many women are killed as men, but characters are treated so summarily that sexual differences seem irrelevant. When Fra Andrea, a Franciscan monk, became too friendly with people of the Moslem faith, he found himself charged with "conspiracy and the practice of magic." He was "thrown straightway into a cell where they tortured him for a few hours. Finally someone impaled his body on a lance." When the beautiful Sol ran away from her husband's home, a crowd caught her and, to conclude the tale, "A tall mokhazni unsheathed his sword, raised it high in the air, and beheaded her." Punishment does not vary by sex; neither does reward. In Bowles's accounts of the history and people of Spain and Morocco, chance and whim are as influential as cause and effect. The montage opens with the epigraph which also closes the sequence: "The river runs fast at the mouth where the shore is made of the sky, and the wavelets curl inward fanwise from the sea." Bowles closes the book with these lines, followed by the objectively phrased warning, "For the swimmer there is no warning posted against the sharks that enter and patrol the channel. Some time before sunset birds come to stalk or scurry along the sandbar, but before dark they are gone." Nature is beautiful, healing, ageless; but humankind quickly, and without precaution, becomes only its prey, the delicate prey of the 1950 stories, and sensitive and indecisive prey of *The Sheltering Sky*.

Judging from *Midnight Mass* and *Points in Time*, what has changed in Bowles's fiction of the 1980s is the tendency to set character against character, to create a dialectic that somehow informs the reader. Bowles's late stories are so spare, so objectively reported, that a reader would not attempt to draw inferences. Sol is a beautiful, homesick woman, but leaving her husband's house is a crime, and for that crime she is killed. Bowles's intention is not to portray Sol as a person, but rather to set in motion forces that remind the reader of inexorable laws, to create a truly moral narrative. In these late tales, and in many of his fictions from *The Delicate Prey* and *The Time of Friendship*, Bowles may be said to have written what Richard M. Eastman calls the "open parable," the narrative that cannot be "closed" and given a simplified interpretation. Because the author's rhetoric allows opaque details, "irreducible" hints that will not lead to any single reading, the narrative remains open to several interpretations.

Despite its reputation as Bowles's most important nihilistic novel, *The Sheltering Sky* limits the reader. Port and Kit and their relationship must be dealt with, inferences must be drawn, sides chosen. But by the time of Malika in **"Here to Learn,"** Bowles has dissociated his reader from real involvement with either the woman or her lovers. Characters act as centers of interest, not as "real" people; and the fiction itself works more on the model Wayne C. Booth describes as those "in which the search for truth is answered with the discovery that truth is found not in concepts but in the reality of artistic activity."

Perhaps that skillful distancing of reader from character is the single most noticeable quality of Bowles's later stories. Astute critics like Joyce Carol Oates have commented that "Bowles's people tend to be our very distant kin, shadowy and remote, unclaimable. . . . The reader is usually outside Bowles's characters," and in one sense, Oates confirms Tennessee Williams' view of Bowles as the creator of the "blindly explosive world that we live in so precariously from day and night to each

uncertain tomorrow." But in a less character-centered view, what Bowles manages to achieve in his terse yet resonant stories, is the impact of an action, a force that creates some dynamic among creations we recognize as characters, whether they be opportunistic women, drug dealers, or tortured professors. We remember Bowles's late *stories*, in short, perhaps more readily than we remember the *characters* from those stories. To create the whole image, and suspend it, and make it, then, memorable is no small feat. It is, indeed, a delicate balance. (pp. 21-3)

Linda W. Wagner, "Paul Bowles and the Characterization of Women," in Critique: Studies in Modern Fiction, *Vol. XXVII, No. 1, Fall, 1985, pp. 15-24.*

JOSEPH VOELKER

It is to his fiction . . . that one must turn to find the Bowlesian *mythos* of travel, for the meeting of place and imagination. What follows is an attempt to derive a central Bowlesian plot from the specific novels and stories. Admittedly, there is variety among Bowles's many accounts of the confrontation between the Western mind and the alien culture, and this derivation distorts things somewhat through oversimplification and selectivity.

The Bowlesian protagonist (male or female) is a spiritual drifter who has come to North Africa (or Central America in *Up Above the World*) in flight from the centerlessness of his prior life. He is not a tourist because he holds no return-trip ticket. His drifting provides the only clarity available, that which comes from a movement away from his past. His itinerary is always a deeper penetration into the alien, which is perceived as closer to some ultimate origin—the absolute atavistically defined in terms of earliness. Port Moresby, in *The Sheltering Sky*, frantically pushes deeper into the Sahara as the typhoid bacillus overcomes him. When he dies, his wife Kit continues his trajectory and loses her identity in sexual enslavement at the hands of the merchant Belqassim. Dyar, a refugee from American mechanized labor in *Let it Come Down*, initially attempts to negotiate Tangier, then commits a theft that cuts him off from both European and Moslem communities, and moves irreversibly toward the hashish-saturation that precipitates the act of murder from which there is no return. In **"A Distant Episode,"** a tiny crystal of the Bowles myth, a linguistics professor allows himself to be led out of the European sector of a town and into ritual enslavement by Reguiba tribesmen. In *Up Above the World*, Taylor and Désirée Slade, peculiarly directionless vacationers, wander inextricably into a murderous trap. In every instance, the movement is begun in an urban setting and shifts to a rural one. The Moresbys and the Professor are drawn from town to desert; Dyar from Tangier to the hills of Spanish Morocco; the Slades from city to plantation. The urban-to-rural movement is accompanied by a corresponding linguistic decay—with each step toward the absolute, the possibility of decipherment erodes further—labyrinthine alleyways and the rich babble of the Souks give way to the empty space and the silence of the irrational. When the Reguibat capture the Professor of linguistics, they cut out his tongue. Kit Moresby closes her formerly penetrating eyes and refuses to speak.

The initial stage of the journey, prior to the protagonist's loss of language, is an act of reading. The North African city-as-text provides a complex means for the European to get himself both physically and morally lost. In *The Sheltering Sky*, Port Moresby leaves his hotel and loses himself in the town, where an Arab leads him to a young prostitute with whom he willingly betrays his wife. When he must escape her protectors, he climbs a ladder and hurls a boulder at his pursuers, possibly killing one. In the early stages of his adventure, he finds himself unable to negotiate the town, and a vertiginous symbolic confusion ensues:

> Everything looked unfamiliar: the houses, the streets, the cafés, even the formation of the town with regard to the hill. Instead of finding a summit from which to begin the downward walk, he discovered that here the streets all led perceptibly upward, no matter which way he turned; to descend he would have had to go back. The Arab walked solemnly along with him, now beside him, now slipping behind where there was not enough room to walk two abreast.

The labyrinthine streets are a metaphor for the disintegration of control in the centerless self-hood of the Westerner. In *Let It Come Down,* Dyar, an American who travels lightly, has only his own American opportunism to help him decode Tangier, and Bowles builds the maze-like texture of the novel out of detailed accounts of Dyar's movements in the streets—the following instance records Dyar's walking to meet the prostitute Hadija:

> This time Dyar was determined to keep track of the turns and steps, so that he could find his way up alone after dinner. Through a short crowded lane, to the left up a steep little street lined with grocery stalls, out into the triangular plaza with the big green and white arch opposite, continue up, turn right down the dark level street, first turn left again into the very narrow alley which becomes a tunnel and goes up steeply, out at top, turn right again, follow straight through paying no attention to juts and twists because there are no streets leading off, downhill to large plaza with fat hydrant in center and cafés all the way around (only they might be closed later, and with their fronts boarded up they look like any other shops), cross plaza, take alley with no streetlight overhead, at end turn left into pitch black street. . . . He began to be confused.

Such passages are the dominant motif of the initial stage of the Bowlesian journey, for his protagonists, on their way to the point of intersection with the alien culture that leads to their immersion in the absolute, instinctively try at first to maintain their bearings—consciousness, though hateful, is so tenacious in them.

There are characters in Bowles's fiction who succeed in remaining at this initial stage and do not succumb to immersion in the absolute. Demonic pseudonyms for the author himself, they are survivors, symbolically as well as literally bilingual. They find their way into and back out of the urban labyrinth. In *The Spider's House,* only one character negotiates the streets of Fez with unqualified success, and that is the American novelist Stenham. The only creature who negotiates a spider's web is a spider, and such seems to be Bowles's quasi-autobiographical characterization. Stenham remains in Fez during the early stages of the Arab revolt to watch in bitterness as the city he loves for its atavism (it is medieval in architecture and puritan in Islamic practices) is destroyed by colonial violence. With no allegiance of his own, he can move nimbly among Arabs and Frenchmen, and he can speak French, English, and Moghrebi. Once again, Bowles presents the city streets as a text, and Stenham is an adept philologist. . . . Stenham represents the closest proximity to comprehension of the other culture a character can achieve in Bowles's *mythos.* It is a Faustian

position. Stenham befriends a Moslem boy, Amar, whose precocious wisdom is as remarkable as his ability to negotiate the labyrinthine city during the violence. But at novel's end, Stenham abandons Amar, leaving him behind despite his status as a symbolic son, and drives away from the trouble with Polly Burroughs, an attractive American communist who denies all validity to the city's history. The severing of symbolic generational ties to Amar and the abandonment of the atavistic city for an ahistorical consciousness mark Stenham as a sterile bearer of anthropological knowledge.

This myth of the adept as demonic author receives the clearest treatment in *Up Above the World.* Grove Soto is the son of a rich Central American businessman and a Canadian mother. He moves between the two worlds with facility. When his mother contrives to pay him a visit, he arranges to have her murdered (a gory parable of the denial of origins). Then he burns down the hotel in which her poisoned body is lying and takes the Slades prisoner because he fears that Désirée may have witnessed the murder. He hosts the Slades graciously while surreptitiously loading them with hallucinogens and playing tape recordings during their delirium, explaining to them in their lucid moments that they are suffering from a tropical virus. The violation of all continuity with the past, symbolized by the murder of his mother, gives Grove a God-like, authorial power. He literally writes the script for the Slade's reality on a typewriter.

The novel is an existential fable of deracination. . . . In *Up Above the World,* Bowles allows Grove Soto to usurp the place of God—author of reality's original script—in order to work out a cosmic model for his *mythos* entirely on the human level of the psychothriller. In the other novels and stories, the existence of a divine script remains problematical. In **"He of the Assembly,"** for instance, one of the hashish stories in *A Hundred Camels in the Courtyard,* Ben Tajah receives a cryptic letter before smoking kif. It is never entirely certain that the letter exists, although it appears at one point that it has been burnt and the ashes scattered.

The Bowlesian protagonist faces one of two fates—if he is not an adept (purchasing survival on the margins at the cost of a betrayal of origins), he is a victim. For the latter category, an initial failure to read leads inevitably to an ambiguously welcome loss of the centerless Western self that is both horrible and perversely fulfilling.

The second stage of the symbolic journey is motion across great expanses of space. Kit and Port Moresby and their friend Tunner travel by bus and automobile into less and less hospitable regions of the Sahara. In *Let it Come Down,* Dyar commandeers Thami's boat for his escape to the Spanish zone and is forced to listen to the Jilali boatman's endless chanting. Bowles carries off his victims by camelback, airplane, and even streetcar. Motion through space provides the right narrative rhythm for Bowles's characteristic rendering of consciousness adrift.

At some point on the journey, European and Moslem reach equilibrium, as the protective structures of French administration recede. This is the moment of intersection between integer and surd. Typically, an act of outrage or violence, usually inflicted by the African on the Westerner, precipitates the loss of rational consciousness, the collapse of the self, and the loss of the linguistic capacity that keeps existence provisional. Belqassim and his elderly companion share Kit Moresby sexually. A Reguiba tribesman pinches the Professor's nose, and when the professor opens his mouth to breathe, the tribesman slices off his tongue with a razor. Dyar witnesses religious acts of self-mutilation among members of an extremist Moslem sect; he returns to his hideout, awakens from hashish-induced dreams and drives a nail into Thami's brain.

The distance covered in the journey from normal Western linguistic modes of consciousness to entrapment in the alien absolute is captured in Bowles's account of the murder of Thami through the use of interior monologue in the scene. No character who crosses over into the surd presence is accessible to the reader—even interior monologue inspires no recognition on our part. As a fictional murderer, Dyar is at the farthest possible remove from Raskolnikov:

> A mass of words had begun to ferment inside him, and now they bubbled forth. "Many Mabel damn. Molly Daddy lamb. Lolly dibble upman. Dolly little Dan," he whispered, and then he giggled. The hammer was in his right hand, the nail in his left. He bent over, swayed, and fell heavily to his knees on the mat, beside the outstretched door. It did not move. The mountain wind rushed through his head, his head that was a single seashell full of grottoes; its infinitely smooth pink walls, delicate, paper-thin, caught the light of the embers as he moved along the galleries. "Melly diddle din," he said, quite loud, putting the point of the nail as far into Thami's ear as he could. He raised his right arm and hit the head of the nail with all his might. The objects relaxed imperceptibly, as if someone had said to it: "It's all right."

Dyar's nonsense syllables seem to lie on the very edge of significance; but they provide no explanation for his motive, and the reader must uneasily dismiss the murder as an *acte gratuite*.

Typically, Bowles uses motifs of imprisonment to render the spiritual condition of his lost Europeans. After the murder, Dyar finds himself trapped inside the farmhouse with Thami's body. Outside are Thami's kinsmen and possibly the police. In **"A Distant Episode,"** the Professor is slung horizontally in a series of metal hoops. In *The Sheltering Sky,* Kit first suffers a kind of imprisonment in the furnitureless room where her husband dies slowly, and then allows herself to be held in a tiny chamber of Belqassim's house, away from his other wives.

Strangely, physical pain, humiliation, literal and symbolic loss of mobility, and the inability to speak or understand speech are a price Bowles's protagonists are willing to pay, rather than return to consciousness. (pp. 30-4)

Bowles remains somewhat equivocal on the condition of his regressive victim protagonists. The reader does not conclude with certainty that they have penetrated the alien culture or discovered the script that was written for them. It is just as plausible to say that no contact has been made, that they have simply broken down in the presence of the other, reduced their own repertoire to the fewest possible gestures, and cast off the burden of provisional self-hood.

And yet Bowles's fictional world is never so dark as its anthropological superstructure. Not every protagonist reaches the extremity of the Bowles *mythos*. In the confrontation between Westerner and Moslem, there is often comedy when they do not understand one another, and a sense of friendship when they mistakenly think that they do understand one another. Beyond the comedy, there is Bowles's supreme artistry in the creation of his Moslem characters, especially of the boy Amar in *The Spider's House.* Few readers are equipped to judge the

socio-cultural accuracy of Bowles's characterization, but certainly Amar is vital, consistent, and recognizably non-Western. Most outsiders in literature are mainly inversions of the culture's tropes: Amar has a provenience. In him a Western writer appears to have imaginatively understood the psyche of a Moslem. His very creation argues against Bowles's anthropological pyrrhonism. Finally, Bowles has sustained his inquiry across a large body of work and designed an unfalteringly precise linguistic texture for its medium. No matter how dark the story, there is pleasure in its unfolding. (pp. 35-6)

Joseph Voelker, "Fish Traps and Purloined Letters: The Anthropology of Paul Bowles," in Critique: Studies in Modern Fiction, *Vol. XXVII, No. 1, Fall, 1985, pp. 25-36.*

GEOFFREY O'BRIEN

[Paul Bowles's] novels are a recapitulation—in terms at once apocalyptic and exhausted, as if all this were going to end soon and a good thing too—of the West's most ancient dilemma, its simultaneous desire for and horror of the Other. What singles out Bowles is that from the outset he seems to have moved beyond both horror and desire. He tells the old tale with the detachment of the disembodied spirit who scrambles the brains of travelers in his story **"The Circular Valley."**

That detachment exacerbates rather than allays the anxiety that flits among the crevices of his elegant, schematic prose. It's the primal anxiety of the civilized, hinging on an uneasy balance between *here* and *there. Here* is neat, sealed, cordoned off, an empty room whose floor has just been swept. *There* is everything else: the whole hidden order of reality. In his hotel room the tourist dreams of the native quarter; in the native quarter he becomes nostalgic for the vacuousness of the hotel room. He has come for an entertainment which at every step risks becoming too intrusive, too threatening; yet to retreat is to reject the content of his own desires. He is the product of a culture that looks restlessly outside itself for its dream material. The craving for security around which civilization constructs itself requires the absence of subject matter: no floods, no quicksand, no murderous animals, no barbarians. Consequently the genres of European culture tend to be vacant forms for which exoticism provides the content. Nubians and elephants are imported to fill the geometric arena. Otherwise, what would there be to look at? (p. 10)

[The] subjective exploitation of a foreign place is fairly universal, but Bowles reveals its mechanisms with unusual frankness. He is like Stenham, the protagonist of *The Spider's House,* who does not pretend that he has come to Morocco to study or to teach, to imitate the Moroccans or to supply them with a role model. Stenham's only apparent goal is to savor certain solitary aesthetic thrills, keenly experienced intervals of displacement. He enjoys the fact that he can never fully understand or be fully accepted by the culture that surrounds him. He walks the empty hills outside Fez to indulge in the rarefied pleasure of *apartness*, as if he could immerse himself in a place by not being there: "It was the knowledge that the swarming city lay below, shut in by its high ramparts, which made wandering over the hills and along the edges of the cliffs so delectable. They are there, of it, he would think, and I am here, of nothing, free." This is hardly the most politically respectable stance toward the realities of the third world. Indeed, *The Spider's House* can be read as a lament for the Moroccan revolution, conceived as the final phase in the cultural Europeanization of the country: by becoming a modern nation in the same sense as France or Spain, Morocco makes an ultimate surrender to its former colonial masters. At the same time the radical untenability of such a viewpoint is clear even to Stenham, who admits that the political fate of the nation concerns him only insofar as it impinges on his idiosyncratic pleasures.

The pervasive hedonism of Bowles's heroes (although to some it would appear a masochistic pursuit of discomfort) carries over to the books, which overtly seduce the reader with a promise of new spaces, unexplored paths. The kicker, of course, is that what lies at the end of those paths tends to be unalloyed horror. The characteristic rhythm of Bowles's stories coincides with the gradually deepening paranoia of the tourist in over his head. Smiling guides have hidden motives; quaintly primitive bus rides start to go sour; minor errors of interpretation lead to hideous consequences. Oddly, these nightmarish intrusions occur in a stylistic context of almost Mozartean grace and balance, a context which they do not so much rend as fulfill. Most horror writers, impatient to get down to business, shuffle unconvincingly through their preliminary scenes of tranquil normality; after all, we know very well that the facade will shortly be ripped aside. But with Bowles we never know quite what will happen: maybe death, maybe nothing. He accords as much weight, as much aesthetic intensity, to someone waiting for a bus or to a couple half-heartedly bitching at each other in a hotel room as he does to whatever baroquely lurid destiny may await them. The banal is just as solid and relentless as the unanticipated violence that emerges out of it; banality and violence are part of a continuum.

Bowles's characters live in a state of anxious attentiveness. For them, drinking tea or purchasing a bus ticket is already a portentous act. In *The Sheltering Sky*, a traveler wanders through the ground floor of a Moroccan hotel, as if boredom were a paradise of vacuity.

> He went to the writing tables, lifted the blotters, opened the drawers, searching for stationery; there was none. Then he shook the inkwells; they were dry. A violent argument had broken out in the kitchen. Scratching the fleshy part of his hands, where the mosquitoes had just bitten him, he walked slowly out of the room through the foyer, along the corridor into the bar. Even here the light was weak and distant, but the array of bottles behind the bar formed a focal point of interest for the eyes. He had a slight indigestion—not a sourness, but the promise of a pain which at the moment was only a tiny physical unhappiness in some unlocatable center.

Many pages later this man will die, abruptly and arbitrarily, of typhus. In discussing the genesis of *The Sheltering Sky*, Bowles relates that he came to an impasse over that death scene. A dose of *majoun* (a potent cannabis cake) apparently enabled him to fully imagine his protagonist's death. In the texture of the novel, the death becomes just another moment, part of the same neutral series that includes the tiny stab of indigestion in the hotel bar. The horror of Port Moresby's death is the effort of consciousness to save itself by somehow leaving the body, an effort we watch both from within and without:

> It was in the silence of the room that he now located all those hostile forces; the very fact that the room's inert watchfulness was on all sides made him distrust it. Outside himself, it was all there was. He looked at the line made by the joining of the wall and the floor, endeavored to fix it in his mind, that he might have something to hang on to when his eyes should

shut. . . . So as not to go. To stay behind. To overflow, take root in what would stay here.

What Port cannot do, the disembodied narrative voice can. It survives the death of Port's consciousness in a wrenching shift of viewpoint which seems almost an act of cruelty, of abandonment. It's as if a torture victim convinced himself that the pain was happening to someone else. This fictional breaching of the barrier of death is like the assumption of an alternate body, in a rite of schizophrenic magic. The hard luminosity and edgy clarity of Bowles's prose describe a divergence, a splitting away. The sharpness of focus itself becomes a kind of blur: the blur of intense heat and light. The narrator doesn't run from the scene of horror; instead, he vanishes and the scene remains, like the room that outlives Port Moresby. Since a reader moves through a story by identifying with its characters, the effect of this abrupt transfer is a bit like losing one's own body. At the same time, the seamless charm of the fictional structure, its lithe resilience, makes the loss seem like a harmonic resolution implicit from the outset.

In the anesthetized silence that follows, death is as sharp and bright as the Saharan sky—or as a sentence in a story by Paul Bowles. A pair of innocent tourists are drugged into madness and casually murdered (*Up Above the World*); an errant linguist has his tongue cut out by nomads ("A Distant Episode"); a nail is driven through a skull (*Let It Come Down*); a man's penis is severed and shoved into a slit below his navel ("**The Delicate Prey**"). The final term, at least implicitly, is always annihilation. An arid soundless terrain survives the extinction of consciousness. . . . (pp. 11-12)

In his travel book *Their Heads Are Green and Their Hands Are Blue*, Bowles writes of the Sahara that "here, in this wholly mineral landscape lighted by stars like flares, even memory disappears; nothing is left but your own breathing and the sound of your heart beating. A strange, and by no means pleasant, process of reintegration begins inside you, and you have the choice of fighting against it, and insisting on remaining the person you have always been, or letting it take its course." It's as if the last pilgrim from the West had come to the edge of the void to have his personality surgically removed. Like the hero of *Let It Come Down*, who "had never known it was possible to take such profound delight in sheer brightness," he wants to remove the last barriers between himself and a sky that shelters by burning away.

Bowles has written a book to describe what that discarded personality was like: an autobiography, although one of the oddest specimens of the genre I have ever read. Perhaps, having demonstrated the dismantling of the ego in his novels, he wished to show the process by which it was built up in the first place. Although frequently fascinating, *Without Stopping* is an unsatisfying book, the only real aesthetic misfire of Bowles's career. It features an extraordinary index: glancing down a random column one encounters Tallulah Bankhead, Samuel Barber, Djuna Barnes, Béla Bartok, Cecil Beaton, Marlon Brando, Benjamin Britten. We catch tantalizingly truncated glimpses of '20s Modernists, '30s Communists, '40s forerunners of the international hip underground. We get a useful recap of Bowles's earlier careers: as a young poet, published in *transition* but deterred by Gertrude Stein's criticism of his writing, and as a successful composer of theater music, working with everyone from Orson Welles to Tennessee Williams. Yet despite his having evidently known—and collaborated and lived and traveled with—every well-known artistic figure of the century, Bowles's autobiography has a weirdly depopulated air.

Far from offering a portrait of his times, he doesn't even say much about his own intimate acquaintances. The most crucial individual, his wife Jane—a near-mythic figure whose emotional abandonment was diametrically opposed to Bowles's cool self-control—enters the book so obliquely as to be barely there. This sense of absence extends to the author himself. Since Yukio Mishima had already appropriated the title *Confessions of a Mask,* perhaps this one ought to have been called *Memoirs of a Mirror.* A consciousness zeroes in on itself only to find that it isn't there.

In Bowles's account of his childhood—by far the most shaped segment of *Without Stopping*—the reflexiveness has a dizzying, coiling power. In tones of absolute frankness he reveals a personality of absolute evasiveness—thereby casting doubt on the frankness. . . . The notion that literal meaning can so utterly conceal provides the key to Bowles's aesthetic. Posted at the beginning of his own self-portrait, it serves as a warning. This was a child who "at the age of five . . . had never yet even spoken to another child or seen children playing together," who "regularly settled into protracted illnesses with a shiver of voluptuousness at the prospect of the stretches of privacy that lay ahead," who after being beaten up at school "stealthily launched punitive attacks on loners who had got separated from the pack" and puzzled over why this was held to be dishonorable. He describes his youthful self as "a species then rare, now the commonest of contemporary phenomena, the American suburban child with its unrelenting spleen." Self-revelation never revealed so little: the disguises and misdirections he admits to may conceal countless others a little more artfully hidden. The voice—dry, chatty, endlessly pouring out anecdotes and observations—becomes a buzzing sound distracting us from the abyss it camouflages.

The implied perpetual motion of the title suggests a complex juggling act. Only occasionally, as in a letter written in 1951 and quoted by Millicent Dillon in her biography of Jane Bowles, does a hint of raw feeling escape:

> Inside I am waiting to escape to somewhere else. I don't quite know where. Naturally one always wants to escape if one has no reason for being anywhere. And I have no reason for being anywhere, that is certain. . . . When one feels that the only reason for working is in order to be able to forget one's life, one is sometimes tempted to consider the work slightly absurd, like the pills one takes to make one's digestion easier. There should be something else in between, but what it is, is anyone's guess.

In this light, Bowles's work is a meditation on the double meaning of the sentence "I have hidden nothing." He has shown the contents of the world, in the most meticulously detailed and concrete fashion; and within that display he has secreted a sense of terminal vacuousness.

His presentiment of hollowness at the core of human personality has proved an invaluable tool for charting the collision of cultures. By temperament Bowles may be, as he avows, a Romantic, but unlike his predecessors he makes no attempt to plumb the depths of the "Arab soul" or "primitive mind" or anything of the kind. Depths are not a matter of great concern for him. He sees the alleged profundities of character as lying a good deal closer to the surface. . . . Given Bowles's concern for the boundary states and pressure points of personality, it's not surprising that in *Up Above the World* he accurately forecast the use of LSD by Charles Manson and others to disassemble the identities of their followers. His collected stories resemble an encyclopedia of fragilities and fault lines, as registered by the tiniest of indicators: glances, gestures, sudden inexplicable resentments or retreats. The understanding kindness of a European woman toward a young Moroccan in **"The Time of Friendship"** becomes unwitting cruelty. **"Here To Learn"** tells of a village girl desperate to leave home who in Cinderella fashion is catapulted into wealth. But when she returns years later to flaunt her riches, the village has disappeared, a victim of progress, and in consequence her identity is effectively destroyed: "There was no longer any reason to do anything."

Bowles is not so much interested in "grief" and "indignation" and "love" as in the marginal areas between them, which have not been honored with a name. In *The Sheltering Sky,* he describes with extraordinary cold-bloodedness a woman's reaction to her husband's imminent death:

> It was not a whole life whose loss she was mourning there in his arms, but it was a great part of one; above all it was a part whose limits she knew precisely, and her knowledge augmented the bitterness. And presently within her, deeper than the weeping for the wasted years, she found a ghastly dread all formed and growing. She raised her head and looked up at him with tenderness and terror. . . . The wind at the window celebrated her dark sensation of having attained a new depth of solitude.

This lizard's-eye view of human behavior enables Bowles to deal with the most delicate of feelings. His desiccated, sun-whitened language can touch on emotion without being touched by it. The narcissism and self-pity so evident in his poetry are subjected in the fiction to a rigorous drying out. (pp. 12-13)

Ultimately, Bowles's writing is not about the individuals trapped in the situation, nor about the Morocco within which the situation unfolds and which he has transcribed with such fidelity. Musician that he is, Bowles wants to notate the abstract shape that their interaction resolves itself into. Just as the winding street in Fez "would slowly disclose its own design," the isolated minds of his characters gradually lay bare the impersonal space between them: the heartless locus of an event. It could happen anywhere—anywhere *else,* anywhere distinct from that other place which is the self's cocoonlike starting-point. Bowles has written only a handful of stories set in America, and as nearly as I can determine they all deal with extreme psychosis: if the place is not fled from without, it must be fled from within. Morocco for him becomes the place where actions are irrevocable.

It is the country where one is severed from one's origins and becomes, fully, an isolated being: hence a magic country. The act of cutting, that frequent motif of Bowles's fiction, is intimately connected to birth and healing. The razorlike keenness of his prose represents yet another cutting edge, linked to a different sort of healing. The harmonic balance of his spiky disjunct sentences magically resolves the unresolvable. The distance between here and there, between the mask and the face, between feeling and action, is bridged—however illusorily—in the integrating ritual of articulation. Saying it does somehow make it so—and make it bearable. Take everything away from words, give them nothing to feed on but sand and heat and blinding light, and they still proffer an unreasonable reassurance. . . . The melodic intensity of Bowles's writing originates in a desperate assertion of physical presence. One can ask for no more than the sheer blind fact that things are there: "Below, the harbor lights came into view and were distorted in the gently moving water. Then the shabbier buildings loomed, the streets were dimmer. At the edge of the Arab quarter the car, still loaded with people, made a wide U-turn and stopped; it was the end of the line.''

The exotic turns out to be constructed of perfectly ordinary elements: lights, buildings, streets, people. What's exotic is merely the existence of the world. The self, which senses its fundamental emptiness, gawks in amazement at shrubs and sidewalks and pebbles. It wants to make contact: but between the I and the Other a wedge has been driven. That jagged fissure is the world. Whatever reunion takes place can only occur elsewhere, in the mediating domain of sentences which are both here and there, part of oneself and outside oneself. ''The broken domes stood out black and jagged against the limpid night sky.'' ''The sheer cliffs rose upward and were lost in the low-hanging cloudbank.'' ''The fine rain slanted through the air outside the arcades and hit the ground silently.'' The music of language posits a perpetual forward movement. There will always be another sentence unfolding. You can travel through syntax as you would travel through space: but if you suddenly stop moving, you might realize there's nothing there. (p. 13)

Geoffrey O'Brien, "White Light White Heat," in VLS, No. 44, April, 1986, pp. 10-13.

PAUL KEEGAN

Bowles is interested in the paradoxical and inscrutable formalities which attend all human arrangements in primitive societies. Many of the stories in *Midnight Mass and Other Stories* (two-thirds of them written since the *Collected Stories* appeared in 1977) concern relations between mothers and sons, masters and servants, husbands and wives, and these are all used to posit the larger interdependence between rational and superstitious practices in any culture. Morocco obsesses Bowles because it so clearly displays such polarities—the undermining of Nazarene medicine by native superstition is one of his favourite comic themes—and because he perceives deviance to be the central social fact, rather than a direction chosen by the individual. Bowles has steered his course in the conviction that ''certain areas of the earth's surface contained more magic than others'', and his return to Tangier after the Second World War was decided by a dream that expressed his sense that lives are fatefully determined by place. . . .

Norman Mailer praised Bowles for opening up the world of hip: ''He let in the murder, the drugs, the incest, the death of the square.'' Bowles has made use of drugs; many of the stories and novels contain hallucinogenic setpieces. *Up Above the World*, his finest novel, concerns the efforts of a rich young Mexican to erase, by systematic drug-induced amnesia, from the possible memory of two American tourists their unconscious witnessing of the contract murder of his mother in a hotel. But far from increasing narrative freedoms, such methods or episodes re-establish a formal distance from character and leave circumstantial selfhood intact and unknowable. That Bowles takes for granted a privileged access to the irrational is less remarkable than his refusal to know his characters socially, or for the most part to communicate details of their physical appearance. Minor characters are exactly rendered, while the protagonists are blurred where introspection might be expected to begin. Bowles's kif-inspired fantasias seek reticence as much as revelation.

The last story in *Midnight Mass*, **"In the Red Room"**, is obliquely about story-telling, and offers a clue to Bowles's aesthetic. An elderly American couple visit their son who is living in Sri Lanka. During their stay they go to the botanical gardens in Colombo, where they are waylaid by a hospitable but sinister local who insists on showing them around the garden house in which, as the son later discovers, he had murdered his bride many years before. The son resists the urge to tell his parents the coda to the story, on the grounds that they had sensed the core of the mystery ''without needing the details''. When, in *Without Stopping*, Bowles recalls being once referred to as a ''devious young man'', he considers this as a comment on his manner of relating stories:

> When I begin to recount an incident, my first intention is to give a bare report of the principal events and nothing more and eventually allow extensions of that material. It must become increasingly obvious to the listener that I am withholding information; this can hardly be an endearing characteristic to observe in a friend.

This cultivation of distance extends to Bowles's use of dialogue. The couples and familiars of his fiction communicate in interchanges of frozen, amnesiac banality. In part this reflects his resistance to the confessional urges of speech, and in part his musical (rather than dramatic) sense of speech as being most expressive when suffused with irritation and bafflement.

Bowles's natural-historical imagination has been praised for its unerring conviction, but his sense of place is primarily aural. This is significant in explaining why his casually exact settings so completely oppress and marginalize their inhabitants; in his world speech is the prerogative of landscape and the natural world, not of man. Nor does Bowles ever offer an account of human will, though his language of appetite and obscure compulsion is subtle and suggestive. Purposelessness—often a central theme—is invariably punished, hence the tendency for violence to become the normative gesture in his fiction.

There is a group of stories in which Bowles takes the transfiguration of violence a step further and writes calm, animistic conceits about possession and violation. It is remarkable that the nature of his material has so rarely compromised his linguistic tact; also, that the ordinary is always present within his other, stranger perspectives.

Paul Keegan, "Magic, Marriage and Murder," in The Times Literary Supplement, No. 4364, November 21, 1986, p. 1326.

STEVEN E. OLSON

With the exception of James Baldwin, Paul Bowles is perhaps America's most distinguished living expatriate writer. Since 1947 Bowles has lived abroad, primarily in Tangier. Virtually all of his fiction is set abroad, either in North Africa or Central or South America; only three of his thirty-nine short stories are set in the United States. Critics have emphasized Bowles's ''foreignness,'' his fascination with the non-Western mind and remote, often inhuman landscapes. Lawrence Stewart calls North Africa Bowles's ''home territory.'' Gore Vidal claims that the triumph of Bowles's art can be traced to the fact that he laudably ignored ''that greatest of all human themes: *The American Experience*. . . . Bowles is still odd man out; he writes as if *Moby Dick* had never been written.'' Leslie Fiedler comes nearest to identifying Bowles's persistent psychological themes when noting the writer's obsession with ''images of alienation, flight, and abysmal fear.'' Yet Fiedler relegates Bowles to a circle of "minor novelists" writing in the gothic tradition of "highbrow terror-fiction" that runs from Charles Brockden Brown through John Hawkes, ultimately dismissing Bowles as a kind of voyeuristic peddler of "horror-pornography."

Stewart, Vidal, and Fiedler are all equally drawn to three of Bowles's most shocking stories. All three discuss **"The Delicate Prey,"** which depicts castration, torture, and murder. Interestingly, Stewart and Vidal choose that story and two others, **"Pages from Cold Point"** and **"A Distant Episode,"** for the focal point of their arguments. The latter two stories describe homosexual incest, violence, and madness. While there is no gainsaying that the fictional world of Bowles is often one of violence and aberration, we must recognize that that is but one aspect of Bowles's imagination. Though they may at times seem gratuitous, the elements of horror in Bowles's writings rarely are. Beneath the violent surfaces of the novels and many of the stories lies a persistent anti-patriarchal stratum that is characteristically American. Indeed, I would argue against Vidal's position, by claiming that Bowles most certainly writes in the Antinomian tradition of the greatest American novelists: he writes, that is, as if *Moby Dick had* been written.

The main source of Bowles's anti-patriarchalism stems clearly from his own childhood, where he met with recurrent humiliations and cruelties from his father.... (pp. 334-35)

Bowles's fiction is peopled with unhappy Americans who "didn't ask to be born" and who are not particularly happy to be alive. In *The Sheltering Sky* (1949) unhappiness arises in part from "the whole horrible thing that happens after every war, everywhere." The progress of Western civilization is treated even more contemptuously in Bowles's third and finest novel, *The Spider's House* (1955), which dramatizes the dissolution of traditional patterns of life in Fez during the Moroccan revolution. Yet Bowles's characters do not derive their unhappiness chiefly from a cultural consciousness nor from the anxiety of living in the Atomic Age. Cultural uprootedness functions nearly always as effect rather than cause in Bowles's fiction. Expatriatism and deracination are by-products of a much deeper alienation, an alienation of self. Security and happiness have not been destroyed by World War II, but have vanished far earlier, in childhood. Bowles's characters are expatriates manqué, individuals who inhabit alien terrains of self. The vertiginous landscapes of Morocco, like those of Central or South America, provide a projected topography of the psychic fissures, cliffs, and abysses formed in a vanished geological age—the age of childhood.

Bowles first depicted the violent failure of a parent-child relationship in **"The Echo"** (1946). In this early story a college-aged American girl, Aileen, visits her mother, who has recently moved from Washington, D.C., to live in Colombia in a large house perched on the side of a cliff. With the mother lives Prue, a masculine, blue-jeaned artist who is clearly lover as well as housemate. Aileen's neurotic behavior within Bowles's erotically charged landscape reveals the daughter's sexual repression and estrangement from her mother, both of which eventually fuel a savage attack upon Prue. Aileen's mother has insisted that the daughter behave civilly toward Prue because "she's my guest and you're my guest." To reduce one's child to the category of "guest" is a decided act of parental betrayal; Aileen's subsequent outrage, directed at Prue, constitutes a displaced assault upon the mother. More significantly, Aileen's assault represents a child's rebellion against patriarchal authority, for the masculine and aggressive Prue functions as both substitute-father and phallic aggressor. That this is so is made

clear by Prue's twisting of Aileen's arm and her flicking of water into Aileen's face on the morning of the daughter's departure. The water-flicking duplicates an earlier incident wherein a male peasant had emptied a mouthful of water into Aileen's face after she had paused in curiosity before his hut. Only by attacking the father-substitute can Aileen, the child, lay claim to a viable identity. (pp. 335-36)

Bowles's most notorious depiction of a perverted parent-child relationship occurs in **"Pages from Cold Point"** (1947). The story depicts the seduction and blackmailing of a father, Mr. Norton, by his sixteen-year-old son, Racky. Less a sordid tale of perversion than a nihilistic allegory of Western civilization, **"Pages from Cold Point"** dramatizes Bowles's deep hostility to the intelligentsia. Like the Professor in **"A Distant Episode,"** Mr. Norton is a benighted and cynical product of his vocation, university teaching, a career he himself admits had always been "an utter farce." The death of his wife, Hope, has plunged Mr. Norton into a disillusioned hedonism, lived out upon the remote point of a small Caribbean island. "After Hope's death" there is no redemption:

> Our civilization is doomed to a short life: its component parts are too heterogeneous. I personally am content to see everything in the process of decay. The bigger the bombs, the quicker it will be done. Life is visually too hideous for one to make the attempt to preserve it. Let it go. Perhaps some day another form of life will come along. Either way, it is of no consequence.

Possibly Mr. Norton's new life form *has* come along. That form, of his own creation, is his son Racky, corruption and hopelessness incarnate. (pp. 336-37)

In *The Sheltering Sky* Bowles voiced what would continue to be the major themes of his fiction: loss, alienation, and flight. To say that these have been the persistent themes of such other male American writers as Cooper, Melville, Twain, Hemingway, and Faulkner is to remove the Bowles canon from the Fiedleresque purlieu of "horror-pornography" and to set it where it more deservedly belongs: in the mainstream of American fiction. In the fiction written after *The Sheltering Sky* Bowles turned more directly toward voicing his themes in terms of "vanished innocence" and lost or destroyed childhoods. In fact, between **"The Echo"** and **"The Frozen Fields"** (1946-1957) Bowles displays an increasingly romantic interest in children. (p. 339)

The concept of child-as-redeemer which Bowles adumbrates in *Let It Come Down* receives full and tragic expression in his third and most brilliant novel, *The Spider's House* (1955). It seems ironically appropriate that Bowles dedicated the book to his father, for the novel brings together the author's most persistent filial and anti-patriarchal themes concerning the adult betrayal of childhood innocence. Set in Fez during the days of the Moroccan Revolution of August 1954, *The Spider's House* contains effective shifts in point of view which intensify the sense of intrigue and uncertainty generated by political events; the absence of the aberrant or sensational enhances the reality of the characters and their plight; and the superbly rendered portrait of Fez—political, social, religious, domestic—provides a Balzacian richness to the panorama of a city and its people. Though Bowles emphasizes in his preface to the 1982 Black Sparrow Press edition of the book that *The Spider's House* is about the "dissolution" of a medieval way of life in Fez, the poignancy of the novel derives more from Bowles's depiction of the timeless tragedy of mankind's fall from innocence.

In a very real sense, it could be said that *The Spider's House* is a parable of the Fall: the seduction of the protagonist John Stenham by the conniving Lee Burroughs brings about corruption and expulsion; an automobile carries the fallen couple away from the now-destroyed purity of Fez to the decadence of Casablanca. Left in the adults' wake is Amar, a fifteen-year-old Moroccan youth trapped between two worlds—worlds as much those of childhood innocence and adult duplicity as the warring worlds of Moslem and European cultures. By deserting Amar, who begs to stay with him, Stenham repudiates that which might save him. The tragic vision of *The Spider's House* relies less upon the historical destruction of medieval Fez than upon the destruction of childhood itself. In effect, Amar *is* Fez: his childish innocence is synonymous with the city's purity. By dramatizing the dissolution of Amar's private and familial world, Bowles symbolizes the dissolution of the larger culture—the technique is similar to Faulkner's in *The Sound and the Fury*.

The Spider's House opens (following a suspenseful prologue introducing John Stenham) as the young Amar resignedly returns home to be beaten by his father. The precise nature of Amar's crime remains murky; we know little more than that his older brother Mustapha has seen him in a "forbidden" area of Fez. Mustapha tries unsuccessfully to blackmail Amar, threatening to report him to their father, Sri Driss, if Amar does not pay. Amar knows that he will be beaten by his father if reported. He does not fear the pain of such beating, but resents its *injustice:* "what was unbearable was the thought that he was innocent and that he was going to be humiliated by being treated as though he were guilty." From Amar's thoughts, we can infer that he is actually innocent of the crime which Sri Driss accuses him of—stealing the household money needed for food to spend on himself in the forbidden European quarter of the city. Amar, however, is no thief. It seems likely that Mustapha himself stole the money for his kif habit, knowing that circumstantial evidence (Amar's being away from home for several days) would condemn the younger brother.

The injustice of Sri Driss's beating of Amar certainly owes much to Bowles's own memories of being arbitrarily and unfairly punished as a child. Indeed, Amar's entire relationship with his father recalls Bowles's relationship with his own. Locked into a protracted struggle with a patriarchal tyrant, the imaginative son knows that he can attain victory only through a creatively active "hostile silence." As Sri Driss mercilessly beats Amar with the buckle-end of a belt, screaming "I hope I kill you!," the son silently ponders whether it is "a consuming hatred or an overpowering love" that he feels for his father. Amar respects his father's unwavering sense of duty, yet at the same time he recognizes an unbridgeable gap between their two worlds. As the son of a Cherif, or descendant of the Prophet, Amar, like Sri Driss, possesses the *baraka*—the gift of healing. The son's power, however, unlike the father's, is derived from the spirit rather than the letter of the Koran. Sri Driss's world is static and dead. The father has no understanding or intuition of his son's private nature, which perceives a living world of constant revelation. A visionary romantic, Amar is the Blakean or Emersonian poet-sayer, the artist who perceives the miraculous in the mundane:

> The thought that his own conception of the world was so different from his father's was like a protecting wall around his entire being. When his father

went out into the street he had only the mosque, the Koran, the other old men in his mind. It was the immutable world of law, the written law, the written word, unchanging beneficence. . . . Whereas when Amar stepped out the door there was the whole vast earth waiting, the live, mysterious earth, that belonged to him in a way it could belong to no one else, and where anything might happen.

Amar, we will soon learn, is the opposite of the American Stenham, the rationally detached and introverted novelist whose powers are failing him.

Amar's innocence rests upon the integrity of his imagination, which daily re-creates the world. Uneducated and illiterate by choice, constantly spinning fantasies, Amar is considered "crazy" by his friends. For his part, Amar takes great pride in being different—it signifies to him his status as one of the Chorfa—he possesses a benevolent strain of the Hawthornesque ability of knowing "what [is] in the hearts of other men." Amar's father has come to regret his decision to let his son remain out of school; consequently, there is a constant struggle at home to force Amar to work. Because a Cherif does not work in any ordinary sense of the term, Sri Driss's efforts to apprentice his son constitute efforts to destroy the son's gifts. Like Claude Bowles, the pleasure-hating father is committed to ending his son's childhood. Catching Amar outside the house several days after beating him, he orders his son to prepare for a job interview as a potter's assistant: "This is not a world just to go for a walk in. You're a man, not a boy any longer."

Like Port Moresby and Nelson Dyar, John Stenham inhabits a cage of self. In Fez, he dwells appropriately in the *tower* of the Merenides Palace hotel. His forced descent from that tower by the intrusion of political events thrusts him into an unwanted and unwonted arena of moral choice. Only once before did Stenham face a similar dilemma of choosing sides—when he chose to join the Communist Party in the Thirties. That choice—the wrong one—has paralyzed "the part of his consciousness which dealt with the choosing of sides," even though he resigned from the Party in 1940. Stenham opposes both French occupation of Morocco and a Nationalist victory. He would prefer that time stand still, that Fez remain somnolently medieval and pure so that he might continue to write without disturbance in his tower. Bowles will not leave his hero alone, of course. Stenham will be able to avoid making a political choice, but he will face a much tougher choice, a moral one: he will have to choose between Amar and an American woman, Lee Burroughs. For the second consecutive time, Stenham makes the wrong choice. In choosing Lee Burroughs over Amar, Stenham chooses badly: he chooses evil over goodness, death over life. To read the novel in any other light, I believe strongly, is to misread Bowles's intention. Amar possesses the key that can unlock Stenham's cage, perhaps even freeing his creative energies as a writer. Stenham, however, chooses a woman he neither loves nor really admires—he locks himself into a yet smaller and more constrictive cage. Clearly, Bowles is commenting upon his own decision to live unfettered in Tangier, where few if any restraints were imposed upon his aesthetic choices.

To minimize or disregard Lee Burroughs' corrupt vacuity is to misread *The Spider's House*. A joyless and mannequin-like bitch, Lee "had become an adult early" following the deaths of her parents in a plane crash. A former worker for UNESCO, she spouts the empty rhetoric of progressivism while valuing human life only in the abstract. Indeed, her Dorothea Brooke-like concern for a whipped carriage horse during her initial outing with Stenham surpasses any concern she ever exhibits for specific Moroccans. Enraged at Stenham's praise for Amar's ability to see "an untainted world" during the festival of Aïd el Kebir, Lee gives the boy money for a revolver. Her motives in doing so, lamely justified on the grounds of pushing Amar into the struggle for Moroccan independence, are completely selfish and irrational—she is attempting only to punish Stenham by destroying Amar, someone he has come to care for and admire. Stenham tells Lee that "there's a four-letter word" for her potentially tragic action.

Only by separating Stenham from Amar can Lee succeed in seducing him. The adversarial relationship which had existed during the festival heretofore had depended upon Amar's proximity to Stenham, for the youth's Islamic gift of *baraka* had provided Stenham with some insight into the substance of Lee's moral corruption. Lee "doesn't know anthing about the world," Amar tells his American benefactor; "she wants to be something powerful." Whereas Amar's friend Mohammed denounces Lee for failing to behave chastely, Amar criticizes her for nothing less that her hubris—her arrogance and pride. Rather than surrender to the world, Lee would see it changed, made over in some ephemeral image of man. As such, Lee is the spider who, according to the Koran, builds "the frailest of all houses." Into that house, from his tower, Stenham descends.

From the moment of having first met Amar at the Café Berakne, where the boy was standing in a pool trying to rescue a dragonfly, Stenham's complacently insular conception of Moroccan life became challenged: "Moroccans just don't do things like that," he tells Lee. Subsequently, when he sees Amar cry with emotion over the beauty of a woman's song at the feast of the Aïd, his convictions are further undermined. Amar, that is, has violated what Stenham always unquestionably assumed: that for a Moroccan "to be touched by beauty was shameful." Though Amar hurriedly checks his emotional response so that his companion Mohammed will not notice it, his spontaneous outburst has a profoundly disturbing effect upon Stenham. Until this moment the American writer has never conceived Moroccans to exist except as a faceless aggregate:

> But now, perhaps as a result of having seen this boy, he found himself beginning to doubt the correctness of his whole theoretical edifice . . . that such a person as Amar could be produced by this society rather upset Stenham's calculations . . . if there were one Amar, there could be others.

Amar's intrusion into Stenham's world approaches a moment of what Mircea Eliade terms *hierophany,* a manifestation of the sacred in everyday life. In Amar's company, Stenham is challenged to renounce or question his nihilistic cynicism. Less an agent than a potential catalyst for Stenham's redemption, however, Amar proves to be no match for Lee Burroughs' duplicity or Stenham's own moral spinelessness. Having stood at the brink of a revelatory instant, Stenham defers further epiphanies: "it required too much effort to go on from there." He returns to Lee. The Knight has turned away from the Chapel Perilous.

Once returned to Fez, Amar becomes dangerously embroiled in the accelerating events of the Revolution. He cannot return to his house to ascertain the safety of his family, but must seek refuge with the Nationalist Moulay Ali and his band of Istiqlal youths, members of the "Friends of Freedom." When finally able to escape Moulay Ali's house after a raid, Amar finds himself "cut off from his home." He seeks the American stranger Stenham, "whose existence in the world meant the possibility of hope." Stenham, who has tousled Amar's hair as well as fed and protected him, represents the affectional father the child needs. Unlike Sri Driss and others, Stenham has never sought to impose rules or dictate behavior, nor has he been judgmental toward Amar. Such shared characteristics as a distaste for hedonism and a distrust of knowledge gained solely through the intellect bond Stenham and Amar together.

Following a number of risks and dangers, Amar succeeds in locating Stenham in Fez's Ville Nouvelle. By this time the Moroccan youth is faint and dizzy:

> He saw his friend in the doorway, his arm raised in a gesture of welcome; then a cloud came swiftly across the sun and the street shot into its dark shadow. He leaned against one of the small dead trees to keep from falling. . . . But then the Nazarene was at his side, leading him into the cool shade of the hotel . . . he was happy. Nothing mattered, nothing terrible could happen to him when he was in this man's care.

Amar's belief that "now everything is well" proves, of course, to be wrong, for Stenham and Lee Burroughs (the evidence of their intimacy displayed in smears of lipstick and odors of perfume) are fleeing Fez for Casablanca. With his world in ruins around him, Amar wants only to be with Stenham. Under a ruse that he intends to visit his mother in Meknes, Amar rides into the hills beyond Fez with Stenham and Lee. There, Stenham orders him from the car. As the car resumes speed, Amar runs after it in the hot tar, his sandals kicked aside: "he had the exultant feeling of flying along the road behind the car. It would surely stop. . . . He ran on. When he got to the curve the road was empty." Like Sal Paradise's auto-desertion of Dean Moriarty at the end of *On the Road,* Stenham's desertion of Amar symbolizes both betrayal and an irremediable fall from grace for the protagonist and a stinging indictment of fathers who rob their sons of happiness.

That Bowles's imagination was deeply moved by the writing of *The Spider's House* can be measured by the first story he published after the novel appeared, **"The Frozen Fields"** (1957). One of only a handful of stories set in America, **"The Frozen Fields"** makes explicit what is only implicit in *The Spider's House:* an abused son wishes his father dead. Bowles's story, similar to Conrad Aiken's "Silent Snow, Secret Snow," recounts an otherwise idyllic family Christmas rendered nightmarish by the neurotic and tyrannical behavior of a parent. (In the Aiken story, however, the suspect parent is mother rather than father.) In the Bowles story, Donald, a highly sensitive and imaginative boy approaching his seventh birthday, is forced to bear the unwarranted humiliations and cruelties visited upon him by his father, Owen, a destroyer of all magic, privacy, and delight. Owen is hated and despised by all who know him. He tyrannizes over both his wife and his son, causing another character, Uncle Ivor, to comment that "it would have been better for everybody if he'd stayed single." Donald's father's raging insecurity explodes in an attack upon his son, who has received many expensive gifts from the wealthy Mr. Gordon, a sexually suspect character. Despite his possible societally condemned propensities, Mr. Gordon is a compassionate and affectional father-figure for Donald. The older man understands Donald's feelings. In giving him gifts, he relives and cherishes his own childhood.

Donald's father, Owen, is about to have a heart attack over his rage at Mr. Gordon's unsolicited largesse toward his son. Owen corners his son in the henhouse, insisting that he and Donald have a snowball-throwing contest, the target to be the trunk of a large tree at the edge of the woods. Because he has dreamed about a large wolf who has seized his father by the throat and carried him off, however, Donald is afraid to throw snowballs into the woods. Enraged at this act of filial disobedience, the father rubs snow into his son's face; for good measure, he also shoves some snow down Donald's neck.

In a state bordering on detachment and coma, Donald endures his unjust punishment, much as Amar endured the injustice of his beating by Sri Driss. Bowles's description of Mr. Gordon's departure from the family farm makes the meaning of Donald's punishment clear. Wearing a "thick beaver collar" and "heavy fur gloves," Mr. Gordon *is* the wolf of vengeance lurking in the woods. Kind and powerful, the wolf is Donald's imagined protector against parental tyranny. As Donald falls asleep after Mr. Gordon's departure, he dreams of the wolf falling asleep in his lap: "Donald leaned over and buried his face in the shaggy fur of his scruff. After a while they both got up and began to run together, faster and faster, across the fields."

As lost son in pursuit of affectional and protective father, Donald duplicates Amar's pursuit of Stenham at the end of *The Spider's House*. Moreover, "**The Frozen Fields**" anticipates Bowles's depiction of parricide in *Up above the World* (1967). Bowles's persistent themes of familial and filial discord, traceable to his own childhood, are decidedly within the mainstream of American fiction. As such, his reputation stands in need of reassessment. After all, American literature has no nuclear families to speak of (except perhaps in the South). In the rare instances where a parent does exist, he or she tends to be savage, misanthropic, or despotic. Consider Irving's Dame Van Winkle, Huck Finn's Pap, James's Mrs. Newsome, and Faulkner's Thomas Sutpen. Captain Ahab and Willy Loman have hardly served as exemplary father-models either. Even Melville's Mrs. Glendinning becomes enemy and parental victim/tyrant when she forces her prodigal son Pierre to opt for annihilation in the world rather than suspect happiness at home.

Adult protagonists in American literature have generally been so severely scarred in childhood or adolescence that their very survival poses a threat to themselves and those around them. Bowles's characters share with those of Faulkner, Farrell, Aiken, Fitzgerald, O'Neill, and Dreiser a crippling familial past. Although his landscapes are exotic and his more familiar scenes shocking, Paul Bowles writes generally of the country within—the topos of promise betrayed, childhood destroyed. (pp. 342-49)

Steven E. Olson, "Alien Terrain: Paul Bowles's Filial Landscapes," in Twentieth Century Literature, *Vol. 32, Nos. 3 & 4, Fall & Winter, 1986, pp. 334-49.*

PAUL KEEGAN

Most striking about this world [in *Call at Corazón and Other Stories*] of North African and South American gothic is its insistence on a single theme: the irreducibility of cultural difference. Other peoples are the great mystery story and, by an often brutal extension, other people—families, neighbours, couples. . . .

Bowles's laconic and brooding vision of difference makes for a chaste narrative style, largely uninterested in psychology and unflinchingly external in its presentation of things either enig-

matically ordered or on their way out of control. The more gothic of the tales might sound Kiplingesque—*contes cruels* which try by this means to seize the imponderable strangeness of an alien culture—but Bowles has nothing of Kipling's knowingness or his sense of a captive audience.

Bowles's own stories are . . . tilted away from the private life. His Americans in foreign parts submit to sheer contingency, their past selves jettisoned; his South Americans or North Africans are beyond reach, their otherness inviolate. With differing emphases, all of Bowles's characters inhabit a narrative world without individual recollection; they are held in its present moment. The Americans are prey to mood—an unbroken series of contradictory impulses—and to irritation, a human static which shuts out its own source. In the story "**Call at Corazón**", set aboard a cramped paddle-steamer in Central America, a wife is unfaithful to her new husband somehow "because" he has purchased a small monkey at their last port of call. The extended honeymoon trip is a favourite theme of Bowles, a drama of last straws which shows small nameless emotions swallowing big authenticated ones. His characters are possessed by whim, fecklessness, a boredom which does not preclude terror, and, above all, the spirit of place.

Physical setting is the real protagonist of these stories. In the preface to *Call at Corazón*, Bowles describes his characters as dominated by backdrop and "almost entirely improvised, as is the action in which they become involved". That does little to suggest the remarkable totality of effect he achieves. One reason why landscape matters so much is that it replaces history. If his stories do secrete explanations of their events they do so "conjecturally", aligning the atavistic regressions of the rational mind with the persistence of primitive belief systems into the contemporary world. The result is a kind of landscape, in which all layers are simultaneously present to view. And though Bowles's landscapes are gothic—this place is about to become dreadful—they are also rooted in an exact natural-historical attention. In "**The Echo**", an American college student visits her mother in Colombia, where the latter has set up house with a sculptress. The house is a post-modernist folly perched over a gorge, and the sculptress a possessive, role-obsessed aggressor. Relations between lover and daughter deteriorate daily through a sequence of numb exchanges ending in violence. Yet the story's madness is modulated almost entirely through place. In "**At Paso Rojo**", set in Costa Rica, two spinsterish sisters visit their countrified brother on his ranch. The less fastidious of the two makes advances to one of the ranch hands, is rejected, and exacts a revenge which brings in train the destruction of the brother's paternalist idyll. Again, the story's surfaces describe a ranch, but leave behind a study in sexual hysteria.

Miscegenation recurs in Bowles, epitomizing the fraught nature of all relations contracted between Americans and the cultures they may think they understand. Several of the stories are about the expatriate community in Morocco, over whose cosy eccentricities in the face of the surrounding strangeness Bowles casts a very cold eye.

Paul Keegan, "Americans in Foreign Parts," in The Times Literary Supplement, *No. 4441, May 13-19, 1988, p. 526.*

William Boyd

1952-

English novelist, short story writer, scriptwriter, critic, and nonfiction writer.

Considered among the most talented contemporary authors writing within the comic tradition of such English novelists as Evelyn Waugh and Kingsley Amis, Boyd often depicts alienated British expatriates who search for personal identity in foreign cultures. He has consistently garnered praise for his detailed evocation of place and character, strong command of language, and perceptive and imaginative wit. Jonathan Yardley observed: "[Boyd] is a biting satirist and social commentator, yet he regards his characters with an affection that is too rare in such fiction. There's hardly a writer around whose work offers more pleasure and satisfaction."

Boyd's first two novels, *A Good Man in Africa* (1981) and *An Ice-Cream War: A Tale of the Empire* (1982), earned critical accolades for imaginative rejuvenations of situations derived from earlier comic fiction. *A Good Man in Africa* centers upon the farcical mishaps that result from the alcoholic and sexual impulses of an obese British diplomat in West Africa, while *An Ice-Cream War* makes use of multiple narrative voices to explore the effects of World War I on the simple, happy residents of a remote East African town. Reviewers regarded both novels as amusing and poignant, commending Boyd's insights into the lives of transplanted Englishmen and their relations with native Africans. *On the Yankee Station and Other Stories* (1981) is a collection of diverse short pieces that most critics viewed as the experiments of a talented young author developing his craft.

In his next novel, *Stars and Bars* (1985), Boyd follows the misadventures of a shy London art appraiser who travels to New York City hoping to overcome his reticence. The Englishman is intimidated by brash New Yorkers and thoroughly confounded by a family of Southern eccentrics, however, before experiencing a moment of self-knowledge while stranded virtually naked on Park Avenue. Although several critics faulted Boyd for a stereotypical approach to the premise of a foreigner abroad, others applauded his shrewd satirization of English and American peculiarities. Boyd also received favorable reviews for *School Ties: Good and Bad at Games, and Dutch Girls* (1985), a volume of two television scripts based on his experiences in the English public school system.

The New Confessions (1988), which Antony Beevor described as "Boyd's most ambitious and most successful novel," parallels *The Confessions,* a volume of autobiographical reminiscences by eighteenth-century French philosopher Jean Jacques Rousseau that greatly influenced the English Romantic movement. Boyd's work presents the recollections of an aging Scottish filmmaker, who recounts his life story from the time of his birth at the turn of the century through his silent film career, his blacklisting during Joseph McCarthy's House Committee Hearings on Un-American Activities, and his self-imposed exile on a Mediterranean island. Although several critics unfavorably compared the psychological intensity of Boyd's novel to that of Rousseau's *Confessions,* others praised his incisive and amusing portrayal of a man who succumbs to twentieth-

century uncertainty. Thomas R. Edwards commented: "[*The New Confessions* is] a novel that can be read with pleasure for its story, and also one that grows in the mind as you think about it afterward, the most ambitious and the best work this interesting writer . . . has yet produced."

(See also *CLC,* Vol. 28 and *Contemporary Authors,* Vols. 114, 120.)

CAROLINE SEEBOHM

William Boyd's novels *A Good Man in Africa* and *An Ice-Cream War* were greeted with cries of approval from both literary critics and readers, so *Stars and Bars* raises more than the usual anticipation. It is about an eager but shy Englishman, Henderson Dores, who comes to New York hoping to lose what he regards as his terminal Englishness in the brash, open, unreserved world of America. . . .

Henderson works for an art auction house (not unlike Sotheby's), for whom he is sent on a mission to obtain a potentially valuable art collection from a reclusive Southern millionaire named Loomis Gage. Much of the novel concerns Henderson's efforts to claim these paintings, which are kept in a locked room in a house in Luxora Beach, Ga., amid one of the most eccentric families one is likely to encounter. . . .

Nothing is what it seems. To complicate matters, Henderson is involved with two alluring but demanding women in New York—his former wife, Melissa, whose teen-age daughter, Bryant, attaches herself to Henderson and ends up in the Gage mansion too, and Irene, whose attraction for Henderson hinges on her resemblance to a Spanish girl who worked in a butcher's shop and around whom he spun a "tingling sexual fantasy" on a boring holiday some years earlier.

After many farcical adventures in Luxora Beach, Henderson returns to New York. The plot then has him staggering up Park Avenue . . . , for reasons too complicated to relate here, dressed only in a cardboard box. On this occasion, as the busy pedestrians avoid him, muttering about yet another lunatic, he enjoys a brief epiphany. "Of course, Henderson suddenly realized with tender elation, they think I'm *mad*. . . . It was a moment of true liberation. A revelation. He felt all the restraints of his culture and upbringing fall from him like a cloak slid from his shoulders."

Henderson is a changed man, make no mistake. There are, however, problems with the novel. Stories abound about an agreeable but hopelessly incompetent fellow's search for identity in an irrational world, and Henderson's virtues do not particularly distinguish him from the crowd. Books about the English experience in America, or vice versa, are not uncommon. This is splendid territory to mine, but it does require an original viewpoint when you enter the lists with novelists ranging from Henry James to Alison Lurie. Mr. Boyd has some funny and perceptive things to say about English shyness as opposed to American spontaneity. . . . But the author seems also to latch on to what are now fairly well aired differences between the English and Americans—pronunciation, for instance, and that old cliché about Americans ruining whiskey with ice.

The major scenes in *Stars and Bars* take place in Luxora Beach, a place of unremitting bleakness and despair. Mr. Boyd's talent in evoking a place, which worked for him so well in his earlier two novels, serves him brilliantly here. In fact, the reader is forced to ask why on earth Henderson, wimpish though he is, does not get out when he can. One remembers Evelyn Waugh's version of the civilized man's descent into primitivism in *A Handful of Dust*. In that case, poor Tony Last, desperate to escape, is condemned to read Dickens aloud to his mad captor for the rest of his days. Mr. Boyd is more charitable to Henderson, but there are times when it seems that charity is not what the benighted twit needs. The point about Henderson's liberation from his roots is well taken, and his adventures through the jungle are amusingly narrated, but the "new clarity" with which he views the world at the end remains, for the reader, a lingering fog.

*Caroline Seebohm, "The Treasures of Luxora Beach,"
in* The New York Times Book Review, *April 14,
1985, p. 17.*

JONATHAN YARDLEY

[*Stars and Bars* features] Henderson Dores. He is 39 years old, English, a bit on the timid side, not terribly sure of himself and not so happy with himself into the bargain. He's come to New York, where he works as the "Impressionist man" for a small art gallery that has hired him "to get things moving, whip up some trade, start making a name for the firm." But neither art nor career is the real explanation for his move; he has left Britain "in a conscious and deliberate flight from shyness," has "come to America for the cure" because "here, shyness was banned; shyness was outlawed, prohibited." Everywhere he goes he sees new evidence of it, as when he goes out for lunch with an American colleague:. . . .

> He looked about him at the fabulous lunchers. Pruitt shouted clear strong welcomes to people he knew. I want to be like you lot, Henderson thought, as he felt his shoulders round and his chest concave; I want your confidence and purpose, I want your teeth and tans, he pleaded, stepping out of the way and apologizing to a waiter. It's not fair.

Indeed it is not, and it does not get any fairer as Henderson Dores stumbles his way through *Stars and Bars,* which is in every respect a thoroughly accomplished and beguiling piece of work. Like William Boyd's first novel, *A Good Man in Africa,* his third is comic in tone and intent; though it is not without its serious aspects, there is in it none of the darkness to be found in his previous novel, *An Ice-Cream War.* Yet though Boyd returns here to comedy, it is with a considerably surer hand than in *A Good Man in Africa,* the hilarity of which is thrown somewhat off track by an unexpectedly sombre conclusion; in *Stars and Bars* Boyd has a more confident hand on his material, with the happy result that the novel's serious side emerges naturally and unobtrusively from the comedy that is its essence.

And comic it most certainly is. By way of introducing Dores to America—"This is his problem: he loves America, but will America love him back?"—Boyd quickly moves him out of Manhattan and into the distant South. He goes there, to an inland hamlet mysteriously called Luxora Beach, in order to assess the paintings owned by one Loomis Gage, a "reclusive, Southern millionaire" who has "a small but very select collection.". . .

[Dores travels south] with dangerous company: Bryant Wax, the nymphetic 14-year-old daughter of his former wife, Melissa, who has divorced her second husband and is now entertaining the possibility of remarrying Dores, though not to the extent of permitting "pre-remarital sex." This helps explain why Dores has involved himself, on the side, with the aggressive Irene Stein, even though in saner moments he cannot imagine why he is flitting uncertainly from one woman to another, tangling himself in a web of deception that only promises to get more messy now that he has Bryant on his hands. Melissa thinks a Southern excursion will be good for her darling daughter; it certainly proves to be no good for poor Dores, her reluctant chauffeur and chaperon.

Arriving at Luxora Beach after an unsettling drive with Bryant, Dores finds himself in enough fixes to keep any comic novel percolating for hours. Loomis Gage turns out to be a spry octogenarian who is oddly reluctant to let Dores see the paintings; his elder son, Freeman, is a hulking lout who warns Dores, in most emphatic language, not to try to sell the paintings and, for that matter, to be off the premises within 24 hours; Cora Gage, the master's only daughter, is a raving Anglophobiac, and his younger son, Beckman, indulges himself in hallucinations about Vietnam. . . . (p. 3)

"Out here he felt weak and unprotected, alien and unfamiliar," Dores quickly realizes. . . .

"He had an awful foreboding nothing was going to work out."

Which is why soon enough he finds himself skulking around New York in darkest night, clad in nothing save a cardboard carton that once had held 2,000 "Marymount No-Slak Sanitary Napkins." But how he gets there, and what he learns from it all, are not to be disclosed herein. Suffice it to say that along the way Boyd stages several splendid setpieces, among the most memorable of which are a dinner at the Gage mansion during which Dores becomes miserably sloshed on a potent local brew called Henry's Goat, and a disastrous weekend stay in Atlanta. . . . (pp. 3, 9)

All of this is so funny that it's easy to lose sight of the skill with which Boyd has brought it off. He is an Englishman who has spent precious little time in the United States, yet he re-creates American speech with the aplomb of a born mimic—I did not detect a single false phrase or inflection—and he has got the American landscape, both physical and psychological, exactly right. Beyond that, and of far greater importance to the book's success as a work of fiction, he has populated it with people so convincingly real that even when the action borders on the fantastic, the reader never loses the sense of being in an entirely human world, one that seems familiar even when it seems bizarre. Rich though the comedy is, it never once lapses into excess; this, as much as anything else, keeps the novel within its human scale.

With four books—the three novels plus *On the Yankee Station*, a collection of remarkably diverse, surprising short stories—Boyd has firmly established himself as a writer of impressive, original achievement. He writes more often than not about the conflict of alien cultures, but he invariably does so in ways that are unpredictable and imaginative; he is heir to an established tradition of English comic fiction, yet within it he is clearly his own man; he is a biting satirist and social commentator, yet he regards his characters with an affection that is too rare in such fiction. There's hardly a writer around whose work offers more pleasure and satisfaction. (p. 9)

Jonathan Yardley, "William Boyd's Brits and Grits," in Book World—The Washington Post, *April 28, 1985, pp. 3, 9.*

GARRETT EPPS

[Boyd] has approached the New World with—dare I say it?—un-British humility. The result is an uneven but rewarding comic novel. The theme of *Stars and Bars* is one the two sides never grow tired of discussing in private: What is the difference not between our two political systems or societies but between our characters, our very selves? Henderson Dores, Boyd's appealingly klutzy central character, has made his judgment: Englishmen are shy, Americans are bold, and Henderson wants to become an American.

Henderson isn't unintelligent, unsuccessful, or even unattractive; he is nearly 40 and just under six feet tall. . . .

But Henderson is paralyzingly timid—so timid that he has ruined his dream marriage to an American girl because he couldn't bring himself to tell the unattractive next-door neighbor that he didn't want to go to bed with her. Now, after some solitary years as a Grub Street art critic in London, Henderson has left England and come to New York in a "deliberate flight from shyness, in a determined escape from timidity." Henderson expects America to make him a new man. . . .

America thrills and intimidates him. . . . He admires the people, "the crowds of Americans—neat, well dressed—strid[ing] past him purposefully, unheeding, confident." And he tries his modest, self-deprecating best to blend in, taking an apartment in the East, studying Zen fencing with a black swordsman named Eugene Teagarden, and entering into an uneasy liaison with Irene Stein, a New York bitch goddess who captivates him at a gallery opening by remarking, "I'm not the fucking hatcheck, numbnuts."

But try as he will, Henderson just can't get into the swing of things. . . .

Then the art auction firm he works for gets a call from a Southern millionaire who wants to sell a collection of Impressionist paintings, and Henderson is packed unwilling off to the land of cotton. In a moss-grown backwater named Luxora Beach, not far from Atlanta, he is subjected to the tender mercies of the Gage family. . . .

What happens thereafter is, as in all good comic fiction, at once intricate and trivial. But before it's over, Henderson has been nauseated by Southern cooking, humiliated in an Atlanta hotel, rejected by Irene, and threatened graphically by Mafia dons. As we half expected, he comes through it all beautifully, until he reaches the moment when, robbed of his clothes, he must wander the predawn streets of New York dressed only in a sanitary napkin packing case. As the first rays of sun touch his half-naked form, Henderson, for perhaps the first time in his life, feels accepted. . . . (p. 41)

All comedy, of course, takes as its subject the integration of the individual into a society that is at least half-mad. So Henderson's epiphany is exhilarating for the reader as well, a fitting close for a drama of transatlantic identity crisis. But a good deal of *Stars and Bars* isn't up to that mark. Boyd's view of smart New York life is precise if not entirely original. His satire of Atlanta . . . is fresh and hilarious. My favorite moment comes when Henderson checks into a mammoth downtown hotel called the Monopark, then finds that to reach his room he must paddle a canoe across the moat in the atrium.

But much of the Southern comedy isn't really up to its setting. For one thing, it is very hard to write a comedy of manners about a group of eccentrics. Boyd evidently means us to take the Gages as a nearly incredible gang of zanies; in fact, by Dixie eccentric standards, they're rank amateurs, and they never quite pull off a memorable slapstick scene. Second, Boyd gets a few details just plain wrong. I don't mean factual mistakes, which don't really matter in comic fiction, but errors of manners, which do: for example, T. J. Cardew, the preacher whose parishioners call him "Father" and who serenely drinks sour-mash whiskey, was plainly created by someone who hasn't spent much time with Southern Baptists.

So in the middle of this book, the laughs are few and far between. Its beginning and ending, however, are just shy (so to speak) of brilliant. And *Stars and Bars* is oddly good-natured in its satire, which is unusual for comic fiction and even more unusual for transatlantic raillery. I hope Boyd will venture South again someday. Unlike many English writers, he seems like a good guest, one who would make his bed, tidy up, and do his best to fit in with native ways. He's even sent America a gracious thank-you note. (pp. 41-2)

Garrett Epps, "Innocent Abroad," in The New Republic, *Vol. 193, No. 2, July 8, 1985, pp. 41-2.*

JUDITH WYNN

English writer William Boyd is a master at broad, knockabout farce and surely possesses one of the most inventively sadistic senses of humor since Jonathan Swift's. But if you have read his two earlier novels, you already know that. Who can forget the fat, sweaty hero of *A Good Man in Africa* getting sexually besieged by the girl of his dreams—the moment he learns that his scorned mistress has given him a venereal disease? Then there's the British East African settler in Boyd's World War I saga *An Ice Cream War* stoically contemplating his baby daughter's desecrated grave only to fly into a passionate rage a few minutes later, when he discovers that the beastly huns have also stolen his Finnegan & Zabriske Sisal Decorticator. In Boydland, be it darkest Africa or grungy old England, whatever can possibly go wrong will, while every man skips to his own demented drummer.

Boyd's latest opus *Stars and Bars,* while adhering to this stranger-in-a-strange-land preoccupation and breaking no new territory so far as the conventional, straightforward narrative goes, ought to net him the world title for hilariously accelerating bemusement, nevertheless. In it, a thirty-nine-year-old Englishman, one Henderson Dores, embarks upon a bifurcated odyssey in quest of (a) the father he never met, and (b) spiritual Americanization. (p. 27)

As the great white hope at the New York offices of Mulholland, Melhuish, Fine Art Auctioneers, Dores yearns to be like the broad-shouldered, firm-voiced yuppie gods who descend upon opulent Manhattan restaurants at noon to consume vast quantities of grilled plaice and filet mignon with butterscotch sauce. (An interesting sidenote in this typically mordant travel novel is that the English, long notorious for their bad cooking, find American cuisine equally bad as well as absurd.) He seeks verve. Confidence. An end to genteel English namby-pambyness. He wants America to work him over.

America does her best. Dores encounters American urban rage, New York looniness . . . , treacherous colleagues, and not one, but *two,* assertive American girlfriends. . . . (pp. 27-8)

With deft and witty sleight of hand, Boyd moves his transplanted Englishman to the Deep South on a treasure hunt for a cache of Impressionist paintings. . . . Of course, Boyd has placed a wild and wooly collection of Dixie grotesques in Dores's way. Without going into an extensive catalogue of these characters—they are drawn from southern-gothic literature, movies, TV, and so forth—suffice it to say that nothing is what it seems.

Boyd is at his best when he has a lot of action, a lot of conversation packed into one small space. The pivotal comic scene is a vegetarian feast at the Gage mansion—turnip greens, hoppin' john, corn dogs, avec California plonc—where a half-dozen topics are discussed at once. . . .

Particularly biting is the way in which Boyd has his hero glom onto any American simplicity and turn it over and over before his eyes as though it contains the keys to American success. . . .

Boyd does some wonderfully funny turns with the parent-child motif. The image crops up again: Dores and boss, Dores and client, Dores and prospective daughter (one of his girlfriends saddles him with her chain-smoking fourteen-year-old for the journey south). One painting in Gage's priceless collection depicts the goddess Demeter frantically seeking her lost child and being comforted at last by the servant-wench Baubo's ludicrously lewd gesture. Is human sexuality a regenerating

force or the whoopee cushion of man's existence? When Dores posts a letter to a British officer for information about his father's mysterious death in the Burmese jungles during World War II, *Stars and Bars* enters Graham Greene country, a world of dark "entertainments." Other Greene entertainments—*The Third Man, Our Man in Havana*—have made for first-rate film scripts. *Stars and Bars* would quite likely adapt well to the movies too. Boyd has a keen ear for dialogue and colloquialism, a first-rate sense of comic timing, and a very good eye for the way people carry themselves—particularly when they think that they are unobserved. (p. 28)

Judith Wynn, in a review of "Stars and Bars," in Boston Review, *Vol. X, No. 4, September, 1985, pp. 27-8.*

JOHN RAE

Public school criticism as a literary genre flourished for about 100 years, from *Tom Brown's Schooldays* in 1857 to the final, inferior blossoms of the 1960s. . . . After Waugh's *The Loom of Youth* [in 1917] almost every serious account of public school life was hostile. The critics raged against the iniquities of the total institution. To W. H. Auden the boarding school was a fascist state. To others it was synonymous with philistinism, snobbery, sadism and the shrivelling of emotion. But in the last decade the critique has changed again: the charge is social divisiveness rather than sexual disorientation.

William Boyd's *School Ties* is in this sense something of a period piece. In his introduction to these two film scripts, Boyd anticipates this criticism. After the films had been shown . . . he visited a number of public schools. 'It was clear to me,' he states, 'that beneath the cosmetic alterations life in boarding school went on pretty much unchanged.' I think he is wrong. The films ring true as accounts of what could have happened in a public school not in the Eighties but in the late Sixties. I am not an unbiassed witness and in fairness to Boyd I recall that the critics of *The Loom of Youth* also argued that it was just a story about a bad school at a bad time.

The two film scripts make marvellously entertaining reading. The dialogue catches exactly the flavour of the frustrations and hang-ups of the inmates of a total institution. The ineffectiveness, even the irrelevance of the staff, is overplayed; from the point of view of the real life of the boys, the staff are indeed peripheral, but surely no headmaster in his right mind would appoint a man like Mole in *Dutch Girls*?

In *Good and Bad at Games* a boy, cruelly persecuted at school, gets his own back ten years later. The circumstances of his revenge are melodramatic and unreal (on the cricket pitch, where else?) but it is a legitimate and effective dramatic device. Cox—the tormented boy—plans and almost succeeds in executing the murder of his chief tormenter. The text cuts back and forth between school and adult life, pointing the way in which experience of the former freezes public schoolmen in a state of permanent immaturity.

At the centre of this immaturity is their inability to develop adult emotional responses, particular in relation to women. . . . How their wives, such as Frances, the wife of the Chief Tormenter in *Good and Bad at Games,* tolerate it is hard to understand, but perhaps the reason is that in this, as in other matters, the private girls school encourages its pupils to have modest expectations.

Dutch Girls is also about sexual immaturity. Allowed out of their boarding school for a hockey tour of Amsterdam, the boys of the story behave with loutish disregard for the feelings of their hosts.... Their pursuit of the Dutch girls is gauche and ineffective; their expedition to the Red Light district a predictable failure. It is light and funny but sad too. We do not see what these boys will be like in ten years time but we can guess.

Writing about adolescents, particularly the public school variety, is an invitation to cliché. Boyd is much too good a writer to accept. I would not have thought it possible to re-work the public school theme with such originality and sharpness of insight.

> *John Rae, "Bad Guys," in* Books and Bookmen, *No. 360, October, 1985, p. 19.*

DONALD CAMPBELL

What use is a public-school education in the modern world? Not much, William Boyd tells us in the excellent essay that introduces [*School Ties*], arguing that 'most public schoolboys have to start a stringent programme of re-education almost as soon as the school gates close behind them'. This would appear to be the premiss that informs the two screenplays that make up this volume. In the first, *Good and Bad at Games,* Boyd approaches his theme from the point of view of the passing of time, demonstrating that an attempt to murder an army officer has its roots in a schoolboy bullying incident. The play revolves around three characters, each of whom resembles one of the stock figures of much schoolboy fiction. In dealing with them, however, Boyd develops a line that runs contrary to expectation. As the action switches back and forward between 1968 and 1978, we find that Niles, hero of the sports field, becomes a second-rate car salesman, while the put-upon weakling, Cox, becomes a pathetically vicious employee of the gutter press. Each represents some kind of failure, and this is equally true of the third character, Mount.... While the other characters in the play serve mainly to provide background colour, their collective presence enhances the play with many insights into the inadequacy of their education.

The second play, *Dutch Girls,* is much less concerned with such insights. This is a comedy, pure and simple, about a group of boys from a Scottish boarding school who go to Holland on a hockey tour. Although it is extremely funny, the fact that the boys come from a privileged background is almost irrelevant. Almost, but not quite. While this good-humoured send-up of the sexual fantasies of the adolescent male could have been written about any group of boys, it is the educational ethos that gives the humour its distinctive flavour. In other words, Boyd is simply drawing on his own experience for material. In neither play does he seek to expose or celebrate the public school system, being quite content to 'tell it as it was'. As in his novels and short stories, Boyd displays a confident assurance that borders on the bland, but never fails to impress with his high degree of skill and thoroughgoing sense of style.

> *Donald Campbell, in a review of "School Ties: Good and Bad at Games, and Dutch Girls," in* British Book News, *January, 1986, p. 54.*

DAN TUCKER

Calling [*The New Confessions*] the story of a life would be both accurate and misleading. It is a life, all right; the book takes John James Todd, a Scot with a rare talent and several bad habits, from his birth to his old age, both out of the ordinary. It makes a richly entertaining, crowded carnival of a novel, stretching from turn-of-the-century Edinburgh through both World Wars and the repellent comedy of the "Hollywood Ten" blacklists.

On the other hand, Todd's life is not a story in any conventional sense. Its whole point is its storylessness—the utterly random nature of the happenings that shape Todd's life and, by implication, all our lives.

Uncertainty and incompleteness are its themes, as they are of today's advanced mathematics (another theme). And as the aging Todd discovers to his pleased surprise, that isn't all bad.

Boyd's fictional hero and the 20th Century are roughly the same age. As his opening sentence tells us, his first act on entering the world was to kill his mother; "the date of my birth was the date of her death, and thus began all my misfortunes." Right there are a couple of our hero's keynotes—a cranky, aggrieved view of the injustices done him, and accurate hindsight. He's quite right: One of the determinants of John James' life is that his father and pompous older brother cannot help seeing him as the cause of his mother's death.

Todd's vision rearward is remarkably clear. After each of his follies, ... he can always see how fatheaded it was, but he never quite masters the trick of seeing it beforehand.

The title refers to the *Confessions* of Jean-Jacques Rousseau, a book that becomes the leading passion of Todd's life. He discovers it as a newsreel photographer imprisoned by the Germans in World War I; the book, smuggled in by an obliging guard, obsesses him with the idea of turning it into a movie epic. The ambition propels him through triumphs and disasters.... (p. 5)

Eventually it takes him to Hollywood, where he becomes, for no special reason, a target of the House Committee on Unamerican Activities. We leave him an old man, hiding out on a Mediterranean island from a Commie-hunting fanatic who may or may not be alive and looking for him.

An odd but fitting sub-theme in all this is the mathematical mystery of prime numbers, an obsession of Todd's school friend Hamish Malahide. Such numbers are fascinating precisely because they don't seem to fit any rules—a comment that Todd intends for his own life as well.

These events make splendid reading. Boyd shares with Canada's Robertson Davies an ability to make the least important of his characters three-dimensional. And he has the knack of plausibility, a way of supplying the unexpected detail that makes a novelist sound like an eyewitness.

If these happenings add up to a story, it is one that even its author professes not to understand. Things happen just because they happen; coincidences that look significant ("John James" is—aha!—the English equivalent of Jean-Jacques) don't seem to signify anything. The elements of Todd's life bump and twine and part as randomly as noodles in a soup pot. But that seems to be Boyd's point: If even mathematics doesn't always make sense, why should life? (pp. 5, 9)

Dan Tucker, "The Random Walk: Life in All of Its Haphazard Twists and Turns," in Chicago Tribune—Books, *May 8, 1988, pp. 5, 9.*

MICHAEL WOOD

English comic writing specializes in scrapes and escalations, mild spots of bother that turn into mounting catastrophes.... The unfortunate hero is usually either disagreeable or brainless, morally either a blank or a little on the seedy side, but we come to like him for his lamentably bad luck. He is not a victim, doesn't rise to such dignity, more like the comic who gets spattered by the pie aimed at someone else. We laugh—we laugh a lot—at his modest and unavailing gestures toward introducing order into this confusion.

Morgan Leafy, the central figure in William Boyd's first novel, *A Good Man in Africa,* is a fine instance. "Selfish, fat and misanthropic," a perspiring English diplomat, he has to cope with the thoughts of dressing up as Father Christmas for a children's party, disposing of an African corpse that cannot be moved for religious reasons, temporizing with an African politician who is blackmailing him and fending off the young woman he fancies but can't give in to because he's caught a dose of gonorrhea. Nastiness is important in English comedy too.

Mr. Boyd has written two very good novels in this comic vein, *A Good Man in Africa* and *Stars and Bars,* the romp of a chronically timid Englishman in America. *Stars and Bars* is more genial, farther from Evelyn Waugh, more Mr. Boyd's own book and written in a wonderfully quick and crackling prose. His other two novels, *An Ice-Cream War,* his second, and now *The New Confessions,* his fourth, are something different—intermittently funny, but after bigger game. They seek to shift the comic vision I've evoked to more earnest territories, to map the absurdities of an often violent, thoroughly historical world.

They achieve quite a bit of success in this line because Mr. Boyd's homework is diligent and sound, and he has a great knack for conjuring up times and places.... But both of these books are slightly predictable in their design, a touch too well made. Their characters are not caricatures, they do hold our interest, but they rarely surprise us. *An Ice-Cream War* tells of 1914-18 hostilities on an African front. *The New Confessions,* which has much to do with film and Hollywood, offers as news, or at least without any noticeable freshening up, everyone's clichés about movies, the only two events in their history no one ever forgets: the advent of sound and the blacklist.

The New Confessions is a very ambitious book, a remake of Rousseau and an application of Werner Heisenberg's uncertainty principle; a fictional mathematician is drafted into the plot so that he can talk theorems and theories and work with Kurt Gödel himself, and is then virtually forgotten.... The hero's name, John James, is a kind of prophecy, a match with that of the Jean Jacques whose work he will not discover until he is 18 and a prisoner of war in Germany. His last name is Todd, and he is the seemingly untalented son of a Scottish surgeon and professor of anatomy....

We should see him, I think, as something like a mixture of D. W. Griffith and Orson Welles, although with rather fewer achievements than they had—and with a Scottish childhood, a European war and an early career in Germany thrown in.

There is much film history here; there are some interesting ideas concerning hand-held cameras and split screens and the like, although they tend to have a rather literary flavor.... John James has awkward sexual escapades that recall those of Mr. Boyd's earlier heroes, except that they are not funny. He is not aggressive, merely impulsive, but he seems to attract enemies and the kind of persecution that ought to be comic but here seems just a rather dogged embodiment of bad luck. He is a failed great man—or perhaps a man whose greatness was very brief and without consequences....

John James is the genius foiled by a lifetime of mischances, some of them major, many of them trivial. But even the trivial becomes important if it goes on and on, and John James himself rails eloquently against the comfortable moralizing notion that we make our own fates. We have our faults, of course, and we make mistakes, but we pay prices out of all proportion to our errors, and quite often we pay for no reason at all. "Filthy luck" does exist, and not every loser deserves to lose. "In reality there is nothing *but* luck."

The pace of this novel, so packed with historical action and personal adventures, is curiously sluggish and dutiful. Each chapter ends with John James in the present (which is 1972), having marched chronologically through its allotted chunk of the century. The general effect is like that of reading too many sentences with the same structure, or seeing a movie made up of almost unvaried medium shots. This is a first-person narrative, as Mr. Boyd's other novels are not, and he seems to have felt obliged to check in his wit and verve and awareness of cliché in order to go in for an impersonation of the stolid John James.

This can't be right, though, since John James is supposed to be flamboyant and reckless. What, then, is he doing with this clean, functional, virtually jokeless prose? No verbal action here, no linguistic performance, no texture, to use a word John James himself likes. "Do I sound delirious?" he asks at one point. "Do I sound overwhelmed, engrossed, utterly trammeled up? Do I sound in love?" Too bad he should ask, because he doesn't sound like any of these things, even faintly. To be fair, the prose is not entirely jokeless, but the jokes, oddly, seem to belong to Mr. Boyd rather than his character, who parodies *The Waste Land,* for example, six years before it is published and finds *The Hands of Orlac* playing in a Mexican cinema, just as it is in *Under the Volcano.*

The aim of this novel is admirable: to take, as Rousseau does, a weirdly exceptional life and claim it is merely representative, that of the naked creature, the thing itself. But for this we need the buzz and color of the exceptional character, and the disconcerting sense that his strangeness is not so far as we thought from our ordinariness. John James is too much of a plodder for this to happen. The publisher's blurbs suggests he is a grandiose figure undercut in the writing, seen ironically in his vanity and posturing. But you can't undercut "this emptiness at the center of myself" or "I seemed to stand before a high looming cliff of despair."

It's tough being a funny writer.... What I've called the specialization of English comic writing reflects a truth of feeling about a foolish and unkind and runaway world, a place where, in the dizzying simplifications of our helplessness, there really does seem to be nothing but luck. But the joke itself is a part of this truth. The truth isn't there if the joke isn't there. All we have then is banality, the grin turned into a grimace. John James at the end of this book stands on a beach on his island, not knowing which of six alternatives in the plot awaits him, a programmatic emblem of the uncertainty principle: . . .

> I look back at my life in this gravid tensed moment and I see it clearly now. . . . It has been deeply paradoxical and fundamentally uncertain. . . .

We feel the wavering bid for irony here, but even the irony seems to be asking for favors, a little too winsome. The scene isn't funny and isn't really serious. It doesn't show an acceptance of uncertainty either, merely the new certainty of indifference. Rousseau himself was not a barrel of laughs, but he was more restless than this, racked to the end by dreams of the earthly paradise he thought he had lost.

> Michael Wood, "Rousseau, Hollywood and the Uncertainty Principle," in The New York Times Book Review, May 29, 1988, p. 5.

VICTOR KANTOR BURG

"My first act on entering this world was to kill my mother." These are the opening words of John James Todd, the narrator/protagonist of William Boyd's *The New Confessions,* and they refer to the fact that Todd's mother died in childbirth. The chronicle of a life in our times, the novel begins vigorously with Todd's birth in 1899 and concludes wearily at an unshown turning point, in 1972.

Todd is a prototypical, contemporary narrator/protagonist—risk-taker, secular fool, heartbreaker, heart weary, obscene, wise, baffled, intuitive. His life is set against both the macro-events of the century, and against *The Confessions* of Rousseau. . . .

Todd is meant to be a wayfarer of history, reflecting the uncertainty of the past several decades. He appears in Berlin in the twenties and forties, in Southern California during World War II, on blacklists in the fifties, at the Mediterranean in the seventies—all the best historical hotspots.

But his book reads a lot like the notes for a Masterpiece Theater or a preliminary version of a high-minded mini-docu-something.

The book contains much good writing: descriptions of faces and meals, moments of grimness and humor, fine perceptions, vivid pictures, a robust ambition to contain a great deal. The sense of being in a hot-air balloon before people were frequent flyers; watching a nanny gently cradle her mouth over her infant son's penis and so ease him into sleep; discovering a soldier with pockets full of human fingers and their rings. . . .

What perplexes the reader is why these and other moments don't hold; why any number of patently well-made characters don't resonate throughout. Part of what causes these failures is that Todd's drama, in an important sense, is over. He recollects the life from an apparently secure present, and a sense of risk and danger is missing. We know that things will turn out relatively all right; after all, Todd is still among the living, writing his book. And when at its conclusion he attempts to place himself in an inconclusive jeopardy, it's too late. Too often have we seen his pattern of leaping gaily into a honeytrap only to have to squirm out. Too often he is scratched by the experience but not scarred.

Another distancing factor is that Todd, like his camera, remains removed. He does not take the opportunity of entering into the minds of others. We see too much from a single, if entertaining, point of view.

More importantly, the book fails to connect Todd with the times and factual personalities to whom he alludes. The places, the history, the people are accurately portrayed, but they do not persuade the reader or animate the plot. Todd need not be a major player in his time, but he needs to be much more than an observer in the scenes of his life.

What is needed is the kind of imaginative translation that can happen when a book is made into a film. . . .

[An] imaginative expansion is needed in *The New Confessions.* . . . Then these confessions—as good as they are in bits—will warrant the full comparison with Rousseau's and will fully realize themselves.

> Victor Kantor Burg, in a review of "The New Confessions," in Boston Review, Vol. XIII, No. 5, June, 1988, p. 28.

THOMAS R. EDWARDS

William Boyd is a young novelist who has attracted considerable attention in Britain lately. *A Good Man in Africa* (1981), about the mishaps of an overweight and underdutiful minor English diplomat in present-day West Africa, recalls how Evelyn Waugh, Joyce Cary, Anthony Burgess, and Graham Greene depicted their countrymen abroad, as well as the domestic social malice of the early Kingsley Amis; that is to say, the book succeeds in being intelligent and funny without seeming especially new. *An Ice-Cream War* (1982) goes back in time, to the small-scale campaigns in British and German East Africa during World War I. Here colonial comedy verges on underplayed tragic farce . . . in a novel that seems more innovative, though a little out of focus. *Stars and Bars* (1984), which has recently been made into a movie, deals with an English art dealer trying to buy a private collection in the backwoods of the American South; he's beset by rednecks who owe something to Faulkner or Caldwell or more recent practitioners of the Southern Grotesque (or, for that matter, to Burt Reynolds movies). It's all managed quite well for a foreigner, but it's not better than the homegrown competition has been doing.

Expatriation, physical or spiritual, seems to be Boyd's major subject, as it has been, at least on occasion, for so many British novelists since Kipling and Conrad and Forster. (p. 32)

Boyd's latest novel, *The New Confessions,* is another fiction of expatriation, but it complicates the genre. Longer and more ambitious than its predecessors, it traverses the present century from its beginnings to the 1970s in a first-person narrative by an artist-intellectual of considerable sophistication. The structure is moderately complex, a consecutive life story interrupted by glimpses of the autobiographer writing and pondering implications in his old age; and it puts that life into ironic play against a model or myth, the self-revelatory precedent of Rousseau's *Confessions.*

Boyd's new Rousseau even bears his precursor's first names. John James Todd was born in Edinburgh in 1899, to an emotionally frozen professor of anatomy and a mother who, like Rousseau's, died in giving birth to him. His miserable childhood found few objects for affection: his father's illiterate housekeeper, Oonagh, who first stimulated his sexual imagination; his father's English friend Donald Verulam, a kindly but rather distant bachelor who introduced Todd to his life work, photography; Hamish Malahide, his pimply, unpopular schoolmate whose genius for mathematics touched the only intellectual talent poor Todd possessed—his instinctive, essentially visual sense of numerical pattern. Both sex and math seemed to promise "secrets" that could be learned, ones that would make sense of the world by revealing order in its apparent randomness. But Todd's gift for numbers soon faded into mere proficiency, and he was never to have much talent for love. His search for patterns was to be conducted through an art, or creative obsession, that is literally concerned with seeing order, the art of cinematography.

First, however, the younger Todd, half speculative observer and half fevered voyeur, tries to see through the merely personal surfaces of his pitifully limited youth, with disastrous consequences. Infatuated with his widowed Aunt Faye, and rightly suspecting that she and Verulam are falling in love, he runs away from school in 1916, . . . hoping to "interpose himself" between the lovers. Humiliated by Faye's shocked rejection of his sexual overtures, . . . Todd flees again, enlisting in a "public school" infantry battalion and finding himself on the Somme just in time for the butchery.

By what seems, in hindsight, the kind of hidden patterning he's looking for, these failures to learn true secrets lead Todd to his career. His experience of trench warfare, whose horrendous absurdity Boyd memorably captures, makes him entirely receptive to Verulam's invitation to serve as a cameraman in the special unit he commands. . . . Here, at last, is Todd's métier. His talent for it leads him beyond the fraudulent jingoism his masters have in mind, and toward finding and composing images whose truthful horror can serve only the purposes of pure, apolitical vision. Boyd finds a metaphor for this liberating disengagement in a culminating episode: near Passchendaele, "shooting" the action from a balloon whose moorings are severed by gunfire, Todd drifts beyond the British lines into German-held Belgium, where he's imprisoned (at first for being a spy) and meets the great friend of his life, a cynical, homosexual young German guard named Karl-Heinz Kornfeld. In exchange for a kiss, Kornfeld smuggles him reading material in ten-page wads. The text is, in fact, Rousseau's *Confessions,* which Todd later thinks he immediately understood was "going to change my life."

After the Armistice, Todd finds a job as a junior cameraman for a London film company that makes trivial comedies, [and] marries not very suitably. . . . [He begins making his own films, but when] his studio goes bankrupt, he can find no other work in England, and in 1925 a vague postcard invitation from Karl-Heinz—who reports that he's "making lots of films and plays," although he is in fact only a movie extra and costume assistant—leads him to Berlin.

Like Rousseau, who struggled to make it as a composer of operas in Paris, Todd at first does miserably in Berlin. But Weimar Germany is the right place for him. He conceives and makes a modern-dress version of Rousseau's *Julie* for Realismus Films Verlag AG . . . and he falls permanently and hopelessly in love with the star of *Julie,* the unresponsive American actress Doon Bogan. The picture, released in 1926, is an international sensation, enriching Realismus and establishing Todd as a world-class director. He begins at once to plan his masterpiece, an enormous three-part film of Rousseau's *Confessions. . . .* (pp. 32-3)

At this point in Todd's life, the novel is half over, and a certain decline sets in, both in the life and in Boyd's book. Personal and public history begin to work against Todd's ambitions. Though he finishes *The Confessions: Part I* . . . the advent of sound-pictures makes it obsolete even before its release in 1931

to sparse and unresponsive audiences. . . . The Depression and the Nazi ascendency ruin the German film industry, at least for non-Aryans, and Todd's nominal membership in the Communist Party, which he joined almost absent-mindedly to endear himself to the radical Doon, makes continued residence in Germany unadvisable. Paying almost all the money he has to Realismus for the negative of *The Confessions: Part I,* he returns to England in 1934.

The rest of *The New Confessions,* though Boyd makes it eventful and entertaining enough to hold readers who like to finish what they've started, seems not to add significantly to what's already been well established. (p. 33)

The novel, that is, turns episodic in its latter half, where Boyd seems less concerned with further explorations of how art and life betray each other, and more with making Todd a figure in modern history—a kind of Flashman who keeps on going even after the thematic implications of his role have been made more than evident. Parallels with Rousseau himself still appear . . . but the device now seems rather perfunctory.

It becomes increasingly clear that Todd really is not like Rousseau at all. He may have had genius as a director (lacking the films, we'll never know for sure), but as a writer he lacks Rousseau's irritatingly unanswerable egotism, his absolute conviction of the overriding importance of his own states of mind, his power to make us care about him almost against our better judgment. And of course *Emile, The Social Contract,* the *Dialogues,* and the rest of the books are always there, should our faith in his genius waver. The Todd we know from his own words is not a genius but a victim. Despite his repeated warnings not to trust his account of himself, we have to trust most of it; and what emerges is a picture of a man who, like most people, lacks some important quality that he wishes he had, and who has indeed been treated shabbily by most of those whose love and respect he's sought.

Here the familiar figure of the expatriate Briton expands into a larger and potentially more poignant figure, that of the homeless person. Though John James Todd keeps leaving places to go somewhere else, it's never clear to him or to us that he belonged anywhere in the first place, that any earthly location can be commensurate with his need to create and to suffer. The aged, defeated Todd at work on his story is the most engaging version of the man Boyd gives us— . . . convinced (quite wrongly, I take it) that he is "at last . . . in tune with the universe." As a comic hero, the person who at least endures and keeps talking in a world that makes no sense in itself, Todd is appealing. Still, I don't feel sure that comedy is what the novel—funny though it often is—mainly has in mind.

The New Confessions shows Boyd, like most of the good British novelists of our century . . . , to be primarily interested in "telling a story," following characters and their fates through consecutive narrative scenes that aim to represent "life" as most of us know it. Boyd may have a Sternian kind of interest in tracing the associational grooves Todd's mind runs in, but I doubt that they're peculiar enough to distract many readers from the story as such. Boyd seems to share the national suspicion of "writing" as the French, the Irish, the North and South Americans, and various other foreign and colonial breeds have been doing it—that is, putting unseemly pressure on language and form to see what significances they may have been keeping from us all this while. Modern British fiction is frugally determined to do the job only with the means that lie readily to hand, and of course there's something admirable, if also limiting, about this restraint.

There's also something readable about it, and I would expect Boyd to become popular with intelligent general readers in America, as in varying degrees have writers like Waugh, Powell, Greene, [and] Burgess . . . , whose serious gifts may be obscured for some by their practive of ''unserious'' fictional genres. Boyd isn't yet quite in this league, and *The New Confessions* has its problems of scale and focus. But it's a novel that can be read with pleasure for its story, and also one that grows in the mind as you think about it afterward, the most ambitious and the best work this interesting writer in his mid-30s has yet produced. (pp. 33-4)

> *Thomas R. Edwards, ''A Child of the Century,'' in* The New Republic, *Vol. 198, No. 24, June 13, 1988, pp. 32-4.*

Raymond Carver

1938-1988

American short story writer, poet, and editor.

Carver's works have placed him at the forefront of the popular resurgence of the short story. Usually set in the blue-collar communities of the Pacific Northwest, Carver's fiction features despondent protagonists whose struggles for survival fall outside the mainstream of American society. Although Carver often portrays alcoholics who are unemployed or trapped in unskilled occupations, his realistic descriptions of their lives are rarely cynical, and the emotions and concerns he evokes are universally recognizable. Michael Foley observed: "What Carver excels at is creating a mood or atmosphere . . . , and, luckily, it is not always an atmosphere of menace. In [his] better stories the mood is of aimlessness, worthlessness, insubstantiality, indecision or regret—our all-too-familiar contemporary demons."

Carver's background is often reflected in his fiction. Married and the father of two children before he reached the age of twenty, Carver endured sundry menial jobs and moved frequently between small towns in the Pacific Northwest. He also battled against alcoholism, which nearly destroyed his professional relationships and provoked bitter personal turmoil until he brought his disorder under control in 1977. Carver's first major short story collection, *Will You Please Be Quiet, Please?* (1976), received much favorable critical attention and was nominated for a National Book Award. The pieces in this volume depict jobless, melancholy protagonists whose unremarkable lives reflect emptiness and despair. Several of the stories in Carver's next significant book, *What We Talk about When We Talk about Love* (1981), are regarded as masterpieces of minimalist writing. Adam Begley noted: "Carver has often been called a minimalist, a term he disliked, but which nonetheless aptly describes his brief stories, and his tightly focused prose. Patterns of speech and incidental gestures dominate, along with an occasional highlighted object; setting as traditionally conceived is all but absent." More unified than the stories in *Will You Please Be Quiet, Please?*, these works focus upon individuals involved in turbulent marriages who understand only that they are unable to change their lives. Michael Koepf asserted: "[The] clear, contemporary vision [that *What We Talk about When We Talk about Love*] gives of the American soul is at once chilling and unforgettably powerful."

Toward the end of his career, Carver began revising and expanding old stories while departing from his minimalist style to experiment with a more detailed, descriptive prose. The pieces collected in *Cathedral* (1983) are longer, more fully developed, and not so relentlessly grim as his earlier fiction, and his protagonists occasionally acquire the personal insight and redemptive qualities that Carver believed he himself gained after he stopped drinking. Many critics commented on the sense of hope displayed in "A Small, Good Thing," which won the O. Henry Award in 1983. This work is a revision of "The Bath," a story that appeared in *What We Talk about When We Talk about Love*. In the original version, the parents of a young boy who dies following an automobile accident are tormented by telephone calls from a baker who has been left with the child's birthday cake. The narrative concludes ambiguously

with a menacing message from the baker. "A Small, Good Thing" begins similarly but continues past the point where "The Bath" ends, with the baker helping the boy's parents to cope with their grief after they confront him with the news of their son's death. The pieces contained in *Will You Please Be Quiet, Please?*, *What We Talk about When We Talk about Love*, and *Cathedral* were reprinted in *The Stories of Raymond Carver* (1985).

Reviewers noted a distinct refinement of vision in the psychological character sketches contained in Carver's last short fiction collection, *Where I'm Calling From* (1988). In this volume, Carver often utilizes his unpretentious prose style to detail short periods of time in the lives of protagonists who are reconciled to unfavorable circumstances. "Errand," for example, which received much critical notice, blends fact and fiction to chronicle the last days of influential Russian author Anton Chekhov. Another story, "Elephant," depicts an elderly man who continues to offer financial support to the indolent, greedy family that abandoned him years ago. At the story's end, divine intervention rescues the man from his oppressive situation. In a review of this volume, John Clute commented: "[In] speaking the thoughts of those who cannot themselves speak, Carver never exploits the ironic gap between himself and his subjects. There is no condescension. . . . The final effect of a Carver story is of humility."

Carver composed much of his poetry during the early part of his career. Many of these pieces were published in the collections *Near Klamath* (1968), *Winter Insomnia* (1970), and *At Night the Salmon Move* (1976). Carver's verse garnered wide critical attention with the publication of *Where Water Comes Together with Other Water* (1985). The largely autobiographical poems included in this volume expose Carver's personal fears and his preoccupation with death. The pieces in *Ultramarine* (1986; published in Great Britain as *In a Marine Light*) reflect the minimalistic style of his fiction. These poems are generally regarded as more optimistic than his earlier verse, with the most highly acclaimed pieces focusing on the courage needed to cope with life's misfortunes. Commending Carver's use of understatement in his poetry, Vincent Sherry noted: "Saying the least is not a deficiency but an art: the verbal spareness is consonant both with the sense of adventure and the terse, virile affection he permits himself."

(See also *CLC*, Vols. 22, 36; *Contemporary Authors*, Vols. 33-36, rev. ed., Vol. 126 [obituary]; *Contemporary Authors New Revision Series*, Vol. 17; and *Dictionary of Literary Biography Yearbook: 1984*.)

DAVID ST. JOHN

Raymond Carver is best known to most readers as the author of three superb collections of short stories: *Will You Please Be Quiet, Please?*, *What We Talk About When We Talk About Love*, and most recently, *Cathedral*. Yet many West Coast readers know something about Raymond Carver that many Eastern readers have only recently discovered—that, for the whole of his writing career, Carver has been a highly respected and widely published poet as well as distinguished writer of fiction.

Though he'd published several limited edition books of his poetry, it was last year's major collection, *Where Water Comes Together With Other Water*, that brought a wider recognition of Carver's work as a poet. His new volume, *Ultramarine*, demonstrates the same precise craftsmanship and deep humanity that his many fans have come to admire.

Not surprisingly, the impulses in the great majority of Carver's poems are often narrative and anecdotal; he is, after all, a consummate storyteller. What we find in *Ultramarine* are aspects of narrative and voices lifted delicately (and intact) from the human pageant Carver so loves.

As in his prose style, understatement is the hallmark of Carver's poetry. There is a directness and conversational ease that recall William Stafford's best work. Although many of the poems display Carver's love of the natural world, his best poems touch upon the constancy of human pain and human courage.

At times, baldly autobiographical and, at times, allowing his figures to speak for him, Carver champions the resilience and perseverance of people; his characters are sometimes broken-down and broken-hearted, but they are rarely broken in spirit. In this way, like Philip Levine, Carver chooses to give his words to those who otherwise would have no one to speak for them.

Each of Carver's poems has a powerful meditative center. Scenes are sometimes violated by past scenes, memories that flood the poem until the speaker is forced to some new reckoning with his situation or his past. Recalling a childhood breakfast and his parents arguing, Carver thinks of his now dead father and says, "We're both far away / from there, and still someone's crying. Even then / I was beginning to understand how it's possible / to be in one place. And someplace else, too."...

Ultramarine is filled with many of the richest and most powerful poems Carver has written. They are poems of great eloquence and passion; this is a highly companionable and sonorous volume of poetry.

David St. John, in a review of "Ultramarine," in Los Angeles Times Book Review, *December 28, 1986, p. 3.*

PATRICIA HAMPL

If sanity best displays itself as gratitude, Raymond Carver's superb book [*Ultramarine*] is good medicine. The collection is suffused with gratitude, sometimes muttered, a form of humility. He has the astonished, chastened voice of a person who has survived a wreck, as surprised that he had a life before it as that he has one afterward, willing to remember both sides.

Mr. Carver understands that the worst complexion you can put on your past is not necessarily the most honest, no matter how tempting it is to be horrified by a former self.

Carver's brilliant stylistic habit, his use of striking juxtapositions, takes the place of weighty explanations....

What Mr. Carver notices (past and present) and chooses to tell undermines shame. This is the book's greatest gift. To call this voice merely honest would not evoke the quality of surrender implicit in the collection's best poems, nor suggest the lyric grace of the writing.

Ultramarine, if it gets the reading it deserves, should be greeted with the same enthusiasm that met Gerald Stern's *Lucky Life* several years ago. There is a kinship between the two books, a midlife second wind, a buoyancy in the midst of regret. Mr. Carver is heir to that most appealing American poetic voice, the lyricism of Theodore Roethke and James Wright.

The collection is perhaps overstuffed—too many poems about death that do little more than repeat that it's coming down the line, a couple of small-spirited poems about a former wife....

But, so what? This book is a treasure, one to return to. No one's brevity is as rich, as complete, as Raymond Carver's. And his wisdom is as much about the necessary distance between people as it is about love:

> We're extraordinarily calm and tender with each other
> as if sensing the other's rickety state of mind.
> As if we knew what the other was feeling. We don't,
> of course. We never do. No matter.
> It's the tenderness I care about. That's the gift
> this morning that moves and holds me.
> Same as every morning.

That tenderness is not sentiment. It is the profound intelligence which informs these graceful poems.

Patricia Hampl, "Surviving a Life in the Present," in The New York Times Book Review, *June 7, 1987, p. 15.*

ROBERT B. SHAW

I wonder why fiction writers, who have at least a slight possibility of making a living with their talents, should feel the urge to write poems. It may be that poetry appeals to them as a more personal form than fiction, a sanctioned mode of self-disclosure. Certainly [in *Ultramarine*] these poems by the well-known short story writer Raymond Carver present themselves as swatches of autobiography. Our response is bound to hinge to a great extent on the persuasiveness of the poet's voice, on his projection of a sincere persona. On this score Carver generally succeeds. He is skilled in his portrayal of lives dogged by grimy misfortunes, and we aren't inclined to doubt that these are the authentic memories of one who has come up and through being down and out. But a gap opens, as we read on, between the human interest he sparks and his artistic treatment of it. The dispiriting material—centering on alcoholism, failed marriages, deaths of friends, discord between parents and children—loses its force when recurred to so many times with no additional insights accruing. We hear many times over about his mother's decline into senility, for instance, only to feel that once would have been enough. Carver is an unsparing recorder of life's baffling hurts, but they never become any less baffling, to him or to us, as he proceeds. This book of 140 pages would have been more effective at half the length, and would have lost nothing of its essential flavor.

In his handling of the individual poem, too, Carver could have used some further editing. He has a nervous habit of ruining otherwise strong performances by tacking moralizing or over-explanatory summations to them. . . . A brief, pungent poem about lovers quarreling and making up, **"The Little Room,"** becomes . . . [a] casualty in its three last, suddenly vapid lines: "Rooms where people yell and hurt each other. / And afterwards feel pain, and loneliness. / Uncertainty. The need to comfort." Even the syntax comes to be predictable in such cases: almost always it is a series of tight-lipped, wistful, incomplete sentences, a Sylvester Stallone mannerism. Carver should hire someone to lean over his shoulder and cross out endings like this.

All this aside, there is absorbing reading in this volume. Carver's voice is likable enough to keep us with him, even when the form of this or that poem fails to satisfy. And in some cases even a carper like me can find nothing to criticize. Some of the better pieces are those in which he strays from his customary quotidian details into a more visionary consciousness. . . . [Poems] which succeed by overlapping trance with reality, or by resisting the temptation to dispel all touches of mystery, are **"Bahia, Brazil," "Mesopotamia," "The Window," "Vigil,"** and **"The Rest."** If Carver can continue to write poems like these he won't owe his readers apologies for taking furloughs now and then from fiction writing. (pp. 230-31)

> *Robert B. Shaw, in a review of "Ultramarine," in*
> Poetry, *Vol. CL, No. 4, July, 1987, pp. 230-31.*

STEVEN PUGMIRE

[*Ultramarine*] is a portrait of the artist in blue-grey middle-age, and it is blunt, simple and complex; in other words, a paradox.

Carver's poems are episodes from his life. They are stories told by an avuncular sort of fellow, sitting on his porch tying flies and spitting in the flower bed. This is amusing for the first dozen pages, until you begin to grow fond of him. Then the characters in his stories start to take on dimensions: his ex-wife; his children, who fill his mailbox with demands for money; his half crazy mother, who blames him when it snows; his drinking buddies. Eventually the images from the poems become cinematic—one image leads to the next, and you keep turning pages to see what happens next as if you were reading an adventure novel.

About the time you begin to think that these poems are not only simple, but simple-minded, Carver throws a hook into you—a line that is strikingly profound and beautifully stated. It's like finding Uncle Lou, who works at the gas station when he's not fishing, sitting on the porch reading Lao-Tse. There is something unsettling about this. Much of the strength of the poems is visual, and at times it seems that Carver hides behind this strength until it becomes a weakness. What is revealed doesn't seem to be enough. The depth of the insights jar against the simplicity of the characters as drawn, including the character of the author himself. This may be an intended paradox, for the blue themes of *Ultramarine*—death, love, choice, and the nature of relationships—tend to make simple stick figures of us all. (pp. 177-78)

> *Steven Pugmire, in a review of "Ultramarine," in*
> Western American Literature, *Vol. XXII, No. 2, August, 1987, pp. 177-78.*

VINCENT SHERRY

[In *In A Marine Light,* published in the United States as *Ultramarine*], Carver writes in the tradition of good prose, though not in the Flaubertian mode of Pound or Ford: Carver is studiously unliterary. He would be original, aboriginal: **"My Crow"** dismisses literary images of that creature, from Ted Hughes's to Homer's. He keeps his language close to the folk idiom of the Pacific Northwest, where he lives. His special gift is the narrative in the vernacular, its relaxed manner at its best when conveying a gratuitous, apparently casual memory: "Where this floated up from, or why, / I don't know. But thinking about this. . . .". From one standpoint rhythmically inert, this laconic style has the effect of forcing our interest away from the verbal surface of the poems, allowing us to focus on the event recalled or to experience the feeling invoked. These events and feelings are rich, moreover; a picaresque youth now owned by memory and a mature response. Carver knows the character and the value of this material. Saying the least is not a deficiency but an art: the verbal spareness is consonant both with the sense of adventure and the terse, virile affection he permits himself. He is also a funny poet, relaying the absurd as a matter of course with a kind of dead-pan hilarity.

Carver's use of idiom gives traction to the airiest of fancies. Talking to the dead in **"Radio Waves"**, for example, he relies entirely on the common sense, the innate gravity of the common tongue. James Wright exposed the dangers of this strategy even when he succeeded with it: "Suddenly I realize / That if I stepped out of my body I would break / Into blossom." A flatly vernacular verse risks the absurd when it seeks the heightening of poetry, and Carver's voice sometimes fails to support the fantastic event. Nor does he handle multiple or intersecting narratives with skill; his syntax and linguistic sensibility do not sustain the complexities attempted in **"Ask Him"**, a walking tour through a graveyard filled with stories as varied as the dead. Despite his casual air, there is a single-mindedness, indeed a relentlessness about Carver's narrative instincts. When he settles to one memory, he can draw an extraordinary power from it.

Vincent Sherry, "Lessons of the Flat Style," in The Times Literary Supplement, No. 4414, November 6-12, 1987, p. 1229.

CATHERINE PETROSKI

Like a painter's retrospective, Raymond Carver's new and selected stories are arranged chronologically, and as we read **Where I'm Calling From** we see themes and techniques interweave, grow, or sometimes disappear. Before our eyes, the writer's palette forms an overall harmony, just as reunited work does in a painter's retrospective. In the present volume, the earliest copyright date goes back 25 years, and selections from Carver's three collections . . . are joined by seven new stories. Where Carver is calling from, in literal terms of the title story, is no museum, however, but a detoxification unit. From that harrowing center **Where I'm Calling From** surveys the situations and people of Carver's stories, and we are spectators to the evolution of his fiction's obsessions.

Understandably, the years have brought changes to Raymond Carver's work. The most portentous of these is the stories' growing lengths and their increasingly more complex, explicit and penetrating focus on a main character's situation. Carver has not, with time, deserted his trademark utilitarian language—the "Carver voice" it seems all writing students must try for themselves. We observe as that voice progresses toward maturity; the prose has become elegantly controlled, a significant contrast to the chaotic subject matter. No longer do we find the jarring slips in diction that in some early stories shattered the fictional illusion. Later narrators do not persist, fortunately, in rendering dialogue with the tag "she/he goes." Readers should thank author and publisher for allowing youthful infelicities to stand. For they make clearer than all the hypothesizing in the world how it is an artist grows.

Carver writes often of relationships between men and women, and the collection reminds us how many of his stories are written from the point of view of female characters. (He can also characterize an infuriating male emotional zombie, as in **"Menudo."**) Finally, for those who can recognize it, the collection may serve as an emotional history of the generation that was born during World War II and grew up in the '60s. Through his characters, Carver documents what it was like to come of age in the '60s, attempt to settle down in the '70s, and try to come to adult terms with oneself in the '80s.

Carver's people are those whose "luck had gone south on them," according to the narrator of **"Elephant,"** the most powerful of the new stories. "Things were bound to change soon," this latter-day Micawber affirms, though the story hardly supports his hope or ours. Carver's characters live (and are usually written about) in the present tense; they struggle with memories that almost always hurt, and they have little real prospect for better days. Carver's vision is dark, often very dark, and consistently so.

If that is the case, why do readers willingly consume such bleak and painful stories? Perhaps because the stories streamline and order and heighten experience in such a way that makes everyday life look both chaotic and relatively benign, and so, in its way, Carver's fiction reassures. . . .

Whether we ourselves live in squalor or affluence, or misery or joy, **Where I'm Calling From** makes panoramic the fundamental human crises of Carver's fictional vision. Who does not know, first or second hand, the rise and fall of hope, the endless puzzle of marriage and children, the inerradicability of intense relationships, the responsibilities toward aging parents, and the effects of alcohol or drugs?

Carver's stories struggle valiantly to order the most disorderly and show us our common humanity as our lives brush against each other, whoever we are.

Catherine Petroski, "The Flip Side of Yuppiedom in All Its Gritty Dimensions," in Chicago Tribune—Books, May 8, 1988, p. 7.

JOHN CLUTE

Since the publication of **Cathedral,** Carver has published relatively few stories, and is reportedly at work on a novel. The seven tales assembled in **Elephant** [published in the United States as **Where I'm Calling From**] (which will be published in Britain on July 4), however, show no slackening of intensity, and strengthen the conviction that he is the finest writer of short stories now active. The inaccurate definition of his work as minimalist may now have been generally discarded, but it may be worth reiterating the argument that in paring his style of easy turns of rhetoric, and in eschewing the sententious ironies of narration from hindsight, he has opened his readers' eyes to all the mute plentitude of the world. At their best, as in **"Intimacy"** and **"Blackbird Pie"** from the current volume, his stories permit no back-talk from the reader. They are simply unanswerable.

Never in these tales of anguish and torpor is the larger *malaise* of an America adrift directly adduced. Carver rarely if ever mentions the United States by name. In the language he allows the middle-aged divorced men and women who populate his region, America is perhaps too huge to address. It is nevertheless the ambient fluid within which each character swims, starved of oxygen. In **"Boxes",** an elderly widow skitters from town to town, desperate for an unattainable rightness, where the mall will be clean at all hours, the sun temperate, the neighbours loving but not intrusive; when she lands on her son's doorstep he cannot begin to cope with the unuttered metaphysic of her search, for there is no chance of discerning within the pattern of his own difficult life a road to Paradise. They part. They will not meet again, anywhere. In **"Blackbird Pie",** a man's wife leaves him. He cannot understand why. He cannot even recognize the handwriting in her note. He only understands that his history has left him, that from this point he will have "to go on *without history*".

In the immensity of a continent, boundaries are of course difficult to perceive, and the significant tales of history may seem phantasmal to the inhabitants of unnamed regions. Carver's entrapped protagonists . . . are creatures of the hinterland, and as such may be ideally suited, just as so much of America seems ideally suited, to the short story form. As Frank O'Connor once famously said, "The short story has never had a hero. What it has instead is a submerged population group." If America is in fact a continent of hinterlands, and if its citizens inhabit territories outside of history, then Carver is indeed a bard.

But in speaking the thoughts of those who cannot themselves speak, Carver never exploits the ironic gap between himself and his subjects. There is no condescension, no moment of epiphanic wisdom couched in terms to which his subjects could never lay claim. The final effect of a Carver story is of humility.

John Clute, "Reports from the Regions," in The Times Literary Supplement, No. 4441, May 13-19, 1988, p. 532.

JONATHAN YARDLEY

[Where I'm Calling From] encompasses precisely a quarter-century of Carver's work and thus provides a welcome opportunity to reassess that work.

Perhaps the first point to be made about Carver is that although he has achieved the status of literary guru, he is not in fact a "literary" writer. He may be the high priest of minimalism, the genre currently so much in vogue in the writing departments, but neither in style nor subject matter does he conform to conventional definitions of the literary. His prose is spare, terse, devoid of showy effects, stripped clean of all but the most inescapable adjectives and adverbs; his subject is the daily life of the American lower-middle class—the flip side, as it were, of the American dream.

The second point is that even as the disciples and acolytes of minimalism flood the classrooms and bookstores with wan imitations of the style Carver pioneered, Carver himself has taken it in quite the opposite direction—if not abandoned it altogether. This was made clear five years ago with the publication of Cathedral, a collection that bordered on repudiation of minimalism, especially in the masterly story, "A Small, Good Thing"; it is emphasized all the more strongly by the new stories in Where I'm Calling From, stories in which Carver permits himself an expansiveness of description and feeling that is only hinted at in his earlier work.

Whether this change is actually an improvement is as much a matter of taste as of objective literary judgment. My own preference is for fiction with ample flesh on its bones, which has much to do with the strong admiration I expressed for the stories in Cathedral upon its publication in 1983. Yet the seven more recent stories seem to me somehow less satisfying. . . .

Now he seems rather less confident of the reader's ability to follow his oblique leads, or perhaps of his own ability to make those leads clear enough to avoid plunging his stories into obscurity.

But it is admirable for a writer of Carver's accomplishment and reputation to continue to test himself; Carver has declined the temptation—and a most alluring one it is—to repeat himself in familiar ways. At this advanced stage of his career Carver is still growing, not merely writing new stories in new ways but also going back into his previous work: fiddling with his older stories, trying to make them even better than originally they were.

That will take some doing, for Where I'm Calling From does nothing so much as remind us how fine, and how inimitable, those stories are. In them Carver has created a world that is as distinct and immediately recognizable as any in contemporary American fiction. Set in the Pacific Northwest, the stories offer little in the way of natural landscape, but much richness of domestic and psychological detail. Taken altogether they add up to what one of Carver's characters calls "a long line of low-rent tragedies," a procession of stories about people whose youthful hopes are dashed against the hard realities of American life—people who find themselves saying "so long to good times and hello to bad."

It goes without saying that they are bleak stories, yet so much bleakness would be unbearable had Carver not ameliorated it with humor and, of even greater importance, with the redeeming presence of love. On the one hand there is despair: "Two things are certain: 1) people no longer care what happens to other people; and 2) nothing makes any difference any longer." Yet on the other there is hope: "This woman broke a man's nose once. She has had two kids, and much trouble, but she loves this man who has her by the arm."

Carver has an acute sense of the singularity, the endearing oddity, of each human being; to each person he grants a measure of dignity because, if nothing else at all, this person has the sure distinction that no one else is precisely like him—no human life can be replicated, therefore each, however flawed, is precious. Carver's people drink and smoke too much, they fall in and out of love, they connect and disconnect; they "don't know what's going to happen to me or to anyone else in the world," yet in their quirky ways they keep on keeping on. The love with which Carver regards them is powerfully moving, and anything except "minimalist."

Jonathan Yardley, "Raymond Carver's American Dreamers," in Book World—The Washington Post, May 15, 1988, p. 3.

MARILYNNE ROBINSON

I take [Where I'm Calling From] to invite a new look at Mr. Carver's career, a conviction encouraged in me by the fact that I would like to offer one. To be blunt, I propose to abduct Raymond Carver from the camp of the minimalists. (p. 1)

Assumptions about what writers must or should be doing tend to preclude curiosity about what they are doing in fact. Raymond Carver is generally taken to epitomize this arid tradition, to spearhead a new version of it called "minimalism."

Including him in this canon is intended as high praise, the assumption being commonplace that a serious writer cannot have any higher object than to make these bones walk yet again. So, on the basis of the strength students and critics sense in his work, Mr. Carver has been more or less dragooned. Then other critics berate in his person the hopeless and diminished landscape they find in contemporary fiction, seeing him through the eyes of his imitators and admirers.

In fact, Mr. Carver stands squarely in the line of descent of American realism. His weaknesses are for sentimentality and sensationalism. His great gift is for writing stories that create meaning through their form. Much attention has been paid to his prose, and to his preoccupation with very ordinary lives and with disruption, divorce, displacement, sadness, the thankless business of cadging income from small and unlikable jobs. He should be famous for the conceptual beauty of his best stories, and disburdened of his worst, which could then pass into relative neglect.

The narrative foreground in Mr. Carver's fiction is typically muted or flattened. The stories have in common a sort of bafflement, justified in the best ones by the fact that their burdens are truly mysterious. Anecdotes—for want of a better word—looming and untranslatable like remembered dreams (which they sometimes are) figure so largely in these stories as to suggest that they are analogues to fiction itself, and also to consciousness, specifically to consciousness as it is shared, collective or bonding. . . . The bafflement in the best of these stories does not render an absence of meaning but awkwardness in the face of meaning, a very different thing.

Mr. Carver uses his narrow world to generate suggestive configurations that could not occur in a wider one. His impulse to simplify is like an attempt to create a hush, not to hear less but to hear better. Nothing recurs so powerfully in these stories as the imagination of another life, always so like the narrator's or the protagonist's own that the imagination of it is an experience of the self, that fuddled wraith. It is as if the replication of the conditions of one's life in another's rescued one from the terrors of accident and randomness, as if the germ of myth or archetype were found at work in the tepid plasma of unstructured experience. This seems to me to express the rationale of Mr. Carver's own artistic practice. (pp. 1, 35)

"So Much Water So Close To Home" is about the marriage of a man terrified of his own insensitivity and a woman of great emotional fragility, whose fears are focused around the undercurrent of violence in the husband's character. The husband, Stuart, has had a part in an incident involving neither guilt in law nor guilt as it is measured by finer instruments, at least so far as he can bring himself to acknowledge. He and three friends have gone deep into the mountains to fish, and have found the body of a young woman floating face down in the stream. After a little liquor and reflection they tether the body to a tree by a wrist and leave it as they found it, for three days, until they are done with their fishing. The story is told by Stuart's wife, who describes the men cooking and drinking and playing cards into the night while to one side the white body floats on the cold water. It is nightmarish, and the tranced state of the men, lingering there, is full of dark suggestion, which, in the wife's mind, shades into the crime itself. Clearly Stuart knows before he tells her about the incident—as he must since it is reported in the newspaper—that she will be deeply disturbed by it. He attempts expressions of love, but they are crude, and they reinforce her fears rather than comforting her. As she becomes more disturbed and withdrawn she becomes more dependent on his loyalty and love, which are real, though intermitted by anger and frustration at her recoil from him and at his own clumsiness.

The story is pure Carver. It establishes a very simple and striking visual paradigm, the woman in the fishing stream, which it is the work of the rest of the story to explicate. The center of the narrative is profound and emotional identification of the wife with the drowned woman, and also between husband and wife. Stuart knows early that his wife is again sliding into illness. She sees his fear and pities him. Marriage is the most characteristic and complex form of these imaginative extensions of the self that so preoccupy Mr. Carver. . . .

In **"Bicycles, Muscles, Cigarettes,"** a man comes to the defense of his young son, who is in trouble with neighbors. The boy expresses his affection for his father by telling him that he hopes not to forget his grandfather, and he wishes he could have known his grandfather at his father's age, and his father at his own age, yearning to imagine himself into their lives, simply to intensify his pleasure in his own. In **"Distance,"** a divorced man tells his grown daughter, whom he sees only on rare occasions, a story about her infancy, calling himself and her mother "the boy" and "the girl." At the end of the story they both regret the loss of the galled, warm, commonplace life they have conjured. (p. 35)

An interesting, though problematic, story is titled **"The Calm."** A man has violated the *comme il faut* of deer hunting, having

"gut shot" a deer and then failed to stalk it down and end its misery. The story about the hunt is told by the man himself, who seems unaware of the impression he is making on his hearers. Apparently the man has neither read Hemingway nor absorbed enough of the local ethos, though he is local himself, to understand how his revelations reflect upon him. No reader will suffer a moment's doubt, however.

The calm of the title is created by a barber, who quiets the indignation of the others. At the end of the story, in a sort of coda, the narrator, who has watched from the barber's chair, says it was during all this he decided to leave his wife. This ending seems arbitrary, but it is not, if his leaving her is a violation of the way things should be, like the miserable business with the deer. Mr. Carver is as obsessed with marriage as any writer since William Blake, and he never treats its disruption lightly. The calm brought on by the absolving neutrality of the barber, in which judgment is dispelled and ugliness dissipated, allows the narrator to make his choice. The barber looks into the mirror at the narrator's face, "but if the barber saw something, he didn't offer comment." There is just such a calm in society, not to be disparaged, very much to be marveled at, though it permits most forms of betrayal and self-disgrace. It is the condition of moral autonomy. (pp. 35, 40)

The last seven stories here, previously uncollected, are more rueful and humorous, written in more elegant prose and more elegiac than the earlier ones. . . . **"Whoever Was Using This Bed"** is about a couple, awakened by a phone call, who talk through the night about the aches and anxieties that press at such times but are lost in the amnesia of daylight consciousness. Finally they come to the question of whether or not the plug should be pulled if one of them were hopelessly ill. It is a funny, very natural conversation. Their insomnia, and the rumpled bedclothes, bring to mind the extreme of intimacy their marriage implies, even to the point of one possibly choosing to end the other's life.

In the story called **"Intimacy,"** a writer visits his former wife, a woman furious that her life with him has been cannibalized to make fiction and that he has become a success publishing the darkest passages of their marriage. She is aware of giving him new material, even in her wrath, and the story, with the writer as narrator, means she has done just that. But he falls to his knees in her living room and stays there immobilized until it occurs to her to say she forgives him. Then she can send him away. Divorce never really takes in Mr. Carver's stories. Marriage is, in essence, an innocent friendship, desperately vulnerable to derangement and bad luck, but always precious in itself, its lost pleasures always loyally remembered. (p. 40)

"Elephant" is a wonderful little story that should put paid, if anything ever will, to a clamor in certain quarters for a Carver story about grace and transcendence. The narrator, a sort of suburban Père Goriot, is being bled of his substance by a former wife, a mother who is "poor and greedy," a shiftless son, a shiftless daughter with two children and a live-in good-for-nothing, and a brother who calls with hard-luck stories. The man is impoverished, exhausting his credit, working and worrying, trying to meet their endless demands. Then he dreams that his father is carrying him, as a child, on his shoulders. The image brings him a great release. He thinks of his daughter, "God love her and keep her," and hopes for the happiness of his son, and is glad that he still has his mother, and that his former wife, "the woman I used to love so much," is alive somewhere. Then perhaps he dies. He is carried past the place where he works at astonishing speed in a ''big unpaid-for car.'' Whether it is death that has stopped for him, or an uncanny freedom, the exhilaration of the ending has a distinctly theological feel. (pp. 40-1)

Raymond Carver is not an easy writer to read. His narratives are often coarse. Sometimes he seems intent on proving that insensitive people have feelings, too. And while the impulse is generous, the experience of looking at the world through the eyes of a character as crude as the narrator of ''**Cathedral**,'' for example, is highly uncongenial.

In ''**Feathers**,'' a story centered on a fine moment in which an ugly baby and a bedraggled peacock frolic together under the dinner table, the reader's attention is drawn to an annoying plaster cast of terribly crooked teeth, displayed like a trophy in the living room of this strange household. In this story, as in ''**Cathedral**,'' characters are overcome by an esthetic experience or realization. *Mutatis mutandis*, it is Henry James— beauty is the mode of address of the world to the human soul.

But there is lump as well as leaven in Mr. Carver, and the lumpishness is more irksome because it feels intentional. The characters sometimes seem set up, or condescended to. It is this condition from which they are rescued in the course of the story. Mr. Carver is rather like the poet William Carlos Williams, who declared their were ''no ideas but in things,'' and who turned banality's pockets out and found all their contents beautiful.

The process of Mr. Carver's fiction is to transform our perception. Perhaps what he does cannot be done in another way. And, viewed from sufficient distance, an interesting problem can take its place among the beautiful things. (p. 41)

> *Marilynne Robinson, ''Marriage and Other Astonishing Bonds,'' in* The New York Times Book Review, *May 15, 1988, pp. 1, 35, 40-1.*

DAVID LIPSKY

In the record industry, they're called compilation albums: best songs from early albums, many no longer available, plus a smattering of new ones, available nowhere else. When a singer changes labels, the new company generally releases one, to show off their catch and also to remind record buyers that the singer's still around.

Raymond Carver's fourth collection, *Where I'm Calling From,* is a compilation album. There are two reasons for its being released now. First, Carver, 49 and widely considered America's foremost short-story writer, has recently changed labels, from Knopf to Atlantic Monthly Press. Second, Carver was inducted this spring into the American Academy and Institute of Arts and Letters. For ten years, he's been a fixture in the literary cosmos, visible to trained professionals but not easily spotted by the naked eye. Now, Carver is officially a star. (pp. 50-1)

Where I'm Calling From includes three hundred pages of stories from his first three collections, stories that still possess a shocking newness. The narrator's voice in ''**Fat**,'' for example, is an uncanny mix of choppy reticence and perfect focus:

> This fat man is the fattest person I have ever seen, though he is neat-appearing and well-dressed enough. Everything about him is big. But it is the fingers I remember best . . . They look three times the size of

a normal person's fingers—long, thick, creamy fingers.

Carver's early stories work by reduction. As readers, we feel the pressure of what his narrators aren't mentioning, the force of unsaid things weighing down on what they are able to say. Even the titles alternate between statements reflecting inarticulateness—''**Nobody Said Anything**''—and questions that are never truly answered in the bodies of their stories—''**Why, Honey?**'' ''**What's in Alaska?**'' ''**Are These Actual Miles?**'' The surprise of *Where I'm Calling From* comes in the later stories, when Carver begins putting the unsaid stuff back in. With most ''minimalists,'' one suspects the assumed terseness of hiding a very real lack of substance. In stories like ''**Feathers**,'' ''**Cathedral**,'' and ''**A Small, Good Thing**,'' we see that a prolix Carver is at least as good as a laconic one. Indeed, these stories, appearing back-to-back, set a standard the rest of the book can't really match.

Which is not to say the new stories in *Where I'm Calling From* are unsatisfying. But ''**Boxes**,'' which follows ''**A Small, Good Thing**,'' is a letdown. It shows what happens when Carver gives himself too much latitude. The narrator's peripatetic mother, living in her son's town for eight months, is going to move again. Carver allows himself a realization scene the earlier Carver would have edited away without a second's thought. . . . (p. 51)

Two of the new stories, the Kafkaesque ''**Intimacy**'' and the baleful ''**Whoever Was Using This Bed**,'' . . . are as good as anything else in the collection. One, ''**Elephant**,'' may be Carver's best. They share an air of earned, masterly confidence; the author isn't struggling to get your ear, he knows he deserves it. Yet one can't help wishing Carver had waited longer to put this book out, gotten more stories together. The early stories have a density to them; they've been mulled over for years. A new story like ''**Blackbird Pie**,'' in which Carver uses a sort of unreliable Edgar Allan Poe voice, would never make a cut like that. The best of Carver's new work deserves a book of it own; tossing in stories like ''**Elephant**'' and ''**Errand**'' at the end of a compilation is teasing.

Still, *Where I'm Calling From* has been arranged cleverly, the stories dovetailing into one another. . . . Bringing the stories into such close contact reveals strengths we otherwise wouldn't have recognized. No one begins stories better than Carver, and no one, certainly, has a better handle on our American style of eating. Consider this, from ''**Cathedral**'':

> We dug in. We ate everything there was to eat on the table. We ate like there was no tomorrow. We didn't talk. We ate. We scarfed. We grazed that table. We were into serious eating . . . We finished everything, including half a strawberry pie. For a few moments, we sat as if stunned. Sweat beaded on our faces.

In the front-page *New York Times Book Review* article on this collection, Marilynne Robinson promised to ''liberate Raymond Carver from the camp of the minimalists'' [see excerpt above]. Excited by her own intepretation of the stories, however, she forgot to go back and do this. Reading *Where I'm Calling From,* one realizes that Carver has been not a minimalist but a precisionist, setting down, as precisely as possible, the exact words for things. He has brought news of his world into ours. One imagines that the title does not so much highlight the story of that name as reflect Carver's whole enterprise. We now know where Raymond Carver has been calling from—it's a place that would have gone unremarked, in a style that would have gone undiscovered, had it not been for him. (pp. 51-2)

David Lipsky, *"News from an Unremarked World,"* in National Review, *New York, Vol. XL, August 5, 1988, pp. 50-2.*

LORNA SAGE

That clichéd remark about Raymond Carver's writing being pared to the bone takes on a new macabre appropriateness now [following his recent death]. Whatever he might have written, it's for these taut, condensed stories and his poems—so obstinately short of epiphanies, or the consolations of metaphor, or terminal revelations—that he'll be remembered. Brevity was the name of his game: the people he spoke for, the white working-class Americans whose voices come over on the page, haven't got too many words, or too much of anything else.

The stories collected in *Elephant* occupy his distinctive territory, the world of domestic panic and chronic insecurity where couples and families fall apart seemingly by a law as inevitable as gravity. In ["Elephant"], a grim comedy of attrition, a solitary middle-aged man finds himself propping up one by one, his mother, brother, ex-wife, daughter, son . . . all miles away and (emotionally speaking) getting further away with every handout. His baffled Archimedian efforts to find somewhere to stand in order to change things, take on, as so often with Carver, a quality of physical, muscular tension. It's not possible for these characters to rest in one's life, to feel at home in it or find an end: 'No destiny,' says another laconic narrator, 'Just the next thing meaning whatever you think it does. Compulsion and error just like everybody else.' . . .

The marriages focus [upon a] sense of betrayal most keenly. **"Intimacy"**, a story about a writer (who could easily, awkwardly enough, be the writer himself) revisiting his ex-wife, is full of a blunt, nameless emotion very like shame, 'She says . . . We were so intimate once upon a time I can't believe it now . . . We were so intimate I could puke." The word stands out on the page like an obscenity. And in a sense it becomes one when you link it with the routine ruin of people's attempts to stay close to each other. What they wanted was, after all, something that's supposed to be commonplace:

> In his better moments, Mr Baxter is a decent, ordinary guy—a guy you wouldn't mistake for anyone special but he is special. In my book, he is. For one thing he has a full night's sleep behind him, and he's just embraced his wife before leaving for work. But even before he goes, he's already expected home a set number of hours later.

This is as near as we come to nostalgia, and it is quite close. The final story here, **"Errand"**, breaks the pattern with a quiet, third person tribute to Carver's acknowledged mentor Chekhov. He's pictured in his last days surrounded by love and solicitude and no nearer to any metaphysical explanation (despite a prosletysing visit from Count Tolstoy) than he ever was. Chekhov's capacity to stay stubbornly puzzled to the end was, one imagines, precisely what Carver so treasured about him—certainly the thing he emulated most loyally.

Lorna Sage, *"The Art of a Doubter,"* in The Observer, *August 14, 1988, p. 41.*

ANNE BOSTON

It was a shock to hear of this fine writer's death, before he reached 50 and a week before this collection [*Elephant*] was published. Raymond Carver has described in *Fires* his hard apprenticeship as a writer, when lack of thinking time constricted him to short stories and poems, which could be drafted at a sitting, at the expense of full-length fiction. Later his circumstances changed, but through choice and possibly, he speculated, through habit he continued to write in the medium which made his reputation. And within the strong tradition of American short-story writing his are among the most accomplished, as this final brief collection bears out.

Carver was a minimalist, with the ability not only to observe the exceptional moments in ordinary lives but also to inhabit his characters, so that they are present in every inflexion of speech. The tension in his earlier writing is often maintained through a powerful sense of menace, of threatened if not actual violence. The seven stories in *Elephant* have lost this aggression, though their characters are still carried helplessly beyond the bounds of safety, to a danger point they never intended to reach. . . .

Like Philip Larkin, Carver writes best about failure, through narrators forced to come to terms with things not working out; like Larkin, again, the relentless gloom is held back by humour, sometimes consciously verging on self-parody. . . .

Shift work, cigarettes and alcohol (or avoidance of it) pervade the pages. Hindsight brings the stories' autobiographical content to the surface; the recognition makes **"Intimacy"** particularly disturbing. Perfect pitch makes Carver's dialogue savagely authentic; here it's accompanied by the uncomfortable suspicion that it was lifted from a real incident. A woman recklessly pours out her grievances against her ex-husband when he visits her years later, now an established writer (and also the narrator). She accuses him of remembering only the "low, shameful things"; then she speculates (accurately) that he'll turn this awful visit into another story. Finally she accepts the worst: "Maybe it'll make a good story," she says. "But I don't want to know about it if it does." Carver's story is horribly convincing—and it reads like eavesdropping; like life paraded as art.

The final story, **"Errand"**, is unlike any other in *Elephant* or in [*The Stories of Raymond Carver*]: a part-factual, part-imagined account of the last days of Chekhov, whom Carver greatly admired. It is also an epitaph, Carver's awareness of his own lung cancer echoing Chekhov's lost battle with tuberculosis. In it, he quotes Chekhov's observation that, lacking "a political, religious and philosophical world view . . . I'll have to limit myself to the description of how my heroes love, marry, give birth, die, and how they speak."

The feeling of having lost a sense of order runs through these stories, and paradoxically it's what gives them their desolate strength; they offer no explanations, but mystery, sometimes, and a tenacious insistence on "truth". Carver himself described his craft with characteristic minimal accuracy in his essay, **"On Writing"**: "The words can be so precise they may even sound flat, but they can still carry; if used right, they can hit all the notes."

Anne Boston, *"Breaking Points,"* in New Statesman & Society, *Vol. 1, No. 11, August 19, 1988, p. 36.*

ADAM BEGLEY

Carver has often been called a minimalist, a term he disliked, but which nonetheless aptly describes his brief stories, and his tightly focused prose. Patterns of speech and incidental gestures dominate, along with an occasional highlighted object; setting as traditionally conceived is all but absent. A simple story [collected in *Elephant, and Other Stories*] called **"Chef's House"**, in which a married couple who have been separated for some time decide to spend the summer together in their friend Chef's seaside house, successfully conveys the feel of a happy house without describing the house at all. When the couple is forced to leave, the woman assures the man that they will find another place. 'Not like this one,' the man replies: 'It wouldn't be the same, anyway. This house has been a good house for us. This house has good memories to it.' Amazingly, the reader knows that this is true.

Sparing with detail, Carver also dispenses what other writers might consider vital information in small, carefully measured doses. In an essay that might pass for his manifesto, **"On Writing"**, he explains the importance of judicious omission: 'What creates tension in a piece of fiction is partly the way the concrete words are linked together to make the visible action of the story. But it's also the things that are left out, that are implied, the landscape just under the smooth (but sometimes broken and unsettled) surface of things.' This tactic Carver shares with Hemingway, who used it to great effect in stories like "Big Two-Hearted River", in which the meticulous description of a fishing trip is charged with tension generated by the unmentioned fact of the fisherman's recent traumatic experiences. In **"The Cabin"**, a very early Carver story replete with echoes of "Big Two-Hearted River", a man goes on a fishing expedition without his wife. Mr Harrold cannot manage to explain why his wife is not with him; it seems there has been some rupture, or at least some undefinable shift in their relations. The central action of the story, a menacing encounter with a group of young hunters, is but a dramatic reaffirmation of the looming threat, implied by his wife's absence, to Mr Harrold's way of life.

What Carver does choose to present he depicts with a clarity born of a devotion to accuracy. Ezra Pound's dictum, 'Fundamental accuracy of statement is the ONE sole morality of writing,' strikes him as hyperbole, and yet he adopts it as a guiding principle. The precision of his language shows most clearly in the remarkable voices that make up so much of his fiction. The monologue is his characteristic mode: men and women telling stories the meaning of which lie just beyond their ken, for the meaning very often resides in the intersection of the substance of the tale with the manner of the telling—that is, the particular pattern of the character's speech. In those stories written in the third person, dialogue most often propels the narrative, provides the key to the story. As Carver says: 'It is possible to write a line of seemingly innocuous dialogue, and have it send a chill along the reader's spine.'

Carver's accuracy is the source of his impressive authority. Because it seems so real, the fictional world he creates also seems inevitable, each action the necessary consequence of the situation at hand. Authority allows him to take risks, to write scenes that hover on the verge of melodrama, or that seem just barely probable. . . .

The first six stories [in *Elephant*] are monologues, of which two are among Carver's most successful. **"Boxes"** is the story of a man helplessly aware of his widowed mother's crazy inability to stay put, to make a home for herself. Permanently dissatisfied, she wanders from town to town, settles briefly near her son, then prepares for another move. He himself is insecurely settled; divorced, he lives with a woman, Jill, who has been twice divorced. The mother sees Jill as an intruder, Jill finds the mother a nuisance, and the two compete for his attention. He is baffled and resigned: 'They could tear me apart in no time at all.' Not only is the man's voice convincing and compelling, but framed within the monologue is the mother's endless carping. . . .

In **"Elephant"**, one of Carver's funnier stories, a man who supports an entire absent family, sending cheque after cheque through the mail, sinking gradually into debt, bemoans the weight of his burden—and at the same time, half consciously, reveals the reasons for his perplexing willingness to assume it. As in **"Boxes"**, the narrator's monologue frames a chorus of other voices. . . . The family knows what the reader learns only gradually, that he is driven by complimentary urges: he dreams of stability and harmony, tries in vain to provide them, and wants to atone for his sins, to repair the violence done in earlier, drunken years. . . .

[In **"Errand"**] Carver depicts Chekhov's last moments, the very stuff of melodrama, with . . . dignity and reserve. At the end of the story, however, an emotionally charged scene transforms an elegant historical anecdote into a potent Carver story. Olga, Chekhov's wife, addresses a young and bewildered hotel porter who has offered to bring breakfast on a tray:

> No breakfast, the woman said. Not yet at any rate. Breakfast wasn't the important thing this morning. She required something else. She needed him to go out and bring back a mortician. Did he understand her? Herr Chekhov was dead, you see. *Comprenez-vous?* Young man? Anton Chekhov was dead.

The porter's inability to grasp the substance, let alone the significance, of Olga's fantastically detailed explanation of the errand she has in mind (she goes so far as to describe a hypothetical mortician) provides a dramatic recapitulation of Chekhov's own unwillingness to face death.

Great writers, Carver once said, leave their 'particular and unmistakable signature' on everything they write. In **"Errand"** he demonstrates that his signature is neither brevity nor the bleak realities of damaged working-class lives, but rather the accuracy and authority of his prose. (p. 17)

Adam Begley, "Less or More," in London Review of Books, *Vol. 10, No. 16, September 15, 1988, pp. 17-18.*

Paul Celan

1920-1970

(Born Paul Antschel) Rumanian-born poet, essayist, and translator.

Celan is regarded as among the most important poets to emerge from Europe after World War II and, with Rainer Maria Rilke, is considered the finest German lyric poet of the twentieth century. In his verse, Celan explored and attempted to reconcile the anguish of the Jewish experience following the Nazi Holocaust. Celan's poetry, which is often described by critics as obscure and hermetic, draws on elements of symbolism, expressionism, surrealism, and Hasidic mysticism while featuring inventive vocabulary and bizarre, dreamlike imagery. As Celan's career progressed, his verse became increasingly cryptic and fragmented, reflecting his search for new ways to express the ineffable horrors of the Holocaust. Rika Lesser commented: "Celan's language—peculiar, idiosyncratic, transformational, at times almost incomprehensible—seems the only one capable of absorbing and expressing a world changed by the Holocaust. His language and poetry issue from the urgent need to communicate, to speak the truth that lies in deeply ambiguous metaphors."

Celan was born in Czernovitz, the capital of the Rumanian province of Bukovina, to German-speaking Jewish parents. As a youth, he became proficient in several languages, including Hebrew and French. After beginning premedical studies in France, Celan returned home prior to the outbreak of World War II and witnessed the Soviet occupation of his hometown. His parents were captured and killed following the German invasion of Czernovitz in 1941, and Celan himself was interned for eighteen months in a Nazi labor camp. The sorrow and anguish resulting from the Holocaust pervades much of Celan's poetry and is especially evident in his most famous poem, "Todesfuge" ("Death Fugue"), a hallucinatory depiction of a concentration camp from the viewpoint of the inmates. "Death Fugue" appears in both of Celan's first two poetry collections, *Der Sand aus den Urnen* (1948) and *Mohn und Gedächtnis* (1952). Characterized by such lyric elements as rhythmical repetition, surrealistic imagery, and rhyme, the poems in these early works combine paradox, negation, and intricate word association to convey the psychological trauma suffered by survivors of Nazi atrocities. With his next book, *Von Schwelle zu Schwelle* (1955), Celan began to move away from somber personal reflection toward a more optimistic outlook and developed an increasing interest in the language of poetry. The verse in *Sprachgitter* (1959) marks an even greater stylistic departure from Celan's early work, as evidenced by its ruptured syntax, unusual diction, enigmatic imagery, and condensed lines. A prevalent theme of this volume is the inadequacy of language to convey profound misery.

In *Die Niemandsrose* (1963), Celan again focuses on Jewish themes, lamenting the persecution and suffering that Jews have endured throughout history and presenting a negative theology derived from Jewish and Christian mysticism. The longer lines and rhyme in this collection signal a return to the verse style of *Mohn und Gedächtnis*. *Atemwende* (1967) is predominantly devoid of Jewish subject matter, focusing instead on poetic language itself. In his last three volumes, *Fadensonnen* (1968),

Lichtzwang (1970), and the posthumously published *Schneepart* (1971), Celan's poetry became progressively more hermetic, featuring further constricted and fractured verse lines, sarcasm, and irony to underscore his heightened sense of isolation and hopelessness. In 1970, Celan committed suicide by drowning himself in the Seine River.

In his prose writings, Celan elaborated upon his aesthetic and poetic theories. *Edgar Jené und der Traum vom Traume* (1948), ostensibly a study of the surrealist paintings of Edgar Jené, develops into an investigation of what Celan termed the "deep sea" of the writer's consciousness, the psychological realm where poetry originates. In the essay "Gespräch im Gebirg" (1960; "Conversation in the Mountains"), Celan engages in an imaginary dialogue with philosopher Theodor Adorno about such topics as language, nature, perception, and God. In "Der Meridian" (1960; "The Meridian"), his acceptance speech for the 1960 Georg Büchner Prize which is constructed as a dialogue with his audience, Celan attempts to find meaning in the world and describes poetry as the process of freeing oneself by searching for a utopia. Celan's essays and speeches were published in *Collected Prose* (1987). In addition to his poetry and nonfiction, Celan translated into German the work of such writers as Arthur Rimbaud, Osip Mandelstam, and William Shakespeare.

(See also *CLC*, Vols. 10, 19; *Contemporary Authors*, Vols. 85-88; and *Dictionary of Literary Biography*, Vol. 69.)

REX LAST

[The] figure who towers above all the other [Austrian] metaphorical poets is that of Paul Celan, . . . a Rumanian Jew best known for one single much-anthologized poem **"Todesfuge"** (**"Fugue of Death"**), which, as has frequently been pointed out, is somewhat untypical of his work at large, in that it is rhythmical, fluent and relatively accessible: image succeeds image in bold and fluent patterns which contrast strikingly with the sparse and almost inscrutable verses of the more mature Celan. In one very significant respect, however, **"Todesfuge"** is typical of Celan; namely, in its obsessive preoccupation with the Jewish race and its persecution throughout the ages.

Celan's parents were interned in a concentration camp, where they met their deaths; but although Celan himself managed to escape, the experiences of the war left an indelible scar on him and constitute one of the dominant themes of his poetry, which also owes a great deal to the rich variety of cultural traditions to which Celan was exposed by virtue of his origins and the situations into which fate brought him. As [critic Siegbert S. Prawer] aptly expresses it:

> Out of his experience of exile and horror, out of his wanderings in German, Jewish, Slav and French cultural and ethnic regions, Paul Celan has managed to fashion a German poetry whose compelling force has been acknowledged even by those who are most disturbed by its occasional preciosity and its sometimes all-too-wilful obscurity.

It is this compelling force, this obsessiveness which communicates itself irresistibly to the reader, even though the meaning may remain elusive to the point of inscrutability.

His first important book of poems, *Mohn und Gedächtnis (Poppy and Memory)*, appeared in 1952; as its title suggests, it is preoccupied with the painful past and with an attempt to come to terms with it. Celan is concerned with his own past experiences, and too with a sense of guilt about what happened to his parents; but he reaches out far beyond his personal sufferings to consider the fate of the Jews under National Socialism and, too, the broader issue of the relationship between Judaism and Christianity. The incantatory tone of the collection is established in the opening poem, **"Ein Lied in der Wüste"** (**"A Song in the Wilderness"**). . . . The language is intense and difficult, the associations largely biblical and Jewish, but often of such obscurity that critics are forced to admit defeat and dub them 'surreal'.

The pessimism of this collection is further heightened by the celebrated **"Todesfuge,"** about which a great deal of critical ink has been spilled. The poem, which concerns the sufferings of the Jews in a Nazi concentration camp, but which some observers regard as partly a love poem, is deliberately couched in a highly stylized mode; it is in essence an attempt—and a highly successful one—to translate into poetic terms the musical form of the fugue. A number of independent images are established and then repeated with variations in order and emphasis up to a climactic point, after which the poem fades away on a dying cadence.

"Todesfuge" also parallels a device from the visual arts: it is a kind of poetic collage, in which graphic images are juxtaposed in a series of 'pictures' without any attempt to fuse them together; in addition, most of the individual images contain their own internal contradictions: the prisoners drink 'black milk'; they are made to dig 'a grave in the sky'; the camp commandant (or one of the guards; his exact identity is not specified) splits into two contradictory people, the gentle lover who writes home and the vicious warder; and the golden-haired representative of German womanhood, Margarete, is set against the ashen-haired Sulamith. Only at the climactic point of the poem is there an end-rhyme, stressing both the inevitability of death and destruction, and also the key significance of colours to the poem:

> Death is a master from Germany his eye is blue
> he strikes you with the lead ball he strikes you true

Only when the colours refer to the Germans are they used in their normal application: blue eyes, golden hair, leaden bullet—the references to colour in the context of the Jews are, however, distorted: black milk, and ashen hair for Sulamith. These two latter are also distorted biblical borrowings: milk is a symbol for purity in the Old Testament and Shulamite is raven-haired. Beyond this, the whole poem represents a negation of the promises of the Lord to the people of Israel. Not least among the bitterly distorted images is that of the smoke of the crematorium chimney rising into the sky like incense; instead of the Jews sacrificing to their God and the sweet smoke ascending like a prayer, they themselves are victims on the altar of the Third Reich.

This incantatory, hypnotic fugue of death is one of the pinnacles of twentieth-century German poetry, and as such has, not surprisingly, attracted an excess of exegetic endeavour; but it is not the precise meaning of the less obvious images that hold the key to the poem (the snakes, for example, with which the commandant 'plays'), but rather the overall impact of repetition and variation with its unusual rhythmical patterns and bleak message to the victims of oppression.

Towards the end of *Mohn und Gedächtnis,* there is a suggestion that Celan is beginning to move away from the intense bleakness of **"Todesfuge"**; and this incipient optimism moves cautiously forward in his next collection, appropriately entitled *Von Schwelle zu Schwelle (From Threshold to Threshold*; 1955), although it is clear that his starting point is such that he has no choice but to take a positive direction. . . . The lines grope their way towards a dimly-seen awareness of the possibility of attaining a new synthesis, of being able to command the all-embracing but extremely elusive forces of language in order to reflect the infinite. Equally, they indicate a shift in emphasis away from personal issues into the direction of recognizing his broader mission as a poet.

But his message . . . is far from unambiguous, since what he is trying to grasp and convey is so complex, remote, and far beyond the confines of rationalistic thought patterns. His poetry, in essence, operates on the brink of silence, on the outer limits of significance. In **"Stimmen"** (**"Voices"**), the first poem of his most celebrated collection *Sprachgitter (The Grid of Language*; 1959), half-perceived voices speak of the Jewish past, of death, and finally no voice speaks of a suffering that will never cease.

The imagery is compressed and oblique, the language sparse and unwilling to yield up its secrets:

> *Voices* from the nettle path this way:

Come on your hands to us.
He who is alone with the lamp,
only has his hand to read from it.

Here the voices speak of the *via dolorosa* of Jewry, of the nettle-grown path which has marked the hands of all those who have passed along it and who now, in solitary bereavement and anguish, cast their eyes on the scars and can yet feel the searing pain which derives not only from the specific sufferings of individuals in the concentration camps, but also from the centuries of persecution which have burdened the Jews since the death of Christ.

Not surprisingly, the motif of the tear appears time and again, in the first instance as a recollection of Jewish guilt in the voice of Jacob. . . . The theme of guilt is carried through to a stanza which deals with the voices in the Ark, and to those outside, sinking, doomed to perish in the Flood for their sins. Ultimately, there is no voice to speak, only the resinous secretion of a plant, oozing 'large as an eye' its own unending grief. . . . (pp. 146-50)

These key themes of the tear-brimming eye and of silence are also central to an understanding of the title poem of the collection. . . . The eye's search for heaven fails, dimmed with tears, and ends downcast, making two pools of water, two mouthfuls of silence. In its endeavours to attain a measure of comprehension of the world beyond the self, the eye had tried to penetrate through the 'bars' of its lashes (a not untypical juxtaposition of a round shape and a straight line in Celan's poetry); but, in a refutation of Gottfried Benn's confident view of the power of the word, Celan takes over his notion of 'gitter' (grid) and transposes it to the eye which peers out into the world, employing the cilia of its lid (again the image is Benn's) as sensory organs. However, all that transpires is greyness and silence; there is no flash of illumination, no insight into the self or the world beyond, as lines from the poem that comes after **"Sprachgitter"** obsessively underline:

Eyes, world-blind,
eyes in the abyss of death,
eyes eyes.

This immensely difficult and painstaking search characterizes the whole of *Sprachgitter,* as the title of the collection, with its ramifying and ambiguous sweep of connotations, implies. It has been variously interpreted in terms of the two-way flow of significances through the grid of language . . . which both filters and inhibits the flow of concepts and their expression; or as the grille through which the members of a closed order communicate with the outside world (a kind of parallel to Rilke's 'schmale Leier', narrow lyre); and it has also been accorded a variety of more exotic and less plausible connotations.

In his next collection, *Die Niemandsrose (Nobody's Rose),* Celan concentrates his attention once again on Judaism. It is no coincidence that the volume is dedicated to the Russian Jewish poet Osip Mandelstam. Once again, the title—as happens so frequently with Celan—contains an inner contradiction, the nature of which becomes clear in the poem **"Psalm,"** which contains within itself the title of the collection:

Praised be thou, No one.
For thy sake
we will bloom.
Towards
you.

Once more, as these lines demonstrate, negation within a religious frame of reference plays a prominent rôle. The psalm is directed not, as one might reasonably expect, at the God of the Jews, but at 'no one'. Like the rose, man grows and blossoms and fades in the service of a deity who remains unknown to him. The precise significance of the 'no one'—and this should come as no surprise to the Celan reader—is caught up in an inextricable web of complexities. It has been pointed out that, in the Old Testament, the rose is identified with Israel; but now, after all the sufferings of the Jewish people, the rose is no longer God's but nobody's; and it is therefore only appropriate that psalms should now be directed not towards God, but to this no one.

Given such a bleak assessment of the present spiritual condition of the Jews, it is almost inevitable that Celan should return to the concentration camp motifs of **"Todesfuge,"** and, indeed the collection *Niemandsrose* opens with lines that develop the motif of 'digging' a grave in the sky. . . . Their digging leads to the unearthing of no positive solutions; its meaninglessness as an activity is reflected in the poem's recitation of the present tense of the verb. Meaning has shrunk back into the word, the supposed bearer of significances.

This drift into silence is reflected also in the poem **"Man-dorla,"** which depicts an almond-shaped glory from whose centre the expected figure of Christ is absent. Once again God has vanished, leaving nothing in His place.

Only in the collection *Fadensonnen (Thread-suns,* 1968), are there to be found some strains of optimism, in poems relating to the 1967 Arab-Israeli war; but, in general, Celan's later poetry becomes ever more obscure, lacking in inner unity, a fact which seems to indicate that he has given up all hope of even searching, let alone identifying a goal. (pp. 150-53)

*Rex Last, "Paul Celan and the Metaphorical Poets,"
in* Modern Austrian Writing: Literature and Society
After 1945, *edited by Alan Best and Hans Wolfschütz, Oswald Wolff, 1980, pp. 142-55.*

KATHERINE WASHBURN AND MARGARET GUILLEMIN

Celan, even for German readers, is baffling, elliptical, paradoxical. Even before you begin, in Celan's words, to "plait and unplait" the strands of associations, obsessions, allusions, and the personal, historical, and literary data which may unite in a single poem, you feel that these are *bent* poems. The syntax goes through more loops and coils than even the agility of German generally allows; some of the neologisms are barely decipherable, or so close to their punning counterparts that a sort of textual *trompe-l'oeil* results; the poetic line, with all its fits, starts, and stuttering halts can scarcely be re-stated in plain prose. Like a wild vine, intensively cultivated, the thrust of Celan's imagery expands, contracts, and proliferates anew, from poem to poem, from book to book.

How are we to read these poems? [Biographer Israel] Chalfen, seeking an interpretation of a certain poem from Celan was told, "Read! Just read again and again, the understanding comes by itself." The advice is less gnomic than it seems. The reader who seeks the full reward for his attention begins a long scrutiny of the poem by leaving no word unturned, by holding it up to the light, by fingering the text for references, familiar and obscure. But at last, he sleeps on it, dreams on it, meshes his own thought processes with those of the poem, and comes thereby to the long-sought gloss. In the silences in and around the poem, there is room for entry. The poems are not hermetic nor the door sealed shut forever.

Celan wrote one poem which contains an imperative intended not only for himself, but for the reader too:

> With a variable key
> you unlock the house in which
> drifts the snow of that left unspoken
> Always what key you choose
> depends on the blood that spurts
> from your eye or your mouth or your ear.

Eye, mouth, ear. To cherish the word in Celan and give it its full value, it must be seen, sounded, heard. Only thus can we penetrate the landscape of pure language created by these poems. The titles, nine in all, of the volumes of Celan's poetry in Michael Hamburger's collection [*Poems*] were rigorously established by Celan, foreshadowed, and echoed throughout each book, to serve as signposts over all the terrain. One by one, Celan embeds the name of each book in the lines of individual poems where the Germanless reader may or may not locate them. These titles are Celan's programs; they require translation along with the texts.

In "Corona," a famous poem from the 1952 volume *Mohn und Gedächtnis,* Celan spills every letter of his private alphabet: autumn, leaf, mouth, eye:

> My eye moves down to the sex of my loved one
> We look at each other
> We exchange dark words
> We love each other like poppy and recollection.

Mohn und Gedächtnis: poppy and recollection. For Celan, the opiate flower represents the intoxication with pure poetry which he shared with a circle of Surrealist poets and artists in postwar Bucharest. The conflict in Paul Celan, "caught in that sensual music," yet possessed by the memory of the Holocaust, produced a poetry of anguished paradox. The problem of maintaining the fierce equilibrium which the paradox demands was . . . never abandoned. (pp. 35-6)

"Todesfuge," "Deathfugue," Celan's most celebrated poem, speaks for itself, and for Celan, who later repudiated it as too particularizing, too direct, speaks all too straightforwardly. The pull toward silence dominated Celan's later relationship to this poem, it took on for him the flawed character of history, more difficult and more "slippery," as Aristotle says, than poetry. In its directness, however subtly wrought, Celan may have seen a heightened risk of perishability. Yet it remains for many readers the centerpiece of Celan's early work, his *Guernica,* however much it violates Celan's conviction that *"La poésie ne s'impose plus, elle s'expose."*

Celan's next book, *Von Schwelle zu Schwelle, From Threshold to Threshold* is in truth a book of passages, its transitions foreshadowed in these lines from is predecessor:

> He's the one who has what I said
> He carries it under his arm like a bundle
> He carries it as the clock carries its worst hour
> From threshold to threshold he carries it, never throws it away.

These poems, with their legacy of guilt and terror, concern themselves with language. They examine the act of writing itself, the course of the journey. Celan has already seeded his path with his primary images—here they increase by fusion,

multiply by fission, gathering power, momentum, richer accretions of meaning. Compare:

> EYES
> shining with the rain that poured
> when God made me drink

with this:

> This is time's eye:
> it squints out
> from under a seven-hued eyebrow
> Its lid is washed clean by fires
> Its tear is hot steam.
>
> Towards it the blind star flies
> and melts at the eyelash that's hotter;
> it's growing warm in the world
> and the dead burgeon and flower.

Rain in Celan is sometimes the bitter draught of god's grace, sometimes the flood of the tears of the living, sometimes the source of the rainbed, the moist place of human sexuality where rebirth is possible. In "time's eye," rain and tears have turned to steam. The pair of eyes is halved to one eye and its photonegative: the blind star. The star is blind; its light blinds the eye. In their union, in a volcanic world of fire and steam, is the hope of regeneration, of a flowering of the dead. Every image in Celan is doubled and redoubled, taken through endless transformations to its nth power. As word is to stone, incandescent stone is to star, star to world. Words are pried apart, forced to yield the sum of their parts, conjugated, babbled, stammered, endlessly recombined in a "piling on of words, volcanic, drowned by the sea's roar." (pp. 37-9)

In *Matière de Bretagne,* we see the vanishing trick, the folding of the page, within the poem itself. The poem is made, and with the maker's sleight-of-hand, unmade. . . . Celan wrote a number of poems set in the maritime landscape of Brittany. Here, the title *Matière de Bretagne* has at least two possible associations. *Matière* is the French word for suppurating matter, for the products of physical decay; to the medievalist, the *Matière de Bretagne* means that class of myths from the Arthurian cycle, including the Grail legends, which has its source in Brittany rather than England. The first stanza treats the physical and mythical topography of the region as one: it ranges from slopes where the bloom of yellow gorse suggests not growth but decay to the thorn courted wound by which the *calvaire* at every crossroad in this Catholic province reminds us of the Passion and death of Christ. The tolling of bells at evening evokes the Celtic legend of the drowned city of Ys, where churchbells are said to ring beneath the waters at sunset, as well as the passage of time.

Time, and the erosion of myth, both sacred and secular, by time is the matter of this poem. As the Void rolls its oceans to vespers, we are near the edge of the great *Nichts* which Celan is to summon over and over in his poetry, reminding us that myth, or religious faith itself, is become a little shrunken place bounded by nothingness. The bloodsail, driven from another shore, draws its color from the setting of the sun, from the stained shroud of Christ, and from our memory of the sail in the Tristan legend announcing (falsely) the death of the loved one. We are left with stagnation and silence, a place like the realm of the Fisher King, dying for lack of rainfall. Rain and snow alternate in Celan, speech and silence, life and death: here, there is a terse allusion to snow and its shadow. What relieves this desolation is the twinning image of the star above and the stone-borer below. The star is a Celanian token of the absolute; the stone, its earthly counterpart. In Celan, the action of boring into stone through geological strata represents his search for the pure word beneath its damaged counterfeits. The poem reverses its tempo; speeding up and reducing its images, it closes with a wish for the repose of hands, a rest from prayer and writing. *You teach your hands to sleep.* For Celan, sleep is the irrational realm in which truth can be perceived anew. To sleep, to dream—the dream, like a lattice, filters waking experience, creates a mesh of wordplay, free association, and memory through which we drift and fall and rise once more. Thus, from **"Snowbed,"**

> Eyes world-blind
> eyes in the lode-break of dying
> eyes eyes
>
> . . . The snowbed beneath us both, the snowbed
> Crystal by crystal
> latticed time-deep, we fall
> we fall and lie and fall. . . .

Like its companion poem from a later book which ends, "We, we are the rainbed, may he come and drain us," this is a poem of *eros* and *thanatos*, half-echoing in its opening lines the terms of a weather report to suggest the climate of the inner and outer worlds. We have the faint outline of a bed, the landscape of a body, the reflection of an underworld "in the lodes." Stone has turned to crystal, a particle of snow. In the latticework, time-deep, the snow crystal is a flake of silence.

In Celan's outer landscapes, references to personal experience are dwindling. When they appear, they are lightly coded. Almost no animals inhabit these spaces, we are in the realm of vegetable and mineral, where the eye dwells, the wandering "I" which sees everything. There are birds, but the birds often seem little more than emblems of a kind of aerial vision. Their names, however, are richly suggestive. When starlings appear, we remember that in German starlings are *Stäre,* identical with the word for cataracts, which induce blindness. (pp. 40-2)

The snow is thickening in the country of *Sprachgitter.* You think of Conrad Aiken's story, "Silent Snow, Secret Snow," of a drift into schizophrenia, you think of a poet and the whiteness of blank pages, you think of Celan, subject to frequent and severe breakdowns and the risk he took travelling so far into what a German critic calls "the nomansland between language and silence."

Celan's next book, *Niemandsrose, No One's Rose,* is dedicated to Osip Mandelstam. The dedication is underscored by a broken quotation introducing a poem near the end of the book where he quotes Maria Tsvetaeva's remark, "All poets are Jews." What Tsvetaeva actually wrote was, "All poets are Jews in a Christian world," an epigram bonding the otherness of the Jew with the otherness of the poet. *No One's Rose* celebrates that otherness; in its argument with god from the ashes, its negative theology, is perhaps the most affirmative statement we find in Celan's work. Names of poets—Heine, Hölderlin, Nelly Sachs—reverberate throughout the book, but it is dominated by one name upon which Celan, in a preceding book, has begun to ring the changes: Mandelstam. Almond is *Mandel*; the name rises from almond-shaped eyes, from almond trees, from references to the almond as the ancient Hebrew unit of counting, and has, muted though Celan keeps the association, the flavor of bitter almonds, the hiss of cyanide. Celan gives the word full weight as it sounds from poem to poem, a splintering echo, a homophone.

In *No One's Rose,* the vocabulary and traditions of Jewish mysticism seem more available to Celan than in the past, sug-

gesting to some commentators a period of integration and acceptance of his religious heritage. There is indeed a mastery in these poems of the canons of formal verse, suggesting a new ease with the German language, and there is at the same time an intimacy, a blasphemous ease with Jewish and Christian theology. Look at the release and energy of the following:

> O one, o none, o no one o you:
> Where did the way lead when it led nowhere?
> O you dig and I dig and I dig towards you,
> and on our fingers the ring awakes. . . .

Digging in the earth summons up the image of the dead, in particular the Jewish dead, clawing their way back to life through layers of earth, and the concept, which Mandelstam frequently employs, of digging in the earth as a groping for the *word,* the immutable words, by which these dead might be remembered. The two actions, one from above, one from below, join hands, make a circle, form a ring. . . . The ring is a symbol in Celan and in Jewish tradition of God's compact with his people, but it also recalls Lorca's lines from a poem about a mute boy:

> I will make a ring of it
> so that he may wear my silence
> on his little finger.

From Mandelstam to Lorca, murdered Jews, murdered poets? Which is subject, which is metaphor? *No One's Rose* is an object where meanings converge: it stands for the Jewish people, it stands for the *logos* of God, the *logos* of man. It is the book of things destroyed, where Celan speaks of the calyx of the great "ghetto-rose" with "reed-choked lips" in lines recalling Petrarch in exile, Mandelstam lost in the far north of the Gulag Archipelago. (pp. 43-5)

In his polyglot career as translator, he not only translated the work of Mandelstam, with whom he felt such deep affinity, but also that of Blok, Lermontov, Rimbaud, Shakespeare, and Pessoa. But whether or not his identification with Mandelstam or his retrieval of what mattered for him in his Jewish heritage provided the freedom and unity of this cycle of poems, the result is a consolidation of his poetic gifts. What followed, signalled by its title, *Atemwende,* or *Breath-Turning,* proved less accessible and for many readers, almost alienating. Breath-units, as Michael Hamburger observes, rather than metrical or syllabic ones, begin to govern the movement of the poem. As the metre shifts, the struggle for expression seems to go into an almost "acute phase." Images of writing, of style, book, and letter are receding. We are back to speech, to mouth over hand.

The German edition of *Atemwende* begins with a short poem wherein we hear, muffled but distinct, Mandelstam's name, once more. (There is a *Maulbeerbaum* or mulberry tree instead of Mandel*baum,* almond tree.) It closes with a shriek of a leaf. The landscape is more severe, its associations more private. We are moving closer to the visionary landscape of Celan's late poems where familiar things have fallen away, where, as the inscription on the cover of the second volume in the German edition of Celan's poems says: *"Die Welt ist fort, ich muss dich tragen."* "The world is gone, I must carry you." This remains:

> Deep in Time's crevasse
> by the alveolate ice
> waits, a crystal of breath,
> your irreversible/witness.

We don't know which personal crises, deepened and prolonged as they were by Celan's history, rekindled the distrust of language that flares up again with such brilliance in these poems. Celan, who described himself as *still geworden,* as "becoming silent," is rejecting language, as betrayer and betrayed.

NO MORE SAND ART, no sand book, no masters

Nothing won by dicing. How many dumb ones?
Seventeen

Your question—your answer
Your song, what does it know?

Deepinsnow
      Eepinnow
        Ee-i-o

The repudiation of "sand art" is threefold. In *No One's Rose,* the Jews are people of the clouds, people of smoke—a reference to the near past and the far, to the fate of those once led by a pillar of fire only to disappear in the air in a column of smoke. Here, given their desert origin, they are the people of the sand. "Sand art" suggests the transience of art, but more specifically, Celan's first book, withdrawn from print by Celan himself, *Sand From the Urns.* The reference to "Seventeen" has been glossed as part of a chain of allusions to the "Eighteen Prayers" of the liturgy, a prayer of Thanksgiving broken off before completion. In the last line, the Hebrew practice of removing the vowels in written texts is burlesqued by removing consonants, utterly annihilating meaning.

Celan is erasing the tablets, as we travel from sand to snow. The first volume of the German edition of Celan's collected poems bears a line from an early poem: ". . . at the eastern window, the slender wanderer-phantom of feeling appears at night." With the breath-turning of the second volume, we are now pointed due north. We are inside a snowscape: When houses appear, they are windowless. But

   . . . A handful of sleep grain wafts from the mouth
   stammered true
   out to the snow conversations.

In the language of sleep, snow-conversations grow. Words are formed like great crystals of ice, transcendent and pure. The word games, the breaking-down of meaning to release more meaning, increase geometrically. The language is more wintry, more exigent, and Celan's English translators begin to lay down their pens. . . . Filaments of meaning from poem to poem grow tauter as the conventional measures of the poet become sparer. Celan's diction begins to lock in the words "delusion" and "madness" while compressing his past into images of shadow and smoke. Over all this austerity, his words of choice assemble like stars into fixed constellations, their patterns sharper, their light more brilliant for the gathering darkness around them. . . . *Fadensonnen, Thread-Suns* is the title of Celan's 1968 collection. (*Lichtzwang, Schneepart,* and *Zeitgehöft,* scrupulously edited and arranged by Celan before his death, are posthumous issue.) The poems seem enigmatic, fragmentary, given to riddling fits and starts. The use of adverbs of space and time is highly idiosyncratic, the better to inform us that:

           Vincent's posted ear
           has reached its destination.

Celan is burrowing in. The poems are now conducting a dialogue, powerful and intact through all their leaps and reticences, with each other. The poems sometimes respond to their younger selves, as in

High-world, lost, the journey of madness, the journey of day
what's askable from here
with the rose in a year of draught
is the Nowhere, interpreted home. . . .

Here is a counter-poem to the famous **"Psalm"** of *No One's Rose.* The bitter reproach to God, in **"Psalm,"** contained in the word *himmelswüst,* "heaven-wasted," is echoed by "High-world, lost." The journey of madness is not the usual poetic trope of a night-journey, but the journey of day: the madness of everyday life in dark times, the terrible deed done in broad daylight. The rose of this poem, like that of **"Psalm,"** is a double symbol for the Jewish dead and for literary creation "over the thorn." The allusion to dust in **"Psalm"** is conserved in "the year of draught." The flower of **"Psalm"** blooms towards Nothing and No One; these converge in this late poem into a metaphor of direction, the Nowhere, on its way home.

The place, Celan tells us in a poem from *Schneepart,* "can't be named." (*"The Snow-Part,"* technically the vocal part of snow as if in a musical composition: Celan's silence is polyphonic.) It is the *ou topos,* Utopia:

   I HEAR THAT THE AXE HAS FLOWERED
   I hear that the place can't be named

   I hear that the bread which looks at him
   heals the hanged man
   the bread baked for him by his wife

   I hear that they call life
   our only refuge.

The paradoxes are not trivial. Nor are they stated merely to drive us to the correct and excruciating reading of the last line. The poem was probably written, under the mandate of Celan's language-economy, as an oblique response to the events of the 1968 student revolt in France which recalls an earlier revolution in which the axe and the Fleur de Lys become one. The place, like the God of the Hebrews, "can't be named"; the axe blooms toward the Not-Place. The triad of "hanged man," "bread," and "wife" is an allusion so obscure as to be almost encoded to the history of the French Revolution: the dethroned monarchs of the *ancien regime* were alluded to, in Parisian revolutionary argot, as "the baker" and "the baker's wife." There is another symbolic triangle here: we think of Celan's reference in another poem, to "delusion-bread," we think of the Christian mystery of Transubstantiation, the conversion in the Eucharist of bread into the body of Christ, the hanged man. We think of the central paradox of Christianity: the death of the Redeemer, whereby "others he saved, himself he could not save": once more, Celan has reversed a paradox, stood it on its head. There it stands, legible to one who gives each word its utmost extremity of meaning.

In *Lichtzwang (The Force of Light)* the process of "wintering over" continues. Celan was committed a number of times during his last years to a French asylum where

     . . . you're being re-educated
     they'll turn you back into he.

Here, for once, Celan's shadowy pronouns, generally non-referential outside the poem itself, are clear enough. The I, the you, the she, he, and they, of Celan's poems are unstable particles: sometimes they address the reader, sometimes the dead. The pronouns unite, split, couple, uncouple, abruptly shift gender in mid-line. They are shards of mirror, reflecting Celan's divided selves: Celan the living poet, Celan the survivor, back from the dead; Celan the observer, Celan the observed. They speak to the world, invoke the absolute. They address enemies and friends: in the case of the contemporary philosopher Heidegger, friend and enemy are one. Celan was fascinated by the Heideggerian thesis of a loss of Being in factual being; he found Heidegger a model for the practice of taking a word in its most literal meaning and then breaking it down etymologically. However, his relationship to Heidegger, whose attitude toward the National Socialist regime was compromising and unrepentant, was double-edged: love and loathing conspire. Heidegger's name and his ideas are trailed through many of the late poems, sometimes openly as in **"Todt-nauberg,"** sometimes cryptically, as in **"Largo."** (pp. 46-51)

In these last poems, Celan has unified what Gerard Raulet calls a "linguistic cosmogony." By forcing the flood of colors, images, and tonalities of his early work through a series of narrowing locks, by submitting the German language to so intense a reduction that he is, in effect, writing German *like a foreign language,* Celan took German poetry through a process of willed decomposition, in which a stylistic devolution creates out of its own wreck the thing it contemplates. When what it contemplates is sacred, then it is bound by Mallarmé's injunction that, "Whatever is sacred, whatever is to remain sacred, must be clothed in mystery." For Celan, Mallarmé's warning was repeated in German by the German disciple of the Symbolists, Stefan George, but his own paradoxical relationship to the German tongue, his shuttle between trust and despair carried him beyond the almost monkish hermeticism of George, past the danger of a purity at times indistinguishable from frigidity. Celan spoke of the German language as having to "pass through its own unresponsiveness, pass through its own fearful muting, pass through the thousand darknesses of death-bringing speech." His response was the creation of an anomalous language, its purity without innocence, reclaimed from the darkness yet capable of addressing it. (pp. 52-3)

Who writes in German as Celan did, damaged by the past and despairing of the present, has at his back the figure of Hölderlin, a poet on the threshold between delusion and prophecy, trusting the numinous power of his evocation to lead him to a creation that lasts, beyond the language of men into the absolute, "the language of God." Hölderlin looked from the apocalyptic social context of his own time into a desired middle future, while his contemporary audience, estranged by his violent departure from plain linear progression and his wrenching of German syntax into more sharply concentrated forms, slowly ebbed away. Hölderlin is the poet turned away, anticipating the exploration of "positive irrationality" by one hundred and fifty years. Celan entered those luminous currents of force when they broke forth again in the poetry of German Expressionism and of French Surrealism, but like Hölderlin before him, he chose the most narrow and arduous course. In the **"Meridian"** speech, he says clearly enough: "Release art? Not at all. Let yourself be led by your art into that which you experience as the most narrow straight and liberate yourself."

The slow demolition of his own lattice structure was his instrument to that end. After *Niemandsrose,* as the heavily diambic rhythms fade from his texts, the genitive metaphors with their accents of Eluard and Goll are replaced by negative metaphors which turn the world upside down, the rich deposits of Rilkean compounds are crossed by more jolting syllables, and the Apollonian music of Rilke, a strong influence on Celan's earlier work, is increasingly paid the ironic homage of mockery. Amid a rising dissonance, the notation itself changes: punctuation, with the clarity it affords a complex syntax, dwindles. There is, above all, a visible disorder in placement values,

in the location of individual parts: units of meaning are smaller, less uniform in shape, more widely placed. Here and there are great rents in the grid itself. Until *Atemwende,* Celan was the skilled practitioner of the art of the *Wideruf,* the refutation of a given poem (often Rilke's) in the lyric canon by one of his own. The late poems dismantle even that scaffolding. The argument with poetry is done, the argument with silence continues, its cherishing frugality leaving only individual words as the substance of a lexicon for exiles, far from the homeland. The words are transparent, poised between existence and nonexistence. You are free, in the end, to make what transfer you will with them. (pp. 53-4)

In a last poem, published six years after his death, Celan wrote with who-knows-what conscious fatality:

> They are throwing gold after me
> the one drowning
> perhaps even a goldfish can be
> bribed.

It is easy, but false, to read into Celan's suicide by drowning the necessary end of his quest for silence, for we fail, by focusing on his personal tragedy, to acknowledge the full extent of his vision. Another artificer of language, fifty years earlier, has given us the words that encompass Celan's destiny: Joyce's hero chose the triple strategy of "silence, exile, and cunning." Celan's was the silence of the unutterable, his exile was a flight from the unforgivable, his cunning was the craft of high art. (p. 56)

Katherine Washburn and Margaret Guillemin, "Threads of Vision, Threads of Meaning," in Parnassus: Poetry in Review, *Vol. 9, No. 1, 1981, pp. 33-56.*

CLIVE WILMER

[*Poems*] contains 120 poems, . . . including a few from the last of Celan's three posthumous collections, *Zeitgehöft* (1976). At last the reader with little or no German can glimpse the full curve of his development; and necessary it is to do so, for the *oeuvre* is strikingly homogenous and much of Celan's meaning is likely to be elicited with the help of cross-reference. The later poems in particular are dauntingly obscure, and the English reader who has some knowledge of German poetry in translation will find the going smoother if he approaches them by way of the early work. The first collection, *Mohn und Gedächtnis* (1952), is much the most accessible of Celan's books, if only because the route is signposted by his more evident models and influences. Rimbaud and Eluard provide a key to the use of imagery. But the rhythms and the density of feeling are inalienably German, with roots in Hölderlin, the later Rilke and, above all, Trakl. A reader's guide to Celan would also make mention of Heidegger (particularly in his insistent etymologising), medieval mysticism (both Jewish and Christian) and the Lutheran Bible and hymnal. The early poems tend to make use of a long, cadenced line which owes much to the hymns of Hölderlin. This line Celan soon abandoned, but the rhythms one associates with it, though broken, re-echo throughout the book and are still audible in the brief, pared-down, fragmentary utterances that precede his suicide. To the foreign reader, such echoes provide something of a lifeline.

The poem which most clearly indicates Celan's departure from the broadly Expressionist mode of *Mohn und Gedächtnis* is **"Speak, You Also,"** which comes near the end of his second book, *Von Schwelle zu Schwelle* (1955). The use of the second person in the title—'thou' would be the ideal translation—is reminiscent of Rilke, but personal pronouns in general are crucial to Celan's strategy and often occur in his poems without named or specified antecedents. They make signals out towards particulars in the world but, being without referents, remain pure functions of language. In this way they focus the central riddle of Celan's work, which concerns the relation of language to the world. Who is this 'you'?—we inevitably ask. Is it God or a lover or the reader? Or the poet himself, addressed in internal monologue? Or is it, as [translator Michael] Hamburger suggests of the piece in question, not so much the poet as his poem, his own speech? If this last interpretation is correct—and I think it is—then the theme of **"Speak, You Also"** is what Celan was to call (in the title of his third book) 'the language mesh'—*Sprachgitter*. **"Speak, You Also"** illustrates the power of words to enmesh—capture, entangle—features of objective reality. But *'Gitter'* is broader in meaning than 'mesh': it seems also to represent language as the grid or framework through and by means of which we perceive, structure and makes sense of the world. . . . In the poem called **"Language Mesh,"** the notion is introduced through an image of eyelashes filtering perception of the 'you', the loved other. But then anything that filters in this way may also be said to exclude and insulate, so, while language may be regarded as a window on reality, it is also the grille that removes the world from its observer.

It is with the line 'Thinner you grow, less knowable, finer' that the direction of **"Speak, You Also"** becomes apparent. One has only to flick through the rest of the selection to confirm the accuracy of Hamburger's judgment that 'the poem anticipates the whole of Celan's subsequent development.' The poems visibly thin out on the page. First line-lengths and then whole poems seem to waste away, as the language becomes more opaque ('less knowable') and the perceptions more tenuous and remote ('finer'). Even in translation the depth of paradox is unignorable; does 'thinner', for example, mean slimmer, pared down to essentials, or does it imply some lack in body or imaginative substance? Language itself has become the focus of Celan's poetry, but the poems have not ceased to concern themselves with the world. It dawns on the reader that this process of verbal reduction and negation, this deliberate narrowing, is ontologically reflexive. The poem is not the only 'you' that grows thinner, less knowable, finer; we must reconsider our first interpretations of the pronoun, this time aware of them as bound within the language mesh.

'Every particular Thou,' wrote Martin Buber, 'is a glimpse through to the eternal *Thou*.' Celan's use of the second person, though notably less serene than Buber's, has roots in the same tradition of Jewish mysticism: according to which, anything that is both 'other' (therefore *far*) and at the same time capable of address (so *near*, at home) becomes the object of devotion, a lens through which the love of God is refracted. Yet Celan's world seems tragically empty of God. He was, after all, a survivor of the death-camps, and his experience there of moral void gives a particularising anguish and urgency to the standard questions of modern ontology. (See, for example, **"Death Fugue," "Psalm," "There was earth inside them," "Tenebrae," "Think of it"** and a number of lesser poems.) His is a world in which 'God', like 'you', is merely a function of language. The mesh is, in part, a metaphor for the disjunction of meaning and being, the indivisibility of which in traditional Jewish and Christian thought is axiomatic: 'In the beginning was the Word.' As the being of man depends ultimately on the absolute fullness of being that is God, so human speech is

validated by the originating Word. Thinner, less knowable, finer: God, surely, is the 'you' who has most notably suffered such a reduction in our time and all other such reductions are dependent on that first one.

Celan's sensibility, Hamburger confirms, was 'profoundly religious'. This becomes clear in what I take to be the core of his achievement, the two volumes, *Sprachgitter* (1959) and *Die Niemandsrose* (1963). The second of these takes its title from **"Psalm,"** an ironic song of praise, a poem of negated devotion in which 'No one' is substituted for 'God'. Nihilistic though it may seem, the poem 'has been shown to have antecedents in both Jewish and Christian mysticism'—so Hamburger tells us. (pp. 26-7)

The anguish of Celan's poetry lies in his need to express the inexpressible and to speak of the unspeakable. Or, to put it another way, his work exists between silences: the perennial silence of God, approached by the mystics through the *via negativa*, and the historical silence induced by the unspeakable crimes of the Nazis.

In the five volumes that follow *Die Niemandsrose,* these silences invade the poems themselves. I am reminded of a paradox of János Pilinszky's which Ted Hughes has quoted: 'I would like to write as if I had remained silent'. In Celan's case, however, the invasion gradually erodes the field of reference that makes such a poem as **"Psalm"** accessible. It is not that Celan abandons the religious and poetic traditions his early work plainly belongs to, but that systematic association is discarded. The allusions become so fragmentary that to pick them up becomes almost a matter of luck. Certain images—of light and darkness, stars, crystal, books, parts of the body—are indicative of continuity, but few poems could be said to communicate from beginning to end. When references are traced in [Michael Hamburger's] Introduction, however, they often illuminate poems that would otherwise remain obscure and one sees quite clearly why Celan so disliked being called 'hermetic'.

A case in point occurs right at the end of the selection. **"The Trumpet Part,"** Hamburger argues, is based around images from the eighth chapter of *Revelation*—the chapter in which the Lamb opens the seventh seal and there is 'silence in heaven about the space of half-an-hour'. The poem alludes to the seven angels with trumpets, the third of whom causes a great star to fall from heaven, 'burning as it were a lamp'.

> The trumpet part
> deep in the glowing
> lacuna
> at lamp height
> in the time hole:
>
> listen your way in
> with your mouth.

In other poems from the last books there are images that suggest a preoccupation with the Apocalypse—something else which Celan shares with Pilinszky. For Pilinszky, who was a witness to the camps Celan survived, Armageddon becomes a metaphor for the sufferings of Europe in the Second World War. It is also an event which is unleashed by the opening of the scroll—in effect, the opening of a book, the unfolding of meaning. This is literally *revelation:* the visionary identification of meaning and being, word and flesh. For Celan as a Jew it carries additional weight, for the opening of the scroll is the fulfilment of the Law. That the scroll was in his mind in this case is clear from the word 'lacuna', which translates the German *'Leer-*

text'. As we have seen in **"Zürich, the Stork Inn,"** Celan habitually disrupts the empiricist sequence of knowledge—from seeing to reading to understanding. Instead he suggests both the failure of cerebration and the involuntary leaps of intuition by ascribing to each sense organ the function proper to another. In the Zürich poem he seems to hear with his eye; in **"The Trumpet Part"** he listens with his mouth. In both cases the images *can* be logically interpreted, but the initial confusion seems to direct us to another level of meaning. Here we may think of the poet as song-maker, as the Orpheus-figure to whom and through whom being is disclosed in the act of singing. Inevitably such a view of the poet's function recalls Celan's debts to Rilke and to Heidegger—the latter in particular, as the verb 'to listen in' *(einhören)* confirms. It is as Heideggerian a verb as one could imagine, with its suggestion of a patient waiting upon being and the re-entry of man, through language and song, into his primal reality. (pp. 27-8)

"The Trumpet Part" is one of many poems by Celan that appear to question the opposition of language to the world. On the one hand is an awareness of meaning as a property of language: as such, meaning has no place in the world. As Wittgenstein puts it, 'The sense of the world must lie outside the world. In the world everything is as it is, and everything happens as it does happen: *in* it no value exists—and if it did exist it would have no value.' But on the other hand is Celan's awareness of man as a speaking animal. It is in the nature of man to try and make sense of the experiences that matter to him, and he makes sense of them by speaking of them. When we speak of the world we confer meaning on it, even if we are convinced that it possesses none. (This is the burden of **"Psalm".**) Celan's silences and negations are strategies for bridging the gap between language and the world. The act of attention that dwells upon *Leertext* and *Zeitloch* (time hole) risks the removal of being in the hope that meaning will be disclosed, even if the meaning is that there is no meaning.

I cannot honestly say whether I have understood **"The Trumpet Part"** or any of the poems in the last three books. Strange to say, they do not bore or frustrate, for Celan was almost incapable of rhythmic or verbal dullness. I am, unaccountably, moved by them, but that is all. And therefore the nub of the matter is likely to remain, for the time being, the middle books: *Sprachgitter, Die Niemandsrose* and, possibly, *Atemwende* (1967). As Celan recognised so early in his career, the 'thinner' the poems become, the 'less knowable' they are: which may be a way of saying that, in them, language begins to resemble the world. I am aware that my admiration for Celan is inconsistent with the view of poetry I have expressed in this journal at other times. I have argued that a poem is, in Yvor Winters's phrase, 'a statement in words about a human experience', that words do not function unless they denote, that language and meaning stand apart from experience. Celan's poetry, as I understand it, recognises the force of such an argument, but he seems to have felt that words could not encompass those experiences that carry most weight for us. The descent into obscurity was therefore inevitable. Theoretically such poems ought to be impossible. The fact that they even begin to communicate is largely due to their author's extraordinary semantic awareness. The poems in *Zeitgehöft* are the logical outcome of the theory of poetry that informs *Mohn und Gedächtnis* and which descends by way of Trakl and Expressionism from a Symbolist tradition of 'pure' poetry. But Celan could not content himself with purity. Even the **"Death Fugue,"** which he came to dislike, is an ironic exploitation of Mallarméan ideals: poetry aspiring to the condition of music and the purification of the tribal language.

It seems to me probable that Celan will prove for the present generation of British poets what the greatest of his masters, Rilke, was to an earlier generation: not a direct influence—that would be nothing short of disastrous—but the most important of contemporary exemplars, a poet who has extended the frontiers of poetic possibility. (p. 28)

Clive Wilmer, "Between Silences," in PN Review *23, Vol. 8, No. 3, 1981, pp. 26-9.*

HANS-JÜRGEN HEISE

The most successful poems in [*Mohn und Gedächtnis*] reveal a decidedly modern author, if one still bound to a conventional vocabulary. He achieves this modernity by providing a musical structure for the emotional content, using his own surrealistic associative technique. To be sure, Celan turns to the past, to the atrocities of the war and the murder of his parents in some of his poems, including the all-too rhetorical **"Todesfuge"** (**"Death Fugue"**). But in most of the poems the elegiac mood is thematically divorced from what might have caused it. It is life—but life as a whole, life in the totality of its ontological relationships—that causes suffering. History, civilization, technology, class struggle—none of these is a significant factor in Celan's lyrics. Celan suffers from the daily banalities of life around him and the deep loneliness within him; and since everything becomes unfamiliar and painful, even love itself cannot offer refuge.

Even if Celan still appears to be relatively "open" in *Mohn und Gedächtnis,* to be concerned with people and things, he is already building around himself those barriers of reserve and ceremoniousness behind which he will later construct his hermetic fortress. An external frame of reference is no longer a goal; it is merely a point of departure for the poetic word, which leads away from mankind, down towards the dark, death-filled vessels, towards an epigram similar in its severity to that epitaph which Rilke composed for himself in 1925, as a means of withdrawing from the company of mankind: "Rose, oh pure paradox, desire / To be no one's sleep under so many / Lids."

This cool formulation often shines through Celan's work from this point on. "Nobody's voice, again," to cite a line from *Sprachgitter (Language Lattice,* 1959). In *Fadensonnen (Thread-Suns,* 1968), a poem cramped in painful isolation appears: "the high-world—lost, the madness-journey, the day-journey. // What can be asked, from this point, / with the rose in a fallow year / No-where, interpreted home." The most striking signs, however, that point to Rilke's epitaph are found in *Die Niemandsrose (The No One's Rose,* 1963), which pays homage to its model not only overtly in the title, but also in the poems: ". . . no one's / root—oh, ours . . . ," "No one kneads us again out of earth and clay / no one blesses our dust. / No one. // . . . A Nothing / we were, we are, we will stay / a Nothing, blooming: / the Nothing's, the No-one's rose." This metaphorical material, however, is given an essentially different meaning in the lines of the last quote, since what was in Rilke narcissism, the ethically unconcerned attitude of the artist, suddenly becomes in Celan a cipher that establishes bonds with the collective.

Die Niemandsrose was Celan's most heterogeneous book. Here the poet reaches back once more to an outworn romantic vocabulary; even though he avoids the all-too-arbitrary genitive metaphors common in the early poems, he now allows constructions which are almost more obsolete and sugary to creep in: pistil bright as souls, stamen empty as heaven, grey-beaten heart-hammer-silver. Even rhyme suddenly appears again. Although in a poem like **"Selbdritt, selbviert" ("The Three of Us, the Four of Us")**, which is deliberately reminiscent of Hans Arp, rhyme has a legitimate parodistic function, in other poems it appears to be a regression, an attempt to hold together all of the unrhymed elements of today with the formal structure of yesterday.

There is no doubt that Celan enters into a crisis with *Niemandsrose*, a crisis that could in no way have been foreseen after the concise texts of *Sprachgitter*. The feeling, the fear, the despair—all of those elements which had also been present in works like **"Sommerbericht" ("Summer Report")** and **"Engführung" ("The Straitening")** but had been artistically perfected and thereby, at least to some degree, neutralized—emerge now once again: the eruptive and chaotic grasping at old forms and searching for new ones, without finding them. *Sprachgitter* presents the lyrical protocol of a life which, even though it fails to capture reality, has, nevertheless, in the realm of the verbal been able to give expression to its failure so that this life, after all, does succeed—albeit in an indirect way. In **"Jakobs Stimme" ("Jacob's Voice")**, a poetic fragment from the introductory cycle **"Stimmen" ("Voices")**, his frustration is conquered; these verses lend dignity to suffering, but they still point back to life: "The tears. / The tears in the brother's eyes. / One hung there, grew. / We live in it. / Breathe, that / it may loosen."

For the most part, however, the poems in *Sprachgitter* deal with a world wherein the lines of communication are destroyed: the world is something that separates. All that remains to do is to report what has already transpired. The isolation seems complete; there is no succor, no hope, no future. . . . All human beings, even lovers, have drifted apart. The self-evident, because it is not self-evident anymore, emerges as something uncertain, something divisive. To be sure, every once in a while a penetrating perception occurs, but then, when confidence arises and when the poet, separated from his fellow men, at least feels himself to be one with inanimate matter, "as if, because of stone, there were still brothers," then questions arise: is this palpably growing transcendence something that really exists? Or is this transcendence only a reflection of the emotion that sifts through the "language lattice," hallucinatory and illusory, similar to those faces painted by van Gogh that provided inspiration for two of Celan's poems?

That which had been mastered in *Sprachgitter* loses almost all of its sharp contour in *Niemandsrose*. It flows apart, reaches back to old patterns of expression, to strange as well as to familiar rhythms, which, even if they had stood the test of their own time, are now no longer adequate; they could be repeated and reeled off not as if a poet were speaking, but rather as if vocabulary and grammar had joined forces to produce lines like: "There came a stillness, and there came a storm, too / there came each and every ocean. / I dig, you dig, and the worm digs too, / and the singing out there says: they dig." Artistic consciousness and insightful intensity—both are suddenly lost here and the words begin to skid around; they only act "as if." In reality, however, they do not communicate, but instead suppress what meaning resides within them or create deaf neologisms. (pp. 36-9)

Celan is not a poet of essences and facts; he is a poet of words and concepts. His poetry is, to a high degree, abstract, but not because he is an abstract poet or—nonsensical term—a concrete

poet. Rather, he writes as he does because his reality has been taken from him: his parents, the city of his birth, Bukovina, the Eastern landscape. ". . . Speech-scale, word-scale, home-scale, exile. . . ." What remained, what he was able to add, was his poetry, which can only be a substitute, and not a restitution. No new literary style, no modern direction is introduced by Celan. He attempts to make existence possible in a situation that would have silenced all of the word technicians or caused them to reconsider the worth of the existent pool of language.

Mohn und Gedächtnis is Celan's first artistically successful book, although still romantically articulated. The vocabulary still has aroma, the metaphors flesh, the sound consolation. Even **"Todesfuge,"** however horrible its theme, resonates with the faint hope that the world can be set aright, as though poetry could conquer, save, and transcend if only it were rhythmical, whispered magically, and pleasant sounding.

Sprachgitter, on the other hand—after the early style fades out in the weaker volume *Von Schwelle zu Schwelle (From Threshold to Threshold,* 1955)—was a book which in subject no less than tone expressed the concept that intense reflection in conjunction with a shocked sensibility could achieve neither trust in life nor contact with one's surroundings.

Niemandsrose, then, was a regression, a fragmentation, which called previous achievements into question. At the time of its appearance no reader could have recognized, given the presence of the old repertoire, which was sometimes employed in a downright dilettante manner, that here several extraordinary themes and revelations were hidden. Today, viewed with hindsight, these themes can be seen as keys and codes: "so / much / is asked of the one / whom hope carts up and down / the hump-backed heart-way—so / much."

Atemwende (Breath-turning, 1967), when Celan had found a new mode of expression in a poetry of fragments ripped apart by feelings of guilt and moral hysteria, it was still not possible to discern that something irreversible had taken place, that communication was being attempted—but no longer with human beings. . . . Rather, the dialogue is with those transcendental realms in which it was so difficult for Celan to believe: "Thread-suns / over the grey-black wasteland. / A tree- / high thought / grasps the light's tone: there are / still songs to be sung on the other side / of mankind." From this point on, Celan does not find his way back into the realm of human communication.

His plunge into a solipsistic world can no longer be halted. The remaining island of the Ego is swamped by the unconscious and what still exists of concrete reality, what still stands as secure knowledge, fades into the unreal. Even though the poet tries to flee through ever new labyrinths of word and feeling, he does not succeed in escaping his moral hallucinations. On the contrary, this conflict grows to gigantic proportions, and Celan—in penance, as it were—now wants to carry the responsibility on a cosmic scale; in fact, he feels himself to be responsible for what does not even exist: "The trace of a bite in the Nowhere. / It, too, / you must battle, / from here." The psychological landslides that are at work changing the personality occur during full consciousness. "The ounce of truth deep in delusion. . . ." Celan perceives both: the truth and the delusion. Like Hölderlin before him, he notices his feeling being buried under a glacier. . . . Love is now characterized as "strait-jacket-beautiful," and Kafka's infamous sentence "for the last time psychology" is quoted in this mood, in this atomized state of mind. The poet ponders the presence and the necessity of normative regulations, the mechanics of interchangeable but, in the final analysis, unrepealable laws and prohibitions: "The broken-up taboos, / crossing and recrossing the borders between them, / world-wet, on / the hunt for meaning, / on flight from / meaning."

The last volume of poetry Celan put together himself, *Lichtzwang (Light-Compulsion,* 1970), begins once again with a cool statement of his position. His personal situation is recognized, the way to deliverance is seen and ironically described: "Remnants of things seen, of things heard, in / dormitory one thousand and one, // day-nightly / the Bear Polka: / they retrain you, / you are once again / he." But only two poems later the darkness returns and life becomes an irredeemable promise: "Lemmings burrow. // No Later." Celan is no longer able to withdraw. The Other, Stronger entices, compels: "Foreknowledge bleeds / twice behind the curtain, // shared-knowledge / effervesces." Shared-knowledge. Presumed complicity. The poet turns against himself more and more; he accuses himself not only of being-so-and-not-different, but he also accuses himself because of the roles he plays: "Gradually clown-faced / . . . the make-up truth frozen blue / in the mouth's corner." The allusion is, possibly, to poetry readings—the exhibition of the most intimate of impulses spoken in public. Celan's words are often only apparently obscure. The truth is that he is revealing his shame and his indignation. Proof of this extraordinary moral sense of responsibility can be found in the poem **"Sink,"** in which Celan does indeed ask the loved one to part from him; however, at the same time he lets solicitude reign and tries to offer protection: "Sink away from me / from the bend of the elbow, // take the One / pulse beat along, // conceal yourself in it, / outside."

The pieces of the world cannot be put back together in this fractured heart. Compassion and despair have increasingly muted voices. The wish to return to lifelessness and to become one with the earth grows immeasurably: "If I were to eat the track of the cart / I would be there." Now it is not far away; the horizon recedes from his active mind, which, in turn, is closing in on him. New perspectives, monstrous abysses open up: "Now, as the prayer-hassocks are burning, / I eat the book / with all the / insignia." Only death can quench such fire, such hunger for the absolute. Death, however, is not yet ready, and so it must be pre-empted. Paul Celan drowns himself in the Seine at the end of April, 1970, seven months before his 50th birthday: "That death, / which you still owe me, I / will carry it / out."

The poems in *Schneepart (Snow-part),* which appeared a year after the suicide, were written between December 1967 and October 1968, in all likelihood before the texts in *Lichtzwang.* In this volume, Celan analyzes his inner situation, the increasing frigidity of his feelings, his isolation. Over and over again the focus is on snow, ice, hail, and—stone. To be sure, the author offers resistance. He confronts the emotional glacier formation, but the attempt to remain victorious, using only the metaphoric capabilities of poetry, is no longer successful. Even when the poet endeavors to hew away the "word shadows,"his efforts produce relationships only within the realm of language, and none on the communicative level: "Two fingers, hand-distant, / row towards the swampy / oath."

Like Mallarmé, who, in order to imagine himself as the high priest of a sacred realm of words, endeavored to degradate to absolute nothingness that existence which tangled, hidden emotions precluded him from accepting, Celan, too, increasingly

separated himself from his surroundings by creating a hermetic cult language. But this Eastern European poet, longing for annihilation, was not able to let his feelings cool off and formalize the misery. Celan, in contrast to Mallarmé, was unable to attain any lasting tranquility. Celan's despair did not allow itself to be stylized into a telling silence, thereby excluding the essential conflict. Celan's ontological perceptions were not those of a man who had to imagine coldness and emptiness from the haven of a materially secure, middle-class existence. The vacuum came to Celan of its own accord; it came to be through the erosion of all things, concepts, feelings. . . . (pp. 39-43)

*Hans-Jürgen Heise, "Paul Celan," translated by
Linda Kraus Worley and Jeff Worley, in* Sulfer, *No.
11, 1984, pp. 36-43.*

HANS RICHTER

The often seemingly dark poetry of Paul Celan does emit its own unique light. Thus it is capable of offering insights even when it seems to defy concentrated efforts to understand it: its transfigurations and associations for the most part allow the reader to sense their inner necessity and logic without having to subject them to rational analysis. Celan's verse exerts a strong appeal even when its meaning remains more or less hidden, since its use of language nearly always expresses its own poetic legitimation. In his early works this was achieved essentially with the aid of suggestive rhythmic and melodic patterns, such as those seen in **"Todesfuge" ("Death Fugue"),** and occasionally by means of rhyme (which was almost totally avoided after the mid-1960s). Subsequently, this was often achieved by presenting lyrical language as a seeking, groping, developing process that now and then appears to result from the interplay of impulses and restraints. Finally this is attained through the strict interlocking of polysemic elements to form a harmonious whole. However, one element in Celan's poetry transcends the many stylistic developments and remains the primary and ultimate creative force, continually renewing itself even when it on occasion seems seriously endangered: namely, the guiding principle of dialogue. To be sure, Celan's poetic concept is already formed before being confronted by Gottfried Benn's apotheosis of the absolute poem, i.e., the apodictic positing of a poem without faith and addressed to no one. But Celan's poetry develops specifically in opposition to Benn's position: Celan conceives of an emphatically communicative poem, a poem addressed to someone. And while Benn maintains in one of his poems that only two things are real, the void and the marked Ego, a realm to which he withdraws in complacent melancholy, Celan insistently refuses to withdraw his marked Ego from the world and replace the world with it; instead he makes the contrary attempt—sometimes hopefully, sometimes despairingly—to establish a worthy relationship of this Ego to the world, no matter how unworthy this world may often appear. As a poet and in his poetry he continually seeks a humane world.

For all its continuity Celan's poetry has in the course of the years indeed undergone considerable change. When one compares the sonorous, rhythmically and melodically unfolding verse of his early period—often excessively ornate and embellished with rhyme—to the later short poems with their tendency towards pointed sarcasm, short lines, retarding division of words, and enjambment, one may easily arrive at the conclusion that one is dealing with the works of totally different authors. If, however, we read Celan's poems as the process of an unrelenting, self-regenerating reaction to the world (and do not neglect to count the poems themselves as part of the world), we will, for all that, sense the unity of Celan's work and will be able to discern the unifying conditions which underlie the diverse components of his oeuvre. It is, in the final analysis, the same historical basis, the same experience in the world and in life, that give rise, for example, to poems such as the lyrically structured **"Todesfuge"** from Celan's first book, as well as to these lines from *Schneepart (Snow Part,* 1971), which are technically so different: ''The world whose stuttering is to be mimicked, / whose guest I / shall have been, a name / sweated forth from the wall, / upon which a wound oozes upward.''

The central noun names precisely that world which will transcend the lyrical Ego, a world that the Ego views from both sides of death, a world to which the Ego, ''wounded by reality,'' is inevitably bound. What seems here to be but an undercurrent comes clearly to light in other poems and is on occasion explicitly mentioned; Celan's manner of observing the world is marked by a process of constant memory and remembrance; even events of the distant past remain omnipresent, and thus there is no past and no forgetting. To be sure, to combine time and space in his poems has always been the sovereign right of the poet and his genre; however, when Paul Celan asserts ''All places are here and now,'' this key statement signifies that his Here and Now includes all of the traumatizing moments of his experience, and it is precisely these which determine his perspective on life, and thus the—in his mature poetry quite unsentimental—elegiac tenor of his works. (pp. 44-6)

> *Hans Richter, ''On Paul Celan,'' translated by Donald Hamilton and others, in* Sulfur, *No. 11, 1984, pp. 44-6.*

RICHARD EXNER

Studies of Celan have proliferated in the last thirty years. Next to Rilke, he is doubtlessly the poet about whom the most has been written. A major portion of this literature addresses the concept of negative poetics, of silence and speechlessness. And it is my theme as well, because I am convinced that Celan's death marks the conclusion of an epistemological act that has been ''reversed'': the recognition that occurs and is experienced through language is suspended by a gradual falling silent and by a renunciation of normal language. ''Silence'' and ''speechlessness'' should not be misunderstood here: Sieghild Bogumil correctly points out, particularly in the second half of her essay ''Celan's Roving in the Word'' (1983), that Celan was not interested in speechlessness itself, but rather in ''that which is silent in language because it is repressed, not expressed, or subject to taboo.'' As Bogumil concludes, a new language arises as such, a statement I will not dispute, and I definitely object to her thesis that art and nature are reconciled in Celan. (pp. 71-2)

In spite of sustained productivity following publication of *Atemwende (Breath-turning,* 1967), we can identify an increasing tendency—as much consciously as unconsciously controlled—toward brevity, alienation, hermetization, and decontextualization of lyrical language and its metaphoric. In Celan, it concerns, I believe, the *German* language: not just any language. It represents the act of undermining one's own and the recipient's comprehension, of bringing that which is historically and personally understood and known to a halt (''zum Stocken''). An act is rendered incomprehensible; it is disas-

sociated, and thereby becomes retroactively impossible. The absolutely unachievable is attempted: i.e. obliteration and making-undone, by the successive revocation of the very language in which the act was executed. This is *one* complication in all Holocaust literature, and it is partucularly—and, due to its inefficacy—the absolutely tragic theme, the *condition créatrice* of the writing person Paul Celan. In brief, from legend and myth we know that through the word and through language creation took place. Thus the world was formed and since that time words and language have brought creation and life to a standstill, even to annihilation. Neither speaking nor silence, deciphering nor muteness can extinguish this knowledge. The ''Death of Speech'' and the ''Hope of Silence'' are, I believe, no longer interchangeable today, though that was not always true. (p. 72)

We shall briefly examine this ''Death of Speech'' in several texts from *Atemwende* and in Alleman's ''broadest possible'' autobiographical sense. We are concerned with texts such as those indicated in the poem **"Fadensonnen"** (**"Thread-suns"**) that seem ''to sing beyond / mankind,'' in the sense, then, of texts to be sung outside an historical (contemporary) context, not songs, but at most ''singable remainders,'' twofold delineations of what broke through the sickle-script, far off in the domain of snow, something ''interdicted lips,'' (literally, ''lips with the mouth removed''—this is only one of Celan's many ''disembodying'' metaphors) which report what occurred only once and a long time ago, something that *was* light and could have meant rescue, just because it *was* once; now, however, *it is not.* These are things robbed of value which are ''nothinged'' by expression, as this neologism from **"Weggebeizt"** would have it.

Individual observations and interpretations seem to be inadequate in Celan's case, more so that in other modern poets. Basically they prove unreliable because each poem appears autonomous in itself, and the entire oeuvre is a single poem, as it were, with a field of associations and vehicles of meaning that both camouflage and reveal. That which can be gleaned from a reading of **"Weggebeizt"** can also be inferred for similar poems in the extremely carefully composed volume, for the volume itself, and even beyond, into the entire oeuvre. The frozen state of **"Weggebeizt,"** the reduction of the written text *per se* to an ice crystal (of the genuine or the mendacious poem, or of writing altogether) is *also* an attempt to silence language, i.e., the *German language,* to make language mute from within: e-i-o. What remains is a crystal of breath that, although inorganic, seems biologically capable of reproduction. It becomes the material for speech, which is frozen in purity, virginal, untouched by the Holocaust, and, more importantly, untouched by those who, with and through their language, had set the Holocaust in motion. This is language attempting to be ''pure'' poetry, if such a reduction to one crystal of breath were possible. But (and one almost hears Kafka's voice from ''An Imperial Message'') never, never will this take place and, if it did, nothing would be gained, because language would again become contaminated.

Thus the ''Atemkristall'' signifies salvation, a rescue which, as it is spelled out, denotes salvation, but, in its hypothetical context, cannot be salvation. It is therefore a rescue of which the reader, perhaps even the author, holds the hope that it exists, such as Thomas Mann's high ''g'' in *Doctor Faustus.* It controls his behavior, as if it existed, though it does not. The proof, the crystal, the one waiting, the final witness is unimpeachable, immovable, and therefore the reader of this poetry is doomed to wait. Unimpeachable, since it is not-yet-language, unimpeachable, since, as immovable ice it can not be done away with, and it is also unimpeachable in the sense of "irrevocable." One is tempted to identify a dualism in the texts mentioned: destroyed/salvation; singable remainder/interdicted lip—a dualism or even a dialectic, or perhaps even the structure of chiasma (the organic and the inorganic overlap in honeycomb/ice and breath/crystal). But this is a deceptive temptation. In a very late poem, Celan says: "as though without us we could be we"—another statement of disembodiment. As if we could, one is tempted to say, speak a language without language. But we cannot. It is of little consequence whether this meta-language which turns what we say into "no-ems" belongs to God, to the self-aware poet, or to this century's nuclearly "radiant wind." Time-crevasse, sickle-script, snow, ice, darkness (actually an almost random series!) are the elements of a suicidal rhetoric of silence (George Steiner), of a rhetoric by which language 'disembodies' itself.

As this suicidal rhetoric becomes more pervasive, almost narcotically melodic in **Mohn und Gedächtnis (Poppy and Memory)**, haltingly and almost shrill in later volumes—the collapse in the poet's house of language has become predictable: particles of negation, reductions, negations from object to nonentity; the demolished corpuscles of speech take over: literally and figuratively, cohesive language stops at the point where human communication ceases. As in Revelations, in the Apocalypse, creation and destruction converge and reciprocally cancel each other out. Linguistic crises, mis-understandings, normally used to be the ingredients of comedy, in refined or crude fashion, or at least of tragi-comedy. But in the Holocaust, not only individual communication, but also the potential for all kinds of communication has perished in the flames. We are not dealing with a misapprehension of whatever origin, extreme or grotesque. Those speaking do not hold anything back. They are not silent by choice; they are forced into muteness because they have been murdered—"ent-mündigt"—deprived of a mouth, of speech in the ultimate sense. After this insight, which is thematized particularly in **Atemwende,** after such a "Death of Speech," how did Celan continue to write? I am prepared to face contradiction, even ridicule, but will assert that he did *not* continue to write—not in the sense that one can *continue to write*. But he wrote. He wrote and knew that nothing that he had experienced historically and linguistically could ever be encoded in comprehensible linguistic symbols. In this one sense and specifically for this poet, Adorno's view that, after Auschwitz, it has indeed become impossible to write poetry, takes on frightful authenticity.

Once language has been thus undermined syntactically, grammatically, and semantically, once speech has died and has taken on the image of decapitated interpersonal communication, an author is naturally deprived of exactly that, which Dante, Eichendorff, Keats, even the late Rilke, Berry, and Snyder drew from the "Hope of Silence": life itself. This is not a frivolous statement. I believe that poetry, even the translation of foreign poetry meant more to Celan than to any other modern poet. It is language which reminds us of what has come into the world through language. For Celan this was the individual and the thousandfold death, the Holocaust. Through language he attempted to remember it and, at the same time, to remove it from all memory, so that the world could continue. The event proved ineradicable, however, and language itself, by means of which it could be eradicated, is, despite all hermetization, hebraization, decontextualization, and reduction to sickle-texts, just as ineradicable. (pp. 76-9)

Let us take a final look at the formidable unity of this Celanian oeuvre which poets from other languages, aided by at best precarious translations, experience as an erratic block. I am thinking, for example, of Jed Rasula's commentary in the Celan issue, edited by James Lyon, of *Studies in 20th Century Literature* (VIII, 1983). There it is asserted that Celan has made use of the German language as if it were an instrument of terror. Celan wrote in German as a Rumanian residing in France. Through understated linguistic gestures he expressed his affinity with the victims of the Holocaust and executed, as it were, language from the inside out. He has consciously, as Rasula asserts, overseen and practiced the syntactic disintegration of the German language. Language matter thus vanished in direct proportion to his growing fame. In Celan's hands the German language became the instrument of its own disembodiment. Little by little, it went up in smoke. Rasula completes this progression of thoughts with the words, "Nothing similar exists in any language known to me." And so we face the "Death of Speech" *without* the "Hope of Silence." (pp. 80-1)

Richard Exner, "Paul Celan's 'Atemwende': About the 'Death of Speech' and the 'Hope of Silence'," translated by Suzanne Shipley Toliver, in Sulfur, No. 11, 1984, pp. 71-81.

JED RASULA

Celan's writing is one of the clear, unarguable limits of modern poetry. In all its facets it composes one single sign, a solid piece of rock bearing the inscription, "Past this point your language disintegrates from anguish." Its relation to a broader tradition of European nihilism is minimal, as Celan's work is closest to the tiny gestures—the shrug, the loose wave of a hand—that indicate with awesome peremptoriness "this one lives, that one dies." Except for a few of the earlier poems there are not even cries of anguish or lament. The later work shows Celan conscientiously applying himself to the German language as an instrument, as though it were an instrument since it has been used as such, of terror. He elected to write in German, while being Rumanian and living in France, because his affinities with the victims of the Holocaust declared themselves most explicitly in the smaller linguistic gestures with which he *executed* the language from within. His work is radical insofar as it is a helpless conscious choice. Very few writers have so openly allowed the language of their poems to be helpless, to be written from a condition of abrupt syntactic disintegration *consciously* attended to. The great difficulty—and thus his greatest example for later poets—is in practicing a craft on material that disappears in proportion to the success of the poet. Celan's invasion of the German language is only possible after the Second World War. The First had incited violence of a different kind; the medium, the language, was a means and not the object of attack. With Celan, the German language itself becomes the means of its own disembodiment. In his hands, more and more of the language simply goes up in smoke. There is nothing at all like it in any other language that I know of.

There is certainly nothing to compare with it in English. For all the interesting graphic propositions (still largely unexamined) in cummings, there is no ground for comparison. . . . I suspect the lack of absorption of Celan into American idioms and attentions arises from a simple enough error, which is the assumption that every notable poet has some kind of "equivalent" in another language. So the most profuse records of verbal injury in such poets as Vallejo and Artaud possibly disguise the distinctness which is Celan's. It may also be that Celan is not fun to read. His poetry may be the most singular contemporary instance of the harrowing, unreadable, prototypical "modern poem" that had manifestations for earlier sensibilities in such work as *The Waste Land*, Dada sound-poems and simultaneities, Expressionist works and more. The singularity of Celan's images, the sensual purity and the sense of hermetic or private meaning, also make his work less approachable in the richly imagistic public domain of American poetry. (pp. 82-3)

Celan's attraction to the German language is bilateral. On the one hand he is decomposing the language of the barbarians from within: on the other, he is conducting a hermetic (*tightly sealed*) passage toward the inviolable hieratic visionary language within German that Rilke made his own. It is as if Celan, in order to come into his own as the German poet after Rilke, could only approach the realm of such a practice by passing through many rings of enemy lines drawn around it. So Celan's work is full of stealth and intentional sabotage. And by the time—or in those instances in which—he is close on the Rilkean purity, the scars of what he has experienced en route peel off in scabs indistinguishable from the exaltation of being there. A prick from a rose killed Rilke. Celan writes as if an entire crown of roses were being held in place in his mouth. Beauty is bloody.

So the position of Celan is in the end twofold. He marks a certain boundary to horror, the response to horror in language, and the assimilation of it in a poetic practice. On the other hand, he is always approaching a beauty which it is terrible to contemplate. This has been the substance of much melodramatic poetry and fiction, but Celan writes with the massive historical evidence pervasive in his chosen language and racial affiliations. And I would suggest that it was as a poet that he most clearly gravitated toward the holocaust as inevitable topos. Each slightest sound of German resonated with bone and ash. Suffocation the condition of the script. Every poem written as the last word, terminus of a race. (pp. 83-4)

> Jed Rasula, "Paul Celan," in Sulfur, *No. 11, 1984, pp. 82-4.*

GEORGE STEINER

The definition of what constitutes a great poet will include several components. Though it may arise from extreme intimacy, from the local and private particular, his or her poetry will, directly or by compelling implication, address itself to those matters which men and women experience as primary. However secular in reference and context (major poetry in a rigorously secular vein is, in fact, rare), the work of a great poet will point to the first and the last things. It will engage the radical commonplaces of human life and death, of the commerce of love and of sorrow between human beings, it will set memory against time.

Secondly, great poetry will establish the need of its own expressive form. Good prose works close to the grain of its particular vocabulary, grammar, cadence. But in great poetry, this unison, this specificity of communicative life within a unique form (the organic metaphor) is closer than in prose. A fully realized piece of prose loses something of its strength in paraphrase or translation, but only something. Ideally, the major poem is so wedded to its linguistic-metrical totality that paraphrase or translation are, at their best, a kind of exegesis,

of unfolding commentary on their source. A poem which could be otherwise is not a great poem.

It follows that the writings of a great poet alter the surrounding fabric of general feeling and of discourse. It is not only the literary canon and the syllabus of cultural reference which are modified by the presence of a new master; it is the more diffuse but pervasive landscape of emotional and sensory recognitions, of self-representation and of the social and public code. More immediately, the poems produced by a truly great poet will change certain features of the language in which they are composed. They will purify and simultaneously enrich the vocabulary, the syntactic possibilities, the phonetics, the tonal and rhythmic modes of speech. Although the actual process whereby such change makes itself felt in the current vernacular may be a slow one, great poetry will have provoked mutations in the evolution of the language.

On each of these counts, the poetry of Paul Celan is to be included with the very greatest in Western literature.

Coming out of a polyglot matrix, out of the hideous particularity of the Jewish experience of near-extermination and exile, expressive of a fiercely guarded privacy—the poems are sentinels of some last citadel—Celan's verse, from the early, suppressed *Der Sand aus den Urnen* to the posthumous *Zeitgehöft*, speaks to the heart of things. The immediacy is of the order which Auden had in mind when he said that what Dante and Shakespeare had been to their centuries Kafka was to ours. We are too much in the net of our time to be certain: but it does look as if political bestiality, aloneness within mass-culture, the condition of the self-estranged and the refugee, the brutalization of communicative media, are its dominants. It does look, to cite one of Celan's most famous images, as if death is, peculiarly, a master in our affairs. To this realization, to these motifs, Celan's poetry speaks directly. But there is in Western, perhaps in world-literature, no greater love poetry than that of the "Jerusalem" sequence in the posthumous collection. And no greater, more universal poetry of the terrors of need and of parting between generations.

Celan's poems are so intransigently themselves, that they rebuke paraphrase (the academic industry of explication is already a vast one). Even the best attempts at translation are, until now, only a distant dialogue. As it happens, Celan's prose was masterly. The *Gespräch im Gebirge* of 1960, with its affinities to Büchner and to Kafka is, stylistically, a classic. But the poems are of another place. Scholars to come will construe an occasional ancestry for their revolutionary vocabulary, grammar, metrics. They will draw notice to those more general elements in modernity, in the poetics of linguistic crisis and linguistic experiment after Rimbaud, Mallarmé and the surrealists. But such genealogies will tell us little. I am not certain that any poetry we know comes closer than Celan's to the being of music, which is the conceptually and formally indissoluble embodiment of meaning within form, of form within meaning. . . . A Celan poem is only itself; the immensity lies in the need.

Imitators are now numerous. Some of Celan's neologisms and emblematic turns are passing into literary German and into the practices of those French poets and thinkers who were among the first to recognize his genius. At certain points, the poems gathered in [the five volumes that comprise *Gesammelte Werke*] *have* touched nerve-centres in the German language. Celan's German contains, as it were, the lineaments of a German tongue "north of the future". . . . By this I mean a renewed language in which the catastrophe of Nazism and of enforced division between East- and West-German could be made a source of truth. Whether this ''stone-written'' shadow language will come into the light, is not yet ascertainable.

The general point is, however, clear. Limiting one's judgment to the history and to the achievements of German poetry, Celan is the poet after Hölderlin. Between them stands Rilke, some of whose music is subtly present in Celan's, and whose famous epitaph is reborn in Celan's equally famous *Niemandsrose.* But it may be that there are in Rilke's prodigal outpourings too many poems which might or might not have been, which have no compulsion beyond their wondrous technique. And even in the *Duino Elegies,* Rilke's vision and argument are of a seductive, indeed magical rhetorical fluency. Celan's meaning, like Hölderlin's, taxes the utmost of our response. Interpretations and debate, intellectual and moral, will return, so long as poetry is read and lived, to the counter-theology of Celan's death-camp poems. . . . No poetry asks more insistently of language whether it can register, let alone make accessible to reason and to imagination, the enormities, sometimes kindred, of human evil and of love. Dante and Celan are the great familiars of love's ways in hellishness. The poetics of temporality and of remembrance, of image and object, in Celan, are often of a Shakespearean intensity (it is precisely these motions of spirit in Shakespeare's sonnets which Celan translates best). In brief, the poetry of Paul Celan is, as is Hölderlin's, and rather more than is Rilke's, a truly metaphysical poetry, the quality of whose philosophic, moral, aesthetic suggestions corresponds to its lyrical means.

Celan is among the most difficult of poets; difficult as is Pindar and, again, Hölderlin. Like other great poets, he works at the far edge of language. He elides, fragments, reverses normal lexical-grammatical-semantic usage and categories in order to test, *in extremis,* the capacity of language to contain and communicate new necessities, new commandments of truth. In Celan's case these commandments took on a special dimension. Could language say that which *had* to be said after the apocalypse of the 1940s? Ought the poet, on the contrary, to be silent in the face of the unspeakable? Both the imperative and the inhibition generate Celan's art. His characteristic solution—after the outright eloquence of the **''Todesfuge,''** the poem which brought him fame and on which he came to look back with some suspicion—was the formulation of that language ''yet to come''.

Abstractly put, such semantic futurity is almost impossible to define. In the poems themselves, however, it is manifest. The predominant speech-image, particularly from *Atemwende* (1967) onwards, is that of words, of phrases, emerging, only imperfectly, from the inchoate pull of night, of water, of tangled vegetation and of ash. Time and again, Celan qualifies his idiom as runic, as stone-born (literally ''lithographic''). But the runes are not incised *on* the stone; they ramify from *within* the stone, from within an integrity of silent, uncompromising witness so authoritative, that their externalization always remains partial, compromised, or as yet resistant to decipherment.

One further aspect must be noted. Knowing Romanian, Russian, French, English and German, Celan chose to write his poetry in the latter tongue. He can have had little doubt as to his stature (high honours came to him and his work). Yet he was adorning, revitalizing, deepening towards futurity, the very language of ''master death'', the very language which had called for, proclaimed, organized the murder of his parents,

the destruction of the culture and community from which he himself came. The internal contradiction is scarcely imaginable. It is the burn-mark, both as haunting light and as ''death-ash'', in everything Celan lived and wrote. (p. 1093)

George Steiner, ''Songs of a Torn Tongue,'' in The Times Literary Supplement, *No. 4252, September 28, 1984, pp. 1093-94.*

ROBERT KELLY

It was the peculiar genius of Paul Celan to be able to strip language of is normal socioeconomic occasions without cutting the lines that lead language to the heart. For all the celebrated difficulty of Celan's poems—dense constellations of morphemes, word elements packed like molecules—they are hard only when you try to think about them. At first touch (what William Carlos Williams called, in a noble phrase, the poem's ''intention to impress'') Celan's poems come to us from a warm sense of life, of paying attention and taking care.

It is unlikely that any translator could match the subtlety of Paul Celan's stock of words; a few words recur again and again, at times with severely different ranges of association. We can ask the translator to be conscious of Celan's own lexicon, his idiolect, and make us aware of it. The translators of [*Last Poems* and *Collected Prose*] are generous with their understanding, and guide us through the sensuous intricacy of Celan's vocabulary.

It is the delight and torment of the translator to try to develop structures that will accommodate the deft hallucinations of Celan's assemblages. Celan's ability to touch us and penetrate to the core of language, where it continually arises to guide, cajole, mislead and console us, produces a poetry of immense expressiveness. The notorious clenched hieroglyphic abstruseness of Celan's poetry is not so much a product of poetic theory as an irreducible consequence of his way of attending to the world. He disparages a certain seense of artifice, saying in a 1960 piece from *Collected Prose:* ''There are exercises—in the *spiritual* sense. . . . And then there are, at every lyrical street corner, experiments that muck around with the so-called word-material. Poems are also gifts, gifts to the attentive.''

Celan is famous above all as the poet of exile, for whom exile was not only linear displacement or geographic event, but a multidimensional domain from which he could never free himself. Born in Rumania (in 1920), speaking Rumanian and Yiddish, he came to be the greatest German poet of midcentury, while all the years of his celebrity were spent living in Paris. Fleeing war and concentration camp, the permanent anguish of the Holocaust, Celan turned to language with an immensely lyrical skepticism; the speech he gave when he was awarded the Bremen Prize for German literature is often quoted: ''Only one thing remained reachable, close and secure amid all losses: language. Yes, language. In spite of everything, it remained secure against loss. But it had to go through its own lack of answers, through terrifying silence, through the thousand darknesses of murderous speech. It went through.''

He died an exile's death in 1970—abandoning the element of our common lives, he committed suicide by drowning himself in the Seine.

The three books Celan left unfinished at his death have been collected in *Last Poems.* . . . They are *Force of Light, Snow-Part* and *Farmstead of Time.* . . .

These are poems from the culmination of Celan's career; a measure of hope and even a joyous, imperiled playfulness return. To say Celan is the most important German poet since Rilke is not to maroon him off on Comp Lit Island. His greatness reaches into English and American poetry, leaving its mark on our poetry; it's hard to think of any contemporary foreign poet who has cast such a spell on our sense of what a poem is.

A fitting and most useful companion to any reading of Celan's verse is his *Collected Prose*. The slimness of the book tells its own story of Celan's love affair with silence. It is one of the wellsprings of his work, and of his influence. Silence is a dominant issue in modern poetics—silence as elision of speech (Celan, Anne-Marie Albiach, the American "Language" school), or silence as a strategy of music (Robert Creeley, the Black Mountain poets, John Cage). The addresses and responses that make up this volume are translated by the poet Rosmarie Waldrop, whose German is native. Her English (now her working language) has an idiomatic adroitness that catches the pauses and suspensions in Celan's *breath*—his prose often seems breathed rather than thought into place.

[*Collected Prose*] includes the haunting prose dialogue "Conversation in the Mountains," which appears as well in *Last Poems*—two translations are none too many for this important extravaganza of language, inventing characters who turn out to be memorably real. Celan's "Conversation," for all its appeal (like "The Meridian") to the work and example of Georg Büchner, will remind us of the dialogic form that his hated and loved Martin Heidegger restored to modern philosophy; it bears here on the inextricable knot of Jewishness and the *word*. We recall that the dialectic is rooted not only in the Platonic dialogue but in the Mishna.

In our time, poets have taken up *philosophieren*—doing (not studying) philosophy. Celan is the loftiest of them, surely, teaching poetry to fashion awareness out of "words which seem," he says in "The Meridian," "something that listens, not without fear, for something beyond itself, beyond words."

> Robert Kelly, "*A Love Affair with Silence,*" *in* The New York Times Book Review, *November 9, 1986, p. 21.*

BENJAMIN HOLLANDER

Paul Celan's *Collected Prose* is an incitement to the poetic intelligence. Scored with a lyric impulse and imagination, these writings could only have emerged with radical necessity out of the occasions which provoked them.

As a Romanian Jew who saw his parents sent to their deaths and who himself spent a year inside a Nazi labor camp, Celan had his faith in the stability of place uprooted at an early age. Following his detention, he returned to his native Czernowitz in 1943 and stayed for two years, before leaving for Bucharest to work as an editor and translator. In 1948, he travelled to Paris and worked there as a poet and translator until his suicide by drowning in 1970.

Celan's poetry, for which he has too slowly come to be recognized as *the* seminal post-war European figure, is similarly informed by these fractured signs of an existence estranged from its source, as they recover a dialogue with place from the condition of exile; all, as he says in "The Meridian" speech, "for the sake of an encounter."

This is encounter as restorative response, both to the Nazi annihilators and to a language which, as he formulates it in his "Speech on the Occasion of Receiving the Literature Prize of the Free Hanseatic City of Bremen," "remained secure against loss" but which "had to go through its own lack of answers, through terrifying silence, through the thousand darknesses of murderous speech."

What comes through this "lack" is an "enriched" language in which the poems and prose writings become coded, distressed, and intimately pressured messages—Celan's image of the poem is "a letter in a bottle thrown out to sea"—both direct and elusive in their desperate address, *en route* to a site from which Celan's voice will locate a language that will speak, as with a felt duration under duress, toward "something open, inhabitable, an approachable you, perhaps, an approachable reality." And yet when Celan's prose approaches this "something open," when his language recedes deeper into its self-consuming dialogue with itself only to seek this other, this "approachable you," it is often projected from a place which is itself an open forum. Thus, in "The Meridian" speech, given upon his acceptance of the George Büchner Prize for Literature, Celan's ostensible subject is the work of the nineteenth-century German writer, George Büchner, yet Celan's vocabulary and syntax, twisting and returning to their source in Büchner while emptying out to a future, absent reader (a thou), become subject to Büchner's several narrative voices and themes: the artist as pariah in search of himself, his place, his language and the fate of his language pressured either by his madness or the culturally vacuous and politically authoritarian discourses around him.

What is rare about "The Meridian" is that the occasion of a prepared speech issues the discovery of an engaging dramatic and particularly lyric form. Like some other writings here, it crosses toward and moves inside its subject, not over it.

Other pieces worth noting in this slim volume . . . include the brilliantly evocative "Conversation in the Mountains" between two Jews, strangers to nature and themselves and speaking with a borrowed language as if they were blindly tapping sticks to silent stone; a selection of insightful and inciting aphorisms called "Backlight"; and Celan's moving "Letter to Hans Bender" on craft as spiritual exercise. In all they represent "a unique, mortal soul searching for its way with its voice and its dumbness"; a prose as radiant and "wholly other" as "the mystery of an encounter"; a gesture toward the reader as precisely and sincerely engaged as a poem, or a handshake. . . .

> Benjamin Hollander, "*Artist as Pariah,*" *in* The American Book Review, *Vol. 9, No. 3, May/August, 1987, p. 20.*

Austin (Ardinel) C(hesterfield) Clarke

1934-

Barbadian novelist, short story writer, essayist, autobiographer, and scriptwriter.

In his work, Clarke portrays the plight of impoverished blacks in Barbados and the problems encountered by Barbadian immigrants in Canada. While his writing is suffused with humorous observations, Clarke's social commentary is often scathing and pessimistic, reflecting the anger and frustration of victims of economic, political, and racial oppression. He makes frequent use of irony and symbolism to emphasize the predicaments confronting characters who wish to escape injustices in Barbados but discover equally oppressive conditions upon relocating to North America. Clarke is especially praised by critics for his skill in rendering the nuances and rhythms of Barbadian dialects.

Like most of the characters in his fiction, Clarke was born into the Barbadian lower class and emigrated to Canada in search of a better standard of living. His autobiography, *Growing Up Stupid under the Union Jack* (1980), evokes the milieu in which he was raised as well as the sense of alienation he experienced in advanced colonial schools that were structured in accordance with British systems and curriculums. Cyril Dabydeen noted: "As the narrator shifts from a childhood to an adult perception of himself, he is confronted by a constantly nagging desire of wanting to prove himself against having his self-image defined for him by his colonial master; contrariously, too, it leads to the obsession of wanting to live up to the standards set by the colonial master, and results in a burning insecurity."

Clarke's first two novels, *The Survivors of the Crossing* (1964) and *Amongst Thistles and Thorns* (1965), are tragicomic depictions of life among indigent residents of Barbados. The former work centers on the unsuccessful efforts of a plantation laborer to organize a strike for better wages. The protagonist of *Amongst Thistles and Thorns* is an illegitimate nine-year-old boy who attempts to find his father after receiving cruel treatment from his headmaster and his mother. This book was particularly praised for its evocation of a Barbadian community from the perspective of a bewildered youth. Clarke's next three novels, *The Meeting Point* (1967), *Storm of Fortune* (1973), and *The Bigger Light* (1975), collectively known as the "Toronto Trilogy," chronicle the experiences of a group of Barbadian immigrants in Canada. *The Meeting Point,* which introduces Bernice Leach, who works as a domestic servant for a wealthy white couple, features characters who are unemployed or perform menial tasks with little hope for advancement. Clarke symbolically links the struggles of the immigrants with the cold and intimidating social and natural environments of Canada. *Storm of Fortune* further details the demoralizing experiences that Leach and her friends undergo in their struggle to assimilate into a society that continuously exploits and demeans them. *The Bigger Light* focuses on an immigrant who attempts to overcome feelings of alienation and emptiness by acquiring material possessions.

The Prime Minister (1977) is based upon events following Clarke's return to the West Indies in the mid-1970s, when he served as an official in the Barbadian cultural ministry. The

protagonist of this novel becomes involved in several farcical incidents, including a widespread political conspiracy. *Proud Empires* (1986), set during the 1950s, contrasts the bitter homecoming of a man who left Barbados for Canada with the hopeful expectations of a young man on the verge of emigrating. Clarke's short stories, collected in such volumes as *When He Was Free and Young and He Used to Wear Silks* (1971), *When Women Rule* (1985), and *Nine Men Who Laughed* (1986), examine the indignities and alienation experienced by Canada's West Indians.

(See also *CLC*, Vol. 8; *Contemporary Authors*, Vols. 25-28, rev. ed.; *Contemporary Authors New Revision Series*, Vol. 14; and *Dictionary of Literary Biography*, Vol. 53.)

PHILIP STRATFORD

[*The Survivors of the Crossing*] deals with a labour dispute on a backward cane plantation and describes the confusion of hope and fear, passion and resignation that seizes the workers when they stage an abortive strike. The characters, as we have come to expect in West Indian fiction, are powerfully realized. They have a Dickensian vigour. The plot is rugged but ragged, and yet in its slowness and its erratic, sometimes improbable movement, Clarke has captured the rhythm, complexity and comedy of the life of this uncertain society. (p. 26)

Philip Stratford, "Six Ways to Escape the Canadian Winter," in Saturday Night, Vol. 80, No. 2, February, 1965, pp. 26-7.

KILDARE DOBBS

[Austin Clarke's] first novel, *The Survivors of the Crossing,* set in his native Barbados, gave notice that he was a writer to be reckoned with, a writer with a gift for a new kind of savagely sad comedy. *Amongst Thistles and Thorns,* his new novel, shows once more that he possesses a wild poetic talent that seems all the more forceful for the control with which it's contained.

The hero is the nine-year-old byblow of a washerwoman who, at the violent outset of the action, is far from being the wise child that knows his own father. In fact the man Milton Sobers thinks is his father turns out to be no one of a kind. Everything that happens in the novel is shown through the eyes of young Milton, but he is no New-Yorker child intrigued by the quaintness of his surroundings. He sees all—and we are made to see and experience all with him—with a strange doubleness, with anger and hatred, but also—and this is what makes Clarke's book extraordinary—with love, with an incontinent appetite for life.

Milton is cruelly flogged by his headmaster, Mr. Blackman. . . . Seeing young Milton's scars from the flogging, his mother is enraged and, taking him with her, sets out to visit Mister Blackman and, as she says, to "get satisfaction".

But she's awed by the headmaster's house, the biggest one on the side road where all the rich black and the poor white live. And it's easy for Mister Blackman, so close to the prestigious white world, to blarney her out of her purpose—a purpose she hasn't the heart to even mention. Instead of satisfaction, she gets a present of a rose. And on the way home, realizing she's betrayed her boy, she gives him another flogging.

Night has fallen and Milton has run away from his mother's home. His adventures during a night of storm and disillusion teach him who he is—but the knowledge comes less like a reconciliation with reality than an encounter with madness. The thunder and lightning outside are hardly more terrible than the storm of despair within him. The drama ends with his putative father and his mother deciding that school is over for him. It's time for him to face life, time for the chain gang.

Told baldly like this the story can only be depressing. But thanks to the author's fierce eloquence, his loving mastery of a vivid and powerful and (to us) exotic idiom, it's exciting and satisfying. There must be autobiography in it, yet it's not a story of a childhood distorted for purposes of vengeance on a cruel environment. The author is so much of an artist that he can't help showing his characters whole. Willy-Willy, the good-for-nothing; Blackman the cruel schoolmaster; Girlie the whore—they're all real. And the prose moves with an impetuous gait, like a black sermon, like a phillippic against a cruel colonial regime, a phillipic against the cruelty and meaninglessness of life itself; and troubled and made more profound by a gusto for reality, a sensuousness and swagger that contradicts the desolating import of the action it describes. As a child's grief

in a storm of tears is contradicted by the strong beat of his own heart. (pp. 59-60)

Kildare Dobbs, "Caribbean Renaissance," in Saturday Night, Vol. 80, No. 11, November, 1965, pp. 59-60.

THE TIMES LITERARY SUPPLEMENT

Bernice is from Barbados, come to Toronto as domestic to rich, Jewish, horrible and pathetic Mrs. Burrmann. Her protests are mostly whistles in the dark, mere gestures against her employer's rude commands, and she puts up an ambivalent resistance to the uneasy spell of the eternal Beethoven Sixth from Mr. Burrmann's record-player. *The Meeting Point* is a threnody, melancholic, angry and savagely funny on Bernice's mesmerized dependence on Mrs. Burrmann's hideous, off-white universe. Mrs. Burrmann relates to "this, this—this—*woman*" with the blundering love-hateful assertions of an insecure *ubermensch*. . . .

Bernice and Mrs. Burrmann make common emotional cause when Bernice (falsely) believes her mother has died. They weep together, sentimentally, rather disgustingly "joined in grief as they had never been united before, by love". But they never in fact discover the bond which really unites them. Mr. Burrmann's furtive, misty affair with Estelle, the younger sister Bernice fetches from home, persists in front of them, flourishing as a mocking reflection of their common ignorance and inadequacy. . . . For [Bernice] and all the other West Indians who have "come up" to Canada there are two irreconcilable, tantalizing ways out of—or deeper into—their frustrations. They can latch on to the placard-line "mumbling . . . a very bad and lugubrious melodic line", embarrassedly supporting banners reading CANADA IS NOT ALABAMA AND BLACK EQUALS WHITE, or they can succumb to another image, join a different queue. On her big day, Bernice phones her friend Dots; "Child, I got it! I got the thing, man. You must come and see it!" She has attained her first chequebook (with her own name printed) from the Royal Bank of Canada—"*My* Bank, to 5m. Canadians". Either way they don't win. The marchers only get wet and the depositors end up like Henry, one of the book's sad heroes, in an unfurnished bed-sit adding noughts to the derisory figures in his bankbook.

Mr. Clarke has a great flair for catching the passwords, patois and special idioms of a particular, beleaguered social group. These people speak not only like Barbadians but, very convincingly, as Barbadians ghettoed in Toronto. It is something of a burden for the reader, though, that the centre of the tale is Bernice rather than someone else. She is a character of impressive but rather bovine complexity, and there are several others present who could have given the book a more entertaining focus without any sacrifice of weight or truth.

"Barbados in Toronto," in The Times Literary Supplement, No. 3402, May 11, 1967, p. 404.

B. POMER

A sociologist reading [*Amongst Thistles and Thorns*] would find confirmed its every conclusion about the serpent-eating-its-tail nature of the unbreakable chain of poverty. Sociological findings are, after all, drawn from observation of life, and life, in an unsentimental and anything but clinical treatment, is exactly what Austin Clarke has created. He has in fact succeeded in setting you down, invisible, in the midst of people and events, with the feeling that you are seeing and hearing without even the printer's pence intervening between yourself and what is going on. His book is bursting with vitality, alive with pictures that fairly leap off the page, and bubbling with streams of natural dialogue in a West Indian idiom that reveals sensitivity both to the musicality of language and its potential for comic extravagance. And the story, for all its hard realities, is told with an irreverent and irrepressible humour that results in unforgetably funny figures and scenes. Brilliant is the word for Clarke's depiction of his highly ebullient people; as a re-creation of shanty life in the West Indies, his novel is true and rich and deep beyond the sum of its . . . pages. (p. 119)

B. Pomer, in a review of "Amongst Thistles and Thorns," in The Canadian Forum, *Vol. XLVII, No. 559, August, 1967, pp. 118-19.*

LLOYD W. BROWN

Clarke's major themes are similar to those of most West Indian novels during the last thirty years—black awareness, national identity, the hateful ambiguities of the West, and the heroic potential of the black peasant. But the emphases and contexts through which he develops these topics are shaped by his experience of the Afro-American consciousness that has been gaining momentum during his stay in Canada and the United States. He has, in effect, helped to contribute a North American dimension to the characteristic identity motif of the West Indian novel; and as the major West Indian writer on the continent at the present time, he provides an invaluable perspective on an aspect of British Caribbean literature that has too often been minimized or ignored in the past. His significance in this respect is increased by the fact that he is among the few West Indian artists of any note to have lived and worked in North America, for any considerable time, since the beginning of the new 'black revolution'.

In fact 'revolution' is the major theme of his first novel, *Survivors of the Crossing* (1964). It presents the abortive attempts of Rufus, a sugar-plantation labourer, to effect an economic and political revolution in Barbados. He tries, unsuccessfully, to break the repressive powers of a white establishment by using the strike as his main weapon, and when that fails, resorts to equally ineffective terrorist tactics. But in spite of the very obvious political motif of the work, the real import of the revolution in *Survivors of the Crossing* is cultural and emotional, rather than constitutional. Hence the portrayal of Barbados in the mid-sixties as a politically deprived society, lacking even the fundamentals of a labour union movement, is an ironic rather than literal anachronism. All the constitutional, political, and economic trappings of the West Indian independence movement have been reduced, by Clarke, to the level of relative insignificance, in the face of the black apathy and self-hate that have traditionally stunted cultural and racial self-identity. The native government and its leaders are conspicuously absent from the main plot of *Survivors of the Crossing,* and are occasionally just referred to in passing as rather vague and irrelevant details of the background. The real powers in Rufus's world are the white plantation owner and a white-controlled police force, both exercising their influence through native sycophants. Rufus fails, then, not only because of his opponents' power and his own incapacities, but also because of the hostility or indifference of other blacks who actively or passively support the *status quo*. Whippetts, the black school-teacher in Rufus's village, is a representative figure in this context; his violent hatred of Rufus and his contempt for mem-

bers of his own race not only make him an effective opponent of the ill-fated revolution, but also demonstrate the educational and class barriers to an effective kind of racial self-identity in his society.

However, the theme of political and economic revolution is more than an ironic exposé of the emotional hollowness of West Indian constitutional development. It is also an allegorization of that spiritual revolution, that self-identification, which alone can impart emotional meaning to political evolution, and which is Rufus's real strength. It is because of this new awareness that Rufus is able to perceive the wider implications of what he originates as a purely economic crusade against a tight-fisted and vindictive system. His revolt provokes an alliance of whites and middle-class Negroes, which demonstrates to him that the ensuing conflict is one of poor versus rich, black versus white. Once gained, this insight heightens his sense of racial and social identity.

But the new experience also alienates him from his society, for it sets him apart from (and in conflict with) the apathetic poor as well as the privileged. The barriers between Rufus and his reluctant followers are symbolized by the treachery of his mercenary girl-friend, Stella (who deserts to the side of the plantation owner and overseer), and by his rapid descent from the role of an ineffective revolutionary to that of a feared outlaw who is finally imprisoned for assault and robbery. In *Survivors of the Crossing,* as in Clarke's subsequent works, the experience of self-identification does not bring transcendental resolutions. Instead it results in alienation, and in the intensification of unresolved conflicts between the new awareness and the old order. (pp. 90-2)

At the same time, however, there are highly suggestive parallels between Rufus's experiences and Clarke's North American background. Indeed, North America always hovers in the background of the novel. Rufus's ill-fated designs, for example, are partly inspired by a smattering of information on the reputed wealth and social justice of Canada and the United States. Similarly, the paradox of his triumph and tragedy is comparable with the major developments in social and racial relationships in the United States: first, the so-called militants in the black community who emphasize the shaping of an Afro-American identity as their primary goal, tend to be alienated from concepts of full integration with a society that they regard as traditionally and inherently hostile to the very nature of their racial identity; and secondly, the emergence of this new black self-consciousness has intensified, not ameliorated, the conflicts initially precipitated by the civil rights movement.

The identity theme with its attendant conflicts also appears in Clarke's next novel, *Amongst Thistles and Thorns* (1965). Both the coherent structure and psychological complexity of this work attest to the rapid development of Clarke's narrative techniques. He treats his racial and cultural subjects on a less exclusively external level than he has Rufus's political misadventures: the moral and emotional conflicts become more coherent and psychologically interesting by being presented as the experiences of a single character whose introspection provides the work with a kind of subjective unity.

Amongst Thistles and Thorns portrays a week-end in the life of Milton Sobers, a young schoolboy in Barbados, who runs away temporarily from both school and home. Milton's truancy is developed as a psychological quest, a search for identity that has racial as well as psychological overtones. He has run away from a sterile educational system represented by a servile and sadistic black teacher, an impersonal and detached white in-spector, and the irrelevant offerings to a white 'Motherland' during the colonial rites of Empire Day. At the same time, he is detached from the society of his village, for only his father, Willy-Willy, shares his interest in the topic closest to his heart—Harlem. Milton's Harlem assumes the dominant symbolic pro-portions it has in [Claude McKay's] *Home to Harlem,* and his day-dreams of the famous black community at once testify to the importance of American symbolism in Clarke's fiction, and indicate the unifying subjectivity with which Clarke is devel-oping his themes: 'I was looking at my mother holding the Book, but I was seeing the green pastures in our village stretch-ing far far out to sea all the way across the ocean to Harlem New York City America'.

The day-dreaming episode takes place after Milton's short-lived 'exile', and emphasizes the degree to which his week-end escapade has been a kind of catalyst for the rapid devel-opment of his insight and self-identification—both of which are symbolized by the racial and cultural 'facts' of Harlem. He also dreams of Harlem during the escapade itself. While he hides beneath the village church one night, the service con-ducted by the Rev. Best becomes a part of Milton's vision of his village as a kind of Barbadian Harlem, and he seems to have been transported across the sea to what he has come to regard as 'Willy-Willy' country. The immediate effect of Mil-ton's short-lived rebellion must therefore be found in the emo-tional and spiritual transformation embodied by the aspirations at the end of the novel: he dreams of 'discovering new worlds and countries and happiness like Columbus; and perhaps, if the day was long enough, I could ever reach as far away from this village and from Nathan and my mother, as Harlem New York, America'.

This last soliloquy is significant for the obvious sense of alien-ation that accompanies Milton's newly-found identity. His mother and Nathan, her lover, are apathetic figures, far removed from Milton's imaginative world, and limited to love-making and the daily drudgeries of making a bare living, he as a rarely-employed labourer, she as a white prostitute's washer-woman. Milton's estrangement from both is dramatized in the evolution of his relationship with Nathan. He has gradually discovered that Willy-Willy, not Nathan, is his real father, that Nathan had been duped into his paternal role as a substitute for the utterly destitute Willy-Willy. Hence Nathan is initially pre-sented as the strong father-figure who is asked to avenge the savage punishments that his 'son' receives at school, but is eventually dismissed by Milton as a contemptible and irrelevent boor. The discovery of Milton's real father is therefore linked with the Harlem symbolism of the novel, for in a real sense Willy-Willy, a former emigrant to the United States, has also fathered Milton's transformation by his stories of black Amer-ica. Both the parental and racial themes thus cohere in the psychological experiences of Milton's rebirth.

But Willy-Willy's own personality and experiences stress the tragic irony that underlies the awakening of consciousness in *Amongst Thistles and Thorns* as well as in *Survivors of the Crossing.* His own transformation during his stay in the United States has alienated Willy-Willy from the apathetic and self-hating society to which he returns, and this is illustrated by his role as the village drunk and local eccentric. Willy-Willy's awareness, like Rufus's, is not translated into transforming action, in the manner of George Lamming's Fola Piggott. It simply heightens a sense of futility, the frustration of being unable to communicate the new consciousness to an insensitive

environment. This failure is shown by his inability to acknowl-edge or support Milton as his child, and by the eventual ig-nominy of drowning in a rainstorm, after being refused shelter by Milton's mother.

At the end of the novel Milton has inherited, not only the triumph of his father's racial pride and awareness, but, by implication, its ironically painful consequences also. Hence the aspirations expressed through his final vision of Harlem are undercut by the realities of the present: his weak-willed mother has sacrificed her earlier ambitions for Milton, in order to safeguard her own sexual interests. She seeks to appease (and hold) Nathan by consenting to the latter's 'plans' for Milton's real future—an abbreviated school education, fol-lowed by the lifelong futility of a semi-illiterate labourer like himself.

In Clarke's subsequent work there are further important de-velopments in both the psychological complexity and the North American motif in his identity themes. One of his best short stories, **"Four Stations in his Circle"** (1965), is set in Canada, and describes the immigrant experiences of a Barbadian, Jef-ferson Theophilis Belle, in Toronto. The identity theme is reversed in Belle's character, for his unaccustomed status as the member of a black minority has intensified his latent self-hatred. His quest is not for a black, but a white, identity. He hates and shuns other West Indian immigrants, and is obsessed with his dreams of owning a house in a wealthy, predominantly white, Toronto district. It is a self-destructive course that ends with the nightmare of total isolation in his coveted but empty house; he is surrounded by kindly neighbours who assume that he can only be the caretaker of such a sumptuous dwelling, and haunted by the memories of a dead mother whom he had previously spurned in his pathological hatred of other West Indians.

Belle's character is really an in-depth psychological study of black self-hate, of the suspicious doubts and fears that thwart any meaningful communication between Rufus or Milton and their respective societies. Because of this, **"Four Stations in his Circle"** is an apt prelude to *The Meeting Point,* for in this . . . novel Clarke draws together all the major psycholog-ical themes of his previous works. As already noted, in the works discussed thus far, the emotional and racial conflicts of Clarke's identity themes have been gradually internalized. First, there are the external symbols of economic and social strife in *Survivors of the Crossing.* Secondly, *Amongst Thistles and Thorns* depicts the psychological and emotional barriers between two or more distinct and exclusive attitudes, each embodied by separate individuals or groups: the imaginative awareness of Willy-Willy and Milton versus the apathy of Nathan and Mil-ton's mother; and similarly, **"Four Stations in his Circle"** portrays the obsessive self-hatred of Belle in conflict with his family and fellow-West-Indians.

Psychologically Clarke's themes evolve a stage further with the incisive irony of *The Meeting Point.* Familiar clashes with the external world of the *status quo* persist, but the more in-teresting conflicts are wholly internal: the actual process of black self-identification is itself being more closely scrutinized, and is revealed as a painful, and often unresolved, series of conflicts *within* each awakening consciousness—the tension between nascent blackness on the one hand, and the old self-hate or apathy, on the other. Moreover, this is the fundamental ambiguity that proves to be the source of much of the novel's irony.

The Meeting Point is the story of Bernice Leach, a Barbadian immigrant working as the maid of the Burrmanns, a Jewish family in Toronto. The title of the work is itself ironic, for the novel dispels, rather than confirms, the optimistic connotations of the familiar phrase. 'Meeting point' really indicates, not reconciliation and harmony, but the collision of hostile attitudes: the black sensitivity of Bernice and her friends meeting the coldness and antipathy of Canadian society. And there is also the personal conflict within each immigrant. On the external level, there are the usual symptoms of inter-racial hostilities. (pp. 92-6)

On the economic level, Bernice interprets Mrs Burrmann's role and attitudes as symptoms of her employer's inability to accept her fully as a human being: in spite of Mrs Burrmann's show of affection, Bernice 'always saw herself as a servant; a sort of twentieth-century slave. It was mainly the amount of hard work which reminded her of her status. And also, the small wages'. On her side, Mrs Burrmann begins to feel 'at ease with "this, this—this—*woman*" (that's how she first described Bernice to her friend, Mrs Gasstein)' and celebrates by allowing Bernice to take the children for walks. The tension is heightened by Bernice's resentment at the exclusive 'whiteness' of her environment. . . . (p. 96)

Bernice herself and her fellow domestics tend to pride themselves on their superior detachment from the excessive and heartless materialism that they attribute to North American society in general, and Canada in particular. Yet they are equally single-minded in the pursuit of the goals valued in an affluent society—the conspicuous display of expensive goods that are sometimes returned to the stores without being used, and the fascinating mathematics of a growing savings account. On the one hand, the racial awareness that leads Bernice to resent white exclusivism also makes her receptive, for a while, to the black individualism of the American Black Muslims. Thus before she begins reading the Muslim newspaper, *Muhammad Speaks,* Bernice does not 'like the word "black" used to describe her colour'. On the other hand, Harlem is the source not only of her black newspaper, but also of the 'complexion lighteners' that she uses in futile attempts to 'alleviate' her blackness. This latent self-hate eventually becomes more overt and dominant, as is demonstrated by her decision to desert the Toronto Negro Baptist Church in favour of the Unitarian Congregation. . . . (p. 97)

Henry White, another member of Bernice's circle, is portrayed in equally ambiguous terms. He views his past career, as a railway porter, as a means of asserting a kind of racial pride, of proving his worth and competence to a hostile society; but paradoxically, he also tends to view his successes as 'white' achievements, as signs that he has 'made it' in the white world: one of his proudest possessions is a photograph of himself 'shaking hands with the Prime Minister of Canada. It was taken a long time ago when he was chosen Porter of the Year. At the bottom, he has written, in pencil, "Mister Henry White, Porter of the Year, shaking with the Prime Minister"'. In one sense his love-affairs with white women are an expression of 'revenge' for racial injustice, a means of asserting his human identity through the very manhood that has been vilified and distorted by fearful superstition and prejudice. (p. 98)

Henry's intense black awareness is matched in the novel only by that of Estelle Shepherd, Bernice's sister, whose Black Muslim sympathies are far less superficial and unstable than Bernice's. But her fervour also seems only to intensify the eventual disillusionment of her self-contradictions, particularly

the humiliation she suffers from her compromising liaison with the treacherous Mr Burrmann. Both Henry and Estelle therefore exemplify the central irony of *The Meeting Point:* the internal conflicts of self-identification are heightened in direct ratio to the intensity of emergent blackness. Moreover, their disillusionments never quite succeed in undermining even the qualified triumph of their self-awareness. This is a triumph that must be contrasted to the placid contentment represented by Boysie, for he is the archetype of black apathy, whose primary concerns (cars, sex, and drink) leave him far removed from the exciting turbulence of Henry or Estelle. Finally, the apparently inconclusive ambiguities of *The Meeting Point* are no less realistic than the trenchant ironies of the two earlier novels: like Rufus or Milton Sobers, Henry and Estelle are satiric reflections of psychological and social conflicts that are vividly dramatized by, though not exclusive to, the current Afro-American revolution.

But to acknowledge the essential universality of these conflicts is not to deny the very strong North American themes through which they are developed in *The Meeting Point.* Henry's character, for example, is dominated by the Harlem consciousness that pervades his 'hip' personality and language. (p. 99)

Another typical Afro-American theme is the novel's portrayal of the ambivalent relationships between the restive black community and other minority groups, particularly Jews. From an economic point of view, Bernice Leach and her fellow-domestic immigrants are dominated by the Jewish presence, for most of them are employed by wealthy Jewish families. Moreover, the love-hate experiences of Estelle and Mr Burrmann, or Henry and Agatha, are partly indicative of the ambivalent Black-Jew relationships in North America. As the member of a minority that itself has been persecuted, the Jew in *The Meeting Point* frequently tends to identify himself with the causes of black people. Hence the black protest march that arouses Bernice's scorn and Estelle's admiration is led by 'a Jewish man, wearing a pair of glasses that had one eye-lens darkened, holding hands with a black woman'. Similarly, Agatha tries to persuade Bernice and other West Indians that she is not prejudiced, primarily because of her own Jewish background.

But Agatha's claims on behalf of some special kind of Jewish tolerance are undercut by her parents' bigoted reaction against her black boy friend; and the brotherly demonstration by the Jewish marcher is counterbalanced by the lessons that the Gassteins (neighbours of the Burrmanns) teach their son on race relations: 'My Mummy says you people are nasty', young Gasstein informs Bernice. 'And my Mummy says you shouldn't live among us. You're different from us.' It is this identification with the prevailing norm of white prejudice that undermines the claims of Agatha, the Burrmanns, and other Jews to some special status of brotherhood in suffering. Even a consummate hypocrite like Bernice is repelled by the insincere imitations of Negro spirituals and civil rights songs at the Burrmann parties: 'Hearing them now, she could not at first recognize them as the same beautiful melodies.'

Mr Burrmann is the central figure in Clarke's treatment of Jewish ambivalence towards blacks. As a youth, 'he had had his share of Negro culture. He had thrown dice with the Harlem-like men, and had even consciously imitated their mannerisms, and a few of their diversions, such as smoking their marijuana'. But as he achieves social and professional success, his relationship with blacks changes, and instead of being friends and social equals, they can enter his new environment only as servants like Bernice, or as back-street mistresses like Estelle. In a very real sense, then, Mr Burrmann's career typifies the ambiguities that nascent blackness in America (typified in varying degrees by Bernice, Estelle, and Henry) attributes to the Jewish role on the continent. Not surprisingly, therefore, Bernice is sufficiently envious of her employers to imitate some of their habits, including Mrs Burrmann's favourite magazine subscriptions, but is also contemptuous of the sterility that seems to have been the inevitable price for Mr Burrmann's success—the sterility that she senses in the obvious emotional emptiness of the marriage.

Mr Burrmann's affair with Estelle becomes a kind of quest for the recapture of a lost vitality, a search that is centred on a woman whose race and social background recall the environment of his forgotten past. As he embraces Estelle on one occasion he recollects the sights and sounds of his Harlem-like youth, and after their love-making, he 'has a new power and a new glory', a sense of freedom from sexual inferiority that leaves Mrs Burrmann and his marriage in a 'background of impotence'. But at the same time, the liaison with Estelle is really a love-hate relationship for both of them; even as they whisper endearments to each other, 'she hated him more deeply, the closer he came', while he mocks himself for being the lover of this 'big black nig-Negro woman'. The Jewish image projected through Mr Burrmann in *The Meeting Point* suggests that the very nature of his economic and social successes has tended to violate the special historical bond that the Jew tries to emphasize between himself and the blacks.

This convoluted Black-Jew relationship is not only part of the multiple ambiguities that dominate the structure of *The Meeting Point*, but also reflects the social tensions of Clarke's North American background. (pp. 100-02)

[The] writings of Jews and Afro-Americans demonstrate the deep-seated ambiguities of the social and economic relationships between both sides—and these are the tensions that Clarke has translated to the West Indian-Canadian themes of *The Meeting Point*. Moreover, this translation is typical of the way in which Clarke's novels have contributed to the North American dimension of the identity themes that characterize most West Indian fiction. It is a contribution that can hardly be ignored, for the increasingly cosmopolitan and universal emphases of the current Afro-American quest for a black identity can hardly fail to have a widening effect on black experience, and literature, beyond the borders of the United States. (p. 103)

> *Lloyd W. Brown, "The West Indian Novel in North America: A Study of Austin Clarke," in* Journal of Commonwealth Literature, *No. 9, July, 1970, pp. 89-103.*

MARTIN LEVIN

A dazzling variety of style and substance glitters from this collection of 11 short stories [*When He Was Free and Young and He Used to Wear Silks*] by Austin Clarke. They range from Barbados, his birthplace, to Toronto, where he has lived, and from interior to exterior monologue. Wherever you look, there are treasures. . . .

"Leaving This Island Place" effects a dramatic juxtaposition between a young man's gray-flannel-and-cricket ambience and the almshouse in which his father lies dying. In **"Griff"** a veneer of phony mannerisms is ruptured by primal anguish.

"The Motor Car" describes what happens to a car washer in Barbados who becomes a car washer in Toronto.

Mr. Clarke is plugged into the fixations, hopes, loves and dreams of his characters. He converts them into stories that are charged with life.

> *Martin Levin, in a review of "When He Was Free and Young and He Used to Wear Silks," in* The New York Times Book Review, *December 9, 1973, p. 48.*

ROB COLTER

When, after living in Toronto for 20 years, John Moore returns to his native West Indies to take on a job as director of culture, he finds that paradise is a state of mind. His newly independent country is governed by suppression and suspicion, its people are impressionable and fumbling, its intellectuals and politicians crude and opportunistic. Alienated, and buffeted by the contradiction of an observable paradise lost and his own poetic image of a paradise regained (symbolized by a real and an imagined lover), he is helplessly drawn into a revolutionary plot where betrayal is a matter of convenience. . . .

Austin Clarke knows his subject well. The dialogue [in *The Prime Minister*] is generally superb, the nuances of character finely observed. But there are some maddening flaws. At times the pace is startlingly out of step, and the point of view is sometimes mishandled and confused. A couple of *deus ex machina* devices—upon Moore's arrival a newspaper "gallivanted" to his feet, presenting a headline announcing his arrival—should have been buried. A proposed cultural festival has the unlikely acronym CRAPPO, and the author is often more didactic than he need be.

> *Rob Colter, in a review of "The Prime Minister," in* Quill and Quire, *Vol. 43, No. 14, October 13, 1977, p. 7.*

DAN HILTS

Most of us find our own lives an endless source of amusement and fascination. We are often all too eager to share these feelings with others. Sometimes, however, we will relinquish time to one whose life seems particularly adventurous, well-connected, or profitable, expecially if it is told with charm and wit. Austin Clarke's memoirs [*Growing Up Stupid under the Union Jack*] have some of these ingredients. Their concern is one pivotal year between 1944 and 1945 when the author came of age in his native Barbados.

The details of family life, the smells and sounds of the island, are caught in sharp focus. The basis of fundamentalist religion is revealed as a search for moral superiority and as an outlet for creative energies. Clarke recalls both the pride in and resentment about being taught in an imitation English private school in a colony that prided itself on being known as "Little England." Even discounting the natural tendency to exaggerate childhood traumas, the schools he attended sound dreadful. Arbitrary and heavy-handed corporal punishment was common. Learning by rote British history, Latin, and French without any reference to local culture was hardly calculated to make education anything but painful drudgery.

The long-range view of the Second World War from a peaceful tropical island is evocative. . . .

Despite some interesting aspects, however, the book is not compelling reading. It's a bit like looking at someone's random collection of childhood photographs. Most of the individual pictures are composed well enough and some are even arresting, but they lack any sort of unity or coherence. There is also a curious lack of emphasis; most of the vignettes are presented in the same desultory manner. The lack of chronological or emotional structure combined with a point of view that is firmly placed in the past are limitations the book does not overcome.

Dan Hilts, "Little England Made Him," in Books in Canada, Vol. 9, No. 6, June-July, 1980, p. 23.

EDWARD BAUGH

Near the end of **The Bigger Light,** the last novel in Austin Clarke's Toronto trilogy, the protagonist, Boysie, gets an unexpected letter from a friend who has returned home to Barbados for a visit. Boysie is at a point of extremity. Having lived in Canada for many years, he has become increasingly withdrawn as he experiences frustration in his comic-pathetic attempt to become a truly integral part of Canadian life. His inner confusion is increased by memories of the Barbados of his youth. At this crucial point in Boysie's life, the friend's letter puts a decisive damper on any hankerings he may have after Barbados. It paints a disillusioning picture of a sordidly tourist-oriented society in which colonial exploitation from without has given way to an equally rapacious exploitation from within, in which the biggest culprits are the ruling politicians. So Boysie, alienated from his homeland no less than from his adopted country, from his fellow West Indians in exile and from his wife, gets into his shiny black Buick and secretly "cuts loose," heading across the border into the United States. But it is doubtful that he will find there whatever he is searching for.

Unlike Boysie, John Moore, the protagonist of **The Prime Minister,** Clarke's latest novel, does return home to Barbados, thereby providing the novelist with the occasion for taking up the cue given by Boysie's friend's letter and elaborating on the scene described in it. A poet of some repute, Moore returns after twenty years, at the invitation of a Minister of Government, to a new post—Director of Culture. It soon turns out that the post is only a political "face-card." Moore is not able, nor even expected, to do anything. Instead, he quickly becomes enmeshed in a plot, concocted by politicians of the Other Party and various other power-seekers, abetted by treacherous Government ministers, to overthrow the Government and seize power. To his consternation, Moore learns that he, whom the plotters had seemingly wished to be their confidante, is to be used as the scapegoat, because of his supposed radical views and intentions. But the plot misfires. The Prime Minister outfoxes the conspirators and uses the pretext of the failed coup to declare a state of emergency and set himself well on the way towards dictatorship. He proves to be the supreme *jinnal* (Jamaican for trickster, crook).

The novel is an angry expression of disillusionment with the management of affairs in the post-Independence West Indies. It gives a version of what Derek Walcott in a recent interview (*Contemporary Literature,* Summer 1979) has referred to as "a profound political betrayal of a people." Clarke paints a basically true, if purposefully exaggerated, picture of a society rabidly resistant to any attempt to change of its bad habits. A mercenary life-style glorifies the tourist dollar, promiscuity, the use of chicanery and toadyism to gain privilege, the use

of power for exploitation, and the use of violence (whether of deed or word) as the most convenient way of dealing with any challenge to the life-style.

Unfortunately, Clarke doesn't go deeply into anything. The picture seems hurried, done in broad strokes. Very little happens under the surfaces of the words. Every detail shouts itself on to the reader's attention. The aim is partly satirical, but the edge of wit and humor is blunt. In aspirations to artiness, Clarke waxes poetic with flat, tiresome overworking of the vague epithet "beautiful," and with vague, soppy evocations of the beauty of the land and of negritude—"his black blessed women" and a daydream motif of the vision of a heavily symbolic black female who appears intermittently and enticingly to the protagonist constitute a rather obvious and facile structural device.

Still, there are one or two nice touches. The opening sequence, recording John Moore's arrival, effects a reasonably skillful interplay of suggestions and feelings, anticipation and delight tempered by uneasiness and an almost elegiac note in the resurgent memories of the island as a sad little place which its people were always leaving. The point about the society's characteristic violence of language is shrewd and well made. But the cleverest feature of the book is the way in which the figure of the Prime Minister is presented. Ironically, given the title, the reader like the protagonist hardly ever sees him, and then only fleetingly and tangentially; nor is he given a name. But that is the point: his absence, so to speak, from the novel attests to the power of his presence in the system (shown in the recurrent references to him, whether awed, obsequious or critical) and heightens the effect of his dramatic and masterful counter-strike against his would-be supplanters at the end. Altogether, it is as if in his shady, impersonal presence he embodies all that is corrupt about the society. (pp. 465-66)

Edward Baugh, "Prime Ministers Unlimited: West Indian Literary Report," in Queen's Quarterly, Vol. 87, No. 3, Autumn, 1980, pp. 465-73.

CYRIL DABYDEEN

In a sense all writing is memorial. In the same vein, too, one can say that fiction is never really fiction at all; that what stems from the creative well of the imagination has its inevitable roots in one's actual life experiences. The case of Austin Clarke, the Barbadian-born Canadian novelist, is no exception, for in nearly all his works he has been plumbing the sources of his background; this search would be inevitable in one aware of his integrity in expressing fidelity to the place in which he was born; it is also significant in terms of identifying a specific ethnic point of view in a pluralistic Canada.

Growing Up Stupid Under the Union Jack, which won the Casa de las Americas literature prize given in Cuba in 1980, spans the author's life from 1944 to 1950 and indicts his colonial educational system which fostered the virtues of the British and the glories of the empire. In Barbados itself, such an educational system became part of the structure of a society, and ultimately became responsible for much of the self-alienation and self-contempt among its recipients. Thus, an overriding sense of futility is seen in Clarke's irony, in which the central character grapples against becoming a "learning fool" in his growing up—all this with a backdrop of the Second World War in Europe, the very place which was supposed to be the fount of civilization and learning. As the narrator shifts from a childhood to an adult perception of himself, he is confronted by a constantly nagging desire of wanting to prove himself against having his self-image defined for him by his colonial master; contrariously, too, it leads to the obsession of wanting to live up to the standards set by the colonial master, and results in a burning insecurity. (p. 156)

Clarke's accurate depiction is spiced, as always, with his humour and sense of irony. The narrator omnisciently looks back and sees himself as a "running fool," the sprinter. Later he joins the Cadet Corps, becomes a corporal, and carries a wooden gun in earnest preparation for soldiery in case Britain calls upon the reserves in the empire. In one of the best comical settings in the novel, we see young black boys executing manoeuvres with wooden guns while the Second World War wages on; while, too, these same boys lustily sing "Rule Britannia, Britannia rule the waves," and pray for the King and the Royal Family. Additional irony is underlined with everyone aspiring and hoping to live in America—primarily because the educational system had not placed any value on anything indigenous.

Clarke continues in this ironic vein when he describes Belleville Avenue, "the ironical showpiece of my country: clean and white, clean and black," with its tennis clubs, yet containing the road sweeper "efficient as a starved dog," in sharp contrast to the coachmen "dressed like fat cockroaches."

Clarke combines his irony with an unusual penchant for dialogue which cuts short long-winded introspection. Thus he aptly creates his scenes, yet can be playfully mocking (*"Je suis, tu suis"*) when the young narrator cannot pass French. He juxtaposes the Queen's English with Barbadian dialect to make his point with compelling effect, using all the nuances of both languages at his disposal, thereby showing his tremendous versatility. Name irony is also used—as with Milton, that of the narrator's, compared with the English poet's, with compelling naiveté and charm: "I asked this new Milton whether his name was real or a nickname. How could someone so close to me, someone I saw walking barefoot everyday . . . ," how could he be named Milton "like that blind man who talked about paradise?" But later the young narrator becomes a "dreaming fool," who constantly carries in his head ideas of English history and culture while aping poetry in the manner of Milton and Keats—as "all this stuck in my mind and I lived this Union Jack time as if I were in an English countryside."

Growing Up Stupid Under the Union Jack is further testimony of Clarke's immense talent. It has all the ingredients of his previous books; here, perhaps, Clarke is simpler, but more direct—having fun at history and at himself (no doubt) in a fictional-memorial genre which the best sociologist or historian would find hard to match. (p. 157)

> *Cyril Dabydeen, in a review of "Growing Up Stupid under the Union Jack: A Memoir," in* The Dalhousie Review, *Vol. 61, No. 1, Spring, 1981, pp. 156-57.*

KEITH GAREBIAN

The eight stories [in *When Women Rule*] deal with the passions of West Indian immigrants to Canada. The tensions and motifs are certainly familiar to anyone who has read Clarke's novels and earlier short fiction, but they do not lose their force because of this familiarity. Brutality dominates the mood of most of the stories, for it penetrates the social milieu the characters inhabit and distorts perceptions and responses. The world evoked is one of hard-luck, downtrodden victims, lost in illusions of their fallen past and present. Sometimes the stories are trite; Clarke depends too often on the ethnic flavour to engage the

reader's sympathies. Sentimentality—even on the side of justifiable anger at social humiliation—is always a danger to fine writing because it can tilt fiction too far in the direction of stock moral responses, weakening the work's aesthetic structure.

However, there is some fine work in the book. **"Griff,"** a story about a Barbadian man who wreaks vengeance on his adulterous wife, has a strong sense of rhythm and musicality. **"The Man"** is a touching but ultimately explosive story about a man who fights time and his own insignificance. And **"The Discipline"** crystallizes a collision of two antithetical worlds posited on contrary concepts of moral and psychological control. Here Clarke uses language to satirize his protagonist and to politicize opposite sides. (pp. 59-60)

> *Keith Garebian, in a review of "When Women Rule," in* Quill and Quire, *Vol. 51, No. 7, July, 1985, pp. 59-60.*

NEIL BISSOONDATH

When Women Rule is a book about impotent men and victimized but strong women—women who, while remaining very much in the background, still rule the roost, all living together in the little hothouse of their ethnic camp. . . .

["**Griff**" is] the most powerful story in the collection. At the end of the story, Griff, "a black man from Barbados who sometimes denied he was black," apparently strangles his wife, and it is in a way surprising that this is the only murder in the book. In many of the stories men contemplate violence against women. They are men groping at ideas of masculinity, luckless gamblers—they spend much time at the horse races or the card table or dreaming up scams—with dreams too large for their abilities, dreams that do not so much feed the ambition as haunt the imagination.

As reflected in the stories, this ethnic camp has little contact with the larger society in which it is based. The police are always seen as a threat, social agencies as interfering busybodies. . . .

The larger society, in this case Toronto, is brashly ignored, the rules violated. Clarke's characters do not form part of the society, live in a camp within it, have no long-term stake in it; and the society, largely unknown, is seen to be alien, hostile, racist, a constant threat to the camp itself rife with tensions. (p. 21)

> *Neil Bissoondath, "Flaws in the Mosaic," in* Books in Canada, *Vol. 14, No. 6, August-September, 1985, pp. 21-2.*

KEITH S. HENRY

Of the four gifted and established West Indian-North American novelists, Frank Hercules, Paule Marshall, Rosa Guy, and Austin Clarke, Clarke is the only West Indian-Canadian. The very small native black population in Toronto, the locale of his North American novels, has allowed his to be the most single-minded focus on the exploration of the special West Indian experience in North America. (p. 9)

[Clarke's] first work, *Survivors of the Crossing,* deals with the lives of men and women in a post-mid-twentieth-century Barbados village dominated by a sugar plantation. The plantation regime here is brutal enough and omnipotent enough for at least some of the prevailing realities here to seem anachronistic for their time. The armed overseer on his horse, for example, well deserves his reputation for bloodthirstiness. The civil government in Bridgetown is of no apparent importance, except as helpful auxiliaries to the plantation in the form of police ''interrogators'' and merciless judges. The villagers mostly live in destitution, relieved only by an uncertain access to sex and rum and sometimes a resort to religion. However, a letter from a former laborer recently emigrated to Canada sets off an unexpected chain of events. His reports of a superior quality of life for black people in his new home inspire in the fevered mind of laborer Rufus an attempt to organize a revolutionary strike. The author's scene-setting in the early pages, dense, grim, humorous, pathetic, full of subtle personal exchanges and brutal ones, heavy with portents, may be the most brilliantly variegated pages of his entire corpus. The attempt at revolution fails. The apathy and treachery of the villagers and the vigilance of the plantation management are serious impediments, and Rufus' inadequacies are too severe to surmount them.

Many of the lasting characteristics of Clarke's work are apparent in this novel. His humor is sly and, as in most of his works, very effective. Humor is often, in Clarke, a brief and unexpected, not necessarily happy, turn amidst disquieting proceedings. (''Swing low sweet clubbio'' is the author's refrain in a later work as police truncheons sail into black Henry White's body—the beating itself partly the result of a serio-comic misunderstanding.) His humor is also commonly a by-product of his exceptionally subtle observation of interpersonal relations between close acquaintances. In the early pages of *Survivors of the Crossing,* we see a number of examples of the troubling humor Clarke extracts from relationships between ''friends.'' Illiterate Rufus, for example, urgently asks Boysie to read to him a letter from his old political comrade, Jackson. Jackson had left for Canada six months earlier, and Rufus feels certain the letter contains momentous news about the means to a better social order in Barbados. But Rufus has to stand impatiently while Boysie chooses only to read the letter silently to himself and without comment.

Clarke is remarkably skilled also in the creation of simple, uneducated characters, women no less than men. In later novels they retain our attention even when they are not merely poverty-stricken but also often unperceptive, even stupid, and leading very physically confined lives. Clarke's use of the ''Bajan'' (Barbadian) dialect is extensive and effective. His recall of the minutiae of Bajan social detail and rural custom is impressive and, over the body of his work, even dazzling. These alone lend a formidable authenticity to the portrayal of his characters.

In Clarke, unlike in Paule Marshall, we never quite achieve a vivid sense of physical presence in the characters or, for that matter, in the landscapes and artifacts. Its absence is not a major failing, however. . . . Clarke exploits this very characteristic in his writing to achieve a second and distinctive artistic success. This absence notwithstanding, Clarke's characterizations are without doubt very successfully achieved as amalgams of textually evolved and textually elucidated personality, verbal style, and accoutrements. In this first novel, we think easily of Rufus and his fork, Clemmie and her salty religiousness, Mr. Whippetts and his slyness, Biscombe and his cunning and cowardice. But they lack an enriching physiognomic resonance. The rare treatment in Clarke of physical encounters, of combat or lovemaking, may, to some extent, explain this neglect. It also helps to explain how little we miss this quality in his novels.

We learn also from *Survivors of the Crossing* that Austin Clarke is very skilled at developing suspenseful plots and that, indeed, he has a predilection for suspense and mystery. From this penchant for suspense flow several characteristics of his novels, some happy, others undoubted failings. (pp. 10-12)

There is a mild irresolution at the end of the novel, a half-closing of ranks over free drinks as Rufus' fate is sealed. This ambiguity is satisfying, in fact, in this novel. For despite their desperate poverty, the ultimate advantage to the villagers of what Rufus crudely envisioned remains as evident as does the weight—to which they have clearly succumbed over their free liquor—of immediate temptation and opposing power. And although the villagers clearly need a respite, the potential for upheaval is patently too great for present conditions to endure. But as our familiarity with Austin Clarke grows, it is easy to suspect that other considerations, along with his artistic instinct, may have induced him to close the novel on this inconclusive note. Clarke has [a] predilection for tension and unpredictability in his plots and an aversion to imposing special teleological meaning on human events. Usually detectable in his work is an implicit moral condemnation of the rich white world, but no expectation of a righteous chastening of that world is encouraged.

In essence, Clarke's second novel, *Amongst Thistles and Thorns,* is a narrative by nine-year-old Milton Sobers, punctuated by reveries, revealing the state and progress of his life over a few hours in his native corner of Barbados. In Milton's company over these few hours, we are in effect taken on a comprehensive tour of daily semirural life in black Barbados. The fundamental characteristic of that life is a deadly poverty scarcely distinguishable from destitution. A grown man begs a loan of one penny.

The main thread of Milton's narrative is his growing resentment of the quality of life, both at school and at home. In both, a sustained lack of interest, even cruelty, is only rarely interrupted by a passing, sometimes feigned, concern. By the end of the tale, Milton's mother's lack of interest in him becomes fully evident as she endeavors to ensnare an old flame. Milton's distaste for his mother, Ruby, previously unarticulated, grows correspondingly great. Her superstition, empty religious obsessions, cowardice, gullibility, feeble maternal concern, and her responsibility for his father's death disgust him.

As in *Survivors of the Crossing,* much remains unresolved, appropriately unresolved, at the close of the work. Milton's final flight is imminent but to what? And it is unlikely, despite her efforts, that Ruby's uncaring paramour will tarry in her leaky shack beyond the morrow.

We have observed that in Clarke's fiction there is little moral judgment beyond the singular implicit moral condemnation of the rich white world. The observation remains true of this novel, as it is of Clarke's later work, with the exception of *The Prime Minister.* There are few enhancing attributes among the lowly or the victimized, and there is certainly no hint of unfolding purpose, of misfortune justly befalling the rich or powerful. . . . There are no genuine compensations for being poor or black.

By the end of *Amongst Thistles and Thorns,* Clarke's command of the major novelistic skills seen in *Survivors of the Crossing* is confirmed. The distinctive achievement of Clarke's second novel, however, is his special evocation of atmosphere throughout the work. Our fugitive glimpses of the figures and landscape are gained, it seems, through muslin. It is an achievement not entirely absent in some of Clarke's later works, but it is certainly most sustained in this novel. He takes brilliant advantage of what is often, elsewhere in his work, a minor failing, i.e., a lack of physical profile. The half-lit, half-submerged, helpless figures of Ruby and Milton, of Nathan and Willy-Willy, seem to share the texture and color of their landscape, a landscape that is, like them, without much definition or substantiality.

One reason that we see this novel's events in an arresting half-light is that they are filtered through Milton's sensibility. The presence of a highly introspective, imaginational dimension in the character Milton is an extremely creative aspect of the novel. Milton's vivid imagination binds him to Willy-Willy, who, as a favorite storyteller and a sometime brief resident in America, is his spiritual link to Harlem. Harlem has become, because of Willy-Willy's stories, the subject of Milton's chaotic daydreams. . . . Willy-Willy, a parasitic loafer, is somewhat redeemed by his Harlem experience and by Milton's imagination, for his ignominious existence and, finally, death in the village may be interpreted as symbolic of the village's failure—except for Milton—to assimilate from him the liberalistic meanings of the black city in America. Willy-Willy's redemptive significance is teasingly indeterminate, however, for he remains a wastrel, and his treasured memories of Harlem are primarily a wastrel's memories. Nonetheless, both Willy-Willy's central meaning in the novel and his spiritual links to Milton do become in various ways more emphatic in his last hours. This is especially the case when Willy-Willy takes the major step of blowing up the barren house of "the Book"—the village evangelical church.

By the end of the novel, we also begin to detect what may be some sources of concern regarding Clarke's work. Foremost among them is an occasional willingness in this writer to go to the very edge of credibility, usually for no compelling reasons. In this novel, semiliterate or thieving teachers, including a headmaster, reappear, a reappearance that does violence to the reputation of West Indian teachers. And in school-conscious Barbados, adult Willy-Willy regales a nonplussed Milton (who, we recall, is nine years old) with a lengthy exaltation of sexual debauchery: "Come outta [headmaster] Blackman' school, and help me breed the womens in this village. . . ." (pp. 13-16)

The Meeting Point, Storm of Fortune, and ***The Bigger Light*** form a trilogy progressively exploring the lives of a small circle of Barbadian migrants in Toronto. In ***The Meeting Point,*** whose events take place in the mid-1960s, we encounter all the main characters. There are Bernice and Dots, two live-in domestics approaching middle age. There is Estelle, Bernice's younger, more attractive, more intelligent, and self-reliant sister, staying in Bernice's cramped apartment. Boysie is Dots's wayward husband. Henry, unlike the others who together have fewer than ten years in Canada, left Barbados some twenty years ago, but, like Boysie, is apparently now among the permanently unemployed. Henry's girlfriend is Agatha, a wealthy, liberal Jewish graduate student. Bernice's employers are the discordant couple, Sam and Gladys Burrmann. Sam and Estelle carry on a mutually exploitative affair, Estelle seeking Sam's influence to enable her to acquire landed immigrant status.

Although a novel, ***The Meeting Point*** is clearly meant to be a social document as well. It provides us with a substantial tour of black Toronto's haunts and makes lavish use of the real names of many of Toronto's personalities, places, and institutions. Many incidents in the unhappy lives of the characters replicate ones mentioned in Clarke's published views on race relations in the same city in the same years. In addition, many incidences of antiblack racism are simply mentioned in passing by characters in the novel where it would overburden the novel to insert them as ongoing events. We are spared little of the degradation black Toronto is forced to endure even in the bountiful and relatively enlightened midsixties. We witness discrimination, unemployment, scorn, and self-hatred. (pp. 17-18)

The fact of ethnicity is all-pervasive in ***The Meeting Point,*** and it is the first identification both author and reader assign to every character and to every event. The work is also in fundamental respects a political novel in that we are constantly made aware of unequal power relations between racial groups expressing themselves regularly and unequivocally. Yet, ***The Meeting Point*** is much more than a fictionalized political tract or sociograph. For one thing, the characters in the novel are fully aware of the unequal power relations, and this awareness is employed to impart a good deal of added but unspoken tension to human relationships which are already sufficiently freighted with other difficulties. For another, the novel is skillfully constructed and developed, proceeding to a number of simultaneous resolutions, some unexpected and even exciting. The black characters have the ring of authenticity, as does the immigrant experience. Clarke's major achievement in this novel, indeed, may well be his successful depiction of his unpromising main character, Bernice Leach. Bernice is physically unattractive, of small intellectual means, and living a physically highly monotonous and constricted life. But Clarke utilizes the few live, thin elements in her existence, without unconvincing drama or artifice, to construct a character that retains our interest permanently.

Of some interest is the novel's suggestion that a West Indian upbringing is a very slender moral resource among these migrants in a white world, an idea contrary to what we have learned to expect from sociologists and economists like Ira Reid and Thomas Sowell or a creative writer like Paule Marshall. Both Boysie and Henry have apparently suffered total defeat. And Bernice's weapons are puny and even contemptible. They range from crying and vain religiosity to morbid self-delusion about conditions in both Barbados and Toronto.

By the end of ***The Meeting Point*** we begin to wonder whether Clarke's vision may be essentially misanthropic. Except perhaps for Estelle, who is hardly a winning personality but who is commendably calculating, not a single major character in any of his first three novels possesses lasting appeal. Of the likeliest candidates, Agatha and Milton, the former is ultimately too naive. And the life of nine-year-old Milton is largely without engaging qualities of childish innocence, charm, and possibility. His life is too brutalized for that. Moreover, Clarke consciously magnifies our difficulties. On the same page that we hear Milton being told that learning is the only escape from his deadly village existence, we also discover that he is apparently also backward at school. Finally, his flight—undoubtedly into swift adulthood and, despite his dreams of Harlem, quite conceivably into delinquency—is imminent at the close of the novel.

Misanthropy of a limited nature, such as we seem to see in early Clarke, is of course a valid literary perspective, one whose proper test is artistic functionality. In Clarke's first two novels, it is an enhancing perspective, and its insistent hold approaches the disagreeable perhaps only in ***The Meeting Point.*** In his last works, it has clearly ceased to be a ruling passion. Clarke's touching and affectionate portrait of his own grandmother is her declining years, in the memoir ***Growing up Stupid under the Union Jack,*** is a telling example of the change. She is mildly vagrant, dependent (even mendicant), and a trifle un-comprehending, but these aspects of her life are, with her love, all part of the allure of the portrait. (pp. 19-21)

In *The Meeting Point* we encounter again the nagging problem of credibility. Admitting her romantic attachment to "black-ness," it remains difficult to see attractive, very wealthy, highly intelligent, and educated Jewish graduate student, Agatha, a woman of twenty-nine, being in love over a period of years with Henry White. Henry is black, over fifty, long unem-ployed, penniless and without prospects, uneducated, is neither handsome nor especially considerate, is indeed thoroughly feckless. Agatha later marries Henry, cheerfully accepting manifold rejections from friends and family that her liaison with Henry initiated and that her marriage multiplied.

The Meeting Point, although by no means a failure, is not Austin Clarke in the fullness of his powers. It is perhaps too unrelievedly distressing, too much a social document, too much in harness to political and social fact. Noticeably, Clarke's comic gift is a great deal less in evidence, his comic moments less successful, than in his earlier novels or his next.

We follow the lives of these Barbadian immigrants in *Storm of Fortune,* an absorbing sequel where lives evolve and develop with less reference to the claims of the power structure. There is certainly social comment but the social documentation is more relaxed, less consistently emotionally involving. All the same, the major revelation of the novel's closing pages is an unmistakable social insight. We are by now very familiar with how straitening and emotionally exhausting it is to be a live-in domestic. But the liberated feeling, following their departure from domestic service, of Dots and even of Bernice—who is a little self-dependent and who has been quite abruptly dis-missed and been forced to live on her rapidly dwindling sav-ings—is still surprising and is emphatic. The lives of Boysie and Henry remind us equally, however, that black life is lived under siege, even when domestic service is not involved. (pp. 22-3)

As the novel opens, Estelle lies in a hospital ward recuperating from an attempted abortion, the results of her liaison with Sam Burrmann. She is befriended during her few days there by a fellow-convalescee, a white northern Ontario woman, Gloria Macmillan, who invites her home to the town of Timmins to mend her life. Mrs. Macmillan is friendly, down-to-earth, and brilliantly persuasive. After leaving the hospital, she even sends money from her slender purse to Estelle to assist her in coming north. Estelle takes up the offer and travels north at great expense only to discover, by the most astonishing of coinci-dences, that Gloria Macmillan lives at North Bay, a town very far away from Timmins. This Macmillan episode is so bizarre, so much without further consequence in the novel, Gloria Mac-millan so strangely unembarrassed during their accidental en-counter at being revealed as a liar, Estelle so unembittered—she is still pregnant and now very out-of-pocket—that we won-der what Clarke's motive could be in developing it. Mrs. Mac-millan is apparently an otherwise normal personality, but her lying is aggressive, sustained, motiveless, profitless, indeed costly. Grateful as we are for Clarke's brilliant demonstration of his facility with working-class characters, male or female, black or white, and for the entree provided by the Macmillan episode into Estelle's essentially reclusive personality, the reader is left with the feeling that the excursion is pointless. The reader fears that any new coincidences of the magnitude seen in this episode will at once deprive the novel of any further credibility.

It should be said that the excessive autonomy of the Macmillan affair and its ancillary scenes (notably Estelle's eventful jour-ney to North Bay) being conceded, this particular excess rather strangely belies one of *Storm of Fortune*'s main virtues. For in this, the most cinematic of Clarke's immigrant novels, an integrated development of the plot is on the whole very happily combined with an impressive succession of varied and inde-pendently arresting dramatic scenes. Those involving Henry are especially interesting and important: by their dramatic char-acter, by their air of progressive desperation, and by their tranquil capitulation, they impart to the novel an element of tragedy beyond the larger one of black immigrant life in To-ronto. This more closely visible tragedy is an undoubted em-bellishment to the work.

The explanation for the Macmillan cul-de-sac in *Storm of For-tune* is partly, it seems, that Clarke's confidence in his powers is now so great—justifiably great—that he becomes a trifle careless and gratuitous. There are other small signs of these tendencies in the novel. Inconsistencies and improbabilities begin to creep into Clarke's world. Of thematic importance are Boysie's great prosperity in his new janitorial business and his new ambition: they are decidedly unexpected in view of what we have seen of Boysie's personality, but they are, above all, implausibly sudden. So is Henry's devotion to poetry. We have already noticed Agatha's unfathomable marriage to Henry.

We begin to recognize also some features of Clarke's novels as clichés, recognizing also, however, that no prolific novelist will escape clichés. The semiliterate and unbelievable Barba-dian schoolteacher, this time a headmistress, is again present: "'One buns billing!' the headmistress screamed . . . 'One bag o' buns missing! Who thiefed a bag of buns?'" She is remem-bered by Bernice in one of those reveries that we are now familiar with, reveries lightly triggered by events and in which lonely characters frequently converse with themselves. We now know, too, that the unsettling letter or newspaper article is a favorite Clarke device. It is now possible to think, too, that Clarke's relentless pursuit of his characters, to visit them in their bathrooms, even to notice Dots's discarded dirty under-clothing, is not only in the service of realité. It is a technique chosen, it seems, to enable us to feel total familiarity with his characters. It fails. For, as we saw, Clarke's characters do not acquire the physical presence they easily could, considering how effective he commonly is in constructing their personal-ities. Except for very limited descriptions of major female characters, Clarke in fact rarely takes any trouble to leave us with lasting physical images. It may be added, finally, that despite the sunlight of the last few pages of *Storm of Fortune,* the voids, viciousness, and fecklessness we encounter remain numerous. Interestingly, some disconcerting examples come near the close of the novel.

The Bigger Light concludes the trilogy on Bajan immigrant life in Toronto. The focus is now very much on Boysie's and Dots's prosperous household and on Boysie's mental state. Themat-ically, Boysie's mental drift away from and again towards mostly the former West Indians, his wife, Barbados and Bar-badian memories, his difficult early days in Canada, is the novel's core. The techno-structural device to suggest Boysie's faltering grip on his environment, his mental sclerosis and narrowing yet blurred vision, is the *idée fixe,* a tightening cycle of recurrent and essentially trifling thoughts and events. (pp. 24-6)

The Bigger Light obviously differs much from the earlier novels of the trilogy. The social environment is a great deal less oppressive and intrusive. The lessons of Boysie's life and his fading marriage may well suggest the perils of attenuated ethnic links in an isolated community, but they are intelligible also well beyond the imperatives of ethnic and racial conflict. For the first time we have concluded one of Clarke's novels without feeling that most of the major characters are, at one time or other, repulsively vicious, brutish, stupid, or juvenile. Bernice's new employer is excellent. Bernice herself is almost vivacious. Gladys Burrmann is absent and Sam Burrmann is behaving admirably, supporting and welcoming his and Estelle's child. The Boysie of *The Meeting Point* is now unrecognizable.

The resolution of *The Bigger Light* is, as we now expect, not very final and, as we also expect, not quite what Clarke carefully prepares us for. Regrettably, Clarke succeeds in not being predictable at the cost of being anticlimactic. Boysie's impulsive crossing of the American border in his powerful car, instead of dying in the suicidal car crash he appears to be courting, simply does not seem to resolve very much. Clarke's habit in the trilogy of raising people and events to centrality, making them seem to be auguries of major events, then letting them slide into nullity, is finally largely wasteful. It is disappointing even in this novel where typically sterile developments do help to demonstrate Boysie's failing hold on reality. Such are, notably, Boysie's peculiar relationship with his neighbor, Mrs. James, and his hunger for the sight of the mysterious woman trudging to the subway every morning.

The collection of short stories *When He Was Free and Young and He Used to Wear Silks* and the autobiographical memoir *Growing Up Stupid under the Union Jack* display Clarke's familiar skills in heightened form and constitute some of his most brilliant and unblemished work. They are thematically an integral part of the body of work already treated. Some of the short stories are, in fact, with only the minutest changes, passages in the novels. Others, such as the title story, are in part, subtle intimations of themes developed in the novels. And Clarke, in any case, seems to be at pains to emphasize the thematic relationship of his stories to much of the rest of his work: old characters from the novels reappear, or new ones with old names, such as Nathan, Henry, and Lonnie. The observations above notwithstanding, Clarke does on occasion explore minor themes and moods absent or rare in the novels. In Calvin and in Jefferson Theophillis Belle, for example, we encounter single-minded and ferociously hardworking male immigrants, driven, admittedly, by ambitions that we are not permitted to regard as wholly admirable. And the very first tale, "An Easter Carol," the relatively innocent forerunner to the later stories of more complex, usually grimmer, temper, has an almost impishly funny climax. Omitting the title story (where most of the classical attributes of the short story are deliberately forsaken for the more chaotic vigor of twentieth-century consciousness), the collection confirms Austin Clarke's mastery of the traditions of this genre. Economy, control, irony, moral distance from the action, expectancy, surprise, and climax are all enviably present.

In the memoir, it becomes evident that much in Clarke's fiction about Barbados life recalls his own life or that of his neighbors and acquaintances. This memoir, the first volume, we are told, of the author's autobiography, is suspended as Clarke enters the Classical Sixth Form of Barbados' prestigious Harrison College. It is a wide-ranging remembrance of a milieu judiciously viewed through the lens of maturer perception and a remembrance of young "Tom" Clarke's evolving place in it. . . . The memoir is at once literarily felicitous and socially alert.

Growing up Stupid under the Union Jack supports the view, despite the many fine literary moments in his immigrant Toronto, that Clarke's art is surest and subtlest in his treatments of semirural Barbados. The richer dialect, thicker custom, more universal cast, and deeper access to the recesses of life and landscape allow him to weave a tapestry especially dense in atmosphere, action, and nuance. It must immediately be said, nonetheless, that many of the memorable passages and scenes in his Toronto novels and stories have no parallel in his Barbados tales. And it should be added that the Toronto work marries—successfully on the whole and brilliantly in places—artistic ambition and artistic opportunity, which would be unavailable to the self-limiting Bajan storyteller.

The Prime Minister stands apart from the rest of Clarke's corpus. It, too, is heavily autobiographical, the fruit of his two-year stint as General Manager of the Barbados Government's Broadcasting Company, a position from which he was unceremoniously terminated in 1976. Condemned as "vindictive" by some Caribbean critics, *The Prime Minister* was written, as Clarke himself concedes, in the "bitter" days following that experience, written about "real people," he points out. It is a work very uncomplimentary about the official elite. The locale is, of course, Barbados.

As a Caribbean novel, *The Prime Minister* is unusual in several ways. It is a suspense and mystery novel, for one thing—its most uncharacteristic feature—and its action takes place indoors. Its focus is almost exclusively middle-class. The sexual attachments are not designed to have a primary sociological meaning. Finally, it is a novel also of political intrigue in the postcolonial world. Clarke's novel is faithful, nonetheless, to the traditional passion of West Indian novelists for explicit or implicit social commentary. (pp. 27-30)

The novel is replete with social commentary on the new, independent Barbados, pertinent and pointed, rarely flattering, but smoothly integrated. Even the romantic interludes are far more effective, it turns out, in recording the collapse of shade consciousness in John Moore's light-skinned lover than in fulfilling their more technical, novelistic objectives. The reader is left to make the important deduction, crucial to an understanding of modern West Indian history and sociology, that her experiences as a secretary in New York are the probable source of this liberation. For "the woman's" confidences to John Moore are not important and could just as easily have been provided by a maid or a male friend. Their bedroom encounters are not engrossing enough to be more than a makeweight: at best they help to maintain the controlled pace of the novel.

The Prime Minister is a final testimony to Austin Clarke's versatility and assurance as a novelist. The imaginative recall of his own and proximate experience is undoubtedly the sustaining resource in much of his work. But this resource is of unusually great range and is enriched by an outward vision and a genuine artistic, poetic sensibility. It is a final testimony, too, to his place as a West Indian intellectual, able to reflect productively on that region outside its established intellectual conventionalities. (pp. 31-2)

Keith S. Henry, "An Assessment of Austin Clarke, West Indian-Canadian Novelist," in CLA Journal, Vol. XXIX, No. 1, September, 1985, pp. 9-32.

DIANA BRYDON

When Women Rule would more properly be titled "When Money Rules." Clarke's inappropriate title shows the confusion of values that mars these stories. Women rule in none of them, but to men insecure about their manhood in a new northern setting, their women appear to rule because they remind the men of how little control they have over their own lives. In each of these stories, Clarke's men feel their manhood threatened through lack of ownership (of houses, cars, or women) and lash out at the nearest targets—usually women—in self-destructive despair. The melodramatic endings—a murder and two fires—show how all this frustration leads to violence, but also reinforce the reader's feeling that Clarke is not really in control of his material. In a defiance of logic, his narratives, as well as his characters, equate the authority of the grandmother in the Caribbean home with the authority of the law, the job and the school in Canada. A real hatred for women sweeps through these pages, yet the capitalist bureaucracy that dehumanizes all his characters would seem to be the chief object of his criticism. (pp. 160-61)

Diana Brydon, "Cultural Alternatives?" in Canadian Literature, *No. 108, Spring, 1986, pp. 160-62.*

PAUL WILSON

In his heyday . . . Austin Clarke was a true pioneer, one of the few writers around dealing with the life and times of Caribbean immigrants in Toronto. His earlier work crackles with an energy, an inventiveness, and a sly, ironic humour that still reads freshly today. (I recommend **When He Was Free and Young and He Used to Wear Silks**). His characters—mostly Bajans, or Barbadians like himself—were lovable, roguish, marginally honest, upwardly mobile people trapped in a society and a subculture from which they sought, in ways both devious and direct, to escape. (p. 20)

Though it apparently inhabits the same territory, Clarke's new book of nine short stories [*Nine Men Who Laughed*] is to his earlier work as bitter lemon is to sugar cane. His characters are older, more worldly wise, more cynical. His men, most of them from the upper classes of their own societies, tend to have unrealistic and thwarted ambitions. They have got so used to blaming the world for their misfortunes they have lost the power to reflect upon themselves. Several are engaged in elaborate con-games directed against women, and the women themselves are almost invariably seen either as objects of sexual desire, financial advantage and security (Clarke says that the "system" is a woman), or disgust and loathing (they are frequently seen scratching their scars, wiping their eyes and picking their noses). Love is absent, calculation has filled the void, and relationships have dwindled to empty routine. Where Clarke once attacked real problems, like police violence, that have real solutions, he now seems to have given up, and given in to a kind of vague, catch-all condemnation of "the system" that leads to a "what's the use" attitude. And even when his characters do show normal human emotions and perceptions, they still can't behave in significant ways. It is not just that they feel helpless—they actually decline to act. When the female bank teller who narrates one of the stories receives a panic-stricken phone call from a colleague she is desperately trying to befriend, she makes no effort to help, with tragic consequences.

Clarke's literary universe—Toronto seen through Bajan eyes—has apparently undergone a deep and disturbing change. Once a world of magic newness, where wonder combined with pain and laughter, he now shows us a place that is more akin to Graham Greene's noxious portraits of fading Third World capitals. The pain has become chronic, the laughter hollow, and the primary emotions are disgust, hatred, self-loathing. His humour—the title notwithstanding—has soured. And where there was once lilt and lyricism in the speech—a melodic representation of Bajan English—there is now a duller, clunkier, and far less consistent tone.

What has gone wrong? What is at the root of such a fundamental and disturbing change in such a skilled writer? Is it the world that has altered so radically, or has something tainted the inspiration Clarke originally found in the life of the people around him?

Clarke has written an introduction that provides a few clues, some more revealing than others. He says, for instance, that the stories were written "as a means of escaping the physical and mental torment skeined by the prepossessiveness of the new culture," but that could be said of his earlier work too. He also says that the nine men of the title are, metaphorically, himself. That makes more sense, and helps to explain the sensation of being thrust into a series of dark, brooding self-portraits that mirror a state of mind more than any "objective reality." But Clarke obviously intends those metaphors to stand for a reality outside himself, for he says that he wrote the stories "to destroy the definitions that *others* have used to portray so-called immigrants, black people. . . ." (pp. 20-1)

His vision is certainly crueller and less palatable, but is it really clearer? In his earlier work one felt the author's deep love for his characters; now one feels a sense of ennui and impatience, as though they had become less important to him than some message that—as metaphors—they were meant to convey. Somewhere in this "clear vision," Clarke's middle ground has collapsed, leaving only polarized, paralysed extremes. Even the best story in the collection, **"The Smell"** (a gripping and skillfully told tale of incest), is crippled by an abrupt and inconclusive ending, as though the author, having broached the subject, declined to go into it any further.

Clarke is clearly going through a troubled period in his creative life, and it may not be too fanciful to suggest that the author's public position in our society may have something to do with it. As a vice-chairman of the Ontario Censor Board, Clarke has assumed over his fellow citizens a position of power which, I believe, contains the seeds of corruption. In a recent interview with *Now* magazine in Toronto, he had this to say about his work:

> Censorship is not just snipping the films. It is making the decision to state that a scene should not be shown because [it] represents a skewed representation or characterization of a group or a class.

To my mind, Clarke's view of his job goes far beyond his mandate, but in any case, I don't believe a writer should ever have anything to do with censorship, period.

Scissors can be an honourable tool of the writer's trade, but only when they are used to cut and rearrange his own work. Could it be that Clarke's power as an official censor is playing havoc with his power and integrity as a writer? If it were, it would certainly not be the first time in the history of modern literature. After all, suppression and creation are irreconcilable forces, and though they are constantly at war within us all, the illusion that they have nothing to do with each other or, even worse, that they can somehow be made to co-exist peacefully, is dangerous and debilitating. Clarke clearly believes that political censorship is justified, and though he couches his views in the rhetoric of social concern, his attitude is arrogant and elitist. It is also proto-totalitarian. As George Orwell once pointed out, the effect of such an attitude on literature is almost always bad. (p. 21)

Paul Wilson, "Hollow Laughter," in Books in Canada, *Vol. 15, No. 7, October, 1986, pp. 20-1.*

VALERIE WILSON WESLEY

The men and women in [*Nine Men Who Laughed*] are West Indian immigrants in Canada, people without roots who yearn for power and money in a land that denies them both. Their stories are tales of failure, self-deception and impotence; laughter is their weapon against despair. Two of the most successful stories, **"Doing Right"** and **"Canadian Experience,"** examine the pressures, often self-imposed, that haunt black men trying to survive in a white world. **"Doing Right,"** as told by a narrator who laughs "'cause I couldn't do nothing more better than laugh," is a humorous account of the get-rich-quick scheme of an ambitious "green-hornet," the Canadian equivalent of a male meter maid. **"Canadian Experience"** tells of an unemployed bank clerk who is driven to suicide by his paralyzing fear of failure. Unfortunately most of the nine stories in this collection are disappointing. The author offers little insight into why his characters act as they do. . . . Most of the female characters are one-dimensional; the male characters are chauvinistic. And the plots, for the most part, are predictable. Despite these shortcomings, Mr. Clarke . . . offers a glimpse into the lives of immigrants whose experiences are rarely examined. (pp. 16-17)

Valerie Wilson Wesley, in a review of "Nine Men Who Laughed," in The New York Times Book Review, *August 23, 1987, pp. 16-17.*

William Demby

1922-

American novelist, short story writer, translator, scriptwriter, critic, and editor.

An author whose works have earned critical praise but scant popular attention, Demby regards blackness as a facet of human existence that is capable of providing strength and wisdom in an increasingly chaotic world. He views his characters not only within the perspective of the black American experience but in relationship to humanity as a whole. Nancy Y. Hoffman has commented that Demby's characters "are bigger human beings, whole human beings, that the white world—*and the black*—must confront humanistically." Greatly influenced by European modes of thinking, particularly the evolutionary theories of French Catholic philosopher Pierre Teilhard de Chardin, Demby addresses the struggle between good and evil, defining good as the ability to evolve beyond past artistic and social structures toward a transcendent new order, and evil as the tendency to remain stagnant. For Demby's protagonists, their African heritage, Christianity, and love act as catalysts for evolutionary change.

Demby's education at West Virginia State College was interrupted by two years of service in Italy and North Africa with the United States Army during World War II. Following the war, he attended Fisk University, where he served as assistant editor of the *Fisk Herald,* a student magazine to which he also contributed short stories and criticism. After graduating in 1947, Demby returned to Italy to study art at the University of Rome. During the next twenty years, he wrote screenplays for film and television and translated film scripts into English for Italian director Roberto Rossellini.

While residing in Rome, Demby completed his first book, *Beetlecreek* (1950). Described by Edward Margolies as "a novel of defeat and death," *Beetlecreek* portrays Johnny Johnson, a black youth sent to live with his aunt and uncle in the southern backwater community of Beetlecreek. Johnny and his uncle soon befriend Bill Trapp, a white recluse living in the town's black section. Although temporarily able to surmount the prejudices of Beetlecreek through their friendship with Trapp, Johnny and his uncle are ultimately forced into betrayal by the oppressive nature of the community, and the novel concludes when Johnny sets fire to Trapp's house to gain acceptance among a black gang. Although faulted for oversimplification, *Beetlecreek* received predominantly positive reviews for its reversal of the conventional scenario of a black man in a white world, through which Demby transforms racial isolation into a symbol of alienation within American society. While John F. Bayliss asserted that *Beetlecreek* is best viewed as "a human document," several critics defined the novel's theme as existential. According to Robert Bone, *Beetlecreek* moves thematically "toward an existentialist definition of evil" because Johnny and his uncle prove unable to transcend the moral and spiritual vacuum of the town or to resist the negative influences of the racist community and the gang. Demby also drew praise for his realistic style and his cinematic focus on particular objects or actions to convey the hopelessness and stagnation of Beetlecreek.

Demby's second novel, *The Catacombs* (1965), is a self-reflexive work that blends realism and imagination in the story of fictional author Bill Demby and his sexual and spiritual relationship with Doris, a black dancer who becomes pregnant after an affair with an Italian count. Demby often interjects his authorial persona into this novel, commenting on its structure and progress or interweaving news items concerning national crises as well as personal incidents derived from letters and diaries. Reviewers were initially bewildered by *The Catacombs,* and some lamented Demby's departure from the more traditional narrative form of *Beetlecreek.* Later commentators, however, have contended that Demby is successful in his stylistic experimentation and have placed his novel in the modernist tradition exemplified by James Joyce's *Ulysses.* Often maintaining that Demby's treatment of the circular and parallel nature of time is derived from cubist models, critics have also noted such influences as modern art, contemporary scientific and social theory, and the cinematic experiments of such Italian film directors as Federico Fellini, Roberto Rossellini, and Michelangelo Antonioni.

Demby's third novel, *Love Story Black* (1978), has been alternately regarded as an examination of the redemptive power of the archetypal black woman and a latent critique of black feminism. In this book, a middle-aged professor pursues relationships with several women, including Mona Pariss, an aging singer whom he interviews for a black journal. Although a virgin, Mona introduces the professor to a simultaneously sexual and spiritual love as she intertwines the development of their relationship with the story of her unrequited past desires. While largely ignored by critics, some of whom contended that the novel lacks the thematic and structural intricacies of Demby's earlier work, *Love Story Black* garnered praise for its uncommon evocation of the innocent, Edenic quality of love. Addison Gayle commented: ''For Camus's doctrine, 'I rebel, therefore I am,' Demby would proclaim I love, therefore I am, thus raising the existential equation beyond romanticism to touch the most profound longings and utterings of the human soul.''

(See also *Contemporary Authors*, Vols. 81-84 and *Dictionary of Literary Biography*, Vol. 33.)

ERNEST JONES

Except that it is not deliberately complex and probing, *Beetlecreek* brings to mind Carson McCullers's *The Heart Is a Lonely Hunter*; for it is about the barriers—only temporarily surmountable—which separate human beings. The immediate foreground is the Negro quarter of a small town in West Virginia. The central figures are an old and half-crazed white man, a hermit tempted to give himself ''the right and power to reach out and touch people, to love,'' and a sensitive and imaginative adolescent Negro boy, the immediate cause of the temptation. The action the hermit takes, after a propitious beginning, is disastrous. The innocence of his feeling for the boy—he seeks a son as the boy a father—is beautifully conveyed. But to the Negro suburb he rapidly becomes a ''sex-fiend.'' Ultimately, in a fit of hysteria, the boy kills him, demonstrating Mr. Demby's gloomy views on the racial problem and the universal impossibility of any lasting communication between two human beings.

I like this novel very much, though it has an entirely predictable and banal ending. Unlike Langston Hughes and Richard Wright and William Gardiner Smith, Mr. Demby has avoided the inevitable pitfalls which beset the American Negro who writes out of his own experience. His book is only in a secondary sense about ''the Negro problem''; it is no *roman à thèse*, except for the general gloomy view about *all* human relationships. To put it very tritely, he is interested in his characters first as human beings and then as black or white. For all his painful awareness of what it means to be a Negro in a small Southern town, he never merely exploits his subject. (pp. 138-39)

[Demby's use of] the individual scene [is] perfect in itself and often informative in ways not strictly related to the purpose of his fiction, but fitting also into the general pattern. The self-betrayal of the boy, who turns on the old man so that he may be accepted by a peculiarly unpleasant gang of teen-agers, is wonderfully realized. The double treachery, to friend and to self, which is one of the more distressing phenomena of adolescence, is especially harrowing in a Negro society in which, as Mr. Demby sees it, the need to be identified with a group is even stronger than among whites. Mr. Demby displays, I might add, a passionate contempt for those institutions of Southern Negro life which minister to this need, for the church and the Ladies' Aid, the gang and the barbershop. Human folly, black and white, as well as the economic system, is the

villain of this piece—an unusual and, some will think, an inexcusable lapse in judgment on the part of a Negro writer. (p. 139)

> *Ernest Jones, in a review of ''Beetlecreek,'' in* The Nation, *New York, Vol. 170, No. 6, February 11, 1950, pp. 138-39.*

AUGUST DERLETH

Novels about Negroes in white communities are legion, but in *Beetlecreek* young novelist William Demby turns the tables. This one is about Bill Trapp, a lonely old white man who lived in the midst of a colored community.

Mr. Demby constructs his story along the parallel lines so often discovered in tales of colored people in white communities. Actually a lonely, misunderstood old fellow, perfectly content to live his life out in the shanty in Beetlecreek, Bill Trapp excites the suspicions and distrust of the neighbors when he attempts a kindness. Making his first break from the shell of isolation in which he had lived for 15 years, Trapp gives a little picnic for a group of children, white and black. Harmless as it is, one of the girls peddles a tale of molestation, which the community picks up and exaggerates, precisely in the manner of any community, regardless of color.

Crossing the story of Bill Trapp are the accounts of young Johnny Johnson, a colored boy visiting in Beetlecreek from Pittsburgh, and of his uncle, David Diggs, who takes the opportunity a local death affords him to run away from his family and his town with the prodigal wench briefly home for her mother's funeral. That Johnny Johnson, the first person whom Bill Trapp befriended, should be the instrument of the destruction of Trapp's home and of the assault upon Trapp, is Mr. Demby's chosen irony. . . .

[Summed up], *Beetlecreek* is a comparatively simple cross-section of life in a Negro community complicated a little by the presence of the lone white man in its midst. It is skilfully done. Mr. Demby is by no means heavyhanded, nor does he belabor scenes or characterizations; his people are credible, their actions likewise, and his story has evenness of pace, whatever it may lack in significance and depth.

As a first novel, *Beetlecreek* offers something different in its situation; competently and well done, it may give many readers pause to reflect that people are fundamentally very much alike, regardless of color, which is a basic truth far too many people need to learn.

> *August Derleth, ''This Racial Novel Turns the Tables,'' in* Chicago Tribune, *February 12, 1950, p. 4.*

HORACE CAYTON

[In *Beetlecreek*], Bill Trapp, a white man, lives in the midst of the Negro section of a rural Southern town. He is a frightened man. He lives alone and no one has visited him in fifteen years. Through a coincidence he meets Johnnie, a Negro from Pittsburgh, who acquaints him with Negro people. There among the rejected, Trapp finds warmth and understanding—a discovery that gives the author his opening situation in this unusual novel. . . .

The fault of this book is that it does not hang together; it lacks a central focus. Yet William Demby, a young Negro writer, has succeeded in this, his first novel, in illustrating the sufferings of both Negroes and whites under the present system of race relations. His sensitivity and fine poetic style mark him as a writer of promise. ***Beetlecreek*** is worth reading for those who want to know more about Negro-white relationships in the back-country Southern town.

Horace Cayton, "Defeated Lives," in The New York Times Book Review, *February 26, 1950, p. 4.*

EDMUND FULLER

Beetlecreek is the name given a small Negro community hung on the flank of a larger white town in a region not precisely identified but which might be West Virginia. But if you think this is the wind-up for presenting another routine race novel you are mistaken. A story possessing a unique and original flavor of its own is offered us by William Demby, a new writer of distinct ability and quality. [*Beetlecreek*] succeeds remarkably well with certain delicate and difficult relationships, barely skirting sentimentality—the kind of thing Saroyan and Steinbeck sometimes have mangled horribly. But it has strength and range beyond this single aspect, as well.

By one of those unexpected but possible miracles of human change, old Bill Trapp, the white hermit who has lived in isolation in the midst of Beetlecreek for fifteen years, chips his shell and emerges into human warmth. His emergence is most heartwarming and amusing.

But human nature is such that sometimes a man's change for the better crystallizes suspicions and animosities in others that had lain dormant while the familiar pattern remained. . . . Perhaps, then, it was only a matter of time, inevitably, before the web is spun around poor old Bill Trapp much the way the skein of malice was woven in Lillian Hellman's *The Children's Hour.* And this is the core of the book.

Bill Trapp is vividly realized, deeply conceived. There is fine work in the tracing of his lonely life, his carnival wanderings. There are a few moments, now and then, when Mr. Demby gets sloppy with him, but these are relatively unimportant in so generally excellent a characterization.

But the richness in the book's people is scarcely tapped. Among the Negroes are several unusual studies. The boy, Johnny Johnson, who shares the center of the stage with old Trapp, is created with beauty and understanding. One cannot forget quickly the recoil of his gentle and ethically sensitive nature from the cruelties and juvenile obscenities of the Gang. It is terrible to see this nature—yielding to the fear of not "belonging"—succumb to their destructive vitality as the story mounts to its appalling climax.

David Diggs, Johnny's uncle, is another complex portrait, in his frustrating, tortured link with his wife, Mary. Altogether, there are a host of well-realized personalities. . . .

At the end I feel that Mr. Demby, to some extent, has shirked his obligation to the reader, ducked out on his denouement at the critical moment, avoided showdowns which, if faced, might have magnified the book's stature immensely. This, however, is opinion. There exists a school to defend his choice. As it stands, it is a book of interesting and original qualities.

Edmund Fuller, "Hermit with Blacks," in The Saturday Review of Literature, *Vol. XXXIII, No. 9, March 4, 1950, p. 17.*

MAGGIE RENNERT

Reviewing this non-novel [*The Catacombs*] is as melancholy and fruitless a proceeding as writing a report on a miscarriage.

And that's my last respectable English sentence, too, unless I commit one absent-mindedly. "Cinematic style" is what Mr. Demby uses, and it sounds like strung-together notes. All those flowing thoughts are fun and easy, and I want to play too. . . .

[*The Catacombs*] has an air of literary cafe society that makes me wrinkle my nose, especially when two characters tell each other, apropos of nothing much, that Jimmy Baldwin is coming to Rome—which is where they are. . . . Worse still is the fate of Elizabeth Taylor, who gets dragged into the jacket copy by way of Doris, a fictional character. This Doris is supposed to be working in the movie *Cleopatra* but what we're interested in is not her work, actually, but the people she sleeps with. Who are an Italian count (fictional, I think) and Bill Demby, who quizzes her about what goes on, with the count on behalf of the new book he's writing about her, which exists in snatches within the book we're reading—in which he goes around discussing the plot with his wife. . . . Despite this comfy mixture of real wife and imaginary mistress, poor Doris looks rather kissed and told on. . . .

William Demby, the one on the cover of the book, not the lover of Doris, wrote a novel [*Beetlecreek*] admired by some of my respected colleagues—that is, other book reviewers. . . . Though I didn't read it, I can see traces of what they must have found, still discernible in the welter of newspaper clippings and desultory ruminations on Being an Intellectual and Being a Negro and most of all Being a Writer. Maybe Demby's agent . . . ought to start a fund to float talented novelists who are in a slump so that they won't try to hit up the public for the privilege of reading loose leaves from their notebooks. Because, Maggie Rennert said to Bill Demby, if your talent isn't good enough to overcome your ennui, why the hell should you expect it to overcome mine?

Maggie Rennert, "Write One, Splice Two," in Book Week—New York Herald Tribune, *June 27, 1965, p. 22.*

PETER BUITENHUIS

There really are limits, I think, to the form of the novel. It can take almost everything, and repeatedly does. One seems to see it coming out of its corner, a battered fighter, scarred by many grim battles with thousands of novelists, yet squaring once more gamely to the fight. William Demby, in his second book, seems to have knocked it out. To put it more fairly, he wasn't writing in the same class.

The Catacombs should be labeled not as a novel but as an autobiography or pastiche or rag-bag, according to the amount of one's tolerance, for surely a novel has to have a guiding principle, or central idea, or at least an attitude. "When I began this novel," writes Mr. Demby, half-way through,

> I secretly decided that though I would exercise a strict selection of the facts to write down, be they 'fictional' facts or 'true' facts taken from newspapers or directly observed events from my own life, once I had written something down I would neither edit nor censor it [myself]. . . . Novels, in theory anyway, are supposed to be slices of life, slices of plum cake. So once the cook has created and stirred up the mixture he has no moral right or obligation to censor, or

select: all the cook-writer can do is taste and smell and say 'Yum-yum' or 'This stinks!'

Well, of course, the novel precisely *isn't* a plumcake. . . . This is why I have to say, regretfully, dishwasher-critic that I am, that most of this book, to use Mr. Demby's own term, "stinks."

He can write extremely well. The first few pages of *The Catacombs,* in which he describes a sexual encounter between Doris, a Negro actress working in Rome, and an Italian count, is first-rate and promises well. But as I continued, I had to check the blurb to find out what the novel was supposed to be about. (By the way, that's an ingenious piece of expositional writing. Full marks. Its relationship to the contents of *The Catacombs,* however, is problematical.)

Bill Demby, as he refers to himself in the narrative, is supposedly writing this novel about Doris. She resents his continual prying and apparently aimless snooping. One can't blame her for that. It must have been very irritating for her to have had this writer hanging around. Doris surely wouldn't have minded if Demby had gone at the job systematically, casting her in a starring role, with looks, passions and ideas all portrayed, like a black Emma Bovary. But she is always getting pushed to one side to make room for newspaper cuttings and random, stream-of-consciousness remarks. (pp. 4, 32)

Impatience sets in for his reader as much as it does for poor Doris. Mrs. Demby's life has apparently supplied him with interesting material for a novel. He is a Negro writer who has lived for some time in Rome and other European cities. He is clearly sensitive to history and his own place in it. But all issues, great and small, all characters, dull and exciting, get mixed into this unleavened cake of a book until they lose identity and meaning.

It's the book that William Demby, with his considerable talent, could have written that one yearns for. With this one, with its shadowy zombies walking through above-ground catacombs, one simply yawns over. (p. 32)

> Peter Buitenhuis, *"Doris Is Always Getting Pushed Aside," in* The New York Times Book Review, *July 11, 1965, pp. 4, 32.*

ROBERT BONE

[*Beetlecreek*] is an existentialist novel whose central characters come momentarily to life, only to return in the end to somnambulance. It is, moreover, an expatriate novel, whose tone is dominated by pessimism and disgust, flowing from a robust rejection of American culture and of Negro life in particular. Viewed psychologically, it is a novel of cramped desire, considerably illuminated by a knowledge of the author's personal history.

William Demby grew up in Clarksburg, West Virginia, in the heart of the mining region which provides the setting for his novel. His education at West Virginia State College for Negroes was interrupted by two years with the American Army in Italy, where he wrote for *Stars and Stripes*. With the help of the GI Bill he completed his undergraduate career at Fisk (Class of '47). Interested in painting as well as literature, he returned to Italy to study art at the University of Rome, where he has remained to write screen plays for Roberto Rossellini. From Clarksburg to Rome is a good many spiritual miles, and this distance is primarily responsible for the tone of *Beetlecreek*.

At Fisk, Demby wrote short stories for a creative writing class, some of which saw print in the *Fisk Herald*, the official student publication. (p. 191)

One of his undergraduate stories, which appeared in the *Fisk Herald* of December 1946, contains the germinal idea of *Beetlecreek*. The story, entitled **"Saint Joey,"** is strongly antifascist in intent. It concerns a white teen-age gang led by a young religious fanatic, which is suggestive in its attitudes and activities of the Ku Klux Klan or the Christian Front. In vigilante fashion the gang decides to murder an old recluse who has violated the racial mores of the community. Much transformed (for example, the gang becomes colored), this material provides the main action of the novel.

At its narrative core, *Beetlecreek* is the story of Bill Trapp, an eccentric old white man whose belted attempt to reach out to his neighbors is doomed in advance by the town's instinct for death. . . . As the novel opens, he terminates fifteen years of silence and solitude by an act of will, thereby displaying the celebrated "courage to be" of French existentialism.

His first awkward contact is with Johnny, a young colored boy whom he catches in his apple orchard, and with Johnny's uncle David, with whom he drinks beer in the local Negro tavern. . . . [Later, Trapp] is unjustly accused of sexual molestation, whereupon he becomes the scapegoat for all of the town's frustrations and animosities. It is Johnny's gang which vindicates the honor of the colored community through a wanton act of arson and murder. To this martyrdom there are distinct religious overtones, for Bill Trapp is variously compared to a biblical shepherd, a saint, and Christ himself. He represents the positive values of kindliness, sympathy, compassion, and love.

Against Bill Trapp's rather ineffectual strivings toward life, Demby sets the deathliness of Beetlecreek. It is conveyed dramatically through the barbershop crowd (narrowness and defeatism), the funeral scene (shallowness and hypocrisy), the persecution of Bill Trapp (cruelty), and above all the church festival, with its petty money-grubbing in the service of a venal clergy. It is conveyed symbolically, too, as the town is compared to a coffin or a hearse. . . . Nor does Demby neglect the socio-economic dimension which has made Beetlecreek a kind of death trap. Mined out long ago, what remains is a ghost town where Negro life in particular is even more circumscribed than usual. As a symbol, then, Beetlecreek represents life without fulfillment. Beetlecreek is a place where life crawls, with a kind of insectile loathsomeness.

The dramatic conflict of the novel develops not around Bill Trapp but around Johnny and David, or more precisely around David, for Johnny is essentially an echo. Through their relations with Bill Trapp, both are brought to the brink of a decision; each evades his responsibility at the crucial moment, choosing the way of death rather than of life. David, one suspects, is Demby's other self, who chose not to be.

David is a frustrated artist, trapped in the deadly backwater of Beetlecreek by circumstances which he regards as inevitable. . . . A summer romance, a pregnancy, and a hasty marriage have trapped him in Beetlecreek. Here he has stagnated, until the advent of Bill Trapp, and of Edith.

Edith is a college sweetheart, who has returned to Beetlecreek for her guardian's funeral. Symbolically, the touch of death is upon her; though she has fled from Beetlecreek, hers is a big-city deadness. David, in his weakness and cowardice, is attracted to her strength and defiance: "But most of all he liked the daredevil in her.'' In a pathetic ''daredevil'' gesture he decides to run off with her for a week, seeking at least a furlough from the spiritual death of the town. But Edith is not the path to life; she represents his dream of the past rather than a positive commitment to the present. It is his relationship to Bill Trapp which demands of David a genuine act of moral courage.

David's basic philosophical error lies in his conviction that ''There was no way, really, that he could shape himself.'' At the climax of the novel, therefore, when Bill Trapp becomes the victim of mass hysteria, he simply drifts, acquiescing in the poisonous prejudice of Beetlecreek. Intimidated by the jeers of the barbershop crowd, he refuses to defend his friend. In the clutch, David lacks the courage to be. . . . This is the meaning of David's symbolic choice between Bill Trapp and Edith: in the face of the terrifying responsibility of freedom, he capitulates; in the face of the urgent decisions of his ''now-life,'' he retreats to the dead past.

Like David, Johnny is alone and afraid, restless and ashamed, and in desperate quest of his own identity. Man and boy share a spiritual state which is, in the existentialist view, the natural condition of man. . . . [Johnny] is a strange boy in a new town, wanting above all to be accepted, to belong. His feelings of alienation draw him first to Bill Trapp, another outcast, and then to the gang.

In Demby's portrait of the gang, the political overtones of the original story persist, and perhaps they intrude to a degree upon his larger thematic concerns. The Nightriders, with their initiation ceremonies and their black robes, with their nameless Leader, brutal and sadistic, offer to Johnny a fascist extreme of ''other-direction.'' Here is strength in which his weakness can seek refuge. It is thus that Johnny, who was the instrument of Bill Trapp's awakening, becomes the instrument of his death. He is compelled by the force of events to choose between Bill Trapp and membership in the gang, and from this decision the denouement of the novel flows. (pp. 192-95)

Thematically the novel has been moving toward an existentialist definition of evil; if no other confirmation of his existence is possible, man will attempt to assert himself in negative and destructive ways. It is so with Bill Trapp, who even as a child preferred to be tormented than ignored; it is true of the townspeople, who find in their malicious persecution of Bill Trapp relief from their empty lives. It is true above all of David and Johnny, who suffer their creative powers to be perverted, rather than endure a spiritual vacuum. Edith and the gang bring movement and excitement into their lives, but it is movement without direction, without purpose, without meaning. The question from which all of Demby's characters shrink is ''What do I want of life?'' In the absence of positive goals their attempts to assert themselves lead to their own destruction.

In an exposition of theme, style should not be slighted, especially when the two are closely entwined. Demby writes well, and in a functional, not merely decorative, sense. His style is appropriately realistic, for existentialism is nothing if not tough-minded. But literary realism is only a point of departure: ''Hair began growing on his soul,'' Demby writes of Bill Trapp's retirement. It is realism transformed by an active imagination in pursuit of higher ends. Demby has a good eye for the image, and this visual quality enriches his descriptive passages: ''In the yard, the shadows under the trees were like jigsaw puzzles suddenly broken.'' But beyond their descriptive

content, such passages may point toward the larger meaning of the novel. . . . (p. 195)

Recurrent images assume symbolic value and are used extensively to buttress the theme. The frantic, swooping birds, for example, provide an objective correlative to David's and Johnny's feelings of restlessness and dissatisfaction. The mirrors (each of the main characters studies himself in a mirror) underscore the problem of identity, while the swinging bridge [on which Johnny often sits] suggests the social separation between colored and white in Beetlecreek. The season in which the action takes place (Indian summer) is converted into a particularly rich symbol. On one level, it helps to dramatize the necessity of choice, of decision. . . . On another, it suggests that the crucial decisions faced by Bill Trapp, David, and Johnny represent their last chance for life.

In the last analysis, Demby handles race symbolically, too. It is in part a question of ''realism,'' of rooting his characters in a recognizable social milieu. But on a deeper level he succeeds in transforming race into a universal symbol. Throughout the novel his readers experience racism chiefly on the rebound, through the antiwhite sentiments of Negro characters. It is a white man, for example, who becomes the victim of a colored ''mob.'' Yet at the same time Bill Trapp is *identified* with the Negro. . . . Man is an exile, an outcast in a hostile universe. The recluse and the Negro become in this view only special instances of man's estrangement from his world and from himself. (pp. 195-96)

> Robert Bone, ''The Contemporary Negro Novel,'' in his The Negro Novel in America, *revised edition,* Yale University Press, 1965, pp. 173-212.

EDWARD MARGOLIES

[It is a] paradox that the more estranged the black intellectual [is] politically, the more a growing number of his literary works appear to be falling into the main mood of American writing. Marcus Klein, in an excellent study of mid-century American novelists (*After Alienation,* 1962), calls this mood ''accommodation''; that is, despite a feeling of impending apocalypse, the omnipresence of evil, the hopelessness of human nature and human society, there persists in American letters a sense of ''the possibility of human community.'' Klein places James Baldwin and Ralph Ellison among exemplars of this mood but one might today cite other less well-known Negro authors for whom accommodation means as well an acceptance of their blackness, not simply as a stigma to be borne in a racist society, but as a source of strength and composure in a world gone awry. (p. 251)

Without question the best example of the new ''accommodation'' is a scarcely noticed novel that appeared in 1965, *The Catacombs,* by William Demby. Significantly, Demby makes scant use of any American background, the novel being set for the most part in Rome. . . . *The Catacombs* deals with a novelist, Bill Demby, who is writing a novel about a love affair between an Italian count and an American Negro girl who is working in Rome as an extra in the shooting of the film ''Cleopatra.'' In effect, Doris and the Count who are truly fictional (real life and imaginary characters stalk in and out of Demby's novel) assume allegorical importance in Demby's mind as Life and Death figures. Doris, luxuriantly sensual, who possesses a terrific inner vitality (and a faintly world weary cynical exterior) is capable of love, growth and martyrdom. In the course of the novel Demby identifies these as being both African and

Christian attributes. The Count, conversely, possesses all the accomplishments, the polish, the veneer and sophistication of a once vital European civilization whose soul has atrophied. He is afraid to give himself entirely to Doris. There is something cold and inert about him. Demby tends to identify these qualities as Caucasian. . . . Ultimately Demby determines to return to America. He is not deluded that the air of violence he feels everywhere about him in Europe is any the less present in America, but he has recovered (presumably through his imagined Doris) his African life force. He has projected for himself a vision of life at once both Christian and African that will enable him to survive.

The bare sketch scarcely does justice to this novel. Demby's language is brilliantly visual and his rhythms haunting. And the very structure of the novel is beautifully interwoven with an imagery and a narrative line that shuttle back and forth in real and imagined time, suggesting an ever shifting battle of Good and Evil, an eternal cycle of Death and Resurrection. That Demby manages to convey these as existing within the mind of his narrator as well as in the external world is part of his achievement.

Although Demby's theme is less sensational than some of the shriller expressions of négritude, he may be more representative of a newer generation of authors than is generally supposed. Which is not to say that his style or methods have influenced others—it is most probable that his novel is unknown—but that his tone, a kind of contained passion, extending beyond anger, implying a deep racial wisdom, is something he shares with the younger writers. It is almost an underground "cool" in these days of "soul" and funky jazz and emotional wear-it-on-your-lapel black letters. If James Baldwin and Leroi Jones shriek at us that black knows best, we cannot quite believe them because we hear the hysteria behind the printed word, but the new authors are credible almost because they do not care whether we listen. They relate in one way or another the stages through which they have had to pass—despair, self-doubt, humiliation, suffering and an awakened knowledge of the sickness of white society—to arrive at their peculiar black sophistication. (pp. 251-53)

> *Edward Margolies, in a review of "The Cata-*
> *combs," in* American Quarterly, *Vol. XX, No. 2,*
> *Summer, 1968, pp. 251-53.*

EDWARD MARGOLIES

Since the 1920's, a considerable number of Negro authors have gone abroad to live and work. Some have returned, dissatisfied and weary at what they have found. But a surprising hard core have remained overseas, determined, in one way or another, to fashion a better life for themselves. As Negroes, they say, they are made constantly aware of their status in America, and race consciousness cannot help but influence the character of their work. Here, then, they write as Negroes first and artists second; hopefully, in a "raceless" milieu they might avoid such difficulties.

Unfortunately, in the vast majority of cases, they do not succeed. (p. 173)

One remarkable exception is the novelist William Demby. Demby's works [*Beetlecreek* and *The Catacombs*] reveal a thoroughly unself-conscious immersion in European modes of thinking, conditioned by a profoundly American outlook. He is, like his literary ancestors, Melville and Hawthorne, ob-

sessed with the problem of evil, but he expresses his concerns in philosophical terms akin to Christian existentialism. He has appropriated techniques ranging from Joycean stream of consciousness to modern cinematography, and incorporated these as instruments of his philosophical quest. (p. 174)

[Biographical] data can scarcely provide any major insights into Demby's creative psychology. What does become apparent, however, are the obvious extremes of his experiences. He was brought up in the relatively confining atmosphere of the Negro ghettos of Pittsburgh and a West Virginia mining town. Even as a college student, he attended all-Negro institutions. As an adult, on the other hand, living a cosmopolitan life among film directors, writers, artists, and the like, his life assumes an altogether different character. These opposing patterns are reflected in his work, where they are pitted against one another as the central conflict of his novels.

In a very real sense the drama in Demby's works revolves around an ever-shifting battle between Life and Death. Death, or evil, is equated with the static, the inert, the stultifying qualities of existence—and judging from the allusions in his works to his American years, one would gather Demby regards this period as having been deadly and constraining. Life, for its part, implies creative evolutionary energies, love and reason. These, presumably, Demby discovered in the European phases of his career.

Although its setting is a small Negro community in a forsaken Depression mining town in West Virginia, Demby wrote *Beetlecreek* in Italy and published the novel three years after leaving Fisk. The novel is related in the third person from the point of view of four characters, each of whom is struggling to extricate himself from the death grip the community symbolizes. The story deals primarily with Johnny Johnson. . . . Johnny, feeling lonely and unloved, befriends a white hermit named Bill Trapp, who lives on a ramshackle farm on the edge of Beetlecreek. (pp. 175-76)

Bill is an enigmatic creature, whose presence in Beetlecreek has seldom disturbed the general torpor of the community. But after fifteen years of self-imposed silence, he determines to communicate and love the world, mainly through Johnny. . . . Alternately imagined in Johnny's dreams and fantasies as a saint and a shepherd, he becomes something of a martyr when Johnny, succumbing to the deathlike atmosphere of Beetlecreek, turns on him and attempts to burn down his house.

Interwoven with Johnny's relationship to Bill are accounts of David and Mary Diggs. David, Johnny's uncle, represents a somewhat older version of his nephew. He, too, as the novel opens, feels alienated and alone, but has come to accept the passive drift of his life. He is awakened momentarily by his friendship with Bill, whom he has met through Johnny. But when an old college sweetheart returns to town to attend a funeral, David forsakes Bill and decides to run away with her. In so doing, David pursues an illusion. Edith is a death figure, having been hardened and corrupted in the big-city Negro ghettos.

Mary, David's wife, is the least defined of Demby's characters. Her vitality has been drained by a loveless marriage and the stifling environment of Beetlecreek; her principal spiritual resources are the odd tidbits of gossip she gathers in the kitchen of the white folks she works for, and a driving ambition to become president of the Woman's Missionary Guild of her local church. Ironically, though, her success in gaining the latter is attended by the desertion of her husband and the murderous arson of her nephew, Johnny.

Thus *Beetlecreek* is a novel of defeat and death. Beetlecreek is itself a metaphor of death, a dreary and sluggish town whose inhabitants have lost all desire for change or hope for improved circumstances. Even its name suggests an arrested form of the evolutionary processes. (pp. 176-77)

Demby employs a kind of stark, refined realism to seize his effects—not unlike some film directors who focus on seemingly prosaic objects in order to register a meaning that might otherwise be overlooked. Johnny, standing on the swinging bridge that spans the creek, observes, in the course of a conversation with some of the gang members, "a hole in the bottom plank of the bridge and in it was a waxy beetle struggling to get off its back." Demby depends more on closely realized visual elements than most novelists. The physical atmosphere of Beetlecreek informs the moral and spiritual dilemma of Demby's characters as much as anything they say or do. Thus Demby will focus on the light that falls over the town at certain hours of the day, or the wind-swept leaves and candy wrappers as they scatter along an empty street, or the freakishly warm weather of an Indian summer night. (p. 177)

Sometimes these images will become more obvious, as when Nature appears to suggest portents that hover ominously beyond the horizon. Indian summer weather lingers on well into autumn, out-of-season earthworms surface to the ground, birds swoop around the roofs and chimneys of houses as if "undecided what to do"—just as, in a fashion, Johnny and David remain suspended in moral indecision regarding what actions they will take concerning Bill Trapp, whether indeed they will save or betray him.

On an even more specific level, Demby will set a critical scene in a junk yard or cemetery, or he will describe a hearse as "shiny and low-slung like a super enameled beetle," or Bill Trapp's fingers "moving back and forth slowly like the antennae of insects." But these literal images are only part of the effect. The impact of the novel lies generally in the contrast between the vaguely looming violence that hangs over the town and the callowness of the townsfolk, the triteness of their talk, the superficiality of their behavior, the narrowness of their vision. In effect, Demby is saying that by the inert and passive qualities of their lives, they have chosen (by not choosing) evil for good, death for life, as revealed by the very essence of the physical atmosphere that engulfs them.

The images convey far more of the message of the novel than the dialogue. The sentences the characters utter are tired, flat and prosaic—as if the very act of expression were a spiritually exhausting experience. What the reader remembers best are scenes where scarcely any words are spoken. . . . Demby shifts his scenes back and forth dramatically among his characters, viewing them, analyzing them at simultaneous moments wherever they may be. (pp. 178-79)

Although *Beetlecreek* is by no means a "Negro novel" in any provincial sense, its existential themes are particularly applicable to the Negro experience. The stifling and frequently destructive atmosphere of the ghetto has been portrayed many times by Negro authors, but here it is shown more as a kind of human condition than as a symptom of a specific social dysfunction. Moreover, such an atmosphere must intensify those universal existential feelings of dread and despair and terror that sociologists relate as being particularly prevalent among Negro slum dwellers. Demby himself recognizes as much when

he represents David's thoughts of "how Negro life was a fishnet, a mosquito net, lace, wrapped round and round, each thread a pain. . . ." The nice little paradox of Demby's novel, however, is that this view of Negro life is not particularly Negro. The white man, Bill Trapp (the name is significant), is as much a Negro as the others—a pariah, an outcast, all his life he has known shame and fear and self-contempt. And the circle becomes complete when the Negro community persecutes him *because he is a white man*. Thus Negro life in all its deathly aspects is the mirror image of white society. (p. 179)

Demby's second book, *The Catacombs,* published fifteen years later, is about a novelist named William Demby living in Rome, who is writing a novel about a Negro girl named Doris. . . . Demby has introduced her to an Italian count with whom she proceeds to have an affair for the next two years. Doris sees Bill frequently and gives an account of herself which Demby will presumably incorporate in the novel.

In the course of her affair with the Count (who is married but living apart from his wife), she takes Bill as an occasional lover. . . . [At] one juncture in the novel, she does not know whether Bill or the Count is the father of the baby to whom she is about to give birth. Doris determines the child is the Count's, but the baby is born dead. . . . [Finally, Demby] prepares to leave for New York, where he has been offered a position in an advertising agency. In the final passages of the book, the Count has taken Doris on a tour through the Catacombs, Rome's ancient cemetery for Christian martyrs. He loses her in the gloom, and as he pursues her along the maze of cold, dark corridors, calling out her name, the novel abruptly ends.

For Demby, plot in the conventional sense is an artifice that conceals the realities he endeavors to express. The fortunes of no one person can be isolated from any other's—indeed, all of existence, animate and inanimate, bears on the essential realities of the individual portrayed; hence any attempt to project the true life of a character in a novel must attempt to project at the same time the multifaceted elements of existence that constitute that life. (pp. 179-80)

Demby construes time-existence as being cyclic—as revealed in the cycle of the seasons, as expressed in the death and resurrection of Christ on the Christian calendar, as imagined in the periodic eclipses of the sun, and as symbolized by the two-headed god Janus whose month January looks both backward on death (winter) and forward to renewed life (spring, Easter).

In order to reinforce what Demby . . . describes as "illusory motion, the dreamlike sense of progression and progress," images, events, colors, puns, patterns of speech, dreams, and mythological, literary, and historical allusions reappear in startlingly different contexts, as the characters proceed along their way—themselves experiencing spiritual death and rebirth. As in *Beetlecreek,* death as opposed to life is related to will-lessness, a failure of courage to act and to love. Its manifestations are violence and nonfeeling. . . . Life and death are thus locked in immemorial struggle as are good and evil in individuals. (p. 181)

[Demby] describes the intellectual as one engaged in the "new warfare of ideas." . . . (p. 182)

Demby's methods of warfare are at first mystifying, but it is warfare directed not against the reader, but against evil. The key to Demby's tactics may be found on the opening pages of the novel. It is morning and he is in his studio awaiting Doris, who will tell him about her night with the Count. The sun shines on his Rotella collages ''that have begun to dance like gorgeous jungle flowers.'' Before Doris arrives, he will read from a number of newspapers that lie on his desk.

From here on in the novel achieves something of a collage effect in which at odd moments the newspaper accounts Demby reads and quotes superimpose themselves, however precariously, on the narrative—the effect is a hovering sense of world and time on even the most private situations. But the various strands of the novel crisscross in other places as well. Demby may intrude on his story with seemingly vagrant thoughts of his own . . . or more frequently he may break into any dramatic action of his principals by projecting what some of the other major or minor characters may be doing or thinking at the precise moment. This simultaneity of presentation is presumably what Demby means when he speaks somewhere of ''cubistic time.'' It is something almost animate. . . . Actually, although the narrative generally unfolds in chronological order, Demby will, on occasion, shuttle back and forth in time in personal recollection or fantasy, or in a kind of Jungian race memory in which some odd newspaper item or disparate event suddenly assumes symbolic or archetypal importance. And yet the fragments do piece together. The novel begins and ends at the Easter season, and themes of death and resurrection become everywhere apparent like spirals within spirals.

If Demby's technique makes *The Catacombs* sound like something of a jigsaw, it is surprising to discover what intensely good reading the novel is. Part of the reason is Demby himself, around whom all the threads of the novel are bound. The prose is informed by a passion and honesty wherein the author tries to come to grips with himself in a world wracked by violence and stress. His principal means are his two ''imaginary'' or fictional characters, Doris and the Count, whose life-and-death confrontation is a reflection of Demby's own inward spiritual struggle. (Real-life characters stalk in and out of this novel as well—among them Demby's wife and son.) The Count, for all his sophistication and elegance, is a death figure. Centuries of inbreeding have left him spiritually debilitated. He endeavors unsuccessfully to reach out of himself, to act toward Doris according to his feelings, but his entire conditioning inhibits him. For social reasons he is afraid to bring Doris with him to Hong Kong, and it is significant that the beginning and end of their relationship takes place in a restaurant near the Catacombs. In contrast to the will-less Count, Demby poses another aristocrat he had once regarded as ''dehydrated'' who, as a journalist, defied the threats of French Algerian terrorists and remained in North Africa to record the terrible struggle for freedom. Thus Demby is saying that by an act of will, of courage, it would not have been impossible for the Count to transform himself had he so desired.

If the Count represents one segment of Demby's nature, Doris represents another. When the reader first meets her, she is all energy and live. . . . Later Demby says there is something about her that suggests fertility. . . . Throughout the course of the novel, Doris stands opposed to the Count as a kind of life force. When she tells him she is going to have his baby, he is angry and terrified at the prospect.

What is perhaps most interesting about Doris is that her creative energies become intimately associated with her Negroness, her African ancestry. Demby speaks of her ''forest-tapered legs,'' her ''dream-secret Negro laughter.'' Beyond that, her négritude begins to assume a kind of saintly quality. . . . The Count's

sister, a nun who has returned from the Congo, says that Africa is an ''idea,'' a dream, where people still speak a ''human language that the rest of humanity has forgotten,'' and that if society is to survive, it will have to become like Africa again and face ''the realities of the tom-tom bed, the subtle clucking of the Bantu tongue.'' The Count himself admits to his wife that embracing Doris is like embracing ''a girl in a dream.''

Doris's symbolism is further enhanced by her Christlike sufferings. She accuses both Demby and the Count of being vampires; in drawing their sustenance from her, they suggest in involuted fashion worshippers at Communion. Doris's plight is made symbolic of the plight of all women who are used and suffer (and die) that their men might survive. . . . [It] is clear that Demby intends his Christian symbolism mainly for Doris. He likens her afterward to Mary, Queen of Scots, and her disappearance in the Catacombs suggests the death of another Christian martyr.

Yet Doris and the Count, for all their symbolic status, ring true as people. Doris talks and sounds like a slightly worldly, slightly exuberant American college girl who pretends to brook no sentimentality. . . . She manages to keep up her skeptical, vaguely amused façade throughout the novel—especially with the Count, about whom she really entertains no illusions. The Count, for his part, always maintains his aristocratic demeanor. . . . (pp. 182-86)

Demby casts his characters in remarkably real settings—cafés, clubs, barbershops, beaches, drawing rooms, country estates. As in *Beetlecreek*—but now with greater skill—he focuses his camera on the seemingly irrelevant to provide an authenticity that might not otherwise be caught. . . Demby cuts swiftly, impressionistically, in and out from one scene to the next, back to the brooding Demby who is imagining his novel—catching his characters in unguarded moments, infusing an air of reality into the dreamlike fragments of the structure.

It is a long way from the Beetlecreek of the Depression era to Europe in the 1960s, but in some respects the distance is not so great. For Doris and Demby, the entire West begins to assume the character of a Beetlecreek deathtrap. . . . The degradation of Europe is imaged in terms reminiscent of the primeval ooze and slime of Beetlecreek. The levels to which life has now descended are fishy and reptilian, and Demby introduces these metaphors unobtrusively. (pp. 186-87)

There is, in addition, a considerable graveyard imagery. Demby attends the funerals of the Pope and of close friends and relatives, and observes on television the stiff, unreal ceremonies following the death of the American President. Rome and Greece, the foundation stones of Western civilization, are now viewed as cemeteries. (p. 187)

But if the West is a graveyard, there remains the expectation of rebirth. Although death images predominate, there are hints of resurrection. A new Pope is elected and makes a pilgrimage to Palestine, the birthplace of Christ. There is even some hope that the Count's flight to the East may rehabilitate him. Demby himself, secure now in his faith, in the sanctity of all existence, decides to fly back to the United States on Easter Monday. (pp. 187-88)

But for all his fond hopes, Demby is aware that the life-and-death struggle will persist, and that troubled days lie ahead. His is an almost Manichaean vision of being and nonbeing locked in timeless combat, and the shifting fortunes of the combatants fluctuate like the ebb and flow of the tides. Within this eternal pattern, it is the business of men to assert their life forces so that the battle may not be lost. And it is especially in America that the battle has been very nearly lost. He tells Doris about an earlier visit to America, where the raw hatreds and underground tremors of social and racial violence portended for him the conquest of Death.

Yet Demby in the novel returns to America a fulfilled man. In part, of course, his deeply religious outlook has discovered for him the role he plays in the cosmos. But in part too, by means of his Christianity, he has recovered his identity as a black man. For Doris has provided him with the example of Christian martyrdom. And it is Africa, lush, green, and fertile, that gives him the sense of Christian life. As the nun, the Count's sister, has put it, here lies the source and redemption of the human race. In contrast, Europe, white, cold, and sterile, has all but exhausted its spirit. (pp. 188-89)

Demby's resolution is a very private one, as any spiritual conversion must be. Yet there is something beyond the privacy of his vision that makes this book so striking. Demby is one of those rare Negro Americans, immersed in the culture of the West, who has discovered himself at home in a civilization that has deeply wounded him. His acceptance of the West has not negated his Negro identity but has enhanced it. (p. 189)

> Edward Margolies, "The Expatriate as Novelist: William Demby," in his Native Sons: A Critical Study of Twentieth-Century Negro American Authors, J. B. Lippincott Company, 1968, pp. 173-89.

ROBERT BONE

> The day is not far distant when humanity will realize that biologically it is faced with a choice between suicide and adoration.
>
>   —Teilhard de Chardin

The writer who succeeds, against all odds, in expanding contemporary consciousness must be prepared for baffled readers and irascible reviewers. The unprecedented stratagems that are required create their own resistance, and the writer's audience grows restive, out of a natural desire to organize experience along familiar lines. It is precisely this familiar order that is challenged by the serious writer, and often enough the price that he must pay for innovation is indifference and neglect.

Such has been the fate of a recent novel by William Demby. Launched by Pantheon in the spring of 1965, *The Catacombs* orbited briefly, encountered a thin cultural atmosphere, and parachuted soundlessly into a deserted sea. What is now required is a search and recovery operation. For Demby's novel, which is entirely a product of the Space Age, has probed to the outer limits of contemporary consciousness. What follows is an effort to substantiate this claim. (p. 127)

[Demby's first book, *Beetlecreek*], is a young man's novel: rebellious, but thoroughly controlled in execution. The point of view is existentialist, the tone expatriate. The style, thick with images of revulsion and disgust, reveals a man in desperate retreat from the smug parochialism of mid-century America. But if *Beetlecreek* is Demby's myth of disaffiliation, *The Catacombs* is his myth of reconciliation and return.

Demby's growth, between his first and second novels, was nourished by a wide variety of intellectual and literary interests. First and foremost was his participation in the great flowering of contemporary Italian cinema. To be on the scene when Fellini and Antonioni broke through the limits of postwar neo-

realism was to witness the creation of a new esthetic, hostile to naturalism and mythic in intent. The aim of these directors was to reaffirm the primacy of the imagination; their method, to require an act of collaboration from the cinematic audience. Demby's recent novel makes a comparable demand.

In his early years abroad, while still searching for his own metier, Demby studied art history at the University of Rome. He remains an ardent viewer, a collector, and a connoisseur. His interest in Italian painting and statuary, both classical and contemporary, is everywhere apparent in *The Catacombs*. (p. 128)

Given Demby's background in literature and painting, and his work in a medium where the two arts intersect, it was natural that he develop a concern with communications theory. The pioneering media studies of Marshall McLuhan appeared during the years of composition of *The Catacombs*, and there is ample evidence to show that Demby was familiar with McLuhan's work.

To these concerns must be added an intelligent layman's interest in contemporary science. Demby is curious about the recent developments in physics and mathematics which have altered our notions of causation and hence our theories of time. . . . Time is not linear in Demby's fiction. He is fascinated by the space between the frames of a motion picture. In *The Catacombs*, he slips into that space and explores its formal possibilities.

Demby's philosophic speculations were given a direction and a form by his discovery of the writings of Pierre Teilhard de Chardin. Father Teilhard's Catholic evolutionism supplied him with a cosmic perspective from which to view the biological dilemma and the cultural crisis of contemporary man. Many puzzling passages and mystifying symbols in *The Catacombs* will be plain enough if placed in the context of Teilhard's thought. The cone, the spiral, and the Omega Point, for example, may be found on the famous medallion designed by Teilhard to illustrate his concept of convergence ("Everything that rises must converge").

One preliminary task remains: to place Demby in his literary tradition. It is not so much American as cosmopolitan and European. Above all it is modernist: *nonrepresentational* is the metaphor that comes to mind. Like the postimpressionists, Demby forgoes a surface realism, in order to create a more compelling reality. He is the direct descendant of that pioneering generation whom we associate with the origins of modern art. His esthetic is derived from the cubist painters and their literary allies.

The American writer whom Demby most resembles is Gertrude Stein. Consider the affinities: like Demby, Stein was a highly Europeanized expatriate. . . . Both writers are inclined toward radical experimentation with the novel as a form. Both abandon the conventional plot-line based on linear time and replace it with a matrix of mosaic, essentially timeless, which Stein has called "the continuous present."

Finally, in the context of literary influence, mention must be made of the works of Isak Dinesen. Demby was introduced to *Seven Gothic Tales* and *Out of Africa* by his wife, who made an Italian translation of the latter volume. He was plainly captivated, for both books have left their mark on *The Catacombs*. Between the Danish baroness, who spent some eighteen years in Kenya, and the American Negro, living abroad in Rome, the immediate affinities are obvious enough. They have to do with the poignancy of exile, a cosmopolitan world-view, and a fascination with things African. They extend, however, to include such literary matters as a penchant for pastiche and an antipathy to naturalism.

On more than one occasion, Demby describes the present epoch as a Gothic age, requiring commensurate devices to render it in fiction. *Seven Gothic Tales,* with its absurd and fantastic elements, must have struck him as a valid image of the times. From the African memoir, by way of contrast, comes the inspiration for his central situation. That fusion of primitive and aristocratic virtues which is the theme of *Out of Africa* is a principal concern in Demby's novel. It is dramatized through the love affair of an American Negro dancing girl and an Italian count. But let us turn at this point to the surface texture of the novel. (pp. 129-30)

The setting of **The Catacombs** is modern Rome. The title recalls us at once to the epoch of early Christianity and the decline of Roman power. Demby thus establishes a parallel perspective, and invites us to consider the fate of modern Europe in the light of ancient Rome. Hunted, persecuted, driven underground, the early Christians retreated to subterranean chambers where they continued to celebrate the Eucharist and the Agape. In what quarter shall we seek their counterpart: a saving remnant holding forth the promise of redemption to the modern world?

Rome, moreover, is a symbol of imperial power, of the white man's historic depredations into Africa. . . . In Demby's novel, contemporary Rome becomes a stage on which a great historico-religious drama sweeps to its final act. For as Africa awakens from twenty centuries of stony sleep, a crisis of staggering proportions is thrust upon the Western world.

Rome, above all, is the Holy City of Western Christendom. Insofar as Europe responds to the challenge of a resurgent Africa, that response will be manifest in the religious councils of the Roman church. Demby is therefore fascinated by what might be called the symbolic gestures of Vatican II. (p. 131)

The action of the novel takes place over a period of two years, from March 1962 to March 1964. Action must be redefined, however, to accommodate Demby's theory of cubistic time. Just as in a Picasso the artist may present us with a head simultaneously drawn in profile and three-quarter view, so Demby strives for simultaneity in the design of his novel. Along with the traditional narrative dimension he attempts to convey, through a stream-of-consciousness technique, the writer's state of mind during the period of composition, including his awareness of historical events.

The novel moves forward simultaneously through three planes of reality. Headlines, news items, and miscellaneous excerpts from a dozen newspapers provide the texture of contemporary history. Musings, free associations, and entries from a kind of spiritual diary supply the subjective dimension. Embedded in this matrix is the fractured story line which alone must satisfy our cravings for a plot. The historical and biographical materials are never merely background, but are held in metaphorical relation to the fictive episodes. The result is a series of illuminating insights, a brilliant crystallization of contemporary consciousness.

The biographical material is paradoxically an expression of the author's antinaturalism. It is precisely to demonstrate that art is *not* a slice of life that Demby introduces this material. Directly observed events from his own life are reported almost casually, only to be processed into art before our very eyes.

The process is the important thing, as the writer selects and arranges from the welter of experience those elements that will enhance his theme. What it amounts to is an upgrading of the imagination. "True" facts and "fictional" facts are given equal status, out of deference to the creative act.

These are the strategies of Pirandello, adapted to the novel form. Their success depends upon a special brand of whimsy. One has to see the playfulness, for example, in Demby's approach to the technical problem of characterization. In the opening scene, a writer named William Demby is waiting in his studio for Doris, an attractive dancing girl who is to be the heroine of his new novel. It is some pages before we discover that Doris is an *invented* character, and still longer before we realize that the putative William Demby, who is after all a character in Demby's novel, is invented in precisely the same way.

The object of this playfulness is to tease the reader into an examination of his own metaphysical assumptions. When the putative William Demby invites his "fictional" mistress to have dinner with his "real" wife, the effect is to dissolve our conventional notions of reality. If the familiar categories of the actual and the imaginary are systematically destroyed, then a proposition will emerge about the nature of human existence:

> I am beginning to have the strangest feeling that we are all nothing more than shadows, spirits, breathed into life and manipulated by Pirandello's fertile mind.

The fertility of the imagination is precisely Demby's subject; throughout **The Catacombs** it is set off against contrasting images of sterility and barrenness. Man is the inventor of his own reality: that is the sum and substance of Demby's fictional technique. (pp. 131-33)

[**The Catacombs** begins in Rome] in the spring of 1962. The Algerian War is mounting to a climax, and the newspapers are filled with the terrorist activities of the European Secret Army. Against this backdrop of life-denying violence, the love affair of Doris and the Count begins. . . . [By August, 1962, the] world is moving toward the Cuban missile crisis, with human life itself perhaps at stake. On an isolated beach in Tuscany, Doris and Bill Demby are making love. (p. 133)

[The novel then shifts to] the month of the twin-faced Janus, 1963. Doris finds herself with "the dilemma of the century to solve." . . . [She] is pregnant, but cannot say whether the white man or the Negro is the father of her child. Her personal crisis is the crisis of the epoch. Just as she must choose between abortion and illegitimacy, so contemporary man must face nuclear suicide, or transcend his present moral categories. Demby sees this choice in the evolutionary perspective of Teilhard de Chardin. If we choose unwisely, all of human history may become a vast abortion.

From this point forward, the novel is concerned with birth: a birth that doesn't happen and a birth that does. The period of Doris' pregnancy is one of stasis, in world affairs, in Demby's personal life, and in the progress of his novel. The mood is one of lassitude, as we await the birth of what is ever more explicitly a symbolic child. Doris, we are told, is expecting her child in August. . . . [But] Doris does not give birth, at least to a literal child.

Toward the end of the novel, Doris confides to Demby:

> I wanted to name the baby John, you know, because of Pope John, and John Kennedy, for what they both did. Giving birth to whatever it was you mean by

the "third thing," using the manly weapon of dialogue instead of the old womanly weapon of poison and the bargain basement gun.

The child that refuses to be born, in short, is a symbol of sanity, reason, *dialogue:* the triumph of the life force. This force was embodied in world politics by the old Pope and the young President.

In the final episode, a symbolic birth occurs. It is the Easter season, 1964. . . . The Count will soon abandon [Don's], having been transferred to Hong Kong on company business. Doris pleads to be taken with him, but is denied. They pay a final visit to the catacombs, and as a young priest describes the sepulture of those who have "died in the Lord," Doris vanishes from sight. It is the Count's turn now to suffer, but through the loss of Doris he is born again. . . . (pp. 134-35)

The Catacombs is an ambitious book, whose themes are drawn from every sphere of contemporary culture. Science and technology, art and literature, sex and race, politics, morality, religion: all are woven into Demby's tapestry. The danger posed by this diversity of theme is a lack of focus, but Demby has surmounted it. Crucial to his unifying vision is the evolutionary creed of Teilhard de Chardin. The ligature which binds together these discrete levels of experience is Teilhard's philosophy of change.

Here is Demby's poetic statement of the matter:

> Doris too must conform, must submit, to that most sacred of universal laws, that first and only law which forever has taught, shall in all eternity teach, that life is existence and existence is sacred, . . . the embarrassing, the terrifying, the unembalmable law of changeless change.

What Doris must submit to is the law of evolution. That law, which is grounded in a paradox, perpetuates the life force by altering its forms. Essences persist, even as forms are modified: that is Demby's fundamental insight. When lower forms give way to higher, we describe the process as evolution. To evolve is to transcend, to outgrow the old forms which once possessed survival value but now are rendered obsolete. Man's highest wisdom is the willing acceptance of evolutionary change. (p. 135)

Conversely, to refuse the evolutionary challenge is to deny the will of God. This is the embalming heresy: the attempt to preserve dead forms. All that is conservative in the social organism, all that resists change and innovation, balks at the new imperative. Forms are mistaken for essences, and the loss of cherished forms is viewed as a catastrophe. Emotional attachments to the past cannot be transcended and the organism, perversely enamored of its own dead forms, perishes. This is the crux of Demby's novel. Modern man, as a result of his atomic technology, faces an evolutionary imperative. He must grow or die. The necessity of our epoch is to dare everything, to accept whatever risk may be entailed in the next stage of human evolution.

If there is a technological threat, there is also a technological transcendence. Modern man is living through a period of transition from the age of the machine to that of cybernetics. . . . Through the improvement of human communications systems, the global unification of human consciousness will be accomplished. A universal language will evolve, based on the stop and go pulsations of the binary computer. (pp. 135-36)

All forms, including linguistic forms, which derive from the machine are doomed. That is the burden of an elaborate image

pattern which persists throughout the novel. Machine production and the spiritual values of rationality and efficiency which it promotes are associated in Demby's prose with squares and rectangles. (p. 136)

The electronics revolution, however, which is based on circuitry and the principle of feed-back, will supplant the square with the circle. The latter form is associated in *The Catacombs* with love, art, and religion. This image-pattern, taken as a whole, amounts to an assault on Western rationalism. The square and rectangle represent the subordination of man to machinery; the circle embodies Demby's hopes for a more human world.

Nowhere in contemporary culture is the transcendence of dead forms more apparent than in the plastic arts. A tradition of five centuries, stemming from the Renaissance, is being overthrown, as representational art is superseded by non-objective forms. . . .

Demby dramatizes this cultural revolution by juxtaposing two art objects. The first is a statue by Michelangelo; the second, a contemporary painting by Losavio. . . . (p. 137)

In the case of the Michelangelo, the meaning of the statue depends upon its *placing.* If we alter the spatial relations of the object to its surroundings, we alter the meaning, however imperceptibly. The object exists, in short, in a state of *contingency.* This is the result of certain preconceptions concerning space, and the conceptual model, wherein all parts of a spatial field are related to each other, is the machine.

In the case of the Losavio, however, the state of contingency is explicitly repudiated, and space is organized in a radically different way. Instead of contingency, we have ambiguity; instead of mechanical determinism, uncertainty, probability, indeterminacy. . . . (pp. 137-38)

The idea of indeterminacy is particularly crucial to Demby's theory of the novel. In naturalistic fiction, the hero's actions are determined by environment and circumstance. Action in the present is contingent on the past, and the role of choice in human destiny is minimized. In Demby's work, however, the element of choice is central. Neither the outbreak of atomic war nor the outcome of a novel is a foregone conclusion. The freedom of a novelist to shape his denouement is emblematic of mankind's freedom to affect the future. Man is the first organism capable of intervening by conscious choice in the evolutionary process.

What are the implications of indeterminacy for the novel as a form? They will become manifest, above all, in the novelist's treatment of time. The naturalistic novel has attempted to imitate or reproduce or represent *natural* time. Demby's "non-representational" fiction, by way of contrast, attempts to free human action from the tyranny of time. It breaks with natural time, much as the cubist painters broke with natural shapes and natural colors. It replaces natural with fictive time—that is, with time relationships entirely of the artist's fabrication.

A fiction that stresses choice and indeterminacy can exert a liberating influence upon the human psyche. . . . [The] function of the artist is to liberate the imprisoned memory of the race, to free man from the dead forms of the past. By his constant invention of new forms, the artist serves as an instrument of sacred evolution.

The preservation of old forms, and more precisely the forms of power, is the unifying theme in Demby's treatment of sex, race, and politics. Male supremacy, white supremacy, and the political rule of the capitalist class have everywhere been challenged in the modern world. On the sexual plane, the challenge to male power from the emancipated woman has produced a severe disorder:

> The crisis of the bourgeois male of this century is a crisis of the absolute power of the man in the family. The bourgeois male, no longer "King," suffers from so-called complexes and neuroses: . . . it is then that the famous crisis of the male whose crown has been taken away occurs.

Demby goes on to discuss "the vendetta of the dethroned King." The male's quest for revenge takes the form of sadism. . . . Having established the psychological principle, Demby proceeds to apply it to other crises of absolute power. He compares the position of the *independent woman* to that of the *independence movement* in Algeria, and discerns in the terrorism of the European Secret Army a parallel to the vendetta of the dethroned male. By metaphorical extension, he moves from the violence and sadism of the French "colons" to that of Mississippi racists and Northern mobs participating in the white backlash.

Demby wants to isolate for our consideration a certain type of violence, grounded in hostility to change. Adherence to the old forms no matter what, a blind commitment to the past, a determination to destroy rather than accommodate have produced a mood of hysteria and a rising tempo of violence in the modern world. The name of this violence, projected on the political plane, is fascism. From his vantage point in Rome, Demby reminds us of that earlier convulsion when the European middle classes, frightened by the specter of a rising proletariat, turned to fascism as a bulwark of the capitalist order. He characterizes this act of self-betrayal as a dinosaur response—a suicidal effort to resist change even at the price of extinction.

When Demby returns to America for a few months in 1963, he is appalled by the high pitch of violence and hatred. (pp. 138-40)

[From] images of violence and criminality, the novel moves toward a definition of evil and, by implication, of God. Demby's concrete representation of the demonic principle is a total eclipse of the sun. . . . (p. 140)

If the Devil exists, then God exists: such are the terms of Demby's spiritual dialectic. If eclipse, or non-being, is synonymous with evil, then "life is existence and existence is sacred." Reverence for life is thus the cornerstone of Demby's values. In the eternal contest between birth and death, growth and decay, he turns in a mood of adoration to all that is life-enhancing. God becomes a kind of choreographer, inviting man to join the dance of the universe. . . . In responding to this invitation, Demby overcomes the skepticism which is the birthright of the modern intellectual. With religious art forms as his intermediaries, he moves toward reconciliation with the Christian faith.

The Catacombs is finally a drama of reconciliation. Neither facile nor sentimental, however, the reconciliation that Demby has in mind takes full account of man's capacity for evil. The modern world is haunted by a death-wish, a morbid fascination with non-being. Men have everywhere succumbed to the spirit of vendetta, or entrapment in the hatreds of the past. (pp. 140-41)

To break the chain of evil, to rise above his ancient animosities, and to defeat the cult of death, it is imperative that modern man assent to change. . . .

It is on this note that Demby's novel ends. We return in the last scene to the catacombs, that dark underworld which was at once the burial vault and the womb of historic Christianity. There, in the person of the Count, the soul of Western man is reborn. The redemptive agent is a dark Madonna, in whose veins the blood of Africa still flows. (p. 141)

Robert Bone, "William Demby's Dance of Life," in TriQuarterly, *No. 15, Spring, 1969, pp. 127-41.*

JOHN F. BAYLISS

Already we have had an assessment of the novel [*Beetlecreek*] by Robert Bone in his *The Negro Novel in America* (1965) [see excerpt above]. I would tend to disagree with this critic's over-emphasis on the existentialist nature of this interesting work, and, instead, I would like to stress its human content.

Biographical details supplied by Bone have some bearing on the novel. William Demby was born in Clarksburg, West Virginia, in the heart of the mining region which provides the setting for *Beetlecreek.* His education at West Virginia State College was interrupted by two years of army service in Italy. On his return, he was able to finish his degree at Fisk University, thanks to the GI Bill. He graduated in 1947. Being interested in art as well as literature, he returned to Italy to study at the school of art at the University of Rome, where he has remained to write screen plays for Roberto Rosellini. (His recent novel, *The Catacombs* (1965), strikes one as reminiscent of the Fellini world of Roman Society.)

Of deeper significance, Demby's creative writing contributions to the Fisk Herald while at the University have a cosmopolitan, strongly GI, anti-fascist flavor. (pp. 70-1)

While understanding the relations between the life and the art of Demby, Robert Bone overstresses the existentialist core of *Beetlecreek.* Judging by his criticism, the novel is an elaborate framework for the main characters to ask themselves the question, "What do I want of life?", and then, because they have no positive goals, the attempts at assertion following the questioning lead only to their own destruction. Without doubt, this kind of patterning is apparent in the story, but one's interest is absorbed far more by the unusual situation of white recluse, Bill Trapp, living as the white minority in a Negro settlement, and more especially, by the very human way in which the recluse tries to break through the barriers a lifetime had erected and which kept him aloof from human companionship. In the last analysis, *Beetlecreek* is a human document, not an existentialist one.

To substantiate this last point, one may first assemble the existentialist evidence of Robert Bone and then show how the novel goes beyond this philosophical base in its impact.

At the beginning of the novel, Bone explains, Bill Trapp terminates 15 years of solitude, and thus displays the celebrated "courage to be" of French existentialism. Set against this striving for life is the deathliness of the Beetlecreek community. . . . The community is a ghost town in a more profound sense than its having exhausted its coal deposit. For Bone, the plot itself revolves around the frustrated Negro artist, David, with whom John is staying.

The boy is meant to be only a shadow of his host, although it is hard to see how this description fits one so lifelike. Continuing the existentialist explanation, Bone shows that David is trying to break out of the stagnation of Beetlecreek by attaching himself to a childhood sweetheart who is visiting the town, but she has the death kiss of the big city upon her. For a moment he makes the right choice by supporting Bill Trapp against the prejudices of the community, but he gives in before the mass hysteria of the other townsfolk.

John, who has left his sick mother in Pittsburgh, is lonely like David, but one feels that Bone is overstressing the likeness when he equates the adult loneliness of David with that of the boy. John also supports Bill Trapp until he later betrays him under pressure from the ''Nightriders'' gang. The similarity with David's betrayal seems merely situational, unless one wants to fit everything into an existential framework. Bone's summing up of the affinities between the two cases seems farfetched in the light of the evidence. He states: ''It is true [the existentialist definition of evil] above all of David and Johnny, who suffer their creative powers to be perverted, rather than endure a spiritual vacuum.'' But the boy's humanity is being squeezed out by Bone's cerebral interpretation, not by the actual story; for, instead of being an existential cut-out, Johnny appears in the story as a very real human being.

In order to put the philosophical base in the background, where it belongs, one should note the evidence in *Beetlecreek* that makes it stand as an ordinary story, without the props of existentialism.

The picture of the old recluse at the start, trying to open the chrysalis of solitude, is not overpainted, nor superficially rendered. . . . (pp. 71-2)

[While Johnny Johnson and the old man become friends], Mary, David's wife, is having her own battle with a self-image. This character is consistently portrayed as truly feminine in her hopes and fears. Her life centers around the Womens' Club of her church. . . . Throughout the novel, Mary's anxieties concerning her standing at the club, and for her stall at the upcoming parish fair, afford an extra human background to the main plot. . . .

To see John and the recluse merely as existential figures is to miss the warmth of feeling displayed by the old man towards the boy, and the latter's own troubled reactions towards Bill Trapp. The old man centers his return to companionship around the young Negro. . . . (p. 73)

Johnny, on the other hand, is torn between a poetic world in which he sees all nature, and all men, as kind, and the other world of harshness but solidarity in the gang. True, in the end he succumbs to the pressures of the gang. . . . But his previous mixed feelings are very much those of the young adolescent; they do not need the existentialist philosophy to prove them true. Demby writes well of this younger consciousness; from the time John shows compassion for the beetle to the time when the youth feels that other irrepressible feelings are stirring in him. . . . David, the frustrated artist, has similar troublings of spirit in which the consciousness feels that other forces are beginning to stir. . . . But one does not have to see both John and David as examples of the same existentialist patterning. In Demby, both survive as human beings.

Even the subsequent betrayal of David's renewed artistic yearnings is not to be seen as caused by some inhuman force, crushing him. The author uses a convincing irony to show David's being trapped by his own aspiration. Not surprisingly, the artist, David, finds Beetlecreek a womb in which one is suffocated, and this feeling of being trapped throws him upon Edith. In his frustration, he sees her as different and really alive. But

his charged emotion has caused him to misjudge the situation. . . . He has given up one painful situation for another.

Sufficient evidence has been introduced to show that the human content of *Beetlecreek* far outweighs the existentialist patterning that is brought in by Bone as interpretation. (pp. 73-4)

John F. Bayliss, ''Beetlecreek: Existential or Human Document?'' in Negro Digest, *Vol. XIX, No. 1, November, 1969, pp. 70-4.*

WILLIAM DEMBY (INTERVIEW WITH JOHN O'BRIEN)

(The following interview was conducted in late 1971. It forms part of a planned book of interviews of black authors that John O'Brien has edited.)

[O'Brien:] *Are there any authors who have affected your writing?*

[Demby:] Well, I think that Virginia Woolf did, for some reason.

Perhaps because of her use and treatment of time?

Yes, time. Certainly it came out in *The Catacombs,* the way she was able to slow down time, or stretch it, or treat time as though it were something that one touched, and could mold. . . .

What about non-literary influences?

Music. (These are comparatively recent influences. I was writing my first novel over twenty years ago.) But in music, Schoenberg and Berg, everybody who was fooling around with ideas of time. I think that that was one influence that really, really profoundly influenced me in ways that I still am not sure of but which certainly influenced the whole structure of *The Catacombs.* (p. 1)

The achievement of **The Catacombs** *is that you are able to incorporate things that are happening in the outside world and mold them into some artistic framework and give them some meaning. . .*

That was a deliberate effort on my part. I was speaking at Rochester a couple of weeks ago, and all this came up. We were discussing all these problems of being bombarded by all these events which come into our consciousnesses electronically or otherwise, at a fantastic speed, almost the speed of light. How can the novelist give this somehow to, . . . how can he recreate this feeling? I was with some Russian writers—I belong to the European Community of Writers—this was in Florence, Italy. We were having an international meeting. . . . And there was a big tapestry on the wall, and a friend of mine from Iceland and some other people were watching this and saying. ''that's the way a novel should be.'' Not linear, not in a kind of horizontal sequence of events, but as one perceives reality looking at that enormous tapestry upon which any number of things were happening. . . . So that is what I tried to do. First I thought, why not try to start a novel at a certain point and, instead of going forward in time, go backwards? Why was it not possible? I never really found out. It was from that idea, that liberating idea, that I conceived of writing a novel, but without any of the controls that a novel usually would have. That is, that I would begin on a certain day and continuously go forward. Every page or every day's work would reflect what has happened to me in my personal life and the lives of the fictional characters who moved around at the same time as the so-called real characters, the people in real life. So each day should reflect all of these things: what I perceived from the newspapers that I was reading, or the things that were happening in other countries, or in the southern part of Italy. Anything. My wife's family. Anything that was going on. All of this was reflected. What astonished me was that there was a real pattern that you perceived. What created this pattern, I don't know. Was it in the consciousness of the author, or was it that any event that you would see happening anywhere, were you to turn your consciousness on it, it would fall into some kind of order? I'm not sure yet how it works but I knew that it worked in *The Catacombs*. And in that novel there was never any turning back, nothing was ever rewritten. It just went forward from day to day until some instinct would tell me that that would be the end of it. That went on for two years.

This may raise the question of whether the artist imposes order or whether he reflects it. Is it resolved in **The Catacombs** *whether the order is created by you or whether it exists and you are finding it?*

I think that it gets to the deeper truth that there is no such thing as chaos perhaps. There may not be. . . .

You try to make connections out of everything in **The Catacombs.** *You don't just try to create an individual, private order.*

I agree with that. I totally agree with that. I mean that that obviously is the function of the novelist. The novelist must have this function of seeing connections. He also has the responsibility (and this may be true for all artists,) to make some connection with the past. (p. 2)

Would **The Catacombs** *have been written had you stayed in this country?*

No. I don't think so. I was lucky to be in Europe at that time. In Rome you were always at a kind of center for ideas. I might have fallen into the naturalistic novel had I remained in this country. I might have.

Do you think of **Beetlecreek** *as being a kind of naturalistic novel?*

No. I don't think so. Not *Beetlecreek*.

I think Herbert Hill made the point that the novel tended towards naturalism.

Well, the truth is those scenes were written in Salzburg, in Austria. And what had happened was that I had fallen in love with a woman. . . . And one night she went out with somebody else and I was pissed-off. That's when I wrote that pathetic closing scene in *Beetlecreek*. So, how do we know where these inspirations come from? I know that it is not a naturalistic novel. I wouldn't call it that at all. The reality of the novel is not naturalistic. The movement that each of the characters has is much more secret than any cause and effect relationship. Johnny certainly wasn't reacting to any . . . it wasn't that he wanted to be in a boy's gang or anything like that. I think that it was the imperative to act, to do anything. I think that all the characters came into something like that. Everyone did something and we say how these doings had a pattern and I suppose you can do that with any group of people. But it is only when they do something, when they move, and the movement is on the level that is perceivable, then I guess at that moment it is worthwhile to write about it. What happened in the novel? Not very much.

Would you accept a term like "existential" to describe the novel?

I always was a little wary of that until two weeks ago. I was up in Rochester reading and talking. A young lady who had been my classmate at Fisk University and worked on the literary magazine I edited, showed me a number in which I had written a review of Camus' *The Stranger*, in which I was also discussing existentialism. Now I had thought that I had been interested in existentialism in Europe when it was fashionable at the time. I know now that I had been interested in it in college, though I had forgotten about that. It appealed to me very much, though I was not quite sure what existentialism means, and I am not sure I am now. (p. 3)

What form of existentialism affected you do you think?

What has always astonished me was how little minor movements on that great tapestry or landscape there, how minor things are interconnected. So that, if you are doing something . . . and this is how the characters in *Beetlecreek* were moving existentially. That is, the things they did seemed in themselves of no importance and yet they moved or touched other lives. . . .

Is there any hope at the end of **Beetlecreek**?

Well, . . . hope. I think the only movement in my novels (and the novels I will be working on) will be more and more a trying to understand the relationships between small movements. That is, people think they move in a meaningful way, that they have come to a decision: they get on a bus. That is only movement without any real . . . I don't know why people expected that in the novel there should be something resolved. . . . [Hope] means that you still have options of movement. I suppose that that is the only thing hope can be. You cannot conceive of yourself changing, because you cannot change. Not only will that character who went North on the bus . . . bring with him the experiences in Beetlecreek, but all his life he'll carry that bag around with him. . . . Hope? I don't know. Is it desirable for the characters to change? I don't know. (p. 4)

Who does the determining, either in life or literature, as to what is to be designated as evil?

Oh, I believe in a moral universe. That is, a universe in which there is movement, where people are born and they die. These are basic things. The world we must live in has a kind of intrinsic order to it. And occasionally there will be gestures which are presumptuous in that they pretend to make things happen when the truth probably is that they are only acting in accordance with something over which they have no control. . . . If this is true, then it means that a lot of the movements, the revolutionary movements, are just expended energy. They are not leading to anything that will be a change. In one period, at least the period I try to demonstrate in *The Catacombs,* there is no change. There is only the illusion of change. It's an idea I will have to think about in the future. (pp. 4-5)

[In regards to the structure of **The Catacombs:** *had other actual] events taken place, would they have worked themselves into the novel and have influenced the outcome?*

I think so. It's a weird experience. But, yes, all these things were included in. And it seemed to me that sometimes I would be sitting down and it seemed to me that events (and this is real paranoia) were being dictated to fit in with the novel, when of course, it is the other way around. But, using this technique creates paranoia. You begin giving attention to things which didn't merit all that attention. But it occurred to me that any time that anyone gives attention to certain things . . . you get unbalanced by placing too much . . . you know, you really could.

I guess now there is a possibility that you could write a novel about how that novel was written.

In writing it, I think I said this at one point or another in the novel, I felt as though I were boxed inside the novel and would never get out. And I remember, I think there is a Zen story of a painter who painted a picture and couldn't get out of the painting. I really felt boxed in.

Is that why the real life characters worked themselves into the novel and why your fictional characters would come out of the novel and become real?

There's a lot of that. Sometimes some people who knew . . . some nutty girls who knew how I was working on this novel would try to invent things so that they would get into the novel. But, of course, I would put them in or not put them in. One of these girls committed suicide, so she was in the novel. . . .

I think that it was Joyce who had a great fear of the written word, that once it was said it would occur in life . . .

Yes. And I was sensing that too. On the other hand, if you are going to assume that type of magic, you could go to the other extreme and say that just by writing it down, it will not happen. But . . . there's ideas of magic there. (p. 5)

> John O'Brien, "Interview with William Demby," in
> Studies in Black Literature, *Vol. 3, No. 3, Autumn,
> 1972, pp. 1-6.*

NOEL SCHRAUFNAGEL

Beetlecreek (1950) revolves around a fourteen-year-old boy who leaves Pittsburgh, where his widowed mother is hospitalized, to stay with his aunt and uncle in Beetlecreek, West Virginia. Life in the small town is depressing for a boy from the city, though, and Johnny Johnson becomes as disenchanted as most of the people who live there. He is trapped by the provincial attitudes of both whites and blacks, and in attempting to accommodate himself to the mores of the community he commits an unpardonable act of inhumanity.

The characters who have the closest contacts with Johnny are his relatives, Mary and David Diggs; Bill Trapp, an old white man who lives alone at the edge of the black section of the community; and several black youths who are part of a gang that Johnny eventually joins. All of these people are trapped in the village, which tends to stifle the lives of its inhabitants. . . . The Nightriders, Johnny's gang, reflect the prejudices of Beetlecreek by applying pressure on Johnny to sever his relationship with the old white man. (pp. 74-5)

Enthralled by the sharing of his life for the first time in years, [Trapp] invites a number of children of both races out to his home in rural Beetlecreek. This rather pathetic attempt at communication turns the village against Trapp. . . . Johnny does not believe the rumors about the immorality of Trapp, but he succumbs to the influence of the Nightriders and sets fire to the recluse's house as a part of the initiation rites that are necessary for acceptance by the gang.

Johnny's act is representative of the hatred and the moral depravity of a community dominated by people who are primarily concerned with conforming to a perverted sense of decency. The efforts of a man to express his love for people are misinterpreted because any positive action in the morally dead town is suspect. An outsider to begin with, Trapp is tolerated as long as he exists in his personal vacuum, but the minute he transgresses the border of the citizen's morbid version of respectability by inviting a mixed group of girls to a party, he is in for trouble. Rumors spread that he is a child molester, and not even Johnny, who had at one time mentally equated Trapp with Jesus Christ, can withstand the pressures exerted by the bigots. His fiery feat is a symbolical crucifixion performed by all of Beetlecreek, which is itself a miniature replica of the modern world. In attempting to adjust to the conventions of the village, Johnny commits himself to immorality.

Robert A. Bone [see excerpt above] suggests that the novel presents an existentialist definition of evil in which man attempts to express himself in negative and destructive ways if no other confirmation of his existence is available. Demby leaves little doubt that the inhabitants of Beetlecreek, both black and white, embrace evil without considering an alternative. Racism, although it exists in abundance, is only an aspect of the general sickness of the community. . . . [In] Beetlecreek no one commits himself to the side of virtue. Even Bill Trapp spends the greatest part of his life in denying his own humanity. His friends, Johnny Johnson and David Diggs, surrender to the mediocrity of their surroundings.

Demby attempts to convey his vision of the world through the use of recurring images and symbolic actions. However, he stresses too much the idea that Beetlecreek is a village of death. The descriptions of the thoughts and feelings of the characters are designed to reveal that Beetlecreek is responsible for the plight of its inhabitants. They are unable to escape from the trap that society creates. In displaying the despair of the more sensitive individuals of the town, the author suggests that those who possess the capacity for constructive action are doomed to failure. Demby proclaims the guilt of mankind, but his deterministic manipulation of the characters detracts from the total effect of *Beetlecreek.* (pp. 75-6)

William Demby's second novel, published fifteen years after *Beetlecreek*, is a story of the development of race pride in an American expatriate. *The Catacombs* (1965) takes place in Rome against a background of newspaper reports telling of racial violence and hatred in the United States. The narrator, in relating the details of a romance between a black actress and an Italian count, is actually exposing his own needs for personal fulfillment. He associates the racial incidents in America with the activities he observes in Europe, and decides that he prefers to be a part of his native country. He favors an active participation in life to a sterile existence in a foreign country.

The narrator is a friend of the young black actress, Doris . . . . Doris realizes that the narrator is in love with her. She carries on two affairs at once, then, and eventually becomes pregnant, presumably by the Italian. The baby is born dead and shortly afterward the disenchanted nobleman informs the girl that he is leaving the country. Doris somehow becomes lost in the Catacombs and the narrator, given impetus by the disappearance of the girl, returns to the United States to assume his racial identity.

Doris, who engages in a personal struggle with the Count, matching her animation against his stagnancy, represents the vital aspects of life to the narrator. She possesses the vitality of Africa and the tempestuous nature of America. The Italian, on the other hand, signifies death and the moral decay of Europe. The triumph of the Italian over the American girl illustrates the necessity for the narrator to return to the United

States before he, too, is destroyed by Rome. On his decision to return, the death images associated with the city are replaced by hints of resurrection, as a new Pope is elected and Easter approaches. Even the racial bigotry of the narrator's native land is preferable to Rome once his religious convictions have given him the courage to face again the prospect of being an American Negro.

Demby's stylistic improvisations are impressive as he attempts to convey a sense of illusory motion reflecting the thoughts of the narrator. His symbolism and imagery revolving around death and the promise of resurrection comprise the most effective aspect of the novel. On the whole, the author's talent is wasted on a flimsy plot and a vapid thematic line that appears to be almost an afterthought. A modern version of Hawthorne's *The Marble Faun,* the book is nevertheless more of a literary exercise than a significant artistic contribution or social commentary. (pp. 128-29)

> Noel Schraufnagel, "Accommodationism in the Fifties" and "Accommodationism in the Sixties," in his From Apology to Protest: The Black American Novel, Everett/Edwards, Inc., 1973, pp. 69-98, 121-46.

JOSEPH F. CONNELLY

Two novels very different in theme, setting, structure, and tone account for the total opus of William Demby, an expatriate Black living in Rome. The fifteen years between *Beetlecreek* (1950) and *The Catacombs* (1965) contribute to these differences and give the appearance of a hardly productive author. . . . In viewing the latter work, the reader traces its theme to a secondary character and to the theme of the earlier one and to the life of their author as he sought his own identity in a hostile milieu. A glimpse into William Demby's personal life helps explain the long duration between novels. As the writer William Demby sought his place in America and then in Europe during the fifties and sixties, his character in *The Catacombs,* Bill Demby, quests for the elusive muse so he can complete his novel and be at peace with himself. Peace—like the muse—eludes him, but he does convey to the reader why she is not achieved.

On the surface, the numerous events and the lost story line make *The Catacombs* appear chaotic. It ends on an unsatisfactory note as the heroine, Doris, disappears in the catacombs. . . . Doris is not dead, though; she has merely gone underground as the early Christians did to practice the religion of Christ. She is William Demby's symbol of his elusive muse hidden among world events that have become too much for him and her. . . . Like Demby, who is both author and character of the novel, Doris plays a dual role, that of character in the novel and inspiration or muse to the author.

As the novel opens, Bill Demby awaits Doris' arrival. . . . As a dancer in the film *Cleopatra,* Doris assumes the extra dimension of an artist herself and fulfills an important link with the Black tradition begun at the Nile and the cradle of civilization. To Bill Demby, the fictional character, she is part of a personal past, being the daughter of his former lover from college days. In recording and writing her story, the artist-character is seeking the female principle from his immediate past and from the far reaches of Black tradition. When Doris goes underground, he is without story line, inspiration and muse. He becomes an unproductive artist.

The novel's composition indicates reasons for disappearance of the muse and for William Demby's lack of artistic production. Contemporary events . . . overwhelm the character-muse, Doris, as well as the author. Doris is left by the Italian Count, and William Demby puts aside fiction for translating films and advertising. Both businesses have drained him by redirecting his creative energies and demanding his full time. Like Doris, he needs a reprieve from massive and violent events. The catacombs are a well-drawn symbol of apparent pause or, in the author's sense, silence. As the early worshippers of Christ went underground to practice their faith unmolested, Demby's muse has sought protection from an unfeeling and hostile world. Release may come when proper conditions prevail.

The settings of both novels become important to the temperaments of the artists portrayed and to the aesthetic conditions and atmosphere prevailing in each place. In *Beetlecreek,* the painter David leaves his West Virginia town because he is trapped there by a wife and the conditions imposed on Blacks by the white community. David is reduced to a sign painter, and, as a result, flees town with a woman from the past. Though this theme is a secondary concern of Demby in *Beetlecreek,* it introduces a concept that dominates his second novel fifteen years later. (pp. 100, 102)

In *The Catacombs,* Rome is the setting and serves well the purpose of the artist because it is the center of Christian art and carries the awe of the Eternal City in its traditions. This spiritual atmosphere appeals to the creative mind and works in conjunction with the growth principle associated with woman. Demby employs many Madonnas in the novel as images of the female principle. Doris is the contemporary image of the traditional Madonna. Rome is unlike Beetlecreek, the place where the artist is strangled by his social and economic condition. On the other hand, Rome seems to foster the artist's abilities; but due to world conditions, between the years 1962 and 1964, the creative ability is overcome by chaos.

Much of *The Catacombs* is concerned with violence and death, especially suicide. As the most prominent examples of suicide, Demby portrays two women whose deaths through suicide project his thinking on sacrifice and human involvement. Marilyn Monroe is his major example of the woman who sacrificed herself for the man she loved. (p. 102)

In another instance of a more personal nature to Doris and Bill Demby, Laura, a West Indian beauty, has taken her life because her husband whom she supports has driven her to it. The suicides of Marilyn Monroe and Laura are the sacrifices of the female principle or growth factor necessary to the artist-husbands of both women. Both have yielded their lives so that the creative man may live. In the case of Laura, human involvement is incomplete because her husband took her for granted. Their relationship parallels that between Doris and Count Raffaele, except the separation is different because Doris has escaped underground and has not surrendered her life. William Demby implies a direct relationship between world conditions and individual relationships. The chaos of the world will remain until man makes personal interactions his goal. Dominating the novel in the guise of great social events and technological and scientific achievements, are actions of an impersonal and empty nature. Man has lost his way in a milieu of clutter. The novelist and main character of *The Catacombs* has lost his inspiration and muse, as he has become temporarily impotent.

In *Beetlecreek* this theme is resolved in another fashion. Separation and alienation occur differently. David, the frustrated artist-as-sign-painter, leaves the town and the wife who imprison him. He flees with his muse Edith Johnson, a former co-ed from his undergraduate days who stands for hope and liberation. . . . David is trying to fulfill his artistic promise from the past and still holds to a female principle which may well be his further undoing as was his wife who brought him to Beetlecreek. David still clings to the elusive muse as the artistic pursuit possesses him.

William Demby's life is much a part of both novels. Like the hero in *Beetlecreek,* he left Pittsburgh for Clarksville, West Virginia, the town transformed into racially divided Beetlecreek. Between the novels, he moved to Rome where the struggle to remain an artist and to make a living continued. . . .

[In Italy, Demby's] family may live without the racial pressures prevalent in his native country. But other forces continue to frustrate the artistic and humanistic temperaments. These forces of violence, upheaval and chaos are dramatically depicted in *The Catacombs* through the author's use of headlines, news releases, TV coverage, and excerpted magazine articles. The two years of the novel's duration are marked by hostility to such an extent that the tradition and inspiration of the Eternal City are overwhelmed by it. Indeed, *The Catacombs* is the documentary of these years and, more importantly, of a segment of William Demby's life. (p. 103)

> Joseph F. Connelly, ''William Demby's Fiction: The Pursuit of Muse,'' in Negro American Literature Forum, *Vol. 10, No. 3, Fall, 1976, pp. 100, 102-03.*

ADDISON GAYLE

> She had taken off her Chinese embroidered robe and revealed her wasted child-like body as in an ancient ritual of puberty, shyly, a profound sense of the rituality of what she was doing. And . . . she placed a cushion under her head and in the innocence and frenzy of first love she touched my fingers tentatively and then seized them with the force of the passionate grasping to life that is both birth cry and death rattle and motioned me to hurry, hurry, hurry. . .

So William Demby concludes, *Love Story Black,* one of his best novels. The hurrying is necessary, both for Mona Pariss and Edwards, the novel's narrator. Both—the one time famous black singer, ''now pushing ninety'' years old and the interviewer, writer, Professor of English—are about to undergo a love/religious ritual in which the myth becomes first truth, then understanding, then revelation: Edwards recalls a nightmare/myth in which he has encountered an old woman in a hut; he seeks water and the answer to a riddle. . . . [He believes that the] old woman in the hut, ''the prophetess,'' will surrender the answer, reveal ''the meaning of the riddle, if I make love to her—''

Love Story Black is then a novel about making love, about truth and revelation, birth, rebirth and death, and though the symbolic import of the novel is borne by Mona Pariss, the tale is as much of the young Professor as it is that of the old woman. . . . If his detractors are to be believed, Edwards and his fiction are Europeanized; thus the writer must undergo his own odyssey, seek a clue to many riddles, search for clarification, meaning. He does not find either when he travels to Africa. . . . Ironically, what he finds in Africa is not the mystery of his roots, but sickness. The answer to the riddle, not so much identity, but the meaning of identity, can be discovered only through Mona Pariss.

Mona is the not so grim ferryman, capable of ushering others across the river Styx, because of the learned lessons of her own tragic experience. In her youth, she became infatuated with ''Doc,'' itinerant minister, railroad porter. She was Doc's discovery. It was he who started her on the road to international acclaim and success. Yet, what she wanted most from the preacher, he could not deliver. . . . Doc, as Mona is to discover, has been castrated. Thus for almost ninety years she lives the agony and suspense of the experience that never was. There is some small recompense gained, when, in exchange for the interview that stretches over time, she orders Edwards to lie naked with her in bed.

Neither Edwards nor the reader is aware of the coming consequences of this act. Neither could have foretold that Edwards [would] . . . disrobe yet another time and become the surrogate lover, mistaken by the old woman for her ''Doc'' of long ago, and fulfill the demand of the prophetess of the nightmare/myth. Yet the thematic import of the novel demands an ending no less existential, mysterious, or satisfying. For the love of Mona Pariss is a child-like love. . . . It is like a religious conversion, passionate, instantaneous, soul-consuming. It is a love that has transcended time, one infused with need and desire, becoming—and this is not too strong a word—a conflagration, sweeping Mona to death and Edwards to a new birth. Hers, however, is what Albert Camus would have called a happy death.

The symbolism in *Love Story Black* is as telling as that demonstrated heretofore by Demby in *Beetlecreek* and *The Catacombs,* revealing the writer's continuing preoccupation with life, death, and love. These have remained his trinity: these givens in the life of every human being. Life as Demby knows must end in death, but neither life nor death is meaningful without love. Love makes both acceptable and one gathers from this work, that Demby pities those who have never achieved it. For Camus's doctrine, ''I rebel, therefore I am,'' Demby would proclaim I love, therefore I am, thus raising the existential equation beyond romanticism to touch the most profound longings and utterings of the human soul. Such are exemplified in the life and times of Mona Pariss and the old woman herself in her quest and in her achievement, exemplifies humankind at its best.

> Addison Gayle, in a review of ''Love Story Black,'' in The American Book Review, *Vol. 2, No. 6, September-October, 1980, p. 10.*

A. ROBERT LEE

[Demby] left America for Europe in the fifties, settling in Rome . . . shortly after the publication of his first novel, *Beetlecreek* (1950), a close-wrought, existential parable, set in a West Virginia hill-town. A decade later followed *The Catacombs* (1965), a venture altogether more 'modernist' in kind, and an experiment as much in its view of human consciousness and its perception of time as its narrative means. The two novels read very much as a diptych, linking visions of human loss and subsequent recovery. (pp. 233-34)

In *Beetlecreek,* Demby's mode is insistently naturalistic, a controlled linear accumulation of images of death made over into a story. The novel depicts a triangle of characters, each in his own way the victim of small-town suffocation. . . . The novel derives its claustrophobic impact from Demby's dense imagery of entrapment, stasis, closed doors and windows, coffins and beetles, a catalogue of death and ways of suppressing the instinct for life. The final act of arson, particularly, serves the novel as an emetic, a violent terminal act of release from the town's racial paralysis. Demby has acknowledged in interview that **Beetlecreek** signified his own leave-taking from America, a society he then believed impossibly locked inside its racial myths and dead-ends. The deliberateness of Demby's prose and the care with which his novel uses major images of death were sure signs of promise.

The Catacombs more than fulfilled that promise, a novel which bids for, and in my judgement achieves, genuine new ground, especially in exploring human connections which run greatly deeper than race. Demby himself calls his novel an experiment in 'cubistic time', narration which seeks to bind different levels and kinds of consciousness one into the other as if time were a shared, simultaneous present, and by which he confirms his affinity with moderns like James Joyce and Virginia Woolf. . . . The novel in fact draws upon a range of modernist sources: foremost Demby's interest in the visual arts. His considerable training in art history and collection shows in the novel's pattern of allusions to painterly form. He also borrows from different post- and neo-realist film strategies, having done translation and screen-writing for Italian directors like Antonioni and Rosellini. Given that the novel was being written in the early sixties, and is actually set between Easter 1962 and 1964, it reveals in Demby an alert response to the then new accounts of a post-Guttenberg Galaxy being explored in Marshall McLuhan's writing and to emerging developments in the mathematics of time-theory and probability. The philosophical roots of his novel he readily acknowledges to be Teilhard de Chardin's evolutionary Christianity, the credo of human ascendence and convergence. Hence, his novel's most resonant touchstone, Rome's ancient sites of Christian sanctuary, the catacombs, serve as points of spiritual and temporal meaning in a manner which recalls E. M. Forster's Marabar Caves. Demby's second novel is self-avowedly 'complex', and runs the risk of mystification, but it controls with great sureness the ambition behind the form.

Though in part a self-reflexive composition (Demby intervenes several times to advise his reader of the kind of novel he is reading), **The Catacombs** keeps steadily in view the world external to itself. It is organized as montage of sorts, a careful inter-working of the 'facts' of world news and change with the 'facts' of its imagined author's life. In one sense it is a book about the world, and about historical process; it is also a book about a book, about its own imaginative provenance. The centre is a work-in-progress being written by one 'William Demby' about his muse and lover, Doris. . . . She sleeps with both the 'author' and the Count he has introduced her to. . . . The novel's last picture is of Doris pregnant, unsure which man has impregnated her (and thus unsure whether she has 'white' or 'black' seed in her body), fleeing like the muse she has become to the further edges of the catacombs. She carries within her the author's fugitive vision, his commitment to a greater kind of human consciousness.

Around this triangle, Demby constructs a narrative which reflects the high-speed technological world of transaction and change. His novel uses extracts from newspapers, weeklies, diaries, personal journals and letters, to re-capture the bewildering speed with which history can now be seen to be in process. He alludes thus to the newly fought Algerian war; the neo-Fascist backlash in France and Italy; . . . and recurrently his belief in a philosophy of time and human redemption which transcends the events of any one immediate now. The novel abounds in these mutual echoes and refractions, mirroring patterns of cross-reference, and holds them to a credible narrative rhythm—not least because there is always to hand a perceptible line of story in process of being discharged.

The climax of these different shifts of energy and contrast takes place when the Count, long habituated to pain and doubt about his own meaning, finally sees through time, both as he himself has known it and as it is reflected in the new media, and grasps that the catacombs, where death has been stored for centuries, is also a means back into life—that Doris, in truth, incarnates the life-principle. His epiphany is also the 'author's', and the reader's, a final point of clarification in a novel which throughout has explored the fatal costs of compartmentalizing human consciousness along simple lines of nationality or race, or to a single measure of time. It makes for a singular moment in a singular novel. **The Catacombs** offers an important endeavour to 'make new', a fiction whose ambitions are matched in the overall achievement. (pp. 234-36)

A. Robert Lee, "Making New: Styles of Innovation in the Contemporary Black American Novel," in Black Fiction: New Studies in the Afro-American Novel Since 1945, *edited by A. Robert Lee, London: Vision Press, 1980, pp. 222-50.*

Margaret Drabble

1939-

English novelist, critic, essayist, biographer, editor, short story writer, scriptwriter, journalist, and dramatist.

A respected editor and writer, Drabble is best known for her novels that chronicle the negative effects of dramatic changes in contemporary British society on the lives of well-educated women. Critics generally distinguish two phases in Drabble's career as a novelist: her first five works focus on young women who struggle with professional, sexual, maternal, and social conflicts as they attempt to establish careers and discover their identities, while her later novels combine commentary on women's concerns with panoramic views of modern England. Fundamental to Drabble's work is an emphasis on predeterminism; her fiction repeatedly dramatizes through fate and coincidence the importance of understanding and accepting individual destiny. In her novels, Drabble blends literary allusions, recurring symbols and characters, witty epigrams, and attention to order and detail. While occasionally featuring such unconventional elements as self-reflexive narratives and direct addresses to the reader, Drabble's books are generally categorized within the mode of realism, and she acknowledges the influence on her work of such realist novelists as Arnold Bennett and George Eliot.

In her early novels, Drabble draws upon her personal experiences to present psychological portraits of intelligent, sensitive young protagonists in the process of adjusting to social roles and fate. Her first work, *A Summer Bird-Cage* (1963), concerns a recent college graduate who experiences setbacks while attempting to begin a professional career and must come to terms with ambivalent feelings toward her glamorous and self-assured older sister. The central character of Drabble's next novel, *The Garrick Year* (1964), is a bored young mother who is tempted into an extramarital affair. Following accidents involving herself and her daughter, the woman realizes that her maternal love is stronger than her attraction to her lover, and she renews her commitment to her family. *The Millstone* (1965; republished as *Thank You All Very Much*) focuses upon an introverted, unmarried graduate student who learns the meaning of responsibility and compassion after she bears an illegitimate child. As in her other works of this period, Drabble describes the biological processes of gestation and birth in intimate detail, portraying this experience as arduous but spiritually enriching.

Drabble's next novel, *Jerusalem the Golden* (1967), which was awarded the James Tait Black Memorial Prize, centers on a young provincial woman who becomes infatuated with the cosmopolitan lifestyle of London through relationships with a college friend and her attractive brother. Following a series of poignant events and coincidences, the protagonist confronts her romantic illusions of life in London and the dreariness of her past, which is reflected in her strained relationship with her puritanical mother. In *The Waterfall* (1969), Drabble's characteristic topics of maternity and sexuality are united in the story of an unconventional love affair. The heroine, an unfulfilled housewife who has been abandoned by her husband, is nursed through childbirth by her brother-in-law. Through the brief, passionate romance that develops, the lovers are awakened to a stronger sense of freedom and self-awareness.

The Needle's Eye (1972) initiates Drabble's use of more varied themes, concerns, and characters. Rose Vassiliou, the altruistic, upper middle-class protagonist of this work, hopes to achieve spiritual grace by renouncing material wealth and embracing a working-class lifestyle in a poor section of London. Although fateful events continually frustrate her plans for salvation, Rose's verve and idealism, coupled with her self-analysis, which is rendered through interior monologues, allow her to gain a sense of direction in her life. In a review of *The Needle's Eye*, Joyce Carol Oates stated: ''[Drabble] is not a writer who reflects the helplessness of the stereotyped 'sick society,' but one who has taken upon herself the task . . . of attempting the active, vital, energetic, mysterious re-creation of a set of values by which human beings can live.'' Frances Wingate, the heroine of *The Realms of Gold* (1975), is a feminist paragon who combines a successful career as an archaeologist with single parenthood. As with other of Drabble's characters, however, Frances's personal freedom is restricted by fate, as represented by her maternal responsibilities and her inability to leave her married lover.

Drabble's interest in social issues is particularly evident in her succeeding novels, *The Ice Age* (1977), *The Middle Ground* (1980), and *The Radiant Way* (1987). *The Ice Age*, her first work of fiction to feature a male protagonist, concerns Anthony Keating, an unsuccessful businessman suffering a mid-life crisis who serves as the catalyst for an examination of British society during the 1970s. The personal tragedies of Keating and his friends underscore larger social problems, for England is presented as a bleak, alienating environment where sudden calamities and random violence are commonplace. *The Middle Ground* offers a similarly apocalyptic vision of contemporary Britain from the perspective of a journalist whose dissatisfaction with her comfortable, middle-class existence is exacerbated by her distress at the decay of modern society. *The Radiant Way* further expands on themes of social decline and personal destiny in its portrayal of three former classmates at Cambridge University whose youthful idealism has been tempered by ineffectual political policies, particularly those of the 1980s. While relating the friendship among the three female protagonists and their various career, personal, and romantic crises, Drabble presents a sweeping indictment of England in which the grisly crimes of a serial murderer symbolize the country's social chaos. Gayle Greene lauded *The Radiant Way* as ''an extraordinary work, a major literary event. Like the nineteenth-century novelists she admires, Drabble offers a panorama which encompasses the whole of English society, and takes on the hardest questions confronting that society, such issues as the relation of England's past to its present, the possibilities of progress (individual and collective), the responsibility of the individual.''

In addition to her novels, Drabble has published several volumes of literary biography and criticism, including *Wordsworth* (1966), *Virginia Woolf: A Personal Debt* (1973), and *Arnold Bennett: A Biography* (1974), and has edited *The Oxford Companion to English Literature* (1985).

(See also *CLC*, Vols. 2, 3, 5, 8, 10, 22; *Contemporary Authors*, Vols. 13-16, rev. ed.; *Contemporary Authors New Revision Series*, Vol. 18; *Something about the Author*, Vol. 48; and *Dictionary of Literary Biography*, Vol. 14.)

GAYLE WHITTIER

Both the tension between motherhood and sexuality and that between motherhood and career appear as themes throughout Margaret Drabble's novels. Her treatment of the two tensions is unique in that she finds the motherhood/career dichotomy easy to resolve, even in her first novels, whereas the darker, more mythically suggestive conflict between the maternal and the erotic aspects of womanhood persists, varied and extended, even in her latest works.

In *The Millstone* (1965) Drabble's narrator successfully integrates unmarried motherhood with the brilliant completion of her dissertation on Elizabethan poetry. True, Rosamund Stacey enjoys the fortuitous privileges of a vacant family flat in London and a reliable babysitter or two. But Drabble emphasizes the psychic, rather than the practical, aspects of her protagonist's status as a working mother. Rosamund disproves the cliché [pondered by Esther Greenwood, protagonist of Sylvia Plath's *The Bell Jar*,] that motherhood places a woman in ''some private, totalitarian state,'' for maternity enhances her work, giving substance and immediacy to scholarly abstraction. . . . Reciprocally, her professional status compensates for the stigma of her unmarried state: ''my name would in the near future be Dr. Rosamund Stacey, a form of address which would

go a long way towards obviating the anomaly of Octavia's existence.''

However, Rosamund Stacey proves much less successful in the limited, but crucial area of eroticism. Still a virgin in her mid-twenties—and in an academic milieu where chastity itself is exceptional—she dispassionately, almost theoretically, loses her virginity with an innocuous young radio announcer. The sexuality of even this situation is undercut by Drabble's presentation of George as sexually ambiguous. . . . Of course her ''choice'' of George reflects Rosamund's own uneasy attitude toward heterosexual pleasure, an attitude which she explicitly defines near the end of the novel, dichotomizing maternal and sexual loves:

> It was no longer in me to feel for anyone what I felt for my child; compared with the perplexed fitful illuminations of George, Octavia shone with a faint, constant and pearly brightness quite strong enough to eclipse any more garish future blaze. A bad investment, I knew, this affection, and one which would leave me in the dark and cold in years to come; but then what warmer passion ever lasted longer than six months?

A second early Drabble novel, *The Garrick Year* (1964) also engages the two tensions between motherhood and career or sexuality, respectively. At first Drabble seems to emphasize the competing demands of a job and a family, as Emma Evans resists her actor-husband's assignment to repertory company in Hereford because it threatens her own delicate balance between children and marketplace. . . . But the thematic signal to the reader proves falsely prophetic. Once Emma resigns herself to following her husband, Drabble develops her much less manageable turmoil between her role as a mother and her potential as the mistress of Wyndham Farrar, an older actor in her husband's company. (pp. 197-99)

But while offspring impede this affair, even practically, Drabble simultaneously presents motherhood as a sexually alluring condition, one which, by fulfilling and energizing a woman psychically, almost paradoxically attracts the man that it must exclude. (pp. 199-200)

Drabble draws motherhood as a condition which requires the *presence* of the mother herself—not her surrogate—to insure the physical safety of her children. Thus Emma's offspring are exposed to accidents and harm in direct proportion to their mother's growing involvement with Farrar, which absents her from them literally or figuratively. For example, Emma arrives home from one abortive assignation to find her house reeking of gas, her husband and the French *au pair* girl oblivious of imminent suffocation. Unlike the actual mother, Emma, the nursemaid shows no deep concern over the children, even when she herself is aroused from near coma in the gas-filled rooms. '''Oh. They will be OK,' she said, lying back on her pillow, with a pale and guiltless smile.'' In effect, while there may be substitutes for some of a mother's domestic functions, her presence is unique and irreplaceable. (p. 200)

Precisely because he diverts her from this crucial maternal vigilance, the lover endangers mother and child. When she and Wyndham meet in public, Emma redirects her attention to her children in time to see young Flora disappear into the waters of the River Wye. . . . Her children are dwellers in her psyche (''I have seen this happen so often in imagination''), and therefore she is in perpetual readiness. Emma literally leaves the side of her lover to rescue Flora, to save, if not the affair, the child. And Wyndham Farrar himself is compelled to acknowledge that the two registers of experience do not mix, writing that "he hoped my children were well, and that he would never fall in love with a woman with children again."

Through *The Garrick Year*'s depiction of the dangers inherent in motherhood and intensified by the mother's distraction by sexuality, we begin to understand why Drabble is able to resolve the career conflict, but not the erotic one. There is a sociological dimension to this resolution as well. Although Drabble presents less advantaged mothers, such as Janet Bird in *The Realms of Gold* and unmarried Eileen in *The Needle's Eye*, her central female figures tend to be educated women who, when they do work, enjoy interesting and flexible jobs. They move in a comfortable, if not wealthy, stratum of society in a country where nannies have long been an acceptable custom, even a privilege, and where young children often leave home for boarding school at what Americans would consider a shockingly early age. In such a climate, the nanny may even come to represent a healthful personal freeing of the mother from an intensively close bond with her children—for we can see, in effect, that the potential for such closeness is intrinsic in maternity as Drabble views it, and that motherhood easily "overreaches" from the natural to the neurotic. . . . But at the same time, ironically, that social custom helps free a woman from the tension between motherhood and career, the resolution of one dilemma shows the residual conflict between motherhood and sexuality in a more rigid pattern: No practical or social expediency can eliminate the uniqueness of the maternal bond or the differing demands on a woman's psyche exerted by her role as a mother or a mistress.

There is an archetypal pattern of maternity in Drabble's works, and it is one which must be acknowledged if we are to understand how the mother/mistress pattern moves as myth and theme in her later works. Typically, Drabble describes motherhood as the result of a conception which is accidental, half-decisive, or casual; it evolves through a pregnancy which, far from being glamorous or euphoric, brings the first intimations of age and death; it culminates in childbirth, an experience always perceived by Drabble as a kind of physical mystery rather than a rational skill, and one utterly transformative of the mother's psyche. Thereafter, motherhood dominates her life in the paradoxical mixture of resentment and joy, exposure and security. There is nothing of the sentimentality of the Victorian "angel mother" in this portrait, however: "I often think that motherhood, in its physical aspects, is like one of those prying disorders such as hay fever or asthma, which receive verbal sympathy but no real consideration, in view of their lack of fatality; and which, after years of attrition, can sour and pervert the character beyond all recovery," Emma Evans says (*The Garrick Year*). But the accidental conception (Drabble's is no country for planned parenthood), the wearying gestation, nevertheless climax in an alchemy of the heart, the rebirth of the woman as well as the birth of her child, and, indeed, the beginnings even of a social conscience. . . . (pp. 200-02)

The magnitude of this transformation *requires* that the woman enter it unknowingly, herself in need of consciousness as the child is in need of life. Rosamund Stacey's attitude towards her body signifies the casualness not only of the virgin, but of one uninitiated into the hostage condition of real life. "I got out my diary and started feverishly checking on dates, which was difficult, as I never make a note of anything, let alone of trivial things like the working of my guts," she comments on her first suspicion of pregnancy (*The Millstone*). And she does

not even *think* about the decision to continue the pregnancy itself: "Once I had thus decided to have the baby—or rather failed to decide not to have it—I had to face the problem of publicity." But if the body itself seems a "trivial thing," the commitment to the child negative, inertia, pregnancy itself awakens Rosamund Stacey to her membership in humanity, in that "commonness" of which Emma Evans was "proud." It even initiates her into consciousness of social class, as she visits a prenatal clinic where mothers suffering from the neglect and malnutrition of poverty present a completely demythicized picture of motherhood. (pp. 202-03)

Finally, however, not even "commonness" or fellow-feeling exhausts social potential of maternity. For the mother stands, throughout Drabble's novels, as the epitome of the "hostage to fortune," the *acknowledged* gambler who risks for us all. The women who conceive children without "planning" them in Drabble's novels do so less from obtuseness or ignorance than from the accidental nature of life itself. No woman can imagine the profound alchemy of the birth experience before the fact; nor can she envision the education in feeling and vulnerability which maternity insures that she will undergo. Such a definitive *rite de passage* must be entered into half-consciously or unconsciously. For in creating another being, the mother doubles her own human vulnerability and brings it to light along with her child. She thus "universalizes" that unspoken half-concealed and profound vulnerability of us all.

Drabble often dramatizes this vulnerability through actual physical harm or congenital accidents inflicted upon the innocent young. Unlike most children in modern fiction, Drabble's seldom suffer from psychological ills or neuroses. Instead, they seem to belong to a nineteenth century milieu where infant mortality is really general, and where nature errs. Octavia Stacey, for example, is found to have a congenital heart defect, as if to suggest that "accidents" not only create life, but shape it prenatally as well. The defect itself is found almost accidentally, too, as if epitomizing a danger so deep that it may strike fatally without symptoms. Rosamund calls in a doctor for what she supposes to be a cold. The affected organ is, significantly, the heart, mover of the blood of life but also symbolic seat of its feelings, for this kind of threat serves something like a moral purpose, breaking the mother to an altruism and a wider human sensibility: "now for the first time I felt dread on another's behalf." It is Rosamund herself whose "heart" has been found "defective," and deficient in a sense of reality. . . . (pp. 203-04)

The Waterfall (1972), published almost at midpoint in Drabble's career so far, can be viewed as a pivotal work reflecting some of the thematic resolutions of her earlier novels and forecasting some of the thematic experiments of the later ones. For example, Jane Gray's maternal experience is virtually paradigmatic, recognizable from the histories of Drabble's earlier heroines. . . . (p. 204)

Jane Gray also represents the motherhood/profession conflict successfully resolved in Drabble's earlier heroine, Rosamund Stacey. Her productivity as a poet actually increases despite her husband's desertion and the expected birth of another child. . . . Significantly, it is not the trials of single parenthood, but the presence of the male, which seems to undercut such creativity. Jane Gray conceals her rush of poetic energy from her lover, even as she also conceals the actual blood pouring onto her sheets after childbirth. And once she and James begin their affair, she *stops* writing, as if to suggest that eroticism, not maternity, usurps woman's creative force. The affair itself becomes material for fiction, the story she recounts in *The Waterfall,* but only after it has ended. Thus Drabble indicates that the creativity behind poetry and the gestation before childbirth are harmonious experiences for a woman; there may even be some mythic connection between her bodily children and the "brain-children" of art. Yet both these ways of creating remain at odds with sexual passion.

The Waterfall opens on an extended note of thematic deception, for in this novel Drabble appears to resolve the mother/mistress tension from the first page onward. She describes Jane Gray's childbed with her characteristic lack of euphemism, her accuracy including the bloody sheets, damaged flesh, sweat, pain, and the peculiar exultation as labor ends. . . . The birth itself assumes a dreamlike quality, taking place as it does in an overheated room during a snowstorm; its ordinariness—the baby is bathed in a pudding bowl from the kitchen, for example—contributes to the newly confined mother's sense of immediate, accessible transcendence, experience resolving itself as painting or music, art forms. . . . Jane Gray's isolation is so peacefully profound that she dreads even the arrival of the midwife who will interrupt her communion with herself and with the mystery of labor. Entering into this arena of female rites, James, her cousin's husband, comes first to look after Jane, then to fall in love with her.

It is one of literature's least likely seductions, precisely because Drabble plays off the taboo of the parturient woman against the stereotype of the seductive adultress. James accepts the uncosmetic realities of birth and its aftermath; for example, he is not put off by stitches, afterpains, or blood. Even as Jane nurses her newborn child, so he in turn "nurses" her with the simple gestures of necessities provided and needs answered. The "commonness" of the event seems contagious, as if James has stood too near the fire of female mysteries. And precisely because Jane is not now *superficially* attractive, he must see her in her "true sexual beauty." Having slept alongside her chastely, like a child himself, he desires her wholly. They consummate their passion at the insection of the maternal and erotic experiences, shortly after Jane's postnatal gynecological examination. She herself sees no distinction between the childbearer and the sexual ecstatic, her desire "so primitive (it) could flow through her, like milk."

Even the sexual abstinence imposed by her confinement—and reminiscent of the "taboo" of the unclean childbearer in myth—works to the deepening of sexual love between Jane and James. For it demands a protracted and unglamorous caring, a *real* and homely knowledge easily lost in the hurry of less impeded affairs. (pp. 205-06)

But this idyllic integration of motherhood and sensuality collapses before the end of the novel. In a climactic scene, James, Jane and Jane's children, off on a "clandestine holiday," crash in a highway accident. The "accident" forces Jane to acknowledge that she cannot love James and her children separately but equally; not only must she choose between them, she *has* chosen: "All I cared for was the survival of the children." . . . (p. 206)

In these early novels, Drabble prepares the way for the heroines of her later works, women who *have been* married, *are* mothers, and who find that one of a lover's prerequisites is his willingness to "father" their already born children. Indeed, we might almost say that, lacking this propensity to care for another man's children, the lover cannot be considered at all. Rose Vassiliou and Frances Wingate (*The Needle's Eye* and

The Realms of Gold, respectively) demonstrate how Drabble continues her resolution of the career/motherhood conflict, while experimenting with new options in the motherhood/sexuality dichotomy.

Rose, a former heiress disinherited for an "improper" marriage, raises her children in a comfortable poverty which arises from her literal belief in the scriptural admonition to "sell all thou hast." Her relative poverty is philosophical, not really social, and while her work includes menial jobs meant to make ends meet, Rose still indulges in a charity uneasily like that of the society matron she was once meant to be. Professionally, Frances Wingate triumphs further, orchestrating the demands of several young children, her academic career as a well-known archeologist, and her wide-ranging travels in North Africa. As if to symbolize her integration of the personal and professional aspects of her life, she takes with her such relics as her children's photographs and the false teeth of a former (married) lover. But while the motherhood/career conflict heals, Drabble's heroines must experiment with possible resolutions of the mistress/madonna tension.

In both *The Needle's Eye* (1972) and *The Realms of Gold* (1975), the mother-with-children meets her prospective lover in a situation of domestic emergency which "tries" his mettle as a potential mate. In *The Needle's Eye,* however, Drabble appears to be practising a turn of plot not yet perfected. When Rose Vassiliou brings home Simon Camish, a married (and disenchanted) barrister, the scene shapes up as a stock seduction. As she confides that her estranged husband is attempting to win custody of her children or to make them wards-of-court, the careful reader of Drabble's earlier works, (especially *The Waterfall*) senses that hers is the specific lure of the mother-in-trouble, and in trouble which cannot be separated from her very maternity. Yet at the end of the recitation, Rose does not go to bed with Camish. Instead, she sleeps with her middle child, neatly substituting a maternal for an erotic comfort—and risk: "Rose, lying awake in bed after Simon Camish had left, got up in the end and got a child and took it to bed with her . . . She held on to it both for comfort for herself and to protect it" (*The Needle's Eye*). By the end of the novel Rose, her children, Simon, and her estranged husband, all convene at the house of her alienated parents; Simon and his wife remain married; and Rose and her husband reconcile. Thus while Simon Camish may provide an interim father for Rose's children, and may tantalize the reader (if not Rose herself) with the prospect of an antisocial affair, Drabble never delivers conventionality's coup de grâce. Instead, the book closes with the restored, if battered, nuclear family intact, an eleventh hour conservatism having reconstituted all.

In *The Realms of Gold,* however, the same mother-in-trouble gambit ends differently indeed. At first Frances Wingate appears to follow the earlier script, arriving home with Karel Schmidt, a married academician who will become her lover, and introducing him at once into a household full of the crises of the single mother. An ambulance greets them at her door, her somewhat incompetent baby-sitter having panicked when the baby put a bead in its ear. Karel is adequate to this occasion, and, indeed, Frances succumbs to him less on sexual grounds than in homage to his recognition of the "malice of (parental) chance." . . . (pp. 208-10)

Like *The Waterfall*'s James, Karel Schmidt strikes the reader as an unresolved child himself. Disorganized, curiously helpless in the stereotypical manner of the "absent-minded professor," he needs the kind of "center" which maternal women are traditionally supposed to provide. And he enjoys children, both his own and Frances's. (This last attribute is virtually a prerequisite of an affair with the husbandless mother in Drabble's works; even when both parties have families, the mistress's brood dominates, either by narrative default, since the woman often delivers the first-person account which is the novel, or by matriarchal emphasis.) Drabble carefully steers the lover/father surrogate through the Scylla of incest and the Charybdis of the "good provider." But the father figure never obviates the dangers which mother and child face through their very existential bondage as a kind of unique "couple" themselves. Paternal risk is somehow more *invented*, "harassed embarrassed anxious," than the vigil-participation of the mother. And a man shares this blood bond only at *his* own risk. (p. 210)

In *The Realms of Gold,* too, Drabble successfully extends her range of parent-child relationships, but only Frances Wingate succeeds in integrating motherhood and eroticism. She does so, however, through a negative counterexample, as it were, since Karel's wife Joy "liberates" herself into lesbianism. The mistress marries the lover, or, on another plane, the husbandless mother marries the wifeless father, setting up a variant modern version of the nuclear family with its complexities of stepsiblings and stepparents. Unlike Rose Vassiliou and Emma Evans, who revert to their earlier personal decisions, to their spouses, Frances Wingate moves in a climate where the "past" is richer and more generous than any individual history. While her sense of the human condition remains deeply historical (involving her move back to Tockley, and, more interestingly, the non-English past of prehistory, her object of study) and while she is able to marry her lover, Drabble nevertheless can only parley their union into a procreative unit. (p. 211)

With the publication of *The Realms of Gold,* Drabble's thematic evolution appears distinctly. Having resolved the motherhood/career conflict in her earlier works, she still contemplates the more stubborn tension between maternity and eroticism. But she is now able to "socialize" the mother-child couple, to see their vulnerability as less mythic and unique, more general and even political in its implications. She has moved from a narrow but deep sense of maternal experience to a broader sense of what constitutes "family," "history," even collective identity itself. She still avoids a full integration between mistress and mother, for while Karel and Frances marry, they do not reproduce. Given the "universalizing" quality of motherhood, however, Drabble turns this personal dross into the social gold of parenthood by proxy. Very probably Drabble's future work, like that of Doris Lessing, will increasingly engage the social questions which have come out of her first, matricentral works into the light of human community. (pp. 212-13)

> *Gayle Whittier, "Mistresses and Madonnas in the Novels of Margaret Drabble," in* Gender and Literary Voice, *edited by Janet Todd, Holmes & Meier Publishers, Inc., 1980, pp. 197-213.*

JOHN HANNAY

Margaret Drabble receives much praise, and condemnation, for writing more like George Eliot or Arnold Bennett than James Joyce. One example of her traditionalism can be seen in her almost quaint belief that the word *fate* will carry conviction for the modern reader. But she also plays with this word in a self-reflexive manner that reorients its traditional meanings and generates new levels of irony regarding the self-awareness of characters. While several critics have commented

on the theme of fate in Drabble's works, they have missed her textual irony and so have failed to comprehend a major aspect of her originality. (p. 1)

Freud believed uncanny experiences reawakened childhood memories, and we might say analogously that fateful moments reawaken memories of familiar stories. As structuralists are quick to point out, these associations derive from the elemental patterns that stories share with one another. Stories of childhood tragedies surfacing late in life, star-crossed lovers, heroic confrontations that end with hollow victories, fortune always coming to one brother and not the other: not only our literary heritage but also our general culture abounds with such paradigmatic plots. Events we term fated seem to emerge from and to conform to this common culture, as if they had been foreordained. The term *intertextuality* describes this sense of life repeating a previously heard story, of life predestined by the patterns that have shaped our consciousness.

The intertext of a given story is the set of plots, characters, images, generic codes, and literary conventions it calls to mind for a given reader. The term *intertext* allows one to speak of these elements as a totality, creating a general sense of a work of art reflecting a tradition, without limiting that sense to individual elements. The intertext is not simply another text to which a work alludes directly or indirectly. Multiple texts or verbal messages are present in any given text through shared elements, and *intertext* refers to these shared aspects rather than simply to the texts themselves. (p. 2)

Clearly the concept of intertextuality presumes a reader's general literacy and competency in interpreting texts, but specific aspects of the intertext will vary, as do all critical interpretations, with each reader's particular background. We need not argue that an author has a specific work in mind that establishes the intertext. Certainly an allusion in the text or a reference in interviews, letters, or journals may provide helpful clues. But allusions are only beginning points for seeking common elements between texts. A reader constructs an intertext, whether or not such specific references are available, out of the codes and the conventions governing the form, genre, and style of a given text.

Since literary works incorporate these conventions self-consciously, we must go beyond simply identifying them and decide how they contribute to the aesthetic ends of the signifying system.... We read the literary work and construct in our minds a sense of the intertextual models governing its structure and its language. From this initial sense, we test and refine our model, finding ever-changing relationships and combinations in the dialectical opposition between the text and the intertext. From this continual interplay, we may infer a third level at which the text, in commenting on the intertext, comments on how literature relates to reality through conventions. [Jonathan] Culler illustrates this dialectic in [*The Pursuit of Signs: Semiotics, Literature, Deconstruction*] while discussing the intertextual theories and methods of Julia Kristeva and Harold Bloom, both of whom insist on identifying "pretexts" or intertexts with which the work wrestles. These critics find in the opposition between a text and the discursive space of language and narrative structure that surrounds it a commentary on the tradition within which it generates its meaning.

Realistic fiction often creates its intertextual dialectic by displacing plots from earlier genres, such as the romance tradition or moral parables, into the realm of the ordinary. Hardy's *Life's Little Ironies* takes fablelike stories and adds twists of fate that create a sense of realism and inevitability out of ironic deflation. (pp. 3-4)

These short stories of Hardy comment on their intertexts by implying that reality is harsher and more degrading than they allow. Drabble adapts their dialectic in *The Millstone* and makes Hardy's *Life's Little Ironies* itself stand for an intertext. Rosamund's friend Lydia refuses to write in her novel about her accident (being hit by a bus and thus spontaneously achieving the abortion she had been unsuccessfully seeking) saying, "It's so unconvincing. Far too unrealistic for my kind of novel. It sounds like something out of Hardy's *Life's Little Ironies*." She cites the Hardy text in order to acknowledge, but then reject, the class of stories for which her accident would be suitable, stories with strongly ironic, sudden twists of fate. We see here how much an intertext depends on the reader's interpretive stance: Lydia feels her accident would seem contrived if used in her "realistic" fiction. But Lydia's rejection is dialectically countered in the passage as a whole, for Lydia's denial of Hardy's twists of fate is spoken in the context of an accident that would fit his conventions and that really did happen. Moreover, Rosamund, clearly Drabble's spokesperson, counters with, "'I've always thought *Life's Little Ironies* had rather a profound attitude to life.'"

Frequently Drabble's novels repeat this pattern, first denying conventions in the name of realism and then reaffirming them by suggesting that "realism" should be broadened to include such conventions. The denial disarms criticism by assuring the reader that the narrative will not force a belief in extraordinary happenstance. All will go according to familiar laws of reality. The reversal of this denial usually takes the form of "truth stranger than fiction." This phrase succinctly describes a two-stage logic that says, first, "realistic" fiction does not contain strange or highly significant coincidences, the stuff of melodrama; and, second, "truth" in real life does contain such amazing coincidences. "Fate" often implies the possibility of a "truth stranger than fiction," a truth whose design and implications seem more symbolic than most "realistic" fiction would permit. Drabble pushes dialectically at the boundaries of realistic novels so as to reorient traditional paradigms of fate and to generate new levels of philosophic and poetic meanings. (pp. 5-6)

While Drabble resists excessively literary fiction, maintaining that she wants to tell stories based on real life, she acknowledges that real life often structures itself according to patterns familiar from literary tradition. Drabble often has the characters themselves become conscious of their fate in intertextual terms that implicitly claim the models are real, and not just literary convention. Of course, as we saw above with *The Millstone*, the denial of convention in the name of realism is itself a convention and as such has multiple intertexts associated with it. One never escapes entirely from the cultural encodings that shape our language; they are our fate. But we may manipulate the codes for various effects, with varying degrees of self-awareness. If our resistance to one model inevitably creates conformity to another, still such conformity may bring a more complete, even more profound viewpoint. (p. 7)

[Drabble's] novels do not present a merely static opposition between fateful intertexts and realistic detail; rather, they present a true dialectic whereby the whims of destiny gradually take on structure and form. The climactic scenes in . . . three novels. . . . (the car accident in *The Waterfall*, the chase after Christopher in *The Needle's Eye*, and Anthony's imprisonment in Walacia in *The Ice Age*) all introduce unexpected, yet somehow predestined, developments in character through chance occurrences. They fulfill the intertext at the moment they very nearly elude it.

Fate labels and by that labeling equates a logic of mysterious causality or chance with cultural and literary norms. Lydia objects to including her bus accident because it depended on chance to bring good fortune and to wrap things up neatly. She calls this model mechanical, but ironically her expectations have derived from a much more mechanically deterministic model: the naturalistic novel's assumption that chance invariably causes misfortune. Drabble's ironic presentation of Lydia's critique makes life's little ironies all the more compelling. Drabble challenges the reader to find an intertext that will create a harmony out of coincidence and accidental occurrences yet not constrict them to lifeless mechanism. (pp. 8-9)

While the conventional patterns of fate underlying Drabble's novels do not fit simply into a small number of categories, neither are they totally amorphous. Drabble tends to repeat a few general paradigms associated with the word *fate*.

My categories form a sequence that suggests one major line of development in Drabble's career to date. I begin with the model of tragic romance—in which a passionate, illicit love fatally draws two characters together in a union that seems destined to end in death—because much of her earlier fiction centers on the choice of love as a solution to characters' existential dilemmas. Drabble's first four novels (*A Summer Bird-Cage, The Garrick Year, The Millstone*, and *Jerusalem the Golden*) all treat young women tempted into extramarital or adulterous affairs, yet withholding physically and emotionally from an erotic relationship and generally finding little satisfaction in sex. Ellen Rose sees Clara Maugham's problem, in *Jerusalem the Golden,* as one of autonomy rather than of sex and gender, but Clara does find her sexual initiation disillusioning. The pleasure she derives from her lover, Gabriel Denham, originates more in her sense of illicit adventure than in any physical desire she feels.

Jane Gray, in Drabble's fifth novel, *The Waterfall*, starts out sexually stymied, but she learns the powerful attraction of love from James Otford, her cousin's husband. She experiences a deeply satisfying orgasm that marks the culmination of her sexual initiation as well as marks the high point of Drabble's preoccupation with sex. Jane's love for James remains illicit and comes near to causing their deaths. In subsequent novels, Drabble appears to have passed on to other concerns, and her heroines all take it pretty much as a matter of course that sex can be pleasurable when the right lover comes along. None of her later heroines fears sex or has significant conflicts about it.

The power of sexual attraction has so often been the theme of literature that one cannot write about it without invoking one of several familiar models: love as salvation, love as curse, love as both salvation and curse, love as disillusionment, and so on. . . . The subject of *The Waterfall* is sexual love, not society, family, or even compassion. It presents the search for existential honesty and the language of self solely in terms of romance, rejecting the claims of children. "Fate" appears more often (and it appears quite often) in this novel in relation to her initiation into love than anything else. Jane worries about her effect on her children and the fate they will inherit from her, but her concern for them remains peripheral to the main plot.

Following *The Waterfall,* Drabble turns her attention much more to the responsibilities of motherhood as providing the terms and structures by which she defines fate. Although continuing to write plots based on adultery, she emphasizes the claims of the family. In *The Waterfall,* Jane's husband, Malcolm, does make an isolated attempt to exert a claim on the children, but he steps back quickly and, it seems, gratuitously. He fits the role of cuckolded and outraged husband from romance stories much more than a model of family concerns. But Christopher Vasiliou, Rose's husband in *The Needle's Eye,* is quite a different case. His reappearance and his attempts to reclaim their three children centrally govern the plot and lead to the climactic scene in Rose's childhood home. Christopher's marriage to Rose has something of the flavor of Malcolm's to Jane and likewise leads to separation because of physical abuse as well as sexual conflict. But Christopher pursues Rose, and she finally accepts him back, resigning herself to the fatality that led her to marry him in the first place.

Rose's children, especially Konstantin, display much more personality and claim more of the reader's sympathy than any of the children in Drabble's earlier novels. We hardly get to know anything about Emma Evans's or Jane Gray's children, and though Rosamund Stacey's baby quickly gains our interest and sympathy, she remains more a symbol of Rosamund's maturation rather than a member of a family. Each of these mothers experiences a crisis of responsibility, indicating that Drabble's deepest moral principles lie with family. But this theme finds its fullest expression in Rose Vasiliou's motherhood, which comes alive in such rich and convincing detail. Furthermore, a narrative structure based on a return to origin—in which a character returns home and rediscovers his or her destiny in determining family influences—allows a broader scope and a deeper examination of the theme of motherhood. In acknowledging her inherited family ties as determinative of her search for self, Rose accepts the necessity for remarrying Christopher.

Drabble moves beyond, though she never abandons, the symbolism of the family for defining fate as universal design. In *The Realms of Gold,* Frances Wingate's children never seem very real, and her commitment to her family appears to demand little self-sacrifice and to yield little self-knowledge. Frances combines comic romance with a return to origin by finding in Karel the solution to both her love and her family inheritance. More important, Frances's anthropological training leads her to become preoccupied with her ancestral depression on a more general, sociological level than Rose's concerns about her parents.

Drabble continues to move beyond the individual in *The Ice Age,* as its title, epigraphs, and allusions to Providence and contemporary problems of English society attest. The adulterous affair between Anthony and Alison leads to no permanent or even compelling solutions, and Anthony's return to his origin is briefly sketched. The children are significant, to be sure, but more symbolic than Rose's children. Molly, Alison's second child, born with cerebral palsy, serves as a touchstone of the compassion and the humanity of the other characters (her older sister, her mother, and Anthony) and as a measure of the justice of Providence. Jane, while an interesting teenager in her own right, figures as symbol of cultural and spiritual imprisonment. The structure of the controlling Providential model—in which the guilt of a protagonist is linked with the ills of society, which are healed only when that guilt is expiated according to divine justice—focuses on the fate of England and Anthony's attempt to "justify the ways of God to man."

Drabble continues her sociological perspective in *The Middle Ground* and expects her next novel will extend this journalistic vein. In *The Middle Ground,* she again presents the possibilities of the tragic romance in the form of adulterous love and a return to origin in Kate's return to Bromley. But neither model adequately defines the plot, which pushes toward the Providential model as it emerges from the book's presentation of London. (pp. 9-13)

Drabble seeks in her later novels, and will undoubtedly continue to seek, a broader perspective that places less emphasis on individual characters than on the destiny of her society. The conflicts do not disappear, and her attitude toward fate remains the acceptance of, not rebellion against, inherent limits. But the narrative structures consist more of a dialogue between the individual and a wider community than between internal aspects of the self. (pp. 14-15)

By investigating the intertextuality of fate, we can suggest the dialectical opposition by which Drabble defines self-knowledge and grace. Her characters achieve wisdom, to greater or lesser degrees, by recognizing the intertext of their fate and, in different ways, by accommodating its demands. One might think this wisdom would bring hope that grace would relieve or lighten the burden of fate. But for Drabble, wisdom alone cannot alter one's destiny. In fact, awareness of fate and attempts to avoid it often ironically become the means for its fulfillment. Drabble's text imitates this irony by reflecting on the plot conventions that emerge from the characters' struggles with their fates. In both the text and the characters' imagined lives, resistance to a model ironically ends by affirming its universality. Drabble's intertextual play suggests that the terms for articulating conflict are embedded ineradicably in the cultural codes and conventions that shape one's consciousness.

Jane Gray, in *The Waterfall,* finds the intertext of tragic romance plaguing her even at the end, where she partly accepts and partly resents paying the price for her sexual liberation. She cannot recast the story of her life wholly in the form of tragic romance, but neither can she reject this model. Her ambivalence becomes her fate, leaving her dissatisfied, though wiser. Rose Vasiliou, in *The Needle's Eye,* claims at most a heroism, at worst a resignation, in accepting back her husband, but she knows more about why she must do it as a result of her visit home. Though her consciousness of the intertext of a return to origin contributed to her acceptance and makes her more admirable because more self-aware, it is not what accounts for the moments of grace that dignify her simplicity and ennoble her suffering. Anthony Keating, in *The Ice Age,* justifies the ways of God to man, we are told, but he cannot communicate his vision from his prison in Wallacia, and we suspect he will find it disappears if he is freed and returns to England. The Providential model remains incomplete, depending on our judgment of Anthony's ambiguous and possibly ironic revelation. All these characters come to a greater understanding of their fate by recognizing and by identifying the intertext controlling their consciousness. But consciousness alone, in Drabble's world, cannot bring freedom from the determinants of personality. (pp. 16-17)

John Hannay, in his The Intertextuality of Fate: A Study of Margaret Drabble, *University of Missouri Press, 1986, 112 p.*

LINDSAY DUGUID

Of the eight novels Margaret Drabble has published since 1963, the first five were notable for their slenderness and jaunty self-confidence. Since *The Needle's Eye* (1972), her books have spread, becoming more solid but less certain, and abandoning the singular perspective (typically that of a bright, attractive woman graduate) for a wider view. *The Radiant Way,* her first novel for seven years, is replete with these characteristic signs of age; pessimistic, diffuse and anecdotal, it charts the fortunes of three women and their circle, and takes for subject the state of the nation.

The book opens on New Year's Eve, 1979. At Liz Headleand's party at her house in Harley Street we meet Liz's old friends Alix and Esther, and mix with the media folk. "Liz moved from group to group, surveying from the stairway, engaging and disengaging, tacking and occasionally swooping, was pleased with what she saw. They were mixing and mingling, her guests; the young were speaking to the old, men were speaking to women, Left was speaking to Right." This rather sardonically presented set-piece suggests that we are to expect a panoramic novel of society, and the feeling is reinforced by the Trollopean device of introducing characters from the earlier books (Kate Armstrong, Anthony Keating, Gabriel Denham) to join the crowd.

Coincidence, fate and overlapping lives pervade the book. Brief career-résumés (including those of the three heroines, their lovers, husbands and children), case histories (Liz is a psychiatrist, Alix teaches in a women's prison), anecdotes, childhood reminiscences, snippets from newspapers, accounts of television programmes: all connect or proceed in parallel to produce a picture of present-day England; the struggles of Liz and her relatively well-heeled friends are compared with the lives of the inhabitants of tower blocks and squats or the men who sit on benches with bottles and roam the wastelands beneath flyovers. The novel touches on the far reaches of the Harrow Road, and also returns to Northam, Liz's birthplace, the grim, denatured, all-purpose Northern town in which is felt the leaden weight of a deprived childhood.

The Radiant Way is studded with revelatory incidents, often recounted after the event or given in indirect speech. It sometimes has the tone of stage directions. . . .

Against a background of cuts, strikes and general decline, the *malaise* of Britain is exposed by means of a series of carefully planned epiphanies (a breakdown on the motorway, a visit to the hospital morgue, a Christmas with stepchildren in St John's Wood, an encounter with a drunk in an aeroplane), and some political conundrums about the decline of the old liberal Left and the rise of Militant are articulated—at one point with the help of a curious neo-Socratic dialogue.

What links the poor and the rich and is common to the lives of all Drabble's characters, however, is not nationhood but madness and death. The dark fantasies of Liz's disturbed adolescence are merely one point on a map of mental states which range from anxieties and perplexities through phobias to full-blown psychosis. Of the genuinely mad, one girl, an ex-prisoner, manifests a chillingly perverted religious mania, while an Italian professor dabbles on the fringes of Transylvanian lycanthropy and a quiet young man is revealed to have committed a series of particularly horrible murders. Parents, husbands and colleagues die; there are precise evocations of bad faith and a virtuoso description of a severed head.

Drabble's selective technique and highly wrought prose—full of inversions, repetitions and rhetorical flourishes—militate against realism, so that despite her evident honesty and concern, the socio-political elements of the book seem strained and unconvincing. Where her vision does come into focus is in its iconographic fusion of squalor, decay, wounds, evil, sex, death and madness—seen as part of 1980s life but also belonging to a darker mystical world. Even the book's title (the title of a childhood reading primer) takes on a tinge of the numinous. Seen in this light, *The Radiant Way* is less like the familiar, warm, baggy panoramic novel of the nineteenth century and more like the paintings of the Neapolitan School mentioned in the book: a large, allegorical canvas scrupulously filled with writhing bodies and conveying, in a highly sophisticated frame of reference, images of horror and messages of dire import.

> Lindsay Duguid, "Icons of the Times," in The Times Literary Supplement, *No. 4387, May 1, 1987, p. 458.*

ANITA BROOKNER

The Radiant Way is Margaret Drabble's longest and most ambitious novel to date, and the one which leaves the reader most unsure of its status. The title refers, in the first instance, to a reading primer produced for children in the 1930s: its deeply evocative cover showed a small boy and a small girl skipping downhill, with a stylised sunburst behind them. In due course, *The Radiant Way* was the title of a pioneering television programme on education made by Charles Headleand, one of the many supernumerary characters in this long chronicle of changing manners: the evocative sunburst of the 1960s was educational expansion and the belief that such expansion would be the new birthright of the nation. And *The Radiant Way* is finally the title of Margaret Drabble's novel, but its use in this context is ironic, for the author has a story of decline and disillusionment to record. Since the story opens on New Year's Eve, 1980, and ends up close to the present day, it could be seen to be a panoramic view of Mrs Thatcher's England, but should this be too daunting, too factual a brief, it is filtered through the lives of three women (yes, again) who met at Cambridge during the 1950s and have been friends ever since. One is a psychiatrist, one an art historian, and one teaches English literature in a remand centre. All, therefore, are highly qualified to take up challenging positions in the years of female endeavour.

These professional women reveal enormous gaps in their reasoning capacity, and I am not sure how intentional this is. Liz Headleand, the psychiatrist, starts off the new decade by giving a party for 200 people in her Harley Street house. After the party she is stupefied to learn that her husband, the television producer, wants to divorce her and marry another woman. Apparently she has been too busy to notice any signs of this, although a gossip columnist of her acquaintance is always happy to tell her the news. This psychiatrist also has difficulty in relating to her, admittedly reclusive, mother, whom she has not seen for three years when the story opens. In addition to this possible flaw in her emotional make-up, she has never solved the mystery of her absent and unremembered father, although in her professional role she is an authority on parenting. All of this suggests a certain lack of credibility which, in so prominent a character, is something of a drawback.

Certain lapses of attention can also be traced in the other members of the trio. . . . In any event one feels that these women could do better, try harder. And in case their activities should not prove sufficiently diverting, it may be noted at this stage that the action of the novel also incorporates a series of decapitations perpetrated by a murderer known as the Horror of

Harrow Road, and a revelation, in the form of a bundle of newspaper cuttings found in her mother's desk, that the psychiatrist's father was in an interesting situation himself: further details would spoil the story for the reader who has already had to surmount a sticky beginning and 396 pages solid with talk and action before coming up against this meaty climax. The novel ends with the three women taking a picnic in Somerset, and demonstrating in every way that they have changed very little since their first meeting at Cambridge 30 years earlier. (pp. 29-30)

I found [the novel] readable but inauthentic, and at one point wondered how serious it was meant to be. Perhaps the intentions behind it are a little too undifferentiated. Or perhaps the problem, for a novel of this kind, is one of style. Margaret Drabble mixes the quiddities of contemporary English detective fiction—notably a familiarity with London street names—with a billowing and almost redundant use of adjectives and qualifying clauses. The heroine, Liz, stares into 'the white flaming chalky cracked pitted flaring columns of the gas fire'. . . .

Even one of the vowels in Liz Headleand's surname seems superfluous.

The result is an over-generous abundance of words to match a great deal of activity. There is material here for several novels: the three women saga, the condition of England saga, the severed heads mystery, and Liz Headleand's own family romance. Since the women are in their fifties, a certain capaciousness, a certain untidiness seem to be in order. Their conversations mix intimacy with extravagance, as do their relationships, for the London characters mix with the Northam characters in a complicated web of intermarriage that rather strains the memory. There are nods towards up-to-date fashions, with tenses slipping knowingly between past and present, yet the desire, I take it, is to write a traditional novel. Perhaps for this purpose the characters are not sufficiently built-up, or, alternatively, taken apart. The women, despite being so deeply serious, have a veneer of frivolity which militates against their being true and accurate portraits. The husbands and lovers remain marginal, and there is a modish indication, in the character of Esther, the art historian, that she will end happily in the arms of another woman.

I do not know whether real life is like this, for I cannot claim to have a closer knowledge of real life than that possessed by Margaret Drabble, but somehow I doubt it. And I cannot help feeling that the headlong style militates not only against the internalisation of opinion that the author seems to entertain but also against the broad concerns on offer. To deal with the condition of England, as many contemporary writers seem to feel called upon to do, requires a certain passionate estrangement which is missing here. . . . But perhaps these comments are unnecesarily captious. There is much here to admire, not least the peculiar stamina that keeps a long and detailed novel in play. For those who like their story-telling unmediated and their fiction abundant, *The Radiant Way* will certainly be their book of the year. (p. 30)

> Anita Brookner, *"Too Much of a Muchness,"* in The Spectator, Vol. 258, No. 8286, May 2, 1987, pp. 29-30.

HERMIONE LEE

Three women meet at Cambridge in 1952, drawn to each other by a shared sense of being 'on the margins of English life.'

Liz has got out of a working-class Yorkshire home (in 'Northam'), horrifyingly overshadowed by an eccentric, parsimonious, agoraphobic mother and an obscurely shaming, absent father. Alix, the embarrassed child of an old-fashioned Fabian in a northern Tory boarding-school, is now finding her political (left) feet. Exotic, secretive Esther left Berlin as a baby with refugee parents. Their ambitions: Liz's 'to make sense of things,' Alix's 'to change things,' Esther's 'to acquire interesting information.'

[*The Radiant Way*] begins with Liz's 1979 New Year's Eve party and ends in June 1985. The three are in their mid-forties, all living in London. . . . The three meet frequently, take long country walks together, observe and share each others' lives.

But, early appearances to the contrary, this is not a Mary McCarthyish post-university satire or a study of middle-class relationships, 1960s Drabble-style. Like her last two, *The Ice Age* and *The Middle Ground*, it is a large-scale historical novel, which uses the lives of the three women, 'Northam' and London, for a magisterial and profoundly pessimistic analysis of the two nations, the divided family, the waste-land that is Britain in the 1980s. . . .

'What is History'? In E. H. Carr's book of that name (read by Esther in the novel), historians are seen as relativists, of their time. To 'tell things as they really were' is thus impossible. If so, the novelist may be the best historian. Drabble takes on that responsibility, on behalf of the white middle classes, by way of a clever, practised, carefully worked-out parallel between manner and subject.

Her narrative believes, explicitly, in pattern and order; it makes cogent connections, controls coincidences and discoveries, likes to use a cool historical present, is prophetic and knowing, often to an irritating degree (there's a great deal of 'It might have been expected' and 'It will readily be perceived'). But pressing up under the rational articulacy and social realism are obscure symbols, vestigial relics of old myths—werewolf, headless corpse, floating wounds—arousing psychic unease and superstitious fear. . . .

Just so, these three competent, intelligent women all have a dark, repressed connection—Liz to her harmful parents, Esther to the demonic Claudio, Alix to a drug-taking girl criminal—which bides its time, and will out. Just so, again, the national 'psyche,' bent to the yoke of the 'new light' of rationalism, erupts in violence, cruelty and fear. An old Northern history is invoked of the battle between the Brigantes and the Romans; defeated by treachery, the Ancient Britons retreated, but their relics remained.

That the novel's chief image of repressed irrationality is a severed head may make for difficulties. The book is such a conscious literary construct—symbols out of Iris Murdoch, parties courtesy of Virginia Woolf, Hard Times after Dickens—that it feels as though it's lining itself up, somewhat portentously, for the 2085 edition of the Oxford Companion, as an 'Important Mainstream Novel of the 1980s.' And the reviews of national events ('these were the years of rising unemployment,' etc) can seem slick and banal by comparison with the sharp-eyed social encounters (Esther and a very drunk Dutchman on a plane) and the vigorous, sardonic family scenes (Shirley and her trying in-laws). I suspect that Margaret Drabble is not so much another George Eliot (as perhaps she believes) as another—say—Thackeray.

But the novel grows and grows. I began it suspicious of the familiar *milieu*, and ended it deeply depressed, but I was won over to its way of seeing. The lasting female friendship is a strongly-felt consolation (this doesn't look like a feminist novel, but its women are the survivors). And the narrator's belief, spoken by Liz, ('I don't believe in good and evil. I believe in suffering, and the alleviation of suffering') stands for a kind of hope, however equivocal and compromised, against the terminal apocalypse prophesied in the book's fine last words.

Hermione Lee, ''Three Women,'' in The Observer, May 3, 1987, p. 26.

DONNA RIFKIND

Margaret Drabble has been writing novels for about twenty-five years, and she has produced enough work to prove beyond doubt that she is a smart and talented writer. This said, it must be acknowledged that her novels, read together, are rather a tedious lot. Her protagonists practice different professions, are of different ages and temperaments, respond differently to their circumstances. But her novels suffer from a constraining sameness which keeps Drabble as a writer wandering around the same circle, treading the same ground. The fact has been clear and becomes clearer with the publication of her newest effort, *The Radiant Way*: Margaret Drabble stays where she is as a novelist because she has no place else to go.

The Radiant Way shares with Drabble's other fiction a central ambivalence toward her London world: on one hand, she echoes the ingrained, tiresome notion that modern life in England is an industrialized nightmare, breeding a universally crushing despair. On the other, her characters manage to live quite nicely in this allegedly doomed society. Their houses are comfortable, their children go to good schools, they themselves have enjoyed fine educations, and their pocketbooks, if not overflowing, have enough money in them to allow them to keep their lunch appointments in good restaurants. It is hard to imagine that such malaise and such ease could co-exist so companionably within these characters. (pp. 70-1)

Drabble draws [her] three main characters with an uneven hand. When Liz's husband announces he wants to divorce Liz to marry an aristocratic bore, Alix and Esther react with ''a critical curiosity that was not entirely comfortable or comforting,'' finding ''something almost satisfactory in watching her plunge and flounder and skitter off course.'' Elsewhere, however, these two seemingly coldhearted women show an unexplained excess of sentimentality; in several slightly absurd scenes, Esther fusses maternally over a potted palm. Esther, as a matter of fact, is an entirely disappointing character. Drabble wants us to believe that Esther has pared down her life so that she gets by with only the most necessary human attachments, that she wants little from life and offers little of herself to anyone. What we feel as a result, however, is that Drabble does not seem to care much about Esther and has therefore emptied her of most sympathetic qualities. The author is much more successful in presenting the messy vitality of a less central character, Liz's sister, a housewife in the dreary northern town where she and Liz were raised.

If Esther is a difficult character to believe in, an even more problematic case is Alix's husband, Brian. Brian is a man of lower-class origins who has become too bourgeois to be able to write the great working-class novel that once burned in him. He now spends his time teaching at a local college and fretting over various union strikes around the country. Although he

occupies an important position in the novel, Brian is so sketchy that we are unable to form an opinion of him; we glimpse him usually only when someone else speaks of him, or when Drabble, in a sociological mood, provides a few facts about his past.

Brian fails to come alive as a character for a more significant reason than Esther, who is merely a victim of the author's apparent apathy toward her. Brian fails because, although his interests are almost exclusively political, Drabble appears to have no sympathy at all for his struggle over the issues with which he is preoccupied. Except for a faintly cynical attitude toward progress and idealism, Drabble's tone toward Brian and toward her other characters is almost maddeningly dispassionate. . . . As Drabble shows herself to be aware, Brian's habit of pursuing a comfortable life while rejecting the society that makes this life possible (he is teaching Dickens's *Hard Times* to his university students while showing strong support for a steelworker's strike in the north) is a deeply hypocritical position. It is a position that has the potential for comedy, but this novel bears no trace of comedy, nor of tragedy, nor indeed of anything but Drabble's willful neutrality. This is not apathy on her part, but a deliberate refusal to do anything with her own understanding of this contradiction, and it paralyzes her ability to provide her characters with sufficient depth, and nearly everything in her fiction suffers as a result. I am not arguing here that Drabble ought to have written a novel seething with political biases. It is important, however, that a book so full of ideological conflicts should make us feel strongly about the characters who worry over these conflicts. Drabble is unwilling to do anything more than report on the situation and then retreat.

As a result, there is a patchwork quality to the narrative as it shifts from one character's preoccupations to another's, with no one event or idea given pre-eminence over the others. (pp. 71-2)

The most dramatic of the book's situations arrives after a good deal of preparation, but it nevertheless seems rather disconnected. Jilly Fox, one of Alix's more menacing prison students, is found murdered, her severed head resting on the front seat of Alix's car. Among the various warnings Drabble provides for this scene are Esther's dreams of decapitated heads, newspaper reports of a crazed killer of women on lonely streets, and Alix's extra-sensory fears for Jilly's safety. Despite the many portents, however, and despite the grisliness of the murder, this scene does not occupy a particularly key place in the narrative, nor is it meant to bear any significant thematic freight. One gets the sense that Drabble provided it because she felt required to come up with a melodrama to rescue the book from her own monotonous neutrality as a narrator.

Other elements in *The Radiant Way* make it a typical Drabble production. One is her habit of inserting the names of minor characters who have served as protagonists in her previous books. . . .

Also evident throughout Drabble's work is her excessive literariness. . . . Throughout *The Radiant Way* are references to Mishima and Maugham, Hardy and Orwell, Angus Wilson and Edmund Blunden; there are few Drabble novels wherein a character is not reading something by Iris Murdoch. (p. 72)

The best parts of the book are those in which Drabble stops neutrally narrating, drops the balanced, overtly literary presentation, and writes, as the cliché goes, from the heart. . . . But there are not enough of such passages, and the gloppy, transcendental ending ("The sun bleeds, the earth bleeds. The sun stands still") does not make up for their marginality. Drabble spends most of her pages chronicling what in *The Middle Ground* she described as "the tatty diversities of tatty distracting modern life." Yet these diversities do not seem quite as tatty as Drabble would have us believe, and her insistence that the British way of life is less than radiant adds up to a wearisome piece of novel-writing. If this is all there is, why take such cautious, precious care to get it all down? Surely there *is* more to contemporary British life than a list of well-digested complaints about quotidian existence, with a few murders and infidelities thrown in for variety. One goes to a newspaper morgue for recitations like this, not to a novel.

More serious, however, is Drabble's refusal adequately to confront the contradictions of modern life that she outlines so carefully throughout her books. She makes sure that she meets certain ideological goals in her narrations—vaguely leftist sentiments are always somewhere in the air—yet goes out of her way to prove that she does not wholly accept that ideology by producing in her tone a slightly sarcastic distaste for it. But since one cannot possibly believe that this hint of sarcasm constitutes a criticism of any sort, one finds Drabble retreating into an antiseptic, passionless narration that destroys any imaginative power her books might otherwise have had. One wonders how long a writer can go on rehearsing these evasions in novel after novel—and how long readers can continue to be interested in that writer's constant bumping up against a dead end. (pp. 72-3)

Donna Rifkind, "No Way Out," in The New Criterion, *Vol. VI, No. 3, November, 1987, pp. 70-3.*

JOHN UPDIKE

The Radiant Way, Margaret Drabble's new novel, forms a panorama, in its glancing way, of life in England from 1980 to 1985. Beneath its many personal incidents we feel not so much the triumph of Thatcherism as that dubious triumph's underside, the decline of the Labour Party—the ebb and fall of an idealistic socialism that for generations of British intellectuals and workers served as a quasi-religious faith.... Education, both enforcer and surmounter of the English class system, lies at the novel's heart: the novel's three heroines—Liz Headleand, Alix Bowen, Esther Breuer—all met at Cambridge, as bright scholarship girls, and in adult life Alix teaches English to young women in prison, Esther lectures on Italian art, and Liz is a psychiatrist, dispensing self-knowledge.

Though Liz, of the three, bulks largest, in her complicated vitality and in the closeness with which the author renders her thoughts and tears and panic and lust, Alix most plainly bears the novel's political burden, moving from an undoubting socialist activism to a political despair that finds comfort in sifting through the papers of an old avant-garde poet, a friend of Joyce and Pound, Duchamp and Man Ray.... She is the child of old-fashioned socialists—"not left-wing political extremists, not loony vegetarians (though they were vegetarians), but harmless, mild, Labour-voting, CND-supporting, Fabian-pamphlet-reading intellectuals." (p. 153)

But England . . . is the site and background of *The Radiant Way,* and not its essential theme. Miss Drabble is ever less a political theorist than an anthropologist, and the sprawling, dazzling pluralism of her novel is meant to illustrate the glimmering interconnectedness of all humanity.... The novel abounds with subtle connections—with names that recur after many pages, with coincidental meetings after many years, with semi-hidden threads between the South of England and the North, between the upper and the lower classes, between the public and the private realms, between individual lives and the great archaic rhythm of the national holidays. On New Year's Eve, "all over Northam, all over Britain, ill-remembered, confused, shadowy vestigial rites were performed, rites with origins lost in antiquity; Celtic, Pict, Roman, Norse, Anglo-Saxon, Norman, Elizabethan, Hanoverian, Judaic rites." (pp. 154-55)

Esther Breuer, petite and Jewish and Berlin-born, is the least English of the three central women, and the one about whom the most mystical lights glimmer in the vast human web. Her scholarship consists of flipping back and forth between books pursuing stray connections—e.g., "a connection between the nature of quattrocento pigmentation, and lichenology as a method of dating the antiquity of landscape"—and her lectures are known for "making startling, brilliant connections, for illuminating odd corners, for introducing implausible snippets of erudition." Esther claims that "all knowledge must always be omnipresent in all things." Her life as it develops bears witness to a connection between the Harrow Road Murders and the quiet young man above her flat in Ladbroke Grove, and to a link between her long-standing love for a married Italian anthropologist, Claudio Volpe, and the faltering vitality of a potted palm he has entrusted to her. Claudio, too, believes in a web, in an overarching world of spirit, in a hidden league of demonic powers: "He spoke . . . of the *spiritus mundi,* the *anima,* the *stella marina,* the *deus absconditus* . . . of Gorgon and the Medusa and Géricault and Demogorgon and Salome and the Bessi of Thrace." He believes that Esther has powers she does not recognize, and, uncannily, on an airplane, she meets and befriends a handsome wild Dutchman with whom Liz, long ago, had sexual intercourse on a North Sea crossing in a Force 9 gale. Esther is the spookiest of the three heroines, the most detached and exotic and the least heterosexual and, to this reader, real. She is a lovingly assembled bundle of bohemian costumes and odd facts about Italian painting, but her charm is more ascribed than conveyed.

It is not easy to dramatize the comforting fascination that some women have for each other. The increasingly frequent novels about the friendship among three or four or five women (for instance, this year's *Hot Flashes,* by Barbara Raskin) tend to be thin where thickness is alleged; the women, and the female author, keep *saying* how intense and meaningful the companionship is, but few actions actually illustrate it. The contacts are intermittent, giddy, and chatty, and leave each woman, in the end, alone with her life—her love life and her family life. Novelists presenting a multiple heroine commit themselves to a strenuous program of keeping a number of independent life stories going, and of summing up the high moments of mutuality and community with word pictures like "They [Liz, Alix, and Esther] would eat, drink, and talk. They exchanged ideas" and "They eat, drink, talk, lie there in the sunshine."

Another triangle of women exists in *The Radiant Way*: Liz Headleand; her sister, Shirley Harper; and their mother, Rita Ablewhite. Interest, psychological and narrative, so naturally gathers about this blood-related threesome that one suspects that Miss Drabble's youthful instinct in her joyous, prattling first novel, *A Summer Bird-Cage,* was sound when she placed her sisters in the center of the narrative and let the female friendships be peripheral. In *The Radiant Way,* the unbreakable kinship between Liz and Shirley serves to connect the two Englands—the thriving, entrepreneurial South and the depressed, working-class North. Liz, the older sister, slaved at her schoolbooks, got a scholarship to Cambridge, and escaped to London and her radiant big house on Harley Street; Shirley, the more rebellious as a girl, "trusted sex," seduced a boy and married him, and stayed in Northam, becoming "a middle-aged housewife, mother of three . . . with nothing before her but old age." Yet Shirley, in the very constriction of her life, is somehow more vivid and sympathetic than Liz, who is half lost in her larger but more amorphous and shallow world; the London scenes are full of chatter asserted to be delightful, while the scenes of Northam have that strong authenticity of something loved in spite of itself. To Shirley, the rebellious child, has entirely fallen the task of caring for the peculiar mother, who for as long as the girls can remember almost never ventured out of her house in Northam, fed her daughters on stale bread and fish paste, and perpetrated a fictitious tale about their absent father. This father, of whom Liz has no conscious memory, and the strange round silver object in the front room, engraced with the monogram SHO, are mysteries—connections not yet uncovered. They make Rita Ablewhite, lying in her bed and listening to the radio and cutting up her newspapers, the most fascinating character in the book, the keeper of its secret.

The initials SHO, we slowly discover, are those of three intertwined aristocratic families, . . . members of which are dotted throughout the book. This glint of silver in the lowly, gloomy house, together with the many brisk socioeconomic biographies offered in these pages, sparks the novels' noblest attempt at interconnection: the attempt to show, in the manner of, say, *Bleak House,* that no Englishman is an island, that the classes and regions are so woven together that manor house and palace impinge on rural hovel and urban slum, and the fates of a junkman like Krook and an orphaned street-sweeper like Jo can touch and alter those of Sir Leicester and Lady Dedlock. Alix Bowen gropes after such a democratic unity when she reflects,

> Sometimes she had a sense . . . that there was a pattern, if only one could discern it, a pattern that linked these semi-detached houses of Wanley with those in Leeds and Northam, a pattern that linked Liz's vast house in Harley Street with the Garfield Centre towards which she herself now drove.

But in the grand attempt to illustrate the pattern Miss Drabble is handicapped by her relatively small canvas and by the artistic embarrassment, which has set in since Dickens, about melodramatic coincidence and two-dimensional psychologies. For all the talk of connection, her novel portrays disconnection—between husbands and wives, parents and children, government and governed.

The Radiant Way is exasperatingly diffuse. Scores of characters are named and never recur; dozens of scenes we would like to witness are relayed secondhand or tersely alluded to; a modernist jumpiness and diffidence undermine the panoramic ambition. The novel feels both scattered and boiled-down—as if an editor had stepped in to speed things up when its first twenty-four hours took over eighty pages. The marriage of Charles and the woman he leaves Liz for, the aristocratic Henrietta, is left almost entirely to our imagination. The Headleands' adult children are evoked but not, as it were, set in motion. Charming, lively apparitions like the bosomy Irish cook Deirdre Kavanagh are not followed into any more adventures. A number of London characters seem to exist for no more urgent reason than that Miss Drabble knows people like them. Liz and Alix have suitors who are carefully groomed for leaps that never

come; Alix's marriage heads for a crisis and veers away. Even Liz's cunningly foreshadowed confrontation with her mother's secret, when it occurs, seems, at least to this reader, cursory, ambiguous, and sour: the long agony of Rita Ablewhite is laughed off as the bad smell from a jar of old pickles, while her daughters clean her house. . . . More than once in the novel, the banality of the human adventure, its every crisis so repeatedly charted and analyzed, dulls passion:

> And as Liz spoke and listened she was aware of a simultaneous conviction that this was the most shocking, the most painful hour of her entire life, and also that it was profoundly dull, profoundly trivial, profoundly irrelevant, a mere routine.

Well, a writer must be true to her bent, and Miss Drabble's is for the deft hint, the impulsive surge, the shrugging surrender to shapeless life. Her novel has a luxurious texture and wears a thousand beauties of expression and insight. . . . Liz's reaction to Charles's desertion warrants the novel's most extended and exploratory treatment; the interplay of her psychic and social and physical selves elicits details of a startling intimacy. . . . Miss Drabble is formidably knowledgeable: she received a double first at Cambridge and, in the five years coincidental with the era of this novel, edited and revised *The Oxford Companion to English Literature.* **The Radiant Way** makes self-conscious bows toward *Great Expectations* and the novels of Jane Austen ("three or four families in a country village," "a few families in a small, densely populated, parochial, insecure country"). Miss Drabble can be as chummy as Trollope with the reader. . . . One of the pleasures of her fiction is the companionship, on every page, of a lively mind showing its incidental erudition, its epigrammatic flair, its quick-witted impatience and impudence. But all this would be brittle were it not for her earthiness—her love of our species and its habitat—and her ability to focus on the small, sweaty intersections of mind and body, past and present. This latter gift is so much hers she takes it a touch too casually. The maze of human interaction she creates has many paths she declines to explore, or explores with a glance. *The Radiant Way* is a rare thing—a long novel we would wish longer. (pp. 155-59)

John Updike, "Seeking Connections in an Insecure Country," in The New Yorker, *Vol. LXIII, No. 39, November 16, 1987, pp. 153-59.*

ANN HULBERT

Margaret Drabble's long and ironic novel [*The Radiant Way*] about the early years of Margaret Thatcher's reign reads like a fat book with a thin book inside, dying to get out. . . .

Drabble was at work revising *The Oxford Guide to English Literature* when Thatcher began revising just about everything else in Britain during the first half of the '80s. Not surprisingly, Drabble was thinking big by the time she surfaced from the classics in 1984. What the decade needed was a Dickens or a George Eliot—an ambitious, imaginative social portraitist. In the '70s Drabble's formerly trim, Austen-like novels about trim young women had already begun to spread and blur as she grasped after greater scope. Now the time had come to undertake the state-of-England novel, and Thatcher's conservative revolution conveniently seemed to call for a large canvas. . . .

In the foreground she puts not one but three of her familiar protagonists, smart middle-class women from the north who graduated from Cambridge in the late '50s, then struggled gamely with men and professions in the '60s and '70s. "Amongst the *crème de la crème* of their generation," Liz Headleand, Alix Bowen, and Esther Breuer have been the beneficiaries of "the brave new world of Welfare State and County Scholarships, of equality for women; they were the elite, the chosen, the garlanded of the great social dream." When the novel opens in 1980, the three friends, all living in London and still regularly in touch, are apparently no longer feeling so elite, so chosen, so garlanded. (Drabble forever multiplies nouns, verbs, and especially adjectives, as though one word could never be sufficiently weighty.)

Drabble studiously distinguishes her middle-aged threesome. Liz "would like to make sense of things. To understand," Alix "would like to change things," Esther wishes "to acquire interesting information. That is all." Their predicaments, like their temperaments, are carefully complementary. (p. 38)

In fact, all three of Drabble's protagonists are curiously self-absorbed and unsympathetic, trapped in minds as meandering as the novel they inhabit. They meet monthly—"They would eat, drink, and talk. They exchanged ideas."—but are disconcertingly opaque to one another, and to the reader. Their creator picks them up and drops them as she pleases; and while she's got them, the usual treatment is to tell rather than show. Or simply to ask. At a turning point in Liz's life—when her shadowy family past rises up to unsettle her—the narrator interrupts with a quiz. . . .

But Drabble misses the most pertinent question, Does anybody care? When the narrator—who favors the 19th-century intrusive style—isn't treating her readers to rhetorical summaries of her heroines' lives and crises, she inundates them with details. One specialty is the slow, significant close-up; Alix spends a page (the second in the book) applying Fluid Foundation, makeup with a name that's meant to resonate. Another is the allusive scan that assumes familiarity with local landmarks— of British politics and media, of London street names and neighborhoods: Should Liz live in Harley Street, Kentish Town, or Kensington?

As if aware that her heroines' dilemmas risk becoming dull, Drabble assigns them each a threatening mystery—Liz's father haunts her; a disturbed inmate has a hold over Alix; an eccentric companion of Esther's grows increasingly strange—but these don't succeed in stirring them much below the surface. Drabble also aims to put her men in more dramatic predicaments; on either end of the political spectrum, they're supposed to be taking England's trauma more to heart. And they do: Charles and Brian, portrayed as childlike compared with their mature mates, are likably impressionable and passionate. They react to the public and private crises Drabble arranges for them, rather than merely ruminate about them. But even Charles's disillusionment with his past idealism (in the '60s he made a TV documentary, called *The Radiant Way,* in support of comprehensive education) and Brian's illusions about radical solutions are packaged into patronizing stereotypes: "Unlike Charles Headleand, Brian was a good man, and instantly recognizable as a good man."

Drabble's protagonists are women who muddle in the middle, avoiding extremes—of right and left, of height and depth. That might seem to make them the ideal center for a comprehensive portrait of a tumultuous era, but in fact their perspective proves to be disappointingly provincial. What Drabble dramatizes is her version of the emerging Social Democratic sensibility. The style, as she both evokes and projects it, is portentously de-

tached and cliquish. She and her protagonists may well be "in some kind of representative position of representative confusion," but it's a rarefied one—especially for anyone who lives outside of England, or even outside of Drabble's ex-Labourite, anti-Conservative ambience. The cluttered foreground invites insiders in search of self-portraits and is likely to daunt others; Drabble's sweeping background seems designed with aloof observers in mind.

But that is the exclusive audience of spectators whom Drabble means to address, as becomes clear in one of the novel's rhetorical panoramas. The narrator aspires to George Eliot-style gravitas and scope, updated with a self-conscious, knowing tone. Instead of empathy, the result is smugness: (p. 40)

Drabble has commented that "sometimes my book is more sociology than fiction, but I don't care." In fact, it isn't really sociology either. Drabble has made the laudable, rare effort to be comprehensive; she sees to it that her book includes north and south, rich and poor, country and city, public and private, young and old, men and women. But instead of bringing these categories to life, she often does little more than label them. Nor is her book more than superficially historically, even though she has ambitiously appointed herself chronicler of half a decade. Drabble's aerial surveys and frozen close-ups effectively undermine any sense of motion. The novel opens in 1980 amid apprehensive confusion and closes in 1985 amid fatalistic confusion, and it's only by resorting to an awkward plot contrivance that Drabble conveys any momentum at all.

Abandoning politics, sociology, and history entirely, she calls on hackneyed symbolism to rouse suspense and sum up her message. There are violent hints all along, alluding to the recurring exploits of the Horror of Harrow Road, who has been cutting off women's heads. He is finally discovered to be Esther's upstairs neighbor, and while the three women chatter downstairs, the police surround the house and the murderer surrenders. It's hard enough to take the severed heads seriously as an image of irrational darkness ironically counterposed to the "rational, radiant light" of the new regime. Drabble pursues the theme to the point of parody when the unremarkable murderer quietly emerges, an emblem of the banality of England's evil; it's as though he's meant to evoke reflections on the tragic normalcy of the official rash of cutting and slashing. (p. 41)

Ann Hulbert, "Maggiemarch," in The New Republic, *Vol. 197, No. 24, December 14, 1987, pp. 38, 40-2.*

GAYLE GREENE

Margaret Drabble once described Doris Lessing as "one of the very few novelists who have refused to believe that the world is too complicated to understand." The same may be said of Drabble, whose tenth novel [*The Radiant Way*]—her first since *The Middle Ground* in 1980—is an extraordinary work, a major literary event. Like the nineteenth-century novelists she admires, Drabble offers a panorama which encompasses the whole of English society, and takes on the hardest questions confronting that society, such issues as the relation of England's past to its present, the possibilities of progress (individual and collective), the responsibility of the individual. Set in the first half of this decade, spanning the time from New Year's Eve, 1979, to the spring of 1985, the novel takes England through 1984, the year of George Orwell's dreaded dystopia; and "1984" is repeatedly referred to, as is "brave new world"—grim portents in a work which asks what the future holds. . . .

On the simplest level, *The Radiant Way* is a novel of female friendship, in the genre of Mary McCarthy's *The Group,* Alice Adams' *Superior Women,* Marge Piercy's *Braided Lives;* but whereas typically in such novels women are differentiated in terms of their attitudes toward men, Drabble's protagonists are differentiated according to their interests and intelligences. Though marriage is important to them, their main efforts are directed at trying to understand the world, their plots center on something other than the making and unmaking of relationships. They are (like the most interesting of Doris Lessing's protagonists) intellectual rather than sexual adventuresses.

We meet them in their forties, living in London. Though parts of the novel take place in the industrialized North of England, *The Radiant Way* is (like *The Middle Ground*) set mostly in London, a London richly and variously rendered. As in the city of Dickens' novels, public squalor contrasts with private cosiness, interiors made comfortable by human effort and ingenuity—islands of "colour and light" in a "landscape of nightmare, an extreme, end-of-the-world, dreamlike parody of urban nemesis"; a "strange, surreal landscape" made menacing by graffiti ("kill the Mozart," "CLASS WAR NOW") and by a violence never far from the surface. Like the city of Eliot's *Waste Land,* Drabble's London has an apocalyptic cast, and Drabble evokes this imagery to suggest a similar question about the future: will this destruction issue into new creation?

The Radiant Way also has affinities with contemporary feminist fiction in its exploration of new choices and opportunities for women. Liz is the most obviously successful of the three, an "accomplished woman" who has achieved a brilliant career, marriage, a family and a house in Harley Street. Like other protagonists of contemporary women's fiction, her ambition is fuelled by matrophobia, "the dread of reliving her mother's . . . loneliness," a mother she has left ("long mad, imprisoned, secret, silent, silenced") in a cold, dark flat in the North (having somewhat unscrupulously turned her over to the care of a sister less successful than she at escaping their dismal background). As a psychotherapist, Liz is interested in what makes and motivates people—"what a mystery it is, the way we carry on"; and the trajectory of her career has affirmed the belief in progress which is essential to her practice—the assumptions that effort and knowledge lead to self-betterment, that understanding the past will improve life in the present.

Though the least ambitious of these women in terms of what she does (her part-time social work barely supports a life above the poverty line), Alix is the most ambitious intellectually. . . . One of the "connections" she aspires to is that between past and present—her own and England's; for, like Liz, she sees the past as a means of understanding the present. She tries to relate her Cambridge education to her present life and contemplates, more generally, England's literary past in relation to its present crises, asking what is the relevance of Shakespeare or Blake to the delinquent girls she teaches. (In a poignant scene she tries—unsuccessfully—to get them to see the connection between a Blake poem and their lives.) Alix's consciousness is filled with literary allusions, with quotes and misquotes that remind us that Drabble herself has spent the last several years editing *The Oxford Companion to English Literature.*

If Liz represents the "personal" and Alix the "political," Esther's response is a sort of combination of the aesthetic and scholarly. . . . Esther makes terms with life early on, using her flair for style to create a "halo of mysterious privilege" about herself, an aura which protects her from commitment to relationships, to work or to politics. Unlike the other two women, she never seriously questions herself. . . . (p. 4)

Though *The Radiant Way* is, like all Drabble's novels, a "good read," firmly anchored in social reality and in social realism, it is also interestingly self-reflexive in ways that make Drabble more than anachronistically "realist" at a time when "serious" (i.e. male) fiction is post-modern and experimental. None of the three women is a writer, but their ways of interpreting and ordering reality offer analogues to the making of narrative. Esther's belief that the whole may be seen in the part illuminates Drabble's own investigation of representative women, families, marriages, professions. Liz's interest in the personal past as a way of understanding the present provides a version of what the novelist does as she tries to make sense of the individual life, to construct the "sequence" of events which determines their "consequence" (the pun is Drabble's). Above all, Alix's aspiration to a "comprehensive vision" epitomizes Drabble's efforts to render the larger pattern: events are filtered through dozens of perspectives in a way that emphasizes relationship, the "intersecting circles" and "kinship networks" of society, connections both known and unknown. Though *The Radiant Way* is a "realist" novel, this narrative structure implicitly challenges a basic convention of realism: by scattering the interest over a myriad of consciousnesses, it thwarts identification with the striking individual and subverts the individualism encoded in realism—it "breaks the story" in Rachel Blau DuPlessis's phrase [as developed in her critical study *Writing Beyond the Ending: Narrative Strategies of Twentieth-Century Women Writers*].

The brilliant opening scene of the novel—the glittering, "up-market" New Year's Eve Party thrown by Liz and Charles Headleand—represents the high point of Liz's personal "accomplishment" and the potential of a certain kind of community as well. From all over London their guests assemble—young and old, men and women, left and right, art and science, "representatives of most of the intersecting circles that make up society." . . . The party does turn out to be a landmark, a "sign," but not of what Liz anticipated: in the course of the scene she realizes (what everyone else already knows) that Charles is about to leave her. The scene puts the reader through a process of misreading like Liz's, for only when we reach its end can we see that nothing meant what it seemed to.

The question of change on a personal level mirrors the question of change on the collective level—of transformation, renewal, progress, for England. The marriage and household are microcosmic; and their dissolution at the beginning of the novel and the beginning of the decade marks the end of a dream of unity, of transcending barriers, not only for individuals but for England. As in *The Middle Ground,* the lives of individuals reflect the times. . . .

The Radiant Way is a political novel: its characters think politically, see all issues politically, fall in and out of love on account of politics. But its politics are bleak. Events of the eighties put an end to the hope of social unity; the defeat of the miners' strike leaves England divided as never before and the Labour movement in ruins. Alix withdraws from political activity; Esther leaves England; so does Otto, convinced that "the whole thing has been an unmitigated, irreversible disaster." Liz continues her private therapy practice, made prosperous by the measures of a government she disapproves of, even though she has more or less demolished the moral and intellectual underpinnings of her profession, her progress having demonstrated that self-discovery is not necessarily "consequential."

Drabble's "Radiant Way" is an ironic title, as the exchange between Alix and Esther suggests: "You would have expected us to have marched forward into the new light by now? The rational, radiant light?' asked Esther. 'Well. Yes, I would,' said Alix. 'Wouldn't you?' 'I suppose I would have expected a little better,' said Esther. 'A *little* more light.' She sighed."

Esther, wandering through a desolate London landscape, reflects "one day they would rebuild . . . but when? There was a lot to flatten first." The question recalls that of *The Waste Land*, but Drabble does not expect destruction to issue into new creation. Nor does she hold out much hope for individual reform as a means of social progress. Nor does she make modernist claims for "art," for the civilizing powers of the artistic imagination (Alix's capitulation to "high art" notwithstanding), for she calls into question the assumptions on which narrative (and indeed most human effort) is based—that effort leads to enlightenment, that reason makes progress, that knowledge is power. Her narrative offers, rather, anticlimax, the disruption of causality, and an unsettling repetition, at crucial points, of the word "nothing." Like Shakespeare, who

refused to "play in wench-like words with that which is most serious" (a line that keeps recurring to Alix), Drabble turns on her own aesthetic structures.

The novel documents the end of "a great social dream," the dream of progress which emerged from post-war England. As Alix concludes, "there is no hope, in the present social system, of putting anything right. The only hope is in revolution, and Alix does not think revolution likely." But if political revolution is unlikely, another sort of "revolution"—the revolution that has returned Alix's poet employer to eminence ("Time has passed him by, and by its natural revolution, has caught up with him again") is not only likely but inevitable: things continue to continue, the wheel will grind on, and though its processes are "not yet finalized," neither are they susceptible to volition, intention, or comprehension.

Alix finds her conclusions "unsatisfactory," Liz finds hers "unsatisfactory," I find them unsatisfactory, and I imagine that Drabble does too. I can imagine the criticism Drabble's politics will incur; but her pessimism emerges convincingly, compellingly, from her depiction of contemporary England. (p. 5)

Gayle Greene, "The End of a Dream," in The Women's Review of Books, *Vol. V, No. 4, January, 1988, pp. 4-5.*

Nuruddin Farah

1945-

Somalian novelist, dramatist, short story writer, and translator.

An important figure in contemporary African literature whose fiction is informed by his country's turbulent history, Farah combines native legends, myths, and Islamic doctrines with a journalistic objectivity to comment on his country's present autocratic government. He also addresses the difficulties faced by Western-educated Somalians in coping with restrictive ancient customs and traditions. Because his novels often contain anti-government sentiments, Farah has lived in voluntary exile in England and Nigeria. J. P. Durix commented: "Farah combines the persuasive power of the propagandist with the lucid and paradoxical analysis of the genuine artist assailed by doubts; his mastery of a complex indirect form of narration based on echoes, symmetry and musical patterns makes his an original voice."

Farah's initial novel, *From a Crooked Rib* (1970), was the first work of fiction to be published in English by a Somalian author. This book presents the story of a rural Somalian girl who flees her family to escape her impending marriage to an elderly man. Seeking refuge in Mogadishu, the capital of Somalia, the girl is unable to adjust to the city's fast-paced environment and is eventually forced to become a prostitute in order to survive. *A Naked Needle* (1976) revolves around a British-educated young man whose search for a comfortable existence in post-revolutionary Somalia is complicated by the arrival of a former lover from England who intends to marry him. Reinhard W. Sander observed: "Next to Wole Soyinka's *The Interpreters*, [*A Naked Needle*] is perhaps the most self-searching [novel] to have come out of post-independence Africa."

Farah's best-known novels form the trilogy "Variations on the Theme of an African Dictatorship." These works document the demise of democracy in Somalia and the emerging autocratic regime of Major General Muhammad Siyad Barre, referred to as the "General" in this series. The first volume of the trilogy, *Sweet and Sour Milk* (1979), focuses upon a political activist whose attempts to uncover the circumstances of his twin brother's mysterious death are thwarted by his father, a former government interrogator and torturer. *Sardines* (1981), the next installment, depicts life under the General's repressive administration and examines social barriers that limit the quest for individuality among modern Somalian women. This novel centers on Medina, a young woman who loses her job as editor of the state-run newspaper for refusing to support the General's domestic policies. Medina must also contend with her mother-in-law's insistence that she allow her eight-year-old daughter to be circumcised, as decreed by tribal law. Critics admired Farah's realistic evocation of his heroine's tribulations, and Charles R. Larson stated: "No novelist has written as profoundly about the African woman's struggle for equality as has Nuruddin Farah." *Close Sesame* (1982), the final volume of the trilogy, concerns an elderly man who spent many years in prison for opposing both colonial and postrevolutionary governments. When his son conspires to overthrow the General's regime, the man's attempts to stop the coup cost him his life. According to Peter Lewis, "*Close Sesame* analyses the betrayal of African aspirations in the postcolonial period: the appalling

abuse of power, the breakdown of national unity in the face of tribal rivalry, and the systematic violation of language itself."

Farah's next novel, *Maps* (1986), is set during Somalia's war against Ethiopia in the late 1970s. In this work, Farah examines conflicts between nationalism and personal commitment through his story of Askar, a Somalian orphan who is raised by an Ethiopian woman. As Askar approaches adulthood, he is forced to choose between enlisting in the army and caring for his ailing adoptive mother, who is suspected of being a spy. Although some reviewers faulted *Maps* for awkward prose and confusing shifts in chronology, Christopher Hope concluded: "[It] is always the sincerity of the emotions and [Mr. Farah's] ability to make them palpable that distinguish this tantalizing and original novel, and make it a journey into what [he] calls the 'territory of pain' and what we, rather loosely perhaps, call Africa."

(See also *Contemporary Authors*, Vol. 106.)

KIRSTEN HOLST PETERSEN

Nuruddin Farah sifts the modern Somali experience through an exceedingly sensitive mind, and it is not surprising therefore that he eschews easy solutions and instead poses a set of questions. The questions he asks are to a very large extent the questions asked by the majority of modern African writers, and his authorship is very much part of the established African literary tradition in which the educated élite takes a "critical-and-yet" view of their societies.

Nuruddin Farah's three published novels, *From a Crooked Rib, A Naked Needle,* and *Sweet and Sour Milk* as well as *Sardines* (to be published shortly) deal with the role (or perhaps plight) of women in a Muslim society, the role of the educated élite, the corruption of the political élite and the repressive nature of the Somali revolution. Both by virtue of his educated background and his themes Nuruddin Farah conforms to the established canon of African writing, and a useful angle from which to investigate his work would seem to be to try and discover if he has added any new insight to it. Looked at in that way he is at least interesting when he discusses the tribalism and corruption of the military/political élite. His description of the alcohol, cars and fast women syndrome adds nothing to the already existing picture, except perhaps a well-chosen quote from Clemenceau to the effect that America "in only one generation" had "ceased being referred to as a barbaric nation and had qualified itself to be labelled decadent." The quotation is used with reference to Africa, but maintains the characteristic ambiguity found in all of the novels. (p. 94)

The naked needle in the book of the same name is Koschin, a young Somali, living in Mogadiscio during the early days of the revolution. In the prelude, which is written in first person narrative, he states the two events which are causing him his present concern and which are the two interwoven themes of the book. They are the revolution "to which I am loyal" and the fact that an English girlfriend, Nancy, whom he has invited to Somalia "on the whim of a day" has just sent a telegram announcing her arrival. These two events on their different levels are forcing him to make decisions, a thing he has never been able to do. This state of affairs is not much improved in the course of the book. On the political level he assesses means and ends by way of an image: "A revolution, y'know, is a pill that tastes bitter, the benefits of which are felt only when one has gone through the preliminary pain and pestilence." Loyalty to the revolution is considered necessary, and towards the end of the book a somewhat toothless and pompous stance is made. "Whoever will do any good for this country and for Africa, I shall back till I die. Go up to the pulpit, do something good and I shall certainly be on your side. If these fail to do what they owe us, I shall declare war against them, single-handed even though I am." The author is, of course, hiding behind his character, and there is no precise indication of his attitude towards him. On the personal level Nuruddin Farah discusses the problems of a small group of Somali/white couples to which Koschin belongs. This is given a political dimension, not in relation to Somali, although it is stated that white wives are a handicap, but in a wider perspective of sexual power-relations between races. However, here also there is a lack of a final point of view. The first half of the Somali man/American woman love story is very much in the vein of Armah's *Why Are We So Blest,* but the second part blames the man for trapping the woman in an alien society by not telling her the truth beforehand. The moral, as pronounced by Koschin is to make sure not to be trapped. "I prefer whoring to marrying, I, for one, feel free." There is nothing wrong with that as a solution, but the whole incident is yet another example of an irritating tendency in the book to touch on vital topics only to drop them in an offhand manner. The style also suffers from

this indecision. Sentences like "I . . . blinded to his wishes by a belief that may be killed no sooner than to-morrow" leave one visionless.

Although some of these flaws are still present in *Sweet and Sour Milk* the higher degree of firmness in both character development and statements of opinion makes it a more rewarding book to read. The book centres on a pair of identical twins, Soyaan and Loyaan, and their different attitudes to the revolution. The tone of the book is much more sinister, and arrests, imprisonments, tortures, informers and generally an atmosphere of fear prevail. Soyaan dies mysteriously in the beginning of the book under circumstances which indicate that he has been poisoned by the regime. Trying to ascertain the truth his brother traces Soyaan's movements using the few clues left to him—cryptic notes and coded messages found in his pocket. This is reminiscent of the detective story technique, but as well as finding out some facts about his brother. . . . [Loyaan] is driven by a personal wish to vindicate his brother, but the insight he gains into the machinations of the regime eventually force him to accept the validity of his brother's vision and try to incorporate it into himself. In a situation of stress he tells himself, *"you must help encounter and then fuse the talents of Soyaan and Loyaan; in you must encounter the forces of life (Loyaan) and death (Soyaan)."* To a reader who is used to more heroic stances against oppression, like, for example, Armah's *Two Thousand Seasons,* Loyaan's political maturing may seem excessively slow and naive, but Nuruddin Farah shares with Ngugi a concern for the doubts and failings of ordinary people who find themselves in extraordinary situations with which they cannot quite cope. Unlike Ngugi's characters, however, Nuruddin Farah's do not reach a definite point of view as a result of their deliberations. At the end of the novel Loyaan, despite his new insight, is still unable to act and the reader is still not certain just how much insight he has gained. The two novels represent a small and somewhat timid beginning of a crucial awareness which, however, in the Somali context, is enough to keep Nuruddin Farah in exile.

A critical view of present political powers, whether black or white, is a theme which in modern African literature is often combined with a search for roots, an affirmation of the validity of traditional society and its potential as a source for a new beginning which should replace the society under attack. One could mention writers like Achebe, Soyinka, Kofi Awoonor, Armah, and Ngugi. In this respect Nuruddin Farah differs radically from the established canon. He finds no virtue in traditional Somali social organization: indeed his two pet hatreds seem to be the patriarch in the traditional Somali Muslim family and the concomitant subjection of women. The patriarch or head of an extended family group as represented by Loyaan's and Soyaan's father is a petty tyrant with unlimited power over the members of his family, and in the larger context of the society he is a cowardly police informer. In [*Sweet and Sour Milk*] Nuruddin Farah connects these two social levels through a quotation from Wilhelm Reich: "In the figure of the father the authoritarian state has its representative in every family, so that the family becomes its most important instrument of power." This juxtaposition of negative aspects in traditional and modern society amounts to a heresy in African writing. It is closely connected with Nuruddin Farah's unique sensitivity towards the situation of women in traditional Somali society. Ironically, he would seem to be the first feminist writer to come out of Africa in the sense that he describes and analyzes women as victims of male subjugation. . . . The detached view of Nuruddin Farah's book, which coincides with the ideology and anger of the Western feminist liberation movement, has only become possible in West Africa with a second generation of writers, some of whom have gained enough self confidence to question and reject aspects of their heritage. The Nigerian writer Buchi Emecheta's description of the subjugation of women in traditional Ibo society is a result of this development and so far the only approximation to Nuruddin Farah's work. *From A Crooked Rib* will I think go down in the history of African literature as a pioneering work, valued for its courage and sensitivity.

Due to a mixture of Islamic law and the needs and hardships of nomadic life the position of women in traditional Somali society would seem to be extremely low. A woman is the property of a patriarch. As such she has no individual rights, but she is protected as a member of her lineage group against outside abuses. Thus blood compensation in slaughtered camels is demanded if she is murdered, even though the amount is only half of the blood compensation demanded for a man. Marriages are arranged by the patriarch who also settles the bride price. Nuruddin Farah incorporates into *From A Crooked Rib* the ethnographical information which is necessary for an understanding of the dilemma of the main character. This information coincides with what one can learn from reading an ethnographical survey, but his use of it is strongly coloured by his attitude. The information that "the engagement and marriage are ratified by a series of presentations" is expressed in the following way in *From A Crooked Rib*:

> From experience she knew that girls were materials, just like objects, or items on the shelf of a shop. They were sold and bought as shepherds sold their goats at market-places, or shop-owners sold the goods to their customers. To a shopkeeper what was the difference between a girl and his goods? Nothing, absolutely nothing.

The main character in the novel, Ebla, a young nomad girl, is sold several times in the course of the story, and when she understands the connection between her human value and money she draws the logical conclusion. "She scratched her sex, then chuckled 'This is my treasure, my only treasure, my bank, my money, my existence.'" This realization is made probable by the story. In order to avoid a forced marriage to an old man, Ebla flees from her nomadic kinship group to the city. By doing this she becomes a woman who is not owned by anybody, and as such she has no legal protection. She joins the marginal group of widows, spinsters and divorced women whose only means of survival is prostitution or shades of it. Ebla marries a student who soon after leaves for Italy, and she is left to fend for herself. Marriage is the purpose of her life, but she has confused ideas about it, and the book is somewhat contradictory on this point.... After the consummation of her marriage (which, incidentally, according to tradition is preceded by her husband beating her up), Ebla wishes that she were either an old woman or a man so that the experience would not have to be repeated. None of her problems are solved in the course of the book, but the reader is left with a very clear vision of the narrow space within which a Somali woman can define herself, and the virtual impossibility of breaking down the walls of tradition and widening the space.

With no sympathy for traditional society and a critical attitude towards the Revolution, Nuruddin Farah must be a lonely man in Somalia. Pushed by his own sympathy and sensitivity, but not pushed too far, anchored to a modified Western bourgeois ideology, he battles valiantly, not for causes, but for individual freedom, for a slightly larger space round each person, to be filled as he or she chooses. It is a thankless task, and Nuruddin Farah stands guard over liberty in Somalia like the camel owner of an anonymous traditional Somali song:

> One of my she-camels falls on the road
> And I protect its meat,
> At night I cannot sleep,
> And in the daytime I can find no shade.

(pp. 95-100)

> *Kirsten Holst Petersen, "The Personal and the Political: The Case of Nuruddin Farah," in* Ariel: A Review of International English Literature, *Vol. 12, No. 3, July, 1981, pp. 93-101.*

JOHN MELLORS

Nuruddin Farah was born in Somalia and now teaches English in a Nigerian university. His protagonist in *Sardines* is a young journalist, Medina, who has just been sacked from the editorship of Somalia's only daily newspaper because she would not print in full the speeches of the General, the ruling dictator. In Nuruddin Farah's 'beloved country' a man gets a life sentence for saying 'the General wasn't God', and a woman shows her independence by keeping her public hair 'untrimmed—curly and unshaven and shocking'.

Nuruddin Farah has a remarkable ability to see things from a woman's point of view and to express the relationship between mother and daughter and between women friends. A victim describes to another woman what it is like being raped: 'It is the element of surprise that is so shocking . . . being caught unprepared, unaroused, dry.' Medina is determined that her eight-year-old daughter will not be subjected to circumcision. She herself had endured infibulation, and she tells a friend, a younger woman, that 'if they mutilate you at eight or nine, they open you up with a rusty knife the night they marry you off . . . Life for a circumcised woman is a series of de-flowering pains, delivery pains and re-stitching pains.' *Sardines* gives the European reader fascinating glimpses of a strange, exotic way of life. Not the least strange thing about it is the language of conversation, in which almost every sentence is embroidered with colourful similes or metaphors. (p. 828)

> *John Mellors, "Beloved Countries," in* The Listener, *Vol. 106, No. 2741, December 31, 1981, pp. 827-28.*

FAITH PULLIN

With this new and extremely ambitious novel [Farah's novel *Sardines*] Farah continues with several of his major themes, but the texture of the work is more densely packed than ever before. As is often the case, Farah writes from a woman's point of view and with a committed sympathy for that woman. His protagonist here is Medina, a cosmopolitan journalist who has been sacked by the Somali authorities because of a confrontation about editorial policy. Medina is not only in conflict with the authoritarian regime itself but with traditional religion, as represented by her mother-in-law, and this double dilemma is also associated with her resistance to the second-class status of women in her society. All these problems become focused on the issue of her eight-year-old daughter's circumcision. . . . The novel reveals a whirlpool of influences—Arab, Somali, Italian, British and Russian—which create no synthesis but merely cause danger and disillusion. Medina herself is the archetypal westernized African who is seen, and sees herself, as a 'guest' in her own country. She has become emancipated from Islam and subscribes to a new political philosophy but she remains, as an individual, essentially dispossessed. The 'story' of **Sardines** is that of Medina's progress towards full commitment: 'No, she wasn't a guest any more. She was a full and active participant in the history of her country.' Farrah is a disturbing writer whose linguistic inventiveness sometimes overpowers author and reader alike; but, in terms of vitality, compassion and the ability to take literary risks, his talent demands recognition.

> *Faith Pullin, in a review of "Sardines," in* British Book News, *Spring, 1982, p. 320.*

CHARLES R. LARSON

[**Sardines**] continues the attack against the current Somali government begun in **Sweet and Sour Milk** (1979). **Sardines** is in fact a sequel to that earlier novel. The foreground of the story is dominated by the ominous power of a fascist general who runs the government: the secret police are everywhere, security thugs trail the innocent, people disappear at random—these are the ubiquitous forces of "the paranoid government which had forced itself upon them by seizing power and then constituting itself as the only legal authority in the country." Yet, with material which might seem heavily didactic in the hands of a less-skilled writer, Farah has returned to a subject that has interested him since the beginning of his career: the role or roles African women play in their contemporary societies.

Sardines is thus a novel largely about women, particularly women who play influential roles within the government yet nevertheless find themselves locked within a masculine power structure, confronting the age-old questions of sexual liberation. Perhaps one example will suffice. When one of the main characters visits a local burial ground, she muses, "Girls were discriminated against as usual and weren't buried there; they were buried outside the family cemetery." No novelist has written as profoundly about the African woman's struggle for equality as has Nuruddin Farah. (p. 59)

> *Charles R. Larson, "Third World Writing in English," in* World Literature Today, *Vol. 57, No. 1, Winter, 1983, pp. 58-9.*

VALENTINE CUNNINGHAM

Nurrudin Farah mythicises recent Somali politics [in **Close Sesame**]. History chose old Deeriye when his birthday coincided with the African National Congress's foundation and the writing of Dervish Sayyid's poem about the death of a British Camel Constabulary officer. Opposed nowadays by his own countrymen's oppressiveness, Deeriye relives past loves and ancient stories, asserts the merits of madness, Mullahs, cryptic prophets, and takes eventually to violent action. Much of which may occasionally read like dilute Salman Rushdie. But in it all the extraordinary mystiques of African-ness and the inevitable if crab-like powers of enigmatic African utterance are most captivatingly presented.

> *Valentine Cunningham, "Biggles and the Murks," in* The Observer, *November 6, 1983, p. 31.*

J. P. DURIX

Close Sesame concludes Nuruddin Farah's trilogy, **Variations on the Theme of an African Dictatorship**. . . . [This] last volume centres on an ageing asthmatic patriarch, Deeriye, who has spent most of his life in prison, first in the colonial period, then under "the General" for his opposition to the President's methods of government. . . . [The] protagonist is a self-avowed Pan-Somalist and Pan-Africanist; he has always defended freedom and state-administered justice against exploitation and tribalist politics. Now that he is reduced to a frail creature over-protected by his children, he can only perceive reality through rumours or indirect reports. . . . Yet, when he senses that his son, together with friends of his, are plotting to overthrow the dictator, he suddenly fears for their lives and begins to wonder whether he has not unduly imposed his political ideas on them. Plagued by doubts, he seeks reassurance in the affection of his family and friends, in the strict observance of the Muslim rituals and in his favourite texts, the Koran, the Sayyid's poems and the Wiil-Waal traditional stories which he tells his grandson Samawade. He becomes increasingly absorbed in visions of Nadiifa, his dead wife, and less and less sure about the borderline between reality and dreams, between vision and political action.

Khaliif, a high civil servant who has suddenly become insane after a brief sojourn in the hands of the secret police, is the only man who can speak openly about the political situation. When Deeriye is hit by a stone thrown by Yassin, the ten-year-old son of his neighbour, a supporter of the General, his fate parallels that of Kaliif, since the narrator reminds the reader that, in the Muslim tradition, only dogs, adulterous women, crows and madmen can be lapidated. This event becomes more significant when, at the end, Deeriye, who has decided to leave his protected seclusion in an attempt to kill the General, is riddled with bullets by the Presidential Guard and left lifeless on the ground with a copy of Ya-Sin in his pocket. Thus Deeriye, in his mission as dreamer, visionary, prophet of Truth and sacrificial victim, evokes Allah's envoy who, in the thirty-sixth sura of the Koran, was nearly stoned to death for preaching the Divine Word.

Close Sesame confirms Farah's reputation as one of Africa's major writers, and as the creator of a new language, strong, poetic and possessing great rhythmic qualities, which, like the author himself, is cosmopolitan yet rooted in the Somali tradition. There is none of the stridency and occasional self-indulgence which mars some passages in earlier novels such as **A Naked Needle**. Farah combines the persuasive power of the propagandist with the lucid and paradoxical analysis of the genuine artist assailed by doubts; his mastery of a complex indirect form of narration based on echoes, symmetry and musical patterns makes his an original voice, for which the opposition between the committed writer and the aesthete has become obsolete.

> *J. P. Durix, "Through to Action," in* The Times Literary Supplement, *No. 4211, December 16,1983, p. 1413.*

PETER LEWIS

Close Sesame is a novel about contemporary African politics and it is set in Mogadiscio (Farah's Italian spelling), the capital of Somalia. The recent history of the Horn of Africa is unlikely to be at everyone's fingertips, and although Farah clarifies aspects of Somalia's colonial and postcolonial history in the novel, intending readers would benefit from a little preliminary research, if only an entry in a good, up-to-date encyclopedia. At the centre of this tragicomic novel is Deeriye, an elderly and humane Somali of national renown who has devoted his life to liberating his country from British and Italian colonialism and to establishing a free society in an independent Somalia. The price he has paid for his nationalist activities and political idealism is many years spent in prison, and the so-called Somali Democratic Republic of today, a quasi-military dictatorship masquerading as a one-party Islamic and revolutionary socialist state, is a grotesque parody of the country he struggled to create. . . . The title of the novel, reversing Ali Baba's magic command, points to the historical irony that the novel confronts: for a number of African countries, liberation has produced tyranny. As one character puts it: 'We Africans did not struggle against the white colonialists only to be colonized yet again by black nincompoops'. No sooner has the cave been opened than it has been closed again. *Close Sesame* analyses the betrayal of African aspirations in the postcolonial period: the appalling abuse of power, the breakdown of national unity in the face of tribal rivalry, and the systematic violation of language itself, so that such words as 'democratic' and 'socialist' are as perverted as 'pacification', for example, was in the colonial era. Farah's acute sensitivity to the distance between official language and actuality in a totalitarian state is remarkably similar to Dovlatov's. (pp. 104-05)

> Peter Lewis, "Closing the Cave," in London Magazine, *n.s. Vol. 23, No. 11, February, 1984, pp. 101-05.*

J. I. OKONKWO

Perhaps it was inevitable that in their presentation of African society, most African writers, being males, have tended to project an exclusively male, distorted view of that society, although one of the earliest Caribbean novels, Claude McKay's *Banana Bottom* (1933), has a woman, Bita Plant, as its central character. Since the proclaimed objective of African writing, especially in its early manifestations, was a reclamation of an African world view that was already on the eclipse, few had sufficient knowledge of the genuine society to question seriously, at the time, the authenticity of the executed re-creations in literature. . . . One aspect of African social existence whose portrayal remained unchallenged for a long time is the life of women within the societies depicted in these creative works. Not only were women characters few, but when they appeared they did so in subservient and insignificant roles. Even then, very little effort was made to illuminate their lives in any detail within the circumscribed role assigned them in traditional society. (pp. 215-16)

It is remarkable that two of Africa's leading creative writers, Chinua Achebe and Wole Soyinka, have been unable to conceive of a woman except in terms of an appendage to man (in the case of Achebe) or as a prostitute, disguised or undisguised (in the case of Soyinka). One sociology researcher has actually discredited the validity of the view of women conveyed in Achebe's fiction in the light of sociological findings that women in traditional society wielded great power and functioned in a greater variety of roles than those ascribed in Achebe's novels. In a novel like *Arrow of God* (1964), for instance, "there are only three females, two of whom are quarrelling wives, and the third, a daughter who is a battered wife." Even in those novels which Achebe sets in modern African society, *No Longer at*

Ease (1960) and *A Man of the People* (1966), the women are merely sex objects. . . .

If Achebe prefers to suppress his women, Soyinka, like Cyprian Ekwensi before him, gives her liberty, but liberty of a dubious quality. From the flirtatious, inexperienced Sidi of *The Lion and the Jewel* (1959), Soyinka's women graduate into Rola or Madame Tortoise of *A Dance of the Forests* (1963), Seji of *Kongi's Harvest* (1967), Simi in *The Interpreters* (1965) and Iriyise of *Season of Anomy* (1973)—the seductive siren, at once desirable and potentially dangerous, but always playing second fiddle to man. (p. 216)

The African writer who has done the greatest justice to female existence in his writing, in the number of female characters he projects and the variety of roles accorded them as well as in the diversified attitudes toward life represented, is the Somali author Nuruddin Farah. . . . The perspective from which Farah projects his women is almost unique within the context of African creative writing. With the possible exception of Ousmane and Armah, whose women possess some vision on which they base their actions, Farah seems virtually alone among African writers in depicting the progress which women have made within the constricting African social landscape. Problems there may be, and for some they are insurmountable. Nevertheless, a good many women are succeeding in scaling the hurdles; and Farah exhibits them, together with their achievements and the challenges with which they are confronted. So pervasive and consistent is his espousal of the female cause that he has been described as "the first feminist writer to come out of Africa in the sense that he describes and analyses women as victims of male subjugation" [see Kirsten Holst Petersen's excerpt above].

Farah's championing of the cause of women is part of his crusade against tyranny and victimization not just of women, but of all who are denied their legitimate rights—social and political, private and public. . . . With his novels *From a Crooked Rib* (1970), *A Naked Needle* (1976), *Sweet and Sour Milk* (1979) and *Sardines* (1981), we are introduced to yet a new trend in the large corpus of modern African creative writing, particularly the novel. The central feature of this new trend is the demythification of the traditional and communal concept of African life, the generally glorified African past, which overidealized the beauty, dignity and excellence of African culture. Farah, like Ekwensi and Soyinka (in his novels), is completely immersed in the present. His novels offer an incisive picture of contemporary African realities compounded with vestiges of tradition and elements of modernism. He sees his function as the molding of opinion (through authentic information) against social and political oppression. He champions the cause of individual freedom and exposes such aberrations as nepotism, misused tribal allegiances, female suppression and stifling materialism, which are responsible for the debasement of humanity and the standard values of the modern African. The first novel, *From a Crooked Rib*, discusses the feminine plight and the general odds which weigh against the female in a traditional Islamic cultural environment. The first two books of his proposed trilogy, *Sweet and Sour Milk* and *Sardines,* give prominent places to women and highlight the repressive and horrifying aspects of the Somali military regime.

The basic female problem, the uncomplimentary status accorded her in African society, is given a general treatment in *From a Crooked Rib.* Although the major character of the novel, Ebla, sets out to extricate herself from the imprisoning women's role in traditional society, her reflections on the matter delve into the general female predicament which exists in modern societies. The novel deals with Ebla's moral and intellectual growth, detailing her progress as she quests for personal freedom and dignity. Escaping from the imminent imprisonment of an arranged marriage to Giumalel (who is old enough to have been her father, and whose two sons had earlier courted her), she is nearly pawned to another consumptive man. But she has sufficient intelligence and strength of character to gradually work out her own destiny.

Ebla is introduced in a prologue through her grandfather's musings about her flight from home; we also learn that she is a member of a Jes (a unit of several nomadic families living together). She and her brother were orphaned early and were entrusted to their grandfather's care. . . . She is presented as intelligent, philosophical and self-willed. Her revolutionary outlook on life makes her question the application of Koranic teachings to every detail of social life. One is surprised that, despite her rural nomadic background, she is capable of examining not only her individual plight, but also the place of women vis-à-vis the male in society. Ebla ponders over many issues.

Such intelligence and individualism are at complete variance with the prescribed confinements of Ebla's cultural and religious environment. Her flight from home is not just a simple matter of not wanting to marry Giumalel; it is her desire to assert her individuality, and also to be understood and appreciated as a human being. (pp. 217-18)

Farah tells the story of Ebla's journey to discovery in a straightforward narrative style. His adroit manipulation of the naïve narrator through whose voice we hear Ebla's story is impressive. The focus on Ebla unveils the deep recesses of her mind in this picaresque adventure. Her innocent ingenuity is conveyed not only in her own thoughts and utterances, which pervade the novel, but also in the naïveté of the narrative voice itself. . . .

The action of [*From a Crooked Rib*] takes its cue from an epigraph, a Somali proverb which emphasizes the subordinate existence of women: "God created Woman from a crooked rib; and any one who trieth to straighten it, breaketh it." Ebla's revolt is aimed at the refutation of this guiding proverb, a male-chauvinist slogan. The title, like Buchi Emecheta's *Joys of Motherhood,* is ironic, for Ebla succeeds in demonstrating the feminine capability of self-assertion and independence. This subtly ironic device, curiously unobtrusive though pervasive, stems from Farah's detachment, which allows the style slowly to reveal the deeper meaning of the novel. (p. 218)

Asha, the landlady with whom Ebla comes in contact after her marriage to Awill, presents another face of woman in this novel. Although she is immoral and greedy, her strong personality is striking. She is a confident and psychologically stable matron who has fought her way to survival in the modern, urban, dog-eat-dog environment. Farah creates a strong feminine independence in Asha in order to portray the potential of individual female achievement in a world dominated by men. Asha has a house in town which she rents on a tenement basis. Apart from the maternal role she adopts toward her tenants, like Awill, she also controls them, manipulates their love lives and purse strings. She tutors Ebla on how to take her revenge for her husband's infidelity.

The widow and Aowrolla, on the other hand, are victims of the rigid Muslim culture. Both appear passive and indifferent to the plight of women. The widow has been subjected to

Muslim peremptory divorce, and Aowrolla experiences the painful, agonizing chastisement of childbirth. Together they represent all women who have accepted the age-long inequality of the sexes, with a reward that comes only through children.

Female characters in *From a Crooked Rib* are relatively few, but their varied outlooks and roles are sufficient to illustrate Farah's ability for comprehensive portrayal of women's roles and characters. In his fiction generally, it is possible to identify three distinct categories of women: the traditional African, the emancipated modern African and the foreigner or West European.

The traditional woman has already been observed in the persons of the widow and Aowrolla of *From a Crooked Rib.* Further characterizations are Qumman, Ladan and Beydan of *Sweet and Sour Milk* and Idil (Medina's mother-in-law) and Fatima bint Thabit (Medina's mother) of *Sardines.* They play a striking part as instruments whereby the repressive regimes of their setting are highlighted. They are the suppressed, second-class citizens of traditional Muslim culture, presented in the stifled protests of their private home backgrounds. Qumman is the typical mother, loving and all-caring, patient and wearily self-sacrificing for her family. Deeply superstitious and religious, she upholds the family reputation against what she considers an importunate assault from Margaritta's relationship with her late son Soyaan. The victim of physical abuse by her husband Keynaan, she exists solely for her children. Because of them, she endures Keynaan's mistreatment and neglect of her. The influence of Qumman and her kind ensures the perpetuation of the social status quo, for they assist in stifling any type of deviation from the pattern they know and accept. Qumman is already bringing up Ladan to be like herself; and through loyalty, service and emotional hold over sons and husbands, Qumman's generation of women, deeply conservative, militate against individual freedom and progress. Loyaan, for instance, determined to demonstrate his aversion to the General's regime by exempting himself from the hypocritical show of solidarity symbolized in communal sweeping of the "Rendezvous of the Brooms," is persuaded by Qumman, Ladan and other women of the clan to conform. (pp. 218-19)

Beydan is a helpless victim, the second wife who acts as the perennial enemy and scourge of the first. She is aptly used by Keynaan to further divide and rule his family. Completely abandoned by Keynaan in her state of pregnancy, her only succor is her co-wife's grown sons. Her life is sacrificed during childbirth. Beydan is a pathetic figure in her helplessness. Suspected by Qumman of poisoning her son Soyaan, deprived of money and attention, she was already haunted by her tragedy in dreams.

Idil and Fatima bint Thabit react to the restrictions of Muslim religion and the traditional cultural norms by channeling all their emotional resources toward the nurture and protection of their children. Their emotional ties to these children work as a type of blackmail. Idil, for instance, is domineering, and her love for Xaddia and Samater is overbearing. Her interference is responsible for the breakup of Xaddia's and Samater's marriages. She is so obsessed to have a grandchild from Xaddia that she consults an herbalist on Xaddia's behalf and goes into an uncontrollable rage when she discovers that Xaddia has been taking pills to prevent pregnancy. Her insistence on having Ubax, Medina's daughter, circumcised drives Medina and Ubax away from their home. In Medina's absence, she takes complete control of the household and attempts to marry off an uneducated and, in her view, more docile and malleable wife to her son—a move similar to the ploys of the mothers-in-law in Mariama Bâ's *So Long A Letter* and one which ultimately estranges her from Samater. Hers is the typical, traditional mother-in-law syndrome.

Fatima, Medina's mother, is obscure and quiet.... She is firmly rooted in tradition, sanctified by name and property. She is chained ankle, wrist and foot to the solidity of her homestead—a typical matriarch born into a slave-owning family. Fatima is of the opinion that the younger generations, no matter how hard they try, can never create any "culture-substitute as faultless and whole as the one Somali society has developed in the past few centuries, any substitute with which to replace the traditional culture." Economic dependence on their men is shown as partly responsible for the submission of these women. Beydan is constantly in need of money. Aowrolla's husband Gheddi takes care of the purchasing of foodstuffs himself. Idil's dependence on her son Samater and even on Medina helps to check her excesses. Psychological factors also contribute, because it is difficult to purge oneself of ideas that have been imbibed throughout one's life. Therefore the Qummans and Fatima bint Thabits cannot release themselves from their bondage. (p. 219)

Farah carries the fight for women's rights into the corridors of power in *Sardines,* a novel which highlights the activities of ... [the] new breed of Somali women. The novel revolves around Medina's search for "a room of one's own. A country of one's own. A century in which one was not a guest." This type of woman character has already been encountered in Margaritta, Soyaan's mistress in *Sweet and Sour Milk* who, with independent means of livelihood, pursues her own interests—intellectual, social, romantic and political. She does not even make any claims on Keynaan for the son she has by Soyaan (a cause of anxiety for Qumman). Margaritta is engaged in research, which absorbs most of her time and energy. After a disastrous first marriage, she has avoided any permanent attachment to a man. This, to a large extent, ensures her freedom. Mulki, Soyaan's secretary, also belongs to this class of women.

Needless to say, this new type of woman is thoroughly rejected by the Qummans and Idils of society.... With Western education, public employment and economic self-sufficiency, these emancipated Somali women hold their own through public and political activity. They are very much at home in the so-called corridors of power through their own merit. Farah's female characters in *Sardines* reach out, each in her characteristic way, for freedom of expression and action. These women of various ages and sociocultural backgrounds engage in unique and intricate systems of relationships and search for new meanings and social definitions of themselves. Their efforts symbolically represent Somalia's search for freedom. The enslavement of Somali women is analogous to the political repression of the people, and until women are completely emancipated, Farah sees no political freedom for the country. As Joyce Cary observed, the root cause of Africa's stagnation is the backwardness, ignorance and suppression of its women. Since women's influence upon the young is enormous, how these future leaders of society are brought up will determine their capacity for handling their country's destiny.

Through his portrayal of educated women like Medina, Sagal, Amina and their associates, Farah presents a penetrating study of the conflict between traditional Muslim culture and the encroaching Western influence. Medina, from all indications, is very emancipated, as are the other female characters in her group, to a certain extent. They all enjoy some degree of personal freedom, having been liberated from ignorance of the intellect—a major effect of education. They are also free from economic dependence.... Medina has the benefit of a university education and the exposure consequent upon the fact that she is the daughter of an ambassador. She is privileged to have been uprooted early from her traditional background and nurtured in the glittering society of many European capitals. She is lucky to enjoy the love and understanding of a humane husband and her country's recognition of her talents, which earns her the editorship of Somalia's national daily newspaper. Indeed, Medina has a country, and an enviable identity. Her efforts, therefore, are for the silent majority who submit to the oppressive laws of the fascist state. She regards her mother-in-law, her clan's traditions and the General as obstacles in her ideal world. They are as much her enemies as the General's militiamen or the security services. As an active member of a revolutionary group that is not only critical of the General's regime but also actively opposed to it in *Sweet and Sour Milk,* her finest hour comes when she is made the editor of the government's main propaganda machinery. Her genuine revolutionary tendency propels her to challenge the editorial policy of daily singing the General's praises. (p. 220)

From Margaritta, Medina and their like, it is only one step forward to the total freedom of Western women, first encountered in Barbara, Mildred and Nancy of *A Naked Needle.* These white women, attached to African men through marriage and friendship, are having difficulty in adjusting to African realities, especially those which concern the position of women in society. One distinctive feature about them is their sexual freedom, which makes them extremely permissive in their relationships with men. The meeting between Nancy and Koschin [of *A Naked Needle*], for example, is illustrative. Koschin met Nancy accidentally in "a crowded pub, in London. She had been looking for her boyfriend in the pub." She is presented as a stereotype of the liberated woman of modern Western society as she competes favorably with men in the pub: "She drank lavishly, almost crazily, until in the end, when she was ready to leave, she ordered another drink. I saw that the contents of her Mexican straw-bag wouldn't settle the bill." Koschin settles her bill. They meet by chance some days later in a jammed discotheque "near the University." Nancy is again stood up by another boyfriend. It is unusual, according to African culture, that Nancy, after a few dates with Koschin, suggests marriage. It is her permissiveness that makes her accept, "at a whim of a day," to return to Africa to marry Koschin, should both be unmarried after two years.

The meeting between Mohamed and Barbara is equally casual; and even though their marriage is stable, Barbara, in a fit of revenge, sleeps with Barre, Mohamed's friend. Mildred's sexual infidelity has become scandalous and a source of concern and dishonor for her husband, Barre. These women, as well as Sandra the American lady, storm every citadel that men consider sacred to themselves.

One fact about Medina [of *Sardines*] is that in spite of her commitment to her freedom, she is never shown as indulging in irresponsible behavior. She is circumspect in her relationships with men and is amused at all the speculations of friends as to the reason for the temporary separation between her and Samater. Invariably, some sexual conflict is suggested. But for Medina, a woman's freedom does not necessarily involve an acceptance of sexual promiscuity. Even Margaritta, who as a single woman feels free to keep lovers, is still portrayed as applying restraint in her associations with men. The other Western types make one dizzy in their relentless pursuit of the male. With them the man has become the sexual victim. But they have drive and exhibit great acumen in the discharging of their duties. In the Somalia of *A Naked Needle,* Somali men, or at least the elite among them, seem to prefer these Western white women to their own women as wives—a fact which arouses the discomfort of Koschin. (pp. 220-21)

The realistic feature of Farah's portrayal of women is that they are seen to take active part in various forms of life around them. Even when they are cast in the traditional mold, like Qumman or Idil, they are active in those areas where they are permitted to operate.... More than this, Farah illuminates the changing role of women in a changing society. He even shows some of the men discussing the plight of women.... For such a commitment to the cause of women, Nuruddin Farah is unique among African creative writers. (p. 221)

> *J. I. Okonkwo, "Nuruddin Farah and the Changing Roles of Women," in* World Literature Today, *Vol. 58, No. 2, Spring, 1984, pp. 215-21.*

REED WAY DASENBROCK

Any collective sense of future directions and possibilities, whether that sense is shared by a nation, a community, an institution, or a family, rests upon a collctive sense of past achievements and failures. Conversely, to have no vision of one's past is to have no vision of a future, ultimately to have no identity at all. *Where are we going to be?* is a question indissolubly tied to the question *where and who are we?,* and that question can only be answered by having an answer to the question, *where and who have we been?*

This interpenetration of past, present, and future constitutes one of the enduring reasons for the power and social importance of literature. A group's sense of its own past is less a matter of an empirical record than a matter of received stories, myths and images. For example, though the Spanish settled New Mexico eleven years before Jamestown was settled and twenty-two years before the Puritans arrived at Plymouth Rock, it is the arrival of the English that seems central to American history. Moreover, the Puritan arrival in Massachusetts looms far larger in our consciousness than the prior and probably historically more important Virginia settlement because—so I would argue—the Puritan flight from the religious persecution of the Old World fits our sense of America as a land of freedom from persecution much more closely than our received image of the slave-owning, mercantile Virginian cavaliers. (Never mind that the Puritans soon set up their own religious oppression in turn.) Thus, later generations selectively create or re-create a sense of the past, largely—though not totally—through art, and this created, simplified past in turn helps to create a sense of what the future could be. To paraphrase Stephen Dedalus, artists do forge the uncreated conscience and consciousness of their race. If that collective consciousness is sometimes a forgery, it is no less potent for that.

These are some very general considerations to begin with, but I begin with them because they take on special force in the newly freed (and in some cases, recently created) countries of the third world. Particularly in an Africa where European powers created states without any regard for traditional borders or tribal enmities, a national consciousness has seemed an urgent need. These countries have had a united experience of colonialism but widely differing pre-colonial and colonial influences on their society. They have, in short, no common col-

lective sense of the past and in turn no collective sense of the future. A wide range of contemporary third-world writers have responded deliberately to this dilemma by trying to create for their societies a usable sense of the past. This does not mean that they respond in the same way any more than the societies they depict have responded in the same way. But they have all been alert to the same dilemma, and if this makes these writers sound more didactic and engaged than is fashionable in the "post-modern" west, it may also be taken as an important source of the value and importance we find in these writers. Contemporary African, Asian, Caribbean, and Pacific writing in English is far more exciting and will come in time to be seen as far more important than either contemporary American or English literature. And that is above all because these writers are traditional in the sense that Stephen Dedalus would have wanted them to be, affecting their societies' sense of themselves at an important and profound level. (pp. 312-13)

In the work of [such writers as Chinua Achebe, V. S. Naipaul, and Wole Soyinka], a progression can be traced from direct treatment of the historical past to a more indirect concern with how the past continues to shape the present through tradition and custom. In each case the aspect of the past seen as most important is the communal organization of pre-colonial African society. Nuruddin Farah's work logically completes this progression, and though all his work is set in contemporary Somalia, it is centrally concerned with the ways the institutions of clan and tribe shape Somali society. Farah is the youngest and least known of the writers discussed here, and my discussion will focus on his major achievement to date, his trilogy *Sweet and Sour Milk* (1979), *Sardines* (1981), and *Close Sesame* (1983), which he has collectively titled *Variations on the theme of an African dictatorship.* What needs stressing in the title is Farah's conviction that it is an *African* dictatorship that he is depicting. Each of the three novels concerns opposition to the rule of the General who has ruled Somalia since 1969. Like Soyinka's Nigeria, Farah's Somalia is under a repressive rule that has successfully appropriated Somalia's heritage in order to buttress its rule. But Farah doesn't have Soyinka's faith in an alternative unsullied past. He sees that the General—as he is always referred to in these novels—has stayed in power for so long because he really does represent something authentically Somali, as difficult as this may be for Farah and his characters to accept. Authentic, genuine Somali institutions do buttress the General's rule, and his authoritarianism is little more than the authoritarianism of the Somali family, clan and tribe writ large. It is true that the outside world (first the Russians, later the Western powers) has been generously helping the General stay in power, but that is not to absolve Somali institutions from blame.

This explains one initially curious feature of Farah's novels, which is that for ostensibly political novels, they spend a great deal of time delineating how the families in the novels work and make decisions. This is because the politics of the nation are the politics of the family, and an authoritarian state depends upon a nation of authoritarian families. As the young swimming champion Sagal tells her feminist friend Medina in *Sardines,* "in an authoritarian state, the head of the family (matriarch or patriarch) plays a necessary and strong role; he or she represents the authority of the state." Thus, overthrowing the General is not enough; to transform Somali society, to remove the possibility of there being a General, one must overthrow that which is like the General in Somali society.

Different aspects of this overriding theme are treated in each of the novels in Farah's trilogy. *Sardines* is above all concerned with the position of women in Somali society, the relation of mothers and daughters, and Farah is exceptional among male African novelists in his concern for the position of women. The other two novels, *Sweet and Sour Milk* and *Close Sesame,* in a sense frame *Sardines* as they focus more on sons and fathers. But in each of the novels, all of the family relationships are important in building up a collective sense of the oppressive nature of traditional Somali family structure and the possibility of alternatives to it.

At the beginning of *Sweet and Sour Milk,* Soyaan, a young economist who has been working for the government but also secretly opposing it, dies in mysterious circumstances, possibly—though not certainly—poisoned by the Government. His twin brother Loyaan supports Soyaan's opposition to the regime; his father, Keynaan, is a pensioned ex-torturer for the regime. And the plot of the book is basically a struggle between these two to control what is made of Soyaan after his death. Keynaan's beliefs are clear and simple. As he himself says, "I am the father. It is my prerogative to give life and death as I find fit. . . . I am the Grand Patriarch." Acting on this premise, he helps the regime make Soyaan into a Hero of the Revolution, a mockery of everything Soyaan stood for in life. And the father, which is to say the General and his regime, wins out over the son, the opposition to the regime. Loyaan's own efforts to demythologize the new hero of the revolution only lead to him experiencing much the same fate: against his will, he is made Somalia's Councillor in Belgrade, and is forced out of the country into exile.

If the male patriarch, Keynaan, is a miniature General, we learn from *Sardines* that matriarchs can be just as authoritarian. Every novel in this trilogy is focused on a struggle, and the key struggle in *Sardines* is between Medina, a Western-educated journalist opposed to the General, and her mother-in-law, who rules her son, Samater, with an iron fist and enthusiastically supports the General. Medina has left her husband, at least partially because he is a minister in the government. But he is no supporter of the government: he became a minister only after threats were made to eliminate many of his fellow tribesmen if he didn't accept. Thus the question in *Sardines* is not whether to oppose the General as much as it is whether one is strong enough to stand free from entanglement with him, and those who value the lives of their family and community too strongly may not be able to do so. Medina and Samater have a daughter, Ubax, and the public reason Medina has left her husband's house is that she is afraid that Samater's mother will have Ubax circumcised. The two reasons aren't so very different, for a society that circumcises women is the same society that produces a dictator like the General. Medina shocks her mother and her mother-in-law by treating Ubax as her equal, her friend. And just as the authoritarian father or mother helps the General preserve his authoritarian rule, Medina sees her un-authoritarian way of rearing Ubax as a way to break down the authoritarian, clan structures of Somali society. What Medina wants is "a home in which her thoughts might freely wander without inhibition, without fear; a home in which patriarchs . . . and matriarchs . . . were not allowed to set foot."

Such a home is depicted in *Close Sesame,* where we are shown three generations living together in a non-authoritarian manner. The protagonist of *Close Sesame,* Deeriye, is a devout Muslim who is an old veteran of the anti-colonial struggles against the Italians. His son, Mursal, is obviously involved in conspiracies against the General with other young men his age but not of his tribe, and Deeriye respects his son's autonomy enough to

let him go his own way (ultimately, to be killed) despite his compassionate love for his son's family. One of Mursal's co-conspirators, Mukhtaar, has a rather different relation with his father; they fight over Mukhtaar's opposition to the regime and Mukhtaar is killed in the fight. Deeriye's strong but non-authoritarian role is implicitly contrasted to that traditional, Keynaan-like sense of the father as the giver and taker of life, the absolute dictator. After Mukhtaar's death, Deeriye is ashamed that he had warned his son not to trust Mukhtaar because of his different tribal associations. Again and again in these novels, the point is made that the diversity of tribes is one of the ways the General can divide and rule, and the traditional organization of Somali society into hostile clans and tribes, each with its own absolute ruler, makes it almost impossible for a sustained opposition to form. But the friendship of these younger men shows that such divisions are not all-powerful, as they can be challenged just as the power of the Patriarch can be challenged. None of these challenges is successful, however. At the end of the trilogy, the General is still in power (as he is today), and authoritarian families still predominate. But we have been given a model of how a different arrangement could exist, and that is Farah's only seed of hope.

Farah thus criticizes African society for its communalism from a perspective that seems close to Naipaul's individualistic critique of traditional society. There are some crucial differences, however, between the two critiques. First, though most of the young protagonists opposing the General in Farah's trilogy are Western-educated and Westernized, Farah criticizes the effect the West has had on Africa as harshly as Soyinka. The African dictatorships he attacks may be African, but they are certainly supported by the West. Second, and more importantly, Farah differs from Naipaul in that he wants to delineate and praise those currents within Somali society that do oppose—if ineffectually—the rule of the General. If it is true, as Deeriye says, that the Somalis are "easily governable," not all of them are. Deeriye, easily Farah's most appealing character, is the crucial figure here, for he is a devout Muslim, a traditional Somali in his manner of life, and an old veteran of the anti-colonialist struggle. And the portrait of Somali culture that emerges from *Variations on the theme of an African dictatorship* is not one of a totally authoritarian culture. The heritage of the anti-colonial struggle, the strength and vitality of Somali women, and the ideology of brotherhood contained in Islam are some of the aspects of Somali culture Farah wants to praise. These may not suffice to overthrow the General, but Farah's notation of their existence means that he is not urging a sweeping rejection of the past in Naipaul's fashion. Like Soyinka, Farah urges that there is much to value and much to reject in the African past, but he is perhaps more realistic in refusing to see the part he wishes to praise as authentic and the other as inauthentic. The African past has good and bad aspects, and the task to undertake is not to reject or embrace that past in toto but to sift and to analyze, to reflect critically in exactly the way this fine set of novels does.

Farah's work, thus, can be linked with Soyinka's in as much as both can accept the necessary biculturality of the contemporary African situation. Both can imagine a blending of old and new that would be better than a total rejection of one in favor of the other. But Farah can be seen as inclining to Naipaul's side in his critique of communalism and Soyinka to Achebe's in his (admittedly qualified) celebration of it. There is, therefore, very little agreement among these four writers, and if we expanded the discussion to include some of the many other fine writers from the third world who are grappling with these issues, we would find even less agreement. This is not to fault these writers; on the contrary, what should be praised most about their work is its critical reflection on the myths their societies live by, including the myths advanced by other writers. Each writer has his own vision of the past and how that past shapes and should shape the present and future of the societies with which he is concerned. This is one measure of the vitality of this body of literature: one of the most important things literature can do is to reflect critically and independently on the myths and notions we live by, and such critical reflection—if almost dormant in American literature in a heyday of formalism—is alive and well in literature written in English outside the dominant Western countries. (pp. 327-31)

> Reed Way Dasenbrock, *"Creating a Past: Achebe, Naipaul, Soyinka, Farah,"* in Salmagundi, *Nos. 68 & 69, Fall, 1985 & Winter, 1986, pp. 312-32.*

KIRKUS REVIEWS

[In *Sardines,* Farah] offered a dense, demanding close-up of a half-dozen intellectual Somali women. Here, in [*Maps*], a somewhat less ambitious yet frequently opaque (and sometimes belabored) sociopolitical character study, he scrutinizes the childhood and adolescence of . . . Askar—an orphan who is raised first by an Ethiopian foster-mother, then by his cosmopolitan Somali kinfolk.

In narration that shifts regularly (and often annoyingly) from second-person to first-person to third-person, we learn that Askar's father—a Somali freedom-fighter in the rebellion of the Ogaden province against Ethiopian rule—died in prison a few months before Askar's birth; that his mother died virtually in childbirth; and that Askar was taken in by kindly, earthy Misra. . . . Askar recalls his intense one-ness with Misra, his jealousy of her lovers (one of whom was a Koranic priest), the changes in their relationship that followed his circumcision at age five. . . . He remembers his parting from Misra at age seven, when he went to Somali's capital city to live with his worldly sensitive, childless uncle and aunt. . . . But now, at 18, Askar must decide whether to join the Western Somali Liberation Front, returning to fight in the Ogaden—or whether to choose an academic career. And this dilemma is complicated by the arrival in Mogadiscio of Misra, a fugitive from the Ogaden—having been accused of betraying the Somali freedom-fighters to her Ethiopian-soldier lover. Should Askar befriend Misra (who may be ill with breast cancer), reopen his heart to her? Is she guilty of betrayal—or, falsely accused, guilty only of being a foreigner? (pp. 1092-93)

Farah weighs down this potentially forceful scenario with stylistic and thematic layerings of every kind: the fractured, you/I/he, past/present narration; folktale-ish descriptions of Askar's dreams and fantasies; verbose imagery involving blood, water, and sky; convoluted, heavy-handed musings on sexual identity, the politics of language, and the "truth" of maps. So the result, though intermittently fascinating in its evocation of the Somali culture and its identity crisis, is for a very limited audience only: readers keenly interested enough in the issues involved to persevere through the verbal and conceptual thickets. (p. 1093)

> A review of *"Maps,"* in Kirkus Reviews, *Vol. LV, No. 15, August 1, 1987, pp. 1092-93.*

PUBLISHERS WEEKLY

Like an exotic fruit requiring a certain taste, [*Maps*] is a worthy read from a prize-winning (*Sweet and Sour Milk*) Somalian writer. Set during the long fight for Somalian independence, it is a chronicle of consciousness invoking the plasticity of memory and the ambiguity of interpretation. The development of a rich and complex perception is skillfully created in the history of Askar, a Somalian orphan. Askar, whose mother died in childbirth and father in a skirmish, is raised by an Ethiopian woman, Misra, who carries a mysterious past. . . . It is obvious that English is not [Farah's] native tongue; his use of the language reads like a translation, with overblown prose and awkward phrasing. On the other hand, he constructs a deft narrative that reflects an oral tradition. The story jumps back and forth and is interrupted by surreal dream sequences, all of this slowly filling in the details and giving shape to a full and dense tale.

> A review of *"Maps,"* in Publishers Weekly, *Vol. 232, No. 7, August 14, 1987, p. 95.*

CHRISTOPHER HOPE

This is a novel about the politics of desire as well as a lyrical evocation of childhood—but above all, *Maps* is a book about borders, boundaries and territorial ambitions, what Nuruddin Farah calls "pastures of the imagination." The novel sets out to delineate, with a cartographer's scrupulousness, the anguish of living on a continent where national boundaries have been drawn by foreign hands, where geography merges with politics and where, even though the old imperialists have departed, their successors have inherited not only their powers but their maps. In short, this is a novel of modern Africa, in which the growing pains of the orphan boy, Askar, and his inchoate, fragmentary memories of his dead parents reflect the wider tragedy of a dismembered Somalia—a country split among the competing owners of its various territories. . . .

The most notable feature of this strange, poetic, passionate narrative is the extraordinary way in which Nuruddin Farah transforms what might in other hands be an angry political treatise into a sensitive account of an orphan of the storms that in Africa pass under the name of politics. And although the novel is set in the Horn of Africa, it has applications that reach as far as my own country, South Africa, where questions of "homelands" have violent political repercussions, and where the drawing of lines between people, the making of maps and the meaning of words are ultimately matters for the police and the army.

Among the powers possessed by the boy Askar is his ability to move backward and forward in time, to be present at his own birth and to peer into the future. His relationship with Misra, the woman who adopts him, is described with savage tenderness and a brilliant accumulation of intimate detail. Mr. Farah, who was born in 1945 and has written several novels, has considerable lyrical gifts. Askar is a kind of wonder child, a boy-man, in some ways the Somali messiah, the "wise child of his people," obsessed with the circumstances of his birth, possibly his own midwife, perhaps even his own creator, since the existence of his parents is problematical. Askar enjoys a relationship with Misra so close as to be almost incestuous and sufficiently powerful to cut them off from the rest of the world.

However, it is Askar's growing recognition that he must begin to discover his own independence that sets him on the path to political awareness and maturity. It is no coincidence that Misra is not a Somali but an Ethiopian, and it is Askar's destiny to fight against Ethiopian domination of his mother country. Such personal and political consonances are handled with great delicacy and imagination. Misra herself is a remarkable creation, warm, motherly, shrewd, but at the same time sexually submissive, devious and possibly a traitor to the Somali cause. Even so, the intense relationship between orphan and foreign mother provides the underlying strength of the novel and knits the whole together. Among the richly woven incidents of their mutual dependence, Askar's observation of an abortion performed on his stepmother is one of the outstanding moments in the novel, a description spare, pungent, unforgettable.

But their relationship is doomed by geography and politics. Two events begin the inevitable separation of Askar and Misra; there is his circumcision and the presentation to him of an atlas in which the topography of his desire becomes clear. Askar begins deliberately to reunite the sundered sections of his "homeland," redrawing "the map of the Somali-speaking territories, copying it curve by curve."

Both as a child, and then as a young man in Mogadishu, by now a supporter of the Western Somali Liberation Front, Askar must contemplate the personal tragedy of the Somali people, scattered across Africa, delivered by geographers into the hands of foreign armies. And he must also confront the wider, equally familiar struggle in Africa between the new imperialists, the Russians in Ethiopia or the Cubans in Angola, and live with the bitter knowledge that Africa is once again little more than a "playfield," where African armies are simply part of the "reserve," to be drawn on by the major powers in their new scramble for Africa. Of course this is true and has a familiar ring to anyone alarmed by the spectacle of African countries caught in the trap between domestic incompetence and international interference.

Such is the force of Mr. Farah's anger that it sometimes overshadows the delicate portraits at the heart of the novel. And his allusive, playful style in which the narrative moves between past and present with great rapidity, is not always easy to follow. But it is always the sincerity of the emotions and his ability to make them palpable that distinguish this tantalizing and original novel, and make it a journey into what Mr. Farah calls the "territory of pain" and what we, rather loosely perhaps, call Africa.

Christopher Hope, "Boundaries of Desire," in The New York Times Book Review, *November 15, 1987, p. 40.*

Penelope (Ann Douglass) Gilliatt

1932-

English novelist, short story writer, scriptwriter, critic, editor, and dramatist.

In her fiction, Gilliatt examines difficulties involved with initiating and maintaining relationships. Employing an understated prose style complemented by terse dialogue and sparse settings, Gilliatt portrays characters who search for security and significance in their lives amid the confusion of post-World War II British society. Gwen Kinkead observed: "[As readers of Gilliatt's works], we are spectators to involvements formed in invisible pasts, to conversations already three-quarters finished, situations interrupted, of endings not yet complete."

Gilliatt's first novel, *One by One* (1965), concerns a troubled young doctor and his pregnant wife who are forced to live apart when a mysterious plague terrorizes London. After his wife and newborn child return to the city, the doctor, tormented by the unrealized career expectations that his mother holds for him, withdraws from his family and eventually commits suicide. *A State of Change* (1967) dramatizes a complex romantic alliance between a female Polish refugee and two Englishmen that endures two decades of personal and career crises. Considered by most reviewers to be less a novel than a sociological study of the shifting sexual and social mores of postwar England, *A State of Change* was described by Hilary Corke as "an outstandingly sane exposition of a *human* point of view." In *The Cutting Edge* (1978), Gilliatt focuses upon a man who competes with his brother for the affections of his former wife. *A Woman of Singular Occupation* (1988) portrays a married Englishwoman's brief affair with an American banker.

Many critics maintain that Gilliatt's elliptical, concise prose is best suited to her short stories. These pieces frequently feature refined protagonists who contend with aging, stagnating marriages, and loneliness. Gilliatt's short fiction, much of which was first published in the *New Yorker,* is collected in *What's It Like Out? and Other Stories* (1968; published in the United States as *Come Back If It Doesn't Get Better*), *Nobody's Business* (1972), *Quotations from Other Lives* (1981), and *They Sleep without Dreaming* (1985). In addition to her reputation as an author of fiction, Gilliatt is well known as a drama and film critic, and she has also written the screenplay for the motion picture *Sunday Bloody Sunday* (1971), for which she received honors in the United States and Great Britain.

(See also *CLC,* Vols. 2, 10, 13; *Contemporary Authors,* Vols. 13-16, rev. ed.; and *Dictionary of Literary Biography,* Vol. 14.)

THE TIMES LITERARY SUPPLEMENT

Poets do not have this problem about clothing some personal statement, some experience belonging to the secret world of emotions, in a formula of outside, observable events; each word can convey a precise image, and an image which each reader is free to play with as his conscious and subconscious suggest.

But the novelist, wanting to write subjectively and to explore private emotions, must choose either to create characters and confuse himself in their private lives, or invent some symbolic situation which so intensifies a private experience that it can be treated objectively.

Having chosen to write a novel about married love, Penelope Gilliatt has attempted [in *One by One*] to use both these methods at once, and the result, although not entirely successful, is at least more searching than most first novels about so battered a theme. She has invented a situation, a plague which attacks London and kills not only thousands a week but also the whole metropolitan merry-go-round of daily-breading, and which exposes in particular the relationship of a young couple, Joe and Polly, awaiting the birth of their first child. Joe is a vet—to the shame of his rich, ailing, Bournemouth-based mother—and at once volunteers to help in the emergency hospitals set up in old underground V.D. clinics. Terrified of infecting Polly or endangering the baby, he insists on her complete quarantine. His deliberate refusal to notice that in so doing he is driving her into a panic of fear and loneliness suggests that he needs, for quite selfish reasons, to be cut off from her love and to hurt her in case she shall in some way debilitate his identity. He sends her to stay with his mother, and is unmoved by the fact that on the way she is set upon by angry crowds whose only thought is that she might infect them. Nor is her lonely,

terrified confinement surrounded by hostile faces and her subsequent flight with the baby back to London enough to break
his obsession. She is thrust into an isolation hospital and there,
by trying to communicate to him how badly he needs love,
provokes his final act of despair.

The plague scene is built up with journalistic skill; coolly and
with memorable detail, like the policemen in masks, the recorded announcement of closure playing on the telephone numbers of the big stores, the prostitutes now out of work turning
to collecting corpses, the author almost persuades us that this
is how it could happen, in some unending August heatwave,
while the Government was away on the grouse moors. But the
object of all this scenery, which is to create a crisis in which
a man and a woman can no longer know enough about each
other to be happy or loving, is less smoothly achieved. Jerkily
interspersed with the sequence of events, the descriptions of a
dinner party, a local repertory performance, a burglary, the
newspaper tycoon and his plots, are long, angry, painful monologues by Polly and Joe. Their love comes across all right,
even if some of the private jokes and joys may seem to some
readers embarrassing in the way the bears and squirrels were
on Mr. Osborne's stage. But Joe, holding forth like a hunted
man against all the forces of society who refuse to let him
alone, is too disjointed, too incoherent in love and hate for
Polly's patient and brave devotion to tame into a convincing
lover. . . .

Moreover, to intensify the claustrophobia of Joe's despairing
situation, the press, that old arch-enemy of private love, is
brought in to expose a homosexual incident in his past. Polly's
jeering lies are soaked up by the reporter; even here, it seems,
she cannot communicate to Joe the need to fool vultures by
suggesting that since both he and she are outcasts, at least they
may be left in peace.

Too much of a rag-bag of protest, comic observation, emotional
analysis, fantasy and cleverness—the language is prickly with
sharp, self-conscious phrases—*One by One* does not quite gell
into an effective novel. But the passion and intelligence which
produced it are far too rare and ambitious for one to wish that
it had been written in any other way or to forget the impression
it leaves.

> *"In Time of Plague,"* in The Times Literary Sup-
> plement, *No. 3296, April 29, 1965, p. 324.*

ROBERT TAUBMAN

First and last, though not for most of the story, [*One by One*]
deals with a representative case of domestic hysteria. Driving
home from work Joe Talbot is so possessed by dread that he
rings up his wife but can't bring himself to speak. Arriving,
he sees her 'standing in panic in the drawing-room, splayed
against the glare from the garden.' The situation between them,
in spite of love on both sides, ends in Joe's suicide; and we
leave Polly at a point when she hasn't been able to go out for
two years. It's a situation brilliantly rendered but somewhat
under-explained, with a resemblance to themes used by other
women novelists: Penelope Mortimer, Bernardine Bishop,
Margaret Drabble. Characters paralysed as if a Gorgon's head
had been turned on them, but still able to think—providing
irony, for they're highly intelligent and vacillate between hysteria and wit: this view of domestic relations has become fairly
current.

There are hints of reasonable explanations—for instance, that
Polly is pregnant, or that Joe, a vet who does medical research
as a hobby at an East End hospital, is the sort of gentle and
upright Englishman for whom England makes life impossible.
I don't suppose Mrs Gilliat wants such hints ignored, especially
when they contribute to her criticism of the state of England:
but they never look like a sufficient explanation of what is
wrong between Polly and Joe. The intense nervousness that
afflicts this relationship—expressed in play-acting, evasion and
mutual protectiveness—makes particular causes seem unimportant. Their nervousness is compulsive, of the kind that trips
over circumstance but doesn't often get realistically involved
with it; and another version appears in their friends Coker and
Moke in the same Twickenham terrace.

But as the situation develops Mrs Gilliatt makes a radical change
by giving them all something to be nervous about. *One by One*
also deals with London in the grip of a plague. This nearly
turns it into a grandiose moral fable; but if it steers clear of
one danger, it encounters others. The delicacy of the writing
gives way, and the plague scenes reach after effect—the sort
of effect Mrs Gilliatt was the first to object to in Antonioni's
films. . . . Her plague is more of an extravaganza corresponding
to private moods of anger or disgust—which also show openly
in the incidental animus against the English press and English
speech-habits and hospitals. But mainly the plague strikes me
as a huge irrelevancy; the interest of Joe and Polly doesn't
depend on it, and putting them in a special plight only obscures
their real one.

> *Robert Taubman, "Particular Plight,"* in New
> Statesman, *Vol. LXIX, No. 1781, April 30, 1965, p.*
> *692.*

MARTIN SHUTTLEWORTH

Penelope Gilliatt tends to look at the world through a telescope:
her observation is precise; her epigrams are sometimes even
profound, but *A State of Change* is chopped into innumerable
separate parts. It runs by as jerkily as a half finished film
through the editing machine. Kakia is Polish. There are three
main men in her life, Andrzej, a Catholic Marxist; Don, a
forceful man of the theatre; Henry, a doctor. She herself, Poland, England, wars, brutalities and the issues of the day pop
by like ping-pong balls in a fountain. The book's implied centre
is not its written centre so it is at once disappointing and
tantalising. Mrs. Gilliatt can analyse better than she can create.
Kakia's Polishness is hardly dinner party deep, but Kakia's a
somebody for all that, for what Mrs. Gilliatt analyses no one
else has created and so one is left at the end with a whole
necklace of insights, yet only wisps, somehow, of contemporary attitudes, not flesh and blood characters to hang them
on.

> *Martin Shuttleworth, in a review of "A State of*
> *Change," in Punch, Vol. CCLII, No. 6610, May 17,*
> *1967, p. 736.*

HILARY CORKE

'Kakia Grabowska, aged twenty-three, cartoonist and citizen
of Warsaw' is the heroine of Penelope Gilliatt's *A State of*
Change. She is thin, simian, wry, observant, unchippy, and
very careful about honesty of thought. Soon she is in England,
in a climate perhaps more congenial than Poland's towards
such characteristics, though one that finds her brand of satirical

caricature, wrung from her by tension and suppression, incomprehensible and more violent than meets the temperate British case. She becomes involved with two men, Don and Harry, already life-long friends of each other and as unlike as can be. Don is 'brilliant', quick, flashy, basically unsure; in entertainment, mass-communications, the perfection of techniques for the conveyance of nothing. Harry is a doctor, steady, idealistic, a merry mind but apparently less sure than Don, less swift; but it does not take us long to see that his unsureness proceeds from a will-to-honesty as fanatical as Kakia's, and that he is slow because on every occasion he hunts and captures the exact word, the exact idea, rather than settling quickly for what sounds smart and will get by.

Kakia soon runs through Don, and the book is really about how she and Harry arrive with long pains at what Don dismisses sneeringly as a 'monogamy' but what they define as a 'constancy'. . . . In fact, the rather formalized scheme that I have drawn up for *A State of Change* falsifies with simplicity. Miss Gilliatt has the inclusive sympathy of high intelligence, and shows herself to be a very different person indeed from all those brassy contenders for the title of Miss World's-Most-Intelligent-Woman: who appear to equate intelligence with contempt and intolerance (both, incidentally, so patently founded upon misplaced self-confidence that they horribly boomerang), and seem to struggle rather to be acclaimed Miss World's-Bitchiest—hard honour indeed to gain, in view of the competition. That is to define her by what she is not. And she is not, for that matter, a 'feminist'; no more than you and I, *cher lecteur,* but not presumably *chère lectrice* are masculinists. I mean that she is a woman and a novelist, but *not* a woman-novelist. I found *A State of Change* extraordinarily rewarding, both as a highly subtle piece of construction, marvellously well written, and as an outstandingly sane exposition of a *human* point of view. If possibly her Harry and Kakia are just a little bit too good to be true, then that is a mistake so very much on the side of the angels that I hope all the trumpets will sound for it, on both banks.

> *Hilary Corke, in a review of "A State of Change," in* The Listener, *Vol. LXXVII, No. 1991, May 25, 1967, p. 693.*

ROSEMARY DINNAGE

I see from the [book jacket of *Quotations from Other Lives*] that previous reviewers have used up most of our precious stock of reviewerish adjectives on Penelope Gilliatt's last two books of fiction: brisk, economical; crisp, splendid; deft, believable; breathtaking, spare; witty, rapier-sharp; delightful, whimsical. This is a pity because Miss Gilliatt is clearly choosy, even fanatical, about words, and while I would endorse at least some of those accolades, it only leaves me with wry, spry and rather swanky for this collection of short stories. Wry, because under the surface of these sketches are intimations of pain; spry, though, because despite such intimations the surface remains impeccably polished; and swanky because of her settings—very English, very grand. English-English, mind you, not British-English; I doubt if there is a Welsh shepherd or an Ulsterman or even a Scottish laird among her characters. (p. 6)

She has lovingly preserved some posh English expressions—"blithering," "go a bust on it," "one does wonder," "your usual sweet self"—that I had almost forgotten existed. She is a connoisseur of verbal oddities and will toss them about like Ping-Pong balls, the faster the better. In her stories secretaries

ponder the meaning of "wanhope" (why not "hope despite everything" rather than "despair?"), knotty Polish proverbs suddenly bob up ("A potato in the ground dreams only of the vodka it will be made into") and a story's themes work themselves out in fortune-cookie mottoes thought up at a conference ("Happiness does not lie in restraint from grief").

Like the messages in fortune cookies and Christmas crackers, though, Penelope Gilliatt's stories depend a good deal on the wrapping and the reader's mellow mood. On the morning after the feast, at a second reading, things can fall a bit flat and the nervy, clipped brilliance seems contrived. We wonder if it isn't all a little fey, whether we can still see the joke, whether the whole thing stands up without those slender columns of hostess gowns and calf-skin loafers in The New Yorker propping it on either side of the page. Reading between the lines is all very well, but we'd like something fair and square *in* the lines. Never mind. She is a stylist above all, and at its best the style makes everyone else's look anxious and overblown. (pp. 6, 15)

As for plot, it's too coarse a concept altogether. Situations sketch themselves in; people—lovers, families, solitaries—approach and retreat, suffer (probably), joke (obliquely); backgrounds are hinted at. Not slices of life, these, so much as elegant slivers. (p. 15)

> *Rosemary Dinnage, "Stylish Sketches," in* The New York Times Book Review, *April 11, 1982, pp. 6, 15.*

LEWIS JONES

The people in [the stories collected in *Quotations from Other Lives*] have conversations about dictionaries and make a great fuss about the differences between English and American usage, but the language in them is a fantastic confusion of the two. Most of these people are upper-class. They go to Oxford where they read Modern Greats and drink claret. . . . Then they go and live at one of their 'three family seats' and worry about the furniture 'the places were not originally architected to be furnished that way'). They keep body and soul together by 'barbecueing steak on the toasting grill', with occasional pause for 'a large dollop of the very best sherry'. They wear lorgnettes. They all talk as Ms Gilliatt writes, with a strained sensitivity positively groanin' with book-larnin': 'All those French housewives now are more Napoleonic than Proustian'. Many characters are presented as Greek scholars, and one actually demonstrates her knowledge of that language by referring to 'the hoi-de-polloi'. The cumulative effect of all this is that of an English-for-Foreigners book written as a practical joke.

The stories are ostensibly about the love-affairs of these preposterous people but they seem to me to be more about the aesthetic arrangement of different sorts of possessions (language, clothes, houses, jobs) than passion. Ms Gilliatt has one of her characters say that these are hard times for writers, as all they have to write about is the unpleasant spectacle of capitalism at bay. If she believes this, as a few other vaguely socialist remarks would suggest, why does she take refuge in a fantastical snobbism? (p. 21)

> *Lewis Jones, "English for Foreigners," in* New Statesman, *Vol. 104, No. 2683, August 20, 1982, pp. 21-2.*

VICTORIA GLENDINNING

On a quick first reading Penelope Gilliatt's latest stories [in *Quotations From Other Lives*] seem incoherent. Undoubtedly, they are lucid, well-crafted, deliberate; the apparent incoherence comes from a startling rejection of one of the cosier assumptions of short-story writers, that a situation or incident is to be captured and given meaning in isolation, by exclusion of the sounds of other voices in other rooms. Penelope Gilliatt's characters live footloose in the global village, or in Babel, wanting to belong somewhere and finding a frail security, or an imperfect love, in arbitrary encounters. In **"When Are You Going Back?"** an American girl in London, feeling excluded by the "ungentle" British and their well-bred silences, feels suddenly happier in a Pakistani restaurant with a doctor she met in a shop who is actually working as a waiter (all the lovable, "unfretful" men in these stories spend a lot of time not doing the thing they were trained for). In the polyglot restaurant, "languages got mixed in her ears." ...

There are urgent communications scattered through these tales like notices in a surreal railway station. "Exits important. Cleave to choice." Perhaps that's also why there are so many cats around. "The cat sat daintily, poised for exit, watching." Penelope Gilliatt's people keep their balance by listening to music—mostly "early music", played on a clavichord, but also, in a dentist's surgery, John Cage—and by using old adages, newspaper headlines, proverbs, as points of reference. There are "words to be saved" in Babel, and one story is set at a meeting of a Christmas-cracker company, thinking up new—or rather old—riddles and mottoes, "It's not the thought, it's the words that count." Food counts too. In more than one story, people irrationally stock up with chocolate bars like emergency rations, as if for a Himalayan expedition. A great many meals are described and eaten and washed up; garlic seems to have a significance beyond the usual.

Those that cling to their original roots—aristocrats in reduced circumstances in English country houses, for example—find coherence no more easily. Mothers die, or run away. **"In Trust"**, which is written as a playlet, has a girl who is bullied by her grandparents all through her childhood into accepting that their beautiful old house in a London square is her sacred heritage, to be cherished and preserved when they are gone. When inflation makes them change their tune for their own convenience, it is the girl who, uncomprehending, is betrayed.

Very old people play a large part. One arbitrary but temporarily happy conjunction is between a doddering professor and a nineteen-year-old student; elsewhere, octogenarian lovers who have fretted for years against circumstances are presented with the possibility of being together. Living with someone, for most of Penelope Gilliatt's people, is just about as painful as separation, especially for the old who remember only the language of complaint and compromise.

But loneliness is the shared terror. When in **"Seven O'Clock of a Strange Millennium"** an aged man poisons the aged husband of his aged mistress, and the plot miscarries, and everyone is writhing with stomach pains as in the last act of *Hamlet*, it is the cat that they all worry about, and all three share the bill from the social worker for his food and cat-litter. "The cat seems to have been major", a puzzled policeman says, and is told: "Loneliness can't be ignored, can it? Isolation being another matter, because often chosen."

Penelope Gilliatt is funny about her deaf geriatric lovers, as she is about upper-class English people and horrible dinner parties, but I don't think it is for their social observation that these stories are chiefly valuable. Many writers in English are capable of that, and of little else. Most fiction comforts and amuses by imposing some sort of order—even order of a perverse kind—on the chaos of experience. These stories face disorder comically and head on, which is why they seem at first incoherent.

Quotations From Other Lives adds up to a provocative book, even if you do have to strain your ears to pick up what is going on in the hubbub of history and accident. The alternative is a worse accident, silence: "I mean, you let a conversation go off the rails and then there are casualties and people getting killed because the carriages are on their sides by then and you don't have the slightest idea how to hoist them up again and the hell with it."

Victoria Glendinning, "Sharing Loneliness in Babel," in The Times Literary Supplement, *No. 4142, August 20, 1982, p. 910.*

LISA ZEIDNER

Not all the characters in [*They Sleep Without Dreaming*] are as dotty as the bag lady talking to herself in **"Purse,"** but all of them are eccentric—the kind who recite Latin verses while doing backbends or still use lorgnettes with ivory handles. Most of the characters are English, with names like Grania Byam. Many are old, nostalgic for better times. Even the younger characters exude an air of fallen nobility as they cheerfully make do with jobs as accountants or proofreaders for needle-point magazines. In [**"They Sleep Without Dreaming"**], a middle-aged woman who is Minister of Transport survives the drudgery of committee meetings by reminiscing about her happy childhood with five siblings and an energetic governess. The pleasures of such people are small, domestic, often culinary. Two old friends from Warsaw, one of whom survived Auschwitz, share tea and a rare chocolate cake; they do not discuss their pasts. A famous scholar meets five dons in a Chinese restaurant and talks not of literature but of parking. ... As in past stories, Penelope Gilliatt's voice is mannered and wry. ... Her decision to report the daily surface of lives, rather than exploring more private emotions, is occasionally disappointing—too much dinner chatter with not enough sense of why a reader should be invited to this particular party. In the better stories, like **"Dame of the British Empire, BBC,"** the characters have depth as well as quirkiness, and behind their studiously charming repartee is loneliness, need—the stiff upper lip trembling, if only a little.

Lisa Zeidner, in a review of "They Sleep without Dreaming," in The New York Times Book Review, *October 27, 1985, p. 40.*

ROZ KAVENEY

One of the best of reasons for using the short story form is to exhibit, by their close juxtaposition, the important links of causality or feeling between elements that might in any longer form seem merely contingent. There are times in the short stories of Penelope Gilliatt when her yoking together of people's richly eccentric childhoods and their useful later lives might seem sentimentally preachy or whimsically ironical, but, at her best, her command of the form enables her to skirt the traps that her tendency to the facile, and her favourite market—*The New Yorker*—might seem to push her towards. That, and her ear: an ear not infallible with lower class modes of speech, but perfectly tuned to the shabby-genteel intellectual world which seems to be her stories' natural milieu.

There is a close link between the results of that commanding grasp of what it is that people actually say, and her habit of making us look hard at the development of a life by sudden cuts and shifts over twenty years. Her characters jump suddenly and radically in their speech as well, moving from one idea to the next in a way which makes it possible for their imagined hearer and—just—the reader to follow, but which defies strict logic. Two of the least effective stories in *They Sleep Without Dreaming* are those in which she depicts mental imbalance; the trick she uses so effectively to make dialogue real has been for so long a way in which lesser writers represent uncontrolled battiness that for her to do so seems like a failure of imagination or nerve, or both. In "The Purse", for example, her upper-middle-class bag-lady prattles on with such rapidity that the story reads as if too easily written, though sentence by sentence her talk is good. Too much of a good thing, perhaps; part of the strength of the several stories here about the life of the mind is that in them the good things the characters say have more of a sense of lived pain and effort behind them. . . .

[The] emphasis on work and on difficulty prevents the stories from falling into the chocolate-box sentiments that their material might have invited from a less careful hand; Gilliatt's astringent humour also helps. "Addio" might have been merely farcical and even distasteful in its picture of a famous soprano, well past her prime, giving a master-class in her old Cherubino costume, slightly let out. The sudden epiphany when she finds a perfect voice among her pupils and the realization that broadcasting makes the young woman's unstageworthy build an irrelevance might have been a cheap piece of O. Henryism. The way our perception of all this is mediated through the slight sexual unhappiness of two musicologists in the audience might have been a rather easy alienation effect. In the event, what keeps the story thoroughly focused is the way Gilliatt makes us believe that the business of making music is of supreme importance to all of these otherwise faintly absurd people; modulation and control are important to her art as well.

"The Hinge" shows two Polish exiles on the loose in Warsaw, friends long parted and not at this stage to be reunited—Wanda, assimilated to British life and merely visiting, and Boleslaw, the stormy petrel, always tempted home to meddle. This is a story of two irreconcilable types and nothing more; its placing in a particular contemporary situation involves the reader in making a political judgment between the two which, however objectively correct, has little to do with the natural bent of Gilliatt's art. But then, how can she avoid writing about Eastern Europe, where the habit of politically tactful or subversive ellipsis makes conversation even more Gilliatt-like than ever? Again, ["They Sleep Without Dreaming"], with its picture of the odd childhood and student years of a Minister of Transport dedicated to the job as one worth doing could do without its over-emphatic condemnation of ambitious colleagues with no sense of value; the political point, if Gilliatt wants to make it, is made effectively by the simple creation of the character.

What that story in its finest moments, and other stories like "Broderie Anglaise" and "On Each Other's Time", do have is a sense of the private, of a shared world within families or within couples, that looks at once banal and bizarre to the outsider. Gilliatt is capable of making us see those invisible long-term games and unspoken compacts from the inside and the outside at once, and of seeing how they belong so totally

in the sphere where she shows them, how little elsewhere. . . . At her best, Penelope Gilliatt is as good as anyone at showing us these things; her limited but well-deployed battery of stylistic and narrative tricks means that she rarely has to descend to telling us.

Roz Kaveney, "Speaking for the Shabby-Genteel," in The Times Literary Supplement, *No. 4313, November 29, 1985, p. 1353.*

VALERIE SHAW

Practitioners of the modern short story often achieve striking effects by remaining silent where writers of an earlier period would have offered explanation and naturalistic detail. The result is a kind of fiction that involves readers in a process of interpretation and judgement, allowing them, as Penelope Gilliatt's stories in *They Sleep Without Dreaming* undoubtedly do, to draw their own conclusions. Silence is both a deftly used technique and a theme throughout this new collection. . . . In general, Gilliatt's characters are more chic than shabby: they are university dons, cosmopolitans, businessmen or, more often still, journalists of one sort or another. This milieu gives the author opportunities for some clever dialogue in which remarks fly off one another at a tangent; and it permits many allusions to non-literary arts such as painting, music and opera. One story, "Addio," concerns an ageing prima donna who enjoys a moment of renewed glory during a master class.

But it is not always clear just how mocking Gilliatt means to be of the fashionable world she depicts so vividly. Sometimes the drift of her narrative does not fully engage the moral attention she wants from her readers. So, while a discriminating awareness is evident in the title story, "They Sleep Without Dreaming", with its exposure of a 'generation of mediocrities', it comes over too obliquely in a piece like "On Each Other's Time", where a character thinks he has gone blind but has merely set his typewriter at blank. Such faintly surrealistic touches appear in other stories, too, notably in "Cliffdwellers", which is set out in the form of a play and where Gilliatt's off-beat humour, her capacity to blend the wry and the touching, can be seen to fine effect. Indeed, her narrative techniques frequently lie close to those of the drama, and if the story "Purse" recalls Beckett, then this perhaps demonstrates that Gilliatt's most valuable contribution to the twentieth-century British short story is her adventurous use of prose to convey the quirky rhythms of people's speech—as well as their silences.

Valerie Shaw, in a review of "They Sleep without Dreaming," in British Book News, *May, 1986, p. 309.*

PUBLISHERS WEEKLY

Culled from previous collections published over the past two decades, [the short fiction contained in *22 Stories* is] representative of the sophisticated vignettes with which readers of the *New Yorker* are familiar. Gilliatt, author also of the award-winning screenplay for *Sunday Bloody Sunday*, is eminently successful in capturing the fussy details with which people often mask deep concerns. . . . The drama that exists in complexities among the generations, the humor in some very English class situations and the absurdities that people endure are viewed in these polished stories from a cosmopolite.

A review of "22 Stories," in Publishers Weekly, *Vol. 230, No. 5, August 1, 1986, p. 70.*

RITA D. JACOBS

Gilliatt knows that people often trip and fall into their lives instead of choosing the patterns that come to rule them. Then it takes a revelation, an insight, a loss to stir them to action. In the most delightful of the stories in her latest collection [*22 Stories*], such as **"Autumn of a Dormouse,"** the urge to save another results in self-salvation. Seventy-four-year-old Mrs. Abbott, usually thrifty and careful, needs to make a vivid impression on her grown son about the way he ignores his own son Alexander. She spends her savings on eighteen roundtrip tickets from New York to Rome and uses them in making daily trips with Alexander. In the end her extravagance allows her to escape her tedious existence, and she gives Alexander the knowledge that change is possible.

Often it is the eye for detail and the ear for conversation rather than any semblance of plot that makes the stories work. In **"Catering"** the soap opera of one family's life is played out through small bits of dialogue as background while the foreground is filled with the business of catering a wedding. Despite the cacophony of the wedding preparations, the reader is quite certain that the background bits are most important.

Quirky characters populate Gilliatt's world: cellists who can't play, accomplished and published writers who can't pay their phone bills, parents who love too much or too little. What an odd lot of people she presents in tales that are often well crafted but not always engrossing and sometimes definitely depressing. These are stories that cannot be read one after another. A reader needs space between and time to adjust to the very different worlds presented in each.

Rita D. Jacobs, in a review of "22 Stories," in World Literature Today, *Vol. 61, No. 4, Autumn, 1987, p. 630.*

HUGH BARNES

It is strange to find history beginning to unfold in small talk as it does in Penelope Gilliatt's new novel [*A Woman of Singular Occupation*]. An Englishwoman leaves Paris a few weeks before the outbreak of the Second World War, crossing Europe to Istanbul. Although larger events rumble away just below the surface of the plot, nobody takes much notice. Here the cutting edge is chat, usually lunch-related.

Not a low-level sort of tourist, Catherine de Rochefauld makes her way to the Bosphorous on board the Orient-Express, which halts and breaks, like the novel itself, having eliminated the direct route through Germany. The story opens with allurement in the restaurant car replete with *maitre d' hotel,* Dresden china and a bulky wine-list.

At times Gilliatt seems uncertain about her central character to whom she gives a whirling beauty and remoteness. Over lunch, Catherine meets two unattached Americans. After some desultory talk about Fascism, she moves on to the subject of her marriage to a French diplomat, older than her 'by the usual European amount', as if this were another constraint making her escape necessary. Is Catherine on the verge of becoming an exile or a refugee? Gilliatt leaves the question unanswered for a long time after the journey ends.

Set in 'a tangled part of Europe' in tangled circumstances, *A Woman of Singular Occupation* reaches deeply into the clutter and vacuity of suspended lives. But the novel doubles back on itself, turning away from the awkwardness of asylum in Turkey (hot pavements and chilly receptions) to deal with an unrestricted European fancy. Gilliatt has come to occupy the shifting ground between past and present where, because nothing actually happens, it's all talk, in small orbits, and old anxieties absorb the shock of the new. It is, in the best sense, a frustrating novel.

Hugh Barnes, "Bosphorescence," in The Observer, *May 1, 1988, p. 43.*

AUSTIN MacCURTAIN

This winsomely absurd novel [*A Woman of Singular Occupation*] opens with the heroine, Catherine de Rochefauld, boarding the Orient Express in Paris in July 1939, and meeting a long-standing acquaintance, an American married to a Turkish business man. In the course of their first conversation we are introduced to Catherine's dumb keyboard, her Paisley notebook and, in this characterization by her friend, herself: "My darling Catherine, what gifts. A composer on the quiet, a friend beyond compare, the perfect diplomat's wife. And such a dresser. How do you afford the time to shop?" A young American banker, bound for Istanbul, introduces himself. Ann Wisner, the American friend, drops a hint about her Paris *cinq-à-sept,* then quotes her husband to the effect that love affairs can be conducted without damage to a marriage, but political opinions are in the husband's hands. Catherine's husband, *en poste* at the French Embassy in Ankara is, it is intimated, loyal to Daladier's government, soon to be Pétain's Vichy. Thus deftly adumbrated, the plot turns out to be perfunctory. Penelope Gilliatt's preferred method is to demonstrate, through clever, glancing dialogue, where few thoughts are completed and all allusions are taken, the brilliance and excruciating sensitivity of her characters. Once in Istanbul, Catherine quickly annexes Thomas, the young American banker, as her lover, then torments him with her secrecy about herself, her husband, her family and her activities. She is shown throughout as a person of such acute intelligence and fine-tempered sensibility that both her friend Ann and her husband, the dubious diplomat, indulge her without question.

Her secret is that she has worked out a wizard wheeze to do down the Hun. Through various unspecified contacts in New York and Europe she learns useful things about fluctuating prices on the commodities black markets which she encodes in her Paisley notebook into musical modulations. She then plays them on her dumb keyboard, which registers the notes on its tracing paper. This is transmitted, disguised as musical composition, to de Gaulle's office in London and, *voilà!*

Not that any of this is confided to anyone. It all takes place against a background of small-time intrigue at and around diplomatic functions. One such, held at the American Consulate, lets us know how seriously Catherine is to be taken. An unknown woman, apparently in league with a local palmist, takes a shot at her from a gun with a silencer attached. But a watchful aide-de-camp has pushed Catherine to the floor just in time, and the bullet shatters the palmist's glass. Catherine's saviour, we are told, "quickly pocketed the bullet"—presumably it had dropped at his feet—and went on to attribute the shattered glass to the soprano's having hit high A. Why the soprano, "a pupil of Nadia Boulanger's'', was spending her talent on a roomful of chatterers we are not told.

It scarcely matters. The book is full of characters who are lightly introduced and forgotten as soon as they have supplied the little twirl which keeps Catherine's top spinning. The spinning consists almost entirely of nervous, competitive dialogue. . . .

When the narrative has petered out with Thomas's departure for Istanbul, we are suddenly transported from the 1940s to the 1980s. Thomas has, since the war, become a renowned nuclear physicist, then, when that became unfashionable, a ''concerned ecologist''. But ''Catherine remained unforgettable'', we are told, so that he has not remarried. He goes to find her, and learns that her husband, just dead, has written an anti-Fascist history that has been honoured by the French Academy. Catherine has become a famous composer, though the ''young knew her best as a campaigner for nuclear disarmament''. He glimpses her from the top of a London bus ''playing the piano at an open-air concert for people before they went to work''. All this in two-and-a-half pages. Honest.

Austin MacCurtain, "Talking of Travel," in The Times Literary Supplement, *No. 4440, May 6-12, 1988, p. 500.*

(Margaret) Rumer Godden

1907-

English novelist, poet, short story writer, nonfiction writer, scriptwriter, editor, dramatist, autobiographer, biographer, and author of children's books.

Godden is a prolific popular author whose fiction combines finely crafted plots, vivid settings, and sensitive psychological portraits to examine the effects of time and change. Her diverse novels focus on familial, social, and spiritual conflicts and crises, and she is perhaps best known for her portrayals of cultural friction involving British characters living in colonial or independent India. Several of Godden's works depict innocent characters who develop stronger senses of identity as they struggle against vain and callous individuals. Many of Godden's novels have been adapted for film, television, or theater.

Godden spent her early childhood in India and has returned there for periods of her adult life. Her experiences inform several of her novels, in which she examines problems within English families in India and cultural conflicts between British and Indian characters. *Breakfast with the Nikolides* (1942), for example, concerns a young English girl living in India who matures during an ongoing clash with her selfish mother, while *The River* (1946) delineates a teenager's attempts to come to terms with her initial feelings of love, mortality, and artistic creation. Similarly, *The Peacock Spring: A Western Progress* (1975) presents a young woman's coming-of-age through her romance with an Indian poet. Contrasts between British and Indian cultures are explored in *Kingfishers Catch Fire* (1953), which details a widowed Englishwoman's endeavors to live among the hostile inhabitants of a Kashmiri village. When her daughter is injured by inhabitants of the district, the woman abandons her ideals of peaceful coexistence and seeks revenge.

The process of transformation from innocence to maturity is explored in several of Godden's novels. *An Episode of Sparrows* (1955) concerns two street urchins who attempt to cultivate a garden amidst the ruins of post-World War II London. In *The Greengage Summer* (1958), a group of English children living in a French country house learn about the darker side of adult life by observing the sexual and criminal exploits of their disreputable neighbors. *The Battle of the Villa Fiorita* (1963) portrays two siblings who attempt to reconcile their separated parents by interrupting their mother's adulterous tryst in an Italian villa. As in most of Godden's novels, the values of innocent characters triumph over those of corrupt individuals.

Godden has also written several works that revolve around themes relating to Christianity. For example, *Black Narcissus* (1939), her first popular and critically acclaimed novel, centers on a group of nuns who attempt to establish a religious order in the Himalayas. Conflicts between the nuns and area natives, a series of natural disasters, and the incipient madness of one of the sisters contribute to the failure of the order. *In This House of Brede* (1969), which details the daily thoughts and activities of a group of Benedictine nuns in England, presents a realistic portrait of convent life. The lives of nuns are again examined in *Five for Sorrow, Ten for Joy* (1979), which depicts

an unusual French religious order whose members counsel criminals and drug addicts.

Godden's diverse topics are evident in several of her other respected works of fiction. In *Take Three Tenses* (1945; published in Great Britain as *A Fugue in Time*) and *China Court: The Hours of a Country House* (1961), she employs nonlinear narrative to express the shifting natures of time and memory. *Take Three Tenses* details the effects of war, romance, and changing society on the relationships and personal lives of several generations of a wealthy London family. In *China Court*, an aging character relates his memories of the former inhabitants of a country house, reflecting on the personal and social significance of the events he describes. *Gypsy, Gypsy* (1940) is a young woman's account of her sadistic aunt's scheme to bring about the spiritual degradation of a handsome and virtuous gypsy. *A Candle for St. Jude* (1948) depicts the struggles and triumphs of a small London ballet ensemble as they prepare for an opening-night performance. *A Breath of Air* (1950), an updated version of William Shakespeare's play *The Tempest*, is set on an island in the Orient and depicts a group of sophisticated Londoners who confront their feelings about love, relationships, and problems of the modern world.

In addition to her novels, Godden has published books in a number of other genres. Of these works, she is best known for her award-winning children's fiction, which includes *The Doll's House* (1947), *The Mousewife* (1951), *Miss Happiness and Miss Flower* (1961), and *The Kitchen Madonna* (1967). Godden is also the author of *A Time to Dance, No Time to Weep* (1987), an autobiographical account of her early life that centers on her childhood in India.

(See also *Contemporary Authors*, Vols. 5-8, rev. ed.; *Contemporary Authors New Revision Series*, Vol. 4; and *Something about the Author*, Vols. 3, 36.)

EDITH H. WALTON

The plot of *Black Narcissus* can be reduced, bleakly, to a very simple formula. It is the story of what happens to a little band of nuns when they attempt to found a convent on the north frontier of India. Not, on the face of it, a very alluring theme nor one likely to hold much quality of excitement. One would never anticipate—certainly I did not—that a tale along these lines could prove so irresistible. For *Black Narcissus* is a real discovery. Not only has it charm, humor, subtlety, and a shining kind of freshness, but it is actually almost without flaw. It would be hard to say how Miss Godden could have improved upon this bizarre and exquisite little novel. If I seem effusive, I am so deliberately. This is not a book to miss. (p. 5)

What eventually happens, how and why the Sisters are driven out . . . , it is not my place to tell. The plot, anyway, is not nearly so important as the atmosphere which Miss Godden builds up and the feeling of palpitant tension which she creates. It is the Palace which one will remember, hanging on the edge of space, with eagles wheeling and screaming in the gulf which divides it from the Himalayas, and the great white peak, Kanchenjungha towering over all. Because this background is so real and so brilliantly strange, what happens to the Sisters also becomes credible. One believes in every step of their tragic-comic fall, as they are softened, altered, corrupted by a wholly fantastic environment.

In the end, however, it is quite impossible to define the charm of *Black Narcissus.* Its setting alone accounts for only a part of it, as does the freshness and piquancy of its story. Perhaps it is the special blend of dry, delicate humor and very real feeling which makes it seem so unique. Perhaps it is merely Miss Godden's gift for creating a series of captivating characters. For the point is that these people are individual and alive, each sister sharply realized, each native deftly drawn. . . . Miss Godden needed to be good to tell so strange a story. She is good, and her book is a lovely one. (p. 10)

Edith H. Walton, "A Bizarre but Exquisite Novel," in The New York Times Book Review, *July 9, 1939, pp. 5, 10.*

HARRY SYLVESTER

If you like the taste of slightly over-ripe fruit, you may very well like [*Black Narcissus*]. You may use your intellect in reading it, but for the full enjoyment of it you must suspend your critical judgment, for Miss Godden is not above deliberately warping facts to make her point.

A group of Anglican nuns takes over a palace in the Himalayas at the invitation of the ruling prince, to try to make of it a

school and a convent. The palace had formerly been the seraglio of the Prince's uncle, and Miss Godden makes a great to do about how its former atmosphere militated against its being turned into a convent. She tells us that this is so, but gives no evidence or demonstration of it. (p. 342)

The nuns do a very good job overcoming the obstacles which Miss Godden, rather than nature, puts in their way. One example is enough to show Miss Godden's method. The sister in charge of the kitchen sends food down with some guides who are to escort a new nun to the convent through the mountain passes. The new nun arrives weak and hungry because the last day of her journey was a Friday in Lent and the cooking sister had sent for her fare principally meat-pies. Now anyone who knows even a little bit about such things knows that under the circumstances of travel, the sister or anyone else could eat meat. The rules of fasting and abstinence do not apply under the circumstances of a long journey and particularly one as desperate as the nun's. But it suited Miss Godden to make the nun—by no means unintelligent—abstain from the meat and thus make the cooking sister feel bad.

Since Miss Godden is convinced that nature triumphs over all, the nuns accordingly admit defeat and abandon the palace. Why, only Miss Godden knows. The circumstances in which she places the nuns are not particularly difficult, especially for people trained in the way of life of religious. But here again Miss Godden completely ignores the effect of such training. It is true that one of the nuns goes slightly mad and dies unpleasantly, but convents and monasteries have been founded and maintained under far more difficult circumstances than those Miss Godden depicts.

Miss Godden writes well enough, but the book is nudging and sly rather than subtle and Miss Godden's prejudices show through so strongly that little of the book except the scenery is convincing. Only the product of a declining English Protestantism could have written this book. . . . (pp. 342-43)

Harry Sylvester, in a review of "Black Narcissus," in The Commonweal, *Vol. XXX, No. 14, July 28, 1939, pp. 342-43.*

FRANCES WOODWARD

[*Black Narcissus*] gets tangled up with your personal emotions, this tale of the nuns in the Himalayas, and you resent its being common property. If you like it at all you like it very much, and are convinced that only you and perhaps a few carefully chosen friends can appreciate it.

We personally like it very much; so to those who call it thin we reply that no, it is delicate and fragile. To those who say it is 'just a *tour de force*' we reply that it is as lovely a piece of quiet, humorous, sustained imaginative writing as we have seen in many years. And to those who compare it to this other book or that we say well, if you must compare it, think of *Mr. Fortune's Maggot.* The short time span which Rumer Godden has chosen for her characters is perfect for her purpose. Their first impression of the great house clinging to the hill's brow is tranquil and serene, like anyone's first impression of an unknown town. It is only when the people begin to come in on you—as they did on the sisters—that adumbrations of disaster stir.

None of these disasters are fortuitous or impossible, since each of them springs directly from the seeds long dormant in personalities the reader has been led to understand more intimately, perhaps, than he understands his own deviations from the man he seems to be.

Black Narcissus is small and clear and fine, like a Dürer etching. And, like a Dürer etching, it will not be put aside and forgotten; you will come back again to look at the figures walking in the bright high wind, eternally alien and mysterious against the alien and mysterious Mountain.

> *Frances Woodward, "Storm Jameson and Rumer Godden," in* The Atlantic Bookshelf, *a section of* The Atlantic Monthly, *Vol. 164, No. 3, September, 1939.*

ROSE FELD

A new voice, a new idea are rare and precious things in the world of fiction. Rumer Godden holds claim to both. We first became acquainted with her through *Black Narcissus*. Her language is muted in a minor key entirely suited to the strange tale she tells in *Gypsy, Gypsy*; the core of her story is profound and original. Aunt Barbe and the Gypsy are persons one does not meet in ordinary life but each has a sentient kinship with the essence of evil and of good in all mankind. Brilliantly paced in a macabre rhythm, the story unfolds with driving purpose and intensity. It is at the same time a devastating psychological study and a powerfully dramatic tale.

From the very beginning one is swept into the mood of catastrophe through the medium of nineteen-year-old Henrietta, niece of Aunt Barbe, fifty-year-old widow of Louis de Longuemare. For centuries dating back to William the Conquerer, the de Longuemares had lived in the Chateau at St. Lieux in Normandy. . . . Until Aunt Barbe came, the relationship between those in the Chateau and those living in its environs was simple and good and mutually respecting. Aunt Barbe, beautiful, domineering, self-indulgent and essentially cruel, had changed all that. With deft strokes, Miss Godden presents the woman in all her evil, proud of her strength, scornful of others' weakness. . . .

But with the death of her husband, Louis de Longuemare, whom she had humiliated and betrayed, whom she had despised for his weakness, she finds an anchor taken from her. Something akin to fear enters her heart, a conviction of sin and a threat of consequences. The coming of the Gypsy to St. Lieux brings the solution to her diseased mind.

There is a superstitious belief among many peoples that one can cleanse one's self through defilement of the pure. Aunt Barbe carries this madness into the field of the spiritual. If she can find a virgin soul, one that has never known sin, whom she can coerce into an evil act, she will be purified. How great is Miss Godden's art is evidenced by the fact that the reader is caught and held in the development of this idea. . . .

The darkening events of the book move swiftly and inexorably to the end.

Gypsy, Gypsy is an unusual book on every count. The writing is distinguished for somber beauty, piercing as a ray of moonlight on black waters; the characterization sensitive and subtle, the story poignant and enthralling. Miss Godden knows her French peasant, fierce in his loyalties and fierce in his hatreds. She portrays all of them with unerring hand, but the best of them, perhaps, is old Bac, the octogenarian who dares speak up to Aunt Barbe and scorn her tardy bounty. . . .

A gentle love story unfolds in the shadow of the tragedy and comes to peaceful ending. But it is the central theme, striking and violent, which gives this book its distinction.

> *Rose Feld, "A Profound and Original Macabre Story," in* New York Herald Tribune Books, *August 11, 1940, p. 5.*

KATHERINE WOODS

Rumer Godden's curious and beautiful *Black Narcissus* has already made its author known for work of unusual character and for fresh yet polished skill. Her new book [*Gypsy, Gypsy*] is marked like its predecessor by pervasive originality, by sensitiveness and haunting power. But it would be hard to think of two novels more different in setting, story and theme. In *Black Narcissus* story and setting presented with a remote and lovely elaborateness a theme which was essentially simple; in *Gypsy, Gypsy* a Norman farm and fishing village form the scene of simple events which work out to its full conclusion a theme which might have sprung from the involutions of an age-old diabolism to actuate a horror story today. . . .

[The] story runs a flawless course of plot and portraiture, through a succession of incidents, in a beautiful setting. And all the more because the scene is so natural is the sinister power of evil and distortion felt in its persistence and ruthlessness. (p. 5)

Many small, significant things happen before the novel is brought to its culmination of catastrophe and from that to its swift, surprising end. And although the reader can certainly not be promised a happy ending to the gypsy's story, the larger ends of justice are not wholly unserved. Henrietta, from childhood, has been too sophisticated to be the victim for Aunt Barbe's sacrifice: she has in herself, and knows it, something of Aunt Barbe's shrewdness and tenacity. She can turn these to good instead of evil, in her own life and René's, and for the people, and the ancient life of the land. And René, who is like Uncle Louis but stronger, need not face Aunt Barbe's husband's sad defeat. Aunt Barbe, one knows, will be exorcized like a wicked spirit of old legend, struck suddenly with failure when she thought her triumph was sure. There is personal tragedy in the novel, of course; but not only that.

And it is always a fascinating story. One is held by it, so, in reading—even before one stops to realize the subtle perfection of form, the natural awareness and troubling suggestion, the strangeness and penetration and beauty, that make it an extraordinary achievment, and leave its echoes calling in one's mind. (p. 17)

> *Katherine Woods, "A Haunting Tale by the Author of 'Black Narcissus'," in* The New York Times Book Review, *August 11, 1940, pp. 5, 17.*

HARRY SYLVESTER

Miss Godden achieved some small reputation last year with *Black Narcissus*, a book about Anglican nuns in the Himalayas. The fact that Miss Godden knew practically nothing about the principles of monasticism and that her book's structure was predicated largely on this ignorance did not prevent a number of equally ignorant people from praising it excessively.

Miss Godden's second book [*Gypsy, Gypsy*] is less pretentious and is peopled with those almost stock characters which generally inhabit the novels of the talented amateur novelists whose name in England seems legion. There is the neurotic niece, the faded and wicked beauty of an aunt, the French fiancé, the various servants. The fact that the scene is the coast of Normandy seems to make little difference.

What saves the book from complete mediocrity is the aunt's quite conscious design superstitiously to relieve herself of the evil she has done in life, of the evil in her, by creating evil in the lives of other people. It's an ambitious book and Miss Godden almost pulls it off. Certainly this is a truer, if less sensational novel than her first one, and her flair for creating the mood of a country and giving her reader the feeling of a place is still strong.

Harry Sylvester, in a review of "Gypsy, Gypsy," in
The Commonweal, *Vol. XXXII, No. 18, August 23, 1940, p. 372.*

ROSE FELD

The scene of [**Breakfast With the Nikolides**] is laid in India, in East Bengal. This is practically native soil to Rumer Godden, for at the age of six months she was brought there from Sussex. Not the least impressive feature of this deeply moving book is her feeling for this part of the world. She writes not as an outsider making notes, but as one who is describing the elements of life that nurtured her body and her mind. The sounds, the smells, the caste differences among the East Indians, their philosophy, form natural and seemingly effortless part of the background she creates. Her talents are peculiarly adapted for telling a story placed in this exotic land, or perhaps it is that her talents are product of the years she spent there. For it is not for story alone one will remember this book but for its pervading mood of mystery that touches scene and character alike. The word "mystery" is used in the sense that she commands by her portrayals that a human being is a creature who can rarely be known by his fellow beings.

And especially is this true in the case of a sensitive child protecting itself against a domineering and arrogant adult.

On the morning that Emily Pool and her younger sister, Binnie, were sent to the Nikolides for breakfast, a joyous event to them, Louise Pool, their mother, got Naroyan Das, the young Hindoo veterinary surgeon to kill Don, Emily's small black spaniel. In insisting upon this, Louise gave deep affront and pain to three persons, to Das, who, in spite of his Western education, found it difficult to kill, and particularly since he was uncertain that the act was necessary; to her husband, Charles Pool, who wished the child to be informed of the deed before it was over, and to Emily, to whom the act held not only the loss of something dear but personal betrayal as well. That Louise believed the dog had hydrophobia justified her in the eyes of neither of the adults, who begged for time to make certain that the animal was actually rabid.

This is the incident which makes the core of Rumer Godden's sensitively probing tale. The flesh of the story lies in events that precede and follow it. . . .

There is a magnetism of beauty in Rumer Godden's work that cannot fail to hold a reader responsive to writing that goes beyond the factual. The act and the spoken word are important to her, but only as outer manifestations of mental and spiritual ferments that lie hidden. It is in her delicate searching of these things, of the soils that nurture the blossoms that she excels. **Breakfast With the Nikolides** adds another high mark of distinction to the fine record of this extremely talented writer.

Rose Feld, "The Sounds, Smells, Soil of India," in
New York Herald Tribune Books, *February 8, 1942, p. 2.*

EDITH H. WALTON

Possibly because she has once again turned to India for her setting, **Breakfast With the Nikolides,** Rumer Godden's third novel, has much the same quality of enchantment as **Black Narcissus,** her first. There seems to be something in the air of India to which Miss Godden's fragile and exotic talent is particularly attuned. Thus, though it had its points, **Gypsy, Gypsy**—the scene of which was France—fell far short of **Black Narcissus** and lacked the peculiar magic which both that book and this one possess. Not in the strict sense a realist—a dealer, rather, in the strange, the romantic, the subtle, the bizarre—Miss Godden perhaps needs a background which is alien and remote if the spell which she can cast is to hold. True, she never falsifies that background, which she knows with great intimacy, but its very glamour and strangeness heighten her effects. India is the perfect setting for the tale she has to tell. . . .

In her new novel the specific scene is the small town of Amorra on the plains of East Bengal—a town which boasts both a Government Farm and an Agricultural College. At the head of the farm is an Englishman named Charles Pool—a lean, dark, reticent, piratical-looking man—whose work has always appeared to absorb him quite completely and who lives in a queer but beautiful house in the midst of the bazaar. . . . The natives like him, but know little about him. This does not prepare them, however, for the shock which they experience when, after eight years of solitude, Charles not only produces a very lovely wife but also two young daughters. . . .

Whatever the reason—and the reader soon guesses that there has been violence and turbulence in the past between Charles and his Louise—the latter stays on in stiff constraint at Amorra together with 11-year-old Emily and her younger sister, Binnie. Pretty like her mother, Binnie is otherwise colorless, but Emily, the plain and gawky one, is a secretive, intense, and most unusual child who senses the hidden conflict dividing Charles and Louise and who becomes ardently her father's partisan. She is a child, as Charles recognizes, who must be handled with care and with respect for her intelligence, not alternately babied and bullied. This, however, Louise does not see. Accordingly, when Emily's beloved spaniel falls ill and is suspected of hydrophobia, Louise makes the fatal error not only of having him killed without proper inquiry but of doing it in Emily's absence—which she has disingenuously arranged—and of lying to her about it afterward.

This incident, trivial as it seems, is the pivotal incident in the book and has wide-spreading repercussions. . . . Emily sets herself to break Louise's spirit and to force her to admit the truth. This she accomplishes by refusing to admit that the little dog is dead, by keeping up an eerie, disturbing and unrelenting pretense that he is still frolicking happily at her side.

This macabre play acting of Emily's not only shatters Louise's nerves—already shaken by loneliness and by proximity to Charles—but it also has its effect upon the superstitious townsfolk. Gradually strange rumors begin to filter through the bazaar and even to invade the student body at the College. There is talk of a ghost dog who leaves ghostly footprints, and of a kind of bewitchment which has befallen Amorra. . . . How it all turns out, and what climactic disaster purges the tense atmosphere, it is not, of course, my province to say. The pattern of the story is so cunningly woven, so brilliant with suspense, that to divulge too much would be unfair.

In any comparison with **Black Narcissus, Breakfast With the Nikolides** must, I suppose, yield a slight edge. Its background is neither so haunting nor so romantic. . . . On the other hand, its greater closeness to ordinary living makes the magic which invests it if anything more remarkable, and certainly it is written with the same charm and delicacy and deftness as its predecessor. Again, Miss Godden penetrates sensitively the mysterious, hidden life of India, reveals it in all its raw strange colors, its ugly racial conflicts. Again she builds up subtly an atmosphere of tension, yet lightens her tale with a dry, elusive wit. The art which Miss Godden practices is, perhaps, a minor one, but in this book, as in **Black Narcissus,** she has brought it very nearly to perfection.

> *Edith H. Walton, "Rumer Godden Brings Her Magic to a Tale of India," in* The New York Times Book Review, *February 8, 1942, p. 7.*

THE TIMES LITERARY SUPPLEMENT

The setting of **Breakfast with the Nikolides** is a small town in eastern Bengal by the name of Amorra, where there is a flourishing agricultural college and research station. This is largely the creation of Charles Pool, a brown, hairy, commanding Englishman. . . . Various odd stories are current about him, and an extra fillip is given to them when he is joined in Amorra by an unsuspected wife. . . . With her came the two children, Emily and Binnie, the elder of them eleven. And Emily at eleven, a watchful, passionate child with a disturbing gift for silence and a weak stomach, is both her father's and her mother's daughter. The tension of the hostility that she feels always about her, the tension of the instability of Charles's and Louise's renewed life together, is dissolved in the more poignant tension of her discovery of herself and of India. A single small incident hastens the process. The black spaniel that Charles has given her is thought to be suffering from rabies and is promptly destroyed, without her knowledge, on Louise's instructions; in her loss, in an outburst of obscure jealousy also, Emily contemplates the face of mystery, touches extremity, and possibly restores Charles and Louise to one another.

It will be gathered that the story is of the delicately implied and rarefied kind, touched not so much by the common breath of life as by a quivering sensibility. It is, nevertheless, a good story, poetically suggestive and at times to be described as exquisite, though somewhat self-consciously exquisite. That self-consciousness has been Miss Rumer Godden's failing in earlier novels, which cultivate beauty too assiduously. Here, however, although in the soliloquies which thread her glancing style of narrative there is a degree of preciousness, the pursuit of beauty is less strenuous. This is partly because the depths of Charles, Louise and Emily are made most sharply apparent in their feelings for the Indian scene, and in describing the Indian scene—landscape and characters—Miss Godden seems to be looking for truth rather than the beauty which in a poetical sense may be truth. Her method, as always, is allusive and a little fluttery, but there is a quality of immediate pictorial evocation in the thing achieved.

The story does produce, in fact, the "feel" of Amorra, the hot sunlight and the dust, the animals and the children, the monotony of the fields and the bright colours of the bazaar and the emptiness of the wide landscape beyond the river bank. . . .

Miss Godden draws together the several threads in her story with a firm hand. True, the cave-man tactics that finally settled Louise's fine-drawn and effulgent hash might have been adopted with some success earlier, but the delay, no doubt, is one of those literary and unlifelike devices without which story-telling would perish.

> *"Tension in India," in* The Times Literary Supplement, *No. 2089, February 14, 1942, p. 77.*

ROSE FELD

To say that Rumer Godden is a romantic poet who writes prose is one way of classifying her. But this is not enough, although the word "poet" encompasses superior qualities of beauty and cadence of expression. It is not expression alone that makes her unique among contemporary novelists. That is only the raiment that clothes the heart and the spirit of the story she tells. Reading her, one is caught in a sort of enchantment when, for a brief and poignant period, not wholly real, one looks into a mirror that throws back images which hold a personal nostalgic meaning. The tale she weaves may be completely divorced from the reader's experience but, always beneath it, there is a deep chord that strikes a note of memory.

In her new novel, **Take Three Tenses,** Miss Godden tells the story of an English house and of the family who, for one year less than a century, have lived there. The subtitle is "A Fugue in Time," and that more accurately describes it. For, like a fugue in music, its pattern is one of starting and retracing a theme, of several life histories, like melodies being carried on simultaneously in a unified harmony. . . . To the house, to the solitary man who lives in it at the time the book opens, the past, the present, the future have no clear division of years. Memories and present-day events crowd each other for recognition and attention.

What this house, its lease now run out, had witnessed in romance, in heart-break, in births and deaths and tragedy, make the story of the book.

Three major romances overlap each other in the book, the story of John and Griselda, of Rollo and Lark, of Grizel and Pax. They weave in and out of each other without respect to chronology. . . . Miss Godden will be writing of Rollo and Lark and something that happens or something that is said carries the story to John and Griselda or to Grizel and Pax. It sounds confusing, but so excellent is her way of carrying mood and quality into scenes that ring the same notes of tenderness or fear or desperation that the reader follows with small sense of a break in the individual stories.

Miss Godden portrays Griselda in her moments of self-examination. She knew that she was wiser than her husband, but she realized that he was the stronger.

The fugue of lives lived and loves lost or destroyed comes to a close with the assurance that the house on Wiltshire Place which has been doomed to die will remain to assimilate the histories of new generations.

Take Three Tenses is a rare book indeed. Apart from its quality, apart from the story it tells, it possesses the gift of personal experience for the reader, not through identification with its characters but through charging his own memories with life.

> *Rose Feld, "The Haunting Memory of Lost Dreams," in* New York Herald Tribune Weekly Book Review, *March 11, 1945, p. 3.*

ANNE FREMANTLE

Take Three Tenses opens with the statement: "the house, it seems, is more important than the characters. 'In me you exist' says the house." And with these words also [Godden] ends her story, which she subtitles, "A fugue in time." Actually, even more than the 99-year-leased house, it is the stream of consciousness that is her novel's hero, as she emphasizes in her repetition, no less than three times, of the same lines from Mr. T. S. Eliot's "Four Quartets." This gives the reader, by the time he meets the same chunk of verse from East Coker, a slight sense of being shouted at. "Yes, yes," he exclaims, "I read it on the first page. I know we must be still and still moving, but let's get to the story, since that too must move.". . .

Miss Godden's characters are the Eye and Griselda, she seventeen, he twenty-nine, new-married in their big London house with their six servants. They have nine children; the twins die; the ninth child costs Griselda her life. The Eye, mournful, consoles himself with a travelling singer, who with her husband is killed in the Tay Bridge disaster; he brings up their orphan daughter, Lark, in his house. Lark is ill-treated by the Eye's eldest daughter, Selina, who dies a bepugged spinster; Lark bewitches Pelham, the Eye's eldest son, but falls for Rollo, the penniless youngest. He gets a commission in the Indian Army, and asks her to wait five years for him, when he'll return and marry her. But Lark can't wait, her position in Pelham's household is too uncomfortable, so she elopes with a minute Italian marquis. . . . (p. 73)

Take Three Tenses ends with Pelham's American granddaughter, Grizel, a WAC officer in this war, and married to Pax, Lark's nephew, whom she meets in "the" house, living there with their baby daughter, Verity. So the wheel has come full circle, the serpent's tail is securely in its mouth, and, as Mary Stuart said before Mr. Eliot plagiarized her, "in my end is my beginning." Miss Godden is a pointilliste, a perfectionist, building up her effects with the lightest of touch, without shock; she uses the simplest things, food, servants, scrubbing brushes, children's clothes, linoleum, smells, sounds, as materials for her magic. And her reader believes, in the hat and in the rabbit, in conjuror and conjured, and in every conversation. There is nothing to stretch either the faith or the imagination: the instant reaction, is, of course it must have been like that, *is* like that. Evocation, invocation, can do no more; here, in perspective as solid as Piranesi's, is a conversation piece executed in the subtlest of monochrome wash.

But, as Swinburne once remarked, a primrose by the rivers brim, dicotyledon was to him, and it was nothing more. . . . Miss Godden's characters are etiolated, unreal, sprouting damply in basements, or in the rarified air of attics—anyway, indoors: they are never exposed to sun, and therefore not to shadow. She gives herself away by prefacing her book with a sentence by Lawrence Abbott describing a Bach fugue. And her characters are indeed notes, chords, sounds; for her, human relationships are simplified by the family, are reduced by a sort of unitary method to phrases in the Book of Common Prayer, children are arrows in the hand, man is cut down like a flower. (pp. 73-4)

Anne Fremantle, "Whose Fountains Are Within," in The Commonweal, Vol. XCII, No. 3, May 4, 1945, pp. 72-5.

THE TIMES LITERARY SUPPLEMENT

Miss Rumer Godden has miscalculated badly in the design of this latest novel of hers [*A Fugue in Time*]. She introduces an old gentleman, General Sir Roland Ironmonger Dane, on the very last lap of a ninety-nine years' lease of a house in London, and after that she sets about building up a personality for the house during the ninety-nine years it has been occupied by the Dane family. Unfortunately, Miss Godden has thought it best to do this by wandering incessantly back and forth in time, intertwining the generations of Danes and their butlers or house cats or charwomen with what seems to be excessive satisfaction in her not too difficult method of narration. The result, at any rate, of her prolonged and unvarying trick of movement backwards and forwards across the years, with the actual experience of those years reduced to the airiest sort of allusion only, is more tedious than she can have bargained for. The effect she intended might have been achieved with a higher degree of poetic imagination, such as gives its haunting quality to, for instance, the evocation of the passage of the years in *To the Lighthouse*, but the fact is that Miss Godden has at best only a literary habit of prettiness to fall back upon. . . .

Miss Godden has her virtues of feminine observation and deftness of touch, but has fallen victim here to an unoriginal and somewhat sentimental device of construction.

"House and Inmates," in The Times Literary Supplement, No. 2260, May 26, 1945, p. 245.

NONA BALAKIAN

There is a certain quality of elusive wisdom about Rumer Godden's novels that, apart from their usual exotic setting, intrigues and charms the reader who comes to them in a receptive mood. She has the gift—no doubt borrowed from the mental climate of her adopted country, India—of isolating the eternal element of existence from the ordinary and familiar, and a poetic awareness of the relative meaning of time that lends fragile, parable-like overtones to her stories. One has the impression of something profound being hinted at, but never wholly revealed.

In **The River** the impression is more than ever pronounced, because Miss Godden is writing about childhood and that time of life when the understanding is still tenuous enough to absorb ideas intuitively. There are moments when her almost-adolescent heroine—borrowing a leaf from Wordsworth—has sudden intimations of immortality, and the framework of this simple story seems to expand to draw into it a larger vision of life. But most of the time it is difficult to know what to expect of this precocious, romantic child who is still young enough to play with mud and insects, though old enough to write mystical poetry.

Miss Godden's real heroine, one begins to suspect, is not Harriet at all, but the source of Harriet's inspiration—the River, with its suggestion of timelessness and of a continuous, detached presence. With her usual deftness she has built around that dramatic symbol a scene containing its own particular flavor and mood. In the background is the great River itself, flowing leisurely between banks of mud and whitestone, alive with a traffic of jumping fishes and crocodiles. In the foreground is the Big House of the jute-pressing works (where Harriet's family lives), lush with exotic garden plants, trees, flowers and birds. Between the two are Harriet—and the problem. . . .

Harriet's inner world is growing faster than she can keep up with it.

In a story of this sort, where the interest centers on delicate sentiments and feelings, it is not a little startling to come upon such elemental happenings as birth and death. Driving her point too hard, Miss Godden has got both, with the result, I think, that she almost spoils the essential simplicity of her theme. Harriet has to learn too much in too short a space. And because she becomes more like a child prodigy than the very human child Miss Godden started to create, *The River* seems, in the end, a little more pretentious than wise.

> Nona Balakian, *"Of Time and the River," in* The New York Times Book Review, *November 3, 1946, p. 20.*

EDWARD WEEKS

In the tone and quality of her writing Rumer Godden is in direct succession to Katherine Mansfield: In Miss Godden's novels, as in Miss Mansfield's short stories, there is an apprehensive interest in time and the change which it is effecting in the character, and in each case the characterization is made luminous by details chosen with skillful, feminine intimacy. In comparing Miss Godden's new novelette, *The River,* with either of Miss Mansfield's famous stories "To the Beach" or "The Garden Party," one notices the same natural nervous flush in the prose.

The River tells the story of one decisive winter in the life of Harriet, an adolescent English girl, half child, half woman, beginning to write, on the verge of calf love, deeply shocked by a death for which she is partly responsible, the sensitive, eager, curious youngster caught at the turning point in her self-revelation. . . . Harriet is learning fast from her mother, from her critical older sister, Bea, from her clear, composed Indian nurse, Nan, and most of all from the sympathy of Captain John, a young soldier crippled and imprisoned by the Japs, who is searching, as Harriet is searching, for the key to life.

The India background is pastel and incidental. What concerns us in the foreground is the series of turns—the publishing of Harriet's piece, the cobra in the garden, the snatching of her diary, the flying of a kite, the last walk with Captain John—with which Harriet emerges from her cocoon.

> Edward Weeks, *"The Girl and the River," in* The Atlantic Bookshelf, *a section of* The Atlantic Monthly, *Vol. 179, No. 1, January, 1947, p. 106.*

NONA BALAKIAN

Miss Godden's kindly, indulgent feeling for her I-Know-Where-I'm-Going heroine [in *A Candle for St. Jude*] is much like that of a nostalgic pupil who loves her teacher more for what she represents than for what she is. In this case, it is the lively, hardworking, hardly glamorous little world of the ballet, where whims and caprices flourish as naturally as the affections. Miss Godden appears to know that world intimately, and not only the details of that way of life, but its very texture: that slightly giddy, breathless and wide-eyed atmosphere which a lesser writer than the author of *Black Narcissus* would have found simply "cute." As the subtle, delicately ironical novelist she is, Miss Godden's success depends, as usual, on her ability to deal with essences—the elusive essences which make up a person's life.

The characteristic essence of Madame's life was its contradictions—its vacillations between generosity and selfishness, vanity and sheer devotion, willfulness and understanding. Like many an aging ballerina, she was soft and sentimental, reluctant

to part with the tiniest testimonial of the past, yet she embraced the present just as passionately; she gave of herself to others, but what she gave she got back with interest—not like Miss Ilse, who gave her mind and heart to Madame, her soul to God, and then had nothing left for herself.

The contrast between these two characters is only quietly emphasized as the story moves on, as other characters—now a variation on Miss Ilse, now on Madame—appear and momentarily take the stage. . . .

Despite the story's undercurrents of agitation and meaning, the plot wears thin toward the end. Yet Miss Godden has a way of making you feel the presence of her characters constantly; like the recurring themes in a piece of music, one looks for them all. . . . Miss Godden doesn't search for depth where it doesn't exist, but neither does she scorn her characters' lack of it. Ordinary as they are, they are none the less individuals who . . . give a sparkling performance.

> Nona Balakian, *"The Anatomy of Balletomania," in* The New York Times Book Review, *August 22, 1948, p. 4.*

ORVILLE PRESCOTT

To my mind, the most successful novel of the summer was one of the least ambitious. It doesn't attempt a major theme, broad scope, many characters, or profound significance. But what it does do it does beautifully. It is Rumer Godden's *A Candle for St. Jude.*

Rumer Godden is one of the finest living English novelists, as readers of her *Take Three Tenses* and *The River* know. Her books are subtle and precise in their craftsmanship, written in a pure, limpid, delicate style, serenely wise and deeply moving, witty and compassionate. Most of them have Indian backgrounds; but *A Candle for St. Jude* is about the world of the ballet in London.

Primarily it is a superb character study of an elderly woman who had been an international star in her youth and who was an impresario in her old age. In her own small theatre, Madame Holbein staged ballets danced by her own pupils. This novel concerns two days of crisis before the opening of a new season. The urgency, dedication, and self-centered passion of ballet are admirably conveyed. The lesser characters who revolve around Madame like minor planets are beautifully realized. And Madame in all her imperious pride and capricious temper is quite wonderful. A modest little book this, but undoubtedly another of Miss Godden's triumphs. (pp. 191-92)

> Orville Prescott, *in a review of "A Candle for St. Jude," in* The Yale Review, *Vol. XXXVIII, No. 1, September, 1948, pp. 191-92.*

IRWIN EDMAN

Rumer Godden writes fiction that moves very close to poetry, and not simply in the sense that her very language is at once melodious and pictorial. Her novels are evocations of a variety of backgrounds, natural and social, but also of the subtler nuances of private feeling. She celebrates at once varied scenes, varied sensibilities, but likewise the common substance of human experience. Sometimes one is reminded of other British writers, particularly women writers of the present or the recent past, Elizabeth Bowen, Virginia Woolf, for instance. But the note struck by Rumer Godden is always her own, even when, as in [*A Breath of Air*], she frankly borrows her plot from Shakespeare. It is almost impossible to refrain from calling this book "The Tempest in Modern Dress," though it and its own title, *A Breath of Air,* suggest the clarity, the luminous magic of Prospero's island. . . .

Rumer Godden has written a parable, an entertainment, a gay and delightful sermon of which *The Tempest* is the text. She has given us a "world elsewhere" that, like Shakespeare's, illuminates the one in which we live.

> *Irwin Edman, "Rumer Godden's Gay, Poetic Parable, with a Bow to 'The Tempest'," in* New York Herald Tribune Book Review, *January 28, 1951, p. 5.*

EVELYN EATON

[In *A Breath of Air*] *The Tempest* has been taken and turned into a lesser island, peopled by puppets conscientiously repeating bowdlerized lines.

Miss Godden's cast is curtailed to six stars: Ferdinand, Stephano, Prospero, Miranda, Ariel and Caliban, played by Valentine, McGinty, Mr. Van Loomis, Charis, Filipino and Mario, and some subsidiary characters which, being Miss Godden's own and she a fine creative artist, are more interesting. . . . The six main characters seem oppressed by a need to conform to Shakespeare's pattern without Shakespeare's help.

Mr. Van Loomis has his good moments, notably in his scenes with Charis and in his soliloquies, but he has none of Prospero's strength. He has not been allowed to believe in the power of his magic—and so he is not the forceful figure appropriate to *The Tempest* in this modern dress. Valentine is an amiable puppet, handsome enough in his stuffed shirt, Charis makes an adequate Miranda—and Miss Godden's Caliban is obligingly monstrous. But the true charm is lacking in all these people. All are much too careful to explain away any aura of the supernatural—even to apologize to the reader when they come in contact with it.

All good writers are allowed at least one not-so-good publication. . . . So far this is Miss Godden's only "thing of naught." Her style is a pleasure, as usual, and there are passages which remind us of the Rumer Godden capable of writing *Black Narcissus, A Candle for St. Jude,* and *The River.*

> *Evelyn Eaton, "On a Lesser Island," in* The New York Times Book Review, *January 28, 1951, p. 4.*

EDWARD WEEKS

Take Three Tenses, A Candle for St. Jude, and *The River,* the novels of Rumer Godden I like best, are each of them a guidebook to an emotional experience—the first in wartime London, the second in a ballet studio, and the third in India. Miss Godden does her writing with a rich palette; like Kipling, she spent her most impressionable years in India and is happiest when depicting the conflict and color of that baffling place.

Sophia Barrington Ward, the heroine of her new book, *Kingfishers Catch Fire,* is an English widow, an attractive romantic who with the best intentions succeeds in doing almost everything wrong. She and her husband were living precariously in Kashmir when, on his sudden death, she was left with a desk full of debts, a minute pension, and the drafty security of a houseboat in Srinagar. As the winter comes on she is pulled down by typhoid and pneumonia, and with her young daughter Teresa and her small son Moo she is carted off to the English Mission. On her convalescence, had Sophie been sensible she would have thrown in the sponge, returning to England to the care of her aunts and the protestations of her old suitor Toby. But Sophie is a fool, impulsive and improvident. While still unsteady on her feet she takes a five-year lease on Dhilkusha, a remote summer house on the mountain: here she and the children will live "as peasants," cultivating the garden and dealing generously and intuitively with the Hindu and Mohammedan villagers who, though she seems not to notice it, are as predacious as hawks. . . .

It is a tribute to Miss Godden's skill that we can follow the escapades of such a ninny with the feeling that all this is inevitable and true to life. The natives; Sultan, the houseboy; Pundit Pramatha Kaul, the wise landlord; Profit David, and Nabir are wonderfully well drawn. Indeed, it is they who carry the story—they and the beauty of Kashmir.

> *Edward Weeks, "The Vale of Kashmir," in* The Atlantic Bookshelf, *a section of* The Atlantic Monthly, *Vol. 191, No. 6, June, 1953, p. 78.*

DACHINE RAINER

The author of the best-selling novel *The River* has written another book [*Kingfishers Catch Fire*] with the same qualities—convincing local color, sympathetic characterization, humor and dramatic irony—and what, for lack of a more adequate word, we must apologetically call charm.

Miss Godden, like Kipling and Forster, prefers Indian to Western culture, and her book is an eloquent testimonial to her preference. Sophie Barrington Ward, mother of two small children, who is suddenly widowed and left with very little income, must make a decision. Should she return to the security of a bourgeois life in England, or remain in India? She chooses eventually to leave westernized India and its English colony, and go to Kashmir. She makes a heroic and moderately successful effort to rid herself of the psychological trappings of her former environment and establish her own way of life—just what that way is, is a trifle obscure; she rather makes it up as she goes along. In that respect, it is bohemian, and since her income is still high compared to the standards of the Vale of Kashmir, she is able to live like a rich bohemian rather than an impoverished one. . . .

What Sophie does give up is the comfort and security of middle-class convention. (p. 256)

However, both Sophie and Rumer Godden are altogether too sanguine about the future. Sophie hasn't tempered her desires with discretion, nor has she acquired the degree of subtlety and sophistication necessary for a Westerner's survival in the East.

What, precisely, has Sophie learned from her melodramatic, but extremely plausible, experiences in Kashmir—from the ground glass in her food, from the aphrodisiac administered her, from the disappearance and near-loss of her daughter, Teresa? Is she in any way better equipped to go on to Lebanon, with its beauties, adventures, and probable treacheries? The main thing wanting in this novel is that, apart from the slightly increased awareness of the existence of her children, there is no evolution in the character of Sophie. (pp. 256-57)

Dachine Rainer, "Bohemia in the Orient," in The Commonweal, *Vol. LVIII, No. 10, June 12, 1953, pp. 256-57.*

VIRGILIA PETERSON

"It's not old-fashioned to say God is good," remarks Mr. Wix, the minister in this latest and loveliest of Rumer Godden's novels [*An Episode of Sparrows*]. "Remember, not one sparrow can fall to the ground—"

"But they fall all the time," protests Miss Olivia Chesney, as the pain of the world's injustice stabs through and through her frail, middle-aged heart. . . .

If any one among our writers today was meant not only to see and care herself about the fall of human sparrows but also to make all who read her books see and care, too, it is Rumer Godden. In story after story—*Breakfast With the Nikolides, The River, Kingfishers Catch Fire,* and now, most poignantly, in *An Episode of Sparrows*—this English novelist who never raises her voice above the muted note of understatement speaks yet so surely and so piercingly of pain and beauty that her words drown the shrill outcry and drum beating of most contemporary fiction.

Rumer Godden knows the world and has shown us, in earlier works, many of its exotic corners, but in this new novel she ventures no farther for background than the shabby but still respectable Mortimer Square in London and squalid Catford Street behind it. Like the narrow communities in India or Kashmir that she has described before, this London quarter, with its handful of comfortably secure people on the square and its host of crowded, struggling families along the old, sooty, bombed-out adjoining street, becomes a microcosm.

What happened on the square to start the whole heated episode must have happened a thousand times before in a thousand cities and might not have even ruffled the nerves of a single inhabitant, had it not been for the conjuncture of character and circumstance Miss Godden has invented. All that actually happened to prompt such tense drama was the removal of some earth from the shrub bed at one end of the square's gardens and the discovery, by the Garden Committee, of this theft.

Who stole it? Who dared to leave twelve telltale round holes behind the railings? Could it have been those awful gangs of children—those "sparrows"—from the street? Could mere children have carted away so much earth? (p. 1)

At the heart of this story of stolen earth are two children whom, once you have come to know and understand them, you will neither want nor be able to forget. . . . (pp. 1, 16)

Only a Rumer Godden could make the simple tale of a forbidden garden pulse with suspense, could avoid the pitfalls of sentimentality, could breathe into such ordinary adults and ordinary children the quickness, the hope and the hopelessness of life itself. Rare indeed are the mind and the pen which wrote *An Episode of Sparrows.* (p. 16)

Virgilia Peterson, "Miss Godden's Tense, Quiet Tale of Some Folk in a London Square," in New York Herald Tribune Book Review, *November 27, 1955, pp. 1, 16.*

ELIZABETH JANEWAY

[*An Episode of Sparrows*] is a charming fable by Rumer Godden dealing with the triumph of the sensitive and the disregarded over the insensitive who command the established order of things. Like all Cinderella stories, it affords us the pleasure of seeing the haughty get their come-uppance and the meek inherit at least a bit of the earth. Like all Miss Godden's books, it is subtly and delicately written.

Taken as a novel, it is also preposterous. But is it quite fair to take as a novel what is really a moral tale? When Miss Godden has made us a very pretty silk purse, it would surely be captious to ask why she did not start with a sow's ear. To make a silk purse at all requires skill and talent, and Miss Godden has used both. Only when reality creeps in does the author's artifice appear artificial, and reality does not creep in very far, and is soon hustled out when it does. And rightly so, for it does not belong in a moral tale. A novel wishes to explore a situation, but a moral tale wishes to make a point, and that it can only do by creating a controlled and therefore artificial situation which will make the point clear.

There are of course all kinds of moral tales. Some of them are dull as ditch water, and some of them have enchanted readers for years. There are big ones and little ones, for the form has been vital and useful enough to have produced classical transmutations that run from *Pilgrim's Progress* through *Paradise Lost* and *A Christmas Carol* to *The Tale of Peter Rabbit.* Miss Godden is no Bunyan, Milton or Dickens. She is, as a matter of fact, a good deal closer in spirit to Beatrix Potter—a Beatrix Potter who, having created Peter Rabbit and Jemima Puddleduck, had decided to translate her dear creatures into human form. (Indeed, those who are interested can discover in Miss Godden's book new avatars of Peter, Mr. McGregor, The Two Bad Mice and Mrs. Tiggywinkle.) But the works of Beatrix Potter *are* classics—little ones, yes, but precise in form and delightful in content. Miss Godden has written a little book too, and it is also precise and will delight many readers. . . .

Except for providing an ending that is so sentimental and so neat as to give even a Dickens pause, Miss Godden makes this all very satisfying. It is two-dimensional but it is touching and what is to be said is said not only clearly but entertainingly. While one cannot believe that Miss Godden's story happened, one can sympathize with her thesis and be pleased to see it worked out so cleverly.

What is true of the plot is true of the characters too. They are not human beings, but then human beings would drag a fable out of proportion just as a messy, unsolvable, realistic situation would. Peter Rabbit and Mr. McGregor and Mrs. Tiggywinkle belong here, for they are types who do not have to be explored but who bring with them their own recognizable and familiar constellation of attributes. They are dexterously drawn, and they engage our sympathies and interest us in the working out of their predicaments.

In a world where the future of the novel is bothering everyone but its audience, there is something to be said for a writer who takes an old form and frankly puts artifice to work—who turns out, in short, such a very pretty and finished silk purse as this.

Elizabeth Janeway, "A Clandestine Garden in the Heart of London," in The New York Times Book Review, *November 27, 1955, p. 46.*

EDMUND FULLER

The pleasures that Rumer Godden brings [in *The Greengage Summer*] as she goes to work in what is for her a new setting, are of a subtle and delicate order. They may hover, at times, at the brink of the precious, but they do not stumble and fall over it, for her essential artistry and control of her materials are safeguards.

The story tells of the summer adventures of a group of English children, in somewhat shadowed circumstances, at a second-rate hotel on the Marne, near the forest of Compiègne. The five Grey children are ranked from Joss, who is 16, through Cecil, 13; and Hester, 10; to the two "Littles"—Will, called Willmouse, and Vicky. Each of these is realized with sharp individuality and distinctive appeal. Cecil—a girl, there is but one boy—is the narrator, from the vantage point of some years after the events.

Their mother is taken seriously ill as they are en route to the hotel Les Oeillets, at Vieux-Moutiers. Upon arrival, she is rushed to the hospital for a long stay. The disconcerted children are stranded at the hotel where neither the proprietress, Mademoiselle Zizi, nor her henchwoman, Mme. Corbet, want them. It is the somewhat mysterious Englishman, Eliot, apparently romantically involved with Mlle. Zizi, who takes them under his wing and casually superintends their stay.

The summer is filled with the special responses and perceptions of childhood, which Miss Godden understands magically. . . . From the first, we feel the specific stresses of crucial maturing, of a physical order for Cecil and an emotional order for Joss. The involvements with adult lives become increasingly complex, acting as precipitants to drastic events, the secret of which belongs to Miss Godden. I think the book would have had greater depth if those events had culminated in some less flamboyant way—the effect now being to make a particular fictional invention of something basically universal.

It is an experience to share the impact upon these middle-class English children of the less inhibited ways of France, especially as they encounter them much in the company of servants and without the protective supervision that would ordinarily have shielded their lives. Realities, some of them ugly and potentially dangerous, advance upon the five Grey children. The basic soundness of their often bewildered responses lend the substance to a slight, but warming, sometimes joyously funny, and exquisitely wrought tale.

Edmund Fuller, "Unprotected Nest," in The New York Times Book Review, *March 23, 1958, p. 4.*

ALICE SAXON

Wit being the soul of this story [*The Greengage Summer*], it is, appropriately, wit that gives it brightness and a consistent quality and at the same time limits its power; ease and cleverness predominate, while a sense of the genuine—and a genuine concern on the part of the reader—is forfeited.

But for one more child and different names, the cast of characters is that of Miss Godden's earlier novel, *The River,* even to certain identical speeches. This is curious but unobjectionable since the children are still very appealing and so are their speeches. The viewpoint is again that of a pre-adolescent girl placed effectively in the midst of a large family—two little sisters, cherubic and placid, and a whimsical, self-contained little brother (these serve to emphasize her own vanishing se-

renity) and an older sister of maturing beauty who has passed disturbingly over a threshold before which the younger girl hesitates resentfully and longingly.

The Greengage Summer depicts, as did *The River,* a season of change, significant events, the discovery of good and evil unfathomably mingled, a season of gently inexorable growth. (pp. 162-63)

In *The River* the same theme of discovery and growth emerges naturally, almost organically, out of its own setting, with a quiet, believable dignity that is truly moving. In *The Greengage Summer,* it is a matter of gimmicks; the devices being so extrinsic and so unlikely—even the necessity of removing the children to a foreign habitat in order to introduce them to "life"—that acceptable or not they necessarily reduce the scope and impact of the book.

It will appeal to some as sophisticated fare, because it gets around a fairly tender theme with a light touch. Yet with respect to the various raw elements involved—passion, murder, homosexuality . . . the reader gets neither an adult's treatment nor the vivid observations of a Colette ingénue, and these elements emerge as if from a milk bath, not very alarming or real. That the narrator and protagonists are wide-eyed English children could, of course, have a particular advantage, but this point of view is not notably handled in *The Greengage Summer,* largely because, as happens more often than not, the whole device of the precious, unexpected naiveté of the child is pushed too relentlessly and ardently.

This is not to complain but only to try to place the book carefully in its own category and to offer some resistance to the wrong kind of praise. It *is* in a way delightful, but it is certainly nothing *more* than delightful. It is difficult to say of this kind of book that it is superficial because it is far too knowing, because it avoids superficiality so adequately (it is filled with appropriate profundities and the correct insights into motivations) and yet the total effect is, nevertheless, superficial. At its best it is very funny; at its worst it is never really moving unless one good-naturedly allows oneself conditioned reactions. *The Greengage Summer* would, in fact, make an excellent movie; the plot is symmetrical and picturesque from all angles, and it employs the kind of sensitivity that could be translated to the screen in its entirety without loss or injustice to the original in the process. (pp. 163-64)

Alice Saxon, "The Godden Cast," in The Commonweal, *Vol. LXVIII, No. 6, May 9, 1958, pp. 162-64.*

VIRGILIA PETERSON

Rumer Godden by now has a sizable body of work behind her. Looking back at her more than a dozen books, what emerges most strikingly is that each of them, unique and complete in itself, nevertheless constitutes a variation on the same major theme—the interdependence of person and place. In any one of them, what happens could only have happened precisely on whichever river or in whichever houseboat or garden or ruin she has chosen, and at some other juncture of time and place could not have happened at all. But in none of her books is one so conscious of the influence of place as in this latest of her novels.

In *China Court,* the place itself, the house with all its appurtenances and surroundings, plays the predominating role. . . .

In a little foreword to the novel, Miss Godden quotes Chaucer as saying that life is a "thinne subtil knittinge of thinges." No description could better fit this book. Gathering up the tenuous threads of suggestion and implication, she knits time now to time past and creates a living fabric. As in her much loved earlier novel, *Take Three Tenses,* here again in *China Court,* she conjugates in verbs to love and hate, to hope and despair, to rebel and accept, in terms not only of five successive generations but of the various periods in each. It requires a certain patience, as she warns the reader at the start, to distinguish and keep in mind the many threads. One has to submit to her premise of the simultaneity of time in order to follow, for instance, the various stages of Mrs. Quin that appear side by side, and to realize that the philosophical old lady, the eager waif, the passionate mistress, the resigned wife, the fertile mother, and the gifted gardener are one and the same.

Rumer Godden knows, better than almost any other contemporary novelist, what children are like, and she knows too what time does to them and how to portray the child that lingers on in the adults they become. But in this book she is less concerned with the people than the place they live in. What she has written is a book-of-hours for China Court, and from laudes to vespers, her prayers and contemplations are fixed upon the house.

Virgilia Peterson, "Rumer Godden's New Novel Subtly Knits Time Now to Time Past," in Lively Arts and Book Review, *March 5, 1961, p. 29.*

ELIZABETH JANEWAY

Reading a novel by Rumer Godden is always an interesting experience. She is so good at what she does, and what she does is so unimportant, that one is left openmouthed as one sometimes is at the circus, contemplating the infinite care and skill with which a performer balances himself on one finger atop a teetering pile of furniture. An astonishing feat! And even more astonishing is the realization that someone has gone to all that trouble to learn how to do it.

In *China Court* Miss Godden is telling the story of a Cornish family, resident for five generations in a Cornish house of that name. And, with the greatest deftness, she is telling it all at once. This is no clumsy, labored exercise in "and then this happened, and then that happened." Miss Godden has grandly done away with the ordinary passing of time, and allowed the generations to mingle in the rooms of China Court, so that we see the house through a flashing shimmer of images nodding to each other across a century and more. . . . It must have been great fun to write.

Is it great fun to read? The answer depends on whether or not you like romantic fantasy, for all Miss Godden's artful and intricate apparatus is employed to set forth a sentimental story in which five generations of stock figures step through one hundred and twenty years of predictable episodes. . . .

They break their hearts and marry the right man. Happy wives are betrayed. Spinsters grow sour and sly. Crusty characters show hearts of gold. There is a great deal of gardening. There is much interesting information on housekeeping in the nineteenth century and on domestic manners, for Miss Godden has done her research well and thoroughly. The happy ending is so neatly contrived that it is positively dazzling, and there is always someone about to have the right emotion and to express it, so that the reader need be in no doubt as to how to feel.

I should fault Miss Godden only with her contemporary young lovers who are really thrown together in too slapdash a manner for even an ingenue and a juvenile lead. The plot, moreover, *requires* them to fall in love at first sight; and though one is inclined to agree that they will, one still would prefer that they had had a bit of choice. Otherwise, this novel is a most skillful and craftsmanlike example of its genre.

It is a tough and long-lived genre, which must obviously give considerable pleasure to many readers: the sentimental romance. These romances have their own conventions and create their own world in which the flux and chaos of life are replaced by order, the terrors by turnip-ghosts, and the range of the unexpected narrowed.

How such conventions differ from those of art—why melodrama, for instance, is not drama—has been and will be argued for centuries. The romances go on. Indeed, they have been written and read for so long that one must really be dogged and determined to quarrel with them; to maintain in humorless irritation that novels should not be cheapened so, or formal talent as superior as Miss Godden's wasted; that fiction is serious, is a way of understanding to the full. Let us drop such out-size and irrelevant arguments and agree that fantasy and daydreams have their place today as much as they did when Jane Austen laughed at them in *Northanger Abbey*, and they and Jane both survived. Then it's simply a matter of whether or not Miss Godden's daydreams suit you. If they do, you'll enjoy her book.

Elizabeth Janeway, "Five Generations and How They Grew," in The New York Times Book Review, *March 5, 1961, p. 4.*

L. P. HARTLEY

Rumer Godden has an innate understanding of the problems, especially the moral problems, of childhood, which has been at the center of many of her novels. Her latest, *The Battle of the Villa Fiorita,* is no exception.

The Villa Fiorita is the temporary love nest of a guilty pair, Fanny Clavering and Rob Quillet, a film-director who has swept Fanny off her feet. Her husband Darrell has divorced her and been granted custody of her two younger children, Hugh, 12, and Caddie, 10.

Fanny and Darrell's elder daughter, Philippa, who had interests outside family life, took the divorce in stride. Not so Hugh and Caddie. Feeling that the bottom has dropped out of their world they resolve to leave England, to go to Italy, foil the honeymoon and fetch their mother back.

Whether such children would really carry through on such a project is a doubt that lingers in the reader's mind. They might contemplate it, but that they would be resourceful and purposeful enough to put it into action strains credibility. Nevertheless, Hugh and Caddie raise the money for their journey by selling Caddie's pet pony, overcome the perils and complications of foreign travel, and finally reach the Villa Fiorita—greatly to the consternation of their quarry.

This is a story in which one is bound to take sides, and it must be said that Miss Godden holds the scales of sympathy remarkably even. Morally, of course, or at any rate by Christian principles, the children are in the right to want their mother back. We ought, perhaps, to be on their side, and it would have been easy for Miss Godden to load the dice in their favor.

Yet Fanny is deeply in love with Rob, who is a forceful and likeable man (even the children come to like him) and we know so little of Colonel Clavering he seems no more than a cipher; we cannot believe that Fanny ever really cared for him.

It is to Miss Godden's credit that she doesn't sentimentalize the children. Hugh is a rather ill-mannered, opinionated boy and Caddie, despite touching qualities and a capacity for self-sacrifice, is no charmer. (p. 4)

The Battle of the Villa Fiorita is an enjoyable novel, even if one cannot quite accept the central situation. Its plot is full of surprises, and its evocation of the Italian setting is vivid—so vivid, in fact, that at the start it threatens to steal the picture and turn it into a landscape with figures. (p. 32)

> L. P. Hartley, *"Spoil-Sports in the Love Nest,"* in
> The New York Times Book Review, *September 29,*
> *1963, pp. 4, 32.*

HAROLD C. GARDINER

[*The Battle of the Villa Fiorita*] is a superb novel. It deals with an important theme, the characters are vivid and strongly limned, the style is a fascinating blend of extremely original phrasing and good old-fashioned story telling, and throughout the whole there sounds a note of absolute authenticity. Yes, you hear yourself saying, this is just as it ought to be—this is real, this is life.

The theme? A rather plain but strangely attractive English matron, mother of three children, wife to a somewhat unimaginative public servant, at the age of 43 falls deeply, blindly in love with a movie director, who is a widower with a young daughter. She starts divorce proceedings against her bewildered husband and goes with her lover to a villa in Italy, to await the final separation that will free her to marry. Her children are left in England under the custody of their father.

Or so, at least, the mother thinks—until the day two of them, a boy about 14 and his smaller sister, show up at the villa. . . . The children have not come to settle in, but to unsettle the dream of love by taking their mother back home.

The magnificent tale ends with the mother on her way back to a shattered home with the two young missionaries. If there is triumph at the end, it is a rather sad one: what will the future be for the disillusioned husband and wife? Many readers, I am sure, would prefer another ending, but this is precisely where Rumer Godden shows her splendid integrity. Having established the character of the mother as a person deeply convinced of the reality of sin (though she desperately tries to smother the conviction), no other ending could have been honest. And it is all the more convincing because the love affair was no cheap pickup; we are convinced that real love motivated the liaison.

The two children, but especially the young girl, are masterpieces of character delineation. One of the most touching facets of the tale is the gradual awareness on the boy's part of the elements of sex involved in the whole matter. He grows wonderfully in maturity as he faces those facts with innate modesty and good sense.

This tale, in short, is a thoughtful comment on the fact that even our little triumphs carry within themselves a knot of sadness; if we win, someone inevitably loses. But the triumph of the book is that the lovers, who are the losers, lose with dignity—a dignity almost forced upon them by the innocence of the children. I think Rumer Godden is saying that the undoubting loyalty of the boy and girl made them grasp, almost unconsciously, that sacramental quality of marriage which their mother had tried so hard to put out of her consciousness.

> Harold C. Gardiner, in a review of *"The Battle of*
> *the Villa Fiorita,"* in America, *Vol. 109, No. 15,*
> *October 12, 1963, p. 432.*

MILLICENT BELL

Popularity is not discreditable, as we surely know in an age of both pop art and the instant exploitation of originality. Even genius—that emanation of energy which sets the critic's Geiger counter chirping—is no bar to general success. So one must not hold it against Rumer Godden that for 30 years her books have been enjoyed by a lot of people with plain tastes, that her fiction frequently runs in the women's magazines and is a book-club choice. Everything she has written has had polish and charm; the best of her works possess a fresh child's vision of reality which is captivating. If the verdict on her books is finally that they are "light" harmless things (whereas veritable art somehow has to hurt), it would be ingratitude not to recognize the pleasure they afford. In the present novel [*In This House of Brede*], her 15th and most ambitious to date, however, she makes it clear that she is asking us to take her more seriously.

Her first success, *Black Narcissus,* which must be remembered by millions in the movie version, was a whimsical little tale about the attempt of a band of English nuns to establish their house in a remote Himalayan village. Given the airy and humorous thing it was, her narrative had a forgivable silliness. Now she has written another novel about a community of nuns, but in a very different spirit. Complexly organized, so that it contains not one but perhaps a dozen stories, and impressively full of realistic detail, it has been announced as a study of the contemplative life; it is not simply, one is led to expect, about some members of a contemplative, that is "enclosed" order, but an exploration into the nature and the reasons for their mode of spiritual life. A theme demanding both high art and penetrating insight.

Miss Godden's publishers say that she worked for three years on this novel, living at the gate of one of the English abbeys in order to observe and consult its inmates. Thus, she has been able to acquaint us with a world hidden from common view; we are initiated into the complex rhythms of the Benedictine rule in a self-contained family of about a hundred females—the rituals of each day, of which six hours are spent in prescribed prayer and chant, and the changing observances of the liturgical year. We become familiar also with innumerable homely details of the monastic household; we are taken literally from cellar to roof. . . . I doubt if there is another work of fiction so full, as the jacket blurb puts it, of the "uncommon and fascinating 'shop'" of convent life.

The effect of this strenuous documentation is a little ambiguous. At times, one is reminded of nothing so much as of those novels that include a large bonus of informational interest about life inside a big city hospital or a prison, or about the inner workings of a Grand Hotel or a major airport. Believer and unbeliever will have an identical curiosity, I imagine, about life "behind the grille" of the cloister. And as in all such novels there is always the danger that the novelist may be so distracted by the independent appeal of his material, that he stops off to write nonfiction instead of a story in which factuality is at the service of theme.

Miss Godden has not altogether avoided this danger, because her sense of theme, despite her sincerity and laboriousness, is simply not as strong as she may think it is. To state it baldly, this is not a religous novel, though intended to be. Many a work of fiction purely secular in scene and characters—I think of some by Hemingway, Faulkner, even Henry James—has more of spiritual struggle and search, more of the sense of sin and redemption than this one whose personages are all habited *religieuses*.

Yet even more ambitious than the presentation of her monastic content is Miss Godden's handling of the intertwined stories of her nuns. How vividly and individually some of these identically-clad women emerge! One remembers Abbess Catherine Ismay in her struggles to attain wisdom and leadership; Agnes Kerr, the noble yet jealous scholar; Maura Fitzgerald, the devoted choir mistress whose love of beauty precipitates her passion for the gifted novice Cecily; the pitiable and repellent Veronica Fanshawe, with her small talent and her large vanity, her alternation of spite and repentance.

Among the "postulants" or novices (whose long journey towards final vows occupies the length of the novel), there are two most fully presented, their past history deftly recalled as their former lives continue to play a part in their present: Philippa Talbot successful career woman in her forties, and the nubile seraph, Cecily Scanlon, a good middle-class daughter who was expected to make a "good" marriage until the inexplicable sense of vocation descended upon her. And yet, despite the successful exhibition of such characters in individual scenes, there is, too frequently a banality and a contrivance about the stories that hold them in place. It is this weakness of conception that keeps Miss Godden's novel plodding around in some weary outer orbit of her subject, keeps her and us a long way from the heart of her matter.

Take the frame-story, as one may call it, of Brede Abbey itself, which encounters a crisis that is not solved until the book has proceeded nearly three-quarters towards the end. In somewhat familiar mystery-story style, the old Abbess dies, muttering "sorry . . ." to her bewildered "daughters," who only discover later that she has compromised Brede's finances by her "stone-fever," her mania for restoring the buildings. What significance does Miss Godden give this situation? Does she exploit the possible spiritual ironies in the Abbess's action, or discover some moral interest in the legacy of confusion which her action might be imagined to have left her successor? Not at all. The crisis that the House of Brede experiences is purely a practical one.

The monastery is now so strapped for funds that it must water its soup and consider selling its park. And a simple miracle overcomes the nuns' difficulties, the discovery of a valuable ruby in an old wooden cross—a denouement which will not seem fortuitous only to the most naive piety. That God works in most mysterious ways is well known. But for the purpose of meaningful literature, at any rate—take Milton's "Samson Agonistes" as an example if you will—miracles are occurrences that demand the full participation of the suffering, striving human spirit. None of these psychological conditions accompany God's miracle at Brede, and one is singularly unstirred by what is surely meant to be a moving climax.

From this point on to the end of the novel, the enveloping story of Brede Abbey becomes episodic. . . . Miss Godden's imag-

ination is working on the lowest level of formula in these last chapters. . . . (pp. 4-5, 34)

Though summary exaggerates the banality of these stories and slights Miss Godden's considerable skill in handling their development, it is essentially true for this reader that they remain glossy and depthless, without that exploratory touch of mental and spiritual issues which might retrieve them.

More than this labored failure to be important, I would have preferred to have had from Miss Godden one of those unpretentious and engaging works such as she has produced in the past, deservedly popular and never contemptible—the exquisite *The River* or *Breakfast With the Nikolides* which utilized her memories of her childhood in India, or the imagistic poetry, like that of a lesser Virginia Woolf, of *Take Three Tenses* and *China Court*. Quaintness and sentimentality were permissible moods in those popular successes that aspired to no great profundity, *A Candle for St. Jude* and *An Episode of Sparrows*. But "the contemplative life" requires another order of vision.

That theme might have had possibilities in an age like ours—when active virtue is so often misdirected, when the young find the appeal of mystic self-perfection (whether achieved by drugs or other means) a valid alternative in a world in which strenuosity has grown ugly. In the 9th and 10th centuries, when the great Benedictine abbeys were founded in Western Europe, after the brutality and chaos of the Dark Ages, something of the same impulse towards inward search and improvement must have been felt. But these are reflections for a book Miss Godden did not choose to write. (pp. 34, 36)

Millicent Bell, "Rewards and Perils of the Contemplative Life," in The New York Times Book Review, *September 21, 1969, pp. 4-5, 34, 36.*

AUDREY C. FOOTE

It is a truism that one can be too smooth, too accomplished, too "good" a writer, but it is a failing for which the general reader has a natural indulgence and for which even those who read much current fiction professionally must have some gratitude—so we should all heartily thank Miss Godden for yet another attractive, well-made novel free of violence and vulgarity [*In This House of Brede*].

While the virtues of this new novel about an English Benedictine monastery for nuns and the lives of the women cloistered there are predictable—an informed, sensitive picture of monastic life, a collection of sympathetic characterizations— the faults are equally obvious and usually also the result of the "good" or professional qualities of the writing. Miss Godden's style is so suave as to seem often facile. Her mastery of the tricky art of transitions in time *seems* gratuitous in this externally static world. The care with which she develops the plot and the events themselves are uniformly mechanical and slick: for example, the turning point of the story and the fortunes of the House of Brede, bankrupted by the building obsession of a previous director, occurs when the present Lady Abbess, in a moment of impatience (the irony of it!), breaks the crude wooden cross inherited through generations of Abbesses and discovers a valuable ruby. In this context above all, an outright miracle, a flagrant coincidence would have seemed more appropriate, less glib. . . .

Yet if Rumer Godden's skills are her flaws, her limitations appear as virtues in this book. She may be popular, but she is not fashionable. She is not merely a woman's writer, but a *lady's* writer, feminine, aristocratic, conservative and discreet, tuned less to social problems than to spiritual predicaments. Her nuns are truly cloistered, their vocation is prayer and praise of God, rather than teaching or good works. Her sympathies and theirs are with Mary, not Martha, Pope Pius, not Pope John. It is a real and quite daring achievement to espouse with conviction such a point of view today.

Rumer Godden is not a writer of power or intensity on a grand scale; such epic virtues would have been quite out of place in a novel about women who are neither sinners nor saints. Their central problem is one of total dedication, self-discipline against the appeal of legitimate worldly values: she indicates that pride in leadership, pleasure in intellectual growth, love of beauty, desire for children, loyalty to family, interest in social reform—all are real and insidious temptations to the contemplative nun. We are made to consider the possibility that these very human sacrifices are more typical, prevalent and subtle in the cloister than the renunciation of flamboyant sins or even the abnegation of spiritual doubt.

Audrey C. Foote, "A Preference for Things Not of This World," in Book World—Chicago Tribune, *November 23, 1969, p. 11.*

ROSALIND WADE

The novelist who chooses the convent for a setting and the nun as a leading character . . . confronts a hurdle from the outset. So many plays, films and novels have been centred around the 'holy' domain that its trappings have become a cliché. Very few writers have been successful in penetrating the mysteries of this—the ultimate of withdrawal symptoms. Whether because of unrequited love or a genuine religious conviction, a rejection of the real world tends not to be exciting.

Has Rumer Godden in *Five for Sorrow, Ten for Joy* done better than her predecessors? Does she satisfactorily explain the phenomena of suppressed sexual desire and personal ambition? The answer remains debatable. Her fictitious 'order' is the French 'Bethany'. The sisters of this community certainly do not exclude the uglier aspects of the human condition for their work is among whores and drop-outs from the Paris slums. Lise, the novitiate with whom the story is mainly concerned, was herself a prostitute during the confused period immediately following World War II. She is known as *La Balafrée* on account of the livid weal on her once beautiful face, the result of an attack by her lover, Patrice. Lise loved Patrice, yet murdered him. It was when she was released from prison that the sisters of Bethany came to her aid.

Much of the important development of Lise's past is conveyed by frequent flashbacks. The precision with which events are tailored to fit neatly into prepared slots is sometimes rather too contrived. They are linked by conversations with Fathers and other nuns in formal, stilted dialogue, presumably as a reminder that the characters are speaking French. Rumer Godden adroitly surmounts these self-imposed limitations. Lise and her sordid story emerge as entirely credible; and the novel's final triumph is that she is seen to accept the closure of all outlets to the normal world and becomes a full and willing member of the order of Bethany.

Rosalind Wade, in a review of "Five for Sorrow, Ten for Joy," in Contemporary Review, *Vol. 235, No. 1365, October, 1979, p. 214.*

JULIA M. KLEIN

For Rumer Godden, freedom flows from submission to authority, and true identity is the product of the willful erasure of ego. These precepts, which underlie all her works, place her among the most conservative of contemporary authors. But hers is a deeply romantic conservatism. In her novels, sacrifice is painted as not only necessary but ennobling; yielding oneself up to others and to God invariably affords her characters a profound and otherwise unattainable joy.

Five for Sorrow, Ten for Joy represents the triumph of this peculiar vision. The novel's title refers to the beads of the Catholic rosary, which slide through the story as a symbol of the mixed nature of its heroine Lise's life. Having plumbed the depths of the Parisian demimonde as a prostitute, madam, and finally a murderess, Lise finds fulfillment as one of the Dominican Sisters of Bethanie, an order of nuns dedicated to redeeming women like her from French prisons.

Godden has written about nuns before, most fully in *In This House of Brede*. Indeed, nuns, with their lives devoted to the beauty of sacrifice (and the sacrifice of beauty), are her natural subject. Even in her overtly non-religious novels, women, especially, discover their duty and identity through renunciation. But for Godden's nuns, renunciation is only a starting point, a way station on the path to spiritual ecstasy.

In the introduction to one of her short stories, Godden said about religious monastics: "Theirs seems to me to be a love story that transcends all ordinary love stories." This romantic premise inspired *In This House of Brede,* which asked us (with limited success) to believe that an upwardly mobile career woman, once married and much loved, would suddenly embrace the chillingly ordered life of a contemplative. In her latest novel, Godden takes care of the problem of credibility, in part, by emphasizing the contrast between the debauched meaninglessness of street life and the tranquil discipline of the convent, with its pageantry of prayer and feast days. She is aided by the fact that, unlike the Benedictines of Brede, the Sisters of Bethanie do more than pray; they work in prisons, saving lives as well as souls. Even an atheist and a liberal can appreciate that.

It is true that Godden's view of both convent and brothel life remains romanticized. Lise herself is the proverbial whore with the heart of gold, murdering not for gain or from lust but out of a special sort of love. Still, her spiritual suffering seems real enough. And so, too, thanks to the power of Godden's poetic prose, does her subsequent happiness, along with its fragility.

Godden has gained a reputation as a consummate craftswoman. Here again she combines a characteristic simplicity of language and muted tone with great narrative complexity. In breaking down the barrier between dialogue and exposition in the long, flowing sentences that have become her trademark, she has always aimed at conveying the seamlessness of past, present, and future. In *Five for Sorrow, Ten for Joy* her use of interpenetrating time levels—flashbacks and flashforwards interweaving in a spiraling narrative which never loses its coherence—has reached a peak of mastery. (p. 40)

Finally, the entire novel is cast in the form of a moral lesson, an allegory told to the reader through the stand-in character of Father Marc. Marc is an activist priest who, in the book's opening pages, snobbishly chafes at what he views as an exile to one of the houses of Bethanie. In the course of this exquisitely told story—as witness to the spiritual beauty he finds there—he, with the rest of us, learns better. (p. 41)

Julia M. Klein, in a review of "Five for Sorrow, Ten for Joy," in The New Republic, *Vol. 181, No. 20, November 24, 1979, pp. 40-1.*

JANETTE TURNER HOSPITAL

"I have always thanked God we did not have sensible parents," writes the English novelist Rumer Godden at the very outset of [*A Time to Dance, No Time to Weep,* an autobiographical account of her first 40 years], and indeed we can only be grateful that there has never been anything remotely sensible or orthodox about her astonishing life and times. She belongs in that small and exclusive club of women—it includes Isak Dinesen and Beryl Markham—who could do pretty well anything they set their minds to: hunting tigers, bewitching men, throwing elegant dinner parties, winning literary fame. . . .

Much of Ms. Godden's irresistible perversity came straight from those not-at-all-sensible parents, who were known as Fa and Mam to the girls. Instead of following the accepted custom of sending their daughters home from India to boarding school in England, Fa and Mam put them in local Indian schools and carted them all around the country to a different hill station every hot season. There was little of the Raj ghetto mentality to this family. Fa was manager of a river steamship company. He spoke Hindi, Bengali and Assamese. He was dashing and handsome (Lady Curzon, Vicereine of India, once described him as an Adonis), a daring sportsman, a bit feckless, invariably blithe and charming. He was already engaged to someone else when he proposed to Mam, and early in their marriage took her duck shooting on the Brahmaputra River. . . .

Even parents who are not at all sensible cannot quite escape the cultural expectations of their era. After their untrammeled Indian childhood, Rumer (aged 12) and her older sister, Jon (13), were sent "home" to boarding school. The culture clash was considerable. They were removed or expelled from five schools in the space of two years. They were wild, yet ferociously intelligent and always polite. When Sister Gertrude, headmistress of their first convent school, snapped: "You must learn that there is a place and time for everything," Jon replied with wide-eyed earnestness: "But it takes time to learn the places." When Jon, suffering from recurrent bouts of malaria, was accused of faking illness and was forced to drag herself to classes, the 12-year-old Rumer beamed a silent vow of perpetual hatred at Sister Gertrude. "'One day I shall write a book about you,' I thought with darkest intent."

At a subsequent school, a teacher was prompted to write of Rumer at age 15 that she had an "intolerance of ordinariness in people or situations," and Rumer herself acknowledges of herself and her sister that "we have always been intransigent and farouche." "I liked extremes," she confesses—and on another occasion, "I did not want to be protected, I wanted adventure."

Adventure was what she got. . . .

She eventually married. Her husband, Laurence Sinclair Foster, was a charming stockbroker, a sort of less honorable clone of Fa, who lived extravagantly and embezzled great amounts of money from his firm in Calcutta. Overnight he absconded, signing on with the British Army (this was during World War II), and leaving Rumer with two little girls, a small income from her dance school, and vast debts. . . .

[Because] of the war, first she was forced to relocate within India. She headed for the mountains of Kashmir, where she and the children were billeted in cramped quarters with other army wives. The trip precipitated a miscarriage. Ms. Godden was attended by a mission doctor whose only equipment was a kitchen knife and a pair of scissors. She survived with her usual panache, found the cramped quarters and the company of army wives unendurable, and located a cottage high up in the mountains above Srinagar. It was almost inaccessible, it was drafty, it had a dirt floor; it was also beautiful, had been built by a Muslim poet, and had a magnolia tree brushing one window. It had, as everyone told her, "every possible drawback." And so, of course, she rented it for five years.

There she taught her own and other people's children; she raised herbs and dried them and made herbal teas that she sold in Calcutta; she wrote books. In fact, between her first book and this one (whose publication marks her 80th birthday), Rumer Godden has produced a staggering oeuvre of 20 novels (some of which have been international best sellers and several of which, including *The Greengage Summer* and *Black Narcissus,* have been made into movies), 7 works of nonfiction, 5 volumes of poetry and 21 books for children.

Despite this awesome output, Ms. Godden is more a first-rate storyteller than a major literary figure. Indeed, the style of this autobiography is best characterized as pell-mell and more than a little artless. It is as though we are getting breathless anecdotes on the run, though naturally we are more than willing to keep running alongside such a mesmerizing and vibrant raconteur. Even so, the reader is aware of frequently clumsy locutions, of a number of grammatical blunders, of sloppy syntax, of a punctuation style that can only be called quixotic. There are, in addition, moments when Ms. Godden's family history veers close to a name-droppng exercise, and there are occasional clichéd reactions to India's "teeming distress" that make one cringe. The assumptions of imperial right, even in the mindset of an unorthodox, highly idealistic and very unstuffy family, are clear, for example, in this description of a woman friend:

> She had been a Lawrence and no two men have done more for India and the prestige of Britain than the Lawrence brothers, John and Henry, especially during, and after, the mutiny of 1857. Sir Henry died in the siege of Lucknow while John, later Lord Lawrence, succeeded Lord Canning as India's second Viceroy. Bim was of the same calibre. . . .

The siege of Lucknow or the liberation of Lucknow? It all depends on one's station in life and viewpoint in history. But it is that era of the Raj, in all its vivid detail, that Rumer Godden captures for us. Somehow it seems superfluous to wish such an indomitable woman, as she celebrates her 80th birthday, many happy returns.

Janette Turner Hospital, "Adventure Was What She Got," in The New York Times Book Review, *January 3, 1988, p. 13.*

ANNE CHISHOLM

With this book [*A Time to Dance, No Time to Weep*], her fifty-sixth, the best-selling novelist Rumer Godden makes her contribution to what is perhaps becoming a minor genre, autobiographical writing from gifted writers brought up in India in the heyday of the British Raj.

As in other recent, comparable books (those by Alan Ross and Raleigh Trevelyan come to mind), certain themes and episodes recur. One is the intense, revelatory, almost mystical sense of natural beauty which the flowers, birds, landscapes and people of India evoked in observant children; another is the shock and pain experienced through separation from their childhood world on long visits "home". It was a multiple shock, since not only were the warmth, light and space of India replaced by dark, cold, cramped England, but conscientious and often chilly relatives or teachers took over from loving parents. . . .

Because her father had a passion for fishing, he chose to work for an Indian steamer company and live in small towns on huge rivers. The family explored India by travelling to a different hill station each year to escape the heat. Godden, though, is too truthful to pretend that all was idyllic; they lived surrounded by squalor and disease, and she recounts a terrifying brush with rabies. She was considered less pretty than her sisters, and felt overshadowed by her talented sister, Jon. One of the delicate personal themes of this book is the complex relationship, part adoration, part competition, between them, particularly when in due course Rumer became a far more commercially successful writer than Jon. . . .

Dispassionately, with affectionate disapproval of all concerned, she describes how she and her sisters became caught up with various "suitable" young men and made "a series of ill-fated weddings in the Cathedral". Her own doomed match was with a young stockbroker whose ruling passion was golf. They married because she was pregnant; he disliked her teaching ballet to "half-and-halfs" and begged her to be less stiff with his cronies. She bore him two daughters, continued to struggle to write, and found out too late that he had gambled away the considerable sums of money she made in 1939 from her first successful novel *Black Narcissus.* By the time the Second World War began, Godden was separated from him, living with her children and their Italian nanny in a remote village in Kashmir. Here, both the beautiful and the darker aspects of India acquired a new intensity for her. . . . But soon after, she and her household started to become unaccountably ill and it emerged that a psychopathic servant was putting ground glass and poison in their food.

A Time to Dance, No Time to Weep ends as Godden sets sail with her daughters once again for England, her marriage over, penniless, taking with her only a treasured Agra rug and the manuscript of a new book. Her autobiography is written with much of the skill that has earned her fiction huge sales and devoted readers. Occasionally she assumes too readily that details of her life and previous work are familiar; but with this book, at the age of eighty, Rumer Godden has reclaimed with moving honesty and precision the lost India she loved.

Anne Chisholm, "Escape from the Hill-Station," in
The Times Literary Supplement, *No. 4430, February 26–March 3, 1988, p. 266.*

Robert Harling

1951?-

American dramatist and scriptwriter.

Harling's first play, *Steel Magnolias* (1987), is set in a Louisiana beauty parlor where six women routinely congregate to exchange local gossip and discuss the vicissitudes of their lives. Praised for its witty, acerbic dialogue, multifaceted characterizations, and realistic blend of humor and pathos, Harling's work elicited comparisons to Beth Henley's comedies about small-town Southern life. Although several critics faulted *Steel Magnolias* as maudlin, Thomas M. Disch observed that the drama establishes "a sure-footed balance between sentiment and buffoonery that many seasoned veterans might envy."

HOWARD KISSEL

At first the denizens of a beauty parlor in a small Louisiana town in Robert Harling's superb first play, **Steel Magnolias,** seem vain and silly. As the title promises, Harling shows us the strength beneath their fluttery exteriors.

Harling has given his women sharp, funny dialogue. "Time marches on, and eventually you realize it's marching across your face," one of the women observes. Unlike other writers who use a mundane locale for stringing together bits of humor, Harling has a sense of structure. The play builds to a conclusion that is deeply moving.

He creates a genuine feeling of community and gives us a powerful understanding of the sometimes ironic, sometimes rueful, unflinchingly honest sense of themselves these women have. Harling's writing may become subtler, steadier but it is already very solid.

> Howard Kissel, *"Showing the Metal inside These Belles," in* Daily News, *New York, March 24, 1987.*

CLIVE BARNES

There is a special kind of "regional" comedy that is highly popular now. It has been encouraged by the Actors' Theater of Louisville, and can be seen at its best in the work of Beth Henley.

In basis it is Norman Rockwell with a freshly acerbic look. The inhabitants of this new dramatic territory—bordered by Broadway on one boundary and Hollywood on the other—make wise jokes, never wisecracks, in an elliptic fashion popularized by *The New Yorker.*

For example: "When it comes to suffering, she's right up there with Elizabeth Taylor."

Or: "I think it is the worst possible taste to pray for perfect strangers."

Or: "An ounce of pretension is worth a pound of manure."

Or: "I'm not crazy—I've just been in a very bad mood for 40 years."

Or: "We enjoy being nice to one another, there's nothing much else to do in this town."

All of these quips come from Robert Harling's new play **Steel Magnolias.** . . . Although they obviously need to be heard in context, these typical quotes (and the play is full of them) are funny, but also cute.

After a whole evening in their company, they start to get more cute than funny. And eventually, more wearing than cute.

Harling's play is set in Chinquapin, La. The social center for the ladies of the town seems to be Truvy's beauty parlor; and here, over the space of two-and-a-half years, and two-and-a-half hours, we watch Truvy, her born-again Christian assistant, Annelle, and four of their clients.

There is Clairee, the widow of the former Mayor; M'Lynn, a well-to-do matron, and her pretty, diabetic daughter Shelby; and Ouiser, a rich character.

This story of everyday folk getting their hair cut, shampooed, and styled, with a little manicure thrown in on the side, is suffused with humor and tinged with tragedy.

The humor is folksy, the tragedy sincere, the play inconsequential. It has all the defects of its merits, and even the bravely borne tragedy, with its glints of humor shining through, has all the humanity of sentimentality about it.

These people are too true to be good, and too good to be true. One smells a film script amid the scent of hair spray.

Clive Barnes, "Humor & Hair Spray," in New York Post, *March 24, 1987.*

MEL GUSSOW

In [*Steel Magnolias*], his first play, Mr. Harling is careful about setting its own atmospheric detail, introducing us to the proprietor of the saloon, Truvy; her eager new assistant, Annelle, and a quartet of regular customers. Over a period of several years, people come and go for wash and set. While waiting for their turn, they thumb through back issues of *Family Circle* and *Southern Hair* and they gossip about each other's lives and those of their neighbors. There are apparently no secrets in [Chinquapin, La.].

Much of this, especially in the first act, is gently amusing, and the play ends on a tender note of loss followed by a feeling of community. But . . . *Steel Magnolias* does not succeed in gathering its resources and transcending its existence as a slice of Southern life.

While seeing the play, I was reminded of the late comedian Herb Shriner, who used to tell stories about sitting in the barber shop in his hometown, watching haircuts, the most exciting event in that sleepy locale. After a while, . . . one realizes that we are sitting in a theater watching haircuts and shampoos.

Within those boundaries—and they are limited ones for a theater-goer hoping to be stimulated—*Steel Magnolias* is ingratiating. . . .

Mr. Harling has a grasp of local language, as in [Truvy's] remarks, many of which seem filtered through the imagery of her profession. "I always wanted to go to Baltimore," she says, "because I heard it's the hairdo capital of the world." . . .

Steel Magnolias is at its most perceptive in offhand moments, as when one woman, caught up in her own problems, says, "I just can't talk about it," and the others reflexively respond in unison: "Of course you can." *Steel Magnolias* is an amiable evening of sweet sympathies and smalltown chatter.

Mel Gussow, "'Steel Magnolias', a Louisiana Story," in The New York Times, *March 27, 1987.*

JOHN SIMON

Often when men write plays with all-female casts, the result is patronizing and false. Such was the case with [P. J. Barry's] distasteful *Octette Bridge Club,* but it is not with the charming *Steel Magnolias,* by Robert Harling. . . . Hitherto, the only men who knew what women say and do in beauty parlors were hairdressers; now it is hairdressers and Mr. Harling. The author follows the facials and fortunes of six women in Miss Truvy's beauty shop in Chinquapin, Louisiana, during a year and a half, and convinces me utterly that he knows their heads inside and out, hair by hair and thought for thought. And, above all, their feelings.

Besides tough, outspoken, hilarious Truvy (her motto is "There's no such thing as natural beauty"), there is her dithering young assistant, Annelle, a sweet, mixed-up thing who doesn't know whether she is married or not ("I swear to you my personal tragedy won't interfere in any way with my doing hair!"); there is Miss Clairee, the town's aristocratic millionairess, who makes a disgustingly rich dessert, "but I serve it over ice cream to cut the sweetness"; there is Ouiser Boudreaux, the town's rich curmudgeon . . . ("I will support art, I just don't want to see it!"); and M'Lynn Eatenton, who is married to a rich bully whose gospel is "either shoot it, stuff it, or marry it," and is a good mother to her two boys and her daughter, Shelby, about to marry a good ol' boy. Shelby is spoiled and imperious, but also generous and spunky—a fountain whose play lifts all surrounding spirits.

But she is also diabetic and shouldn't have children, yet becomes a mother. This will have serious consequences, but Harling's play, which until then is frothy, frivolous, and full of southern exoticism, has a steady undercurrent of fortitude that enables it to rise to drama. The women get teased more than their hair as they feud or gently mock one another; but it always ends in fondling and forgiveness. Underneath their occasional flutters and felineness, they are also staunch comrades, more savvy than sappy. . . . These emotional women are also steely; they cry, but hair-dryers will also dry tears.

The play is often only one jump ahead of soap opera, but always manages to see a bit farther and deeper. The women do have natural beauty, even if it is not necessarily at skin level. . . . There is love among these characters, and love from the author for all. (p. 94)

John Simon, "Wall in the Family," in New York Magazine, *Vol. 20, No. 14, April 6, 1987, pp. 92, 94.*

JULIUS NOVICK

All of the ladies passing the time at Truvy's beauty shop in Chinquapin, Louisiana, are nice. When Annelle, Truvy's new assistant, blurts out that her not-quite-husband is a wanted criminal, the ladies surround her with sympathy, and Truvy offers her a place to live. Shelby, the only young woman we see among Truvy's customers, invites Annelle to her wedding reception, where Annelle meets a man she eventually marries. "We enjoy being nice to each other," says Truvy. "There's not much else to do in this town."

Evidently not. When everybody is nice, possibilities for action, tension, conflict, are limited. When gunshots are heard, it's only Drum, Shelby's father, trying to frighten the birds out of the yard in order to protect the new patio furniture. This makes a neighbor lady named Ouiser very angry; she insists that the noise is causing her mangy dog to lose his hair. Oh, the drama of life in Chinquapin, Louisiana! Were it not for Shelby's medical problems, which are planted in the first scene and blossom into sentimental pathos at the end, that would be about it for event and incident in *Steel Magnolias*.

What makes the play entertaining, in its placid way, is that these nice ladies have sharp tongues. "Whitey Black is a moron. I'm not even sure he has opposable thumbs." . . . "Of course I remember him. He had the longest nose hair in the free world." "Sammy's so confused he doesn't know whether to scratch his watch or wind his butt." (pp. 86-7)

I'm of two minds about *Steel Magnolias*. There is something refreshing in Mr. Harling's refusal to abide by the convention that any small town, especially a small southern town, must be a hotbed of something or other—at least narrowness, stupidity, and bigotry, if not vice and horror. Shelby is a pretty blond whose favorite color is pink, and who wants only to get married and have children and grandchildren, but Mr. Harling refuses to make her vapid and shallow. Her mother is protective and carping, but turns out to be courageous and loving. (The "steel" in *Steel Magnolias* evidently refers not to metallic rigidity, hardness, and coldness, but to sheer strength of character.) And yet . . . how incurious this playwright seems to be, how little he has to tell us about Chinquapin. Nobody in the play has any serious money problems except Annelle, and hers are quickly taken care of; the oil boom and bust have done a lot to Louisiana, but Chinquapin has evidently missed it. No black people are seen or mentioned in the play. Nor is there even a real attempt to explore the mystique of womanhood that beauty parlors represent. Like the three monkeys rolled into one, Mr. Harling seems determined to see, hear, and speak no evil. What is he holding back?

Still, it's surprising how much amiable, sentimental fun *Steel Magnolias* is, considering its marked deficiencies in character, plot, and what Aristotle called "thought." This is Mr. Harling's first play. It would be interesting to see what would happen if he could put aside some of his niceness and really see *into* some aspect of human existence, in Chinquapin or elsewhere. (p. 87)

Julius Novick, "Southern Comfort," in The Village Voice, *Vol. XXXII, No. 14, April 7, 1987, pp. 86-7.*

EDITH OLIVER

[*Steel Magnolias*], a commendable first effort by Robert Harling, is about a beauty shop in a small town in Louisiana, where all the action takes place, over the course of about two years, and the six women of the dramatis personae are the proprietress, her assistant (shampoos and taking out rollers), and four of the steadiest customers—daily communicants is more like it—ever recorded. Their peculiar names are Truvy, Annelle, Clairee, Shelby, M'Lynn, and Ouiser, and they are a wisecracking lot, tough on the outside, soft on the inside, and many of their cracks, expertly delivered, are funny. Underneath all the banter, though, runs a sad, not to say sentimental, story. The story begins on the day of Shelby's wedding, when she persuades the proprietress to put baby's breath in her hair, to the mild protests of her mother and the comments of the other ladies. . . . There is a shadow over the wedding; Shelby has a mysterious seizure, and we learn that she is a diabetic and has been told that she may never have children. (The fit is so unsettling that I thought for a while that the dramatist was using "diabetic" as a synonym for "epileptic," but no.) Shelby is pregnant in the second scene, eight months later, defiantly telling her worried ma that no adoption agency would consider anyone with her medical record, so she and her new husband have decided to chance it the real way, and later on come reports of a dialysis machine and an unsuccessful kidney transplant. The pathos, though, does not determine the tone of the play, which is more a matter of salty chatter than damp tears.

Comparisons may be invidious, but comparison with Eudora Welty's incomparable *Petrified Man*, a short story about another Southern beauty shop, this one in Mississippi, seems inevitable. No wisecracks, no one-liners here, but a humor that probes and reveals the shoddy lives of the mean-spirited characters and subtly camouflages the horror within. *Petrified Man* is an indelible classic; *Steel Magnolias* makes an amusing evening—much of it does, anyway.

Edith Oliver, "Under the Dryers," in The New Yorker, *Vol. LXIII, No. 26, August 17, 1987, p. 63.*

DAVID RICHARDS

About 20 minutes into *Steel Magnolias*, a rollicking and altogether endearing first play by Robert Harling, there is a sudden shifting of gears that signals the presence of a gifted playwright and indicates that he is very likely to make good on the evening's abundant promise.

Up to that point, the play . . . has been robustly funny. Harling is obviously an observant writer with a sharp eye for the idiosyncrasies of Southern womanhood.

Steel Magnolias begins by chronicling a particularly busy April day in a small-town Louisiana beauty shop. . . .

Truvy, the good-hearted proprietor, has just hired an assistant, who in her goggle-eyed nervousness tends to produce hairdos that are overly "pouffy" even by Southern standards. The customers will soon be coming in to get teased and fluffed, and the morning promises to be chaotic.

It is, you see, the wedding day of the town beauty, a certain Shelby, and excitement is running high. The bride-to-be insists on a bouffant, sown with baby's breath—just like Princess Grace in the photo she's brought with her.

Shelby's mother, M'Lynn, is understandably edgy and frets that the all-pink wedding motif "makes the sanctuary look like it was hosed down with Pepto-Bismol."

As the women trade gossip, good-natured jibes and reflections about men, marriage and the latest styles in *Southern Hair*, *Steel Magnolias* is off to a hilarious start. Then Shelby abruptly turns ashen and slumps over in her chair. She's having a diabetic attack.

She has them often, so none of the characters is unduly alarmed by her spasms. They pat her hand, hold her head, try to get her to sip some orange juice and wait for her to come out of it.

In short time she does, and the merriment and ribaldry resume. But in that momentary surcease of high spirits, Harling has deftly served notice to his audience: His play is not to be just another caricatured romp through a redneck backwater.

Comedies about the South—of which there seem to be a plethora these days—tend to paint it as the land of rampant eccentricity, not to say heat-induced retardation. There are usually dead animals on the road and pistol-packing loonies in the garden. The food is as sweet and syrupy as the accents. . . .

Women, I suspect, will instinctively acknowledge the truth of Harling's play. . . . Men can see what they've been missing. We have the barber shop, I suppose, but after watching *Steel Magnolias*, I was obliged to admit the barber shop is just a hollow, blustery place for a shave and a trim. Then you're back out on the street again.

David Richards, "Short Cut to the Big Tease," in New York Post, *September 2, 1987.*

Paul Horgan

1903-

American novelist, historian, biographer, short story writer, critic, essayist, poet, editor, librettist, and dramatist.

The recipient of Pulitzer Prizes in history for his nonfiction studies *Great River* and *Lamy of Santa Fe,* Horgan is a prolific author of works in several genres who is probably best known for his historical novels set in the American Southwest. Although Horgan has been alternately characterized during his career as either a Catholic or a regional writer, most contemporary critics share James M. Day's opinion that he "is more devoted to explaining human dignity achieved through experience than he is to specifically 'religious' answers." Reviewers also agree that Horgan transcends provincial concerns through his insightful character studies and diverse thematic interests. While some commentators contend that his fiction lacks the originality and profundity of his historical works, Horgan is praised for his depth of knowledge, craftsmanship, and lyrical style.

Raised in a devout Catholic household in Buffalo, New York, Horgan moved with his family to New Mexico when he was twelve years old. This relocation provided the settings and subject matter for many of his novels, which, according to Robert Gish, often address "the great American themes of the East's contact with the West." Horgan launched his writing career by winning the Harper Prize Novel Contest for 1933-1934 with his first work of fiction, *The Fault of Angels* (1933). Described by Edith H. Walton as "a witty, adroit, rather precious comedy of musical life in a middle-sized American city," this book centers on the eccentric Russian wife of an opera conductor who is rejected for trying to reform the passionless, materialistic values placed on art and music by an upstate New York town. Although this novel received mixed reviews, Horgan was generally praised for his convincing portrayal of New York's artistic milieu and his blend of satire and tragedy. His next novel, *No Quarter Given* (1935), centers on an introspective composer whose estrangement from his narcissistic wife and imminent death from tuberculosis lead him to initiate an affair with a sensitive actress and renew a relationship with his alienated stepson. Their love and sympathy enable the composer to complete his greatest symphony. Sean O'Faolain commended *No Quarter Given* as "an admirable piece of work, and a convincing picture of sophisticated American society, told with feeling and . . . imaginative beauty."

Horgan's next novel, *Main Line West* (1936), initiates his concern with the history of the American Southwest. In this story of the tramps, evangelists, and other individuals who traversed the trail running west from Kansas to California early in the twentieth century, Horgan reflects on the American heritage of restlessness. *Main Line West* relates the brief marriage of a traveling salesman to an unworldly woman whom he subsequently abandons. Determined to raise Danny, their newborn son, the woman becomes an evangelist; years later, she is stoned to death by an irate mob for preaching nonviolence following the sinking of the *Lusitania* by a German submarine. The novel's sequel, *A Lamp on the Plains* (1937), is a coming-of-age story in which Danny travels by boxcar to a small town in New Mexico, where he comes under the influence of a

devious confidence man posing as a learned professor. He is eventually adopted by a wealthy rancher and learns the meaning of honor and morality at a military academy. Although some reviewers objected to the extreme length and dense poetic language of *Main Line West* and *A Lamp on the Plains,* both novels received praise for their solid craftsmanship and vivid evocation of the American Southwest.

In *Far from Cibola* (1938), a short novel originally published in the 1936 fiction anthology *The American Caravan,* Horgan portrays impoverished residents of a small town in New Mexico during the Depression, exploring the dynamics of mob violence after the United States government pronounces that the community is ineligible for federal relief. *The Common Heart* (1942) is a romantic and philosophic novel in which an unhappily married man's love for his disturbed wife is renewed after she attempts suicide. Following a tenure as Chief of the Information and Education Division of the United States Army Information Branch during World War II, Horgan published *The Devil in the Desert* (1952), a short novel which had originally appeared in 1950 in the *Saturday Evening Post.* This work centers on an aging, infirm priest who undertakes a hazardous journey up the Rio Grande River to administer sacraments to pioneers. Although this prideful decision results in a fatal rattlesnake bite, the old man reaffirms his moral worth before he dies by engaging in discourse with the devil, which he envisions in the snake.

In addition to his novels, Horgan established a reputation early in his career as an author of narrative histories about the Southwestern United States. *The Habit of Empire* (1939), a prose rendering of Captain Villagrà's epic verse account of Juan de Oñate's colonization of New Mexico, garnered mostly positive reviews, although some critics questioned his celebration of the Spanish conquest of the Pueblo Indians. Following World War II, Horgan's output of historical works increased. His major nonfiction study, the two-volume *Great River: The Rio Grande in North American History* (1954), confirmed Horgan as an important and influential chronicler of the Southwest. The result of fourteen years of research and formulation, this book represents Horgan's attempt ''to bring to the reader a survey of the historical life—pre-Spanish, post-Columbian, pre-technological, and proto-modern—of the American Southwest.'' Although faulted for disputable historical interpretations and a tendency to omit some sources to avoid ''diverting the attention of the reader,'' according to Horgan, *Great River* was widely praised for its painstaking combination of research and dramatic narrative.

Horgan attracted wide critical attention with *A Distant Trumpet* (1960), an epic historical novel set in the 1880s that revolves around the attempts of Lieutenant Matthew Hazard to revitalize the fighting forces of Fort Delivery, located in the territory of Arizona, in preparation for a Chiricahua Apache uprising. Based on historical records concerning Fort Bowie and the capture of Apache leader Geronimo, this work begins with a long factual summary and concludes with Hazard's arrest of the Apache renegades. Although some reviewers faulted the novel's exorbitant length and stereotypical treatment of Apache culture, most praised Horgan for his extensive research and characterizations, and Paul Engle called *A Distant Trumpet* ''the finest novel yet on the Southwest in its settling.''

During the 1960s, Horgan began a series of semiautobiographical novels, often designated by critics as his ''Richard trilogy,'' in which an elderly man looks back on his struggles with guilt, betrayal, and loss of innocence. The first book of this series, *Things as They Are* (1964), relates Richard's childhood in New York and his first awareness of sin, which he experiences after drowning a beloved pet. Richard's adolescent intimations of the human impulse toward tragedy is further developed in *Everything to Live For* (1968), in which a visit to the house of his mother's cousin in Philadelphia culminates in the suicide of her admired son, who is unable to bear his guilt over a childhood accident that resulted in the amputation of his mother's arm. Although some critics complained that the tendency of Horgan's characters to overintellectualize restricts reader sympathy, Frank Littler asserted that the novel ''is expertly told, and what must have been a difficult pace is always under control.'' In the final volume of the trilogy, *The Thin Mountain Air* (1977), Richard reflects on his life at twenty years of age, when his family was forced to move from New York to Albuquerque after his father contracts tuberculosis. While working on a sheep ranch, Richard learns of moral weakness when a fellow hand with whom he fraternized murders the farm owner and rapes his wife.

Although Horgan's prolific output diminished during the 1970s, he achieved popular success with his novel *Whitewater* (1970), an elegiac and lyrical treatment of the perception of time and reality in which three sensitive adolescents discover the relationship of past to present. Horgan's next major work, *Lamy of Santa Fe: His Life and Times* (1975), is regarded as a significant and original contribution to historical scholarship for its insight into the life of Jean Baptiste Lamy, the first archbishop of Santa Fe, whom Willa Cather fictionalized in her novel *Death Comes for the Archbishop*. The significance of Horgan's book stems from his extensive research into Catholic archives stored at the Vatican, which allowed him access to previously unavailable information about Lamy's early life. In *Mexico Bay: A Novel of the Mid-Century* (1982), Horgan shifts between the American Southwest and Washington, D.C., to explore various reactions to World War II. This novel relates a talented woman's marriage to an opportunistic playwright, her passionate but nearly fatal love affair with a frustrated artist, and her redemptive relationship with a young historian who is researching a novel on the Mexican War that began in 1846. Robert O'Connell maintained that in *Mexico Bay*, Horgan displays ''the compelling powers of a great novelist: ease and fluidity of narration, classically clear and simple description frequently laced with evocative imagery and incisive character delineation.''

Horgan has published works in several other genres. *The Return of the Weed* (1936; republished as *Lingering Walls*), *Figures in a Landscape* (1940), and *The Peach Stone: Stories from Four Decades* (1967) collect much of Horgan's short fiction. Horgan's literary endeavors also include the libretto for *A Tree on the Plains: A Music Play for Americans* (1942), an American folk opera featuring music composed by Ernst Bacon; *The Centuries of Santa Fe* (1956), a blend of factual and fictional portraits of individuals from over three centuries of Santa Fe society; *Citizen of New Salem* (1961; published in Great Britain as *Abraham Lincoln, Citizen of New Salem*), a highly praised biography of Abraham Lincoln's early life in New Salem, Illinois, that first appeared in the *Saturday Evening Post;* and *Songs after Lincoln* (1965), a collection of poems. *Of America: East and West, Selections from the Writings of Paul Horgan* (1984) contains pieces that reflect the dual geographic settings and subject matter of his fiction.

(See also *CLC*, Vol. 9; *Contemporary Authors*, Vols. 13-16, rev. ed.; *Contemporary Authors New Revision Series*, Vol. 9; *Something about the Author*, Vol. 13; and *Dictionary of Literary Biography Yearbook: 1985*.)

EDITH H. WALTON

The world of art eludes the writer, and especially the American writer, with fatal persistence. It is apt to be peopled, in fiction, with wayward, incredible children, addicted to threadbare poses. The ''temperament'' with which they are credited, the ideals which they are presumed to serve, have a hollow air of falsity. Few novelists are capable of viewing a musician, a poet or an artist with a detached and realistic eye. Their pictures of bohemia usually conform to an attenuated Trilby pattern and are bathed in a pseudo-glamour which is remarkably unconvincing. . . .

[Mr. Horgan] has not succumbed, however, to any such pitfalls. Partly because his tone is lightly satiric and partly, perhaps, because he is so very sure of his ground, *The Fault of Angels* somehow persuades one that even its flagrant absurdities bear some relation to truth. . . . [The novel] is a witty, adroit, rather precious comedy of musical life in a middle-sized American city. . . .

As the book opens, [the city of] Dorchester has just acquired a conductor for its new opera company in the person of Vladimir Arenkoff. John O'Shaughnessy is delegated to look after Vladimir's welfare and is, therefore, one of the first people to meet his beautiful Russian wife when she comes on from New York to join him. Nina is intelligent, impulsive, warm-hearted, glamourous. It is characteristic of her that she attaches china hearts to the pull cords of the window shades (in an effort to make her apartment *gemuetlich*). It is also characteristic that she cries quietly and exquisitely throughout her first lunch with John—because America has no heart, is cold, is without gayety or life.

Had Nina been content to let well enough alone and to savor placidly her success with the artistic and social luminaries of Dorchester, that one mad Winter of her stay there would not have been so desperate and dizzy an experience. But she was afflicted with ambition, "the fault of angels." She wanted to change people's souls and to remedy all the heartbreaks that she found about her. . . . Naïve as a child, she created countless disturbances and left behind her a trail of desolate admirers (female as well as male) when the stifling air of America at last became too much to be borne.

Oddly enough, this Nina, with her strange broken English and her snatches of French, is more credible than a mere description suggests. So are her satellites, and the other slightly frenzied figures in Mr. Horgan's comedy. . . . All these portraits are delicately exaggerated, subtly burlesqued, but they have a kind of inner fidelity to truth. . . . Although there is less bite to his satire, Mr. Horgan reminds one a little of William Gerhardi at his best. Certainly he is as careful never to flounder out of his emotional depth.

Whether one could honestly call *The Fault of Angels* a first-rate novel is another and more questionable matter. Mr. Horgan is amusing; he has exploited a fresh and bizarre vein of native American material; he has caught the flavor of that self-contained little world whose parties and concerts and opera goings he chronicles. Nevertheless, his book is at times a little tedious and a little long-winded. Nina's weird patois—faithfully copied by her admirers—tends to grow tiresome, and toward the end of the book one party begins to seem astonishingly like another. Perhaps it takes a robuster talent for satire to vitalize such exotic fare and to prevent a full-length novel of this order from appearing a trifle monotonous.

Edith H. Walton, "A Comedy of Musical Bohemians," in The New York Times Book Review, *August 27, 1933, p. 6.*

SOUTHWEST REVIEW

The Fault of Angels is laid in a city in upstate New York called Dorchester (which is easily understood as Rochester), where a solitary and beneficent millionaire, Mr. Ganson . . . , has founded a municipal opera. The hero is a young man named John O'Shaughnessy (which is just as Irish a name as Horgan), a sort of factotum about the establishment. The other characters are a very mixed group of the actors and musicians connected with the opera, Mr. Ganson himself, a society matron or two from among Dorchester's wealthiest, a bluestocking, two landladies, and above all Nina, the Russian wife of Vladimir Arenkoff, director of the orchestra. It is a comedy of manners.

Very little happens except that John falls in love with Nina, and that Nina, failing in her charming and sincere effort to convert Mr. Ganson to her own childlike enthusiasm for doing good in this world, finally leaves Dorchester to return to Paris. A murder is introduced somewhat as the murder is introduced into [Aldous Huxley's] *Point Counterpoint,* in order to add movement and some sort of a climax.

It is not the structure of the book, then, that counts, but rather the satire, and the character of Nina. Mr. Horgan is able to draw her as completely charming and a little ridiculous at the same time. . . . Once in a while Mr. Horgan suggests that John is about to become fatuous, but at the end he escapes being drawn into Nina's train as a satellite. And on the whole, it has been very good for John to have been overcome and to have wept a little.

But the book is most notable for its gallery of characters grouped about an institution which even in its tendency to collect foreign artists and Russian refugees is inescapably American. Mr. Horgan is never bitter, and the futility of life lived under these very special conditions (for art in America always seems special) does not strike him as tragic. This is a young man's book in most respects—in its passages of fine writing, in its occasional uncertain wavering between comedy and pathos, and in the pure romantic aura which surrounds Nina—but in its habitual gaiety it seems the work of an older man. It is a refreshing performance, giving evidence of considerable powers of observation, and presenting its numerous characters with no blurring of outlines. There have not been many American writers with the gift of sophisticated comedy; Mr. Horgan has it. His accomplishment is the more surprising because he invites comparison with a talented company, from Petronius to Meredith and to Aldous Huxley. . . . Mr. Horgan is all but alone in his shrewd ear for the amusing turn of speech and his delicate sense of the ridiculous, together with his realist's eye for life and character as they are. (pp. 7-8)

H. S., "Comedy of Manners," in Southwest Review, *Vol. XIX, No. 2, Winter, 1934, pp. 6-8.*

FRED T. MARSH

Paul Horgan's new novel [*No Quarter Given*] might be set down as a contemporary comedy; but comedy flourishes best at the tag-end of a stable, placid and stupid social order which it holds up to scrutiny. The modern temper is too troubled and unstable, but too personal and too socialistic, steeped in Freud, Marx, pessimism and the new physics, all at once, to be amused at pictures from Society (capitalization is mine). And Mr. Horgan sicklies o'er his irony with the cloudy cast of personal sentiment. He indulges in too many heart throbs. And he does not seem to know or care what his long, very long and awkwardly organized, novel intends.

He writes of a world in which several Societies clash. There is the Society of the established celebrities—artists, musicians, writers, etc.; the milieus of Broadway and Hollywood; a dash of Bohemia and a soupçon of Park Avenue. And, of course, all these moving circles frequently become concentric. All the people emerge directly out of Meredith's *Book of Egotism* and of every one of them might be said: "Through very love of self himself he slew." These are all Sir Willoughbys with a vengeance—as befits the scene, an amorphous society. But Mr. Horgan, at heart a sentimentalist, seems not to realize it. He has tried to pin his book down to crude reality and to tradition by bringing in the Mexicans of the Santa Fé artist colony, and by bringing into his tale the symbolism, beauty and history of Roman Catholic mythology. But his people are not good Roman Catholics; they move in the aura of their own detached talents and personalities.

But there is good story-telling here, some excellent character sketching, some high and engaging humor, and a personal tragedy which is both moving and restrained and delicately fashioned. There is material for any number of short stories. . . . And there are passages as nicely dramatized as a Behrman stage comedy.

Edmund Abbey, promising modern composer, passes through the many stages, the ups and downs, of a tubercular exile in Santa Fé. He is the third husband of a woman to whom social intercourse and the excitement bound up with it is the breath of life. And in Santa Fé, during the period of the story, is Maggie Michaelis, the actress. . . . Maggie, too, is seeking recuperation in New Mexico. Mrs. Abbey, Georgia, restive under the restraints imposed on her as caretaker of an invalid, finds a variety and a long series of excuses to absent herself from the home in Santa Fé, which her money supports—or rather the money settled on her by her two previous husbands—and the inevitable happens. The composer and the actress find solace and happiness in each other's company. Edmund makes rapid strides toward recovery and takes up again the symphony he had started, his Opus 18. Involved in the plot is Georgia's son, David, a youth at prep school, a boy who is realized here with some of the best strokes in the novel, a superior and intelligent youngster, troubled and unhappy. David has come almost to despise his mother; and his loyalty is centered on Edmund and Maggie, with whom he finds friendship and comradeship. This is the situation and the unfolding of the drama follows.

But incorporated into the novel are long passages dealing with the past of the various characters, particularly with the past of Edmund Abbey, which is a novel in itself. And in some of these sections Mr. Horgan is at his best. The story of Lillian Remusat (born Roemke), greatest prima donna of her day, whom Edmund Abbey once, through a lucky fluke, accompanied on concert tours, shows Horgan at his best. In Lillian he has created an extraordinary, memorable and convincing character.

No Quarter Given strikes the reviewer as a novel of little relevance, significance or intention in a modern world. But its virtuosity is undeniable. It is a long novel displaying an unusual talent. A few of the fifty-five sections are of the stuff of that "high" comedy which is a part of our literary heritage. Fewer still are inept, for Paul Horgan is an accomplished tale-teller. But the first duty of the novelist of social comedy is to know, even if he does not directly deal with it, his background, the body out of which rises the froth and the flavor. Meredith, like Henry James and Proust, was instinctively aware of it. In our present age "high" comedy, to be significant, must take a new and original turn.

> *Fred T. Marsh, "A Novel of Contemporary Social Comedy," in* New York Herald Tribune Books, *February 3, 1935, p. 4.*

MARGARET WALLACE

[Horgan has followed his novel], *The Fault of Angels,* with a work even more mature and carefully wrought. *No Quarter Given* is a long and fairly complex novel. Although it wanders at times from the main theme, although we occasionally lose sight of it entirely—and we suspect the author also does—although our attention is divided among a half-dozen characters whose lives are detailed with extraordinary care, still *No Quarter Given* must be accounted a successful and stimulating book.

In most respects Paul Horgan is thoroughly modern. Yet, unlike the average modern novelist, he has an abundant fertility, an inventive faculty which seems virtually inexhaustible. Where most of his colleagues in the ranks of fiction writers, when they are fortunate enough to hit upon an original character or a fresh situation, seem determined to spin it out as far as possible, Mr. Horgan apparently has space to develop only a fraction of the notions that suggest themselves to him. This quality permits him, as it permitted his robust predecessors of the eighteenth century, a good deal of literary license. He can take liberties with our attention. He can leap from this point to that without excuse or warning.

The main figure of Mr. Horgan's story—and the person of all his characters who seems to us most fascinating and least real—is Edmund Abbey, a brilliant young composer already dying of pulmonary tuberculosis when the story opens. Married to a wealthy woman several years his senior, and financially dependent upon her, Abbey lives in her enormous house in Santa Fe, while Georgia travels in search of amusement.

Maggie Michaelis, the actress, who becomes Abbey's mistress—and during the last weeks of his life his wife—and his young stepson, David, a sensitive boy just emerging from adolescence, are his only sympathetic companions, though his friends and admirers are scattered over the musical world. . . .

As a study in genius, the portrait of Edmund Abbey is more than usually satisfying—an effect to which its brilliant unreality possibly contributes. We never get inside Abbey's mind, or know him, in the sense that his actions have become to us clearly predictable. But his outward characteristics fall as neatly into place as the fragments of a jig-saw puzzle. He is charming, impulsive and incapable of compromise, at once rawly sensitive and callous to the point of heartlessness. His selfishness is so complete and lacking in self-consciousness that it bears no trace of ordinary meanness. His external life forms a pattern which seems magnificently inevitable—if this is not an attribute of genius, it ought to be.

Mr. Horgan is even more skillful as a story-teller than as a creator of character. This is saying a good deal, for, long as his novel is, there are many characters of whom we would willingly know more. . . . Even such minor figures as Miss Trimble, the trained nurse, have a tantalizing vitality.

Without being in itself a work of the first importance, *No Quarter Given* displays talents which may easily become so. Mr. Horgan writers skillfully, in a fresh and honest and illuminating style. Although one cannot help feeling that the narrative as a whole falls somewhat short of his initial concept, there are parts of it—dramatic scenes and graphically rendered incidents—which will remain vividly in one's memory.

> *Margaret Wallace, in a review of "No Quarter Given," in* The New York Times Book Review, *February 3, 1935, p. 6.*

STANLEY YOUNG

Those readers who were moved to applause by Mr. Horgan's gayly knowing novels, *No Quarter Given* [and *The Fault of*

Angels], . . . will be thoroughly surprised to find his present book [*Main Line West*] stocked with blunt, heavy, pre-Main Street types—with evangelists, traveling salesmen, tramps and farmers who lived on the main line west from Kansas to California, 1900-1918.

In a prefatory note to his brother, Mr. Horgan has indicated his new intentions: his almost lyrical desire to show the West he knows as a "country of beginnings," . . . where, under wide horizons, there is a constant restlessness and curiosity about life that makes a man unable to "sit down to rest or lie down to die until he knows where he's at." . . . [Mr. Horgan] is frankly inclined to believe that out of "restless beginnings" may come those characters who will nourish the flagging life of the nation.

None of the characters of this book, however, can stand as the doers or visionaries of tomorrow. This novel, it seems, simply lays a background for succeeding books which will follow the career of young Daniel Milford, if I interpret Mr. Horgan rightly, to its roving end. Daniel was the son of Daniel, a traveling salesman, and it would take no prophet to foretell that as his father's son he would be unlikely to settle down. His father, bland and successful, the roué of hotel lobbies, trots his horse across the flat country of Kansas one afternoon and reins in at the Kinneyman farm. The unworldly freshness of Irma Kinneyman so intrigues him that he finally succumbs to marriage. But traveling with his shy bride somehow takes the edge off his exciting life. (pp. 7, 15)

As heaven is not his destination, he gets rid of his ties by the simple process of depositing his wife in Coronilla, Calif., and abandoning her on the eve of childbirth. With this gesture he disappears early in the story, and with him goes a great part of this reviewer's interest. Although we see Irma facing life bravely with her infant son in Coronilla, and young Danny running wild in the shaggy life of the town, the experience seems to come to us as something recounted rather than felt. Irma is finally bitten by the restless spirit which was her husband's and she feels "called" to evangelism. With young Danny she tours the country and fills the churches, but her character seems inconsistent with our earlier understanding of her as a farm girl in Kansas. Even as a mother she fails to awaken any recognition in my experience of Western mothers as every one from Rolvaag to Cather has written of them.

In the final scene, in which Irma is stoned on the platform while she pleads for peace before an audience still inflamed with the news of the sinking of the Lusitania, Mr. Horgan is reassuring. There is a high emotional quality to the writing which is to be found nowhere else in the book. Here, as at no point after Daniel Milford Sr. leaves the story, he conveys with force the confusion and restlessness of the American scene.

What more he does is to give a slight lyrical impression of the West, but even here he strains for effects. . . . Somehow Mr. Horgan's picture of the country seems flat and one-dimensional. And there is nothing very urgent in the lives of the characters, in spite of the traits attributed to them. The figure of the Chinese restaurant keeper, that lonely, desolate type of Oriental who sits forever dreaming on his stoop in Western towns, is the most memorable character in the book and yet he is certainly outside the general intention of the center of interest.

It would almost seem that this highly gifted author had been urged to write in materials which are not yet entirely his own. He approaches with passion the country he knows, yet some-

how the wry, intellectual attitude which strikes through his earlier work has given his readers a far better product. Every one who believes in Mr. Horgan will look with eagerness not unmixed with fear to the publication of the further flights of Danny Milford's heritage of restlessness. (p. 15)

Stanley Young, "West of Kansas," in The New York Times Book Review, *March 22, 1936, pp. 7, 15.*

DORIS CUNNINGHAM

In *Main Line West,* [Mr. Horgan] propounds the thesis that the Western American has imagination and restlessness. Symbolic of the one is the white wooden church, and of the other the railroad tracks. The story centers about these two symbols.

Daniel Milford, a traveling salesman, stops overnight at a farmhouse to get under cover from a driving Kansas rain. Here he meets Irma, pure, beautiful, smoldering, who marries him much to his own surprise, and takes to traveling with him. . . . They reach a small town in California where Dan buys a store with living quarters above it, presents the deed to Irma and quietly disappears. Danny is born; Irma struggles to make a living and several years later takes to the road as an evangelist. Success is hers for a time, but with the coming of war to America she finds herself preaching an unpopular doctrine—peace. She is attacked and stoned by a hysterical mob while she is conducting a revivalist meeting, [and dies]. . . . Danny, her son, is left filled with bitterness, rootless.

Mr. Horgan has written an interesting novel but that he has truly portrayed the "moving" Western American is open to question. Certainly Daniel Milford is not a phenomenon peculiar to America. He is an international and irresponsible rover. Irma, it is true, could hardly have happened elsewhere. One can well believe that she "got religion" in California, and that when she started out preaching she hadn't the faintest notion what it was all about. Yet her religion is pure emotionalism and the hysteria which caused her death is the direct result of her own revivalist methods. Surely this is not the achievement of the little wooden church. A bit of imagination might have led Irma to preach "Love thy neighbor as thyself," rather than "Thou shalt not kill." (pp. 220-21)

There is a coldness in Mr. Horgan's style which generally keeps one from being much concerned about his characters. But certain incidents stand out vividly. For example, his description of the Kansas landscape and evening in the farmhouse. Or again in scenes of horror he succeeds almost too well. The tramp who tortures Danny, and Brother Trainor are two of the most loathsome characters imaginable. One detects a rare sensitiveness in the author and a genuine distaste for cruelty, but one ends by wondering whether he himself is rooted in the soil because the settings are all one setting: they might just as well be Connecticut or California. (p. 221)

Doris Cunningham, "Imagination and Restlessness," in The Commonweal, *Vol. XXIV, No. 8, June 19, 1936, pp. 220-21.*

MARGARET WALLACE

It would be an exaggeration to say that *A Lamp on the Plains* is a major novel. It is no exaggeration, however, to make another statement not exactly equivalent—that its appearance marks Paul Horgan, potentially at least, as a major novelist. . . . [None of his previous novels] had as much real fullness and vitality as this outwardly simple story of a boyhood in a New Mexican town.

A Lamp on the Plains strikes one as simple only in certain obvious respects. The time of the narrative is brief and its action compactly integrated. Too many novelists have described the years of adolescence to leave much freshness in the material. A boy wakes to consciousness of himself, begins to speculate about the world, falls in love for the first time, feels a stirring of undefinable ambition, experiences the excitement of hero-worship and the flatness of inevitable disillusionment and slowly begins to emerge as an individual in his own right. This story is as old as the subjective novel itself, as new as the imagination of the artist can make it.

For the purposes of Mr. Horgan's novel it might never have been told before. Each experience of the waif, Danny Milford, who crawls miserably out of a box-car and goes foraging for food in the ugly little town of Vrain, has something of the sense of newness, even of wonder, with which it might really strike upon the mind of an adolescent. The year is 1918 and the wartime hysteria at its height. . . . [Following the death of his mother], Danny took to directionless flight—riding in freight trains, living like a small predatory animal on the outskirts of Vrain, snatching food from backdoors, finding companionship in a dog as dirty and homeless and starved as himself.

Definitely, though, there is something about the boy. Mr. Horgan expresses this less through the workings of Danny's formless young mind than through his effect upon other persons. Danny gets caught at his thieving and finds shelter with his captor—a mechanic at a filling station. One by one he finds other patrons, each adding something to the fragmentary pattern of the world he will one day possess. Earlene and Myrtle, the waitresses at the station lunchroom. Mr. Hopeman, the meddlesome and rather pathetic Protestant clergyman. . . . The wealthy rancher, Wade McGraw, who casually adopts Danny and sends him to school with his own sons.

Each of these persons, loosely yet intimately linked to Danny's growth, has been drawn by Paul Horgan with a sharpness which seems related to poetry on the one hand and to caricature on the other. For that matter, the scenes of the story . . . are carved with similar vividness. Mr. Horgan is not far from having invented a language of his own in which to tell this story. Sometimes his prose moves with a spaciousness which suggests the vast landscape itself. Sometimes it drawls and twangs with the very accent of the people he describes. Now and then, in striving for an effect, he tortures a word too far out of its common meaning. But nearly always he attains one quality far more usual in poetry than in prose, the quality of suggesting far more than he seems to say.

It would be impossible to guess, from the evidence of the present novel, whether Mr. Horgan means to continue Danny Milford's history in a subsequent volume. It is to be hoped that he will. The story of Danny's youth, by reason of its self-imposed limitations, is not a novel of the first rank. If it were matched as splendidly by the story of his manhood it might well become so.

> *Margaret Wallace, "A Novel of Youth in Arizona,"*
> *in* The New York Times Book Review, *March 14,*
> *1937, p. 6.*

EDA LOU WALTON

[*A Lamp on the Plains*] is a psychological study of youth and adolescence done against the background of a very small New Mexico town, Vrain, not very far from Roswell. In many ways it is one of the most interesting stories Horgan has written, packed with characters who are fully created. The narrative would move more rapidly were it not for the author's tendency, present in all his books, to overwrite and to poetize his materials. Nevertheless, the novel is well constructed and worth reading.

Danny, the protagonist, is met first hidden in a box car on a cattle train. . . . A sensitive, frightened lad, Danny gets out in Vrain to stretch his legs while the little town busies itself about watering the cattle on the freight. He misses the train and becomes a fugitive in the little town, stealing to eat and hiding in the hills, his only companion a dog who has picked him up.

Thereafter his life is closely tied up with that of the village. We come to know the half-starved, rebellious or completely indifferent people of the town in its crescent of low hills. We know, through some fine descriptive passages, the significance of the trains passing this little settlement; we have felt the heat of the coming summer and the accumulated tenseness of the long years of the war. . . . All the smells and sounds and sensations of this place are vividly before us.

And the town takes an interest in Danny, a stranger in its midst. Then suddenly comes the news of the armistice. And out of the blue another stranger appears and makes a patriotic speech. His name, the townspeople soon learn, is Professor W. Winston Burlington. He is, obviously, a good deal of a fraud, but he pretends to enormous knowledge and has a real passion for literature of which he himself has made nothing. He now becomes Danny's guide. And the *Lamp of the Plains* is seen as a symbol of knowledge and of beauty.

The "Professor" literally pushes Danny into contact with books, sets him to reading all he can get in the Santa Fe reading room for the trainmen. . . . The portrait of the "Professor," a perfect scalawag, is one of the finest characterizations in this novel. He is improbable, but Mr. Horgan makes him completely real and understandable. And Danny, too, likes the old man, although he soon begins to learn that his leader has feet of clay.

The whole latter part of the book is concerned with Danny's life on the McGraw ranch, for Mr. McGraw, a well-to-do rancher, genteel, tolerant and wise, adopts him. Here the study in adolescence becomes completely rounded out. Kitty, McGraw's daughter, and Steve and Hank, his two sons, represent other phases of youth's growth into maturity. Paul Horgan is at his best in realizing for his readers the significance of the adolescent dream world of these youngsters.

We are not told how manhood is finally reached, or womanhood. And this book, though it contains love and tragedy, is not a mere love story. We leave Danny thinking of heroes and of men; youth wishing to follow the heroism of the past, not aware that his own occasions of heroism will resemble nobody else's, and will have to be met not with repetitions of lovely actions out of the past, but with the resources and wits that dwell in the character of the present.

A Lamp on the Plains is most valuable for its portrayal of a variety of Western characters, for its rich sense of atmosphere. There is no doubt that Horgan uses his people as symbols, but he succeeds, in this book, in making them live. The author's style, his delight in poetic details and in descriptions, the occasional artificiality of his own personal observations concerning his characters may annoy the reader. The book, to be sure, need not have been broken into so many little sections designed like lyric poems. The growth of the child mind from sensitive animal awareness to intellectual and emotional maturity could have been done without the titles and subtitles which rather overemphasize the author's intention. The novel, however, is interesting, and the characterizations, especially of the men, and more especially of the young boys in the book, are excellent. With his women characters Mr. Horgan is somewhat less successful. As a psychological study, however, the book has much to commend it, nor is it lacking in narrative interest. And where descriptive writing is used to advantage and not overused, Mr. Horgan's style is effective.

> Eda Lou Walton, "Adolescent in New Mexico," in New York Herald Tribune Books, *March 21, 1937,* p. 6.

OTIS FERGUSON

[*A Lamp on the Plains*] is solid and simple, a little overwritten, altogether quite fine. The story is about young Danny, who got out of a box car into the town of Vrain one night and stayed there; it is about the New Mexico town as well, and the people in and around it who had an influence on Danny.... (p. 81)

There is a special evocative quality to the prose here that makes atmosphere real and reality a ground for the illusion of truth and feeling to grow in. Not only the sight and smell as described, but some suggestion of the body's answer to that time of day or season: "The air drew into chill ... in this earliest likeness of spring, under its sparse snow, with its cows and brown hills ... washed sky and cold mud sweet and crisp with the evening's ice...." Sometimes it is simply a tonal delicacy in the choice of one word, as when he speaks of pigeons whuttering out away from the eaves, the train stopping with a wince of steam and metal, the brooding hoot of cows. Sometimes the selection of one detail, to bring the reader back through memory into a whole scene: "There was a scent a little like candy in the house always; not too sweet, very clean, somehow the savor of the family's habit in its house." And the same touch applies to the characters, each standing clear and sharp by virtue of a sudden picture of how he looks, what he does. They become clear and knowledgeable in all human complexity without ever the feeling of the writer's labor.

Paul Horgan is one of the true creators of a dialogue medium (as opposed to the dese-and-dose school of phonetic slipshods); he has a good understanding of speech rhythms in all sorts of registers, all of them quick and natural. (pp. 81-2)

[*A Lamp on the Plains*] is a serene book, working to neither hope nor despair; it doesn't pretend to be the story of Man in America. Yet it has such a strong taste of what we who live in it simply call this country, is so completely without need of explicit generality and prophetic statistics to those of us who just live here and even think about it without putting much stock in the "Man in America" books, that I shouldn't be surprised if some well tempered historian of the future could reconstruct for himself an awful lot from it about the condition and shape of the time, "somehow the savor of the family's habit in its house." (p. 82)

> Otis Ferguson, "American Rural," *in* The New Republic, *Vol. LXXXXI, No. 1173, May 26, 1937,* pp. 81-2.

ROBERT VAN GELDER

[One morning in *Far From Cibola*], farmers and townspeople were to meet in a little county seat in the State of New Mexico to hear the decision of government representatives on whether or not the district was sufficiently impoverished to warrant extra Federal relief. Before breakfast that morning Ellen Rood was called into the yard by her two small children to kill a rattlesnake and in those moments of protective fury found a release and exaltation greater than anything she ever had known before....

Down the road nearer town old man Lark resolved that morning to end, if he didn't die trying, his wife's fretful complaints against the noise of the windmill. The chains had not been greased for months. For a man of Andrew Lark's age and none too certain health the climb to them was dangerous. While his wife, fearful and intent and proud, stood watching, old Andrew climbed the steep ladder, strongly held his balance and greased the chains.

Through a dozen episodes such as these Mr. Horgan explores some of the individuals who made up the mob that gathered outside the courthouse to hear the decision on Federal relief. Looking beneath the words, the routine actions, the automatic violence and hardness and sentiment, he discovers and shows these people as they are in themselves, alone and exiled from the mob surrounding them, separated except in moments of great intensity even from those most intimate to them. Grouped as a unit they are little more than a problem of economics and law enforcement. But the drama of the mob is small compared to that greater drama as individuals fuse and part.

Mr. Horgan writes with feeling, he is a truly talented stylist, a natural rather than a "made" writer. But though his novelette ... may be to some unusually discerning readers a triumph in composition, in architectural design, to the majority it will seem formless. Many of the episodes are strikingly vivid, and with most of his characters Mr. Horgan has had marked success. But the final impression of most readers will be of formlessness that obscures the ultimate meaning, the final point.

> Robert Van Gelder, "The People in the Mob," *in* The New York Times Book Review, *March 6, 1938,* p. 7.

OTIS FERGUSON

The Harper people could at least have mentioned that Horgan's very short novel [*Far from Cibola*] is a reprint from *The American Caravan* of 1936, instead of sliding it over as a new book. It is a minor work beside *A Lamp on the Plains;* it merely takes the hard-up citizens of a Southwest farming town, examines them for their private mechanisms, shows them in an abortive mob action before the courthouse at noon, and follows them back into their homes and routine pursuits that evening. The action has been a sort of temporary release; directly or indirectly it has affected several lives. What we get from it is a small but typical fragment of American life in the thirties, a certain equipment for understanding.

Paul Horgan's style, here as elsewhere, should be recognized for more than its sustained cadence and its just enrichment of folk poetry.... There is in it that almost alchemic trick of calling up in a breath the scene, the mood of it or of people, morning and evening, kitchens, sheds, the town square; pride in simple skills, the dull anger against poverty and the years. In this he is apt to extend the image into something too tenuous for the best large effects, so that the reader lives in his world but finds it somehow trancelike and removed. But in this (not to mention his delight in the forms of life) he is one of the most sensitive and acute writers working today.

> Otis Ferguson, "Two in Fiction," in The New Republic, Vol. LXXXXIV, No. 1216, March 23, 1938, p. 200.

EDA LOU WALTON

Paul Horgan's scene has always been New Mexico and his knowledge of the country and its history and legends is extensive. He uses this knowledge again in [*The Common Heart*], and his sensitivity to the strange skies and landscapes of the Southwest plays over his story. As for the story, it is, as almost always for this author, romantic. Not that Dr. Rush, the typical scientific man, need be romantic. But Mr. Horgan makes him something more than a doctor. He is a man deeply in love with his native land, scholarly in his research as to its lore, sensitive as the author himself to its beauty. He is married to a woman caught in a psychological difficulty which disrupts their life together and allows her to live only in cheap romantic magazine stories, if she lives at all.... His son is aware too of some strangeness in his mother, but is very busy growing up in typical Western-boy fashion together with his best friend Wayne, a poor widow's boy.

Wayne's sister is just budding into adolescence and love. Her love affair is used as a deliberate contrast to Dr. Rush's mature search (against odds) for a woman who understands him and his interests.... [Every] one in this tale is an idealist, and every one behaves with rather extraordinary kindness and acts finally on high moral principles.... Mr. Horgan always tends to idealize human beings, and if he didn't have the ability to put them into plot and action and scene quite realistic one would be less inclined to believe his tales. But for him, obviously, the "common heart" is good.

Paul Horgan writes well. This book is planned in pieces which, deliberately used, show contrasts between one set of lives and another. We drop one set of characters and pick up another again and again—a trick which keeps the suspense high. Even the introduction of old legends and historical tales does not stop the flow of the story. Nor does the weather stop it. Rather, it enhances drama—much as it does in the movies. The book would, indeed, lend itself admirably to the requirements of the screen.

The Common Heart is easy to read. It will not move the heart too deeply, nor call for too much thought. It will give those who love New Mexico fresh memories and those who do not know it knowledge of a strange country which ,if any country can, does command the lives of its people. The story is thickly peopled, but the main characters are definitely in the limelight all the time. This novelist knows how to tell a story, and keeps the close attention of his reader to his characters, be they Western doctors or aged Mexicans filled with their own type of wisdom.

> Eda Lou Walton, in a review of "The Common Heart," in New York Herald Tribune Books, November 22, 1942, p. 21.

WILLIAM DU BOIS

Paul Horgan has been a white hope in American letters ever since he stepped into the ring some ten years ago.... Since

that date, not to prolong a metaphor, he has stolen more than one decision on points alone. Mr. Horgan is always an honest craftsman, with a true grasp of an author's importance in a rapidly changing world. In *A Lamp on the Plains, No Quarter Given* and *Main Line West* he has given us novels of understanding and beauty.... If his writing lifts the reader high and then leaves him somehow unfulfilled the reason is often as elusive as this writer's own quality.

In *The Common Heart* Mr. Horgan returns to the Southwest of some twenty years ago to tell us the story of Peter Rush, a philosophical doctor of Albuquerque, who marries Noonie Larkin at the close of his New York internship and brings her home to start a family beside the Rio Grande....

But after the birth of their son, a strange *malaise* comes over Noonie's spirit, causing her to withdraw into a cottonwool heaven of her own. When we meet Peter and Noonie both are emotionally becalmed: the rift between them is deep, though neither of them can put the trouble in words. Now Peter meets Mary Carmichael, a lady novelist who is wintering in New Mexico. He falls in love with her; they are on the point of eloping when Noonie takes an overdose of sleeping pills and is rescued from death just in time. After her recovery she regains her emotional balance in a way that Mr. Horgan does not explain clearly. With this new maturity her love for Peter is mysteriously revived. As the novel ends they are securely wed again, completely dedicated to the task of raising their son.

Mr. Horgan fills in his classic scenario with many overtones. Donald Rush and his best friend, Wayne Shoemaker, are developed with all the author's well-known skill. The parallel story of two star-crossed, adolescent lovers is used for effective counterpoint.... Throughout we are made subtly aware of the timelessness of time, the merging of past and present in this open, sun-steeped country. Peter, as an amateur historian of the region, is forever poking among old land grants and soldiers' diaries. A chunk of musty history is brought bodily into the novel, burnished into an odd reality of its own and then tied into the present through Peter's musings....

[All] the ingredients of the novel are here, the superb scenic background, the elements of rich emotional conflict. Yet the conflict is never realized; as a story *The Common Heart* does not resolve itself. When one has put it aside its desert is still a magnificent backdrop; its characters, for all their surface reality, are still nebulous, forever avoiding the head-on collision that would make the sparks of true drama fly.

At this date it is needless to underline Mr. Horgan's great gifts. He is lyrical and earthy with equal ease; his pages are exquisite blendings of man's atavistic memories and his eternal groping toward a higher plane. But he is more the painter than the story-teller, after all; more poet than novelist. In *The Common Heart* he has outlined a series of apparently related crises that should add up to a novel, and don't. For *The Common Heart* lacks the dramatic underpinning that might have sustained it through its many pages. For all its translucent moods, for all its splendid imagery, it will disappoint more readers than it satisfies. It is a hard thing to say, but in this reviewer's opinion Paul Horgan is still no more than a white hope in our literature. He has everything it takes—except a knockout punch.

> William Du Bois, "The Elements Are Here," in The New York Times Book Review, November 22, 1942, p. 40.

DIANA TRILLING

[In *The Common Heart*], Mr. Horgan has written a book with a thesis. The thesis is implied in the title: what we all have in common is the heart, and this is a novel that argues for love. But what Mr. Horgan means by love is rather complicated. He means sexual love, but he also means religious love; above all, he means family love—sexual and religious love can meet.

Not that *The Common Heart* is a work of homiletics or in any explicit way a call to piety. Mr. Horgan refers to the Church only tangentially, and his feeling for the Southwest country, though charged with religious emotion, is certainly as pantheistic or pagan as it is Christian. But it is not without point that Dr. Rush, the leading character, is a physician attached to a Catholic hospital (he himself is given no denomination), nor is it an accident that his amateur researches into local history so often lead back to an ancient faith. It is significant, too, that when he speaks of the mental sources of ill health, he uses the word "spiritual" instead of "psychological." On the other hand, without ever mentioning Freud, Mr. Rush is given to quite psychoanalytical exhortations on the subject of no happy children without sexually happy parents. In short, one gets the impression that, in the nineteenth-century fashion which has recently shown signs of becoming the twentieth-century fashion, Mr. Horgan is concerned to justify science and faith and is reconciling them in this figure of his physician. For science he has turned to medicine in its psychiatric aspect, and love is the common ground he has found for the teachings of the Church and the teachings of modern psychology.

It is love that is missing in the Rush household and so abundantly present in the Shoemaker household: Mr. Horgan's novel, with many excursions into the more distant past, takes place in Albuquerque some twenty years ago and the difference between the Rush and Shoemaker families makes up its main outline. There is Mrs. Rush, who married her husband after his internship in the East. Resentful at having had to follow him to New Mexico, she neurotically refuses to find contentment where her husband is content, and after the birth of her only child, her neuroticism grows into a deep fear of their sexual partnership. There is Dr. Rush, robbed by his wife of a larger family, who is almost sent into the arms of another woman. There is Donald, their son, who in all the small ways children have, smells out the miseries of his parents. (pp. 831-32)

But Mr. Horgan's novel is not the bleak record of case histories that a bald statement of its theme would indicate. A linear story, in which very little actually happens, it is made rich and various not only by Mr. Horgan's lucid and supple prose, but by a wealth of insight. There are many passages, such as the wanderings and imaginings of the two thirteen-year-old boys, that have an accuracy of observation which is the best stuff of fiction. As a close investigation of the springs of family life and in its awareness of what goes on in the minds of children, *The Common Heart* is reminiscent of Elizabeth Bowen's *Death of the Heart*—but without Miss Bowen's grit.

That Mr. Horgan's novel should lack grit is especially interesting in the light of his previous books. *The Fault of Angels*, for example, is a novel that one remembers for its author's remarkable satiric gift. Now, in *The Common Heart*, though there is still the gift that will not completely be downed, Mr. Horgan appears to be doing his utmost to destroy it. Only minor figures in the story—Lisette, the Rochester glamor-girl, or Rollie, the drug clerk—are drawn satirically. With his major characters, Mr. Horgan does not permit himself this method of attack, although, even when he is being most "good," his

eye is certainly still the eye of the satirist, if only because he sees sharply and accurately rather than much. And it may be that it is just because Mr. Horgan fears his satiric eye that he is so concerned with love and so self-conscious about his goodness. (p. 832)

Diana Trilling, "Novel with a Thesis," in The New Republic, *Vol. 107, No. 25, December 21, 1942, pp. 831-32.*

THOMAS SUGRUE

[*The Devil in the Desert*] is a brief, tender little story about an old French priest named Father Louis, who a hundred years ago lived at a mission in Brownsville, Tex. For thirty years Father Louis made two trips yearly to the upriver country of the Rio Grande, carrying the sacraments to scattered settlers in the brush country. . . .

When Father Louis got old, Father Pierre, his young superior, wrote to the bishop in France asking for power to keep the aged veteran off the trails, where heat and snakes and lack of water made travel dangerous even for the young and those who were armed. He received power just before Father Louis was about to depart on a trip, but the old fellow, sensing what was coming, tricked the younger man into looking for a pair of sun glasses and rode off in haste, fearful that he would be kept from doing what he felt was his privilege—serving God in the wilderness until he met death.

This time death was waiting for him, coiled in the shade of mesquite bush. He would not have crawled into the shade had he not been so tired from the fast he put upon himself as penance, and he would not have put the penance upon himself had he not succumbed to anger when his old friend Guerra suggested riding for a few days with him. . . .

It was the sin of his life, this anger; he had never been able to overcome it, however sorry he was after committing it. So in the end it killed him, and then suddenly the devil appeared and the dying padre had to discuss with him the division of the soul which was about to be liberated from its flesh. Father Louis wanted to go to heaven, but evil is not allowed there, and part of him, the anger at least, was in this negative category.

From the way the novelist and historian Paul Horgan puts it, one doesn't know how the argument came out, but in Texas the belief is that the good in Father Louis was released through all of the Rio Grande country, and stays there, while the evil in him went into the rattlesnake which killed him. One way or the other it makes a provocative tale, with less of the devil than one might desire, but not too much of the goodness of Father Louis, and just the right amount of Texas in the decade following the Mexican War.

Thomas Sugrue, "Dialogue at Death," in The New York Times Book Review, *March 23, 1952, p. 14.*

PAUL ENGLE

[*The Devil in the Desert*] is the sort of simple story, uncomplicated by many characters, by subtle motivation, or by rapidity of action, which depends for its success on a perfectly sustained tone of language.

This Paul Horgan has accomplished, as he has in other books not half as widely read as they should be. And for all its simplicity of incident . . . , the story has a great richness, the demonstration of Father Louis as the human shape of divine faith.

The story concludes with a dialog between Father Louis and the devil in the form of the snake who had struck him. In this, Father Louis shatters the snake with his straight logic, proving the evil that is in the animal which had killed him. And what the story proves is that it was actually God in the desert, working thru his own dark way, which takes the form of what we call evil, which is therefore blessed.

We need 10,000 legends like this, and can hope that Paul Horgan will write at least a handful of them.

> Paul Engle, *"Fine, Simple Legend—The Kind Needed,"* in Chicago Tribune, *April 6, 1952, p. 5.*

MARGARET L. HARTLEY

In *The Devil in the Desert* Paul Horgan has managed, in a small space and with an economy of materials that matches his admirable economy of style, to talk about the greatest questions that exist—life and death, good and evil—against a southwestern background that does not remain simply a background but becomes one with the events of the story.

For thirty years the French missionary priest, Father Louis Bellefontaine, had ridden out alone, twice a year, from Brownsville into the arid country up the Rio Grande to minister to the few families whose homes were scattered in that wilderness. Finally he has become so old and ill that his superior knows he should forbid him to go on another such journey. But in the face of the old man's inner strength and of his eagerness which is both for duty and for escape, the younger man finds himself unable to utter the words that would keep him from going.

So Father Louis starts out on the hard journey through the dry heat and the hotly shimmering light, with the thorny mesquite catching at him. At the isolated home of Encarnadino Guerra, whom he has watched grow from a ten-year-old boy to the father of six, the old priest encounters the evil which still, in spite of his years of faith and endurance, remains within him. He loses his temper and becomes violently angry when Encarnadino hints that he ought to give up and return to Brownsville. The tongue-lashing he has given his friend came, he knows penitently after he has left the Guerras, from his lifelong besetting sin of pride.

Exhausted by the heat, by his self-inflicted penance of not eating or drinking until nightfall, and by the shrilling of a great swarm of cicadas, Father Louis falls asleep under a mesquite tree. There a diamond-back rattlesnake seeks his shade and falls asleep by his shoulder; and when the priest wakes and moves, the snake strikes him.

As the poison works in his body, Father Louis has a vision of the snake returning to him as the personification of evil. "I do not hate you," he says to it. "It is enough that I recognize you." And the snake replies, "That is my damnation." The embodied evil is unable to bear the self-knowledge to which Father Louis inexorably leads it in the dialogue which follows. This dialogue, brilliant and convincing, is the central point of the book. (pp. 347-48)

The Devil in the Desert is not regional in any limiting sense; but in it the southwestern landscape and the human characters are blended in such a way that the significance of their rela-

tionship is immediately perceived and is in turn related to universal meanings. For this good and valid use of regionalism Paul Horgan has a particular gift. Here he has exercised it to the full within the strict boundaries of the novelette. (p. 348)

> Margaret L. Hartley, *"The Old Man and the Desert,"* in Southwest Review, *Vol. XXXVII, No. 4, Autumn, 1952, pp. 347-48.*

PAUL ENGLE

It was certain that Paul Horgan would write [*A Distant Trumpet*]. . . . [After] his early novels, his short fiction and his other books on New Mexico, it became not only natural but necessary for him to write the finest novel yet on the Southwest in its settling.

Given the debauchery of meanings which television has added to the word "West," a reader must approach any book set in that gun-loud, Hollywood-happy region with firm suspicion. Can anything new, authentic, ever again be written about an area that has become as mythological as ancient Greece, in which a frontier outpost now has as standardized a sequence of heroic actions as ever doomed Troy had?

Mr. Horgan has found some newness. He has skillfully blended much that is traditional about the Southwest—such as a cavalry officer's beautiful bride following him to his desolate post in the Eighteen Eighties against the wishes of her family—with a fine power of fresh detail. Only a person with a close and enthusiastic knowledge of the indigenous life of the region could conceive such a character as the Apache scout White Horn, called by the soldiers Joe Dummy. There is no more trite figure in our writing than the Indian, and yet Horgan has created an individual, a character, who is believable and alive, while remaining wholly Indian.

This is the story of Lieut. Matthew Hazard, United States Army, of his ordeals, glories, ideals and disappointments. In the earlier portion of the book we follow Matthew from a boyhood encounter with President Lincoln, through his West Point career, his refusal to give up an assignment to the desolate and dangerous post in the Indian country of Arizona for a safe appointment in the East, and his marriage with Laura, an Army daughter—an event to which Matthew brings not only his warm love for the girl but his solid devotion to duty as a young officer sees it.

All of this is, of course, the merest preparation for one of the most dramatic episodes of the story, a battle between the troopers and the Apaches, as a result of which Matthew and the scout, Joe Dummy, are sent to follow a retreating band of Indians over fierce, fantastic country into Mexico. . . .

After a ride that earlier writers on the West would have described as "epic," they reach the Apache band. Here follows a fine scene, as Matthew treats with Rainbow Son, through Joe Dummy, and persuades him to bring in his people and surrender. Later, in the novel's climactic pages, Matthew rejects a decoration out of loyalty to Joe Dummy, unjustly imprisoned with the Apaches he had helped to capture, and his Army career is abruptly ended.

The book plays off the romantic gloss of the West against the honest reality. Here is the pretty Eastern girl starting her family in a bare, sun-baked adobe building, but with the inevitable fine glass brought out at great trouble, and replaced when broken, because it is the symbol of the secure and comfortable life back home. And here also is the fine grit of sand in the steady wind, the sifting force that erodes the massive rock, and will erode the gentle personality unused to raging violence, of weather or of man.

It is the quality of the author's control that he keeps these two forces in balance, and actually makes each support the other. When a patrol rides out and finds the hideously mutilated bodies of a man and a woman, the true horror is spread out before us on the ground, and the odor of fear is tangible in the breathed air. Contrary to regulations, the soldier and the woman had ridden off alone into the desert and had died for their folly. . . .

It is in the latter part of the novel that we especially note the author's feeling for the Southwest: its shattered stone; its distances to which clarity gives an extra dimension; its colors that surpass in variety and permanence, on the harsh ground, any ever seen in the colorful sky; and the powerful effect all of these have on the people living in that mad, magnificent country. Place becomes as energizing a force in this story as time, as love, as courage, as duty, as supreme a factor as the north of England for the Brontës, northwest France for Flaubert, New England for Frost, Yoknapatawpha County for Faulkner. People act the way they do because, in part, of where they are. It is not simply air that the women and men of this novel breathe; it is Southwestern air, tanned, sparkling, tangy with sage and clean with emptiness. . . .

The novel is not without flaws. One of these is the excess of comment by the author, heavily emphasizing the obvious. Of Laura, he writes, "Her heart seemed to take flight from her breast, like a spirit freed." The Civil War was "changing lives suddenly and remorselessly." But such weaknesses are minor and do not block the long flow of the story.

This book is like a distant trumpet calling us back to a gone time.

Paul Engle, "Horsemen Who Ride on Forever," in The New York Times Book Review, April 17, 1960, p. 1.

MARGARET L. HARTLEY

The reading of Paul Horgan's *A Distant Trumpet* sent me back to a favorite of mine among his books, *The Habit of Empire,* published over two decades ago, to look at the two accounts of journeys and battles in the Southwest together, as a person might stand with a miniature in his hand looking at a great wall-covering canvas by the same artist. This seems to me an instructive analogy, for the characteristics of the six-hundred-page *A Distant Trumpet* are those of a tremendous painting of a battle scene, with its requirements and also its limitations, so different from the requirements and limitations of a miniature like *The Habit of Empire*'s close-focused picture of Oñate at Acoma. . . . (p. viii)

The scene of *A Distant Trumpet* is huge and stark—the Arizona territory of the 1880's, at the time of the final subduing of the Apaches. It is the dry, harsh, clear-skied southwestern country that Paul Horgan knows so well and has written of so memorably. The great sweep of such a land necessarily dwarfs the people who come to it. And in the sort of canvas to which this book may be compared, populated with many characters engaging in scenes of organized violence, there is little chance for the painting of the subtlest lines engraved on a face by complex emotions; the positions and expressions of the figures in such a composition must make clear the basic reasons for

their standing and acting as they do, with an economy of line that shall not confuse matters. So, perhaps, something is lost that can be found and mused over in a miniature. But in the feeling of space and sun and clear, splendidly composed action, with characters drawn so that the eye can appreciate at once the appropriateness of their being and doing precisely what they are, something is also gained. Much is gained in *A Distant Trumpet,* where the sense of time and place is developed through the descriptive passages that are Horgan's strong point, and the whole is held together by his splendid ability to organize.

The characters divide themselves into two groups: the officers and men of isolated Fort Delivery, with Lieutenant Matthew Hazard in the foreground, and the Chiricahua Apaches, of whom White Horn, or Joe Dummy, is seen most clearly. With Matthew is his wife Laura, gently reared but brought by her love for her husband to this desolate frontier post. . . . These and a number of minor characters demonstrate the various ways in which human beings of many different dispositions react to the highly special conditions of time and place; and if we seem to have met the same types—delineated with less skill—before, it is because the numbers of such reaction patterns are limited by the gigantic forces faced by any man or woman who, for any purpose, entered that forbidding frontier in those perilous years.

At the other side of the canvas (except for Joe Dummy, who is with the people of the Fort) stand the Apaches. The decisive character here is Rainbow Son, who takes the place held in historical fact by Geronimo. (The author, in a postscript, says, "As a work of fiction this book invokes appropriate indulgences in respect of historical fact.") . . . Rainbow Son's final submission, brought about through a plan conceived by General Quait from his ruminations upon human psychology drawn from Caesar's *Commentaries* and other classics wedded to observations in the field, is not historical fact and to some may not seem completely convincing, though the scene in which it is presented is an absorbing one.

Rainbow Son is not, however, the most clearly seen of the Apaches. While most of them are quite simply brutal savages, against whom the Army is entirely justified in acting with any necessary severity, there is one unquestionably human being among them—White Horn, who becomes Sergeant Joe Dummy, faithful scout and friend of Matthew Hazard. One of the most sensitively detailed passages of the book is contained in the early pages in which White Horn's childhood, training, and winning of his name are described. It would be taking the whole story on a different philosophical level than that on which it is set forth to inquire too deeply into the fact that the insights shown in this passage, not followed through for the Apaches as a whole, are applied to the one Apache who deserts his tribe to work for those who are, in fact and regardless of their advanced civilization, alien invaders of the Apache lands.

A Distant Trumpet is, all in all, a romantic novel written at a time when this enjoyable genre is not the most fashionable. It is good reading, and will take its own place, unlike that of Horgan's *Great River* and equally unlike that of *The Habit of Empire,* in the literature of the Southwest. (pp. viii-x)

Margaret L. Hartley, in a review of "A Distant Trumpet," in Southwest Review, Vol. XLV, No. 3, Summer, 1960, pp. viii-x.

THOMAS F. CURLEY

It's a strange feeling to have about a novel that is some six hundred twenty-five pages long, but when I finished [*A Distant*

Trumpet], I felt there should have been more. It's hard to say just why I felt this way but I think it's worth a try.

First of all about the book. The hero of the story is Matthew Hazard, born in 1856 and left fatherless when his father, a soldier in the Union Army, was killed at Chickamauga.... He was his father's child and he was going to be a soldier in the U.S. Army. He grew up in a time, as Mr. Horgan states, when "two prevailing visions" appeared above the lives of Americans: one was the Civil War; the other was the West. The one made memories; the other promises....

When Matthew grew up he went to West Point, graduated, fell in love and was engaged to Laura Greenleaf, a colonel's daughter, whose mother fought the marriage, unsuccessfully, with every resource at her command. Matthew's first assignment was to Fort Delivery in the Arizona territory. After about a year, he was given leave, returned East and married Laura who accompanied him back to Fort Delivery.

I have skipped innumerable episodes, not because they are without interest, but rather because all the way through Mr. Horgan seems to be slowly and carefully building up to a grand and awesome climax. Finally the climax comes. A General Alexander Upton Quait, a memorable eccentric, but an efficient officer, is assigned to the western territory. His aim is to put an end, once and for all, to the troubles with the Indians. The hundred odd pages of Book Three, entitled "Trial at Arms," are by far the best in the book....

A hero's welcome is given Matthew in Washington. But he learns, just before receiving the Medal of Honor, that his Indian scout, White Horn, who had accompanied the captured Indians to Florida, had been detained himself by order of the Adjutant General. All Indians were to be treated alike.... When Matthew Hazard realizes that the order is not to be countermanded, he takes the medal from around his neck, places it upon the desk of the Secretary of War, salutes and leaves the room. The next day he resigns.

This is the bare bones of the story. Mr. Horgan, who has written much on the West, has done, it seems to me who am no expert, thorough research on his novel. And no doubt there are many readers who will enjoy the rendering of the era in the drawing rooms of Washington as well as the deserts of Arizona. I do think, however, that Horgan's chief purpose was to reveal a man's character....

Now, since I'm sure that Horgan knew what he was about, what's my complaint? Just this: Matthew Hazard knows himself so well that his character is never articulated. He is a good and honorable man, yes; an heroic soldier, yes; but the texture of his character never comes through. As General Quait said, given the givens, Matthew had to act as he did. Yes, but the point is that we should not know that until afterwards, and we know it all along. Matthew Hazard is never fully alive because he is never quite free. That is why I said that I wish *A Distant Trumpet* had been longer. An older friend of Matthew's, an Army widow, "saw ahead for him what she had seen in other soldiers, old and young, who had for whatever reason left the service. They were clothed in the past, brave and yet lost in the present." I'd like to know that Matthew Hazard, too.

That's my complaint—a small one if what you want is a good historical novel, but not so small if you are weighing the claims of a "major American novel."

Thomas F. Curley, "Claims of a Novel," in The Commonweal, Vol. LXXII, No. 13, June 24, 1960, p. 332.

JOSEPH COWLEY

[In *A Distant Trumpet*, Horgan] has returned to the desert regions of the Southwest for the historical setting of this big sprawling novel about one small phase of winning the West. In it Horgan does a commendable job of recreating the desert country just north of the Mexican border and the life that must have existed on a frontier Army post during this Indian-fighting phase of American history. Unfortunately, the novel's pedestrian style, its superficial, wide-ranging treatment of both characters and incidents, and its cloyingly "genteel" tone seriously mar it for any but the most durable book-club reader.

A Distant Trumpet is essentially the story of Lieutenant Matthew Carlton Hazard and his young bride, Laura, and their Army service at Fort Delivery, a lonely outpost deep in Apache country in Arizona Territory during the 1880s. The climax of the novel is a show-down between Matthew and the Apache Chief, Rainbow Son. But we have to plow through many pages of trite writing before we reach that point. The style of writing is of the "she laid her head upon his manly breast" variety, and doesn't vary much from one page to the next.... The effect, needless to say, is at first cloying sentimentality and finally deadly monotony.

A full third of the book goes by before it even begins to get off the launching pad.... [An] overlong biography of Matthew is bad enough (inasmuch as it's not really germane to the central story), but the author does the same for each of the principal characters—and some who are not so principal. Presumably, he is trying to show us just what it is that makes everyone tick. But the mountains of background detail fail to take the place of real characterization.

Another reason the novel fails is that so much of it is *told* instead of just being permitted to *happen*, and told in obvious detail. Nothing is left to the imagination. There are no ambiguities here. The reader doesn't have to stretch his mind to understand anyone or anything that goes on. He always has the author to comment on the action and the people, to tell him what to think and feel....

Thus every emotion is strained through rather coarse sensibilities, and we seem to be viewing most of the action and people once removed. One result of this predigestion of the material is that nothing gets through that is likely to shock or upset even the most tender-hearted or genteel of readers. Everything is softened, watered down—brutality, fighting, love, sorrow, the commonness of the soldiers. Even the adultery of Kitty Mainwaring, one of the officers' wives, first with Matthew and then with Corporal Rainey, is not given us as direct experience. We learn about it through a haze of words and polite talk. And when Kitty dies we are spared the sight of her.

This is not to say that *A Distant Trumpet*, overlong and trite as most of it is, does not have its moments. Horgan has a real feeling for the open plains of the Southwest, for its shimmering, empty distances, its dust and heat and monotony, and for its beauty, too. And there is a very creditable job of delineating the Indians. Despite their brutality, they are not just the bad guys, but a real people. Scenes involving them in their natural setting are the best in the book.

Despite its romantic tone, *A Distant Trumpet* tries to treat honestly one important phase of American life and history. As such, it is not a conventional novel of the "old" West with stock characters. The people, events and setting are much as they must have been during a time when America was still westering. As it now stands, the superficiality of the novel's style and treatment of character, scene and incident will prove insuperable to the serious reader.

        Joseph Cowley, "Winning the West," in The New
        Leader, Vol. XLIII, No. 26, June 27, 1960, p. 25.

JOHN K. HUTCHENS

[*Things As They Are*], says Paul Horgan, is to be regarded as fiction, and not—save for a single, unspecified chapter—as autobiography, and naturally he is to be taken at his word. At the same time it is one of the significant delights of *Things As They Are* that more readers than not will find in it, if not Mr. Horgan's early life as such, much of their own. This has, I suppose, something to do with the universality of art. Mr. Horgan is an artist.

For this is an episodic chronicle of childhood, composite as it may be, up to that point where innocence shockingly and inevitably encounters actuality: an end and a beginning. A boy in an upstate New York town—Richard—loves and is loved by his parents. Still, he lives within an inner world of his own fashioning that they cannot possibly know, for all their love of him, and that only a rare adult, like Uncle Fritz, actor and drunkard, can really share.

So the worlds of imagination and reality interweave, and it is the essence of Mr. Horgan's tale that the former is quite as real as the latter in a child's life—in young Richard's as, once upon a time, in yours and mine. What could be simpler, and at the same time more complex?

He kills a pet, and does not know why, and experiences guilt. Already the innocence is fading. . . . The horror of threatened perversion brushes him, but, since he does not understand it, some innate wisdom keeps him silent about it. In all, subjective honesty he has a religious experience, is not believed, but is not crushed or embittered. With a child's pure fervor he loves, and learns what betrayal is, or what seems like betrayal, and, with that, the years of innocence are gone forever. He has learned too much. He has been pushed into what is, for better or worse, that world in which innocence will be a memory of joy and terror.

As the piper who pipes that familiar song once more, Mr. Horgan writes as a poet and as the biographer of us all. His prose sings but does not chant. He is both lyrical and muscular as he evokes the lights and shadows of a common ordeal. He is, as I say, an artist.

        John K. Hutchens, "A Gentle Shove by the Hand of
        an Artist," in Book Week—New York Herald Tri-
        bune, August 2, 1964, p. 6.

VIRGILIA PETERSON

[Mr. Horgan] has an imposing body of work behind him, but nothing he has written before quite foreshadows the piercing beauty of this latest novel [*Things As They Are*]. It is the story of a small boy's first encounters with "things as they are" inside and outside himself. The theme is scarcely new. Contemporary fiction abounds in sensitive children and contains almost as many variations on the loss of innocence as there are writers who have lost it. Yet Mr. Horgan manages—perhaps in part because he is writing about childhood, unlike most who do, in the full maturity of his years and of his art—to make the morning of life as pristine as the dawn of creation itself.

Things As They Are is not a remembrance of the author's past. In the note with which he prefaces the book, Mr. Horgan explains that his use of the autobiographical "I" is no more than a device "to invite the reader's belief." So the boy, Richard, whose shocks this seismograph so delicately records, is to be taken as a child of the author's imagination. But Richard is also a child whose own imagination, in reach and quality, might well have been the author's.

Richard's story dates back to before World War I. His home, a pleasantly spacious house in the hypothetical upstate New York town of Dorchester, was—*mirabile dictu*—a happy one. He and his handsome, youngish parents loved one another neither too little nor too much. . . . Yet the realities Richard met with were not pretty. No amount of care or loving kindness could keep him from knowledge of the cruelty, violence, injustice, fear and forbidden longings which, whether or not we believe with Paul Horgan in the wages of original sin, we all recognize as the dark side of the facts of life.

The first evil Richard came face to face with was . . . within himself. His grandfather had taken him to stay on a farm where he had no one to play with except a kitten. One day the kitten vanished. No one paid much heed to its disappearance except Richard, who from then on seemed, as his grandfather told his parents later, unusually downcast about it. Indeed, all the way back to Dorchester on the train . . . the cloud of gloom enveloping him did not lift.

It was only when he found voice enough to tell his father what had happened to the kitten that the weight fell from his heart. But even then, even after the promises he had made to God and parents to be good forevermore, he felt again as he lay in bed the thrill of the kitten struggling under the water in the creek and wondered how he could be sure he would sin no more.

Between the time when Richard drowned the kitten and the time, some five years later, when he discovered in the family drawing room his two beloved friends—a married lady who smelled of violets and an army captain who owned a sword— locked in the trance of a mad embrace, he had to adjust his vision of reality continually. . . .

He had to accept murder and suicide and death. He had to learn from the anger of a priest how unacceptable to God, how blasphemous, was his attempt to prove his vocation for the priesthood by a night-long vigil before a statue of the Infant which seemed, to his overheated imagination, to open its arms to him and speak.

Despite this succession of discoveries, however, Richard's innocence is still far from lost when, with sorrow and affection and no little pride, we have to take leave of him on the last, lovely page. Few books are harder to put down than *Things As They Are*.

        Virgilia Peterson, "Learning about Evil," in The
        New York Times Book Review, August 2, 1964, p.
        4.

HAROLD C. GARDINER

[In *Things as They Are,* a somber note sounds] almost inaudibly under all the adventures and escapades, the parental love, the very young friendships and partings, the fun and the sorrows of young Richard. Mr. Horgan states that of the book's ten chapters, only one touches on a direct experience of his own life; so we cannot well call the whole book autobiographical.

But young Richard's experiences come through with such a stamp of truth upon them that we must surely say that Mr. Horgan has lived them all deeply in his imagination—they are truer than if each of them had actually happened in "real" life.

Guilt was certainly the first knowledge of the young protagonist of these ten tales; and it was a guilt that sprang from a deliberate act of wanton cruelty. . . . He experienced the first revelation of the attractiveness of sin. And this dark knowledge is what he gains in most of the other episodes of his life here recounted.

But again—is this dark knowledge? If it is, it is still the knowledge that is proper to our human condition; for it implies that its darkness is lighted by the operations of the free human will. Richard's "loss of innocence"—like that of anyone else—means at the same time a growth in a sense of responsibility.

Some of the episodes do not strike this note very deeply; some are funny, such as the one on "The Spoiled Priest." But even under the fun (as is true in all real humor) there is a little echo of sadness, of regret for the passing of youth's simplicity. And every one of the chapters is beautifully appealing in its depiction of a warm and loving home and the lovely relationships between the boy and his parents.

Mr. Horgan has given us a gem of a book that is shot through with Christian and humane soundness, without once raising its voice to make a theological or moral point. Implicit throughout is the idea that growth into manhood means, for fallen man, an awakening to the awful attraction of evil and simultaneously (perhaps priorly?) to the quiet attraction of the good, and that along with this goes the responsibility to make the choice, under God, that one must make if he is to be an integral man.

To achieve all this under the guise, if we may call it that, of a little boy's remembrances of times past is no mean feat. Mr. Horgan has done it superbly. (pp. 323-24)

> *Harold C. Gardiner, in a review of "Things as They Are," in* America, *Vol. 111, No. 12, September 19, 1964, pp. 323-24.*

TOM GREENE

[In *Memories of the Future*, Horgan] relates an almost old-fashioned story of two extremely wholesome American families. These people apparently accept life's hard knocks without whimpering, they pay their dues in the human race and they earn a reasonable share of life's pleasures and treasures largely through courage and thoughtfulness, good manners and a deep appreciation of the beauty and rarity of lasting friendships.

Their love and sacrifice, their faithfulness and sense of honor, are all tested through two World Wars. Their tragic losses are borne only through possession of the ancient virtues of forgiveness and understanding. Young Naval Lieutenant David Hopkinson, a convert to Catholicism, gives witness to these values amidst the filth and suffering of a Japanese prison camp during the closing days of World War II. . . . David forgives his captors despite their cruelty, the idiocy of their vanity, the outrage of their estimate of human life. He begs a fellow prisoner to carry home to David's family the truth that he died without hatred in his heart for anyone.

It is puzzling that such a talented writer, in his weaving of these elements, should resort to casting the fellow prisoner as David's best friend from Annapolis days. A reader's frustration

increases when the best friend returns home and is caught up in a love that will lead him to marry David's widow.

Horgan's skillful alternation of past and present helps us to understand this situation with some compassion. . . . But one gets the unsettling feeling that we have here more of a plot outline for an interesting motion picture than a living, enduring novel.

Even so skilled an artist as Paul Horgan—and much of this writing shows real artistry—is unable to help us know these people and share and experience some of their lives and loves in a mere 216 pages. Mind you, there are several subplots interspersed that go back to Wilson's "War to end all wars."

The novelist, in serving as a bridge to our union with real and whole human souls, must touch on at least portions of the evil that exists in them or their environment. The only evil in this yarn is pinned on the "bad guys," the Japanese prison guards and officers. There's a lack of completeness in this portrayal of three decades in the lives of a few of our Naval officers and their families and fortunes.

On the credit side, the book possesses many scenes that are deeply moving filled with feeling and warmth and life. A couple of episodes are unforgettable.

But the distinguished author of *A Distant Trumpet* and *Things As They Are* knows that every champion has an off night. It is to be hoped that Paul Horgan is at work on something more durable and vital. (pp. 747-48)

> *Tom Greene, in a review of "Memories of the Future," in* America, *Vol. 114, No. 21, May 21, 1966, pp. 747-48.*

PETER BUITENHUIS

The novel is moving so fast in so many new directions that to come across such a highly traditional one as this naval story by Paul Horgan [*Memories of the Future*] is almost like visiting a museum. Mr. Horgan is of course a highly-skilled professional writer, and *Memories of the Future* is a beautifully written, well-organized piece of work. But it depicts a world of order, ceremony, almost of innocence, that seems at odds with all that we know and feel at the present time. In other words, *Memories of the Future* is a curiosity, like its enigmatic title, a tour de force that stands polished and glistening in the pale January sun of Annapolis, Md., where it is largely set.

The characters, all somehow related or old friends, are stuck in the United States naval service, like barnacles to an old hull. They have names like Avy, Doro, Wick and Dinny, yet these names accompany flag rank, so that the book is woven together with gold lace and "charm," informality and punctilio. I suppose that it is dedicated to the ideas of service, duty and sacrifice, unfashionable qualities, unfortunately, in these days.

The characters and their sons all go to Annapolis and to sea as if there were nothing else in the world to do. Vice Adm. Avy Thayer is the Superintendent of the Naval Academy, the genial host to the party that gathers to celebrate the end of World War II but also to commemorate those who have suffered and died in it, particularly David, the young son of Avy's sister-in-law, Doro, a naval lieutenant who has died agonizingly in a Japanese prison camp.

The novel moves back and forth across the lives of the characters from graduation on. Mr. Horgan has managed to avoid most of the sentimentality to which this sort of literature lends itself, largely by a tight control of tone and an almost classical purity of language. The trouble with the sort of distancing to which this treatment gives rise is that it makes for a kind of impersonality, suitable to an epic, perhaps, but not to the easy bonhomie of the novel form.

The characters do not spring to life, but remain in the distinctive poses of their rank and elegance. The novel is full of gestures—salutes, slight bows, flashed smiles. Only in isolation (which is rare) do the characters give way to displays of emotion. . . .

One consequence of all this is that for a long time the reader is not sure who Avy is in relation to Doro, or Doro to Dinny, or Vivi to Hoppy, or Deedy to anyone. What is worse, he doesn't much care. It's something of a relief to move out of the relentless, elaborate, cheerful ceremoniousness of the Superintendent's quarters to the recalled prison camp, where David—a real name at last—in blood, mud and excrement, suffers and dies. Here the novel comes to life on the level of felt experience from which it departs only at its peril.

The sad fact is that a coterie novel cannot really exist in this harsh world unless it contains some qualities of universal experience. This *Memories of the Future* does not have. It may be lapped up by the old and new brass of the Navy, but I can imagine it being given the boot even at West Point.

> *Peter Buitenhuis, "Old and New Brass," in* The New York Times Book Review, *June 19, 1966, p. 3.*

FRANK LITTLER

In a previous work, a fragmented study of childhood entitled *Things as They Are,* Paul Horgan named his principal character Richard, and placed him—a 4-year-old child—in the imaginary town of Dorchester, N.Y. The Richard of *Everything to Live For* is also a Dorchester boy, a youth of 17 who would have been born in the same year. The duplication is puzzling, there being no suggestion that the present story—hardly more than a novella—is a sequel to *Things as They Are. . . .*

The story is narrated by Richard in adulthood. It is a skeletal but steely account of youthful tragedy in upper-crust Pennsylvania a few years after World War I. Richard is invited to spend a weekend with the Chittendens, his mother's cousin and her husband, on the occasion of a house party. His parents urge him to go, partly because the Chittendens' son, Max, is an unusually handsome 21-year-old on whom they vicariously dote, and also because they are frankly taken with their cousins' opulence. A young man's freedom to pick and choose among social functions, however infrequent, generally comes a few years before he reaches his majority, and this is an invitation Richard would be glad to decline. He is persuaded to the contrary and boards the train for Pennsylvania.

The atmosphere that greets him is baronial. Mr. Chittenden's accent is American patrician, of a kind that would be uncommon today, and he owns a library of first and special editions of Byron. His wife has lost an arm, in circumstances that reflect contrastingly on herself, her husband and Max. (p. 5)

It is not the author's purpose to festoon his framework with the ephemera of 1921, though there are references to bootleg whisky and Max's "motorcar," evocatively, is an Isotta Fraschini. This ends Mr. Horgan's resemblance to another American novelist of Irish extraction, and his attitude to the rich is considerably more detached.

The title of the book may uncover too much; but granted that the story will end in tragedy, the car becomes an important instrument of it. The reasons for the tragedy are seen through Richard's well-mannered prose to be feasibly Byronic. Unfortunately, he analyzes his hosts with a mind to which maturity has given balance without complete understanding. And the reader's sympathies may be less than fully engaged.

It is often hard to find a deeper meaning in the personal calamities of the landed gentry than in what befalls those of a less rigid upper-lip; and while the author sketches out the emotional interactions, he refrains from filling them in. In fact, he seems to be leaving it to us to decide who suffered the most from the climax to his tale.

Everything to Live For will therefore provoke more thought than feeling. But it is expertly told, and what must have been a difficult pace is always under control. (pp. 5, 23)

> *Frank Littler, "A Weekend in the Twenties," in* The New York Times Book Review, *August 25, 1968, pp. 5, 23.*

ALFRED C. AMES

In a format almost as tightly disciplined as a Greek tragedy, Paul Horgan has developed [*Everything to Live For*], a story both modern in its psychological penetration and its exemplification of the new social mores, and classical in its deliberate, chiseled phrasing and the simple directness of its plotting.

The setting is the estate of the Chittenden family outside Philadephia in 1921. The protagonist is Max, twenty-one, a Harvard undergraduate and heir apparent to millions. The narrator is his second cousin Richard, seventeen, from upstate New York, and there are Max's parents and his fiancée, Marietta Osborne.

The irony of the title is so quickly evident that the nature of the climax is an open secret long before one arrives at it. Yet Horgan keeps the reader from looking ahead; for the slow relishing of the writer's careful style is more important than the satisfaction of curiosity about how matters will be worked out.

Among the mixed-up characters in *Everything to Live For,* even the apparently equable narrator suffers from tension between the outer and the inner person. The public role is of course especially demanding of the extremely rich. Being a Chittenden means being host to the county, even at home being on perpetual display before the servants. . . .

Poor cousin Richard, thrust for the first time into baronial splendor, makes a natural foil to Max. But the novelist's scheme requires him to be exquisitely perceptive and gifted with total recall. At best, Richard is implausible. An omniscient point of view would have permitted him to be less precocious, but then the story would have unfolded less gradually and convincingly than it does.

The few motifs recur repeatedly, with variations and resonance. When the last thread is neatly tied, we can look back on an expert and elegant work of art. If what it has to say about life is conventional, that is a price often paid for skillful artifice.

> *Alfred C. Ames, "An Echo of Greek Tragedy," in* Book World—The Washington Post, *September 8, 1968, p. 20.*

MICHAEL O'MALLEY

To see Paul Horgan's talent pumped fruitlessly into this flaccid pudding of a book [*Everything to Live For*] is depressing. The idea was, according to the jacket, to tell, "among other things, a parable of an encounter between the spirit which denies and that other which affirms." But what you get is more of a parable about the spirit which is Crybaby and that other which pats soothingly upon the back. Richard, the nice young square-jawed Catholic narrator, does the patting, and his cousin Maximilian Chittenden is the absolutely stupefying Crybaby. What's more incredible is that Mr. Horgan seems to *like* Max Chittenden. . . . I think the author got too close and made the fatal mistake of falling in love with one of his own characters. Max is actually beyond human bearing—a smug, arrogant, selfish oaf, who happens to cry a lot. The crying is supposed to show his sensitivity and make us love him, I suppose. To my mind, the advice given Richard by Max's mother, "Richard, don't get too fond of Max," is one of the most hilariously unnecessary warnings in literature. . . .

The entire Chittenden family is gone on Lord Byron. . . . The Chittendens are immensely rich: Max never turns off the engine of his Isotta-Fraschini; "They'll do it," says he. Max is, of course, handsome, brilliant, a Harvard senior at twenty-one, keeps his room like a pig-pen, wears secondhand clothes . . . , and has this girl friend he's been sleeping with for simply *ages*. Her name is Marietta Osborne and she gets to exclaim things like "—Oh, the *thingness* of everything!" and like that, and at times to give "a small rapturous groan of appreciation." If the novel is meant to be a study of the Byronic personality, it does not come off. In fact, the more you read of Max, the more he seems the archetype of today's bored campus rebels, heaving rocks at the local cops because . . . in their exquisite ennui—there seems nothing much else to do. Max pores over Byron's letters, becomes more and more dramatically tragic, and goes to his inevitable sad end. Speed kills. So do massive cases of self-afflatus. Before Max's body is cold, Richard is bedding Marietta in her car, and we're forced to think of Bus Ad students shouting from classroom windows to the beards: The Square will inherit the earth. Ol' Richard makes out all right.

I can't see that anything about anybody is proven by this novel—except, perhaps, that an artist, when he moves in too close, can easily get mired in his own paint.

> *Michael O'Malley, in a review of "Everything to Live For," in* The Critic, *Chicago, Vol. 27, No. 5, April-May, 1969, p. 74.*

ANNE FREMANTLE

[In *Whitewater*, Paul Horgan is concerned] with the here flowing, there simultaneous (*nunc fluens-tunc simul*) together and total aspects of time. He takes the lives of a group of people living in a town he calls Belvedere, in East Texas, in the 1940's. More specifically, he tells of the lives of three teenagers: in order of appearance, Phillipson Durham, William Breedlove and Marilee Underwood. They are very different. Phil, whose parents have not long come to Belvedere, is an introvert; Billy is a golden glorious creature, a born leader, a marvelous mimic, who dominates his friends and especially Marilee. . . . [As] their omniscient narrator sees them, each [is] unique and complete, that is, complicated, contradictory, complex and wholly unaware of what makes them tick, or even of the fact that they are ticking.

In his prelude—and much in the marvelous construction of this novel recalls a musical composition . . .—the story's themes are sounded by a flash forward. Phil, now a happily married professor in an Appalachian college, when asked by a student the best way to reach perception, replies "You often see more by looking at an upside-down reflection in water than you do if you look at what casts it." This reflected sign, he adds, can seem like the past "about which there is so much to learn and remember." While the direct sign "is like the present," which "we hardly notice by living in it."

The Whitewater of the title is now an artificial lake, eighteen miles long and six at its widest. Created because the railroads needed water for their locomotives, it took ten years to fill up: the former inhabitants of the town (now sunk some three hundred feet in the lake's depth) moved to Belvedere or Orpha City. Whitewater lake, and the drowned town, since "nothing is gone," act and react on each other throughout the novel, and the double image, like the double vision by which it is seen, records without repetition, like a theme in a symphony.

In the beginning, Phil and Billy, in a canoe on their way to camp one night on Whitewater's best island, hear mysterious voices, one heavy, one light. To hear what is being said, they strip and swim, but only make out that one voice is asking, one answering. Swimming still nearer in the moonless dark, they are shot at, twice. Next morning no one is around. The first sign of Belvedere they see on their return home is the silver-painted municipal water tank "shining with a soft glow against the horizon haze" caused by the smog from nearby oil fields. This water tank is the nemesis for all three of the story's protagonists. Yet it is no external thing, but their own natures which bring them to their separate destinies: everything that happens to each one is inevitable, and, given causality, unavoidable.

As Paul Horgan's major theme is the double vision of reality, the "now and in the hour of our death" that make up the always 'only now,' so his minor one is the double vision of good and evil, beauty and ugliness. On the one hand there is the shoddiness and vulgarity of "most everything" men try to make, that hurts Phil so: on the other, there is the "incomparable pomp of eve" as Robert Louis Stevenson called it, that pours over the tawdry and the trivial. So Phil admires the accidental industrial beauty, produced by the vapor lights on tall aluminum poles over the highway, when the sky is still brilliant and the earth a lilac gray. (pp. 52-3)

Rabindranath Tagore declared all reality to be relationship, and in *Whitewater* the relationships are built up delicately, stroke by stroke, as in a Seurat painting, so that each is essential to every other. . . .

There are two main triangles in *Whitewater:* first Phil discovers Marilee, then Billy does, but Billy also discovers Phil. Marilee is a unique girl, but Phil is like no other boy, so Billy promises that the three of them will be something new in Belvedere. It is Billy's will that leads them, but he "never felt what Phil's friendship was made of—of how much resentment, unwilling love, envy, curiosity, admiration, self-hatred." Yet Billy knew that "all you've got to use in this world is yourself." The other, older triangle, is made up of Tom Bob, the bank manager; his exotic mistress, Thyra, who works in a beauty shop and salvages her conscience by doing good with all the money Tom Bob lavishes on her; and Tom Bob's wife. Thyra gives him the "belly-comfort" denied him by his snobbish, childless wife. . . . Yet the wife "alone of the three had passion," and when she thinks she is dying of cancer she takes a gun to kill her rival. Billy's mother persuades her to forgive . . . , and Thyra, brought low by such magnanimity, gives up Tom Bob. Paul Horgan is not sentimental: the result is that Tom Bob has a stroke and dies, his mistress fades into addled old age, and his wife has hysterics over Billy's death. . . .

"Everybody's end is sad" Vicky tells Phil, and so it is. Billy's terrible death, literally at Phil's hand, and Marilee's lonely, watery exit: badgered by her mother, preached at by priests, loved by Phil, she goes to Billy who has "called to her through their child."

Paul Horgan, as W. H. Auden wrote of his Maker "is affectionate to all his creatures." But his courage is not less than its compassion: one is cheated, "not even the world of its triumph," and it is not easier for Phil to live than for Billy and Marilee to die. What is most satisfactory is the clarity of line—as in a great draughtsman's work or a great dressmaker's; this story is, for all its richness, beautifully uncluttered.

William Blake prayed:

> may God us keep from single
> vision and Newton's sleep.

In *Whitewater* this prayer is answered: as above, so below, the two worlds, interior and exterior, of reality and reflection, are both admirably viewed and recorded. (p. 53)

Anne Fremantle, in a review of "Whitewater," in Commonweal, *Vol. XCIII, No. 2, October 9, 1970, pp. 52-3.*

PAUL K. CUNEO

[*Whitewater*] is basically the story of three young people, high school students, in Belvedere, a small town on the vast plains of Texas, and of a number of the town's inhabitants whose lives influence or intersect theirs.

William Breedlove, Phillipson Durham and Marilee Underwood are the three rather improbably named young people who, for a year or two, seem to live in or near the center of the town's activities. Their days and those of a number of other citizens of the town . . . all contribute to a sort of mid-twentieth century *Our Town*.

As with many of these efforts to capture the lives and atmosphere of a typical American town, the author of this one has felt the need for some sort of frame in which to present his picture, and that is readily at hand in the mature memory of one of the three youthful friends. But then to add another dimension to the story, Mr. Horgan introduces the town of Whitewater, a town not far from Belvedere as distances are measured in Texas, but now at the bottom of Whitewater Lake. . . . The town and the lake seem constantly to be rising in the course of the story, apparently to give some extra meaning to it.

Perhaps the author merely intends the ghostly town at the bottom of the lake to add a greater reality to the everyday life he is chronicling in Belvedere, but somehow the name of the novel and the ways in which the town and the lake are introduced, and keep re-occurring in the story, would seem to indicate that there is more meaning to them than this. What the meaning of Whitewater is, however, I must confess escapes me. The fault may be mine for missing what Mr. Horgan has made clear, or Mr. Horgan's for making his intention too obscure or for seeming to intend something that actually he does not intend. But

somewhere there is a fault. Obviously Whitewater—the town, the lake, or an idea expressed by either or both—has a bearing on the story or the novel would not be named as it is. Yet I miss the point.

To add to my confusion about the novel, a young college student who glanced at my copy of the book commented, "What an old-fashioned looking dust jacket!" That is the kind of impressionistic judgment one cannot argue about—especially across the generation gap. But it led me to wonder if anyone under thirty might not be inclined to render the same sort of verdict on the novel itself. If I were not bothered by the meaning of Whitewater in the course of the novel, I would be inclined to say that this is one of Mr. Horgan's best. As it stands, I don't know quite what to say about it. (pp. 293-94)

Paul K. Cuneo, in a review of "Whitewater," in America, *Vol. 123, No. 11, October 17, 1970, pp. 293-94.*

L. J. DAVIS

Anyone who dislikes [*Whitewater*] has got to be some kind of snob. This is not to say that it is a good novel or even a clever one; it is neither, but it is certainly very friendly and full of good intentions. The relationship of its characters to persons either living or dead is purely accidental, and its relationship to observable reality is idealized, highly selective, and fortuitous at best. Paul Horgan appears to believe that it is really neat to be young and that most people, down deep, are pretty darn decent. These are venerable American myths, and it is quaint and a little sad to encounter them today.

Horgan's sentimental protagonists are three teenagers—two boys and the girl they both love—who live in a small town on the Central Plains of Texas in the late 1940s. They are by no means your average teenagers of that or any other era. They are downright wonderful. . . . One boy is the golden—literally—hero of the high school, the captain of all the teams, the most beloved of all his tribe. The other boy is scrawny and dark, but with the heart of a poet. And in her own way the girl is every bit as marvelous as the one that got carved up in Capote's *In Cold Blood*. Despite the accidental death of one of them, the suicide of another, and a certain amount of incidental faggotry, mortal illness and adultery, this is a curiously static tale. . . . Horgan is far too much the romantic humanist to open the windows and let in the furies.

There is, of course, a certain validity in this viewpoint. . . . [Horgan uses his protagonists'] characteristics for his own purposes but is otherwise almost totally reluctant to consider their implications. The truth is that he simply likes his people too much to view them with a true novelist's vision, and his eye is all too often dimmed by a tear. His teenagers don't talk like real people, they talk like someone's fondest memories, and at times his descriptive writing sacrifices the better part of clarity for the sake of lyricism. Everyone in the book will go to heaven when he dies.

Horgan's faults are serious but they are ones of affection and goodwill and perhaps not too much should be made of them. If his powers are limited, they are still sufficient to bring back what it was like to be seventeen on a summer night and high on moonlight.

L. J. Davis, "Fond Memories," in Book World— The Washington Post, *January 31, 1971, p. 10.*

WEBSTER SCHOTT

In this tender but tough work of art [*The Thin Mountain Air*], . . . Paul Horgan tells us his mind on love and lust, mercy and moral erosion. It is his declaration of humane alternatives: Feel, think, change.

The perspective is strange. A 70-year-old man of sensibility and passion (his biography corresponds to Paul Horgan's) looks back on his life at 20. As he tells his story of love and death, he senses that the moral design of everything ahead seemed to be forecast in the upheavals, breakdowns, and sensual tides that engulfed his mother and father while much of the United States was rocking to sleep with Calvin Coolidge.

We've met Richard, the narrator, at earlier ages in two previous Horgan novels, *Things As They Are* (1964) and *Everything to Live For* (1968). If they were about the loss of innocence, *The Thin Mountain Air* confirms the cost of that loss and extends its possibilities. Adultery, murder, and political crime are perversions of sex, rage, and aggrandizement.

Richard leaves college in the spring of around 1923 to help his father campaign for lieutenant governor of New York on a Democratic ticket headed by a florid judge once indicted for bribery. His father wears responsibility as if by divine right. He carries the election. Shortly after inauguration Richard's father collapses with a tubercular hemorrhage. Richard and his parents leave their Henry James mansion in Dorchester, which looks like Horgan's native Buffalo, for a sanitarium in Albuquerque and a society much sicker than anyone in a hospital.

Appearances continually split from reality in *The Thin Mountain Air*. The elegant, phlegmy society of Anglo-tuberculars in Albuquerque contains deceits and bigots whose empathy for one another is [frail]. . . . Richard's father draws information from a network of agents in the New York senate to nourish his fantasy of succeeding the corrupt governor who must be evicted from the state house. Richard himself, puzzled witness to "corruption . . . everywhere" and the "differences between visible style and invisible character," is drawn into a charade of love and a stupid murder for sex that becomes the dramatic center of the novel.

Richard too begins showing signs of T.B. and is sent by his father's physician for a month of toughening up on a sheep ranch owned by an ancient patrician. Don Elizario Wenzel has taken as his wife a beautiful girl 55 years his junior. She is angelic property, a statue to clothe in silk, and respectability to guard by night. It is only a matter of time before one of the sheep-dipper ranch hands tries to give Concha what Don Elizario barely remembers.

Handsome as a stud horse, radiating energy, Buz Rennison "shed good will with smiling indifference." The women of the world await him, and he is always ready, as he shows Richard during a weekend orgy in town. . . . Concha denies Buz's simple gonad universe. She loses, and Don Elizario dies in a trough of sheep dip. The catastrophe moves Richard further toward maturity. . . .

In the fiction of young men and women, emotions are at war with the way things are. In the fiction of older men and women, emotions have been brought to a truce. Inner negotiation stabilizes the drain of energy. Wanting more yields to taking less. While *The Thin Mountain Air* unwinds events like a reel of crises . . . , all the events are twice filtered. Once through the vivid imagination of a young man sensing possibilities; and

once again through the wisdom of a much older man knowing their consequences.

You can't read *The Thin Mountain Air* with indifference. Paul Horgan's language ripples with elegance. It also runs toward flowers. He assumes the attitude of a professor of life. Egos of an assertive nature may take offense, and probably should. Richard has one foot in Babylon and the other in the Century Club. I responded to Horgan's novel for familiar reasons. It is beautifully written and layered with thought. I was reading it as I turned 50. It told me about what I had learned so far and still had to come to terms with.

> Webster Schott, "One Foot in Babylon," in *Book World—The Washington Post*, *October 23, 1977, p. E6.*

ANNE FREMANTLE

[It] may well be, that a hundred years hence, what will seem [Horgan's] most valid and valuable works will be the three "Richard" novels [*Things as They Are, Everything to Live For,* and *The Thin Mountain Air*], a trilogy written, perhaps significantly, in the first person. These are accounts of three stages in one boy's growing up, partly in New York State, partly in the Southwest, the later venue of the third volume. In these three books he has recorded, brilliantly and lucidly, the "agony and ecstasy" of one young life in these United States during the first quarter of this century.

What, exactly, is his theme? Richard notes, in the very first paragraph of *Things as They Are* that: "the loss of innocence is a lifelong process—the wages of original sin." And the first pages describe Richard's deliberate drowning of a beloved kitten—his first conscious sin.

A second question to which all three novels address themselves is whether what you gain is worth what you lost? In all three novels the answer, described in a relentless sequence of events, is always perceived at the level of the perceiver, whether Richard is six, or seventeen, or twenty.

For example, Richard, going to school for the first time, is asked by the mother of the boy next door, John Burley, to accompany him. . . . The school, run by Catholic nuns, was only a few blocks away. But when the boys reach it, and the teacher is introducing herself to the class, the other boys, aware that John is retarded, start chanting rude remarks. . . . When John and Richard start home together, they are waylaid by five other boys who take John into a garage belonging to the rich parent of two of them, strip him and hose him down with cold water. Richard flees and fetches John's mother, who rescues him. But John dies of pneumonia as a result of his treatment.

Richard is sent for and given John's toys. . . . John's mother tells him, "We wonder if perhaps it is not better that God took him." Richard tells her, "You never sent for the doctor." She asks, angrily: "Don't you believe we loved him?" To which Richard replies, "Did you have him die?" Richard, clutching John's power boat, escapes as John's mother lunges at him. But his parents wonder why John's parents never again spoke to them or to Richard. . . . Richard has learned the power of truth. And Paul Horgan begins the next chapter with the comment: "All growth is the discovery of power—or powers."

In the second novel, *Everything to Live For,* Richard, now seventeen, goes to stay with some cousins who are immensely rich. Their only son, Max, is about to celebrate his twenty-first birthday at their annual mammoth Fourth of July party. . . . [Max] has lovely manners and a lovely girl-friend, Marietta, daughter of the local doctor. She tells Richard the reason for Max's mother's disability—she has an artificial hand. When Max was a child at a rustic birthday party for him, Max, disguised as a scarecrow, carried a big rake. Dancing a square dance, he reached out to change partners and dance with his mother, hitting her hard with the rake. Later she developed a tumor, and in a two-hour operation while Max waited at the hospital and Marietta's father was in attendance, her hand was amputated.

Max's father could not cope, retiring into his library. Marietta knows that Max, who adores his mother, feels guilty. . . . [He finally] drives his fancy sports car onto a railway crossing as the express arrives, and is killed. The night after the funeral Richard has his first sexual experience with Marietta, who next day dismisses him. He is shocked and anguished, having fallen in love. But she tells him: "We made love for Max as much as for each other last night. You will realize that later if you don't now." She has made him see he is a boy in his last year at school and she is, in effect, Max's widow.

Here the ache of growing up, of death and destruction, is mitigated by the basic goodness of all the protagonists. In the third volume, **The Thin Mountain Air,** Richard, who has been able to face the evil within himself as a child, meets evil all around. . . . [When his father develops tuberculosis], Richard opts to leave college and move with his parents to the Southwest, where the "mountain air" is recommended. Here he meets Don Elizario Wenzel, an old, rich man, and his lovely young wife. Richard seems thin, pulled down: the local doctor, a friend of Don Elizario, arranges for Richard to be sent for six weeks to work on Magdalena, the Wenzel ranch, where the annual sheep dipping requires the hiring of extra hands. Richard finds himself sharing a bunk with Buz, a foul-mouthed, totally valueless human being who (of course) instantly determines to "make" Wenzel's wife. (pp. 123-24)

The descriptions of working on the ranch, of the sheep dipping in the opaque, ill-smelling, yet necessary slime, day after day in the boiling sun, are superb. Buz, for the heck of it, tries to drown a sheep, forcing it under the poisonous dip, but not releasing it. Tom, the preacher-turned foreman, saves it, and tells Don Elizario to "fire the no-good runt." But instead, since Buz is needed to finish the dipping, Don Elizario ducks him in the slimy dip, then makes him apologize to Tom. Buz explains to Richard that he only apologized because he needed the money. A few days later, finding Don Elizario outside at night, Buz throws him backwards into the dip, where he drowns; Buz then goes to Don Elizario's house and violates his wife, who is a virgin. Since Buz's amulet is found in Don Elizario's dead hand, Buz is clearly guilty, and is eventually condemned to death, after trying to persuade Richard, who was guarding him, to let him go. . . .

The third question then seems to be: what does that really mean? What has Richard learned? That, as Oscar Wilde said "each man kills the thing he loves"? That "we are born in other's pain, and perish in our own"? That "Even the weariest river, winds somewhere safe to sea"? Etcetera, etcetera. The poets have tags for it, doubtless. But whatever the answer is, the reader has learned to relive Richard's growing pains, and what it meant, some of the time, perhaps all of the time, to be young between 1905 and 1925 in a happy, loving family in the USA. (p. 124)

Anne Fremantle, in a review of "The Thin Mountain Air," in Commonweal, *Vol. CV, No. 4, February 17, 1978, pp. 123-24.*

JONATHAN YARDLEY

Mexico Bay is a praiseworthy novel, but first a few words of praise for its author. . . . [Horgan's] books have won a respectable degree of popular success, but he has never achieved it at the price of lowered standards; in everything he writes he is at the least a solid craftsman, at the most a vivid stylist. Over the years he has received an array of honorary degrees and appointments, teaching positions at several prestigious colleges—and the high respect of his fellow writers. . . .

In **Mexico Bay** Horgan wanders a bit beyond his customary territory, taking in not merely the Southwest but also the nation's capital. The book is set, in large part, in the early days of America's entry into World War II, and it is my guess that in tone if not in actual incident it is heavily autobiographical; it has an air that is at once nostalgic and elegiac, as though Horgan were harking back to a lost time that has particular and profound meaning for him. In the best sense of the term it is an "old man's book," one that looks to the past with affection, pride and clarity.

It is primarily the story of two people. Howard Debler is a young historian who is researching a study of the Mexican War, with the hope of writing a book that will capture the human and intimate aspects of combat. Diana Macdonald is the daughter of a prominent newspaper publisher and the former wife of an equally prominent playwright, Jack Wentworth; now she is living on the Texas Gulf Coast with her lover, a talented and charismatic artist named Ben Ives.

Howard and Diana knew each other slightly before the war, when he spent several days examining her father's collection of Mexican War documents. Now, after the war, they meet again on the coast. . . . This new encounter triggers extensive flashbacks to the early years of marriage to the suave and self-important Wentworth, a marriage that evidently was one of mutual convenience and no passion. Soon after Pearl Harbor, in that hour of "the mammoth heavings of a new national spirit stirring alive," Wentworth maneuvered a place in the wartime government and headed for Washington. . . .

[The] Wentworths entertained official Washington and Jack acquired a reputation as a witty and gracious host. But when he attempted to arrange a friendship—an affair?—between Diana and Ben Ives, his tactics backfired; they ran off together, and he was left with a considerable embarrassment. Now, in the present, all are reaping the consequences of their actions. Diana, who has moved to the center of the novel, is caught up in a grand passion that eventually proves excessive; the tempestuous Ben commits a dreadful folly, and she is left to put the pieces of her life back together, to make "a choice between nothing and possibility."

The story of these people and their tangled lives is interesting and Horgan tells it with characteristic skill. But the real strength of **Mexico Bay** is its evocation of wartime Washington: the excitement of uniting behind a "just war," the fierce competition for social standing, the hectic and often mysterious comings and goings, the tension and the giddiness. Only in some of the novels of John P. Marquand—notably *So Little Time* and *B. F.'s Daughter*—is that vibrant time and place so keenly depicted. Horgan has a sharp sense of the city. . . .

Paul Horgan is not a flashy writer. His prose is quiet and modest, yet insistent; its rhythms move the reader through the story more forcibly than one realizes—past, in fact, a few excessive, but forgivably so, twists and turns of plot. *Mexico Bay* is not one of the larger works in his imposing canon, but it is unfailingly interesting and arresting.

> Jonathan Yardley, "Paul Horgan's Wartime Washington," in Book World—The Washington Post, February 21, 1982, p. 3.

JOHANNA KAPLAN

[Although it] is set in Washington, D.C., during World War II and is subtitled "A Novel of the Mid-Century," *Mexico Bay* suggests the ambiance of a much earlier time and the flavor of a really old-fashioned novel—the kind of book you might come across by chance on the shelves of a comfortable New England summer house. In this quality lie its strengths and its weaknesses. Picking up such a book in a heedless summer daze, you might let your eyes coast over its extremely civilized beginning pages, not immediately gripped by an urgent authorial voice; but then, gradually, you find you've given up your demanding disbelief and have given yourself over to the particular world—and particular conventions—of this very courtly, intelligent novel. *What happens to these characters?* you want to know, once Mr. Horgan has set them in motion. For, above all, though somewhat swaddled by less than vivid language and by distinctly mannered locutions, what this novel offers is a wonderful story.

Diana Macdonald, the focal point of the narrative, is the beautiful, oddly vulnerable, greatly adoring—and adored—daughter of a long-widowed, powerful upstate New York newspaper publisher. Their tie to one another is the most authentic and poignant emotional connection in the novel; the stilted, stiff-upper-lip conversations between father and daughter are always shadowed with a near-desperate, unexplained melancholy. One of Diana's earliest admirers in the novel is the young historian Howard Debler, but when Debler first sees her, Diana is already married—self-condemned into the icy, imprisoning arms of clever Jack Wentworth. Wentworth, a venal successful playwright of drawing-room comedies, is a kind of John Barrymore villain—a man you love to hate—and Mr. Horgan's portrait of Wentworth is wickedly funny. . . .

Wentworth is a monster of egotism, a nasty snob and cynic; he wants Diana only as an adornment, having previously evinced no interest in women (except as unwitting providers of risible material for his plays).

During World War II, Wentworth goes to Washington to work for a wartime information agency connected with the State Department, and in these precincts he flourishes. . . . Always a man to embrace surface, Wentworth considers it his unique patriotic duty to set up a "suitable establishment in Georgetown" "for in times of privation, drabness, personal losses, was it not all the more necessary to keep up the graces of life at home?" So all through the dull years of national peril, he stages perfect dinner parties in his Georgetown mansion, and Diana—witty, unhappy, enigmatic Diana—perseveres as his elegant hostess, exciting admiration and mild puzzlement in everyone.

At the war's end, Diana comes to excite more than admiration from Benjamin Ives, a brilliant, brooding young painter whom her husband has taken up and brought home. Jack Wentworth's attempts to insinuate Ben into the life of his household are deftly evoked by Mr. Horgan; so, too, are the ensuing scenes of subterranean and, later, actual violence. Finally, Diana and Ben run away together to a beach shack on the Gulf coast, but when Ben's unfortunate temperamental violence once again erupts, and this time with a tragic result, Diana must be rescued by her old prewar admirer, the morally coherent historian Howard Debler. One of the curious sidelights of this novel is its rather vehement positing of art against history. For art, in this view, is a monster: shallow, cruel and greedy when false (Jack Wentworth); seductive, guileless and unpredictably destructive when genuine (Ben Ives). History, on the other hand, in the person of Debler, is everything humane, decent and sensitive. If all this seems a bit odd coming from a novelist, then it must be recalled that Paul Horgan is also a prize-winning historian.

At the very end of the novel, Debler and Diana are married and happily settled "in one of those wonderful old California mansions, enormous and fancy" in Berkeley, where Debler is a full professor of history. This is comic only in the light of history; for the unfairly advantaged reader knows exactly what rough beast in baby shoes was already slouching toward Sproul Hall.

> Johanna Kaplan, "Diana and Admirers," in The New York Times Book Review, March 28, 1982, p. 15.

ROBERT O'CONNELL

Nearing 80 years of age, Mr. Horgan continues to display in his new novel, *Mexico Bay,* the compelling powers of a great novelist: ease and fluidity of narration, classically clear and simple description frequently laced with evocative imagery and incisive character delineation.

There are five major characters in the novel. The story's focal center and heroine is Diana Macdonald Wentworth, "so young and beautiful, so intelligent and friendly," who endures deep anguish as the wife and hostess of the charmingly deceitful Jack Wentworth and more agony as the live-in lover of the nomad painter, Ben Ives. Diana's father, George Macdonald, is a prosperous upstate New York newspaper publisher who devotes his life fully to his daughter when Diana's mother dies shortly after giving birth to her and from whom Diana first severs her ties. . . . Howard Debler, one of Diana's early admirers, is a young university historian who first makes her acquaintance while researching materials in her father's library for his book on the Mexican War of 1846-48. His loving care and compassion for Diana during her darkest hours after her tragic loss of Ben Ives moves her to discover in Debler her true deliverer.

The main settings of the novel's action shift back and forth between the urban social, political and military atmosphere of Washington, D.C., during World War II and shortly after, and the extensive, sometimes deserted, wind-creased dunes along the southwestern Texas coast of the Gulf of Mexico. . . . Since the heart of the story is about Diana Macdonald Wentworth's struggle to liberate herself from what ultimately becomes a painful facade of happy marital life with her husband, Jack Wentworth, the title of the novel—*Mexico Bay*—at first appears to be puzzling.

However, the suggestive power inherent in the novel's title gradually emerges. For the massive Gulf of Mexico acts as if it were some gigantic "character" profoundly human in thought and feeling. It experiences both deep serenity and fierce anguish in its vast waters. It vividly reflects Ben Ives in his drunken, brawling and lethal mood, ending in brutal murder and in headlong flight into the wrath of the storm-aroused seas of the Gulf. It placidly mirrors the joyous freedom and contentment of Diana, unfortunately short-lived, after she escapes from Jack Wentworth to a new, unfettered life with Ben Ives. "At the Gulf of Mexico," Horgan writes, "the sea itself seemed a vast meditation." (pp. 59-60)

Robert O'Connell, in a review of "Mexico Bay," in America, *Vol. 147, No. 3, July 31, 1982, pp. 59-60.*

ROSEMARY BOOTH

[*Mexico Bay*] is a novel dramatically constructed. In it, Horgan's characters move through scenes of south coastal Texas in the 1950s; back into Washington, D.C. during the Second World War years; and forth toward a California future, always with a sensed backdrop of century-old occurrences. The four main figures themselves bring different attitudes to bear on the events in which they take part. . . . (p. 538)

The characters are defined in their responses to the main event of the story—World War II—and also to its scenic analogue, Mexico Bay itself. . . . Like the bay, the war evokes a spectrum of reactions.

To [the playwright] Wentworth, the conflict is an opportunity for advancement and conviviality on a dutifully grand scale. . . .

Ives, as an artist, observes the war first-hand and portrays it directly in sketches of soldiers and others in the struggle over-

seas. The solitude of his stark vision disturbs the painter, who at times yearns to belong to "a working world alongside other men."

It is left to the scholar-writer Debler, who serves in the war, to span the gap between Wentworth's opportunism and Ives's visionary art. From the outset the historian knew that he "already had most of his facts. What he quested after . . . was the sense of men in a particular place." This search forms a framework for *Mexico Bay,* while Debler as protagonist resolves the contradictions posed by the other two men. Horgan depicts Debler's power as an ability to unite landscape with human activity, to enliven landscape with meaning. . . .

Diana Macdonald is a more anemic character than any of the men, depending on them for security and self-definition. She is, however, believable as a woman of the 1950s reared under fairly restrictive circumstances.

All of this analysis can be taken too seriously, of course. *Mexico Bay* is primarily a story, full of speed and energy as it spins to a finish. In addition to rich and precise details of setting, the novel is strewn with artful descriptions of people, as, for example, Howard Debler's mother, who kept a shoe box marked "Pieces of String Too Short to Use." . . . (p. 539)

Like Paul Horgan's other writings and like the great river of his study—the story runs swiftly and surely over its course to a full conclusion. A satisfying read. (p. 540)

Rosemary Booth, "Swift & Sure," in Commonweal, *Vol. CIX, No. 17, October 8, 1982, pp. 538-40.*

William (Joseph) Kennedy

1928-

American novelist, journalist, editor, scriptwriter, critic, and nonfiction writer.

An author of regionalist literature whose works examine universal themes, Kennedy is best known for his novel *Ironweed*, for which he received a Pulitzer Prize in fiction as well as a National Book Critics Circle Award. Drawing on his extensive knowledge of the history, idiom, and people of his hometown of Albany, New York, Kennedy depicts the outcasts, vagabonds, derelicts, and gangsters that he encountered in his childhood and, later, as a journalist. Kennedy often embellishes the stark realism of his settings with surrealistic events and imagery, prompting many critics to link his approach with magic realism, a technique in which fantastic events are presented within the scope of rational experience. Kennedy's focus on such concerns of the typical Irish Catholic novel as sin, suffering, and redemption has prompted critics to compare his works to those of novelist James T. Farrell.

Kennedy began his writing career during the early 1950s as a journalist for the *Albany Times-Union* before accepting editorial positions on various newspapers in Puerto Rico and Florida. Following several unsuccessful attempts to use San Juan as a fictional setting, Kennedy returned to the *Albany Times-Union* in the 1960s. Although nominated for a Pulitzer Prize for a controversial series of articles on Albany's slums that he wrote during this period, Kennedy realized that his hometown provided the natural setting and material for his fiction and abandoned his journalistic career. In his first novel, *The Ink Truck* (1969), Kennedy introduces the city of Albany from the perspective of a mentally unstable syndicated columnist whose unsuccessful efforts to disable a newspaper firm culminate in a desperate attempt to drain an ink truck of its cargo. Although this book initially received mixed reviews, Joel Conarroe described the 1984 reprint of *The Ink Truck* as indicative of "an energetic but as yet undisciplined artist working his way somewhat clumsily to the flexible style that would become his trademark, a style indebted to Joyce, Fitzgerald, and Beckett, yet very much his own."

In the 1970s Kennedy initiated a trilogy of novels set in Albany during the Depression that interweaves related characters and events in the manner of William Faulkner's works about the fictional region of Yoknapatawpha County. Although Kennedy garnered several positive reviews for *Legs* (1975) and *Billy Phelan's Greatest Game* (1978), the first two volumes of his triad, both books failed commercially. Kennedy's subsequent novel, *Ironweed* (1983), was rejected by thirteen publishers before Viking reconsidered its decision at the request of novelist Saul Bellow. Interceding with editor Corlies Smith, Bellow commented: "These Albany novels will be memorable, a distinguished group of books." This remark gave Smith the idea of marketing the books as Kennedy's "Albany Cycle" and prompted the reissue of *Legs* and *Billy Phelan's Greatest Game* upon the publication of *Ironweed*.

In *Legs*, Kennedy uses multiple viewpoints and a pastiche of styles to examine the gruesome facts and legends surrounding the life of Jack "Legs" Diamond, an actual Albany gangster.

In his six years of research, Kennedy discovered so many conflicting facts and myths that the novel finally emerged as a study of American responses to criminality. Although some reviewers objected to Kennedy's unsentimental acceptance of American crime and violence, others commended his suspenseful narrative control. Peter S. Prescott called *Legs* "a shimmering, witty story that [combines] fact and myth to prod at our national ambivalence toward celebrity criminals." *Billy Phelan's Greatest Game* is based on the actual 1933 kidnapping of the nephew of former Albany Mayor Dan O'Connell. This work centers on a gambler and hustler who must decide between preserving his street image and satisfying the demands of Albany's political figures by informing on the kidnappers. *Billy Phelan's Greatest Game* initially received mild reviews but was favorably reassessed by commentators following Kennedy's completion of his Albany Cycle.

With *Ironweed*, regarded by many critics as the outstanding work in the Albany Cycle, Kennedy garnered acclaim for his command of historicity and setting and his use of varied prose styles. Written in an ironic, elegiac mode, this novel compassionately yet unsentimentally relates the story of Billy Phelan's alcoholic vagrant father, Francis, a haunted but resilient man who returns to Albany after having accidentally dropped and killed his thirteen-day-old son twenty-two years earlier. Using language and imagery suggestive of classical myth, as well as allusions to James Joyce's epic novel *Ulysses* and the *Purgatorio* of Dante, Kennedy shifts from past to present and from brutal realism to lyrical fantasy as Francis confronts the ghosts of friends and family members. Like Ulysses, Francis visits the spiritual underworld and feels compelled by a sense of fate to face mortal dangers and the vengeful furies of his past in hopes of atoning for his guilt and shame. Robert Towers praised *Ironweed* as "a kind of fantasia on the strangeness of human destiny, on the mysterious ways in which a life can be transformed and sometimes redeemed."

Kennedy's next work, *O Albany!: An Urban Tapestry* (1983), combines a nostalgic memoir of his youth in Albany with a nonfiction examination of the city's neighborhoods, ethnic history, and Irish-American political dominance under Mayor Dan O'Connell. Christopher Lehmann-Haupt commented: "Even if one doesn't give a damn for Albany, it is always interesting to watch [Kennedy's] imagination at play in the city and its history, for one is witnessing the first steps in a novelist's creative process." In his recent novel, *Quinn's Book* (1988), Kennedy examines the history of Albany from the perspective of a young orphan who witnessed the progress of the Underground Railroad, the chaos of the Civil War, and the New York City draft riots of 1864. This picaresque work blends fact and fiction with prose styles ranging from melodrama to newspaper reportage to describe, among other fantastical events, communication with the spiritual world and the resuscitation of a dead woman through necrophilia. Although some critics regarded Kennedy's use of historical idiom as unconvincing, many applauded the novel's humor, originality, and witty, ironic style. T. Coraghessan Boyle asserted: "*Quinn's Book* is a revelation. Large-minded, ardent, alive on every page with its author's passion for his place and the events that made it, it is a novel to savor. One puts down *Quinn's Book* with a sigh, ever envying Mr. Kennedy his roots."

(See also *CLC*, Vols. 6, 28, 34; *Contemporary Authors*, Vols. 85-88; *Contemporary Authors New Revision Series*, Vol. 14; and *Dictionary of Literary Biography Yearbook: 1985*.)

CHRISTOPHER LEHMANN-HAUPT

[In *O Albany!*]—which is part memoir, part history and part celebration of the Empire State's frowzy capital, the second oldest chartered city (after New York) in the United States—Mr. Kennedy sounds every note that his multioctaved voice can reach.

He is by turns reverent and cynical, boastful and defensive, angry and sentimental, wistful, witty and proud—so proud of Albany's course along the mainstream of American history that he wonders, as residents of Albany have apparently done for generations, whether John Wilkes Booth and President Lincoln might have made eye contact on a day in February 1861 when they were both in town. . . .

Mr. Kennedy, who once tried to leave Albany, but quickly saw the error of his ways, seems to know everything there is to know about the city. . . . He knows that the first living thing that passed through the newly mingling waters of the Erie Canal and the Hudson River on Sept. 25, 1823, was a three foot eel, which was skinned and exhibited in Albany's Lyceum of Natural History.

He knows the neighborhoods and the ethnic history of Albany, and he probably knows more than anyone alive about who might have killed the gangster Jack (Legs) Diamond in an Albany rooming house on Dec. 18, 1931. He knows Albany's literary history: Melville was schooled there, but left. Henry James spent his childhood there, but left. Bret Harte was born there and left almost immediately. Dickens read from *A Christmas Carol* there, and left. . . .

Does Mr. Kennedy know—and tell—more about his Albany than a reader wants to hear? A sign or two might seem to point that way. . . . There are occasional memories of childhood friends that only other childhood friends may want to share.

But his passion for important detail and his eloquence nearly always compensate. . . .

Even more absorbing than the detail and the enthusiasm is the raw material of Mr. Kennedy's fiction, present on every page. Even if one doesn't give a damn for Albany, it is always interesting to watch the author's imagination at play in the city and its history, for one is witnessing the first steps in a novelist's creative process.

A worn-out old joke has it that a commentator on American cities once said, "Now, you take Albany, New York." To which his listener responds, "No, *you* take Albany, New York!" William Kennedy takes Albany, New York, and makes of its character, its people and its history something that all of us can take.

> *Christopher Lehmann-Haupt, in a review of "O Albany!" in* The New York Times, *December 23, 1983, p. C24.*

THOMAS FLEMING

In *O Albany!* William Kennedy sets out to prove his native city is "centered squarely in the American and human continuum." There is no question that he succeeds marvelously. So well, in fact, that I could have sworn at various times I was reading a chapter in an unpublished treasure I happen to possess, *The Autobiography of Frank Hague*, or a slightly modernized version of that 1903 classic by Alfred Henry Lewis, *The Boss: And How He Came to Rule New York*.

That opus contains the rules that all the bosses, including Albany's satrap, Daniel Peter O'Connell, faithfully obeyed to perpetuate their unholy reigns—"Never interfere with people's beer . . . give 'em clean streets. . . . Kape the street free of ba-ad people.". . .

[Mr. Kennedy] knows Irish-American machine politics was not funny, although there were lots of laughs. In *Billy Phelan's Greatest Game*, the second of his three very good Albany novels, a newspaperman named Martin Daugherty realized he was a powerless Albany Irishman, a condition that "ate holes in his forebearance." He saw himself as a "martyr to the hypocritical hand-shakers . . . the lace curtain Grundys and the cut glass banker thieves who marked his city lousy." He saw Albany as "One of the ten bottom places of the earth."

In *O Albany!* Mr. Kennedy, a former newspaperman, has repaired those punctures in his forbearance. He writes about his native city with a nice blend of nostalgia and serious history. He makes no attempt to conceal Albany's iniquity. On the contrary, he emphasizes what makes his city unique—the amazing durability of its Irish-American political machine. For 64 incredible years, from 1919 to 1983, Albany remained firmly in the grasp of Dan O'Connell and his smiling WASP front man, Mayor Erastus Corning. (p. 11)

Mr. Kennedy ends his personal reminiscence of growing up in North Albany by describing how he walked out of church during "narrowback" sermons, refused to sing "Too-ra-loo-ra-loo-ral" and registered to vote as an independent. Eventually he discovered the only thing he could not shed was his Irishness, although two trips to Ireland and one visit to the Ancient Order of Hibernians' St. Patrick's Night Dance convinced him to abandon trying to write about the Emerald Isle.

This remnant of Irishness has led Mr. Kennedy into history and a fresh view of American reality. In many ways, *O Albany!* is his acceptance of the power of the past. This vision has carried him far beyond the bitter naturalism of James T. Farrell's *Studs Lonigan,* the moral anguish of Harry Sylvester's *Moon Gaffney,* the ambivalence displayed by Edwin O'Connor in his comparatively neglected but superior novel, *The Edge of Sadness.* You can almost hear William Butler Yeats chanting in Mr. Kennedy's ear, "Cast a cold eye / On life, on death." Except that his eye is anything but cold. He has given a lot of thought to death; he has also noticed life's habit of dancing on graves.

For example, in *O Albany!* his recounting of the joint careers of Dan O'Connell and Erastus Corning ends with two funerals, each reported in careful detail. Francis Phelan, the drunken-bum hero of Mr. Kennedy's third novel *Ironweed,* a man who spends a lot of time talking to the dead, would have no difficulty getting the point of this denouement of six decades of ruthless chicanery. . . .

With its nostalgic recollections of vanished neighborhoods bearing names like Gander Bay, Pluck Hollow and Cabbagetown, *O Albany!* also reminds us how much of life is beyond or above politics. It recalls how many incarnations Albany and the rest of America have undergone in the 370 years since a handful of Dutchmen sailed up the Hudson to open a fur trading post and ended with a city on several hills. So many flourishings, fadings, deaths and rebirths. Albany has been counted out a dozen times—with the disappearance of the fur trade, the waning of the Erie Canal, the collapse of the railroads, the evisceration of its downtown section. Each time it has returned to improbable life. . . .

Downtown Albany now is strutting again, thanks to a new generation that has grown weary of suburban boredom and expensive gasoline. . . .

Mr. Kennedy freely admits that this latest resurrection may not prove durable or even genuine. But you have the feeling that another one, even more improbable, is sure to be around the corner. Maybe that is why you come away from this book's fascinating view of the American experience, the human experience, feeling hopeful. You may not like it all, but there is something here for everybody. (p. 12)

> Thomas Fleming, *"A City and Its Machine,"* in The New York Times Book Review, *January 1, 1984, pp. 11-12.*

MICHAEL E. PARRISH

[In *O Albany!: An Urban Tapestry,* Kennedy] has produced a splendid social history . . . and a compelling urban history that transcends the uncritical veneration so common to the old genre. Utilizing extensive oral interviews, historical archives, news-papers and a sure, personal grasp of Albany's many neighborhoods and peoples—past and present—Kennedy has written a book distinguished by intellectual depth and a vibrant prose style. His is a rich feast that bubbles with the humor, nobility and pathos of the men and women who lived, worked and played in New York's capital city from the 17th Century to the present.

O Albany! is the story of how a city and its diverse people survived tumultuous economic and social changes from the age of the sailing ship and flintlock rifle to the computer chip. . . . Somehow, by virtue of its political influence and the creativity of its citizens, the city managed to absorb assorted economic shocks and to remain an important center of trade, administration and intellectual life. Each turn of the economic wheel left a deep impression upon Albany's landscape and mentality, which Kennedy recounts with telling statistics and memorable anecdotes.

Like other cities of the Northeast, Albany also became a stage for acting out America's central social drama in the years from 1840 to 1960—the integration of millions of foreign-born immigrants and Southern blacks, most of them pre-industrial rural people, into a modern, urban political economy. Each of Albany's immigrant groups . . . faced the resentments and fear of those who came before them; each fought to achieve dignity and security through ethnic solidarity, and each left an important legacy to the city's political and social history.

Kennedy is at his best evoking the rich flavor of distinctive neighborhoods, rituals and beliefs. The Young Men's Italian Assn., for example, attempted to eradicate the negative image of the organ grinder as Italian beggar by pushing legislation through the state legislature to prohibit anyone from publicly playing any "street piano, hand organ or music box unless such person is incapacitated for labor." . . .

Kennedy has written a fascinating account of a most durable political machine: Through a combination of ethnic-religious piety, brazen tax-assessment and iron discipline, the Dan O'Connell organization controlled Albany from the Roaring '20s to the late 1970s. . . .

From the days of Al Smith to Hugh Carey, New York politicians and those aspiring to national office paid tribute to the Albany machine. "Did Harry Truman really say you could have the door-knobs off the White House?" a reporter once asked O'Connell. "No," replied the venerable Boss of Albany, "but he was friendly. Very."

> Michael E. Parrish, *"Immigration to an Ongoing Urbanity,"* in Los Angeles Times Book Review, *January 29, 1984, p. 2.*

GEORGE W. HUNT

William Kennedy's *O Albany!: An Urban Tapestry* is a grandly entertaining book about a seemingly hopeless subject: Albany, N.Y., source of endless inspirations—along with Bayonne and Burbank—for Johnny Carson's writers. William Kennedy . . . tells vivid tales of his native town with humor and enthusiasm.

The subtitle "An Urban Tapestry" describes the book's structure. Kennedy interweaves a personal memoir of an Irish-Catholic boyhood and a tour of the city's ethnic neighborhoods with an engaging history of Albany's prominent place in America's past and present. . . .

Events like the completion of the Erie Canal, the romance of Union Station and the Twentieth Century Limited, rum running and its offshoots in Prohibition, the chicaneries connected with Nelson Rockefeller's grandiose scheme to construct the Capitol Mall . . . provide the shifting backdrops to Kennedy's drama. But his novelist's eye and ear are delightfully alert to the emblematic anecdote of days gone by. . . .

[The] most vivid portraits are those drawn of Mayor Erastus Corning (many Albanians thought his first name was Mayor) and of Boss Dan O'Connell. . . . (p. 189)

In addition to these endearing charms, *O Albany* is a refresher course for anyone who grew up in the 1940's and 1950's and retains nostalgic sentiment for urban grittiness and innumerable neighborhood characters, as well as fond memories of Swing music, soda joints and strait-laced girls. . . . Do you remember when your neighborhood boasted about having a look-alike of first Bing Crosby and then Frank Sinatra? If so, this is just the book for you. (p. 190)

> George W. Hunt, "William Kennedy's Albany," in America, *Vol. 150, No. 10, March 17, 1984, pp. 189-90.*

GEORGE W. HUNT

[Kennedy's] *Ironweed* gathered exceptionally enthusiastic reviews, has already won the Pulitzer Prize, the prestigious National Critics Circle Award for Fiction and as "novel of the year" is likely to sweep the field of fictional awards. . . .

What is all the fuss about? To answer that question, one must begin at the end, with *Ironweed.* The action of the novel takes place within the lower regions of a Depression-beset Albany, and its central character is Francis Phelan, the "ironweed" of the title, a name that "refers to the toughness of its stem" and also its resiliency. Francis, an ex-big league third baseman, has finally returned to the hometown he left 22 years ago because of his shame and guilt at having accidentally dropped and killed his 13-day-old infant son in April 1916. Francis, by most definitions, including his own, has been and is a bum and, as Kennedy's epigraph chosen from Dante's *Purgatorio* suggests, the hobo world he inhabits is hellish, and yet it is also potentially purgatorial and so eerily purifying. Though this bleak setting first strikes the reader as relentlessly somber, Kennedy's compassion, ironic wit and resourceful style enliven *Ironweed* and eventually elevate everything of apparent lowly circumstance.

Catholics, alert to the liturgical cycle and doctrinal belief that subtly shape much of the story, should appreciate particularly the complex optimism that is the novel's subtext. The action begins on Halloween 1938, "the unruly night when grace is always in short supply and the old and the new dead walk abroad in the land," and reaches a climax on All Saints' Day. . . . The novel ends on All Souls Day, and the events described correspond with that day's liturgy wherein the story of Job is joined with St. Paul's challenge to death ("Where is thy sting?") and with Jesus' promise of a final resurrection in John's Gospel. Throughout, Kennedy artfully exploits dramatically what this liturgical cycle enacts: The Catholic belief in the communion of saints, the conviction that the living are linked spiritually and truly with all the dead, with those suffering still and those successful, and that their mysterious unity and mutuality transcend the limits of heaven and earth.

The most impressive feature in *Ironweed* is the ease with which Kennedy moves between the realms of the living and of the dead, and from brutal realism to lyrical and symbolic resonances. The novel opens in a cemetery where Francis visits the dead in his family as they simultaneously visit with him, and such mutual encounters—generally unasked for—continue throughout the story. The dead here are far more than hallucinatory visitors; instead, they are vivid characters themselves, observers with keen perceptions, who talk with a peculiar serenity about the passing show and yet, if angelic, impose obligations of expiation on Francis, and if not quite angelic yet, are accusatory in a relaxed way. . . . (p. 374)

Kennedy's skill is especially impressive in that he so constructs the reader's point of entry that such intrusions do not seem stark or bizarre or oddly fanciful but natural, even neighborly. The reason is that his artistic control throughout is so deft that, as novelist George Stade noted, "the words do not feel as though they were spoken (or written) by anyone. They feel, rather, as though they somehow emanated from the events they described, as though the events were becoming conscious of themselves as they occurred." In a fine novel every episode should be surprising and yet not seem so. This artistic aim is present everywhere in *Ironweed* but is especially evident in the sensitively wrought chapter where Francis screws up his courage to visit his old home and the wife whom he still dearly loves and whom he abandoned in confusion so long ago. The scene is memorable for the restraint of its telling and for the affection and realism and complexity of feeling it captures. Honesty is Francis's most cherished virtue, and its artistic equivalent is obviously the same for his creator.

Ironweed is distinctively Irish in its emotional rhythms and attitudes. . . . But to an even greater degree, it is also distinctively American, finally betraying that brash buoyancy and inexplicable hopefulness that characterize so much of our literature. . . . (pp. 374-75)

By a transformative updating [Kennedy's] Albany trilogy reexplores the "classical" themes in American literature: From Emerson's accent on self-reliance to that of Whitman's innocent orphan, ever "on the road" in simultaneous search for a self and in quest of a father, who remains all the while prey to the conflicting impulses of memory and hope, freedom and commitment. All three of Kennedy's central characters are misfits in urban society, not so unlike Melville's Ishmael and Twain's Huck Finn and their offshoots, "running, finally, in a quest for pure flight as a fulfilling mannerism of the spirit." Legs Diamond, to all appearances, is just a rogue and an outlaw, but from the perspective of *Legs*'s rather jaded narrator, his defense lawyer Marcus Gorman, Legs is a picaresque saint and but another version of "the Great" Jay Gatsby. . . .

Few authors could successfully navigate the shoals of such potentially windy sentiment, but Kennedy's keen ironies allow Legs's story to sail free toward mythic entertainment, reminiscent of a rich American archetypal tradition that for some time has gone untapped. Billy Phelan, the hero of *Billy Phelan's Greatest Game,* is a more peaceable Legs Diamond, a boyish adult who is honorable and compassionate and "who accepted the rules and played by them, but who also played above them." Like *Legs,* Billy's tale is narrated in vivid, cinematic fashion; it should be a gripping movie, replete as it is with crisp, funny Runyonesque dialogue, a host of eccentric characters, clever surprises and farcical turns that pivot around the complications consequent upon the kidnapping of the nephew of Albany's powerful political boss. Billy, the oldest son of "ironweed" Francis Phelan, is both a gamester and a sportsman, and his jaunty expertise in bowling, pool, poker and betting is rooted in a world of gamy saloons, dusky billiard halls, murky gambling dens and the city's mean streets. In this romantically tinged, realistic world, comedy and tragedy not only collide, they intermingle; and none of these characters nor any of us readers would expect otherwise.

William Kennedy has made his Albany a wonderful place to visit and dwell in imaginatively, and he has populated it with friends and other kinds who keep popping in unannounced throughout his trilogy. A fine accomplishment and great fun too: Who could ask for anything more from any writer, Celtic or no? (p. 375)

George W. Hunt, "William Kennedy's Albany Trilogy," in America, Vol. 150, No. 19, May 19, 1984, pp. 373-75.

TERENCE WINCH

Any student of 20th-century American fiction has heard of the Southern novel, the black novel, the Jewish novel. But in spite of its long and illustrious history, almost no critical attention has been paid to the Irish-American novel. . . .

This void does not seem especially significant until you begin to catalogue some of those writers whose work owes something to their Irish-American identity: James T. Farrell, Scott Fitzgerald, Eugene O'Neill, Mary McCarthy, Flannery O'Connor (though she denied it), [and many more]. . . .

William Kennedy's work has been extremely well-received by the literary mainstream and no doubt few readers have thought of him as specifically Irish-American since, to a great extent, the existence of this particular tradition in our fiction is unknown and as yet undefined in any systematic way. Yet it is reasonably safe to say that not since James T. Farrell has an American writer so successfully translated his Irishness into a major work of American fiction.

That work consists of three novels that have come to be known as The Albany Novels. . . . Unlike Farrell's three Studs Lonigan books, Kennedy's novels do not comprise a seamless narrative. Each novel is distinct and independent, though all of them are connected.

The novels are set primarily in Albany in the 1930s. That city is very much a microcosm for the Irish in America. By the late 19th century, "with the help of Jesus, and by dint of numbering forty per cent of the city's population," [as Kennedy remarks in *Billy Phelan's Greatest Game*], the Irish had replaced "the Dutch and Yankees" as the rulers of the city. But in spite of political power, Irish-American consciousness has been, and still is, dominated by a tension between the demands of rural Ireland and urban America. . . .

The Irish may run the city, but "Irish Catholic" and "nigger" are the "Same thing to some people." The struggles and yearnings of the Irish in America have often required the use of alcohol, Catholicism, violence, and humor. And Kennedy's Irish-America is no exception.

Legs is compulsive reading. The life of Legs Diamond is the story of a one-man crime wave pouring out in prose that never lets up. Violence, love, sex, and comedy are all part of the story and Kennedy's versatility proves more than capable of telling it all.

One of the notable features of *Legs* is that it is, in some ways, an unconventional, innovative work (scenes are foretold before they are depicted, points of view shift continuously, narrative voices are multiple and require a large repertoire of language styles, and the overall tone of the book segues back and forth between realistic and metaphoric modes), while at the same time its powerful narrative momentum and the vivid writing brought to all its parts make *Legs* as much a page-turner as *The Great Train Robbery*.

You come away from *Legs* feeling you know more about this "Philadelphia mick" than any biography could ever tell you. Jack Diamond is not only a flashy, dramatic character in Kennedy's novel; he also takes on a heavy symbolic burden. But Kennedy manages to preserve the tension between Jack the real-life, crazed, violent criminal, and Jack "the grand confusion of our lives," the magical product of our "collective imagination." Jack never becomes a vague abstraction, an allegorical figure stripped of his particulars. He is a contradiction, sometimes larger, sometimes smaller, than life: "accuracy about Jack wasn't possible." . . .

In both *Legs* and *Billy Phelan's Greatest Game*, a somewhat cynical, detached and even envious observer is played off against the magical man of action. In *Legs*, Marcus is foil to Jack. In *Billy Phelan*, Martin Daugherty, world-weary fifty-year-old reporter, plays the passive, urbane counterpart to Bill Phelan, a tough, thirty-one-year-old ex-street kid. These two pairings-off serve Kennedy's interest in balance; that interest quite possibly has its source in the split values of Irish-America mentioned earlier. . . .

Billy Phelan's Greatest Game owes more to the hardboiled school of detective literature than the other two Albany novels, although Kennedy's impressionist and symbolist tendencies are still in evidence. The city of Albany and the rough terrain of the working-class Irish are more prominent features of this second novel. Once again, balance is crucial as the novel seesaws between Martin [and Billy]. . . . All appetites for serious fiction and for the classic "good read" are satisfied: the kidnapping of a politician's son, and Billy's quest to salvage his reputation for integrity on the streets of Albany, give the novel its fast pace and suspense; while Martin Daugherty's more contemplative desire "to love oneself and one's opposite" provides a counterweight to Billy's adventures.

Billy's fifty-eight-year-old father Francis is the hero of *Ironweed*. Francis, once a major league fielder, is guilt-ridden and haunted by the ghosts of his "lifetime of corpses." . . . When the novel opens, Francis has returned to Albany after more than twenty years as an itinerant bum on the run from his past. His return to Albany forces him to choose between his two lives: the wife and children he left long ago and the new wife and friends he has accumulated during his years on the bum. Francis' divided loyalties, and his life in exile, are emblematic of Irish-American history.

But with *Ironweed*, Kennedy abandons the contrast between active and passive characters. There is no narrative dialectic as in the first two books. This novel is all Francis Phelan, with no detached onlooker to balance his vision of life. Francis carries on dialogues with the dead as much as with the living, and with himself most of all. In fact, Kennedy gets more inside Francis' interior life than he does with any of his other characters.

And that is part of the problem with this novel. It is too much a one-character book, without the balance that makes *Legs* and

Billy Phelan so successful. . . . *Ironweed* is also considerably more contrived than the other novels. It opens, e.g., on Halloween "when spooks make house calls and the dead walked abroad," and the relentless use of the dead as characters becomes tiresome. None of which is to say that *Ironweed* is a terrible novel. Although the book lacks the skillful structural complexity of its predecessors, Kennedy's portrait of Francis and the hobo underworld is extraordinarily vivid.

Terence Winch, "The Albany Novels," in The American Book Review, *Vol. 7, No. 4, May-June, 1985, p. 19.*

LOXLEY F. NICHOLS

The Ink Truck, Kennedy's most atypical work, contains many of the elements that later became his trademark. In this first novel we are introduced, obliquely, to Albany, New York, and are initiated into a predominantly Irish(-American) world of unsuspected heroes, lost causes, and errant pookas. Here we see Kennedy's first attempts to re-establish twentieth-century man as a social being, inclined to congregate in coffeehouses and taverns. And through an outrageous protagonist we become aware of Kennedy's understanding of character as an attribute of style, and the relevance of articles of clothing as extensions of one's anatomy, as means of self-creation, as signs of kinetic existence. . . . (p. 46)

Such sentiments of self-affirmation abound in one form or another throughout Kennedy's work, but they engage his undivided attention in his second novel, *Legs,* a fictional account of nonfictional gangster Jack (Legs) Diamond. In his effort to evoke the spirit of the arch-criminal, Kennedy depicts a murdered Diamond doubting his own mortality. And indeed in death Diamond does not stop being, he merely undergoes a "sartorial mutation" of sorts and "goes away," pulled sluggishly by an oversoul that seems to have come "on little cat feet." . . . (pp. 46-7)

In staking out the dimensions of his fictional world by limiting it to a literal, familiar place, Kennedy gains freedom through restriction. For this second novel, Albany not only gives Kennedy place, but it also gives him subject, and through subject he acquires time, the 1930s, a period to which he has adhered in his last two novels. By using Albany, a place already created, and Diamond, a story already told, Kennedy is relieved of the burden of certain rudimentary aspects of invention and is free to concentrate on redefining preconditioned responses to known stimuli.

In *Legs,* however, Kennedy's goal is greater than his accomplishment. Jack Diamond takes three pages to die, and during those three pages he is more alive than in the preceding three hundred. The story is encumbered and finally collapses under a weight of inconsequential details and innumerable dimly defined characters. Perhaps Kennedy asks too much from the historical figure, or maybe he is too intent on objectifying the cool distance of a ruthless killer. Whatever the mechanical malfunction, the effect is that Diamond never captivates the reader the way Kennedy means for him to.

Written when Kennedy was fifty years old, *Billy Phelan's Greatest Game* marks a transition. In *Legs* a single character acts upon and thus creates Albany, whereas in this third novel the place itself molds and ultimately identifies the characters. As in *Legs* its plot is built on an excerpt of Albany's history, but here the nonfictional element provides context rather than focus, and

instead of one central figure there are two. Billy Phelan, a "kid" of thirty, a gambler and a sport, single and untested, is balanced against Martin Daugherty, a fifty-year-old newspaperman, a husband and father, a man weighted with responsibility.

While *Legs* is often murky, meandering, and gruesome, *Billy Phelan* is lucid, controlled, and humorous. . . . Kennedy's grasp of the male world of pool halls and bowling alleys, so apparent in this novel, seems only natural considering what he afterward wrote about an early sojourn away from Albany: "I was incapable of writing a transient's novel about Puerto Rico . . . I cared more about the shape of the ball returns in the Knights of Columbus alleys in Albany. For I remembered those ball returns. They were artifacts out of a significant past." Kennedy's ability to compose vivid portraits and taut, witty dialogue does not extend to female characters, however. Billy's assignation with his girlfriend is off-key, trite. The love scene between Martin and his father's former mistress with its contrived echoes of Baudelaire ("Hypocrite! Lecher! My Boy!") is only slightly more successful. Also, while Billy cuts a flashier figure, Martin, who has the greater potential for sustaining our interest, suffers from the divided attention.

This dichotomy of focus is resolved in *Ironweed,* a book devoted to Billy's hobo father, Francis, who in 1938 is approximately the same age as the author in 1983. While Martin attempts to expiate past sin by physically repeating the transgression, Francis reenacts his past by communing with ghosts who lead him on a Dantean tour of his own underworld.

Ironweed's commingling of past and present, dream and reality, is expertly orchestrated. Kennedy's virtuosity of technique is well illustrated in a scene in a skid-row bar when Francis's companion is invited to sing for the crowd. The magic of the moment . . . ultimately descends to reality—"Some odd-looking people were applauding politely, but others were staring at her with sullen faces"—in a manner reminiscent of Bierce's "An Occurrence at Owl Creek Bridge." Such double visions and the tentativeness of the book's ending might also call to mind a writer like John Fowles. In Fowles, however, the ploy is an authorial intrusion; in Kennedy it emanates from the character's own perception.

Mythical allusions are readily discernible in *Ironweed.* There are the names Helen and the Ulysses-sounding Aloysius (Francis's middle name). And it happens that after a twenty(-two)-year absence, Francis returns home to find a grown son, a faithful wife, and friendly dog. Such details, plus Kennedy's exploration of the father-son relationship, immediately identify him with Joyce; however, placing Kennedy in a *tradition* of writers like Joyce and Proust and Faulkner is ultimately more to the point. His imagination, like theirs, is firmly planted in native soil. His books, like theirs, are filled with "presences" often felt more than seen. And he, too, writes "family" novels, on-going histories of characters that extend from one book to another. In addition to these and other thematic similarities, Kennedy's use of stream of consciousness, interior monologue, and development by association links him to these writers. For example, the memories conjured by the sight of a "clean, soft-colored, white-on-white shirt" recalls Proust's account in *Swann's Way* of the past revived by a *madeleine* dipped in tea.

The pervasive vitality of the past lies at the heart of *O Albany.* Though incidental in *The Ink Truck,* place becomes increasingly prominent in each book until it becomes the subject itself. In concluding this history/memoir, Kennedy demonstrates that talk is indeed ''an animating principle'' and that nothing is ever past, nothing ever ends. An example of the on-going dynamism of story-telling also frames ''North Albany: Crucible for a Childhood.'' In this lyrically fluid chapter, twenty pages in a single paragraph, Kennedy moves by association through the picture-book pages of memeory transforming neighborhood into paradise, reminiscence into myth. . . . Kennedy's personal search is fulfilled in this book, and in this section particularly. North Albany, a place where ''You were never solitary for very long anyway, for it was an Irish neighborhood that believed in overpopulation,'' is Kennedy's antidote to the existential void. Here Kennedy, a writer who is by turns eloquent, poetic, slangy, and schmaltzy, a writer who favors words like ''nifty,'' who occasionally lapses into phrases like ''a terrific neighbor, with a marvelous but sad smile,'' comes to terms with the ''mawkish essences of my life: the syrupy, sappy sentimentality that chokes in my gorge and makes me laugh and weep against my will, against all that is intelligent and genuinely holy.'' (pp. 47-8)

Whatever Kennedy's weaknesses, we have to admit that his joyous, whole-hearted acceptance of the contradictions of his nature is the triumph of a writer of substance and a man of singular style. (p. 48)

Loxley F. Nichols, ''William Kennedy Comes of Age,'' in National Review, *New York, Vol. XXXVII, August 9, 1985, pp. 46-8.*

PETER P. CLARKE

William Kennedy's *Ironweed* must be seen against a protean mythological background. In the patterns of his journeys and in the nature of his struggle, Kennedy's protagonist, Francis Phelan, resembles a number of familiar figures from classical myth. Most obviously, Francis is a wanderer like Odysseus and Aeneas, and a long wanderer at that: he has been on the bum for twenty-two years. Like Odysseus, he returns to his faithful wife after long absence; like Odysseus in Book XI of the *Odyssey* and Aeneas in Book VI of the *Aeneid,* he visits the underworld and talks to the dead; like both heroes, Francis faces mortal danger and embraces tempting women; like both, he is pursued by relentless, vengeful deities or spirits; and like Aeneas, Francis is compelled by a strong sense of fate. Moreover, Francis' roots seem to reach to Menelaus and perhaps even to Agamemnon. He is like Menelaus in his relationship with his own Helen, particularly when Helen is lost and Francis feels that he must find her. . . . And he may resemble Menelaus' older brother Agamemnon in one important way: it was Agamemnon's sacrifice of his daughter Iphigenia which propelled him to Troy and which sealed his tragic fate just as it was Francis, ''killing'' of his son Gerald which launches him on his apparently degenerate adventure and which prevents him from seeing himself as anything but a bum.

This association between Francis Phelan and classical heroes is reinforced by Kennedy's use of language and imagery drawn from and suggestive of classical myth. . . . Katrina is ''This goddess, who had walked naked across his life.'' Francis is not only Katrina's ''beautiful Adonis of Arbor Hill,'' but also a ''warrior'' facing a ''phalanx of men in Legionnaire's caps.'' (pp. 167-68)

[The] general importance of myth in the novel has not gone unnoticed by critics and reviewers, who often resort to the language of epic and myth to describe Kennedy's work. One reviewer refers to Francis as a ''ragged hero,'' another [for

Publishers Weekly] mentions his ''quest'' [see *CLC,* Vol. 28], and a third [George Stade] discusses *Ironweed* under the heading of ''mythifications'' [see *CLC,* Vol. 34]. This last critic also notes that Annie is ''a disappointed Penelope'' and compares the novel to Sophocles' *Oedipus at Colonus.* Even the comments on the book's dust jacket connect the novel and myth. Alison Lurie is cited as observing that ''*Ironweed . . .* gives an almost mythic dimension to the final wanderings of two completely down-and-out characters,'' and Saul Bellow is quoted as remarking that ''Francis is also a traditional champion . . . a type out of Icelandic or Irish epic.'' The general mythological background of *Ironweed* is clear, and the general function of that background is clear as well. Kennedy's use of myth serves both to elevate apparently degraded bums to heroic stature and to transform the simple, desperate search for a place to sleep—for a home—into an adventure equal to the greatest quests of all time.

However, Kennedy does not confine his use of myth to the general associations established thus far. He makes his most specific mythological connections in characterizing the women of the novel and in indicating the nature of their relationships to Francis Phelan. Most of the women in *Ironweed* are at one point or another depicted as goddesses. We have already seen that Kennedy refers to Katrina as a naked goddess and to Francis as her Adonis. Herein lies the key to all the many goddesses in the book, for if Francis is Adonis, not only is Katrina Aphrodite or Venus, but several other mythological pairs are invoked as well. The story of Venus and Adonis is a ''rendition of a recurrent theme: the Great Mother and her lover who dies as vegetation and comes back to life again.'' Remember that Francis is ironweed, tough stemmed vegetation that struggles back to life despite regular attempts to destroy it. Moreover, Venus and Adonis are also Cybele, the great Phrygian Earth Mother, and her lover Attis. . . . Clearly, Francis is driven by the earth mothers of the novel: by Kathryn, his mother; by Katrina, his neighbor; by Helen, his bum lover; by Clara, Jack's ''crazy bitch''; and by Annie, Francis' wife, not necessarily as she really is, but as Francis has assumed her to be—a hard woman who has never forgiven him for letting Gerald slip to his death. And we know that Francis, if not castrated, is impotent and that he willfully cuckolds himself by taking Helen to sleep in Finny's car.

There is ample evidence in the novel that its women can be seen as variations of the goddesses whom Robert Graves subsumes under the name of the White Goddess. Kathryn, for instance, is ''Queen Mama'' and a perpetual virgin like Artemis. . . . In fact, the name Kathryn or Katherine means pure or unsullied. The late October moon (associated with Artemis and the White Goddess) presides over the landscape of the novel, and, through their association with the moon, Clara and Katrina are connected with Artemis as well. (pp. 168-69)

Despite her obvious sensuality, Katrina is disturbingly like Artemis, too. . . . Kennedy leaves no doubt of the dangers posed by such a goddess. To her poet-husband, Katrina is ''a caged woman ripping apart the body of a living rabbit with her teeth.'' . . . Is it Katrina who destroys Francis by making him a wino, a bum? Certainly, Francis is in the presence of a powerful creature, destructive and creative of life at the same time. . . . (p. 169)

The image of Clara on the chamber pot is striking and disturbing. When Helen observes, ''She's got the runs,'' Clara shoots back, ''I'll tell people what I got.'' Her diarrhea and her bitchery foul the atmosphere and ruin Francis and Helen's chance for food and shelter. . . . Clara is moon-goddess, but she is also something more. It is tempting to see her as a Harpy and Francis once more as Aeneas. In Book III of the *Aeneid,* Aeneas describes his stopover at the Strophades to get food. The island teems with cattle and goats, but the Harpies inhabit the place, and they are "incontinent." When Aeneas and his men sit down to feast, the Harpies come "To seize our banquet, smearing dirtiness / Over it all . . . / And a stinking smell." Clara's presence fouls the feast that Francis and Helen would enjoy just as the Harpies foul the Trojans' feast. (pp. 169-70)

To complicate matters even more, there are suggestions that Clara is to be seen in terms of another fearsome female deity from classical myth: "She shook her head . . . and the greasy, uncombed stringlets of her hair leaped like whips." Here Clara seems to be a Gorgon, with whips rather than serpents for hair. The point of all these shifting mythological allusions is to establish the women as powerful and awful presences in the novel. (p. 170)

Although it is difficult to make much of Clara as a Fury, Kennedy clearly wants us to see Kathryn Phelan that way. In Greek myth, the avenging Furies are three in number: "Alecto, 'the uneasy,' Tisiphone, 'the blood-avenger,' and Megaera, 'the denier,'" . . . As "denier of life," Kathryn Phelan is associated with the third of the Furies, and there is no doubt that Francis' mother is a denier. She is a denier of all pleasures, from the pleasure of noncreational sex to the morbid pleasure of eating weeds in the grave. . . . Other characters function as Furies, as well. If Francis' daughter Margaret is not a Fury, she certainly is furious when Francis returns home with a turkey in Chapter VI. Even Francis serves as a Fury when he fulfills his role as an avenger: "Francis got 'em. He avenged all scars." Ironically, it is his own "crime" that demands vengeance most. . . . One of the fine ironies of the novel is that Francis is the most relentless pursuer of vengeance on himself.

Another of the great ironies of the book arises from the fact that the major women in the novel are not only White Goddesses and Furies who exact retribution, but they are at the same time Fates. In the central mythographic passage in the novel, which is also the climactic scene, Francis has a vision which functions as an epiphany for him and for the reader. He is in Mrs. Fennessey's flop house after the reunion with his family. Francis has run once more, but up in the dormitory-like room he sees "three long-skirted women who became four who became three and then four again." In the paragraphs which follow, Kennedy names five women in Francis' life: Annie, Helen, Peg, Sandra, and then "Francis saw Katrina's face among the five that became four that became three." After he Hectors the other bums in the flop house, Francis' vision resolves and focuses itself. . . . This passage constitutes the clearest use of myth in the novel, for the picture of Kathryn "crocheting," Katrina "measuring," and Helen snipping connects the three women with the classical Moirai or Fates. . . . The implication is clear. Francis sees here that the direction of his life—his destiny or fate—has been determined by the women in his life. (pp. 170-72)

Further examples of allusions to fate or the Fates abound. When Francis says that Sandra's "time was up," Helen says, "That's fatalism." . . . After making Helen go to spend the night in Finny's car because "It's what there is," Francis walks "with an empty soul toward the North Star, magnetized by an impulse to redirect his destiny." It may be significant that he steers by the North Star, and not the moon, here. At any rate, redirect his destiny he does. He finds a safe place to sleep "because

he needed to confront the ragman in the morning." He works for Rosskam the ragman long enough to earn the money for the turkey he feels he must bring to the reunion with his family, an action which will ultimately rid him of his Furies and settle on him a kinder fate.

But that ultimate fate is not sure until the end of the novel. In the meantime, Kennedy asks, "Why the hell should Helen always make Francis feel dead?" Among other reasons, Helen makes him feel dead because he is Attis, the dying and resurrected god, to her Cybele, and because she is Atropos, the inflexible shearer of the thread of life. . . . We learn that Helen's fate has been determined by a father who squandered his money and committed suicide and by the cruel manipulations and "duplicitous thievery" of her mother. Momentarily, we see Helen as Fury, too . . . , and she wonders about herself: "Dare you be so vindictive?" Then she contemplates her own fate again. . . . [Yet] Kennedy leaves us to decide how much of Helen's life has been fated and how much self-determined. (pp. 172-73)

Francis, it seems, is more fated than is Helen, for his hands are "artificers of some involuntary doom element in his life." He reviews many of the things he has done which he never intended to do, from killing to running away. He goes home with the turkey, kisses Annie. . . . Once again Katrina functions as a Fate, or a determiner of fate. Finally, "the question on the table" at the Phelan house is why is Francis home? Francis gives an answer: "'You might say it was Billy,' Francis said. . . . Perhaps Annie's answer is more to the point: "It was the woman, wasn't it?" Questions of fate and women once more occur together, as they do again which Francis says, "Helen's got me on the bum." Kathryn, Katrina, Helen (Clotho, Lachesis, Atropos—the Fates) have determined the course of Francis' life, Francis' nearly tragic life.

Ultimately, however, that life is not tragic, for Francis' Furies retire, the White Goddess relents, and Fate smiles. That this salvation is possible for Francis is indicated by the passage in which Kathryn, Katrina, and Helen are resolved into Annie. . . . The rest of the novel is expiation, which is nearly complete when Francis returns home with the turkey. Annie opens "the door wide" for him, grandson Danny idolizes him, Billy likes him, and Peg finally accepts him. . . . All the expiation that remains for Francis is to share his food from home with a bum named Michigan Mac and with "the guy in the piano box" with a wife and baby, to confess his sin to his fellow bums, to battle the invading Legionnaires, and to try to save Rudy by carrying him to the hospital. Rudy dies, and Francis runs again, as he had after killing Harold Allen during the trolley strike. The novel seems to have come full circle, and Francis seems launched on another round of aimless, alcoholic wanderings.

But then he thinks "of Annie's attic." . . . [Francis] is reborn, reintegrated into the family and life, particularly by Annie, who assumes the benign role of the Great Earth Mother "through whom resurrection and new life may be attained." This redemptive pattern resembles the pattern of Aeschylus' *Oresteia:* responsibility for the death of a close family member, pursuit by Furies, trial or expiation, acquittal, and transformation of Furies to the Eumenides or Kindly Ones. Thus, in the central mythographical passage, the three women "all become Annie," the kindly one who welcomes Francis back and hides him in the attic.

The mythological background of *Ironweed* is a rich kaleidoscope of shifting images which elevate and ennoble the people and action of the novel. Francis is Odysseus, Aeneas, Mene-laus, Agamemnon, Adonis, and Orestes. The women are Fates and Furies, Harpies and Gorgons—White Goddesses all. To recognize these elements from classical myth is not to deny elements from other mythologies which may also be present. There is no doubt, for example, that the terms and rituals of Christian salvation become increasingly important as the novel progresses. . . . However, Francis' assignment to an attic (one is tempted to find an allusion to Attica here) residence is as much the apotheosis of classical myth as it is the salvation of Christian dogma. Greek and Roman heroes from Hercules to Oedipus to Aeneas to Augustus Caesar are deified at the ends of their lives. Thus Kennedy leaves Francis a somewhat un-comfortable demi-god, eager to descend to Danny's "mighty nice little room" where he can be merely human again.

Ultimately, the power of *Ironweed* rests on Kennedy's ability to take what seem to be subhuman bums, transform them into heroes, and then reveal their basic humanity. That ability de-pends on the use of myth in the novel. In one of the most moving scenes in the *Iliad*, Homer shows us Hector saying goodby to Andromache and Astyanax before returning to battle. The strength of the scene, its ability to move the reader, lies in Homer's revelation of the common domestic situation behind the great hero of the great city of Troy. William Kennedy's *Ironweed* seems to reverse that process, taking the vulgar re-lationships of bums and the lapsed domestic life of the Phelan family and revealing the epic, heroic struggle involved in main-taining the former and in reestablishing the latter. Kennedy's depiction of the reuniting of Francis and his family is as moving as Homer's rendering of the parting of Hector and his family. To this end, Kennedy uses myth in the novel, and uses it effectively. (pp. 173-76)

> *Peter P. Clarke, "Classical Myth in William Ken-nedy's 'Ironweed'," in Critique: Studies in Modern Fiction, Vol. XXVII, No. 3, Spring, 1986, pp. 167-76.*

CHRISTOPHER LEHMANN-HAUPT

Strictly speaking, William Kennedy's audacious new novel *Quinn's Book.* is not an addition to his Albany trilogy. . . . The characters are wholly different, and since the plot is set in the 19th century instead of the 20th, there is not even an echo of the previous three books.

Yet like those earlier novels as well as Mr. Kennedy's first one, *The Ink Truck, Quinn's Book* explores the history of Albany and its environs, and attempt to transmute such basic matter into a vision of the human imagination in its search for creative freedom. Again the characters aspire to that apotheosis experienced by Francis Phelan in *Ironweed* when, upon falling asleep on a freezing night in a deserted barn, he heard "ethereal trumpets." . . .

The Quinn in *Quinn's Book* is Daniel Quinn, a young Albany boy orphaned by cholera, who begins the novel working for a Hudson River skiffman. At the story's spectacularly tragic opening, set in 1849, a boat is struck by an ice floe, drowning "the great courtesan, Magdalena Colon, also known as La Ultima, a woman whose presence turned men into spittling, masturbating pigs." . . .

Magdalena's perils attract a huge crowd to a nearby bridge, whereupon "with a flagitious roar and an agonized whine, the old wooden span" collapses, plunging a hundred-odd citizens into the icy water. At this moment, a freak of nature causes

"a rush of ice like none in Albany had ever seen," which in turn produces a tidal wave that somehow sets fire to a block of stores along the quay frontage: "fire rising out of flood—the gods gone mad."

After this apocalyptic start, it seems almost anticlimactic that over the succeeding decade and a half, Daniel witnesses labor strife among local iron-foundry workers, class warfare fo-mented by a secret society of oligarchs, the operation of the underground railroad for escaped slaves, the waging of the Civil War, the outbreak of the New York City draft riots of 1864, . . . and the running of a racing meet at Saratoga Springs. . . .

And given Mr. Kennedy's taste for language, we are not sur-prised that *Quinn's Book* is written in a pastiche of 19th-century styles, ranging all the way from bombastic melodrama to a wonderfully comic bit of sportswriting. . . .

But where *Quinn's Book* is most ambitious is in trying to connect the souls of its characters to a vision of American history, and here Mr. Kennedy wobbles a little. The story's opening scenes are successful. Following the catastrophe of fire and ice, Magdalena Colon, the drowned courtesan, is loved back to life by Daniel's necrophiliac boss, whereupon she re-ports a vision that is almost a comic version of Francis Phelan's dream in *Ironweed*: "When I first died, I saw a child looking up at me from the bottom of the river as I was slowly sinking from above. . . . 'I welcome you,' she said, 'to the birthplace of dreams, where even dolls live forever.'" . . .

Mr. Kennedy works hard to fuse these Coleridgean visions with his plot. He endows various characters with the power to commune with the spirit world, and he gives Daniel the am-bition to become a writer as well as equipping him with a magic disk that seems to egg people on to second sight.

But despite all this hocus-pocus the plot of *Quinn's Book* pro-ceeds in one dimension while the spiritual development of the characters progresses in another. It's true that Daniel grows into the writer who narrates *Quinn's Book,* and it's equally true that *Quinn's Book* can be said to represent the fulfillment of Daniel's dream to "fuse disparate elements of this life, however improbable the joining."

But a connection is never really made between the disparate elements and Daniel's dream of fusing them. On the one hand, there are crazy, cataclysmic events, and on the other, there are possessed people. But all that mediates between them is the author's rhetoric, which too often produces such greedy but undernourished passages as the following:

> And in such privileged moments his life became a great canvas of the imagination, large enough to sug-gest the true magnitude of the unknown. . . . In Maud's presence . . . , the canvas became unbearably valu-able and utterly mysterious, and he knew if he lost Maud he would explode into simplicity.

Unfortunately, *Quinn's Book* never does "explode into sim-plicity." The result can be a great deal of fun. But at heart it doesn't make much real and satisfying sense.

> *Christopher Lehmann-Haupt, "'Quinn's Book', William Kennedy's New Novel," in The New York Times, May 16, 1988, p. C18.*

PETER A. QUINN

With *Quinn's Book*, William Kennedy adds another installment to his Albany Cycle of novels. . . . *Quinn's Book* should add to that renown. It carries the Cycle back in time to its mid-nineteenth-century origins but is neither mere genealogy nor a clone of stories already told.

Quinn's Book proceeds with the force of a cyclone: the Cycle as spinning helix. A boat ferrying La Última, one of the world's great courtesans, across the Hudson is crushed by ice. Four of the five occupants drown. A bridge collapses from the weight of spectators to the drowning, with another forty or so fatally dunked. . . .

Maud, La Última's niece and the sole survivor of the incident on the Hudson, is taken by her rescuers to the house of the Staats, an ancient Albany Dutch family whose saga encapsulates much of New York's colonial history. Here the corpse of La Última is resurrected by the lovemaking of John the Brawn, her boatman/rescuer, and what begins as necrophilia ends as revivifying fornication. Meanwhile, much of Albany is burning to the ground, a blaze caused by a washerwoman whose bonnet was set afire by sparks from the burning quay. All this—and more—in the first thirty pages!

Most of these events really happened. Not on the same day, and not in exactly the same way as Daniel Quinn, the book's narrator, recounts them. But the riots, floods, fires, drownings, wars, and conspiracies that fill Quinn's story are all the stuff of history.

Is *Quinn's Book,* then, a historical novel about Albany? Yes, in the same way Joyce's *Ulysses* is a historical novel about Dublin. The purpose is not to fool the reader into thinking he or she is seeing through a glass clearly what is now departed (although Joyce enjoyed creating that effect as one artistic device among many). Instead, it is to play with the mirrors of place and time, to mingle fantasy with fact, the recorded event with the mythical, the improbable with the impossible, piling one atop another until we see reflected in the resulting phantasmagoria the human truths that chronologies can never give us. . . .

Stephen Dedalus tells only a half-truth (at best) when he says, "History is a nightmare from which I am trying to awake." As he understood but left unsaid, history is also part wet dream, part mummery, part Punch and Judy. We resist these several truths. We abhor not vaccums but absurdities. We want our history as our textbooks and most historical novels gave (and continue to give) it to us: settled, decorous, purposeful.

Quinn's Book won't let us have it that way, all neat and dignified, hair combed, pants pressed, shoes shined. It will let us look for a moment at this illusion. . . .

But take notice, *Quinn's Book* warns us: The dead are not dead. Nor have they fallen asleep, awaiting the encore of the Last Judgment. The dead walk among us. The consequences of what they took for truth continue to shape our world; their saintliness or silliness will be forever felt. (p. 308)

Daniel Quinn begins, as we all do, by assuming the meanings of life can be searched out, handled, possessed. He believes those meanings are as available as the past he sees displayed at a patriotic bazaar in Albany during the Civil War. . . . This is the past that everyone can be comfortable with. A collection of curios.

Quinn's search also has a metaphysical dimension. The age he lives in sees to that. America at the middle of the last century was incandescent with the bright lights of seers and clairvoyants, with . . . doctrines that fudged the line between the ma-

terial and the spiritual, and offered a view of the eternal reality as near as the mysterious tapping ("as of someone gently rapping") first overheard by the Fox sisters in upstate New York.

The echoes of these spiritual communications surround Quinn. The love of his life, Maud Fallon, whom he pursues from line two of the book until its last words . . . is a reluctant practitioner of spiritualism, her career as a danseuse interrupted by the thunderous rappings of an insistent spirit. Quinn has visions of his own. He sees his first in the eye of the dead (but-soon-to-be-resurrected) La Última. He is also in possession of an ancient Irish disc ("his Celtic potato plate") that his parents brought over from Ireland and whose secret usefulness he is never able to figure out.

Finally, he doesn't have to. Quinn takes to heart the advice of Will Canaday, the editor of the *Albany Chronicle*: "Remember this, Daniel. The only thing worth fighting for is what is real to the self. Move toward the verification of freedom, and avoid gratuitous absolutes."

Quinn eventually does. He stops trying to find the Ultimate Truths and starts creating his own individual meanings. Searcher becomes progenitor. Daniel has found the craft of words. (pp. 308-09)

Lucky Quinn. In Maud's arms he will set the Cycle spinning. . . .

Lucky us to have an artist like William Kennedy to regale and entertain, telling his tales with such wit and verve and in the process creating something so memorable and true.

The luck of the Irish, I suppose. (p. 309)

> Peter A. Quinn, "Incandescent Albany," in Commonweal, *Vol. CXV, No. 10, May 20, 1988, pp. 308-09.*

T. CORAGHESSAN BOYLE

[Following] the now legendary success of Kennedy's Albany cycle . . . , the historic little city on the Hudson is as firmly established in the literary geography as Joyce's Dublin or Faulkner's own Yoknapatawpha County.

Quinn's Book, like its predecessors, is set in Albany. The action spans a period of 15 years, from 1849 to 1864, a particularly tumultuous time not only for Albany but for the country at large; the Civil War, the New York draft riots and the workings of the Underground Railroad are all given play here. Against this historical backdrop, the narrator and protagonist, Daniel Quinn, struggles to liberate himself from "life's caprice," establish his career as a journalist and win the hand of Maud Fallon, a heroine as magical and elusive as Dickens's Estella. Indeed, *Quinn's Book* does have a decidedly Dickensian flavor to it, particularly in the opening chapters. As the book begins, Quinn is a 14-year-old orphan, his parents and sister having succumbed to the cholera epidemic of the preceding year. Like Dickens's child heroes, Daniel is at the mercy of the adult world, apprenticed first to a canal man who beats him and refuses to pay his wages and then to a boatman, John the Brawn McGee, who, while less brutal, is hardly more scrupulous.

Together, McGee and Daniel come to the aid of La Ultima, a renowned danseuse-courtesan, who piques the fates by trying to cross the ice-swollen Hudson in December. A floe crushes the skiff, and down go La Ultima, her maid and her 12-year-old niece, Maud Fallon. While the mercenary McGee recovers the courtesan's precious baggage and apparently lifeless self . . . , Daniel rescues Maud. "It's you who have first right to my life," she tells him, and thus begins the love affair that becomes central to Daniel's life and the book's development.

But if Mr. Kennedy manages brilliantly to evoke Dickens, he does so through a sensibility informed by the age of Gabriel Garcia Márquez and the school of magic realism. La Ultima (a k a Magdalena Colón) is a character of such fine, lusty and absurd proportions that she might have wandered into town with the gypsy troupe from *One Hundred Years of Solitude*: "'It ees a pleasure to meet a rrreal mon,' she said in her fraudulent, Hispanicized English (she was of Hibernian stock and spoke the language perfectly)." Her twitting of the powers that be brings instant retribution and cataclysmic woe down upon the heads of Albany's hapless citizens. No sooner have Quinn and McGee returned to the pier with Maud and the inanimate Ultima than the span itself collapses, plunging "a hundred or more" [feet] into the torrent. (pp. 1, 31)

Quinn, John the Brawn McGee and Maud manage to escape this scene of devastation, John hauling La Ultima's corpse and baggage with him. Maud, remarkably self-possessed considering what she's been through, directs them to the mansion of Hillegond Staats, widow of Petrus, a man who traced his lineage to the time of the patroon. Hillegond is a capacious woman, in physique and spirit both, and she takes them all in, though Maud's only connection to her is tenuous: she and La Ultima had stayed with Hillegond during their last tour of Albany. It is here, in the *doon-kamer,* or "dead chamber," of this ancient august mansion, that La Ultima is laid out. No need to mourn her, though. For John the Brawn, besides being broad of back and opportunistic, seems to be something of a necrophiliac as well.

In a bawdy and very funny scene, he manages to resuscitate La Ultima through the act of coitus, and she comes alive in his arms. Aroused, Hillegond joins in, while, unbeknownst to the participants, Quinn and the prepubescent Maud look on. A short time later, after witnessing a second and even more astonishing resurrection, Maud and Quinn fling themselves at each other in a fury of oscular passion, until they are rudely separated by a scandalized Ultima. The separation is emblematic of their relationship, which is not resolved till the last page of the novel.

It is this house, the Staats mansion, around which the remainder of the book revolves. Quinn and his friends become Hillegond's guests during the period of La Ultima's recovery, and, as a result, the young Daniel gets his first taste of newspaper work, which will become his education and profession both. . . . Unfortunately, he soon finds himself separated from Maud—through the machinations of John the Brawn—and embroiled in other adventures. When next he meets Maud—two years later, in Saratoga, where she has become essential to her aunt's stage performances—he is just shy of 17, a working journalist, and his part in delivering Hillegond's son from his kidnappers has earned him a lifelong annuity. The two come together again, only to be parted once more, and cruelly.

Quinn's Book now leaps 15 years into the future. Hillegond is dead, a victim of murder; La Ultima, still a beauty in her 50's, is succumbing to the ebb of time; . . . [Quinn has become famous] as an unsparing Civil War correspondent; and Maud, delectable and mysterious, has earned herself a certain notoriety in the theater for a risqué act involving an on-stage horseback ride. The war itself is conducted offstage, but in a riveting

speech delivered to the beautiful people gathered for the races at Saratoga, Quinn brings its reality home. He has grown confident, no longer the orphan buffeted by the winds of fate, but a man able "to alter existence, to negate life's caprice and become causality itself." In the finale, he must fight to win Maud from her fiancé, Gordon Fitzgibbon, the new lord of the Staats manson.

As a writer of historical fiction, William Kennedy is unparalleled among his contemporaries. Rooted firmly in Albany, he sees "an archetypal as well as an historical context in which to view the city's mutations," and asserts that the "task" of his fiction is "to peer into the heart of this always-shifting past, to be there when it ceases to be what it was, when it becomes what it must become under scrutiny, when it turns so magically, so inevitably, from then into now." The books of the Albany cycle are a testament to this *ars poetica*, books and live comfortably in their history, convincing and true. **Legs,** Kennedy's fictional life of Jack (Legs) Diamond, Albany's most notorious bootlegger, illuminates with equal grace the dark country lanes of Catskill and the mean streets of Albany, presenting, in the process, the most sympathetic gangster since Gatsby. And **Ironweed,** justly celebrated for its haunting, elegiac prose and its vision of the man crippled by the past, reinvents historical fiction. **Quinn's Book,** especially in its harrowing riot scenes. . . . and its look at boxing and the races at Saratoga, is a lively addition to the canon.

On the negative side, **Quinn's Book** does seem occasionally to warp under the weight of its history, sacrificing narrative drive and cohesion to the historical sidelights. Then, too, the author's use of an ersatz 19th-century idiom often rings false, as in the 12-line opening sentence. . . . After John Barth's *Sot-Weed Factor* and its sendup of the false idiom of the historical novel, it is difficult to take such locutions seriously.

Fortunately, however, the language of **Quinn's Book** rises above the occasional lapses, and Quinn, as the book progresses, becomes increasingly eloquent, dropping the convoluted syntax in favor of the cleaner, more contemporary line. And if the history sometimes overwhelms the story, it is always fascinating. There are marvelous divagations on the lineage of the Staats family and the Underground Railroad, and a colorful sample of the age's sportswriting. Mr. Kennedy does indeed have the power to peer into the past, to breathe life into it and make it indispensable, and Quinn's battle to control his destiny and win Maud is by turns grim, amusing and deeply moving. In an era when so much of our fiction is content to accomplish so little, **Quinn's Book** is a revelation. Large-minded, ardent, alive on every page with its author's passion for his place and the events that made it, it is a novel to savor. One puts down **Quinn's Book** with a sigh, ever envying Mr. Kennedy his roots. (pp. 31-2)

> *T. Coraghessan Boyle, "Into the Heart of Old Albany," in* The New York Times Book Review, *May 22, 1988, pp. 1, 31-2.*

RHODA KOENIG

Either William Kennedy has lost his mind, or it has been taken over by a succubus named Joyce Carol Oates. **Quinn's Book,** an account of the fortunes of a mid-nineteenth-century upstate orphan, is replete with torture, mutilation, eye-gouging, impalement, spirit manifestations, and necrophilia, none of which is as much fun as it sounds. The backdrop for Daniel Quinn's adventures is the era of Irish immigration, anti-slavery agitation, and Civil War, a scene peopled with a cast of shifting multitudes. To and fro they wander, speechifying, rubbernecking, bursting into song, and sticking the odd shiv into one another. It's a production of intolerably baroque excess, from which you come away with a memory of squirming buttocks or spilling entrails but little impression of feeling and character.

Orphaned by the cholera plague, Quinn is apprenticed to an Albany boatman in December of 1849, when the town turns out to see Magdalena Colón, the celebrated exotic dancer and courtesan, cross the icy Hudson in a skiff.... An ice floe caves her boat in, and Quinn's master, John the Brawn, immediately sets out to rescue—not the dancer but her trunk. By the by, he fishes out the drowned Magdalena, commenting, "One dead slut." Quinn reaches into the water and saves Magdalena's young niece, Maud....

The tragedy on the river, though, is just an opening act.... After the bridge breaks, a tidal wave sweeps other spectators from the pier. Through a shrieking, moaning crowd, John and Quinn make their way . . . to the mansion of Hillegond Staats, where little Maud claims they will be well received. Indeed, the huge crone welcomes them and shows John to a chamber where, after laying Magdalena out, he proceeds to lay her, period. "John the Brawn climbed aboard Magdalena Colón and began doing to her gelid blossom what I had heard him boast of doing to many dozens of other more warm-blooded specimens." . . .

The night, however, is young. Next, a demented criminal hangs himself in the mausoleum outside Hillegond's house, and she orders the coffin of her ancestor, damaged in the process, to be brought inside. Curious Maud lifts the lid, and the body, no longer interested in a bit of fun, explodes and turns to dust. This excites Maud so much, says Quinn, that she "ground her pelvic center against my own and kissed all of my face with a ferocious gluttony." . . .

Turning away from the . . . gelid blossoms, Quinn sets out on an odyssey to become a man and recover Maud, who vanishes for as long, and as mysteriously, as the heroine of a novel with a paper cover and flock title. He digs up a birdcage his mother hid and discovers, under a false bottom, a bronze Celtic disk engraved with a hideous face. . . .

Enough. This farrago of violence and hormonal shenanigans seeks to stagger and astound us, but it just belabors us into apathy with its clotted language, its posturing and absurdity. Strange Celtic disks aren't all you find at the bottom of a birdcage. (p. 93)

> *Rhoda Koenig, "Search and Destroy," in* New York Magazine, *Vol. 21, No. 21, May 23, 1988, pp. 93-4.*

SVEN BIRKERTS

[With] *Quinn's Book,* Kennedy has attempted a novelistic fusion of history and fancy. Alas, even Homer nods.

To begin with, not only is Kennedy mesmerized by the possibilities of his chosen setting, he is also showing signs of the Balzacian itch: he seems to want his novels to link up through character-crossover until a whole imaginary world has been populated. Billy Phelan, for example, is the son of Francis Phelan, the protagonist of *Ironweed*. In the new novel, a deeper ancestral link is forged. Daniel Quinn, the hero, is grandfather

to his namesake Danny Quinn, also of *Ironweed*. As Kennedy affirmed in an interview in a recent *New York Times Book Review*: "They're all interconnected. I've worked out the genealogies. New lines are established that I hope will be part of future books. It's inexhaustible...."

The link between the earlier works and the new novel seems merely expeditious, however. For while the trilogy is sharply naturalistic, *Quinn's Book* may be viewed as Kennedy's flirtation with genre fiction—specifically, with the sort of parodic extravaganza attempted by John Barth in *The Sot-Weed Factor* and by Erica Jong in *Fanny*. Historical circumstance is the springboard, the source of situations and stylistic inventions. The general idea is to filter period material through an authorial presence rendered ironic by much historical hindsight. The result, at least in this case, is an awful conspiratorial winking in the tone, a prose incessantly parading around in some silly costume. Here is Kennedy's opening:

> I, Daniel Quinn, neither the first nor the last of a line of such Quinns, set eyes on Maud the wondrous on a late December day in 1849 on the banks of the river of aristocrats and paupers, just as the great courtesan, Magdalena Colón, also known as La Última . . . boarded a skiff to carry her across the river's icy water from Albany to Greenbush, her first stop en route to the city of Troy, a community of iron, where later that evening she was scheduled to enact, yet again, her role as the lascivious Lais, that fabled prostitute who spurned Demosthenes' gold and yielded without fee to Diogenes, the virtuous, impecunious tub-dweller.

These first words, I have already read in reputable places, herald a narrative that is Dickensian in amplitude and García Márquesian in its magical animation. Certainly we are to applaud the ambitious blending of the ribald and picaresque with the matter-of-fact. But there is nothing original here. The passage is pure pastiche, a rip-off of the Colombian master that is not made clever or excusable by the play with a Latino name. In García Márquez, the complex manipulation of tenses and the shuffling together of image-laden clauses is done in the service of an awe-struck narrating sensibility—a sensibility invaded and transformed by the visions it would relate. There is nothing of the kind in Kennedy's book. The grown-up Quinn who is looking back to tell his story is supposed to be a journalist and war correspondent of some repute. But he is posing when we first shake hands, and, as a result, we never trust him again.

The García Márquez lead also proves to be a red herring, for after a few trial shots at magic realism—a prophetic vision descried in the open eye of a corpse, an ice jam that grows into a mountain—Kennedy jettisons the mode. It's almost as if he decided in mid-chapter that a more native prototype would be better suited to his needs. Would that he had gone back and erased his footprints.

The other big name invoked is, as I said, Dickens. But that's not quite accurate, either. Kennedy's prose has nothing of the richness of detail or comedy; nor can he even approximate the flash and sparkle that Dickens elicits from his collisions of characters. No, in its thin superficiality and deus-ex-machina improbabilities, *Quinn's Book* is better compared to those quickly concocted dime novels that eviscerated Dickens for devices and played to the public's enormous appetite for sensation and melodrama. (p. 41)

Kennedy is evidently enraptured by the legends of Albany—its rough river-men, its power politics, its formative ethnic clashes. And, truly, the materials for a major historical novel are all there. But *Quinn's Book* is not that novel, not by a long shot. Kennedy has rashly assumed that a set of type-cast dime novel characters are sufficient pretext, and that the swirl of history around them will provide color and content in abundance. But the flatness of these cartoon figures—Quinn as do-gooder and blank slate, La Última as gold-hearted old bawd, Brawn as lovable scoundrel, and Maud as the ultimately virtuous prize—ensures that the events will be registered with equivalent flatness. The history cannot live apart from the consciousness that perceives it. All of the brawls and catastrophes and glimpses into the dark cog-works of power politics read like scene sketches from a novelist's notebook.

Here, quite randomly excerpted, is Quinn's recounting of how he came upon Dirck, the kidnapped son of Hillegond Staats:

> I found Dirck in the farthermost stall, face down in soiled hay, wearing the same ill-fitting clothes he'd been wearing when abducted. On close look it was not animal droppings but his own blood that had soiled the hay. I rolled him over to see his face and found it a total wound, a horrifying smear of blood, gash, and swelling. His eyes told me that he was still alive, but not for long, I judged. . . .

Nothing wrong with this, you might say. Not technically, no. The sentences follow in order, provide the basic clues for a reader to visualize. But that's all—basic clues. There is no precision, no conveying of shock or fear, no fastening on the quick, living details. The passage is representative. Kennedy rarely gets any better, or worse, than this. The story slogs on in just such undistinguished, tired sentences. Open to any passage in, say, *Ironweed* and you will see how far the stylist has fallen.

And the reason? Hard to say. It may be that the historical distance was just too much for the author to bridge in imagination. But the problem may also have to do with Kennedy's recent exposure to screenwriting and its less arduous demands. I suspect that the writing of *Quinn's Book* coincided, at least in part, with Kennedy's work on the screenplay of *Ironweed*. The pace and exteriority of the new novel are patently celluloid. Indeed, the screen, rather than the page, might be the destined home for these slight lives. For the camera inevitably enriches stereotypes, and it catches the grain of concrete details that prose cannot always reach. Kennedy would not have to change much—just the second word of the title. That job done, he could get back to what he ordinarily does so beautifully: real writing. (p. 42)

Sven Birkerts, "O Albany," in The New Republic, *Vol. 198, No. 26, June 27, 1988, pp. 41-2.*

Francis (Henry) King

1923-

(Has also written under pseudonym of Frank Cauldwell) English novelist, short story writer, poet, dramatist, biographer, travel writer, critic, and editor.

One of Britain's most respected contemporary authors, King writes detailed, realistic works of fiction which exhibit a pessimistic view of modern humanity and a fascination with life's injustices. Many of King's novels and short stories are populated by immoral and hypocritical characters whose perceptions of isolation and inadequacy are considered by critics to be the strongest attributes of his fiction. A British Council officer for fifteen years, King has lived in Greece, Italy, and Japan, and he often sets his works in such exotic foreign locales. He has stated that his favorite protagonist is the expatriate who is simultaneously exasperated and enthralled with his adopted country. James Kelly observed: "Mr. King is at home with the raw tragedy and pathos of life—. . . he is a forceful writer who can make you respect what he has to say."

King's first two works, *To the Dark Tower* (1946) and *Never Again* (1948), were published while he was a student at Oxford University. *To the Dark Tower* concerns a self-centered retired army general who suppressed his troop's fanatical commitment to him in wartime but forces his family to succumb to his egocentricity. *Never Again,* a largely autobiographical portrait of King's years at foreign boarding schools, introduces the isolation and frustration that has become a recurring theme in his works. *The Dividing Stream* (1951) was King's first novel to be published in the United States. Critics regarded this tale of vacationing foreigners in Italy as a revealing commentary of cross-cultural relations, particularly in his portrayals of wealthy American teenagers and impoverished Italian youths. *The Dark Glasses* (1954) is set on the Greek island of Corfu and chronicles a love triangle involving a married English botanist, a Greek girl, and her homosexual brother, whose attraction to his sister's lover results in her murder. A reviewer for *Time* stated: "King overexposes and underdevelops his hapless English hero, but his color shots of Corfu are snapped with the eye of a Matisse." *The Man on the Rock* (1957) is a complex portrait of an attractive young man whose compulsive actions destroy his benefactors.

King's next novel, *The Custom House* (1961), is considered by many critics to be his finest work. This book draws heavily on his experiences as a British administrator in Japan during the early 1960s. Primarily related from the perspective of Knox, a British teacher, *The Custom House* recounts the murder of an exotic dancer and its repercussions on those who hardly knew her. Knox also expounds on the differences between Western and Oriental cultures. *The Last of the Pleasure Gardens* (1965) depicts the tribulations of a middle-aged couple following the birth of their retarded son. Aware that the boy will never be self-sufficient, the father kills him. Of the novel's sustained sense of foreboding, Kenneth Allsop commented: "The Wagnerian chords are held precisely muted by the plainness, almost the nullity, of Mr. King's expertly controlled vernacular." The plot of *The Waves behind the Boat* (1967) recalls that of *The Custom House* in its story of Bill and Mary, a British couple living in Japan, whose lives change following

the death of an acquaintance. Their ensuing relationship with the dead woman's sibling housemates and the amorous advances made toward Mary by both individuals prompted critics to fault King for abandoning the complexities of human relationships in favor of melodrama.

A Domestic Animal (1970) is the most autobiographical of King's works. His candid attitude toward homosexuality is reflected in the story of Dick Thompson, a middle-aged homosexual writer, who falls in love with Antonio Valli, an Italian philosopher on sabbatical in England. King contrasts the irrationality and shifted priorities of unrequited love with the earlier placidity of Thompson's life. A critic from the *Times Literary Supplement* observed: "[*A Domestic Animal*] is often painful and occasionally silly, but the author has created an oddly touching figure in this middle-aged man roused to self-destructive emotion after a lifetime of indifference, restraint and discretion." In *Danny Hill: Memoirs of a Prominent Gentleman* (1977), King assumes the role of "editor" of a bawdy spoof of John Cleland's novel *Memoirs of a Woman of Pleasure.* Although critics noted numerous historical inaccuracies, this tale of the adventures and conquests of the libidinous brother of Fanny Hill garnered praise for King's skillful use of parody. *Act of Darkness* (1983), set in British-occupied India during the 1930s, examines the hypocrisy of the elite. This novel revolves around two upper-class English lesbians who kill a six-year-old boy after he discovers them in bed. The women then disguise the murder to appear to be the work of the Dacoits, a band of criminal Indians. *Act of Darkness* received largely negative reviews; some critics viewed the lesbians' reaction to the child's innocent discovery as an authorial attack on women, while others contended that their motive is tenuous. *Voices in an Empty Room* (1984) also garnered marginal reviews for its story of three bereaved women who attempt to communicate with deceased loved ones through parapsychology. King's recent novel, *The Woman Who Was God* (1988), details a woman's search in Africa for information about the death of her son, a member of a mysterious cult. "To say too much would be to spoil things," Christopher Hawtree commented, "for the succession of events is itself one of the novel's main delights."

King's short story collections share many of the themes of his novels. *The Brighton Belle and Other Stories* (1968) resembles a novel, as its concentration on what a critic from the *Times Literary Supplement* termed "[the] freakish eccentricities in Brighton" connects the separate tales. Critics praised King's warm but unconventional characters and his startling conclusions to the stories. Many of the pieces in *Indirect Method and Other Stories* (1980) focus on the adventures of expatriates in their adoptive countries. Of this collection, Sylvia Clayton commented: "What makes all the stories a pleasure to read . . . is Francis King's talent for summoning up a person or a scene in a single striking phrase that lies somewhere between poetry and gossip." *One Is a Wanderer and Other Stories* (1985) features a selection of King's short fiction published between 1949 and 1983. *Frozen Music* (1987) is a novella that explores a British family's disillusionment upon returning to India to visit the grave of their matriarch and finding nothing as they remember it. This work was lauded for its admirable balance of humor and sensitivity. In addition to fiction, King has also written poetry, plays, travelogues, and a biography of E. M. Forster.

(See also *CLC*, Vol. 8; *Contemporary Authors*, Vols. 1-4, rev. ed.; *Contemporary Authors New Revision Series*, Vol. 1; and *Dictionary of Literary Biography*, Vol. 15.)

DAN WICKENDEN

Immune to the blandishments of preciosity and symbolism, a young English writer makes his American debut in a refreshingly vigorous novel of human relationships. With a postwar summer in Florence as backdrop, *The Dividing Stream* plays intricate and eminently readable variations upon the not unfamiliar theme of love's fitful power to bridge the void separating one human being from another.

The central octet includes an Anglo-American couple whose marriage is in crisis, an extraordinary old woman, an adolescent brother and sister, a pair of Italian street boys, and a war hero from Burma who emulates T. E. Lawrence. Assorted tourists, expatriates, and Italians almost innumerable, furnish a full orchestral accompaniment, and because Francis King has a gift for character, the least of them is almost as vivid as the most important.

He is able, too, to keep a story moving rapidly through a series of unexpected convolutions, and his range of moods extends

from outrageous comedy to sudden violent drama. Not one of his pages fails to convey a palpable atmosphere or lacks a brilliantly visual quality, and episodes tumble from his sleeves with such spontaneity and profusion that it is surprising how well-knit his plot proves to be.

It is true that Mr. King disregards technical niceties, makes lavish use of acrid detail, and draws pessimistic conclusions about love, and his story occasionally seems as implausible as real life so often does; but if these are flaws, they are outweighed by the exuberance with which he writes. Nor does it greatly matter that many of his people appear unsympathetic and a few of them abhorrent, for they are interesting, individual, and sharply alive; and Mr. King himself has perceived them with an understanding that amounts to compassion.

Dan Wickenden, "Here's a Bright Newcomer," in New York Herald Tribune Book Review, June 17, 1951, p. 5.

THE TIMES LITERARY SUPPLEMENT

The Dividing Stream is not an altogether successful book; Mr. King is not equally interested in every member of his considerable cast, and his manner shows sometimes a distinct resemblance to that of Mr. Aldous Huxley's early work. Nevertheless, this is a novel written for the most part with fine assurance, and reaching a quite exceptional level of imaginative intensity in some scenes and portraits.

The author is at his best in writing of the several adolescents who play with doom-laden gaiety in the shadow of their elders' frustrations and miseries. Pamela and Colin are the children of a wealthy American business man named Max Westfield; their lives are linked, in a way that is made to seem perfectly plausible, with those of two wretchedly poor Italian boys named Rodolfo and Enzo. There is some sharp and subtle counterpointing of social relations here, in such incidents as that of Enzo's quite casual arrest for the theft of a brooch which has in fact been taken by Colin, and the brief glimpses of Enzo's wretched home life are admirably treated. Perhaps the most memorable scene in the book is that describing an unbidden visit paid by Pamela, Colin and Rodolfo to the villa of the old eccentric Englishwoman for whom Enzo works, and their excited opening of forbidden rooms and drawers.

The insight with which these four adolescents are distinguished is lacking in the portraits of the two or three sets of adults with whom Mr. King is principally concerned. Max Westfield is tolerant, good-natured, unimaginative; his second wife Karen, stepmother of Pamela and Colin, is possessed by the brittle and restless dissatisfaction that marks many women approaching middle age. Their married life is complicated also by the fact that, while Max was serving in the forces, Karen had an illegitimate child by another man; and she is unable to forgive Max his stony lack of sympathy on this occasion, or to feel anything but contempt for the consideration he shows in almost all other matters. Karen, in fact, has the subconscious desire to be dominated which marks the heroines of so many books; and she seems to find what she needs in a cold-natured hero of the war, a minor Lawrence of Arabia named Frank Ross. The working out of this relationship, and Karen's final acceptance of her dismal life with Max, is the book's central situation which is reflected, or distorted, in the lives of the other characters. . . . Some of these characters are a little more than Mr. King can yet manage; both Max and Karen seem rather often to be less people seen and understood than read about and copied. *The Dividing Stream* is, however, a considerable achievement for a writer not yet 30 years of age.

"Flashes of Insight," in The Times Literary Supplement, *No. 2577, June 22, 1951, p. 385.*

J. D. SCOTT

The number of post-war novelists is very large, but if you can name six within a minute you are doing very well. Nor has any single writer of the post-war generation achieved either the prestige which Aldous Huxley had in 1924 or the kind of success that Norman Mailer has had in America at the present time. The well-known new novelists of the Fifties—making the assumption, in all its hubristic optimism, that the Fifties are going to run to well-known novelists at all—have perhaps still to publish their phenomenal first novels. Yet there are a few post-war novelists who are emerging, with more recognisable names, more completely established themes, with personalities that grow harder at the edges, with tricks that become more obvious and irritating, but also perhaps with subtleties and profundities which at long last claim our aberrant, myopic attention. Of these Mr. Francis King is one.

His name is already recognisable (*To the Dark Tower, An Air That Kills*) and his literary personality has always been pretty hard at the edges. It is marked off, for one thing, by a striking capacity for presenting widely diverse types of character. He is particularly good with spartan, Fascist-minded, soldierly men—there is a very telling portrait in [*The Dividing Stream*] of an ex-Burma hero—but he can do children and old people, Italians and English, rich and poor, with such sympathy that for once one really needs the information—often so painfully unnecessary—which is provided by the publisher. (Mr. King was in fact born in 1923 and went to Shrewsbury and Balliol.) It is perhaps more relevant to Mr. King's cosmopolitanism as a novelist that he seems to have spent much of his life abroad, but his ubiquitous unsentimental sympathy gives the effect, not of reporting, but of a kind of professional creativeness which is unusual and impressive. In *The Dividing Stream*, it is true, this isn't quite perfect; Max, who is American, is never convincingly American as the diverse English are all convincingly English and the diverse Italians all Italian.

But that doesn't matter very much. A novel that opens with style and pace, that gathers momentum as it gathers weight, that combines insight into character with brilliantly restrained evocations of place, that is voluptuously readable without ever being merely expert, can carry a few imperfections. *The Dividing Stream* is a formidably ambitious book—Mr. King is, with reason, a formidably ambitious writer—and the theme is on a formidable scale. Briefly, it is a theme of reconciliation, of the reconciliation of a group of diverse antagonistic characters after the faithlessness and cruelty, the heat and the dust and the spiritual luxury of a long Florentine summer. Formidable indeed; a theme of love beyond the reach of talent to convey. Something more than the Americanism of an American has eluded Mr. King, and when I reached the end of this impressive piece of work my impression was of its falling between two stools—although perhaps one might say between a stool and a throne—in achieving neither the authority of a major novel nor the neatness of a minor one. (pp. 722, 724)

J. D. Scott, in a review of "The Dividing Stream," in The New Statesman & Nation, *Vol. XLI, No. 1059, June 23, 1951, pp. 722, 724.*

THE TIMES LITERARY SUPPLEMENT

Mr. Francis King in *The Dark Glasses* is never able quite to accept the simplicity and savagery of the young Greeks Stavro and Soula. . . . Mr. King writes, it is true, from the point of view of an extremely timid and innocent middle-aged English botanist who has come out to Corfu with his Greek wife: but the effect is still somehow artificial, and Stavro and Soula seem to be less genuinely primitive characters than standard models in a modern convention of primitiveness. The story in which they are the central figures is coolly and delicately told. The tragedies in it take place off-stage, while Patrick and his wife are convalescing in Naples from the emotional ardours of Corfu. The dark glasses are the occasion of tragedy. They are the glasses through which the botanist Patrick Orde looks at Corfu, seeing it untruly through their mild light: but they are also, in a literal sense, the glasses he gives to Soula with whom he is carrying on an affair, rather than to Stavro who is in love with him. Mr. King always writes well, and his perception of scenes and people is acute: but in *The Dark Glasses* his sensibility seems to be operating rather uncertainly.

"Black and White," in The Times Literary Supplement, *No. 2734, June 25, 1954, p. 405.*

TIME, NEW YORK

Take an Anglo-Saxon with an ailing love life and plant him under the Mediterranean sun. Will the change kill or cure him? . . . In *The Dark Glasses* the atmospheric catalyst is the Greek resort island of Corfu, and the inhibited patient is a 39-year-old crew-cut Englishman named Patrick Orde whose eleven-year marriage to a Greek woman is not so much on the rocks as thoroughly becalmed.

Patrick is a kind of dilettante snowman. . . . Corfu thaws him out—first with a throb of color from its sapphire sea and sky, orange groves and olive trees, then with the pastoral charm of tinkling goat bells and squat white stone houses, and finally with its people, who teach him a language of the heart that is puzzlingly Greek to him. Biggest puzzle of all is his Venus de Miloesque wife Iris, who plunges into the thankless chore of running a local clinic without an outward trace of pity for the poverty and peasant ignorance of her fellow islanders. What she is trying to smother in work, Patrick belatedly discovers, is a long-smoldering love interest in the humbly born manager of the family estate, who happens to be dying of cancer.

Patrick soon runs an erotic fever of his own over a nubile, neo-pagan teen-ager named Soula. Little more than fugitive kisses and caresses, the affair with Soula is tragically complicated by the fact that her brother Stavro, a boy with cryptohomosexual longings, feels he should rank first in Patrick's affections. By novel's end, Soula has died at her brother's hand. Resignedly estranged from each other, Patrick and Iris leave Corfu chewing the bitter rind of memory, all that is left of their brief repast of the juices and joys of the sensuous life. . . .

[King] has scraped the marrow of his Greek characters. He recognizes their fortitude under real pain, their histrionics over emotional trifles and their bristling pride. Above all, he captures their gift for draining each passing moment of life as if it were a glass of their own villainous *retsina* wine. Author King overexposes and underdevelops his hapless English hero, but his color shots of Corfu are snapped with the eye of a Matisse, and Patrick's departure from the Ionian isle seems like expulsion from a demi-paradise.

"Island Interlude," in Time, *New York, Vol. LXVII, No. 13, March 26, 1956, p. 112.*

RICHARD WINSTON

"Do you think that I can't see that you're hard, and selfish, and mercenary?"

These words are addressed to Spiro, the unheroic Greek hero of [*The Man on the Rock*], Francis King's tale of the eternal, ambivalent love affair between the Anglo-Saxon and the Mediterranean temperaments. Here this affair takes place both inside and outside the novel, between the characters and between the writer and his subject. Mr. King has strong feelings and incisive opinions about the vanity, hypocrisy, wantonness and unscrupulousness of many Greeks, and he does not hesitate to express them bluntly. He is equally candid, if somewhat more forbearing, about the fatuousness, ineffectuality, hollowness and effeteness of his American and British characters.

Spiro, the narrator, has grown up in shattered, poverty-stricken post-war Greece—a land where even today, after a year of unprecedented prosperity for most of the world, one and a half million out of a population of eight million are unemployed or underemployed. . . . [His] one asset is his striking beauty, which effortlessly attracts the love of men as well as women. With an opportunism too natural to be really base, he deceives, exploits and finally destroys those who love him. Yet his wrecking of lives is done offhandedly, without especial malice. Unless— and Mr. King leaves this for each reader to decide for himself— there is a deeper unconscious viciousness in Spiro's childlike refusal to foresee the consequences of his actions. Thus, by a carelessly dropped word he ruins the career of the American relief administrator who raised him out of starvation and ignorance, and attempted to mold his character. By angling for a rich marriage, he makes his mistress, a middle-aged Englishwoman, commit suicide. By letting his disinherited wife work during her pregnancy, he brings about her death. Yet in each case he is not solely responsible; his victims are also the authors of their own destruction. And Spiro is not callous: in his way, and after he has lost them, he loves those whom he has betrayed or doomed. . . . Francis King has a feeling for the violence of modern life that we associate with American rather than British writers. But his force drives deep. He has written a novel interesting in technique, colorful in setting, fertile in incident, rounded in form. This is a courageous and mature book that should be widely read.

Richard Winston, "The 'Hero' as Troublemaker," in New York Herald Tribune Book Review, *January 19, 1958, p. 3.*

FRANCES KEENE

Certainly [*The Man on the Rock*] is not a "nice" novel about Greece today. Nor is the protagonist, Spiro, a "nice" person. As Lord Russell says, "To be a nice person it is necessary to be protected from crude contact with reality." What Spiro has had all his life is crude contact—and little else.

A Greek boy of classic proportions and incandescent power, snatched from the war and subsequent civil strife, Spiro has survived by the shrewd use of all available help. For a start he was picked up by an American welfare agency employee of unexpressed homosexual tendencies, who proceeded to educate the boy above his intelligence. Later Spiro passed from his tutelage to that of an aging matron with too much money

and the inevitable need of the unlovable to be "loved." Almost without need to say so, Spiro confirms his own incapacity to love when he recalls the murder of his parents before his eyes and the butchering of his older brother. The flat narrative of the bloody civil war, the partisan reprisals, the flights to the hills, the youngster's increasing inability to react to pity or fear—all carry a conviction that makes Spiro's plight a fit subject for the most serious fiction.

That Spiro goes on to act at least as the instrument of destruction for his young Greek wife is a part of his predetermined fatality. . . .

At this point, the author evokes Blake's Promethean image of a boy nailed to a rock. But this man-child is also a Spiro, realistic, opportunistic, crafty. The rock is not the women who seek in vain to bind him, but the faceless profile of our time.

Francis King's . . . *The Dark Glasses* held promise of probing insight and cauterizing power. He is a young writer with intensity of purpose skillfully concealed behind a facile style, swift-paced dialogue and a spoofing surface-irony. But the purpose is there, foremost. In *The Man on the Rock* he has written an engrossing book.

Frances Keene, "Modern Prometheus," in The New York Times, *January 19, 1958, p. 27.*

THE TIMES LITERARY SUPPLEMENT

[*The Custom House*] is a story about foreigners living and working in Japan. It is perhaps a contribution to our understanding of the Japanese and our relations with them; but it is largely spoilt by the author's apparent distaste for both communities. When the characters act ignobly this seems natural, because we have been given some insight into their ignoble motives; when they act generously we are surprised—the springs of action are mysterious. This is a reflection of our everyday experience, but it is not endearing in a novel.

The scene is Kyoto, among a missionary group, with the limelight on an Australian neurotic called Welling, who has terrible memories of his own past cowardice, and a sense of uselessness in his mission. A set of Japanese characters is centred on the disagreeable tycoon Furomoto—his family, employees, and female victims. The story is partly told by Knox, a middle-aged university teacher, through pages of his journal which are remarkably similar in tone to the rest of the book: an inept man, easily disgusted, unable to "make" the Japanese woman whom he loves.

Two acts of violence provide the main climaxes of the plot. A Bible-class student, unjustly dismissed by Furomoto, tries to blow him up, but ridiculously blows up himself instead. A strip-girl, one of Furomoto's mistresses, is murdered, and the blame falls on Welling, whom she has unsuccessfully tried to win as a lover. In the last few chapters, when Welling is struggling in the mesh of accusation, the book achieves dramatic unity and at last begins to grip. The earlier climax seems less relevant, through lack of proper build-up; but Welling's character has been so thoroughly investigated that his cowardice and nobility in an extreme situation gain our assent. The book ends in pathos, emotional confusion, and a sad feeling of defeat on almost all fronts.

There are several reasons for the relative failure of this novel. One is that [Mr. King] has experimented with a technique of using many points of view. It is a relief to come back to the chapters where Knox is "I", even though one is repelled by his emotional ineffectiveness. There are so many minor experiences scattered through the book, and the interior views of the characters are so brief and superficial, that the reader often cannot remember who experienced what.

Another reason is that the author has apparently not enough faith in his plot and characters to tell the bare story: it is bolstered out with an enormous amount of general comment and detail about Japan. When an author finds himself in foreign parts, with a keen eye for externals and an intelligent surmise about motives, he may be tempted to give us the lot. Mr. King seems to have taken this line. The result is that we are often reminded of our externality. . . . Externals replace insights, too, in the delineation of character. Sometimes Mr. King gets his knife into one of his people and cannot leave the externals alone; for example, an Englishwoman called Colethorpe. Poor girl, we are told time and again what gargantuan buttocks she had, till her character seems merely gluteal.

The style of writing is rather thick, and this sometimes heightens the squalor. The style in the conversations is often particularly prosy and priggish, uninfluenced by the modern tendency to imitate real speech. . . .

Defects of technique would be forgiven at once if the book showed real compassion. Or even if it were inspired by generous indignation or savage hatred. Instead, we are brought to share the author's irritations. Are these a sufficient basis for art? In the latter part of the book our attention is held, but many readers will find it hard to get there.

> *"Seen from the Outside," in* The Times Literary Supplement, *No. 3108, September 22, 1961, p. 625.*

JAMES KELLY

For those who have wondered from time to time what life in Japan is really like since the war, this acid, unsparing novel by an Old Japan Hand may fill in some blank spaces. *The Custom House,* received appreciatively in England, is Francis King's ninth novel, and one gets a strong impression that it has been distilled directly from the author's own disenchantment while serving as a British administrator in Kyoto.

One possible subtitle for his book might have been: "A resident Occidental surveys and interprets everyday life among the inscrutable, mysterious, quaintly lethal Orientals." Mr. King's style is a skillful mixture of querulous social comment and true-toned dialogue which carries him far and wide in an effort to serve up the flora, fauna and flavor of a civilization not likely to be understood from the window of a tourist bus. Roaming al fresco among the Japanese and Caucasians who are attached to a mission on the outskirts of Kyoto, the author achieves an informative, tumultuous and thought-provoking novel which at times becomes as confusing and unidentifiable as the subject it explores. The reader, left to shift for himself among entwined subplots, may agree with the derelict newspaperman who drifts through *The Custom House*: "There's no * * * country in the world where people are so much like each other—not good, not bad, like *like*. There are no individuals in Japan; or damned few. Just a race."

The story begins in the diary of Bill Knox, a middle-aged university teacher from England, who views existence in Kyoto with a jaundiced eye. We follow his bleak, mostly unrewarded romance with Setsuko, an Anglicized Japanese girl who lives with her unsavory rich uncle. Now and then we skip to the

problems of a cowardly missionary who has become obsessed with the charms of a young strip-teaser. There is also a peripheral English artist who rooms with the girl by day and fills the rest of her time with a tepid physical-culturist attached to the mission staff. . . .

Tangled plot threads pull tighter when the teaser is found murdered in circumstances which implicate the missionary. A great many people lose face before this scandal concludes, but it does give the missionary a chance to preach one final parable which, in turn, gives the novel its title:

> If in this world, things be found in a man's luggage which do not belong to him, what does it matter? He cannot be cheated out of the life eternal. And if in this world someone escapes punishment by passing off his contraband on another, let us not vex ourselves. He may blind the customs-officers of this world; but the customs-officers of the next world cannot be blinded, and he will be found out and punished according to his deserts.

In lugubrious closing passages, Knox thankfully packs for Athens, and Setsuko seems implicated as a Communist spy or worse. . . .

Despite its precarious construction and scatter-shot attention, *The Custom House* nevertheless gives evidence that Mr. King is at home with the raw tragedy and pathos of life—and that he is a forceful writer who can make you respect what he has to say.

> *James Kelly, "Vignettes of Kyoto," in* The New York Times Book Review, *June 3, 1962, p. 26.*

BRIGID BROPHY

Mr Francis King's new novel [*The Last of the Pleasure Gardens*] confronts a question most people must have glanced at and glanced quickly away from: what would one do and feel if one had an idiot child?

Ostensibly, Mr King offers a sympathetic, documentary reply. His middle-class couple in Battersea (*those* are the gardens of the title) are as ordinary as their names, Barbara and Peter. Their sole eccentricity is to have a third child when they are already middle-aged—and that lends plausibility, at least in folklore terms, to the child's being an idiot and gives external conviction to the hysteria of his mother's love for him. Mr King establishes the pair in family and social relationships just odd and complex enough for verisimilitude.

And yet this is not, I think, a naturalistic novel. Because his use of words is largely unmetaphorical and without bravura, Mr King passes for a much more literal transcriber of appearances than he is. Examined close to, the texture of the information he gives resolves itself, like some paint surfaces by Titian, into a series of mordantly selected observations rendered economically and in ambiguous isolation, each a tiny scene in itself. The seeming solidity of Barbara and Peter is done by brilliant sleight of hand. They are enough there for one to assert that their marriage would have met some disaster if not this one, but not quite enough for one to be sure they could hold attention for their own sakes in a different situation. That is quite enough for Mr King's purpose—which, however, I take to be less decriptive than dramatic; he is concerned with the act in which their situation disintegrates.

The apparently naturalistic surface is in this book a structural necessity. Only by stretching over it a very everyday-looking catwalk could Mr King entice a reader to cross the pit of pessimism he is opening up. . . . Only after one has been led into it does one realise one is imaginatively participating in a martyrdom.

And indeed Mr King has set himself the very problem, in relation to his readers' feelings, which Renaissance painters were set by a commission for a gruesome martyrdom. He solves it with Old Master painterly skill—and even an Old Master device of design. The story is told in violent temporal fore-shortening. The book opens after the culminating destruction has happened, then goes back to the start of the story and proceeds chronologically until it catches up with itself. This is not quite fluently done—the first section is a touch over-crowded with allusions the reader cannot yet take. But it mar-vellously makes its main effect: because the reader partly knows the outcome in advance, it transfers to him some of the char-acters' agony of foreboding—for, of course, the unspoken hor-ror the parents face all through is not knowing what will become of the idiot when he is grown-up and orphaned, a horror which forces at least one of them to the unconscious resolve that he must not be allowed to grow up. Because the reader knows from the start that he won't be, Mr King's narrative can, as it approaches its climax, make more and more daring omissions and syncopations. . . . In its last effect the book seems the very opposite of a fabrication to answer the question 'What would it be like if . . .?' Rather, I surmise, some passionate despair in Mr King's imagination sought out the question as a means of articulating a violent shriek against those who, as the her-oine's thoughts put it, 'refused ever to admit that life was, for the most part, hideous and cruel and unjust'. (pp. 530-31)

> *Brigid Brophy, ''A Martyrdom,'' in* New Statesman, *Vol. LXX, No. 1804, October 8, 1965, pp. 530-31.*

KENNETH ALLSOP

A low-key modulation strikingly brings off Francis King's dreadful domestic *Götterdämmerung* [***The Last of the Pleasure Gardens***]. Upon the middle-class, reasonably liveable, Batter-sea marriage descends the thunderbolt of an idiot child. The parents' confusion of disgust and furious, pitying love destroys them and the child: murder, prison for the husband. The Wag-nerian chords are held precisely muted by the plainness, almost the nullity, of Mr. King's expertly controlled vernacular. I balked only at the last-minute transference of the story into the husband's mouth, his explanation. Unnecessary. We know al-ready. Mr. King is the invisible author: without intruding, he opens the door upon his scene, soft and slippered.

> *Kenneth Allsop, ''Clapped by Love,'' in* The Spec-tator, *Vol. 215, No. 7163, October 8, 1965, p. 456.*

THE TIMES LITERARY SUPPLEMENT

''What the hell is Nishimura doing?''

''Exchanging meaningless politenesses'', I an-swered.

The very first sentence of Mr. King's new novel [***The Waves Behind the Boat***] is characteristic of all his work. He is an expert on the minor social emotions: irritation, embarrassment, resentfulness, spleen. Ask a cross question, and his novels will give you a cross but authoritative answer: really these people are impossible, unpunctual, dishonest, lazy, even if stupid En-glishmen also say so.

But one should not confuse Mr. King's narrator (the wife of a young English lecturer in Japan) too easily with her creator. She is often the mouthpiece for the kind of barbed observations which littered the gloomy pages of *The Custom House* with the corpses of Anglo-Japanese relations. But basically she is in this book to be educated, not to educate us. She and her husband are asked by the Japanese police to identify the corpse of an Englishwoman whom they vaguely know. Through a fog of bureaucracy and foreignness it emerges that she was not all she might have been. Not only did she sponge off all comers—as the young couple had found to their own cost—but she slept with some of them too. Mr. King has always been a dab hand at parasites, and there is a pleasing symmetry in the dead woman's ability to use up Bill and Mary's time and emotions, in death as in life, without being a close enough friend to justify such demands.

But at this point the novel becomes more ambitious. The dead woman was drowned while staying with a mysterious family of White Russians, whose reluctance to take any responsibility is one of the reasons why the Japanese police dragged Bill and Mary into the case. This couple, domineering Bibi and her elusive brother Sasha, seem completely uninterested in a trag-edy which may have been partly their fault, but very interested indeed in the English couple. Mary stays alone in their ex-traordinary home, whose quarrelling occupants give her what must be one of fiction's least idyllic holidays since the narrator of Isherwood's *Down There on a Visit* rashly went off to his Greek island.

Forsterian mini-drama is at least civilized, and it is a medium Mr. King knows very well; but exotic melodrama is something else. Skeletons rattle in the Akulov family closet, storms break out in stone gardens, the predictable shadow of murder rises and falls, both Bibi and Sasha make equally predictable sexual assaults on poor Mary. Such bald summary is inevitably comic, but it is unlike Mr. King to lend himself so easily to bald summary. He has perhaps overdone the empathy for an un-sophisticated narrator. . . . The author has gone slumming a bit in his portrayal of naive decency, and stretched things a bit in the exotic milieu with which he confronts her.This serious, skilful, intelligent book is better than many, but not Mr. King's best.

> *''Minimelodramatics,'' in* The Times Literary Sup-plement, *No. 3402, May 11, 1967, p. 404.*

DAVID REES

Few English novelists have written with more insight and as-surance on life in Japan than Mr Francis King, and ***The Waves Behind the Boat*** is one of his best books. We begin with the report of a death of an Englishwoman in a remote part of Japan; the nearest British consul isn't able to investigate the tragedy, so he dispatches a young British couple, friends of the dead Thelma, to the scene. From the very outset Mr King success-fully establishes the maze of ambiguities from which his story is made. . . . (p. 618)

[Once] Bill and his wife, Mary, the narrator of the story, arrive at the scene of the death, their troubles have only begun. Before they leave with Thelma's ashes packaged 'in their traditional container' they have met not only an enigmatic chief of police, but Bibi Akulov, a rich White Russian woman with whom Thelma had been staying when she died, and who only in-creases the sense of mystery attending the death. The novel explodes during a further visit to Bibi's house by the sea where an entire tapestry of complex, sinister events and passions interact to change Mary's life for ever. The deployment of character and incident is beautifully wrought and there are revealing references to the confusions of Anglo-Saxon expatriate life, such as the delights of steak-and-kidney pie at the 'English' pub in Kobe. Best of all, over and above the drive of superbly organised narrative, is the way in which Mr King conveys the mood, manners and customs of a country which perhaps of all the lands of the modern world remains a mystery to the foreigner, whether traveller, journalist, consul or council lecturer. (p. 619)

David Rees, "Sense of Mystery," in The Spectator, Vol. 218, No. 7248, May 26, 1967, pp. 618-19.

STANLEY REYNOLDS

Francis King in another day would be a literary star; a Maugham? a D. H. Lawrence? something big anyway, and prized. He has written 11 novels and a book of verse, and *The Brighton Belle* is his third collection of short stories. In them one sees a rare structural talent at work, able to twist an ending without disjointing the framework, able to shape a plot without becoming unrealistic. When he is not-so-good, which is, say, three times in the 13 stories of this collection, it is obviously because he is a natural storyteller and able to make a tale out of anything that comes to hand. He is a first-rate talent and at his best when dealing with death and destruction rather than mere palpitations of the heart. All the tales are of Brighton, town of decaying middle-class gentility, con men, perverts, aristocratic flotsam and working-class jetsam. Because of the unity of subject you could say it may be read like a novel; better to liken it to an eerier sort of day trip. (p. 556)

Stanley Reynolds, "Dreaming," in New Statesman, Vol. 75, No. 1937, April 26, 1968, pp. 555-56.

THE TIMES LITERARY SUPPLEMENT

[In *The Brighton Belle*] Francis King deals with freakish eccentricities in Brighton, concentrating on lonely old people, sexual deviation and juvenile delinquency. The exception to this generalization is the last story, surely the best, about a Japanese scholar and his English girlfriend, who is jealous of his work. This is concentrated and original: it could not have been . . . inspired by a news item. They are all thoroughly accomplished and readable, if occasionally too neat to be taken quite seriously. Mr. King appears in person, as it might be Mr. Isherwood. The early stories of Angus Wilson are also brought to mind, notably in the insistence that lonely, frightened old people can be very cruel, and in the cool, sharp stares at homosexual stirrings. One of the homosexual stories, though, **"The Performance of a Lifetime"**, is exhilarating, lyrical.

"In the Flesh," in The Times Literary Supplement, No. 3463, July 11, 1968, p. 721.

THE TIMES LITERARY SUPPLEMENT

Unrequited love has lapsed recently as a subject for fiction; the pangs accompanying sexual performance have become more familiar. So perhaps it is not surprising that [*A Domestic Animal*] should be about the homosexual feelings of a middle-aged novelist for a married Italian whose energies are exclusively directed towards women. Antonio is a philosopher teaching temporarily in an English university and he takes a room

in Dick's elegant house. From something very like love at first sight, Dick's infatuation develops predictably and the novel turns on his jealousy when he discovers that Antonio is having an affair with a sad, blonde girl who is not worthy of him. Dick's jealousy is debilitating, a torment and impossibly demoralizing, and the portrait of Antonio that emerges through it is of a love object whose qualities are blurred by the feelings he arouses. . . .

There is no such thing as a completely hopeless love, and Francis King is at his best when suggesting those moments of irrational optimism and the lowering of other standards which can go with a possessive, sexual love. . . .

Mr. King has written a strange romance which manages to be truthful about love and the ravages of jealousy too. If the object of the love and the characters who watch it in postures of sympathy or ridicule seem sometimes too formalized and unreal, this can be accounted for by the transforming ways of passion, which are seen to blinker, befog and distort the judgment as well as the senses. The novel is often painful and occasionally silly, but the author has created an oddly touching figure in this middle-aged man roused to self-destructive emotion after a lifetime of indifference, restraint and discretion.

"Ravaged," in The Times Literary Supplement, No. 3582, October 23, 1970, p. 1213.

PATRICK COSGRAVE

[*A Domestic Animal*] is a bad, pernicious book by a writer of obvious integrity and talent who sees only through a glass, darkly. . . .

King's narrator is a sad, queer, English, novelist, who falls helplessly in love with his Italian lodger—a beautiful, wholly unrealised footballer turned philosopher, himself torn between the demands of a eupeptic wife and an attenuated mistress: there is a great deal of sex here. . . .

The distinguishing mark of King's book is the poignant juxtaposition of the ordered and delicate life of its narrator with the primitive character of his passion: Dick tries to live in his antiqued home, waiting for Antonio to return from sessions with Pam in her battered Volkswagen; he is consumed with jealousy, rescued occasionally by an objective realisation that others might be almost as unhappy as himself. Within the inevitably, and deliberately, narrow existence of the selfish, if civilised, homosexual, gradually degrading himself through a necessarily degrading passion, King is brilliant. But that inverted world is very far from enough; for us, for King's talent; for the novel as an art form, as a realisation and judgment of human value. . . .

Every detail in this novel is beautiful and its whole strategy is wrong. In the most brilliant and objective piece of contemporary novel criticism in England since the war, P. H. Newby wrote of King . . . that 'intensity of experience' was his forte and that his characters were among 'strangely foreshortened figures . . . giants and grotesques'.

King's narrator suffers, but nobody else in his book lives: they are all grotesques. His footballer-philosopher has scarcely an intelligent word to utter. He is not only inarticulate in the presence of other philosophers (even when they are queer), he is incapable of sensing or seeing a single intellectual notion or moral feeling: he is a beautiful body, a few words in Italian set in italics and, in the author's recurring word, 'unfathomable'. Yet King—one of the few young writers in Newby's list who is still writing well and usefully—chooses to confine himself within the narrow range of a pervert's limited experience when he, with his talent, could go public, give the novel back its true social dimension and treat of what Denis Donoghue called 'the ordinary universe'.

Patrick Cosgrave, "Three Lapses," in The Spectator, *Vol. 225, No. 7427, October 31, 1970, p. 525.*

SYLVIA CLAYTON

Francis King is the anatomist of expatriates, a writer who brilliantly records their misadventures in a strange environment. While Somerset Maugham shaped from lives in exile extended after-dinner anecdotes, King goes beyond reportage to reveal that clash of expectations which can turn the difference between two cultures into embarrassment, anger, or even hate. In [*Indirect Method*] he moves with confidence, a genuinely cosmopolitan writer, from Japan to Greece, to Italy, to America and back to London, observing how trapped individuals flounder and fail, and registering their behaviour in supple, caustic but never heartless prose.

His best stories pivot on a sense of justice and responsibility, an equilibrium he achieves wittily and without strain. The title story, **"Indirect Method"**, illustrates the cleverness of his technique. It catches the stifling atmosphere of a hotel in Kyoto, where a woman medical lecturer has come to stay, ostensibly to revisit the university where she worked fifteen years earlier, in fact to look up the handsome former student who had been her family house boy and her lover. The reunion is not a success. Osamu is now a business man, married with two children, and the contentment of his marriage is unexpectedly hurtful to Liz, whose husband irritates her. The stratagems that the former lovers adopt to save each other from losing face are described with the utmost neatness and economy. Theirs was always an unequal relationship, and his gift to her of an expensive antique snuff-bottle makes the break between them final. It ends his feeling of obligation; it closes the account.

In another taut, memorable story, **"Sundays"**, a disagreeable English family—father, mother, teenage son—turn away from the sunlit landscape of Lake Como, where they have a villa, to concentrate on a trivial, peevish, conversational brawl. The grandmother, who is treated with no consideration and simply expected to be useful, achieves a certain personal satisfaction as she makes her way to Como by hydrofoil to buy the Sunday newspapers. There are no dramatic events, but there is once again a deep-rooted conflict of standards and expectations, this time between the generations.

Perhaps because Francis King is so quick to detect dangerous tremors in a relationship, even though all on the surface may be calm and bright, he is less successful when his material is in itself sensational. In **"Little Old Lady Passing By"** the elderly Russian woman living in poverty and squalor, befriended by a West Indian woman hospital orderly, turns out in the final paragraph to be a world-famous ballerina; the news comes as a shock of the wrong kind, for this accurate, wakeful style of writing is not suited to romantic fiction. . . .

What makes all the stories a pleasure to read, though, is Francis King's talent for summoning up a person or a scene in a single striking phrase that lies somewhere between poetry and gossip. The sister in hospital who trots up ''like a mettlesome, broadbeamed pony'', the woman psychiatrist ''wearing a leather jacket that had the sheen of pork crackling to it'', the voice of the bouzouki singer, ''its gears stripped from her reckless exploitation of its phenomenal range'', are all instantly fixed in the memory.

Sylvia Clayton, "Culture Shocks," in The Times Literary Supplement, *No. 4050, November 14, 1980, p. 1280.*

ANDREW MOTION

Act of Darkness: the title is teasingly associative. This thing of darkness? Heart of darkness? Even—perhaps—art of darkness? These echoes, like everything else about Francis King's new novel, direct our attention beyond the narrative surface and force us to concentrate on the motives which underlie it. They make us judge the book less as an exotically located detective story—which on the face of it, it is—than as an analysis of the psychology of crime. They give us the thrills of a murder story not as ends in themselves, but as a means to investigating an obsession with death and concealment.

The obsession is introduced with slow relish in "Omens", the first of the novel's six sections, in which all the main characters are given a chapter each. First is six-year-old Peter Thompson, a solitary, tale-telling boy living (in the 1930s) with his family in India, brooding on the murder of his Uncle Jack, who was hacked to pieces by a demented Gurkha. The same event haunts his half-sister Helen, and its effect is intensified by the grief she feels for her dead mother Eithne. Peter's young Eurasian governess Clare—rescued from tedious hotel work by his father Toby—suffers the gloom by adoption, refracting it into frustration with her job and unhappiness at being pursued by her employer. . . .

These intimations of mortality are horribly confirmed by the novel's second section (the "Act") which contains its pivotal incident. Peter's body is discovered in the servants' lavatory, stabbed, with his throat cut from ear to ear. A bra (yes, that's right, a bra) is discovered beside him in the slime—and this, it turns out, is the murder weapon: he has been suffocated with it, then knifed. Dacoits are credited with the crime, but evidence suggests that someone in the household is in fact responsible.

Thus far, the novel creates a sense of emotional enclosure and restricted geographical range—in spite of the vastness of the country in which it is set. In the third and fourth sections the locations become more wide-ranging and the atmosphere, consequently, grows less intense. This is unfortunate, since the mood of the central characters remains guiltily claustrophobic and their existence circumscribed. Helen returns to England to live with an aunt in Earls Court, and endures a series of metaphorical and literal imprisonments. Her movements are governed by consideration for the aunt, she is stuck in London during the Blitz, and when her father, Isabel and the new baby return from India at the end of the war, they burden her with obligations and fears. Not even her training as a doctor, and her love for a young Jewess, Ilse, can alleviate her sense of oppression—which culminates in her confessing to the murder of Peter. . . .

Helen's time in jail is relayed in the novel's weakest and most disruptively discordant section: "an unpublished, private memoir" kept by the Prison Governor. Helen is pictured as clever, withdrawn, and capable of inspiring regular outbursts of lesbian love—in the Governor herself among others. Not only does the memoir's tone imply an unease on King's part about the likelihood of the Governor's falling for Helen—"one of the strangest and most painful episodes in my life"; it also prepares us too well for the book's final revelations. On a visit to Australia following her release, Helen bumps into Clare, and it transpires that they had an affair in India. When Peter accidentally caught them in bed, Clare suffocated him with the nearest thing to hand—the bra—and Helen stabbed him to make it seem the work of Dacoits.

After the evasions and secrecies which preceded it, this final disclosure is meant to have the ring of truth. But does it? For the most part, the story-line of the book is handled with the professionalism one would expect of King. . . . Yet its attempts to wed the fictional events to convincing psychological motives are often unsatisfactory. This is largely because King is at pains to build a tension between the highly detailed and realistic presentation of certain circumstances (the murder, the flat in London), and a studiedly vague account of others (the Indian home and the prison are unnamed). The point, presumably, is to produce a feeling of generality and potential mystery; the effect, though, is to create a sense of permanently impending imprecision—and therefore also of implausibility. And this crucially damages our readiness to accept and understand the reasons for the murder, by which the book stands or falls. It is not just that we worry about how easy it in fact is to suffocate someone with a bra—nor simply that we think a six-year-old seeing two women in bed together would not know enough to accuse them of lesbianism—but that the reasons for Clare's doing so are not psychologically justified. It is hard not to feel, indeed, that the murder's symbolic value distorts its narrative credibility. Decoded, it reads like an attack by women on men (or boys, anyway) which, because it is so cruelly and unnecessarily extreme, implies the author's disapproval of women. And put like that, it leaves one feeling that inside *Act of Darkness*—for all its calm control—is a much more disturbed and disagreeable, not to say actually offensive, novel trying to get out.

Andrew Motion, "Keeping It in the Family," in The
Times Literary Supplement, *No. 4199, September
23, 1983, p. 1011.*

ANITA DESAI

While [*Act of Darkness*] is said to be based on an actual child murder in Victorian England, Francis King has not transferred it to the colonial India of the 1930's without reason. He has used every possible means to underline his theme of pervasive deceit and heighten the atmosphere of threat and destruction. Every object mentioned is employed to further the effect. Mr. King creates extraordinary tension and maintains it as the tale winds its way up to not one but three climaxes. There are no light interludes, no comic characters. From start to finish, one hears the same insistent drumbeat as in those old films about trouble in the tropics—sex-and-death, say the relentless drums, death-and-sex.

The Thompson family lives in ease and luxury in its Eden—summering in a large villa in a hill station surrounded by lakes and forests, within reach of the club and with access to the excitements of the city where Toby Thompson owns hotels and runs his extensive business. Yet this is not the India of Kipling or Rumer Godden. The sun does not illuminate, the space does not liberate, the sounds have no harmony. This Indi glowers

in a fitful light, it cowers beneath an approching thunderstorm, and omens crowd the pages. . . .

Mr. King does not, however, see the menace as an external one, imposed by history. He clearly does not share the impression of the Eurasian governess, Clare, that the Thompson household is clean, gracious and desirable, in contrast to her own home, which is distressingly squalid and mean. He is agonizingly aware that the superiority of the English family's home is founded on a veritable sewage pit of immorality. Again and again, he writes of the disparity between the lives of the self-indulgent rulers and those of their dark-skinned servants.

Indeed, gross exploitation involves the whole land, its government, business and society. Exploiter and exploited, plunderer and plundered, all struggle in a morass symbolized by the pit of ordure in the servants' outdoor lavatory, to which the child Peter is forbidden to go but does.

Apart from brutal collision, there is no meeting point between East and West. But when the most repulsive murder of all is committed, the killers are not those who have reason to commit it; the criminal instinct erupts from the whitest and purest bosom. Evil is not safely distanced, external; it lies within, in terrifying proximity. The corruption is not in the land but in the uncontrolled urges of its rulers. . . .

That was an unacceptable proposition at the time, and the crime is passed off as the act of untraced terrorists. Yet guilt pursues them all like an ineradicable disease. Ultimately it leads the heroine to "confess" in order "to atone." But here we come to another of Mr. King's unexpected subtleties. Although he makes us recognize evil in a palpable, almost physical way, so hotly do we feel its breath, so close is its bitter stench, he does not pretend it can be exorcised or vanquished by the cleansing act of confession. His conflict is not between right and wrong but between good and evil, an altogether different matter, transcendent rather than merely social. . . .

However evil man may appear to be, Mr. King seems to say, he is a hundredfold more evil still. In the steaming Garden of Eden he has painted, there is sin without redemption and the Devil is never vanquished by the Saviour. It is as stark and disquieting a theory when applied to private lives as when applied to public affairs, and Francis King's achievement in *Act of Darkness* is to make the one a metaphor for the other.

Anita Desai, "Evil in an Indian Eden," in The New
York Times Book Review, *December 25, 1983, p. 7.*

MARY HOPE

Francis King's craft is now such, that embarking on his latest novels is like getting into a superbly engineered car, driven by a daring but faultless chauffeur, for a destination unknown but never in doubt. You know that you will hardly be conscious of gear changes; that curious, surprising and sometimes alarming detours will never mean that he has lost his way, merely that they will enlighten the arrival. He is now writing at the height of his powers, using his skills to treat of matters disturbing to a modern reader. A rush of creativity, which last year produced a compulsive study of evil and atonement in *Act of Darkness*, now throws up an examination of the emotional undertow which affects those faced with bereavement.

At least, that is one way of reading *Voices in an Empty Room*, and for the rationalists among his readers it is perhaps the only way. But the book is also a deliberately ambiguous account—

how, indeed, could it be otherwise?—of the search for communication with those on the Other Side, leaving the reader guessing until the last pages—and beyond—about the validity of paranormal experience.... *Voices in an Empty Room* is set in the familiar, safe south-coast and London milieu, and it is the characters themselves who carry the load of oddness and shock which leads from revelation to revelation.

The groundwork is immaculate. Sybil, the poised, confident and groomed headmistress of a smart south-coast girls' school, retires to her study to write, hanging on the door a 'Do Not Disturb' notice from the Stratford-upon-Avon Hilton about which she has always felt rather guilty, being obsessively honest in details like paying for an extra *Guardian*, leaving her bus fare with fellow passengers, and so on. Her staff and girls assume she is working at the edition of Meredith's letters on which she has long collaborated with her beloved brother, Hugo, recently dead as a result of—according to the coroner—'a stupid and tragic accident'. Then, with a chill, we realise that she is, in fact, giving herself up to automatic writing. The journey begins.

From now on, in a brilliant series of characterisations and narrative legerdemain, Mr King takes us backwards and forwards in time, between Sybil's quest to contact the adored Hugo, and Hugo's disastrous attempts to demonstrate the paranormal: so-called mind readings carried out between the disturbing twin nephews of his friend Henry's housekeeper. Hugo's experiments lead him not to the paranormal, but to only too human weakness and catastrophe: what has previously been hidden from him is not the supernatural, but the truth about his own suppressed nature. His emotional obtuseness ends in disaster: his researches have been attempts to run before he can walk.... Hugo's life is finally seen as a series of Chinese boxes in which no one is playing straight, either with themselves or with him: emotional trickery is mirrored by crookery, blackmail and deceit.

So, gently, Francis King apparently leads into one blind alley after another in the search for communication with the dead. One fake paranormal experience after another is exposed until the reader feels, comfortably, that this is a simple, worldly mystery story. But that is to reckon without his masterly narrative tricks: it is much more than that. Along the way, Sybil, by apparent chance, meets two other women who are also trying to establish longed-for contact with lost loved ones. Lavina Trent is a brilliant actress, in voluntary retirement after the hideous death—accident or suicide?—of her only son whom in the eyes of the world she has always adored and cherished, but whom, it becomes clear, she has always used as an adjunct to her own image. Bridget Nagel is desperately trying to get through to her journalist husband, killed during the Falklands conflict, without whom she is perilously adrift, prey to the cruellest of con tricks. (pp. 22-3)

As I have said, the reader is kept guessing throughout, as false trail follows false trail; the curtain is tantalisingly lifted and then, again, lowered. Poltergeist manifestations in an East End flat seem real enough but Bridget's revelation turns out to be a cruel trick. Or is it? Has the Other World oblique ways of manifesting itself? Revelations may get through, but to the wrong people in the wrong place. As Lavinia says, 'That's what is so infuriating. People get something; all the time they keep getting something. But the something is not what one wants. It's all so incalculable and uncontrollable.'

The book ends with the possibility of some such askew revelation, but the characters are cheated of it and thrown back

on desolation and shreds of faith. Only the omniscient author has let us into the secret, to decide whether it is a real revelation or just coincidence—just another monkey with a typewriter. (p. 23)

Mary Hope, "Conjuring Tricks," in The Spectator, *Vol. 253, No. 8146, August 25, 1984, pp. 22-3.*

JULIAN SYMONS

Hugo is a literary gent working on a monumental edition of Meredith's letters. He is married with two children, but has homosexual urges or twinges. Lavinia is a successful, highly regarded actress. Writing in the *TLS*, Hugo said her Hedda was the finest he had seen. Bridget is "a small, pretty woman of forty-eight" whose husband has been killed in the Falklands. What joins these three characters? The belief in an afterlife, or at least in the possibility of reaching beyond the material world through psychic phenomena. When Hugo falls to his death from the balcony of a Brighton hotel, his devoted sister (and Meredithian collaborator) Sybil tries to reach him through automatic writing. The suicide of Lavinia's son Stephen moves her to similar activities, and Bridget longs to be in touch with her dead husband Roy.

Francis King's *Voices in an Empty Room* tells these separate stories very cleverly, shifting from past to present through sections called "Was" and "Is" (shifting tenses too, in a way that occasionally makes for awkward reading), and ending with the three women meeting for the first time. This final passage is called "Will Be?", the interrogation mark presumably meant to suggest that this may not happen, although use of the future tense here rather curiously makes the tone assured rather than tentative....

Skill, ingenuity, some phrases finely turned; yet this is not a successful novel, in part because the three stories remain essentially separate, so that there is a distinct and uncomfortable change of gear from one to another. More important than this, though, is the fact that King has chosen, in psychic belief, a linking theme unsuited to his talent. He operates most successfully by indirection, so that, for example, we are never positively told until Stephen's death of his sado-masochistic inclinations. Such obliquities are not suited to accounts of activities like automatic writing. In life intelligent people may be deeply credulous—Conan Doyle believed in those photographs of fairies at the bottom of the garden—but in this respect life won't do for fiction....

The book's final suggestion, that although much trickery exists in the psychic field, some kind of communication outside logical knowledge is possible to minds with a particular fine tuning, is rather anticlimactic. What are essentially three clever and at times moving stories have been stitched into a novel that is less than the sum of its parts.

Julian Symons, "Believing in the Beyond," in The Times Literary Supplement, *No. 4248, August 31, 1984, p. 964.*

ROXANA ROBINSON

Francis King's editors are not really his friends. Why, otherwise, would they allow this English novelist and critic to publish a collection of 21 stories so wildly uneven in quality? Mr. King's last novel, *Voices in an Empty Room,* showed him master of a subtle, melancholy style, rich and understated. At his best he achieves this in his short stories, but it occurs rarely in [*One Is A Wanderer*]. "**Indirect Method**" is a poignant story about an Englishwoman who returns to Japan and visits her family's former houseboy, now a married businessman, who had been her lover. The great chasm between them, and the failure of emotion to bridge it finally, is beautifully rendered, as it is in "**The Festival of the Dead**," about an Englishwoman whose Japanese lover mourns the death of his young son. . . . But the rest of the stories are crude and heavily ironic, lacking depth, perception and finesse. We have the feeling that he is dashing these off. In three of the stories, for example, there appears a woman whose hair is "an improbable shade of orange." Using the same trite phrase three times in the same book is not a criminal offense, but it makes the author's position clear: Mr. King simply can't be bothered to think up a new phrase, one that startles and delights and brings a character into vivid focus. Instead we are rushed and rattled through these stories, thick with clichés, thin with ideas, as if Mr. King has other things on his mind—not fiction, unfortunately. And his friends are no help to him at all.

> *Roxana Robinson, in a review of "One Is a Wanderer," in* The New York Times Book Review, *March 2, 1986, p. 24.*

D. J. TAYLOR

Although Francis King has been writing for over 40 years—the pieces brought together in *One Is A Wanderer* go back to 1949—the themes of his fiction endure. Mr King's impulse stems, I should say, from a conviction of the impossibility of establishing a satisfactory relationship, and also from a deep-rooted disgust of human inadequacy. These stories display a characteristic assortment of second-rate egotists to their worst possible advantage; the terrible family of "**Mess**," complacent, sponging Eleanor in "**Home**," the self-centred Japanese professor of "**Loss**." So painstakingly are human defects conveyed, so sharp are the physical sensations engendered, that you end up hating large parts of the *dramatis personae*: a characteristic, possibly, of all the best-regulated fiction.

It is an oddly narrow perspective, compounded by a uniformity of subject-matter. Mr King specialises: he writes about decaying old queens whose voices can be heard fluting above the chinking glasses; about queer, resourceful old women, psychic phenomena, and inscrutable yet vulnerable orientals. His strength is his dialogue, which reflects the turns and cadences of everyday speech and instantly pins his characters down, conveying their boorishness or irresolution in a few brief sentences. "**Sundays**" is as representative of Mr King's talent as any. An old woman, staying with her ghastly daughter, son-in-law and grandchild on Lake Como, undertakes an expedition to collect the English newspapers. Brought back, they remain unread: but still she feels a sense of achievement, of small barriers overturned. It is a tiny epiphany.

For all this skill, so cunningly deployed, it is worth asking why—in the light of comparisons with Chekhov—these stories are not quite of the highest quality. The answer lies not in the absence of charity, or in the obvious hooks, or even in the echoes of Maugham and Mansfield, but in the fact that they are almost *too* complete. Writers like Joyce convey in their stories an otherworldliness, the sensation that each story is a pinpoint of light in the centre of nebulous haze. There is about them an air of fragmentation, of randomness which does not exist in Mr King's sharp, tightly-ordered intimations of disgust.

However, it is futile to criticise a writer for not being like another writer. Francis King has written some of the finest short stories to have appeared in English since the War. It is a pity that all the collections from which *One Is A Wanderer* is drawn are out of print. (p. 54)

> *D. J. Taylor, "Artefacts & Art," in* Encounter, *Vol. LXVII, No. 1, June, 1986, pp. 53-6.*

ROSALIND WADE

[Francis King's *Frozen Music* is] set in India, a scene already explored by him with such memorable effect in the vivid and terrifying *Act of Darkness*.

In *Frozen Music,* the action is contained in a strictly limited time-span, during the visit of three ill-assorted people and their Indian driver to the unattractive small township of Balram. The expedition has a special purpose. The oldest member of the party, Philip, wishes to inspect his wife's grave, which he has not seen since she died just before World War II. He is a frail and ailing man, not really up to the gruelling journey. With him are his disillusioned and recently divorced son Rupert, who, by means of intuitive reportage and numerous flashbacks, serves as narrator, and Philip's attractive Finnish wife, Kirsti, many years his junior. There is little comfort to be had on arrival at Balram for the main hotel is too full to accommodate them and the alternative is an unsavoury place in which to eat and sleep. Nostalgic expeditions follow, including a visit to friends who had 'stayed on' and come to love the unlovable Balram.

For both the father, Philip, who lost his wife so many years ago, and the son, Rupert, bereaved at such an early age, it is a painful period of readjustment and for Kirsti could have been one of embarrassment, had she not possessed a resilient and resourceful spirit. Not unexpectedly, Philip soon succumbs to an indigenous bug, thus throwing Kirsti and Rupert into closer personal proximity. Their clandestine visit to the local cemetery is conveyed with notable sensitivity and all that is revealed by the headstone and its immediate neighbour would be almost unbearably poignant but for the sharp humour with which the torrid and deteriorating situation is observed. Of course, Rupert and Kirsti have by this time become deeply attracted to each other; of course, they are deeply concerned about the pain this will cause Philip—yet in the final chapter all is resolved—how, where and when is not revealed and perhaps the reader's unsatisfied desire to know more about the transition period is the only casualty of the restricted novella length. (pp. 213-14)

> *Rosalind Wade, in a review of "Frozen Music," in* Contemporary Review, *Vol. 251, No. 1461, October, 1987, pp. 213-14.*

RALEIGH TREVELYAN

The chilly title of [*Frozen Music,* a] beautifully constructed short novel . . . conceals a story of torrid emotions in the plains of central India. Around 1960 an oddly assorted family trio sets out from England to visit the grave of Philip's long-dead first wife in a small town called Balram, near Indore. Philip, an elderly ex-publisher and failed writer, kind and vague, has recently married an attractive and scrupulously efficient young Finnish woman, Kirsti, who nursed him after his prostate operation. *Frozen Music* is the title of the book on architecture he always meant to finish. That he should have wanted to embark on this quest with Kirsti, only four months after their marriage, is indeed surprising. They are accompanied by Philip's son Rupert, the narrator, a somewhat calculating individual recovering from a divorce and haunted by the memory of his mother's death from tuberculosis. . . .

Francis King has always shown himself a master of conveying the undercurrents of half-truths and tentative expressions of love and irritation within a family. As in his previous novel with an Indian setting, *Act of Darkness,* there is a mystery, leading up to an unexpected climax. In this case the mystery, gradually peeled away, concerns the horror of Rupert's mother's death. . . . The squalor and seediness of the new, industrialized India that has crept over and submerged the old British cemetery at Balram comes as a shock after the romantic Lake Palace at Udaipur. . . . Philip gradually and confusedly has to accept the reality of the fact that this spot where he might have liked to have been buried (and what about Kirsti? Rupert wonders) has become hideous. He is taken ill, and Rupert and Kirsti are left alone to go off on their fatal drives around Balram.

One of Francis King's typically sharp vignettes occurs in a hotel dining-room. Rupert hears a furious voice behind him: "What the hell's going on here? Do we have to wait all night?" That's a voice from my childhood, he thinks. He turns and sees that the speaker is not "some puffy, crimson-faced relic of the Raj, but a beautiful young Sikh, his curly beard in a net". In contrast, later, there is the sight of the shabby figure of the once powerful maharajah, unshaven, with trodden-down heels. . . .

Some of us may have an urge to seek out places of a lost past: places of happy childhood memories perhaps, or connected with people we have loved. Nearly always it turns out to be a mistake. There is a cruelty in this book, but at its heart is the moving and strongly felt theme of return and disillusion.

> *Raleigh Trevelyan, "Indian Summer," in* The Times Literary Supplement, *No. 4409, October 2-8, 1987, p. 1074.*

CHRISTOPHER HAWTREE

Francis King's twentieth novel opens verbosely, with "runnels", "raceme", "prehensile" and "entablature" all in a three-page chapter which depicts a night-time death by water and rock; but then, the first, italicized line of the book is, *"she imagines it as a novelist might imagine it"*. Lest this be taken as a work announcing itself as "post-modern", it should be said that *The Woman Who Was God* then whips along. As in other books King has written since the late-1970s digression of *Danny Hill* and *The Action,* a mystery appears to lie at the centre. Its full meaning strikes from another quarter, one which readers might anticipate but which takes them no less by surprise (rather more satisfactorily than it did in *Act of Darkness*).

To say too much would be to spoil things, for the succession of events is itself one of the novel's main delights: events by which the divorcee and dodgy restaurateur, Ruth St Just (puzzlingly, the opening sentence calls her Ruth St John), is brought to the pit of the mind as she confronts each obstacle set in the way during her attempt to discover the true circumstances of the death of her only son, Jim, a non-swimmer who has holed up in a strange Community in the charge of Mother on an island off the African coast. With relish, King describes the behaviour of Ruth's oafish ex-husband, an estate agent. . . . Ruth duly becomes one herself, Whitehall's procrastination

being such that she puts the Cotswold restaurant behind her and heads for Africa, press alerted.

Africa is evoked not so much vividly as genuinely. Scene after scene remains in the mind; notable is the curious incident of the food harvested from the coconut-trees which overhang a swimming pool: "something moved at the crest of one of them. A bird, she thought, a huge ungainly bird." It proves to be a man, his task one of cutting away the fruit and letting it fall waterwards, while her fascination with it brings about a priapism which, perhaps punningly, arouses her "devouring curiosity". The narrative, in which one senses so much waiting beneath its surface, seethes all the more when Ruth reaches the island of Ellampore. Perplexity and mistrust provoke an increasing claustrophobia which stops nothing short of devastation—all the greater for final evidence of the dual egotism latent in the novel's title.

All this carries one along, but there are moments when vocabulary is stretched a little too far, blurring the image. Enjoyable as King's novels always are, it is in his short stories that he is at his most incisive: perhaps more of them will be reissued (and written) as a result of the success this novel is sure to enjoy.

> *Christopher Hawtree, "Into Africa," in* The Times Literary Supplement, *No. 4439, April 29-May 5, 1988, p. 471.*

ROSALIND WADE

There are some authors, such as Charles Dickens and Sir Walter Scott, who were prolific, and often condemned on that account: others as for instance E. M. Forster or Jane Austen, whose high reputation rests on a relatively modest number of published books. Both situations have much to recommend them. It is always satisfying for a writer to feel that his or her form is maintained throughout the years, even if the performance is occasionally uneven. On the other hand, a small, highly-polished output often remains embalmed in a kind of unalterable perfection. Francis King belongs in the former category. He has published, with astonishing frequency, a large number of novels as well as biography, travel and poetry. It is not many months since his novella, *Frozen Music,* was reviewed in these pages [see Wade's excerpt above] and now comes a new major work, *The Woman Who Was God.* The 'woman' of the title is not the central character. Events centre round a rejected wife and mother bent on investigating the mysterious death of her eighteen-year-old son in Salloum, a semi-fictitious African state.

It is much to Francis King's credit that he invests the depressed, neurotic female with genuine integrity and common-sense. Ruth St. Just is obsessed by her doubts about the circumstances in which the tragedy occurred. Understandably, as the official verdict that young James St. Just died after diving into a half-empty swimming pool fails to take account of his congenital fear of water and the fact that he could not swim. After drawing blank in terms of sympathy or assistance from her ex-husband and various foreign and commonwealth officials, Ruth sells the restaurant through which she has maintained her self-respect and an independent income and journeys forth into unexplored territory to discover the truth for herself. The inefficiently administered travel arrangements and the peculiar people encountered *en route* provide excellent opportunities for the display of Francis King's seemingly inexhaustible fund of information about far-away places. A comedy this certainly is, if in somewhat macabre terms but, as the story progresses, sinister under-currents begin to surface, although these are soon submerged by the exploration of other assorted characters and of Ruth herself. Saloum is, indeed, a law unto itself and only the foolhardy would venture there to stir the muddied waters.

Each revelation heralds a fresh complexity of motive for the boy's death. Needless to say, no relevant information is forthcoming, yet Ruth continues her fearless probing into the very core and heart of the tragedy—the unconventional, run-down community presided over by 'Mother', (the Woman who was God), of which James had unaccountably decided to become a member. Here, where the truth should have been readily discovered, it proves more than ever difficult to establish the facts, yet boldly she persists until, reluctantly, she admits defeat and returns home. However, that is not the end of the story. Francis King is adept at providing startling *dénouements* to his novels and ***The Woman Who Was God*** is no exception. A posthumous 'suicide' note left by James presents a new and sensational twist to the affair, one which must not in fairness be disclosed although for the astute reader, a careful reappraisal of the novel, with its many illuminating comments and subplots, will almost certainly reveal the clues. (pp. 45-6)

Rosalind Wade, in a review of "The Woman Who Was God," in Contemporary Review, *Vol. 253, No. 1470, July, 1988, pp. 45-6.*

Jerzy (Nikodem) Kosinski

1933-

(Has also written under pseudonym of Joseph Novak) Polish-born American novelist, nonfiction writer, and scriptwriter.

Best known for his novel *The Painted Bird,* Kosinski is a controversial writer who employs explicit violence and sexual scenes in his fiction to delineate the importance of maintaining individualism in a society in which, he believes, traditional values and morality are no longer valid. His protagonists are often victims of conflicting social codes who become persecutors in their quests for identity and control over their own lives. Although critics agree that his novels are frequently disturbing, Kosinski is lauded for imaginative, lucid writing and penetrating thematic exposition. Eric Korn commented: ''The clarity of Kosinski's prose leaves one no chance of escaping from its dense, demanding moral perplexities.''

Many of Kosinski's works are regarded as autobiographical. Born in Lodz, Poland, Kosinski was separated from his parents shortly after Nazi Germany's invasion of his homeland, and the fear and violence that he experienced during World War II became a dominant element in his fiction, most notably in *The Painted Bird.* After the war, Kosinski was reunited with his parents in Lodz. As a young adult, he studied sociology and political science at the University of Lodz. In 1957, Kosinski emigrated to the United States, where he taught himself English in four months. During the early 1960s, Kosinski published two sociological studies, *The Future Is Ours, Comrade: Conversations with the Russians* (1960) and *No Third Path: A Study of Collective Behavior* (1962), under the pseudonym of Joseph Novak before concentrating on writing the unorthodox fiction for which he is best known.

Kosinski's first novel, *The Painted Bird* (1965; revised, 1970), chronicles an unnamed boy's struggle to survive in an Eastern European country during World War II. For his own protection, the boy is sent by his politically active parents to live with a foster mother, who dies shortly after his arrival. He wanders the countryside alone, tormented by villagers who mistake him for a Jew or a gypsy because of his dark complexion, and he is struck mute from the atrocities that he witnesses and endures. The boy loses his innocence as well, for when religious faith proves to be futile, he resolves that only evil can combat evil. By the novel's end, reunited with his family, the youth begins to express this belief by becoming the tormentor in his relationships with others. Elie Wiesel asserted: ''Written with deep sincerity and sensitivity, this poignant first-person account transcends confession and attains in parts the haunting quality and the tone of a quasi-surrealistic tale.'' *Steps* (1968), a sequel to *The Painted Bird,* won the National Book Award for fiction. In this work, the boy has become an adult who is unable to conform to accepted social norms and inflicts cruelty on others in retaliation for the viciousness and debauchery imposed on him as a child.

Being There (1971), which is unique in Kosinski's fiction for its absence of sex and violence, satirizes American popular culture and the role of the media in contemporary politics. The hero of this novel is Chance, an illiterate, simple-minded gardener who is forced to enter the outside world after the death

of his reclusive, millionaire benefactor. Unable to understand the complexities that result from his independence, Chance assumes the mannerisms and dialogue of the personalities whom he constantly watches on television. A succession of absurd events thrusts Chance into the political arena, where his gardening theories are taken as ingenious metaphors for the state of the nation, and he is eventually heralded as a potential Presidential candidate. Acclaimed for its subtle, balanced humor and guileless protagonist, *Being There* was adapted for film in 1979, and Kosinski received awards from organizations in Great Britain and the United States for best screenplay.

The Devil Tree (1973; revised, 1981) focuses upon the exploits of a self-centered young heir to a business empire. While some critics faulted Kosinski for excessive use of clichéd dialogue, most maintained that his denunciation of the distorted values of young elitists is well directed. Reception of his following work, *Cockpit* (1975), was more enthusiastic. This novel centers on Tarden, a former government agent who erases all records of his background and creates alternate identities. He tests the authenticity of his new personas by destroying or aiding strangers as he desires. Tarden is the first of Kosinski's protagonists to control his own destiny as well as the fates of others. Jonathan Baumbach observed: ''An abrasive and risky book, *Cockpit* defines itself . . . by the suicidal chances it takes, carrying throughout . . . the lethal pellet of its own destruction, brilliantly defying the limitations of its form.''

In *Blind Date* (1977), Kosinski borrows thematically from the writings of French biologist Jacques Monod, whose work *Chance and Necessity* suggests that human existence is merely a succession of random chances. The hero of Kosinski's novel embodies Monod's beliefs by enjoying a privileged, self-indulgent lifestyle, oblivious to the repercussions of his willful actions. Fabian, the protagonist of *Passion Play* (1979), is a manipulating, libidinous polo player and author who travels throughout America for athletic and sexual challenges. In *Pinball* (1982), which critics generally consider his weakest novel, Kosinski examines the ease with which society can eliminate individuality through the story of an artistically frustrated composer and his girlfriend who track down a reclusive rock star in hopes of disclosing his actual identity. Several critics faulted Kosinski for melodramatic dialogue and one-dimensional characters while contending that his inclusion of graphic sex and violence—pivotal elements in *The Painted Bird* and *Steps*—is merely gratuitous in *Pinball*.

Kosinski defined his recent novel, *The Hermit of 69th Street: The Working Papers of Norbert Kosky* (1988), as ''autofiction,'' which encompasses but does not adhere strictly to fact or fiction. Kosky is a famous and controversial author whose integrity is threatened when a literary journal accuses him of plagiarism. This charge was likewise brought against Kosinski in 1982, when Geoffrey Stokes and Eliot Fremont-Smith suggested in an article published in the *Village Voice* that certain passages of Kosinski's works had been written by others. Kosinski's novel contains over five hundred pages of quotes, footnotes, newspaper clippings, and other documentation in support of his contention that one cannot compose a novel without outside input. Larry McCaffery observed: ''*The Hermit of 69th Street* is a peculiar blend of intimate revelations and abstract musings on the nature of the self and the sources of artistic creativity. It is Kosinski's most ambitious, experimental and nakedly confessional work to date.''

(See also *CLC*, Vols. 1, 2, 3, 6, 10, 15; *Contemporary Authors*, Vols. 17-20, rev. ed.; *Contemporary Authors New Revision Series*, Vol. 9; *Dictionary of Literary Biography*, Vol. 2; and *Dictionary of Literary Biography Yearbook: 1982*.)

ROBERT E. ZIEGLER

The way a man's sense of self is defined and articulated in his interactions with other people is a central concern in the novels of Jerzy Kosinski. In his works, one consistently finds two opposing types of characters: the protagonists, who deliberately make their identities obscure, and the secondary characters, who link their identities to their jobs, or who believe that the power they exercise of the position they occupy legitimates their actions and tells them who they are. The heroes, rather than belonging to a group, prefer to lead self-contained lives, like the itinerant polo-playing Fabian in *Passion Play* or the free-lance agents and assassins in *Blind Date, Steps* and *Cockpit*. . . . Kosinski's protagonist is drawn to his enemies, who feel their identities are grounded in some underlying ideology of which they believe themselves to be representatives. Often the main character will challenge the mythical identity of these others, confronting them with a document, a photo-

graph, or a tape-recording which isolates them from the security of their social and political context and forces them to acknowledge their personal vulnerability. The Soviet officers, the wealthy industrialists, the aloof women, who, in Kosinski's books, are blackmailed, their true identities threatened with exposure, are made to see that their superiority is not grounded in nature, that their prestige does not issue from the correctness of their ideology, the evidence of their business acumen, or their physical attractiveness. Contrary to the function of the posed ''electoral photograph'' which, according to Roland Barthes, promotes identification between voter and candidate and ''tends to spirit away 'politics' to the advantage of a 'manner of being,' a socio-moral status,'' Kosinski's photograph deciphers the myth, forces the subject of the photograph to dissociate himself from his symbolic role, and reveals him to be an impostor. (p. 99)

Myth, Barthes says, ''abolishes the complexity of human acts, it gives them the simplicity of essences . . . , it organizes a world which is without contradictions, because it is without depth, a world wide open and wallowing in the evident, it establishes a blissful clarity: things appear to mean something by themselves.''

The businessman in **Blind Date** who engages in industrial espionage, the Soviet official at the Palace of Science and Culture in **Cockpit** who harasses those whose actions bring them under his purview, cite the mythical legitimacy of their ideological system as justification for what they do. The invocation of the ''natural'' truth of their mythical values forecloses the possibility of any appeal on behalf of the victimized individual. Personal responsibility for another man's welfare or happiness is rejected; his aleatory existence is constantly subsumed to the tenets of the ideology whose truth goes without saying.

It would seem that a myth cannot be impugned except in terms of another myth. In **Blind Date**, Levanter, the protagonist, is out skiing in the Alps one morning when he catches sight of a woman struggling desperately to make her way down the slopes. The three men who seem to be accompanying her pay no regard to her precarious situation. After taking photographs of each of the members of the party, Levanter approaches the woman and begins to question her. Having discovered that the woman, an inexperienced skier has only known her companions since that same morning, he advises her of the danger, telling her that she will likely never make it to the bottom alive.

> ''You've no right to scare a person like that,'' one of the Englishmen intruded.
>
> Levanter turned to the men. ''Now you all listen,'' he said. ''This young lady will walk all the way down, and you will carry her skis. I'll be around to make sure that nothing happens to her. If she is hurt, I have taken enough photographs to have all three of you arrested and charged by the authorities in ValPina.''
>
> ''And in whose name are you doing this?'' snapped one man.
>
> ''Simple humanity will do for the moment,'' Levanter replied. Then, raising his camera, he quickly photographed them again before they could raise their hands to cover their faces. Without a word, the girl took off her skis and handed them to her companions. They all started the long walk down.

Here Levanter uses the camera to interrupt the myth-making process. And when the three men attempt to reintroduce to the discourse a reference to an authority ''in whose name'' people act and which relieves them of personal responsibility, Levanter threatens to produce the photographs which serve as an objectified accusation of their guilt, as they are frozen in the picture and isolated from the context which they have trusted will exculpate them. The photograph is a denunciation of their alibi; it shows where they really are, by reproducing their images as simple signifiers which have no excusatory meaning attached to them. (pp. 100-01)

Kosinski's characters exhibit a corresponding need to gather information on others. *Cockpit* opens with a description of Tarden going through the wardrobe of the hostess whose party he was attending, examining her underwear, and looking through her checkbook. "In the bathroom, I surveyed your cosmetics and studied the vials of pills in your medicine cabinet. I wrote down the name of each doctor on the label, the prescription date and indicated dosage, then took a sample from every bottle." Tarden himself always goes under an alias and arranges his life in such a way that, should circumstances require it, he can disappear without leaving a trace, without feeling himself a captive of his own past or history. As the restrictive myth of Stalinism had encompassed everyone and everything and had stated its principles as both its explanation and justification, Kosinski's characters betray a kind of ideological claustrophobia in their need to know that an escape route is always open to them. . . . In order to safeguard themselves against the prying of bureaucrats and policemen, Kosinski's characters resort to creating phony, ready-made identities for their own use. Unlike the essentialist man of myth, whose actions are condemned to represent the evident "truth" of the myth which supports him and whose only role in the world is "characterized by an endless repetition of its identity," Kosinski's hero is free, through the use of pseudonyms and disguises, to invent his identity anew at all times. He is not, like the existential man, a sum of his own actions, required to assume the burden of responsibility for what he has done before. Having executed in a steam-bath an Eastern European agent whose mission was to denounce potential defectors, Levanter in *Blind Date* discards the image of the corpse from his mind, forces himself to forget his necessary but now insignificant act. With no document as evidence, the memory of the dead can be erased.

> Back in his apartment Levanter felt safe and secure. Scarcely an hour had passed since the clerk had entered Levanter's room at the baths. But what had taken place there had already receded into a remote corner of his memory. It was nothing but an old Polaroid snapshot; no negative, photographer unknown, camera thrown away.

In addition to concealing his real identity through destroying all records of his past acts, Kosinski's character avoids all but the most casual and short-term relationships with other people. He often assumes an empty identity as a mental defective or a deaf-mute as a means of encouraging others to act toward him with the least inhibition and the greatest spontaneity and indifference, thereby inducing them to reveal their true identities to him. While playing the role of a handicapped person, capable of neither hearing, speaking nor understanding, the protagonist in *Steps,* whose name is never given, can observe people and can function as though he were virtually invisible and unsignifying; the response he elicits, the need for others to react to him in a contrived or artificial way is reduced to a zero-degree.

He can also adopt a mythical identity himself, like that of the military officer whose generalized uniform Tarden has made

for himself in *Cockpit.* Such an identity leads others to a particular manner of reading. . . . Once the tailor has established that Tarden is not buying the uniform to impersonate a real military officer, nor to wear as a costume in a play or masquerade, he is instinctively led to ask what the uniform is meant to say: "Exactly what mood do you wish your uniform to convey?" (pp. 102-03)

The carefully balanced interaction between myth-producer and myth-consumer, between the exhibition of power by the one and the contemplation and self-effacement of the other, is raised to a ritualistic level during those ceremonies (academic processionals, policemen's balls, retirement dinners) at which members of a group, whose identities are formally expressed by their distinctive dress, award to their colleagues prizes, trophies and medals in honor of some particular achievement. . . . The pleasure arising from the repetition of these ritual convocations results both from the ostracism of those who exist outside the rigid structure of the fraternal order and from the recognition granted by members to one another that they belong to an organization whose primary function is to constitute itself in opposition to those it keeps out.

The narrator in *Steps* recounts such an event, "a spectacular reception given by the Party for carefully selected local, political, military and scientific dignitaries and delegates from foreign countries." What was unusual about this occasion was the appearance of a scientist, formerly in disrepute within the Party and recently released after having spent years in a labor camp. . . . Along with the other guests, the newly rehabilitated scientist moves among the officials, accepting the medals presented to him and pinning his own on them in return. Then the narrator observes something peculiar happening:

> I was just about to leave when I saw him embracing one of the most highly decorated marshals of the country. Leaning toward the Marshal's glittering chest, he fastened the golden badge to his uniform, piercing it and the fabric with the pin he held in his right hand.

> I approached the marshal for a closer look, and instantly had to restrain myself: the badge was a foreign-made prophylactic. The condom was wrapped and pressed into shiny golden foil, and the name of the foreign factory stood out clearly in small letters embossed around its edges.

> On my way out I saw the results of the scientist's activity: almost all of the high Party and government officials displayed foil-wrapped contraceptives pinned to their lapels. After I left the reception, it occurred to me that only when the dignitaries had reached home and removed their heavy badges would they discover the lighter one. I wondered whether they would remember who had decorated them this way, and if they did, what their reaction would be.

Tarden and Levanter are motivated by a similar need to denounce the falseness of these ceremonies whose only purpose is to affirm the mythically privileged status of the group in power. The reason Kosinski's characters are deemed so subversive or dangerous is that they actively oppose any ideology that expropriates from the individual his prerogative for self-creation and forcibly integrates him into a system in which his acts can do nothing but iterate that system's values. In order to avoid being captured and subsumed to the group's collective image, the character will try to remain anonymous so that others will never be able to relate to him in any ritualistic way. For this reason, his effort to slough off a self whose only function is to curtail the possibility for creative change implies a rejection of the meaning of the word "consequence" both in its causal and temporal senses, and a cultivation instead of the freedom to remain available for whatever life may offer. In this way, he is no longer obliged to react to what he has done before; the present moment is not constantly weighted down by the need for a retrospective accounting for previous deeds. (pp. 104-06)

Kosinski's characters also assume disguises because they require those who encounter them to react in an equally creative way. Whereas the frequency of contacts between people whose relationship is of long standing precludes spontaneity and encourages them to respond only to the conventionalized image they have formed of each other, the newness of the false identity demands a fresh effort from them every time. . . .

Whether it be the disguise or the photograph which reveals the truth of the other person or refocuses it in an unexpected way, the images and documents which Kosinski's characters accumulate and present to those they meet are designed to counteract people's beliefs in the comfortingly mythical positions they occupy and the undemanding nature of the relationships they maintain with those they know or might get to know later. (p. 106)

Occasionally there are passages in Kosinski's novels which express the ontological isolation of the man stripped of his official identity, liberated from the files and dossiers that tell him who he is, and cut off from the people who share with him a preference for engaging in only the most ritualistic types of interaction. The retiree who for decades has hated his job and despised his employer, the political prisoner who is suddenly released from his cell in jail or an asylum, longs to return to the structured familiarity of his captivity. With no more need for dreams of retribution or plans for the redress of personal or social wrongs, they are cast out into freedom, magically absolved of their past and left alone in the present, identical only to themselves. (p. 107)

When entering into relationships with others, with lovers or casual acquaintances, Kosinski's character seeks to preserve this same anonymity. Even when his encounters with the other take place frequently or over a long period of time, he will often suddenly drop out of sight before the two merge into a mythical "we" whose transpersonal unity absorbs the freedom which derives from their respective individualities. He tends to subordinate all relationships to the need to cultivate an identity whose authenticity depends on an ability to step out of his past. He is shown always ready, with luggage packed, to catch a flight to a different country at a moment's notice. Being there, as himself, necessitates leading a life that is ahistorical and apart. On the one hand, Kosinski's novels illustrate a compulsion to attack and expose those who conform to any underlying ideology, who develop a factitious view of themselves, like the Communist committeemen whose status Tarden and Levanter try so hard to demythify. In opposition to them, the protagonist performs an act only when it erases all its traces, when it delivers him from all its antecedents. That is why Kosinski's characters find it so important to live without the burden of any image others may have of them or that they may acquire of themselves. Each of their deeds intends the simultaneous destruction and recreation of that image as the means of attaining the freedom they so ruthlessly seek to exercise. (p. 108)

Robert E. Ziegler, "Identity and Anonymity in the Novels of Jerzy Kosinski," in Rocky Mountain Re-

view of Language and Literature, *Vol. 35, No. 2, 1981, pp. 99-109.*

JACK HICKS

Kosinski's work is a fictional construct, a textual triumph of the imagination, but it is also a literature of moral witness that contains testimonies by those who survive the burning and return, scarred and purified, to insist that we recognize and remember our own darkest potentials.

In America, this literature of moral witness survives most richly in the Afro-American fugitive slave narratives, songs, autobiographies, poetry, and fictions, the written legacy of coffle and yoke. Jerzy Kosinski's work, however, has European roots in the genocide committed by the Nazis and (for Kosinski) by any collective group larger than one, and in other attempted exterminations of Jews, gypsies, and many faces of the scapegoat Other. Kosinski's novels circle back constantly over that dark land and share the memories of others who escaped the Holocaust to create art from their waking nightmares: Tadeusz Borowski, Elie Wiesel, Wolfgang Borchert, Heinrich Böll, André Schwarz-Bart. Like the morally hysterical narrator of Borowski's *This Way to the Gas, Ladies and Gentlemen*, a man who processes countrymen to the gas chambers and crematoria and is at once victim and executioner, Kosinski's fiction underscores the terrible price of survival and relentlessly poses the question: "Are we good people?"

The responses to this central question, couched in the scalding experiences of Kosinski's heroes, are complex and indirect, and their sum finally offers little comfort to readers and critics who require a literature nourished by liberal humanism, who ask of fiction a sense of man's essential decency or his ability, through reason, to improve his moral and social lot by acts of personal or collective integrity. The author works a much more radical, consciously antihumanist, modernist, and postmodernist vein of literature; he is one of a chorus of Artaud's "voices from the flames," writers whose visions of modern social life are essentially pessimistic and devolutionary in experience. He possesses the sight of dark prophets: the Europeans de Sade, Artaud, Céline, and Genet; the Japanese Mishima; the American William Burroughs; all of whom would view what human civilization has become as "one disaster created to solve another."

Indeed, most alarming in Kosinski's version of the Holocaust is the fact that good and evil are inextricably coiled. The work confronts us regularly with paradoxical scenes, charged with a brutal tension and ambivalence, in which the torturer and the tortured require, even *demand,* each other for human definition. The medieval world of the peasant village [depicted in *The Painted Bird*] is a demonic fairy tale set in an ignorant, superstitious land, but the modern ruthless Nazi counterpart scarcely offers the painted bird any more comfort or humanity. (pp. 185-86)

Here too Kosinski's writing is a witness to modern terror, to the impersonal dystopia of the Stalinist State. Though his vision is at times Kafka's paralytic nightmare of the modern self lost in an endless corridor, he shares a willingness to offer, however grudgingly, testimony to the threat of collective socialism and his escape from it, along with Alexander Solzhenitsyn, Yuri Daniel, Andre Sinyavski. Here again he is the man on the fence. Although they escape and witness the same psychic archipelago, Kosinski does not share Solzhenitsyn's "old fashioned" humanism: his belief in a supreme being, his stubborn faith in man's potential goodness, his fondness for Russian (as opposed to Soviet) culture, his enthusiasms (albeit waning) for democratic capitalism since he settled in America in 1957. Although Kosinski's early success was very much connected with his value as a political prize—the quick winning of a Ford Foundation grant with little proficiency in English and the publication and acclaim of the Novak books were no accidents, coming at the height of the cold war—he has refused to advertise the virtues of his adopted society. As president of American P.E.N. (Poets, Essayists, and Novelists), he emphasized his distrust for all collective causes in a 1973 inaugural address:

> If, in spite of my mistrust and fear of collectivity, I have accepted the presidency of American P.E.N. for the coming year, it is because the aims of P.E.N. match my own: freedom to write, to oppose any form of censorship, to promote the exchange of ideas and the meeting of intellectuals of diverse origins and views, to foster translation of works of merit, always aware that in today's atomized societies, literature—above all—triggers imagination, mobilizes emotions, and ultimately arms its reader to face his very own self and cope with the unknown in his very own existence.

Literature is a defensive weapon because it "triggers," "mobilizes," "ultimately arms" the reader against those forces around him that threaten to diminish or obliterate his consciousness. Thus Kosinski extends the enemy line: the peasant village and the modern socialist commune, nazism, communism, Christianity, capitalism, the aggression of war, and the benign malignance of apparent peace. They are all coconspirators against the self, and he has most recently indicted the mass culture of the United States as "no less indoctrinated by the Polyanna values of popular culture than are, let's say, their Russian counterparts by the decades of dehumanizing ideology of omnipotence of the Party." His most explicitly critical observations on technological America are reserved for sections of *Being There* and *The Devil Tree,* but he has been most vehement and most repelled when we were at the height of social protest against involvement in Asia. He writes then in strained rhetoric about contemporary young Americans as manipulated and unthinking "dead souls," who are as dangerous as his medieval peasants, priests, or Russian bureaucrats, the social herd at its worst. . . . (pp. 187-88)

In a more recent novel, *Blind Date,* he skips the stone westward from Polish village to suburban Los Angeles, a morphic dreamland in which "strings of invisible sprinklers sent up fine sprays that turned sunlight into rainbows." The narrator Levanter and author Kosinski recall the life and death of their mutual friend Woytek. The memories are painful, an attempt to preserve in text and release from memory the slaughter of Woytek Frykowski at the hands of the Manson Family in 1969. The Cancerous gangs are the "Crabs of Sunset . . . out of balance with the world . . . the missing link between man and robot." Unknowingly speaking of his killers shortly before his murder, Woytek pronounces Kosinski's ultimate unicellular American horror:

> Had California been an independent country, it would have long ago gone fascist—Left or Right, it wouldn't matter. For the Right, Crabs of Sunset would become the fuel for the final draconic measures that would be used to get rid of them; for the Left, they would be the ignition for the revolution that would swallow them later. As it is, the state of California has become the embodiment of their mental state: neither Right

nor Left, with no shape or direction, a giant amoeba. Here, everything stretches—nature and people.

I suggest that Kosinski's vision is blackly Hegelian, which is fitting given his communist education as a social scientist, and that he constantly struggles in his work between the impinging shapes of society and the dream of the self. Though his writing is firmly rooted in the detail of his own psychic past and is an act of self-definition related to the fiction making of biography and history, it contains its own antithesis, a countermovement. "It was and it was not": projections of the author's will, his works break loose from him. His imaginings have their own life as textual constructs and seek to lure him away, like a bird from its cage.

On the most basic level, Kosinski's fictions are dominated by actors and protagonists, and one may see a strong emphasis on the liberating qualities of the independent self. The nature of his protagonists follows a path of evolution. The boy of *The Painted Bird* discovers the necessity of the self as the only fixed point in a chaotic world; Jonathan Whalen of *The Devil Tree* is a retrograde image of the dangers of the damaged self; and Tarden and Levanter are protean selves, modern confidence men who enact the fullest, ambivalent potential of the free consciousness. The painted bird's most powerful dreams are those of metamorphosis, of release in wind and fire from the earth of the peasant village, of being Levanter—as his name implies, a shifting wind blowing through the lives of others, the realized spirit of change itself.

Against this core of central character, there is an equal pressure exerted by the author wary of containing his fiction's development, of holding Proteus to the rack. The jail of the social body is transferred to the text itself; and there is a desire in seven novels to deny plot and to resist the gradual accumulation of episodes into "lines" intersecting in any causal pattern. At their strongest, his protagonists manifest a fierce desire to create themselves through their selective memory of the past, yet memory hardens like dead skin and restricts the play of the self in the present. Thus the narrators shape themselves like contemporary sculpture, asserting their negative spaces, the uncreated pockets of their existences, and their potentiality. They wrench their memories free from time and place, describing Robbe-Grillet's ideal "double movement of creation and destruction." (pp. 188-90)

The protagonists of the works following *The Painted Bird* seek full consciousness, and they embody a world of anxiety in the record of that quest. Recorded language is a confession, a self-indictment, and thus, as Robbe-Grillet declares, they seek an enormous and dialectic present, "which constantly invents itself, as though in the course of the very writing, which repeats, doubles, modifies, denies itself, without ever accumulating in order to constitute a past—hence a 'story,' a 'history' in the traditional sense of the word." Kosinski uses interviews often to establish his poetics of disruption. He writes of *Steps* that it "has no plot in the Aristotelian sense. In Aristotle's terms for the revelation of the action, the end fulfills the beginning and the middle determines the end. But the aim of *Steps* precludes such an ordering of time." Speaking later of *Blind Date,* he continues in a more moral strain: "That's why in fiction I stress an incident, as opposed, let's say, to a popular culture, which stresses a plot. Plot is an artificially imposed notion of preordained 'destiny' that usually dismisses the importance of life's each moment. To bypass that moment, to dilute it in the gray everydayness, is to waste the most precious ingredient of living: the awareness of being alive." Thus in the Novak books, he has sought in the cinematic montage and the literary episode his ideal means of preserving those spurts of experience; he has drawn on the paradox of film, in which the perception of movement issues from the steady progression of fixed frames.

Céline, Burroughs, Kosinski: they are pseudonymous brothers. The works of all three are haunted by the fear of a totalitarian state and a loathing for mass existence. Detroit, Freeland, Poland—these landscapes are hallucinated in paranoia, their citizens repelled by and finally drawn toward the character and nature of *power*. The protagonists are burnished or consumed by it, perhaps even fascist in its self-defense, and they go forth into labyrinths of conspiracy and hatred, as if there were evil inherent in the physical world itself. They are abnormally armored counteragents sealed against the hidden and open corrosives of modern life. But they also share the postmodern anxiety of contemporary fictional characters, sensing that the forms giving them birth will, at every turn, bring on their extermination. Thus the corpus of their work is self-mutilated, as if to dispel a monster with a totem of its own menace. The putrifying corpse of modern life in Céline's *Journey to the End of Night* and *Death on the Installment Plan* is rent repeatedly by ellipsis, "my damned three dots." Burroughs's resonant image of the junkie nodding in "the grey fibrous wooden flesh of terminal addiction" is finally a metaphor for the imprisonment of modern consciousness. The piercing of flesh by the needle, the body by the phallus, the rending of the text, and finally the shattering of the physical cosmos itself, these are transformations. Burroughs's endless cranky experiments with cut-ups, fold-ins, and breakings of sentence, image, and word are his attempts at fiction making as an antidote to corporeal addition, as an attempt to dismember the text to release the will, turn off the machines, and undo the entire physical world. In Kosinski's work we see the same paradox, the narrative yearn for omnipotence and release from the body (depicted in the feats of his protagonists) contradicted by the impermanence of the surrounding world, the skin of the text, the body of meaning.

Working against this structural spirit of disjunction is Kosinski's spare presence in language. Although Irving Howe speaks for many in praising him as a stylist, "a master . . . [who] has few equals among American novelists born to the language," even comparing him with the senior emigres Conrad and Nabokov, we should note more precisely the severe nature of that style. At its best, it is a ruthlessly disciplined, cold, detached instrument.

Style is a reflex of consciousness, and Kosinski's spartan vision forbids certain indulgences of language. He in no sense shares the comic linguistic exuberance shown by Barth or Barthelme, nor does he fashion the baroque interiors of a John Hawkes or a William Gass. Unlike his countryman Conrad, whose hothouse English grew like a thicket, Kosinski prunes and espaliers his language. The vocabulary is limited, the syntax simplified, the conceits as direct as possible. His strength is in conveying disquieting scenes with absolute lucidity, and his language, to that end, must be transparent as water. "It is the opposite, for instance, of what Nabokov does," he notes; and continues, "his language is made visible . . . like a veil or a transparent curtain with a beautiful design. . . . My aim, though, is to remove the veil. . . . For me the novelist is not a displayer of stylistic bonfires; he is primarily conveying a vision." Thus the language is direct: with its icy mechanical body of nightmares and obsessions, it inscribes many variations on a few deep patterns and, precariously allied with the prose instru-

ments of pornography, becomes a sublime vehicle for freezing, fixing, entombing—and thus preserving—human experience. (pp. 190-92)

Kosinski exhibits a "double movement" of the man on the fence. That man is a body, a protagonist, a text-active and quiescent, declaimed and undone, omnipotent and imprisoned—and is propelled through the buried literary geographies of myth and archetype. Traditional mythic and archetypal forms possess implied unity, growth, order, and evolution, but in this novelist's hands they become plastic molds that are handled ironically, parodied, inverted, and shaped to his own very different ends. *The Painted Bird* is a demonic fairy tale, Jung's child voyager passing from the dark unconscious to the light of self-realization. But Kosinski twists the conventions of folklore and mocks the traditional reconciliating assertions of psychic wholeness and social continuity in the conclusion. *Steps* is a contemporary, inverted *Metamorphoses*. *Being There* is a cosmogenic parable, a biblical allegory of the seven days of creation that is used to indict the perversion of the American Eden by mass media and popular consciousness. *The Devil Tree* issues from our dream of success: Horace Whalen, steel magnate, is Horatio Alger, and his son Jonathan is an inversion of that myth, a devolution who takes down empire, father, and self. Tarden is an international agent who has transcended national causes and *Cockpit* is his deceptive contemporary confession. Levanter, his most recent romantic hero, is a wind and a merchant and a mythic place—an archetype of metamorphosis itself—a picaresque god who trades in the essences most tempting to us: youth, beauty, passion, power. *Passion Play* is a failed medieval drama. (pp. 192-93)

I speak of Kosinski as writing within a tradition of antihumanists, aligning him particularly with his pseudonymous brothers Louis-Ferdinand Céline and William Burroughs. All share chthonic visions as well as the kindred paradoxical gestures of pseudonymy: to write under a pen name is at once a disclosure and a hiding. Destouches became Céline only in 1932, with publication of *Journey to the End of Night*. Burroughs assumed the mask of William Lee with *Junkie* in 1953. In this sense, the "Novak" who stands behind the two sociological works of the 1960s is an ambivalent fictive persona, a paradoxical figure at once revealed and cloaked. Though the name "Novak" vanishes with those two works, the voice and consciousness do not. There is a rough art in the early efforts, and Kosinski's imaginative powers seem to undercut the "truths" offered by social science. Noting the deft shuffling of materials in *The Future Is Ours, Comrade,* one reviewer suggests it "should not be read uncritically." Kosinski/Novak is surrounded by anxious Kremlinologists. They introduce each work with a tentative air and are clearly anxious with their covey, as newsman Richard C. Hottelet's self-assurances betray: "In a book like this . . . everything depends on a reporter's credentials. Joseph Novak . . . is certainly a serious person, and there is nothing to suggest that he has not honestly recorded and summarized the remarkable material on everyday life and opinions in the USSR."

European pedagogue that he is, Novak concludes stiffly that "the fundamental intellectual goal of this study is to reflect through individual human experiences a picture of mass processes, to discover the mechanism of the formation of the distinctive *social yardsticks* by which the people of the USSR measure themselves and others, their criteria of social evaluation." Clinical and dispassionate, he is analytical and conclusive as well, and if his efforts are made suspect by the closet novelist, he has lasting revenge.

The Novak books mark a watershed for Kosinski's novels and are the precursors of his fiction. They offer a detailed picture of the menace of the collective state—the psychic backdrop of the novels—and reveal early techniques of composite, episodic narration. They are a fund of sketched anecdotes and metaphors (the painted bird, the skier), and characters like Gavrila in *The Painted Bird* and Romarkin in *Blind Date* have a first ghostly life in these pages. But Novak does not vanish. He is not fully eclipsed by the novelist Kosinski and occasionally surfaces as a distracting, explanatory presence in the novels. His voice is instructive—drawing conclusions, underscoring ''meaning,'' and undercutting the cinematic power of carefully established scenes. Kosinski's best art is one of understatement, of withheld judgment, of emotion implied in action or image, but Novak is a noisy guest. As Gerald Weales rightly notes, his ''greatest weakness as a novelist is his desire to explain things—his symbols, the significance of his scenes, the political and philosophical implications of the action. One corner of his mind seems never to have gotten on that plane that let him escape from a society in which ritual self-examination is the norm.'' His denials to the contrary (''I never talk about a book''), the author is an incessant, artful critic of his own work. Novak steals only a corner in the novels but takes the center light in orchestrated interviews and the long explanatory essays, *The Art of the Self* and *Notes of the Author*. (pp. 193-95)

We find, while examining his nature, that Kosinski's unique mode of contemporary American fiction is that of philosophical examination. The shapes and energies of his work are generated by a constant dialectical inquiry, an examination of the magnetic tensions between related sets of oppositions: fate and the independent will, collective society and the elected self, history and the renewing existential moment, the tomb of the body and the energetic play of mind, the illusion of myth and the reality of the broken pattern, the permanence of art and the evanescence of experience. His protagonists and their distorted images are created in the posing of these oppositions. Their beings are force fields describing the contradiction, ambivalence, irony, and temporary reconciliation between the polar forces that shape modern life and Jerzy Kosinski's seven romances of modern terror. (p. 195)

Jack Hicks, ''The Romance of Terror and Jerzy Kosinski,'' in his In the Singer's Temple: Prose Fictions of Barthelme, Gaines, Brautigan, Piercy, Kesey, and Kosinski, *The University of North Carolina Press, 1981, pp. 177-267.*

PAUL R. LILLY, JR.

Reviewers of each of Jerzy Kosinski's seven novels—from *The Painted Bird* to *Passion Play*—have been quick to point out this writer's fascination with violence. A random sampling of his books will involve the reader in scenes as grisly and varied as a Manson-like multiple killing in a Beverly Hills estate, a man eaten alive by rats, a trussed-up Russian spy dispatched with a dueling saber, a decapitation by a slammed car door, a rape of a school girl at a summer camp. Add to the list scenes of seemingly gratuitous cruelty: a child fed bread balls filled with fish hooks, an injured horse strangled by its owner, birds painted grotesque colors to ensure that they will be torn to pieces by other birds. Finally, some of Kosinski's own comments draw further attention to the place of violence in his books. In an interview with Joe David Bellamy in 1974, Kosinski theorized about the aggressive nature of fiction itself. ''Fiction assaults the reader directly, as if saying: It is about you. You are actually

creating this situation when you are reading about it; in a way you are staging it in your own life.'' What Kosinski says about his manipulation of the reader is not surprising; all reading involves conscious deception on the part of both writer and reader. But his candor about arranging words so as to assault the reader's imagination completes the picture of the writer as aggressor, the reader as victim, the word as a weapon. (p. 389)

The issue of violence in Kosinski's work, then, is a complex one, and one which he knows touches the center of his achievement as a writer. Whatever that achievement is, his books are not so much a preoccupation with violence as they are complex studies in the shifting identity of victim and oppressor. Power, not violence, is what fascinates Kosinski. All of his main characters—the boy in *The Painted Bird*, Tarden in *Cockpit*, Levanter in *Blind Date*, Fabian in *Passion Play*, indeed Kosinski himself—have known powerlessness and victimization. Their natural impulse (and here is where Kosinski is most compelling as a writer) is to transform themselves from victim to oppressor. . . . In the world of Kosinski, there are no other options open to the victim: he must seize power through deception or remain powerless. Divesting one's self of the identity of victim means assuming the identity of the oppressor. Or, as Mitka the Cuckoo explains to the boy in *The Painted Bird*, ''Man carries in himself his own justice, which is his alone to administer.'' Since each person is intensely alone, everything that is outside the individual self—political structures, nation states, business institutions, friends, lovers—represents a potential enemy, and must be constantly deceived or destroyed before it transforms that person into victim.

For Kosinski, violence is neither an abstraction nor an isolated event without a meaning. It is instead a relationship between two role-playing agents—the victim and the oppressor. The act of violence is the end result of a dynamic flow of power between these two agents. Kosinski is interested less in the outcome of this flow, that is, the act of violence itself . . . than he is in the special dynamics of power that define the identity of victim and oppressor. Neither role is a static one; each may become the other, and it is this unpredictable transformation of victim into oppressor or back into victim that characterizes his best novels. Identity is all. The identifying marks of the victim are sometimes easily determined (the Jew in German-occupied Poland), sometimes not (the wealthy guests in a Beverly Hills estate). Violence is sometimes planned (Jews carried in box cars to their deaths according to railroad timetables), sometimes random (the killers turning up at that particular Beverly Hills estate). But the violence occurs only after the roles of victim and oppressor are sorted out and the power of will begins to flow. In a sense, the novels are a compendium of cautionary fables, warnings, admonitions: the self must establish the role of oppressor simply to avoid the only alternative, victimization. Kosinski himself, discussing his intention in writing *Blind Date*, sees the book as a ''warning.'' ''It is a warning that, given the staggering proportion of violence in our society, life is, at best, uncertain—we might not live through the very next moment, our next blind date, so to speak.''

Although violence in Kosinski's fiction appears in a variety of guises—political, racial, and sexual—each scene tells us something of his vision. But it is his use of violence between writer and reader, or, as Kosinski puts it, the ''assault'' on the reader's imagination, that is perhaps the most unsettling.

For Kosinski, every political system works against the integrity of the individual, forcing that individual to assert himself in an act of self-preservation. Whatever violence is committed is justifiable retribution for the initial violence done against the self. Here, for example, is what the boy in *The Painted Bird* learns from Gavila, his Soviet Army tutor: "In the Soviet world a man was rated according to others' opinion of him, not according to his own. Only the group, which they call 'the collective,' was qualified to determine a man's worth and importance." But this determination of the worth of the individual by the collective does violence to the self. The boy wonders about the implication of Gavila's teaching, and asks himself the question, What if the collective decides he is best suited for deep-water diving? "Would it matter that I was terrified of water because every plunge reminded me of my near-drowning under the ice?" Already the boy senses that the collective's decision—whatever its high-sounding intentions—represents a physical threat, a forced venture into an area that the self, were it free, would not go. The boy's sense of the implicit threat of the collective (the image of being pushed into deep water) prepares him for the violence he must do to preserve himself. In *Steps,* another narrator, also unnamed, recalls his first defiance of the state. Assuming the voice of the commander of a university unit in the national guard, he orders the current officer, a fellow student and personal enemy, to attack the city arsenal. The attack takes place and the student officer is arrested for treason. Later, the same narrator is cited by his student branch of the "Party" for the crime of "lack of involvement." Sensing he cannot victimize the state indefinitely, he plots his revenge on the state, escape. (pp. 390-92)

What we call the Free World is for Kosinski no less an enemy than the Communist collective. Rampant consumerism is the counterpart of the Marxist state and it presents simply another collective assault on the self. (p. 393)

Consumerism's deadly weapon is what Kosinski calls the "Master Charge attitude to life," and thrives on a society of "parrot trained consumerists" who take their models from the mass media, especially television. Kosinski's *Being There* satirizes what he sees as the popular religion of consumerism supported by a steady diet of televised blandness. Chance, the main character, is the victim of TV. All he knows of life comes from the garden he tends and the language of television he learns to mime. But Chance is also the unwitting deceiver of the consumer society that looks to television for meaning: news center commentators, newspaper editors, the FBI, the KGB, the President—all are gulled into thinking that Chance is what they want him to be. . . . [The] tension between oppressor and the victim still holds: consumerism is a political system that victimizes the individual. And because the individual is frequently unaware of his role as victim, such as Chance in *Being There,* the power of this system is perhaps even deadlier than the more overt power of the Communist state.

Kosinski's experience as a child in war-time Poland provides *The Painted Bird* with some of the most graphic scenes in which victimization is established by racial identity. Because the boy in *The Painted Bird* is "olive-skinned, dark-haired, and black-eyed" he resembles a "Gypsy or Jewish stray" and must play victim first to the local peasants ("fair-skinned with blonde hair and blue or gray eyes") and then to the German soldiers, including an SS officer with "smooth, polished skin" and "bright golden hair." Then, as the Soviet Army closes in on the German occupiers, the Kalmuks appear suddenly on horseback to reinforce the boy's—and the other villagers'—role of victim. Their skin, the boy says, is "even darker than mine"; but their arrival transforms the role of the villagers, whose blondness and blue eyes have now become the identifying

marks of the victim. Finally the Soviet soldiers arrive and hang all the Kalmuks, whose dark skin is easily distinguished from the peasants. Throughout all these transformations of oppressors and victims the boy learns that the only escape from victimization is to adopt the disguise of the oppressors, now the Soviet soldiers. At the conclusion of the book the boy has managed to establish this new role with *élan.* Wearing the uniform of a Soviet soldier, he tests his new power on a four-year old child adopted by his own parents. He grabs the child's arm and squeezes it until "something cracked and the boy screamed madly." Because he is a victim of his racial identity, he does violence to that identity in order to escape from it. In *Passion Play,* Kosinski's latest book, a young girl by the name of Stella passes herself as white and enjoys the life of a Southern horsewoman, whose racial hallmarks she had adopted. When the main character, Fabian, discovers her secret, she becomes his victim. Only minutes before Stella had been commanding a black servant working in a riding stable. But with Fabian's sudden knowledge, Stella is transformed from oppressor into victim. (pp. 393-95)

It is Kosinski's treatment of sexual violence that troubles most readers. Racial and political violence seem forces that loom large in life, and if they provoke the individual into acts of vengeance, such provocation is understandable. But sexual violence stems more from a personal whim, a conscious pose. Irving Howe, commenting on *Steps,* objects to "the immorality of the spectator whose detachment is from the other side of the moon." Not only in *Steps* but in the rest of Kosinski's novels we find main characters and narrators all too willing to detach themselves within a sexual relationship, to take part in, as Fabian states it in *Passion Play,* "a spectacle of which he was both protagonist and solitary witness." But even with this said, sexual violence nevertheless has its own relentless logic, stemming from Kosinski's belief that the individual is alone. To avoid being victim, each person must strive to become the oppressor in the relationship. Thus every sexual partner in his fiction (and there are many combinations: man-woman, woman-woman, man-man, a number of *ménage à trois* variations, woman-goat, man-rabbit, and so on) is involved in a war of wills: who shall be the oppressor, who the victim?

Deception is the single constant in all these relationships. One lover poses as victim, for example, then, at the right moment, transforms himself into the oppressor. Sexual activity for a typical Kosinski character resembles not so much a passion play, to borrow one of his titles, but a power play. Here is Tarden again, this time boasting of one of his sexual triumphs. He recalls how as a youth he taught himself to retract his "member," hiding it by means of a "plastic-edged clamp, which made it look as if I were recovering from an amputation." He invites a girl to his house and, after assuring her that he is incapable of penetrating her, they begin to make love. "As long as the clamp remained in place, I felt a bit of pain, but the sense of harnassed power made orgasm crude by comparison. Later, when the girl was too aroused to be aware of what I was doing, I surreptitiously removed the clamp and shot into her without warning." Tarden poses as victim of sexual mutilation, lures his partner into a state of vulnerability, then attacks, his missing member appearing suddenly as a weapon of vengeance. . . . In *Cockpit,* Tarden, involved in a liaison with Valerie, decides that he has been victimized by her. After he had arranged for her to marry a wealthy suitor, she wishes to break with Tarden. Determined to direct the flow of power back to himself, he brings her to his apartment, ties her to a chair, and goes out into the night to hire three derelicts to rape her. While the men perform Tarden's vengeance on Valerie, Tarden records it all with his camera.

One of the most sustained and graphic scenes of this kind occurs in *Blind Date*. At a youth camp in East Europe, a 15 year old Levanter listens avidly to his friend Oscar, who is an accomplished rapist, formulate a new grammar of sexual violence. Oscar calls rape "breaking the eye," and applies his personal vocabulary to every part of the female body he intends to violate. . . . Armed with this new vocabulary, Levanter decides to experience "breaking the eye" himself. He sees a girl at the camp who attracts him, and he secretly calls her "Nameless." Levanter not only figuratively rapes her of her personal identity by such a naming, he later succeeds in literally raping Nameless in the woods. His power play, learned from Oscar, is so effective that her scream of terror and pain seems to articulate victimization at its most extreme: "There was something unnatural about the sound. He imagined an inner spring had snapped inside her." The young Levanter shows no remorse at snapping this inner spring, and when, a year or so later, he meets Nameless (who never saw her attacker) he begins to date her. But a certain gesture gives him away, and she suddenly knows Levanter is the person who raped her. Levanter is chagrined not at what he had done, but at being discovered. His knowledge of her is no longer superior to her knowledge of him, the flow of power begins to reverse itself, and so Levanter breaks away.

This whole scene might well stand for the sexual violence that has received so much comment by Kosinski's critics. Irving Howe's word, "detachment," is at the heart of the problem. When Kosinski claims that his fiction is "about you," the reader, and that the reader is a co-creator ("you're creating this situation when you are reading about it"), he is positing much more freedom to his readers than the actual reading experience can justify. The "you" cannot create a situation outside the sequence of words that Kosinski has arranged with such craft. In fact, the reader is more an observer than a creator, and his evaluation of what he is observing is generally at variance with that of the narrator. Take, for instance, the scene in *Cockpit* in which Tarden ushers into his apartment the three derelicts he has chosen to rape Valerie. As Tarden coolly photographs the scene, his detachment is a model for Kosinski's detachment as he creates the voice of Tarden. The voyeur-like nature of this special reader-writer relationship is perhaps what one critic, Raymond Solokov, referred to in his review of *Blind Date*: "This collusion between writer and reader is obscene, but that is its point."

Kosinski's reply to all these objections is that his novels are neither amoral nor immoral, but that they explore the possibility of an entirely new morality, one based on the scientific discoveries of Jacques Monad, whose work, especially as summarized in the book, *Chance and Necessity,* demonstrates that nature has no plan, no scheme for the future, no destiny. . . . Kosinski insists on the moral nature of Levanter. He speaks of Levanter's "development of soul" and his deep concern for "moral issues." He dismisses the rape of Nameless by pointing out that Levanter "was willing to suffer the legal consequences for the rape, but that the authorities refused to believe he was the rapist." But surely his willingness to suffer the legal consequences is not the point: the reader's experience of Levanter's rape of Nameless is disturbing because Levanter experiences no feeling, no emotion, neither remorse nor elation. He remains detached, clinical, and his willingness to admit publicly to rape might well be a sign of perverse pride—Oscar's pride, say, in being a rapist.

Kosinski's personal vision, his insistence that we should develop "an awareness of life as it happens in each of its moments, and that man must treat each of those moments as unique," is consistently and convincingly portrayed in his novels. But if the vision is new, it is not a moral one. A code of behavior that treats each moment as unique but excludes an evaluation of the meaning of that moment, especially the moment's possible ramifications of pain and suffering for others, can not also be a moral code. . . . The problem with the vision, and with the code of behavior derived from the vision, is that it is too simple: life is reduced to a series of unique moments that elude evaluation. Human relationships are reduced to power plays between victim and oppressor. But a moral vision implies awareness of complexity, the presence of doubt, ambiguity, involvement, despair, joy. Kosinski offers sequences of moments, each unique and powerfully narrated, but with all the complexity of life simply abstracted (Tarden's words came back: "I could abstract myself from its power") until the moment is nearly a hollow shell. (pp. 395-400)

Paul R. Lilly, Jr., "Vision and Violence in the Fiction of Jerzy Kosinski," in The Literary Review, *Fairleigh Dickinson University, Vol. 25, No. 3, Spring, 1982, pp. 389-400.*

JOSEPH McLELLAN

Most of *Pinball* takes place in the South Bronx, as desolate an urban landscape as any this side of Pompeii: burned-out buildings and empty streets haunted chiefly by predatory juveniles. Also burned out, as the book opens, are its hero, Patrick Domostroy, and the battery of his car, which he takes to a garage for recharging. Clearly, we are wandering through a forest of symbols.

Domostroy (who resembles Jerzy Kosinski about as much as a washed-up composer can resemble a successful novelist) lives in this wasteland, all alone, in an abandoned dance hall named the Old Glory (another symbol). He was a composer of serious music, widely acclaimed at the height of his success 10 years ago, but his battery has gone dead and he has dropped out of society. Now, he earns a scant living as an accompanist, playing the piano (or accordion, harpsichord, even a synthesizer) in small, out-of-the-way nightclubs frequented by solitary men who watch television or play pinball and electronic games while waiting to pick up women. . . .

This quiet life is disrupted as the novel begins by a young woman named Andrea Gwynplaine, a student at the Juilliard School who seems to have plenty of money and is willing to spend it on an odd quest: to track down and identify a mysterious rock star known only as Goddard who never appears in public but has enjoyed enormous success on records. She enlists Domostroy to find him partly because Goddard's record company, Nokturn, is affiliated with [Domostroy's], but also because it seems appropriate to use one reclusive musical genius to catch another.

She succeeds, after a fashion and with disastrous results, in a plot as highly convoluted as the novel's symbolism. Ultimately, this doesn't matter much. What matters, I suppose, it that Kosinski, who has managed to do very well by writing what is essentially the same novel over and over again, has come up with a significant variation on his standard themes and personalities, a few new twists in the almost inhuman behavior patterns of his protagonists. His modality this time is a transfer of the writing business into the music business. Domostroy, for example, has been an officer in an international musicians' organization much like PEN, the writers' organization in which Kosinski has served with distinction. And some of the details about the elusive Goddard may remind readers of the only slightly less shadowy Thomas Pynchon.

As part of his very detailed background for *Pinball*, Kosinski displays an uncommon familiarity with music and the music business, particularly the compositions of Chopin and some advanced problems in performance practice and technique. Clearly, he is profiting from the fact that his mother was a concert pianist, but he also uses his wide friendship among musicians—notably the late Goddard Lieberson, who was an accomplished composer as well as the head of CBS Master-works records. The mysterious Goddard in *Pinball* owes something to Lieberson—not only his name but some motifs in his music. He also owes something to Karlheinz Stockhausen, as does Kosinski, who has constructed his novel, in a way, like a Stockhausen composition and derives some of his mystique from the German composer's philosophy of indeterminacy:

> To Karlheinz Stockhausen, whose electronic compositions so clearly influenced Goddard, a musical event was without a determined beginning or an inevitable end; it was neither a consequence of anything that preceded it nor a cause of anything to follow; it was eternity, attainable at any moment, not at the end of time.
>
> Weren't life's events like that too? Domostroy wondered.

Whether or not they are in life, they certainly are in a Kosinski novel. The characters wander about—not aimlessly but still more or less blindly, bumping into one another and into miscellaneous obstacles that may or may not have a meaning, achieving a real human contact only briefly, more or less by accident and with a fear or revulsion that quickly drives them apart.

Like the game that gives his novel its name and some basic motifs and techniques, there is something inhuman about Kosinski's writing and his characters—an inhumanity that he himself recognizes and emphasizes. His style of writing is dry and sometimes slightly awkward. He makes no real effort to enliven his scenes by standard techniques known to anyone who has taken an elementary course in creative writing. His characters are remote (even—perhaps especially—when they seem to be representing the author), viewed with pitiless objectivity and through a sharply focused long-distance lens.

Kosinski treats his characters (and they usually treat one another) as objects. Not that the story lacks intense feeling—quite the contrary—but it is intense feeling fixed on a slide to be examined under a microscope. Below the cold-seeming exterior, the feelings in this story seem too hot to be approached closely. And so the author retreats (like his hero in the Old Glory) into a kind of abstraction. And he writes mostly about people who are able to relate only in terms of trickery—hiding secrets, telling lies and callously manipulating one another. As it has been so often in Kosinski's books since *The Painted Bird*, the most pervasive human relation in *Pinball* seems to be that of victim and victimizer. . . .

The book's final paragraph shows Domostroy turning to pinball to kill time and perhaps indulge in a bit of symbolism.

> He dropped a coin into the slot. Where GAME OVER had been a second before, BEGIN GAME now began to flash at him. He pressed the button, and the first

ball popped up into the shaft, but for a moment Patrick Domostroy could not make up his mind whether to play it or not.

Or can it be an image of Jerzy Kosinski deliberating whether to start writing the same novel yet again?

Joseph McLellan, "Playing at Life," in Book World— The Washington Post, *March 7, 1982, p. 7.*

DOUG FETHERLING

Patrick Domostroy, the pivotal figure in Jerzy Kosinski's *Pinball*, is like a character out of Graham Greene who talks like one out of Anthony Burgess. Domostroy is a burnt-out case, a middle-aged musician whose talent has disappeared, a once-famous composer of orchestral works reduced to playing in the South Bronx in "a pinball joint that tries to pass for a nightclub." The combination of his hard luck and his technical knowledge of composition makes him a sitting duck for Andrea Gwynplaine. She's a well-off co-ed who buys his erudition with money and sex and puts it to a peculiar use. Thereby hangs a complicated and disturbing tale full of what could be mistaken for profound statements on urban anthropology—specifically, the maze of cheap sex, fickle celebrity and psychological gamesmanship that has informed the seven novels of this least starry-eyed of immigrants. Unfortunately, these strengths are undermined by a disintegrating plot in what amounts to an ersatz mystery. (p. 64)

Because of the bald nature of his prose and his love of episodic construction, Kosinski manages to make the plot more plausible than it sounds. He builds up the story a layer at a time, in the manner of a journeyman bricklayer. The problem is that Kosinski maintains the narrative flow for only the first half of the book, where everything is sharp and tightly controlled. But then, as though unsure of the story, he lets the whole thing get away from him and rematerialize as silly coincidences, broken mainspring pacing and panting conclusions. It's not a virtuoso performance, but perhaps half of one. Although the format is that of a mystery, the appearance is deceiving. Nothing is let out of the bag, for instance, by the early revelation that Goddard is actually James Osten, a ne'er-do-well whose father owns a classical record label that Goddard secretly subsidizes with his filthy rock lucre. Only in the last few pages is a crime suddenly committed, and then just as quickly resolved, as part of a contrived trick ending unworthy of the author.

What the reader can salvage from *Pinball* is Kosinski's vision of New York and California as nightmares more fascinating than any dream. At one point, young Osten, son of an East European immigrant made good, is "touched by his father's naïveté, his unflinching belief in things American—even when they were so patently absurd." Not so for Kosinski himself, who becomes caught up in the money-grubbing, desensitized world of pop culture to the point that he loses all perspective. The subject of the book overwhelms its style: what was intended as a muted satire becomes a wallow in sensation and triviality. (p. 65)

Doug Fetherling, "Sex and Dreams and Rock 'n' Roll," in Maclean's Magazine, *Vol. 95, No. 10, March 8, 1982, pp. 64-5.*

LESTER BANGS

Pinball is practically unreadable. Jerzy Kosinski is muzzing around after some Big Statement on how celebrityhood destroys artists, but he never makes it (except, didactically, in the last 10 pages), because the plot is ludicrous, the characters (especially the women) unbelievable cartoons, and the dialogue leaden and melodramatic (''And now you have graduated to crime. What's the ending of this cruel play?'' sounds like something out of ''Dudley Doright'')....

Kosinski (or someone) has done his homework, as we're all too painfully aware: instead of absorbing and employing it in dramatically effective ways, he just regurgitates it in huge blocks like a cramming student, so we get lots of sentences like: ''In the song 'What's Become of the Baby,' on their album *Aoxomoxoa,* the Grateful Dead modified keyboard and percussion sounds, mixing and modulating natural and artificial tones by means of electronics.'' Despite such diligence, Kosinski obviously knows nothing about rock 'n' roll, and has even less feel for it (''Thrilling as rock culture was, it was riddled with an excess of human trauma ...''). His descriptions make Goddard's music sound like a cross between Emerson, Lake and Palmer and Meatloaf, with lyrics lifted whole from (I swear I'm not making this up) Yeats, Joyce, and Archibald MacLeish, spizzed up for teen consumption with zingy song-titles like ''Acne Lady'' and ''Pornutopia is Utopia.''...

Really, though, rock is just one more source for trendy exploitation, like Candypants, Mood Undies, the National Vasectomy Club, John Lennon's assassination, Jack Henry Abbott (turned into a singing cowboy), and Kosinski's own film debut in *Reds,* all of which turn up named outright or flimsily disguised. None of them saves *Pinball* from being dead and plodding, any more than the prolix sex scenes between his two nigh-interchangeable male protagonists and the Barbarella-like floozycuties capering their way. Which brings us to the real point: ''Explicit sex!'' as Kosinski beamed at the giggling ladies on *Live at Five,* explaining that it's the only freedom left in Iron Curtain countries and ''the highest form of communication between human beings.'' Especially if they're dirty old men who wouldn't know a funkadelic from a frijid pink or, finally, care.

Lester Bangs, in a review of ''Pinball,'' in The Village Voice, *Vol. XXVII, No. 11, March 16, 1982, p. 43.*

THOMAS S. GLADSKY

In a *Paris Review* interview, George Plimpton asked Jerzy Kosinski, ''Could you see yourself starting all over again—new country, new language?'' to which Kosinski replied, ''It's a nightmare, but ... yes, I could.'' Starting over characterizes all phases of Kosinski's life and art—from his youth in Poland to his residency in the United States, from sociologist to novelist, from an East European writing in Polish to an American writing in English. Starting over aptly describes his protagonists as well from the Jewish Pole of *The Painted Bird* to the universal selves of the subsequent novels—the everymen who ''begin again'' in a strange new world. Kosinski's major fictional interest, the survival of the self in the post-war world, dramatizes the point that Kosinski also transcends geographic, ethnic, and cultural boundaries as he starts over. In this sense, he joins the family of twentieth-century Slavic writers (Conrad, Nabokov, Milosz) who, starting anew, earned their literary reputations in a language and cultural setting other than their own and who created characters and themes native to all grounds.

As we intuitively, if not intellectually, know that some part of Conrad's art must be Polish, Nabokov's Russian, and Milosz's

Lithuanian, so too we know that Kosinski's novels must also reflect his own Polish-Jewish-East European background, the place from which he starts. On this subject, Kosinski provides little help. He is reluctant to identify himself as either a Pole or a Jew and has sometimes deliberately distorted or disguised the facts of his life in Poland. The result is a public self (gregarious, cosmopolitan, witty) that contrasts sharply with his idiosyncratic private self—a fear of sudden arrest, an obsession with secret hiding places and false identification papers, and a habit of storing food and weapons in the trunk of a car. Moreover, his attempts to make a life from his fiction and a fiction from his life have resulted in a web of autobiographical fictions and fictional selves so tangled that Kosinski the man is thought of as ''a kind of Polish James Bond'' and his works are classified as ''literary disruptions.'' (p. 121)

Despite the Americanized settings and protagonists, the novels are unmistakably informed by an East European presence. Six of the eight protagonists, for example, have East European backgrounds; most are political refugees from socialist Poland. Four of the novels include scenes in Eastern Europe, usually Poland, and a fifth, *The Painted Bird,* is set entirely in Poland. With the possible exception of *The Devil Tree,* all of the novels include Slavic characters—Poles, Russians, Ruthenians. In addition, the works are laced with frequent references to Slavic customs, place names, institutions, and history—many of which remain obscure to the general reader. Taken together, these seemingly random and often disjointed references constitute a short course on contemporary East European politics, the Polish temperament, and Polish culture, including Polish-Jewish relations. Kosinski's Polish roots have shaped his fiction in even more important ways. His themes, his eccentric protagonists, his thematic coherence, and even his development as a writer are directly related to his own struggle to come to terms with his Polish past—a struggle which, as a common thread in all the novels, offers a way to understand Kosinski's artistic growth.

Kosinski's novels are studies of the deracinated self, cut off from time and place, divorced from a cultural context and native tradition, trying, as it were, to protect and defend itself against the threatening forces that exist in the post-war world.... Describing his novels as portrayals of men ''desperate to find out who they are,'' Kosinski has been preoccupied with this quest throughout his career. As early as 1968, he outlined in *The Art of the Self* what would become the pattern of his novels when he wrote that ''the self must constantly get clear from its past in order to live fully in the present.'' (p. 122)

Early discussions of Kosinski's fictional evolution and the structure of his work have ignored the influence of Eastern Europe. In 1975, Kosinski described his art as a ''five-book cycle [that] would present archetypal aspects of the individual's relationship to society.'' With the advantage of hindsight, he noted that his first novel [*The Painted Bird*] deals with the most universal of social metaphors: the vulnerability of a child in the context of a war-ravaged society. Inflamed by the controversy surrounding *The Painted Bird,* Kosinski never fully explains the structure of the entire cycle, but Jerome Klinkowitz picks up where Kosinski leaves off. For Klinkowitz, the first five novels are to be read as a movement from self-detachment to autobibliography which he defines as a mixture of historical, fictional, and personal material. The physical maturation and experience of Kosinski's later protagonists, Klinkowitz notes, match Kosinski's personal growth as fiction and biography merge. Norman Lavers follows Klinkowitz's lead, reading the novels as essentially parts of a ''spiritual biography.'' The limitations of these views become obvious as Kosinski continues to publish novels. Has he begun a new cycle? Modified the old? Recycled? The publication of three more novels, particularly *Pinball*, makes it clear that Kosinski's fictional "cycle" has yet another dimension. Representing a major change in Kosinski's treatment of Eastern Europe, these novels cause us to re-evaluate the earlier ones, especially in the context of Kosinski's attitudes about his Polish self. To do so is to conclude that Kosinski's fiction falls into three, not entirely distinct, periods: rejection of the East-European self, the impulse toward accommodation, and the reconciliation of old and new world selves.

Given the horrors of war-time Poland and the civil strife and political oppression that followed, it is no surprise that Kosinski's first two novels totally reject everything associated with Eastern Europe. In both novels, the singular aim of the protagonists is to slough off the old skin and "to get clear of the past" as Kosinski phrases it. Needless to say, Kosinski's portrait of Poland is devastating. Reminiscent of Isaac Singer's *The Slave*, *The Painted Bird* portrays Poles as sadistic animals; superstition, anti-Semitism, violence, and ignorance characterize daily life. Ultimately what emerges is a nation indicted for its part in the Holocaust.... So alienated is Kosinski's young narrator that he will not identify his own cultural-religious background, refer to his ethnic traditions, or even mention the name of the country despite the obvious Polish setting. The narrator's state of mind mirrors that of Kosinski who tells us that having left Poland, he was determined "never again to set foot in the country where I had spent the war years."

Although not formally a sequel, *Steps* functions that way: *The Painted Bird* describes physical torture; *Steps* documents mental torture; the former condemns war-time Poland; the latter denounces post-war Polish socialism. (pp. 123-24)

Kosinski emphasizes, moreover, the destruction of the self begun by the Nazis in the concentration camps, and continued in post-war Eastern Europe through "unspecified" policies that resulted in mental collectivization or, as Czeslaw Milosz expresses it, "the captive mind." Trapped by a mindless bureaucracy, the narrator must join a paramilitary organization at his university, conduct "self-evaluations," attend obligatory party meetings, and live on a collective farm as a punishment for political dissent. Eventually he flees Poland by inventing fictitious identities, other selves, if you will, who recommend him for study abroad. Although the final third of *Steps* records the narrator's "first steps" in his newly adopted country, the novel is thematically finished much earlier. Leaving his European self behind, the narrator reflects on his departure from Poland and presents himself as one waiting to be reborn. Like Whitman, he is "timeless unmeasured ... suspended forever between my past and my future." Later Kosinski would comment that, had he stayed in Poland, "preserving the self in a totalitarian society would have been his aim."

Having successfully shed his old world skin, Kosinski, in his next two novels, *Being There* and *The Devil Tree,* offers new selves in the form of typically American protagonists without any roots at all. Outside of time and place, suspended between the past and the future, Chance and Whalen are true successors to the nameless protagonists of *The Painted Bird* and *Steps,* who must discard their old world selves before discovering genuinely new ones.... Frank Chance embodies the American desire to be undeservedly famous; Jonathan Whalen reflects our wish to be undeservedly rich. Both represent the "suc-

cessful" culmination of the first stage of Kosinski's fictional cycle—the self getting clear of its East European past.

A conscious denial of the past figures prominently in both novels. In *Being There,* one of the characters succinctly comments, "A man's past cripples him, his background turns into a swamp." What makes Chance a desirable vice-presidential candidate is that he owns no past.... In *The Devil Tree,* Whalen has masterfully concealed his own past by "tailoring my reminiscences to the person I'm talking to."

Despite Kosinski's attempt to stay free of "the swamp," Eastern Europe intrudes itself into both novels in seemingly incidental ways. Chance meets, of all people, the Soviet Ambassador who, mistakenly believing that Chance speaks Russian, discusses Russian literature with him.... [In *The Devil Tree*] Kosinski introduces a minor character who has a conversation with a grocery manager, "An older Jewish man ... with a heavy European accent." Richard wants to know why the insecticides are kept so near the vegetables. When the grocer calls Richard a nut for suggesting that someone would poison vegetables, Richard responds, "You are a Jew. Millions of your people died poisoned by gas. Why would anyone kill Jews?" Richard, we learn, witnessed Nazi massacres in White Russia even before "the gas chambers were established." What these incidents make clear, of course, is that the Holocaust, Jewishness, the Soviets, and Eastern Europe are never out of Kosinski's mind nor ever far away from even the most American of his protagonists.

After *The Devil Tree,* Kosinski returns to an East-European-born-protagonist whose ongoing struggle with the self occurs within the background that Kosinski knows best: a Polish landscape, Soviet-style politics, the war in Europe, and ethnic identities. Although *Cockpit* and *Blind Date* feature Kosinski's familiar theme and the ever-present rootless wanderers about whom we know little or nothing (they even use aliases), the novels represent a shift in Kosinski's treatment of Eastern Europe and thus mark a major step in his long journey home. For one thing, the presence of Eastern Europe is more intense in these novels than in *Being There* or *The Devil Tree.* For another, Kosinski reveals an impulse toward accommodation with his native land. His protagonists express similar ambivalent feelings: one impulse is to seek revenge; another is to seek accommodation. Their response parallels, one might say, Kosinski's own.

In both novels, the survival of the self is directly related to the past which, Kosinski seems to conclude, recreates itself even as it is destroyed. In *Cockpit,* Tarden, for example, believes that he exists in a "curious time warp," "completely cut off from my past." His life depends, he insists, on his ability "to instantly create a new person and slip out of the past." Juxtaposed against this rational formulation is Tarden's rambling monologue in which a single memory picture evokes another so that unconsciously, "the montage of a past self will emerge." Tarden's compulsion is to disguise the past as he desperately tries to reveal it. His behavior is analogous to Kosinski's hide-and-tell method of giving partial information about Poland to a reader who must then identify the specifics for himself. (pp. 124-26)

Like Tarden, Levanter [in *Blind Date*] is a transplanted Slav who uses his position as an intelligence agency operative to revenge himself on the totalitarian regimes of Eastern Europe. Despite the fact that Levanter hides as much as he reveals and that the reader must once again piece together Levanter's history, we learn, as we do in *Cockpit,* that the struggle features old and new world selves. Almost a private dialog in *Cockpit,* this struggle becomes more prominent in *Blind Date* as Kosinski adjusts his methods to focus his developing insights.

Although he is not specific about Levanter's birthplace, nationality, or religion, Kosinski, for the first time since *The Painted Bird,* strongly implies that his hero may be a Polish Jew. Levanter explains that his parents emigrated from Russia to somewhere in Eastern Europe before he was born. He also talks about his experience in a Soviet-style army where he was abused because he was thought to be Jewish. On another occasion, he recalls a boyhood game called "Name the Jew" and how he was ordered to play by a gang of neighborhood toughs. More important, Levanter is the first Kosinski hero to recognize that his European past cannot and will not disappear and that he must, in fact, reconcile his ethnic past and amorphous present—his eastern roots and western inclinations. (p. 127)

For the first time, Kosinski's protagonist is at least somewhat comfortable with his East European roots. He admits to being pleased by "the influence of his European upbringing." Compared to the brutal portraits of Poland in earlier novels, *Blind Date* betrays a touch of sentiment for the homeland as Levanter fondly remembers boyhood escapades with good friends, skiing in the Tatras, and Chopin's Nocturnes. (p. 128)

Another exile whose childhood was "spent in the stony rural life of one of those marginal old countries," Fabian, the protagonist of *Passion Play,* harbors the usual resentment toward his past in Eastern Europe, where his playmates often "turned on him in the bond and unity of their family kinship." . . . What differentiates Fabian from his predecessors, however, is his ability to reflect upon his alienation. Through Fabian, Kosinski examines his own ambivalent feelings about the old world and, like his protagonist, moves one step closer to reconciliation.

Still an outsider, this Kosinski hero surprisingly thinks of himself as an immigrant, one of many to whom dual identities have been a natural, even desirable, condition. He senses that he is not necessarily trapped between two worlds, that he is not unique, and that, instead, he shares "a dual past with many Americans of his generation." Whereas Kosinski's earlier protagonists actively conceal their multiple selves even from themselves, Fabian recognizes that all "the skins that he shed, phases of the body and the mind" were alive in memory—that his quest, in effect, is a search for the buried past. The itinerant polo player, Fabian, thus rides toward a knowable, although unknown, destiny. (pp. 128-29)

If the impulse toward reconciliation is a faint but constant glow in *Blind Date* and *Passion Play,* that impulse becomes a bright star in *Pinball,* Kosinski's most hopeful statement. At first glance, the novel follows the familiar Kosinski pattern. Predictably, the hero, who grew up in Eastern Europe and studied in Warsaw, still bears the scars of World War II; and predictably, he represents the alienated self in conflict with the threatening modern world. Within this formulaic pattern, Kosinski makes crucial changes. Although Domostroy is another example of the deracinated self, Kosinski blunts Domostroy's alienation by dividing this theme between the Slavic Domostroy and the American rock musician, Jimmy Osten, who retreats into an anonymous private world after each performance. (p. 129)

Although Patrick Domostroy is in many ways an atypical Kosinski hero, he is not associated with politics. He is neither a spy nor a self-appointed avenger; he hardly refers to his days in Eastern Europe. Quiet and retiring, he is Fabian without a van home, a middle-aged deracinated self looking for roots. Kosinski makes this point early when Domostroy talks about a car he had bought fifteen years earlier, now a worn-out "symbol of his own mobility and affluence." Laying the journey aside, he moves into the Old Glory, once the South Bronx's largest ballroom and banquet center that has formerly hosted a mostly Jewish clientele, and serves as the guard and custodian of this symbol of his assimilated, ethnic, Jewish old-world self and his newly adopted American identity.

Although the struggle with self is the major concern in *Pinball,* Kosinski develops this theme differently, by creating two protagonists whose contrasting views toward music illustrate the self in turmoil and the self in harmony. The rock musician, Jimmy Osten, believes that private and public selves must remain forever disjointed. The elaborate methods he uses to hide his identity associate him with Whalen, Tarden, and Levanter. The classicist Domostroy, on the other hand, sees music as a transcendence of self. As he explains it, "To compose music was for me, to belong to everyone, to speak every language, to convey every emotion." (p. 130)

For the first time in his fiction, Kosinski compliments his native land whose name he could not bring himself to mention in preceding novels. And for the first time, he seems at ease with his cultural past and with himself. Now he can even joke about Poland. In the novel, he names a law firm that represents musicians "Mahler, Strauss, Handel and Penderecki," associating the avant-garde, lesser-known Polish composer with the more recognizable masters. Kosinski's more relaxed posture is especially evident in the conclusion, which, in previous novels, had been typically foreboding, or, at best, problematic. Snug in his new home, aptly named "The Old Glory," Domostroy plays pinball as "Game Over" gives way to a flashing "Begin Game." Although he cannot decide if he will "start over," we are led to believe he will. Similarly, *Pinball* leads us to believe that Kosinski, having at least partially reconciled old and new world selves, like his surrogate protagonists, may also be ready for a new game. Kosinski's private life footnotes his fiction—in 1980 he participated in a tribute to the Polish union—Solidarity. (p. 131)

Thomas S. Gladsky, "Jerzy Kosinski's East European Self," in Critique: Studies in Contemporary Fiction, *Vol. XXIX, No. 2, Winter, 1988, pp. 121-32.*

PUBLISHERS WEEKLY

[*The Hermit of 69th Street: The Working Papers of Norbert Kosky* is presented] as the "working papers" of a deceased writer whose life and times mirror Kosinski's own. Set in New York and Hollywood, the story is hobbled by its form, a relentless homage to Vladimir Nabokov. Almost every page is studded with footnotes and documentation, some consisting of newspaper leads and some culled from imaginary sources. Quotes from a panoply of writers are strewn throughout the text. It is as if Kosinski is obsessed with proving that in the hands of a gifted writer anything can be given meaning and relevance. There is much mystical hocus-pocus over the recurrence of the number 69 throughout these pages; the conceit includes incessant asides to the printer and the reader, signed N. K. and J. K. Kosinski makes thousands of allusions. In a reference to the Charles Manson murders, for example, he calls Sharon Tate Ophelia and the other victims Rosencrantz and Mr. and Mrs.

Guildenstern. This is a clever tour de force, but difficult to define as a novel, not to be compared with *The Painted Bird, Steps* or *Being There* for sheer quality of writing. It's a self-conscious demonstration of technique, delivered with a wink and a smirk.

A review of "The Hermit of 69th Street," in Publishers Weekly, *Vol. 233, No. 18, May 6, 1988, p. 93.*

JOHN CALVIN BATCHELOR

"Good poison is hard to find," sighs Norbert Kosky, the unhappy middle-aged hero of Jerzy Kosinski's clever new satirical novel, *The Hermit of 69th Street.* Norbert Kosky is said to be a *most* famous and brilliant Polish émigré novelist, author of some eight startling fictions that not only have made him wealthy, distinguished, celebrated and endlessly serviceable by statuesque, orgiastic women, but also have created in him a need to write one more amazing book that will illustrate his "inner terror"—his soulful pilgrimage from a childhood in the Holocaust to a well-appointed hermitage on New York's West 69th Street.

Unfortunately for Norbert Kosky, his victories with the pen suddenly poison his life ruinously when a local journal accuses him of being a plagiarist, creep, whoremonger—and just about every other way the yellow press can say impotent liar. The charge: Norbert Kosky did not write his own books; he jobbed out his work; he is a "floater" not a "swimmer" in the ocean of literature—he is not Norbert Kosky.

This may remind you of the squall some years back when two literary journalists at *The Village Voice* published a piece suggesting that Jerzy Kosinski had not written all of his own books, that he had employed assistants who contributed significant ideas, scenes, energy. The allegation was rebutted in *The New York Times* and the waters calmed, though apparently not for Mr. Kosinski. Norbert Kosky is less a stand-alone character than a stand-in for the impugned author. Jerzy Kosinski has worked up an elaborate scheme to revenge himself against what he calls "docu-slander." He also seeks to demonstrate that no one ever wrote a book without the hands of others living and dead, and to exhibit the mystical notion that if Kosky/Kosinski is not what he says he is—a gifted, hard-working Polish émigré novelist—what writer is what he says he is? What writer is not an impotent liar?

Accordingly the book is built as "autofiction," which Kosky/Kosinski defines as neither truth nor fiction. It purports to be the unfinished manuscript left behind by Norbert Kosky when he is lost at sea, and the author Jerzy Kosinski has annotated it with eccentric, intriguing footnotes and bibliographical citations that make the text resemble biblical exegesis. The text is layered with boldface quotations from every imaginable learned source: famous writers (Maugham, Conrad, Dostoyevsky, Kafka, Bruno Schulz, Jerzy Kosinski); famous books (the Talmud, the Tantras, Genesis); famous promoters (Lenin, Diane Arbus, Samuel Goldwyn, Nietzsche, Kinsey); famous villains (Pilate, Goebbels, Stalin, Chaim Rumkowski of the Lodz ghetto); famous religionists (Abraham Heschel, Henry Ward Beecher); and the simply famous (Garbo). The hoped-for effect of all this, according to Norbert Kosky when he is asked at one point what he is working on (*"roman à tease,"* he jokes), is to render the subtext worth the price of admission.

Nevertheless Kosky is a winning *luftmensch* whose personality is consistent with the charming, fumbling characters Jerzy Kosinski has favored in such earlier books as *Being There, The Devil Tree* and *Pinball....*

He is not the nasty fellow he would like to be, nor is he crude enough to be believed when he promotes himself as lecherous. He does have this "inner terror" like 10 extra pounds around the middle, and it is carefully revealed in flashbacks and footnotes that Norbert Kosky, like his literary executor Jerzy Kosinski, survived the German and Russian vivisection of Poland to escape eventually to America. Worst of all, he does not know why.

The ambition of this novel is not to answer such an incomprehensible question, but rather to commit a poison-pen letter that will serve as an antidote to an over-examined life. Jerzy Kosinski writes fluidly and wittily, explores his privileged world like a Conradian adventurer, soldiers worldwide for literature and makes a first-rate prosecutor of the 20th century's true criminals. It is also possible that he is not the best mockingbird for himself. Cynthia Ozick's stunning short story "The Mercenary" remains the high-performance aircraft of Kosinski-pricking. For now, Kosky/Kosinski has yet to reach such a height, weighed down as he is by being the pilot and ordnance of his Stealth bomber of a soul.

John Calvin Batchelor, "The Annotated 'Roman à Tease'," in The New York Times Book Review, *July 3, 1988, p. 11.*

LARRY McCAFFERY

The appearance of [*The Hermit of 69th Street*], Jerzy Kosinski's ninth novel and his first since a sensationalized *Village Voice* article six years ago alleged that he had misrepresented his writing methods and his life, indicates what we should have known all along: Kosinski, a spiritual child of the Final Solution, is a survivor. Indeed, he has emerged from the Great Kosinski Furor (which resulted from a scrupulously researched, but misguided distillation of rumor and innuendo that Kosinski himself had helped perpetuate) with a vengeance, creating a defiant, highly personalized literary response to the charges leveled against him. *The Hermit of 69th Street* is a peculiar blend of intimate revelations and abstract musings on the nature of the self and the sources of artistic creativity. It is Kosinski's most ambitious, experimental and nakedly confessional work to date.

The basic aim of this massive, unclassifiable text... is to allow readers a myriad of entryways into the mysteries of his own personal writing habits and the alchemic processes of all literary creation. *The Hermit* is designed to be a vast labyrinth of words, a dizzying series of textual passageways that must be negotiated individually and which ultimately all lead to a final destination: Kosinski's inner self, his soul. It is the confused welter of fears, memories, fantasies, factual knowledge and personal experience that comprise his identity and are the source of his creativity.

The most fascinating aspect of *The Hermit* is watching Kosinski develop an utterly original form to express this "self" without reducing it to the formulaic simplicities implicit with both autobiography and realism. Finally abandoning the masks, disguises, false beards and wigs he and his characters have favored until now, he invents a novelistic alter ego (the Norbert Kosky of the book's title) whose life and works are blatant extensions of Kosinski's own; he then provides for the reader dozens of accesses and perspectives into the complex processes involved in his creation of Kosky and the fictional world he inhabits. (pp. 1, 9)

Naturally many features of Kosky's existence bear a striking resemblance to what we know about the outlandish realm that Jerzy Kosinski appears to have lived in these past 55 years. But Kosky's world is also a realm of words governed by esthetic structures, so clearly it is different as well, which is at once the most obvious and most profound point of this autofiction.

Norbert Kosky is a 54-year-old survivor of the Holocaust who emigrated to America from Ruthenia, an East European realm that Kosinski uses to explore his deeply ambivalent, painful links with his native Poland and his Jewishness. Propelled into the status of literary superstar after writing a number of controversial but widely respected novels, Kosky for a while hobnobs with the elite . . . and engages in a series of peculiar sexual encounters. He also enjoys immersing himself in water and then levitating in public—an ability that becomes a central metaphor for the artist's need to ''float'' above the currents that make up his existence, to at once be a part of but always the master of his elements lest he drown.

Gradually we begin to see how Kosky has transformed the elements of his ''real life''—which includes his private obsessions, fantasies, personal problems, traumatic memories, metaphysical musings and reading, as well as the actual events he experiences—into the controversial, autobiographically based novels that have established his reputation. These novels are, of course, notable for the same sorts of things Kosinski's works are: their cool depiction of shockingly violent and erotic scenes, their focus on the needs of individuals to take refuge within a shifting series of disguises in order to survive the massive brutality and dehumanization of modern life, their fascination with the way the media are able to infiltrate and influence even the most private reaches of our sense of identity and value systems. Exploring Kosky's obsessive, haunted, yet playful literary sensibility therefore allows Kosinski to expose the inner theater of his own mysterious identity more openly than he has ever dared to in the past. . . .

[Any] plot summary greatly distorts the actual experience of reading *The Hermit.* At every turn, Kosinski impedes our progress through the work by his constant textual interventions. The result is a vast, convoluted book whose different planes of existences interact with one another to embody the mysterious processes that somehow combine to produce a novel. It also functions as an elaborate vindication of Kosinski by relentlessly laying siege to the concept of authorial originality, by exposing the provisional, intertextual nature of all ''meanings'' and by pointing out the dangers implicit within any society where the ''ownership'' of language is rigidly defined and the free play of creativity and collaboration are unable to function.

Georges Bataille once made the useful distinction between the avant-garde novel whose experiments seem to be made for the sake of experiments versus the work whose peculiar features seem born out of necessity. *The Hermit of 69th Street* is a work so excessive and self-involved, so obviously written by Kosinski for himself, that it seems born out of precisely that sense of necessity and compulsiveness. It is a sense that is rare among writers—but common among survivors. (p. 9)

Larry McCaffery, ''Kosinski's Mask behind the Mask,'' in Book World—The Washington Post, *July 10, 1988, pp. 1, 9.*

(Frederick) Louis MacNeice

1907-1963

(Also wrote under pseudonym of Louis Malone) Irish-born English poet, critic, translator, dramatist, scriptwriter, editor, and novelist.

A member of the "Oxford Group" of poets of the 1930s that included W. H. Auden, C. Day Lewis, and Stephen Spender, MacNeice is best known for verse in which he examines social concerns and the vagaries of the human condition. Envisioning the poet as an extension of the common individual, MacNeice often employed colloquial speech to address current events and everyday experiences of urban life in vivid, journalistic detail. While his poetry has been faulted for superficiality and flatness of style, MacNeice is admired for his ability to capture the specifics of time and place with cinematic imagery, lively rhythms, and inventive language. Samuel Hynes commented: "[What MacNeice] could do best was record feelings, and especially the sad side of feelings—the regret, the melancholy, the nostalgia, the helplessness and hopelessness of ordinary existence in an ordinary world."

Born in Belfast, Northern Ireland, MacNeice soon moved with his family to Carrickfergus, where his father served as minister and, later, bishop of the Anglo-Irish Church of Ireland. MacNeice led an isolated existence during his childhood as a result of his father's vocation, his mother's early death, and his family's subsequent relocation to England, all of which influenced the elegiac tone of his verse. MacNeice attended Oxford University, where he studied classical literature and philosophy and met Auden, Day Lewis, and Spender. Although these writers espoused various left-wing doctrines, MacNeice never fully committed himself to any political or philosophical programs, opting instead for a skeptical, agnostic, humanistic outlook. From 1941 until his death, MacNeice worked in the Features Department of the British Broadcasting Corporation, producing numerous scripts and writing several radio dramas, among them *Christopher Columbus* (1942), *The Dark Tower* (1946), and an abridged translation into English of Goethe's *Faust, Parts I and II* (1949).

The poems in MacNeice's first collection, *Blind Fireworks* (1929), center on childhood experiences and reveal his facility for striking imagery and diverse stanzaic forms. MacNeice's second volume, *Poems* (1935), established him as one of the most promising English poets of the 1930s. In this work, which was accepted by T. S. Eliot for the publishing firm of Faber & Faber, MacNeice comments on contemporary social and political issues from an aloof, ironic perspective. In the collaboration *Letters from Iceland* (1937), MacNeice and Auden blend travel poems and prose with light verse to discuss their adventures in Iceland as well as their lives and homelands. *The Earth Compels* (1938) examines domestic troubles, including MacNeice's painful divorce from his first wife. *Autumn Journal* (1939), which many critics consider his most ambitious piece, documents in impressionistic verse MacNeice's observations of personal and political events of the late 1930s while weaving memories of childhood, education, marriage, and travel. Samuel Hynes observed: "[*Autumn Journal*] is a poignant last example of that insistent 'thirties theme, the interpenetration of public and private worlds."

MacNeice's verse of the 1940s and 1950s relies less on energetic rhythms and powerful imagery, as the mood of his work becomes more somber and meditative and his themes increasingly allegorical. In *The Last Ditch* (1940), *Plant and Phantom* (1941), *Springboard: Poems, 1941-1944* (1944), and *Holes in the Sky: Poems, 1944-1947* (1948), MacNeice focuses on love relationships, philosophical and religious matters, and the consequences of World War II. *Ten Burnt Offerings* (1952), described by MacNeice as "experiments in dialectical structure," consists of ten long stylized and allusive poems on religious and historical subjects. *Autumn Sequel: A Rhetorical Poem* (1954) resembles *Autumn Journal* in style and theme but is considered to lack the poetic and historical impact of the earlier poem. In *Visitations* (1957), MacNeice returns to the short lyrics and conversational tone of his earlier work. *Solstices* (1961) and *The Burning Perch* (1963) are generally acknowledged as marking a renewed vitality in MacNeice's verse. In these volumes, he ruminates on death, the end of love and ambition, and the debasement of the spirit in hostile times.

MacNeice also earned respect for his literary criticism. *Modern Poetry: A Personal Essay* (1938) outlines his criteria for what constitutes skillful verse, stressing the importance of rhythm, rhyme, and technical innovation. *The Poetry of W. B. Yeats* (1941), considered the first major posthumous study of Yeats, explores this influential Irish poet's aesthetic and spiritual tenets. *Varieties of Parable* (1965) examines the use of parable in the work of a wide range of authors, including Edmund Spenser and Samuel Beckett. MacNeice also wrote *The Strings Are False: An Unfinished Autobiography* (1965); the novel *Roundabout Way* (1932), under the pseudonym of Louis Malone; and translated into English *The Agamemnon* (1936), which is regarded as one of the finest modern renderings of Greek drama.

(See also *CLC*, Vols. 1, 4, 10; *Contemporary Authors,* Vols. 85-88; and *Dictionary of Literary Biography,* Vols. 10, 20.)

SAMUEL FRENCH MORSE

As a political poet, MacNeice has been slow to "progress". He has not, in other words, been willing to make a rather hasty burnt-offering to any single group; instead, he has kept his integrity and gone only as far as his somewhat skeptical gaze on "future good" has let him go. And having to cope with a powerful inclination towards the quotidian, towards "milestone and curio," painting, "the expected response," he has attempted to make a significant order which will include the quotidian, and which will permit him to retain hs own identity in this order. This, of course, is what any serious poet must do, but it is just this lack of identity (or, in some cases, a too insistent identity of the poet with his poems, resulting in an overwrought eclecticism) that accounts for so many poetic failures. There is no way to accomplish this order; it remains a problem for the individual poet. There is, for example, a poem in *The Earth Compels,* called **"Circus,"** in which MacNeice seems to have adopted, consciously or unconsciously, the method of *The Airman's Alphabet:*

> Zanies by royal
> Charter and adept
> At false addition
> And gay combustion
>
> With bladders for batons
> And upright eyebrows
> Flappers for feet
> And figs for no one.

The matter is not so much one of influence here as it is a failure on the part of the poet to identify his method with himself to the extent that the reader does not think first of another poet, in this case, Mr. Auden. The method of *The Airman's Alphabet* is not, of course, Mr. Auden's private property, but at present, no other contemporary poet has so firmly identified himself with it.

MacNeice can, and fortunately, does create his own surface, his own line of attack, and his own methods, in the greater part of his poetry. These identifying qualities were perhaps most apparent in his 1935 volume in such poems as **"An Eclogue for Christmas," "Train to Dublin," "Birmingham," "Sunday Morning,"** though they appeared throughout the book, and gave it distinction among the volumes of that year. The later poems, which provide the text of **The Earth Compels,** continue largely in the same vein; the few apparent modifications come in an increased soberness, in a greater variety of technique, and in a solidification of point of view. MacNeice still re-iterates the position he had taken in **"Valediction,"** but less often now. . . . For the most part, however, a sense of impending disaster, of a threat to the loved familiar, drives the poet further into action. "Minute your gesture but it must be made," appears as a theme more than once. Yet it does not upset the balance. It may be this realization that gives part of the impetus to **"Carrickfergus," "Christmas Shopping," "Rugby Football Excursion," "On those Islands," "Leaving Barra,"** and the remarkable translation of Horace, poems which are more than landscape without pretending to be more, as well as the more "active" poems, **"Iceland," "Epilogue," "Eclogue between the Motherless,"** and **"Eclogue from Iceland."**

The ability to see the present in terms comprehensive enough to make the present of more than temporary significance, not to a small group "on the inside" merely, but to an increasingly large audience, is rare, and is something MacNeice possesses to a high degree. (pp. 281-82)

Samuel French Morse, in a review of "The Earth Compels," in Poetry, Vol. LIII, No. 5, February, 1939, pp. 280-83.

CONRAD AIKEN

["We stand convicted," MacNeice says in a poem from **Poems: 1925-1940**] called **"Men of Good Will,"** "votaries of the topical and transitory, we put in words what is topical and transitory, anyone can detect it." He will make a virtue of precisely that, and of allowing himself no nonsense, no romantic pretense, no vision. His own life is ineffectual and trite; he will report it so. But the entertainment, yes, that is another matter: he can at least be entertaining. And indeed he is.

For sheer readability, for speed, lightness and easy intellectual range, Mr. MacNeice's verse is in a class by itself. Open it anywhere, whether in narrative, eclogue or lyric, and at once you are swept away by the tireless and effortless enumerative pace, the bright rush of nominal images, the gay prodigality of scene, the so easily caught tune and mood. Yes, this is the world we know, all right, and this too is a fellow we can like, here are pubs and football games and Freud and the dreary economic muddle and the confused political ideologies through which we try to think, or feel, our way, and the sad glad conquests and vapors of love too, the whole great blooming buzzing confusion (to quote William James)—it's all here, bright and quick as a river to swim in. And so, in we go; and out we come; and it is only then that we find how little of all this has stuck to us. Not a thing—practically not a thing. For the trouble is, it is *too* topical, *too* transitory, *too* reportorial— it has that sort of merit and vividness which is good in the presence of the object, and by virtue of the object has a kind of quick and momentary magic; but it has, one fears, very little *residual* magic, very little of that quality of intricate and teasing wroughtness which sends one back to a poem not for the meaning but to see how the meaning was said.

No, Mr. MacNeice writes as he runs; he is always in a hurry; we catch the delightful fragments of speech which he addresses to us, as it were, over his shoulder—but we cannot help thinking that he would be better if he could take more seriously either the function of the poet as *genus irritabile vatum* or the virtue of the artifact. Even the best of the lyrics—and they are very good—such as **"Meeting Point," "A Toast,"** with their very skillful use of vernacular refrain to dignify a sentimental theme, suffer from that sort of carelessness about the fine points of form which indicates an essentially barbaric attitude toward art. If only all that brilliance could be put to better use! But then, Mr. MacNeice professes indifference to this, believes that nowadays only a more off-hand method can be natural or true, and prefers to be merely entertaining. We must therefore leave it at that. (pp. 830-31)

Conrad Aiken, "Poetry as Entertainment," in The New Republic, *Vol. 104, No. 24, June 16, 1941, pp. 830-32.*

STEPHEN SPENDER

Evasiveness and scepticism are not the two sides of the same medal. The question of whether the sceptic is being evasive only arises when he is dealing with 'ultimate facts' of experience. For better or worse. MacNeice did write some long poems in which he tried, in a deliberately haphazard way, to state a view of life. The first of these was **Autumn Journal,** written in 1939, a considerable tour de force, in which the poet records in vivid impressionist verse, his reactions to private and public experiences. The view of life here is deduceable rather than explicitly stated. It is that the attitudes of *'l'homme moyen sensuel',* whom the poet here represents, survive in the 'low dishonest decade' of the Thirties. The hero of MacNeice's poetry, as of Orwell's prose, is the individual who (to adopt Orwell's phrase) is 'decent'. **Autumn Sequel,** a poem of twenty-six cantos in Dantesque *terza rima,* is far more ambitious than the earlier poem, but less heartening. Like its predecessor, it is skilful, vivid, honest and journalier. (Detractors might, I suppose, call it journalistic, but this is surely only because journalism includes some of the best as well as much of the worse modern writing.) In **Autumn Sequel** MacNeice intensifies his vision of *l'homme moyen sensuel* of the earlier poetry into that of certain individuals who embody what is really a humanistic philosophy. Certain of his friends, although in no sense leaders of humanity, nevertheless are a kind of elect, possessing qualities which make MacNeice recognise them as such and enabling them also to recognise one another. They form a kind of secret society of those who are really human among so many people who are bureaucrats and automatons, MacNeice's elect are a scholar, a poet, a man of action, lovers—they have a kinship with Yeats's lechers, drunkards and saints. Some of them exist on a less exalted level. (pp. 20-1)

So in **Autumn Sequel** MacNeice embodies humanist values in his portraits of subdued heroes who exhibit civilised values of love and wine and books and acts of courage against the dreary background of modern routines. . . .

MacNeice is more successful in his generalisations about the *condition humaine* than in his particularised characterisations of his friends. He sees those whom he regards as heroes as roles personified. These roles are partly created by themselves, partly they exist in the minds of beholders. One does not dispute them, for one supposes him to have chosen his heroes and girls with fine discrimination. My criticism is not that he sees only the positive, creative and demonstratively human side of his characters but that his selective way of presenting them lays him open to the same objection as he himself makes to people with public and routine personalities. He substitutes for the political and officialised view a superior kind of public relations of the public-private kind and not too far removed from a Third Programme documentary. (p. 21)

His sense of life is of the tragically heroic. Nevertheless he never seems to get at the centre of tragedy which is the heart of the tragically afflicted individual. He only sees the external display which such a person, if he is courageous, puts up.

MacNeice was probably influenced by Yeats in attaching such importance to the show, parade, performance, the courageous defiant act of living. Yet Yeats even when he is in a Nietzschean mood of non-compassion almost compulsively sees the horror beneath the glory of the scene:

> Yet they, should the last scene be there,
> The great stage curtain about to drop,
> If worthy their prominent part in the play,
> Do not break up their lines to weep,
> They know that Hamlet and Lear are gay;
> Gaiety transfiguring all that dread.

I do not mean that MacNeice fails to be moved and moving. He is aware of cruel juxtapositions:

> But Gavin's cradle sank and the dark defiled
> Atlantic scrawled its flourish of cold foam
> Above him, while on shore we drank our mild
> and bitter, wondering when he would come home.

There are depths here—the depths of the Atlantic, the black spaces of passionate loss. Nevertheless the general effect of MacNeice's longer poems is of cinematic images moving across a screen.

Particularly when he writes about people—whether his anti-hero heroic friends or some girl he is passionately in love with, he lacks some dimension. It is this lack which gives his poetry the impression of superficiality. To put it in contemporary jargon, he lacks 'psychology'. He sees people as their images moving across screens. I do not mean that he doesn't perceive beneath the external display of eyes, lips and noses, flickering darknesses filled with hob-goblins, witches and demons—like the DT's in Dylan Thomas—but he sees these too from the outside, as part of the show. He does not experience any other person from within. Least of all, does he know himself. (pp. 21-2)

Although MacNeice touches gingerly on his childhood, as on an exposed nerve, the material of his early life remains simply an area of dark pain at the centre of his poetry. In the beautiful short poem **"Autobiography,"** he writes:

> My mother wore a yellow dress:
> Gently, gently, gentleness.
>
> *Come back early or never come.*
>
> When I was five the black dreams came;
> Nothing after was quite the same.
>
> *Come back early or never come.*
>
> The dark was talking to the dead;
> The lamp was dark beside my bed.

This is deeply moving, and makes poetry out of reticence: the lamp sheds darkness instead of light. Terror remains absolute, silent:

> When my silent terror cried,
> Nobody, nobody replied.

Plant and Phantom, a poem to which MacNeice seems to have attached importance, tells us a lot about Man, but does not mention that every individual is some one who calls himself or herself 'I':

> Man: a riot of banners,
> Bulge in the wind, a prism,
> Organ-pipes in the sunset,
> Orgy of brains and glands,

> Thunder-crackle and the bounce of hail,
> Wink of wings and fog's delusion,
> A rampant martyr, a midnight
> Echo, a forest fire. . . .

[MacNeice] had some Romantic trappings, for example a certain nostalgia, but a Romantic is someone (whether Wordsworth, Keats or D H Lawrence) who asserts in his work his own essential being. Louis stood outside everyone, including himself. The qualities of his sensibility are those of a secondary 'I', an elegant and observant poetic person, that records and responds. As such a persona, MacNeice is too protected and defensive to be a 'modern' like Joyce or Eliot. His persona, as his poetry, is conditioned by his manners, the company he keeps, his culture, his education. If he appears 'superficial', it is because he so rarely, either in ideas or feelings, seems to get beyond his classical learning and his Oxford culture. . . .

If not a Romantic, MacNeice does not, despite his knowledge of the classics, have the objectivity—or pseudo-objectivity—of the modern Classicist either. He does though have a certain aristocracy of attitude and feeling. He is a one-man aristocracy, all by himself, surrounded by his little court of the elect. . . .

MacNeice was neither Romantic nor classic because he was neither completely subjective nor completely objective. For the purposes of writing his poetry he interposed between his fundamental subjective self or its opposite—a fundamentally objective non-self—a secondary self or persona which he maintained in his life as well as in his work with most remarkable, and remarked-on, consistency. This secondary self was very idiosyncratic. What he had, to a degree unparalleled among his contemporaries, was a temperament, that of one who certainly did not wear his heart on his sleeve, but was intelligent, educated, fantastic, witty and possessed of some inner tuneful rhythmic sweep, a throbbing colour of sensibility that swept through his language. His best poems are those lyrics which are events struck off this temperament. The poems in which he tries, or half-tries, to make philosophic statements about life, reveal a certain shallowness because they do not spring either from an original intellect or from his deepest experiences. On the other hand, they have their place in an honourable tradition of poeticising about the journalier preoccupations of cultivated men living in their time, like much of Matthew Arnold's poetry or like Arthur Hugh Clough's *Amours de Voyage*. He is better than Clough. They are poetic 'documentaries' and people a hundred years hence may well turn to *Autumn Journal* and *Autumn Sequel* with interest and to get some sense of a very gifted poet's reactions to public and private living in the second quarter of the twentieth century. (p. 22)

> *Stephen Spender, "MacNeice: Poet of the Passing Show," in* Books and Bookmen, *Vol. 20, No. 11, August, 1975, pp. 20-2.*

ELTON EDWARD SMITH

Like Chinese fireworks, the poems [in *Blind Fireworks*] go through their light random popping antics against the somber background of secular holiday or religious festival, then fall and go out. Quite expectedly, many poems are about childhood experience: the pleasures and dangers of sleep, reminiscences of life in rectory and church, and many references to classical deities. But even so early a collection grants two glimpses of social concern. In the foreword MacNeice charmingly expresses his admiration for the Chinese because they invented gunpowder not to kill people, but to entertain them with fire-

works. He links the "Time-God" Thor with the "Man-of-Science" Pythagoras by having them both serve as figures for the passage of time. But the selections make clear that something more is meant than the ordinary passage of time. This is the final or end-time which theology calls eschatology—a theme of doom introduced early (1929) and coming to maturity in the radio-drama *Out of the Picture* (1938).

"This Tournament" evokes the delicate imagery of moths jousting in the sun, smashed by the descending hammer of Thor. Even Pythagoras, who explains and supports the universe mathematically, is warned, in "A Lame Idyll," that his own era is coming to an end and that he too will fall into the dustheap along with Adonis and Proserpine. The dead gods circle about the contemporary symbol of an industrial chimney in "Twilight of the Gods." The abacus of Pythagoras is broken; he can no longer keep the world steady by counting. "Coal and Fire" is topically concerned with the industrial revolution, but thematically points to a revolution in which the "damned" middle and the golden mean will find no place at all. "Adam's Legacy" contains only two possible choices: stand before a door that will not open, or quietly await the trump of doom.

"The Court Historian (A Satirical Composition)" metes to the scholar the same short shrift MacNeice had already given to Pythagoras. The historian sits godlike, inscribing the dates of dynasties, oblivious to a figure about to tap him on the shoulder and usher him into past history. "Candle Poems" innocently describe shrinking cylinders standing in increasing islands of wax. But a breakwater of wax is inadequate protection for an island against the tides of a troubled time. Candles are more appropriate to the foot of a single casket, or to the demise of a total culture. This theme of dying culture is further developed in "Neurotics" as the poet compares Aeneas fleeing successfully from burning Troy with modern man who is destined to perish along with his moribund culture. (pp. 69-70)

Poems (1935) is insistently contemporary with an emphasis upon wireless, factory chimneys, policemen, and buses fulfilling Michael Roberts's prescription: "it was inevitable that the growth of industrialism should give rise to a 'difficult' poetry . . . abrupt, discordant, intellectual."

But if the circumference of MacNeice's language and imagery is determinedly social, the center is warmed by personal characterization. And whereas for many proletarian poets the singing voice grows strident and the intellectual tone doctrinaire, MacNeice was saved by the coolness and virtuosity of his performance. The complex meanings and the large issues tend to be expressed in delightful doggerel with childlike naïveté. The result is a cool distancing of sentiment and doctrine that makes both palatable.

Poems begins with "An Eclogue for Christmas," a form much favored by MacNeice, the dialogue precursor of his later verse plays. *A* is the urban half of a personality which is *B* in the country. His world is so full of nonessential sweets that it might be called a "diabetic" culture. Drums and Hawaiian guitars drown the cry for identity. Like modern art, his life has been splintered and abstracted; symbol, or pastiche, but is never just itself. Full of liabilities, with no assets, there is hope of no new beginning; there is only the certainty of an end when the "Goths" will again "come swarming down the hill." Flats, clubs, beauty parlors—all the trivia of contemporary culture, will be mowed down by young men with machine guns.

B, the rural side of the modern personality, is a grim Hardy protagonist rather than a hearty Fielding squire. Every place is simply a spot to die. The county gentry have declined into male alcoholics and tweedy women who still attempt to hunt and farm although factory smoke pollutes the air and settles down on field and forest. Eventually all these private manors will be socialized, and the survivors of the gentry will be talented buffoons or prostitutes. The countryside evokes only memories of the past and the wisdom of nonassertive animals and stones. So from his rural attempt at escape, *AB* must return to London, to be anesthetized by saxophones, xylophones, canvases in galleries, canvas sails on rich men's yachts, and the final technical perfection of a grilled steak.

Culture is in decline; escape is impossible; modern life is intrinsically trivial; and the hopeless truths may be made only grimly acceptable by witty statement. There is much use of rhyme to make the poetry sound childishly singsong and somehow parodic. The vocabulary is more frequently the words for material things than for philosophic concepts. The total effect is an adult critique of what is wrong with England and a Stoic courage in the face of despair.

The substitution of things for theories is noticeable in **"Train for Dublin"** when the poet toasts "incidental" things rather than symbolic images of painted wood. The search for meanings is abandoned for the simple experience of each thing "exactly" as it is. The eschatological vision of *Blind Fireworks* is continued and amplified in *Poems*. In **"Morning Sun,"** the radiant splashing of the fountain in the square is quickly transformed to dust-grey powder. In **"Persons,"** the Greek hero swings the Gorgon's head wide, everything living is turned to stony death and an empty earth spins like a mad moth around a blackening sun.

"To a Communist" is an antidoctrinaire toast. Before the Party member preens himself on his dialectical solution to all society's ills, he should remember that the snow which purifies everything overnight may also melt in a single day. **"The Wolves"** is a sad and hopeless warning of danger. The enemies of freedom howl about England's coast. All that the liberal and conservative politicians can think of is to form a circle and join hands, or to build ineffective little sand castles on the beach, temporarily blotting out the howls with talk and laughter. In **"Aubade,"** the poet remembers the dreams of youth when he assumed that the unnecessary mythologizing of life would end in an enlightened *Götterdämmerung* and the consequent exaltation of humanity. But now in maturity he sees only the stark light of early dawn falling on urban brick facades, and hears only the voices of newsboys announcing war. **"Spring Voices"** warns the suburbanite that even while he putters about in the garden, gambles on horses, or buys cigars, he may "loiter into a suddenly howling crater" or fall over backward "garrotted by the sun." Using the imagery of a circus, MacNeice barks that laboring men are no longer obedient; respectability has come to an end; we live on sufferance awaiting disaster. The world is a trapeze with the ropes wearing thin, and we all know that circus jobs, sooner or later, spell death. (pp. 70-3)

Louis MacNeice indicated his membership in a group of working poets by publishing a strange travel book, *Letters from Iceland*, in 1937, written in collaboration with W. H. Auden. . . .

Auden was drawn to Iceland by his Scandinavian ancestry and an interest in the Norse saga. Under contract to Faber and Faber to do a travel book, he arrived in Iceland first and was later joined by MacNeice and other friends. Lest they brood over the *ultima Thule* of the ancient world, he brought along

a breezy satirical volume by Lord Byron. Five chapters of the travel book (1, 5, 8, 13, 16) become the racy installments of a *terza rima* letter from the twentieth-century British poets isolated at the world's end to the nineteenth-century Romantic poet exiled in Greece. (p. 75)

The book is quite self-consciously a collage: photographs, press clippings, statistics, graphs, gossip, natural scenery, men and women, the arts, the European news—and, above all else, Auden and MacNeice themselves. (p. 76)

Nineteen thirty-eight was Louis MacNeice's *annus mirabilis* in which he had four volumes published: *I Crossed the Minch,* another travel book; *Zoo,* chatty comment on animals and people; *The Earth Compels,* a volume of poetry; and *Modern Poetry,* prose criticism of modern poetry. Because MacNeice knew no Gaelic and the Hebrideans spoke nothing else, *I Crossed the Minch* was condemned to be "a tripper's book written by someone who was disappointed and tantalized by the islands and seduced by them only to be reminded that on the soil he will always be an outsider." (p.78)

MacNeice chose to go to the Hebrides for a reason analogous to Auden's decision to go to Iceland; he hoped the Celt in him would be drawn out by a primitive culture which went deep into his forbears. But oddly he was unprepared for the wholesale emigration from the islands, a phenomenon that Dr. Johnson had noted in the eighteenth century. He was also sadly disappointed to discover that instead of insularity guaranteeing the continuity of the primitive culture, the islands were themselves the victims of cultural invasion from the mainland. The primitive culture was dead; the engrafted culture had not yet taken firm root: "More than one generation is required before a man can be a capitalist with grace."

In a very controversial section about the effect of the Soviet Union upon indigenous cultures, MacNeice accepts the oftenrepeated praise that the Soviets maintained local traditions and cultures wherever possible, although always within the framework of subservience to the new order. This pattern appeals to MacNeice as the ideal way to link conservation of the old with radical zeal for the adventurous new. But instead of producing this rich cultural brew, it seems to him that his leftwing comrades in England "suffer from the masochism of the puritan." Instead of personal enrichment, party membership permits no frills, comforts, or luxuries for the body or the mind. Individual persons and unique communities must be liquidated for the sake of economic cooperation and the united statement of the Marxist creed. To MacNeice so bleak a social philosophy looks like a "future of Esperanto, Sunday School treats and homage to the Highest Common Factor" (cf. **"Eclogue from Iceland"**). But again he reminds himself that Lenin recognized the necessary role of differentiation. . . . (pp. 78-9)

In an important and topical, but also whimsical interview with his Guardian Angel, MacNeice is asked if he has read *Forward from Liberalism*, that "nice" book by his friend Stephen Spender. Besides, isn't it about time he took some definite position on political issues? The divided poet replies that his sympathies are leftist, both intellectually and spiritually. "I would vote Left any day, sign manifestos, answer questionnaires. . . . My soul is all for moving towards the classless society." But so far as heart and "gut" are concerned, "man for me is still largely characterized by what he buys. . . . I am both a money snob and a class snob." Even in his attitude toward women, MacNeice likes them better if they are rich and perhaps have "Honourable" before their names. He especially values the gestures, poise, and intonations which are "imitated from snobs by a snob and practiced for the seduction of snobs." This dividedness is not a tension to be released, but a sign that the poet is irrevocably one of the lost intelligentsia. Thus, to the precise and probing penultimate speech of the Guardian Angel: "Are you going to, partly out of pique, partly out of vanity, but mainly because you are just darn bone lazy, wilfully espouse a life of outmoded triviality and inaction—" the poet who is weary of fighting and always losing the same battles can only mutter "Oh, go to hell."

"Bagpipe Music" swishes its kilts and skirls its tune but ends with the same ominous peal of doom. In this fast-moving, slangy bit of cynicism, modern man is seen to care nothing for Eastern spiritual disciplines or new world religions, but he manages to get by with a bank balance and "a bit of skirt in a taxi." (pp. 79-80)

The last poem in *I Crossed the Minch*, **"On Those Islands (A Poem for Hector MacIver),"** observes that the old culture survives to some degree in the smaller fishing villages of the islands where no one hurries, fires are still built of peat, Gaelic tunes are preserved intact, and the parlor photographs of island sons who were successful in the New World strike the only discordant modern note. But this kind of simple peace, made by blotting out the modern world and remaining resolutely in the past, is "not for me," says the poet, and implies probably not for anyone for very much longer. (p. 80)

[*The Earth Compels*] contains very little new work, and the new poems largely deal with older themes. **"Homage to Clichés,"** one of MacNeice's best poems, is both complex in structure and subtle in transformation of image. (p. 81)

"Homage to Clichés" embodies MacNeice's favorite game of the ominous clue lurking in the banal social situation. How pleasant to sit in a bar with an attractive woman and make the kind of conversation that requires no effort and no thought. But through a hidden door, up a belfry stair, hang eight black bells within a womb of stone. We imagined that our manipulation of them as chimes was the only sound they could make. But ringers are removing their coats to toll rather than to chime, and a timekeeper with watch and pistol stands ready to signal the end of the whole delightful world of cliché and refrain. (pp. 81-2)

Modern Poetry: A Personal Essay (1938) represents Louis MacNeice's most important body of literary criticism. The very first sentence of the preface binds the poet to the world: "This book is a plea for *impure* poetry, that is, for poetry conditioned by the poet's life and the world around him." As entertainer, the poet is tempted to fall over into escape literature; as critic, he may become so deeply committed to a particular school of thought that his verse becomes propaganda. The middle course is preferable not because it is the echo in verse of the prose convictions of the community, but because it becomes "its conscience, its critical faculty, its generous instinct." Ideological organizations will press him to "tell lies to order," but his job is to serve up poetic truth.

MacNeice muses that although his generation was profoundly influenced by Eliot and Pound while they were in school, they have turned instead to the writing of popular poetry—not popular because more people read it, but because it deals with man as a political animal with strong physical instincts, needs, and affections. Therefore the poetry of W. H. Auden, Stephen Spender, C. Day-Lewis, John Lehmann, Julian Bell, and William Plomer often deals with the economic, material, social,

and sexual factors that are part of the lives of all modern men. They accept Marx and Freud, with their dialectics of materialistic socialism and the deep role of the physical instincts, as the chief architects of the modern mind. A secondary influence of Marx is the predilection for a world of concrete things rather than a shadowy universe of Platonic forms or Shelleyan ideas. Thus, forsaking the rebellion of the Romantics, the obscurity of the new metaphysicals, poets have now shifted back from withdrawal to involvement in the common life of men.

The poet is not different from other men, "he merely has more highly developed muscles and better coordination. And he practises his activity according to a stricter set of rules." Having restored the poet to normality, he performs the same office for the reader of poetry: "an ideal normal man who is an educated member of his own community and is basically at one with the poet in his attitude to life."

Both of these definitions lead to the famous definition which has aroused the extremes of admiration or castigation: "I would have a poet able-bodied, fond of talking, a reader of newspapers, capable of pity and laughter, informed in economics, appreciative of women, involved in personal relationships, actively interested in politics, susceptible to physical impressions." Thus **Modern Poetry** begins with the subtitle "A Personal Essay," and ends with the definition of the poet that fits no poet more aptly than it fits the author, Louis MacNeice. (pp. 82-3)

In his foreword to **Poems: 1925-1940**, Louis MacNeice pronounced **Autumn Journal** to be "in a sense, a failure; it fails in depth . . . we shall not be capable of depth—of tragedy or *great* poetry—until we have made sense of our world." It is quite natural that a verse diary of the public events and private meanings from August 1938 through January 1939 would be so caught up in the rush of event that the *Journal* would be all foreground and little background, although, with shadows aplenty.

Autumn Journal joins those other diverse and greater works of art—Shakespeare's *Othello* and Eliot's *The Waste Land*—which explore dilemmas without suggesting solutions, and therefore leave both artist and audience with a certain frustration and sense of incompletion. When Julian Symons dubbed the *Journal* "The Bourgeois's Progress," he was making contrast rather than comparison, for the point of Bunyan's great picaresque wandering is that Christian was illuminated by a heavenly vision and reached his goal. **Autumn Journal** begins with the generalized good will of the liberal, records amazement and shock at the political events of the period, and ends with a diffuse restatement of that same good will, badly shaken by events and already recognized by the poet to be ineffectual. That MacNeice was aware of these shortcomings is made clear by the inadequacy of his defense. Concerning the ephemeral topicality of the *Journal,* in a note he simply reminded the critics of the natural limitations of the genre: "In a journal or a personal letter a man writes what he feels at the moment." (pp. 85-6)

Cantos 1 through 4 move from Hampshire to London, from the beginning of August to the end of summer. Then in canto 5, on a beautiful day, Hitler speaks over the radio, and the bloody frontier of Auden and Isherwood is no longer just the theme of a bad play; it is the current reality of Everyman's life. It is no use to take refuge in the prayer of Jesus "Let this cup pass from me." We helped to mix the brew and it is only fair that we should join in drinking the liquor. Irresistably, his mind wanders back to his trip to Spain the preceding Easter (canto 6). He came home and promptly forgot Spain; now Spain has come to him in England.

The newspapers are full of conferences which adjourn before settlement, ultimata delivered by both sides, and over all the mad soprano shriek of Hitler's voice on the wireless (cantos 7, 8). The crisis will be settled in panic, and the resulting international relief will be only self-deception. He returns to Birmingham where he came to teach the Classics eight years before with his first wife. Now he is both wifeless and thrust by the international crisis out of his ivory tower. But the crisis is postponed: Chamberlain has saved the skins of Free Europe at the expense of their souls and the Czechoslovak nation goes down the drain.

In October (canto 9) the poet is back in London, the prey of sad thoughts about classical history. The ancient Greeks played out their little drama of truth and humor between the ''jealous heaven'' of the irresponsible gods and the indifference of the ''callous sea.'' But free speech ended on Lacedemonian pikes, and Athens became a wall-less university town. The great talk went on for another thousand years, but it was no longer the epic of heroes. When the professor of Greek sought to recall the great free citizens of Greece all that came to mind was late Hellas, with crooks, opportunists, fancy boys, splitters of hair, demagogues, quacks—borne on the impatient backs of all those slaves!

The return to his teaching duties (canto 10) reminds him that British education initiated the pupil into normal life—and of course it was assumed that things would always be normal in the British Isles. He is haunted in canto 11 by the girl of canto 4. Then it is Tuesday, October 25, 1938 (canto 12), and the golden weather reminds the classical scholar of a Roman mob crying for bread and circuses and caring nothing about freedom.

Perhaps one of the difficulties of a British classical education is that the graduate is all general, with no particularities, whereas, says MacNeice, the man on the street tends to have particular items of information but no general conceptual frame in which to fit them. Unfortunately, an Oxford graduate is left with an incapacity to ever believe anything again. The next evening (canto 14), the poet goes down to Oxford to vote and to help drive voters to the polling places. He goes partly for the fun of reunion, but also partly because he is coming to realize that the parliamentary system is the only defense of the citizen of a free society against the legionnaire's eagles of militarism and the lictors' axes of fascism. Perfectionists wait forever in a London fog; it is necessary to make crosses and blanks on votes even for unideal candidates. Unfortunately the best people are the very ones least likely to make solidarity of cause, but they must line up now against the beast.

Canto 15 describes the frenetic activities into which a pleasure-loving people throw themselves in order to blot out the thought of war. The poet (canto 16) recognizes that intellectuals, like Yeats, may become too aware of the cross-currents of motivation to take any appropriate action. Yet Yeats's beloved Maude Gonne saw it all and was still capable of purposeful action. Sitting in the November sun (canto 17) the poet recalls that just as Aristotle claimed that the heart of drama was in action, so man-in-action is the essential and only existent man. Once men held convictions with blood, bone, and pulse (canto 18); now they simply juggle possibilities in the brain. December brings bad news of the revival of the ghetto for the Jew,

the gagging of free speech in the German universities, the growth of concentration camps for the enemies of the state.

At last, in canto 19 he can think of the lady of cantos 4 and 11 with no passionate reaction of resentment. He hopes she is busy, wishes her luck, and thanks for the party. On a visit to the National Gallery (canto 20) the arrogant Old Masters seem to affront the tentative systems of values of the modern world. They had such confidence, and we ask only to be left alone. A week before Christmas the poet thinks about the luxury gifts brought by the Magi to the very child destined to totally devalue them. The herald angels sing on the street corners, but not to announce peace to the waiting world, only to cadge for small coins.

A man ought to be like a fire (canto 21), spent recklessly but giving a good return; burning silence into sound, laughing at the dark, jumping into blaze from a single spark to purge and warm the world. On December 19 and the first snowfall in London (canto 22) the poet plans a visit to France for the trivia of eating, drinking, and a sophisticated but casual woman. He will not remain in Paris; he will cross the Pyrenees into the ''pain and pride'' of Spain (canto 23). The planes from Majorca, ''modern Valkyries,'' bomb the city, while the matter-of-fact faith and courage of the populace shame all those who would dissolve truth in niggling petty distinctions.

Canto 24 begins with an invocation to sleep. May the conflicting selves the poet finds within wake up from that sleep healed and united; may his former wife sleep serenely beyond the Atlantic. But his dream is interrupted by coward doubts. The New Year is ushered in by bombs as well as bells, and tomorrow he must make decisions that call for action. Later on he can audit all the old accounts; later on he can sit in the sunshine; later he can see the whole design from its ending.

Autumn Journal records an indecision, which although lucidly mirrored, is not therein resolved, and thus continues to haunt his later work. Besides being a skillful poet, MacNeice is a very honest man. Therefore he recognizes that the gentle hedonism which he met in rectory and school, the bequest of nineteenth-century altruism, is too delicate a plant to survive long in the coming clash of the classes. Loathing fascism, and clearly dissatisfied with things as they are in England, he still cannot quite go all the way to the Communist position. Because he was part of the old world order that provided the forcing-frame for fascism, he therefore shares its guilt. But he is kept from doing anything constructive about the political threat, first because he feels helpless before the vastness of the problem, and second because he is hopeless about building a better future.

Beneath all the technical brilliance of the twenty-four cantos of this extraordinarily sustained long poem, there lies a blunt question which receives a bald answer: ''What can my kind of person be expected to do, in this kind of a world, at this terrifying moment? The obvious fact that the *Journal* fails to make sense of the world and therefore resolve the particular problems raised makes the answer unavoidable: nothing. It is pleasant to be assured that the river he will cross will not be the Styx of death, nor the Lethe of forgetfulness, but the Rubicon of decision. When? Oh, tomorrow. All accounts will be audited *later;* the sun will shine *later;* the answer to the problem equation will come out at the *last.*

And so, as John Peale Bishop put it, the Anglo-Irish poet plays out that bathetic tragedy, ''The Hamlet of L. MacNeice.'' Every bit as irresolute as Shakespeare's prince, he assigns to his leading character in *Out of the Picture* the stabbing of a surrogate Mr. Polonius Chamberlain. He goes down to Oxford instead of to Wittenberg in order to commit a public act which will release his frozen will. He proposes to win an election, which is promptly lost. No nunnery for his Ophelia; it simply takes three cantos to erase her from his memory. The bloody frontier he had sniffed at in the play of friends, now takes focus beside his bed, but he is as helpless before it as Hamlet in the face of Fortinbras's troops. Both Louis MacNeice and Prince Hamlet are haunted by father-ghosts, by soldier-ghosts, and most of all, by the ghost of a kingdom's dead greatness. (pp. 86-90)

[The poems in *The Last Ditch*] are not "heroic," they lack the power that comes from coherent and passionate belief. The poet is "rich" technically and intellectually; he is "not rich" in terms of affirmation, confidence, and faith. The poems are slight "odds or ends." Among them the "thief" of contemporary history may be located bundled up "in the last ditch," an ex-liberal with his back against the wall of his self-imposed limitations.

"**Prognosis**" is an elegant literary ballad concerning the possibilities of the coming spring. After *Autumn Journal* the poet has both sharpened and wiped his pen in order to write lines which are witty with slant rhyme, and lyrical with restrained passion and sadness. A tea leaf in the cup heralds the arrival of a stranger. Will it be John the Baptist to herald a new Incarnation, or will it be the prophet Jonah to announce that in forty days the world will end?

There are sixteen poems which the author groups under "**The Coming of War.**" Four of the group have Irish settings: "**Dublin**," "**Cushendun**," "**Sligo and Mayo**," and "**Galway.**" Generally they draw the contrast between the idyllic landscape and the coming of war. The relics of the past tell a story of ancient wars which were survived by the people, but today the populace goes about business and pleasure as usual while "doom" laps at the door.

"**London Rain**" is one of MacNeice's metaphysical poems, perhaps suggested by the famous "wager scene" of Pascal's *Pensées*. The warning beacons on the English Channel become God and No-God playing at pitch and toss. And unlike Pascal, it makes no difference which one wins. If God wins, He will simply pardon the sinner; if No-God wins "nothing will matter at all." (p. 90)

This quiet, pleasant collection ranges in style from the jog-trot rhythms of "**Dublin**" to the lyricism of "**Cushendun.**" The artist has clearly moved ahead technically; he makes many successful experiments in style, metric, and rhyme pattern. But there is a certain embarrassment at the point of maturation, for too many of the poems are juvenile in topic, mood, and intention. The major tension in the collection lies between the settled, safe past and the threats of war. But it is a dialectic which never proceeds beyond the tension of thesis-antithesis to synthesis. The thought is still arrested at the shock level of *Autumn Journal*. The poems say three things exceedingly well, but the total effect is lost by the complete lack of formulation of the necessary fourth. MacNeice is charming and even poignant at "When I was young"; his nostalgia is most persuasive in "This is the old England I loved"; the shock is much more muted than in the previous diary-journal of "These are the pieces of the past after the bombs burst." But instead of a true climax, with the restoration of order, this is simple catastrophe which leaves the pieces and the audience scattered everywhere.

The pieces might be picked up and restored to the old, settled pattern—and this is manifestly impossible. Or they may be put together by a new logic to make a new and better pattern. But the poet doubts that they can be put together in a new pattern, and even more he doubts that such a new pattern would be better than the old one which was bombed. Thus the pieces lie scattered on the floor and the absence of a structure of logic gives the delightfully and eminently readable verse a note of irrelevance and frivolity. It is a mistake to let surface rhythms blind us to the shadow of defeatism in, appropriately, *The Last Ditch*. It is a good thing for a competent artist to re-oil his tools, but where does one go from "the last ditch?" (pp. 91-2)

Elton Edward Smith, "Louis MacNeice: The Circular Movement," in his The Angry Young Men of the Thirties, *Southern Illinois University Press, 1975, pp. 69-92.*

TOM PAULIN

MacNeice is always crossing the water, and the feeling of unease and displacement, of moving between different cultures and nationalism, which he paradoxically returns to in his poetry, means that his imagination is essentially fluid, maritime and elusively free. He cannot identify himself exclusively with one or other part of the island: the North of Ireland is 'devout and profane and hard', while the South is 'a gallery of false tapestries.' And in *Autumn Journal* he asks

> Why should I want to go back
>   To you, Ireland, my Ireland?
> The blots on the page are so black
>   That they cannot be covered with shamrock.
> I hate your grandiose airs,
>   Your sob-stuff, your laugh and your swagger,
> Your assumption that everyone cares
>   Who is the king of your castle.

Ireland, he concludes, is 'both a bore and a bitch'. Her children 'slouch around the world with a gesture and a brogue / And a faggot of useless memories.'' His dismissive celebration is wild and melancholy, gay and sober—a series of passionate Irish contradictions.

Of course the lines are deliberately journalistic, and MacNeice's technique of setting clichés dancing to a hurdy-gurdy rhythm can be tedious. This throwaway lyricism—'the beer-brown spring / Guzzling between the heather, the green gush of Irish spring'—often resembles a commercial jingle and the images are frequently stale or received, like the contemporary surfaces he was so fascinated by and on which they are partly modelled. In "**When we were children**" he compares laburnum blossom to scrambled eggs, and his witty copywriter's eye often pins down such slick gimmicky images. The urban rootless world of rootless urban clichés, consumer durables and advertising hoardings is an essential part of his imagination, and while he sometimes recycles images of the Irish landscape like a tourist board official eager to woo 'the sentimental English', few Irish writers have totally resisted the temptation to export their Irishness. And in any case Irishness is a sometimes clownish commodity which depends on being transported elsewhere.

It's wrong to condemn MacNeice for this deracinated, even at times ersatz, quality because it's something which is implicit in the Irish landscape—the West of Ireland, for example, is strewn with derelict cottages abandoned by emigrant families and it's also covered with breezeblock suburban bungalows built with money brought back from abroad. Landscape and journeys fray against each other, and it is a shore and a seascape crossed by a journey which is at the centre of MacNeice's imaginative vision. From his first mature poem, **"Belfast"**, to his last poem, the stoic **"Thalassa"**, his imagination is caught by ships and 'the salt carrion water':

> Down there at the end of the melancholy lough
> Against the lurid sky over the stained water
> Where hammers clang murderously on the girders
> Like crucifixes the gantries stand.

Here the eye crosses Belfast Lough to the gantries in Harland and Wolff's shipyards which stand over the quays where the passenger ferries and cargo boats dock. The image catches the provincial introversion, the puritan work ethic, the cruelty and injustice of the stagnant society MacNeice only peripherally belonged to. The unfinished ships, he implies, stand in their scaffolds, and this fuses birth and death in a manner that is distinctively Irish (like Joyce's puns in his title, *Finnegans Wake,* or like Beckett's gravedigger's forceps). Although the view here is down the lough towards the city, because ships are launched there and other boats leave from the quays the image also looks out towards the open sea and England.

MacNeice responds to an idea of doomed freedom, the emigrant's ship leaving 'the husk of home' as he says in **"The Left-Behind"**, one of a sequence of poems which investigate the dilemma of the displaced exile who is condemned to be a tourist in the land of his birth. With a characteristic mixture of freedom and fatalism he says in this poem that his youth is a 'tall ship that chose to run on a rock', and in **"Death of an old lady"** he makes a most complex image from this:

> At five in the morning there were grey voices
> Calling three times through the dank fields;
> The ground fell away beyond the voices
> Forty long years to the wrinkled lough
> That had given a child one shining glimpse
> Of a boat so big it was named Titanic.

(pp. 52-4)

On the page opposite **"Death of an old lady"** in the *Collected Poems* there is a short and little-known poem called **"House on a cliff"** which is one of MacNeice's finest achievements:

> Indoors the tang of a tiny oil lamp. Outdoors
> The winking signal on the waste of sea.
> Indoors the sound of the wind. Outdoors the wind.
> Indoors the locked heart and the lost key.
>
> Outdoors the chill, the void, the siren. Indoors
> The strong man pained to find his red blood cools,
> While the blind clock grows louder, faster. Outdoors
> The silent moon, the garrulous tides she rules.
>
> Indoors ancestral curse-cum-blessing. Outdoors
> The empty bowl of heaven, the empty deep.
> Indoors a purposeful man who talks at cross
> Purposes, to himself, in a broken sleep.

The hard boxed circling rhythms build a terrible stoic isolation. The voice is variously and tautly cadenced in a cross between stress and quantitative metre—that word 'cross' stretches bitterly in so many directions—and there is a mysterious openness within or beyond the poem's mirror-like reflections of a dead closed universe. If this is one man facing his lonely mortality on the far extremity of an unnamed place, the 'ancestral-curse-cum-blessing', the cross purposes and the broken sleep, suggest that the house is Ireland. Again, the silent moon and the garrulous tides obliquely suggest a Yeatsian reference to cold fanatic ideals and mob action. As in **"Death of an old lady"**,

MacNeice recapitulates some of his favourite symbols—sirens, sea, wind, clock—in a manner that is almost playful. Although the demand for 'meaning' will discover and insist that 'the blind clock' is the pulse of an indifferent and mechanical universe—the earth's compulsion—the poem is best appreciated in terms of voice, atmosphere and a pure symbolism. It is a bitter and tragic poem with a freedom in its intensity that transcends its unflinching sense of cosmic indifference, malignity or mischief—the 'winking signal' of the lighthouse and MacNeice's favouritely ambiguous 'the siren' simultaneously warn and lure. If this poem fits that baffled and contradictory term 'Irish', it also has an asocial, even a derelict, quality which makes it difficult to place. It subverts any comfortable notion of belonging and this is true of all MacNeice's poetry. The anguished sense of displacement that is so fundamental to his imagination means that many readers glance at him and then hurry on. Instead he needs to be read and cherished. There are many places that should be proud to lay claim to him. (pp. 55-6)

> Tom Paulin, *"The Poetry of Displacement,"* in Poetry Review, *Vol. 69, No. 3, March, 1980, pp. 52-6.*

DONALD MOORE

[MacNeice] had an individual perception and skilful craftsmanship that overlaid like gold foil the insistent note of foreboding of his times. Underneath so many of his poems we feel rather than see the "rich flow of fun and fantasy, the mercurial gaiety, the warm vitality and love of life" which, we are told, endeared him to his friends. . . .

MacNeice was born in Ireland, but by education he was an English Public Schoolboy whose imagination and intellectual abilities were fostered among gifted contemporaries. At Oxford he was successful both in his literary friendships and in his scholarship, and there is always a pleasing scholarly aloofness in his work. Because he worked mainly in Birmingham and London much of his poetry is about, or takes its imagery from, the English cities that he came to know so well. In the *Collected Poems*, the two poems on **"Belfast"** and **"Birmingham"** are on the same page, and as we read them we can be in no doubt where his enthusiasm, his critical enthusiasm, of course, really lies. Here is part of his description of Birmingham in the early nineteen-thirties:

> The lunch hour: the shops empty, shopgirls' faces relax
> Diaphanous as green glass, empty as old almanacs
> As incoherent with ticketed gewgaws tierred behind their heads
> As the Burne-Jones windows in St. Philip's broken by
>   crawling leads;. . .

and

> On shining lines the trams like vast sarcophagi move. . . .

The whole poem, with its references to Platonic Form, the Pharaohs, Pentecost and sarcophagi shows how he can bring his wide classical knowledge and the religious influences of his upbringing into the everyday modern world with all its technologies. In **"Sunday Morning"** he recreates for us that moment in the city suburbs when "Man's heart expands to tinker with his car" and

> Down the road someone is practising scales,
> The notes like little fishes vanish with a wink of tails, . . .

And he conjures us to make of this respite from "the week of time / A small eternity, a sonnet self-contained in rhyme." Although the classical, biblical and philosophical references in his poetry may tend to distance him from some of today's readers whose education is so very different, no-one who pauses to look at and listen to a suburban Sunday, even today, can fail to recognise the aptness of those lines, with a guitar perhaps taking the place of the piano which MacNeice heard.

These city images informed his poetry throughout his life. (p. 76)

The first twenty years of MacNeice's writing were over-shadowed by the anticipation of war, by war itself, and by the aftermath of war. Few writers, either in prose or poetry, reflected as sharply as he did what it felt like to live through those times. As early as 1934 he wrote what is for me the most poignant poem of anticipation. It conveys that awful feeling of inevitability that stifles every hope of escape. He called it **"Aubade"**:

> Having bitten on life like a sharp apple
> Or, playing it like a fish, been happy,
>
> Having felt with fingers that the sky is blue,
> What have we after that to look forward to?
>
> Not the twilight of the gods but a precise dawn
> Of sallow and grey bricks, and newsboys crying war.

But it is in *Autumn Journal* that he weaves into one tapestry his childhood, education, work, marriage and travel abroad with his conviction of inevitable war. He knew that we all put "blinkers on the eyes of doubt" as we contemplated "The blue smoke rising and the brown lace sinking / In the empty glass of stout." But he was intensely aware that

> . . . The bloody frontier
>   Converges on our beds
> Like jungle beaters closing in on their destined
>   Trophy of pelts and heads.
> And at this hour of the day it is no good saying
>   'Take away this cup';
> Having helped to fill it ourselves it is only logic
>   That now we should drink it up. . . .

Denied the opportunity to join the forces MacNeice shared the anxieties of a war waged against civilians. . . .

Strangely, if I were asked which of his poems really caught the atmosphere of civilians in wartime I would choose **"Whit Monday"** with its stark contrast of holiday and fear. And when the war was over, no other poet expressed so vividly the incompatibility which men returning from service with the forces felt with the sad and selfish world that was waiting for them. . . .

It is strange that those who revelled in the confessional poetry of the 'fifties and 'sixties should have failed to recognise this element in MacNeice. His personal experiences, his sensory perceptions, his doubts and fears were central to his poetry which contains the autobiography, or the subjective aspect of it, that he never completed in prose. He turned again and again to incidents of his own life as the subject of his poems. **"Star-Gazer"**, dated 1963, is about an incident of his boyhood, like many earlier poems. From the same final volume **"Goodbye to London"** is a resumé of all his contacts with that city, beginning with his schooldays and ending with the intense disappointment at the sad post-war revival:

> And nobody rose, only some meaningless
> Buildings and the people once more were strangers
> At home with no one, sibling or friend.
>   Which is why now the petals fall
>   Fast from the flower of cities all.

But it is in the frightening incantatory poem **"Prayer Before Birth"** that he exposes his deep and lifelong uncertainties. In form echoing the liturgies of the religion in which he was brought up, it is a great and intimate confessional poem:

> I am not yet born, console me.
> I fear that the human race may with tall walls wall me,
>   with strong drugs dope me, with wise lies lure me,
>   on black racks me, in blood-baths roll me . . .

(p. 77)

Donald Moore, "'The Drunkenness of Things': The Poetry of Louis MacNeice," in Quadrant, *Vol. XXVII, No. 11, November, 1983, pp. 76-8.*

EVE WALSH STODDARD

MacNeice introduced the term "parable-art" in 1936 (having borrowed it from Auden), developing its meaning through 1962, when he devoted an entire lecture series to defining the genre and analyzing the parabolic nature of selected literary texts. Because this poetic of the parable became an increasingly strong beacon for MacNeice, leading him to produce dramatically new types of poems and to change his judgments about his literary precursors, we need to understand what "parable-art" means for him, and perhaps whether it adds anything to literary theory in general. MacNeice's evolving use of the term reveals two components: one semantic and one structural. The semantic component came first, adopted directly from Auden's distinction between "escape-art" (epitomized by the products of aestheticism and imagism) and "parable-art."

In 1936 MacNeice introduces "parable-art" as "that art which shall teach man to unlearn hatred and learn love." One can see the appeal of the secularized Christian term for MacNeice, who had grown up in an Anglican rectory. This initial use of the term "parable" contrasts it with "escape," thus placing it in the camp of realism and of social criticism intended to better the human lot. While his impulse toward social criticism is part of a poetic tradition which includes both Pope and Shelley, the question remains how should and can the poet influence his society? Pope, Wordsworth, and Shelley offer quite different answers ranging from direct criticism to beautiful symbols that will indirectly enlarge human sympathies. MacNeice, facing the horrifying destructive capabilities of twentieth-century humanity, latches onto the parable as the prime poetic instrument of social criticism. However, what he subsumes under the genre of "parable-poem" evolves with his own increasing sophistication from a direct, realistic mode of discourse to an indirect, mythic / symbolic mode drawn from folk and literary traditions and well-suited to dramatize the darker forces of life.

The second, or structural component of parable-art is its operation on two (at least) levels of meaning. This is what we mean in ordinary language by "parable" or "allegory." Between the 1930's and 1946, when he openly avows an interest in allegory, MacNeice changes not only his goals as a poet but his interpretation of language, poetry, and experience. In the manifestos of the Thirties, he asserted that poetry could succeed in a literally journalistic, univocal form. However, by the introduction to his radio play, *The Dark Tower,* in 1947, he realizes that "reportage can no longer masquerade as art." He has come to see that "the single-track mind and the single-plane novel or play are almost bound to falsify the world in which we live." The catalyst for this ideological change was MacNeice's study of Yeats, completed in 1941, set against the horrors of World War II. In the introduction to his book on Yeats (1941), he shows a new respect for the poetry previously dismissed as "escapist":

> If the war made nonsense of Yeats' poetry and of all works that are called 'escapist,' it also made nonsense of the poetry that professes to be 'realist' . . . both these kinds of poetry stand or fall together.

The introduction to *The Dark Tower* (1947) has the ring of a new manifesto and as such marks the beginning of MacNeice's mature, post-Thirties poetics. This text suggests a new philosophical stance based on the relationship between language and human experience. In an absolute rejection of his earlier realism, MacNeice states that "man does after all live by symbols."

This linguistic-epistemological rationale for non-realistic art is fully developed in MacNeice's final statement on poetry, *Varieties of Parable* (1963). . . . He explains that there are "two reasons why all fiction is to some extent parabolical. One is the extremely artificial nature of the language." Because the relationship between word and meaning, or signifier and signified, in the terms of de Saussure, is arbitrary and relative, rather than inherent and transparent, in a sense all discourse is allegorical. When we encode our messages into words, on a mundane level we perform the same activity as the allegorical poet who encodes "larger" or more abstract systems of meaning into a symbolic story. Thus MacNeice concludes that even the seemingly most realistic characters and events "will at once acquire a wider reference . . . they will be symbols." Not only has he come to appreciate the use of symbols in art, but also its converse: the reading of "real" experience as a system of signs or emblems with deferred meaning.

Varieties of Parable is chiefly an interpretation of MacNeice's parabolic precursors in English literature, but it also sheds light on his goals for an evaluation of his own poetic career (unfortunately ended by the time the lectures were published). MacNeice's acceptance of the parable as a non-realistic mode of discourse evolved from an increasingly complex view of political realities, while his interest in the double-meaning form of the parable grew out of a dissatisfaction with ornamental images, and a desire to use images to structure poems. . . . In *Varieties of Parable* MacNeice distinguishes between two types of parable poem he aspires to create more of: one is "double-level poetry, of the type of Wordsworth's 'Resolution and Independence,'" and the other consists of "more overt parable poems in a line of descent both from folk ballads such as 'True Thomas' and some of George Herbert's allegories in miniature such as 'Redemption.'" For convenience the two types will be referred to as "Wordsworthian" and "overt."

As a basis for his theory, MacNeice appropriates the *Oxford Dictionary*'s definitions of "parable" as "any saying or narration in which something is expressed in terms of something else" or "any kind of enigmatical or dark saying." The main difference between the two types of parable MacNeice singles out is the weight carried by the surface or literal meaning and the arbitrariness of its relationship to the symbolic meaning of the poem. Because this relationship in the "overt" parable is more arbitrary, the reader must work harder to interpret the meaning, as in solving a riddle or puzzle. (pp. 117-21)

The simpler type of parable, which I have labeled "Wordsworthian," has a more inherent relationship between literal and symbolic levels of meaning, and does not require the listener to be an initiate. In this type of parable, the sign system constituting the initial or literal level of the text is intended to represent "reality." The imagination of the poet reads into the text of his own experience (in "Resolution and Independence" the encounter with the leech gatherer) an allegorical meaning. The poem not only recreates the concrete experience but also suggests its ultimate significance in the poem. . . . In the overt parable the least emphasized level of signification is the surface or literal one. (p. 122)

Most critics who discuss MacNeice's poetics of the parable focus on the overt, mystery type, similar to what has traditionally been called "allegory," in the vein of *The Divine Comedy* or *The Faerie Queene*. This type evolves from MacNeice's pervasive use of the trope of life as a journey or quest and from his lifelong interest in the logic of fairy tales and dreams. Critics agree that his last three volumes of poems, especially the posthumously published *Burning Perch,* demontrate a new, sharply defined vision and voice which draw their strength in part from the world of gothic mystery and nightmare. (p. 123)

The other type of parable poem, the Wordsworthian, has been ignored by critics even though it is the logical outgrowth of MacNeice's early journalistic writing. . . . Because the deferral of meaning is not obviously signaled in such poems, readers often fail to see their point and thus dismiss them as trivial, as was the case with Wordsworth's *Lyrical Ballads*. This type of parable grows naturally out of the progress of MacNeice's career. He always writes about the events of contemporary life, private and public. In many early poems there is a tenuous relationship between anecdote and reflection or commentary. In the later poems the reflections become implicit in the description or story, forming what Coleridge called a symbol, a translucence of the general in the particular. In *Varieties of Parable* MacNeice carefully distinguishes this type of structural parable from naturalistic stories with one symbol, such as the prison in Dickens' *Little Dorritt*. He insists that the text must operate on two levels of signification throughout.

However, as MacNeice himself admits, many of his best and most characteristic later poems do not fit the scheme of the parable poem because they do not turn on the unified structural image he admires. Rather they are predominantly reflective or expository, but radiant with accretions of meaning through the use of individual metaphors, symbols, and allusions to literature, religion, and the classics. *Autumn Sequel* (1953) is a large version of this type of poem. Individual cantos are allegorical quests, but the structure of the whole is journalistic, or realistic, tracing the poet's "journey" through a particular autumn, a season that marks the progress of MacNeice's life in his private symbol system. Like the earlier *Autumn Journal,* the poem uses a diary format, but it tends toward allegory through intertextual reference to Dante's *Inferno*. Loosely conceived of as a dream-vision quest through time, the poem focuses on the role and vocation of the poet. Many diverse frames of reference impinge on the poem, from the parrot symbolizing mechanism to the realm of King Arthur to ideals of the Greek *polis*. Thus although the poem tends to expand beyond its literal recording of events, it does not do so in a unified structure which could be called "allegory" or "parable."

The final canto, however, heralds a turning point in MacNeice's poetic career. It successfully synthesizes not only the threads of the entire work but also the two types of parable poems MacNeice identifies as his goals in *Varieties of Parable*. Like the Coleridgean symbol, or the Wordsworthian type of parable, Canto XXVI recreates a real, ordinary event which yet radiates a higher moral meaning. As in many of MacNeice's parable poems, the poet is on a train journey. It is Christmas day and he has just finished hooking up radio cables as part of his job for the BBC. This literal, humdrum occupation takes on symbolic significance in the context of his philosophical aspiration to transcend selfhood through love and communication, represented both in specific Christmas messages to specific friends and in the communicative function of the radio cables. In the third tercet, having mentioned the completed job and his place on the empty train, the poet asks, ''Is it true / That this is a special day?'' There is an immense weight attached to this seemingly simple question, the weight of two millenia of western metaphysics, of a teleological view of history, both individual and cosmic. The immediate answer is implicitly ''no,'' on the one level because MacNeice is an atheist, and on a more superficial level because it is a workday for him, not a holiday. But the remainder of the canto undercuts, albeit skeptically, the hero's usual cynicism. The poem moves from literal narrative to reflective metaphor in the fourth tercet, in response to the poet's question:

> The telegraph poles
> Endlessly filing past against the blue
>
> Remind me that those wires connect with living souls,
> Some few of whom I know; and as the long
> And backward strand of memory unscrolls,
> The slow wheels gather slowly to a song,
> My private hook-up, and I start to send,
> Wires or no wires, directions right or wrong.

The telephone wires that connect with individuals provide a metaphorical vehicle for the hero's poetic reaching out to his friends with Christmas greetings. The train tracks unreeling from behind the train represent the past experiences of MacNeice's life, his memory.

Carrier pigeons, suggesting communication, send the evil, mechanistic (and non-realistic) parrot slinking away. The parrot serves as a transition from naturalistic, though figurative, description to dream logic as we enter the realm of overt parable or allegory. The empty train suddenly becomes like Dante's *Inferno,* full of the dead, symbols of MacNeice's past sins. This encounter with the nightmarish representative of past errors comes in the context of a comparison between the poet on the irrevocably forward-moving train and Theseus penetrating the maze to defeat the Minotaur. As he enters the overt allegorical passage of the canto, the speaker explicitly parallels himself to Theseus:

> So I today, equally undefended,
>
> Not knowing if we are running fast or late,
> Walk through this empty train. Empty? To my surprise
> Each carriage is full of creatures that look me straight,
>
> If straight is the right word, between the eyes.
> But who or what? Some of them should be dead,
> Yet here they sit four-square in full disguise
>
> Of life. The wrongs that I have done, thought, said,
> Stare back at me. Some of them should be men,
> But why are their hands like claws, their eyes an acrid red?

This section adopts the mode of Dante's *Inferno* to represent the hero's moral / psychological scrutiny of his acts and poems over a lifetime. Since he does not share Dante's Christian hierarchy of values, MacNeice's sins are violations of human relationship, personal as well as political, including guilt for ''the scorch and blast / Of new and clever bombs.'' Suddenly

the atmosphere of the ghosts on the train changes from guilt and hellishness to a balanced vision of both error and hope, the latter represented in particular by the ghosts of Socrates and Blake. The poet-hero smells frankincense, a secularized allusion to the hope of new birth, on one level the birth of a new poetic identity for the quester. Through allusion to the wood of error in which Dante is initially lost, MacNeice concludes on a note of hopeful skepticism: ''The train is getting somewhere.'' (pp. 124-27)

MacNeice's second to last volume, *Solstices,* includes more Wordsworthian-type parable poems than any other volume. Throughout his career he followed precepts similar to those Wordsworth espouses in the Preface to the *Lyrical Ballads:* the poet should be a spokesman for and to ordinary men; he should use ordinary, colloquial language, and he should look steadily at his subject. Like Wordsworth, MacNeice writes poems which appear to describe external objects, places, and events, yet actually reflect on human consciousness.

One poem from *Solstices* which exemplifies this Wordsworthian sleight-of-hand, the translucence of the general in the particular, is **''The wiper.''** On the literal level it starts with a concrete description of the driver's and passenger's perspective of the road from inside a car on a dark, rainy night:

> All we can see a segment
> Of blackly shining asphalt
> With the wiper moving across it
> Clearing, blurring, clearing.

Nothing in the first stanza indicates symbolic overtones. But the second stanza, focusing on the road, refers to ''the mystery / Of its far invisible margins,'' asking ''Will these always be with us?'' Stanza three looks at the cars, ''Boxes of glass and water.'' The fourth stanza turns to the memory of the car's passengers, to the relationship between past and present, while the final stanza looks not very invitingly to the ''black future,'' literally the dark night ahead on the road. Only through subtle double meanings does MacNeice suggest the allegorical or symbolic nature of the poem. The words ''mystery'' and ''always'' in stanza two, and ''black future'' in stanza five are the only obvious indicators of a level of meaning beyond the literal. The poem symbolizes life as a journey with the potential of being a quest, a potential limited by the restrictions of partial blindness. The riders in the car can see only brief snatches of a black road, a mysterious road with unknown dimensions. The darkness of night, of the meaningless void of existence, is broken intermittently by the lights of other people insulated and partially blinded in their own ''moving boxes.'' Significantly, while each car driver is able to see very little through the dark and rain, his or her car gives off light that illuminates the dark for other drivers, if only transiently. Each driver is islanded in a car, but able to bridge the void that separates him from other drivers for fleeting moments.

> The dials in the car measure distance covered and speed,
> But never a gauge nor needle.
> To tell us where we are going
> Or when our day will come, supposing
> This road exists in daytime.

In Aristotle's terms, the speedometer indicates efficient causes, but the final causes, the destination and the daylight, are not indicated. The final stanza completes the picture of the people boxed into cars in darkness, seeing only ''through the tiny segment / Cleared and blurred by the wiper.'' MacNeice agrees with St. Paul that ''We see as through a glass darkly,'' but he cannot accept the Christian hope of eventually seeing ''face to face.'' With a characteristic, pessimistically positive assertion, MacNeice concludes that although we are ''dazzled by darkness . . . Yet we hold the road.'' In spite of our ignorance and clouded perceptions, our living in a world without absolute value and truth, we manage adequately to muddle through the journey of life. **''The wiper''** is without doubt a parable, but the concrete, surface description retains primacy. The philosophical significance radiates out from the images, like a halo around a physical object. In contrast, in the overt parable of **''The burnt bridge,''** the surface words dissolve into the ultimate meaning as they deflect the reader toward the tenor, much as a spectator cannot resist looking in the direction toward which people are pointing.

The Burning Perch, MacNeice's final volume, returns to the gothic riddles of *Visitations,* but with a new style: the harsh, concise, sharply delineated images of nightmare. The essence of MacNeice's career and his attempt to write ''double-level,'' parable poems is expressed in a line from his **''Homage to Horace''** in the final volume. He says he is ''caught between cosmic and comic radiation.'' The words ''cosmic'' and ''radiation'' reverberate with meanings that explain MacNeice's ultimate difficulty in creating parables. Allegory depends on a system of correspondences between different planes of reality, most notably the moral or spiritual and the ordinary. MacNeice is a modern skeptic; his reality is the nuclear bomb. The ever present threat of total destruction makes life and the quest for value comic and tragic simultaneously. ''Cosmic'' refers to his desire for a metaphysics he can believe in and to the threat of wholesale destruction. The older and more skeptical MacNeice becomes, the more he faces the mysterious side of experience without rationalizing. The poems tend not to be able to sustain the unified world parable requires because the poet is caught between skepticism and a desire to believe. Thus, despite his stated aim to write more parable-poetry, his best poems capture this vacillation. (pp. 128-31)

> *Eve Walsh Stoddard, ''The Poetics of the Parable in the Later Poems of Louis MacNeice,'' in* Concerning Poetry, *Vol. 18, Nos. 1 & 2, 1985, pp. 117-31.*

BRENDAN KENNELLY

I was born in Belfast between the mountain and the gantries
To the hooting of lost sirens and the clang of trams:
Thence to Smoky Carrick in County Antrim
Where the bottle-neck harbour collects the mud which jams

The little boats beneath the Norman castle,
The pier shining with lumps of crystal salt;
The Scotch Quarter was a line of residential houses
But the Irish Quarter was a slum for the blind and halt . . .

I was the rector's son, born to the anglican order,
Banned for ever from the candles of the Irish poor;
The Chichesters knelt in marble at the end of a transept
With ruffs about their necks, their portion sure . . .

These lines from his poem **''Carrickfergus''** show that Louis MacNeice felt that in Ireland he was an outsider from birth. He was ''Banned for ever from the candles of the Irish poor''. Sean O'Casey knew poverty from his earliest days in the slums of Dublin; Patrick Kavanagh knew poverty in Monaghan and later in Dublin; and Austin Clarke wrote many poems about poverty, though his view of it tends to be that of a middle-class spectator. Yet, in their different styles, and with varying degrees of imaginative intensity, these three writers were involved in Irish society in ways that Louis MacNeice somehow never quite managed, or perhaps wished, to be. He remained an outsider to that world of seething deprivation, riotous squalor and articulate resentment so intrepidly explored by O'Casey, Kavanagh, Clarke and others. And this sense of being an outsider in Ireland is, in a deeper sense, characteristic of what we may call MacNeice's spiritual life, his developed stance as a poet. All through his poetry we encounter a man who doesn't really seem to belong anywhere, except perhaps in the fertile, mysterious, consoling and challenging land of language itself, where every fresh discovery is inextricably bound up with a new mystery. Yet even there, where a poet might reasonably be expected to feel unreasonably at home, the recurring doubts and uncertainties gnaw away at his mind and imagination. MacNeice is one of the most intelligent of all Irish poets; he is also, in his work, one of the loneliest. And he has, apart from a few loyal followers among the poets of Ulster, such as Longley, Mahon, Heaney, Ormsby, Hewitt and Muldoon, as well as the distinguished critics, Terence Brown and Edna Longley, been largely ignored in Ireland, particularly in the Republic. He is still the outsider, still ''banned'', not only from the ''Irish poor'', but from the anthologies which help to educate the vast majority of Irish children. It is a shame, because MacNeice is an excellent poet, a skilful craftsman, a shrewd critic of both literature and society, a thinker who makes complex thoughts lucid and shapely, a considerable dramatist, a disciplined classicist, an assured translator and an attractive personality. He achieved all this while remaining a loner. . . . [MacNeice] learned to look clearly and critically at himself; and he achieved the hard lucidity of the loner. He writes:

> Speaking for myself, I should say that the following things, among others, had conditioned my poetry—having been brought up in the North of Ireland, having a father who was a clergyman; the fact that my mother died when I was little; repression from the age of six to nine; inferiority complex on grounds of physique and class-consciousness; lack of a social life until I was grown up; late puberty; ignorance of music (which could have been a substitute for poetry); inability to ride horses or practise successfully most of the sports which satisfy a sense of rhythm; an adolescent liking for the role of ''enfant terrible''; a liking (now dead) for metaphysics; marriage and divorce; Birmingham; an indolent pleasure in gardens and wild landscapes; a liking for animals; an interest in dress.

This reads like a somewhat quirky list of influences; in fact, the influences are clearly perceived and accurately stated. One can appreciate how his ''inferiority complex'' due to ''class-consciousness'' may have driven him towards his interests in Communism in the 1930s; one can see how his ''ignorance of music'' may have led him to try to create, often with startling success, a poetry remarkable for its rich musicality, its rhythmical assurance and subtlety: his confessed ''liking for metaphysics'' helped him to work towards a poetry that is often complex but clear in its thoughts; the solitary name ''Birmingham'' brings home to us the fact that MacNeice celebrates and criticises the life of cities such as London, Dublin and Belfast with rare eloquence and insight; and even the final ''liking for animals'' and ''interest in dress'' point towards a poetry involved with ordinary human activities and feelings. MacNeice sees the poet as a spokesman for ordinary people. He believes that poetry should always be in touch with what he calls ''the spontaneous colouring of ordinary speech''.

The clarity of MacNeice's self-knowledge, the precise presentation of influences, the candid statements concerning his views of language in poetry—all this suggests a poet who is honest, unpretentious, undeceived, cultivated, perceptive, relishing the activity and bustle of the ordinary world. And MacNeice is a truly ''worldly'' poet in this sense: he looks closely at society, at people, at his roots, at his present situation, at the complex, changing state of the world in which he has to live. And he moves through that world on his own, alert, watchful, scrupulously recording what he sees and feels. To this extent, he is not a poet of the fascinating past, or the perplexing future; he is neither conventional historian nor aspiring prophet; he is much more the poet of the swirling, urgent present. Many Irish poets are deeply concerned with the past, finding in Ireland's turbulent history images and personalities that, when dramatised and charged with imagination, help to shed light on current problems. Here, as in so many other respects, MacNeice is an outsider. He is a superb chronicler of the contemporary. His most famous poem, *Autumn Journal,* is proof of this. It is a brilliant, sweeping, comprehensive poem.

In a prefatory note to *Autumn Journal* in the 1966 edition of *The Collected Poems of Louis MacNeice,* (a note not included in the first edition of the book), the poet stresses that he is writing what he calls a ''Journal'', and adds that ''In a journal or a personal letter a man writes what he feels at the moment; to attempt scientific truthfulness would be, paradoxically, dishonest . . . It is the nature of this poem to be neither final nor balanced . . . Poetry in my opinion must be honest before anything else and I refuse to be 'objective' or clear-cut at the cost of honesty''.

That, briefly, is a statement of the poet of conscience refusing to surrender to the aesthetic stylist in himself. This is the logic of MacNeice's position as an outsider. He clings to his individual moral honesty with an unrelenting grip even as he is deeply aware of its artistic limitations and defects. He knows that there are overstatements and inconsistencies in his poem; but he leaves them there, in their earned place in the work, because they are valid aspects of his vision of contemporary reality. The poem was written between August 1938 and early 1939; and it is steeped in a grim awareness of the coming war. In the midst of this awareness, MacNeice turns, significantly, to Ireland and broods, with the peculiar intensity of the outsider he is, on the violence and lunacy of the land of his birth. Even though this passage was written in a way which, according to MacNeice himself, was neither ''final nor balanced'', the picture of violence, futility, self-deception, prejudice and chronic unemployment is as true in the eighties as when MacNeice wrote it in the thirties. Because MacNeice honestly describes contemporary Ireland, he is hair-raisingly pertinent half-a-century later. It may be that if a poet has the courage to be passionately true to the passing moment he will be true to all time. . . .

All through *Autumn Journal,* we feel the impact of MacNeice's compulsive honesty. The poem has all the excitement of a long, detailed, lively letter from a friend whose thoughts are worthy of respect and whose perceptions are unfailingly stimulating. Excessive self-consciousness in poetry frequently has a deadening effect on the poem's language because the tone tends to become portentous, laboured and self-important. But MacNeice, reaching for the vitality inherent in ''the spontaneous colouring of ordinary speech'', and determined to speak to his reader as if he were writing him a spontaneous letter, creates a poetry that is natural, chatty and gripping. Themes of extraordinary importance fill the day's ordinary talk. . . . Inevitably this deliberate chattiness leads to weaknesses in the poem. Just as diaries, journals and personal letters are often a

mixture of the trivial and the serious, the irrelevant and the significant, so *Autumn Journal* contains lines, even whole passages, which add little or nothing to the poem as a whole. But this, as already stated, was deliberate on MacNeice's part. These lines and passages, therefore, are most fairly criticised when seen in the context of a flawed, conscious design, and not as weak or slight moments of which the poet is unaware.

MacNeice's stubborn honesty helps to account for his strengths and weaknesses as a poet. He is a celebrant and critic of urban life; he has, therefore, a keen eye for the characters that abound in cities (see **''The Mixer'',** for example, in which he effectively compares a man to a Latin word, ''often spoken but no longer heard''); he has a profound respect for the integrity of the individual and a vehement hatred for the forces which violate that respect (see **''Prayer Before Birth''**); his exploration of time concentrates, for the most part, on the present so that even his most personal poetry, his love-poetry, for example, deals with the present fleetingness, or the fleeting presence of love. Paradoxically, this concentration on the present moment seems to rid him (for the moment) of the burden of time. . . . MacNeice's love-poems are among his best. The more one reads them, the more haunting they become.

These are some of MacNeice's strong points as a poet. If one must point to a weakness in his work, one must concede, I think, that it is closely connected with his concept of the poet as spokesman. Many of MacNeice's poems have a kind of sophisticated literalness which tends to limit his work to one meaning, to deny it the musical, mysterious echoes and reverberations one finds in Blake and Yeats, for example. And since this is a direct consequence of MacNeice's determination to be 'honest', it may be more accurate to describe this 'weakness' in his work as the inevitable limitation of his strength, the necessary consequence of the flaw in his declared artistic intention.

As the years went by, MacNeice became increasingly conscious of this limitation. Accompanying his dissatisfaction with the literal utterance is a growing longing for a symbolic one. The poet is not only a spokesman; he is also an explorer. He is not only a representative voice; he is also a medium for many voices. His job is to find a style and a method that will do justice to all these functions. MacNeice, while retaining his basic view of the poet as spokesman, ('I have grouped the poet with ordinary men and opposed him to the mystic proper. I do not withdraw from this position'), becomes increasingly aware of the fact that language itself is symbolic and will not, when imaginatively handled, permit itself to be restricted to mere literalism. (pp. 96-104)

In his later poetry, MacNeice moves more and more deeply into a symbolic richness and resonance. I shall give one example; it is **''Charon'',** a late poem. Here the literal is enriched by the mythological; the poem is rooted in concrete reality but it also suggests strange worlds, mysterious possibilities. London and the Thames mingle with Virgil and Dante. Charon, son of Erebus (Darkness) and Nyx (Night), ferries the dead across the river Styx to their final abode in Hades. Here we find MacNeice writing from a very deep level of his being; he is no longer a mere spokesman for others; he is exploring the dark underworld of his mortal self. Perhaps the irony of all this is that the poet who writes uncompromisingly of his own experience, in this symbolic way, becomes in the end a more enduring spokesman for others than the poet who consciously tries to speak on behalf of others. MacNeice's poetic self included both kinds of poet; or rather, the literalist was forced, or forced himself to become a symbolist; reluctantly, the symbolist emerged as the one capable of the more complex utterance. I am not suggesting a poetic schizophrenia in MacNeice; I am talking about a slow development. . . . MacNeice's *Collected Poems* comprise almost six hundred pages of skilled, musical and immensely enjoyable poetry. It may well be that his very honesty led him to become the outsider he remained to the end. One thing is certain though: he deserves a more attentive, critical readership. To read through his published poems is to encounter a voice speaking for intelligent, questing, somewhat bewildered people in our modern world that remains unquestionably wonderful and is increasingly threatened. (pp. 104-05)

> Brendan Kennelly, *"Louis MacNeice: An Irish Outsider," in* Irish Writers and Society at Large, *edited by Masaru Sekine, Colin Smythe, 1985, pp. 96-105.*

ALAN JENKINS

MacNeice's poetry at its best is instinct with the 'dailiness' of his life—as a salary-earner (lecturer, broadcaster, freelance journalist and reviewer), and as a husband, lover, traveller and pub-haunter. There is a corresponding emphasis in many of the pieces reprinted [in *Selected Literary Criticism of Louis MacNeice*], an insistence that 'a good poem must have both a relation to "life" and a new life of its own'. Arnold's phrase about poetry as 'a criticism of life' is repeated, without further comment, over and over again, as though it had an almost talismanic virtue; and there is a powerful distaste for 'purists' (Apocalyptics, Surrealists, 'Art for Art's sake'), a deep suspicion of automatic procedures and unadulterated productions. This is fine as far as its goes, and certainly consistent. . . .

MacNeice was an intelligent, learned, common-sense reviewer, and there are some *un*commonly firm insights throughout this book. He can, though, sound merely bluff and opinionated, the straightforwardness descending to a kind of snobbish bluster. The need to elevate one group of writers occasionally makes judgments on others suspect; a particular set of concerns (whether with syntax or the relation of the intellectual to the proletariat) can cause blind spots. Eliot is a kind of touchstone, but an Eliot who wrote 'the wittiest social commentary of our period ("Prufrock" and "Portrait of a Lady")' and the most perfect expression of the defeat of our civilisation ("The Waste Land").' Yeats, another touchstone, is treated with more acumen, Dylan Thomas almost reverentially.

By far the best pieces, though, are those in which MacNeice discusses his own poetry and methods, or his preoccupation with poetic drama (Sophocles performed in Greek, Eliot's verse-plays, Auden and Isherwood), or launches his attack on 'the West End' and its audiences; or, again, the scholarly-historical essays on longstanding enthusiasms, Malory and Apuleius. . . .

The common reader should go primarily not to this book but to the lyrics, the *Autumn Journal* and the unfinished autobiography, *The Strings are False*: in these are the dash and allure and vitality of MacNeice's best writing, the astringency, worldliness and un-frivolous lightness of touch that could make a point about revolution in poetic technique by slipping in an observation on the fickleness of fashions in women's clothes.

> Alan Jenkins, *"Earning His Keep," in* The Observer, *April 5, 1987, p. 24.*

DENIS DONOGHUE

MacNeice's sustained work in literary criticism is three books: *Modern Poetry: A Personal Essay* (1938), *The Poetry of W. B. Yeats* (1941), and the Clark Lectures at Cambridge in 1963, published as *Varieties of Parable* (1965). The new *Selected Literary Criticism* reprints material from 1931 to the year of his death, 1963: mostly reviews of Yeats, Eliot, Auden, Dylan Thomas, Robert Frost, a few cultural pronouncements, comments on translations of Greek tragedies—he was happy schoolmastering Gilbert Murray, R. C. Trevelyan, Robert Fitzgerald, and Christopher Logue—and some lively words on Spenser, George Herbert and Norse sagas.

These pieces are interesting, but it's a pity he didn't take his journalism seriously. I think he was damaged by a theory he held about 'double-level poetry', as he called it in *Varieties of Parable.* He would rather write verse than prose, and he vaguely divined that he could write a kind of poetry which, apparently concerned with surfaces and references, would somehow at the same time gain reverberation by touching patterns of feeling more fundamental than anything specified. He thought Wordsworth's 'Resolution and Independence' a good example of double-level poetry. He thought, too, that he could achieve this doubleness by going in the other direction, starting with parable or allegory, as in folk ballads of the 'True Thomas' kind or George Herbert's little allegories like 'Redemption', and letting the second level, this time a matter of contingency and ordinariness, establish itself mainly because it couldn't be kept out. The Clark Lectures failed to make much of the theory, and they were a mess in other respects, but at least they show what he was after. They show, too, why he couldn't take reviewing seriously enough: it moved only on one level, it didn't have access to the second level, of symbolism and allegory, it was merely news that doesn't stay news.

So he was content to strike attitudes. He scorned Surrealism, for the wrong reason—because Surrealists didn't keep their promises. He was high-toned about the Movement: 'As individuals then, we must welcome some of these New Liners, but as a group or a Movement, let them go.'

Many of his sentences are lazy. Of Auden: 'What cannot be repeated too often is that he is a poet who has something to write about.' (That can easily be repeated too often.) 'Zanies as heroes of fiction have by now, I suggest, had their day. Steinbeck's *Of Mice and Men* was the *ne plus ultra.*' Wrong: there are zanier zanies than Steinbeck's Lennie, and it says something good about Lennie that he wouldn't know what MacNeice's Latin tag is saying. Of Eliot: 'So we got hold of Eliot and, though at a first reading he seemed unheard-of heavy going, we sensed straight away that he filled the bill.' 'Sensed', indeed. Of 'The Love Song of J. Alfred Prufrock': 'At a first reading I saw no form in it and, with the exception of the mermaids at the end, got little kick from it.' If that was your first reading, Mr. MacNeice, could we please hear your second? Of Dylan Thomas: 'I never knew the slim and faunlike figure which was painted by Augustus John and which, when he was barely grown up, had swept through literary London rather like a forest fire.'

The best, most energetic piece in the collection is MacNeice's Introduction to *The Golden Ass*, William Adlington's translation (1566) reprinted in the Chiltern Library (1946). In the presence of a Greek or Latin text, MacNeice took the rare pleasure of subduing himself. Without making a theory of it, he makes much of the fact that Apuleius in turning a man into an ass never forgets that he has a double level on his hands:

it is a man, indeed, as turned into an ass. MacNeice well quotes the passage in *Marius the Epicurean* in which Marius and Flavian read Apuleius's book and relish his 'unmistakably real feeling for asses, with bold touches like Swift's, and a genuine animal breadth'. Distinguishing between Apuleius's syntax and Cicero's, MacNeice doesn't quite explain what the difference means. Peter Levi's recent comments, in the *Times Literary Supplement,* on parataxis, and now MacNeice's on Apuleius's way of making sentences 'often without conjunctions, just adding up and adding up', suggest to me that there's more to the undifferentiating syntax than meets the bewildered eye. But in any case this is the prose MacNeice I care for.

Denis Donoghue, "Denis Donoghue Writes About Louis MacNeice, and the Thrusting of Shakespeare into Touch," in London Review of Books, *Vol. 9, No. 8, April 23, 1987, p. 19.*

(Dame Edith) Ngaio Marsh

1899-1982

New Zealand novelist, dramatist, autobiographer, short story writer, nonfiction writer, scriptwriter, critic, and travel writer.

Together with Agatha Christie, Dorothy Sayers, and Margery Allingham, Marsh is considered among the most prominent female writers to emerge during the Golden Age of British detective fiction of the 1930s. Best known for her popular series of murder mysteries featuring Chief Inspector Roderick Alleyn, Marsh utilized intricate plots and light, melodramatic characterizations to depict multifaceted individuals whose interaction eclipses the central crime and its detection. Jean M. White observed: ''If [Marsh] can be fiendishly clever in concocting murder plots, she never has been content to settle for a flashy puzzle, letting cardboard characters fall where they may. With a single phrase, she can limn a character into the memory.'' Although occasionally faulted for authorial detachment, repetitious subject matter, and avoidance of social and political issues, Marsh has garnered praise for consistent ingenuity and skillful dialogue. Earl F. Bargainnier commented: ''[Marsh] accepted the formulas and conventions of the Golden Age, but, while remaining within their boundaries . . . , adapted them in her own way through five decades . . . , and that is no mean achievement.''

Marsh began her career in the arts as a professional actress with a touring Shakespearean company in New Zealand and Australia during the early 1920s. In 1966, she was awarded the title of Dame Commander of the British Empire, reflecting her achievements as a producer and director of drama in New Zealand. Marsh's extensive knowledge of theatrical milieus is reflected in the fastidious dialogue and dramatic atmospheres of her fiction, while her lifelong affinity for England is expressed in her predominantly British settings and affectionately satirical eye for such figures as squires, country vicars, doctors, nobles, and spinsters.

Roderick Alleyn, whom Marsh introduced in her first novel, *A Man Lay Dead* (1934), is regarded by many critics as a transitional figure between the aristocratic master detective of Golden Age fiction and the hard-boiled procedural police detective who became popular in later years. In such novels as *Death in Ecstasy* (1936), *Artists in Crime* (1938), *Death and the Dancing Footman* (1941), *Opening Night* (1951; published in the United States as *Night at the Vulcan*), *Spinsters in Jeopardy* (1953; republished as *The Bride of Death*), *Killer Dolphin* (1966; published in Great Britain as *Death at the Dolphin*), *Black as He's Painted* (1975), and *Light Thickens* (1982), Alleyn is characterized as a professional detective who relies less on the masterly intuition demonstrated by Sir Arthur Conan Doyle's Sherlock Holmes and more on routine police investigation in his pursuit of murderers. Although he adheres strictly to police regulations, concentrating on physical evidence and opportunity rather than motive, Alleyn retains some traits of the classic British sleuth. An aristocrat educated at Oxford University, Alleyn is literate, authoritative, charming, and exceptionally observant—characteristics that often help him infiltrate the insular communities of the homicides to which he is assigned. Although he occasionally feels empathy toward suspects, Alleyn's duty as a police officer invariably prevails.

In several of Marsh's mysteries, including *Vintage Murder* (1937), *Death of a Peer* (1940; published in Great Britain as *Surfeit of Lampreys*), *Colour Scheme* (1943), and *Died in the Wool* (1945), Alleyn leaves his English surroundings and travels to New Zealand, where he discovers natural beauty amid a new cultural heritage. Although several local critics maintained that Marsh unfairly portrayed the country as inferior to Great Britain, others, including Carole Acheson, praised her richly detailed descriptions of the New Zealand landscape and ''her sympathy for the [native] Maori people, particularly for their difficulties in adapting to an alien culture.'' In addition to her detective fiction, Marsh published *Black Beech and Honeydew: An Autobiography* (1965), as well as several nonfiction works, most notably *New Zealand* (1942), a history of the country written with Randal Matthew Burdon. She also adapted her novels for the stage in such plays as *Surfeit of Lampreys* (1950), with Owen B. Howell, and *False Scent* (1961), with Eileen MacKay.

(See also *CLC*, Vol. 7; *Contemporary Authors*, Vols. 9-12, rev. ed.; *Contemporary Authors New Revision Series*, Vol. 6; and *Dictionary of Literary Biography*, Vol. 77.)

JEAN M. WHITE

In Chapter IV, page 58 of the first edition of *A Man Lay Dead* (1934), Roderick Alleyn, Chief Detective-Inspector, CID Scotland Yard, makes his first appearance on the scene of crime. He strolls urbanely into his initial case . . . to begin a career that has provided many a diverting, puzzling, and, at times, maddening moment for mystery readers over the last four decades.

A few pages after Alleyn's quiet entrance, Dame Ngaio Marsh gives a quick introduction to her sleuth:

> Angela had time for a good long stare at her first detective. Alleyn did not resemble a plain-clothes policeman she felt sure, nor was he in the romantic manner—white-faced and gimlet-eyed. He looked like one of her Uncle Hubert's friends, the sort that they knew would "do" for house parties. He was very tall, and lean, his hair was dark, and his eyes grey with corners that turned down. They looked as if they would smile easily but his mouth didn't. "His hands and his voice are grand," thought Angela, and subconsciously she felt less miserable.

And those of us who cherish an affection for the stylishly-told traditional British mystery, with discreet murder among civilized enemies, also have felt less miserable because of Alleyn and Dame Ngaio Marsh. Every two years or so now, it is comforting to know that Alleyn is due back for another sophisticated duel of wits and that Dame Ngaio again will be viewing the scene with a gently ironic eye to spot human and social foibles. . . . In a world of irrational violence, it is positively cheering to find that tidily-ordered, proper murders still are being committed for such perfectly valid reasons as jealousy, greed, passion, or hate.

As Dame Ngaio recalls it, her sleuth was born on a very wet Saturday afternoon in 1931 in a basement flat off Sloan Square in London, where she then was working for a house-decorating firm. She had finished reading a detective story . . . and began to wonder idly whether she might try the same. So she splashed to a nearby stationer's shop and bought six tupenny exercise books, a pencil, and a pencil sharpener. She already was equipped with a sharp wit, observant eye, inventive mind, and graceful prose style.

Today, at 77, Dame Ngaio is writing as well as ever, which can be very well indeed. Some of her recent novels, particularly *Black as He's Painted* [1975], can stand beside her best, including *Enter a Murderer* (1935), *Overture to Death* (1936), *Final Curtain* (1947), and *Clutch of Constables* (1969). There is none of the embarrassment of those waning latter-day Christies.

"With the passing of Agatha Christie, Dame Ngaio Marsh stands as the undisputed doyenne of mystery writers," proclaims a promotional blurb for *Last Ditch,* published this spring as the latest Alleyn case. The more ardent fans of Dame Ngaio would argue the timing. For Marsh always has been a far better writer and novelist than Christie even as she has worked in the shadow of her slightly older contemporary's incredible mass popularity. Dame Ngaio handles the language with an impeccable sense of style. If she can be fiendishly clever in concocting murder plots, she never has been content to settle for a flashy puzzle, letting cardboard characters fall where they may. With a single phrase, she can limn a character into the memory. . . . (p. 36)

In her fondness for background and character, Dame Ngaio sometimes does neglect to get on with the main business of detection. Then, particularly in the earlier books, she hastens to retrieve with post-murder interrogations and perhaps a reprise of suspects, motives, and movements. It is as if she suddenly has remembered that she really set out to write a detective story and not a novel of manners. Dame Ngaio is an acquired taste, and the leisurely pace is not to everyone's liking. Sometimes she ends up with a forced solution. But even when a Marsh mystery misfires, it is done with style, redeemed by a memorable character or a skewered pretension to recall with relish.

In recounting the story of the birth of her detective-hero, Dame Ngaio recalls how, on that long-distant wet Saturday afternoon of 1931, she decided on "comparative normality" in the face of the vogue for amateur sleuths with celebrated eccentricities in the Holmesian tradition. (pp. 36-7)

Dame Ngaio didn't want to "tie mannerisms, like labels," around her hero's neck. Fortunately, she didn't altogether succeed, for our affection for people and characters embraces their quirks as well as their virtues. Alleyn is an attractive, civilized, compassionate man with an accidental elegance and a witty humor drawn from understatement. In the early days, he is acutely embarrassed when the popular press refers to the "handsome inspector." He uses the affectionate nicknames of Br'er Fox and Foxkins for his aide, Inspector Fox. Alleyn, as Dame Ngaio had hoped would turn out, is "that nice chap with more edge to him than met the eye—a good deal more."

Yet Alleyn, though a professional policeman and a nice chap rather than a snobbish amateur sleuth, still is very much within the mold of the Gentleman-Detective of the Golden Thirties of the English detective story. . . .

Along with her Gentleman-Detective, Dame Ngaio has retained other trappings from the Golden Thirties mystery even as she has moved with the contemporary scene. . . . She delights in bizarre murder weapons, country-house amenities, dotty English lords, vicars, village busybody spinsters, maps and a cast of characters.

Some of Dame Ngaio's murder weapons are diabolically ingenious. A jeroboam of champagne provides a spirited demise for a theatrical producer when it drops on him in *Vintage Murder.* A gossipy spinster is murdered by a pistol rigged to a soft pedal of a piano as she launches into the opening bars of an explosive Rachmaninoff's romantic prelude (*Overture to Death*). . . . A proper murder doesn't have to be bloodless or unimaginative.

The theater, on and off stage, provides the background for some of Dame Ngaio's most successful mysteries. Her "damery," as she likes to call it, came from her contributions to the theater in New Zealand rather than for her considerable accomplishments as a writer of literate mysteries. . . .

Over the years, as Dame Ngaio has refined her talents, Alleyn has matured as a character. He has been promoted to superintendent. A bachelor for the first half dozen books or so, he meets, courts, and marries Agatha Troy over the span of two more novels. A portrait painter of distinction and a woman of independent character, Troy does not intrude on her husband's professional career. But she sometimes does get involved innocently in an investigation. (p. 37)

The Alleyn son, Ricky, is by now down from the university, trying to write a first novel in the solitude of a British channel island, when he becomes a central figure in *Last Ditch*. And it is pleasant to watch as Inspector Fox, that stolid, plain-thinking and worthy companion in Alleyn's investigations, chats up a French maid for valuable information after all those hours spent listening to French on the gramophone in an earlier book.

Somewhere, perhaps it is in her autobiography, *Black Beech and Honeydew,* Dame Ngaio mentions her favorite quotation from Keats: "How happy is such a voyage of conception, what delicious, diligent indolence!" It well might be said of her mystery novels. (pp. 37-8)

Jean M. White, "Murder Most Tidy," in The New
Republic, *Vol. 177, No. 5, July 30, 1977, pp. 36-8.*

EARL F. BARGAINNIER

Ngaio Marsh's detective novels have made her New Zealand's most famous author. However, in spite of her popularity, she has always been reticent about her fiction, saying that there is only so much that can be said on the subject. She has much preferred to discuss her work in the theatre, as is evident in her autobiography, *Black Beech and Honeydew.* Her success as a director, especially of Shakespeare, was rewarded by her becoming Dame Ngaio in 1966 (she refers to the title as her "damery"), but her international fame is the result of Roderick Alleyn and the novels in which he has solved murders since 1934. Beginning in the Golden Age of British detective fiction, Marsh has generally been considered one of the four most significant women writers of what has come to be known as the classic British detective story. . . . (p. 81)

Any study of Marsh's work must begin with Roderick Alleyn. As her sole detective and the protagonist of all her fiction, no aspect of that fiction can be examined without in some way including him. He has been described by Erik Routley as "the last romantic hero of detective fiction . . . [who] makes Lord Peter Wimsey look like a frivolous neurotic" and as "a very satisfying and amiable kind of superman." Alleyn is the epitome of the British sleuth, who surprises everyone by not being a bit like a detective. He hates murders, yet his career is spent in solving them. . . . He exemplifies the later development of the Golden Age British detective. As one of the most significant of the gentleman-policemen, he prepares the way for the police procedural novel so prevalent today. Though Alleyn has the handsome appearance, the aristocratic background—with all its attendant qualities, the charm, the bookishness, and the witty facetiousness—of some other gentlemen-detectives, his attitudes toward others, his authority, and his methods of detection make him something other than the conventional Golden Age British detective.

According to Marsh, Alleyn's name is the result of her family ties, but certainly her involvement in the theatre influenced the choice of his last name, that of Edward Alleyn, Elizabethan tragedian, founder of Dulwich College, and husband of John Donne's daughter. After giving him his name, Marsh endowed him with a striking physical appearance. Known in the newspapers as "Handsome Alleyn" and "The Handsome Super," he is "a monkish-looking person with a fastidious mouth and well-shaped head." This image is developed by a character's thinking that he looks like a "grandee turned monk, but retaining some amusing memories." . . . (pp. 81-2)

In *A Man Lay Dead,* Rosamund Grant observes, "This man Alleyn, with his distinguished presence and his cultured voice and what-not, is in the Edwardian manner," and she is not far

off the mark. Alleyn was born in 1896 into the British aristocracy, being the younger son of a baronet. . . . His upper-class background is, of course, a significant element in both his image and his work. A few details of his personality can illustrate. He set the tone at his Oxford college, but when reminded of that he is horrified. He speaks Latin, French, German and Italian. He seems to be continually and always politely refusing drinks pressed upon him, for he does not drink on duty, yet he is a wine expert, shuddering at the Invalid Port used in the ceremonies of a pseudo-religious cult. . . .

More important than such personal characteristics is the effect of his background on his career as a detective. . . . Members of the upper-class request Alleyn from the Yard when murder occurs in their circles, for he is one of them, a gentleman. At the same time, he has a marked effect on the servants of the rich and well-born. In *Hand in Glove,* Alfred the butler says to the cook that "class is class and to be treated as such. *In the Force* he may be, and with distinction. *Of* it, he is not." . . . (p. 83)

However, it should not be thought that because of his background and connections Alleyn is a snob. He inwardly writhes "under his blatant recognition of his snob-value." Whenever his brother, Sir George Alleyn, is mentioned, his usual reaction is one of "falling over backwards rather than profit by their relationship." Nor will Alleyn allow aristocratic suspects to take advantage of his own position: he refuses to "respond to this appeal from blue blood to blue blood." This refusal is an example of one of the principal elements of Alleyn's character: his personal and professional fastidiousness. In his dealing with others, he is nearly always ultra-polite; the only exceptions are when being facetious with friends and when forced to exert his official authority. (p. 84)

A significant aspect of Alleyn's fastidiousness is his attitude toward his job. He is continually introspective about his work, calling it "indecently preposterous." He considers murder "a crime in bad taste." . . . Alleyn is opposed to capital punishment; he says, "As the law stands, its method of dealing with homicides is, as I think, open to the gravest criticism. But for all that, the destruction of a human being remains what it is: the last outrage." Yet in *When in Rome* he allows a murderer to escape punishment. Such a view for a fictional detective is unusual. At the end of one case, Fox says, "It's the kind of case he doesn't fancy. Capital charge and a woman. Gets to thinking about what he calls first causes. . . . Society. Civilization. Or something." It is at such moments that Alleyn suffers *angst.* . . . [At] times the gentleman is at war with the detective.

Part of his charm is the result of his fastidiousness. . . . His charm causes people to confide in him, trust him, and allow him to maneuver them. When questioning suspects, he suits his manner to whatever the particular person expects of or wants from him, and, as a result, he gets what he wants from them. Both fastidiousness and charm are inherent in Alleyn's personality, but he uses these qualities to be the successful detective he is. (pp. 84-5)

Over and over, Alleyn's extensive knowledge, vast reading and catholicity of taste are emphasized. . . . By far his favorite subject is William Shakespeare; there are allusions to or quotations from his works in all thirty-one novels. In *Killer Dolphin,* Peregrine Jay, a writer and director, thinks that "Alleyn knew as much as he did about Shakespearean scholarship and was as familiar with the plays as he was himself." . . . Alleyn's

Shakespeareanism is obviously the result of Marsh's career as a director of ten of Shakespeare's plays, but, though at times the quoting may seem excessive, it is largely justified by his Oxford education and his general intellectuality.

Related to the bookishness are his theatricality and facetiousness. . . . Alleyn is a firm believer in irony, and he makes such use of it that it is not surprising that Bathgate can explode with "Facetious ass!" or that Fox occasionally casts "his eyes towards heaven" or says, "Come off it, sir.". . . (pp. 85-7)

Alleyn's facetiousness could easily become a weakness in his presentation, but Marsh makes sure that the reader knows he is not malicious: "Alleyn . . . never made too much fun of anybody." Since the "fun" is almost always with his two closest friends, it is presented as being harmless. In fact, whenever Alleyn feels that he has wounded, he apologizes. . . . And so there is charm and fastidiousness even in his facetiousness.

Nigel Bathgate and Inspector Edward Walter (Teddy) Fox are Alleyn's closest friends. . . . (p. 87)

Fox is described by Alleyn as "sane," "nice-minded," "a concealed classicist," "a wise old bird," and "the perfect embodiment, the last loveliest expression, of horse sense.". . . Throughout the novels, there is a running joke about Fox's attempts to learn French from records, and since Alleyn's French is perfect, it is a good illustration of Marsh's technique of contrast between the two. Fox is definitely lower-middle class; he looks like a policeman in his bowler hat; his language is simple, without literary allusions; and he is slow and sure rather than brilliant. Therefore, he is an excellent complement to the aristocratic Alleyn. Marsh never lets Fox take center-stage from Alleyn, but in him she creates a "loveable" and contrasting second-lead to her star.

Of the recurrent characters not actively engaged in crime-solving, the most important is Agatha Troy Alleyn, called Troy by her husband. Marsh has stated that both her agent and publisher were opposed to her introducing Troy to the series of novels; however, she insisted. . . . [Their] marriage is a very happy one, for they are two intelligent people, each prominent in his and her careers, and neither dominating the other.

Among the other members of his family, his son Ricky appears in *Spinsters in Jeopardy* and *Last Ditch*. . . . Alleyn's mother appears in *Artists in Crime* and *Death in a White Tie,* and his knightly brother finally appears in *Black As He's Painted.* Lady Helena Alleyn is a grand dame of sixty-five, who resides in the country, has extensive social connections, raises Alsatians, and indulges in various handicrafts. She and Alleyn are close, and she is anxious for him to marry and happy when he does. The best word to describe her is *sensible,* and Alleyn obviously inherits that quality from her. Of Alleyn's older brother, their mother says, "It's a pity he hasn't got your brains.". . . Sir George is simply the traditional bumbling aristocrat, and a foil for his brother.

For Roderick Alleyn is anything but a comic aristocrat. He is "possessed of an effortless authority," and he is aware of it. . . . This personal authority is one of the effects of his background and one of the elements of his success as a detective, but there are others.

Alleyn's methods of detection are a combination of those of the master detective in the Holmes and Poirot tradition and of those of normal police routine, making him a transitional figure between Golden Age detective fiction and the modern police procedural. As a master-detective, he has abilities the normal policeman does not. . . . His relationship with Troy is given part of the credit for such ability; he has a double vision: "As a stringently trained policeman, he watched automatically for idiosyncrasies. As a man very sensitively tuned to his wife's way of seeing, he searched for consonancies."

Another element of the master-detective in Alleyn, which has already been discussed, is his ability to provide the image people want or expect. By fitting his approach to the individual in his interviews, he wins their confidence. . . . This apparent intense interest in the concerns of those involved in a case of murder is one of his most successful methods of gaining information. Another method is reconstruction of the murder. In *Enter a Murderer, Death and the Dancing Footman,* and *Death of a Fool,* as well as others, Alleyn restages the events of the murder in order to trap the killer. Although he says that he does not do it "out of any desire to figure as the mysteriously omnipotent detective," which would be "impossibly vulgar," the effect *is* of an omnipotent detective stage-managing others. Of course, as a master detective, Alleyn generally knows quite early the identity of the murderer. . . . His usual problem is to find evidence to justify his theory. . . . One method of finding that needed evidence is what he calls a "hag," which is "the ruthless taking-to-pieces of the case and a fresh attempt to put the bits together in their true pattern." Such a recapitulation of everything known also allows the reader to see how brilliant a detective he is, in putting those pieces together.

Other items contributing to the master-detective image are the admiration of other policemen, one of whom describes his textbook on methods as "the Scourge of the Service"; his success in disguise, whether as a communist or a bookish health-seeker; his ability to do without sleep or to tell himself to wake at a certain time and do it; his willingness to use tricks, and his intuition of evil. (pp. 88-92)

In *Vintage Murder,* Alleyn says, "I'm an incurable nosey parker. Detect I must, if I can," and detect he does. Though there are the grand touches of the master-detective, Alleyn believes in routine police procedure and in distrust of conjecture. He defines his professionalism "as an infinite capacity to notice less and less with more and more accuracy." In his comments on detective fiction, he insists that "real" police activity is different and uninteresting. . . . In *Colour Scheme,* Alleyn states most fully his attitude toward the nature of the detective process:

> Police investigation, we protest, is not a matter of equally balanced motives, tortuous elaborations, and a final revelation in the course of which the investigator's threat hangs like an *ignis fatuus* over first one and then another of the artificially assembled suspects. It is rather the slow amassment of facts sufficient to justify the arrest of someone who has been more or less suspect from the moment the crime was discovered.

Such a process does not allow for what Alleyn calls "the hateful realms of surmise and conjecture.". . . (pp. 92-3)

Along with conjecture, Alleyn distrusts motive in determining who is a murderer. . . . The stress on opportunity rather than motive is a principal factor in his method, and it is matched by his belief in a reliance on pattern, the fitting-in of each little piece of evidence to determine what is the odd—and conclusive—piece. (p. 93)

Alleyn's introspection toward his profession has already been discussed, but some additions and qualifications need to be made. At one point, he indicates to Bathgate that nothing must interfere with his professional duties, but on another occasion he says, ''What rot they talk when they teach us we should never get involved. Of course we get involved: we merely learn not to show it.'' Involvement is human, and when lecturing to a police class, Alleyn warns the students not to lose their humanity.... At the same time that Alleyn is required to do things that offend his sensibilities, he has to accept these as part of the nature of being a policeman.... Therefore, whatever he is required to do, he does—no matter what his own likes or dislikes may be, while trying to retain the humanity which he so highly values.

By now it should be evident that Alleyn is a mass of disparate elements. The reason is that Marsh unconsciously created a transitional figure. He has the aristocratic background; the personal charm, fastidiousness, and handsomeness; and the bookish facetiousness of the gentleman-detective of the ''between-the-wars'' school of British detective fiction. But he is also a policeman, using a team of subordinates in ''routine'' police investigation, and in this respect he looks forward to the later procedural novels, for there is more police routine in the early novels than in any other group of British detective novels of the 1930s. Marsh is generally effective in creating a seamless character out of these two quite different strains of detective fiction. When there are inconsistencies or contradictions, they are the result of the forty-six year time-span of the novels, rather than a lack of focus on her part. Indeed, much of the success of Marsh's detective fiction is due to her ability to adapt within Alleyn the many different elements of both types and still make him a character whom the reader both admires and cares about.

The settings in which Alleyn moves and the people whom he encounters are other elements of Marsh's success. She has stated, ''I have always tried to keep the settings of my books as far as possible within the confines of my own experience.'' Since her experience has included being a painter, an actress, and a director, as well as a New Zealander, she has naturally incorporated her other careers into her fiction. Troy Alleyn's profession is the most obvious example of Marsh's use of her painting in the novels. Marsh's theatrical career has contributed to the scenic effect, which is characteristic of her novelistic technique; her fiction is largely dialogue presented in a series of drama-like scenes. In choosing specific settings, she follows the Golden Age closed circle, or isolated, convention. Within that convention, she manipulates a relatively small number of place-types with great ingenuity of detail.

Though some belong to more than one, most of her settings fall into one of five categories. The largest number are the nine which take place in English country houses.... [These] novels are typical of Golden Age detective fiction and are among the best of their kind. Next are the seven which either occur in the theatre or involve theatrical families. No writer has used the theatrical scene for murder as often as Marsh... and her love and knowledge of the theatre is the obvious reason for this predilection. Her experience has enabled her to employ the theatre as an integral element of her detective fiction, involving plot, characterization, and atmosphere, as well as setting. Seven novels are set outside England, four in New Zealand. Why Marsh has not more frequently used her native country cannot be answered. Its combination of the exotic and the British would seem to offer many opportunities for her descriptive skill and for all sorts of misdirection. Certainly, the four set there (*Vintage Murder, Colour Scheme, Died in the*

Wool, Photo Finish) are not only excellent examples of Marsh's detective fiction, but attractive introductions to her antipodean homeland. The fourth group is another particular specialty of Marsh; five novels are concerned with some form of cult (*Death in Ecstasy, Spinsters in Jeopardy, Death of a Fool, Dead Water,* and *Last Ditch*). A cult, whether sexual, religious, or folk-mythic and whether bogus or sincere, provides a colorful background, a cast of eccentric characters, and numerous, and often strange, red herrings to complicate murder, and Marsh has been highly and rightly praised for her ability to manipulate these elements. The last group consists of four novels which take place in London high society. Three are essentially comic novels of manners.... The four works which do not exactly fit these categories are *The Nursing Home Murder, Death at the Bar,* and the two ''in transit'' novels, *Singing in the Shrouds* and *Clutch of Constables.*

Populating these settings with Alleyn, his aides and his family are the victims, murderers and suspects whom he confronts in his investigations. Again, the most obvious statement to be made about her characters is that they are typical of the Golden Age. Her victims are either unlikeable—philanderers, rich and disagreeable elderly people, bitchy or neurotic women, blackmailers, etc.—or unknown, so that the reader feels nothing when they die, the major exceptions being *Death in a White Tie* and *Death at the Bar.* They are always much less interesting than her murderers or, even more, her suspects, who may vary from the comic through the romantic to the eccentric, unpleasant, or nasty.... Twenty-four of Marsh's novels contain a young romantic couple in some way involved in the investigation of murder: as witnesses, suspects, or aides to Alleyn. Neither the young man nor the young woman is ever the guilty person; rather their relationship is used to complicate the case. A few of these couples verge on the silly, but most are attractive types.... Setting aside the murderers, other unpleasant characters abound. Whether engaged in non-murderous criminal activity or just possessing grating defects of personality, they scatter suspicion and make Alleyn's job more difficult.... All in all, Marsh exhibits virtuosity in the creation of varied minor characters, while staying within her own experience. As with her settings, the large number of painters and actors and actresses reflect her other professional interests, as the similar number of New Zealanders and Australians reflects her antipodean origin.

Marsh's murderers are also a varied lot.... [She] is expert in using the least-likely suspect ploy, but she is perhaps even better with its opposite, the most-obvious suspect. Quite often her murderers are not only the most obvious suspects, but also the most unpleasant, yet she is still able to create that essential doubt as to guilt in the mind of the reader. Examples include *Overture to Death, Death at the Bar, Death and the Dancing Footman, A Wreath for Rivera* and *Singing in the Shrouds.* The fact that so few generalizations can be made about her murderers is a compliment to Marsh's versatility in finding opponents for Alleyn.

However, one generalization that can be made is that her murderers employ some of the most bizarre methods ever devised to dispatch their victims. (pp. 93-7)

[Marsh's preference for] bizarre, even outlandish, methods of murder contrasts with her usual moderation in presenting the action of her novels. She apparently believes that the single act of violence which is the impetus of the remaining action must be striking and original. Though that act is more talked about than seen—as is the case with most writers of classic

British detective fiction—she always makes sure that it is so striking that her characters will be shocked, frightened, puzzled and utterly unable to stop talking about it until Alleyn provides the final explanation.

It has already been noted that much of Marsh's fiction is dialogue. Her novels move at a leisurely pace, and most are longer than the average detective novel. She has not escaped criticism for the structure of her novels. . . . [Even] though Marsh becomes more assured in her narration of the central investigation in later ones, she still spends many pages on matters other than detection. (p. 98)

There is also the element of comedy, perhaps most evident in the presentation of the Lamprey family of *Death of a Peer,* a family based upon one whom Marsh knew well, as evidenced by their large role in her autobiography. . . . Some readers may prefer "straight detection," with nothing except a crime and its solution. Marsh will not satisfy them; rather she appeals to the reader who enjoys meeting interesting people involved in a crime within a detailed setting and seeing their relationships and reactions and who is not overly anxious to discover whodunit.

On another level, much of the structure of Marsh's novels is naturally determined by the conventions of classic detective fiction. When she began to write, she modeled her novels on those prevalent in the 1930s. Therefore, her early works reflect the devices and techniques already used by Sayers, Christie and others, and many of these continue into the later novels: maps, connected chapter titles, repeated characters, mention of previous cases, the mid-novel recapitulation, the lists of various sorts (clues, questions, suspects), the detective's laying traps for the murderer, the action stopping with the arrest of the murderer, the final summation by the detective, and on and on. The rule of fairness to the reader was made much of in the Golden Age, and Marsh has been scrupulous in laying out all of the necessary information. A re-check of any novel, after the final summation demonstrates that. . . . In a number of her later novels Marsh uses a device which some may think unfair, but is actually not. Again and again, Alleyn will tell Fox or other characters some discovery or conclusion, but the reader is not privileged to know what is said. . . . Irritating as such omissions may be, they are not unfair, for Alleyn has simply made a deduction which, on the evidence *already* given, *could* have been made by the reader.

The structural feature of Marsh's novels most often criticized is the amount of time Alleyn spends interrogating one witness or suspect after another. The early novels especially are characterized by a long parade of interviews, sometimes repetitious, with chapter titles giving the names of the persons questioned. It can be argued that, though weak from a narrative standpoint, such a series of interviews is a prime illustration of Alleyn's continual insistence that most police work is routine and even tedious. Also, they indicate Marsh's interest in character, since they emphasize the reactions of those involved, and the influence of her theatrical work, for each is a dramatic scene, practically all dialogue.

From these interviews, Alleyn not only pieces together the sequence of the crime, discerns motives and eliminates some suspects, but also obtains verbal clues by his questioning, whether lies or truth. What is surprising, however, is that most of the cases hinge not on verbal clues, but on physical ones. (In this respect, Marsh differs considerably from Agatha Christie, to whom she is so often compared.) (pp. 98-100)

Before he reaches them, Marsh makes his job more difficult by throwing all sorts of red herrings in his path. She is fond of including another crime which complicates the investigation of the murder. . . . It is enough to say that Marsh is never at a loss to find ways of impeding Allyn's process of discovery, which only makes his ultimate success even more brilliant.

After his interrogations and the collection of clues, Alleyn knows the murderer, but on five occasions he employs a reconstruction of the crime with all principal suspects present in order to trap that murderer. The usual explanation is that there is not enough evidence to justify an arrest otherwise. After using this device in her first three novels, Marsh returned to it only twice, in *Death of a Fool* and *Death and the Dancing Footman.* . . . But though a reconstruction may produce a murderer's confession or total collapse and certainly provides a dramatic arrest, Marsh apparently realized that continuous reconstructions to provide final solutions would not only be boringly predictable, but would hardly indicate Alleyn's powers of deduction. Those critics who have accused her of overusing reconstructions have obviously not made an accurate count. (pp. 100-01)

As noted, most of the novels follow the classical formulas—many with individualized distinctiveness—but others do not. *Spinsters in Jeopardy* is Hitchcockian with the Alleyn family accidentally witnessing a murder from a train, the six-year-old Ricky being kidnapped in the Maritime Alps and a subsequent chase to rescue him, and an orgiastic cult in a cliff-hanging castle as a cover for drug-dealing, whose meeting is invaded by Alleyn and the young Raoul Milano in disguise. *Colour Scheme* offers a World War II spy story blended with theatrical satire, a Cinderella-type romance, and the exotic Maori culture and the landscape of New Zealand's North Island. Troy's dominance of the action in *Clutch of Constables* and Ricky's in *Last Ditch* are not typical roles for family members of a fictional British detective. The hysteria and commercialism surrounding the spring of the Green Lady in *Dead Water* is an effective and unusual backdrop for murder. Even more is the Marsh-invented folk-myth of the Mardian Morris of the Five Sons and Betty, Crack and Fool, which is the structural framework of *Death of a Fool*—and nothing less than a fictional *tour de force*. The differences between the absurdly comic antics of the Lamprey family in *Death of a Peer* and the tense four-suspect puzzle of *Died in the Wool* are other indications of Marsh's range, and examples could be multiplied. . . . [In] spite of Roderick Alleyn's always being present, there is *variety of structure,* as well as detail, in Marsh's fiction, a fact that some critics have failed to acknowledge.

The values present in Marsh's novels are those of the upper-middle class, tempered by her career in the theatre. Like most of her Golden Age colleagues, Marsh is a detached observer of the foibles and frailties of her characters. Though they may be treated romantically, there is always distance between them and their creator. This is true even of Alleyn; no one can say that Marsh fell in love with her detective. Her basic view of her characters is one of amusement, especially evident in the numerous satiric portraits scattered throughout the novels. Though conservative in her view of society's need for stability and of the necessity of protecting property, she is liberal, again in comparison with most Golden Age writers, in matters of morals. There are few authorial comments on moral, as opposed to criminal, lapses in the novels, the major exception being the taking of drugs, about which she obviously feels strongly, nor does religious belief play a significant part. However, she does present the police as a moral force. Never is there a doubt that Alleyn, Fox and their aides are on the side of justice; rather they are the exceptional upholders and preservers of what is best in their society. Her presentation of Troy Alleyn's career—and Alleyn's considering it more important than his own—provides an added dimension to her works, one unusual enough in the 1930s to cause opposition to Troy's introduction. In summary, Marsh follows the conventions of Golden Age detective fiction, but her own acutely clear-eyed and sensitive nature has enabled her to incorporate elements of the novel of manners, of romance, of satire, of character and of her personal interests to create a distinctly individual body of work.

When one considers that Marsh has been writing detective fiction for forty-six years, with little sign of diminished power, one can only be surprised by the consistently high level of her accomplishment. Though she has not written as much in that long period as others in her field, she has brought a style to her work which those more prolific must envy. Readers have come to expect and to delight in the distinguishing characteristics of her fiction, including her leisurely plots, with little physical action; her bizarre murders, sometimes more zany than horrible; her clever dialogue which rarely becomes silly; her skill at description which never becomes padding or clutter; her exploration of character and character-types; and her creation of one of the most famous of gentlemen-policemen, Roderick Alleyn. She has accepted the formulas and conventions of the Golden Age, but, while remaining within their boundaries, has adapted them in her own way through five decades into the 1980s, and that is no mean achievement. (pp. 101-03)

> *Earl F. Bargainnier, "Ngaio Marsh," in* 10 Women of Mystery, *edited by Earl F. Bargainnier, Bowling Green State University Popular Press, 1981, pp. 78-105.*

JESSICA MANN

Ngaio Marsh celebrated her eightieth birthday in 1979. That same year she published her thirtieth thriller. Her first novel appeared in 1934. Whether her books have the lasting quality which will make them popular when the author is no longer around to benefit from them time will show, but she is always regarded by those who write about the genre as one of the 'big four'. (p. 218)

Although some of her books are 'more English than the English', Ngaio Marsh has always regarded New Zealand as her home, and the descriptions of it in the few books set there, and in her autobiographical volume, are more evocative and enticing than any of those set in the England of which she is so fond. In these, as in all her work, we are very aware of the scenery. Marsh's training was in painting, and her main interest is the theatre; it is very evident that the strongest of her senses is the visual one. (p. 219)

[In the mid-1920s], Ngaio made friends with a family which was to have a considerable influence on her life, and which she described in her novel *Surfeit of Lampreys* (known as *Death of a Peer* in the USA) written in 1941.

Barzun regards this book as an 'intolerable tale'. Erik Routley puts it in his short list of the very best. It probably depends on whether one likes or loathes the family, whose description is really the whole point of the book. It consists of an earl's heir, his wife and their six children. They dazzle the heroine of the novel, a young New Zealand girl; they enchant many

readers and they clearly both dazzled and enchanted Ngaio Marsh. They are meant to be funny though not witty, unmusical but capable of entertaining an audience, kind but selfish, broke but not poor. Life with them was exciting, and Ngaio fell in love with the whole family; like Roberta in the novel, 'with appalling simplicity, she gave her heart to the Lampreys.'. . . At various stages in the book they are called elusive, vague, flippant, scatter-brained, unstable and reprehensible. But for the fact that they are united in affection for one another and possess that elusive quality, charm, the novel would not seem to be a very flattering portrait of people to whom its author was devoted; in the autobiography she says that they are sweet of disposition, generous, Christian, and nothing if not Irish. (pp. 221-22)

[Marsh] was not a great reader and rarely read crime novels, though she had loved *Sherlock Holmes* as a child. However, one wet Sunday when her mother and her friends were away, she borrowed a detective story from a lending library in a stationer's shop and spent the day reading it. It made so little impression that later she could never recall whether it had been a Christie or a Sayers. In any case, she decided that she could do as well, went back to the stationer's to buy some pencils and sixpenny exercise books, and sat down to start writing. Her story was based on the "Murder Game". It was set at a house-party, and was complete with the obligatory butler and footmen, the silly young ass, the pretty ingenue, Russian conspirators and a glamorous detective. She worked at it in the evenings and was surprised when her mother said it was good enough to publish. Its eventual title was *A Man Lay Dead*, and though it now seems too humdrum to be worth reading, it presaged the qualities which made its successors popular.

Marsh decided that she must have a detective quite different from the eccentrics like Poirot, Holmes and Fortune. She felt that his 'chance lay in comparative normality'. She decided not to tie mannerisms round his neck like labels, and hoped to create an attractive civilised man whose background resembled that of her English friends. So she made him the younger son of a landed family in the Chilterns, who was educated at Eton, was briefly in the Foreign Office, and whose mother bred Alsatian dogs. He was named after the Alleyn who had founded Dulwich College, where Henry Marsh had been to school, and his first name was chosen after a visit to Scotland where Roderick is a popular name. (p. 223)

[A publisher] accepted *A Man Lay Dead*, and brought it out in 1934; the contract was for Ngaio's next three novels also. . . . Marsh was from that time onwards to publish steadily and regularly. She had found her length, as it were, and stuck to it. Her talent was for light, glancing characterisations, excellently realised settings, precise plotting, and for conversation as good as might be expected from a writer whose true love was the theatre.

It is perhaps because Marsh regarded writing as of very secondary importance to her dramatic work that she was able to repeat the same type of book again and again. She never tried to change the kind of novel she wrote as the years went by; never grew irritated with her hero; never wrote anything which touched her emotions more deeply, although she apparently continued to hope until quite recently that she would one day be able to write a serious novel about the early settlers in New Zealand. As well as the odd play, she has written a book about New Zealand for American schools, but otherwise she sticks to detective stories. 'They are most exacting things to write,'she told a journalist. Certainly she works very hard at the research on her novels, partly because she believes that the majority of her readers are professional men, 'the very people who can catch you out.' Consequently she is very careful to be accurate about weapons and wounds, although her books are rarely explicit about gory details. 'I often envy the straight novelist,' she said in 1978. 'A detective story has to be disciplined. It must have a beginning, middle and end. A lot of novel writing at the moment tends to be formless. Also straight writers don't have to do anything like the same amount of grilling homework. You can't afford to make mistakes.'

This disciplined framework on which Marsh constructs her novels is either their merit or their drawback, depending on taste. Those who prefer the puzzle novel enjoy Marsh's stories precisely because they do set out their clues and problems in such a structured way. As reviewers always write, 'Dame Ngaio plays fair'.

To other critics, this very rigidity is a fault. One has the feeling that the novels all begin as a perceptive exposure of certain people and places, but that at the stage when the initial layout is ready to be exploited, the author takes fright. (pp. 224-25)

Ngaio Marsh herself has not said much about her approach to crime writing; but she has written that her books attempt to treat of 'people in the round'. She begins every time with two or three people that she wishes to write about, and often starts to write before developing the plot and its denouement. She recognises the difficulties that this intention creates. 'The more deeply and honestly [the crime writer] examines his characters, the more disquieting becomes the skulduggery that he is obliged to practice in respect to the guilty party.' Her aim is, it seems, to create rounded characters of all but the villain, but in nearly every book one feels that she withdraws from the dangerous process of dissecting her character's emotions, and retreats into discussion of those physical details which will result in the traditional resolution of crime in an ordered society. Her books avoid social judgements and do not question the political basis of society. Alleyn has no doubt about his duty.

All this is evidence of that extreme desire for privacy, that mask, which is typical of novelists who choose to write mysteries. Marsh invents, or describes, characters which are of interest to her, and potentially to her reader, but seems to be unable to force herself into the self-exposure which revealing more about them would entail. In some of the books which adhere too mechanically to the recipe it does not matter; they make excellent puzzle novels. In others, it is a disappointment. The Lampreys, for instance, are potentially as interesting to the reader as to their affectionate chronicler, but we see them too much from the outside. *Opening Night* (1951) (called *Night at the Vulcan* in the USA) presents a varied group of theatre people, portrayed with perception through the eyes of a young New Zealand girl newly arrrived in London. But once the police investigators join the cast the characters lose a dimension. It is not that Marsh is incapable of greater subtlety, merely that she is evidently determined to reserve for herself, or for her work in the theatre, her deeper insights and understanding.

So we are left with a corpus of work which is pleasant and entertaining but not entirely satisfying. . . . [In] Marsh's work one senses withdrawal.

The locales of her books, on the other hand, are vivid and evocative. Naturally, many of them are set in theatres, and several in New Zealand. . . . But the predominant impression of her surroundings is of the same village England as Agatha Christie's, with such characters as squires, spinsters who wor-

ship God and the vicar, the retired colonel, district nurse and tweedy doctor. The heroines have names like Rose Cartarette, Nicola Maitland-Mayne and Camilla Campion. The locals are yokels and use words like 'thikky' meaning 'that', 'dussn't' meaning 'dare not', and such phrases as 'wonderful queer to think of, hearts'. In this use of dialect, as in her picture of upper-class life, Marsh is 'more English than the English'. Perhaps it is because her view of England is inevitably one of a visitor, however devoted, that she retains this idealised view of life in the Northern hemisphere.

No writer can avoid giving away some information about herself. Marsh's passionate affection for English ways and life is merely one example of attributes she cannot conceal from the reader. We learn a good deal about her interests not only in the theatre, but also in art. Alleyn loves, and eventually marries, a world-famous painter called Agatha Troy and, as detective-hero's girlfriends tend to be, Troy is a bit of a giveaway about her creator. . . . [The] likeness between Troy and Marsh has been noticed by several commentators. (pp.225-27)

The one Alleyn child, Ricky, appears occasionally in the novels until in *Last Ditch* (1977) he takes over as detective. Ngaio Marsh is not the only inventor of a series detective who has tried to pass the interest along to the next generation; Michael Innes had introduced Appleby's son Bobby in the same role. In neither case is the device very successful, and both authors returned to their old friends and contemporaries in subsequent books. Alleyn is addressed by his son as 'the Cid' but this, like other similarly whimsical touches—Brer Fox, for Alleyn's subordinate, for example—can grate on the reader.

The whole assumption behind Ngaio Marsh's novels is of an agnostic conservatism, and an acceptance of the value of stability; but the only political point to be made in any detail is about racial discrimination.

It is evident from her autobiography, and from the novels also, that Ngaio Marsh is proud of the way in which New Zealand has adopted the principle of integration from the very beginning—'the intention of our forefathers: that the Maori and the Pakeha shall be as one people.'

She does not deny that friction exists, but regards it as springing from differences in behaviour, and not from past injuries. . . . This interest in the relationship between members of different races appears again and again in her novels. *Colour Scheme* (1943) is a fascinating picture of the contacts between the European and the aborigine in New Zealand. . . . The Maoris are described by Marsh with a quite unsentimental affection, and she is particularly successful with her portrait of the tribal leader, Rua, who has been a warrior, an editor of a native newspaper, and a Member of Parliament. (pp. 227-28)

The respect she has always felt for the Maoris has made Marsh sensitive to the infamies of colour prejudice. . . . In later books she writes again about colour prejudice, though her comment is incidental, for her novels are never propaganda tracts. In *Clutch of Constables* (1968) a black doctor is a fellow guest on a hotel barge with Troy; he is well dressed at 'High Establishment' level, and is almost too cultured, refined and civilised. Those who, like Alleyn and Troy, like him immensely, still think of him as strange. Marsh, like Troy, sees the doctor in visual terms, and there are several descriptions of the light falling on his skin, 'warmly dark, with grape coloured shadows'. . . . (p. 229)

Black As He's Painted (1974) features an African president who had been at school with Alleyn.... Marsh has the opportunity again to use her pen as a brush—'those reflected lights in the hollow of temple and cheek' and a chance also to express the feelings which she has about the Europeanisation of other races.... A liberal, agnostic, tolerant supporter of the status quo: in that at least Ngaio Marsh has revealed herself. (pp. 229-30)

After the war, Ngaio Marsh returned to England and her Lamprey friends. Her novels continued to reflect her experiences: *Swing Brother Swing* deals with another family of eccentric aristocrats in austere post-war London; *Spinsters in Jeopardy*, which like the pre-war *Death in Ecstacy* uses the peculiarities of a lunatic and vicious religious sect as the peg for its plot, is set in a converted Saracen stronghold carved into the cliff face in the South of France—the Lampreys and Ngaio Marsh had spent a holiday in just such a castle above Monte Carlo. From this theme, as from others, Marsh retreats from full exploration; she is amused and sardonic, even a little disgusted, but not really interested, and the irrational urges of the devotees, the corrupt motives of those who batten on them, are seen wholly through a policeman's eye....

In Britain, Marsh had become a well-known and popular writer.... [She] was surprised, she wrote, to find herself taken seriously as a writer, and justified her work, as her colleagues Sayers and Allingham had also done, by saying that the mould into which a detective novel was forced was no more contemptible than that of any other conventional form of writing—for instance, the diamonds, hearts and triangles into which the metaphysical poets fitted their verse. 'The mechanics in a detective novel may be shamelessly contrived, but the writing need not be so, nor, with one exception, need the characterisation. About the guilty person, of course, endless deception is practised.' (p. 232)

Throughout her life [Marsh] has retained that quality of privacy which pervades her fiction. As she wrote at the end of the autobiography, 'I find I have withdrawn from writing about experiences which have most closely concerned and disturbed me. What I have written turns out to be a straying recollection of places and people; I have been deflected by my own reticence.'

In the same way, the author's reticence has diminished the life of her novels. It is this, more than anything, which may determine whether they survive. (p. 233)

> *Jessica Mann, "Ngaio Marsh," in her* Deadlier than the Male: Why Are Respectable English Women So Good at Murder? *Macmillan Publishing Co., Inc., 1981, pp. 218-33.*

BRUCE HARDING

Ngaio Marsh once said that 'All good detective novels begin in Baker Street.'... Like Conan Doyle, she possessed in high degree the gift of word painting and the gift of telling a story. The plots and structures of her novels evidence a carefully cultivated semblance of artlessness, and yet while her choice of language is usually graceful and limpid her style often proclaims its maker's delight in its own exuberance. Indeed, the main reason for the continued popularity of Marsh's novels lies in the sprightliness of her characterisations and her vigorous and elegant style. So, the Holmesian priority remained imperative for her: the supremacy of an arresting protagonist and

the cultivation of a good literary style. In this respect no greater contrast could be imagined than between the work of Marsh and Agatha Christie of whom Erik Routley said:

> [The] beauty of her technique (which is quite compelling) is entirely in technique, never in style. No writer worth attending to has used more stock phrases in dialogue than [Christie] did ... The devotee of Michael Innes would find her style as exasperating as the lover of Ngaio Marsh ... would find her people.

And some years ago a Canadian reviewer [Samuel Marchbanks, a pseudonym of Robertson Davies], was moved to comment that Marsh's detective Roderick Alleyn 'is of even greater interest to me than the well-contrived mysteries which Miss Ngaio Marsh causes him to solve.'

Marsh's own preoccupation with style (which was in itself a major contribution to the evolution of detective fiction) early earned her praise: in 1943 a *New York Times* reviewer wrote that Marsh had by then 'proved that in her ironic and witty hands the mystery novel can be civilized literature', and earlier this year *The Times* declared that she 'was one of those writers who, during the 1930s, raised the detective novel to a high level of literary art.' At the same time Bruce Mason wrote that her novels 'were finely crafted, richly erudite displays, yet [Dame Ngaio] never insisted on her virtuosity, letting one find it for oneself.'... [The] private world of Ngaio Marsh was above all elegant, quietist and refined—generating literary heterocosms in which aesthetic discrimination was a major value, which certainly left her open to Patrick Evans' epithet 'the artist-as-mandarin' who wallowed in what he terms a 'comfortable colonial mentality' in which England could still be called Home.

However, to be fair, this was largely unavoidable, for Dame Ngaio was (whether egalitarians like it or not) a natural aristocrat—a 'queen of the spirit' in Mason's words—who was taught from the cradle to abhor all crudeness and vulgarity and to prefer the formal, the ceremonious and the graceful in art.

Her idealising was perhaps a direct consequence of the [New Zealand] provincial's dilemma, but more certainly because the genre of detective fiction is in essence a hybrid falling between romance and realism and thus is not a firmly realist literary form. So the [*Times Literary Supplement*] noted that Marsh wrote about the lively Lampreys—who 'were very grand for New Zealand' (*Surfeit of Lampreys*)—'with the zest for England of one born and bred a long way away.' And Charles Brady lamented the English manor house setting in *Final Curtain* (1947) because 'the ingredients are not precisely new: the will; the protective mother; the dotty family that has been *de rigueur* in English fiction from Shaw to Waugh.'

The great strength of the Marsh books is her gift of characterisation. As Joan Stevens has observed:

> It is the people whom she assembles for her fictions who make them so lively.
>
> Above all, they can *talk*. The varied and vivid confrontations of their dialogue establish personality and keep the plot moving.

(pp. 447-49)

[Marsh's] choice of a literary career as a crime novelist was not such an odd one if we remember that Ngaio read the work of Edgar Allan Poe as a young child and the Conan Doyle Holmes stories at about nine years of age, and that her education was as English as antipodean conditions would allow. But lest we blithely consign her as one inseparably wedded to the world of criminal literature we should look at a short story called **"Moonshine"** which Marsh thought she wrote for [the Christchurch *Sun*] at the age of nineteen. If this is so, it furnished early evidence of remarkable literary talent. . . . (p. 449)

With **"Moonshine",** a touching little story about a child's discovery that Father Christmas is a mythical figure, Marsh introduced the highly ingenious device of framing her narratives with punning titles. In this case, on the prosaic level the title deals with the placement of the Christmas parcels by Janey's own father while she watches in the moonlight; on the metaphorical level, it conveys the general idea that the Santa Claus business is bogus. In addition, it neatly suggests the playful link between real fathers and Christmas. Warwick Lawrence who compiled the anthology [*Yours and Mine*] in which **"Moonshine"** was republished, described it as "one of Ngaio Marsh's earliest stories, and . . . one of the most beautiful and poignant ever written for children by a New Zealand writer.' To my mind, however, this story reveals a high level of sophistication. What is immediately striking about this story is the pronounced Englishness of its tone, . . . but of far more importance is the artfully simple depiction of the turbulent emotions of childhood and the acquisition of adult knowledge when Jane and her father tenderly discuss the rationale for his innocent deception.

When confronted with such evidence of unusual literary promise we may well ask why Marsh later chose to restrict her energies to the exigencies of the 'International Style' of bestselling fiction. Jessica Mann is surely correct in making the point about Marsh hiding her innermost personality behind a mask, for what makes a . . . story like **"Moonshine"** live is the fact that in it Ngaio Marsh exposed something of herself (albeit very obliquely). But I think also that Marsh realised that she was not a strikingly original writer (in the sense of having greatly profound insight into life) and, as she needed an income, she elected detective fiction which was in that Golden Age a fairly 'highbrow' field. . . . (p. 450)

Although Marsh only set four novels in New Zealand, I would argue that at least three of them contribute something in their own distinctive way to the broader picture of life in this country. In making this claim I take issue with Randall Burdon's contention that 'in a literary sense Marsh was always below par when writing about her native land'; not with the view that London was her spiritual home, but with his idea that this fact 'may explain why Roderick Alleyn and his victims perform to greater advantage in a metropolitan than in a remote antipodean environment.' For this is tantamount to accepting the claim in a British newspaper [the *North Eastern Evening Gazette*] that while it was true that Marsh was born in New Zealand, 'her first book was acccepted while she was in England . . . so we are entitled to consider her as one of us.' (pp. 450-51)

[Marsh's] supreme achievement as a New Zealand-born author was to combine the cosmopolitan outlook of an internationalist with a firm loyalty to her own people (Maori and Pakeha) and their respective traditions. The rub was, of course, that in this process of oscillating between—in Gertrude Stein's terms—the country where she belonged (England) and the one in which she really lived (New Zealand), Ngaio Marsh appeared to some a misplaced English woman. While one can argue that this geographical and emotional tension was a very fruitful one in generating all her artistic attainments, it meant that Marsh was misunderstood as a cultural prig by some of her own compatriots. . . . Marsh's pride in her own unique country is amply reflected in two books (both entitled *New Zealand*) which she

has produced about it. Dennis McEldowney was right to point out that in her stories Marsh 'always continued to write about New Zealand as though she were a visitor, while believing she was a native', but this need not diminish her national pride and loyalty. Indeed, it was precisely in maintaining this stance that Marsh's personal expression of loyalty consisted. Jessica Mann has written that Marsh's picture of England is rather an unreal one [see excerpt above], adding suggestively: 'Perhaps it is because her view of England is inevitably one of a visitor, however devoted, that she retains this idealised view of life in the Northern hemisphere.' Can these two negatives of McEldowney's and Mann's create a positive? I think they can.

Marsh wrote two novels about wartime espionage in New Zealand (*Colour Scheme* and *Died in the Wool*) and two in peacetime with murder among groups of transplanted entertainers (the comedy troup in *Vintage Murder* and operatic *ménage* in *Photo-Finish*). New Zealand provided her with a varied ambience for these detective narratives as well as analogues to the conventional English villages of detective fiction. (pp. 451-52)

Yet it is still important to ask why Marsh only set four out of thirty-two novels here and why so many of the New Zealanders in them are either transplanted English or Kiwis with a strong Homing instinct. Her answer was that it was a matter of diction:

> I think one of the difficulties I find in writing books with a New Zealand setting is that I write very largely in dialogue, and I'm afraid I do think, by and large, that the New Zealand dialogue is monotonous and I do think that the average New Zealander has a very short vocabulary.

Marsh also used the highly sensitive (one might say sensuous and even painterly) consciousness of Roderick Alleyn to register the shades and nuances of the New Zealand environs. In this sense Joan Stevens appears to have misjudged Marsh's tactic when she writes that the New Zealand novels 'are not among Ngaio Marsh's best stories; Alleyn does not have his wonted sparkle among the geysers and the sheep.' It was precisely by keeping Alleyn in an uncertain relation to this new locale (at the risk of toning him down) that Marsh must have hoped that a fresh and objective image of New Zealand could be achieved. (One hardly thinks Alleyn below par in *Colour Scheme* and *Died in the Wool*, surely.) In *Vintage Murder* Alleyn muses upon the sounds issuing from a mountain stream and of a bellbird 'with a note like a little gong' and finds himself bewitched by the bush near Ruapehu:

> . . . Suddenly, close at hand, the bird called again—a solitary call, startlingly like a bell. Then this unseen bird shook from its throat a phrase of notes in a minor key, each note very round with something human in its quality.
>
> The brief song ended in a comic splutter. There was a sound of twigs. Then the call rang again and was answered somewhere deep in the bush, and back into the silence came the sound of running water.

This is a subtle, . . . taut and rhythmically evocative passage of descriptive writing. There is also the picnic episode, sensitively modulated so as to suggest something of the underlying logic of nature in New Zealand and the human response to it.

One of the staple ingredients of . . . colonial novels, according to E. H. McCormick, was that 'When a colonial is introduced it is as a bucolic foil to the god-like principal characters.' Can the same be said in respect of Alleyn in *Vintage Murder*?

Professor Ian Gordon has no doubts that this is generally so, and he writes of

> the idea that there is something to be ashamed of in speaking New Zealand English which still haunts us. We see ourselves as the minor character in one of Ngaio Marsh's own whodunnits who speaks in a way that 'betrays his antipodean origin.' He is always good for a laugh.

From the moment when Alleyn meets the plain and deferential New Zealand detectives ('By cripes sir, I'm sorry. We'd heard you were—we didn't know—I mean') his position as one of authority is unmistakeable. This becomes unbearably embarrassing when young Detective-Inspector Packer oozes forth 'instant and acute hero-worship' for Alleyn:

> 'He looks like one of those swells in the English flicks,' he afterwards confided to his girl, 'and he talks with a corker sort of voice. Not queeny, but just corker. I reckon he's all right. Gosh, I reckon he's a humdinger.'

This is plainly dreadful, and it creates a cruel caricature of a coarse and naïvely oafish colonial—a rustic clown in fact. With phrases like these, Marsh's respect for her own people could be thrown sharply into question. When Detective-Sergeant Cass (perhaps better named Crass) is 'shaken by a stupendous belch' we must ask what exactly Marsh is getting at. The answer, as ever, lies in the detectives' lack of that style and verbal panache which so characterises Roderick Alleyn. It is true that Marsh enjoys displaying the curious antipodean *patois* to her cultivated English readers; [as she] explained, 'What is happening is that in a way the English people in these books—or the non-New Zealanders—are in the position of the reader. They're encountering 'New Zealandisms' for the first time and so is the reader.' (pp. 452-54)

Ngaio Marsh once observed that 'Pakeha [or white] New Zealanders cannot be described as a remarkably spiritual people. They are not given to introspection, and generally speaking there is little mysticism in their make-up.' With this ruthlessly accurate summation of her own stock, Marsh pinpointed one source of that conflict of perspectives between Maori and European (most notably concerning the status and ownership of land), and this is a problem which she dramatised very responsibly in *Vintage Murder* and *Colour Scheme*. (p. 455)

[In *Colour Scheme*, the] real trouble starts when Roderick Alleyn presents Carolyn Dacres with a Maori tiki. Her husband Meyer then facetiously bows to the ornament for good luck, and Alleyn whispers to Dr Te Pokiha 'I half regret my impulse.' Te Pokiha's reply is significant: 'So may my great grandparents have laughed over the first crucifix they saw.' Of course, shortly after this scene Meyer is killed and Te Pokiha tells Alleyn 'The tiki is revenged'. . . . Marsh implicitly vindicates the moral order when the sacrilege of *tapu* objects returns with an unexpected irony upon these reckless and obtuse Europeans.

Te Pokiha's account of the initial desecration of the tiki by a European is a damning piece of narrative, and one of his laments about European colonisation is that Maoris 'have become a sideshow in the tourist bureau—our dances—our art—everything.'. . . Can it be that, in spite of her honourable intentions, Marsh herself unwittingly used the Maori element for plot enhancement? The issue seems to focus around Alleyn's instinctive admiration for Te Pokiha, the Oxford-trained, pureblooded Maori aristocrat with 'the most exquisite manners.' Alleyn's attraction to him is undoubtedly founded on respect, but that respect is itself clearly based upon the Doctor's presence and bearing. . . . We have previously heard Te Pokiha summed up by Wade; that although athletic and brainy ('Best type of Maori'), the Doctor is only 'ninety per cent civilised . . . See him when he goes crook!' True to form, Te Pokiha rises to provocation, his lips coarsen 'into a sort of snarl', his teeth are bared like a dog's and the ever-suave Alleyn purrs, 'By Jove, the odd twenty percent of pure savage.' It was this passage of *Vintage Murder* that so enraged Bill Pearson when he wrote about writers (usually not New Zealanders) who showed in their stories 'that all Maoris, no matter how educated, are incomprehensible savages at heart.'

As if to set the record straight, Marsh tried to present a less ambivalent portrait of a Maori *rangitira* in the next New Zealand story, *Colour Scheme*. In this novel Ngaio Marsh exhibits a deep reverence for Rua Te Kahu, a chief of the Te Rarawas. She is less successful at avoiding cliché with his great-granddaughter Huia, the memorable yet vaporous Maori help whose 'voice was as cool and deep as her native forests.' But in the person of Rua, Marsh wishes to create a symbol for the Maori people over a long stretch of time. . . . Rua's father was a *tohunga* who had signed the Treaty of Waitangi and therefore he is a well equipped figure to declaim on his 'children', like the half-caste ('a bad *pakeha*-Maori') Eru Saul. He remarks that

> The reason may put on new garments but the heart and the blood are constant. From the shaft of the weapon there flows an influence darker and more potent than all the *pakeha* wisdom I have stored in my foolish old head.

This is not a piece of subtle racism (it is far less liable to misinterpretation than Alleyn's 'odd twenty per cent of pure savage'), nor is Marsh using the Maori notion of *tapu* as a sensational bit of superstitious supernaturalism. The affair of Questing (his name being suitably ironic), in search of native relics to sell, serves as a deeply critical comment on the cupidity and lack of spiritual values of the European.

In *Died in the Wool* (1944) Marsh renews the attack on the New Zealand accent in the person of Cliff Johns. The novel abounds with accurate transcriptions of the dialect too numerous to detail, however Cliff tells Alleyn of his experiences as the son of a Mackenzie Country farm manager who was nearly 'taken over' by the over-bearing Flossie Rubrick:

> I liked the way she talked. A bit of an English accent. Crisp and clear and not afraid to say straight out what she thought without drawling 'You know' after every other word. . . .

Cliff is pointing to the way many New Zealanders shy away from clear, direct speech and instead speak with an incredible tentativeness which suggests a lack of confidence in the worth and soundness of their opinions. (pp. 455-57)

The broader strategy hones in on the philistinism and utilitarian bias of New Zealanders, as illustrated in Fabian Losse's remark that Cliff was for a time regarded as a 'freak'; that 'In this country, young men are judged almost entirely on their ability to play games and do manual labour.'. . . When examined closely, *Died in the Wool* is a surprisingly subtle novel about the problem of aesthetic values in a young country like New Zealand. . . . *Photo-Finish* (1980) is a less impressive achievement in terms of the New Zealand element. While set near Kumara at Lake Brunner on the West Coast, as one reviewer declared: 'The setting is incidental; it could be anywhere', and it employs New Zealand colloquialisms with an eye to overseas readers. (pp. 457-58)

But the chief New Zealand policeman, Inspector Hazelmere, is presented as a man of undoubted competence and it is quietly noted that there has been a considerable growth in artistic and cultural appreciation in this country since Alleyn's previous visit. . . . It is also highly significant that in this, Marsh's final leave-taking of the land of her birth, she should return to those special memories of *Black Beech and Honeydew* and in prose which exudes an intense and passionate love for [New Zealand]. . . . It was once disparagingly said of that indomitable character, Flossie Rubrick, that she denigrated critical thinking in favour of a mindless patriotism and an unquestioning loyalty to her country. Fortunately Dame Ngaio Marsh never fell victim to that malady, and I believe our national literature is greatly the richer in consequence. (pp. 458-59)

> Bruce Harding, "The New Zealand Stories of Ngaio Marsh," in Landfall, Vol. 36, No. 4, December, 1982, pp. 447-60.

CAROLE ACHESON

The New Zealand author Ngaio Marsh is one of the small number of detective writers whose novels are as popular today as they were when she began writing in the nineteen-thirties, at the height of the fashion for detective stories. With her English contemporaries Agatha Christie and Dorothy Sayers, she has earned a permanent place in the history of detective fiction, and is certainly New Zealand's best known writer. In New Zealand, however, her international reputation is something of an embarrassment. No young country, earnestly struggling to establish a national literature, wants to be known for its detective, rather than its serious, fiction. On the other hand, Marsh's work in the New Zealand theater has been eminently respectable, and she was officially rewarded by having a theater named after her, and an honorary doctorate and the title Dame Commander of the British Empire conferred on her.

Marsh was well aware that her dual career was rather a liability in New Zealand. She commented in her autobiography [*Black Beech and Honeydew*] in 1966:

> Intellectual New Zealand friends tactfully avoid all mention of my published work and if they like me, do so, I cannot but feel, in spite of it.

The truth of this statement is borne out by a review of the autobiography [by Dennis McEldowney in the New Zealand journal *Landfall*]. It is a wonderfully revealing piece which says very little about the quality of the book, but actually amounts to a carping school report on how poorly Marsh measures up as a New Zealand writer:

> She has always contrived to write about New Zealand as though she were a visitor, while believing she was a native. She has usually been conscious of writing for an overseas audience, but this is not the whole explanation. Her people were English gentry, or upper middle class. . . . Her parents may not even have thought of themselves as exiles (after all they gave their daughter a Maori name), but clearly remained English—which was not too hard to do in Christchurch. Ngaio Marsh was an only child, and shy. It is understandable that when she came to write she could report ordinary New Zealand speech and attitudes with rather less authority than cockney.

The charge that Marsh wrote like an Englishwoman rather than a New Zealander is, of course, part of a far more important and complex issue, that of New Zealand's cultural relationship to England.

Historically New Zealand's ties with England have been of the utmost importance. (pp. 159-60)

At the same time New Zealand has been increasingly concerned to establish a separate national identity and to define ways in which New Zealanders differ from the English. The native Maori culture is often used to lend a touch of Polynesian distinctiveness, but this is largely decorative, a matter of songs and crafts for tourists, Maori symbols for the national airline, a war chant acted out before an important rugby game. There is no question of the *pakehas* (Europeans) seriously adapting themselves to Maori culture; quite the reverse. However, New Zealand's colonial history has provided a more significant source of cultural differences from England, derived primarily from the country's origin as a pioneer society and its consequent pride in being egalitarian, in having rejected the English class system. (p. 160)

Beneath the surface of national pride is a constant desire for recognition and approval of New Zealand's progress as an independent young country. In such a context Marsh's unashamedly middle-class, English, artistic background and outspoken comments on her country's shortcomings could hardly fail to arouse hostility. What was acceptable earlier in the century, when New Zealand's cultural debt to Britain was taken for granted, now grates on nationalistic and egalitarian nerves. (pp. 161-62)

Marsh's first four detective novels, published between 1934 and 1936, closely follow the conventions established by such English writers of the thirties as Marjorie Allingham and Dorothy Sayers. All four are murder mysteries set in England and solved by a gentleman detective called Roderick Alleyn. Alleyn differs from other gentlemen detectives of the period in that crime is not his hobby, but his job: he is a professional policeman working at Scotland Yard. His impeccable social background—titled parents, Oxford and the Foreign Office—is an asset in disarming middle and upper-class suspects, but causes some personal conflict: detection is a duty, not a game, and it is not always possible for him to keep his hands clean or indulge private scruples. He conceals his underlying sensitivity behind a fashionably flippant manner, especially with his "Watson," journalist Nigel Bathgate. The novels are written mainly from Nigel's point of view, and the emphasis is primarily on the presentation of evidence and the process of deduction.

The conventions of the genre, and especially the concept of the gentleman detective, must initially have seemed to Marsh to be incompatible with a New Zealand setting. Other detective writers had used foreign settings, such as Paris, the Riviera or the Nile, but these were all well-known resorts for the smart and wealthy, and were endowed with a glamour the reader could enjoy vicariously along with his problem-solving. In any case, the sketchily-drawn foreign background was rarely more than a device to bring together and isolate the usual group of suspects: it was all treated lightly as part of the detection game. But in *Vintage Murder* (1937), Marsh's fifth novel and her first set in New Zealand, Marsh takes the setting very seriously indeed, and incorporates into the murder mystery not only her love for the landscape but a good deal of social comment about her fellow countrymen and the ambivalent relationship between Englishmen and New Zealanders.

Alleyn comes to New Zealand on holiday and shares a train journey with a touring English theater company; the actors later invite him to a birthday party where the host is murdered. When the New Zealand police learn Alleyn's identity, and that he is acquainted with all the suspects, they ask him to work with them on the case. The procedure of investigation is familiar but Alleyn soon realizes that he must consider the crime with reference to English, white New Zealand and Maori values. Because Alleyn is English, and New Zealand is presented from his point of view, Marsh obviously makes the background more accessible to the non-New Zealand reader. But the theme of Alleyn as outsider, a stranger to both the theater group and the New Zealanders, is an integral part of the novel. Alleyn's changing relationship to the landscape also plays an important role in the development and resolution of the plot.

Initially, the landscape serves to emphasize the contrast between the enclosed world of the touring company, interested only in the next theater, and Alleyn's consciousness of being on his own in a new country. . . . After the murder Alleyn finds himself caught between the English suspects, who try to enlist his support, and the New Zealand police. (pp. 163-64)

Nonetheless, Alleyn finds the New Zealanders pleasantly straightforward compared with the actors' self-conscious sophistication and continual role-playing. Convinced that the leading lady, Carolyn Dacres, is withholding vital evidence, Alleyn deliberately takes her away from the theater and out into the reality of the forest. At first Carolyn is "an incongruous figure in her smart dress," but then she begins to respond to the quiet and beauty of the scene. . . . Leaving her time to think, Alleyn walks further into the forest and away from the *pakeha* world, becoming conscious of the alien giant trees and dense tree ferns as a living force, part of the old, primal New Zealand before the coming of the Europeans. Alleyn laughs at himself for mentally "repopulating the bush with wandering Maoris," but the experience leaves him with a heightened sensitivity to Maori culture and values, and is an important aspect of the novel's Maori theme.

With the help of a Maori doctor, Rangi Te Pokiha, Alleyn has bought a greenstone tiki, a small native carving of a human figure usually worn as a pendant. The tiki is not merely an ornament but in Maori mythology the namesake and symbol of Tiki, the first man and father of mankind. By extension it also "represents a human embryo and is the symbol of fecundity." On an impulse Alleyn gives the tiki to Carolyn at her birthday party, and it becomes the object of facetiousness and coarse remarks from many of the actors. . . . The tiki is later found at the place where the murderer set his trap, and there is a hint that Te Pokiha could have committed murder to avenge the insult to the tiki. This solution seems less fantastic as it becomes clear that Te Pokiha is immensely proud of his Maori heritage, and in spite of his own Oxford education feels strongly about the effects of European civilization on his people. . . . Alleyn is sympathetic: through Te Pokiha he comes to appreciate not only the problems of the modern Maori, but the symbolic value of the tiki, which seems to have "a kind of dark wet smell like the native forest." By the end of the novel, although Alleyn still finds New Zealanders "very anxious that one should admire their country, rather on the defensive about it," he has come to understand and share in the Maori affinity to the land, and has "fallen in love . . . with the country altogether."

Vintage Murder is a far more ambitious detective novel than anything Marsh had attempted before, and clearly incorporates many of her responses as a returned expatriate, particularly her feeling for the land, sympathy for the Maoris, and dislike of defensive and self-limiting colonial attitudes. The problem of combining a serious commentary on New Zealand with the stylized format of a detective story is overcome largely by changing the character of Alleyn, and making him the central consciousness of the novel. His former flippancy is dropped: he is now serious and thoughtful, a sensitive observer with a police-trained eye for detail. His personal desire to understand New Zealand and its people is given impetus by the murder investigation, and the usual tension between detective and suspects gains additional depth and interest by the conflict of three cultures. As a result the New Zealand setting is no mere travelogue but a significant and well-integrated element of the story.

Marsh returns to New Zealand in her tenth novel, *Surfeit of Lampreys* (1941), a curious blend of detective story, gothic thriller and comedy of manners. The opening chapters, describing the eccentric upper-class English Lamprey family in New Zealand, and later their New Zealand friend Roberta Grey's arrival in London to stay with them, are largely autobiographical. Much of the humor of the book is derived from practical Roberta's amazement at the Lamprey's total lack of common sense. (pp. 164-66)

While Roberta marvels at the Lampreys' incompetence, she finds their charm and frivolity, the antithesis of colonial earnestness, deeply attractive. She also realizes that whereas she thinks of New Zealand as an extension of England, the English Lampreys find New Zealand an alien place. (p. 166)

When Roberta arrives in England the Lampreys welcome her with a Maori war dance on the wharf, and, as she walks off the ship, a parody of New Zealand self-consciousness: " 'Tell me,' said Henry solemnly, 'what do you think of dear old England?' " Nonetheless Roberta is conscious of a gulf between their London sophistication and her rural New Zealand background. The murder of Lord Charles Lamprey's brother, in circumstances which suggest that one of the family must be responsible, forces Roberta to reappraise the Lampreys. She retains her affection for them, but from a different point of view, as she matures from being a shy colonial impressed by the Lampreys' English urbanity and elegance, into a resolute young woman who perceives how her level-headedness and practicality can assist her friends. . . . Roberta's changing view of the Lampreys is a reflection of the changing relationship between the maturing colony and the mother country, and the novel offers a gentle satire on the expectations with which the English and New Zealanders regard each other. It is a theme which Marsh develops to its fullest and funniest extent three years later in *Colour Scheme* (1943).

Colour Scheme, set in wartime New Zealand, is essentially a comedy of manners in which the murder/detective element serves only to provide a structure and a climax. The leading characters are an English family, the Claires, who like the Lampreys have emigrated to New Zealand for vague and misguided reasons. . . . They work hard at running a spa resort but are incompetent and unbusinesslike. Clinging to Edwardian standards of middle-class gentility, they turn away socially unacceptable customers as often as possible; unsurprisingly, the spa has financial problems. Although Colonel and Mrs. Clair continue to live in an old-fashioned world of their own, their two children have had to cope with growing up in New Zealand, and neither has found a successful compromise between parental and colonial expectations. Barbara, shy and awkward, has chosen to live in middle-class English isolation with her parents; her brother Simon "had attended the Harpoon State schools and, influenced . . . by his schoolfellows' suspicion of 'pommy' [English] settlers, had become truculently colonial, somewhat introverted and defiantly uncouth."

Simon's New Zealand manners grate on all the family, but most severely on his irritable and outspoken uncle, Dr. Ackrington, who has retired from practising medicine in London. Marsh's theater-trained ear for dialogue is at its best in presenting the contrast between Dr. Ackrington's fluent, formal English, Simon's aggressive New Zealand slang, and the easy-going colloquialism of a particularly vulgar guest, Maurice Questing. (pp. 166-67)

The family's attempt to communicate with Questing . . . [on any] issue, such as his proposal of marriage to Barbara, is doomed to failure because they literally do not speak the same language. Colonel Claire and Dr. Ackrington naturally assume an air of authority because that is what their middle-class English education trained them to do. . . . But the English class system means nothing to Questing, who is a successful businessman: by his standards the Claires are simply old-fashioned and foolish. With unshaken confidence in his own social and business abilities, he speaks a worldly-wise idiom composed of English, American and colonial cliches, which does indeed carry him through situations which leave the Claires speechless.

The one character who sympathizes with Questing is another colonial guest, Dikon Bell. Dikon, a cultivated and well-travelled New Zealander, is in a position to appreciate the cultural gap between Questing and the Claires. However, he has his own problems; his recent return to New Zealand has forced him into the expatriate's dilemma of feeling torn between two countries: "Dikon, who longed to be in London, recognized in himself an affinity with this indifferent and profound country, and resented its attraction." Dikon has an equal affinity with his English heritage, especially the theater; this brings him into conflict with Simon, who has adopted the New Zealand stance of finding the arts effeminate. . . . [Simon] is unimpressed by the Englishmen who come to stay at the spa. Their leader is the aged, patrician Rua Te Kahu; the affected, pedantic Septimus Falls, who is actually Alleyn working undercover as a wartime intelligence agent; and Dikon's employer, the distinguished actor Geoffrey Gaunt. (pp. 167-68)

A different cultural point of view is provided by the large cast of Maori characters. In *Vintage Murder* Marsh was anxious to demonstrate the lack of racial discrimination in New Zealand. Perhaps feeling that she had bent over backwards with the scarcely typical Oxonian Dr. Te Pokiha, in *Colour Scheme* she presents a cross-section of the Maori community living near the spa:

> Rua . . . had witnessed the full impact of the white man's ways upon a people living in a stone age. He had in turn been warrior, editor of a native newspaper, and member of Parliament. In his extreme age he had sloughed his European habits and returned to his own sub-tribe. . . .

(pp. 168-69)

The way in which Rua's people have assimilated various aspects of British culture is shown by the Maori concert which is held to honor Geoffrey Gaunt. . . . Gaunt is greeted outside the meeting-house by a ritual Maori welcome; the entertainment includes Maori songs and dances, Irish ballads and Gaunt's recital of speeches from *Henry V* and *Macbeth*. The Maoris, with their strong tradition of oratory, are especially delighted by the Shakespeare. The concert episode emphasizes that the

Maoris who are secure in their own cultural traditions share none of the colonials' ambivalence towards British culture.

In the relationship between Maori and *pakeha* characters it is the Maoris who behave with the greater tolerance and make the more concessions. . . . Even when Rua discovers that a sacred ancestral adze has been stolen by Questing, he compromises his sense of what is due to restore the adze to its former sanctity, and submits to having it held as police evidence. The extent of his sacrifice is not really appreciated by the *pakehas*; Mrs. Claire murmurs, "'Oh dear. One of those *silly* superstitions. Sometimes one almost loses hope. And yet, you know, he's a regular communicant'." Superstition or not, Questing's death in a pool of boiling mud, the tribal legendary fate of those who commit sacrilege, does not strike the Maoris as wholly unexpected.

Although Marsh paints an observant and sympathetic picture of English, colonial and Maori manners in *Colour Scheme,* the tone remains light and amusing. Her next novel, also set in wartime New Zealand, is a complete contrast. *Died in the Wool* (1945) is a somber book and to some extent suffers from taking itself too seriously. In this novel, Marsh extends several themes touched upon in earlier books, particularly the affinity between land and people, and the cultural problems arising from New Zealand's English heritage.

Died in the Wool is set in the foothills of the Southern Alps, on the remote Mount Moon sheep station. Alleyn, still on his mission to find enemy agents, comes to Mount Moon to investigate a report of espionage, possibly linked with the unsolved murder of Flossie Rubrick, the station owner's wife. Alleyn's inquiries increasingly focus on the running of the sheep station and the Rubricks' attitude as landowners, and Mount Moon becomes the central image of the novel, symbolizing the multiple role the sheep station has played in New Zealand's history: bringing settlers to the secluded hill country; making sheep the backbone of the nation's economy; and creating a new landed gentry out of the wealthy station owners.

Although by colonial standards Mount Moon is an impressive old estate, Marsh satirizes its pretensions as both an English stately home and as a triumph of civilization over the wilderness. . . . Mount Moon is ultimately rendered insignificant by the emptiness and magnificence of the mountains surrounding it.

The accounts of Flossie Rubrick which Alleyn hears describe an ambitious, hard-driving member of Parliament who sees the Mount Moon station and its gracious homestead solely as a fitting background for her political career and social status. As a woman representative of a rural constituency, Flossie is asked to write an article on women in the back country. It is a task she promptly hands over to her secretary. . . . Flossie is quite aware of the reality of a woman's life in the back country but is indifferent to it; she has no sense that her position as landowner and politician entails responsibility to the land and its people.

In her role as gracious station owner's wife she has found a protege, Cliff Johns, the musically talented son of her station manager. Cliff's socialist father resents Flossie's interference, but "his wife, persuaded by Flossie, overruled him and Cliff went off to boarding-school with sons of the six runholders scattered over the plateau." At sixteen Cliff rebels, and although Flossie had planned to send him to England to study music, he leaves school and goes to work mustering sheep. Flossie is furious, not least because Cliff has grasped that her real interest is not in himself or his music, but in her own importance as his patron.

Cliff is now unhappily caught between two worlds: that of the Rubricks, British-oriented, well-travelled and appreciative of the arts, in which he is intellectually at home; and that of his parents, narrow, inward-looking, dismissive of the arts, but sincerely attached to him. On his return to Mount Moon it is some time before the other men will accept him as a fellow musterer. . . . (pp. 169-71)

By contrast, Cliff finds in the English visitor Alleyn a sympathetic audience for his views on music: "'That's what I wanted to do. With music, I mean. Say something about this.' He jerked his head at the vastness beyond the window and added with an air of defiance, 'and I don't mean the introduction of native bird song and Maori hakas into an ersatz symphony.'" . . . (p. 171)

In *Died in the Wool* the New Zealand/British relationship is no longer a comedy of manners but a serious issue in the young nation's search for a national identity. To the older generation, like Arthur Rubrick, England still sets the social and cultural standards, modified only slightly to suit New Zealand conditions. The younger generation, like Cliff, are torn between rejection of England's cultural dominance and recognition that New Zealand is not yet able to offer an acceptable alternative. Cliff's decision to muster sheep instead of studying music is, Marsh suggests, only an adolescent gesture of defiance: in maturity, Cliff's generation will help to create a new national culture.

Died in the Wool reflects Marsh's interest in a matter of increasing importance to New Zealanders involved with the arts: the desire to encourage an indigenous culture without lowering the standards set by the parent country. . . . In future, Marsh's comments about New Zealand would appear in essays, reviews and an autobiography, whereas almost all her post-war novels are set in an unreservedly middle-class English world that scarcely notes the existence of the antipodes. Correctly considering that her earnest fellow countrymen had little tolerance for a New Zealand version of an essentially bourgeois, British form of popular writing, Marsh simply rejoined the mainstream of British detective fiction.

Marsh does return briefly to New Zealand themes in her last two novels, though neither *Photo Finish* (1980) nor *Light Thickens* (1982) shows her writing at its best, and both are reworkings of earlier plots. *Photo Finish* is a more superficial version of *Vintage Murder*, with a group of international opera singers substituted for the English theater company. Once again

Alleyn finds the unspoilt New Zealand scenery a refreshing change from the affectations of his suspects; once again there are hints of Maori vengeance which add to the tension without becoming unconvincingly explicit; but the setting is never an integral part of the story as it is in *Vintage Murder.*

Light Thickens is a sequel to *Death at the Dolphin* (1967) and concerns a London production of *Macbeth.* A principal theme in the novel is the effect of superstition, and Marsh portrays this from three points of view: the superstition within *Macbeth;* that of the actors taking part in what is often thought to be an unlucky play; and that of the Maori actor who plays First Witch. London-trained Rangi Western, whose name indicates his dual cultural background, introduces some traditional Maori gestures into his part to emphasize the witches' primitive and savage nature. Gradually he develops qualms about profaning his Maori heritage, which are reinforced by a series of unpleasant incidents culminating in murder. The Maori element is used partly to increase the characters' fear and uncertainty; and partly to illustrate the Maori dilemma of how far it is possible, or even expedient, to retain Maori beliefs in a predominantly *pakeha* world.

It is fitting that Marsh's last two novels should reiterate the main concerns of all her New Zealand fiction: her love for the land and her sympathy for the Maori people, particularly for their difficulties in adapting to an alien culture. She had considerably less sympathy for the *pakehas'* rejection of British culture, and felt nothing but distaste for the self-imposed parochialism resulting from the mixture of complacency and uncertainty she saw in many New Zealanders. (pp. 171-73)

If her presentation of New Zealand speech sometimes reaches an extreme of colloquialism and inarticulacy, and her colonial characters seem unduly Philistine, it is not because, as the reviewer mentioned earlier suggested, her English background limited her to reporting "ordinary New Zealand speech and attitudes with rather less authority than cockney," Marsh, professional writer, actress and producer, had a keen ear and an observant eye, but she was not purporting to write serious, realistic novels. She was a writer of popular fiction who took the opportunity in her books of saying not only what she liked about New Zealand, but of satirizing what she perceived to be its shortcomings, especially those arising from New Zealand's cultural ambivalence to Britain. (p. 173)

Carole Acheson, "Cultural Ambivalence: Ngaio Marsh's New Zealand Detective Fiction," in Journal of Popular Culture, *Vol. 19, No. 2, Fall, 1985, pp. 159-74.*

Bharati Mukherjee

1940-

Indian-born American novelist, short story writer, nonfiction writer, and journalist.

In her fiction, Mukherjee depicts problems faced by Indian and other third world immigrants who attempt to assimilate into North American lifestyles. Using an understated prose style replete with ironic developments and witty observations, Mukherjee focuses upon sensitive protagonists who lack a stable sense of personal and cultural identity and are victimized by racism, sexism, and other forms of social oppression. Several critics have compared her studies of cultural clashes to the works of V. S. Naipaul, while others have noted the influence of Bernard Malamud on her portrayal of minority individuals who have difficulty adapting to their new surroundings.

Much of Mukherjee's fiction is informed by her personal experiences. Born to wealthy parents in Calcutta, India, Mukherjee earned graduate and post-graduate degrees in English at universities in India before enrolling in the University of Iowa Writing Workshop. At Iowa, she met Canadian novelist Clark Blaise; they married and settled in Canada before moving to the United States. In her first novel, *The Tiger's Daughter* (1972), Mukherjee presents a satirical portrait of Indian society from the perspective of Tara Banerjee Cartwright, a young expatriate who is not yet accustomed to American culture yet is estranged from the morals and values of her native land. The daughter of a wealthy Indian industrialist, Tara studies at a United States university and marries a North American. Returning to her homeland to visit her family, Tara expects to find the city she fondly remembers from childhood, but she is shocked by Calcutta's poverty and squalor and by violent political events, which are contrasted with the comfortable lifestyle of her family. John Spurling stated: ''The book's strength and originality come from its author's subtle use of her heroine, the way she is made to register the frailties and contradictions of her ancestral way of life, so that the reader, aware at first only that he is observing somebody disoriented and floundering, gradually discovers that it is not so much she as the world around her that is crumbling.'' *Wife* (1975), Mukherjee's second novel, is a psychological study of Dimple, a young woman from Calcutta who settles in New York with her new husband. Raised to be passive and dependent according to traditional Indian standards of femininity, Dimple lacks the inner resources to cope with the fear and alienation that she experiences in New York, and she gradually descends into psychotic violence. In this work, Mukherjee depicts the disorienting and dehumanizing effects of urban American society and indicts Indian cultural values that discourage self-reliance in women.

In the introduction to her first short story collection, *Darkness* (1985), Mukherjee charges that deep-rooted racism in Canadian society fosters hostility between the nation's white majority and various ethnic subcultures. The stories in this volume serve to illustrate Mukherjee's argument. In "Tamurlane," for example, an Indian cook who has been maimed in a racial attack remains in Canada despite continual threats and the assurance of a safer environment in the United States. As in several other stories in this collection, confrontations between Indians and whites result in bizarre and violent acts. While *Darkness* fo-

cuses primarily on the problems of Indians in North America, Mukherjee's next collection, *The Middleman and Other Stories* (1988), which won the National Book Critics Circle Award, portrays the experiences in the United States of immigrants from Europe, the Caribbean, and other parts of Asia as well as India. Some of these tales are related from the perspective of white Americans, and the volume as a whole chronicles both the experiences of third world people adjusting to a new culture and the reactions of members of their adopted society. Polly Shulman noted: ''In Mukherjee's books, everyone is living in a new world, even those who never left home. As traditions break down, the characters must try to make lives out of the pieces.''

In addition to her fiction, Mukherjee has written two nonfiction works in collaboration with Clark Blaise. *Days and Nights in Calcutta* (1977; revised, 1986) chronicles a year-long visit that the couple made to India, while *The Sorrow and the Terror: The Haunting Legacy of the Air India Tragedy* (1987) is a journalistic account of the crash of an Air India jet off the coast of Ireland in 1985.

(See also *Contemporary Authors*, Vol. 107 and *Dictionary of Literary Biography*, Vol. 60.)

MARTIN LEVIN

After several years on American campuses the daughter of a Calcutta tobacco potentate returns for a summer to her native city. Tara Banerjee Cartwright [the heroine of *The Tiger's Daughter*] has acquired a degree, an American husband and the makings of dissertation on Katherine Mansfield. None of these is adequate preparation for re-entry into the Brahmin *beau monde*—which, in the author's reflective eye, is reminiscent of the *Cherry Orchard* syndrome. Tara's daddy, known to family and friends as "The Bengal Tiger," belongs to a mercantile aristocracy with its roots in the age of Victoria. This chauffeured, unimaginably-cosseted upper crust is threatened from within by aggressive "new men" of the stripe Chekhov characterized so well in Lopakhin, and from without by militant hordes of the destitute.

Miss Mukherjee's heroine is a perfect instrument for recording the mutations of her time: sensitive, observant and almost spongelike in relation to experience, she is one of those protagonists to whom things happen.... I suspect that Tara's passage to India is a better barometer for 1972 than most of the alleged nonfiction pouring from the presses.

> *Martin Levin, in a review of "The Tiger's Daughter," in* The New York Times Book Review, *January 2, 1972, p. 16.*

J.R. FRAKES

It may seem frivolous, at this moment, for a reviewer to recommend this beautiful novel of contemporary India [*The Tiger's Daughter*] seen through the eyes of a sensitive and confused daughter of Bengali Brahmins returned from a 7-year sojourn in the United States for a holiday with her wealthy family. And yet this is surely much more than conventional "return of the expatriate" fiction, structured on the familiar pattern of trembling expectation, shock of unrecognition, episodic disillusionment, and final sad acceptance of one's alien position between two worlds. The form may be similar, but the substance is freshly complex and enlightening. The comedy is certainly here—brought off with economy and understatement—but beneath its surface lie bitter truth and dread.

As in Forster's *A Passage to India,* the serio-comedy is based largely on disproportion, imbalance, incongruity: Calcutta debutantes swooning over Johnny Mathis, Natalie Wood, and Bob Wagner while children eat rice and yoghurt off the sidewalk; the new manager of a Darjeeling hotel—trained at Cornell—hoping to turn it into a "fun place."

Despite her training at Vassar and Wisconsin, 22-year-old Tara Banerjee Cartwright is not really capable of serving as bridge between these worlds, especially as she witnesses the collapse of all cultural verities in her patrician family and giddy young friends. More and more it seems as if her liberal American husband, who has stayed home, is right in seeing Calcutta as "the collective future in which garbage, disease, and stagnation are man's estate" and in warning her that a bloody caste-and-class struggle is on the way. This witty, charming, ominous novel ends with Tara locked inside a car while a violent revolutionary demonstration surges through the Calcutta streets.

> *J.R. Frakes, in a review of "The Tiger's Daughter," in* Book World—The Washington Post, *January 9, 1972, p. 2.*

PETER S. PRESCOTT

[In *The Tiger's Daughter*, Bharati Mukherjee] has written a novel about a girl named Tara Banerjee, born in Calcutta, sent to Vassar for an education and married to an American. It is really a very nice novel, built on understated irony and wit.

Tara returns to Calcutta, without her husband. She wants to see her family, her city, her friends again; she wants to recapture what she once knew, seven years earlier when she left at age 15. We never learn why her husband did not come with her, but the novel profits from his absence: obvious cultural conflicts are avoided, and Tara regains her innocence, this time an innocence of disassociation. She looks at her own country, at the misery she had once ignored, and is appalled: "How does the foreignness of the spirit begin?" she wonders. (p. 79)

In time, Tara comes to hate Calcutta for its misery, for its children scrabbling for food from the sidewalks, yet she envies her former life "that was more stable, more predictable" than the life she knew in America. Her friends, Tara thinks, are invulnerable to reality, and yet she herself has changed: "The years away from India had made her self-centered." Perhaps there is nothing to be done. The Brahmins have always removed themselves from the misery around them, from the children falling asleep or dead at their gates.

Tara is familiar; like so many heroines in fiction of feminine and vaguely British orientation, she is bright, elegant, alert and ironic—and with much to learn. Above all, she is vulnerable: not because she is stupid or vulgar or imperceptive, but because she finds herself alienated from the naïveté and callousness of those she loves. Boredom is the affliction of her accustomed world, but she cannot be bored; revolution is about to overtake it, but she cares for the revolutionaries. Her understanding of her situation is above all complex: "The misery of her city was too immense and blurred to be listed and assailed one by one . . . it was fatal to fight for justice." So Tara thought. She began by withdrawing from her companions on a train; she ends by huddling in a car that is being stoned by a mob. It is all very neat—too neat, perhaps, in that Miss Mukherjee tends to repeat delicate points that she has already made—but the wit is dry and the perceptions acute. More people would like this book than are likely to read it. (p. 80)

> *Peter S. Prescott, "Lives of a Bengal Lady," in* Newsweek, *Vol. LXXIX, No. 3, January 17, 1972, pp. 79-80.*

THE TIMES LITERARY SUPPLEMENT

For once, the publishers have hit on some apposite adjectives in describing [*The Tiger's Daughter*] as an "elegant first novel", and referring to Bharati Mukherjee's "quizzical" and "off-centre" vision of her native Calcutta. For Miss Mukherjee, like her heroine Tara, left behind a Brahmin family to study in the United States, married an American, and is now Assistant Professor of English at McGill University....

So it is no surprise to the reader although apparently to Tara—who has left her amiably liberal husband behind to write his novel—that the Calcutta she revisits to see her family and smart ex-convent contemporaries provide some pretty depressing shocks....

Tara's westernization has opened her eyes to the gulf between two worlds that still makes India the despair of those who govern it. This is really all that Miss Mukherjee succeeds in saying, but because she controls her emotions with such a skilled balance of irony and colourful nostalgia her novel is charming and intelligent—and curiously unmoving. . . .

Miss Mukherjee is very funny at the expense of the ambivalent snobberies of Tara's contemporaries. Arranged marriages? Perfectly acceptable within their elitist families, although Tara, by daring to choose an American husband, is an admired curiosity. And their peculiar Indian-English idiom—the immediate popularity of Tara's new Americanisms combined with Victorian genteelisms—offers splendid scope for some very funny dialogue. "'You are not satisfied with Pronob's eyemaking?'" says gossipy Reena. "'You want him to be downright lecherous. My God! You are a real fuss-pot.'"

There are elaborate picnics, visits to the shrines that Tara's mother values in spite of her daughter's embarrassment, discussions with the Tiger—a big, simple, handsome father figure—moments of fear and anguish when David's letters make America seem a million miles away, and the bizarre visit of a dazzling Black Panther called McDowell, who deserts his hosts for the "other side" of penniless students. Finally there is what perhaps Tara has subconsciously been waiting for throughout her disturbing stay—a political riot, when the rightist leader who thought she was modern enough to share his hotel room provokes the mob, with its soda bottles and bam-boo sticks, to attack the Catelli Continental.

Yet because Tara herself has remained so ineffectual a focus of distress and is so unwilling a catalyst, it is hard to care whether or not she will be able to return to her cosy hamburger husband. The flashbacks to old Tiger's heritage, the bewilderment of his fat, saintly wife, and the snatches of poetry which, like Cassandra's utterances, echo as the old tea-planter is trampled—all these suggest that Miss Mukherjee's elegant heart is moved by the past, but that Tara's own divided sympathies will do little for any future India.

> *"Oh, Calcutta!" in* The Times Literary Supplement, *No. 3721, June 29, 1973, p. 736.*

JOHN SPURLING

In tackling, in her first novel, the decline of a whole way of life—that of the Bengali Brahmins—Bharati Mukherjee has taken the risk of contributing merely another tract to the endless discussion of what can be done about India. She has actually achieved something more in the tradition of *Buddenbrooks* or *The Leopard*. *The Tiger's Daughter* (the title perhaps a deliberate reference to Lampedusa's novel) is less grand in scale, its vision less dynamic than either of those books, its tone of voice less ironic than Mann's, less melancholic than Lampedusa's, but like them it is a true imaginative exploration of a class in decay rather than a sociological description. The heroine is a young Brahmin who, living in the United States and married to an American, returns to visit her parents in Calcutta. The book's strength and originality come from its author's subtle use of her heroine, the way she is made to register the frailties and contradictions of her ancestral way of life, so that the reader, aware at first only that he is observing somebody disoriented and floundering, gradually discovers that it is not so much she as the world around her that is crumbling.

For this reason many of the fine set scenes—a visit to a slum, a walk by the funerary banks of the river, a picnic by a swimming-pool, a dance in a Darjeeling hotel during the summer season in the hills—seem to begin as random episodes but

unfold slowly in retrospect as sombre portents, places on the road to a catastrophe whose climax is still only heralded at the end of the novel with the brutal death of one of the heroine's childhood friends at the hands of a mob of rioters. But Bharati Mukherjee also has a sense of humour: witness her ear for Indian English ('I'm Joyonto Roy Chowdhury, fast friend of your daddy') and the scene in which a young American visitor to the enclosed world of the Brahmins turns out to be a revolutionary-minded Negro with an Afro hair-style.

> John Spurling, *"Losing Caste," in* New Statesman, *Vol. 86, No. 2207, July 6, 1973, p. 26.*

KRISHNA BALDEV VAID

Bharati Mukherjee's extraordinary second novel [*Wife*] transcends its ostensible occasion on the wings of its excoriating irony and its luminously icy insights. (p. 155)

Being, essentially, a mimetic novel, *Wife* invites the traditional test of plausibility and verisimilitude and passes it without a question. With strict economy and corrosive humor, it portrays its milieu—the mildewed middle class life of Calcutta in Part One and the morbidly materialistic Indian ghetto of New York City in Parts Two and Three—with an admirable richness of implication and in memorable scenes. It catches all the conversational clichés and social inanities it cares to. It offers a variety of vapid characters and engages our interest in them. For her pathetic but puerile protagonist, Bharati Mukherjee reserves a special style and tone consisting of closeness and distance in appropriate measure so that Dimple wins our attention and sympathy despite our distaste for her emptiness—she is a victim of circumstance, as well as her own inner inanities.

Another important aspect of this novel is its refusal to be relegated to the category of those Indo-Anglian novels that are out to sell their exotic trash in the foreign market. Bharati Mukherjee makes no concessions to the so-called common but curious foreign reader who resorts to novels about India primarily for acquiring spurious information about that "fascinating" place and its "strange" people. Such novels are unnecessary and outrageous. They are often dispensable as history and always mediocre as art. *Wife* is good because it is good artistically and not because it offers any *information* about India. It also avoids another familiar flaw of the Indo-Anglian novel: it does not seek to concoct a putatively Indian English, which is often unreadable, under the pretense of adjusting Indian speech rhythms to an un-Indian medium. This is not to say that it doesn't have its Indian flavor, but this flavor is not phony.

Having regarded it as an impressive novel, however, I wish to indicate an area where *Wife* does not fulfill the expectations it initially arouses. Since it straddles two huge cities, and by implication two huge countries, one is tempted to look for a greater variety of international comparisons and contrasts in manners as well as morals. One keeps hoping for signs of an Indian Henry James. Since, again, it is the story of a crackup in exile, one wishes that the novelist had probed the larger matter of anguish and terror inevitable in an alien environment. Perhaps, Bharati Mukherjee couldn't have explored this area through a character like Dimple. Perhaps, in a sense, it is good that she does not introduce boredom and exile as major themes in *Wife*. Perhaps, it was never her intention to make more than a tentative statement about the confrontation of India and America. But one can't help thinking that had she done so, the transcendence mentioned earlier would have been greater and the novel richer. And one can't help hoping that in her future work, Bharati Mukherjee will put her exceptional powers as a stylist and her acute insights into disinherited minds to a more daring use and set more difficult, less mimetic, goals for herself. (pp. 156-57)

Krishna Baldev Vaid, in a review of ''Wife,'' in fiction international, *No. 4/5, 1975, pp. 155-57.*

DIANE JOHNSON

You may have noticed Indian wives, at the market or movie, always looking rather cold in their thin saris, Acrilan sweaters, ankle socks and tennis shoes. You may or may not have thought about them and wondered what they talk about among themselves, but after you read [*Wife*] you will know, and it will give you pause. It is a funny but upsetting account of the conflict of western and Indian cultures, and of modern and old-fashioned traditions of female destiny, as embodied in the life of Dimple Dasgupta, and told with a kind of deadpan comic ferocity that partakes both of the tradition of the English novel of manners and of the fatalism of India.

At the beginning, at home in Calcutta, Dimple is dreaming about marrying—anybody—but preferably a neurosurgeon, and her father is combing the matrimonial ads for an engineer. . . . She is 20 and already afflicted with signs of passive anger. The tension between her actual powerlessness and forms of freedom suggested to her by the changing Indian culture have made her sick. She reads *The Doctrine of Passive Resistance* for her university exams and expects to employ domestic passive resistance, for instance withholding affection, to win the love of the unknown husband, who is the only hope of adult freedom she has. She is so depressed about her flat chest she thinks of suicide.

At last a matrimonial candidate is found, Amit Basu, a consulting engineer, who is ideal in that he has already applied for emigration. . . . Amit is an earnest young man, even a considerate one by the standards of Indian masculinity, but Dimple has lived so long in a fantasy world of advertising and advice columns, that she is emotionally incapable of understanding another human being, and she cannot understand Amit or try to. . . .

The young couple emigrate to New York, and Dimple must adjust to a whole new set of circumstances amid violence and high-rise isolation. Amit, preoccupied with economic realities, is little comfort. They meet other Indians who have adjusted to or reacted to America in startling ways—have taken to wearing blue jeans and short hair, and associating with Americans. Her friends try to encourage her to take up various activities, but she is afraid to leave her apartment, and begins sleeping all day and suffering from insomnia at night. She disapproves of the unbecoming candor and fast western ways of the other women but is too Indian to complain of the increasing disorder of her inner life, sliding into madness with such docility it is hardly noticed. Certainly Amit doesn't take it seriously enough; in his mind only pampered American women have ''breakdowns.'' He explains that she is having culture shock.

This is true in part and the influence of American culture is significant. She was already a victim of her own, caught in a tradition of passivity, female treachery and covert violence; here she learns to turn it outward. Her powerlessness and small acts of cruelty typify women in many societies at some point

in history. She lies, smiles, moons around flushed with her own fantasies, but she always has dinner ready on time. She kills a mouse, flushes goldfish down the toilet. She soothes herself with a litany: nine ways to die—and if she had remained in India she would have committed suicide. In America, she commits murder.

The author, Bharati Mukherjee, has a fine ironic eye for the very details of American life that engross Dimple—television, pizza, plastic flowers, parties. But her strokes are more cutting when she draws Indians themselves. She mocks their confusion and ambivalence, and it is mockery that is serious and deep, though it seems only to concentrate on details of dress and social behavior. . . . One guesses that Bharati Mukherjee finds quite unforgivable in Indians any tendency to be intimated by or attracted to the artifacts and mores of American culture.

It is a scary story, told with malice and charm, and through it one becomes somehow better acquainted with Indians than before. The Indian middle class seen in the horrible muddle of our own society becomes more real and sympathetic than ever it does in those idylls or tragedies of Indian village life or elaborate sagas concerning mothers-in-law. Their plight, in particular the plight of Dimple and the other women, sheds a sinister half-light on our own condition.

Diane Johnson, ''A Sari Predicament,'' in Book World—The Washington Post, *May 18, 1975, p. 3.*

LINDA SANDLER

Television is this year's villain, and sociologists are assembling a formidable amount of evidence to show that TV has replaced the devil and human greed as the first cause of social evil. But no form of technology can be studied in isolation from the rest of society, and it sometimes takes an outlander or a novelist to show why. Bharati Mukherjee is both, and she has an extraordinarily subtle grasp of the effects of the media and the causes of violence—and how they interrelate. Her novel *Wife* is the rarest kind of book, combining artistry, humor, and cultural diagnosis. It's the story of Dimple Basu, romantic wife of a Bengali engineer, who is translated with catastrophic suddenness from Calcutta to New York, where she experiences the psychic dislocation we call ''future shock.'' Dimple emigrates to the electronic age with her traditional values almost intact, only partly modified by the pop culture of modern Calcutta. She is unable to make the transition from Before to After, and chooses violence as a ''problem-solving'' device. . . .

Mukherjee's first novel, *The Tiger's Daughter,* was published and extremely well received in the U.S. in 1971. The style of humour and the cultural ironies in the book recall another story of the returned exile, *Too Long in the West* by Balachandra Rajan. But Mukherjee's action is far more intense; and although her heroine shares much of her own sensibility, she treats her with toughness. (p. 75)

The Tiger's Daughter is an extraordinary book, with material enough for three novels. In *Wife,* Mukherjee simplifies and sharpens her focus. She reverse the pilgrimage, journeying from East to West, she confronts personal and social violence head on, and she splits her complex self into sharp facets, creating characters who shatter like glass.

Dimple Dasgupta is the most unstable of dreamers—she daydreams. She entertains movie stars, she walks through fire for love; and because she takes the myths of her culture for literal truths, life is always betraying her. Marriage, which should bring her freedom, cocktail parties, and love, brings her instead a marriage contract with Amit Basu, an engineer who lacks the wealth and inclination for high life and passion. Under the passive posture of Amit's wife, there is a considerable accretion of violence: Dimple lives with her fermenting frustrations and puts her faith in the New World.

Violence is Dimple's fundamental experience of New York. Newspapers, car radios, and casual conversations announce murders in alleys and ice cream parlours. When the fun of parties and new friends wears off, Dimple finds herself stranded in a fully furnished, fully applianced apartment in Greenwich Village, terrified of the city outside. She kills time in the style familiar to anyone who has been a student or unemployed, watching soap operas and Johnny Carson, gradually losing the ability to separate fantasy from event. Television introduces her to love, middle-American style. Amit, she sees, has betrayed her. In Calcutta he had been an emblem of strength; now he seems weak and vulnerable. He has none of the features of TV heroes, and he is preventing her from metamorphosing from obedient wife into independent Westerner. (pp. 75-6)

Mukherjee develops her theme, the North American education of Dimple, with complex irony and skill, transforming cultural symbols into the surreal images of Dimple's final madness, where television becomes the voice of conscience in her head. But Mukherjee makes it clear that television doesn't make an eagle out of a dove—like most people, Dimple has a subterranean streak of violence. She is uprooted from her family and her familiar world, and projected into a social vacuum where the media become her surrogate community, her global village. New York intensifies her frustrations and unhooks her further from reality: she kills easily, like a sleepwalker.

Wife is the story of a woman who is trapped between two cultures, and who aspires to a third, imagined world. Living in her social vacuum, Dimple is not unlike hundreds of American men and women who believe and are betrayed by the promise of fulfilment offered by the media, and who choose the solution suggested by a violent environment. The meaning of *Wife* goes far beyond its title theme, and the book carries frightening implications about North American society. It suggests that there is a vacuum where once was society, and that violence becomes increasingly ordinary where there is no anchoring community. The global village, as Mukherjee perceives, is a territory where sleepwalkers enact subliminal drives. (p. 76)

Linda Sandler, "Violence as a Device for Problem-Solving," in Saturday Night, Vol. 90, No. 5, October, 1975, pp. 75-6.

GEORGE WOODCOCK

Bharati Mukherjee gives the whole matter of assimilation and multiculturalism a different twist in the introduction to her book of stories, *Darkness*. It is a bitter little piece of writing, and how much of it comes from the writer's temperament and how much from experience one must leave the reader to judge. She tells how in Canada she thought of herself as an "expatriate" because she saw "immigrants" to Canada as "lost souls, put upon and pathetic." She says that "the country is hostile to its citizens who had been born in hot, moist continents like Asia; that the country proudly boasts of its opposition to the whole concept of cultural assimilation," and she even accuses "the nation," by which she presumably means the government,

of "officially" inciting its citizens to "react against" the "visible minority." (pp. 150-51)

Bharati Mukherjee's really important accusation is that "the country proudly boasts its opposition to the whole concept of cultural assimilation." By this she is presumably . . . expressing her opposition to multiculturalism and by implication embracing assimilation. . . . This impression is reinforced by her feeling, on departing to the United States, of moving "away from the aloofness of expatriation, to the exuberance of immigration." Clearly she immersed herself with relief and gladness in the great melting pot, which many of us have not found so welcoming.

This sense of a will to sink into an alien culture, as distinct from remaining a member of a self-conscious minority in a more pluralist society like Canada inspired many of the stories that are collected in *Darkness*. In all but one, the central, experiencing character is of Indian or other South Asian origin, and the basic problems are those of making contact, and of learning the right behavioural signs that will transform one from a "not quite" into a member of that bland and prosperous American society whose inhabitants Mukherjee presents with a strange mixture of envy and contempt.

The agonies of the "not quites" are sometimes terrible, yet they are not without hope, and this is essentially the difference between the stories Mukherjee writes about America and those she writes about Canada. "Tamurlane," tells of a fatal encounter between Asian illegals and Canadian police and immigration officers, is the most terrible story in the book, and the best, because it arouses the most genuine passion. Its anger marks it off from most of the other stories with their social knowingness and their bittersweet ironic tone. It is not accidental that Mukherjee has won major journalism awards (Canadian ones, be it noted by those who take over-literally her accounts of being rejected here) for her stories; they are in fact very good magazine fiction, provocative in tone but not experimental enough to be difficult reading, and—with two or three exceptions—not wiry enough to stand up well to collection. It is surprising she has not yet appeared in the *New Yorker*. But she will, I am sure, and there she may find the great good American place for which she longs. Personally, I think it is a pity she is lost to Canada; stories like "Tamurlane" are full of threats and promises, and the conflict of Canada might have brought them out more formidably than the content of American acceptance. (pp. 151-52)

George Woodcock, "Mulberry Bush," in Canadian Literature, No. 107, Winter, 1985, pp. 149-52.

PATRICIA BRADBURY

Bharati Mukherjee thinks Canada is a very frightening place—more frightening than unknown islands in revolution. In her short story "The World According to Hsü," the protagonist, Ratna, is not afraid of the violence that keeps her and other guests locked inside their holiday island hotel. She is fearful of Toronto, where she might have to live. "A week before . . . a Bengali woman was beaten and nearly blinded on the street. And the week before that an eight-year-old Punjabi boy was struck by a car announcing on its bumper: KEEP CANADA GREEN. PAINT A PAKI." "In Toronto, she was not Canadian, not even Indian," as she is on the island and almost everywhere else. "She was something called, after the imported idiom of London, a Paki. And for Pakis, Toronto was hell."

In 1980, after 14 years of living in Canada and after having taken out citizenship here, Bharati Mukherjee emigrated to the United States. In a *Saturday Night* article, she bitterly declared why. Now, five years later, with her short-story collection *Darkness,* she is declaring why again.

"Canadians are mean as hell," says a character who's been attacked in the short story **"Isolated Incidents."** "I don't know about that," responds a human-rights officer. "If this had happened in New York, you'd have been left for dead." "Correction," the victim's lawyer quickly intervenes. "If this had happened in New York, he'd have been mugged for his money, not racially assaulted."

Violence in America, Mukherjee implies, is ubiquitous and terrible, but at least it's democratic. It offers her and others a bizarre kind of freedom. Nobody is singled out.

Her anger about Canada, which has not waned a bit, and her heightened energy from her stay in the U.S. have vitalized this extraordinary group of stories. With the swift eye and language of a North Americanized Naipaul, she offers us material that feels vividly new.

Mukherjee is a master at suddenly twisting a tale's end so that the narrative collapses with a devastating blow. **"Tamurlane"** is a powerful example of this. Gupta, a tandoor chef in a restaurant that employs mostly illegal immigrants, is crippled from being pushed in front of a Toronto subway train. The illegals he works with have a system of hiding places in case of a sudden raid. They divide the world not into Hindu and Moslem, but into those who have papers and those who do not.

In the restaurant, Gupta is being encouraged to go to the States by an enthusiastic sponsor. The U.S. is another location in which to hide, where "those who can run, do". Gupta, the chef, refuses to yield his ground even when a raid sends everyone else scattering. Leaning against a counter to support his crippled legs, he orders the threatening Mounties out of his kitchen. The horrifying scene that follows resolves itself in a swift but violent struggle that is a ruthless and tragic mockery of his decision to remain in Canada. . . .

The poison, the battles, the agonizing confusion of selves that plague most of these characters, these "not-quites" in American society, are ultimately as brutal as a racial assault. Melting into America opens devastating wounds. As Mukherjee has stated in her introduction, Indianness becomes a metaphor for a partial and, therefore, painful understanding.

Mukherjee's prose is tight and sure-footed, except in the story **"Angela."** "Angela" suffers from an overabundance of characters and from what seems to be a name-dropping of modern issues: Nicaragua, the plight of farmers, the series of rapes in day-care centres. These rob the story of its strongest points: a hospital vigil and the courtship of a Dr. Menezies. In these *Darkness* tales pain usually comes to the characters who bring too much India to America. And this India seems to rise as success peters out. . . .

The final story, a lyrical description of an Indian miniature painting which shows an emperor at the head of an imposing army, leaving his beautiful city, provides a central metaphor for the book. Without this emperor, this vigorous and traditional unifier, the city will be ruined by outsiders. "Give me total vision," the leader asks his artist. "Hide nothing from me . . . Tell me how my . . . capital . . . will turn to dust . . . but tell it to me in a way that makes me smile. Transport me

through dense fort walls and stone grilles and into the hearts of men."

Through these lines, Bharati Mukherjee could be addressing her writer's self. She is listening for America singing, she says, and hears it in the exuberance and psychic chaos of immigration. She is showing identities slowly breaking into pieces, cracked open by raw and totally alien dreams. But she always shows this with artistic grace and with the unstated promise that identities, in new and unimaginable moulds, will soon be rebuilt again.

> *Patricia Bradbury, "Mukherjee Draws Tales from Fear in the Streets of Toronto," in* Quill and Quire, *Vol. 51, No. 8, August, 1985, p. 43.*

ANITA DESAI

One can hardly pay higher tribute to Bharati Mukherjee's collection of short stories, so bleak and aptly called *Darkness,* than to say that everywhere in them are echoes of V. S. Naipaul. . . .

The resemblance is nowhere so great as in one of the two finest stories in this collection, **"The World According to Hsü."** It could have been written by him, this tale of an estranged couple's visit to an island off the coast of Africa suddenly struck by a coup and curfew; it has the same grey melancholy, the same way of picking out the telling detail. . . . (p. 143)

There is a scene at the end in which the motley tourists, confined to the seedy hotel dining room by curfew, dine while listening to each other's conversations and even participating in them. 'Ratna had ordered "The National Dish". She found it a concoction of astonishing crudity.' A touch of sophistication is lent by 'An acceptable red wine—surprising, eh, from such a place?' The worldly-wise Ratna is not surprised and points out 'It used to be French . . . At least the French left palpable legacies, despite the profound underdevelopment.' Then, when her husband defies the curfew and stumbles out to search for the Southern Cross,

> she saw that the label on the bottle read: *Côte de Cassandre.* A superior red table wine that no one had ever heard of: perhaps the lone competent industry on the island . . . She poured herself another glass, feeling for the moment at home in that collection of Indians and Europeans babbling in English and remembered dialects. No matter where she lived, she would never feel so at home again.

This is the point where the two diverge: Naipaul is not merely the expatriate; he is superior to all expatriates, he stands without their circle and is their pained but nevertheless cruel observer; Bharati Mukherjee is an observer too, just as clever, but the superiority is false for she is actually a victim. Naipaul would never have 'felt at home'—to be so would have dealt the death blow to his writing. Mukherjee, with a womanly instinct, ducks into the nearest loophole and proceeds to make herself comfortable.

The other of her two best stories, **"Saints,"** displays the extent to which she has made herself comfortable in what must once have been an entirely alien culture. Although the chief character is a little boy with the grotesque name, Shawn Patel, which betrays his racially grotesque ancestry, there is little in it of the expatriate's bewilderment. It is a perfectly realized piece of work. Here she is in total command of her material and its idiom, and she catches to near-perfection the American tone, the American hysteria, the American *angst.*

It is a mastery that has not been easily won, she explains in her introduction, or without sacrifice. She describes her years as a member of a minority community in a cold, white land, Canada, 'hostile to its citizens who had been born in hot, moist continents like Asia . . . the country proudly boasts of its opposition to the whole concept of cultural assimilation. In the Indian immigrant community I saw a family of shared grievances. The purely "Canadian" stories in this collection were difficult to write and even more painful to live through'. (pp. 144-45)

In her ironic tone, just edged with bitterness, her sharpness of observation, the elegance of both her style and her attitude, somewhat world-weary and cynical, with an undercurrent of genuine pain, she seems close to another woman writer of the continent, Joan Didion. The fact that one can compare the two shows the extent of her success in 'assimilation'. There are of course differences—Mukherjee does not indulge in the bizarre or the voluptuous that Didion luxuriates in, and Didion would have taken good care to keep away from a world as seedy, as sordid as that occupied by Mukherjee's characters. Bharati Mukherjee's world is a small box-apartment that smells of curry and in which her characters—shady accountants, Trinidad-Indian hookers, successful executives, professors, domestics and busboys—live their squalid lives under great pressure, erupting frequently into violence, emerging with the oily sheen of new money upon them and wearing that as justification for all their humiliations. Not that Mukherjee embraces them even if she insists, in her introduction, that 'I see *myself* in these same outcasts'; she is sufficiently detached—perhaps too detached—from the orthodox Indian father who, on discovering his daughter, an electrical engineer, in the throes of morning sickness, brought on not by dalliance with an American boy—'Bob, John, Jimmy or Tom'—but with a bottle, a syringe and a donor's sperm, raises that traditional Indian weapon, the rolling pin; from **"The Lady from Lucknow"** who lolls on her lover's bed, acknowledging 'I was just another involvement of a white man in a pokey little outpost, something that "men do" and then come to their senses while the memsahibs drink gin and tonic and fan their faces'; from the illegal cooks and waiters in an Indian restaurant, barricading themselves against inevitable discovery and expulsion. Detachment seems necessary to her art; the stories like **"Visitors"** and **"Nostalgia"** that one guesses are closest to her own milieu and experience are the least interesting, lacking both weight and shape and betraying somewhat repellent vanity and self-indulgence.

Like any observer, she needs to remove herself, to place some distance between herself and the observed in order to achieve the correct perspective. Unfortunately, her ear for Indian speech is poor; her imaginary dialogues come off best; when she attempts realism she merely succeeds in parodying it.

It is a little surprising therefore to learn, from her introduction, that she feels a kinship with, of all writers, Bernard Malamud. Having moved away from 'the aloofness of expatriation, to the exuberance of immigration', she says she 'joined imaginative forces with an anonymous, driven underclass . . . I see my "immigrant" story replicated in a dozen American cities, and instead of seeing my Indianness as a fragile identity to be preserved against obliteration (or worse, a "visible" disfigurement to be hidden) I see it now as a set of fluid identities to be celebrated', and she sees Malamud's stories 'as part of the same celebration'. She does not see that it cannot be so:

her material is not so tractable, not so accessible to universal tones and simply not in the same class of human tragedy as that to which his Jewish characters belong. This is not her failing but her misfortune: the furtive Indian, uneasy in the sophisticated West, made base by his greed for a share of America's affluence, does not belong with the driven Jew and his sole sanctuary. What is so stirringly human in Malamud's stories is replaced by something essentially uneasy and the tone of Mukherjee's book is wry, not rich and vibrant and glowing as in Malamud's work. Malamud's characters have enriched American literature, his prose has given it new sounds and resonances; the Indian tongue as reproduced by Mukherjee is unlikely to do anything like that for the American language— it may distort, bend and mispronounce, it may bring in that despised 'sing-song' but it cannot be said to have enriched. What Bharati Mukherjee has done, and done admirably, is to stand witness, with honesty, with clear-sightedness and with remarkable distinction. (pp. 145-46)

Anita Desai, "Outcasts," in London Magazine, *n.s. Vol. 25, Nos. 9 & 10, December, 1985 & January, 1986, pp. 143-46.*

HOPE COOKE

In the story **"The World According to Hsü"** (which seems closest to the actual biography of the author, a Bengali immigrant married to a Canadian) a woman vacationing in a tourist island paradise undergoing a revolution listens to her husband read about geology and feels "with effort she might become an expert on the plate tectonics of emotion." In this superb collection of short stories, *Darkness,* Bharati Mukherjee writes of the tearing off of old selves, the collisions of Eastern and Western lives, the wrinkling up of new forms of identity.

The characters Miss Mukherjee describes include maharajas, illegal alien busboys and a bayonet-scarred refugee who sits straight and elegant in an American parlor playing the piano, her erectness "one more civility that makes the immense, snowy Midwest less alarming, less ambiguous."

The newcomers' feelings about the West span a spectrum from marooned expatriation to exuberant identification to momentary nostalgia for old homes. The stories are complex, ironic, uncondescending to expectation. . . .

Several of the stories, particularly those written in Canada, where, the author tells us in a bitter preface, anti-Asian sentiment is not uncommon, deal with the power of politics and society to bruise immigrant lives. The strength of the collection, however, comes from an accumulation of privately realized, often partly blindly realized, experiences. The final story, **"Courtly Vision"** (which might have been better placed at the beginning), provides through the study of a Mogul painting insights into the intricacies of the author's own miniaturist writing. In the painting an emperor leaving Fatehpur Sikri (a unique, even bizarre city whose ruler attempted to unite Hindu and Moslem cultures, and which was abandoned within decades of its founding) commands the artist to give him total vision. The emperor has intimations of infinite calamities, but does not see even the foreign count who crouches in a "lust-darkened arbor," ready to ravish the empress. Neither does the ardent count see the nearby thieves or the Portuguese priests who have "dogged the emperor through inclement scenery" and who now wait, biding their time to proselytize the emperor. "Adventurers all, they guard from each other the common courtesy of their subterfuge."

The characters in Miss Mukherjee's stories often exist in the same plane, juxtaposed, flattened out in a way that is both Mogul miniaturist and modernist. Although failure to communicate—surely our major contemporary theme—is at the heart of this collection, the protagonists in *Darkness,* unlike our sad Western characters, are bright with disappointment. Moments of loss, attainment, violence and yearning for grace explode in what I can only describe as crystalline fixity. The stories are lapidary with detailed objects, even products. American brand names and Indian exotica (invested with an equal power) objectify emotions and yet gleam with an enameled literalness that at once distances and compels the reader. Isolated body gestures—the sister of a dying woman carrying home dinner leftovers in a "shiny package breast-high as if it is a treasure"; an unwed pregnant daughter holding up a copy of *National Geographic* to ward off her enraged father; an immigrant hash cook who holds his Canadian passport in front of his face as a Mountie shoots him; an adulterous empress who holds her fists "in front of her like tiny shields" from which sprouts "a closed, upright lotus bloom"—stick in the mind, and reveal the shifting of continents.

> Hope Cooke, *"Bright Moments of Disappointment,"* in The New York Times Book Review, *January 12, 1986, p. 14.*

PETER NAZARETH

Bharati Mukherjee's third volume of fiction [*Darkness*] is finally out, a decade after the second novel.... And yes, it is different from the first two [*The Tiger's Daughter* and *Wife*]. It is not just that it is a volume of short stories: with *Darkness,* Bharati Mukharjee comes to terms with North America. (p. 184)

[While] she says she has become a North American writer, it is a writer of *the other America,* the America ignored by the so-called mainstream: the America that embraces all the peoples of the world both because America is involved with the whole world and because the whole world is in America. Her cast of characters includes immigrant Indians, white Americans, Vietnamese, Italian Americans, white Canadians, immigrant Lebanese, non-white Canadians, Americanized Indian children, American children born of one white American and one Indian parent, etc. The Indians include Sikhs, Bengalis, Goans, Bangladeshis, Gujaratis, and so on. Among the white Americans, there are New York professionals, workers, busboys, Iowa farmers, John Deere engineers, radicals.... The Canadians include white women bureaucrats, pop stars, academics, and the Mounted Police. These characters interact with one another. Precisely because her canvas is wide, her stories are short. Through short stories, she is able to take on the world and to provide multiple perspectives.

"**Tamurlane**" is first person narration by a male illegal Indian who works as a waiter in a Toronto restaurant and who sleeps three other Indian "illegals" in his apartment. (pp. 184-85)

They are raided by the Mounties. Gupta, the chef, who could only move rigidly with crutches since he had been thrown by racists onto the Toronto subway tracks—hence "Tamurlane," which means "Timur the Lame"—did not respond quickly enough. In reply to a Mountie's rudeness, he suddenly chops the Mountie's outstretched arm.... The sudden violent end works on two levels. Within the story, we see a transference of rage: the Mountie does not realize that his prejudice against Indians will trigger off the suppressed desire for revenge on the part of Gupta, a Canadian citizen. Gupta was unaware he

had this desire: one of the men, trying to persuade the men to leave for New York, says of him, "Like a true Gandhian, he forgave them." The other level is that of shock to the reader. It is difficult for the reader not to wince. There is no catharsis at the end of the story.

Yet Mukherjee provides balance to an unbalanced situation: "**Isolated Incidents**" has a white Canadian woman protagonist in her late twenties who works for the Human Rights Office. Ann is going to have lunch with her old friend Poppy, now "Peppi Paluka," who has made it as a sexy pop star while Ann has gone nowhere with her writing. She is looking forward to the lunch, to connection with exciting faraway places and the world of make-believe, but nothing comes of it and she has to go to lunch at a "Colonel Sanders spot." There she is harassed by Mr. Hernandez, who had come earlier to see her with his sister's immigration problems and refuses to accept her explanation that she only deals with Human Rights issues. The restaurant represents her diminished dreams.... We see the immigrant mythifying the callousness of the white Canadian, not seeing her problems as an individual. The violence here is of another order: Ann is leading a life of quiet desperation, and the story ends with her walking back to her office. The complaints within the story of discrimination against Indians and other immigrants are balanced by Ann's problems as an individual and as a worker of limited power within a bureaucracy.

At other times, Mukherjee achieves balance by referring to characters or things from one story in another. "**Nostalgia**" tells the story of Dr. Manny Patel, a psychiatric resident at a hospital in Queens, married to a white American woman while "**Saints**" is the story of his son after Dr. Manny and his wife have separated. In both stories, the protagonists are actually trying to come to terms with their complex inheritance and to have roots: not "fixed" roots but the feeling of belonging by integration of the diverse experiences, myths, psychic needs and relationships. (pp. 185-86)

[In "**Saints**"], Shawn Patel is American and moves about with a multiracial American group. His parents have separated and he is upset that his mother is being exploited by an American man who, unknown to her, has had sexual relations with a Yugoslav woman. (There is a touch of Freud here.) He does not understand his father, who sends him gifts. One of these is a parcel of two books, an art book, "reproductions of paintings that Dad loves," and a "thin book with bad binding put out by a religious printing house in Madras. The little book is about a Hindu saint who had visions. Dad has sent me a book about visions." (pp. 186-87)

Mukherjee's story is like the "saint" stories by J. D. Salinger: note the bottle imagery of "**Visions**" and the fact that among Salinger's major characters are Franny and Zooey *Glass.* ... But there is a difference between Salinger's adolescents and Mukherjee's: because Mukherjee's have a more complex inheritance, the search is not to preserve innocence but to find wholeness. As such, even a man may also be less than mature. The attraction to sainthood, to a violation of the norms of social behaviour, is an indication of this search, although superficially we would consider the character to be strange or even a pervert. Shawn knows his mother would have been happier to have a daughter so he takes on the feminine side of himself, even using make-up. As an American, born in America, he makes the Vietnamese boat-person, Tran, feel at home, understanding the violence he has been through and not wanting, unlike the teacher, to censor that violence.

"The Imaginary Assassin" also has a young male narrator attracted to saints, a Sikh born in Yuba City, California in 1960. While other American kids "had their rock stars to make life bearable," he had his mythic stories of family members. . . . He talks to his Grandfather, who claims to have killed Gandhi, although someone else was caught for the murder. The Grandfather explains why he wanted to kill Gandhi—because of the brutalization of the Sikhs, particularly of the women, and of others during Partition. . . . (p. 187)

The story explains the psychology of Sikhs while letting us see the other side of the sainthood of Gandhi (and of the portrait of Gandhi in the block-busting movie): the price others pay such that "Gandhi the celibate was the biggest rapist in history." Is the story true? Yes, as a work of the imagination—note the "imaginary" of the title—and of what is real to the psyche. The end connects up with the "real world": a slender, modern houseguest is picked up by the Yuba City police because they say "he'd killed another Sikh in Toronto, Canada. I don't know how, or why, or when."

Sainthood and violence lie very close together, the stories suggest. The saint can be an oppressor of the people and a murderer. Sainthood can be the cause of and justification for violence. On the other hand, as we have seen, certain types of "violence" are commited by people we can call secular saints—people whose actions make survival and growth possible for themselves and for others.

"Visitors" is a reworking of the novel *Wife,* a clue to the fact that each story is meant to have the effect in shorthand of a novel. Like *Wife,* the story deals with the undermining in America of the myths and illusions about marriage with which an Indian woman is brought up. In both the novel and the story, a man comes to the house on the East Coast while the husband is out at work; in both cases the wife's mind begins to snap because the romantic notions of wifehood combined with the Indian elite's idea of the U.S. as paradise do not fit the reality. The protagonist's mind is captured by a "language" of imprisonment. But in the novel, the male is a white American who becomes her lover; in the story, it is a young Indian who has problems coming to terms with America who wants to become her lover but it is unlikely that they have had sexual relations. At the end, in *Wife,* the protagonist kills her husband. . . . In the novel, the wife kills the *Indian* husband: in the story, what is released is the longing to embrace alien, dangerous America. (p. 188)

Within **"Courtly Vision,"** there is a . . . clue to Bharati Mukherjee's writing:

> *Give me total vision,* commands the emperor. His
> voice hisses above the hoarse calls of the camels.
> *You, Basawan, who can paint my Begum on a grain
> of rice, see what you can do with the infinite vistas
> the size of my opened hand. Hide nothing from me,
> my co-wanderer. Tell me how my new capital will
> fail, will turn to dust and these marbled terraces be
> home to jackals and infidels. Tell me who to fear and
> who to kill but tell it to me in a way that makes me
> smile. Transport me through dense fort walls and
> stone grilles and into the hearts of men.*

This is what the literary artist has done: she has penetrated below the surface, found the reality, and told the truth on several grains of rice. The leader wanted to be told the truth, even the bad news. But Bharati Mukherjee does not only focus on the bad news. She also celebrates life, the creative possibilities contained within people, the ability to give up fixed

worlds, to break out of cages and relate to a complex, multicultural world. The painting is a two-dimensional cage. The writer-artist frees the people from two-dimensionalism, the writer-artist sees the meaning and the potential. Even her novels were complex explorations without any of the protective, distancing cynicism of Naipaul. The attraction of Naipaul to Bharati Mukherjee the writer in the early days was not his cynicism but that he provided a literary model different from that of, say, Jane Austen: he showed that it was possible to create a fictional world about one's village far from the colonial metropolitan centre, that the chaos of a once colonized people was a worthy subject for fiction. Her novels are sympathetic attempts to break the barriers of restrictive culture and class. The first novel has a protagonist who returns to India and there confronts not only the radical movements of Bengal but also the other America, as represented by a humorous, Black Power American visitor. Bharati Mukherjee's world as a writer has changed but the new world was always there within the old. (pp. 190-91)

> *Peter Nazareth, "Total Vision," in* Canadian Literature, *No. 110, Fall, 1986, pp. 184-91.*

POLLY SHULMAN

In Bharati Mukherjee's fiction, sex and violence circle each other like twin stars. At best they're universal languages, ways to communicate across cultural walls. At worst, they're gestures that can't be ignored, even when they're not understood. Her subject is the sparks that happen when cultures meet. With rapes and riots, suttee and tender acts of adultery, her characters try to talk to each other in languages they've half forgotten or never completely learned.

Her first novel, *The Tiger's Daughter* (1971), is as autobiographical as the best of them. Tara, the only child of a Brahmin industrialist, has returned to her native Calcutta after seven years in the U.S. . . . Toward the end of the book, one [Indian] family offers to host a student from Los Angeles. McDowell, to their astonishment, turns out to be black (they thought for sure he was Irish). Tara has to act as mediator between the two cultures, but her efforts are in vain. When she interferes, she only confuses everyone further or offends—asking McDowell, for example, if he's from Watts. Left to themselves they get along, oblivious to their differences. McDowell delights the daughter of the family by teaching her new phrases: right on, power to the people. He steers his hosts safely through their own streets; when protesters mob the car on the way back from picking him up at the airport, he gets out and teaches them to chant "Brown is beautiful." After a few days, he goes off to join the rioters, a desertion his hosts, unprepared, see as a terrible betrayal. Tara understands both sides, but can't explain.

It's a position Mukherjee's characters often find themselves in—seeing the same interaction from the point of view of a different culture with each eye. Sometimes the result is paralyzing, a double muddle, but sometimes the images click together to give depth vision. *The Middleman and Other Stories,* Mukherjee's new book, announces this theme in its title, but it's by no means a new subject for her. Foreignness, in all its aspects, has always fascinated her; what's new is her definition of home. . . .

Taking V. S. Naipaul as a model, she wrote with self-protective irony, particularly apparent in her second novel, *Wife* (1975). Dimple Basu, the heroine, is an exile in New York, the bride in a traditional arranged marriage; she's one of the characters for whom double vision means a divided self. Slowly Dimple cracks up, and the book ends in an act of not very convincing violence—Mukherjee keeps Dimple and her world at arm's length. But after moving to the U.S. Mukherjee underwent a transformation. Seeing herself in the tradition of Ellis Island American writers—*Darkness* is dedicated to Bernard Malamud—she shed "the aloofness of expatriation" for "the exuberance of immigration."

The change came upon her suddenly, she says, and it's easy to pick out the earlier stories in *Darkness*. "Hindus" and "The World According to Hsü" seem diffuse, full of frustrated anger. "Isolated Incidents," about Paki-bashing in Toronto, is almost pedantic; like one of her own middlemen, Mukherjee is addressing people she knows aren't listening, so she has to shout a little to be heard. The newer stories, though, make up for these lapses. "Angela," "A Father," "Saints," and just about all the stories in *The Middleman* are as subtle as *The Tiger's Daughter,* and even sharper—either Mukherjee is now confident that she can interpret to her new countrymen, or she's writing for herself. . . .

In *Darkness,* Mukherjee drew her characters from many subcontinental classes and religions. There's a Pakistani Muslim engineer and his wife, a maharaja, illegal restaurant workers from god knows where. In *The Middleman,* she goes even further, gathering protagonists from all over the globe; sometimes she leaves out the Indians altogether. Her writing has a new toughness, the violence both more explicit and more to the point. It's a departure, and a measure of her confidence. She's right to be confident—she's getting better and better.

In "Fathering," a veteran sends for his daughter by a Saigon barmaid, hoping to improve his relationship with his girlfriend. Instead, the daughter and girlfriend hate each other and battle to control him. It's a suspenseful, tightly constructed story. The child is delirious, perhaps from a virus, perhaps from shell shock. Her arms are covered with strange, round bruises. She raves in an eerie (but believable) combination of "ordinary" American child talk—"Dad, can I have a quarter?"—and war vocabulary. The father, who narrates the story, is the middleman, caught between his girlfriend and his daughter, between the pills and tranquilizers of Western medicine and the curse little Eng believes in. . . . When [the] father realizes Eng has been trying to cure herself with money, digging quarters into her arms, he takes her away from the doctor and his knockout shots. "I got no end of coins," he whispers. It's not only the newcomers who have to learn new rules and ways of thinking in these stories—Americans who love them also end up changing.

Successful immigrants hang on to their old selves while taking advantage of the possibilities the new culture offers. In India, marvels Panna, Charity Chin would be a flat-chested old maid; in New York, she's a rising model. Of course, the process of keeping both worlds can be strenuous; an Italian-American remembers her grandmother cooking two Thanksgiving dinners every year, one of turkey and fixings, one of the grandfather's favorite pastas. And at every step, there's someone waiting to exploit incipient Americans. Every third Wednesday, out of gratitude, Charity sleeps with the plastic surgeon who "fixed" her eyes. In another story, Jasmine, a hopeful, enterprising teenager, has herself smuggled from Trinidad to Michigan and spends her first few months as an unpaid chambermaid-bookkeeper for other Indian Trinidadians lucky enough to be legal. Her next job is as a "mother's helper"—actually a 24-hour

nanny-cook-and-maid—in a professor's family. The story ends with the professor seducing her on the Turkish carpet she vacuums every day. . . .

"Jasmine" is particularly chilling because the heroine has no idea she's being exploited. Mukherjee appreciates this sort of irony. The vet in "Fathering," who loves his daughter so much that he's willing to change his whole life for her, is also one of the Yankees who killed her grandmother and destroyed her world. The exploiter is the lover, the destroyer the redeemer.

Perhaps this is the meaning of change. In Mukherjee's books, everyone is living in a new world, even those who never left home. As traditions break down, the characters must try to make lives out of the pieces. New cosmopolitans, suspicious but brave, they run off into the "alien American night," expecting shame, disaster, and glorious riches; they get them, too, though never quite the way the imagined. Immigration for Mukherjee needn't mean assimilation. The melting pot, yes, but it's the lumps that interest her. Assimilation implies forgetting, blotting out the past, but the past is what the present is made of. If she weren't still an Indian, Mukherjee wouldn't be the wonderful American writer she is.

Polly Shulman, "Home Truths," in VLS, *No. 66, June, 1988, p. 19.*

JONATHAN RABAN

When Bharati Mukherjee dedicated her last collection of stories about immigrants, *Darkness,* to Bernard Malamud, she was both saluting an old friend and bedding herself down in a tradition. In modern American fiction, the immigrant has classically been Jewish: Jewish writers, from Abraham Cahan through Henry Roth to Malamud himself, have reworked the facts of their history into a rich body of literary mythology. In *Darkness,* Ms. Mukherjee . . . successfully grafted her own experience as an Indian on to that of the American Jews. Now, in *The Middleman,* she hijacks the whole tradition of Jewish-American writing and flies it off to a destination undreamed of by its original practitioners.

Her characters have a great deal in common with their Jewish counterparts: they're heroes to themselves, a size larger than life, and they see the surfaces of America with the bug-eyed hangover clarity of the greenhorn afloat in a gaudy new world. Yet they're not tired, huddled or even poor: they own motels, work scams, teach in college, breeze through on private funds. Their diaspora is a haphazard, pepperpot dispersal. They have been shaken out, singly, over a huge territory, from Toronto in the north down to a steamy Central American republic. They're in Ann Arbor, Cedar Falls, Rock Springs, Flushing, Manhattan, suburban New Jersey, Atlanta, Florida. With no Lower East Side to keep the manners and morals of the old world alive, they're on their own and on the make. How the introspective and overmothered sons of the ghetto, from David Levinsky to Alexander Portnoy, would have envied Ms. Mukherjee's new Americans—their guiltlessness, bounce, sexual freedom, their easy money and the lightness of their footsteps on the American landscape. Unlike their Jewish literary ancestors, Ms. Mukherjee's people are no more tormented by conscience than butterflies.

The stories in *The Middleman* are streets ahead of those in *Darkness,* fine as that collection was. Not only has Ms. Mukherjee vastly enlarged her geographical and social range (the immigrants in her new book come fresh to America from Vietnam, the Caribbean, the Levant, Afghanistan, the Philippines, Italy and Sri Lanka, as well as from India), but she has greatly sharpened her style. Her writing here is far quicker in tempo, more confident and more sly than it used to be. There's no slack in it, as there was in some of the *Darkness* stories, and no Creative Writing. (pp. 1, 22)

Most of the stories are monologues, spoken by compulsively fluent talkers whose lives are too urgent and mobile for them to indulge in the luxury of the retrospective past tense. They hit the page in full flight, and they move through the stories as they move through the world, at speed, with the reader straining to keep up with them. Throughout the book, the idiom of America in the 1980's is handled by Ms. Mukherjee with much the same rapturous affection and acuteness of ear that Nabokov, another immigrant, brought to the idiom of America in the 1950's in *Lolita*. On one level, *The Middleman* is a consummated romance with the American language.

It is also a romance with America itself, its infinitely possible geography, its license, sexiness and violence. In a story called **"Loose Ends,"** a Vietnam vet who is working in Miami as a hired killer describes the details of his job with offhand boredom, while his attention is fully engaged by the sight of a blond swami levitating on a prayer mat above the roof of a discount clothing store in a suburban shopping mall. Airborne for "two or three minutes," the flying swami is eventually caught by the police in a net and hauled off to jail in handcuffs. The whole incident is over and done with in seven short sentences, but it haunts the book.

For America is a place where the laws of physics are suspended, where people can defy gravity, where magic is an unremarkable part of everyday life. Ms. Mukherjee's characters are levitators who float clean over their tawdry circumstances. In **"Jasmine,"** for instance, an illegal immigrant from Trinidad is employed as a mother's helper by a deadly dull academic couple in Ann Arbor. When the wife's away, the husband predictably takes the girl on the living-room carpet. But Jasmine is in a solipsistic ecstasy. Squirming beneath the man's body, the "Flower of Ann Arbor" thinks of how she has "no visa, no papers, and no birth certificate. No nothing other than what she wanted to invent and tell." In America, only in America, she can make herself up as she goes along.

Jasmine's happy brand of neo-Platonism, her capacity to create and inhabit her own ideal republic is typical—and it is typical of Ms. Mukherjee that she can make one fear for the life of a character just when that life seems to the character to be in a state of perfect order. Jasmine and her fellow immigrants are never going to spend their nights bettering themselves at City College, never going to start up a *Commentary* or a *Partisan Review*, never going to run for governor. The journey to America has turned them into chronic travelers who live, as travelers do, from minute to minute, dangerously free of both past and future. One suspects that a lot of them are bound to end up, like the swami, in the slammer.

Every story ends on a new point of departure. People are last seen walking out through an open door, planning an escape, or suspended on the optimistic brink of a blissful sexual transport. . . . For these birds of passage, America is a receding infinity of fresh beginnings; they keep aloft on luck and grace.

Some fall abruptly out of the sky. A few are in anguish. In **"Fathering,"** Eng, a Vietnamese child rescued by her American father from Saigon and carried home to Rock Springs (Montana? Wyoming? Arizona? we aren't told), tries to mu-

tilate herself by pressing coins into her flesh—the same coins that in Vietnam had been used as amulets for wounds—to protest her forced exile in her father's land. Ambushed by a doctor armed with a syringe full of sedative, she turns on her father, crying, "You Yankees, please go home. . . . Scram, Yankee bastard!" For the young Eng, to be an immigrant is to be invaded, conquered, colonized; she *is* Saigon, cruelly encroached on by an alien small town in the far West, and the story ends with her father joining her in her flight from Rock Springs. The great lesson that the immigrant has to teach the born-and-raised citizen is that being on the run is a native American condition. The Americans in *The Middleman* are constantly being awakened to their own restlessness and fluidity by the newcomers. Like Eng's father, speeding away with his daughter in the "cold chariot" of his van, they too learn to levitate. (pp. 22-3)

Jonathan Raban, in a review of "The Middleman," in The New York Times Book Review, *June 19, 1988, pp. 1, 22-3.*

ELIZABETH WARD

It does not do to think of Bharati Mukherjee primarily as an Indian or an immigrant or a foreigner. . . . For Mukherjee writes prose so indelibly, effortlessly American that I, a fellow-immigrant, occasionally have trouble keeping up with her rapid colloquial patter, in something like the way I could never follow the dialogue in *The Rockford Files* when I first came to this country [from Australia]. . . .

Bharati Mukherjee may be writing in [*Middleman and Other Stories*] from first-hand experience of what she calls "the process of immigration," yet she writes as naturally as one born not just to the language, but to the culture. It's more than a matter of tell-tale little phrases and images—the pickup, the Braves, Ted Turner, finished basements, Tab and Reeboks and Corning casseroles—it's a certain casual, tough-guy inflection that Mukherjee has down pat. "In changing gears," somebody in one of her stories observes of his aristocratic Filipino girl-friend, "she's right up there with Mario Andretti." How long do you have to have lived here before being able to throw off a perfect, all-American sentence like that?

The fact is that Bharati Mukherjee . . . is first and foremost a very fine fiction writer, funny, intelligent, versatile and, on occasion, unexpectedly profound, all of which makes her someone to take notice of, no matter what her theme. On the other hand, possession of these qualities also means that Mukherjee is certainly worth listening to on the subject that seems to fascinate her above all: "the transformation," as she has called it, "of North American society by 'new' faces from Asia, and the transformation of those 'new' people (who are some of the oldest in the world) by the ideas of America."

The stories collected in *The Middleman* are designed and arranged to illuminate, one by one, various facets of this latter-day American melting-pot, incorporating the experiences of Indian, Afghan, Filipino, Vietnamese, Trinidadian and Sri Lankan immigrants and the endless, exquisite ironies of their relationships with older Americans, that is to say, the ones who got here earlier. One of the funniest and most effective stories in the book, **"Orbiting,"** records an awkward, subversively joyous Thanksgiving Day dinner that is used by an Italian-American girl as an occasion to introduce her Afghan boyfriend to her family. The story captures shades, layers, of experience. Rindy's Mom and Dad are, after all, immigrants too, but in comparison with Ro from Kabul they may as well have arrived on the *Mayflower*. Grave, passionate, educated in subtlety, Ro is like a being from another planet. "In my father's world," reflects Rindy, "grown men bowl in leagues and drink the best whiskey they can afford. Dad whistles 'My Way.' He must be under stress. That's his usual self-therapy: how would Francis Albert handle this?" (p. 3)

At once less flamboyant and more poignant are the handful of stories chronicling the immigrant experience from the point of view of immigrants themselves. **"The Management of Grief"** is a quietly stunning story dramatizing the imagined consequences of a plane crash that actually occurred a couple of years ago. An Air India jet en route from Canada exploded over the sea off the west coast of Ireland; sabotage was suspected. Mukherjee is devastatingly perceptive about the effects of the disaster on the victims' relatives in Canada: the isolation and withdrawal of these Indian families, despite clumsy official efforts to help them, and the varying degrees to which they were able to adapt. The question is also raised, whether or not adaptation is necessarily a good thing. "'You see what I'm up against?'" pleads a social worker to an Indian woman who is acting as an informal go-between. "'I'm sure they're lovely people, but their stubbornness and ignorance are driving me crazy. They think signing a paper is signing their sons' death warrants, don't they?' I am looking out the window. I want to say, *In our culture, it is a parent's duty to hope*."

In **"The Tenant,"** Maya Sanyal, a university writing teacher in Iowa, formerly of New Jersey, North Carolina and Calcutta, experiences what it is like to be "an American citizen. But.", which is exactly the no-man's-land inhabited by so many of Bharati Mukherjee's characters. It is a state that Mukherjee, through her characters, experiences—and in the end transcends—with humor, grace and a disarmingly sharp-edged intelligence. Lumped together with other Indians or perceived outsiders by well-meaning American friends attempting to liven up her social life, Maya finds herself living with her armless landlord.

> She has never slept with a man without arms. Two wounded people, he will joke during their nighly contortions. It will shock her, this assumed equivalence with a man so strikingly deficient. She knows she is strange, and lonely, but being Indian is not the same, she would have thought, as being a freak.

In giving such an articulate voice to people who too often are lumped together in contemporary America as "ethnics" or "minorities," Bharati Mukherjee becomes, in *The Middleman and Other Stories*, herself the most valuable kind of middleman, bridging disparate worlds. (p. 9)

Elizabeth Ward, "Notes from a New America," in Book World—The Washington Post, *July 3, 1988, pp. 3, 9.*

Morris (H.) Philipson

1926-

American novelist, nonfiction writer, biographer, and editor.

In his fiction, Philipson examines moral issues among spiritually or emotionally impoverished upper-class Americans. These characters often attempt to escape their unsatisfying lives through legal or sexual transgression. For example, the protagonist of Philipson's first novel, *Bourgeois Anonymous* (1964), joins an encounter group in an attempt to rid herself of middle-class inclinations. She experiences conflict, however, when she falls in love with a working-class man with strong bourgeois aspirations. These characters view one another as agents for entering different social classes.

Philipson's next three novels, *The Wallpaper Fox* (1976), *A Man in Charge* (1979), and *Secret Understandings* (1983), explore aristocratic life in Connecticut. In *The Wallpaper Fox,* an affluent married couple who appear to lead a stable, untroubled existence force an uncomfortable confrontation when they can no longer tolerate the lies and deceptions that they have kept to themselves. Jane Larkin Crain commented: ''[*The Wallpaper Fox*] raises disturbing and complicated questions about the capacity of family life to mitigate an increasingly barren modern experience.'' *A Man in Charge* centers on questions of power and virtue in university politics. In *Secret Understandings,* a woman learns that she has an incurable brain tumor but conceals this knowledge from her family in order to maintain her individuality. Gary Davenport observed: ''[*Secret Understandings*] is a fearless, unsentimental, and philosophically serious treatment of an urgent and even heroic confrontation between self and world.''

In *Somebody Else's Life* (1987), Philipson investigates avarice and subterfuge in the art world. This novel focuses on disenchanted philosophy professor Stephen Cooper, who is jealous of his wealthy half-brother's art collection and decides to write a popular novel about art forgery. Cooper's plans change, however, when his lover, an art conservator, persuades him to collaborate with her on the crime depicted in his unpublished novel. Paul Skenazy remarked: ''[Philipson's] point is fundamental—that in a world where everything from politics and works of art to body parts and the qualities of the past can be created in a near-perfect facsimile of the real thing, so can, and will, one's emotional capacities, will to live and personality.'' Philipson has also edited several books on philosophy and contemporary thought and has written the nonfiction work *Outline of a Jungian Aesthetics* (1963), as well as *The Count Who Wished He Were a Peasant* (1967), a biography of Leo Tolstoy.

(See also *Contemporary Authors,* Vols. 1-4, rev. ed. and *Contemporary Authors New Revision Series,* Vol. 4.)

ALASDAIR MacINTYRE

[A] brilliantly clear exposition of Jungian psychology is given in Dr. Morris Philipson's *Outline of a Jungian Aesthetics.* Dr.

Philipson attempts both to be loyal to Jung and to be fully critical and scientific. The result is that his work lacks the magical quality of some Jungian writing (this is not a hostile criticism); and yet unfortunately he gets no closer to rendering Jung rational. He treats the existence of the Collective Unconscious as an hypothesis, for example, without ever considering the question of its testability. When he comes to explain the Jungian view of art, we are therefore inevitably conscious that the theory which is to explain art to us has yet to be given a specific content. Its credentials remain unclear. The hope is that the theory may become clearer through its applications. It is therefore worth saying that throughout the book the theory is *never* applied. No particular work of painting or literature is discussed for more than a line or two. Names are thrown about and the activity of ''the'' poet or ''the'' artist is discussed. It is perhaps only fair to add that Dr. Philipson is expert at sharp in-fighting with Freudian aestheticians.

Dr. Philipson's book is thus additional confirmation, if any were needed, that Jung's so-called theories belong not in the world of rational thought to which Dr. Philipson valiantly tries to introduce them, but in the half-world of theosophy, astrology, and the like. (p. 6)

Alasdair MacIntyre, "Irrational Man," in The New York Review of Books, *Vol. IV, No. 2, February 25, 1965, pp. 5-6.*

ROBERT PHELPS

[*Bourgeois Anonymous*] is a funny book that will make you laugh out loud; it will also make you think uncomfortably and unconclusively about your life in urban, credit-card America. It is a novel of ideas, cut along early Huxley lines, but for my money better. Here and there, its moral imagination reminded me of *Howards End*; though more often I thought of Shaw: Mr. Philipson is incisive, articulate—and perverse. In fact, what seems to me to be important about this book is its gallant, magnanimous wrongness. It is a pipe dream, but an endearing one. The author is a well-meaning man who, in 1965, still wants to belong to something, a man for whom self-interest, no matter how coolly enlightened or psychiatrically approved, is still not enough; yet a man who can't find any community to join, and who therefore acts quixotically, very imaginatively, but impractically.

Mr. Philipson has written a tract, and an unfashionably sweet love story about Lavinia and Jeffrey. Lavinia is from one of our better suburbs. She has read Sartre at Smith; she has already, in her early twenties, abandoned a first marriage; she has a "creative" job on a fashion magazine and lives with a schoolmate on Sheridan Square. She is restless, miserable and while she waits for a miracle, she attends meetings of the Manhattan chapter of Bourgeois Anonymous, where all ages gather in masks to confess how they are struggling to escape middle-class blight. For in the 20th Century, all America is divided into three parts: the outcasts, the bourgeois, and the incasts. The latter are self-made aristocrats, and it is to their free, unfumbling ranks that Lavinia hungers to rise.

The boy, Jeffrey, is a bastard, therefore a born outcast. But he is also a mathematical genius, therefore in vertically mobile America, he has become an incast. He is as restless as Lavinia, for he cannot bear merely to be free and brilliantly self-absorbed. As Lavinia wants to escape from the cant of her suburban family, Jeffrey wants to escape into rules, patterns, limits, a family, a neighborhood. He wants to become a thoroughgoing bourgeois, and when he sees Lavinia at a New Year's Eve party, he recognizes his perfect mate.

Jeffrey feels about the middle class as someone might feel about the Catholic Church or the Communist Party. There may be insincere Catholics, or cynical Communists. But the ideal is always there, waiting to be embodied. Jeffrey dreams of becoming a *worthy* bourgeois. . . . If most bourgeois are false, it is not the fault of the class. "Don't you see how glorious an idea this is?" Jeffrey exclaims. "How demanding? How exalted? How saintly?"

Lavinia doesn't. But she does see a glamorous maverick, a true loner, a self-made, self-ordaining, idealistic male who can save her from her family, and she falls in love. The courtship proceeds. . . . Jeffrey prevails, presumably retaining his incast individuality and at the same time settling down to station wagons and golf in White Plains.

If I am to take Mr. Philipson seriously—and I do—then I can only say he is wrong. Simone Weil said: "It is wrong to be an 'I', but it is worse to be a 'we'." Aloneness is hard, but it need not necessarily be lonesome, nor barren. In any case, as Auden reminds us, it "is man's real condition."

Robert Phelps, "On Being Middle Class," in The New Republic, *Vol. 152, No. 25, June 19, 1965, p. 25.*

WALTER SULLIVAN

Philipson's [*Bourgeois Anonymous*] is all surface, a hollow bonbon that melts on the tongue. His main character is a young lady who for reasons that she is not entirely clear about does not want any longer to be bourgeois. In an effort to divest herself of her middle-class proclivities, Lavinia joins Bourgeois Anonymous. At meetings of BA, held in the dead of night, members don hoods and robes and encourage one another with tales of personal fortitude and of obstacles overcome on the road to freedom from a bourgeois orientation. The trouble in Lavinia's case is that she falls in love with a young man who is not bourgeois at all, but who wants to be. This involvement leads to some mildly comic scenes: Lavinia, wanting to be unconventional, would like to go immediately to bed; Jeffrey, determined to be conventional, will not take her. Lavinia's mother, father, brother, *et al.* are sketched in predictable fashion, and at the end all comes right when Jeffrey explains that the bourgeois do not really exist: they are a sociological fiction.

Bourgeois Anonymous is billed by its admirers as satire, and perhaps it represents what passes for satire now that all our literature seems to develop on a reduced scale. But it is not a very good book and therefore its satire is not very meaningful. Up to a point everybody writes well these days: everybody has an ear for mother's saccharine dialogue; everybody can convey father's idiotic attachment to his Cadillac and show the way brother smokes and smokes and smokes. But all too frequently these slight beginnings at characterization, these most superficial of all details, are taken as the most profound of existential perceptions. So far have we come in measuring the universe and all that is in it by the yardstick of ourselves. Mr. Philipson is tedious before he is done. (pp. 710-11)

Walter Sullivan, "Updike, Spark and Others," in The Sewanee Review, *Vol. LXXIV, No. 3, Summer, 1966, pp. 709-16.*

JANE LARKIN CRAIN

At first, **The Wallpaper Fox** threatens to be merely a routine chastisement of morally flaccid, upper-middle class America. Soon, however, this solid and serious novel emerges as not just an exposé of what *really* goes on behind the well-groomed facades of the affluent, but a thoughtful exploration of character and the efficacy of moral action in forming and reforming it.

As much as anything else, this is a portrait of a marriage, that of Henry and Kate Warner, he a successful businessman who attaches an almost religious significance to the impeccable furnishings of his existence, she a complete homemaker who relishes but is at the same time uneasy about the ease and comfort of her well-ordered sphere. At the heart of their life together is a profound deception involving the paternity of their oldest child; several lesser lies seem to ripple out around their joint masquerade, until a series of crises undermines lifelong habits of rationalization and compromise, forcing the Warners and those close to them into decisive confrontation with each other and themselves.

Morris Philipson . . . writes with grace and amplitude. Largely free of contemporary cant about the much reviled nuclear family, the novel raises disturbing and complicated questions about the capacity of family life to mitigate an increasingly barren modern experience. The author's vision is a melancholy but compassionate one, seeing no final resolution between the animal urgencies that animate experience on the one hand, and overly civilized forms for survival on the other. But from the isolation of their brainspun and indulgent torments, Philipson's characters *do* manage to break through to some essential sense of reality and communion—and they seem to do so through the power of human love.

> *Jane Larkin Crain, in a review of "The Wallpaper Fox," in* The New York Times Book Review, *December 12, 1976, p. 7.*

THE NEW YORKER

[When Mr. Philipson] talks about current manners and morals, as he frequently does throughout [*The Wallpaper Fox*], he seems a thoughtful and fairly worldly man. How, then, to comprehend the awful coyness and downright silliness of this novel about domestic felicity, in which even the salad dishes "snuggled up against the dinner plates." Small lies and how they threaten to mushroom into major crises are at the center of the soap-operaish plot.... The story takes place in New Haven and gives us a lot of tips about the difficulties of running a large, expensive house and some chilling looks at the dinner parties of the rich and powerful who play on the fringes of university life. (pp. 98-9)

> *A review of "The Wallpaper Fox," in* The New Yorker, *Vol. LII, No. 47, January 10, 1977, pp. 98-9.*

AUDREY C. FOOTE

Morris Philipson's [*The Wallpaper Fox*] is dedicated "For Iris Murdoch with gratitude." At first glance there appears to be no similarity at all, let alone debt, between these two writers, other than an apparently compulsive use of coincidence in their plots. Murdoch's novels are English, aristocratic, Jacobean in their preoccupation with bizarre and often violent sexual relationships. *The Wallpaper Fox* is American, middle class, and suburban in its domesticity. But it is soon evident that Philipson too is of that species of writer, rather rare these days, for whom characters and plot, however interesting or intricate, are quite subordinate to moral issues, paramount and explicit....

The author's low-keyed skill is apparent in the first section; he engages our sympathy for his hero, Henry Warner, so adroitly that we are hardly aware of Henry's first suave peccadillo which, after all, seems to hurt no one but the IRS. But this minor bit of cheating soon emerges as part of a pattern of self-indulgence, vanity, pleasure in excitement and above all deception that riddles the lives of Henry, his upright wife Kate, their son Jonathan and all their impeccable associates. Eventually all the skeletons are trotted out into the open through a series of coincidences which seem naive and amateurish in so neat and realistic a novel of manners. But in fact, as in Murdoch's novels, these coincidences are the writer's signposts to direct our attention to the significance and inevitability of ethical imperatives; morality spits out mere plausibility of plot. Philipson is more optimistic than Murdoch; when confronted with the issues and alternatives, his characters take their medicine with good grace. But Philipson is more sentimental—and less convincing—since that medicine seems to heal with little bitter taste, and with no fatal side effects.

> *Audrey C. Foote, in a review of "The Wallpaper Fox," in* Book World—The Washington Post, *January 30, 1977, p. E8.*

DAPHNE MERKIN

Morris Philipson's *A Man In Charge* is a puzzling and inept novel. Its characters appear to be hacked out of granite. The intricate plot lumbers noisily along, full of bizarre twists of fate that you'd been watching out for from the start, since this is the kind of story where the author steps in and tells fate what to do. Philipson's technique includes such antiquated devices as foreshadowing—not tactful hints of future developments, but the real, stagey stuff.... The puzzling part is that there are interludes of great intelligence in this book, struggling to be noticed amid the debris—the patently unconvincing dialogue affixed to various unconvincing personalities, and descriptions that sound as if they were lifted from a Jacqueline Susann primer.... It is as though Philipson has shackled an observant, even Jamesian mind to a mass-market, obtuse mode of expression.

A Man In Charge is about civilization and its discontents. Conrad Taylor is the vice president of a prestigious Eastern university. A man of learning and integrity, a highly competent administrator and a loyal friend, he is in addition good-looking, sensuous, witty, and a fair skier—in short, a walking advertisement from the *New York Review of Books* "Personals."...

Trouble brews when the provost of the university dies. Despite the fact that Conrad is next-in-line for the job, the President decides to appoint a Search Committee. (This is, you understand, the early '70s, when Search Committees were rampant throughout the land.) Will Conrad obtain the post on the basis of his many years of devoted labor on behalf of the university? Or will it go instead to Grant Hannover, a brash millionaire who is also a trustee and has the contacts necessary to raise much-needed funds? And *who* has been stealing objects from Conrad's oice? Could it be young Tom Spofford, his obsequious assistant, who "had a passion for success but no sense of direction"? These questions—and more—are answered in the course of Philipson's long-winded and resolutely humorless narrative. *A Man In Charge* pulsates with sound and fury—and will leave many readers entranced. When the band has passed, though, not much remains except dim echoes of what might have been. (p. 8)

> *Daphne Merkin, "Privileged Lives," in* The New Leader, *Vol. LXIII, No. 11, May 21, 1979, pp. 7-8.*

CLIVE LAWRANCE

[*A Man in Charge*] approaches greatness when it deals with the author's main concern—power and integrity. Too often, however, it plunges into issues—love, sensuality, hippie awareness—on which Morris Philipson does not have as firm a grasp; then it stumbles toward mediocrity....

The title *A Man in Charge* is ironic, for the main character, Conrad Taylor, a powerful man at a prestigious American university, comes to recognize that we are seldom fully in control of our human lives.

In his relationship to the university, Taylor is a man of towering intellect and integrity. Is he incorruptible? It would appear so, for he brushes aside a million-dollar bribe. Then two events enter his life offering great leaps of power. One is the possibility of a government position; the other is the death of the provost of the university, leaving Taylor the logical successor....

The reader may recognize corruption in whatever guise, but can the tempted? Would we in Taylor's position?

These are absorbing and eternally important questions at any level of power from secretaries to presidents. . . .

Much of the essential elements of the novel take place in Taylor's mind, but Philipson is also a master storyteller. He has many surprise twists as the tale rolls compellingly toward Taylor's final awful decision. On the one hand lies falsity; on the other, loss of much of what makes his life meaningful.

The choice he makes is a tribute to Philipson's artistic integrity.

Clive Lawrance, "Big Man on Campus," in The Christian Science Monitor, *July 30, 1979, p. 19.*

GARY DAVENPORT

[In *Secret Understandings*], Morris Philipson focuses on a married woman who finds her commitment to her husband, her family, and her society confronted by the demands of her private world—but he recasts the formula with great originality. *Secret Understandings*—the title of the novel is wholly apposite to the situation in which his principal character Shelagh Jackman finds herself. She is an intelligent and reflective woman in her early fifties, and her loyalty to her husband—a prominent judge whose life . . . is happily centered on his marriage—is unquestionable. In fact, given the open and authentic relationship that Philipson depicts in the first half of the book, the reader can scarcely imagine either of the Jackmans deceiving the other in any significant way. And yet Shelagh is aware all along that she is cast in multiple roles: she sees herself not merely as "myself" but also as "myself-for-my-sister, which is as different as myself-for-my-husband is from myself-for-my-son." Hence the multiple modes of narration in the novel: Shelagh's letters and diary entries are interwoven with a third-person narrative which, although centered on Shelagh's consciousness, fully renders the social context in the novel-of-manners tradition.

While visiting her sister in London, Shelagh becomes ill, and a medical examination reveals an untreatable malignancy of the brain. Almost impulsively she conceals the truth from her sister, and returns to her husband (who had stayed in America) with the horrible knowledge that she has six to nine months to live. At this point the crisis of secrecy develops, for she decides not to tell him, or anyone else, about her condition. She deceives her husband about the most important truth of their lives, partly out of love for him and partly out of her refusal to be treated as an object—to lose her autonomy and effectiveness as a person.

A reader may well become apprehensive at this point in the action: how can the rest of it (nearly half) survive the maudlin spectacle of this doomed woman heroically struggling to be cheerful for the benefit of her unsuspecting husband? How can it avoid becoming a morbid chronicle of the "passive suffering" that Yeats pronounced an unsuitable theme for literature? After such misgivings it is a real delight to watch Philipson's mastery of what is one of the most difficult problems he could have created for himself. Essentially what Shelagh Jackman does is demonstrate that her love—of living, of her husband, of herself—is a more formidable condition than death. Without a trace of cant, and without immunity to the terror of the situation, she is able to manage death: she makes it so private, she confines it so thoroughly, that all it can do—however absurd this sounds in abstraction—is kill her. She is a rare

person: her husband sees her as having "to an exceptional degree, a sense of the balance between a person's being solitary and being bound to others." But she is also a very typical person with a universal problem: "Mankind as a whole," she says in a letter to her husband, "keeps the central secret from itself—that People Die." The reader has a vicarious sense of triumph that is uncommon in fiction, and it is enhanced by a risky but successful O. Henry ending in which Shelagh's husband is revealed as capable of equally profound and tortuous secret understandings. Philipson's novel is a fearless, unsentimental, and philosophically serious treatment of an urgent and even heroic confrontation between self and world. (pp. 130-31)

Gary Davenport, "The Two Worlds of Contemporary American Fiction," in The Sewanee Review, *Vol. XCII, No. 1, Winter, 1984, pp. 128-36.*

PAUL SKENAZY

[Morris Philipson] knows about academics, art and the world of high culture from the inside. In *Somebody Else's Life,* he takes that experience and turns it inside out with an intriguing question: Can you be other people than you are, or think you are, or have so far made yourself?

That's what Stephen Cooper starts wondering while in Washington for his niece's wedding. He is overcome by the lavish abundance of his brother's mansion. . . . Suddenly Cooper realizes that his own life as a professor of the history of philosophy at Northwestern University was "of no consequence in the world they inhabited." His usual defense—comparing his discriminating sensibility to their philistinism—collapses, and he must admit that he "was profoundly tired of himself."

Perhaps prompted by this ennui, he is overcome by a work of Whistler in a museum and imagines making a lot of money by writing a novel about someone who fakes an antique leather wall hanging. But the literary plans quickly give way to real hopes of pulling off a swindle when his lover, Alice Jensen Chase, makes him realize that as an art authenticator she has the skills to create such a forgery. . . .

Despite its framework of crime and fakery, *Somebody Else's Life* is not just a commonplace thriller. We are, after all, in another social and cultural territory, and Philipson is after other things than the kind of financial payoff that his hero Cooper believes will alter his life. This is a story about authenticity. . . .

His point is fundamental—that in a world where everything from politics and works of art to body parts and the qualities of the past can be created in a near-perfect facsimile of the real thing, so can, and will, one's emotional capacities, will to live and personality.

Given the interesting premise, the frequently fine eye for social graces and gaucheries, the multiple ways duplicity turns back on itself and the carefully researched technical aspects of the art ploy, Philipson's novel should be better than it is. He has a complex problem as a writer: to engage our attention while revealing the inner emptiness of a meanspirited man. Cooper is, as he himself realizes, "hollowed out," and we must both see through and into this singularly boring figure.

But Philipson is not a strong storyteller. He is more a moralist and organizer, something like an ethical bureaucrat of plot. He manages all the angles and twists and turns with admirable facility and control. The pieces of the puzzle fit in their proper order and sequence, but the scenes rarely take on the vivid energy, intense sense of threat, or feel of living in a limbo of identity that one yearns for in a fiction of this kind. The pace falters; the prose too often reads like a song playing at too slow a speed. A well-meaning didacticism—an unnecessary reiter-ation—overcomes the tension of the crime and the insights into character, as if Philipson is explaining his ideas to a slightly cretinous audience. This leaves us feeling mildly entertained and frequently enlightened but unsatisfied. We end the novel knowing a lot about aspects of art forgery and something of the tedium of the life of the mind, but with little sense of having made a real or lasting discovery about anything more substantial than the envy that begins the adventure.

> Paul Skenazy, "A Thinking Man's Crime," in Chicago Tribune—Books, *February 8, 1987, p. 7.*

BENJAMIN DeMOTT

When vanity weakens, dangers swarm. This is one lesson taught by *Somebody Else's Life,* Morris Philipson's fifth novel. The hero, Stephen Cooper, a fiftyish, philosophy-professing bachelor at Northwestern University, is vain of both his intelligence and his ability to please women sexually. He's lived most of his life in a condition of equable self-appreciation, gratified by escape to the academy from the "simple, un-selfconscious philistinism" of the family into which he was born, convinced of the foolishness of permanent human attachments.

Comes a family wedding, though—Cooper attends almost by accident—and his self-love is shaken. The father of the bride, a half-brother Cooper has patronized for years as mindless, steps forth astonishingly as a man of parts—a rich and influential entrepreneur who has somehow also managed to develop an admirably original taste as an art collector. Strolling this relative's Potomac estate, conversing with the man's friends—people with larger agendas and appetites than are found in faculty clubs—Cooper suffers intimations of personal triviality. Why had he not known better than to preen himself on his humdrum academic career, his round of sexual exploits?

Brooding on this and related questions, Cooper conceives the promising ambition of turning his existence around—becoming a genuine Somebody. The main narrative of *Somebody Else's Life* details his effort to prove it's never too late, not even for a philosophy professor, to lay claim to a significantly individual life.

But like many of his contemporaries, Cooper can't shed the assumption that big money is the key to pressing such a claim successfully. For a while he's stuck in hackneyed fantasies of quick riches (writing a best seller, peddling movie rights, etc.). Then his current girlfriend Alice, a conservator at the Art Institute of Chicago, shows him a fresher path. The best seller Cooper is drafting describes an attempt to counterfeit a 16th-century Spanish leather wall hanging possessing an extraordinary history. . . . Alice advises him to drop the book and commit the crime it imagines. The two join forces to bring off a forgery, fabricating an objet d'art with an estimated 57th Street value of $1 million, and resourcefully arranging for its sale.

The themes and interests surfacing in *Somebody Else's Life* have appeared before in Mr. Philipson's writing. He introduced a cast of cheats and liars in an earlier novel, *The Wallpaper Fox,* and has produced at least one monograph in art history, a study of Leonardo da Vinci. Commercial and psychological realities are often well-observed in this carefully plotted tale. Places are finely rendered. . . . We move inside Cooper's chilly satisfaction as he and his lover-accomplice bring off one trick after another in the identity-switching necessary to their scam. . . . And we're also brought close to the pain and rage—"the post-adultery blues, when the lady *can't believe* it's over"—of the women whom Cooper (incorrigible to the end) deceives.

But despite these achievements the book isn't a fully satisfying performance. Persuasive handling of themes such as deception, greed and rebirth calls for moral clearsightedness, and *Somebody Else's Life* frequently seems morally confused. Its hero is presented as a figure capable of envy but not of commitment, treacherous to friends, exploitive of women, respectful of no value. Yet the author appears also to believe that Stephen Cooper's moral life can be taken seriously. . . .

Experienced readers nowadays are schooled in contrarieties; combinations of cool shallow caddishness and melodramatic emotional intensity are not a problem, provided the author seems in touch with the discontinuities and concerned to read their meaning. *Somebody Else's Life* seems out of touch with its discontinuities, oblivious of the ponderable moral vacancies at the core of its central character's ambition. Even though it is readable and intermittently entertaining, it comes across in the end as an opportunity wasted—a more than ordinarily vexing near miss.

> Benjamin DeMott, "Intimations of Triviality," in The New York Times Book Review, *February 15, 1987, p. 31.*

Pierre Reverdy

1889-1960

French poet, critic, editor, essayist, novelist, and memoirist.

An influential literary theorist and poet, Reverdy was closely associated with Cubism, an art movement that emerged in Paris during the years preceding World War I. Defined by Kenneth Rexroth as "the conscious, deliberate dissociation and recombination of elements into a new artistic entity made self-sufficient by its rigorous architecture," literary Cubism paralleled the development of its counterpart in the visual arts, seeking to endow poetry with an autonomous vitality while liberating the genre from strict representation of nature. Reverdy's work, which is characterized by unconventional typography and punctuation, use of both prose and free verse forms, and sparse, unadorned diction, emanates from the Symbolist heritage of Charles Baudelaire, Stéphane Mallarmé, and Arthur Rimbaud. Reverdy's poetry nevertheless eschews Symbolism's emphasis upon mystical and idealized realms in favor of expressing physical reality through unexpected juxtapositions involving commonplace objects and occurrences. Although some critics have noted a detached and dehumanizing quality in much of Reverdy's work, most have praised the clarity of his vision and the multiple implications expressed in his poems. Mary Ann Caws and Patricia Terry observed: "Through his influence on such Surrealist poets as Breton and Eluard, and also directly, Reverdy's work has had a great impact on the American Imagist poets of the middle part of this century. In him can be found both ellipsis and intensity, both informality and care for new forms."

Reverdy was born in the small provincial town of Norbonne, France. In 1910, he traveled to Paris, where he became associated with painters Georges Braque, Pablo Picasso, and Juan Gris and poets Max Jacob and Guillaume Apollinaire. Under their influence, Reverdy began to publish his poetry, and in 1917 he founded the literary journal *Nord-Sud*. A crucial document in the development of literary Cubism, *Nord-Sud* also provided a forum for the early writings of such Surrealists as André Breton, Philippe Soupault, and Louis Aragon. In late 1918, *Nord-Sud* ceased publication, and in 1921 Reverdy and his wife converted to Catholicism, retiring five years later to a monastery in Solesmes, France. Reverdy continued to write during his years at the retreat, and much of his subsequent work explores psychological and religious themes while displaying only infrequent traces of the influence of Cubism. Reverdy eventually became bitterly disillusioned with religious institutionalism, and his pessimism began to affect his experiences within the secular world. Friendships deteriorated, and his writing received less critical notice, which further aggravated his depression. Although he failed to maintain his Catholic faith, Reverdy lived and wrote in seclusion at Solesmes for the remainder of his life.

Reverdy's early poetry, which was deeply influenced by Cubist doctrine and the verse of Apollinaire, reflects disenchantment with the idealism of the Symbolists as well as with objective representation as advocated by traditional art. In these volumes, which include *Poèmes en prose* (1915), *La lucarne ovale* (1916), *Les ardoises du toit* (1918; *Roof Slates and Other Poems*), and *La guitare endormie* (1919), Reverdy creates fragmented por-

traits of musical instruments, tables, windows, and lamps similar to those in the paintings of Picasso, Braque, and Gris, seeking to exorcise these objects from fixed notions of reality. He frequently endeavors to render the simultaneity and multiplicity of perceptual experience by offering successive views of a particular subject or object through contrapuntal themes and images. With *Nord-Sud*, Reverdy provided himself with an outlet for his aesthetic beliefs. Perhaps Reverdy's most widely discussed literary concept is his theory of the image, which he expounded in *Nord-Sud* in 1918 and which Breton later incorporated into his Surrealist creed. Rejecting I. A. Richards's widely accepted definition of literary metaphor, which emphasizes a comparative relationship between the "tenor" and "vehicle" of a metaphoric image, Reverdy developed his own principle, which Robert W. Greene summarized as "the bringing together of two equally important objects of attention not normally associated with each other, a rapprochement that sets off the spark of esthetic response in the reader. Thus, the various fragments of the Cubist poem . . . should, in theory at least, generate by their reciprocal action a whole series of sparks, of fleeting illuminations."

In the years following the discontinuation of *Nord-Sud*, Reverdy experienced profound spiritual uncertainty. His conversion to Catholicism and seclusion at Solesmes exemplified his quest for meaning and is reflected in his poetry from this time.

Such collections as *Etoiles peintes* (1921), *Coeur de chêne* (1921), *Cravates de chanvre* (1922), *Grande nature* (1925), and *La balle au bond* (1928) exhibit the skepticism, despair, and ensuing guilt that permeated Reverdy's life and influenced the development of his personal and artistic sensibilities. Reverdy's later poetry posits that the essence of existence involves perpetual change and transformation. In *Sources du vent* (1929), *Flaques de verre* (1929), and *Pierres blanches* (1930), Reverdy expresses themes of motion in images of physical fragmentation and intense psychological contradiction. *Ferraille* (1937) is dominated by scenes of violence, chaos, and world holocaust, as well as by spiritual and psychological disintegration. Reverdy eschews these aspects in *Le chant des morts* (1948) in favor of a tone of resigned pessimism and an acceptance of the instability of human existence. Many of the poems in *Plein verre* (1940) and *Bois vert*, which was completed in 1940 and published as part of *Main-d'oeuvre* (1949), focus on death as the ultimate consequence of stagnation. Despite the negativism and images of death that pervade many of these later works, art also appears as a central focus, providing a source of identity, stability, and hope. Many of Reverdy's most significant poems are collected in the volumes *Les épaves du ciel* (1924) and *La liberté des mers* (1960), the latter of which contains illustrations by Georges Braque. *Selected Poems* (1969), the first compilation of Reverdy's verse to appear in English, was translated by Kenneth Rexroth.

Reverdy's prose has been published in several volumes. *Le voleur de Talan* (1917) is a novel written in free verse, *La peau de l'homme* (1926) comprises a novel and short fiction, and *Risques et périls: Contes, 1915-1928* (1930) is a collection of short stories. Reverdy's diverse aphorisms and meditations are contained in *Le livre de mon bord: Notes, 1930-1936* (1948) and *En vrac: Notes* (1956), while his theoretical writings have been assembled in the volumes *Self défence: Critique esthétique* (1919), *Le gant de crin* (1926), which also contains personal notes on religious topics dating from his early years at Solesmes, and *Nord-Sud, Self défence, et autres écrits sur l'art et la poesie, 1917-1926* (1975).

(See also *Contemporary Authors*, Vols. 97-100, Vols. 89-92 [obituary].)

W. KENNETH CORNELL

The passage of years has perhaps now given us sufficient perspective to make provisional evaluations of the progress of French poetry in the twentieth century and to turn our attention from the great debt which modern poets owe to Ducasse and to Baudelaire, to Rimbaud and Mallarmé, toward the question of innovations and new poetic manners in our times. The day may well come when we shall view with wonder the richness and variety in poetic expression during the post-Symbolist period, an epoch we are prone to think singularly unreceptive to poetry.

The majority of commonly accepted authors in modern French verse bear either in their form or thought the indubitable stamp of our century. We have seen the evolution of something which may be called "poésie pure," which transcends the narrow limits of poetic schools, and in which lyric art has been given an approach, an existence, utterly different from that of prose. Péguy and Claudel, Soupault and Eluard have invented styles

so personal as to defy imitation. Valéry, in spite of traditionalism in form, has so included the dynamic processes of thought within the framework of verse that he too emerges startlingly original and individualistic.

It is of a poet who has not won general recognition, who is indeed accepted with many reservations, that we wish to speak. His name is Pierre Reverdy, and in talent as well as genuine accomplishment he would seem to be one of the luminaries of recent letters. Born at Narbonne in 1889, Reverdy became a resident of Paris in 1910. About 1917 he attained some prominence as editor of *Nord-Sud*, a magazine which did much to further the understanding of Cubism, and in whose pages Reverdy first stated his poetic creed. It was in this same periodical that the early writings of several of the future Surrealists appeared, among them, contributions by Soupault, Breton, and Aragon, and this has sufficed to associate the name of Reverdy with the Surrealist group. In truth he has little in common with them, save the discovery of relationships between things which seem at first sight utterly disparate, and the sense of mystery surrounding man's conscious and sub-conscious world. But Reverdy never strove to shock; the excesses of Dadaism were impossible in a man of his contemplative mind. When the Surrealists turned toward Communistic and anti-Catholic doctrines, he shut himself away from them. Of deeply religious nature, a person utterly removed from any political interests, he left his erstwhile collaborators when they began to blaspheme and to produce their rather alarmingly Freudian texts and pictures. The "cadavre exquis" experiments or the uninhibited discussions on love which Breton, Péret, and Crevel were publicizing could not interest his thoughtful spirit.

Reverdy's literary history has been a singularly retiring one. He has stated openly that he expects only a small and elite public. This he does not say in a narrow or snobbish sense, but rather because of general belief: "La poésie est exclusivement aux poètes qui écrivent pour eux seuls et quelques hommes doués d'un sens que les autres hommes n'ont pas." Consistently with this article of belief, Reverdy published between 1915 and 1922 his little volumes of poems and prose poems in "éditions de luxe" of from fifty to one hundred and fifty copies, and it was not until 1924 that these rare items were given extensive publicity in the collection entitled ***Les Epaves du ciel***. Following on this came six years of fecund production, but in 1931 the poet became silent and it was not until 1937 that his tragic and beautiful volume ***Ferraille*** appeared. This silence, of which Mallarmé and Valéry furnish comparable examples, is not difficult of explanation in the case of an author who confesses that he has no confidence in his own work.... (pp. 267-69)

But if Reverdy speaks modestly concerning his work, he is not gentle in his attitude toward his readers. He suggests that what the conservatives might call disorder in modern poetic thought is often simply not an obvious and usual alignment of ideas; in reply to those who speak of obscurity in expression, Reverdy insinuates, none too tactfully, that the critics have not brought in enough of their own intellectual powers to illuminate poetic thought. Finally he insists that it is not acceptance by the public, but rather the intrinsic worth of a production, which counts. The problem becomes even more forbidding and complicated when one knows that Reverdy has only contempt for traditional verse forms, which he regards as mere ingenious patterns of words, and when one takes into account the fact that he refuses to submit his compositions to ordinary rules of logic and that he scorns verse which reaches a conclusion.

Like the styles of his contemporaries, Reverdy's literary manner is so personal as to negate the importance of sources. The creation of a group of poets called Cubists is but a vague way of indicating a manner of approach, but neither Guillaume Apollinaire, Max Jacob, nor André Salmon have close points of similarity with Reverdy. The exuberance of the first, the mordant irony of the second, and the fantasy of the third create worlds in which the sober and burning spirit of Reverdy could not live. If there be a link between these poets it is in the absence of ornament, in the complete liberty of form, in matters of method rather than kinship of mind. Reverdy's poetic atmosphere is in truth quite divergent from theirs and is closer to that of a poet of entirely different inspiration and technique, Jules Supervielle.

Yet Reverdy is of course provided with spiritual ancestors. . . . In his own case the influences of Pascal, of Baudelaire, and of Mallarmé emerge. They have nourished but have not dominated him. He writes prose poems, excellent ones in which the theme of the ideal is a poignant theme, but their rhythm and content are not those of Baudelaire; he yearns toward the absolute in poetic expression and employs ellipses and strange verse patterns, but his approach is not Mallarmé's; he is led toward religious faith in part by cognizance of his own frailty, but even more by curiosity concerning the eternal essence of things and by a poetic love of the mysterious.

In his published volumes, though they appeared over quite a span of years (1915-37), Reverdy has changed little. Those who speak of his work say little in adverse criticism save to complain of the curtain of obscurity or more particularly the eternal monotony of his production, and both remarks are not without some justification. . . . [Through] their pessimism Reverdy's endless probings into the mysteries of his nature and of his world do sometimes lead to a sense of vacuity. Yet his thought, winging away toward what the poet cannot hope to know, even if it does at times end in the too rarefied atmosphere of the ineffable, is likely to produce a slight shiver of mysterious pleasure in the reader. This would seem a legitimate goal of poetry.

Reverdy is preëminently the poet of the mysterious. This appears in the very symbols he uses. He is constantly attracted by windows, because they either open on a dark and shadowy world which refuses to yield its secrets or upon the endless space of the universe. The unknown drama on the other side of the partition is as important to him as is the invisible wall which separates two people who are striving to know each other. Perhaps for the same reason the wind, laden with a thousand stories and touching so many things, is dear to him. It is not that the limits of his understanding appear to him a comforting or salutary thing, for menace and portent loom in the shadowy backgrounds evoked in many of his poems. Curiously enough, it is this surrounding mystery, the inability of man to understand others, and least of all himself, which orients the poet toward religious faith. Unable to comprehend the meaning of the tangible world, incapable of bringing his imaginative musing to any sort of conclusion, lonely and misunderstood, Reverdy casts himself at the feet of God, the source of all understanding. (pp. 269-71)

Be it constancy of purpose or limitation of talent, Reverdy has consecrated almost his entire effort in the expression of beauty to poetry. Three critical volumes, *Self Defence, Le Gant de crin,* and *Picasso,* make exception to this rule, but even in them one is aware that a poet is speaking with a kind of impassioned logic which rises at times to the style of Pascal. . . . (p. 271)

Such writing gives proof of a direct and succinct mind. Reverdy's prose is the key to his poetic manner. His prose poems are short and extremely dense in structure; the poems are usually equally brief and even more cleared of excess words. They take on all manner of form, and recognizing no regular metre or rhyme, they appear on the page as isolated phrases mingled with compact groups of lines. Such arrangement is not without its charm, for there is in it a suggestion of the varying speeds of the mind in the formulation of an idea and the importance attached to the concept. The gaps, the isolations of phrase, are part of Reverdy's poetic creed, for in essence this artistry is nothing other than the elimination of the unessential. In this Reverdy's admiration of the Cubist painters played some part and his results stem from painting, just as certain effects of Breton and Eluard emerge from Masson, Tanguy, and Ernst. What isolates Reverdy from most of his contemporaries is a sense of control, a rigid condensation at which he arrives through processes of dream, thought, and contemplation. These last two stages are not always important to the Surrealists or even to the other poets called Cubists and the free rein on the imagination gives their work an exuberance and lack of moderation which are far from Reverdy's effects.

Reverdy rebukes those who love words too much; he even scorns the search for literary sentence-form. All that he strives to do is to search out within himself the true poetic substance. Then he allows this substance to dictate the form his writing is to take.

Beneath the straightforward, almost dispassionate utterance of Reverdy there lurks a vibrant, consuming emotional life which is at once the greatest paradox and the most engaging element of his work. There is, it is true, no extensive baring of the heart, no expatiation on emotions, but there is the infinitely more subtle study of a single moment or aspect in exaltation, or more often despair. With an exactitude and penetration which suggest paragraphs of Marcel Proust, Reverdy conveys in a few lines the agony of awaiting someone eagerly desired, the moments when the clock hands stand as though crucified, the sense of disgust at the enslavement of the senses, the resurgent quality of remembered tenderness, and constantly the urge toward the ideal. . . . (pp. 272-73)

Others of these delicate, tenuous emotional moments, revealed with a clarity which is almost blinding, treat of the inner ravage wrought by a glance or a word, the sudden surprise of a new facet in human nature, or the complete isolation of self. And it is usually the momentary revelation, the terrific force of some unexpected truth, which Reverdy states in his concise and naked phrase. (p. 273)

The plan of the poems in which the theme is the moment of intense emotion is usually very simple. The first part, through a number of images, creates the atmosphere. The emotional result is stated tersely, and in such a way that a maximum of strength pervades the simple utterance. . . . The bridging of gaps between the images is not too difficult in Reverdy and while the reader may be constantly aware that his is only one of many possibilities in forging the links of thought, the totality of effect remains clear and constant. Even if Reverdy, in his poetry, has refused to submit to the ordinary rules of logic, his mind is clear and disciplined. The essential quality of lines and forms, even of thoughts, looms as important, rather than the accumulation of diverse and confusing objects which intrigue the delvers into the realm of dreams. Just as one is struck in Picasso's painting by what has been left out in order to create a more vital and powerful effect, so does he feel in this poetry the careful suppression of the non-essential.

The greater part of Reverdy's poems contains the essentials of a landscape or at least a suggestion of pictorial setting. Here the point of view or the time of day seem to matter little to the poet, some of the pictures being presented as from a train or boat in motion, others from a completely static outlook. The mystery of night intrigues the poet, but he is often attracted by the rich intensity of sunlight. He evokes countryside and sea, village, city, and plain. The forest is the only part of the visual world which seems neglected in his writing, and this is perhaps natural in a poet who is constantly poised for the unknown, for whom the sky and the far horizon constantly attract the gaze. For Reverdy, the sky is a constant invitation to infinity and he has written relatively few poems in which his glance does not make record of birds in flight, of clouds and wind, of serene blue, or of stars. Even within the rooms that are the setting of some of his verse, the window is the gateway to vast spaces. Sounds rise upward and roofs and trees merely conceal a portion of the immense and seductive curtain which conceals the unknown.

The final impression of this poetry is that of complete economy in words. The inner thought of the poet, with connecting ideas weeded out, emerges startling and at first glance too brutally naked. Qualifying adjectives, save those of emotional value, are eliminated; and adverbs play little part in this direct language of the essential. The resultant style, with its powerful and evocative verbs, is vibrant and moving. This is all part of a carefully conceived plan, in which the poet has chosen only the simple, constant things and has refrained from any amplifying description.

Such direct and unadorned poetry does not lend itself to complicated figures of speech; the few similes and metaphors are simple and are taken from banal and every-day objects. . . . Reverdy says that water rises like dust, that at times the world seems to stop like the pendulum of a clock, that a light trembles like a star, that life in the street is like blood coursing through the veins. Such similes do not seem intended as an ornament and disappear into the framework of the idea. Yet Reverdy's style, supported by occasional intense metaphors . . . , gives an impression of constant images and of a richly imaginative mind. This effect is achieved, not merely through his association of objects which attain relationship not through the senses but through the mind, but also by frequent personification of the inanimate and even of ideas. (pp. 273-75)

The willow dips its shining fingernails into the eddies of the stream; the murderous sun leaves the trees ensanguined and the fireplaces devour the light. These hardy flights of the imagination build from the exterior world a subjective universe which is the reflection of the author's own mood. The image becomes inseparable from the sentiment. . . . Reverdy has perhaps conquered the territory of suggestivity toward which the Symbolists yearned and where many of them met defeat. Few poets have accomplished the absolute fusion of picture and mood, but Reverdy nears success in this form of artistry.

Reverdy has said that a poet writes merely to know himself better. Certainly the introspective qualities of his verse are ever in the foreground and reveal a sensitive, somewhat bitter disposition destined to unhappiness and pessimism. The leitmotif of loneliness and isolation runs through all his work. . . . By nature a solitary figure for whom his fellow creatures remain eternal mysteries, Reverdy has been able to sing the delicate melody of the sigh left in the room after the loved one's departure or the gesture of farewell hovering in the air. His sensations are deep and moving but they have no sonority. (pp. 275-76)

Perhaps in *Ferraille* there is a new bitterness, a greater intensity of sorrow than in the days when Reverdy was content to evoke the forms of men without "existence réelle," but this is mitigated in his work by an extreme sense of pity which is not always directed inwardly. His poems are filled with figures of homeless and lonely wanderers. In Reverdy's first volume the little man with the overly big shoes who stands shivering in the light of the street lamp is but one of many succeeding ones, like the wayfarer confronted with the closed shutters and the growling dog in **"Façade"** or the tragic figure of **"Le Coeur écartelé"** whose faith is but a thorny thicket, whose eyes have lost their light and whose hands bleed against his heart. Nor is the poet so removed from reality that he cannot outline a peaceful picture of family life in **"Abat-jour"** or try to seize the spirit of a seaport in a single line. . . . (pp. 276-77)

The recurrence of themes, the pessimism of tone, the unchanging method of presentation have brought against Reverdy the charge of monotony. . . . [But] the reader who savors the poems bit by bit, meditating on some fragment of brilliant insight, some telling bit of imagery or some thought-provoking flight of the imagination is likely to append a modification. . . . When the poet speaks of the avid rust which is eating his heart, when he describes the faces of buildings washed with full buckets of light, even when he sees the setting sun as the slaughterhouse of light, his courage and forceful felicity of expression impose themselves on the mind and heart. The very inquietude of the writer, the author of **"Les Buveurs d'horizons"** and of **"Port,"** is a palpitating and emotional element which has some of the mysterious lure of Supervielle's poems. The unknown may not be of our earth, but it is thereby all the more enigmatical; it is that fourth dimension toward which we see the poet inexorably pushed, his breast slashed by the weapon of time. . . . (p. 277)

Reverdy's accomplishment has been the transposition of physical and moral phenomena to an artistic level and there the creation of a new world. By this alchemy he has come near to the writing of pure poetry, and upon reflective perusal of what he has done, there will likely be some who will be led to cry:

> 'Tis true: There's magick in the web of it.
>
> (p. 278)

W. Kenneth Cornell, "The Case for Pierre Reverdy," in Essays in Honor of Albert Feuillerat, edited by Henri M. Peyre, Yale University Press, 1943, pp. 267-78.

KENNETH REXROTH

The poets associated with Cubism are Guillaume Apollinaire, Blaise Cendrars, Jean Cocteau, Max Jacob, André Salmon and Pierre Reverdy. As the years have passed and *cette belle époque* recedes into perspective, for us today, Pierre Reverdy stands out from his fellows as the most profound and most controlled artist. This is part of a general revaluation which has taken place as the latter half of the century has come to judge the first half. . . . Although time has seldom worked so quickly, I am more or less confident that those revaluations will stand. Certainly Pierre Reverdy's present position should be secure. International literary taste has learned the idiom, the syntax that was so new and strange in 1912. Fortuitous novelty has fallen away and this has enabled comprehension and judgment. Neither Reverdy nor Tristan Tzara can shock anybody any more. And so those values once masked by shock enter into the judgment of a later generation.

Juan Gris was Pierre Reverdy's favorite illustrator, as he in turn was the painter's favorite poet. No one today would deny that they share the distinction of being the most Cubist of the Cubists. This is apparent to all in Juan Gris. But what is Cubism in poetry? It is the conscious, deliberate dissociation and re-combination of elements into a new artistic entity made self-sufficient by its rigorous architecture. This is quite different from the free association of the Surrealists and the combination of unconscious utterance and political nihilism of Dada.

When I was a young lad I thought that literary Cubism was the future of American poetry. Only Walter Conrad Arensberg in his last poems, Gertrude Stein in *Tender Buttons* and a very few other pieces, much of the work of the young Yvor Winters and others of his generation of Chicago Modernists, Laura Riding's best work and my own poems later collected in *The Art of Worldly Wisdom* could be said to show the delibrate practice of the principles of creative construction which guided Juan Gris or Pierre Reverdy. It is necessary to make a sharp distinction between this kind of verse and the Apollinairian technique of *The Waste Land, The Cantos, Paterson,* Zukofsky's *A*, J. G. MacLeod's *Ecliptic,* Lowenfels' *Some Deaths,* the youthful work of Sam Beckett and Nancy Cunard and, the last of all, David Jones's *Anathemata.*

In poems such as these, as in Apollinaire's "Zone," the elements, the primary data of the poetic construction, are narrative or at least informative wholes. In verse such as Reverdy's, they are simple, sensory, emotional or primary informative objects capable of little or no further reduction. Eliot works in *The Waste Land* with fragmented and recombined arguments; Pierre Reverdy with dismembered propositions from which subject, operator and object have been wrenched free and re-structured into an invisible or subliminal discourse which owes its cogency to its own strict, complex and secret logic.

Poetry such as this attempts not just a new syntax of the word. Its revolution is aimed at the syntax of the mind itself. Its restructuring of experience is purposive, not dream like, and hence it possesses an uncanniness fundamentally different in kind from the most haunted utterances of the Surrealist or Symbolist unconscious. Contrary to what we are taught, it appears first in the ultimate expressions of Neo-Symbolism in Mallarmé, in his curious still lifes like "Autre Éventail," in occult dramatic molecules like "Petit Air," and, of course, above all in his hieratic metaphysical ritual, *Un Coup de dés.* It is in this tremendously ambitious poem in fact that all the virtues and the faults of the style, whether practiced by Reverdy, Laura Riding or myself, can be found. (pp. v-vii)

Returned to today, *Un Coup de dés,* or the poems of Reverdy or Laura Riding seem negotiable enough and the similar poems of Yvor Winters seem only passionate love poems or rather simple philosophic apothemes. Reverdy, in fact, in most of his poems is hardly a mystic poet. He simply uses a method which he has learned from his more ambitious poems. It is ambitious enough. He seeks, as all the Cubists did, to present the spectator with a little organism that will take up all experience brought to it, digest it, reorganize it and return it as the aesthetic experience unadulterated. All works of art do this. Artists like Reverdy or Juan Gris sought to do it with a min-

imum of interference. When they were successful their artifacts were peculiarly indestructible. Today, like the paintings of 1910, Reverdy's poems have become precious objects indeed. They have a special appeal now because, although rigorously classical—(I suppose my description of their method could be called a definition of an hypertrophied classicism, which in a sense was precisely what Cubism was)—they are not in the least depersonalized. Quite the contrary—they are rather shameless. So many of the poems are simple gestures laying bare the heart. For this reason Reverdy has influenced personalist poets like Robert Creeley and Gary Snyder and through them whole schools of younger people.

Reverdy was aware of the final deductions to be made from his poetry as a whole and from his poetic experience when in his most illuminated poems he pushed it to its limits. It is not necessary that the poet have any special religious belief, or any at all, but if poetic vision is refined until it is sufficiently piercing and sufficiently tensile, it cuts through the reality it has reorganized to an existential transcendence. In Reverdy's case the consequences were more specific. In 1930 he retired to the Benedictine Abbey of Solesmes and lived there as a lay associate until his death in 1960 with only rare visits to Paris on business trips or to see old friends.

The revolution of the sensibility that began with Baudelaire became in the latter work of Mallarmé a thoroughgoing syntactical revolution in the language because it was realized that the logical structure of the Indo-European languages was an inadequate vehicle for so profound a change in the sensibility. In actual fact, although Apollinaire is usually considered the watershed of modern poetry, no single poem of his represents as thoroughgoing a change in method as Mallarmé's.

The only attack on the language that was as drastic was the Simultaneism of Henri Barzun, the father of the American critic. Unfortunately the quality of Barzun's work leaves much to be desired and his impact was slight. Gertrude Stein and Walter Conrad Arensberg both went further than anyone writing in French, both in their attempts to provide a new syntax of the sensibility and more simply in applying the methods of Analytical Cubism to poetry. Pierre Reverdy is the first important French poet after *Un Coup de dés* to develop the methods of communication explored by Mallarmé. (pp. x-xii)

> *Kenneth Rexroth, in an introduction to* Pierre Reverdy: Selected Poems, *translated by Kenneth Rexroth, New Directions, 1955, pp. v-xiii.*

DAVID I. GROSSVOGEL

There is a Reverdy reminiscent of Verlaine. Occasional refrains in the poems of *Cale sèche* relate and echo through the melody of feminine rhymes and a lulling rhythm, sadness ill-defined, the sentimental nostalgia of time evanescent in its lunar and oneiric landscapes. Such sadness is elicited by only a part of the poet's sensitivity and it calls his attention to only a part of experience. It is not an exclusive note in even this early world of Reverdy, though it is partly indicative of the moment to which *Cale sèche* belongs, a moment still marked by a concern with the outer as well as the inner modalities of the poem. In addition to echoes of Verlaine, a breath of hot-house symbolism occasionally drifts through this verse . . . dammed up quite suddenly by colloquial irony in the manner of Laforgue . . . or enlivened by still more ancient virtuosities. . . . (p. 95)

However, if these familiar sights are striking, it is especially because they intrude upon private grounds; they are alien in a generally unadorned and sober verse. If one is mindful of Reverdy's age at the time of this writing and of his meridional background, his youth spent close to sun and nature (he was born in Narbonne on September 13, 1889, and did not come to Paris until 1910), and if one considers in its totality this already achromatic, lamp-lit world, Reverdy's soberness appears to instance a discipline. The originality of this early verse is that of a personal expression that rejects, more often than it admits them, peripheral concerns and outer dictates. In days of stylish addiction to topical enthusiasms that begin with Diaghilev's advice to Cocteau in 1912, ''surprise me!'' and Apollinaire's ''most modern mainspring, surprise'' in 1914, Reverdy's poetry derives little from the mechanical muses that inspire much of the poetry written thereafter by Cocteau, Cendrars, Apollinaire, etc. Completely unaffected by stimuli of this sort, Reverdy has come to wonder, retrospectively, whether his former associates were actually influenced by it:

> As for those poets who once claimed that there was as much poetry in railroad stations or locomotives as in any other place or object, I wonder what it was they meant other than that a railroad station and a locomotive did not repel them any more than a relay station or a stage coach.
>
> (''**Circonstances de la poésie**,'' *L'Arche*, no. 21, muss. 1946)

If these early poems borrow from the color of their times, that color will be found not in transitory symbols but in the suffused grayness already referred to. Should Aragon's Marxian analysis of cubist esthetics be correct, economic reasons account for the soberness of the tenement-housed art developing at this time. The monochrome of Reverdy's poems is a first indication of cubist discipline. Historical evidence of his affiliation with cubism is provided by the magazine which he starts in 1917, *Nord-Sud*, whose aim was to parallel in literature the cubist experiment. If this circumstance is allowed to illuminate the reading of the antecedent *Cale sèche*, a recurrent trait becomes evident: a disjunctive, terminal chord established in the final verse, called by Aragon ''the definite solution of the problem'' (*Nord-Sud*, May 1918), whose resonance acts as a contrapuntal theme to the rest of the poem. Viewed in pictorial terms, this final verse is an image in a different plane, whose apposition to the body of the poem places the latter in a new perspective and gives it another dimension. ''**Sentiments fanés**'' ... ends with a verse whose typographical separation underscores the difference of a new stylistic and spiritual perspective.... This line, which cannot be read in isolation, shapes anew each image that has preceded it and forces reappraisal of the entire poem.

''**Sentiments fanés**'' does not proceed, as a matter of fact, from a single inspiration. The Maeterlinckian world that breaks upon a stanza reminiscent of Laforgue, illustrates a technique of refraction whereby a single emotion is split according to different though complementary apperceptions. This technique would be of value as a means of stating the fullness of a perception, if it were not that with the mood of each part is recalled a poet more usually associated with that mood—the suggestion of a pastiche frustrates the suggestion intended. In contrast, the counterpoising of the final verse—or image—achieves the same effect more directly and without the dissonances of the literary superimposition. And it is interesting to note that in *Cale sèche* there are already poems such as ''**Crèvecoeur**'' nearly entirely constructed of such fragmentary images.... Reverdy has expressed himself frequently on the nature of his art and of poetry in general. His comments in

Nord-Sud (collected in *Self-defence*, 1919), *Le Gant de crin* (1930), *Le Livre de mon bord* (1948), as well as articles and lectures, have established him as a lucid theorist, though one whose remarks about poetry seem curiously conservative alongside his poetic expression. His thought moves far afield, ranging from the conventional statements of a moralist to the biographical notations of a man undergoing a religious crisis. However, Reverdy fastens repeatedly on a number of assumptions that emerge as the formative lines of his esthetics. Amongst these, his notions about the so-called ''object'' probe deepest into his poetic structure. The previously quoted lines from ''**Circonstances de la poésie**,'' though they begin as a defense of certain poets who came into prominence at about the same time as Reverdy, are a declaration of principles; they conclude with the words: ''For there is no more poetry in a stage-coach than in a locomotive. No more, no less. There is none [in either]!'' And Reverdy broadens his argument to show that poetry will be absent as well from the emotion to which the contemplation of the object might lead. Nor will it be derived from emotions that tradition has ennobled, such as love, or hatred. Whence then is poetry derived? The sense of Reverdy's answer is plain from the aggregate of his writing and is spelled out in *Le Gant de crin:* ''poetry comes from the poet,'' exclusively.

The removal of a poetic inherence from whatever lies outside the poet places Reverdy in the Rimbaud-Mallarmé-Valéry orbit and exposes him to the ambivalences that shaped the thought of his predecessors—ambivalences that spring from their particular views of the form and substance of poetry. Mallarmé tension between ''flesh'' and the ''blue'' is experienced again by Valéry to whose intimate tragedy *La Jeune Parque* gives form. Poetry, traditionally the realm of the seer (whose naming by Rimbaud merely introduces poetry's age of self-consciousness), tempts the poet away from a finite, temporal and partitive state toward the dizzying prospects of totality and the absolute. But this will to utter lucidity, this desire to speak through Mallarmé's ''essential word'' of only quintessences and directly to the sheer consciousness, foretells the poet's assumption into godlike purity and loneliness. This temptation contends therefore with another, that of the impure mysteries of body and soul which preserve the young woman within *Le Jeune Parque*. Words, the bones of poetry, extend this ambiguity that has become definition after frustrating definitions. Moments of mind and music, words define themselves through these two terms as what they are not. The mind—godhead in man—and music are samples of purity that emphasize the impurity of words: to demand for poetry the transcendence of either is in fact to redefine the concept. The idea of the poem, though it aspires to the occult, and the phrases of the poem, though they aspire to melody, suffer too much from the utilitarian taint of words to attain such transcendence: poetry remains impure in essence.

This hopeless quest, tempered by a foreboding of its hopelessness, this sublime aspiration, magnified by its concomitant relapses, is interesting as one of the tragic stances of man: the hopelessness and the urge combine to fashion the poem. However, another way is suggested by the poet Claudel, debarred by Catholicism from assuming this tragic posture. By postulate, Claudel cannot reject the divine creation of which he is a mere but indissoluble part; but neither is his poetic ego so mean as to be hampered by such considerations. Although he acknowledges the lesson of Rimbaud, Claudel also acknowledges certain limitations to the seer's powers which he subordinates to those of God. The principal concession is recognition of God's superior vision which is the measure of all things—including the poet's limitations. Preserved by God from the vortices of the infinite, the poet turns back to the tangible—though god-like—dimensions of the earth whose acute translator he becomes. The object asserts its essential meaning through his vision: the poet creates by naming.

Reverdy shows a similar respect for the object. With Claudel, he is among those poets who believe that reality—"that which has objective existence"—is an absolute that is external to the poet and which it is the poet's job to decipher, in contrast to those who believe that such an absolute must be sought only within the poet's mind, and that the outer reality is in fact an illusion that impedes this search. Reverdy is materialistic to the point of spirituality, a man with an unsated thirst for "le réel"—the tangible evidence of phenomena—demanding for his poetry only that which is "consistent and permanent" (*Le Gant de crin*). But alongside a Claudel who sees a common sap flowing through diversified forms, Reverdy is an analyst for whom the material quiddity of each thing determines its unique spirituality. "The tang of reality," a frequent expression of his, informs what he writes through objects which, though barren of innate poetry, are palpable truth to a poet who is the meridional grandson and great-grandson of sculptors.

This reality is the term of Reverdy's quest, and it is its appropriation that affords him regal arrogance in asserting "la nature, c'est moi" (*Le Livre de mon bord*). But that "moi" appears in the poem only to the extent that it transmutes into the reality of the poem the reality which the object has in the outer world. It is not the "moi" of Valéry for whom the mind, supreme conscience of an all-encompassing self, expresses the totality and the loftiness of a transcendental perception; such sublime romanticism, along with all aspects of symbolism, was rejected quite soon by Reverdy (see his first articles in *Nord-Sud*). Instead, he demanded a "depersonalization" of poetry (one of the many fundamental views which the poet never relinquished, expressing it again in a recent and important article, **"Cette émotion appelée poésie,"** *Mercure de France,* August 1, 1950). Depersonalization is not synonymous with dehumanization. Paradoxically, it is those who demand that the human mind be the catalyst of ultimate truths who eventually soar beyond human levels and comprehension. The materialist Reverdy is in search of a truth that acquires meaning only in human terms, even though the human being is not present here. A comparison with the surrealists' experiment elucidates this paradox.

The objects that enter into Reverdy's poetic world have been likened to those of the surrealists. Such a comparison is encouraged by the pronunciamento which Breton, Aragon and Soupault made in 1924—presumably out of partisan sympathy—declaring that "Reverdy is the greatest poet alive today." The object of the surrealist's world is indeed reminiscent of Reverdy's in that it does not undergo transformation and is not a symbol but remains an instance of "crude reality" coursing at will in the poet's inner (mental) world where it is not limited through logic or convention to aprioristic significance. The object is an instantaneous perception of absolute reality in an unordered totality of such absolute perceptions, with no mutual link or hierarchy to bind them. The surrealists carry to its illogical extremes the dehumanization of the "je" begun by Valéry, in whom the "je" was already a mere performer for the benefit of a greater inner omniscience. The surrealist's process of dehumanization becomes a deliberately anti-human onslaught, the premise of which is that human dimensions are

essentially an expression of the limitations which poetry—or the surrealist's experience—hopes to transcend. Reverdy's devotion to the primacy of the object excludes the human dominant, along with all the notions of romanticism. But the palpable reality of his poems evidences the corollary of "la nature, c'est moi": the intimate texture of Reverdy's self is indeed that of nature. And so his truth remains that of man since it exists as a totality that is at least theoretically within man's grasp, rather than eluding him at the confines of his mind in an unending chase that leads the poet ever further away from the human reality.

Since the humanism of Reverdy disciplines his objects and thereby rejects Breton's autonomous and heterogeneous elements, words, which Breton wanted "dry as numbers" because they are likewise individual precipitates of an absolute reality, will also be of a different kind for Reverdy. True, his words are frugal and plain as are his objects, and enjoy no special status in his esthetics: they too are void of revelation or poetry— "a love of words kills style" (*Le Gant de crin*). But in the same way as Reverdy's poetry creates the reality of the object, his poetry creates words, and the words build the object in its own rhythm—called by Manoll "the rhythm of reality." This is not the poetic emphasis of Claudel which transforms the object into a predetermined Claudelian reality; instead, it is the very pulse and texture of the object informing the Reverdy poem.

This devotion to clean shapes, this essential lineation of prosaic objects that discards sentiment for a palpable texture, transposes into poetry the plastic ideals of cubism: the innermost poet assumes the tangible shape of objects; the poem which is self is matter in the same way as the cubist painting renders material the inner vision of the painter. Such creation is in fact disciplined re-creation. Where Claudel's catholicity conjoined all things through divine grammar and thus reinstated the simile (discarded by Rimbaud), the cubist world of Reverdy is an artistic unity that eliminates simile and metaphor because it exists as an inter-refraction of planes determined solely by the nature and structure of the artifact. "Les ruisseaux sont secs dans la cour voisine" is a fact, not a symbol or the evidence of poetry. It is a plane of reality, whose relation to the total composition determines the nature of that composition. Eventually, the poem is entirely built of such segments of vision, and as the poem on paper is still evidence of the poet's structural vision, the physical transcription of the poem extends that vision graphically. The tactile and visual concerns of the cubist lead logically to an interest in the physical appearance of the poem; Reverdy, a proofreader during his early days in Paris, was all the more sensitive to the latent suggestion of the printed page. He helped to set type for his first published poems and remained conscious of this aspect of their being thereafter. His typographical compositions are restrained, befitting his poetry, and amount to little more than a punctuation that replaces the grammatical punctuation which the new form of his poems has rendered unavailing. He does not strain for the esoteric significance of Mallarmé's typography, the facetious complexities of Apollinaire's *Calligrammes* or the noisy extravagances of dadaists. Simply, in Fumet's words, "the type-setting is to remind the reader, especially in the shorter poems, that the text settles on a mystery, that there is nothing to be gained from turning the page." Thus projected into the sensible form of the poem and the visual dimensions of its typography, the object has been assimilated by the poem to the fullest extent possible: the poem has become an object. . . . Cubism proposes to translate an essential reality through analysis. It rejects the exceptional object which is transitory by definition and hence, in this view, unessential. For the painter, this represents engagement beyond the usual responsibilities of the craftsman, placed as he now is in a world from which have been removed the traditional guideways and which he can render meaningful only through the depth and discrimination of his own vision. For the poet such responsibility is not new since his craft is merely a way of rendering his personal vision. It is another matter, however, to see the poet using for his analysis the particular techniques of cubism. It is this usage that distinguishes the shape and marrow of Reverdy's poetry.

Though it does not appear as a performer, it is the self in Reverdy that arrests and renders intelligible the random flight of the outer world—that "fixes," as hyposulphite the photographic plate, what is "consistent and permanent" in that outer world of transitory forms. Within this random motion, the controlled inner world of Reverdy is immobile—Valéry's "precious zero to which every algebraic expression equates itself." The quality of that inner world is determined by the humble *materia prima* upon which the transubstantiation will be effected: the objects to be spiritualized are neither the magical objects of Cocteau nor are they the shining prototypes of a momentary newness as are Apollinaire's. The objects of Reverdy are outwardly common and drab—as elementary as their truth. And the eye of the inner world that sees them is an object too: a window (like for example **La Lucarne ovale** which gives its shape to an important collection of Reverdy's poems in 1916). Nor should this window be mistaken for a symbol—there are no symbols in this poetry; it is the material aperture that shapes the material object which it views: "a window contrived in a facade and the hole in a damaged wall are unlike; and above all, do not speak of ellipsis" (**Self-defence**). The window must be remembered alongside the prosaic lamp that signifies, as did once Bérard's chandeliers over the house and garden in *L'Ecole des femmes,* the controlling presence of the artist, the stability of the artifact within the illusion.

The window breaks up the outer motion into static segments which are for the cubist the planes of his apperception. It isolates and transfixes (the verb is Reverdy's) individual fragments of reality whose interrelation is meaningful only in terms of the new totality which they define. Each segment of the object thus perceived (and the word "object" designates of course any external reality of which the poet takes cognizance) is a rudimentary and limited gesture, an isolated phase that is twice essential because it is a part of a greater essentialness and because it is thus separated from the contingencies of a conclusion. The elemental objects isolated in this manner are either retainers of time, such as the sky, the sun, day, night, rain, wind, etc.; or they are those that record its passage, such as roads, sidewalks, tracks; or again, they are the physical impediments to that progress, walls, towns, etc.

In a poetry that shuns words and emphases, these visions are neither poetic effects nor images. As early as 1918, Reverdy had rejected the metaphor, expressing in *Nord-Sud* a view often repeated in his writings: "The image is an unqualified creation of the mind. It cannot come about as the result of a comparison but comes instead from the bringing together of two more or less distant realities." This method is not either, as has been suggested, the reasoned derangement of the senses advocated by Rimbaud. Reverdy does not relinquish rational control. The dream, which in the Rimbaud-surrealist poetics frees the mind on its boundless quest, is rejected by Reverdy:

> To dream is to flee . . . To contemplate is to seek,
> to cherish and to caress . . . The dream is a debili-

tating bath, contemplation is a tonic bath . . . The dream is a tunnel that passes under reality. It is a sewer of clear water, but it is a sewer.

(*Le Gant de crin*)

Instead, Reverdy's fragmented vision is simply analysis and construct; these "dismembered sensations" as Raymond called them prematurely (*De Baudelaire au surréalisme*) are regrouped in a synthetic gesture, an artificial vision whose every part is an apperceived instance of reality: it is the process whereby "nature" becomes "moi."

Working with a cruelly unpoetic language, rejecting whatever is suspect of harboring poetry without the consent of the poet, and hence illegitimately, proceeding in his analysis with clinical precision, Reverdy is able nevertheless to suggest through a simple statement the multiple perception of his vision. (pp. 96-103)

But this method—or vision—skirts an obvious danger. Depersonalization is a first step towards dehumanization; effacement of the sentient self behind the analytical self leads to a loss of human warmth. Indeed, the poetic world of Reverdy is endangered by everything that is cold—the gray monotone; the quality of its black sun, chill stars, sky, night, wind, etc.; the emptiness that is the wake of the hand that has withdrawn an incipient gesture of friendship. Every clinical removal is a human loss. However, the precision of a technique that allows the clear apperception of things, controls in no way the implication of things. And though the "je" of Reverdy is seldom stated, it is felt to be anguished beyond the statements that it might make.

Reverdy's is an anxious world because for him, as for Cocteau, poetry is a perilous undertaking. Because the instruments of the analyst operate on a world that is not speculative, the reconciliations of craft and existence lead to an intimate dilemma:

> The poet is in a difficult and often perilous position,
> at the intersection of two planes, each of whose edges
> are cruelly sharp, that of the dream and that of reality.

(*Le Gant de crin*)

At what point does the necessary spiritualization of the self break contact with the equally necessary substance of external reality? Suspicious of heaven and earth, of sterile metaphysics and of unregenerate materialism alike, Reverdy is caught in a metaphysical squeeze and at least one commentator—Fongaro—has suggested that religion may have entered the life of Reverdy through this impasse.

Be this as it may, the anxiety that betrays the human in the analyst has deeper roots. Because of Reverdy's particular lighting, his inner rooms, even when star lit, are bathed in gloom. And the fragmentary forms analyzed by the window are strange in their isolation, frightening in the nakedness of their truth, and oppressive in the timelessness of their statement. And when their aggregate message has been deciphered, it merely confirms the endurance of an eternal mystery.

This anxiety is the pedal point in Reverdy's poetry—the suffused color of this cubist analysis. And although there is a younger poet who calls to mind an equally young Cocteau, in whose writings a star occasionally turns into merely a starfish, and the suggestion into little more than a pun; and although again, at another extreme that starts with *Ferraille,* there is the temptation to allow the "je" to step forward, to seek a human contact which evidence denies, it is the somber underlying anguish which this cold analysis more clearly echoes and which remains Reverdy's most haunting note. (pp. 104-05)

David I. Grossvogel, "Pierre Reverdy: The Fabric of Reality," in Yale French Studies, *No. 21, Spring-Summer, 1958, pp. 95-106.*

ROBERT W. GREENE

Only once did Pierre Reverdy explicitly acknowledge that another writer had influenced his creative life: "Baudelaire, par ses deux préfaces aux *Histoires extraordinaires* d'Edgar Poë, m'a influencé. C'est notre art d'aujourd'hui qu'il a décrit." That he so honored Baudeliare is not surprising, for it was Reverdy's generation which had welcomed *Les Fleurs du mal* and *Le Spleen de Paris* to the public domain. What is unusual perhaps is that he singled out for special mention not poetry but critical and theoretical texts by Baudelaire. Of at least equal significance, while not entirely unexpected, is Reverdy's opinion that the texts in question were prophetic. The second of the two prefaces, entitled "Notes nouvelles sur Edgar Poë," contains—probably for the first time in the French language—the term "poésie pure." Baudelaire used the term in connection with his desire to rid poetry of "heresies" such as didacticism, passion, morality, and truth. Today the phrase "poésie pure" calls to mind Paul Valéry and Henri Bremond, the dominant figures of the "poésie pure" debate of the 1920's and 30's. Yet Pierre Reverdy, a poet and theorist who took no part in the controversy, was perhaps more profoundly affected than its participants by Baudelaire's dream of a pure poetry. (p. 1)

First-hand knowledge of the aspirations and achievements of the Cubist painters was by far the most important single experience in Reverdy's artistic formation. Their rejection of representation in art as an end and of perspective as a means, along with their inclusion of quotidian objects in their canvases, inspired Reverdy to strive for a similar purity and immediacy in poetry. The impression made on the poet by his colleagues from the *bateau lavoir* was so deep that his entire *oeuvre*, imaginative and non-imaginative, illustrates Gaëtan Picon's thesis that creative writers since Baudelaire and Flaubert have steadily lost faith in traditional realistic means and at the same time have become increasingly obsessed with reality. Reverdy's uniqueness lies in his utter lucidity concerning the nature and the far-reaching implications of the new ideal of purity shaping the art of his time. For this reason his theoretical writings constitute an exceptionally illuminating document in the evolution of contemporary literature.

Reverdy's career as a writer began in October, 1912, when he published a short essay entitled **"A un pauvre écoeuré"** in the *Bulletin de la Section d'Or*, and ended in 1960, the year of his death, with the appearance of *La Liberté des mers*, a deluxe edition of poems illustrated by Georges Braque. Most of the books which the poet brought out during the forty-eight years of his publishing life were collections of poetry. It therefore seems quite appropriate that Reverdy should be known primarily as a poet, and perhaps equally appropriate that scholars and critics up to the present time should have devoted nearly all of their attention to that aspect of his writings.

Reverdy the writer of fiction remains virtually unknown, but this is not the impediment to an understanding of the whole artist that it might appear to be. The poet had stopped writing stories sometime before 1930, when he published *Risques et périls*, his third and final work of fiction. As Stanislas Fumet has pointed out, with the "story" in the traditional sense con-

sistently lacking in Reverdy's *contes*, it is likely that circa 1928 the poet simply decided to abandon a genre which he found too constricting for his particular talent. The hypothesis acquires credibility when it is considered in the light of the serious doubts which Reverdy entertained regarding the validity of history, biography, and anecdotal poetry. Furthermore, a close study of the poet's fictional works would perhaps result in their being reclassified, in nearly every instance, as either transposed essays or prose poems.

On the other hand, Reverdy's theoretical writings cannot be dismissed as atypical within his total production or as assimilable to some other genre. Two years after bringing out **Poèmes en prose** (1915), his first book of poems, the poet was already formulating the aesthetic principles underlying his own poetry, the poetry of some of his contemporaries, and the canvases of the Cubist painters. With his articles in *Nord-Sud*, the avant-garde review which he founded and edited in 1917-1918, he made his debut as a theorist of art and poetry. Once started, moreover, Reverdy never tired of probing the assumptions on which his work was based, of discussing the creative act, or of redefining art, poetry, and the poet. Periodically publishing his reflections in article, preface, and book form, by the end of his life he had produced a considerable body of theoretical material. Besides the many uncollected pieces, these writings consist of: *Self Defence: critique esthétique* (1919), *Le Gant de crin* (1927), *Le Livre de mon bord: notes 1930-1936* (1948), and *En vrac: notes* (1956). This work has never been studied in its ensemble. In fact, except for the scattered references to one or another of the poet's definitions which can be found in almost any of the longer articles on his work, to date there have been only two limited attempts to isolate his poetic principles.

As we have already seen, there was no sustained effort on Reverdy's part to produce works of fiction. A similar eventual diminution, though not so radical as in the case of his story writing, can even be observed in his poetic yield. During the last thirty years of his life he brought out only half as many books of poetry as he did during the first fifteen years of his career as a poet. Thus it was only in the realm of theory that the flow from Reverdy's pen remained constant.

Although the poet's theoretical work, a vital occupation for him early and late, has as yet received little critical attention, it has not gone unread. On the contrary, it has been recognized as the utterance of a sensitive and articulate theorist of the new in art and poetry. In 1952 André Breton praised Reverdy [as a] . . . theorist of the image . . . In 1956 Jacques Charpier and Pierre Seghers, in their anthology of *artes poeticae*, suggested the broad outlines of Reverdy's aesthetic with excerpts from *Le Gant de crin, Le Livre de mon bord,* and *En vrac.* And in 1962, Daniel-Henry Kahnweiler, reviewing Reverdy's writings on the plastic arts, extolled the poet's amazing grasp of the Cubist painters' aspirations.

While together these views of Reverdy give some idea of the breadth and import of his thought, it seems inevitable that alone each should focus a narrow light on the poet's theoretical writings. Since Breton had in 1924 incorporated a part of Reverdy's definition of the image in his *Manifeste du surréalisme*, it is understandable that in 1952 he should still associate Reverdy with his "thèses sur l'image poétique." Although the Reverdy texts in *L'Art poétique* constitute more than just a sampling of the poet's statements concerning the image, the anthologists—doubtless for reasons of space—do not quote from *Self Defense* or from any of the poet's many essays and prefaces. Ironically, however, the danger of distortion is greatest with Kahnweiler's brief but searching study. Without gainsaying the role that Reverdy played in explaining Cubism to the Cubists, to himself, and to others, we must nonetheless keep his writings on the plastic arts in proper perspective. Just as it would be wrong to assume that his remarks on the image, as important as these are, convey his entire poetic theory, so also would it be misleading to consider him as merely the explicator of Braque or Gris. (pp. 2-5)

It is possible that in some of its details Reverdy's theory would not hold up well under close scrutiny. So much, at least, may be inferred from Robert Champigny's remarks [in *Le genre poétique*] concerning ambiguities of language in Reverdy's definition of the image. Nevertheless, however accurate criticism of isolated passages in his writings may be, the microscope seems the wrong approach to Reverdy. Considered as a whole, his aesthetic has both internal coherence and historical appositeness. The definition in question reflects the increasing prestige and responsibility which poetic means generally and the image in particular were acquiring in the minds and works of many of Reverdy's contemporaries. And within the theory the importance which he ascribes to poetic means is totally consistent with his notion of the absolute independence of the created work.

Even granting that Reverdy's definition of the image is imprecise in its terminology, it adumbrates an extremely "modern" insight. His misgivings notwithstanding, Champigny sees in the three key sentences ("L'image est une création pure de l'esprit. Elle ne peut naître d'une comparaison, mais du rapprochement de deux réalités plus ou moins éloignées. Plus les rapports seront lointains et justes, plus l'image sera forte—plus elle aura de puissance émotive et de réalité poétique.") a laudable effort to make a radical and thoroughly "modern" distinction between metaphor and analogy, between an essentially poetic means and a prosaic one—an early attempt to explain what Champigny calls "la réaction poétique d'interférence."

There are of course other "modern" features in Reverdy's theoretical writings. His essays on painters and sculptors, for example, have been identified as belonging to the twentieth-century genre of "poésie critique" which Apollinaire's *Les Peintres cubistes* inaugurated. Insofar as the label may connote the impressions of an amateur rather than the reflections of an initiate, however, it is misleading in the case of Reverdy. For the nearly fifty years of his adult life the poet examined, from within, the implications of the Cubist revolution. But in spite of this reservation, there is no denying that, along with Breton, Malraux, Ponge, Char, and several others, Reverdy helped to establish a new kind of art criticism, criticism in which a creative writer sensitive to the plastic arts records his successive reactions (meditative, imaginative, analytical) before a single work or series of works.

Whether Reverdy was analyzing Picasso, defining the image, or discussing any other theoretical point, however, one ideal seems to have directed his thinking. Throughout his life he was obsessed with formulating the principles of a pure art. In historical terms this means that he was involved in continuing the conscious purification of poetry which Baudelaire's essays on Poe had set in motion. Reverdy, moreover, was fully cognizant of his ideological descendence, and consequently of his basic kinship with the ascetic current in modern poetic attitudes. Yet his name has only rarely been linked with that

current, or with its more illustrious exponents, Mallarmé and Valéry.

Reverdy's contribution to the cause of poetic purity deserves to be recognized, particularly inasmuch as it breathes new life into what had become a moribund development in French poetic thought. As T. S. Eliot points out in an address entitled "From Poe to Valéry," the systematic purification of poetry operative in France from the time of Baudelaire's texts on Poe reaches both a climax and an impasse in Valéry. Valéry's extreme self-reflexiveness, Eliot notes, leads him to elevate the creative process above the created work, an attitude that is ultimately fatal to art. Beside Valéry's narcissistic aesthetic, Reverdy's stubbornly work-oriented theory, also rooted in Baudelaire and Poe, assumes the character of an antidote, a means of allowing "the most interesting development of poetic consciousness anywhere in [the last] hundred years" to remain vital and viable.

From an historical point of view the corrective nature of Reverdy's theory in relation to Valéry's is perhaps its most significant aspect. Furthermore, it possesses this identity far more completely than one would at first suspect. The two crucial notions which according to Eliot originate in Poe and culminate in Valéry have their counterparts in the two leitmotifs which we have observed in Reverdy's theoretical writings. Eliot asserts:

> There is first the doctrine, elicited from Poe by Baudelaire . . . 'A poem should have nothing in view but itself'; second the notion that the composition of a poem should be as conscious and deliberate as possible, that the poet should observe himself in the act of composition—and this, in a mind as sceptical as Valéry's, leads to the conclusion, so paradoxically inconsistent with the other, that the act of composition is more interesting than the poem which results from it.

As regards the first notion, the principle (in embryo) of the autonomy of the work of art, Valéry and Reverdy of course agree. But a comparison of the second notion with the other theme in Reverdy's aesthetic reveals the essential difference between the two theorists, and shows as well that the inconsistency which Eliot has noticed in Valéry is not present in Reverdy.

The second leitmotif in Reverdy's theoretical writings contains an implicit distinction between Symbolist introspection and Cubist introversion. To the extent that he was mesmerized by the operations of his own mind, Valéry epitomizes Symbolist introspection. Reverdy's distinction permits him to "relieve" Valéry, to continue the conscious purification of poetry without falling into self-contemplation. Again and again, it will be recalled, Reverdy insists that the poet must be introverted, aware of his means, in the very moment that he draws the elements with which he creates from the raw materials of life-nature-living-reality. In fact, Reverdy returns so regularly to the principle of the poet's dual orientation in the creative act, that one feels in the end that something beyond the principle itself is at stake. It is as if he sensed that a new aesthetic was needed, one which would not *reject* self-consciousness but *transcend* it. Roger Shattuck has shown that just such an aesthetic was beginning to inform the work of a cluster of creative artists in France soon after 1900. It embodied the advances of self-reflexiveness even as it embraced the external world. Shattuck describes it thus [in *The Banquet Years*]: "It is as if, in Edmund Wilson's terms, Axel and Rimbaud could inhabit a single human being who retreats from reality by seizing it in a sustained effort of transformation.'' This is a perfect description of Reverdy's conception of the creative act.

The vitality and the relevance of Reverdy's poetic theory stem from its being situated at the intersection of two lines of thought, the Cubist revolution and its consequences on the one hand, and on the other, the pure poetry tradition emanating from Baudelaire. Though an admitted disciple of Baudelaire in this regard, Reverdy was forever immunized against the temptation of [what Shattuck called] ''stalk(ing) the workings of his consciousness into the reaches of solitude and solipsism'' by an enduring admiration for the artist who ''imagine d'après nature.'' His obsession with poetic purity was always balanced by his passion for objective reality. Precisely because he maintained himself ''au tranchant cruellement acéré,'' Reverdy also resisted the temptation of the object. Unlike Ponge, he never gave up his poet's right to perform ''l'acte magique de transmutation du réel extérieur en réel intérieur,'' to conceptualize objective reality. The ''glorification et la remise en honneur de la matière'' which Reverdy saw as one of Cubism's accomplishments appears carried to its logical conclusion in Ponge. By the same token, one element in the pure poetry tradition, self-reflexiveness, attains its most extreme form in Symbolist introspection. Standing between Symbolism and Ponge, Reverdy at once reconciles them and revitalizes Baudelaire's dream. (pp. 93-6)

> Robert W. Greene, in his The Poetic Theory of Pierre Reverdy, *University of California Press, 1967, 108 p.*

JULIA HUSSON

[*English translations of the poems ''Une eclaircie,'' ''Son de cloche,'' and ''Bêtes,'' included in the following excerpt, are taken from* Roof Slates and Other Poems of Pierre Reverdy, *translated by Mary Ann Caws and Patricia Terry, Northeastern University Press, 1981.*]

In order to understand what the term ''poème-objet'' meant to Reverdy, we need to see it in the context of that new movement with the seemingly contradictory title of Literary Cubism. Far from being the product of a literary school, this movement arose out of a close friendship and association between the Cubist painters and their poet friends at the beginning of the century. (p. 21)

The ideal shared by the Cubist painters and poets alike was primarily to give art its own reality, to free it from its traditional subservience to the real world, which it was supposed to imitate. . . . Their aim was to create a work of art which would exist as an *object,* that is, an autonomous creation which could take its place among the natural things of the world and no longer exist as a reflection of that reality. . . . The poets who most clearly formulated this new aesthetic were Pierre Reverdy and Max Jacob. Their aims are not to be confused with the rather naïve attempts of certain poets at the time to create poetic ''objects'' by writing poems on cubes or folding paper to be suspended from the ceiling in a room or even with Apollinaire's use of original typography in his *Calligrammes.* Such devices in no way changed the poem itself and seem to be equivalent to those of painters who thought that to reduce everything to geometrical shapes in a picture was to be a Cubist. There is something more fundamental in common between the true Cubist painters and poets: the need they felt for a more solid architecture which would be its own justification and not just a

support for a subject or ''story'', and a return to the object as a reaction against, on one hand, the formlessness and fleeting character of Impressionism and, on the other, the equally fleeting and rarefied atmosphere of Symbolism. Of course, the way had already been paved by the Post-Impressionists and by poets like Rimbaud, but Reverdy and Jacob wanted to carry this still further—to eliminate narrative from their works altogether and to fix the reader's attention on the poem itself as a concrete, compact whole. (p. 22)

At the same time the Cubist poets were conscious of redefining poetry and of giving it a new character that would once and for all set it apart from prose. Poetry, they thought, is language, but language used in a different way, to a different end, which is not just utilitarian. Poetry does not come from the use of ready-made verse forms, nor is it inherent in any particular object or scene. As Max Jacob said, it is not enough to write a series of unequal lines with a half-pun at the end and think it is poetry. ''Poetry comes from poets'', says Reverdy, in a disarmingly simple formula. A poet alone is capable of using language in a different way, to a different end, from the prose writer. In a poem every word must seem necessary, immovable, irreplaceable. The poet welds words together into a single indivisible creation from which nothing can be taken away without destroying the poem.

This is where the greatest challenge lay to the Cubist poet— to use words in a different way, words which already had a meaning before he used them. Their purpose had always been to convey a meaning, to express an idea, or to tell a story. Now the poet's task was to remove the narrative from a poem without the words becoming meaningless. Here the technique of the painters came to his aid—he replaced succession by juxtaposition, progression by simultaneity. The ideal of the ''poème-objet'' is static art, a poem in which the most important element is the architecture, the structure. This does not mean traditional verse forms which, indeed, Reverdy rejected. The subject alone, he said, determines the form of the poem. . . . By way of illustration I have chosen the collection of poems entitled **Les Ardoises du toit,** because of the time at which they were written (1918) and because they seem to crystallise the various Cubist aspects of a technique which was modified later. The title itself is significant. As the introductory poem tells us, each poem is written on a slate, therefore is already seen as an object:

> Sur chaque ardoise
> qui glissait du toit
> on
> avait écrit
> un poème

The visual aspect, we shall see, is as important as the aural one. Even the diagonal lay-out in this poem recalls the slope of the roof. This kind of pictorial quality had already appeared in another collection of Reverdy's poems, **La Lucarne ovale,** published two years earlier. There we are reminded of the oval frame of many Cubist still-lifes, for the window constitutes an ever-present frame through which the poet looks at the world.

In order to create a new reality one must first break down the old order and then recompose it in an entirely new way. Juan Gris spoke of a pack of cards reshuffled incessantly into new combinations but with the emphasis on the limited initial elements. . . . The elements used by Reverdy are few, but because they are familiar and elementary—*la maison, la cheminée, la porte, la lampe, le vent*—they are powerful. The poet is not looking for unusual elements but a new, original order. . . .

So, in the first stage of the Cubist process of creation we have the breaking down of reality into separate elements. In writing this means discontinuity, the suppression of logical links between sentences and words, an apparently indiscriminate use of tenses which makes actions seem to happen simultaneously or at some undefined time, the absence of punctuation making each line self-sufficient, the new typography which sets words on a page like so many islands, isolating some, grouping others in a dense mass or in a pattern, or leaving blanks within the body of the poem itself. Each one of these techniques seems designed to separate the elements of the poem and to make any kind of narrative interpretation impossible. The greatest danger to the poet would seem at this point to be *fragmentation*.

It is here that we must look at the second stage—the synthesis or riveting together (since this is the term that Reverdy favours) of these elements in such a way that they become inseparable, one single fabric. (pp. 23-5)

The first step towards giving each poem an individual character, an identity as an object, was the new typography. Reverdy set out his poem on the blank page as a painter might a picture, with a feeling for the masses of words almost as concrete elements. The poem is no longer a dense mass of lines of similar lengths divided or not into equal stanzas. Each poem has its own particular "shape." The lines often start half-way in from the margin, or sometimes a simple word may be isolated in the middle of the page or on the right-hand side. The poems, all except one, are never long enough to take up more than one page and thus the whole poem may be seen at one glance in its entirety, from beginning to end, with its own characteristic form. Because there is no need to turn the page the reader's attention is fixed on the poem by its initial visual impact. Neither in Cubist painting or poetry should we need to search outside the work of art. . . . (p. 26)

Reverdy makes use of blanks in his poems both to replace punctuation and to make the reading of the poem easier. His blanks are never just empty spaces. They mark divisions in the train of the poet's thoughts and feelings, and they are as necessary as the silences in music to the over-all rhythm of the poem in that they are filled, as much as the words themselves, with silent beats. A simple detached word is read much more slowly and often takes as long as a whole line. This means that the word is given a double emphasis—by its length and by its visual effect. A Reverdy poem is never just abstract music—it must be seen as well as heard. Each word has the figurative appearance of a concrete thing. Sometimes the poem achieves an effect reminiscent of Apollinaire's *Calligrammes* where the disposition of the words makes in fact a "picture" of the thing they are describing, as in the poem **"Orage"** in which the diagonal pattern of the lines evokes the lightning itself:

> Et c'est tout
> > Soi
> Sous le ciel ouvert
> > Fendu
> Un éclat où le souffle est resté
> > Suspendu

or in the poem **"Bêtes"** where the assymetrical balancing of the lines suggests the pacing back and forth of the animal in its cage:

> Tu regardes en passant l'animal enchaîné
> > Il part de son élan
> L'exil entre les haies

or the drops of water hanging from the spout so vividly evoked by the indented line:

> Trois gouttes d'eau pendent à
> > la gouttière

On some occasions the whole poem is written around a central blank or space as in **"En Face,"** or seems to be filled with air because its subject is of the same nature, in poems such as **"Air," "Soleil," "Matinée."**

As can be seen from these examples, Reverdy's effects are always discreet and are never arbitrary, never used for their own sake, to stand out in a poem at the expense of the rest. This kind of calculated virtuosity is scorned by Reverdy. . . . The typography is always dictated by the meaning of the poem; it is a structural element, not mere decoration. True to the Cubist aesthetic the detail is always subordinated to the whole, to the "architecture" of the work. This is particularly true of Reverdy's images, which, in spite of their surprising novelty, are absorbed into the fabric of the poem and have a convincing naturalness; in fact we almost pass over them sometimes for they are enunciated with such simplicity that we accept them unquestioningly. . . . (pp. 26-7)

Reverdy's theory of the image has so influenced the poetry of this century that we tend to forget how he first formulated it. . . . The "comme" of comparisons had already been eliminated by poets before him, but Reverdy carried the process further still by his idea of the image being that which welds together seemingly disparate elements with a shock that reveals a new reality. He at once realised the added importance of the image as a structural element through its power of synthesis. It was for his theory of the image that the Surrealists recognised Reverdy as their master, yet they misunderstood its true meaning. They overestimated the shock value of the image, creating arbitrary combinations for their own sake, with no intellectual control over the new reality which these combinations revealed. They did not take into account the second half of Reverdy's theory. . . . (pp. 27-8)

Reverdy's images neither describe nor compare, but present us with the new reality as he has created it, and we accept it as a new truth. . . . In some cases he brings together two separate realities and we ourselves supply the link in our reading—each new line gives meaning to the preceding one or enriches it. . . . Reverdy insists that his words are not symbols—they are themselves, concrete objects that we all know, and it is their juxtaposition with others that gives them new meaning.

The suppression of logical links creates an initial surprise, yet we have no difficulty in understanding. . . . (pp. 28-9)

We have seen how the image can unite separate elements at one point in a poem. But images are also used on a larger scale to give unity to the poem as a whole through the repetition of certain themes and words which create echos and recalls.

In **"Etape"** we are ever conscious of the starry night above a dying man, revolving about his head, through the careful placing at intervals during the poem of images, not descriptions. . . . The same procedure is used in the poem **"Aile"**, where the image of the bird-soul becomes clear only at the end, when we ourselves have linked the first mention of wings . . . with the last . . . although the poet himself has not connected them for us.

At times we can follow the elaboration of two separate sets of images which remain nearly always opposed to each other throughout the poem. The group light/noise/heat is often opposed to darkness/silence/cold, and in the poems **"Patience"** and **"Visite"** we find similar contrasts between weight and weightlessness and the movements of ascension and descent.

A further step in the interpenetration of words and images is a simultaneous presentation of two separate sets of images, one concrete and the other abstract or imaginary. Thus in the poem **"Tête"** we see at the same moment a head and a house and cannot separate them since the attributes of one are given to the other by the poet's imagination. Sometimes a whole poem is written in this way, sometimes the combination of concrete and imaginary is restricted to one ''impossible'' image. . . . Nature is quite often given human characteristics, an independence and will of its own; inanimate objects move of their own accord. . . . (pp. 29-30)

This technique of simultaneous description does in fact create a static poem. Yet though there is no linear development there is movement of a purely internal kind. Reverdy is always conscious of an invisible framework outside of which the poem never extends—it never opens on to anything else. In fact, the most characteristic movement of any Reverdy poem is a reversal in the last half or quarter of the poem, or even in the last line. The last half counteracts the first. For instance, if there had been a movement of hope in the first half, the second will destroy it; the poem turns back on itself towards the centre, which seems to represent an immobile point or axis. The last line nearly always seems to close a circle with the finality of the frame of a painting, which reminds us that Cubist paintings always led the eye back into the picture, never outside of it, as the use of linear perspective and cut-off objects did in traditional paintings. Often this last line seems to sum up what has gone before, as in the poems **"Fausse porte ou portrait"**, **"Sombre"**, **"Clartés terrestres"**; it is a definition of what we have by this time pieced together and understood from the reading of the poem—reminiscent of the solution of a puzzle. (pp. 30-1)

The remaining great unifying factor in Reverdy's poems is the rhythm, which we mentioned briefly in reference to the typography. Although there are never any definite patterns of verse and rhyme, Reverdy often uses traditional verse forms, alexandrines and especially octosyllables; but these are always interspersed with lines of two, three and four syllables or more, which not only give emphasis to the words that compose them, but mark divisions in the text. Often a line seems astride two lines, looking backwards and forwards and giving meaning to both. . . . A common rhythm is the balancing back and forth of lines—both to the eye and to the ear—one half answering the other, like the swing of a pendulum:

> The cry was coming from far away
> > From the other side of the night
> And all that comes forward
> > And all that I flee
>
> > > **"Une Eclaircie"**

Here, a feeling of panic is created, and yet the same asymmetrical pattern can sound completely different in a poem like **"Son de cloche"** with its longer lines slowing the movement down. Here it is the silences that make themselves felt:

> > Look
> The stars are not shining now
> > Or the earth turning
> A head has bowed
> > Hair sweeps the night

Again in the poem **"Bêtes"**, as we showed earlier, the rhythm is an exact echo of the action—first the pacing back and forth of the animal in its cage, then, as it looks towards the sky and freedom, the poem opens out on to one word which seems infinite:

> His astonished eyes plumb the sky
> > His head against the bars
> Toward that hint of the infinite
> > > Immensity

The rhythm carried over through the blanks assures the continuity of the poem and so avoids any effect of fragmentation.

It might seem from this preoccupation with form that the resulting poems would have an impersonal, almost abstract character, and in fact some critics have reproached Reverdy with a certain monotony in his limited elements and a too great austerity or bareness. In defence of the poet and in conclusion I come to the last and no doubt more important element in Reverdy's poetic theory—the subject-matter, as he understands it. . . . (pp. 31-2)

The greatest unifying factor in all Reverdy's poems is in fact the constant presence of the poet, the unity of feeling and personality which pervades them all. Poetry serves the double purpose of revealing the poet to himself—that part of himself which is the most obscure, the most secret and rare—and of conveying it to the reader. And these poems, these never-ending variations on a few limted themes, are in search of that essence. . . . For, paradoxically, it is not the subject-matter alone which can move us, but the finished work of art. It is the transformation of raw emotion through the use of language that puts it on a higher plane, one on which it is more capable of moving us. The actual form is but the most perfect exteriorisation of what the poet feels most deeply. What we see on paper are merely the means he has used to achieve his higher purpose, that mysterious ''soudure d'âme à âme dans le choc poésie.''

The all-important form, paradoxically must pass unnoticed, since it has become the only possible vehicle to express the subject. . . . (p. 33)

The two—form and subject-matter—are so inextricably linked that one cannot exist without the other. . . . What happens between the poet and the reader when the poem is read is something beyond rational explanation, described by Reverdy in terms of miracle and magic—''le mystère.'' But, contrary to the common ideas of inspiration and originality, Reverdy believes that only the most familiar, the most general and most simple things can have a truly powerful and eternal impact. What he calls ''le réel'' is really what the Cubist painters wished to attain by rejecting the superficial and reducing objects to their permanent, essential nature. . . . (pp. 33-4)

As I pointed out earlier, the words are not used as symbols but as themselves, as signs, concentrating within them everything we know about the object they stand for; and the more familiar the object, the greater resonance in the word. . . .

What some critics regard as ''poverty'' is instead extreme concentration and achieves an extraordinary density of expression—''le faisceau d'émotions'' which Reverdy refers to in *Le Gant de crin*. Not a word is superfluous: ''le décoratif c'est le contraire du réel.'' The lack of adjectives, the naming of objects with the definite article, the constant use of vague pronouns (*quelqu'un, on*), or the vague use of normally definite ones (*il, tu, vous*), give a deliberate lack of precision, but at the same time a universal, eternal quality which time cannot change. The poet's relationship with his reader will be never-endingly new and immediate since it is not limited to any precise historical time or situation; it is that mysterious spark which unites two human beings and is beyond their comprehension. . . . (p. 34)

Julia Husson, "Pierre Reverdy and the 'Poeme-Objet'," in Australian Journal of French Studies, *Vol. V, Part 1, January-April, 1968, pp. 21-34.*

ANNA BALAKIAN

Pierre Reverdy has been truly one of the important metaphysical poets of his time. A contemporary of two great nonrealists, Claudel and Valéry, he found spiritual outlet neither in a specific religion nor by reducing life to an abstract purity. Incapable of public adherences, he lived his personal as well as artistic life in the lonely margins of literary coteries. According to him, life is the same for everyone, nothing amazing, nothing unpredictable. His own was free of personality quirks, of mental or physical aberrations. In fact his art so completely invaded the current of his daily living that biographers would have few events to record about him. This is not to say that he "lived" for his art, but on the contrary his art was the expression of that life, comprised its constant pulsation and passage and was integrated with it. Upon the publication of his first major volume of poetry, *Les Épaves du Ciel (Chips of Heaven)*, written for the most part between 1915 and 1918, and collected in 1924, this is all the information which he gave about himself: "Pierre Reverdy, born in Narbonne on September 13, 1889. No travel, no adventures, no story, but what stories." . . . (p. 100)

The major biographical and artistic fact in Pierre Reverdy's life was, at the age of twenty, the impact of his father's death; not just the emotional shock of loss of the dearest being in his life, but the horrifying material reality of the metamorphosis between livingness and lifelessness, the abruptness of the change, and the infinite implications it suggested to him in terms of the myths connected with immortality. On that day and forever after he was obsessed by the fixed and morbid idea of nothingness. His spiritual house of cards collapsed, and it is thereafter futile and deceptive to talk of the poet Reverdy in terms of religious mysticism or dogmatic faith. In his prose maxims (1930-36) collected under the title, *Le Livre de Mon Bord* (1948), he says touchingly and yet bluntly: "One can believe in God without living him . . . but one can love him without believing in him—with a love, insane, rebellious and strong, loving all that he might have been if he could have been." This is the only love of God that one can honestly refer to in speaking of the mysticism of Reverdy.

Yet, his loss of faith is the beginning of his real spirituality, with which his whole poetic work is inextricably involved. As he abandoned the faith of his childhood he felt that for him faith had been a stopgap in his spiritual development. It seemed to him that belief was the end of a crisis and therefore incompatible with his nature and its need for relentless searching. The loss was really a gain, the beyond had lost its determined target, expanding into something larger, in fact the beyond was henceforth "everything that is outside of the skin that is tightly drawn around our body." He took the "metaphysical distress" that arose out of his personal loss of father and of God not with self-pity but as an impulse toward greatness: "it is not a weakness but on the contrary a symptom of quality and force,

for every soul that is besieged by it can henceforth rely only on itself to surmount it."

The loss of faith is also a source of fortitude for Reverdy. He accepts the fact that death is the greatest enemy of man and the invincible one. But this fact creates in him neither a sense of defeat nor of cynical disdain. Disdain of death would be accompanied by disdain of life, and although he admits the tragic basis of life, he refuses to disdain living. The alternative is to transmute life within our limited number of years. How to transmute it becomes the preoccupation of his life and work.

Reverdy's work is the overflow of this metaphysical quest. If he became a writer it was because that happened to be the only means of expression at his disposal at the moment of spiritual awakening. Had he been trained in art (like his father), or in music, his poetic contacts with the physical world would have been represented just as readily by lines or notes.

From 1915 on, the stratifications of his life,—rather eventless from the point of view of social involvements or emotional crises,—are the slow unwinding of his work. After his first volume of collected poems, already cited, there was the exposition of his *ars poetica* in *Le Gant de Crin,* and the eventual collection in three volumes of his complete writings, including the previously mentioned *Le Livre de Mon Bord,* and two volumes that comprise his total poetic writings from 1913 to 1949. Throughout the entire work, whether prose or poetry, the principal theme and thought is the quest for the absolute in the various strata of reality. It is significant to note that although he sidestepped the coterie of the surrealists, he preceded them, then became their contemporary, sharing their metaphysical aspirations; but he evolved his destiny independently and in solitude though remaining on friendly terms with surrealist artists and poets, just as he stayed faithful to his earlier affiliation with the cubists without making it a total involvement. Living in the monastery climate of Solesmes and taking only occasional trips to Paris and its hotbeds of literary theory, he integrated nonetheless within his work the many metaphysical *élans* of concern of the artists of his time.

First of these was the concept of reality. Unlike metaphysical poets of past epochs, Reverdy always considered reality irrevocably involved in mysticism. His *mystique* does not annihilate reality. Because of this he has often been called a "realist." But we must be careful to understand that what he calls reality is not the accepted concept of the real. For him reality is what lies beyond "the deception of the senses." It is neither on earth nor in heaven, but as he terms it "over the roofs." In his sturdy hands he will take the clay of earthly objects and through language transform them. Were he to abandon the plane of reality, he explains in an essay entitled **"Fausses Notes" ("False Notes")** appearing in the art magazine, *Verve* (1952) he would end up in nothingness. The poet must stay in reality, after having first made a "leap toward the heights, like drops of water, surging out of the river," but only to return, the better "to be absorbed after having thrown off darts of diamonds with which light had adorned them."

More than any other of the [major symbolist or surrealist poets] . . . , Reverdy could have shunned and despised exterior reality. If Rimbaud was repulsed by his birthplace, Charleville, and early in life ran away from it, it was Reverdy's destiny to spend his days on earth in the dreariest of environments. The town of Narbonne where he was born is one of the least attractive of Mediterranean cities. There is none of the colorful atmosphere of vegetation or the picturesqueness of Mediterranean villas. It is somber and squalid, a worker's town, lacking the glitter of most coastal cities. The monotony of its houses and streets is depressing (observed as of the late 1950s). Others of Reverdy's meridional colleagues came north and settled in Paris. Reverdy's stay in the capital, which for so many other writers became the city of enchantments, was of short duration. He could not afford to live in Paris, and he went to live in the town of Solesmes simply because it was one of the cheapest places to exist for a poet whose livelihood was precarious and inevitably irregular. If Norbonne is a sad town, Solesmes is positively dreary (observed as of the late 1950s). Its streets lined with solemn, uniform poplars, are inundated by the melancholy bells that toll in the monastery. There is a silence that is almost unearthly in Solesmes, where the transients that come by are mostly attracted there for meditation and devotional retreat. Reverdy talks often in his poems of roads that turn. After seeing Solesmes one might add that they turn and go nowhere. Dreary houses line the streets and are surrounded by farm country. To be stuck in such a desolate spot without possessing the religious power of transcendence that comforts most of the inhabitants living in the shadow of the great monastery, could only have been tolerated by a poet having within him the power of transformation. The monks with whom I spoke at the monastery confirmed the fact that Reverdy never went to Mass although his wife was a most devout and practicing Catholic. But he spent innumerable hours in the monastery reading and particularly talking with the monks whom he admired as lay thinkers rather than for their religious beliefs. These endless conversations were his main distraction from the monotony of his existence. When his need for the companionship of his artist friends became too acute he went on one of his many brief fugues to Paris to recharge the battery of his mental vitality, which burned like a quiet but constant flame in the chill atmosphere of Solesmes. Reverdy's metaphysical power over his daily drab environment becomes the more miraculous when the picture of the two dreary locales of his existence are brought to mind. But if in a similar environment Jean-Paul Sartre's Roquentin has nausea and finds his life absurdly useless, the poet in Reverdy demonstrates the victory of imagination and its power to give elasticity to the view from our window: it is the triumph of inscape over landscape.

In a similar case of incongruity between the poet and his environment, Stéphane Mallarmé had found release in the world of verbal abstractions. In his sonnets he found refuge in metaphors of the void and in rarefaction of objects divesting themselves of their concrete dimensions and weights. Quite to the contrary, Reverdy does not obliterate the reality but transfigures it, endows it with an unwonted, unpredictable quality that places things on the brink of revelation in a posture of expectancy. They convey the moment when the magician touches the object with his wand, just as it is about to but has not quite turned into something else. This transitionary quality injects a vibrancy in the objects and into physical nature that is often more compelling than the actual occurrence of phantasmagoric transformation, just as the present participle of a verb has more power of provocation than the past participle. One might say that the network of Reverdy's imagery presents the earth in transition.

According to Reverdy, man's leaps of imagination are valid only when they meet with an equal degree of linguistic power. The literary image, even as the pictorial, has an existence independent of the natural order of things. It is neither a quality of man who created it nor consistent with the objects of this world. It resides outside both the see-er and the objects of his vision, yet has its own inherent reality. "Poetry is neither in life nor in things—it is what you do with them and what you add to them," he reflects in *Le Livre de Mon Bord*. The only metaphysics possible for him consists in rendering matter dynamic and thereby reaching the absolute through matter.

It can therefore be said that the poet is against reality yet deals constantly with it. When, on the one hand, Reverdy says: "The poet is a furnace in which to burn reality," and in the next breath asserts that "the poet is essentially a man who aspires to the domain of the real," there is not really the contradiction that the words seem to indicate. In a most lively image Reverdy illustrates this apparent contradiction: "The poet is a transformer of current—from the high tension of reality to the incandescent filament which gives light."

In other words, unlike his precursors, the symbolists, he accepts the exterior world just as he refuses to disdain life, but at the same time he constantly affirms man's insatiable hunger for the marvelous. In this quest, the enemy will not be reality but nature. The distinction which he makes between the two has been accepted as fundamental by the surrealists. Reality is what you make it; the rational laws by which we judged physical nature in his time are the inflexible element, and must be surmounted by man's imagination. He says in *Le Livre de Mon Bord*:

> The innermost quality of man is his inexplicable need for the marvelous. And that is his sharpest point of divorce from nature. We no longer believe in miracles—nothing is more obvious. But the miracles in which we no longer believe are as nothing in comparison with those that each man carries in reserve within his innermost self and which his imagination offers him at all time.

In his acceptance of the exterior world he points up better than any critic of the time the point of default of symbolism. He minimizes the importance of the dream, which had been the crux of the aspirations of both the romanticists and the symbolists. For Reverdy it is only a means to an end: the tunnel that passes under reality, a gutter of reality. The poet dreams, but he dreams of life, of his hypothesis of life, in which he learns to love life better: "One learns to love reality better sometimes after a long detour by way of dreams." His dream then is hard and durable, as the studies in concrete which are the dream realizations of the artist. "It was an unheard-of adventure, that of the artists of the concrete, when they extended this domain toward that of poetry, the immense field of the undefinable," he observes in the *Verve* article. It is their example that he chose to follow rather than that of the musician whom the symbolists imitated. In following the techniques of music, poets had met with their most dangerous pitfall, a danger from which we have not yet (1952) liberated ourselves, deplores Reverdy. For by simulating the only art that does not need to evoke reality, they stumbled into a vagueness not only of expression but of mind: an exit out of life leading not to the infinite but to nothingness.

No, the dream and its imprecisions, may be a temporary opiate to the poet, but he must not become addicted to it, for it will lead to sterile fields. Not the musician but the artist should be the modern poet's counterpart. It is the artist that has succeeded in attaining not an escape but a marvelous kind of new reality through the object.

> If man disappears, the earth remains, the inanimate objects, the stones in the road. If the earth disappears, there remains all that is not the earth. And if all that

is not the earth disappears, there remains what cannot disappear—one may wonder why—because one cannot even think it and in the long run this is really what reality is, so far from the mind and mirror of man, who cannot even conceive of it.

(*Verve*)

This ultimate material reality which he defines in old age, is what he earlier named ''surreality,'' and it is upon an approximation of this that he wove the network of his poetry. It is the field of mental perception and physical sensitivity wherein unapparent relationships are grasped between objects. Beyond these relationships lies the infinite, i.e., the realm at whose borders our faculties fail. But within the charmed circle of these relationships, imperceptible to the common breed and attained as if through a mystic chance by those who may call themselves poets for lack of a better word, the artist has the impression of real creativeness. Less optimistic than Saint-Pol-Roux, Reverdy concedes that it is an illusion, but it is the guiding force, nonetheless, of the artist's work and more satisfying to his mystic thirst than any cult.

The test of the quality of a being is then not the degree of inner (dream) or outer (rarefication) escape in which he engages, but the objects toward which he radiates and by which he is represented, or with which he is identified by the immediacy of the image. Otherwise he is unthinkable, nonexistent. In the deserts of nonexistence there is no real art. By his penetration of the concrete, the quality and limits of the mind can be recognized and judged. Man's roots are in heaven but as a tree upturned, whose leaves touch the soil, it is this contact with the tangible that gives promises of illuminations.

Undisturbed by polemics, personal affiliations, or schisms with colleagues—as is the case with the surrealists—Pierre Reverdy came closer to defining the spiritual and aesthetic position of the modern poet than anyone else in France in his time. . . . (pp. 101-09)

> Anna Balakian, *"Pierre Reverdy and the Materio-Mysticism of Our Age," in her* Surrealism: The Road to the Absolute, *revised edition, Dutton, 1970, pp. 100-20.*

MARY ANN CAWS AND PATRICIA TERRY

Symbolist and post-Symbolist French poets have wished to free poetry from whatever they defined as ''literature.'' Verlaine wanted poetry to be ''music'' as opposed to ''eloquence.'' Rimbaud, far more ambitious, believed that poetry could transform life itself by detaching the things of this world from their environment of habit and custom. The Surrealists, not content with Rimbaud's program of ''systematic dis-ordering of the senses,'' tried to eliminate conscious reaction to experience altogether. The result would be an art dictated by the subconscious, and thus independent of craftsmanship. Apollinaire, a beacon, as Reverdy said, for contemporary poets, gave the Surrealists their name but did not join them in reducing, or, as they saw it, exalting the poet to his undifferentiated subconscious. His own poetry introduced a new freedom of vocabulary and the beginnings of nonsequential presentation of the elements of the poem, a primary technique being the elimination of punctuation.

Compared to these predecessors, Reverdy strikes one as simultaneously more austere and more violent. Where Apollinaire, even at his most unorthodox, still used his own emotions as the materials of his poems, Reverdy allows himself to be

apparent, if at all, only as an abstract presence, the mind that both orders and inhabits the still life or the landscape. Very much in the manner of the Cubist painters who were his friends, Reverdy exists in his works as a diffuse intensity by his very refusal of a perspective that would dictate the way in which the elements of the poem or painting are to be perceived. The particular elements Reverdy chose were often the same modest, everyday objects found in the paintings of Braque, Picasso, and Gris: window and table, pipe and playing cards, guitar and newspaper, lamp and wine bottle. These objects occur simultaneously on the undisguised two-dimensional surface of the paintings. In the poems they are juxtaposed in such a way that although they must, by the nature of the process of reading, be perceived one after another, their position on the page, syntactical ambiguities, and the absence of connecting particles force the eye and the mind to grasp them all at once. It is in this sense that Reverdy wanted to make a ''static poem'' which would resemble a painting.

Born and educated in Toulouse and Narbonne, Reverdy moved to Paris in 1910 to live the rest of his life there and in the equally gray climate of the Abbaye de Solesme. But he seems never to have lost a nostalgia for the more brilliant landscapes of his youth, and defined, as the aim of his art, ''to oppose to the ebb and flow of emotion the moving brilliance of the earth's surface, hard, clear and dry, in the bracing air of the heights.'' The essay, **"Note Eternelle du Présent"** (1933), adds that art steals from its contact with the earth the means by which it rises ever closer to the sun.

The son and grandson of sculptors, Reverdy made of his own intangible medium something as physical as possible. . . . Language was to be kneaded like a kind of dough in order to produce a poetry that would ''glorify matter and restore it to a place of honor.'' As Mallarmé aspired to achieve in language something with which to confront the silent purity of the Ideal, Reverdy's no less paradoxical project was to use language as an instrument with which to construct, out of the ''splendid health'' of nature, a durable, and anti-natural object. This he perceived as the aim, not only of poetry, but of the arts of his time in general, and the response of painters is indicated by the affinity they obviously felt for his work.

Reverdy's poems were illustrated by the painters already mentioned, and by Matisse, Derain, La Fresnaye, and Chagall. Modigliani and Picasso, among many others, painted his portrait, and Gris' ''Still Life with a Poem'' is an homage to him, as is Breton's celebrated poem ''Tournesol'' or ''Sunflower.''

In 1917 Reverdy was the director of the influential journal *Nord-Sud,* and he contributed to the ''Now-ist'' or ''Presentist'' journal *Sic,* directed by Pierre-Albert Birot (1917-1918); to the early Surrealist production *Littérature,* directed by Aragon, Breton, and Philippe Soupault (1919); and later to their *Révolution surréaliste* (1925). He was responsible for the first formulation of what Breton took as his own theory of the image: ''The image is a pure creation of the mind. It cannot be born from a comparison, but only by bringing together two distant objects. The greater the distance between the objects and the more appropriate, the stronger the image, the more powerful its emotional force and poetic reality'' (*Nord-Sud,* no. 13, March 1918). Through his influence on such Surrealist poets as Breton and Eluard, and also directly, Reverdy's work has had a great impact on the American Imagist poets of the middle part of this century. In him can be found both ellipsis and intensity, both informality and care for new forms. . . . (pp. xv-xvii)

Reverdy, finally, is the ''plastic'' poet he chose to be: at once static and quietly dynamic. Poems, he said, should be ''crystals precipitated from the effervescent contact of the mind and reality.'' The resulting crystals are neither dark nor brilliant, but rather quietly luminous, not just in the texts themselves, but in their lasting effect. This poetry takes place indeed within a closed space: doors pulled shut, a house not to be entered, a wall blocking off exit, barriers of all sorts—but the smallest detail may lead to a wide interior space.... (p. xvii)

> *Mary Ann Caws and Patricia Terry, in an introduction to* Roof Slates and Other Poems of Pierre Reverdy, *translated by Mary Ann Caws and Patricia Terry, Northeastern University Press, 1981, pp. xv-xvii.*

Anatoli (Naumovich) Rybakov

1911-

Russian novelist and author of children's books.

Rybakov has gained international attention for his novels *Heavy Sand* (1979; also translated as *Heavy Sands*) and *Children of the Arbat* (1987), both of which are critical of past Soviet policies. *Heavy Sand,* an epic tale of two Russian-Jewish families set in the World War II era, garnered praise for Rybakov's implicit condemnation of Soviet atrocities toward Russian Jews during the Nazi Holocaust. Walter Laqueur summarized critical consensus when he maintained that *Heavy Sand* "is not a great work of art, nor does it contain anything new or startling to the Western reader. But in Soviet terms Rybakov had gone as far as he possibly could, and it was a brave thing to do."

Children of the Arbat was written during the 1960s but remained unpublished for more than twenty years because of its negative portrayal of communist leader Joseph Stalin. The recent publication of this novel is generally identified with reform policies promoted by Soviet premier Mikhail Gorbachev, including *glastnost,* which pledges greater freedom of expression, and *perestroika,* an economic and social restructuring campaign. Hailed as an important historical and political document, *Children of the Arbat* achieved immediate popular success following its serialization in the Soviet literary journal *Druzhba narodov.* This work analyzes Stalin's rise to power in the early 1930s, in part through its focus on the semiautobiographical character of Sasha Pankratov, a student living in a bohemian section of Moscow called the Arbat who is exiled to Siberia for making a careless ideological comment in a student newspaper. Using a traditional, nineteenth-century Russian prose style, Rybakov depicts Stalin's consolidation of power through fear and distrust, culminating in the assassination of his close advisor Sergei Kirov in 1934, the year in which the Stalinist purges were initiated. Although some Soviet commentators objected to Rybakov's unsympathetic portrait of Stalin, others lauded his revealing treatment of the former leader's mental instability and its detrimental effect upon Soviet society. Many Western critics faulted Rybakov's avoidance of larger questions concerning the moral failure of communism during the Stalinist era, while others praised his authentic depiction of Stalin's political and personal life. Lauding *Children of the Arbat* as "a triumph of both style and substance," Josephine Woll commented: "[The] depiction of Stalin—which Rybakov deems his greatest achievement—is spellbinding, unprecedented for Western and Soviet readers alike."

(See also *CLC,* Vol. 23 and *Contemporary Authors,* Vol. 126.)

best known as the author of books for children and adolescents. Some ten years ago, however, he published **Heavy Sands,** an extraordinary novel (by Soviet standards) about the sad fate of a Jewish community in a small town under German occupation in World War II. As I noted at the time in a review of the book in *Commentary* [see *CLC,* Vol. 23], **Heavy Sands** is not a great work of art, nor does it contain anything new or startling to the Western reader. But in Soviet terms Rybakov had gone as far as he possibly could, and it was a brave thing to do. . . .

Children of the Arbat, which was originally written in the 1960's but could not appear until now, is in a different literary class altogether, and it has already been highly praised by some of Rybakov's peers. (The weekly *Ogonyok* published some ten personal letters to Rybakov by leading writers and critics in which adjectives like "grandiose," "colossal," and "Shakespearean" abound.) It is the story of a generation: the young men and women who lived in central Moscow in the early 1930's. Arbat, to the west of the Kremlin, is one of the oldest parts of the Soviet capital. (p. 63)

Rybakov's novel has two protagonists: a (fictional) student named Sasha Pankratov, and Stalin. Sasha is handsome, a good son and friend, reasonably intelligent, an enthusiast—terribly naive and a bit of a prig. As a young Communist he commits some minor ideological gaffe when preparing a wall newspaper

---

WALTER LAQUEUR

[The Soviet] literary monthly, *Druzhba Narodov* ("Friendship of the Peoples"), has recently published the third and last part of Anatoli Rybakov's **Children of the Arbat,** a novel that even before it appeared was being hailed as the great political and literary event of the year. Rybakov, now in his seventies, is

at his college. Although normally this sort of thing would be dismissed, or incur a mild admonition, unbeknownst to Sasha the organs of state security have been building up a case against an old Bolshevik and in a roundabout way he becomes implicated in the frame-up. Thus a student's prank is transformed into an act of treason; Sasha is arrested and is sentenced (leniently) to three years of administrative exile in Siberia. (pp. 63-4)

Prison and Siberia cure him only in part of his naiveté. When a machine in the local kolkhoz (collective farm) breaks down, Sasha volunteers to repair it, warning everyone in earshot that it will fail again. . . . [He also inadvertently] calls the chairman of the kolkhoz a fool. The machine duly breaks down again . . . and the chairman brings a criminal action against him for deliberately wrecking the socialist economy—a crime punishable by between ten years and life.

Now the local head of the KGB, a fine person of much experience and originally an enthusiast like Sasha, takes pity on the young man and patiently explains to him some of the ground rules of Soviet society: never volunteer if there is the slightest risk that things may go wrong, never call anyone in authority a fool. . . .

Thanks to this guardian angel, Sasha escapes serious trouble. For there is no doubt that he does need protection. His friends and family (with the exception of his mother) have scarcely exerted themselves to help him. In fact, with two exceptions his contemporaries, the young enthusiasts of 1934, do not appear to be an attractive lot, and the worst character in his circle, an out-and-out careerist, joins the secret police.

In the parts of the novel devoted to these young people Rybakov's description of the mores of Moscow society is excellent. Siberia, on the other hand, he portrays a little colorlessly. But in any case where this novel truly comes alive is as a superb psychological study of its second protagonist, Stalin. . . .

[In Stalin], Rybakov portrays a man who genuinely believes in Russia and in Communism but who also happens to be a lunatic and a criminal; a politician who comes to power not through far-sightedness, oratorical skill, personal charisma, or other qualities of genuine leadership but who simply is more brutal and cunning and morally uninhibited than his colleagues in the Politburo, and who ultimately outmaneuvers and liquidates all but the most servile toadies among them.

Rybakov imitates Stalin's style of speech very effectively, especially the constant habit of posing rhetorical questions. . . . And he has certainly done his historical homework: the story he tells is largely authentic, and it will serve well to replace the Soviet histories of the 30's which were never written. . . .

The tale Rybakov unfolds is all but unrelievedly grim, although it does have its gruesomely light moments. Thus, while relaxing at his villa at Sochi, Stalin suddenly comes down with a toothache; his personal dentist, a man by the name of Lipman, has to be flown in from Moscow. There ensues an inner conflict as Stalin must reconcile his desire to be feared by everyone with his need for a dentist whose hands do not tremble. . . .

Does Rybakov have nothing at all positive to say about Stalin? Actually, there does seem to be an underlying suggestion in the novel that his iron fist was somehow indispensable to the development of the Soviet state, and that "objectively" he may therefore have played a certain positive role. Whether Rybakov himself subscribes to this line of thought it is difficult

to say; pseudo-objectivity of this kind may be the price for the publication of a book like *Children of the Arbat* in the first place. But it could be that Rybakov does believe it, for he is himself a member of the generation of which he writes, a generation of people who, though totally disillusioned, still find it difficult to accept that Stalinism had no redeeming features.

In this respect, *Children of the Arbat,* moving and powerful as it is, falls short of telling the whole truth; it is a story that is not brought to its appropriate conclusion. The novel proper—there is an epilogue that flashes forward several years—comes to an end on the very eve of the Kirov assassination in 1934, an event which triggered off the mass arrests, trials, and executions, and the effect is a little like *War and Peace* ending before the battle of Borodino or the burning of Moscow. (p. 64)

The bittersweet epilogue to *Children of the Arbat* describes a chance meeting at the front toward the end of the war between Sasha, now a major in a Guards division, and his old friend Maxim who early on in the novel had joined the army and now has risen to the rank of general. They warmly embrace and drink to the memory of their less fortunate comrades who did not survive. Sasha confides to his friend that his personal file carries the notation of his once having received a sentence under paragraph 58 (treason and crimes against the state), which is to say that he will remain forever vulnerable. . . .

Not so long ago happy endings were *de rigueur* for Soviet books; if a story or a play did not end well, at the very least the author was obliged to call it an "Optimistic Tragedy." In recent years Soviet literature (and to a lesser extent Soviet movies) has become far more interesting but also far less optimistic. . . .

The Soviet people still have to come to terms with their past, and Rybakov's book is a milestone on this painful road. But they also have to look forward—and this is likely to prove even more difficult. . . .

But where will the inspiration and new idealism come from? Not, one suspects, from the burned children of the Arbat or their offspring. The Soviet Union certainly needs *glasnost,* but it needs a cultural revolution even more. . . . So far, although all sorts of interesting proposals have been advanced, even the most fervent proponents of "openness" would not claim that the Soviet Union is anywhere near such a cultural revolution. (p. 65)

> Walter Laqueur, "Beyond Glasnost," in Commentary, Vol. 84, No. 4, October, 1987, pp. 63-5.

WALTER GOODMAN

Children of the Arbat carries the imprimatur of experience. Like its hero, Sasha Pankratov, the author, Anatoly Rybakov, grew up in Moscow on Arbat Street in a relatively upper-class enclave of a society that he pictures as far from classless. And like 22-year-old Sasha, he found himself exiled to Siberia for trivial offenses as the murderous purges of the 1930's were beginning.

Sasha's story is a Young Communist's Progress. Deeply loyal to the ideals of Communism and the Soviet regime, despite the injustice done to him, he learns as he travels "the endless prison road" and endures much hardship, danger and loneliness how his own rigidity was somehow reflected in the harshness of the regime. But he will not betray his faith. "His path lay with the Party, with the people, with the state.'' Sasha's is the human face of Communism.

Mr. Rybakov has acknowledged that Sasha is something of a self-portrait, and the author has treated himself kindly. . . . We root for him, in his risky encounters with the N.K.V.D. and the Siberian taiga, as we might root for Oliver Twist. And like a Dickens hero, Sasha recognizes belatedly that he loves vivacious Varya, who, back in Moscow, is making her own complicated and brave journey to maturity. Sasha's mother, too, is portrayed as a heroine in her willingness to defy the regime for Sasha's sake. A son's tribute.

This long, absorbing novel is crowded with exiles and apparatchiks, technocrats and time servers, workers and hustlers. The episodes in Siberia and those back in Moscow, which make up most of the book, have a scope and richness of detail that we associate with 19th-century novels. Even in a time of terror, Mr. Rybakov never lets us forget, people carry on with careers and love affairs. Muscovites' grinding concerns about living space, food rations, reputation infuse the story, and the details, whether in a dance hall or on a building site, stamp it with authenticity. . . .

[Rybakov] is no modernist. There is little irony here or ambiguity or stylistic innovation. We are in the hands of an old-fashioned, all-knowing narrator. ''In time,'' he reveals, ''Berezin would pay dearly for this error.'' The writing . . . is straightforward and full of flat-out judgments of a sort that 20th-century novelists try hard to avoid. A good Communist lets us know that Stalin has ''created a regime of fear, lawlessness, and arbitrariness.'' Taking the currently acceptable view of the Stalinist period, Mr. Rybakov argues through his good Communists that Stalin betrayed the ideals of Lenin, about whom no unkind word is uttered. . . .

Mr. Rybakov is not ashamed to deal in moral categories. Not all of his many characters come into clear focus, but most of them, in the tradition of Dickens and Balzac, can be separated into serious and frivolous, honorable and devious, good and bad. One of the more vivid is ''cunning and cautious'' Yuri Sharok, a shaky young man filled with resentment against the better-connected youths of the Arbat, who finds a career with the N.K.V.D. . . . Yuri is a Soviet Snopes.

At the center of the web of terror is the huge shadow of Stalin, presented here as an abstraction of evil. Mr. Rybakov makes only a gesture at fitting him to the human dimensions of the other main characters. (He has problems with his teeth.) This Stalin is paranoia incarnate, cold-blooded by nature and cruel on principle. . . . Mr. Rybakov's account of Stalin's machinations leading up to the 1934 assassination of Sergei Kirov, the popular Leningrad party leader, has the fascination of pure unashamed villainy. . . .

The scenes of the dictator manipulating allies and opponents alike, probing their weaknesses, teasing them, scaring them, betraying them, are rendered with quiet ferocity. . . . The message here, a not entirely persuasive one, is that it was this single malign force that poisoned an entire society.

Even if the monster theory of history seems to slide by Russia's past and the nature of Bolshevism, the publication of *Children of the Arbat* is one of the great events of glasnost. Its appearance in this country is an event, too, one that plunges us into the daily sufferings, compromises and daring acts of defiance of the Soviet people during a grim time.

Walter Goodman, ''Stalin's Evil Shadow in a Long-Suppressed Novel,'' in The New York Times, *May 10, 1988, p. C17.*

IRVING HOWE

This enormously long novel comes to us spattered with the blood and grime of 20th-century history. . . .

Important historically, as part of the Russian people's struggle to recover their past, *Children of the Arbat* is somewhat disappointing, certainly uneven, if taken strictly as a work of literature. The 77-year-old Mr. Rybakov has written honestly and at times with a rough energy, but his gifts as novelist and thinker are limited. *Children of the Arbat* is semiautobiographical; in the 1930's Mr. Rybakov himself was a victim of the purges and was exiled to Siberia. After World War II he was ''rehabilitated'' and went on to write numerous books.

For Soviet readers deprived of historical knowledge (those, say, to whom *samizdat* writing is unavailable), and perhaps for some Western readers who have been depriving themselves, this novel will come as a revelation. In its depiction of the years of terror, it is candid and strong. But insofar as one can distinguish between literary substance and extra-literary relevance in this kind of historically weighted fiction, it must be said that *Children of the Arbat* does not measure up to other Russian novels on allied themes.

Mr. Rybakov's lumbering novel lacks the lyricism of Boris Pasternak's *Dr. Zhivago*, the moral fire of *The First Circle* by Aleksandr Solzhenitsyn, the intellectual audacity of Vassily Grossman's *Life and Fate*. What we have here is a novel that seems made to order, decades in advance, for the Gorbachev moment: tell more than anyone since Khrushchev about the time of terror, but don't stray too far from the party's orthodoxies and avoid the ''delicate'' problem of the relation between the terror and the system. Boldness of presentation fades off into timidity of reflection.

Like other Russian writers untroubled by the subtleties of literary modernism, Mr. Rybakov has mounted a novel in the grand Tolstoyan manner, with many characters and narrative strands. For the better Soviet writers this kind of structure must seem tempting: it promises a return to the great tradition of Russian literature and it might be a way of imaginatively encompassing the torments of their society. But it is a literary temptation with grave risks. Only a writer with Tolstoy's moral and intellectual powers could conceivably pull it off—and even then it's questionable whether *anyone* can successfully transfer the ordered balances of 19th-century narrative to a work dealing with the slaughter and chaos of our age. In any case, Mr. Rybakov has not managed it.

The novel opens with a sympathetic portrait of young people in the Arbat, an old bohemian quarter in Moscow, as they struggle to cope with mounting political hysteria. Sasha, the novel's rather colorless protagonist, affirms his belief in ''the party'' even as the party starts making life miserable for him. The ebullient Varya wants only to find space for personal life. The ''simple working-class boy'' Yuri stumbles into becoming an agent for the N.K.V.D. All these young people are trapped in historical currents they can neither understand nor control, and meanwhile the party *apparatchiks* grow more arrogant.

Sasha is soon in trouble. He has innocently printed a few joking rhymes about colleagues in his student paper, and this brings a charge of political levity. (p. 7)

Sent to a Moscow prison, Sasha undergoes a frightening interrogation, about which Mr. Rybakov aptly remarks that what mattered "was not whether someone was actually guilty. [The interrogator] was concerned with the *general* version of their guilt." Still faithful to "the party" (a faith Mr. Rybakov seems to regard as an unquestioned principle), Sasha ends up in Siberia.

Now, all this ought to be deeply affecting, and the idea of it surely is. But the segment of the novel portraying the young people of Arbat is not, in my reading, very affecting. The narrative seems curiously inert and without personal flavor, the writing sluggish and dry, and the characters lacking in sharpness of definition.... It's as if the dreariness of spirit typical of Socialist Realism, that doubly misnamed Stalinist esthetic dogma, had seeped into the hearts of even its opponents.

The prospect clears and the prose takes on color once Sasha reaches Siberia.... At the novel's end Sasha finds a heroic model in another exile, Lydia Grigoryevna, once a high party functionary, now depriving herself to care for a child she has adopted in Siberia. Reflecting on this woman's penance for the wrongs she had done while in power, Sasha concludes that "above religions and ideas [is] the capacity to sacrifice oneself for others. And the fact that it can take place even here . . . gives me hope: human feeling has not been killed in people and it never will be."

An admirable sentiment; but is it really a sufficient conclusion—Mr. Rybakov offers little else—to a chronicle of falsehood, terror and death? Who, including the architects of the gulag, will declare against "human feeling"? One suspects this is a generality with which to evade the hard political and historical questions thrown up by Mr. Rybakov's story.

The most gripping pages of *Children of the Arbat* take us to the Kremlin as Stalin cements his tyranny. So closely knowledgeable is this portion of the book, it seems likely that Mr. Rybakov had access to high party figures who whispered stories to him about the antics of the Beloved Leader.

The Stalin portrayed here is a monster, pretty much the same monster we have come to know from biographers and historians.... [With] a well-developed taste for blood, the Stalin of *Children of the Arbat* identifies himself with the czars of old Russia and "the historical process" (the grand delusion of Bolshevism).... In an unnerving chapter about Stalin's toothache, the despot "passes on" fear to a poor dentist—quite in "a *tsarlike* way."

Anatoly Rybakov's narrative approaches climax with a detailed account of the clash between Stalin and Sergei Kirov, leader of the Leningrad party. Kirov, in what may be an idealized portrait, emerges here as a decent man, totally loyal to Stalin but reluctant to go ahead with the terror.... Mr. Rybakov hints that it was Stalin himself who arranged for Kirov's murder, a judgment quite in accord with conclusions reached by such historians of the period as Robert Conquest and Roy Medvedev.

The political segments of *Children of the Arbat* have their grisly fascination, yet even here, at his best, Mr. Rybakov reveals limitations of mind and sensibility. At no point does he venture beyond prescribed Leninist orthodoxy or, at best, the recent notion of "Communism with a human face." Neither in his own right nor through his characters (who might be supposed to have a need for sustained reflection about why their lives

have been wrecked), does the novelist ask whether the Bolshevik exaltation of "the party," that totemic "We," smoothed Stalin's rise to power. (pp. 7, 9)

Yet questions persist, questions that a reading of Mr. Rybakov's book forces upon one. Was there something about the system itself that enabled the terror? What kept so many Bolshevik leaders, some of them courageous enough during the civil war of 1920, supine before the tyrant's power? . . .

I anticipate the objection that these are questions about historical actuality, while *Children of the Arbat* is a work of fiction that cannot be expected to provide elaborate explanations. Yes; but Mr. Rybakov has written a work in which fiction and history are completely interwoven, so that the questions I have raised are both relevant and likely to have troubled at least some of the kinds of people about whom Mr. Rybakov writes. The criticism I'm making here, a *literary* criticism, is not that Anatoly Rybakov or his characters fail to provide congenial answers but that they fail to grapple deeply with inescapable questions. Or to put it another way, Mr. Rybakov has an empirical rather than a speculative mind, while the subject he has chosen is one that requires—by the writer himself, by his more thoughtful characters or both—sustained and independent reflection.

In the great Russian novels, there are people who think. (p. 9)

Irving Howe, "At the Mercy of Apparatchiks," in
The New York Times Book Review, *May 22, 1988,*
pp. 7, 9.

JOHN BAYLEY

The novel, as we are often told today, is a trick in which the reader is invited to cooperate. The more talented and original the trickster, the more the reader believes what he is told. He becomes, in fact, a novel reader, which is a status different from that of his ordinary self.... This has been the case in the European novel ever since *Robinson Crusoe*.

The Russian novel, effectively since the 19th century, has always been rather different. Its hero, as Tolstoy said, is Truth.... The Russian "novel" was always closely and conscientiously involved in what society was doing or thinking. Ironically, it was just this expectation of "the truth" that made censorship seem necessary to the authorities, whether czarist or Soviet. So the novel for Russians has always tended to belong to the "Now it can be told" category of literature. Hence its authority and its popularity.

Still, from a Western point of view there are distinct disadvantages. A work that will seem fascinatingly bold and true to a Soviet audience may seem merely rather tame and plodding to a Western one, conspicuously lacking in any element of the "novel." This might seem to be the case with Anatoli Rybakov's *Children of the Arbat*. It follows the reliable old method of assembling a group of young people—who live in the Arbat, a sort of Moscow SoHo or Greenwich Village—and telling the story of their lives and fates in the year 1934, just before the big purges got under way....

Rybakov is very much a traditional Russian writer, with no tricks about him. This novel was written 20 years ago and presumably kept on the shelf in the hope of publishing it in the more permissive times that have now, we hope, arrived. Great times for the "Now it can be told" bandwagon.... Yet there are serious drawbacks to this sort of resurrection. Truth is not only relative in art, as in most things, but it depends on the shock of the new, of immediate authenticity. That is part of the novelist's accomplishment in making us accept the world he creates. Thus the sheer absence of novelty about Rybakov's novel does much to undermine its authenticity, despite its candor and its validity, its 19th-century air of moral seriousness. The book's Western publishers claim, rather desperately, that it "is destined to become a classic." But destiny in this field is not a very reassuring concept, maybe meaning no more than a return to honored obscurity on the top shelves of public libraries.

Certainly Rybakov's novel lacks the impact of style and personality that hit the reader of Pasternak's *Dr. Zhivago* and Solzhenitsyn's *A Day in the Life of Ivan Denisovich*. There may be another, less candid reason for that lack of impact. Although Rybakov, like Solzhenitsyn, tells the story of an innocent man in the grip of an inhuman system, he softens the blow, as it were, in unobtrusive ways. His Sasha is not condemned to a Gulag, but to open exile in Siberia. The Great Purge is just about to begin when the novel ends. (p. 40)

Rybakov's method, again a traditional and time-honored one, is to alternate domestic scenes involving his cast of mostly youthful Muscovites and scenes in the Kremlin where Stalin and his henchmen are talking and planning. . . . Although well done and full of biographical detail, Rybakov's picture of Stalin is too familiar to grip the experienced reader's attention. We have been here too many times before, and Rybakov uses conventions of historical fiction that are equally venerable. (pp. 40-1)

A delightful tenor voice is heard singing a song about nightingales and love at a pleasant dacha outside Moscow, and a visitor next door inquires about it. "Oh that's our neighbor, Comrade Yezhov—such a nice man." As every Russian knows, and most Western readers too, Yezhoz, far from being a nice man, was head of Stalin's secret police. . . . The story of his charming manners and singing voice are also part of folk legend. Why go into the matter, then, with such an elaboration in a contemporary novel? The answer must be that these things can now be made official in the traditional authority of the Russian novel form, the misdoings may now be placed in a public record; and the old devices of the historical novel are there for that purpose.

Children of the Arbat remains an impressive record, however, impressive in its scope, its understanding, even in the somewhat laborious conscientiousness with which the feel of an epoch is re-created. Paradoxically, the Russians love to get things right, to join their history and their culture together. The educated Russian's appetite for knowledge in such directions is far greater than that of his Western counterpart. Rybakov's novel is indeed destined to become a classic in its native land, although its circulation in the West is more likely to be among specialists and Soviet watchers, who would appreciate its wealth of local and historical detail. (p. 41)

Rybakov, like most Soviet authors, would be careful to distinguish our lot from theirs, careful to emphasize that nothing is wrong with the Party, only with Stalin and his henchmen who abused it. . . . "The main thing, Kirov thought, was to protect the core of the Party organizations. As long as the Bolshevik hard core was alive and strong, the Party was indestructible." And the Party proved to be indestructible, no matter what Stalin did, just as the system of Peter the Great was perpetuated by his successors. Rybakov mentions more than once Alexei Tolstoy's novel *Peter the Great*, which flattered Peter and Stalin by open comparison.

But Rybakov's novel is also permeated with Balzac. Sasha manages to get a copy of *César Birotteau* from the Butyrki Prison library. He finds a heartening quote in it:

> "Unhappiness is a step toward the rise of genius, a purifying font for the Christian, a treasure for the deft, an abyss for the weak." He was not a genius or a Christian, nor was he deft or weak. Yet he felt something in these words that was important to him.

And important to Rybakov too. His sense of, and identification with, the decent Russian in Sasha, and his account of the processes of his arrest and interrogation, are clearly conveyed. And even his perception of Stalin's personality, however familiar, is well rendered; so are his descriptions of Stalin's dentist, his soft boots, his taste in wines. Drawn into all these matters, as by Scott or Balzac, the reader even begins to sympathize with the view that Stalin's "line was correct but his methods unacceptable." . . . (pp. 41-2)

Tout comprendre c'est tout pardonner? Not exactly. We have here, rather, the novel at its immortal trick of making us accept the world it offers—a world in which we are delighted to read, among many other things, that young Varya, after setting up with a shady but affectionate Moscow spiv, got her dresses made by Nadezhda Lamanova, her brassieres by Lubenets, her girdles by Koshke on the Arbat, her shoes by Barkovsky, Gutmanovich and Dushkin. Those intimate details are what the good old novel is all about, they are its lifeblood. Rybakov is an artist, as well as an archivist, in the way he provides them. (p. 42)

John Bayley, "The Shock of the Old," in The New Republic, *Vol. 198, No. 21, May 23, 1988, pp. 40-2.*

CHRISTOPHER WREN

Anatoly Rybakov considers it appropriate that his novel *Children of the Arbat* is identified with the campaign of economic and social restructuring that Mikhail S. Gorbachev has begun under its Russian name of perestroika.

"Perestroika helped publish this novel, but I think that the novel helps perestroika too," the Soviet writer said. "Having read the book, people have grasped the truth. People have taken a critical look at their history and themselves."

"This is a bitter book and people read it with great bitterness, but they recognize themselves," Mr. Rybakov said. . . .

"A writer's main tool is his memory—his own memory, the collective memory of his people," Mr. Rybakov said during an interview Monday in his New York hotel suite. "And the strongest memory is the one that is created by a wound to the heart. And the strongest of these wounds was suffered in the 1930's, the most tragic period of our lives." . . .

[Rybakov] said he had not set out to make Stalin one of his principal characters. But, he explained, "Stalin began to grow, he took up space and took over half of the novel."

His depiction of Stalin seemed so knowledgeable in its details that some readers have assumed that Mr. Rybakov had access to some of Stalin's acquaintances or archives closed to ordinary Soviet citizens. Mr. Rybakov said he enjoyed no such advantage.

"I didn't use any materials from archives and I didn't even try," he said. "I used materials available to me—newspapers, records of party congresses, Stalin's own works and the stories of people who knew Stalin personally. After all, I lived through that time. And I was a writer, so I guessed. It is interesting that after the novel came out, people sent me documents that confirmed what I had only guessed at." . . .

The novelist bridles at having his work evaluated against Boris Pasternak's *Doctor Zhivago* or Alexandr Solzhenitsyn's *First Circle.* "These are great writers and I am not trying to equate myself with them," he said. "But their books were published across the border, and mine was the first to be published in the Soviet Union." . . .

Mr. Rybakov said he had rebuffed earlier offers to publish *Children of the Arbat* in the West after it had been rejected at home. "I understood if I published the novel abroad, then it wouldn't be published in the Soviet Union," he said. "And I had to have my people read this book.

"Since I didn't publish abroad for those 20 years, I lost something in the way of fame. But I fulfilled a writer's duty to his people."

Christopher Wren, "For 'Arbat' Author, Novel Is Yoked to Perestroika," in The New York Times, May 26, 1988, p. C34.

JOSEPHINE WOLL

Anatoli Rybakov is relentlessly realistic in his *Children of the Arbat*—a book that has made him, after a reasonably successful writing career spanning forty years, a media star at the unlikely age of seventy-six. *Children of the Arbat* was written more than twenty years ago; the first version of it was supposed to be published in 1967, until the post-Khrushchev clampdown aborted such plans. The second version, due out in the late 1970s, also fell victim to cultural belt-tightening. With each rewriting, Rybakov says, he expanded the portrait of Stalin. Though he was offered many opportunities to publish *Children of the Arbat* abroad, he refused, wanting it to appear first at home. Finally it did—in the spring of 1987, in the journal *Druzhba narodov (Friendship of Peoples).* . . .

Children of the Arbat is a kind of Bildungsroman, though the education it describes is hardly the traditional sort. Rybakov's autobiographical hero, Sasha Pankratov, is an idealistic twenty-two-year-old engineering student who is arrested in 1934 for editing a news sheet insufficiently reverent toward the October Revolution. He is sentenced to three years' exile in Siberia.

The novel has four loci: the neighborhood whose heart is the old Moscow street called the Arbat, in whose alleys and courtyards Sasha and his friends grew up; Stalin's two residences, the Kremlin and his dacha in Sochi; and Siberia, with its population of natives and exiles, whom Sasha encounters en route to and in his village of exile. The first nexus of characters and incident, while necessary to the novel, is the most schematic and the least interesting, especially after Sasha's arrest removes him from Moscow. The exile saga is unusual and fascinating: there have been far fewer descriptions of exile than of camp and prison, even in unofficial Russian literature. And the depiction of Stalin—which Rybakov deems his greatest achievement—is spellbinding, unprecedented for Western and Soviet readers alike. (It is much fuller than Solzhenitsyn's in *The First Circle,* though the two authors view Stalin in much the same way.)

What Rybakov has accomplished is a triumph of both style and substance. In 1934 Stalin should have considered himself to be at the apex of his power, leading a Party finally united behind him after the costly and divisive factional infighting of the 1920s, and ruling over a country eager to be transformed from an agricultural backwater into a great industrialized and modern state. What Rybakov shows us is a man so profoundly distrustful of those around him, and so contemptuous of those he rules, that his postulates can logically lead to only one conclusion and one course of action: a reign of terror. (pp. 103-04)

Rybakov wins our trust in his "reading" of Stalin, his re-creation of his thoughts, by making himself Stalin's valet, as it were. He shares with us intimate knowledge, whispers "secrets": Stalin, when no one could see him, sometimes wore eyeglasses. He mimics the thudding stress patterns typical of Stalin's speech by italicizing Stalin's third-person references to himself, even mental ones. . . . He mimics as well Stalin's repetitive syntax, his demagogic style of answering his own rhetorical questions. When Stalin refers, over and over, to those who displease him as "Comrade Enukidze" and "Comrade Kirov," the very word *comrade* thumps like a chair kicked out from under a dangling body.

By blending Stalin's internal monologues with an omniscient narrative, Rybakov proceeds smoothly from known fact to unverifiable but credible interpretation. It works. We believe in the authority of his version. . . . Rybakov persuasively roots Stalin's sweeping distrust in childhood imputations of bastardy, and his psychobiography is veridical, making sense of Stalin's view of the revolutionary as someone impelled not by the slogans and phrases with which he manipulates a somnolent nation but by personal humiliation.

Rybakov's Stalin was always a humiliated outsider, first as a solitary child eating lamb and corn out in the yard while his mother's rich employers drank wine and laughed among themselves, then as the alien Georgian surrounded by rude, boorish Russian sots, and the singleminded autodidact among finicky intellectuals who—unlike him—understood neither the Russian people nor the nature of power.

For the adult Stalin whose mind we read, power is everything. (He values those writers who understand his two absolute convictions: the constancy of human perfidy and the primacy of power.) He has learned about the getting and keeping of power from the likes of Machiavelli; now he reckons Machiavelli could learn from him. What Stalin understands, specifically, is that to keep his own power he must preserve and even strengthen the *apparat,* while gutting its autonomy with continual changes of personnel. . . .

Stalin owed his power in part to men who distrusted and disliked him personally. . . . Rybakov examines the political and psychological bind such men found themselves in: Devoted to the Party and the ideals they made a revolution and fought a civil war for, they close their eyes to what they know to be lies "for the good of the Party." Having chosen, they do not defy Stalin, because he is their head of state, responsible for transforming Russia into a world power. (p. 104)

Less exalted people use much the same rationale as those at the top. Alferov, the administrative officer to whom Sasha reports in exile, a Party member relegated to Siberia because he lived "too long" abroad, explains that for the good of the country judges convict as "saboteurs" people they know to be innocent. For centuries the Russian peasant has known only one technology: the ax. Put him on a tractor, on a combine, in an automobile, and he will disable it out of ignorance and technical illiteracy. Russia cannot afford to allow the peasant to become technically literate by ruining the machinery he is learning to use. So only one textbook serves: fear, encapsulated in the word *saboteur*. Breaking the tractor is sabotage; sabotage gets ten years. Only then will the peasant be more careful. . . .

It is a subtle and plausible reading of how such a system could function, an object lesson in how ends can be used by honorable people to justify horrible means. It also goes a fair way toward explaining the current reaction against probing and publicizing the Stalinist past.

Those patriots (I do not use the word ironically) who write to *Pravda* and *October* feel that their country is better served by emphasizing successes, even at the cost of falsification, than by lancing the boils of recent history. They fail to connect the present malaise with the Soviet past, and they reject what Rybakov and many others see with absolute clarity: that the Soviet Union cannot move forward on a legacy of lies. Rybakov's *Children of the Arbat* is an important part of replacing that legacy with a heritage of truth. (p. 105)

Josephine Woll, ''Stalin's Ghost,'' in The Atlantic Monthly, *Vol. 261, No. 6, June, 1988, pp. 102-05.*

ROBERT CONQUEST

For the last year or so, anyone interested in Soviet history has been inundated with information. Not that anything like the full truth about the Stalin epoch has been told, but intensely illuminating snippets have been piling up. Most of the facts come not from ''official'' authorities, or even from historians, but from journalists and surviving relatives of victims of terror, writing in a dozen or so Soviet periodicals. But the most forthright revelations have turned up in plays, films—and novels. And the most remarkable of the novels is *Children of the Arbat*. . . .

[The novel's] characters are, to varying degrees, victims of the pervasiveness of denunciation: vigilantes in the institutions, the schools, and the Young Communist League, with their mean and pettifogging interpretation of all speech and action as potentially ''hostile.'' It is in the icy squalor of his exile on the Angara River, though there is treachery there, too, that Sasha finds among the ''former people''—the criminals, the exiled kulaks, anarchists, Mensheviks, social revolutionaries—attitudes that are more humane.

Back in Moscow, his mother, commenting on Sasha's fate at the hands of the new regime, challenges her Old Bolshevik brother: . . . ''If the Tsar had sentenced you Communists according to *your* law, he'd still be on the throne.'' . . .

For the Soviet audience, this is dynamite. And the book has indeed caused a sensation. The story of individuals, victors and victims, caught up in Stalin's creation of the New Class— the police-state privilegentsia typified by Sasha's ambitious classmate Yuri Sharok—has never been so fully told there. But above all, it is the author's remarkable treatment of Stalin himself, and of the most sensitive crux of Soviet history, the Kirov murder, that has made the book an epicenter of the quakes now shaking the Soviet mind.

The picture of Stalin is by far the best ever drawn, in the USSR or in the West. With care and detail, Rybakov builds up Stalin's character and his thoughts in his relentless march toward supreme power. (p. 40)

Stalin emerges, in his way, as a genius, his distended will matched by an unrelenting subtlety of maneuver. Everything becomes a bitter political struggle for the supremacy he claims as his due. Finally, by a decisive though disgraceful act of murder, he achieves the breakthrough that eventually will bring him to absolute despotism.

The murder of Stalin's longtime supporter Sergei Kirov, an exceedingly popular and relatively liberal member of the politburo, is a sticking point in the current struggle for the truth about Stalinism. This underhanded and vulgar murder of a close colleague and potential rival gives the lie to the whole moral underpinning of Stalin's regime. . . .

Rybakov does not quite say in so many words that Stalin procured the assassination. But his account of the sordid and intricate plot behind it makes the point perfectly clear, and Soviet reviewers have accepted this. Rybakov started to write his book during the Khrushchev period, and his information about the case is believed to have come from acquaintances who had given testimony to a commission set up by Khrushchev to investigate the case. Its report was not published, and the book, originally scheduled for publication in 1966, also became a casualty of the re-Stalinization then setting in.

Children of the Arbat, as a humane and extraordinarily well constructed novel, stands on its own merits. Politically, it and similar works may be seen as preliminaries to the full-scale public attack on Stalinism that Gorbachev is expected to launch, sooner or later, as part of his campaign against the reactionaries still deeply entrenched in the system. (p. 41)

Robert Conquest, ''Skeletons from the Closets of the Kremlin,'' in Mother Jones, *Vol. XIII, No. V, June, 1988, pp. 40-1.*

JOHN UPDIKE

[*Children of the Arbat*] concerns a number of young people who grew up in the Arbat region of Moscow, a bohemian quarter west of the Kremlin, and the ways in which their lives intertwine and diverge between the fall of 1933 and December of 1934. In this period, climaxed by the assassination of Sergei Kirov in Leningrad, Stalin is portrayed as corrupting Lenin's idealistic revolution with his own paranoia and power lust. . . . The novel's portrait of Stalin, intimate and lengthy, must constitute its central scandal from the standpoint of the Soviet censors and the principal reason it had to wait for *glasnost* to see print. To the Western reader, who has long had access to a number of unvarnished biographies of the dictator, . . . this aspect is less than sensational, though Rybakov's imagination does pull off some lively strokes, from Stalin's tearful identification of his father, the Georgian cobbler Vissarion Dzhugashvili, with the Charlie Chaplin of *City Lights* to the aging tyrant's gingerly give-and-take with a young Jewish dentist, who succeeds in making Stalin a plastic plate though the dictator insisted he wanted gold. But Stalin's meditations on how to rule Russia, rewrite history, and eliminate even a shadow of opposition within the Politburo are less valuable—less purely Rybakov's to give—than the sketches of ordinary Russian life in its surprising variety and flavor. . . . (p. 112)

The children of the Arbat are called Sasha, Yuri, Lena, Nina, Max, Vadim, Vika, and Varya. Varya, Nina's sister, is seventeen; the rest are in their early twenties. Most are members of the Young Communist League, the Komsomol, and their friendly little world is shaken when their Komsomol secretary,

Sasha, is arrested and sentenced to three years' exile in Siberia. . . . The subtleties of Party organization are not easy to follow, nor are the names easy to keep straight, but a sense of tightening control, pervasive spying, and irrationality descending from on high is conveyed so well that we feel relieved and even exhilarated when Sasha reaches the underpopulated hinterland of the Angara River, between Kansk and Bratsk. . . . The author, who suffered such an exile, evokes the summer atmosphere of Siberia's rough Eden with the tenderness of remembrance. . . . The novel's central theme, if one can be identified, is Sasha's moral education: he arrives, amid the system's outcasts and low-priority citizens, at the conclusion that "human feeling has not been killed in people and it never will be." (pp. 112-13)

Rybakov's prose, though a bit too quick on its feet to be called plodding, comes across as colorless and rarely gets off the ground . . . : in six hundred and eighty-five pages I didn't notice a single simile. [The publisher] reportedly hoped for another best-selling *Doctor Zhivago*, but there is in **Children of the Arbat** nothing of Pasternak's poetry and magical sweep of vision and coincidence. . . . But Rybakov does show some modernist daring in the shape of the book: big as it is, it feels like a fragment, a ragged thick slice of life. Almost all the questions raised by its multitudinous soap opera are left unanswered. . . . Only Kirov, who is assassinated, has his story rounded out; and Stalin's has been rounded out by history. A number of the children of the Arbat, introduced with considerable ceremony, do a single turn and then retire to the wings, waiting perhaps for the next act, or the next opera. Can this drastically unresolved large novel be the mere first installment of a giant roman-fleuve cascading in rough parallel to the author's own eventful life? It is, Rybakov declared in a *Time* interview last year. . . .

But *Children of the Arbat*—whose American publisher gives no hint of anything less than a complete novel—doesn't even tell how Sasha survived his first Siberian winter. On the public level, a climax of sorts is reached in Kirov's assassination, which will set off the historical purges to come. On the private level, things stay up in the air. For all its wealth of characters, the novel feels light and thin. It lacks the increased gravity of history rounding a curve. It dares to enter Stalin's head, but it cannot climb outside Stalin's heritage. It conceives happiness in the traditional Russian way, as something filched from the state—a kind of spiritual sneaking, a defiant privacy and personal freedom. "The state had always seemed to Sasha so all-powerful, all-knowing, and all-pervasive. In fact, it wasn't so. You could avoid the state." Might the state itself change for the better? This question lies well beyond the horizon of this novel, and we scan the daily newspaper for the answer. (p. 114)

John Updike, "Doubt and Difficulty in Leningrad and Moscow," in The New Yorker, *Vol. LXIV, No. 30, September 12, 1988, pp. 108-10, 112-14.*

(James) Ed(ward) Sanders

1939-

(Has also written under pseudonym of Black Hobart) American poet, songwriter, nonfiction writer, novelist, short story writer, and editor.

Best known for *The Family,* a study of convicted murderer Charles Manson and his followers, and for his folk-rock group, the Fugs, Sanders played a prominent role in the transition from the Beat movement of the 1950s to the counterculture of the 1960s. Through his writing, music, and political activism, Sanders advocates ''Total Assault on the Culture.'' In his verse and song lyrics, he denounces war, conventional morality, and government repression while celebrating physical and spiritual liberation and altered states of consciousness. Compared by some critics to such poets as William Blake, Walt Whitman, Allen Ginsberg, and Charles Olson, Sanders blends slang, profanity, and neologisms with archaic diction and Greek and Egyptian hieroglyphs to create verse rich in satire and social commentary.

Born in Kansas City, Missouri, Sanders moved to New York City in the late 1950s and was inspired to become a poet by his reading of Beat literature, particularly Ginsberg's poem *Howl* and Jack Kerouac's novel *On the Road.* In the early 1960s, as an active opponent of nuclear weaponry, Sanders was arrested during a peace vigil at a Polaris submarine base and later sentenced to Montville State Jail, where he wrote his first work, *Poem from Jail* (1963). Following his release from prison, Sanders sought a forum for his radical political and literary ambitions, and in 1962 he founded *Fuck You: A Magazine of the Arts.* This journal, which espoused anarchy and pacifism, published work by many of the important Beat writers of the time before it was shut down by police in 1965 on charges of obscenity. In 1964, Sanders opened Peace Eye Bookstore, which became the focal point for the New York Beat culture. At Peace Eye, Sanders met poet Tuli Kupferberg, and they later formed the Fugs. Described by David Jackson as a ''burlesque rock-folk-poetry satire group,'' the Fugs were notorious for their lyrics about sex, drugs, and politics. The group gained an enthusiastic cult following, which propelled Sanders to the forefront of the American counterculture.

In such early volumes as *Poem from Jail, King Lord/Queen Freak* (1964), *The Toe-Queen Poems* (1964), and *Peace Eye* (1965; revised, 1967), Sanders employs ancient and contemporary language, vulgar diction, myth, and commentary on current events to express disillusionment with the world. Despite his pessimism, Sanders conveys his belief that salvation is possible through communal living and harmonious coexistence with nature. In *20,000 A.D.* (1976), Sanders reveals his fascination with ancient Egyptian culture through translations of genuine hieroglyphics while also emphasizing his interest in the antiwar movement. *Investigative Poetry* (1976) and *The Z-D Generation* (1981) are manifestos in which Sanders demands that writers describe instances of government corruption in their work.

In *The Family: The Story of Charles Manson's Dune Buggy Attack Battalion* (1971), Sanders documents the events leading up to the murder of actress Sharon Tate and six others in 1969

by Manson and his disciples. Sanders conducted hundreds of interviews, attended the trial, read transcripts, and visited Manson's camp and the crime sites in an attempt to explain how the California youth culture that supposedly championed peace and love could produce a ''family'' of mass murderers. Some critics contended that Sanders concentrated too much on minutiae without revealing the motivation behind the killings. According to Phil Tracy, however, ''Sanders *has* managed to rip apart the myth that Manson was an isolated nut, the family a collection of deranged morons and the Tate-LaBianca murders a singular happenstance. He has pierced the underside of hipdom and found it as gory as its counterpart in the straight society.''

In his fiction, Sanders often lampoons the New York bohemian milieu in which he lives. *Shards of God: A Novel of the Yippies* (1970) is a mock-epic tale detailing the political, social, and religious events that culminated in the formation of the Youth International Party during the 1968 Democratic National Convention. *Tales of Beatnik Glory* (1975) consists of satirical vignettes of the hedonistic Greenwich Village Beat culture of the late 1950s and early 1960s. This book focuses on Sam, an autobiographical character, who portrays his rural childhood and his involvement in radical literary and political groups. *Fame and Love in New York* (1980) is an intricately plotted novel set in the near future that burlesques the greed of the

New York art community. Sanders has also edited several anthologies of poetry.

(See also *Contemporary Authors,* Vols. 13-16, rev. ed.; *Contemporary Authors New Revision Series,* Vol. 13; and *Dictionary of Literary Biography,* Vol. 16.)

TED BERRIGAN

Interestingly, there are few images [in *Peace Eye*]. The work is for the ear and the head, the eye free to go about its business (seeing OUT)....[Sanders's] metrics are eclectic and sure (Whitman, Ginsberg, Billy James Hargiss), and his Time/Space woofwarp, in the Pound, Olson tradition, is both effective and (convincingly) accurately erudite. These two stylistic elements, metrics and manner, provide the framework for some of the most exciting, rich, musical magic rhetoric of today. He is, like Allen Ginsberg, emotionally on top of his lines, and he is also and at the same time, like Charles Olson, slipping and sliding geometrically into your brain cells, sensually zapping the senses thru the brain.

The poems are absurd, as befits a total assault on the culture. A shrewd and arrogant hard-nosed innocence pokes itself between the line(s) and the message that is spelled out reads, "EVERYTHING IS OK." For example, lies: "No turning back / no rewrite / no voice!" and for example, the facts: "Peace Eye is open to any who / rip wide the brainvalves, & / fuck the mish system, / be it with wad technique."

> *We shall be exposed*
> *and stand bare ass*
> *in the Kosmos.*

"Accept then / these fantasies / ... / Build then / GOOF CITY / in America / where there are / United States."

The language is abrupt, it is rude and burning cold, as ancient as it is current, as literary as it is (and it is) of the streets. (p. 95)

> *Ted Berrigan, in a review of "Peace Eye," in Kulchur, Vol. 5, No. 20, Winter, 1965-66, pp. 94-6.*

RICHARD DUERDEN

King Lord / Queen Freak, is only six poems, and all short, but I think three of them—**"Prayer to the Lady, Queen Freak;"** **"Crotch Lake;"** and **"Sheep-Fuck Poem"**—are worth whatever reasonable price the book is.

Sanders' language is not simply colloquial. He has swallowed the colloquial entirely, and the language is released—released into and informed by the life within his vision. It is a vision of life as an invisible net, a plexus, that is "freaky" simply because it includes all things plus all persons. The language, by the profound fact of inclusion, re-sees: it, the language, by seeing and touching, is that stream his vision is. It touches and says the same freaky inclusion. All things and persons are acted upon. Vision and compassion are as real as chemistry. The language and the author are acted upon through things and persons. He is changed by the vision analogical (not homological) to a blood transfusion. Or a pill.

The first poem, **"Prayer,"** is simply that, a prayer celebrating continuity, the sun the central organ of plexus, light the first and last unit of it all, and thus up-taken unto Ra, the sun-disc, the it / we shines down "that morning ring true among the Vases".

In the poem **"King Lord / Queen Freak"** the sexual act with woman (earth) is the entrance to "ONE me yet make me scattered . . . gel my viscera forever in the Jars of Death". But it's in the three poems mentioned above that we get to the stream. In **"Prayer to the Lady, Queen Freak"** it is through woman, as through it all, that we go into "the rite of KICKING OPEN THE DOOR . . . the brain-valves ripped open / mind-screens flung away / and all the bits / & hunks boil inward / The direct retinal Flood . . . Brain-valves torn in the WORD STREAM / BRAIN leaking in the cosmos / We enter the FLOOD".

Language and life, when the "brain-valves" are finally "torn", enter the cosmos. Are in it all. (pp. 126-27)

> *Richard Duerden, "Eyes and 'I,'" in Poetry, Vol. CVIII, No. 2, May, 1966, pp. 125-30.*

A. R. AMMONS

Ed Sanders's primary subject matter in *Peace Eye* is: Energy is Holy. Pan is the god, not the devil. Civilization, carrying its freight of repression as hate, is not holy. There is no space to argue how simplistic and one-sided this subject matter may be: at least, Mr. Sanders has taken his side to the limit, and there's bravery and force in that.... My trouble with Mr. Sanders's highly-charged, geyser-fraught world, is that I can't imagine who shops for the groceries. If Energy costs so much, if it diminishes man to a rod, woman to an orifice, if it obliterates all surface and personality, then the good is brutally, devastatingly compromised.

> *A. R. Ammons, in a review of "Peace Eye," in Poetry, Vol. CVIII, No. 3, June, 1966, p. 196.*

THE ANTIOCH REVIEW

In his characteristically apocalyptic voice, Ed Sanders . . . aims to reveal the history, social dynamics, fears, passions, values and aspirations that motivate the members of the Woodstock Generation [in *Shards of God: A Novel of the Yippies*]. His "novel" suffers from pornographic repetition, auctorial intrusiveness and a host of other social and literary offenses, but it doesn't lack energy. Amusing characterization and inventive social situations add vitality if not credibility to a plot that more or less follows the political, religious, psychedelic and totally unbelievable chain of events leading up to the Democratic National Convention of 1968. Despite his literary intentions, Sanders has somehow created a faithful and interesting picture of the Youth International Party.

> *A review of "Shards of God: A Novel of the Yippies," in The Antioch Review, Vol. XXX, Nos. 3 & 4, Fall, 1970 & Winter, 1971, p. 459.*

ROBERT CHRISTGAU

The Family is the first complete, authoritative account of the career of Charles Manson. A small-time thief, forger and pimp who was paroled after seven years in prison at the dawn of San Francisco's 1967 Summer of Love, Manson, hirsute and acid-eyed, was charged with the Tate-LaBianca murders less than three years later. In January, 1971, he was convicted of these seven murders. He must still stand trial for two others—one of them, according to author Ed Sanders, a hideous torture experiment—and is implicated in many more.

The Family tells how an ambitious petty criminal focused some cunning amateur psychology on particularly vulnerable examples of the mass alienation of California's youth Bohemia, and created a "family" of disciples bound together by a macabre synthesis of antisocial pathology and communal ideals. Combining calculated alterations of tenderness and violence with awesome sexual stamina and a line of pseudo-guru babble, he attracted a following of pathetic young women whose sexual favors helped him move his band of lumpenhippies through various crash scenes. He used drugs and sex for blackmail and mind control, developed a doom philosophy influenced by the satanist cults that flourish around Los Angeles, and prepared his disciples for racial Armageddon, which they all believed was imminent, with a battalion of stolen dune buggies equipped with booty acquired on stolen credit cards. The murders that resulted from this runaway obsession with violence seem inevitable in retrospect.

The outline of this story has been known for quite a while—sometimes reliably, sometimes not. Ed Sanders has solidified it, filling in particulars and verifying rumors. Manson's close relationship with hip Hollywooders like record and television producer Terry Melcher and Beach Boy rock star Dennis Wilson, now minimized by the principals, is fully described. His occult connections are detailed. The crimes and their solutions are recounted with great care for sequence and consistency. Sanders's research occupied a year and a half of his life; tens of thousands of pages of data were organized into some 50 subject files and dozens of chronological files. All the allegations he reports have been checked against known facts, and for the most part he refused to use any information that didn't come from at least two separate individuals. This work was extraordinarily difficult, requiring auxiliary investigators and even disguises. Since most of Manson's associates are partisans of violence, it was also dangerous. (p. 2)

In the age of the new togetherness, it isn't just the good guys who get together. In *The Family,* Sanders states this problem once and never makes the point again: "the flower movement was like a valley of thousands of plump white rabbits surrounded by wounded coyotes. Sure, the 'leaders' were tough, some of them geniuses and great poets. But the acid-dropping middle-class children from Des Moines were rabbits."

Sanders doesn't dwell on this idea because his narrative is almost compulsively free of what in a more literal context he refers to as "horse dooky." He refuses to philosophize, psychoanalyze or make excuses. *The Family* is nothing more than a chronological arrangement of all those facts, apparently written direct from the files, rapidly. True, the diction is characteristic Sanders Americanese—in all his work he has a way of coming up with hyphenated coinages like "bunch-punching," "murder-fated" and "hell-creep," and he is fond of words like "tycoon" and "sleuth"—and he will occasionally add a jarring note of boyish sarcasm to some especially grisly disclosure by ending the paragraph with a brief "far out" or "oo-ee-oo." But the book is determinedly non-written. There is no theorizing, and no new journalism either—no fabricated immediacy, no reconstructed dialogue, no arty pace.

This data-mania is itself an anti-middlebrow avant-garde ploy. Sanders is quite capable of normal prose and fictional tech-

nique, and had he deemed the effort worthy he probably could have made *The Family* into something like *In Cold Blood* or even *The Boston Strangler,* but he represents a sensibility that has pretty much rejected such devices and his book is truer and more exciting for it. His terse notebook style, avoiding comment and ignoring conventional standards of rhetoric, functions as a deliberate artistic choice. Although he may mention in passing that arrests for possessing a harmless euphoriant or for "felonious breast-feeding" can be expected to spark dangerous resentment, he clearly feels that the facts about Manson and his followers speak for themselves, and that they are horrible beyond explanation.

The intensity of this feeling, which reflects Sanders's commitment to nonviolence, is the greatest virtue of an excellent book. The Manson case engendered much confusion in the ranks of hip. A distressing minority . . . were unwilling to believe that a long-haired minstrel could also be a racist and male supremacist who used dope and orgasm and even some variety of love to perpetuate his own murderous sadism. In his coverage of the trial for the Los Angeles Free Press, Sanders did his best to protect Manson's presumption of innocence, and he was severely critical of anti-hippie hysteria among straight journalists, but his own research convinced him who was how guilty and ought to convince anybody.

Guilt is definitely the word. Sanders believes that, for whatever reason, the plump white rabbits in Manson's entourage have become "crazed with the willingness to murder" and must be separated from society. His portrayal of Sharon Tate and associates, on the other hand, while tinged with the deep disdain of a genuine psychic voyager for ruling-class dabblers, is temperate. He doesn't conceal their connections with big-time dope and with the occult, but he does withhold damaging but irrelevant information "in respect for the memory of the innocent slain."

The murderers are guilty and their victims were innocent—after years of rationalization and hip irony, such a formulation has a refreshing moral directness. Let others fulminate over co-optation by rich straights. Sanders knows that for the most part the co-opters are only contemptible, and he will return to oppose the death-creeps who rule this society some other time. For now, he is horrified by the satanist coyotes who battle the forces of Yippie for the soul of the disaffected young—the sexist bikers, the cults that traffic in animal and (it would appear) human sacrifice. In order to say this, Sanders has done nothing less than risk his own life, for that's how serious he believes the enemy within to be, and who knows enough to gainsay him? It is only fitting that such a risk should produce such a terrifying book. (pp. 24-5)

*Robert Christgau, "Lumpenhippies and Their Guru,"
in* The New York Times Book Review, *October 31,
1971, pp. 2, 24-5.*

ANATOLE BROYARD

The Family is an attempt to relate Charles Manson and his followers to the freak cults that flourish in California: the devil-worshippers; the drinkers of dog blood; the doom-presagers, acid droppers, occultists, bike gangs and porn lovers. The author, Ed Sanders—a poet and former leader of a rock group called The Fugs—spent a year and a half investigating Manson and the context out of which he came. He conducted 400 to 500 interviews, compiled 50 subject files, read all the transcripts of the cases, visited the sites of the crimes and of the "family's" camps. He risked his life to write the book, he says, "since most of Manson's associates are partisans of violence." Piously asserting that he has played down the more sensational aspects of the Manson story, Mr. Sanders proceeds to drown us in a garbage-truckload of data. Manson was a nomad and we are obliged to follow him not only all over California, but also from room to room, from car to car as he wears them out, girl to girl. We hear what he allegedly said and did, down to the most meaningless minutiae. By the end of the book, we know everything about him except what kind of person he was, why he acted as he did and how he was able to influence so many people. . . .

Judging from the way he held his family together and from the high degree of organization he was able to achieve, Manson must have had charisma, talent and a degree of eloquence— but you'd never know it from Mr. Sanders's account. Apart from hinting that he was a sexual virtuoso who usually instructed his partner to think of him as her father, the author leaves it to us to puzzle out Manson's secret from fragmented glimpses of an antic megalomaniac.

For almost three years, Manson supported his growing family by bartering the girls for worldly goods, by stripping people of everything they owned while they were on acid trips, by using stolen credit cards and by borrowing the houses of people he had somehow befriended offstage. His various pronouncements—all dutifully reproduced—amount to nothing like a coherent set of beliefs, plans or even pretensions. He was always asking people to kill him or let him kill them; beating or making love to members of his family; packing or unpacking his converted school bus before or after a motiveless move. . . .

As he grew more bloodthirsty, Manson gave the girls lessons in throat-slitting and skull-boiling. He also practiced "machete chauvinism": throwing it at them like a vaudeville performer. Since drugs were an integral part of their lives, they were probably sustained in these experiences by one kind of high or another. The general reader, however, is not so fortunate, and has to suffer the machete chops of Mr. Sanders's style as well as he can.

A refrigerator is "emplaced" on a bus; people "clink bodies"; breaking and entering is a "creepy-crawlie"; members of the family "utter" forged checks or credit cards; people are often called simply "humans"; members of a group or persuasion are indicated by the suffix "oid." Looking is translated into "copped a visual"; people's various aliases are relentlessly prefaced by "aka"; one of Mr. Sanders's witnesses "allegedly alleges"; when, out of delicacy, the author employs a euphemism, it's cute enough to make your teeth ache. A sentence begins with "Of irony" instead of ironically; intimidation becomes "several deaths may have resulted to create silence and fear"; the author periodically pauses to whistle at what he has just written with "oo-ee-oo."

Since he himself has gone through some of the scenes he describes, Mr. Sanders may have written this book as a form of penance, a purification rite. Anybody prurient enough to read *The Family* deserves to suffer right along with him.

Anatole Broyard, "More and Less about Manson,"
in The New York Times, *November 11, 1971, p. 45.*

PHIL TRACY

Beyond the ludicrous assumption that all evil in our country is directly attributable to the "straights" or our involvement in Vietnam, there has in fact been very little discussion as to how a group like Manson's could come to be. Certainly not through drugs alone. If everyone who dropped acid regularly was into killing people, the country would already be awash in a sea of blood. Granted acid is a kinetic agent in the Manson experience, breaking down traditional taboos and scrambling acquired value systems. Also granted, Manson chose his family carefully, using time-proven techniques from his little-known career as an L.A. pimp in the mid-'50s; spotting the weak and insecure, those most receptive to his messianic message. But that doesn't explain the active ingredient. Why the slaughter, why the blood path with so many trips to choose from in wicky-wacky California?

In an effort to answer that question Sanders [in *The Family*] spent more than a year and a half trying to trace the life of Manson's family as they ricochet back and forth across the golden state of California for close to three years. The result is a montage of facts, some relevant, some obscure and most completely confusing.

Perhaps the single most important ingredient Sanders has come up with is what he calls "sleazo inputs": the various pain and death cults that were floating around Los Angeles at the same time as the Manson family. . . .

But he is never able to make direct connections between the "inputs" and the family. In this sense *The Family* is a simulation of the pulverized, bewildering L.A. experience. Events appear as isolated incidents without the necessary linkage to place them in perspective. A meeting here, a happening there, with nothing concrete to connect them. You could write it off to sloppy research but few people have invested the time and energy Sanders has to come up with his story. It's not the reporter who confuses you, its the reality he writes about.

Even so, in his opening chapter Sanders confesses that during his investigation "I became a data addict," and unfortunately his addiction carries over into the book. Sanders' tendency to throw every piece of information he's collected into the narrative (including what seems at times half a million aliases) only further beclouds an already hopelessly confused reality. It's as if the author, caught in the web of the L.A. experience, could no longer distinguish between the significant and the extraneous. The result is such a confusing welter of detail that one is left at the end of the book unsure exactly who in the family committed what murders or whether they were ever convicted for them.

Despite its marred presentation, *The Family* is a book that has no trouble holding a reader's attention. Its documented chronology of the Manson family's wanderings is a guide to the California underworld of drugs, sex, madness and pain. Sanders' sometimes brilliant, sometimes ponderous style of narrative guides you back and forth between the various centers of hip insanity. A data king with knitting needles, he tries to connect the elements together into some discernible pattern.

Ultimately, he fails. One is left with three questions for every answer. Sanders *has* managed to rip apart the myth that Manson was an isolated nut, the family a collection of deranged morons and the Tate-LaBianca murders a singular happenstance. He has pierced the underside of hipdom and found it as gory as its counterpart in the straight society.

Phil Tracy, "'Sleazo Inputs' and Psychedelic Madness," in Commonweal, *Vol. XCV, No. 18, February 4, 1972, p. 428.*

ROBERT KEE

[In *The Family,* Ed Sanders] tells us in a frenzied introduction:

> For a year and a half I wrote down literally everything I heard or saw related to the so-called Manson family. I carried with me at all times a tape-recorder and recorded at least one hundred hours of interviews, confrontations and comment. Nothing was too trivial to escape my jotting Rapidograph. Day and night I roamed Los Angeles gathering data. I became a data addict.

He can say that again (and does, incidentally). His book is a mass of conscientiously acquired data, often hooked together by no more subtle literary device than the blank space around new paragraphs. Even the running undercurrent of sexual orgy and the knowledge that the Sharon Tate and other murders are to come serve as poor inducement to keep up with the Rapidograph. Racy as is the style, with sentences like: 'Ugliness was,' 'Ceaseless was the love-making' and 'Oo-ee-oo' (three times by page 148, and on page 178: 'We shall have to pause here for an oo-ee-oo'); vivid as is the phraseology: 'perv is what the LA music scene eats for breakfast'; and contortionist as is the syntax: 'Important in terms of sleazo inputs is to remember that . . .'—the net result is only a sort of manic tedium.

The author is like some facetious steel ball on a pin-table machine, flashing up amazing thousands of nothingness before sinking back to a real zero. . . . But though we are given a great deal of extraneous detail about Charles Manson's world and even the minutiae of his several thousand orgasms a year (before *and* after meals), we get no real clue as to why he's like what he is. We want to know just how the Book of Revelation and the Beatles' music worked on him to this grotesque and barbarous effect, but Sanders hardly begins to explore him as a personality. Only at one point does he briefly dismiss the need to do so by saying that Manson had read all the books on magic and anthropology. But that is like explaining Hitler by saying it is all in *Mein Kampf*. That Manson was what we have to call ill is undeniable. But how ill, and why, and how much his illness tells us about our own 'health', are the interesting questions—here totally obscured. In fact, one is left speculating whether Manson might not be more interesting than this book makes him.

> *Robert Kee, "Perv," in* The Listener, *Vol. 87, No. 2250, May 11, 1972, p. 627.*

JOHN YOHALEM

Tales of Beatnik Glory is a collection of yarns, anecdotes and shaggy person stories—some perhaps true, a few no doubt autobiographical—of the Lower East Side in the period, roughly 1959-62, of High Beat, a time in both the arts and life-styles of a suspicious bubbling that might well pass for ferment. Ed Sanders was there, founding arts magazines with unprintable titles, singing strange songs, radicalizing, effervescing.

Outside the Village, Sanders is remembered for a music group, The Fugs, that seemed to parody rock bands—with digressions into bawdiness, Dada and Egyptian mysticism—and for a book, *The Family,* which might almost have been a parody of New Journalism. In *The Family,* a study of the Manson group and related cults, Sanders wrote as if he were a speed freak delirious with paranoia, clutching you by the collar to whimper the latest revelations of horror. The cumulative effect, as was doubtless intended, was to wrack the nerves.

In *Tales of Beatnik Glory* he has calmed down as befits his gentler subject; he has retreated from shrieks to cackles and sneers. Beatnik glory consisted, we are told, of "ImGrat"—immediate gratification, that old hip hedonism. . . .

There are some good stories and some good lines—a ballet ending in sex is rather prettily described, Washington Square on Sunday and Avenue B at 4 A.M. well evoked. At a poetry reading, besides capsule descriptions of each poetic type, we are treated to samples of work such as "America! robots with shoes made out of living gophers climb from the tv dinner plates to eat your teeth!," which is almost as much fun as the real "Howl."

If Sanders could sustain the anecdotal pleasantries or the satire he would have produced a better book. This one seems to have been dashed off while half asleep and little rewritten. There is no unity of attitude or style, even within individual stories. Sanders can't decide whether he is glorying in decadence like a shopkeeper on a spree, or striking the poses of the self-righteously liberated, or putting the whole scene down from a still more knowing standpoint. His writing, too, is erratic—no longer shrill but of a constant alteration between abstruse intellectual references (the sun is always Ra) and archaic witticisms ("the angst of an empty stomach emptied away—for e'en a nascent Keats is de-ego'd and deprived of depravity by the talons of the food hawk"), homegrown slang and seventh-grade English errors. . . .

Sanders is not difficult to read, he rattles along at a fair clip, but his excesses bring upon the reader a sense of staleness not unlike the morning after some drugged adventure. Worse, he salivates with deprecation, with hipper-than-thou put-downs and sneers at lesser tribes without the flash, in nearly every anecdote. This is unjustified, if only because the beats could never resist the temptations of straight culture. ImGrat, by Sanders's account, seems to include dinners at the Plaza and bank vice-presidencies—such things are undeniably gratifying.

It was an era of good times and of saying much that required saying, but the artistic achievements were not unprecedented, the revelation was not without peer, beatnik glory was subjective.

> *John Yohalem, "Fun and Games in East Village," in* The New York Times Book Review, *November 9, 1975, p. 22.*

BARRY WALLENSTEIN

In *Tales of Beatnik Glory,* Sanders tells an inside story of his years on the Lower East Side in New York, years that included the running of an underground bookshop and press, the emergence and recognition of writers such as Ferlinghetti, Burroughs, and Charles Olson, and a reemergence of political activism. Yet, he talks about it all in a tone of voice not likely to inspire genuine interest in the period or place. In fact, the book seems to be a warning for all those who might be tempted to give the Beats thoughtful attention. In a way, Sanders' *Tales* may be a curious example of Dada fiction, where truth or history is presented through self-contained fictions and exaggerations, in which the medium imitates the message. While the reader has no trouble getting hold of the subject, it is more difficult to grapple with the author's point of view. He seems to have no more interest in committing himself to a consistent vision of the beatniks than the Beats of the time had in accuracy of definition or conventional manners.

The book is unified by its main character, Sam. At college in 1957-58 he reads Ginsberg's *Howl* and realizes that "things will never be the same." The book follows his romantic and ragged adventures: his Greenwich Village poverty, his connections to a rural past, his radicalism. But this is presented in a flippantly casual satire. One wonders if Sanders cares, or ever cared, to ponder the life he describes, as the vignettes tend toward situation comedy and the characters merge into stereotypes of Beat lore.... (p. 543)

Possibly Sanders is saying, by his burlesque of poetry readings, political demonstrations, and people, that the only way to remain true to the spirit of the times is to avoid the analytical processes of evaluation and judgment. His tone, however, implies a judgment nonetheless. At one point in his narrative, a character states that, except for Ginsberg, the Beat movement produced only "a lot of crap." While this is a little surprising coming from a worthy participant, his estimate is shared by many who loved the Beat scene in the late fifties and early sixties, and by even more who, for a variety of reasons, have dismissed the literature. (pp. 543-44)

Barry Wallenstein, "The Beats," in Contemporary Literature, Vol. 18, No. 4, Autumn, 1977, pp. 542-51.

JOHN LEONARD

Although *Fame & Love in New York* is set in the near future, it seems to have arrived by time capsule from the pre-yahoo 1960's, when apocalyptic humor was more in fashion.... [Sanders's] first formal exercise in fiction owes a good deal to Thomas Pynchon, Kurt Vonnegut, Joseph Heller, Ken Kesey and R. Crumb, and nothing at all to Aristotle.

Fame & Love in New York . . . is more about fame than about love. And it is mostly about money. Everybody's ambition in the book is to take "a droll stroll past the pecunia patch" or "down cash cache creek" or "up Buck Flood Boulevard." Everybody includes artists, poets, novelists, scholars, private eyes, intelligence agents, rare-book dealers, gallery owners, critics and journalists, who are known as Starved Foxes, not to mention the Mafia, which is known as "maf-org." . . .

The President in charge of *Fame & Love in New York* is, for reasons obscure to me, named Kennedy. Nevertheless, we have landed on Mars. To walk across the Brooklyn Bridge is to risk being mugged by "air toughs" in "minicopters." (Helicopters are, like tofu, a continuing motif.) The news weekly magazines are called Gorp and Urge, instead of Time and Newsweek. Nobody is safe from the electronic ear of a "surveillance chip," a bug that looks like a discarded wad of bubblegum even as it monitors our thoughts and dreams.

To summarize *Fame & Love in New York* is to risk ridicule. Milton Rosé, an artist specializing in "deconstructions/constructions," is justly famous for his "Homage to the Food Chain," which features a 500-ton frog with a Mona Lisa smile. But Milton goes too far when he includes Beethoven's actual desk in one of his collages. His patron, Sigmund Hammerbank, would like to help him but is too busy trying to corner "the noses of America"—that is, the domestic cocaine trade—on franchise from Count Volpe, who is known for his "Etruscan thumbs." When you cross Count Volpe, he removes your thumbs and puts them in a vase.

Meanwhile the Balzac Study Group is rewriting all 90 novels in the *Human Comedy* series for a contemporary audience, and using the paperback advance money to bankroll a socialist revolution in the year 2000, which revolution is also being bankrolled through benefit concerts by J'Accuse, although another rock band, Dark Pelt, less idealistic, concentrates on defacing Mount Rushmore with unnecessary nostrils. What has any of this to do with the casket scam, or rain capes fashioned out of duct tape and plastic trash bags, or the Barrel Generation? Forgery, like the faces of American Presidents, cocaine-dealing, data-collecting, helicopters and tofu, is a Sanders obsession.

Balzac, of course, also wrote novels about money. But what about Hart Crane? Why has the National Aeronautics and Space Administration adopted a bridge as its symbol? Why does Milton Rosé plan a secret Hart Crane shrine on Mars? If Balzac and Hart Crane are the literary bookends of *Fame & Love in New York*, how come there are so many mentions of Albert Camus? When J'Accuse sings "Then Jesus came among the Geodesic Domes at Daun and the State Police Killed Him until He was carried away on a green Frog's Back Rag," what are we supposed to think? . . .

Mr. Sanders turns everything into money, including socialism. He is the satirist run amok. . . . .

Fame & Love in New York is a very funny mess, like the black novels of the 1960's and unlike history since.

John Leonard, in a review of "Fame & Love in New York," in The New York Times, December 17, 1980, p. C33.

CARL SOLOMON

[With *Fame & Love in New York*, Ed Sanders] has written a strangelovian novel about farce and terror in the New York art world. From Soho to Brooklyn-ho to Queens-ho to Bronx-ho to Staten Island-ho and from their to Ho-ho, Burroughsian and Queneau-like characters (lone Appleton the poetess, Milton Rose the artist, J'Accuse the rock band members) scuffle for bread, pleasure, and integrity while terror in the form of Hunk Forbes, the para-military right-wing nut, lurks in the wings preparing for a sudden apocalyptic appearance. Traditionally in America, the Jack London Iron Heel vision of a right-wing hell has complemented the Orwellian vision of a left-wing hell. In Sanders, these two hells overlap. He has a complex, screwball, Rube Goldberg-like grasp of the technology of the future and fills out his satire with drawings, charts, lists and other devices hilarious at first impact but unfortunately growing a bit tedious with repetition before the novel ends.

Sanders has been a first-rate satirist since at least the mid-sixties when he was the leader of the Fugs and has always had a unique personal idiom and style occasionally reminiscent of satirists of the past but always recognizably Ed Sanders. In his novel, he introduces some of his past experience (like references to William Szabo—an old poet pal—the Fugs, and idiosyncratic verbal constructions redolent of, say, his Toe-Queen poems). Who can deny a man his personal idiom? It's the way he speaks. His dissection of Ione Appleton, poetess, founder of the Balzac Study Group, committer of "public fornication," and an individual determined to make it by hook or by crook, ranks with the best of early Waugh.

However, Sanders does have a few shortcomings. Chief among them is an inability to edit himself and a tendency toward repetition. *Fame And Love In New York* is undoubtedly too long, far longer than his subject matter warrants. Waugh seldom bored and his books had greater entertainment value than *Fame And Love* for that reason. Sanders indulges himself too greatly at the readers' expense. This book is not a satirical classic but is nevertheless head and shoulders above most current fiction. It would be an injustice to Ed Sanders to deny or to fail to mention that his enormous erudition (not as commonplace a commodity these days as one might think) shines through on every page. His prose blossoms everywhere with recondite words and information in a manner rivalling William Buckley or Anatole Broyard.

The barbs he directs at his avant-garde rebels are as sharp as those he hurls at the culture in general. Ione becomes, for a while, the epitome of the irksome female aesthete everybody remembers from his English classes. The rebels reach a peak of absurdity when they consider substituting a poem by Allen Ginsberg for "The Star-Spangled Banner" as our national anthem. Soho and Tribeca are stripped of their in-group glamour and become less intimidating to the uptown layman as a result of Sanders' debunking satire. . . .

His overall weakness seems to be a unidimensionality of subject matter and technique. All comics have a few special identifying routines and Sanders' greatest and most typical comes when he discusses crass aspects of his exaggerated culture boom, like the sale of Proust-brand cork-lined rooms. He is best when he reveals the commercial exploitation of culture generally—for the sake of "mon" and to avoid "pov"—and the madness of selling and collecting memorabilia of great and long-gone cultural names; when he reveals the shallow Darwinian survival bent behind our superficial idealism. . . .

Fame and Love in New York should be read by everybody who loves art, enjoys genuine intelligent humanism and likes good, normal, gritty wit.

> Carl Solomon, in a review of "Fame & Love in New York," in The American Book Review, Vol. 3, No. 4, May-June, 1981, p. 14.

MICHAEL E. BROWN

Ed Sanders' *Fame and Love in New York* is exceedingly funny. It is a swift, pointed, uncompromising, yet strangely reassuring survey of the thing-loving, reputation-making, credential-toting, intelligence agent's dream-world of that fascistically-aestheticized, almost-high-society enterprise sociologists like to call "modern culture." Through it all runs this ex-Fug's uncanny ability to warp the comforts of sacred places and pleasures. . . .

But we are neither disturbed nor embarrassed by the demented ambitions that spot this wall, though we know them as presently in place and at ease where we live. Sanders is making fun; and the fun is, at once, the book's success and its failure. The fun is there, but by the time we finish reading, it is gone because what it is funny about had been made too much figure and too little fact. The satire, typically, overwhelms its content when it succeeds; and this is simultaneously, the measure of the failure of its political intent.

There are three devices that organize this piece. One is the science fictionalist's device of setting a familiar scene in the near future. This creates a sense of imminence and clarity, both necessary for the satiric effect. The imminence retains the moral disposition; clarity gives it its objects. The device simplifies.

It does away with ambiguity, dull edges, and loose ends. In this case, what is left is the otherwise unbearably familiar world of hardware, uniforms, calculations, equipment, positions, names, covers, records, techniques, and sites. Life is language, language is jargon, and all is fad. . . .

The second is a steady undercurrent of allusiveness, provocatively-coded quasi-references to solid figures of contemporaneity: Judy Chicago, the Sculls, Castelli, The Electric Company, Lew Archer, Jean Seberg, conceptual art, high punk, and high class conspiracy. Driving this undercurrent is the technocratic passion for micro-records ("surv-chipping") and macro-control. Governing the packed synchrony of the arrangements are several political-aesthetic pairs which constitute the dizzy morality of Sanders' dunciad: creativity-destruction, art-military, love-investigation, desire-enterprise, intention-accounts. Behind it all is a suspected allusionist named Sanders. . . .

The third organizing device is the story itself, for there is one, and many. It winds swiftly and hilariously along, gothic in its involutions and epicycles, like bebop. It begins with the financial predicaments of one Milton Rosé, artist and entrepreneur, and the problem of peddling a stellar work employing, among other things, Beethoven's desk, an enormous likeness of Betsy Ross's needle, and sundry trinkets appropriate to its title, *Circles of Paradise*. The job of peddling goes to a Sigmund Hammerbank, whose shady connections open to a global conglomerate of porn, dope, and art. This gives way to a series of tangled adventures in which appear, among others, a tough detective named Fitz McIver, a Balzac-inspired group of writers led by the amazing Ione Appleton, famous for her bardiatrics and Duct-Tape Boutique and obsessed by a desire to "Delineate the Age," and J'Accuse, a "Science-and-Technology Rock" group that had remained popular throughout the major musical periods, from "folk-rock" to "Watergate rock," "glitter/decadence/punk rock," and "mea culpa/repentance rock." The search for Hart Crane's trunk, the attempt to solve the theft of Count Raspachi's Balzac manuscripts, and the penetration of the Balzac Study Group's Creativity Bunker, take us through the highways and byways of SoHo, YoHo, BrookHo, HoHo, and a dozen other Hos. The climax is reached at a spectacular "Room Trash Benefit" that turns ugly and bloody. Rosé dies before his masterwork is completed, "And all began to sing:

> Float thou, o soul of the painter,
> out beyond the shoulders of slime
> -----
> while we on earth work on
> The Glorious Deadline"

> Michael E. Brown, "A Story of Fame and Love in New York," in Artworkers News, Vol. 10, No. 10, June, 1981, p. 40.

PAUL BERMAN

The Z-D Generation is a chapbook manifesto in the spirit of Ed Sanders's earlier volume, *Investigative Poetry*. Z-D stands for Zola-Diderot, and the idea is that poets, writers, and everyone else should devote themselves to critical scrutiny of the national government, the way Zola and Diderot did. The Z-D generation will engage in mass muckrakery. . . .

Sanders proposes slogans and formulas to speed Z-D investigations along: for instance, the Three Adverbs, C/R/E, which stands for Ceaselessly/Relentlessly/Ethically. He advocates Full-color Flow Charts, 3-D Data-Grid Hologram J'Accuses, and other slick techniques to avoid "Data-Midden & Boredom." And he is full of philosophical aperçus about the principal enemy, which is state repression. . . .

The climax of Sanders's manifesto is his suggestion for a 30-volume *Encyclopedia of 20th Century American War Criminals*. This is a terrific idea. . . . Sanders observes that anyone who attempts to create such an encyclopedia better be prepared to endure the nasty ill will of the state, the way Diderot and Zola did. That's a good warning. The government does notice this kind of opposition. According to Sanders, the FBI file on Tom Hayden is 250,000 pages long. I wonder how long the file on Ed Sanders is, even without the encyclopedia. Does it contain the complete run of his *Fuck You/a magazine of the arts?* Does it record his warblings for the Fugs? An FBI file is the opposite of Pinocchio's nose: it grows every time you tell a truth. Sanders's is growing even as you read.

Paul Berman, in a review of "The Z-D Generation," in The Village Voice, *Vol. XXVII, No. 16, April 20, 1982, p. 41.*

L. BERK

Any assessment of the cultural and literary avant-garde since the start of the 1960s will benefit from [*Thirsting for Peace in a Raging Century: Selected Poems, 1961-1985*]. The book provides an important view of life on the periphery from a legendary figure who is at once an eccentric scholar-poet in the tradition of Pound and Olson and an outrageous rocker (member of the Fugs) who has also written the most important book on Charles Manson [*The Family*]. . . . Many of these poems sparkle with incisive wit and originality. The less effective poems are too dependent on the technique expounded by Charles Olson, and place too much emphasis on cleverness. Sanders takes the practice of projective verse a step further than most: he includes drawings in the body of many poems.

L. Berk, in a review of "Thirsting for Peace in a Raging Century: Selected Poems, 1961-1985," in Choice, *Vol. 25, No. 8, April, 1988, p. 1247.*

Anne (Harvey) Sexton

1928-1974

American poet, short story writer, dramatist, and author of children's books.

Sexton was one of the best-known and most controversial of the Confessional poets, a group composed primarily of New England writers who rose to prominence during the 1950s and early 1960s. Like such fellow Confessionalists as Robert Lowell and Sylvia Plath, Sexton wrote highly introspective verse that revealed intimate details of her emotional troubles. Reflected in her writings is the severe depression from which she suffered for most of her adult life and which led to her suicide. Characterized by vivid imagery and daring metaphors, Sexton's early work deals intensively with her psychic traumas and her attempts to overcome mental illness. While she began her career as a highly methodical poet who wrote within formal metrical and rhyme schemes and reworked her manuscripts through several drafts, Sexton composed her later poems in various experimental forms, often with little or no revision. In addition to focusing upon her emotional life, Sexton's later work includes frequent allusions to mythology, fairy tales, and Christian motifs and explores such topics as romantic love, motherhood, and relations between the sexes.

Sexton spent most of her life in the affluent, upper middle-class suburbs of Boston. She married at age nineteen and attempted to settle into the role of housewife and mother. During her early twenties, however, Sexton began to experience bouts of depression that eventually led to hospitalization. After the birth of her second daughter, Sexton attempted suicide. During her recovery, she was encouraged by her psychiatrist to write poems as a form of therapy, and after her release she began attending poetry classes and workshops. Among her teachers were W. D. Snodgrass, John Holmes, and Robert Lowell, all of whom were connected with the new Confessional movement. These instructors profoundly influenced Sexton's development as a poet, as did her friendships with classmates Maxine Kumin and Sylvia Plath. Sexton soon began to publish her work in magazines and to give spirited public readings, rapidly gaining a reputation as an important new poet.

Believing that complete honesty and self-revelation were essential to her creative work, Sexton wrote a number of early poems that candidly describe her struggles to cope with her psychological problems. These pieces are included in her first collection, *To Bedlam and Part Way Back* (1960). "You, Dr. Martin," for instance, portrays the desolate daily existence of a patient in a psychiatric ward. In "The Double Image," one of her most acclaimed works, Sexton describes the conflict between her desire to be a loving and devoted mother and daughter and her withdrawal into psychosis. "Elizabeth Gone" and "Some Foreign Letters" concern the death of her aunt Anna, a figure who reappears in numerous works by Sexton, including "The Nana-Hex" and the one-act play *Mercy Street* (1969). Other poems, while thematically and tonally impersonal, focus on the emotional states of fictional narrators. More than any of her later writings, the poems in *To Bedlam and Part Way Back* conform to traditional structural patterns. In her second collection, *All My Pretty Ones* (1962), Sexton began to experiment with a less formal, more intuitive and sponta-

neous approach to composition. In many of these poems, particularly the title piece, Sexton confronts her ambivalent feelings toward her parents and expresses her grief over their recent deaths. Sexton's penchant for vivid imagery is evident in "With Mercy for the Greedy," a vision of Christ's martyrdom in which he is eaten alive by rats, and "Letter Written on a Ferry While Crossing Long Island Sound," in which the narrator's yearning for a heavenly blessing is represented by a surrealistic vision of floating nuns.

Sexton received the Pulitzer Prize in poetry for her third collection, *Live or Die* (1966), which many critics consider her finest volume. While her earlier poems are mostly cathartic outpourings of emotion, Sexton's pieces in *Live or Die* evince a more controlled, analytical approach to the Confessional style as she contemplates possible causes for her psychological anguish. In "Those Times" and "Imitations of Drowning," for instance, she relates some of the traumatic incidents from her childhood. The major theme of this collection involves the choice that Sexton must make between life, with its attendant joys and miseries, and death, through suicide. The final poem in the collection, "Live," affirms her decision to continue living.

Most commentators regard *Love Poems* (1969) and *Transformations* (1971) as the last accomplished collections of Sexton's career. While the pieces in *Love Poems* chronicle an extra-marital love affair, *Transformations* develops a sardonic pastiche of the fairy tales of the Brothers Grimm. In the latter volume, Sexton abandons Confessionalism and adopts the persona of a middle-aged witch who perverts the legends of such archetypal heroines as Rapunzel and Cinderella. Her version of "Rapunzel," for instance, involves a love triangle between Rapunzel, the witch who holds her captive, and the prince who rescues her. In "Cinderella," Sexton cynically compares the well-known fairy tale to equally unlikely stories in which the desires of the downtrodden are miraculously gratified.

In *The Book of Folly* (1972), Sexton returned to the Confessional mode, reiterating themes of trauma, anguish, and alienation. Her occasional interest in religious symbolism resurfaces in "The Jesus Papers," a nine-poem sequence depicting the life of Christ through images of birth, death, and sacrifice. The predominant theme in her final collections, *The Death Notebooks* (1974) and *The Awful Rowing toward God* (1975), is the desire for salvation through a transcendent mystical experience. "The Death Baby," a sequence from *The Death Notebooks,* makes use of the image of the title figure to express a complex range of associations, including Sexton's hunger for spiritual fulfillment. The infant also represents her obsession with mortality, a force that impels her toward self-destruction but which paradoxically provides the chief inspiration for creative endeavors that give meaning to her life. In the poems that conclude *The Awful Rowing toward God,* Sexton envisions a journey by boat to confront her creator; the last poem in the sequence, "The Rowing Endeth," describes the end of her spiritual quest, as God challenges her to a poker game and draws the winning hand.

Several editions of Sexton's writings have been issued posthumously, some edited by her daughter, Linda Gray Sexton. *45 Mercy Street* (1976) contains "The Divorce Papers," written shortly before Sexton's death, in which she describes her divorce and the failed romances that followed. The title sequence in *Words for Dr. Y* (1978), a collection of poems and short stories, recounts in verse a series of sessions with her psychotherapist. *The Complete Poems* (1981) offers a comprehensive retrospective of Sexton's career as a poet.

(See also *CLC,* Vols. 2, 4, 6, 8, 10, 15; *Contemporary Authors,* Vols. 1-4, rev. ed., Vols. 53-56 [obituary]; *Contemporary Authors New Revision Series,* Vol. 3; *Contemporary Authors Bibliographical Series,* Vol. 2; *Something about the Author,* Vol. 10; *Dictionary of Literary Biography,* Vol. 5; and *Concise Dictionary of American Literary Biography, 1941-1968.*)

MAXINE KUMIN

It seems presumptuous, only seven years after her death, to talk about Anne Sexton's place in the history of poetry. We must first acknowledge the appearance in the twentieth century of women writing poetry that confronts the issues of gender, social role, and female life and lives viewed subjectively from the female perspective. The earlier world view of the poet as "the masculine chief of state in charge of dispensing universal spiritual truths" (Diane Middlebrook, *The World Into Words*) has eroded since World War II, as have earlier notions about the existence of universal truths themselves. Freed by that cataclysm from their clichéd roles as goddesses of hearth and

bedroom, women began to write openly out of their own experiences. Before there was a Women's Movement, the underground river was already flowing, carrying such diverse cargoes as the poems of Bogan, Levertov, Rukeyser, Swenson, Plath, Rich, and Sexton.

The stuff of Anne's life, mercilessly dissected, is here in the poems. Of all the confessional poets, none has had quite Sexton's "courage to make a clean breast of it." Nor has any displayed quite her brilliance, her verve, her headlong metaphoric leaps. As with any body of work, some of the later poems display only ragged, intermittent control, as compared to **"The Double Image," "The Operation,"** and **"Some Foreign Letters,"** to choose three arbitrary examples. The later work takes more chances, crosses more boundaries between the rational and the surreal; and time after time it evokes in the reader that sought-after shiver of recognition.

Women poets in particular owe a debt to Anne Sexton, who broke new ground, shattered taboos, and endured a barrage of attacks along the way because of the flamboyance of her subject matter, which, twenty years later, seems far less daring. She wrote openly about menstruation, abortion, masturbation, incest, adultery, and drug addiction at a time when the proprieties embraced none of these as proper topics for poetry. Today, the remonstrances seem almost quaint. Anne delineated the problematic position of women—the neurotic reality of the time—though she was not able to cope in her own life with the personal trouble it created. If it is true that she attracted the worshipful attention of a cult group pruriently interested in her suicidal impulses, her psychotic breakdowns, her frequent hospitalizations, it must equally be acknowledged that her very frankness succored many who clung to her poems as to the Holy Grail. Time will sort out the dross among these poems and burnish the gold. Anne Sexton has earned her place in the canon. (pp. xxxiii-xxxiv)

Maxine Kumin, "How It Was: Maxine Kumin on Anne Sexton," in The Complete Poems *by Anne Sexton, Houghton Mifflin Company, 1981, pp. xix-xxxiv.*

JOYCE CAROL OATES

Criticism of Anne Sexton during her lifetime for the inordinately "confessional" nature of her poetry has, perhaps, been misdirected. Lyric poetry, from Sappho to Sidney, Donne and Shakespeare, from Byron to Yeats and Lawrence and the "confessional" poets of our time, has obsessively analyzed the self and the self's dazzling adventures, usually in love. That the self-absorbed poet is always in danger of exhausting his material, and straining the capacity of his language to say familiar things in original ways, is evident; but the risk is one most poets are willing to take. "Why not say what happened?" Robert Lowell asks in "Day by Day."

The problematic nature of Anne Sexton's poetry has less to do with her admittedly self-entranced subject matter than with how judicious she was in translating emotion into art. If *The Complete Poems* proffers itself, like *Anne Sexton: A Self-Portrait in Letters* (1977), as a kind of memoir to be read chronologically, its impact is unnerving; for, contrary to all expectations, this collection begins with poems of eerily compelling authority, in the superb *To Bedlam and Part Way Back* (1960) and *All My Pretty Ones* (1962), and then gradually disintegrates, through *Live or Die* (1966), *The Book of Folly* (1972), *The Awful Rowing Toward God* (1975) and the painful posthumous work consisting of *45 Mercy Street* (1976), *Words for Dr. Y.* (1978) and *Last Poems.*

It should be recalled that Anne Sexton died, by suicide, in 1974. But as early as the mid-60's, her poetry had begun to lose its scrupulous dramatic control and to be weakened by a poetic voice that, rarely varying from poem to poem, spoke ceaselessly of emotions and moods and ephemeral states of mind. Now the poet is euphoric; now she is depressed; now she toys with the idea of suicide; now she is passionately in love and fulfilled; now she is rejected; now bitter, now resigned, now ready to die; and then again, euphoric, having found God. The emotions are flicked before us like playing cards, and we are invited to think that the instruction of her poetry lies in its examination, as if unconsciously, of the tragic limitations of this kind of life-in-poetry: a curious failure not of *feeling* but of *imagination.*

What powerful poems, however, are in these early books. Witness the splendid heartrending control of the very first poem, **"You, Doctor Martin"** (1960), in which a psychiatrist at a mental hospital is evoked walking "from breakfast to madness," while his patients are "large children," their wild emotions now tamed to the harmless making of crafts. . . .

And there is **"Ringing the Bells"** (1960), miming madness with a poignant equanimity. . . .

"Wanting to Die" (1966), which is, quite simply, about wanting to die, presents the suicide's case in language as austere as Sylvia Plath's, and is remarkable for its dispassionate examination of the helpless "betrayal" of the body. Wanting to die is "the almost unnameable lust," though the poet has nothing against life. . . .

It is disconcerting to move from such masterly poems to this, from **"The Ambition Bird"** (1972):

> So it has come to this—
> insomnia at 3:15 A.M.,
> the clock tolling its engine
> like a frog following
> a sundial yet having an electric
> seizure at the quarter hour.
>
> (p. 3)

The posthumously published poems are almost without exception haphazard and sketchy, swinging from self-pity to a mordant bravado ("Don't look now, God, we're all right. / All the suicides are eating Black Bean Soup; / the Dalmatian, our turnip, our spotted parasite / snoozles in her chair.") that defies comprehension on any level, save the flamboyantly "surreal." Particularly poignant throughout the volume as a whole are the poems addressed to the poet's deceased father and mother— though, as with all such "confessional" (or accusatory) work, the reader cannot really know how valid they are, or how mytho-poetic. Did her mother actually accuse Anne Sexton of giving her cancer? Was the poet truly "the unwanted, the mistake / that Mother used to keep Father / from his divorce?" From time to time, lovers appear, with the force of minor deities; but they disappear all too soon, and the poet is left alone once again, hurt, baffled and resentful. Jesus is evoked, in a somewhat unorthodox manner ("Jesus saw the multitudes were hungry / and He said, Oh Lord / send down a short-order cook. / And the Lord said, Abracadabra.") Constant throughout the decades of poems are images of wounds, broken bones, blood, masks, death ("And death looks on with a casual eye / and scratches his anus"). If there are innumerable disappointments here so far as well-honed complete poems are concerned,

there are also innumerable lines and images that fairly leap from the page, with their unmistakable Sexton ring. . . . (pp. 3, 37)

Though the volume under review is perhaps not so dismaying a publishing venture as the *Self-Portrait in Letters,* which surely does a disservice to its subject (so hasty and careless are many of the letters, so undistinguished in language, ideas, sentiment), one is left nonetheless with the conviction that, Sexton, of all contemporary poets, would have been far better served by a judicious *Selected Poems,* which might have rescued poems of surpassing beauty and power from qualification—or outright contamination—by less distinguished poems. Alas, how risky it is, these days, to die! ("I want to be an important poet more than I want to be a popular one," Anne Sexton said in a letter written in 1973. "Only God knows if the two go together." God may know; but we can guess.)

A word must be said about the gracious and informative foreword by Maxine Kumin [see excerpt above], which touches upon the wildly varying critical responses to Sexton's work, while offering no dogmatic assertions of its own. . . . Mrs. Kumin notes that there were readers "who clung to Sexton's work as to the Holy Grail," and others, primarily male, to whom it was an abomination; but the focus of her wise, sympathetic essay is on the poetry, and on Sexton's intermittent obsession with her craft. (p. 37)

> *Joyce Carol Oates, "The Rise and Fall of a Poet,"*
> in The New York Times Book Review, *October 18,*
> *1981, pp. 3, 37.*

HELEN VENDLER

The unevenness in Anne Sexton's writing makes her work hard to judge, but the publication of the *Complete Poems* demands some attempt at judgment. Many of these poems are by now famous or infamous, but a clear sense of Sexton's talent—its extent and its limitations—has yet to appear. The Sexton legend not only haunts the poems, but is unhappily perpetuated in the ladies-magazine tone of the introduction to this volume by Sexton's generous friend, Maxine Kumin [see excerpt above]. (p. 33)

Sexton, as the earlier poems show, was eager to master all the prosodic and stanzaic variations she could find useful; Sexton's lack of success does not usually (until the latter part of her life) result from lack of labor. Sexton worked hard for her teachers—among whom I include her therapists as well as her mentors (John Holmes, Robert Lowell) and her fellow poets (Plath, Starbuck, Kumin). She worked hard too for her students, who were grateful to her for her intense advice about their writing.

What, then, did Sexton have; and what did she lack? The second question should perhaps be raised before the first.

She did not have an education. Emily Dickinson had no more formal schooling than Sexton but she did have her father's library, and a precocious appetite for poetry. Kumin takes a peculiarly American point of view when she remarks, "Untrammeled by a traditional education in Donne, Milton, Yeats, Eliot, and Pound, Anne was able to strike out alone, like Conrad's secret sharer, for a new destiny." Of course the poets of the past never thought of a traditional education as a set of fetters. Their notion, on the whole, was that in reading your great predecessors you were learning the language of poetry. So Milton read for seven years at Horton after leaving Cambridge; so Hopkins did classics at Balliol; so Keats translated Virgil in high school and read his way, underlining, through Spenser and Shakespeare and *Paradise Lost* and Chapman's *Homer*. It is anyhow an odd view of a "traditional education" that would sum it up as "Donne, Milton, Yeats, Eliot and Pound." In any case, Sexton is said to have read "omnivorously and quite innocently whatever came to hand and enticed her." According to Kumin's list, rather little that enticed her was poetry. Kumin lists "popular psychiatric texts" (Reik, Rieff, Deutsch, Erikson, Bettelheim), and says that after Sexton took a course in Dostoevsky, Kafka, and Mann, she went on to read novels by Saul Bellow, Philip Roth, and Kurt Vonnegut—a sequence that tells something about Sexton's taste, since someone else might have gone on to Tolstoy, Flaubert, and James. Kumin concludes the remarks on Sexton's reading by saying, "But above all else, she was attracted to the fairy tales of Andersen and Grimm . . . ; they were for her, perhaps, what Bible stories and Greek myths had been for other writers." Kumin does not raise the question whether Grimm and Andersen can possibly rival as imaginative sources the Bible and Greek mythology—but the question is important in thinking about Sexton.

It was not the ethical parables of the Bible, or the fertile suggestiveness of Greek myth, but the grim tit-for-tat of fairy tales—where the unsuccessful suitors are murdered, or the witch is burned in her own oven, or the wicked wolf is himself sliced open—that appealed to Sexton's childlike and vengeful mind. The fairy tales and folktales put forth a child's black-and-white ethics, with none of the complexity of the Gospels, and none of the worldliness of the Greeks. It is characteristic of Sexton that she did use the myth of Prometheus—which reads like one of her folktales, with its rebel hero, its avenging father-god, and its grotesque evisceration by a vulture.

Sexton looked, usually in vain, for ways to stabilize her poems outside her increasingly precarious self. She based one sequence on horoscope readings, another on the remarks of her therapist "Doctor Y," another on the life of Jesus, another on the Psalms, another on beasts. The only group that succeeds more often than it fails is the group based on folktales, *Transformations*. The tales—Snow White, Rapunzel, Cinderella, Red Riding Hood, the Frog Prince, Briar Rose, Hansel and Gretel, and others—gave Sexton a structure of the sort she was usually unable to invent for herself, a beginning, a middle, and an end. Her poems tend, on the whole, to begin well, to repeat themselves, to sag in the middle, and to tail off. She had an instinct for reiteration; she wanted to say something five times instead of once. Her favorite figure of speech is anaphora, where many lines begin with the same phrase, a figure which causes, more often than not, diffuseness and spreading of effect rather than concentration of intensity:

> . . . I will conquer myself.
> I will dig up the pride.
> I will take scissors
> and cut out the beggar.
> I will take a crowbar
> and pry out the broken
> pieces.

This is a form of poetic backstitching or, to change metaphors, a way of letting the poem get stuck in one groove. The folktales, by the necessary forward motion of plot, gave Sexton a momentum and shape that, on her own, she seemed to have no instinct for.

The tales, as I have said, matched her infantile fantasy; they gave her a clean trajectory; they turned her away from the morass of narcissism. But most of all, they enabled her as a satirist. Kumin speaks disapprovingly in the introduction of a draft of a poem which she disliked. It had, Kumin says, "what seemed to me a malevolently flippant tone." And Kumin urged that it be rewritten; and it was. But Sexton's aesthetically most realized tone is precisely a malevolently flippant one, however distasteful it might seem to others. Sexton herself preferred the maudlin or lachrymose or (on other occasions) the winsome or the babyish. But in the Grimm transformations all her sharp-eyed satire was unleashed. **"Snow White,"** for instance, indicts the bourgeois cult of hypocritical virginity. . . . **"Rumpelstiltskin"** looks sardonically at the myth of maternal doting. . . . **"One-Eye, Two-Eyes, Three-Eyes"** casts a cold eye on the social role of the deformed. . . .

> When a child stays needy until he is fifty—
> oh mother-eye, oh mother-eye, crush me in—
> the parent is as strong as a telephone pole.

This painfully graphic sketch is written by a person who is not "nice." What is occurring in such writing is not so much the shattering of taboos as the expression of an extremity of non-participatory vision. If Keats took part in the existence of the sparrow at his window with what we might call an objective sympathy, he could not have refrained from extending that same sympathy to the repressed virgin or the nursing mother or the hunchback. But a satirist feels under no obligation to extend sympathy. Sexton feels a slashing glee in her perfect vignettes. . . . Sexton threw off phrases with reckless bounty. The death cricket and the ballistic missile in this passage are shafts that fly straight and true; and the night nurse enters literature. In these fiendish cartoons, Sexton is most unlike Lowell. Too often, in her poems about family members and asylum experiences and exacerbated states, she sounds entirely too much like an echo of Lowell, and a bad one. . . . There is far too much of this sort of thing in the *Complete Poems*, especially in the dreadfully imitative sequence **"The Death of the Fathers."**

Sexton's poems read better as a diary than as poems. They then seem a rather slap-dash journal stuck with brilliant phrases. Even the most formally arranged poems have, underneath their formal structure, no real or actual structure: they run on, they chatter, they moan, they repeat themselves, they deliquesce. Or, conversely (as in the famous **"Her Kind"**), they stop without any particular reason—they could have been shorter, they could have been longer. If, as A. R. Ammons once said, a poem begins in contingency and ends in necessity, the trouble with Sexton's poems is that they lack that necessity—the conviction that they were meant to be just as they are, with just these words and no others, extending to just this length and no other, with each part pulling its weight. Dickinson and Bishop often make us feel that necessity; Edna St. Vincent Millay—like Sexton a facile and prolific writer—does not.

Necessity appeals to some readers more than others, needless to say, and most of Sexton's readers have read her as a gripping journalist of the strained and difficult in life. One knows her very well by the end of this book. In that sense, she succeeded as a diarist, if not as a poet. Through this diary we come to know this third daughter whose two elder sisters laughed at her; she is the daughter of a rich alcoholic father who behaved toward her with sexual possessiveness, and of an unloving mother obsessed with enemas and cleanliness. The daughter defended herself by taking on a wooden lack of feeling, from which she was partially released by therapy after a postpartum depression. But she then thought of herself as composed solely of excrement. If she saw herself as an animal, it was as a rat.

These feelings were never to disappear. Giving up her children while she was in the asylum exacerbated her guilt. She confused poetry writing with therapy, expression with restructuring. The restructuring never seemed to take hold, though the writing, like the analysis, became obsessive. She saw that she was a perpetual, avid child, "a baby all wrapped up in its red howl," demanding that her family and friends mother her. "I need food / and you walk away reading the paper," became her reproach. She recognized, and was cruelly frank about, her compulsions; but she was unable to change her insatiable nature, her "greed for love." She defined herself as "a woman of excess, of zeal and greed," and nobody could have said worse things of her than she said of herself:

> Do I not look in the mirror,
> these days,
> and see a drunken rat avert her eyes?

Eventually, she was able to work less well at revision. The fantasies spun out of control; the dreams and hallucinations began to float around in disorder, and the masochistic poems about Jesus assumed disagreeable proportions:

> Jesus slept as still as a toy
> and in His dream
> he desired Mary.
> His penis sang like a dog . . .
> with His penis like a chisel
> He carved the Pietà.

In the poems, Sexton seems only fraily connected to anything outside herself. Her children, husband, and friends have a shadowy existence here, along with various unspecified lovers, who seem temporarily valuable as means to make Sexton feel loved. There are occasional mentions of war. But the relentless centrality of the "I"—almost always indoors alone, contemplating its own anguish (even if sometimes in farcical terms)—is finally exasperating. It drives us to comparison with other "I" poets of extreme psychic states—Dickinson and Berryman come to mind. Berryman, besides his humor, possessed a perfect, even icy, recognition that Henry, his libidinal self, was just that—one restricted portion of his entire self. Berryman's intellectual self took on the derelict Henry as a case study. Berryman's moral self looked on in disapproval, and offered, in blackface, quiet judgments and calm sympathy for Henry's distracted sins. Sexton's own intellectual mercilessness saves many poems. But she had no moral sympathy for herself; and she, more often than Berryman, lost herself in tragic attitudinizing and melodrama. Dickinson had the great gift of observation—not of the freaks of the world, making common cause with them, like Sexton (the witches, the old, the sick, the winos, the crippled)—but rather of the cosmos, a universe strict, impersonal, beautiful, dangerous, and indifferent. Dickinson felt acutely the scale of the whole creation, the nature of its imperial design. When she saw human beings, she saw them in that frame. . . . (pp. 34-6)

Dickinson's "I," though as insistently present as Sexton's, is always placed in a context—religious, philosophical, cosmic, or social—larger than itself. When Dickinson goes mad, she does not take her madness as normative; she says, "And then a plank in Reason broke." There is a normative sanity present to measure the vertigo of psychic instability. Sexton's fantasies are often self-indulgent; only rarely can she include a plumb line by which to estimate her own slant out of equilibrium. In Sexton's poems we miss the complexity contributed by the

double vision of fever taking its own pulse, being at once physician and patient. This was a double vision especially rigorously practiced by Sylvia Plath at the end of her life. But Plath, unlike Sexton, had a violent need for structure and containment; chaotic inner states, however exciting, did not in her view suffice to make a poem.

As Sexton passes into the anthologies, the more obviously "feminist" poems will no doubt be chosen, and there is no reason not to represent them. . . . But the evil eye (as Sexton put it) should be in the anthologies too. This "evil," unsympathetic, flat, malicious, gleeful, noticing eye is neither male nor female, but it is Sexton's most distinguishing characteristic:

> The big fat war was going on.
> So profitable for daddy.
> She drove a pea green Ford.
> He drove a pearl gray Caddy.
>
> In the end they used it up.
> All that pale green dough.
> The rest I spent on doctors
> Who took it like gigolos.

This is of course superlatively unfair to the doctors and to Sexton herself. But that was Sexton's chief flair—a knack for the flat, two-dimensional cartoon. Some of that shrewd caricature should make its way into the anthologies too. (p. 36)

Helen Vendler, "Malevolent Flippancy," in The New Republic, *Vol. 185, No. 19, November 11, 1981, pp. 33-6.*

KATHA POLLITT

Like Sylvia Plath, with whom she is often paired, Anne Sexton arouses strong feelings of popular adulation and critical unease. How could it have been otherwise? At a time when American poetry was nearly as male-dominated as football, she wrote frankly, extravagantly and without apology about the experience of women. Scarcely less important, she was a democrat practicing the most snobbish of arts. While most of her colleagues were scholars and critics and translators with university affiliations, she was a junior-college dropout and suburban matron who began writing poetry after watching a television program called *How to Write a Sonnet*. With her recurrent bouts of madness, her suicide attempts (she finally succeeded in 1974), her flamboyant sexuality and her vibrant physical presence on the poetry-reading circuit, she fit as no poet since Dylan Thomas the popular stereotype of the self-destructive genius—beautiful, damned and oh-so-sensitive. It was a role she exploited to the hilt. (p. 533)

Time has muted the appeal of this image. Suicide and madness are less voguish these days, for one thing—perhaps the public self-destruction of so many postwar poets, male and female, has been a cautionary lesson. Then, too, the progress of feminism has made the suicide of gifted women seem less a romantic triumph of the will than a sorry failure of the same. (The women's movement came too late for Sexton, who admired its goals but could not internalize its values, a combination of attitudes succinctly expressed in the nickname she gave herself: Ms. Dog.) The 16-year-old girl who slept with Sexton's poems under her pillow in 1972 is probably in law school today.

Finally, thanks largely to Sexton's own influence, it is no longer shocking for a woman to write poems about menstruation or her uterus or abortion—or, for that matter, about erotic joy, of which Sexton also had her share. No doubt many critics still wince in private at women poets who claim for themselves the sexual frankness long ago claimed by their brothers, but they are much less likely to wince in print, and when they do they look squeamish rather than authoritative. When Patti Smith can be compared to Rimbaud in *The New York Times Book Review,* anything goes.

As if to ratify that cultural shift, here is this eminently respectable-looking tome [*The Complete Poems*]. . . . If you are a fan or a library, you will doubtless want to rush out and get your copy. If you are a lover of poetry or a book reviewer, you may try to read your way straight through. I caution against this, though. There are beauties here—Sexton wrote as many tight, precise, brilliantly associative and emotionally subtle poems as any number of poets with more secure reputations. But she also wrote dozens and dozens and *dozens* of poems that are histrionic, verbose, flaccid, mechanical, sentimental, mannered and very, very boring. While this melancholy ratio is not surprising, or even, perhaps, very interesting—it's *hard* to write a good poem—the sheer quantity of inferior work does tend to dull one's response to the gems. One puts down this enormous book with the nagging feeling that all along a slim volume of verse was trapped inside it.

And yet, the gems are there. Sexton's poems are her hospitalizations, for instance, are sadder, humbler, less literary than Lowell's—closer, one feels, to the inmate's sense of infantilization in the face of psychiatric authority and the madness itself. (pp. 533-34)

The sheer range of Sexton's voice is impressive. There is the restrained, formal grief of **"The Double Image,"** with its delicate probings of mother-daughter connections; the dazzling purity of **"The Starry Night"**; the sardonic, precise diction of **"Wanting to Die"**. . . .

She could be witty, too, as in **"Housewife"**:

> Some women marry houses.
> It's another kind of skin; it has a heart,
> a mouth, a liver and bowel movements.
> The walls are permanent and pink.
>
> (p. 534)

All the poems I've mentioned come from her first three books, *To Bedlam and Partway Back* (1960), *All My Pretty Ones* (1962) and *Live or Die* (1966), for which she won a Pulitzer Prize. Most of Sexton's memorable work is to be found in these early books: **"The Moss of His Skin," "In the Deep Museum," "The Black Art," "Her Kind," "And One for My Dame," "The Wedding Night," "Little Girl, My String Bean, My Lovely Woman."** The list goes on and on. And most of this good work pays homage, however faintly, to some sort of traditional form.

Like most poets of her era, Sexton began as an apprentice to poetic tradition. She was a daring rhymester (**"The Double Image"** gives us Gloucester / lost her and cancer / answer) and, on occasion, a brilliantly colloquial reworker of classical forms and themes—see her biting sonnet on the Icarus myth, **"To a Friend Whose Work Has Come to Triumph."** Sexton moved away from form as she matured, as most poets do, but without having worked out ways of achieving in free verse what form makes so easy: the use of structure and sound to delimit a drama, intensify emotion and clarify meaning. With some notable exceptions—**"Housewife"** or **"In Celebration of My Uterus,"** with its high-spirited echoes of "I Hear America Singing"—Sexton's free verse, early and late, is lax and ram-

bling and self-indulgent. She starts a poem pages before announcing its subject, or she starts on one theme and wanders off into another. She uses language carelessly, relying on repetition, that bluntest of instruments, instead of on aural patterns—assonance, off-rhyme, half-rhyme, rhythms and pauses. Rather than use images that relate so as to deepen them all, she uses arbitrary, throwaway similes reminiscent of Roethke at his most annoying ("I . . . brought forth young girls / to grunt like fish"; "My long brown legs, / sweet dears as good as spoons"). (p. 535)

In the late work, Sexton lavishes the same level of imprecise feverishness on anything and everything, from God to her therapist, from the signs of the zodiac to the Vietnam War dead. And one realizes with growing horror that these vastly disparate occasions really *are* all one for her, for they are all merely the flickering projections of a grotesque and seamless solipsism. In Sexton's case, at least, Sartre was wrong and Milton was right. Hell was not other people. It was herself.

Well, perhaps it is too much to ask that her work be larger-spirited and more stringent than it is. Poetry for Sexton was always a matter of half-art, half-therapy. "I hook into my mood and drain it onto the paper," she wrote of her prodigious output of letters, and she might have said the same thing about many of her poems. If one can see her as an artist who squandered her talent by refusing to discipline it—out of vanity or hunger for easy celebrity or sheer self-absorption—one can also see her as an anguished, mentally ill woman who managed out of her inner chaos to make a few poems that work as literature and as safety valves, a few momentary stays against confusion, not just for herself but for the reader as well.

Both of these assessments are right. Critics often find themselves quoting F. Scott Fitzgerald's famous remark that there are no second acts in American lives, and Sexton is squarely in the tradition of writers whose careers are a long downhill slide from early achievement. But Jarrell provides a kinder epitaph. "A good poet," he said, "is someone who manages, in a lifetime of standing out in thunderstorms, to be struck by lightning five or six times; a dozen or two dozen times and he is great." Never mind the numbers, or whether they were evenly spaced out over the course of her life. Anne Sexton did her standing out in thunderstorms. Her rain-soaked poems will vanish. The lightning-struck ones will remain. (p. 537)

> *Katha Pollitt, " 'The Awful Rowing',"* in The Nation, *New York, Vol. 233, No. 17, November 21, 1981, pp. 533-37.*

GREG JOHNSON

At the heart of Anne Sexton's poetry is a search for identity, and her well-known infatuation with death—the cause of her rather notorious fame, and the apparent reason her work is often dismissed as beneath serious consideration—has little to do with this search; in her best work, in fact, it is most often an annoying irrelevancy, however potent it seems in its occasional command of the poet's psyche. Quite simply, Sexton's poetry is a poetry of life, and if her work is "confessional" at times, or even most of the time, this does not mean that the poet's confessions (the word itself is misleading) necessarily describe experiences ridden with guilt or pain. This is where Sexton's poetry diverges so dramatically from that of Sylvia Plath, of whom she is frequently seen as a kind of epigonic follower. Plath mythologizes death with great power and succinctness, and places herself at the center of a myth whose message is "blackness—blackness and silence"; her vision is brutally nihilistic, and she embraces it willingly. Plath's struggle is that of the mythmaker—primarily artistic rather than personal, since the personal self is mercilessly pared away in her poetry (as are all other selves) in deference to the controlling myth. Anne Sexton, on the other hand, speaks longingly and lovingly of a world of health, of childlike wholeness—a world toward which she struggles valiantly and against insuperable odds. To understand her poetry as a record of this struggle, and as a testament to its value and importance, is to appreciate its special relevance to the contemporary world, a world of increasing disjunction between personal and social selves and one whose chaotic, literally "maddening" effect on the individual mind Anne Sexton manages to convey with that blend of craft and vulnerability that is her special magic.

Unlike Plath, and certainly unlike Robert Lowell—with whom her name is also frequently and pointlessly linked—Sexton is a Primitive, an extraordinarily intense artist who confronts her experience with unsettling directness, largely innocent of "tradition" and privately developing an idiom exactly suited to that experience. As Louis Simpson remarked after the publication of her first book, "This then is a phenomenon . . . to remind us, when we have forgotten in the weariness of literature, that poetry can happen." The reader's sense of the direct and seemingly spontaneous quality of Sexton's earliest volumes—*To Bedlam and Partway Back* (1960), *All My Pretty Ones* (1962) and *Live or Die* (1966)—can partially be explained by noting that she first began writing poetry, at the age of twenty-eight, as a form of personal therapy, a way of formalizing past traumas and of coping with an increasing sense of disorientation in her conventional role of suburban wife and mother. Her emotional instability, including her suicidal impulses, contributed to the immediacy, rawness and power of much of the poetry. This kind of therapy no doubt helped the poet in her personal life, but what is heroic in Sexton's case, and particularly relevant to her readers, is the earnestness and scrupulosity with which she mastered her craft, developed her highly original voice, and set about the task of communicating her experience to others. That Anne Sexton herself later succumbed to the "weariness of literature"—her later work, on the whole, is distinctly inferior to her early poetry, and verges at times on self-parody—and finally to her own destructive impulses, does not diminish the value and irresistible power of her finest achievements, which speak to us in a voice by turns inspired and beleaguered, joyful and aggrieved, lost in the confusions of self but found, ultimately, in her masterful articulation of her experience as a whole, a complex experience which serves as a painfully truthful mirror of the age.

Sexton's first two volumes have much in common, both in their multi-faceted handling of the identity theme and in their adherence to rather strict poetic forms. In both there is a constructive relationship between the deeply painful, inchoate materials—experiences in a mental institution, the loss of the poet's parents, and unceasing struggle to define her own selfhood—and the restraining, masterful form of the poems themselves. There is little sense that the poet is arbitrarily forcing her experiences into rigid, inappropriate shapes, primarily because she convinces us that she has pierced to the core of those experiences to discover shapes inherent in them; the formal, measured quality of the verse not only indicates the poet's necessary caution in dealing with her turbulent materials, but also establishes a crucial distance from which she may safely view her continuing struggle and present it to her readers in palatable form. Yet the controlled, meditative voice of these

early poems is frequently mingled with an openly vulnerable, "confessional" voice, one which conveys genuine, childlike experiences of pain and terror. The poems are neither songs of innocence nor experience, but continually oscillate between conflicting states of mind, admitting continued disorientation while simultaneously creating an impressive poetic order.

An important difference between the first two books should be recognized, however. *To Bedlam and Partway Back* comprises an ordering of a specific, urgent experience—the descent into madness and a partial return—while *All My Pretty Ones* broadens from this painful but rich experience to consider more general themes of loss (especially the loss of parents) and upon an explicit need to define the poet's self in terms of the world. Although Sexton's books describe an ongoing personal development and flow naturally one into the other, each of the early volumes has a distinct identity and merits separate discussion. As Geoffrey Hartman has noted, *To Bedlam and Partway Back* is not merely a collection of poems but "truly a *book*," and there is ample evidence that Sexton organized the volume with meticulous care. The shorter lyrics in Part One deal with a cluster of obsessive themes, all related to the poet's search for identity, while the pair of long, meditative poems in Part Two achieve a tentative but emotionally satisfying resolution. (pp. 2-3)

By far the majority of poems in *To Bedlam and Partway Back* explore the poet's identity in terms of other women. There are poems about being buried alive (**"The Moss of His Skin"**), paralysis within a marriage and its "pantomime of love" (**"The Farmer's Wife"**), the literal paralysis of the goddess Diana, changed forever to a laurel tree and noting in despair that "blood moves still in my bark bound veins" (**"Where I Live in This Honorable House of the Laurel Tree"**). In one of the most moving of these poems, **"Unknown Girl in the Maternity Ward,"** Sexton dramatizes the relationship between a mother and her daughter with a typical mingling of tenderness and a hopeless sense of estrangement. The mother can only consider her child a "fragile visitor," her "funny kin," and the reason is the mother's lack of her own selfhood, since she is, after all, "unknown". (p. 4)

In seeking to define her own identity through poetic fictions about other women, and about relationships between women, Sexton merely sees her own identity as inferior and finds that genuine relationship is unavailable. Later volumes will explore the causes behind her failure to "connect" meaningfully with others, but in *To Bedlam and Partway Back,* her failure leads directly into madness. Although she pictured herself, wryly, as "a secret beatnik hiding in the suburbs in a square house on a dull street," any pride she might have taken in her role as poet seems cancelled by this image of herself as a misfit, someone who did not live in that "good world" she envied her great aunt and could not create for herself. One senses that Anne Sexton felt herself forced into poetry, that her inability to find satisfaction in a conventional role made the pose of a "secret beatnik," a rebel—in the sense that both poetry and madness are forms of rebellion—her only means of survival. Unlike Emily Dickinson, who felt that "Much Madness is divinest Sense" and whose extreme self-sufficiency (however "mad" it might have appeared to her Amherst contemporaries) was the sign of a fully realized identity, Sexton desperately needed the approval of others: "I want everyone to hold up large signs saying YOU'RE A GOOD GIRL." Her belief that she had failed to be "good," and that she had no way of finding a "good world," led to a madness that was not divinest sense but hellish chaos, a threatened disintegration of selfhood.

This linking of madness with evil, with the inability to be "good," recurs in Sexton's poems dealing with her experiences in mental institutions. She continues to lament her sense of loss and disorientation: "They lock me in this chair at eight a.m. / and there are no signs to tell the way" (**"Music Swims Back to Me"**). In the first stanza of this poem she pictures herself as an orphan seeking the way home. . . . These lines, like Ophelia's mad speeches, blend irreality and the absence of sequential thought with a terrifying, sane intuition; immersed in a surreal, abandoned world, the speaker nonetheless understands her need to escape, to find "sign posts" back toward health.

Does Sexton imagine any way out of this impasse, any way to escape the debilitating terrors of a consciousness plagued by a conviction of its own evil? One possibility is to replace self-loathing with an open acceptance of evil—even admitting the likelihood that she is "not a woman." What is remarkable, however, is not this admission itself but the lively, almost gleeful tone in which it is uttered:

> I have gone out, a possessed witch,
> haunting the black air, braver at night;
> dreaming of evil, I have done my hitch
> over the plain houses, light by light:
> lonely thing, twelve-fingered, out of mind.
> A woman like that is not a woman, quite.
> I have been her kind.

("Her Kind")

"A woman like that is misunderstood," Sexton adds wryly, but the poem is a serious attempt to understand such a woman—her sense of estrangement, her impulse toward death—by internalizing evil and giving it a voice: a chortling, self-satisfied, altogether amiable voice which suggests that "evil" is perhaps the wrong word after all. Sexton's witch, waving her "nude arms at villages going by," becomes something of value to the community, performing the function Kurt Vonnegut has called the "domestication of terror." Unlike Plath's madwoman in "Lady Lazarus"—a woman at the service of a private, unyielding anger, a red-haired demon whose revenge is to "eat men like air"—Sexton's witch is essentially harmless. Although she remains vulnerable—"A woman like that is not afraid to die"—she rejects anger in favor of humor, flamboyance, self-mockery. She is a kind of perverse entertainer, and if she seems cast in the role of a martyr, embracing madness in order to domesticate it for the rest of the community—making it seem less threatening, perhaps even enjoyable—it is nevertheless a martyrdom which this aspect of Sexton accepts with a peculiar zest.

Poems like **"Her Kind"** and **"Music Swims Back to Me"** help create the famous, fatally glamorous mask of Anne Sexton—part lovable witch, part helpless madwoman—for which she became famous, and which is often discussed as if it were the only self present in Sexton's poetry. Denise Levertov, in her well-intentioned, somewhat patronizing remarks on Sexton's suicide, suggested that Sexton was "too intensely troubled to be fully aware of her influence or to take on its responsibility. Therefore it seems to me that we who are alive must make clear, as she could not, the distinction between creativity and self-destruction." But Sexton did take on a personal responsibility for the interest her work aroused—she sent cheerful, supportive letters, for instance, to the countless victims of mental illness who wrote to her—and much of her poetry, from the first volume onward, expresses anguish over her destructive impulses, with an awareness that they are threatening to her poetry as well as to her personal well-being.

Part Two of *To Bedlam and Partway Back* contains only three poems, but they are long, reflective works which attempt to take stock of the poet's progress, to state a rationale for her kind of poetry, and especially to acknowledge lifelong conflicts that have prevented a healthy development of self. These goals are directly addressed in the volume's longest and finest poem, **"The Double Image."** Here the poet gathers all her themes into a single autobiographical narration, seeking that "certain sense of order" through a careful, measured recounting of her seemingly chaotic and random experiences. Like many of Sexton's more somber, reflective poems, **"The Double Image"** is addressed to her daughter, establishing the crucial dynamic between the poet's desire for an affectionate, healthy relationship with the child, and her yearning toward the madness that threatens to separate them. The poem's tender, carefully modulated voice is firmly aligned on the side of health, but the poet remains aware of her continued vulnerability. She sees her madness as an unknown, demonic force, an "ugly angel" whose voice enchants the poet—much like the "disquieting muses" in Plath's analogous narrative. After giving way to madness and losing her child, Sexton has returned as a "partly mended thing," still unable to assume a healthy identity. . . . The poem's title refers to Sexton's mother and daughter, seen as potent forces pulling her simultaneously in two directions. Sexton's mother (certainly a cold, uncaring figure in this poem) represents "the stony head of death," while the final lines speak of the daughter's inestimable value for the poet's present self, not only as a symbol of the life-force but as a hopeful foreshadowing of her own developing selfhood. . . . (pp. 4-6)

In Sexton's second volume, *All My Pretty Ones* (1962), she broadens her scope from consideration of the specific, urgent experience of madness to consider more universally comprehensible forms of loss. Sexton's parents died in 1959, and though she insisted at the time that she would not write poems about them, she later changed her mind. The first part of this volume contains **"The Truth the Dead Know," "All My Pretty Ones"** and **"Lament,"** poems dealing with her parents' deaths and among the finest she ever wrote. Not surprisingly, the ostensible theme of bereavement is mingled with an examination of the poet's continuing struggle toward identity. In that strange, bitter elegy, **"The Truth the Dead Know,"** Sexton seems to eschew the common rituals of mourning: "Gone, I say and walk from church, / refusing the stiff procession to the grave"; she prefers, instead, to "cultivate myself" and to avoid such a powerful intimation of mortality as the death of both parents within a few months. The poem ends, however, by emphasizing not her own refusals but those of the dead, and into her voice creeps something like envy. . . . (p. 7)

A far gentler, more nostalgic poem like **"Young"** recalls the poet's innocence as a "lonely kid" whose relationship to her mother was not yet perceived as a "funnel"; and in **"Old Dwarf Heart"** she creates a separate, mythical self—again resembling Plath's disquieting muses—who insists upon "the decay we're made of": "When I lie down to love, old dwarf heart shakes her head." Sexton can never escape this destructive self ("Where I go, she goes"), which is perceived as having originated in a vicious Oedipal "tangle," but the loss of her parents does give her a kind of grim new beginning, and the rest of the volume explores various avenues of escape.

In her attempt to counter the truth the dead know with a gentler, more humanizing truth, Sexton seeks out two major sources of comfort: religious belief and domestic love. Her early cluster of religious poems, forming Part Two of *All My Pretty Ones*, initiates a theme that will recur throughout her work—especially in her posthumous volume, *The Awful Rowing Toward God* (1975)—but she seemed to find little solace in her religious ponderings; at times, in fact, they only increase her sense of guilt. In **"With Mercy for the Greedy,"** addressed to a Catholic friend who tried to convert the poet, Sexton says with childlike sincerity: "I detest my sins and I try to believe / in the Cross. I touch its tender hips, its dark jawed face, / its solid neck, its brown sleep." Unlike Emily Dickinson, who saw herself locked in a battle of wills with God the Father, a Puritan Nobodaddy who threatened her own sense of self, Sexton was drawn toward the image of a gentle, redemptive Christ, a God who was palpably human. But she concludes, ruefully, "Need is not quite belief," and explains, with typical Sexton wryness, "I was born doing reference work in sin . . ." In Part Three, which consists of a single poem, **"The Fortress,"** Sexton insists that the love between herself and her daughter has greater redemptive power than any religious belief. The poet has a sense of her own value, however fleeting, in her protectiveness toward her daughter: "What ark / can I fill for you when the world goes wild?" Although she knows that "Life is not in my hands" and cannot promise that her daughter will find happiness, the poem emphasizes their tender domestic alliance, the "fortress" their togetherness forms against the "bombs" of experience.

In one of the volume's most impressive poems, **"Letter Written on a Ferry While Crossing Long Island Sound,"** Sexton makes an ordinary boat ride into the occasion of an optimistic, even transcendent spiritual vision. (p. 8)

With two accomplished volumes behind her, with a blossoming career and innumerable devoted readers, she summoned the courage to bluntly question the value of living—to decide whether, in fact, the pain of life does not outweigh its rewards. In **"The Black Art"** she insisted: "A woman who writes feels too much, / those trances and portents!" Her decision to explore fully those excessive feelings, to relate her mysterious "trances and portents" to her central concerns of identity, poetry and survival, helped her toward *Live or Die* (1966), winner of a Pulitzer Prize and the finest achievement of her career. The volume's title represents an ultimatum; the poems themselves, arranged in chronological order and reading, as Sexton herself noted, like a "fever chart," show the poet moving toward a stark confrontation with her suicidal impulses and with her "portent" that life as a whole—not only for her, but perhaps for everyone—is simply not worthwhile. And yet, as one astute reviewer, Thomas P. McDonnell, noted at the time *Live or Die* was first published, Sexton gives us more than "impulses": "(this) is not a poetry of spasmodic revelation or of occasional incident transformed from similitude to artifact: in its continuing wholeness one perceives the suggestion of a journey." It was a journey, as *Live or Die* makes clear, upon whose outcome rested her life itself, and one she approaches with great courage and her developed artistic powers.

Carl Jung, discussing the obstacles to personal growth, notes that venturing into "obscurity and darkness" is absolutely essential in the quest for a new stage of development, a higher individuation of self. For Anne Sexton, there were two kinds of "darkness"—her madness, which represented personal defeat; and that agonizing uncertainty about her life and her identity which could only be eased through poetry and whose resolution—even if temporary—could represent significant progress toward mental stability and a secure sense of self. In *Live or Die*, Sexton has greatly matured as woman and as poet: she

does not glorify madness, setting herself apart from the rest of humanity, but rather perceives it as an ignoble escape and, most of all, as a colossal waste of time. The most fearsome "obscurity and darkness," Jung suggests, lies in a sane, ego-centered approach toward personal problems, not in a surrender to the chaotic promptings of the id. In her third volume Sexton recognizes this truth, and the recognition helps produce some of her finest poetry. (pp. 9-10)

In **"Wanting to Die,"** Sexton notes that her own body, her essential physical self, is only a "bad prison" that should be emptied of breath, of life. Through poetry she sought liberation from this cruel and unnecessary prison, a liberation that could come only through a compassionate acceptance of her own flawed but redeemable self. Thus her emphasis in *Live or Die* is not upon "confession," with its implication of guilt, but upon compassion for herself and for all those who have influenced her personal existence. Seeking out the origin of her illness in childhood traumas and inadequate relationships with her parents, she is not interested in assigning blame but in bringing to light the dismal facts themselves; there is a new, strong impulse to face past realities and to assess their impact on the present. If this produced only a partial liberation, at least it represented an *earned* freedom that could directly affect the poet's life—acting as a form of therapy—and intensify the honesty of her art as well. (p. 11)

After *Live or Die*, Sexton's personal evolution began to seem increasingly frenetic and directionless. In her later volumes she assumes various effective guises—the witty lover of *Love Poems* (1969), the ribald folklorist of *Transformations* (1971), the religious seeker of *The Awful Rowing Toward God* (1975)—but never again does she achieve the immediacy and fullness of *Live or Die*, a book that shows her largest, most personal issue examined with her utmost energy and clarity. In a sense, her later books are elaborate footnotes to that volume, developing ancillary themes and exploring areas of existence which become important once Sexton has made her crucial decision to live. And, as many critics have noted, she began to abandon the careful craftsmanship so evident in the early volumes, producing a large number of poems but letting their quality suffer a noticeable decline. Increasingly uncertain about the direction of her career, Sexton began to rely on the familiar, melodramatic voice of her earlier work, frequently repeating herself and no longer seeming able, or willing, to hone that voice through a rigorous attention to form, or to deepen its implications through fresh or surprising insights. As an artist, in short, she seems to stop growing. As a result, the American literary myth that a writer is only as good as her last book has been extremely damaging to Sexton, as expressed in the form of harsh or dismissive reviews of her last volumes. The recently issued collected edition of her work, however, should force readers to take another look, and especially to rediscover the value of Sexton's important earlier work.

In a letter written a few weeks before her death, Sexton remarks upon the famous closing poem of *Live or Die*:

> I do not know how I feel about such an old poem as **"Live"** in *Live or Die*. The poems stand for the moment they are written and make no promises to the future events and consciousness and raising of the unconscious as happens as one goes forward and does not look backward for an answer in an old poem.

A typically breathless, headlong statement, one which contains—with the advantage of hindsight, we can see it easily—a veiled warning, as well as a surprisingly harsh contempt of "old poems" representing experiences that are past, dead, no longer available to the poet (and, it would seem, no longer interesting to her). On the surface, it also suggests an unwillingness to *learn* from experience, to assimilate past insights into the vulnerable present consciousness as talismanic reminders, if not as forms of positive moral instruction. But actually the statement is consistent with Sexton's poetry as a whole, and merely states once again the darker side of her belief: one cannot go backward, and the poet can "make no promises" that artistic resolutions can remain valid beyond the experience of a particular poem. "Experiment escorts us last," as Emily Dickinson wrote, and Sexton shared this frightening awareness of the uncertain, friable nature of personal evolution, of the pitfalls lying in wait at every turn of experience. What remains for us, after her death, is to admire her spirit in facing that experience, to rejoice in her momentary triumphs and to recognize, in the poems themselves, her ultimate survival. (pp. 12-13)

> Greg Johnson, "The Achievement of Anne Sexton,"
> in The Hollins Critic, *Vol. XXI, No. 3, June, 1984,*
> *pp. 1-13.*

DIANE MIDDLEBROOK

When Anne Sexton's posthumous *Complete Poems* came out four years ago, poet Katha Pollitt summarized the negative judgment many critics arrived at in their reviews: "the sheer quantity of inferior work does tend to dull one's response to the gems. One puts down this enormous book with the nagging feeling that all along a slim volume of verse was trapped inside it" [see excerpt above]. Contemporary poets tend to be assessed by the carat: prized for glitter, durability and for scale that permits resetting in an anthology. As Pollitt says, "the gems are there" in Sexton, too.

Yet the appearance of a complete poems also presents an opportunity to pose questions about a writer whose entire body of work is the necessary critical context. How are the gems related to surrounding poems? Is the un-gemlike work inferior as art, or does it represent different artistic goals? Sexton's method of writing, which she referred to as "milking the unconscious," often produced a loosely-structured poetry dense with simile, freaked with improbable associations. In a poem addressed to James Wright, Sexton herself acknowledged she knew the effect offended certain tastes: "There is too much food and no one left over / to eat up all the weird abundance" (**"The Black Art"**). Weird: uncanny, magical, unconventional. While some of Sexton's most admired poems work, like little machines, on well-oiled armatures of rhythm or rhyme (such as **"All My Pretty Ones," "The Starry Night," "Wanting to Die"**), others equally powerful depend on manic or despairing or ecstatic cascades of association (**"The Furies," "O Ye Tongues"**) that flow like an open spigot. The gems, or closed forms, tend to be early; the looser style, later. In this collection, the reader can watch Sexton evolve her second style as a way of exploring a changing relation to her subject matter.

Sexton's *Complete Poems* is a compilation of the eight books she saw into print, plus an edited collection of work left in manuscript at the time of her death. . . . The early poetry (*To Bedlam and Part Way Back*, 1960; *All My Pretty Ones*, 1962) holds up very well. But as this volume shows, Anne Sexton made bolder exploration of her lifelong subject—her experiences of madness—in later work, beginning with the volume *Live or Die* (1966). Mining the realm of the unconscious as

she had been taught by both psychotherapy and contemporary writing, after 1962 Sexton became increasingly preoccupied with the psychological and social consequences of inhabiting a female body.

Because Sexton's writing seems so personal she is often labeled a "confessional" poet and grouped (to her disadvantage) with poets such as Lowell, Berryman, Roethke, and Plath. But Sexton resisted the label "confessional"; she preferred to be regarded as a "storyteller." To emphasize that she considered the speaking "I" in her poetry as a literary rather than a real identity, Sexton invariably opened her public performances by reading the early poem **"Her Kind."** These are the first and last stanzas:

> I have gone out, a possessed witch,
> haunting the black air, braver at night;
> dreaming evil, I have done my hitch
> over the plain houses, light by light:
> lonely thing, twelve-fingered, out of mind.
> A woman like that is not a woman, quite.
> I have been her kind.
> . . .
> I have ridden in your cart, driver,
> waved my nude arms at villages going by,
> learning the last bright routes, survivor
> where your flames still bite my thigh
> and my ribs crack where your wheels wind.
> A woman like that is not ashamed to die.
> I have been her kind.

No matter what poetry she had on an evening's agenda, Sexton offered this persona as a point of entry to her art. "I" in the poem is a disturbing, marginal female whose power is associated with disfigurement, sexuality, and magic. But at the end of each stanza, "I" is displaced from sufferer onto storyteller. With the lines "A woman like that . . . I have been her kind" Sexton conveys the terms on which she wishes to be understood: not victim, but witness and witch. (pp. 293-94)

Sexton's *Complete Poems* yields most when read as if it contained a narrative: an account of a woman cursed with a desire to die. Why is she different from other women? Where did the curse come from? A story line with a beginning, middle, and end takes shape in *Complete Poems* as Sexton systematically exhausts a set of culturally acceptable explanations for the condition of her kind. These are, first, a psychiatric explanation; later, a sociological explanation; and finally a spiritual explanation.

The story begins with the discovery of the poet in the sick person. The narrator of Sexton's first book is a woman "part way back" from Bedlam—that is, not yet restored to the family home as wife and mother—contemplating what took her to the mental hospital: the preference for suicide over motherhood as she had learned that role from her own mother (**"The Double Image"**). Bedlam has been a school which taught a valuable lesson: the power of signs.

> I tapped my own head;
> it was glass, an inverted bowl.
> . . .
> 　if you turn away
> because there is no lesson here
> I will hold my awkward bowl,
> with all its cracked stars shining
> like a complicated lie.

("For John, Who Begs Me Not to Enquire Further")

From now on, she will be a poet of the tapped head: the mad housewife.

Condensed into the metaphor of the broken kitchen bowl are most of the meanings Sexton associates with her own liberation into poetry. Before she tapped meanings from her head, the bowl—her womanly identity—revealed but enclosed her (like Plath's bell jar); only through costly breakage did the identity begin to shine with complex significance. Breakage ruined the bowl for kitchen use but endowed it with a more precious moral utility. Further, the act of offering her own breakage as a gift shifted her relation both to her suffering and to the beholder. In the metaphor of the bowl whose cracks become stars, Sexton avows belief that her experience has been redeemed by its transformation into the social medium of language. "Star" in her personal mythology will from now on designate that place— the poetic symbol—where the language of private suffering grows radiant and magically ambiguous.

Sexton began writing poetry as a form of therapy, at her doctor's suggestion. In her first two books, she uses a good many references to this therapy and occasionally speaks of herself almost objectively as a case history. These are her most admired books. They are also her most "confessional" books in that they establish that her maladjustment as a woman is to be her subject as a poet.

By 1962, Sexton's poetry had won a respectful audience. But as a psychiatric patient she had experienced many setbacks and relapses. She had changed as an artist; as a sick woman, she did not change: repetition of destructive patterns was one of the symptoms of her illness. To survive as a poet meant to attain another, a less reportorial relation to the subject of her pathology. Beginning with poems written for her third volume, *Live or Die*, Sexton gradually abandoned the polarity sick/well which gives underlying structure to the poems of *Bedlam* and *Pretty Ones*. In the poetry of *Live or Die* Sexton begins to explore the suspicion that what she suffers from is femaleness itself, and is probably incurable. "—I'm no more a woman / than Christ was a man," she says in a dream (**"Consorting with Angels,"** *Live or Die*). Behind this claim are questions that eventually dominate her last, religious poems: what kinds of social significance has *her* suffering? Is it too specifically female to contain spiritual meaning? Can a woman speak for Man? More and more for Sexton the problematic will not lie between being insane and being healthy, but within being female. To be female is to be defective. (pp. 295-96)

In my reading of Sexton's *Complete Poems, Love Poems* (1969) and *Transformations* (1971) form a dyad. *Love Poems* exposes the dilemma of the female poet trying to write within the conventions of the literary genre of love poetry: *Transformations* explains this dilemma by situating sexual love in its social context: the marriage contract that stabilizes the social order. Both have an unsettling, masochistic tone. The speaker of *Love Poems* experiences her body as a hoard of attributes, desirable only in dismemberment. "Love" is the anxious energy she feels as her body parts come to life under the prospective or actual gaze of a man. . . . (p. 300)

Transformations also presents women as some of their parts; but since Sexton adopts here the plots of fairy tales from Grimm, by which children are instructed in the repression and displacement of libido, the consciousness is perhaps more acceptable than it feels in the radically masochistic *Love Poems*. The tale-teller of *Transformations* is "a middle-aged witch, me"—the woman who has done her hitch over the plain houses but is not a woman quite. She designates as the chosen auditor of these stories a boy of sixteen ("He is sixteen and he wants

some answers. / He is each of us") who has found a gold key and is about to learn the use of it.

> Its secrets whimper
> like a dog in heat.
> He turns the key.
> Presto!
> It opens this book of odd tales.

These narratives are adapted directly from Grimm; what Sexton underscores in retelling is the phallic key. The wisecracking witch supplies prologues which emphasize roles and strategies within the system of exchange where sexuality is the coin circulated among the generations to replenish the family and define differences between masculine and feminine identities. . . . Sexton said *Transformations* was "as much about me" as any of her first-person lyrics, and it is. Yet in neither *Love Poems* or *Transformations* is the pathological conceived as merely personal. If Sexton's *Complete Poems* can be read as a woman's story of her wish to die, these explore the death wish as a response to the emptiness of sexuality experienced as a commodity—its repetitiousness, its fetishes.

In the last three books Sexton saw through publication, another appetite emerges: the hunger for redemption. Sexton reformulates, this time in religious terms, her oldest questions about the origins and meaning of her wish to die. The dyad of mother and daughter, and the oedipal triangle, scrutinized psychiatrically in earlier work, return to these volumes as potential sources of grace. In one of Sexton's most imaginative inventions, regression becomes a metaphor for spiritual quest.

The Book of Folly reintroduces the theme of mother's power of cursing or curing a sick daughter. Sexton had, in effect, two mothering figures in early childhood, and both have roles to play in Sexton's late poems. Great-aunt Anna Dingley, the loving "Nana" of Sexton's early childhood, went insane and was institutionalized shortly after Anne told her about kissing a boyfriend at age thirteen. Sexton thus associated her own sexual development with her spinster aunt's decline, and re-created the episode in numerous poems (see, especially, **"Some Foreign Letters," "Rapunzel," "The Nana-Hex"**) as well as in her play *Mercy Street,* in which the maiden aunt witnesses an incestuous episode with the father. In *Folly*, Sexton's yearning to recover the "good mother" lost first to insanity and then to death takes the form of desire for regression to the period before the heterosexual kiss divided them. (pp. 301-03)

Sexton's real mother, Mary Gray Staples Harvey, occupies another kind of ambivalent symbolism. In the late poems, Sexton locates the possibility of her redemption from insanity— the evil of being female—in the memory of her first connection to Mother Mary through the mouth. . . . Mouthing mother, her original hunger was appeased; yet appeasement was only possible in the infant stage when the female body of the mother was innocent—that is, was a source of comfort, not an object of identification. Redemption from the condition of femaleness resides, by this logic, only in the infant stage before separation has done its work and before the infant knows her name and pronoun.

In this world both symbolic and real, it is no more innocuous to be male, of course. The three ambitious sequences that end *Folly*—**"The Death of the Fathers," "Angels of the Love Affair," "The Jesus Papers"**—can be read as progressive confrontations with father figures, motivated by Sexton's defect-haunted sense of herself as a woman. If to mother a daughter is to press her into female roles, so to father a daughter is to expose her to male desire. **"The Death of the Fathers"** revisits old subject matter—young Anne Harvey's tender fascination with her father Ralph Churchill Harvey—treated in the elegiac lyrics of the earlier volumes, most poignantly in **"All My Pretty Ones," "Young,"** and **"And One for My Dame."** But by the time of writing *Folly*, Sexton has reduced the dead father to a mere symbolic shadow of himself. In *Folly*'s **"Death of the Fathers,"** he stands for the unattainable object of desire, the lover who might give her both safety and sex. But above all, he is the man she can't have: first because he's her father; again because he's a drunkard; then because he's dead; and now, when Sexton is 42, because his authenticity has been challenged by a usurper, a man claiming to have been her mother's lover. By 1971, of course, Sexton's memory of Ralph Churchill Harvey has been much mediated by years of psychotherapy. But in any case by age 42 a woman's relationship to her father, even a relationship disfigured by memories or fantasies of incest, takes its place in a social realm larger than family life.

In *The Book of Folly* this realm is theological. Sexton's most inventive explanation of femaleness in the scheme of things occurs in **"The Jesus Papers,"** the sequence of nine poems that ends *Folly*. Food metaphors dominate this sequence; most particularly, the metaphor of breast milk as a principle of generosity, a form of salvation issuing specifically from the female body. Flowing from the madonna's breast, (**"Jesus Suckles"**) it offers the infant his first knowledge of human connection— and its cognate, knowledge of separation. The experience of separation or the creation of the selfish ego becomes in these poems *the* principal human experience needing spiritual cure. Thus the infant Jesus, separating from the breast, fantasizes himself as a truck, an image that recalls Sexton's guilty happiness at discovering her poetic gift as won at her mother's expense. ("I did not know that my life, in the end, / would run over my mother's like a truck"—**"Those Times . . ."**). (pp. 303-04)

In Sexton's version of Christian theology, Christ's death, like her own deathwish, is meaningful to others as a source of symbolisms. For God does not dispense meaning. He dispenses in infancy the hunger for meaning, and he endows the earth with meaning-makers. In Sexton as in Christ the sufferer and the symbol-maker meet: she is the hungry woman we eat as we read her words.

These, in any case, are the symbolisms carried over into Sexton's last two books: *The Death Notebooks* and *The Awful Rowing Toward God*. (p. 306)

Sexton's firmest poems in the volume *The Death Notebooks* are built on the symbolisms radiating from this infant indentity condensing hunger/sacrifice/poetry. In both the **"Death Baby"** sequence and, further on, in the **"Furies"** sequence, the successes arise from the startling originality and intelligence with which Sexton draws on regression as a source of imagery. **"The Furies"** appears occasionally to owe something to Theodore Roethke's sequence "The Lost Son," and the final sequence, **"O Ye Tongues,"** is modeled after Christopher Smart's "Jubilate Agno." In both cases the models are structural, and have served to free Sexton's characteristic strength: access to the matrix of symbolism, the infant psyche from which she retrieved her subject matter throughout life. (pp. 307-08)

The pair of poems that begin and end [*The Awful Rowing Toward God*] (**"Rowing"** and **"The Rowing Endeth"**) give it a solid structure. Sexton writes in **"Rowing"** that she had passed her life ignorant of God as a destination: "I grew, I

grew, / and God was there like an island I had not rowed to." While writing the poems of *Awful Rowing*, Sexton was preparing to separate from her husband; projected changes in her way of life seem to lie behind Sexton's metaphor of the island as a spiritual destination with the characteristics of a new household. It "will not be perfect, / it will have the flaws of life, / the absurdities of the dinner table, / but there will be a door / and I will open it." Unlike the childhood home, unlike the "cruel houses" of married life (including the mental hospitals she has lived in), this island, she believes, houses the paternal presence who might embrace and rescue her at last.

But when she arrives, in **"The Rowing Endeth,"** "at the dock of the island called God," she does not find the expected door. No shelter; no embrace. Instead, she and God "squat on the rocks by the sea / and play—can it be true— / a game of poker." The hand she's dealt Sexton calls a royal straight flush. Instead it seems to be a run of 9-10-J-Q-K, a suit—or family— of five headed by a King and Queen; presumably, the ace is missing from this straight run, because the winning hand is God's five aces. ("A wild card had been announced / but I had not heard it / being in such a state of awe / when He took out the cards and dealt.") God, like the salesman-father named Ace in Sexton's play *Mercy Street*, is fond of a joke, and the poem ends as loser Anne joins the winner in his "untamable, eternal, gut-driven *ha-ha*."

God's aggressive masculine presence in the poem aligns him with other father figures in Sexton's poetry, including the doctors: those she is doomed to love from a position of compliance, but from whom she will never receive healing care. God's "wild card" signifies the privilege of Him over Her everywhere—the inscrutable possession of dominance. But the poker game with God also seems to stand for a final confrontation of her delusions as delusions. There is no "door" to pass through which will retrospectively transform her history, and no magic embrace, equivalent to God's wild card, which can "get rid of the rat inside of me."

Between the first and last poems of this volume, however, Sexton writes on a variety of themes that may be regarded as "rowing" exercises, or strategies of approach to the redemptive island. In these poems her body acquires a new set of meanings, as a site for the study of the existence of evil. . . . Sexton's *Complete Poems* ends not with a "last word" but with 141 pages of unpublished work in various stages of finish. An epigraph for the book might well have been, "The story ends with me still rowing" (**"Rowing"**). The mysterious curse of her mental illness, and the death wish at its core, could be lifted neither by medical nor by other means; but in becoming its storyteller Sexton achieved an emancipating relation to it. "This is madness / but a kind of hunger . . . Turn, my hungers!" In the leap from madness to metaphor Sexton fled solitary confinement again and again. Arriving at the end of Sexton's *Complete Poems* brings me to the question of merit. Sexton was in many ways an interesting writer; but was she an inferior poet?—Inferior, say, to her mentor W. D. Snodgrass, her teacher Robert Lowell, her friends James Wright and Sylvia Plath, her Boston peers Adrienne Rich and Denise Levertov?

As I have been suggesting, I find Sexton a startlingly original and valuable artist. But Sexton differs from members of this group in two important ways that make it difficult to rank her among these other writers. First, she was not an intellectual. Sexton had only a high school education; she got her training as a poet in workshops. Though she had a quick mind and read widely, her thinking was intuitive rather than systematic. She did not identify herself with a literary tradition, she did not measure herself in terms of precursors, she did not acquire a critical language by which to classify and discriminate. Hers is not a poetry of ideas—aesthetic, political, philosophical, or historical.

Second, she stopped writing the kind of short lyric that remains coin of the realm in American poetry: the lyric of perfect economy composed according to an exacting formal standard, whether in meter or free verse. Critics still praise Sexton's early work for its control of the materials of disorder by means of formal effects she dismissed as "tricks." Manuscripts of early poems reveal that Sexton often began by setting herself a design problem: a stanza template with rhyme positions designated "a, b, c," etc.; then she would write a poem into the mould. She continued this practice, with good results, through 1962: her workshop years. (pp. 309-10, 312-13)

Sexton's later style developed out of the demands of her subject matter: accounting for madness. The exploratory, associational method she devised gave priority to the implacable structure of unconscious processes. This method is most successful in such poems as **"O Ye Tongues," "The Jesus Papers," "The Furies," "The Death of the Fathers," "The Death Baby," *Transformations***—works where the traces of a narrative adumbrate a boundary of reference within which to rationalize the flow of association. For much of Sexton's *Complete Poems*, the horizon or story line is, of course, autobiographical, focused on Sexton's attraction to death. Sexton's *Complete Poems* might be described as a psycho-narrative in verse, to which each poem is a contribution.

Moreover, the type of poem Sexton evolved was probably an inevitable creation in mid-century American poetry. It articulates the dilemma of a female recipient of certain ideas about women's place in the social order; it invests this dilemma in a single persona, a performing voice. The contemporary writings of Sylvia Plath and Adrienne Rich offer perhaps the closest analogues to Sexton's work, since their own dilemmas were equally privileged and middle class. As young *women*, all three had embraced prevailing ideologies about women's roles. All three of them seem to have been excessively susceptible to highly conventional expectations, tormented by questions about whether they were "good" daughters, students, mothers, wives. As young *artists* they had to gain recognition in a prestige system condescending to women, and the conflicts they experienced between the roles of woman and artist fueled their development. In fact, the gender specificity of much of their poetry helps us see how specifically "masculine" were the concerns of peers such as Lowell, Snodgrass, Berryman, Wright, Roethke, Ginsberg—who struggled to attain spiritual authority in the postwar consumer society littered with unusable masculine stereotypes.

But for Plath and Rich, the male-identified literary tradition eventually suggested models for transcendence uncongenial to Sexton. Both Plath and Rich essentially revised, for women's use, the poetics of romanticism which centers the poem in a visionary ego. Plath adopted the voice of a maenad; Rich evolved a powerfully personal voice of informed social criticism.

Sexton's voice remained unembarrassedly domestic. She tested notions about self and God against feelings schooled in repression, and her poems do not transcend, they explore this repression. Sexton's art celebrates word-magic, buffoonery, regression, "milking the unconscious," as inexhaustible sources of resistance to the deadly authority of the stereotypes constraining adult women's lives. Sexton's artistry was to achieve a mode

of expression for this particular female consciousness, expression at once intimate and theatrical. Her audiences, mostly women, responded to that voice as the manifestation of a condition they had previously felt to be wholly personal and interior. Suddenly, poetry had expanded to acknowledge a whole new citizenry; the middle-class American woman beginning to seek liberation from confinement in domestic roles. As American poetry slowly incorporates a feminist consciousness, Sexton's work seems uncannily ahead of its time. It seems bound to endure at least as long as the social and psychological dilemmas that inspired her. (pp. 313-14)

Diane Middlebrook, "Poets of Weird Abundance," in Parnassus: Poetry in Review, *Vols. 12/13, Nos. 1/2, 1985, pp. 293-315.*

DIANA HUME GEORGE

Anne Sexton's poetry tells stories that are immensely significant to mid-twentieth-century artistic and psychic life. Sexton understood her culture's malaise through her own, and her skill enabled her to deploy metaphorical structures at once synthetic and analytic. In other words, she assimilated the superficially opposing but deeply similar ways of thinking represented by poetry and psychoanalysis. Sexton explored the myths by and through which our culture lives and dies: the archetypal relationships among mothers and daughters, fathers and daughters, mothers and sons, gods and humans, men and women. She perceived, and consistently patterned in the images of her art, the paradoxes deeply rooted in human behavior and motivation. Her poetry presents multiplicity and simplicity, duality and unity, the sacred and the profane, in ways that insist on their similarities—even, at times, their identity. In less abstract terms, Sexton made explicit the intimacy of forces persistently treated as opposites by the society she lived in.

I appreciate the intention of statements made since her death that caution readers against becoming enamored of Sexton's illness and that encourage concentration on the celebratory aspects of her poetry. But another cautionary note is perhaps in order: that readers not ignore the expression of poetic and personal anguish for which the celebration is counterpart and foil. "The soul is, I think, a human being who speaks with the pressure of death at his head," Sexton wrote in a 1963 letter. Her poems articulate some of the deepest dilemmas of her contemporaries about their—our—most basic fears and wishes. Although Sexton's canon reaches for the unities of human experience, she did not abandon duality, even dichotomy. Poets must transcend us in some ways to be counted great of mind, but they must also be *of* us. Her poems vibrate in that energetic, passionate area between everlasting certainty and everlasting doubt. When she perceived the sameness of everything, it was against the background of the difference; when she perceived the difference, it was in reference to the sameness—just as metaphor, the imaging of connectedness, always implies a prior discontinuity.

Sexton flashed a sparkling, multiple light on human faces from the beginning of her writing career until the month of her death. For seventeen years she spoke in a direct, intimate way of people she loved. Her concentration on human relationships produced sharp, masterful portraits of people who were worth keeping alive, or worth resurrecting. That they were often "all her pretty ones" creates part of her poetry's poignancy. Her personal relationship to many of those who people the world of her poems amplifies the resounding creation of whole, complicated characters whose compelling presence is perhaps more deeply artful for having been lived. If many of Sexton's people had not so lived, her skill and art would have been solely responsible for breathing the life into them. As it was, she most often worked from the life and perhaps must share her credit with those who died before her and those who have outlived her: her mother, her father, her daughters, her husband, her lovers, her aunt, her grandfather, and her remarkable friends. I am glad there was or is an Eleanor Boylan, whatever name she bears.

When Sexton tells her dead father that she will bend down her strange face to his and forgive him, she is speaking of what we all need to do: to bend down our faces to our fathers, living or dead, and forgive them. When she calls her mother her mocking mirror, her overthrown love, her first image, she speaks for all of us of woman born and first nurtured against "her plump and fruity skin." When she becomes the child of "elbows, knees, dreams, goodnight," she is the child in all of us, recapturing those moments when "love grew rings around me." When she says to her daughter, "Everything in your body that is new is telling the truth," she may be transcribing what she said to her daughter; she is also expressing for the collective mothers of her readership what we all want to be saying to our daughters, what we sometimes have not the courage or attentiveness to say. The mother of "life is not in my hands" tells a terrible truth, but she is also the mother of "Darling, stand still at your door, sure of yourself, a white stone, a good stone. . . ." This is a mother who tells the truth, one who gives you "the images I know."

In her lively, lonely telling of her truth, in her giving of the images she knew, Sexton looked for "uncomplicated hymns / but love has none." So the daughter who has loved and watched her mother closely enough to see "that blaze within the pilgrim woman" will also confess that this most important death does not equip her with grief. The friend who watches Eleanor Boylan talking with God, "as close as the ceiling," will warn her to speak quickly, "before death uses you up." The great aunt who climbed Mount San Salvatore, that "yankee girl, the iron interior of her sweet body," will one day careen into the streets and stop passersby "to mumble your guilty love while your ears die."

In **"Her Kind"** and **"The Black Art,"** Sexton characterizes the poet as one who feels too much, thinks too much, and lives in an atmosphere of "weird abundance." In a 1966 letter she writes about the abundance that "runs wild with love as cancer." Sexton did, in some respects, connect the sources of poetic inspiration with death. Certainly the connections between extremist art and suicide as a form of poetic destiny have been destructively romanticized. My intention in raising the point is not to confirm it but to suggest something that it indicates. The limited extent to which Sexton connected art and self-destruction may have been symptomatic of her illness. I think she would have agreed: "Suicide is the opposite of the poem." That she *might* have felt called upon to fulfill a poetic as well as personal destiny by suicide—and I do not necessarily think she did—is better viewed as symptomatic of the cultural conditions she so clearly perceived and lived with.

Poets are among the few whom our culture still invests with a ritual function. We ask them to speak the unspeakable for us, and when they do, we are capable of effecting a violently negative transference. Critical response to Sexton's poetry seems to me to bear this out. Particularly if the poet has exposed our pain, seen into our darkest selves, we need to purge ourselves of the violating member, to punish the one who has broken boundaries and violated taboos. That Christianity depends for salvation on a sacrificial lamb whose death permits us to abrogate responsibility for the human failings we call "sin" speaks of our need to transfer guilt. Sexton's identifications with the crucified Christ sometimes have the ring of a self-aggrandizing and self-appointed martyrdom. But to whatever extent she may have been martyred, it was at the invitation, if not the insistence, of an exceptionally hungry audience.

Yet we are angry with Anne Sexton for killing herself, partly because she is the same poet who wrote with such commitment and intensity of the delight of being alive. If Sylvia Plath was always removed from her readership by the consistency of her "dead hands, dead stringencies," if she was always somehow beyond the merely human, always "the arrow, the dew that flies / Suicidal, at one with the drive," Sexton was not always so. Before and after she was sometimes that, she was also the mother of **"Little Girl,"** the lover of **"Us,"** the daughter of **"Oysters,"** the child of **"Young."** She spoke to us of celebration of the sun, that "excitable gift," of all the wicked, pure, lovely fun of being alive. Perhaps we could not tolerate knowing that this was the same woman who saw "rats in the toilet." If she was more clearly one of us, then her defection was more serious. It endangered us more deeply. She was an anomaly, a fish with wings.

Many of the qualities of Sexton's poetry so often seen as inconsistent I see as part of the vitalizing struggle to make of her art a salvation both spiritual and bodily. Much like the early Blake, Anne Sexton moved between contraries with equal force, equal conviction, and equal doubt. One can experience disappointment or frustration in the presence of such vacillation and label it a failure of nerve or will or imagination—or one can experience it, as I do, as one's own truth. To make it more concrete: if you think linearly about the building of a body of truth, then you must think only in terms of progress and regress. Anne Sexton comes to happy resolutions repeatedly in her work, from poem to poem, volume to volume. *Live or Die* is structured in just such a pleasing, simple shape: after a struggle with destruction, it ends with the affirmation of life. Yet in subsequent volumes she backslides continuously, seeming to erase her previous truths, to compromise them, or to give them up. In the early *All My Pretty Ones*, Sexton first forgives her father. In later works she sometimes appears to renege on that forgiveness and to exhume the old ghost she had, we thought, laid to rest. In a literary and moral tradition presided over by *Paradise Lost* followed by *Paradise Regained*, and a theological one structured by the external resurrection of a crucified god, the linear progression of truth is denied by the return of the ghost from eternal rest.

The wish that art may carve into permanent perfection either our hope or our despair is understandable but too limiting. There is ample room in my own notion of poetry for the repeated reflections of that imperfectability that separates humans from the gods they create. The repetition of a set of emotional and mental acts is central to Anne Sexton's poetry and represents a striving after personal and poetic catharsis that is never quite achieved, even when it is claimed. Her poetry enacts the repetition compulsion that may justly be called thanatopic from one perspective. From another, the movement that seems repetitive represents an intricate tension between contraries that is at the core of all creative process. (pp. xi-xiv)

Diana Hume George, in her Oedipus Anne: The Poetry of Anne Sexton, *University of Illinois Press, 1987, 210 p.*

Karl (Jay) Shapiro

1913-

American poet, critic, essayist, editor, novelist, and autobiographer.

Perhaps best known for critical essays in which he attacks strict adherence to form and tradition in modern poetry, Shapiro composes verse that defies classification because of his varied and unpredictable approach to theme and presentation. In his poetry, Shapiro explores love, war, religion, and, most notably, the relationship between poetry and prose—a topic that he often addresses by combining the two genres in his works. While some critics maintain that Shapiro's use of such diverse forms as the sonnet, blank verse, and lyric poetry yields erratic results, many regard his extensive output as impressive. In a review of *Love and War, Art and God,* Leo Connellan observed: "In Karl Shapiro's poetry there is a timelessness and grace, energy of the earth. No poet better comprehends the academic, proves it time and time again and then shuns it to write for us about the every day things of our lives."

Although Shapiro's first work, *Poems* (1935), secured him a scholarship to Johns Hopkins University, his verse received little critical attention until the publication of *Person, Place, and Thing* (1942). Composed while Shapiro was stationed in New Guinea during World War II, the pieces in this volume garnered praise for his adroit use of dramatic monologue. Shapiro was awarded the Pulitzer Prize in poetry for *V-Letter and Other Poems* (1944). This collection contains what many critics lauded as the finest war poems ever written by an American. Several selections in *Trial of a Poet and Other Poems* (1947) were written on Shapiro's homeward journey immediately after the war and eloquently communicate the sense of humanity's irrevocable loss during that turbulent era.

In his next major volume, *Poems of a Jew* (1958), Shapiro examines the doctrines of Judaism and Christianity, rebuking and defending both religions while discussing his brief conversion to Catholicism several years earlier. Shapiro experimented with free verse to great critical success in *The Bourgeois Poet* (1964). Considered one of his most accomplished blends of prose and poetry, this self-analytical collection develops a stream-of-consciousness narrative reminiscent of the verse of such Beat poets as Allen Ginsberg and Lawrence Ferlinghetti. In his succeeding volume, *White-Haired Lover* (1968), which consists of twenty-nine love poems dedicated to his second wife, Shapiro returns to traditional verse forms. *Love and War, Art and God* (1984) combines early poetry with new verse in which Shapiro contemplates the eclectic concepts of the volume's title. Critics considered Shapiro's informal free verse better suited to his animated imagination than other styles utilized in this volume. In the pieces collected in *New and Selected Poems, 1940-1986* (1987), Shapiro confronts both contemporary social issues and personal concerns. A critic from *Publishers Weekly* asserted: "Here the poet-chronicler of World War II and postwar society in America—that polished, elegant and smooth commentator on the hypocrisies, prejudices and delusions of our common life—brings himself into our future with exact and telling descriptions."

Shapiro's criticism is noted for its passionate and controversial arguments against traditional poetry. *Essay on Rime* (1945) is

an extended treatise written in verse in which Shapiro comments on the state of twentieth-century poetry. Presenting a survey of past traditions and trends, he argues that the reverence of modern verse for intellectual themes has contributed to its decline as a creative genre. Shapiro concludes that a more emotional and personalized approach should be utilized to restore the originality and vigor of poetry. While several critics faulted Shapiro's analysis as unfocused and tenuous, Louis Untermeyer maintained: "[*Essay on Rime*] is both thoughtful and emotional, packed with complex ideas yet brilliantly lucid. The lines continually cry for quotation." In the essays comprising *In Defense of Ignorance* (1960), Shapiro continues his argument against formality in modern poetry. This volume stimulated controversy in academic circles for its polemical attacks on such seminal poets as T. S. Eliot and Ezra Pound. In *To Abolish Children and Other Essays* (1968), Shapiro maintains that contemporary American poets are overwhelmed by England's distinguished literary past. Critics generally agreed that the most impressive piece in this collection is "A *Malebolge* of Fourteen Hundred Books," an alphabetical homage to Shapiro's favorite authors. Paul Fussell, Jr. declared: "Here we see him not thinking or formulating . . . but recalling, embracing and sentimentalizing, which he does convincingly once he escapes from some aristocratic literary form with which he is uneasily quarreling."

Shapiro has also written a novel, *Edsel* (1971), about an infamous poet who is converted from his immoral lifestyle by the love of a woman. In addition to contributing essays and articles to numerous periodicals, Shapiro served as editor of both *Poetry* and *Prairie Schooner,* and he recently published *The Younger Son* (1988), the first installment of an autobiographical trilogy.

(See also *CLC,* Vols. 4, 8, 15; *Contemporary Authors,* Vols. 1-4, rev. ed.; *Contemporary Authors New Revision Series,* Vol. 1; *Contemporary Authors Autobiography Series,* Vol. 6; and *Dictionary of Literary Biography,* Vol. 48.)

DELMORE SCHWARTZ

Essay on Rime is an attack upon the character of modern poetry and upon the author's own poetry, as Shapiro says with modesty. This modesty would be less distressing were it not uncalled for, and were it not a repudiation of Shapiro's own attitudes and practice as a poet.

The essential vagueness of Shapiro's attack is such that any attempt at an exact formulation of it must omit some ambiguous qualification or apology. To state directly what is actually diffuse and contradictory, Shapiro has discovered a threefold confusion in modern poetry. In prosody, the modern poet depends too much upon scansion by count of ear, which Shapiro confounds with such devices as Cummings's typography and with his own misunderstanding of Bridges's analysis of Milton's blank verse. In language, the modern poet makes a false use of conversational diction, abstract nouns, and like devices—a criticism which is too general to mean very much. In belief, the failure is disbelief, the effort to find beliefs, and an acceptance of the doctrines of Freud—accusations which are soft impeachments indeed. . . .

The wrongness of this new work extends from the writing as such to the governing motives of the entire poem. In particular, the versification is in a rhythm as crude as a rocking-chair's, and the phrasing is full of such items as "traumatic shattering shock," "gross indecency," "brave kids," and "the golden doors of Hopkins' heart." And then in describing the nature of modern poetry Shapiro commits countless errors of fact and interpretation. A passage from Marianne Moore's profound poem about poetry, the ironic remark, "I too dislike it," is cited by Shapiro to show that Miss Moore literally dislikes poetry. Freud's *therapy* is said to be "deterministic" and "deductive." Poe is called "the Lenin of the Symbolists." . . . These details would not matter too much except for the purpose they are meant to serve.

The declared purpose of showing the decline of modern poetry none the less permits Shapiro to praise greatly a few authors—Joyce, Eliot, Auden, and other modern poets. The fault is said to be with the imitators of these great authors, though the imitators are making use of the masters' inventions. . . .

When Shapiro speaks of criticism—by which he means only "self-dependent pride in thought, act, and invention"—and when he attacks intellectuals who practice criticism—which turns out, after all, to be elucidation and evaluation of and commentary upon works of art—the bias and the crucial weakness of his attack seem to become plain. The worst consequence of such attacks as these—Shapiro's is not the first, or the last,

or essentially different from that of Van Wyck Brooks or of J. Donald Adams—is that the false and vicious seesaw of attack and defense is forced upon everyone. To object to this kind of attack upon modern poetry is far from being prepared to deny the excesses and limitations of modern poetry. To feel that Shapiro's anti-intellectualism and philistinism are foolish does not mean that one has to justify the serious defects of the intellectual and the bohemian. In [*V-Letter and Other Poems*], his previous volume, in a poem entitled "**The Intellectuals,**" Shapiro wrote, "I'd rather be / A milkman" and "I'd rather be a barber" than an intellectual, forcing one to wonder what is so wonderful about being a milkman—not that one has anything against milkmen. In this new work he condemns intellectuals more than anyone else, which suggests powerfully that the attack on criticism is a fear of critics, and the hatred of the intellectual a fear of the intellect. There is no other explanation of his horror of glosses, commentaries, translations, and the analysis of poetry. The truth is that the modern poet, critic, or intellectual is not so inferior to the milkman as this depressing and disappointing book makes out.

Delmore Schwartz, "Karl Shapiro's Poetics," in The Nation, *New York, Vol. 161, No. 19, November 10, 1945, p. 498.*

LOUIS UNTERMEYER

[Karl Shapiro's *Essay on Rime* is] the most important book of poetry to come out of the war. It is not only a book *of* poetry but *about* poetry, a straightforward but deeply probing work of contemplation and analysis. Written in the South Pacific, where, for almost three years, Shapiro served as a sergeant in the Medical Corps, it is a stock-taking which is invaluable to the practising poet and richly instructive to any reader. A work of vivid estimates rather than a formal survey—for Shapiro had no access to books during the composition of his seventy-two-page rhymed essay—it is both thoughtful and emotional, packed with complex ideas yet brilliantly lucid. The lines continually cry for quotation. T. S. Eliot is "the strange Pied Piper of despair"; Hart Crane "leaped from the deck-rail of his disbelief to senseless strangulation"; by 1920, "the thin ice of belief had cracked and given way":

> . . . The figure-skater
> Of rime had sunk beneath the lake, and art
> Took a deep and submarine aspect.
> The corpse, the crawling rat, the bones, the wraith
> Arrived in sequence: a whole world lay wrecked
> And inundated Prufrock filled with grief
> And whimsical mockery walked along the beach,
> Envied the crab and heard the mermaid sing.

Apart from its wit, its gusto, and its technical ingenuity, Shapiro's *Essay on Rime* is of vital importance to any lover of poetry today, for it is essentially and first of all a work of belief, a resonant affirmation of faith. (p. 338)

Louis Untermeyer, "War Poets and Others," in The Yale Review, *Vol. XXXV, No. 2, December, 1945, pp. 335-38.*

HARRY ROSKOLENKO

The poet-turned-critic has ideal conditions for the practice of literary legerdemain when exorcising the black arts of criticism. Some of these sharp gentlemen have argued for regionalism and metaphysics while producing very dull examples of that school; others, less rigid, have blasted their trends toward science, nature, dialectic and the sociological muse. Each one has trailed his coteries with much fury and little poetry. As Shapiro says,

> Critics in particular have minced matters
> By acquiring all authority to talk.

This is doubtless a wholesale opinion now that the challenge comes home to the hothouse itself. Divorced from life or the substance of dreams, the critics, for the most part, have submitted tiresome commentaries, substitutions for literature with specialized formulas to back up their lack of original ideas and imagination, so that the flow outward from the critic to the pale poet inwardly has had a poor time of it. But now we are in for new vistas, with a pentametric conscience beating ghosts of English prosody on the doorsteps of American poetry. What the critic has failed to do, Shapiro assails; and if he stumbles over some old bones, new hats or surrealist poker-faces, it is his own literary nightmare he is taking for a walk. For he is examining in . . . [*Essay on Rime*] the source of our Rime, its reason and its ruin. Many faces look in at him through the mirrors on the ceiling.

Our rhythms are unnatural, says Shapiro, except in Whitman, who "shocked polite society." Browning was "hippity-hop"; Milton was pure; Hopkins had only a theology and not even, alas, his invention of sprung-rhythms; of Eliot's "Ash Wednesday" Shapiro says: "for in a hundred years no poem / Has sung itself so exquisitely well." Of course *Ulysses* was a "magnificent failure," a quote borrowed by Shapiro; yet there is fulsome praise for Joyce's "rhetoric of rhyme." To come a bit closer to our scene, Auden "employs Braces of proselike forms" similar to Shapiro's own mixture and mould; Yeats had his great ear, and was not a mathematical dissecter of the line, which was his good fortune; but the Cults have sinned most with their visual practices and aberrations. . . . If the essay makes any sense, one must denounce all *avant-garde* writers, from Rimbaud to Mayakovsky. The Objectivists get the merry morning and an impolite stare; so does Lawrence, who merely sat between the Imagists and the Objectivists and just sat—whereas William Carlos Williams had at least his microscope for dull company. Stephen Spender is where he started, in a circle; and Marianne Moore is a jeweler by trade, according to Shapiro, who has his own blueprint for poetry. Each ingredient of poetry must constantly be checked, he says: so much melody, sense and metre per pound of poem. No wonder the professors beam. It is so mathematical, precise, and as self-contained as a loud drum, even though he breaks through the skin with self-envelopments of ideal situations.

The section called **"Confusion In Language"** has the inherent mystique of the general theme and goes from poetry posturing in tweeds and 57th Street semantics to whimsy, irony, and self-accusation at the services Shapiro rendered before he became the elder statesman. *Obscurantism* is the agile culprit everywhere, alternating with sociology, naturalism, economics, psychoanalysis, and special pleading. The *personal*, even when dedicated to Democracy as in Whitman, is not particularized enough into art; it remains so much bric-a-brac in somebody's linen closet. . . . It is poetry of the mind and not of the heart which Shapiro opposes, but he has on occasion mixed his own biology with the political banisters.

In the final section of this didactic essay, **"The Confusion of Belief,"** all the black flags are out and the lights go green in this concert of crimes in Rime. . . . Shapiro decries the wrangling between the poets, as if there is anything American about that. One has only to recall Catullus in a better age and his

poems to Suffenus if one wants a first-rate brawl. Then too, Shapiro is his own good example, as he well shows. He even objects to competition, which is rather a tender notion in a Christian society, for if poets are not like athletes, they are at least concerned with permanence. And yet the belief of the ordinary-man (as opposed to poet-man)—even if he does not *sing*—can be just as negative after you have examined him for the full growth of his *faith*. It is at best a word with linguistic furnishings of the heart. Shapiro sees all the confusions created by the isolation from an adequate belief, though Lord knows what he favors in this smorgasbord of the sentimental, with his tidbits of Marx, Eliot, MacLeish and Christ; all of Saintsbury and Lanier; Chicago, Sydney, Milne Bay and now, the Connecticut Idyll. Problems of geography can be turned into problems of morality, or into mediums for similar diffusions. It is indeed his *personal mystery*. (pp. 139-40)

The book, nevertheless, has intense interests even though it suffers from surface conceits and values, with alleged public meanings adorning the privacy of usages. What should have been a witty text comes through in a variation of vulnerable ecstasies. The special pleading indulged in by sentimental critics has given a false atmosphere to the book, supposedly written "without sources and texts" in the Netherlands East Indies. This is rather shocking since Shapiro spent most of his New Guinea stay at Milne Bay, with enough books from the library on the hill, near Waga, to fill up a hundred fox-holes. Before a myth grows about this *daring* bit of scholarship without texts (none was needed and it reads like that) it had best be laid to rest. (p. 140)

> *Harry Roskolenko, in a review of "Essay on Rime,"*
> *in* Accent, *Vol. 6, No. 2, Winter, 1946, pp. 139-40.*

DUDLEY FITTS

I happened to read several reviews of Mr. Shapiro's *Essay on Rime* before I was able to get at the book itself. These criticisms ranged in approval all the way from Conrad Aiken's, which placed Mr. Shapiro at the head of his generation, to Harry Roskolenko's [see excerpt above], which brushed him aside with scant courtesy indeed. Somewhere between them was William Carlos Williams, who, in a singularly incoherent article, seemed to come to the conclusion "Shapiro Is All Right." And now, as I reread these reviews in the light of the poem, I can understand Mr. Aiken's enthusiasm, for the book is courageous and alive; and I can sympathize with Mr. Roskolenko's annoyance, for it is seriously marred by misinformation, special pleading, and facile judgments. Dr. Williams's perch is swaying too frantically for me to roost with him there, but somewhere near him is where I take my stand: Mr. Shapiro is just about All Right, let the damns faint where they may.

He is All Right in the first place because he honestly and modestly believes in the rôle of poetry as poetry, not as philosophy or theology or political economy or psychotherapeutics. The best statement of this occurs at the beginning of the last section, in a discussion of the suicide of Hart Crane; but it pervades the book—it is, indeed, the subject of the book, for the basic error is that of "The artist who interprets all sensation, / All activity, all experience, all / Belief through art." In the second place, he is aware of various disturbing tensions in contemporary poetry which he calls Confusions—in Prosody, in Language, in Belief—and he sets himself the task of examining their causes and indicating a remedy. Finally, he has had the courage to choose as a medium what surely must be the flattest, palest verse form ever handled by a poet of repute (the Wordsworth of *We Are Seven* is pyrotechnical by comparison) and has managed it in so unaffected, unselfconscious a way that it is actually compelling. To such all-rightness much must be forgiven, and I have no wish to dwell on the *minutiae* of error and prejudice which so exercise Mr. Roskolenko and which make even Mr. Aiken shake his head. My concern is rather to discover why it is that a treatise which looks so right, which says so many good things and says them so well, carries so little conviction; for the *Essay* leaves me, if not cold, at least chilly in the conviction that something is far from being all right.

My doubts began early. What bothered me was an uneasy feeling, which rereading has only reinforced, that in spite of considerable particularity, in spite of a great deal of the *apparatus* of argument, substantially very little was getting said. I do not mean that there are not names and facts and places. They are here in over-abundance. Nor do I mean that Mr. Shapiro is clumsy or inept with his material—on the contrary, he is a clever (a perhaps too clever) showman. The trouble seems to be that whenever the poem gathers itself together, winds itself up to deliver a telling point, the telling point turns out to be a commonplace. It is for all the world like a debate in which everybody is agreed at the outset. (pp. 39-41)

A fair example is the discussion, in Part I, of the difference between strictly metrical verse and verse moving in the direction of free cadence, "counterpoint." *The Rape of the Lock* is unexceptionably instanced as being typical of the first, and "every rapturous air / That rose from Shakespeare's heart," somewhat less accurately, of the second. A marginal gloss shows us that we are at the core of "confusion in English prosody"; but if all that Mr. Shapiro means is that some poetry scans and some does not, I can not share his alarm. *Nascitur ridiculus mus.* "Nor is it accurate to charge the great / with misconstruing metric," he says. But no such misconstruing has been suggested: indeed, he goes on to observe that "true poets" are not given to the metrical analysis of their own work; and to this he adds the unexpected misinformation, "as a fact of weight," that there has been no "large work" of prosody "in five hundred years of noble rime," and that the study of metric dates only from the middle of the last century. All of which adds up to a shakily documented refutation of a non-existent charge. (p. 41)

Real as these difficulties are . . . , they do not alter the fact of the *Essay*'s many triumphs. The rewards are to be found in the detail, in the passing comment, rather than in the thesis itself. One who wants the best of Mr. Shapiro as a critic should turn to the discussion of *Ulysses;* to the acute analysis of Auden's style; to the weighing of the significance of Crane's suicide; or to the less solid but still illuminating account of the Marxists and Freudians, though the discussion of the latter thins out into a singularly infelicitous carping at Freud himself and ends with an anticlimactic bump:

> I think
> The apogee of this corrupt technique
> Has found its place in Hollywood, the scene
> Of many cultural horrors of our time.

(O daring conjecture!) It is in passages like these, which are definitely touristic, that the poem comes nearest to justifying its title. (p. 43)

Dudley Fitts, "Mr. Shapiro's Ars Poetica," in Poetry, Vol. LXVIII, No. 1, April, 1946, pp. 39-44.

ALEXANDER COLEMAN

Karl Shapiro stated in his other collection, *In Defense of Ignorance,* that "the present essays are intended to be the last criticism I shall ever write." Inconsistency can have its virtues, but he is back again in 1968 with *To Abolish Children,* which in spite of a few fine things (**"The Death of Randall Jarrell," "To Revive Anarchism"**), shows him to be more adept at shock tactics than at rational critical discourse. . . .

Do we really need to be told that "the average graduate student who works a little at it can write a poem as well as Yeats," that there is no "poetry of sensibility" in America (this in an essay which omits mention of Anne Sexton, Robert Lowell, Elizabeth Bishop and W. D. Snodgrass), that "I have nothing to say about Dante. I can't read Italian, and in English he is pure nonsense," that Robert Frost can write rings around John Donne." Really, who needs it?

Alexander Coleman, in a review of "To Abolish Children," in The New York Times Book Review, August 18, 1968, p. 31.

JOHN P. SISK

The simplest way to indicate to Karl Shapiro's public that it will feel at home in his new book [*To Abolish Children*] is to list its heroes and villains. The heroes are Henry Miller, Whitman, William Carlos Williams, De Sade, D. H. Lawrence, Picasso, Rimbaud, Wilhelm Reich, Mailer and (with reservations) Pound and Auden. The villains are Eliot, Tate, Valéry, Yeats, Baudelaire, Wallace Stevens, Shakespeare, Plato and Vergil.

To see how this potential melodrama gets fleshed out and nuanced one might begin with the last and longest piece, which is about the fourteen hundred books in the Poet's library. Here the range is from Aristotle, "the opposite of a poet," to Yeats, in whom "is summed up all the phoniness of the art of poetry." This exercise in "alphabetical criticism" has great unity of theme and tone despite its appearance of being a free-wheeling ramble. It is witty, high-spirited and knowledgeable; the prose is excellent; the appreciation of literature turns out to be a good deal more catholic than one might expect given Shapiro's theories. . . .

Shapiro's lines go back through Whitman to Emerson, particularly to the *American Scholar* essay with its declaration of literary independence from England and from all previous culture. This is especially clear in **"Is Poetry an American Art?"** and **"The Decolonization of American Literature"**: English Literature is a dead literature in America; all things English are foreign; our literature is engaging in a Socratic dialogue with all previous values. To put it in Emerson's words, we have listened too long to the courtly muses of Europe.

Shapiro shares with Emerson the overriding conviction that the past is not a school but a prison in which the masterworks of tradition are the wardens. . . . The only salvation . . . comes from the anti-poet who by writing Bad poetry (that is, authentic poetry) subverts the establishments. Bad poetry will continue to move towards prose and will avoid the official language of poetry (Shapiro has a line to Wordsworth also). The Bad poet will be a poet of situation rather than language; obscenity may be his best means of attack; he will yearn to break out of poetry altogether; culture will not trick him into immorality and permanence; if he is fortunate he will be buried not in Westminster

Abbey but in Potter's Field. Above all, he will not, like Eliot, turn into a Government Poet.

Eliot finally let up on Milton but Shapiro will not let up on Eliot. This is understandable given Shapiro's anarchistic acceptance of change and diversity, his suspicions of establishments and institutions (including his own well-established tradition of dissent), and his rejection of all orientations that assume that value comes from anywhere but the individual. (p. 32)

[Nothing] in *To Abolish Children* more clearly marks it as a book of the sixties than its tendency to overkill. . . . The first and title essay, ["**To Abolish Children**"], much of which would be endorsed by such establishment overkillers as Max Rafferty and Malcolm Muggeridge, opens on a note of overkill: "Hardly a leader, whether president, general, public relations man, professor, publisher, or poet can be held to be honorable in his intentions." (pp. 32-3)

Overkilling, God knows, has always been a thoroughly American pastime that is no more apparent in Vietnam than in the chase scenes in silent movies, in the tall tales of the old Southwest or in Wilt Chamberlain's dunk shot. I sense Shapiro's awareness of this fact in a remark about H. L. Mencken: "What really kept him going was a kind of good-natured anger, frequently fake. He burlesqued every aspect of democracy without ever pausing to consider the alternatives."

Shapiro's own anger is not fake, but like Mencken he often fails sufficiently to consider the alternatives. Perhaps he dare not, for to consider alternatives too closely is to risk becoming a captive of the irony-constipated world he abhors. But other risks remain: for instance, the risk of the square world's self-protective practice of identifying overkilling criticism of itself as humor and enjoying it immensely. Shapiro at his best deserves a better fate than this. (p. 33)

> *John P. Sisk, in a review of "To Abolish Children," in* Commonweal, *Vol. LXXXIX, No. 1, October 4, 1968, pp. 32-3.*

PAUL FUSSELL, JR.

Shapiro has been enacting the role of the not terribly bright village reformer ever since 1945, when, in *Essay on Rime*, he called for "a plainer art." What he wants is a turning from received and thus discredited English and European techniques of focus in favor of honest encounters with the stuff of local experience, which I'm afraid he takes to be uncomplicated. His masters in this enterprise have been Whitman and W. C. Williams, but he has served neither very well, lacking the sensitivity to idiom of the one and the talent for a rude and consistent honesty of the other.

The title piece of *To Abolish Children* is a reactionary put-down of the youth revolution that might perplex but certainly would not offend George Wallace. The quality of both the thinking—warmed-over early Fiedler—and the expression can be gauged from this: "The American adult must battle 'youth' to the death. 'Youth' is a figment of the American imagination which is destroying America itself." *To the death* is pure Shapiro; so is *a figment of the imagination*. Indeed, the main reason Shapiro's Philistine and square-primitivist guise fits him so snugly, the reason he has worn it so comfortably and so long, is that he possesses by nature none of the taste and tact of the literary dandies he has set himself to despise. In *To Abolish Children*, although he is presuming to discourse about poetry

and its relation to public reality, he addresses us sometimes in the idiom of a Pentagon press conference, sometimes that of a small-town PTA meeting, and sometimes that of General Jack Ripper cautioning us against the indiscriminate expenditure of our bodily fluids. We find babu grammatical effects of the sort committed by the nervous genteel: "All the poets sat on the edge of their seats while Jarrell, whom everybody had to admit had earned the right to do so, put together the jigsaw puzzle of modern poetry before our eyes." Throughout are offered a prose texture which innocently achieves a realization of *lumpen-Amerika* itself.

Shapiro manages to install even Randall Jarrell within this world of cliché: we are told quite seriously that he "faced the music of the American Way of Life." Likewise Baudelaire becomes "the alpha and omega of modern poetry," Eliot "hits the nail on the head," and Frost manifests a "disinterest in ideologies." Sometimes a more hep idiom takes over, as when Whitman is described, in the language of the martini suburbs, as "bright-eyed and bushy-tailed." Then the voice will shift to that of the rewrite man on the local weekly, and we hear of "members of the third sex," "the garrison state," and "the world today," or we are informed that "Ours is one of the greatest periods of art in history." We are forced to apply to Shapiro what he says of Hart Crane: "He would have liked to be illiterate but he was only uneducated. He was . . . cursed with a touch of the poison of culture, wanting to be cured and wanting another bite."

The sad thing is that Shapiro's simplistic program for writing commits him—"lock, stock, and barrel," as he would say, and does—to this kind of language and to its shabby simulacrum of actual thought and feeling. Even if his talents were such that he could aspire to accurate exposition, it is logically a part of his program not to write well because the enemy is, as he tells us, "literature." Those who write well are exactly those "stylists," snobs and phonies who populate "the Serious World," and Shapiro's miserable prose assumes the function of distinguishing himself from them.

In their substance, Shapiro's essays against "literature" and "the Literati"—he actually uses that word—are the counterpart of those embarrassing ads for "Conjecturism" in *The New York Times Book Review*, ads suggesting that the common reader is being had by sissy New York critics who design nothing but his humiliation and bondage. Shapiro's implicit appeals to untutored American manliness are similar, as are his suggestions that "art" and "criticism" are largely rackets practiced upon the sturdy autodidacts of the Middle West by the swarming quacks and fairies of the East. (pp. 141-43)

The side of Shapiro that is most likable he shows us in the best piece in *To Abolish Children*, a rambling, readable anti-essay titled "*A Malebolge of Fourteen Hundred Books*." Here he talks about his favorite books in his library, considering them not according to any *a priori* system of groupings familiar in critical practice, but alphabetically, as they stand on the shelves. Here we see him not thinking or formulating, which he does badly, but recalling, embracing and sentimentalizing, which he does convincingly once he escapes from some aristocratic literary form with which he is uneasily quarreling. Honesty and humanity are in this piece, and a relative freedom from his usual embarrassment in talking about "literature." This "*Malebolge*"—odious word—is to the bulk of his criticism what the energetic prose poems of *The Bourgeois Poet* are to his poetry. It is a successful realization of his urge to freedom from imported, un-American forms.

But despite occasional successes like these, Shapiro's career has largely a monitory value. He has dissipated his forces in that old sentimental-egalitarian American game of trying to create art while denying its validity and privileges. He is not comfortable with what he is making: its claims to special status embarrass him. He ends in that same nervous, apologetic relation to what he has made that has embarrassed and perverted countless American writers, including Whitman, Twain and Hemingway. It is ultimately the American terror of participating in a remote and perhaps useless kind of excellence, as well as the fear of being ridiculed at the barbershop as separate and pansy, that has done him in. (pp. 144-45)

> Paul Fussell, Jr., "The Bourgeois Poet," in Partisan Review, Vol. XXXVI, No. 1, Winter, 1969, pp. 141-45.

LAURENCE LIEBERMAN

The longest section of Karl Shapiro's new book of essays [*To Abolish Children*]—over a hundred pages—is a free-wheeling discussion of scores of his favorite books, alphabetically arranged. "When I read criticism I want to meet the author", Shapiro says, and his **"Malebolge of Fourteen Hundred Books"** is conceived as both an intellectual autobiography and a personality profile, modelled, as he tells us, after Henry Miller's *The Books in My Life*. Many authors are named without comment, some are discussed reverently for several pages (Baudelaire, Lawrence, Whitman, Williams, Henry Miller), others are ransacked and plundered, then discarded when they cease to implement Shapiro's poetic theorizing: "It is the excitement of the process of starting over that thrills me." If a good many of the eminent literati are ingested and as swiftly regurgitated like so much nondescript fodder for Shapiro's bellying thought, I, for one, find the **"Malebolge"** to be thoroughly entertaining, as well as enlightening in a number of ways.

As in the prose-poems of *The Bourgeois Poet*, Shapiro is continuing to "kick over the traces" between poetry and prose in this work. Ironically, his earliest celebrated critical work, *An Essay On Rime*, though written in verse, more closely resembled traditional poetry criticism in its content and formal logic than any of the criticism he has written subsequently in prose. With each successive critical work, he has advanced another step in the genesis of what he calls "anti-criticism criticism", acknowledging a large debt to Jarrell as the major forerunner in this mode. Both in his poetry and his prose, Shapiro's principle of form, or anti-form, is "the relevancy of the accidental", since he believes with Malraux that "the fragment is king". Most of the essays in this volume—particularly the extensive **"Malebolge"**—are successful experiments in a viable and richly flowering tradition ranging from Virginia Woolf's *Common Readers* to Lawrence's *Classical Studies in American Literature* and Williams's *In The American Grain:* the conquest of the personal familiar essay—importing the authority of intuitive impulse from poetry or fiction—over a formal, didactic, impersonal criticism. (p. 348)

> Laurence Lieberman, "Poet-Critics and Scholar-Critics," in Poetry, Vol. CXV, February, 1970, pp. 346-52.

LEO CONNELLAN

Whereas most poets achieve, shine, and then fade, Karl Shapiro is writing better than ever and still ahead of him, obviously,

are his best poems, though no one writing poems in America can beat what Karl Shapiro has already written.

A wonderful gentleman, Mr. Stuart Wright, is insuring that we all have Karl Shapiro's wonderful poems, by publishing [*Love & War, Art & God,* a collection of] new poems and the poems we all know are among the best poems ever written.

Sadly, though, the great Karl Shapiro poem **"Nigger"** with some of the best sound and music in our language is not in this collection. Long before the Martin Luthur King victory, this poem screamed at the lynch mentality and ruthless prejudice still only too very frighteningly real and very much with us.

However, there's **"Auto Wreck"** and **"V-Letter"** is *the* love poem we all yearn and imagine but cannot write. There's marvelous **"Adam and Eve"**, too, containing one of the very best images of Eve. . . .

> we turned and saw
> a body swollen as though formed of fruits.

In Karl Shapiro's poetry there is a timelessness and grace, energy of the earth. No poet better comprehends the academic, proves it time and time again and then shuns it to write for us about the every day things of our lives, **"Buick"** or **"Girls Fighting Broadway"**:

> two girls one blond one latin with fixed hair
> in summer dresses hug each other
> in a shallow doorway shove each other
>
> as if playfully on streaming Broadway
> in heavy August it looks like kissing
> to a passerby or some kind of come-on . . .

No American poet has stood by principle and ignored the heavy personal cost for doing this, than has Karl Shapiro, who, just in case the truth is that no "whacked out mind turned on itself," fought "Pontius Pilate's ever being rewarded." . . .

Poets owe Karl Shapiro, first, for creating a sound and music in language that no other poet has surpassed . . . and poets owe Karl Shapiro, many poets first got their work in a textbook anthology because Karl Shapiro put it in for them.

> Leo Connellan, in a review of "Love & War, Art & God," in The Small Press Review, Vol. 17, No. 2, February, 1985, p. 12.

RICHARD TILLINGHAST

Karl Shapiro's name and something of his career as a poet are known to most readers. Now in his early 70's he is the author of more than a dozen books of poetry and criticism including *In Defense of Ignorance, Poems of a Jew* and *The Bourgeois Poet*. Many of his works are controversial, because Mr. Shapiro has always tried to challenge his readers. . . . [It] is fair to say that for most readers he has become more a name than a presence. This lapse should be corrected with Mr. Shapiro's fine selection of his poetry, *Love & War / Art & God*.

His narrative poems based on biblical themes, such as **"Adam and Eve"** and **"Bath-sheba,"** strive too hard for a solemn, elevated tone. Their iambic pentameter is constrictingly unvaried. Mr. Shapiro comes into his own when he launches into American themes in a freer style. Cadillacs, Buicks, New York streets, academic office buildings, poetry readings, drugstores, love in offices and cold-water flats—all these fuel his exuberant, often satirical imagination. He relaxes and has fun in free verse. His fancy soars in prose poems with sentences like these: "From the tropical tree and the Rothko in the Board Room to the ungrammatical broom closet fragrant with waxes, to the vast typing pool where coffee is being served by dainty waitresses maneuvering their hand trucks, music almost unnoticeable falls. The very telephones are hard and kissable." In his bittersweet celebrations of American life, Mr. Shapiro is a son of Walt Whitman, a Charles Ives or Aaron Copland in verse (but with more humor). . . .

I am glad to see much of his early work available again, because in the poetry he wrote during the 40's there is a freshness that represents the best of experimental Modernism. Poetry in 1985, by contrast, reminds me of the Democratic Party in 1985; so segmented by loyalties of region, gender, ethnic group and style of life that the constituency, or potential constituency, is ignored. Mr. Shapiro needles poetry-as-lifestyle: "Established poets are forced to wear beards and bluejeans; they are treated kindly in bohemian zoos; mysterious stipends drift their way. They can trade soap for peyote at specified libraries." His approach to poetry, as seen in the preface to *Poems of a Jew,* is more edifying: "These poems are not for poets. They are for people who derive some strength of meaning from the writings of poets & who seek in the poet's mind some clue to their own thoughts."

> *Richard Tillinghast, "From Comedy to Simile," in* The New York Times Book Review, *March 31, 1985, p. 14.*

DAVID WOJAHN

Of all the poets of the generation of Lowell, Bishop, and Roethke, Karl Shapiro has become the most undervalued. This statement may come as a surprise to readers who remember the acclaim that greeted Shapiro's work in the Forties and early Fifties, but it seems clear that the generations of poets who have developed since then are unconcerned about or unaware of Shapiro's achievement. . . . Much of the neglect that Shapiro has suffered can be blamed on the poet himself: he has made only passing acknowledgement to the changes in poetic fashion, and the glib, dyspeptic stance of his best poems and criticism is something many readers do not have a tests for. Furthermore, Shapiro is a writer who peaked early. His best poems were written during the first decade or so of his career, and, with the exception of the strange and vitriolic prose poems gathered in *The Bourgeois Poet,* little of the work he has published in the last three decades has been of great consequence. *Love & War, Art & God* contains a large proportion of these less successful recent poems, but it is nonetheless a valuable collection, and perhaps it will win Shapiro a new following.

Like so many of the poets who made debuts in the years before World War II, Shapiro co-opted some of Yeats's music, as well as the social criticism of the early Auden. But while Auden could cloak his outrage in a gentlemanly British reserve, Shapiro spat his out with a classically American outlandishness. Like the small group of poets who have been influenced by his work—Louis Simpson and Alan Dugan immediately come to mind—Shapiro is a chronicler of the "American Scene," and he doesn't much like what he sees. **"University,"** one of Shapiro's earliest poems, remains one of the most acute studies of our national hypocrisy, and we can see this even in its opening lines.

> To hurt the Negro and avoid the Jew
> Is the curriculum. In mid-September
> The entering boys, identified by hats,

> Wander in a maze of mannered brick
> Where boxwood and magnolia brood
> And columns with imperious stance
> Like rows of ante-bellum girls
> Eye them, outlanders.

From the very beginning, Shapiro identified himself as an iconoclast, and his outsider's role extended beyond his attacks on social injustice. At a time before it was fashionable to do so, he proudly proclaimed his Jewishness and set himself against the main trends of Modernism. (His essays on Pound and Eliot are garish hatchet jobs.) Yet, for all his stridency, Shapiro could be a wonderfully tender poet. We don't see this side of him in his love poems, which veer toward the sentimental, but it does materialize in empathic portraits like **"The Leg"** and **"The Figurehead,"** as well as in the poems that focus on Shapiro's experience in the military during World War II. (pp. 167-68)

Why Shapiro has failed to fulfll his early promise is perplexing. Perhaps his refusal to participate fully in any of the trends of postwar American poetry has been a liability for him as much as it has been a source of his integrity. What looks like Shapiro's independent stance may in fact be a kind of vacillation. He has sampled styles but never adopted them. He has dabbled in the open forms and thematic frankness that have been the norm in American poetry since the advent of the confessional writers, but he has done so with a certain discomfort. Though his best poems are written in traditional meters, his wild cynicism has nevertheless seemed poorly suited to traditional prosody. Shapiro found his voice very early in his career, but he never found a style. While his persona is always lively, his writing is uneven. This problem is made more obvious than it might otherwise be in *Love & War, Art & God,* for Shapiro has chosen to arrange his poems thematically. He devotes a section of the book to each of its title's abstractions, and, without a chronological arrangement, Shapiro's jumble of manners looks all the more glaring. . . . Shapiro's 1968 *Selected Poems* is a far better showcase of his achievement, and there's enough impressive writing in *Love & War, Art & God* to make an interested reader go back to the earlier collections. Shapiro has been a prolific writer, and there is much for readers to savor besides this new book. (pp. 168-69)

> *David Wojahn, in a review of "Love & War, Art & God," in* Poetry, *Vol. CXLVI, No. 3, June, 1985, pp. 167-69.*

KARL SHAPIRO [INTERVIEW WITH ROBERT PHILLIPS]

[Phillips]: *You were in the army, during World War II, when your first two books of poems,* **Person, Place and Thing** *and* **V-Letter and Other Poems** *came out in this country. When you returned from the War, were you aware of having become the literary spokesman of your generation?*

Shapiro: Words like "spokesman" and "touchstone" took me completely by surprise. For very real reasons. Not only had I been out of the country when my first two books were published, but I have always been "out of the country" in the sense that I never had what ordinarily is thought of as a literary life, or been part of a literary group. What psychiatrists nowadays call a support system. I never had any of that and still don't. I've never been magnetized toward a center like New York. I never even thought of living in New York. When I first started to publish single poems, the place I thought of was Chicago, since *Poetry* magazine was there. And you didn't have to live in Chicago to have something printed by them. I thought *Poetry* was preferable to any magazine that I knew of in New York except perhaps *Partisan Review,* and that was relatively new and wasn't specifically poetry anyway. So when I was in the army in New Guinea and finally got the reviews that people sent of my first book, they were all very heady to me. Using words like "spokesman." I was baffled. I wasn't sure what the reviewers were talking about, because I had no associations with anybody. I had never met a poet in my life before winning the Pulitzer in 1945. Well, that's not strictly true; when I went to Johns Hopkins in 1939, W. H. Auden gave a private reading to a group of special literature students, and I was one. I shook hands with him. As it happened, at that time he was my idol, above all others as a modern poet, and that experience was a very sustaining one. But I could hardly say I "knew" him. (pp. 184-85)

What were the physical circumstances of your writing during the war? Did you have much time off?

I was drafted a year before the war, when it was a one-year peacetime draft that people have forgotten about now. And I was in almost a year when Pearl Harbor happened, so I couldn't get out. But because I was from Baltimore, I was sent to the Medical Corps—all of us who were drafted from Baltimore that first day were sent to the Medical Corps. I guess they knew the war was coming and were trying to build it up. A lot of us were orderlies from hospitals but many were clerks, stenographers and so on. I was studying in a library school at the time, I was going to be a librarian. But I couldn't take the final exam because I was drafted. Nobody had ever heard of a student deferment in those days. Because of my background of two years of college at Johns Hopkins, they put me in the company headquarters office and gave me a typewriter. (pp. 186-87)

But what about the availability of a library? You also wrote **Essay on Rime** *when you were stationed in the South Pacific area. It's full of quotes from Eliot, Auden, Yeats, Cummings, Crane . . .*

There weren't that many quotes. Besides, I had a book. I'd met William Van O'Connor [later a literary critic] in New Guinea and we became friends right away. He was stationed at Fort Morely and so was I. We were waiting to go someplace else and Bill gave me his copy of the *Oxford Book of Modern Verse,* which Yeats had edited. I had that book and I had quotes in my head and there was always a Bible. And that was about it. I later heard there was an army library nearby, but if there was I had never heard of it. Anyway, I wrote *Essay on Rime* to amuse myself. We had been told that we were going to be in one spot for ninety days with nothing to do. So we were just sitting there waiting to be shipped to the Dutch East Indies. Well, I had the office and the typewriter and the paper, so I blocked out a poem. I figured I wanted to write a poem about poetry, an essay like Pope's. And I actually diagrammed it— I had never done that before in my life. But I diagrammed how many sections there would be, how many lines per section, how much on prosody and how much on language, and so on. I figured precisely how many lines I would write a day to get the book done in ninety days, and I did it. It was thirty lines a day, and I went to the office every day and wrote those thirty lines. I had no reports to write. The office was deserted.

It's a prodigious feat.

Well, yes, but you see, I had it all in my head—I had read everything on prosody before I was drafted. Don't forget I'd

been working in a big library and I knew a lot about prosody. Nobody ever read prosody books except me. And the rest of the stuff in the poem was simply my ideas about Auden and Williams and the rest. (pp. 187-88)

*Some of your later poems—"**The Phenomenon**" and "**In the Waxworks**"—seem concerned with nightmares, whereas your earlier work is very rational, almost idealistic. Are you aware of undergoing any personality changes that could account for that?*

I'm not aware of any changes in personality or outlook. "**The Phenomenon**" might be called a war poem, too. I was very surprised when *The New Yorker* accepted it. The other one was about the honky tonk in Baltimore, where the low bars and cheap hotels and burlesque houses are. I was writing about the unconscious part of a civilized city. Of all the stuff that drifts to the bottom. (p. 190)

In 1964, when you published **The Bourgeois Poet,** *you made a clean break—not only with the poems of your past, but it seemed with all European art before the Renaissance. When did you recognize the futility of the well-made formal poem? And did you have a model—Ginsberg?*

Certainly not Ginsberg! Influence is strange. Because one can be influenced powerfully in every way but technique. For instance, I would think Walt Whitman probably had more influence on my whole poetic thinking than anybody, but I never dreamed of trying to write in the Whitman manner. My precedent for the style of *The Bourgeois Poet* is French poetry. When I shipped out overseas, from Boston to Australia, it took forty days. I carried a baggage sack full of books, which is an awful thing to do because I had to carry them. There were no porters for a private or corporal. Among the books I took was Baudelaire's *Flowers of Evil* in a bilingual edition. I also had a French dictionary and did some translations of my own on the ship. I think it was then and there I fastened on the manner of *The Bourgeois Poet* poems. When I got to Australia, I published a privately-printed book in which my first poems appeared. They're in that style. In fact, I still keep two of those poems in my latest collected poems: "**The Dirty Word**" and "**The New Ring**." I liked writing in that style very much, but at the time it seemed a dead end. It wasn't until the early sixties that I returned to the model and did more.

Was **The Bourgeois Poet** *conceived and written as a book, or as individual poems that somehow came together?*

No, no, as a book. I had a Guggenheim, to go to Europe, and I wanted to write a kind of autobiography in verse. But I didn't know exactly how to do it. . . . I was trying to write about becoming a poet, using some of those letters as a basis. I found I could not write in Italy. I've since discovered that I can't write when I'm traveling. Later trips to Rome, London, all ended the same way. I love Europe, but whenever I go there, I feel I'm catching a disease. So I cut that trip short and came home. I lived in Nebraska then and I had a study built in my garage. When it was done, I sat down and wrote *The Bourgeois Poet* poems straight off. I wrote one every day. There were ninety-four in the book, some quite long.

Did you complete more than the ninety-four?

God yes. I had quite a lot I wanted to say then—either about the past or the present or from the point of view of a middle-class American poet, Jewish, and living in the middle of the United States and having come through certain things. (pp. 195-97)

You wrote in that book that you are of the race to whom "the audience brings me news of my death." Have you been conscious of trying to overcome a critical decline, or to live up to your early reputation?

Well, no. When I wrote that I was, you know, very well received. I think I took that expression from Freud. Certain people were wrecked by success, like Dylan Thomas and Delmore Schwartz. I've continued. In fact, I'm not so sure when I used that phrase, in that context, that I meant the race of Jews and not the race of poets.

Oh. I took it to mean poets.

Good. Because I always had this feeling—I've heard other Jews say—that when you can't find any other explanation for Jews, you say, "Well, they are poets." There are a great many similarities. This is a theme running all through my stuff from the very beginning. The poet is in exile whether he is or he is not. Because of what everybody knows about society's idea of the artist as a peripheral character and a potential bum. Or troublemaker. Well, the Jews began their career of troublemaking by inventing the God whom Wallace Stevens considers the ultimate poetic idea. And so I always thought of myself as being both in and out of society at the same time. Like the way most artists probably feel in order to survive—you have to at least pretend that you are "seriously" in the world. Or actually perform in it while you know that in your own soul you are not in it at all. You are outside observing it. You must know exactly what I mean.

I do. What does it mean to you to be a Jew? Christ is certainly one of your myths. What has being Jewish done to your work?

Just everything, in a way. I went through a period like many middle-class Jews in which I consciously drew away from the religion and everything Jewish in my life. And I think for a long time, say in the 1930s, I felt completely cured of the religious virus. And of course at that time, everybody was enveloped in radical politics and nobody really took religion seriously. Even among poets—except Eliot. During the war I became more interested in Christianity. . . . When I came back from the war, I returned to my original position of neutrality. I didn't think about religion and I didn't care. I felt I didn't have any personal stake in that kind of thinking. I had by then become known as a poet and was given very good jobs— teaching in universities, Consultant in Poetry at the Library of Congress. I considered myself above religion.

This doesn't sound like the author of **Poems of a Jew** *speaking.*

The actual turning point in my life was the voting of the Bollingen Prize to Ezra Pound. This sounds real crackpot, but it is true! I was one of the people on that jury, and I was the only one who voted against giving the prize to Pound. There was an enormous amount of publicity about it. It was a great blow to me, the publicity and scandal. I was suddenly forced into a conscious decision to stand up and be counted as a Jew. Jewish organizations got in touch with me, Jewish papers wanted me to write things for them, make me a spokesman. (pp. 197-99)

Let's return to **The Bourgeois Poet** *one last time. That was your first and last thematic book of poems?*

That was the only one of its kind, and I knew when I had come to the end of it too. Actually, there is a plot in that book. It has to do with a female graduate student I was involved with. (p. 202)

A lot of it is the sort of old-fashioned free verse of the King James Bible. It was an unconscious imitation of the Old Testament declamatory poetry. But that is a step backwards from the straight prose style in terms of versification. What I was sure of at the time was that the two traditional attributes of poetry—rhyme and versification—were not only nonessential, but artificial impediments to the poetic process.

But in your next book after that, **White-Haired Lover,** *you returned to traditional verse forms.*

I did and I didn't. Most of them are in conventional forms like a sonnet, but they're not what anyone would call good sonnet form. The meters are too bumpy. And there's no intent to conform to, say, the iambic pattern. There's no inversion in the second foot and that kind of thing. I didn't pay attention to that. In fact, I was doing what Eliot succeeded in doing when he discovered his own kind of iambic and free verse, which he called Websterian. Whether or not Webster was just a bad versifier, or trying to make the line conform to whatever speech was in his time, I don't know. But Eliot succeeded in adapting Webster to get a line which both is and is not iambic. And so, in other words, is loose. (pp. 202-03)

Was writing your novel a different process from writing poems?

Completely. It had nothing to do with poetry and I—never having written fiction, just one short story—didn't have any inhibitions. I wrote *Edsel* so fast, I wrote parts of it sitting on a beach with a portable typewriter in Tampa, Florida. . . .

It's a very inventive novel, very unpredictable. The reader can't guess where he's going next.

That's because I didn't know. It was written that fast. I once read that E. M. Forster said, when interviewed about *A Passage to India,* that he knew when those people got into the cave, something terrible was going to happen. He just didn't know what. I felt the same way about *Edsel.* The fascination, you know. It was a marvelous experience for me—I had something I wanted to say, and I think I said it. (p. 210)

In the novel you say the hardest thing for a poet is to separate his actual feelings from his poetic feelings. Is there that distinction?

There is. I might have had in mind Eliot's statement about aesthetic distance and personal emotion. It's a question of judgement and taste. Suppose I liked Kate Smith and Bing Crosby. At the same time, I'd feel disgusted with myself for liking them. You see? (p. 211)

Edsel described his poems as all jagged glass and rusty nails. Is that how you viewed your own poems at the time?

Some. That's how I viewed American poetry generally. You know Louis Simpson's poem on the subject: "Whatever it is, it must have / A stomach that can digest / Rubber, coal, uranium, moons, poems . . ." (p. 212)

What are you working on now?

For about two years, I've been writing this autobiography of sorts. It's funny how I began the book. My brother, Irvin, who was a child prodigy, asked me on the telephone, "Karl, how did you become a poet?" And I didn't know the answer. So I started trying to find the answer in this book. The first thing I wrote about was meeting a professor in a railroad station, trying to get a scholarship to the university after I'd already dropped out of school. So you can see, the thing has no chronology. It's not thematic. It may even be a new form. I'm doing something which I think is interesting. I didn't want to name people, let alone drop names—I didn't even want to name myself. So I talk about myself in the third person, as The Poet, which I think of as the fourth person, because it's the poet standing outside himself looking at all these other people, which include him. I'm getting somewhere. I've got enough material now to know that I have the making of the creation of a character—the self-creation of a character who becomes a poet and discovers his identity that way. I've read parts of it to audiences and they really like it. Because it's like conversation. It's not like writing. (p. 213)

Do you have a sense of a public for your own work, for whom you write poems?

I'm surprised from time to time when I find evidence that people have learned something from me, or when people tell me they have. I've always tried to achieve a certain tone of voice, which I think I now have under control. It's not simply a question of locution and syntax, it's a question of hearing the tones in which people communicate with each other on various levels. And that generally involves idiom—if idiom is a synonym for a rich, spontaneous kind of language. Randall Jarrell was extremely good at this, although if you try to write like Jarrell, you're only imitating him. And Delmore Schwartz, as in his poem, "The Beautiful American Word, Sure." (p. 215)

The last question: Why do you write?

I don't know why, but it's a compulsion. I feel that after working a long time, I've really learned how to do what I do. I enjoy it. I don't think there's anything more satisfying than turning out a good stanza or a good piece of prose. And when you're satisfied enough, you want to show it to other people. That's called publication. (p. 216)

Robert Phillips, "The Art of Poetry XXXVI: Karl Shapiro," in The Paris Review, *Vol. 28, No. 99, Spring, 1986, pp. 183-216.*

PUBLISHERS WEEKLY

[The] wonder and the value of [Karl Shapiro's *New & Selected Poems: 1940-1986*], revised from the edition published a generation ago, are in its final but few, nearly perfect new poems. Here the poet-chronicler of World War II and postwar society in America—that polished, elegant and smooth commentator on the hypocrisies, prejudices and delusions of our common life—brings himself into our future with exact and telling descriptions of **"Vietnam Memorial," "Retirement"** and his elegy **"At Auden's Grave."** He rounds his own achievement. All the well-known Shapiro classics that precede these ultimate poems bleed their life and our history into their meaning. As for Auden's grave, Shapiro makes it into a symbol for the century—its progress, its struggles, its conscience. This is not a redundant selection of Shapiro's poems. On the contrary, it is a *completed* one, full of compassion and purpose.

A review of "New & Selected Poems: 1940-1986," in Publishers Weekly, *Vol. 232, No. 9, August 28, 1987, p. 73.*

DENNIS SAMPSON

Karl Shapiro, whose second volume of verse, *V-Letter and Other Poems,* won the Pulitzer Prize in 1945, has pretty much remained outside the arena of popular poetry for two decades. His recent retrospective, [*New & Selected Poems: 1940-1986*],

includes all of his more widely anthologized pieces, **"Auto Wreck," "The Fly," "V-letter," "The Progress of Faust,"** and **"Buick,"** as well as several newer poems and work known only to those who have closely followed Shapiro's career. Shapiro has always been somewhat of an enigma to contemporary poets and critics. As a formalist, his poetry appeared out of fashion in the late sixties, despite the publication of *The Bourgeois Poet,* free-verse rantings that should have endeared him to the beat poets but didn't. Because of his refusal to recommend Ezra Pound for the Bollingen prize, he incurred the disdain of his peers: Pound's anti-Semitic poetry and his radio broadcasts during the Second World War were understandably repulsive to Shapiro, who has written as insightfully of the Jewish predicament as any poet in America and who has used his Jewishness and the subsequent alienation the Jew feels as a touchstone for nearly all his work.

Shapiro has consistently thought of himself as the outsider, "a tower of bitterness" as he says in **"Poet,"** suspicious of those who would include him in their literary circle and bitterly denouncing the ineffectual academic life, where the "Old Guard sits in judgement and wears ties, / Eyeing the New in proletarian drag, / Where the Assistant with one lowered eyelid / Plots against tenure." As a poet who will never be accepted or fully understood by the public, as a Jew, born into a world inexplicably distrustful of him, and as a man for whom God is irritatingly mysterious, Shapiro stands as the quintessential American exile. (p. 384)

Determinedly at odds with the powers-that-be, Shapiro can be delightfully acerbic at times, though his diatribes in syllabic verse can grate. At his best is the Shapiro of the love poems and the poems where the moral import of an event is conveyed with precision. **"Adam and Eve"** recounts the fall from grace of those recalcitrant lovers, in a style reminiscent of Dante—both for its lucid rendering of mythological figures and for its rhythm. (p. 385)

Of the newer poems, only a few draw directly on Shapiro as a formalist; the concision is still there, as is his wit and cynicism, but meter and rhyme have frequently been abandoned and his mocking self-effacement (Shapiro is seldom harder on anyone than himself) is tempered with humility and a kind of childlike awe. Visits to the gravesites of Hiram Ulysses Grant and W. H. Auden are the occasions for poems, intimating a desire to put aside his quarrels with the world for a while so that he may, however peripherally, come to terms with the fact of his own mortality.

As with the Arnold of "Dover Beach," the saving grace for this poet, exiled in as many ways as he seems to be, is love of man for woman. All Shapiro's love poems are beautifully conceived, testaments to his artistry and greatness of heart. In his shortest poem to date, **"The Pigeons,"** the writer sees two pigeons on the ledge far above the street, "In the denouement of the beautiful storm." Noticing their reflection in the window, he wonders about their appearance there:

> Is that why they were here
> Or were they blown by chance, these doves,
> Into a momentary conjunction
> By some maker's dream?

This collection charts the spiritual progress of a querulous and compassionate man. (pp. 385-86)

Dennis Sampson, in a review of "New & Selected Poems: 1940-1986," in The Hudson Review, *Vol. XLI, No. 2, Summer, 1988, pp. 384-86.*

Wilfrid (John Joseph) Sheed

1930-

English-born American novelist, critic, essayist, biographer, short story writer, and editor.

Sheed is respected as a witty, erudite novelist of social satire. He draws on his experiences in England and the United States to lampoon inadequate educational systems, the turpitude of the media, the problems of Roman Catholics in a secularized society, and the estrangement of individuals caught between two cultures. Critics often praise Sheed's incisive wit, forceful moral sensibility, and poignant use of British and American idioms.

Sheed's parents were writers, publishers, and religious activists. In 1926, they founded Sheed & Ward, an important progressive Roman Catholic publishing house. At the outset of World War II, the Sheed family moved from London to Torresdale, Pennsylvania. Shortly thereafter, Sheed contracted polio, which led to a more sheltered lifestyle and indirectly contributed to his interest in literature. During the early 1950s, he attended Oxford University, which provided the setting and experiences for his first novel, *A Middle-Class Education* (1960). In this work, Sheed condemns the mediocrity of British and American colleges by depicting a Rhodes Scholar who is more interested in pleasure than classroom achievements but nevertheless wins a scholarship to study at an American university. Sheed's second novel, *The Hack* (1963), details the loss of faith and mental breakdown of a writer of hackneyed inspirational stories and verse for popular Catholic magazines. This work focuses on two of Sheed's major themes: the ineffectuality of the Roman Catholic church in contemporary society and the fatuity of the communications industry. *Square's Progress* (1965) centers on a married couple who seek alternative lifestyles among bohemians and the proletariat. However, they find these options as vapid as their suburban existence.

Sheed's next novel, *Office Politics* (1966), examines the battle for power on a magazine staff after the editor retires. The pieces in *The Blacking Factory and Pennsylvania Gothic: A Short Novel and a Long Story* (1968) explore childhood and adolescence and exhibit a more serious tone than Sheed's previous fiction. *The Blacking Factory* describes the tribulations of an American adolescent in an English public school, while *Pennsylvania Gothic* centers on a twelve-year-old American boy who discovers that he has suicidal impulses after he moves with his family to a small town near Philadelphia. Sheed's next full-length novel, *Max Jamison* (1970; published in Great Britain as *The Critic*), is narrated mainly through the interior monologue of the title character, an influential theater critic whose compulsive need to analyze causes discord in his personal life and drives him to the brink of insanity. Andrew Sarris commented: "Sheed's creative feat in *Max Jamison* is to make us aware of the dangerous tightrope between art and life, career and family, mind and heart we must all walk in order to fulfill our duties and possibilities on this earth."

In *People Will Always Be Kind* (1973), Sheed investigates from a journalistic perspective the idiosyncrasies of American politics in the early 1970s. The first half of this novel chronicles the progress of Brian Casey, an athletic Irish-Catholic youth

crippled by polio, who finds his niche in campus politics. The second part, set twenty years later, relates Senator Casey's campaign for the Democratic presidential nomination from the viewpoint of his speechwriter. An idealist, Casey struggles with religious, ethical, and political realities but becomes disenchanted and eventually drops out of the race. *Transatlantic Blues* (1978) traces the encroaching schizophrenia of a television talk-show host. Schooled in England but working in the United States, the protagonist feels a part of neither country. *The Boys of Winter* (1987) satirizes the American publishing world, exposing the envy, animosity, and bitter competitiveness that exist among writers, editors, and publishers. Christopher Lehmann-Haupt observed: "With many a witty phrase and cutting apothegm, Mr. Sheed has not only dissected artistic pretension but also revealed the profound human need for masks."

Sheed's acclaimed collections of reviews and essays, *The Morning After* (1971) and *The Good Word and Other Words* (1978), display his eclectic interests in such subjects as literature, film, politics, Catholicism, sports, feminism, organized crime, and the labor movement. In *Frank and Maisie: A Memoir with Parents* (1985), Sheed intersperses autobiographical information with an account of the lives of his parents. Sheed has also published the biographies *Muhammad Ali: A Portrait in Words and Photographs* (1975), *Claire Boothe Luce* (1982), and *The Kennedy Legacy* (1988).

(See also *CLC*, Vols. 2, 4, 10; *Contemporary Authors*, Vols. 65-68; and *Dictionary of Literary Biography*, Vol. 6.)

WEBSTER SCHOTT

Brilliant right down to his punctuation, Sheed [in *The Good Word and Other Words*] has found all the current possibilities in reviewing and exploits them like a robber baron. (His detractors, I suspect, will say he has run them to the ground; but that's a different review.)

The key lies in a line Sheed throws away while explaining literary infighting. "Criticism," he says, "is a contact sport." People like Wilfrid Sheed (there are only a few of them) and the rest of us review books because it's such a self-satisfying way of making contact with the great big world outside the study window. And the world can't fight back; it's so much safer than driving a truck. The sport comes in matching the words to the thought.

Where else, except by writing book reviews or reading a collection like *The Good Word,* can you get in touch with and deliver judgment on Norman Mailer, Groucho Marx, Irish saloons, the Beat Movement, George Gershwin, Watergate, Scott Fitzgerald, suicide, Catholic atheists, Dr. Spock, pornography, the 1968 and 1972 presidential conventions, Bonnie and Clyde, the war in Vietnam, and the underlying psychology of Vince Lombardi? Not to mention the other couple of hundred writers, artists, nitwits, events and books that Sheed considers in these 52 reviews and essays. . . .

It's a splendid journey *The Good Word* takes us on through the late 1960s and early 1970s. As readers of his novels (*Transatlantic Blues, Office Politics,* etc.) know full well, Sheed is as curious and independent as a cat, and he handles the English language as if he owned it. Sheed may have thought as a boy he wanted to be a baseball player. But if he wasn't born to write, then the next most likely career would have been as a stand-up comic:

> "It cannot be emphasized too strongly that an evening with Gertrude Stein is just an evening with Gertrude Stein."

> "[E. B.] White's notes to the milkman achieve effects that others sat up all night for."

> "[Henry Luce] played with facts like a cat with a ball of wool, doing everything but digest them. His memory span was just great for a weekly newsmagazine."

But to be glib about the world outside is just window dressing for bigger visions, and Sheed's adroitness of phrase seldom distracts him from giving us his mind. It's worth having.

He writes most seriously about words, women, and sex. Book reviewing gives you opportunities far beyond charting plots if you have the necessary intellectual courage. Sheed does.

Sheed says to hell with the New Journalism as journalism. Tom Wolfe writes nonfiction in the "language of shoes and cocktail spreads and is called a fop for his pains, instead of the heartless moralist he is." "We enjoy Wolfe . . . precisely for the dis-

tortion . . . The real subject is his imagination." Sheed cares so much about our use of language because it's the code of our thought.

Sheed's **"Now That Men Can Cry . . . ,"** is the most sensitive essay I've read on the subject of women's liberation. It's about what's never mentioned in the Movement—love. . . .

As for sex, well, he sees it as it is—a matter of expression. . . . The sexual relationship is adversary and volatile, which places it at the center of fiction.

I don't like everything Wilfrid Sheed writes. He has an assertive taste for certain words: "bourgeoisification," "cineastes," and "weird." He takes cheap shots at Hemingway and probably hasn't suffered enough adultery to know what Mary was saying in *How It Was.* He uses B. F. Skinner's name like a reflex and I don't believe he has read Skinner's books.

None of which alters what Sheed the writer brings to the craft of reviewing books, or Sheed the thinker in engaging the sun each morning. He is one of our brightest reflectors. Let's urge him on in our mutual education. (p. E4)

> Webster Schott, "Criticism: A Contact Sport," in Book World—The Washington Post, *December 24, 1978, pp. E1, E4.*

JACK BEATTY

Sheed is not your usual reviewing hack. He is a novelist—a prolific and accomplished one; nine novels, two nominees for the National Book Award—at large among other people's books. His reviews are the word pictures which the books have stirred in his imagination, an uncommonly droll organ whose productions are never less than interesting, even though to captious readers and slighted authors they will not pass as book reviews. Sheed is disarmingly honest about this. The truths of his kind of reviewing, he says [in *The Good Word and Other Words*], "are the truths of fiction. The books are events that happened to me and are as open to misinterpretation as my neighbors on the Siege of Chicago in 1968. Along with one's novels, these pieces form a mosaic of someone coming of age in a certain time and place and what he made of it."

To judge by the array of first-rate pieces in this collection, Sheed has made the witty most of whatever he has reviewed, and this is certainly worth a salute. But it is also true that he has stayed with subjects some might judge minor, subjects that positively require something to be made of them. Apart from an illuminating glance at Joseph Heller's *Something Happened,* there are no really problematic modern books or authors discussed here: no Pynchon, no Marquez, no Borges, no Nabokov. In short, there are no texts by a really imperial mind—a mind Sheed would have to deal with on its own terms, not on his.

Sheed may shy away from the literary heights, but, on the strength of his novelist's warrant, he ranges compensatingly far into the great unexplored reaches of American culture. He has, for example, written a masterfully thorough and revealing guide to the labor movement and a funny debunking essay on the Mafia. In this collection he waxes wry on an astonishing variety of subjects. There are essays on Orwell, Hemingway, Wodehouse, E. B. White and W. C. Fields. There is a witty rumination on the "I was a vampire for the Chicago Bears" school of football exposé; and there is an extraordinary essay in cultural history which sets our clock for the start of the Beat Movement back 10 years, to the Columbia of Thomas Merton rather than that of Allen Ginsberg. Catholics, ethnics, Dr. Spock, Watergate, are a few of the other subjects on which Sheed has a good, and often a superb word to say. Indeed, from this motley of cultural occasions he has fashioned a book that boosts one's flagging faith in the possibility of literary criticism. For all his waywardness in handling texts, Sheed performs the Arnoldian office of sorting out our moral confusions and modulating our enthusiasms and condemnations, so that we may "see the object as in itself it really is."

Sheed's virtues as a critic begin with his irresistibly engaging opening sentences. "The literature of nausea has come to professional football," is the sprightly start of one piece. Another begins, "If you like to think of fictional art as a branch of magic, authors' jacket photos have to be a terrible disappointment." Try *not* reading a review that begins on that perky note. Finally, imagine the portentous opening most reviewers would write to A. Alvarez's *Savage God*. Here's Sheed's: "Books about suicide make lousy gifts, and many people think it's unlucky, to have them around the house as well."

These first sentences are, I think, emblematic of Sheed's whole critical talent: whatever illumination or instruction he offers— a great deal, usually—will be served up with dollops of delight. So you have to read these pieces twice: once for the funny lines . . . and once for the wisdom beneath them.

Wisdom? That sentence about suicide continues: "So A. Alvarez's excellent *Savage God* may wind up more talked about than bought. A pity, because the book is also about life, just as suicide is about life, being in fact the sincerest form of criticism life gets." That sounds like wisdom to me, and typically it's wrapped up in a throwaway line, which may be the only way we can take such observations.

You get to the bottom of Sheed's wisdom by sorting through his throwaway lines and taking into account the unsentimental but humane understanding he displays toward such sufferers as Dorothy Parker, E. B. White and F. Scott Fitzgerald. (pp. 38-9)

He calls literature "the one subject in the world one cannot be priggish about," and he's singular in this, too, remarkably free of literary spirituality. . . . To Sheed, the English Catholic, the Church has a monopoly on the religious impulse. He looks to literature for what it can give: wit, intelligence, style, and occasionally, some refracted light on reality.

Because Sheed is so free of the higher seriousness himself, he is devilishly adept at spotting it in others. To Irving Howe's complaint that Philip Roth, in not exploring the "real pathos" of Mrs. Sophie Portnoy, has caricatured Jewish life, Sheed's demur is resonantly typical: "But what would have happened to the book's manic drive, its unique tone, if he had done that? . . . Critics should look to these technical problems before they reach for the moral ones." At Richard Kostelanetz's plausible grouse that there is a New York literary mafia—a hydraheaded creature made up of magazines with New York in the title—which is out to get him and his friends, Sheed lets fly with common sense. Picture, he says, the overworked young woman from Jersey who does the bulk of the work at these establishments. "Her job is simply to get literate reviews at bargain prices, free of spite and logrolling ("You mean you don't know they fought a duel at Vassar!"), from unpredictable amateurs and reliable hacks. She is not, whatever the result, out to get you."

There you have Sheed at his best, confronting theory with actuality, moralism with art. You get a little too used to these moves as you read piece after piece in this collection; Sheed goes down better in the magazines where he doesn't have to compete with himself. But that's the only complaint you'll hear out of me. Any friend of sanity must be grateful for *The Good Word*. (p. 39)

Jack Beatty, in a review of "The Good Word and Other Words," in The New Republic, *Vol. 180, No. 3, January 20, 1979, pp. 38-9.*

SAUL MALOFF

Taken all in all Philip Rahv embodied the cultural and intellectual history of his generation, and represents the best of it.

As Wilfrid Sheed represents the best of his. Wilfrid Sheed? How can one possibly get from Rahv to Sheed? Well, the long way around, son.

Only it's not so long as, looking at the two of them standing there, you might suppose. Appearances (I believe it's been said) deceive; and Sheed is a master conjuror of appearances. On the face of it, where Rahv is ponderous (and that is his characteristic voice), Sheed is agile; where Rahv is classic, immersed in the large issues, solemn, Sheed is nothing if not contemporary, regarding the running experience of day-to-day squintingly, his leathery cragged features partially concealed behind the mask of a crooked, mirthless, unforgiving smile. Rahv wrote in Polemic, his native tongue, in a strong residual Russian accent (in fact his native land); Sheed has contrived out of his trans-national migrations a distinctive, perfectly pitched voice, neither quite English nor quite American, cannily combining elements of both and mixing them with a third into a distinctive freshness and buoyancy, an idiosyncratic signature. The language, or dialect, is spoken on a small, self-sufficient island with a population of one: call it Offshore—the language, not the island, which is uncharted and has no foreign policy to speak of. The constable is on duty at all times.

Sheed has been called "witty" so long and so steadily it must sometimes come to seem a term of subtle abuse to him, a veiled insult. Of course he is that, effortlessly, naturally, by a sort of spontaneous combustion: helplessly, on consequence of special chemistry. I mean to say it can't be faked, or got by hard sweaty labor (not that aspect of his writing, which we may call "style," without embarrassment): a writer's head works that way, or it doesn't, and there's an end of it, more's the pity. One can be witty and not a writer. Sheed is a witty writer; he is a writer and a wit; or, if I may strain the point, a writer whose singularity lies in his wit, his wittiness

That's the sort of thing Sheed has to put up with, while gnashing his teeth. But don't be taken in by the affable manner. A strong, supple intelligence is in control around the clock: that constable, wary, on the lookout, unblinking. Few if any current writers on writers and writing can release as much flashing light in a thin (and in many a thick) volume as Sheed does in a paragraph. [*The Good Word and Other Words*] contains the *New York Times Book Review* columns of that name, and they are as sparkling on second reading as on first and will be on third and fourth; and contains as well a scattering of reviews and essays on assorted subjects, literary, political, general-cultural, some of them surprising, as again and again we're made to see where the really interesting and lively subjects unsuspected lie.

Now and again I balk, or pause long, at this or that pronouncement, assessment or observation; in fact I balk rather frequently. But I say this in tribute: how often does one think a writer worth the bother? For one example of many: Writers should attend to their business, Sheed rather peevishly argues, ideologists to theirs, and frontiers never crossed—thus, to my mind, closing a bit too impatiently a complex, bloody question which of its nature will always be with us, and needs to be argued in season and out as the question alters in pressure and form. (pp. 119-20)

The feast awaits you; but I can't bear to leave off without mentioning a wonderfully moving essay in "ancestor worship," a testament in homage to his parents, Frank and Maisie Ward Sheed, written when that noble woman was still alive. The control of feeling is superb—a miraculous balancing-act where a single wrong move would be fatal; but from the first breath to the last Sheed moves along that finest of wires with perfect—with insolent—ease, leaving not a dry eye in the house. Exactly the way a gentleman conducts himself on that island, and an incomparable example of how offshore is spoken there. The man is a civilizing force whose appointed mission offshore and on is to keep us honest. (p. 120)

Saul Maloff, "Keeping Us Honest," in Commonweal, *Vol. CVI, No. 4, March 2, 1979, pp. 117-20.*

MICHAEL WOOD

The Good Word reprints the splendid column Sheed once wrote under that title for *The New York Times Book Review,* and a number of other essays and reviews. The book is long, and some of the topics look a bit tired. The tone is light, sometimes downright breezy, and it can be a liability. What is one to do with a man who writes, "Like Oedipus, we may be sorry we asked"? Not even S. J. Perelman could get away with imitating S. J. Perelman so blatantly.

But Sheed is a writer in the sense that [such reviewers as Irving Howe and Roger Sale] are not. Not because he writes novels (although he does), but because he writes *prose,* cares about what language does as well as about what it says. Casual allusions are his signature. "If one had grants enough and time," he murmurs at one point. At another he speaks of Catholic readers as "plowing their books into diapers," and at another describes the bookshelves of the Fifties as they "groaned with ex-Communists harking to the hound of heaven." I don't want to play the prof about such a graceful and funny line, but please do notice the alliteration and the comic closeness of *harking* to *barking.* Sheed is the master of the glittering phrase—"People who have never tried it have no idea how pleasant being nasty can be"—and surely no one else could identify Evelyn Waugh's college in Oxford as "a social climber's disaster," or Graham Greene's family as "lumpen ruling class." . . .

Sheed has a great appetite for what he calls the "vulgar, subtle sprawl" of America, but his best subjects are English. He is rarely less than funny and lively on any topic, and in his own generous way he is a moralist. But it is all pretty much featherweight stuff, *except* for the essays on figures like Chesterton, Hilaire Belloc, Orwell, Waugh, Cyril Connolly. Sheed writes better than anyone I know on authors who fall just below the first rank, and the clumsiness of that lamentable phrase is an indication of the sort of task that faces him. He claims neither too much nor too little for them, invents discriminations and tributes which no one has ever thought of ("Although I never wanted to meet him," he says of Connolly, "I salute his memory as a friend"; Chesterton, he says, "seldom wrote anything

hopeless and he never wrote anything perfect"), and envelops them in a crisp tenderness which is just what they need.

At such times the breezy tone stiffens, and we read of Belloc, his mind smashed into "brilliant fragments," his gaze fixed on the flickering "masks of boredom" around him: "the faces of rich, restless people, tinkering with customs and beliefs as if they were lawn furniture." Or of Orwell, afraid of his own particular form of the dark: "What he most feared was the blind spot between us and the future, the space between identities where we could get lost forever." Criticism, occasionally, is what reviewers write even when they don't have the time. (p. 36)

Michael Wood, "Harking and Barking," in The New York Review of Books, *Vol. XXVI, No. 7, November 8, 1979, pp. 34-6.*

JOHN GROSS

For many years Sheed & Ward was the pre-eminent Catholic publishing house in the English-speaking world. But the flesh and blood Sheed and Ward—the Frank and Maisie of their son's memoir [*Frank and Maisie: A Memoir with Parents*]— formed a more remarkable partnership still. They were tireless lecturers, doughty street-corner orators, gifted authors: Frank Sheed's theological writings earned him, layman though he was, a doctorate in theology from Rome itself (complete with the right to wear a four-pointed biretta), while Maisie Ward wrote biographies, notably her life of G. K. Chesterton, that are of lasting interest. The two of them were also unique personalities, very different in temperament and background, but bound together, as Wilfrid Sheed says, by "a Siamese twin of a vocation which neither could have pursued solo."

As the subtitle he has chosen suggests, Mr. Sheed has not attempted to provide a full-scale portrait of his parents. Instead, he has written an account of what it was like to grow up as one of their two children; in the course of it we learn a good deal about his own life, and something of his sister Rosemary's as well. But the book is Frank and Maisie's, beyond a doubt, and a very eloquent memorial to them it is—both entertaining and deeply felt, full of wry insights into the contradictions of human nature, a demonstration (if one is needed) that love and what in the end can only be called filial piety are no barrier to the incisiveness that readers of Mr. Sheed's novels and journalism have come to expect of him. . . .

Frank and Maisie is more than a family album—it also contains many interesting sidelights on two generations of Catholic life in both Britain and America. There are glimpses, often from unexpected angles, of figures as different as Hilaire Belloc (a certain reticence here on Mr. Sheed's part, perhaps) and Dorothy Day, of the urbane Msgr. Ronald Knox, whose translation of the Bible was one of Sheed & Ward's great best sellers, and the somewhat less urbane Bishop Fulton Sheen. . . .

Much of the book also reads like a tale of four cultures— English, Irish, American, Australian: of the tensions and permutations among them that the Sheed-and-Ward heritage came to embody, and sometimes the abrasions, too. . . .

If *Frank and Maisie* has a weakness, it is Mr. Sheed's occasional descents into an inappropriately gutsy prose; there are times when you can almost see the bright colloquialisms being pinned into place. But for most of its length it is an exceptionally well-written book as well as an unusually perceptive one—in the best sense, a decidedly stylish performance.

John Gross, in a review of "Frank and Maisie: A Memoir with Parents," in The New York Times, *October 15, 1985, p. C21.*

ROBERT TOWERS

Filial piety is hardly a conspicuous virtue these days, when hostile or disappointed offspring seem eager to give us the lowdown on Mommy Dearest or to reveal, with appropriate ruefulness, the hideous truth about Dad's sexual predilections. *Frank and Maisie,* Wilfrid Sheed's memoir of his embullient Australian father and his downright and unconventional English mother, is redolent of this old-fashioned virtue; when not positively brimming over with affection, the book is saturated with respect—at once awed and humorous—for this doughty marital team, who, as the leading Roman Catholic publishers of their day, helped alter the countenance of the Catholic Church in the United States. Such piety is attractive, though it necessarily imposes certain limitations on the memoir's scope as biography or history. . . .

Mr. Sheed tells, in a deliberately informal way, the story of this incongruous but loving couple and their two children, Rosemary and Wilfrid. The founding of the publishing house, Sheed & Ward, in England and America led to much shuttling back and forth between the very different worlds of English and American Catholicism—between that of Chesterton, Belloc, Evelyn Waugh and Monsignor Ronald Knox on one side and Monsignor (later Archbishop) Fulton Sheen and Father Leonard Feeney (a Sheed & Ward protégé who was excommunicated) on the other. Frank Sheed, his son reveals, was encouraged by British Intelligence officers to come to the United States in 1940 to see if he could "do something" about the isolationist demagogue Father Charles Coughlin, "the Radio Priest." The American church was a shock for the Sheeds. As Wilfrid Sheed puts it, "America's many freedoms have not always and everywhere included the freedom to think. For Catholics before Vatican II, the land of the free was preeminently the land of Sister Says—except of course for Sister, for whom it was the land of Father Says." . . .

The changing face of American Catholicism is of course a subject of great inherent interest. I could have used more information about the role of Mr. Sheed's parents in it, but he clearly has other intentions in mind. The subtitle of his book is "A Memoir with Parents," and indeed young Wilfrid's own story figures largely in *Frank and Maisie*. While this perspective is often useful in evoking his parents in their domestic role, the tale itself—Wilfrid's transplanting to America at the age of 10, the tribulations of the boy with the sissy English accent among the Irish-American toughs of his boarding school, his unpleasant experiences at a very different sort of English school, his fanatical interest in sports and the devastating effects of polio, his cheerfully misspent years as a quasi Yank at Oxford—has been told before; Mr. Sheed's readers have encountered it in such heavily autobiographical fiction as *A Middle Class Education, The Blacking Factory* and *Pennsylvania Gothic,* and *Transatlantic Blues.* Frank and Maisie are simply more interesting figures than Wilfrid Sheed's younger self, and I found myself resenting the fact that this familiar persona occupies so much space in the family photograph.

Even so, the portrait of Frank that emerges is thoroughly engaging—and persuasive. We see him as a tireless but good-natured debater of theological issues, as a natural entertainer who knew by heart all the popular songs of the English-speaking world, as an unpredictable and delightful presence to his children and grandchildren and a devoted admirer of his indefatigable wife. Mr. Sheed writes movingly about his father's old age, when after a troubled period in the late 1960's he accommodated himself to the changes in the church and in his childrens' lives and could even accept Maisie's death with determined cheerfulness.

The treatment of Maisie Ward lacks, I feel, some of the warmth and intimacy with which Mr. Sheed presents his father. As an industrious biographer (of Browning and Chesterton among others), a sturdy Catholic activist committed to social justice, a woman of sudden and vigorous enthusiasms and a street-corner preacher for most of her life, Maisie was not the pie-baking or shoe-tying sort of mother and one occasionally senses in her son's childhood anecdotes about her a degree of the ambivalence the boy must have felt. The history of her upper-class family seems to embarrass the antisnob in Mr. Sheed, who tends to be sarcastic about some of her relatives and harsh toward England itself, dwelling on all that is smug, dank and class-ridden in that country. Yet the overall account of his mother is enormously admiring. He clearly finds much to relish in her personality, including her eccentricities, which were those of a supremely confident (and innocent) Edwardian Englishwoman abroad.

A number of questions that arise from the parents' story remain unanswered. I, for one, would like to know what sort of money Sheed & Ward generated in its heyday. How did Frank function as a businessman—was he really so happy-go-lucky about practical matters as the book suggests? How did the genial Frank and the idealistic Maisie respond to the ugly strain of anti-Semitism in Frank's English idol, Hilaire Belloc, and, to a lesser degree, in G. K. Chesterton? How far—if at all—did their anti-Communism lead them in the direction of Senator Joseph McCarthy? What sort of relationship, if any, did they have with the leaders of the American Catholic hierarchy? Filial piety—or perhaps the focus of the memoir itself—may account for Mr. Sheed's reticence on these and other matters.

Finally, something needs to be said about the book's style. Wilfrid Sheed's addiction to slang is well known. "I am drawn to the demotic," he writes, "and simply pile it onto all the other demotics I've picked up, throwing out nothing." His breezy, sportswriter's approach is useful in conveying the song-and-dance-man personality of Frank at home and in mocking certain pomposities and shibboleths, but too often the writing is merely careless. It is not so much the constant use of slang as the quality of it that I find grating. It has a tendency to fall into cliché ("just what the doctor ordered") or become perfunctory ("she outshone her husband by a . . . mile") or strained ("while I high-tailed it for the Fatted Calf"). "Cute" is a word of disapprobation in Mr. Sheed's vocabulary, yet how else, except as cute, can one describe a sentence such as "She [the young Maisie] might even have become a don, which would have been curtains for little me"? The problem is related to a pervasive jokiness of tone. . . that to some degree trivializes his subject matter and works against the real interest and attractiveness of his story.

Robert Towers, "Faith, Works and Good Clean Eccentricity," in The New York Times Book Review, *November 10, 1985, p. 12.*

J. M. CAMERON

[In *Frank and Maisie: A Memoir with Parents*] Wilfrid Sheed weaves his own autobiography—or rather sketches for it—into the narrative of his parents' lives with skill and tact. How it felt to be a boy, and then an adolescent, and then a young man, now in England, now in the United States, is given to us con brio, and some of the painful transitions are given with an economy that carries its own pathos. This is especially marked in his treatment of his attack of polio and its physical and psychological consequences.

All this is pleasant and worth having, both in itself and as a contribution to the social and intellectual history of Anglo-Hibernian Catholicism in and out of the United States. Those who want to study this history in depth won't be able to neglect Sheed's book or, for that matter, Frank Sheed's own volume of memoirs, *The Church and I*. But there is all the same something a little unsatisfactory about Sheed's treatment of Frank and Maisie. He is sympathetic and affectionate, never rude or curmudgeonly; he attributes no great crimes to them in their ways of bringing him up; he doesn't doubt their qualities as thinkers and scholars. But there is something wrong in the way he comes to his task; and what is wrong is represented by what I can only call his unrelenting facetiousness.

Now Sheed is indeed, as he himself emphasizes, a writer of comedy. . . . It may be that he can't think of another way of telling his story, or telling it in such a way as not to bore the reader. I think he is mistaken. It is true that from time to time the vicissitudes of Sheed and Ward demand a comic treatment and it is also true that American Catholic life in the period in which they flourished offered scope for comedy. Some of it is black comedy. It is hard to smile indulgently at the memories of Cardinal Spellman and Father Coughlin. But much of it is knockabout stuff.

All the same, serious matters were in question. This is the very premise on which the lives of Frank Sheed and Maisie Ward were erected. The truth or otherwise of Catholicism, the nature of the Church and its relations to the men and women who compose it, the implications of the Gospel for matters of personal morality and for questions of social justice, all these are matters of some seriousness. Now, readers who are Wilfrid Sheed's contemporaries or elders know their way around such questions; but those who are younger often lack the elementary information Wilfrid Sheed takes for granted. I am not sure that on all the episodes he touches any reader under thirty-five could pass even a simple examination.

For example, there is a brilliant sketch of Father Leonard Feeney S. J. but the development of his thought and the reasons for his collisions with ecclesiastical authority are not made clear. This is an episode of some importance in the settling of opinion in the pre-Conciliar Church in the United States. A zealous Boston priest, Feeney was condemned by Rome for insisting on an especially savage interpretation of the principle that "there is no salvation outside the Church." Almost certainly there was sympathy with his rigorism among some of the clergy. But the swift Roman action was an uncovenanted piece of good fortune for American Catholicism. Many other persons and events are touched upon with some sharpness, but Sheed doesn't give enough historical information to make the persons and episodes plainer for the contemporary reader. More solid history into which the lives of Frank and Maisie could have been inserted would have made the book profitable and more useful. (pp. 36-7)

I have already mentioned what strikes me as the excessively facetious tone that pervades so much of this memoir. Perhaps it is strong evidence of how Wilfrid Sheed's English education

has shaped him. It is the English, not the Americans, who try to disguise the expression of deep feeling with irony, to diminish excessive praise with "not bad" and "quite good." But when he comes to give us an account of Frank's final days the sheer force of the events compels him to pull out a few more stops and to move us, as he himself is moved. . . .

Despite the facetiousness, and the occasional failure to fill in as much of the historical detail as the picture needs, Wilfrid Sheed's memoir is amusing and in the end affecting, a witness to times that will soon seem as remote as the world before the internal combustion engine. However remote they may be, they are alive in *Frank and Maisie*. (p. 37)

J. M. Cameron, "The Good Life," in The New York Review of Books, *Vol. XXXIII, No. 8, May 8, 1986, pp. 36-7.*

ART SEIDENBAUM

Anyone unfortunate enough to earn or learn a living in the book business will relish the back-biting behind the back-slapping in this artful novel [*The Boys of Winter*] about the wiles of writers, editors, publishers and hangers-on. Every character, as a matter of fiction, is a hanger-on here, trying to survive over somebody else's live body.

Anyone affluent enough to experience an enclave existence will recognize the incestuous absurdity of what happens in the Hamptons where Jimmy's bar functions as a cathedral plaza, with residents assigned their squatting places on the basis of being year-rounders, summer-dwellers or mere weekenders. Similar foolishness—involving in-groups within in-groups—occurs in Laguna, Key West and Carmel.

Many normal people may also enjoy the way Wilfrid Sheed puts his needle to puncturing accepted public wit or attributed private wisdom at the same time. . . .

A real writer is at work here, one with a keen sense of selves—self-worshiping and self-deprecating. He knows how writers band together against the alleged greed and stupidity of publishers and editors. He knows how those same writers also feel superior, each to each, even while banded together. And he knows how the other side feeds, parasitically, off the writers' work: "Luckily," says narrator and publisher Jonathan Oglethorpe, "I have my own little ego to keep me warm. I also believe that I am better than all of them, only with the good taste not to put it in writing."

But Oglethorpe is putting it in writing. While he tends to four odd authors in the Hamptons, he is also writing a novel about odd authors in the Hamptons. And one of those four tended authors—the once-celebrated, now-slipping Waldo Spinks—is also writing a novel about the same people in the same place. This is at first a funny comedy of manners, most of them bad manners, as the real novelist, Sheed, reels around inside two fictional novelists and also publishes a previously unpublished early short story by Oglethorpe. Later, alas, comedy becomes a kind of confusion as the reader must remember to separate Sheed from his creations and the creations from each other. By the end, Sheed has further complicated this business by having Oglethorpe confess that his novel and Spinks' novel blurred into one.

There is enough plot and plotting among the characters to make a serious novel of Russian proportion. But that is not enough for Sheed. He invents a subplot about softball to engage the

Hampton crowd and give them a chance to compete with a team from Hollywood as well as from other Long Island hamlets. The team grows out of a "hot stove league" conversation, concocted during the winter when there is nothing to do but drink at Jimmy's and look for things to talk about besides which writer is lusting after which other writer's wife. Baseball is usually good for a few laughs in fiction, being, like barroom boasting, a sport of so much potential and so little scoring. "The Boys of Winter," however, play a pretty dull game; they are singularly inept while their ensemble is rarely amusing. When Spinks almost kills a Hollywood producer, in fury over another rejection notice, the seams of artifice are showing.

But when Sheed sticks to the game of letters, his calls are much closer. . . .

The boys—and girls—are at their best in the bar, sneering at the locals, savaging each other and trying to make love in the clutch. Novelist, essayist, memoirist Sheed even manages to make his narrator grow up as the seasons change. The talk is consistently sure and swift because Sheed, though he may play uncertainly by construction, plays beautifully by ear.

> Art Seidenbaum, in a review of "The Boys of Winter," in Los Angeles Times Book Review, July 19, 1987, p. 2.

CHRISTOPHER LEHMANN-HAUPT

[In *The Boys of Winter*], Wilfrid Sheed has found a perfect target for the self-loathing that the heroes of his novels . . . sometimes vent upon themselves. This time Mr. Sheed's persona is "the writers' natural enemy, a publisher." He is Jonathan Oglethorpe, editor in chief and junior partner in Williams & Oglethorpe, with a weekend house on Long Island in the Hamptons. Even in the off-season—especially in the off-season—he likes to hang out with a bunch of his writers at the back tables of Jimmy's. . . .

Actually, Jonathan is a publisher who is writing a novel. "Having played the courtesan to" his writers "too long, curtseying to their pretensions . . . I would like to show them who's got the royal blood around here, by beating them to the great regional book—roofing, siding, and all." One of its main purposes will be to score points against Waldo Spinks: "Routine case, no complications. Acclaimed first novel sucked out of his youth and the Korean War. Nothing much since. Terminally overpriced."

Unfortunately, Waldo is also writing a regional novel, partly to get Jonathan. Jonathan will raise the stakes by offering to publish it for a cut-rate advance. Waldo has his resources, too. Other victims get caught in the cross fire: summer visitors to the Hamptons, year-round residents of the Hamptons, painters, writers, publishers, movie people, liberals, conservatives and amateur athletes.

It all gets extremely complicated, with twists and doublecrosses that culminate in a vicious softball game. When the final pitch gets thrown, nothing is as it seems to have been. With many a witty phrase and cutting apothegm, Mr. Sheed has not only dissected artistic pretension but also revealed the profound human need for masks. With the scalpel of satire, he has sliced away the shell that covers up the shell.

> Christopher Lehmann-Haupt, in a review of "The Boys of Winter," in The New York Times, July 30, 1987, p. C23.

HERBERT GOLD

Probably best known as a witty reviewer and tender memoirist, Wilfrid Sheed here deploys some of what he knows about the life of literature through an apparatus of vaudeville gags and magickings, plus a hint of autumnal grief. The subject of *The Boys of Winter* . . . is not so much the life of literature as careerism—also sex and softball—in an exurban Long Island colony.

In an early essay, **"The Minor Novelist,"** Mr. Sheed observed that "the fuel that keeps the new people moving faster than the speed of worry is money." Both elements in that process, the worry and the money of writers, are now being examined, along with how they qualify adjacent matters such as love and sex, family, friendship, and the primitive, never quite abandoned intention to be an Artist—perhaps even arrogantly to be more than a minor artist. Some of the fun of the book comes from the reader's sense that he is getting, to cite Mr. Sheed's essay **"The Writing Condition,"** "heightened, selected, imagined gossip." . . .

A Chinese-boxes plot, with parodic echoes of both Borges and the New Journalism, is a convenient game for the interpenetration of Waldo Spinks, a best-selling novelist on the way down, and Jonathan Oglethorpe, an ironic editor, publisher, secret writer. They are telling the same story, revving up the level of abuse of each other. Other members of the cast include a boring but gifted novelist teetering on the edge of both being recognized and being cuckolded; he's more successful at the latter than the former. Nikki van Dyne bats her eyes on her husband's behalf, but neither talent nor wife will manage to make him famous. The narrator laments Billy's "invisibility" as he produces good books that nobody reads: "How do you explain this to a man? You, sir, are good but invisible." Lamenting poor Billy's fate doesn't stop Oglethorpe from joining the chase after the sexy wife, who only seeks to move her husband's career an inch or two forward. Oglethorpe also knows the answer to writers' deepest moral dilemma: "whether a vile publisher is better than no publisher at all."

And then there are Cecily Woodruff, who writes Park Avenue romances but has principles about the prose she will sleep with; Ferris Fender, a stalwart gay novelist of the Civil War—please call it the War Between the States—who treats the village to frequent lessons in Southern manners; Hollywood people, unpacking their clichés and "moving in the general direction of Deal"; and a few necessary functionaries to speed the progress—a barkeep, a sportswriter, drop-in visitors. In the whimsical way of fiction, which Mr. Sheed as Critic might like to analyze, a sketchy love affair between Oglethorpe and Cecily seems only a sketch, while the sketchy moments of estrangement and reconciliation between Oglethorpe and his son are moving and convincing. The ironic telling hardly flags, yet the miracle of feeling peeks through.

The story—softball game, attempted murder by beaning, a suicide—is knockabout. We're in High Social Comedy country here. "I don't know, maybe you have to take up decency early, like the violin," the narrator says. The resonance recalls a bit of the unmerrie sardonick England of Evelyn Waugh, with some American kindliness thrown in among the fun of the literary and artistic Hamptons, where most art books turn out to be memoirs of Jackson Pollock and the writers trot around carrying manuscripts in their teeth. In the Midwest, where I was raised, I thought the Word was holy and those who performed words must be something like prophets, or at least angels. Mr. Sheed leads us through dark realities.

He is also leading us cunningly through the lighter ones with a record number of shrewd observations about the business and craft of the profession: "A bad year looks pretty much like a good one at a small quality [publishing] house"; "Nobody in the arts, or maybe out of them either, *ever* came to the Hamptons in search of oblivion." . . .

The Boys of Winter is a mocking bird, a singing scavenger, not a system. Too much attention should not be paid its views; how it perches on the branch is its meaning. Hollywooders spraying the countryside with movie options, softball madness and the rules of the local saloon, indecisions about sex (and, in several cases, which sex to have sex with)—this is all broad stuff. But the tale-telling is so chipper and speedy that the reader skips along quite merrily, maybe sometimes pausing to move his lips over an especially cunning turn. There is a light ration of puns. Nor does Mr. Sheed wear his angst on his sleeve. An impeccable comic voice plays out the farce—and what does "impeccable" mean here? The voice doesn't strain or take itself seriously, and yet the character types are nailed down, the dialogue slams the coffins shut. . . .

Incited by tavern indolence, the softball game (boyish, but there are women too) provides not so much suspense as a parody of suspense, a string of knots holding beads of comic scenes and observations. The familiar patriotic habit of playing baseball supports a subtext of comment on American religion, success, amorphous social life, ambition, failure, death and marriage—all the grand subjects in alternating order of triviality. The tone is teasing, not bitter, although most of the characters lie awake in their separate dark nights of the soul. Mr. Sheed also manages to portray Presbyterian strictness with a certain fastidious distaste; no sweat here, either. He plays against middlebrow literary style, while avoiding metafiction, as in: "'. . . .' What is the sound of four dots in real life?" (p. 3)

If satire is what closes on Saturday night, social comedy doesn't normally fill the seats the rest of the week either. *The Boys of Winter* asks to be enjoyed for its play and dance. At some point the question of the novel as satire, the novel as social history, might be raised (but I prefer not to do so). Mr. Sheed's problem here might be to make the lit biz stand for American Malaise, the Human Condition. (There, I'm almost doing it.) How does he face the problem? By laughing it away. The smarm he reports is marvelous for its own sticky self; it doesn't have to be Big World-Historical Smarm. The riffs on friendship, loss, youth and age come in glints of insight through the narrative voice of a martyred but not defeated survivor. (pp. 3, 20)

The Boys of Winter brings Grub Street to contemporary times and the exurbs—and it's funny. Finally it does the satirist's good work of demolition, but it also, alas, tells much of the truth about literary politicking. And for watchful readers, it tells some of the truth about politicking in general, minus the atomic weaponry and massive money movements of statesmanship on the international scale. The gloomy conditions of publishing are not rubbed in our faces, and the implications are among the subtexts adroitly not emphasized. There is a nostalgia for times when the Word really did seem haunted and holy.

Because the book performs a traditional task for the novel—bringing the news of the world—and because of the spirit of its enterprise—wit stirred in disaster—it should surely become the most popular of Mr. Sheed's novels. (p. 20)

Herbert Gold, "'Come On, Big Boy—Let Me See Your Manuscript'," *in* The New York Times Book Review, *August 2, 1987, pp. 3, 20.*

RHODA KOENIG

For *The Boys of Winter* Sheed has put away the fairy dust he wafted over the images of his sainted parents in *Frank and Maisie,* and he is no longer crouching at the hem of Clare Boothe Luce. This is a return to the Wilfrid Sheed we know and love, the wise and dirty-minded old man in the corner who has seen greed, petulance, self-delusion, erotomania, and *Schadenfreude* plaguing the best and second-best minds of his generation. He's not surprised by any of it, but he finds it pretty funny.

Out in Nether Hampton, where the early pumpkins blow, a cast of fictional characters gather at Jimmy's bar to rub egos together while waiting for the softball season. They are the novelists in the stable of Jonathan Oglethorpe, the Scottish-Presbyterian publisher who spends a lot of time on Long Island grooming and currying them and breaking up the bigger fights. Waldo Spinks, the two- and ham-fisted writer hanging on by his thumbs to the big money, has produced nothing to equal his early war novel and measures out his life in bar tabs. Billy van Dyne, the unsalable quality writer, takes it like a man when Oglethorpe turns down his latest book: "He shuts his eyes. They are probably filling up with a hate that he can't afford to show. . . . When he opens them, it is with a warm smile that seems to say, 'Would you like to sleep with my wife?'"

The question isn't entirely theoretical, as Jonathan has had his eye, if not much else, on Nikki van Dyne for some time. Nikki is visually pleasing, but mentally negligible. . . . The rest of Oglethorpe's list is Cecily Woodruff, a somewhat masculine romance novelist . . . and Ferris Fender, a very masculine gay southern novelist who worries that he is becoming artificial. . . .

The ego friction reaches the combustion point when a contingent of Hollywood types muscle in on the best table at Jimmy's and, worse, form a rival softball team. The writers' hostility is tempered by the knowledge that the Hollywooders hold the magic gold of options in their fluffy paws. Even Jonathan keeps his already "stealthy venom" further in check.

Sheed manages a laid-back blend of cynicism and ruefulness that also allows for some genuine sadness. Jonathan has a son, but all his attempts to love the boy only plunge him into stuttering, Presbyterian embarrassment. . . .

The rather gory climax, savoring more of Norman Mailer's Provincetown than Wilfrid Sheed's potato patch, strains credibility, not to mention tone, and the novel-within-a-novel aspect is as tiresome as these things usually are. But Sheed is clearly having fun in this book, and if you have to be a bit of a curmudgeon yourself to enjoy it, you'd be a much bigger one if you didn't.

Rhoda Koenig, "Hard-Ball," *in* New York *Magazine, Vol. 20, No. 32, August 17, 1987, p. 65.*

THE NEW YORKER

Softball—as a game and as a subject for hot-stove conversation—and [a] saloon form the center of gravity of Mr. Sheed's [*The Boys of Winter*]. He is certainly one of the funniest writers alive in the Hamptons, or anywhere. His humor is entirely a matter of style. He writes sentences that explode. . . . (p. 120)

The Boys of Winter is narrated by one Jonathan Oglethorpe, an editor at a "quality" New York City publishing house, and its plot, or gentle momentum, has to do with Jonathan's struggles (amorous, pecuniary, literary) with his several writers and with beautifully composed creatures from Hollywood and the summer fund-raising circuit. Fortunately, we never get far from the literary art: Oh, cries the lovely wife of a novelist, "'Why must writers always be so *envious?*' She suddenly looks as if she's going to cry, as well she might, having just stubbed her pretty toe against an iron law of nature." (pp. 120-21)

A review of "The Boys of Winter," in The New Yorker, *Vol. LXIII, No. 35, October 19, 1987, pp. 120-21.*

Jane (Graves) Smiley

1949-

American novelist, short story writer, and nonfiction writer.

Through detailed character studies, Smiley's fiction explores complex relationships among family members, friends, and lovers. Critics generally agree that Smiley's observations of daily routine and use of sharp, revealing dialogue enable her to define characters and their emotions while expressing larger themes of loss and recovery. In his review of her initial publication, *Barn Blind,* Michael Malone asserted: "Jane Smiley handles with skill and understanding . . . the inchoate, cumbersome love that family members feel for one another."

In her first novels, *Barn Blind* (1980) and *At Paradise Gate* (1981), Smiley examines the powerful bonds that dominate the lives of two families. In *Barn Blind,* the Karlson children strive to match the unrealistic expectations set by their demanding mother, while *At Paradise Gate* centers on the tense relationships between the Robison daughters, who have gathered at the deathbed of their father as their mother prepares for her life alone. In Smiley's third novel, *Duplicate Keys* (1984), followers of a failing New York City rock band react to the murder of two of its members. Rather than approach the story strictly as a thriller, Smiley concentrates on the alternately strained and supportive relationships of the survivors. Although some critics faulted the plots of these books for predictability, Smiley drew praise for her presentation of compelling, well-realized characters and her detailed evocation of place.

Smiley's next book, *The Age of Grief* (1987), is a collection of short fiction in which marriage and family emerge as central issues. The title novella, which Anne Bernays described as "a shameless, unblinking look at the sort of emotional accommodation made by partners in even the best marriage," examines a husband's self-doubt and his decision to avoid a confrontation following the discovery of his wife's infidelity. Critics praised Smiley's meticulous attention to routine situations and her lyrical portrayal of the delicate balance between idealism and reality in marriage. In her historical novel, *The Greenlanders* (1988), Smiley employs the intricacies of the medieval Nordic folktale to chronicle the spiritual and physical demise of Norse settlements established in Greenland by Eric the Red during the tenth century. Smiley relates her theme by gathering the thoughts and experiences of separate settlers into the unifying narrative voice of one Greenlander, Gunnar Asgeirsson. Although some critics considered her epic style cumbersome, others praised Smiley's ability to humanize historical events through austere yet celebratory prose. Howard Norman commented: "Given the vast template of History, it is impressive how Ms. Smiley is able to telescope certain incidents, unravel personalities in a few paragraphs, delve into a kind of folkloric metaphysics—she is a diverse and masterly writer."

(See also *Contemporary Authors,* Vol. 104.)

DORIS GRUMBACH

Jane Smiley has given her first novel [*Barn Blind*] an Iowan background, not the expected soy-bean and corn farms, but a horse ranch, the only one in the state, it would seem. In the foreground she has placed a family, dominated by the rigid and redoubtable convert-to-Catholicism, Kate Karlson, who breeds horses, trains and shows them, teaches children to ride them and puts her own four children through strict equestrian paces. Her hopes for an Olympic team rider are pinned on one son, but she is demanding of the others as well.

Smiley moves behind the eyes of one child, one adult, after the other, allowing us entry into each consciousness, each response to the required life of horses and horse shows. This shuttling viewpoint is one of the novel's flaws, I think. It results in a lack of focus which is disconcerting even as it provides us with far more information about every character than would be permitted if the story had been told, as I thought it might have been, from Kate's point of view, or even the daughter's, the periodically weeping girl who has our sympathy through the height of her adolescence.

The novel comes to a dramatic and terrible climax with a fatal riding accident. We are prepared for it because we have felt that Kate's demands on her family are too great for her loving and dutiful offspring to survive. *Barn Blind* has the advantage of a milieu seldom so well-known by a writer as Smiley knows this horse farm and all its peripheral activities, and the disadvantage of too much documentation, too many facts and details of setting. But most of the time, with the Karlson's and the other horsey people, we are interested in them and concerned for their fates. Jane Smiley is impressive in her fictional debut.

> Doris Grumbach, "A Fanfare for Five First Novels," in Book World—The Washington Post, *June 15, 1980, p. 4.*

MICHELE M. LEBER

Kate Karlson—accomplished, admired, and obsessed—is the hub of the family 40-horse farm, which she runs by strict schedule with only her four children as stable hands [in **Barn Blind**]. But as Pony Club lessons and show preparations start, the family equilibrium shifts: Margaret, 18, is back from college and unaccountably weepy; Peter, 17, with the best horse and training, shows signs of his mother's equine intoxication; John, 15, is furious at Kate's pervasive influence and provokes her anger; and Henry, 12, plans to run away. And Axel, whose bedroom Kate left after her sweeping conversion to Catholicism . . . , is flirting with his wife of 20 years. But Kate is blind to anything beyond her own interests—no one ever asked the children if they even liked horses, Axel realizes with dismay—to the point that the concluding tragedy barely touches her. Richly evocative atmosphere . . . and finely realized characters make this a remarkably involving first novel with a message that lingers. (pp. 1410-11)

> Michele M. Leber, in a review of "Barn Blind," in Library Journal, *Vol. 105, No. 12, June 15, 1980, pp. 1410 11.*

MICHAEL MALONE

Jane Smiley's **Barn Blind** makes one think of those preadolescent girls whose ardor for horses with names like Black Stallion and King of the Wind makes even the passion of a Messalina pale by comparison. Imagine such a girl grown into a self-assured and self-absorbed mother of four adolescents, all or any one of whom she is obsessively (and with blind disregard for their own desires) determined to make into the Olympic equestrian star she herself has failed to become. Imagine not a shrew but "a brisk brown woman" whose neighbors admire her . . . ; [whose] husband of 20 years is flirtatiously in love with her; and whose children honor and obey and seek to escape from her as Old Testament sinners fled Yahweh's sleepless eye. Such a woman is Kate Karlson, the chilling heroine of this pastoral novel of smooth texture and—like the Middle Western summer in which it is set—rich, drowsy pace.

Kept naïvely farmbound, safe from drugs and delinquency, the four Karlson teen-agers labor from dawn at character-building chores and at horse-work under the rigorous Prussian coaching of a mother who apparently feels that the family that rides together abides together. But her children, thrashing about in a hormonal flood, balk at her dream. . . . Jane Smiley handles with skill and understanding the mercurial molasses of adolescence, and the inchoate, cumbersome love that family members feel for one another. By summer's end, Kate's Spartan code that her sons should finish a meet on their saddles or not at all is horribly fulfilled. But blinkered by hubris, Kate is barn blind to grief and loss; she is thrown, but never falls.

> Michael Malone, in a review of "Barn Blind," in The New York Times Book Review, *August 17, 1980, p. 14.*

KIRKUS REVIEWS

Though rather too belabored and talky to match the impact of Smiley's impressive **Barn Blind** debut (1980), this claustrophobic, deathbed study of an edgy Des Moines family [**At Paradise Gate**] reaffirms her acute feel for silent wounds, thwarted affections, and complex domestic tensions. Ike Robison, 77, is severely ill from heart disease, staying in bed except for occasional trudgings downstairs—and so the three 50-ish Robison daughters have come to gather 'round mother Anna (the novel's central focus) during what seems to be a deathwatch. But family unity is hardly the result in the 24 hours covered here. . . . [Her daughters, industrious] Claire and beautiful, cosmopolitan, snobbish Helen continue their everlasting verbal duel. Fat realtor Susanna murmurously bemoans her fate: no children, a husband who left her. And when Helen's young daughter Christine arrives, announcing her imminent divorce, a new subject is up for group discussion. . . . [Anna] rakes over the past: her strict Mama, her marriage and life with demanding Ike on a failing ranch, her 20-year refusal to let Ike sleep with her. . . . And through the dead-of-night hours—the novel's best section—the aged couple sleeps hardly at all: Anna is on edge, especially after a weird phone call (her imagination?); Ike's bed is re-made again and again; she rebuffs his wanderings into her room; they bicker and snipe, with an explosion from Anna when Ike says her long-ago friend Elinor "looked like a piece of beef jerky." But the next day, before Ike dies, there'll be a tiny moment—Anna helping Ike in the bathroom—of new closeness: "For the first time in her life, they overlapped." And brand-new widow Anna finally looks ahead, having worked through the "rules" and "demands" of the past. Most of this is quietly splendid, with plainspoken details, a brooding sense of the house itself, and un-gussied-up dialogue. Unfortunately, however, as if afraid that readers will miss the point, Smiley indulges in flat, repetitious summaries of the feelings involved. And even more marring are the daughters' speechy debates—which escalate when Christine much too neatly (Death and Rebirth) discovers that she's pregnant . . . and which often make this novel seem like an old-fashioned, contrived stage-play. Flawed work, then, but worthy, honest, and—at its best—wry and sternly moving.

> A review of "At Paradise Gate," in Kirkus Reviews, *Vol. XLIX, No. 15, August 1, 1981, p. 963.*

MICHELE M. LEBER

While 77-year-old Ike Robison lies gravely ill [in **At Paradise Gate**] three generations of Robison women gather in attendance. They squabble—about hiring a nurse to relieve Anna, Ike's wife of 52 years, . . . about the divorce planned by granddaughter Christine, whose pregnancy is a somewhat pat balance for Ike's dying. But most of all the Robisons remember, so that . . . readers will know this family, its relationships, and its history, better than their own. Central to it all is Anna, who reexamines her marriage while readying herself for life after it; no less vivid are daughters Helen, Claire, and Susanna, as distinctly different as siblings usually are. This is a wonderfully dense novel, studded with sensuous descriptive passages and marked with slivers of insight—a treat for senses and intellect alike. For Smiley, another quite remarkable effort.

*Michele M. Leber, in a review of "At Paradise Gate,"
in* Library Journal, *Vol. 106, No. 19, November 1,
1981, p. 2155.*

VALERIE MINER

[*At Paradise Gate* is] about families and death and the death-lessness of families.... [Smiley considers] the afterlife of survivors who, in their grief, encounter both sides of mortality—their relatives' deaths and their own continuing lives.... [She also indicates] that death is more than the loss of a life; it is an exposure of human fallibility and an acknowledgment of inextricable kinship.

[In *At Paradise Gate*], Jane Smiley watches the women in a middle-class Iowa family.... [The novel suggests] the mutability of family and [reminds] us of its powerful hold. We witness genetic mirrors, primal imprints and failed strokes of communication.

As *At Paradise Gate* opens, Ike Robison's three grown daughters sit downstairs waiting for him to die. Helen, Claire and Susanna claim they came to help their mother, Anna, and to cheer Daddy to recuperation. But their nervous intensity, like the heavy stillness before an earthquake, is an unmistakable omen.... Their somberness is interrupted by Ike's grand-daughter Christine. Bright, flush-faced Christine presents the family with a further problem—her pregnancy and forthcoming divorce. Jane Smiley strikes delicately all the chords between the women's stolid endurance of Ike's illness and their frenzied attempts to preserve Christine's young family.

So Helen, Claire and Susanna wait in the familiar living room, which is cushioned with unstruck blows, insulated with unsaid words, electrified with decades of family tension. They are decent daughters, available for all the chores, emergencies and rituals of life and death. Reading *At Paradise Gate* is like being confined to an endless Sunday afternoon, anchored at home by too much dinner and too many memories. The women recall their old rivalries, which are not so old after all. They discuss their shared traits and acknowledge that even their differences are the result of their reactions to one other.

Anna, their mother, is the most vital character. Unburdened by sentiment, she is angry that her husband is abandoning her and that her daughters remain so dependent.... Her marriage has been hard—uprooting, violent, cold—but she has grown used to Ike. Who will share the spring lettuce? Anna's tart honesty and acute consciousness hold the book together when the story line dwindles....

At Paradise Gate is not so much about Ike's death as about Anna's life—a retrospective on her difficult past and a resolution of her remaining years. Death's imminence changes the dimensions of time. For Anna, one closely observed day has the complexity of 10 remembered years. As she confronts her finiteness, she achieves a quiet certainty about her right to what's left of her world. (p. 15)

[Smiley views] the next generation with an almost evolutionary optimism. Is it hubris or instinct that draws us forward? Despite the dead, despite the treacherous disappointments of the living, families survive. Perhaps because they provide a continuity for compassion, a place for one more fragile attempt at love. (p. 43)

Valerie Miner, "Domestic Novels," in The New York
Times Book Review, *November 22, 1981, pp. 15,
42-3.*

MALCOLM BOYD

[In *Duplicate Keys*], Alice is part of a group clustered around a rock band; two of the musicians, Denny and Craig, are brutally murdered.

Alice is 31, divorced, lonely, dependent—and once had a brief affair with Craig. She works as a New York librarian. The killing shatters any semblance of security in the circle of friends surrounding the band.

Ray, "brightly flushed in the manner of all pale, pale men, and eternally pudgy," is a highly successful soundman and a homosexual....

Ray, whose "irritating coquettishness" is tolerated by Alice, belongs to the group with her husband, Noah, who has a penchant for saying the wrong thing. Now it turns out that Ray had been sleeping with Craig.

Denny was the lover of Susan, who possesses "Alice's favorite face, pale, peaceful and good, unglamorous, a face that never fell apart with animation like Alice's own."...

As the friends react to the tragedy, as the police move in to solve its puzzle, Alice finds herself in a surprising place. "Somehow the square dance had spun into a new figure, and she was at the center, where she had never been before."...

In the aftermath of the killing and quite by accident, Alice meets Henry Mullet.... She feels her flesh "warm and spread beneath his grasp, beneath his detailed, observant and passionate knowledge."

Yet, in her experience, "lovers were as often adversaries of a sort as they were friends." She is aware of a difference in herself because of the murder, "more emotional, more afraid, less routine."

Murder becomes the backdrop for Alice's emerging relationship with Henry....

In a moment of apparent clarity it seems suddenly true to Alice "that no man would ever do more than kiss her life or her imagination, no man could overcome the quantity of experience she had now accumulated." Finally, however, Henry seems "very familiar, and their affair, though dreamlike in retrospect, bore all the self-conscious constraint of a real and no longer new relationship."

Smiley's third novel, bright and energetic in treatment, is slack and predictable in plot. A fine character study with a lively repertory company, it lingers too close to the surface of feeling. It doesn't take the plunge.

*Malcolm Boyd, "The Song Ends, Murder Lingers,"
in* Los Angeles Times Book Review, *March 18, 1984,
p. 7.*

LOIS GOULD

Wordsworth said it right: "We murder to dissect." He was deploring what books do to life's beauteous forms. *Duplicate Keys* proves his case beyond a shadow. Killing off two characters before page 1 ..., Jane Smiley arrives wielding bright dialogue like a scalpel, disarming us. It takes less than a paragraph before we're on to the fact that neither she nor we are going to care very much who done it, let alone why. We are all in it for the dissection.

Which is as it should be in a novel set in the coolest of places and times—Manhattan, 1980. This may be the anatomy of a murder but only because we happen to be in the neighborhood. More important and far more compelling is the anatomy of friendship, betrayal, . . . and the bittersweet smell of near success that is perhaps the most pungent odor in town.

Jane Smiley's West 84th Street is full of what the city likes to call its affluent young, though in truth they are neither. Already in their mid-20's in the mid-70's, when they blew in from the Middle West, Alice and Susan and Denny and Craig and Noah and Rya arrived in New York full of beans (garbanzo) and beginner's luck (the rock band had a hit record). But they, like the rest of us, have outgrown the 70's, the food, the dreams and the music. Now they have dead-end jobs, plants that need watering and early-30's panic, relieved by Chinese takeout and reruns of old fantasies. . . .

So they go for walks and occasional cocaine. . . . No one has any kids; they have become each other's. No one gets to say no anymore about sharing; they just do—keys, beds, trouble, loss of faith, murder. Jane Smiley knows she's got us where we live.

Meanwhile, what about that double homicide? One of the friends, a young woman with a gorgeous chin who does something vague for a cable television company, sums up the group's feelings: ''I mean, the murder was awful and all that.'' She says this while spearing shrimp toast off another friend's plate. . . .

The operating condition here is affectlessness, formerly known as cool. The author matches her tone to her people with unerring pitch. Images have an elegant, satisfying thwack, like the closing of solid-core doors. . . . In a moment of self-discovery, ''It seemed suddenly true to her that no man would ever do more than kiss her imagination or her life.'' And, most tellingly, expressing emotion: ''I love you,'' Alice says to Susan. ''I know,'' Susan replies, noting that in their lives, this is a phrase that usually means ''you owe it to me to do what I say'' or maybe ''thanks for doing what I said.''

When terror arrives, we are hardly surprised to find ourselves, like them, mesmerized but shockproof. Fear is just another emotion that hangs out, waiting for itself to happen. It drifts through the door like an intruder in overpriced sneakers who has somehow got hold of the key.

This is not an ordinary mystery, but we do get a first-rate cliffhanger. . . . By the way, the detective's name is Honey. He isn't one, of course; he isn't a hero either. A nice touch. Jane Smiley appears to have an unbreakable habit of them.

Lois Gould, ''When the Sharing Had to Stop,'' in The New York Times Book Review, *April 29, 1984, p. 14.*

LAURA MARCUS

The theme of detection in **Duplicate Keys** is seemingly employed to . . . conventional ends. The novel opens with its heroine, librarian Alice Ellis, being questioned by the implausibly named Detective Honey after she has discovered the murdered corpses of her friends Denny and Craig in the New York apartment they shared with Susan, Alice's closest friend and Denny's lover. By relegating Honey's professional activities to the background, however, and recounting the story·from Alice's perspective, Jane Smiley opens the way for rather dif-

ferent forms of exploration—of marriages, affairs, friendships, growing up and growing older.

Alice's relationship with Susan is central, and Smiley demonstrates a considerable sensitivity in the treatment of love and friendship, displacing the forensic impulse into an analysis of feeling and emotion; but although the prose is for the most part lucid and precise, the novel's ethos—early 1970s hippydom grown up in the 80s, or failing to do so—works against it. Alice and Susan's lengthy dialogues require more deserving subjects than failed but ever-hopeful rock-stars Denny and Craig, joint-smoking Noah or fatuous Rya to justify their intensity.

Duplicate Keys makes some intelligent links between detective work and more general forms of perspicacity. The title refers not only to the running motif of stolen and borrowed keys, of changing locks too late, but also to the question of the dangers and the delights involved for women in opening up their lives to others. Miss Marple wouldn't have recognized this novel's territory, but it's convincing for all that.

Laura Marcus, ''Families and Friends,'' in The Times Literary Supplement, *No. 4247, August 24, 1984, p. 953.*

ANNE BERNAYS

If there are still readers who consider the novella a marginal form and a notch or two less worthy than the full-length novel, **The Age of Grief**—a work just under 100 pages long and infinitely satisfying—should change their minds once and for all. The title piece in a collection that includes five short stories, this novella is explicitly about a marriage in jeopardy and, under its surface, a poignant and rich meditation on the nature of love and change. It is artless in the best sense, a triumph of the craft of narrative, for we believe that all written here really happened.

David Hurst, Ms. Smiley's narrator, is a dentist, a profession even less glamorous than that of butler. . . . David is married to Dana, also a dentist; the two met in dental school and now share a practice. They have three little girls: Lizzie, 7; Stephanie, 5; and Leah, 2. David loves his work, loves teeth and even admires fellow practitioners. . . .

Into this more or less idyllic household crawls the worm of discord: Dana, an amateur singer, falls in love with a man in her chorus. David doesn't want Dana to know he knows. He suffers morbidly. . . . Desperate to confront his wife, he can only talk about teeth: ''Mrs. Hilton needs to go to a gum specialist,'' he tells her. As the terms of their marriage shift, Dana grows inaccessible, even defiant, and David mourns: ''I wish my wife loved me. I wish her constant blue eyes would focus on me with desire instead of regret.''. . .

The situation at home continues to deteriorate, for David is as incapable of confronting Dana with her infidelity as she is of confessing to it. Confusion, a state David once thought of as ''gray mist,'' becomes instead ''perfect sight and perfect mystery at the same time.'' At the end, David concludes, about marriage, that it is ''a small container, after all, barely large enough to hold some children.'' **The Age of Grief** has the compactness of a short story, the density and expansiveness of a novel. It is a shameless, unblinking look at the sort of emotional accommodation made by partners in even the best marriage and a glorious achievement for Jane Smiley.

The author of three full-length novels . . . , Ms. Smiley is much occupied with marriage. In **"The Pleasure of Her Company,"** one member of an apparently happy union unexpectedly turns gay. . . . In **"Long Distance,"** the most compelling of the five [stories], a young man has extricated himself from an affair with a Japanese woman and feels both relieved and guilty about this as he visits his married siblings over Christmas. . . .

The stories are fine; the novella is splendid.

> Anne Bernays, "Toward More Perfect Unions," in
> The New York Times Book Review, *September 6,*
> *1987, p. 12.*

MICHIKO KAKUTANI

"I am thirty-five years old," says the narrator in the title story of Jane Smiley's new collection [*The Age of Grief*],

> and it seems to me that I have arrived at the age of grief. Others arrive there sooner. Almost no one arrives much later. I don't think it is years themselves, or the disintegration of the body. . . . It is more that the barriers between the circumstances of oneself and of the rest of the world have broken down, after all— after all that schooling, all that care.

This sadness, these intimations of loss, this sense that one can no longer control or even prepare for the future—this is a state of mind familiar to many of the characters in this finely crafted collection.

Dave, the 35-year-old man who speaks of an "age of grief," is himself trying to cope with a piece of knowledge that has ruptured the bright, cheerful fabric of family life that he has so carefully woven since college—knowledge that his wife no longer loves him, that she has fallen in love with another man.

Kirby Christianson, the hero of **"Long Distance,"** . . . [must] face up to the fact that what he is really afraid of is the realization that his life has taken its "final form"—that he can no longer pretend there are endless possibilities, or shrug off his responsibilities and failings.

A similar epiphany or moment of disillusionment ambushes other Smiley characters as well. In **"Dynamite,"** a radical, who's been hiding out from the F.B.I., suddenly starts thinking about her mother, and she resolves, then and there, to blow up the "firm shape" of the life she's made for herself in the underground, by returning home, after 15 years.

In **"Lily,"** a lonely single woman finds herself abruptly placed in the role of witness (and accessory) to the breakup of her friends' marriage, during a weekend visit. And in **"The Pleasure of Her Company,"** Florence learns that the neighbors she thought of as her best friends have simply used her as a means of deflecting attention from their marital problems. . . .

Marriage and family, in fact, are a central issue in nearly all these stories. Some of Ms. Smiley's characters, like Lily and Florence, find a "kind of attractive complexity" in the marriages they see around them, but they do not understand the rules of intimacy and their tentative efforts to become involved in their friends' marriages have disastrous results, in which they are pegged as interlopers or patsies.

Others, however, embrace marriage as a union that promises protection against the perils of the outside world. . . .

Of all the tales in this volume, [the] title story [*The Age of Grief*] is the longest and most complex, and its commodious

form seems best suited to display Ms. Smiley's talent for delineating the subtle ebb and flow of familial emotions.

While some of the shorter stories (in particular **"Jeffrey, Believe Me,"** a silly, mannered monologue about a woman attempting to seduce a gay male friend) suffer from a certain constriction, as though dialogue and events were being crammed into a neat and preconceived package, *The Age of Grief* opens out, organically, from a comic portrait of two dentists married to each other into a lovely and very sad meditation on the evanescence and durability of love.

In making her narrator a man, who knows of his wife's infidelity but who chooses not to acknowledge it, Ms. Smiley has not only succeeded in creating a thoroughly sympathetic character, but she's also found a narrative voice that moves fluently from the past to the present, from philosophizing to more active story-telling. She sets down, for us, the affectionate, ironic banter that can help bind a couple together; as well as those terrible, skewed communications in which everyday words conceal a darker subtext.

Preparing breakfast before work; getting the children ready for school, driving to the summer house; staying up with a sick baby; watching television after dinner—those "moments in every marriage that are so alike that they seem to be the same moment, appearing and vanishing"—those thoroughly familiar moments are captured by Ms. Smiley with such immediacy and precision that we are left with a sense of having participated in her characters' lives. And we consequently grieve for them when it seems that they are about to lose all that they'd once wanted.

> Michiko Kakutani, in a review of "The Age of Grief,"
> in The New York Times, *August 26, 1987, p. C21.*

LAURA FURMAN

After a reading of Jane Smiley's new collection of stories and her title novella, *The Age of Grief,* it is the characters' delight in the pleasing surface of the world that stays longest with the reader. Some of Smiley's characters are charmingly conceited. Some worry about each other, their children, about themselves. They fear accidents and see dirty windowsills as a sign of creeping chaos. But Smiley's readable prose is at its best when it reminds one of the pleasures of seeing the unexpectedly picturesque and of hearing familiar harmonies. Though there is interest for the reader in the knots that confound the characters, Smiley's people come alive not in the dilemmas that motor the stories along but in the luminous details and sensual observations that the writer gives them.

In **"The Pleasure of Her Company,"** Florence, a nurse, comes home one night to find " . . . the one lovely place on her otherwise undistinguished block—porched, corniced, many-peaked, and recently painted Nordic blond with pique white trim." . . .

The new people on the block are Frannie and Philip, and the unmarried Florence becomes a guest at their marriage. . . . Naive about marriage, Florence is shocked when her friends separate. A little rushed (perhaps by the present-tense narrative), Florence never quite catches up with Frannie and never really gets the full pleasure of her company. What is memorable about the story is not its solution or observations about marriage—it is Florence's naive and willing romancing about her friend.

"**Dynamite**" is narrated by a woman who is underground because of her political activities during the anti-Vietnam War period and who works now as a shift engineer at a fertilizer plant. . . .

The narrator wants to return home to put together her fragmented life but clearly won't. In the end, her longing for her always vague and eccentric mother is so much more authentic and moving than the premise of the character as underground bomber that one wonders if such a foil was really necessary to character or story.

The Age of Grief, the title novella, is about six weeks in the life of a couple (both dentists) and their three little girls. The wife considers leaving her family for a lover. The husband-narrator works hard to avoid a discussion with his wife that would force her confession or reveal his knowledge of her dilemma. He succeeds, aided by the unrelenting current of daily life with children, not entirely convincing details of dental practice, but most of all by his dogged commitment to keeping things going no matter what. . . .

Smiley's thrust as a writer is generous. She wishes to tell us what she knows, to put her best thoughts about living into a pleasing dramatic form. Still, there didn't seem to be much internal reason for the dentist's extended musings to be a novella rather than a short story. In this case, the novella may be either too long or short a form—as many before Smiley have found it—for her to shine in.

The most circumscribed story in the collection is the one in which Smiley's gifts work best. "**Long Distance,**" about an American man and his Japanese lover, was for me the most complete. In it, as in all fine short stories, form and content merged in a thrilling moment for the reader.

> *Laura Furman, "The Barriers of Circumstance," in*
> Los Angeles Times Book Review, *October 18, 1987,*
> *p. 6.*

BRAD HOOPER

[*The Greenlanders* is a] towering historical novel based on the tenth-century settlement of Greenland by Norseman Erik the Red and a band of Norse colonists. After flourishing in Greenland for centuries, the colonists disappeared, leaving behind only their buildings and artifacts. . . . [Smiley] focuses her huge novel on the way these Norse colonists live during the colony's decline, as their world goes wrong. From page one, the reader is engulfed in the thick of detail: customs, flora and fauna, food, history, geography—all the facts surrounding the hard lives endured by the Greenland settlers. The novel is obviously well researched, obviously the product of total immersion by the author in her subject, but ultimately it is more impressive than moving. There is not a lot of narrative drive here. Still, the people who lived in this European outpost and who tried to effect a living there are viably created. Historical fiction must be convincing in its evocation of the past; writers working in this genre must understand the peculiarities and distinctions of the particular time and place being brought to life—and must be able to embrace the reader with a sense of traveling back in time. And Smiley does that superbly.

> *Brad Hooper, in a review of "The Greenlanders,"*
> *in* Booklist, *Vol. 84, No. 13, March 1, 1988, p. 1049.*

HOWARD NORMAN

Fortunately for us, Ms. Smiley, author of the recent, much applauded short-story collection *The Age of Grief* (which could serve as an appropriate subtitle to *The Greenlanders*), has been long intoxicated by [Greenlandic history]. . . . Meditating about her subject, she has said

> Why did the Greenlanders disappear after centuries of relative prosperity? There are some theories: that the northern climate grew colder, that there were attacks by English and Basque pirates. Some people think that the skraelings—Eskimos—laid waste to the settlements. The most general answer is that the Greenlanders were so blinded by their own cultural prejudices that they were unable to adapt when conditions changed. They never stopped looking to Europe for succor, long after Europe had abandoned and forgotten them. Though they could get along fine with a thin lifeline, they could not get along with no lifeline at all.

Ms. Smiley clearly feels great compassion for the Greenlanders, their myriad confusions and bewilderments, yet she is careful not to portray them only as victims of Time and History, but of their own limitations as well. All around them were the original inhabitants, who doubtless had survived astonishing ravages of hunger and isolation. But by and large, to most Greenlanders the skraelings were a species of malevolence, not a source of knowledge toward survival. The skraelings drew into sharp focus the Greenlanders' ignorance and sense of menace. . . .

Like a minutely detailed tapestry, *The Greenlanders* chronicles hundreds of episodes and tributary episodes: the seasonal seal hunts and rituals, the travels over hazardous yet awe-inspiring terrain, the births and deaths of the Gunnars Stead Folk, the Ketils Stead Folk, the Gardar Folk, the Solar Fell Folk, the Icelanders and the Norwegians. Given the vast template of History, it is impressive how Ms. Smiley is able to telescope certain incidents, unravel personalities in a few paragraphs, delve into a kind of folkloric metaphysics—she is a diverse and masterly writer. Each long chapter, "Riches," "The Devil," "Love," has its expansive theme, just as the theme of the Great Extinction runs through the entire novel. But the cadences of day-to-day village life, the larger social dynamics as well as the domestic particulars, comprise the true riches of *The Greenlanders*. Despite the story being set far back in time, it has a certain urgency. Again, in her writing about writing the novel, the author says,

> The experience of these medieval people must speak to us in some fluid and haunting way, for they were our precursors, a branch of our family that lived fully, and indeed richly, even while they moved—as our own civilization may be moving—toward apocalypse.

The Greenlanders employs a "folkloristic" mode—with its stories overlapping other stories, folded into yet others, it all seems more told than written. That is, of course, Ms. Smiley's strategy and accomplishment. At times, however, villagers tend to come off like historical caricatures: their dialogue consists of exchanged aphorisms rather than plain talk, whatever plain talk was in 14th-century Greenland. Sometimes I felt that each conversation was a crisis, or provoked one, that each utterance would sink under its own menace, or wisdom.

In this sense, the dialogue seems a recapitulation of the Greenlanders' thinking, not their thinking itself. This is not to say, however, that the author intrudes; it is in dialogue (as much as anywhere) that the true character of the Greenlander is most forthrightly illustrated. Here, I wish to mention the novel's length, 558 pages, if only because it struck me as almost a separate animation. Each page seemed to attempt to correspond, decade by decade, if not breath by breath, with the slowly evolving Greenlandic tragedy. Therein lies the novel's courage, and its burden. It takes a certain disciplined curiosity to get through this tome, except by incremental readings, perhaps on a hundred winter nights.

The Greenlanders is not simply an epitaph, nor does it solve only one "great mystery"; it solves hundreds of small ones. Also, there's a sense of revelation. Toward the novel's end (it closes with a tale about to be told), the citizens of this bereft country, severely diminished, dazed by events, their collective memory perhaps more somber than ever, realize that

> hunger and disease had come and gone before, and now that the great hunger was over, men saw that such things happen in the natural round of events, for the world is by nature fallen from Paradise, and the Lord has made no promises about repairing it for the pleasure of men, but asks men to use the world as a tool for repairing their own souls.

> *Howard Norman, "They Should Have Listened to the Skraelings," in* The New York Times Book Review, *May 15, 1988, p. 11.*

VERLYN KLINKENBORG

In Jane Smiley's recent novella, *The Age of Grief,* a dentist speaks with the patterned incoherence that marks the voice of truly contemporary fiction. He says,

> Teeth are important. Eskimo cultures used to abandon their old folks in the snow when their teeth went, no matter how good their health was otherwise. People in our culture have a lot of privileges. One of them is having no teeth.

In which culture—the one where loss of teeth is fatal or the one where it is a privilege—would a dentist be more important? For *The Age of Grief*'s narrator, that compact allusion to Eskimos is the relic of a world almost inconceivably more arduous than his own privileged life. (p. 36)

The vulgar moral of history is that people in our culture have a lot of privileges. That may be why historical fiction tends to be pulp fiction these days: it reeks of that complacent moral, according to which hardship is just the necessary foil to romance. Even serious historical fiction seldom has the pungency of novels set in the present, offering an elaborate temporal illusion and the reprise of familiar conventions instead of the news we badly want to hear.

Smiley's new book, *The Greenlanders,* is a wonderful exception, a historical novel with the nearness of contemporary fiction. It is a sobering work set in 14th-century Greenland— barely within the confines of European culture—and closely based on what is known of life in the remnant of the colony established there by Erik the Red, who was exiled from Iceland in the tenth century. The Church survives among Smiley's Greenlanders, as do ecclesiastical and secular law; those artifacts and their workings we can imagine, but who can imagine the country? Greenland is bare of everything but difficulty. And yet, as the gentle Norwegian priest Sira Pall Hallvardsson says, "These Greenlanders declare it a fresh and lovely spot,

in the way that all men look about themselves at the earth and think themselves at home."

The Greenlanders is a chronicle of events occurring within the life-span of Gunnar Asgeirsson, who was born in 1352. The 190 inhabitants of Greenland's Eastern Settlement (a Western Settlement has already perished) live on farms, or steadings, widely separated by fjords and low mountains on the island's southern tip. (pp. 36, 38)

When serious historical novels fail, they usually do so through anxiety of evidence: they tell the joke and have to explain the punch line too. Unlike fictions about the way we live now, they cannot rely on what the reader knows, for the reader rarely knows enough (and sometimes—worse—knows too much). Their rhetoric is not that of persuasive storytelling but of overpleading, so we end by crediting the research, not the characters, the setting and not the plot. Here again, Smiley's novel is a brilliant exception. Of a fellow priest, Sira Pall observes that his impatience lies hidden in the "'ironia' typical of the Greenlanders." "Ironia" is the mode of this book. It convinces by explaining nothing.

Smiley's narrative manner is an expansive imitation of the terse Norse sagas. Near the end of the book we learn that this work was written by Gunnar Asgeirsson, who meant to let "all the folk of the world . . . learn what is really the case with us." Gunnar is proud and intelligent, one of perhaps three literate men in the Eastern Settlement, but he has never been to the world. His voice remains dissolved within the community of Greenlanders; though he is a storyteller within the story, his tales know no first person. He assumes that the reader lives as he does, though in less isolation. . . . What we will need to know, Gunnar assumes, is the nature of Greenlanders. And he is right. This is the news we want to hear.

The Greenlanders has a profusion of plots broken into tiny narrative units. As the narrative advances, the plots begin to cohere the way stories told about any small community do. Some lives arch across the whole of the novel, notably those of Sira Pall and Gunnar's son, Kollgrim, and Gunnar's older sister Margret. (p. 38)

There is assuredly something stonelike but quivering in the character of these Greenlanders. The bitterness of the land forces them into narrow paths, and their hold on life is stubborn. Self-irony afflicts even their spiritual teachers. . . . They have learned that "whatever will happen will be good enough," and that there is no reason to complain if "the winter was no colder than previous ones, Lent no longer, and Easter no warmer." This sustains them when sand drifts over the fields or starvation visits. It allows them to face equally the sure extinction of their race.

The Greenlanders is a grim book, and yet in its austerity and the caliber of its art it is jubilant, its effect that of a prayer composed by one of the priests at Gardar:

> Lord, we lie in our turf houses,
> As in graves covered with snow,
> And our prayers rise to you as loudly
> As the voices of the dead.
> Lord, You break the ice for us,
> And call forth the green grass,
> And so we rise out of our houses
> And come forth singing.

When this was first read to the congregation, "only a few praised it," because it was too true, but it resonates in the reader's mind. In *The Greenlanders,* singing is the sound you hear above the wind.

Smiley's greatest achievement is not the accuracy of her research, the vividness of her characters, or the simple abundance of her story. It is the uncanny movement of the narrative, which radiates a spirit of acceptance. This is partly a philosophical matter (clearly, the Greenlanders are stoic) and partly a technical matter. Contemporary fiction often moves like a man tripping: it loses its balance and stumbles forward, tumbling into cumulative order. But from the moment *The Greenlanders* begins [until it ends] . . . , the narrative is perfectly balanced, never cascading forward or backward, at ease with the way first one thing and then another thing happens in the lives of these extraordinary people.

This grace arises from the stern resignation—reflected in the storytelling—one feels in the speech and conduct of the Greenlanders. Their deliberate acquiescence to the condition they inhabit is itself ironic. . . . Resignation is never more evident than when it cracks, as it does when Margret, who normally dresses in a conservative purplish wool characteristic of her family's steading, wears a gown of red silk to meet her lover,

Skuli. . . . Margret discovers that when the patient, unsurprised "carapace of self" shatters, sin and vanity result. She sees

> that this is how it is that folk are made to desire what they know they should not have, they are made to wait for it, so that when it comes, no matter how dark and full of sin and repellent it is, they are glad enough to welcome it.

The Greenlanders portrays the hard place, the harsh relic of being where tradition is fragile and civilization no more durable than winter hay. The reader encounters so much truth in this novel that Sira Pall's analogy between the Greenlanders and all men seems not trite but inevitable. When the book ends, one remembers well the lives of Gunnar and Margret and Kollgrim, but one remembers most of all Sira Pall's (and Smiley's) compassion for the stonelike souls in his cure, souls that can barely be readied for heaven so resolute is their elemental grasp on existence. (pp. 38-9)

Verlyn Klinkenborg, "News from the Norse," in The New Republic, *Vol. 198, No. 20, May 16, 1988, pp. 36, 38-9.*

George (Edwin) Starbuck
1931-

(Born George Edwin Beiswanger) American poet.

Recognized as an accomplished composer of light verse, Starbuck uses flamboyant phrasings and formal poetic techniques to address social, political, and aesthetic issues. Adept at both traditional and free verse, Starbuck writes poetry characterized by satire, parody, keen intellect, whimsical humor, and unusual rhymes and puns. Dana Gioia observed: "If comedy and satire have maintained a place in contemporary poetry, if light verse continues in some small way to keep the general language free of pomposity and cant, no American poet is more responsible than George Starbuck."

Starbuck's first collection of verse, *Bone Thoughts* (1960), which won the Yale Series of Younger Poets Award, earned him praise as a protest poet with a wide repertoire of technical abilities. In this work, he confronts such topics as sex, war, conformity, and the atom bomb. In *White Paper* (1966) and *Desperate Measures* (1978), Starbuck employs a variety of forms, including sonnets, elegies, and acrostics, to further explore war and the darker side of daily existence. *Talkin' B.A. Blues: The Life and a Couple of Deaths of Ed Teashack; or, How I Discovered B.U., Met God, and Became an International Figure* (1980) satirizes college life in the United States by making use of the folk song tradition popularized by Woody Guthrie and Bob Dylan. *The Argot Merchant Disaster: Poems New and Selected* (1982), for which Starbuck received the Lenore Marshall/Nation Poetry Prize, collects verse from throughout his career. In a review of *The Argot Merchant Disaster,* Peter Porter commented: "Starbuck's extraordinary dandyism and playfulness with words is *sui generis:* he writes a heightened, surrealist light verse as though it was a last desperate remedy for the absurdity of so much contemporary American life."

(See also *Contemporary Authors,* Vols. 21-24, rev. ed. and *Contemporary Authors New Revision Series,* Vol. 23.)

JOHN HOLMES

[*Bone Thoughts*] is not the best title for the book, because the book is infinitely livelier and alive, but so is the title-poem ["**Bone Thoughts**"]. Bones, yes: of snake, bird, chick, owl, elephant, mouse, and poet. But under the live flesh, X-rayed with an ironic flash, they are as beautiful, absurd, and precise as watch-wheels, and as necessary and right for the life they wear. The flesh of the poem is its words, and words are the warm flesh of this book.

Subject-matter is one thing, and a poet uses what he has to. Starbuck uses love; Boston; the lost; war; poetry; Chicago; the found; the seasons; the bomb—and in each of these, some of the others, most often love. But the form is the real thing, the words and the sounds of the words, the pattern of the sounds of words. In this George Starbuck has a rare and brilliant gift. His word-ranging is extraordinary, and his pin-pointing of the

thing itself with the surprising right word is sharpshooting genius. All his targets are centered. There hasn't been as much word-excitement in a book of poems for years as there is in this one. Within the subject-matter there are of course moods, attitudes of mind, shifts of amusement, anger, tenderness, contempt; and there are words for them all, literary words, slang, intimate words, big words, right words, tight words. Starbuck can do anything with words, one feels certain; the question has been raised as to whether or not he attempts to do as much as he is obviously able to do. His wit bothers some people. It bothers his editor, who says, "Certainly there are escapades in these poems, some of them more spontaneous than others, that fade rather quickly once their point has been made." But Dudley Fitts also recognizes, as we all must, that accurate handling of paradox is a "queer rigor that discovers the pity in the horror. This is the saving violence of wit." What all this bother means is that this is a brilliant first book. . . .

Passion, learning, and wit, then, give this book its quality. The bones are warmly fleshed, but the poet never lets us forget the bones are there. This is as true of the four longish poems on Boston, written when Starbuck first moved there from Chicago and California, as it is of "**Cape Cod Autumn,**" "**Ghosts of the Missionaries,**" or "**One Man's Goose.**" Starbuck's subjects are very much of his time and his own age: the bomb is on his mind, so are sex, conformity, fakery, and integrity. The

352

most stirring serious poem in the book is **"Unfriendly Witness,"** sad and heavy with the world's cruelty. In other poems, Starbuck's seriousness comes on a double-take. At first it is merely brash, in the sonnet where he throws the textbook on Keats in the ocean, the text he is boning up on for a summer school course. On the double-take, later, it seems a fine flourish of a gesture, live student vs. dead book. The best double-take in the book is **"A Tapestry for Bayeaux."** Whether this poem is really about war, or not, war is never very far from most of these poems, the deep anxiety of the young these days. . . .

The one thing that is on every page is as Fitts says, "a stylistic flourish, an instance of technical bravura. Reading at random, I was arrested by what seemed to me an extraordinarily handsome complication of sights and noises . . . wherever one enters, the structure here is composed and complete." Starbuck has some of the marks and notions of the best poets, but this parts him from them. He confronts daily life, and structures his response, which brings us back to his great gift with words. Words are more important to him than he is to himself, an extraordinary thing to say truly about a poet, but of him it is true.

> John Holmes, "A New Poet Meeting a High Standard," in New York Herald Tribune Book Review, June 12, 1960, p. 4.

HARVEY SHAPIRO

[Starbuck's *Bone Thoughts* is attractive] because of its witty, improvisational surface, slangy and familiar address, brilliant aural quality (the play with consonant and vowel patterns is sometimes overdone and reads like a thinned and speeded-up Robert Lowell). Starbuck's language is exact and alive, though it can get modish—particularly when he is working his jukebox vein. He describes some city trees this way: "The elms along the drag / so mop and yet so fag." (Later, in a jazzed-up allusion, they become "Bare ruined chorus-lines".)

In a foreword, Dudley Fitts . . . describes Starbuck as "a man awake in the nightmare of our day." For all his lightness, this young poet is registering a protest; war and the Bomb (it figures in six of his poems) are among his subjects. He may become a spokesman for the bright, unhappy young men who have too much wit and style to run with the Beats.

> Harvey Shapiro, "A Quartet of Younger Singers," in The New York Times Book Review, October 23, 1960, p. 32.

JAMES DICKEY

[*Bone Thoughts*] seems a thin, bright, brittle affair to me, despite the writer's skill (here skill appears to be not so much skill as an elaborate form of trickery). I have never liked the notion of a poem as a sort of *performance,* and Mr. Starbuck's book convinces me that my prejudice has some foundation. There are clever parable-poems about dancing mice, and others with the tough-talking cynicism of the literary rather than the authentic tough ("The soft flush / of a cat-house after hours"), as well as a good deal of surface noise such as "Copper grapevines / clickety-clack their telegraphic ragtime / tongues . . . ," and so on. Only once or twice, as in **"Worship"** and in the italicized lines toward the end of the long poem addressed to Jonathan Edwards, do you get the feeling that the things of which Starbuck writes would know themselves, were they to read his poems about them. For the almost trance-like or in-

stinctive quality of authentic poetry, Starbuck's work is content to substitute a knowledgeable chattiness. It seems to me that Mr. Starbuck is another of the many young poets, both American and British, who must wait in company with their skill, as if they were indeed alone in the dark, until the right material or the right change in themselves or in the poetic climate can find them.

> James Dickey, in a review of "Bone Thoughts," in Poetry, Vol. XCVII, No. 5, February, 1961, p. 318.

ROBERT F. CAYTON

The verses in [*White Paper*] sting: "Man don't bug me with your stockpiles and witch hunts" and "Lyndon, I'm sick and tired of demonstrations." While the quality of the sting varies, the poet is surprisingly consistent in persisting his message: the continuous investigations by man of man's relation to his world. He develops his theme in a variety of forms in which the satire is sometimes further enriched by parody. A good example of parody is found in the long poem, **"Poem Issued by Me . . ."**. Starbuck's previous volume of poetry, *Bone Thoughts* . . . was praised for a lavish display of wit and a fine utilization of dramatic elements. Both of these traits are still abundant in this work. The wit is comprehensible, though it has, for my taste, too many macabre tones. Many of the lines here, in spite of the overt primary interest in the evils of today's world in them, are cadenced by subtle rhythms that are not discernible on first reading.

> Robert F. Cayton, in a review of "White Paper," in Library Journal, Vol. 91, No. 18, October 15, 1966, p. 4961.

GARY L. FISKETJON

Desperate Measures, by George Starbuck, is a collection of light verse—it says so, right on the acknowledgements page. I never know quite what to make of light verse; contrarily, I mouth the words "heavy verse" and wonder what *that* might be. In any case, I suppose one expects light verse to be lively and delightful, often whimsical, and Starbuck's is all of that and more. His poems are airy, his verbal resources prodigious, his love of rhyme and pun passionate and outrageous. These poems hop, skip, and jump.

Among the most appealing is **"Tuolomne,"** a poem which celebrates God's grandeur in a playful, mock-heroic fashion. Every now and again one senses the beauty of grass, of trees, of "pebble-brightening water," but the poem is essentially a grab bag of biblical and literary allusion, satire, and Pop culture. . . .

In this volume, . . . Starbuck is more than contented to "scribble side-notes to the fall of nations," to play hit-and-run with the myriad varieties of unwarranted seriousness: the Creative Writing Workshop, Professordom, Politics, Great Poetry in general and John Hollander in specific, and (in the title poem [**"Desperate Measures"**]) "the Oil Crisis, the Mills Crisis, the Grains Crisis, the Hays Crisis, the Butz Blunder, the Lance Matter, the Catfish Hunter Catastrophe and the Peanut Crunch. . . ."

His are indeed desperate measures, and when the rhymes seem merely clever, the humor more quantity than quality, I think of Robert Frost's remark: "If it is with outer seriousness, it must be with inner humor. If it is with outer humor, it must be with inner seriousness. Neither one alone without the other under it will suffice.'' Perhaps this is misapplied criticism. Starbuck is, to be sure, awfully good at what he does: You'll like this sort of thing, if this is the sort of thing that you like. (p. 72)

Gary L. Fisketjon, ''The Chapman Cometh,'' in The Village Voice, *Vol. XXIII, No. 29, July 17, 1978, pp. 72-3.*

MICHAEL McFEE

''I have committed whimsy,'' writes George Starbuck early in his *Desperate Measures,* a headlong collection of light verse virtuosity. For sheer ''verbal razzmatazz,'' as he calls it, Starbuck is the S. J. Perelman of contemporary poesy, with that cynic's fine eye and ear trained into a dazzling display of forms—clerihews, double dactyls, sonnets, villanelles, ballads, ''Pop-Popean ring-a-ding-dinging,'' ''ten arias in search of an operetta,'' and other hybrids, a ''houseful of / Metrical freaks.'' He can manage a manic string of rhymes beside which Skelton would look timid, and he hauls out some breath-wide polysyllables which ''make a feller's fez hurt.''

There will be those who find such ingenuity more desperate than measured, who might find such a collection superficially clever in its parts but hollow as a whole. I disagree. Besides the light versifier's traditional unity and depth of vision—i.e., as satirist of the faddish and pompous and pretentious, from writing workshops to Watergaters—Starbuck's temperament is peculiarly modern and dense in its reflexivity, its obsession with itself. While mock-waiting for a ''call'' or ''the pure Organic Form'' or ''a muse of fire, a sack of dough,'' Starbuck shows us that the words themselves are sufficient ''Apology,'' that the poems, glittering in their artifice like a multipartite baroque invention, are worlds enough. . . .

Michael McFee, in a review of ''Desperate Measures,'' in Carolina Quarterly, *Vol. XXXII, No. 1, Winter, 1980, p. 98.*

DEREK STANFORD

To read almost any page of George Starbuck's volume *The Argot Merchant Disaster* is to encounter a legerdemain possessing the elegance of Wallace Stevens and the divinely comic patter of the librettist Sir William Schwenck Gilbert of the D'Oyley Carte Opera set-up. Take, for instance, these lines from **''The Sixth Fleet Still Out There in the Mediterranean:''**

To be an
Omnibus of immensity with a tin-can retinue
To be cerulean, not herculean.
To shine against the bright blue empyrean
Bright as a dancer's eyelid, bright as the riffraff at a zoo
Crowding the bars with titbits and break through.
What an Odyssean outcome. What a coup.

When irony is as brilliant as this, it has all the rhetoric of a romantic poster. Out of illusion and bombast is engendered a wonderful scintillating beauty.

Derek Stanford, in a review of ''The Argot Merchant Disaster,'' in Books and Bookmen, *No. 329, February, 1983, p. 28.*

R. W. FLINT

Several poems in *The Argot Merchant Disaster* (which, by the way, contains no poem with that title) have the true anthological shine about them. Not to know **''The Spell Against Spelling''** argues oneself an ignoramus, so thoroughly does it exhaust the last comic reaches of academic orthography. Or what better ribbing of the summer workshop madness has ever been conceived and roundly carried out than **''The Sad Ballad of the Fifteen Consecutive Rhymes''**? Mr. Starbuck is not always so parochial. **''The Universe Is Closed and Has REMs,'' ''Magnificat in Transit From the Toledo Airport,'' ''The Great Dam Disaster, a Ballad,'' ''Sunday Brunch in the Boston Restoration''** carry what might thoughtlessly be called undergraduate humor to fresh heights of virtuosity—at least for Mr. Starbuck—in a spirit that X. J. Kennedy, another local wit, aptly calls shameless. Great sport, to be sure, but also something more, though exactly what is fortunately hard to say.

Lorenzo da Credi
Honored the Lord, St. Joseph, and Our Lady,
But not so hotsy-totsily
As did Benozzo Gozzoli.

So begins a poem that wrings all the starch out of art appreciation but with no loss of a fitting profundity. In **''Capital, Just Capital''** he early mapped out his territory:

The Law is
possibly the kindest
form of death.

The Letter
killeth, but the Spirit
deadeneth

to any
but its own mellifluous
waste of breath.

No paltering there, no olive branch extended to hierophants who persist in dancing their metaphysical minuets with the ghost of the late great other George, Santayana. Mr. Starbuck's obsessiveness has paid off, has made him the region's secular antiphon to its starstruck aspirations, a verbal pyrotechnician of very nearly the first order. (pp. 15, 38)

R. W. Flint, ''Debut and Continuity,'' in The New York Times Book Review, *February 13, 1983, pp. 15, 38.*

PETER PORTER

[Anyone] who enjoys the humane baroque of Anthony Hecht and Richard Wilbur will rejoice in Starbuck's work. . . . Starbuck's extraordinary dandyism and playfulness with words is *sui generis:* he writes a heightened, surrealist light verse as though it was a last desperate remedy for the absurdity of so much contemporary American life.

Consider two stanzas from a poem [in *The Argot Merchant Disaster*] dating from the Vietnam War. **''Late Late''** is comic verse but it catches the desperate tone of the homecoming of corpses, as if *Mash* were to be done for keeps. . . . Starbuck's poetry is wonderfully exuberant, and at the same time performs elegantly funny experiments with language. . . .

All through his book, the names and surface peculiarities of American life rear up in litanies and doxologies of love and wonder. He specialises in those jokey double dactyls often set as *New Statesman* competitions. In **''Falling Asleep over Scott,''** he even composes a lengthy poem out of such bits. 'Who in the name of the / Quasihistorical / *Sent* me this houseful of / Metrical freaks?' he asks. The answer must be his loving muse, who stands him in good stead throughout the 100 or so pages of this brilliant book. . . .

Peter Porter, "Charnel House Chic," in The Observer, *June 12, 1983, p. 29.*

WILLIAM HARMON

Those who cannot tell the difference or hear the resemblance between "Argo" and "argot," those to whom language equals Kleenex, only cheaper—those have no business reading *Poetry* and will not be interested in George Starbuck's breathtaking achievement. If, however, you have ears and live with any alertness in an English-speaking society, then you ought to know that Starbuck is among the most talented poets in the world, and you had better buy a copy of **The Argot Merchant Disaster** right away. I regard it as the best book published in 1982.

For one class of reader, nothing I say will disabuse them of their lamentable denseness. For the opposite class, nothing will be necessary to convince them of the great distinction of Starbuck's poetry. Between these extremes, there may be a lukewarm but attentive class who will recognize Starbuck's most obvious gifts—ingenuity, wit, humaneness—but may, deep down, doubt that a poet so lavishly endowed with cleverness, urbanity, and intellect can do his job solemnly and piously enough to be taken quite seriously. (p. 350)

Starbuck is not diabolically clever: he is not wicked or mean with language. No poet is less nasty. Even the victims targeted and skewered by his satire—Secretaries MacNamara, Rusk, and Kissinger, say—get off easy, as though their rascality were somehow cured and forgiven by his attention. Starbuck's is an angelic imagination, and his cleverness has a profound Orphic dimension. As far as can be from idle puns and puzzles, Starbuck's wordplay is like Shakespeare's or Joyce's. It is, like theirs, enormously comic, to be sure, but it betokens, at the same time, an extraordinary, loving measure of attention to the phenomenal anatomy of language and of the whole world as well.

But let me document the ingenuity. Starbuck belongs in some literary counterpart of the *Guinness Book* in any number of superlative categories: most consecutive rhyming syllables (fifteen); longest sequence of lines rhyming with the same sound but with different final letters for each sound (fourteen); best compounding of the Double Dactyl rules (*double* doubles in *both* stanzas, *twice*); finest serious poem in dactyllic monometer (**"A Tapestry for Bayeux"**); ditto in short (or poulter's) measure (**"Unfriendly Witness"**); most entertaining anti-mannerist re-executions of over-celebrated poems by Browning, Hopkins, Blake, Longfellow, and Mother Goose (**"Translations from the English"**); neatest Franco-Russian rhyme (*champagne* and *Do svidanya*); and most engaging instance of cross-alliteration (**"seven-league sea-legs"**).

I could go on, but I want to concentrate on Starbuck's matchless sensitivity to some recent changes in English. Since the time of Poe (who complained that English furnished too few spondees to support what Longfellow was doing in "Evangeline" and "The Courtship of Miles Standish"), the center of gravity in our language seems to have migrated—back, maybe, towards the Germanic genius of Old English. An increasing num-

ber of new words entering English and German seem built on the model of *railroad,* say—two substantial monosyllabic nouns hammered together and, fairly often, clinched by alliteration. . . . Vocabulary affects scansion, and since about 1840 the iamb seems to be giving way to the spondee, especially at the end of an important line ("On the bald street breaks the blank day," "Here I am, an old man in a dry month"). Gary Snyder, in his way, which may be shaped by monosyllabic Chinese, has worked out an answerable verse for space-age noun use; and so has Starbuck, in a different way. (pp. 350-51)

The Argot Merchant Disaster is so organized (in four parts: 1980s, 1950s, 1960s, 1970s) that the contents are bracketed by lively but thoroughly serious poems that are convincingly joyful. (p. 352)

William Harmon, "The Star of the Disaster," in Poetry, *Vol. CXLII, No. 6, September, 1983, pp. 350-53.*

JOHN HOLLANDER

George Starbuck's **The Argot Merchant Disaster** brings together his comic and satiric verses of the last two decades and reminds me, once again, of how dismal the solemnity of much pretentious literary verse is at the moment. Starbuck's indignation is not savage, but civil; he is unmatched in America today at taking the pompously or otherwise exasperatingly thrown ball and running with it, if not in the Harpo Marxist mode of Kenneth Koch (who is playing on a different field, in any case), then in the great choreographic tradition of Praed, Calverley, Gilbert, Samuel Hoffenstein and Ogden Nash. His skill is enormous: he can compose a whole poem on Benozzo Gozzoli's frescoes out of clerihews; he can take a technical problem and turn it into a bit of moral satire, and he can do what only the highest form of wit can accomplish, contriving surprises at two levels at once.

John Hollander, in a review of "The Argot Merchant Disaster," in The Yale Review, *Vol. 73, No. 1, October, 1983, p. R19.*

DANA GIOIA

Our choice for the 1982 Marshall Prize is George Starbuck's **The Argot Merchant Disaster: Poems New and Selected.** Some people will be a little shocked by the choice. Many more, we hope, will be delighted, because Starbuck is not the kind of poet who is commonly considered serious enough for major awards. A master of light verse and satire, he is usually relegated to a second class of literary citizenship. Segregated by the Jim Crow laws of contemporary criticism from all but a few specialized anthologies, his work is not widely known, and until the publication of this volume, all his earlier collections were out of print. But if his audience has not been large, it has been dedicated. Connoisseurs of language have long recognized him as one of the few living masters of satiric poetry.

For the last thirty years Starbuck has steered an independent course in the trendy currents of American poetry. He has written light verse in an age that demanded deep seriousness. He has blithely mastered both free and formal poetry when literary politicians required steadfast allegiance to only one camp. While many poets retreated into the narrow realm of personal concerns, he consistently engaged broader social and political issues. He has savagely satirized the military and the exploiters of the environment while not ignoring the shortcomings of the intellectual establishment to which, however reluctantly, he himself belongs. Treating these themes with objectivity in a distinctly personal manner, he affirmed the public role of the poet without succumbing to the dangers partisanship poses to art.

As the self-deprecating title of this collection suggests, Starbuck has a keen sense of his own limitations as a poet. He is no Prince Eliot nor pretends to be. He cultivates the role of active citizen rather than that of priest or prophet. This modesty, however, does not disguise Starbuck's conspicuous strengths. He has been rightfully praised as a brilliant stylist, a virtuoso of comic rhyme and rhythm, of literary pastiche and pun. He is also an honest and intelligent observer of his age, though less attention has been given to this crucial quality. Perhaps Starbuck has become the unwitting victim of his own inventiveness. The glittering surfaces of his poems have obscured the depth and seriousness of his concerns. Too few readers have noted the essential interdependence of his voice and vision. His humanity has given resonance to his technique just as his ingenious imagination has invigorated his beliefs.

But while Starbuck has often instructed, he has never failed to delight. *The Argot Merchant Disaster* is a hilarious book. Even poetry judges are human, and one deciding factor in our choice was how much he made us laugh and how surprisingly illuminating we found those moments of mirth. Reading the poems aloud to one another, we felt refreshed by the dexterous clarity of his language, enlightened by the sharp accuracy of his wit. His poems recaptured for us that elemental pleasure of hearing and pronouncing memorable speech basic to all poetry. (pp. 369-70)

If comedy and satire have maintained a place in contemporary poetry, if light verse continues in some small way to keep the general language free of pomposity and cant, no American poet is more responsible than George Starbuck. (pp. 370-71)

Dana Gioia, "Starbuck Wins Marshall Prize," in The Nation, New York, Vol. 237, No. 12, October 22, 1983, pp. 369-71.

Robert Penn Warren

1905-

American poet, novelist, critic, short story writer, biographer, essayist, editor, dramatist, and author of children's books.

An important figure in twentieth-century American literature who was appointed by the Library of Congress as the first Poet Laureate of the United States, Warren is the only writer to have received a Pulitzer Prize in both fiction and poetry. His novels and verse are often based on historical incidents and legends of the American South. Instead of examining the events themselves, however, Warren concentrates on the universal moral issues inherent in these occurrences, often focusing on the theme of the immutability of history. Cleanth Brooks commented: "The poetry, the fiction, and even the critical essays of Robert Penn Warren form a highly unified and consistent body of work. But it would be impossible to reduce it, without distorting simplifications, to some thesis about human life. . . . In the best sense, it is inductive: it explores the human situation and tests against the fullness of human experience our various abstract statements about it."

Born and raised in Guthrie, Kentucky, Warren was instilled at an early age with traditional agrarian values and a fondness for storytelling. He attributes much of his knowledge and interest in history, poetry, and oral tradition to his maternal grandfather, with whom Warren spent his childhood summers. Warren attended Vanderbilt University in Nashville, Tennessee, where he studied under poet and critic John Crowe Ransom. At Ransom's invitation, Warren became the youngest member of the Fugitive movement, which brought him into contact with such influential poets and critics as Donald Davidson and Allen Tate. Upholding the values of Southern agrarianism against the North's encroaching industrial economy, the Fugitives honored classical literature and metaphysical verse while advocating the use of formal diction and meter in poetry. After receiving his Master of Arts degree from the University of California at Berkeley and studying at Yale and Oxford, Warren taught English at Louisiana State University and, with fellow faculty members Cleanth Brooks and Charles W. Pipkin, founded the prestigious literary journal the *Southern Review*. Warren also collaborated with Brooks on the textbooks *Understanding Poetry: An Anthology for College Students* (1938) and *Understanding Fiction* (1943), which are based in part on the theories of New Criticism. Favoring close textual analysis of a literary work, New Criticism originated from discussions held by the Fugitives and the group that evolved from them known as the Agrarians.

Warren's early poetry was heavily influenced by the Fugitives. The pieces collected in his first two volumes, *Thirty-Six Poems* (1935) and *Eleven Poems on the Same Theme* (1942), combine folk narratives of Warren's native Kentucky with the metaphysical verse championed by Ransom and Tate. He also makes use of sonnets, lullabies, and lyrics to examine the relationship between humanity and nature. According to James H. Justus, Warren "learned very early [from Ransom] not only the technical resources of strict forms but also the exciting modulations possible in poetic conventions. . . . From Tate, Warren observed how the dissociated modern sensibility, exploited so forcefully by Eliot and Pound, could be accommodated to the

Southern temperament." *Selected Poems, 1923-1943* (1944) includes "The Ballad of Billie Potts," which is based on a Kentucky folk tale about a frontier innkeeper who makes his living by robbing and murdering travelers until he mistakenly kills his long-lost son. This work evidences Warren's evolving interest in narrative form and his preoccupation with original sin, which he details as an inevitable progression from innocence to knowledge and evil. In the extended poem *Brother to Dragons: A Tale in Verse and Voices* (1953; revised, 1979), Warren further addresses the nature of evil in this story of Lilburn Lewis, a nephew of Thomas Jefferson who murdered his slave for breaking a water pitcher that belonged to his deceased mother. *Promises: Poems, 1954-1956* (1957), for which Warren received his first Pulitzer Prize in poetry as well as the National Book Award, reveals a dramatic stylistic shift from narration to introspection. In contrast with the majority of verse written by the Fugitives, the poems in this volume are distinctly personal, and several are dedicated to Warren's children. Peter Stitt asserted: "[Before *Promises* Warren] was more a poet of despair and alienation than one of joy and union. . . . What we see in [*Promises*] is the poet questing to define, to understand, to apprehend, somehow to seize, the meaning of the joyous promise he senses."

Much of Warren's verse published during the 1960s and 1970s continued to express the importance of family and the need for self-examination. *You, Emperors, and Others: Poems, 1957-1960* (1960) offers a variety of styles, including narratives and parodies of nursery rhymes. *Incarnations: Poems, 1966-1968* (1968) is distinguished by Warren's experimentation with typographical arrangement and poetic diction. In the verse ballad *Audubon: A Vision* (1969), Warren chronicles the life of ornithologist and painter John James Audubon while celebrating the artist's ability to transform the brutality of nature into beauty through imagination. *Or Else: Poem/Poems, 1968-1974* (1974) features verse examining both the public and private life of its narrator, identified as "R.P.W." Warren received his second Pulitzer Prize in poetry for *Now and Then: Poems, 1976-1978* (1978). In this collection, he meditates on his life, beginning with his boyhood in rural Kentucky and progressing, in Warren's words, through "sixty years blown like a hurricane past." Warren's later verse is collected in *Being Here: Poetry, 1977-1980* (1980) and *Rumor Verified: Poems, 1979-1980* (1981) and is combined with earlier pieces in *New and Selected Poems, 1923-1985* (1985).

Warren is probably best known as the author of the novel *All the King's Men* (1946). This book offers a revealing examination of the complexities of political demagoguery in its portrayal of Willie Stark, an idealistic country lawyer who becomes corrupt after he is elected governor of an unnamed Southern state. Stark's rise and fall is documented by his cynical assistant, Jack Burden, whose moral beliefs are renewed following Stark's murder by a childhood friend. *All the King's Men* exemplifies Warren's fixation with original sin; in one passage, Stark articulates the state of humanity with his dictum: "Man is conceived in sin and born in corruption and he passeth from the stink of the didie to the stench of the shroud." At the time of its publication, this novel was regarded as a thinly-disguised biography of Huey "Kingfish" Long, the populist governor of Louisiana whose autocratic rule led to his assassination in 1935 and whose political machinations Warren observed during his tenure at Louisiana State University. Robert Gorham Davis called *All the King's Men* "brilliantly done, with magnificent brief set-pieces in which Robert Penn Warren writes prose equivalent to his poems in sound and rhythm and imagery." The winner of the Pulitzer Prize in fiction, *All the King's Men* was adapted into an Academy Award-winning motion picture in 1949 and has also been produced for the stage.

Many of Warren's other novels are based on specific events that took place in and around his native Kentucky. His first novel, *Night Rider* (1939), revolves around the Kentucky "tobacco wars" of 1909. In this work, an association of tobacco farmers utilizes violent methods to force independent growers to join their organization. *At Heaven's Gate* (1943) was suggested by the career of Luke Lea, a Tennessee banker and politician whose unscrupulous activities and violent death generated scandal during the time that Warren attended Vanderbilt University. In *World Enough and Time* (1950), Warren offers an interpretation of an infamous homicide case that took place in antebellum Kentucky. From basic factual information, Warren creates a surrealistic tale centering on a young attorney who faces execution for the murder of a man who allegedly seduced his fiancée. *Band of Angels* (1955) addresses the nature of freedom and the search for identity. This work concerns a plantation owner's spoiled daughter who discovers her black ancestry and is sold into slavery following her father's death. While in bondage, the girl suffers many indignities before realizing her inner strength and resolve. *The Cave* (1959) derives from another incident that took place during Warren's

undergraduate years involving a young explorer who died after being trapped inside a cave for eighteen days. Warren employs this tragedy as an allegory to comment on communal responsibility and moral knowledge. *Wilderness: A Tale of the Civil War* (1961) relates the adventures of a European Jew who emigrates to the United States to join the Union Army.

Warren's next work of fiction, *Flood: A Romance of Our Time* (1964), details the observations of a Hollywood scriptwriter who returns to his decaying Tennessee hometown to gather material for a film documenting the region's misfortunes. In *Meet Me in the Green Glen* (1971), an adulterous woman kills her husband and allows her lover to be sentenced to death for her crime. *A Place to Come To* (1977) dramatizes the efforts of Jed Tewksbury, a renowned classical scholar, to confront his squalid upbringing in order to live comfortably in the present. In his review of this book, Jonathan Yardley noted: "[Warren] is always straining to answer the big questions, to take on the great concerns of human existence."

Warren is also well known for his biographies of abolitionist John Brown and Jefferson Davis, the president of the Confederacy during the Civil War. His literary studies include *Modern Rhetoric* (1949; reprinted as *Fundamentals of Good Writing: A Handbook of Modern Rhetoric*) and *Democracy and Poetry* (1975). In addition, he has edited *Faulkner: A Collection of Critical Essays* (1966) and *Selected Poems of Herman Melville* (1971).

(See also *CLC*, Vols. 1, 4, 6, 8, 10, 13, 18, 39; *Contemporary Authors*, Vols. 13-16, rev. ed.; *Contemporary Authors New Revision Series*, Vol. 10; *Something about the Author*, Vol. 46; *Dictionary of Literary Biography*, Vols. 2, 48; and *Dictionary of Literary Biography Yearbook: 1980*.)

In this volume commentary on Robert Penn Warren is focused on his novel *All the King's Men*.

ROBERT GORHAM DAVIS

In 1935, the year that [Louisiana governor] Huey Long was shot and killed, Robert Penn Warren, a distinguished poet and associate professor at the University of Louisiana, began editing *The Southern Review* with Cleanth Brooks. It was one of the best and purest literary quarterlies in the United States, and it was paid for by a brilliant and unscrupulous vulgarian who had imposed a naked dictatorship of fraud and force on the State of Louisiana, and who was now reaching out, through undercover alliances and Share-the-Wealth Clubs, for national power.

The Southern Review was completely free to print whatever its editors, men of integrity, thought best, and yet by that very fact, and by the presence of such men at the University of Louisiana, Long's ambitions were being served. He had poured millions of dollars into the university with a Fascist's love of buildings, particularly of stadiums. He had some of his happiest moments parading his heavily mechanized ROTC before visiting celebrities and personally conducting the huge bands and the elaborate cheering at football games. But his larger purpose was to win over the ambitious youth of the State and make them leaders in his national Share-the-Wealth program. Half the students at L.S.U. were getting money from State jobs, with all the corruption and intrigue inseparable from such an arrangement in Long's Louisiana.

Moreover, Huey Long interfered in university affairs in characteristic fashion. . . . He expelled honor students for criticizing his rule over student organizations. Such acts naturally aroused great protest. To forestall blacklisting by national educational organizations and to placate intellectuals, Long was shrewd enough to have able writers and teachers brought to the university and given freedom of expression and teaching as long as they let him have his way in politics.

The ethics of collaboration in such a regime, with medicine substituted for education, is the theme of *All the King's Men.* Should Dr. Adam Stanton, the aristocrat, the man of ideas, consent to run the great hospital built by the dictator, the man of action, Willie Stark, whose methods he despises? Should his aloof pride keep him out of living history just bcause it isn't as pure and objective as science? Should a good man refuse to do greater good through the aid of Willie Stark for fear some of Stark's dirt might stick to the goodness?

Warren had been troubled by similar themes in his earlier fiction. *Night Rider,* a historical novel of the organization of the tobacco farmers, told what happened when violence was used as the last resort in support of a just cause. His second novel, *At Heaven's Gate,* was a dress rehearsal for *All the King's Men.* There, too, Warren dealt with political and business corruption; with past and present evil; with the relation of aristocrats and back countrymen. And he used in part the story of a national figure, Sergeant Alvin York. But, rich and complex though it was, *At Heaven's Gate* did not hold together. There was nothing to give it the unity, drive and immediacy that the realities of Huey Long's career give *All the King's Men.*

For Robert Penn Warren is writing about the real Huey Long even more frankly than Adria Locke Langley was in her very successful *A Lion Is in the Streets.* The details of the hero's education, mannerisms and features; of the impeachment proceedings and assassination, put this beyond question. The novel must be judged, then, in political as well as literary terms, for its total effect is to justify Long and the intellectuals who played ball with him; to romanticize him; to have a kind of love affair with him through the three women who adore him, one of them implausibly and inexplicably, the aristocratic heroine. The man of action and the man of ideas yearn toward each other, "each incomplete with the terrible division of their age." In between is the reporter Jack Burden, the thoroughly unpleasant teller of the story, who is able to move freely through the two worlds of ideas and action, of the old and the new politics, because he is nothing in himself.

It is not simply that Willie Stark is made to justify himself in terms that Long might have used: that is, that a job had to be done for the people of Louisiana, and he was willing to play dirty politics if that was necessary to get it done. [At one point in Warren's novel, Stark asserts:]

> Dirt makes grass grow; a diamond ain't a thing in
> the world but a piece of dirt that got awful hot. And
> God-a-Mighty picked up a handful of dirt and blew
> on it and made you and me and George Washington.

But Warren also simplifies and alters Long's career almost in the spirit of Parson Weems. In an early scene in *All the King's Men,* the cynical reporter and the fiery Irish girl secretary, like characters in a Clarence Budington Kelland serial, get hold of the earnest young teetotaling politician who is the dupe of higher-ups and who is boring the people with theories and statistics. They tell him the truth, get him mad, get him drunk, and send him out to make the speech that launches his career. At the end of the novel, as a result of his son's paralysis in a football accident, Willie Stark reforms completely, goes back to his simple, good wife; breaks with his dishonest lieutenants, and tells the reporter with his dying breath that, if he had been spared, things would have been different from then on. The reporter becomes good, too.

All the King's Men is brilliantly done, with magnificent brief set-pieces in which Robert Penn Warren writes prose equivalent to his poems in sound and rhythm and imagery; lyric passages full of wisdom and acute observation about a boy's falling in love; about men growing old; about being a failure; about parents and children; about a cow seen at night; a woman seen from a train; friendships in childhood; changes of season in the slums. In his descriptive passages, Warren records almost too sharply, as if with glasses to overcorrect myopia, so that we stare from a few inches away at shreds of shuck lying in the pig's trough, or at the creping of a lovely woman's neck, or at japonica petals in a pool after rain, or at a man's cortex laid bare by the surgeon's knife.

Mixed with this pure gold is the brass of slick writing and melodrama that comprises the rest of the novel. Warren knows his trade. . . . But his writing can be false, nevertheless, as in the description of Anne Stanton, "that fine, slender, compactly made, tight-muscled, soft-fleshed, golden-shouldered mechanism," or of Burden's first wife, "a mystic combination of filet mignon and a Georgia peach, aching for the tongue and ready to bleed gold." And final drama is attained by extravagant use of Polti's famous thirty-six basic plot situations. Burden, for instance, causes the suicide of the man he did not know to be his father, and saves his mother's soul in doing it. Adam Stanton, later the assassin of Stark, operates on the spinal cord of the son of the man who had seduced his sister.

But it is the political pattern of *All the King's Men* that is really disturbing. The treatment of Negroes, always called "niggers" and given strictly Stephen Fetchit roles, is not surprising, since Warren contributed the piece, **"The Briar Patch,"** to the Southern manifesto, *I'll Take My Stand,* and had written earlier a whole book attacking the legend of John Brown. It is not surprising that he should assume that Long's program would economically benefit the mass of the people, despite evidence to show that, through squandering money, lowering wage rates and imposing indirect or hidden taxes, Long made their situation worse. But it is surprising that *All the King's Men* never really faces the threat of men like Long to the democratic process itself.

Robert Penn Warren is fascinated by the strong man of action, as many of our war novelists were fascinated by romanticized Nazis. And the question of *All the King's Men* is solely whether the man of ideas can work with the dictator in the interests of historic change; whether, in carrying out that change, the unscrupulous vulgarian is not really a better man than the selfish, dignified, discreet and also immoral politicians from whom he seized power. Warren does not ask—the question apparently has no imaginative appeal for him—whether American tradition does not demand that we fight men like Long with the utmost resolution and with all the democratic means at our disposal, in order to preserve in this country and in the world free, open, pluralistic societies in which individual rights are protected by law and in which ultimate control is invested below in the people and not above in Willie Stark. Anyone able to swallow the dictator's tempting logic of *All the King's*

Men will find an instant emetic in a few random savorings of the real Huey Long as described by such reporters as Forrest Davis, Carleton Beals and Harnett T. Kane. (pp. 3, 24)

Robert Gorham Davis, "Dr. Adam Stanton's Dilemma," in The New York Times Book Review, August 18, 1946, pp. 3, 24.

HAROLD C. GARDINER

Humpty-Dumpty was an egg. Whether or not the author intended the connotation, his title [*All the King's Men*] not only recalls that fact, but also suggests that his story is about an egg—in fact, about a number of eggs, and a harder-boiled clutch it has rarely been my misfortune to try to stomach.

Chief egg is The Boss, Willie Stark, political mogul in a State not named. Willie is the third or fourth of recent fictional recreations of Huey Long, complete in all details, even including the final assassination scene in the marble-walled State capitol. He is the same crude-mouthed, unscrupulous, dynamic figure whose love for the "peepul" of the American boobocracy is matched only by his immoral ego-mania. Surrounding him are various other eggs, all of whom were boiled hard in various stages of rottenness. First among them, for the purposes of the story, is Jack Burden, the chief's research man, whose honorable estate it is to dig up the dirt on all whom The Boss wants to rub out politically, and not infrequently, physically.

The story is told by Burden and *is* one—I, for one, put the book down tired out: I was tired of the story, an old rehash of the oft-told tale of political noisesomeness; tired of the sock-feet on the mahogany desks; of the sub-human trigger-men; of the artesian wells of profanity; of the phony theologizing of the narrator.

But most of all I was tired of the casual blasphemy, as when Burden mocks at Baptism by saying that a man who presumably gets a new personality through a delicate brain operation may be considered to have been re-born "in the name of the Big Twitch, the Little Twitch, and the Holy Ghost. Who, no doubt, is a Twitch, too.". . . And I was tired unto yawning at the long scene of frustrated sexual liaison, in which the author takes a page and a half to detail all the preparations. . . .

I review the book thus at length for a reason. First, Mr. Warren is an author of some note, and the novel will attract wide attention; at last, it is safe to say that it will be strongly advertised. Second, the man writes with power, though it must be pointed out that his technique of paragraph-long, meandering sentences makes unduly hard going. It is shame that he has so prostituted his talents. . . .

A study of political and moral corruption may be legitimate and valuable for those interested in civic reform and abnormal psychology. The general reader should keep his nose out of them—at least until the day when publishers will give away, free with every copy of such a book, and in good working order, a gas mask.

The story ends with a dim suggestion that Burden has come to realize that perhaps there is more to life than mankind twitching at the end of a cord like a marionette. Such vestigial spiritual awareness, however, is a niggardly draft after the bleak wastes.

Harold C. Gardiner, "Why Put Him Together?" in America, Vol. LXXV, No. 21, August 24, 1946, p. 503.

DIANA TRILLING

Robert Penn Warren's *All the King's Men* is not the first novel to draw its inspiration from the career of Huey Long. Some years ago there was John Dos Passos's *Number One*, which I have not read, and a few seasons ago there was Hamilton Basso's *Sun in Capricorn*, which, as I remember it, dealt rather freely with the actual biography of the Louisiana Kingfish. Mr. Warren would seem to stay closer to his original: he gives us a complete life-story, from the days when his Willie Stark was just an earnest, urgent, back-country farm boy to his early years in law practice and his first venture into politics, through his flashing rise to political power and the governorship, to finally, his assassination. I say "would seem" because, acquainted with only the broadest outlines of Long's life, I have no way of knowing how much of Mr. Warren's detail is a matter of record and how much supplied by the novelist's imagination. But since Mr. Warren offers his story wholly as fiction, the question of factual accuracy need not be raised.

And a very remarkable piece of novel-writing *All the King's Men* surely is. For sheer virtuosity, for the sustained drive of its prose, for the speed and evenness of its pacing, for its precision of language, its genius of colloquialism, I doubt indeed whether it can be matched in American fiction. Mr. Warren's method is the method of great photography, his poetry an overtone of photographic documentation. Perhaps one must imagine the camera of Walker Evans inching over mile after mile of the South, piling up its record of personal portraits and place portraits and portraits of things, catching fact after fact of the Southern heat and mystery, indolence and venality and despair, in order to begin to have a notion of what and how Mr. Warren sees.

Nor are its imposing gifts of composition the only recommendation of *All the King's Men*. There is also its largeness of intention. Mr. Warren's study of a political leader is intended to investigate the moral relativism inherent in the historical process. One might describe it as a fictional demonstration of Hegel's philosophy of history. For what Mr. Warren seems to be saying, with Hegel, is that spirit or goodness arises only out of the ruck of living and the clash of self-seeking wills. He is questioning the absolutes of good and evil which are so much the assumption of a large part our present-day political morality.

But all relativistic positions are peculiarly liable to misinterpretation, and the Hegelian relativism especially must be read very purely not to be translatable into a justification of means by their end, or not to be understood as the belief that good always, even often, has its source in evil. Yet here precisely is the inadequacy of *All the King's Men,* that it can give rise to just such misconceptions of what I am sure was its very much purer informing idea. It is in fact difficult *not* to infer from Mr. Warren's novel that a Willie Stark's absolute power is justified by such public benefactions as the fine hospital he builds, or that we are to welcome the Willie Stark type of political unpleasantness as a step in political progress.

In part, of course, this may be the inevitable result of translating the hero of history into a hero of fiction. For, concerned with the world historical figure, Hegel was concerned only with his historical or force aspect, not with his ethical aspect; but fiction always deals primarily with individual human beings, and only by suggestion with philosophical abstractions, and when Mr. Warren personifies his abstractions, as the novelist must, he in effect alters a way of viewing history into a system of personal morality from which, then, we evolve a system of political morality. Thus Willie Stark is not an evolutionary force, but first a person on whom his author exercises an ethical judgment; and if only because he is the hero of the novel, we must assume that this judgment is largely admiring or approving. The result is that it is the demagogue's usual dull ambivalence—half the obsession with power and half a soft generosity and idealism—that is made to stand for the dialectical struggle of good and evil in both individuals and society. . . .

All the King's Men is told through the point of view of a young newspaperman-researcher attached to Stark—one of those pre-fabricated figures out of the city room whom Mr. Warren endows with a wonderful eye but with no equivalent gift of inward vision. . . . But although Jack Burden is so essentially shabby a person that he vulgarizes any thought he entertains or acts out, it is to him that Mr. Warren entrusts an idea of history that requires the nicest discriminations. It is Burden's morally ambiguous evaluation of Stark that we are forced to accept as Mr. Warren's.

And if the low quality of Burden's moral awareness is responsible for most of the ethical and political confusion of *All the King's Men,* so must it in some measure account, I think, for the failure of Mr. Warren's novel to achieve the artistic stature commensurate with the author's writing gifts. For one has the idea that were Mr. Warren's narrator to inhabit wider realms of thinking and feeling, he would not only alter our view of the book's central character but also give greater meaning to its subsidiary people, that he would raise all his associates out of the realm of the commonplace and raise their conflicts from melodrama to drama. Certainly the conception of almost all Mr. Warren's characters fails to match the energy of the prose in which they are delineated. While Mr. Warren's language draws upon every resource of actuality, his creation of people lacks all freshness of perception. It is the inner human mystery that Mr. Warren blinks as he pursues the mystery of the historical process.

> *Diana Trilling, in a review of "All the King's Men,"*
> *in* The Nation, *New York, Vol. 163, No. 8, August*
> *24, 1946, p. 220.*

GEORGE MAYBERRY

[*All the King's Men*] is in the tradition of many classics; while it deals with themes and characters that are not confined to its given time, its action is composed of Sunday-supplement history and melodrama. *All the King's Men* is at least the fourth novel to make use of the Huey Long story . . . but the idealization of Long in the fictional Willie Stark is so complete that Warren can hardly mean his novel to be taken as literal history. And when it is said that the action revolves around the adulterous love of an aristocratic Southern girl for the wool-hat boy who became Governor of a state that in many ways physically and politically resembles Louisiana—when that girl's honor is avenged by her brother and when even a mid-Victorian mysterious parenthood is used to provide a major climax, it must be remembered that the great classic writers from the Greeks to Hemingway worked with no more inventive fables.

To reduce Warren's "plot" to its elements and at the same time avoid a dry absurdity is comparable to an attempt to suggest what "Hamlet" is "about" through a brief paraphrase. In his youth Jack Burden of Burden's Landing had been the friend of Adam and Anne Stanton, the children of Governor Stanton. There had been one summer when Jack and Anne had taken it for granted that they would marry—why they didn't

is one of the reasons you will have to read *All the King's Men* practically word for word to find out. Years later Jack, having passed through the corruptions of the university, fruitless marriage and newspaper reporting, is the confidential adviser of Willie Stark, who had come down out of the hills to become Governor and overthrow what was left of the world and traditions of the Burdens and the Stantons. The day came when Jack Burden walked into Anne Stanton's room to ask if she and Willie—"Then I looked into her face. She met my gaze quite steadily. I did not say anything. And I did not need to. For, looking at me she slowly nodded." And inevitably Adam was told, and in the corridors of the monstrous capitol that Willie had built, Adam shot him down to be killed immediately by Willie's gunman.

This, with an Elizabethan prodigality of subplotting and an even older use of *in medias res* and the flashback, is the story Jack Burden is given to tell. For in the first place *All the King's Men* is a story, though it is also an excellent political novel, and a genuinely philosophical novel, accomplishments which are rare enough in the history of our fiction. But it is primarily a superbly written narrative in which the surface of the writing is brilliantly integrated with the character of the narrator and the nature of his experience. The touchstones of such writing in our literature are, of course, *Moby Dick* and *Huckleberry Finn*, and more recently *The Sun Also Rises* and *The Great Gatsby*. The single quality that encompasses these varied books is the use of the full resources of the American language to record with imagination and intelligence a significant aspect of our life. Warren's last novel, *At Heaven's Gate,* suggested that he was one of the few of our writers who knew enough, had thought enough and was blessed with the ability to express his knowledge and his thinking in a dramatic narrative, to produce the really big book *All the King's Men* has turned out to be. (p. 265)

[*All the King's Men*] is a story of some definable people in a certain time and place, and an inquiry into good and evil and the nature of things. All together it is the finest American novel in more years than one would like to have to remember. (p. 266)

> *George Mayberry, "On the Nature of Things," in*
> The New Republic, *Vol. 115, No. 9, September 2,*
> *1946, pp. 265-66.*

LEO KIRSCHBAUM

For one reader, [*All the King's Men*] was dull and callow. The story is aimless until in the last three chapters it explodes into reckless Hitchcock, patched together out of indiscriminate violence and mechanical surprise. The characters are merely reiterated stock types: the good woman who bakes a cake in the midst of disorder, the cartoon politician, the highminded Southern jurist and gentleman who reads the classics and drinks good Bourbon, the idealistic young doctor, and so on. . . . None of them comes alive. For most of the book, the style varies between the turgidly poetic and the flat hardboiled, the latter much like Hemingway and for the same reason—to hide the hero's aching heart. Occasionally there is a flash of superb writing, but by and large the style is oversmart or highflown or semi-hysterical. . . . As for the novel's formal but erratically-presented philosophy, it is under-developed and unconvincing and unrelated to the narrative, both in its first phase (that we are *merely* neural agents) and in its second phase (that we *surely* possess wills). The values of the book are never clear-cut; loose poetry substitutes for intellect. *All the King's Men* can only be called a bad failure as a novel. (pp. 392-93)

All the King's Men is a serious attempt to set forth in the personality of its hero [Jack Burden]—in his constant frustration, in the complete lack of inner security that drives him to hitch on to the substitute father Willie Stark—a valid sensibility of our time, and through that sensibility, a valid image of our world. That, I suppose, is why the critics have given the novel such high marks. They have correctly identified the heart and mind that inform it as undeniably contemporary, and they have apparently considered that this novel represents the best that can be thought and done in American letters today. They may be right. The "I's" of Nathanael West's *Miss Lonelyhearts* and Edmund Wilson's *Memoirs of Hecate County* also suggest that to think and feel today is automatically to be damned. These "I's"—alike in being more-than-average serious, intelligent, observing, sensitive—are neurotics who suffer intensely from the modern world. They are not like the "I" of Juvenalian satire, who looks bitterly upon man's messy kettle of fish; they are in the kettle themselves, and they know it.

Seemingly, then, there could be two disparate judgments concerning the make-up of the narrator in Warren's novel. On the one hand, it could be said that his ambiguity, confusion, and high emotionality turn the book into a kind of case history of delayed adolescence, and that a case history, as American critics in general have yet to learn, is not a novel. Furthermore, since a novel is a construct that always seems to demand a limited and clear moral viewpoint, it may also be said that Warren has written a confused book, because his own relationship to the narrator of the novel is never made clear: what is *his* attitude toward Jack Burden? Does he too surrender to Willie Stark? On the other hand, one could say in reply what could also be said about another seemingly bad but disturbing novel, Hemingway's *To Have and Have Not:* Here is a hero who is sweating it out. He is neither careless nor sure. He sees a great deal and reacts deeply. He truly represents the contemporary ego. If art falsifies this ego, the less art it is.

This last seems true in principle. But I do not see why a truthful depiction of a modern Hamlet need necessarily be presented in bad prose, in a bad plot, and among hackneyed characters. Moreover, it is exceedingly debatable whether the particular neurotic patterns of Jack Burden's personality are truly representative of the situation of man in our time. Jack's inexplicable and hysterical refusal to have sexual relations with the woman he loves, romanticism castrating itself, seems to me a highly individual infantilism, and Jack's final amoral and mystical approval of the American fascist Willie Stark—who brings almost no named objective good to his people, who does not even recognize the presence of Negroes in his state—is a total abnegation of manhood that cannot be regarded as inevitable in any terms: neither the modern world, nor Willie Stark's state, nor Jack Burden's character, requires it. (pp. 393-94)

Leo Kirschbaum, "Leading Pulitzer Contender," in Commentary, *Vol. 2, No. 4, October, 1946, pp. 392-94.*

HENRY RAGO

The publication of *All the King's Men* assures Robert Penn Warren of a place among the handful of novelists in America worth taking seriously. His story moves chiefly through the fabulous but completely credible political career of Willie Stark, a Southern demagogue whose personality and language are a terrifying mixture of good and evil, the scripture and blasphemy, purity and cynicism. But Mr. Warren's hero, to my mind, is not Willie Stark, but the conscience of a people—the novel is about the South, about America, and about all men in "the terrible division" of modern society—and he brings this conscience to its point of greatest awareness in Jack Burden, who is with the Boss day in and day out as intellectual hatchet-man and stooge. It is Jack Burden who tells the story and who suffers in it. Burden (the name is good allegory) is a former newspaperman; he is heir to a respected family tradition in the community; he is deeply sensitive; one of Mr. Warren's skilful touches is in the startling differences in language between Burden's speeches and his thoughts. Burden knows from the beginning that the frustration which drives him to live on Willie Stark's energy worsens in an obscure guilt. But there *is* energy in Willie Stark, there is life there, for good or for bad. And so Burden exchanges the conflict which stifles all action in him for the paradoxes of good and evil in Willie Stark. Values do not conflict in Willie; they destroy each other. His personality is the destructive element in which things are made neutral. There is no value except the dionysiac one of the brute personality itself. Values for Willie are always "just a couple of jumps behind what [we need] to do business on." So Jack Burden suffers from betrayal at the outset, and the story is the intensification of that suffering, as he is led to betray more and more. The pattern here is classic, but the timing and the astonishing climax are new, and genuinely from Mr. Warren's own hand.

The squalor which Mr. Warren reports is given literally and straight with the modest look of mere journalism, but it is saturated with a kind of Greek religious sense. His pivot is the tragic choice between not-knowing and knowing: not-knowing leaves us only the emptiness of the life lived under "the godhead of the Great Twitch"; knowing brings us the anguish of incompleteness in that separation between "idea" and "fact" which is the definition of our age. And between emptiness and doom, Mr. Warren's choice is for doom; it is, in any case, an effort, even if one dies in the effort; it is, at least, a *choice,* and emptiness is not. . . . (p. 599)

T. S. Eliot once complained that most modern novels are not "written." *All the King's Men* is completely written. The language does all the work. It does all the slowing down, and the speeding up; it controls all the tone and volume; and it controls the reader; you read this book not at your own pace but at Mr. Warren's. It is language that gives us not only the characters (even, in an extraordinary way, the most casual characters) but the internal "selves" within a single character. If Mr. Warren gave us only Willie Stark, we should be grateful for an important contribution to American rhetoric. But there are the accents of all the other characters. And in the thoughts of Jack Burden, one sees how Thomas Wolfe would have written if he had had flair and coherence. There is not a sentence in this book that is free of Mr. Warren's writing. For such completeness we can be doubly grateful and commend both his integrity and his generosity. (p. 600)

Henry Rago, in a review of "All the King's Men," in The Commonweal, *Vol. XLIV, No. 25, October 4, 1946, pp. 599-600.*

THE TIMES LITERARY SUPPLEMENT

The problems that confront an American novelist are so different from those with which writers in this country must deal that it is sometimes not easy to find a common ground of criticism. The instinct for dramatizing all events and relationships has become so much part of the American tradition of life that situations which seem to English eyes exaggerated or over-simplified are found on examination to have their own American reality, simply because they are so generally accepted in such terms in America. Thus [*All the King's Men*], based on the Huey Long dictatorship of Louisiana, manages to convey an extraordinarily vivid picture of various aspects of political corruption in the Southern States and elsewhere, without somehow ever putting the subject in perspective; and yet the portrait of Willy Stark, "the Boss," gives such a clear idea of how a third-rate demagogue of this type might look to one of his entourage that it is hard to say whether the author could have made a more balanced approach without altering the whole content of the book. . . .

All the King's Men is an interesting and talented novel, though it suffers from being "over-written" in a peculiarly American way. There are, indeed, signs that the movement of the twenties and early thirties to simplify style is now at an end in the United States, and that American writers—and especially Southern writers—are developing a highly ornamented, and often obscure, idiom that looks back, perhaps, to Herman Melville.

"Southern Dictator," in The Times Literary Supplement, *No. 2414, May 8, 1948, p. 257.*

WALTER ALLEN

[*All the King's Men*] is a masterly rendering of life and government in a backward American state in which heat, dirt, squalor, illiteracy and the remains of a traditionally gracious way of life for the wealthy exist side by side. It is, as it were, the world of the decayed houses of Faulkner, of the moronic poor whites of Caldwell, set in their social and economic context.

But Mr. Warren is not content merely to tell the story of the rise and fall of Willy Stark; through his narrator, Jack Burden, he sets it in perspective. Burden will probably be something of a problem for the English reader. Stark's confidential secretary, he is a newspaperman talking with the tough cynicism that we expect of newspapermen in American fiction. So it comes as a shock to realise that Burden is much more than this, that he has been trained as an historian and a scholar and that almost by second nature he translates events during Stark's governorship into their historical analogies. And, as the book develops, Burden grows in importance, so that by the end it is his story rather than Stark's that Mr. Warren seems to be telling. Yet one is aware of no feeling of strain in Mr. Warren's handling of his parallel stories; they are indeed organically related; for the fall of Stark and his long consideration of the significance of the career of his former chief lead to Burden's redemption from what he calls the dream of the "great twitch," the principles of which are: "First, that you cannot lose what you have never had. Second, that you are never guilty of a crime which you did not commit." It is not until the end of the book that we realise that Burden's redemption, his discovery that "history is blind, but man is not," has been the outcome of events going far back into the past, that Mr. Warren has most cunningly been unwinding a plot of truly Ibsenite complexity. The occasional sentimentalities, the over-simplification of human relations into which Mr. Warren slips, are of the kind that seem inseparable from even the best contemporary American fiction. They do not prevent the book from being a very formidable attempt at a novel on the grand scale.

Walter Allen, in a review of "All the King's Men," in The New Statesman & Nation, *Vol. XXXV, No. 900, June 5, 1948, p. 464.*

MALCOLM O. SILLARS

All the king's men, and the king himself, can be clearly seen to represent the great American tradition of Populism that swept the poorer agricultural areas of the Middle West and the South in the late 1930's. It is surely far more than the narrow context of the life of Huey Long, as too many have mistakenly supposed. The spirit of Willie Stark has reared itself in many states and in many forms; in Bloody Bridles Waite of Colorado, Sockless Jerry Simpson of Kansas, William Jennings Bryan of Nebraska, Alfalfa Bill Murray of Oklahoma, Kissin' Jim Folsom of Alabama and many others. The political elements of *All the King's Men* are rooted in the past and yet are all, in one way or another, degenerative of the tradition they represent.

There are four such elements which should be isolated and their interrelationships known in order to see more clearly the novel's meaning. The hill people of the South represent a particular economic group who are now, as they were in the days of Willie Stark, and earlier in the days of Pitchfork Ben Tillman, set apart from the more aristocratic and proper conservative people of the flatlands. Willie Stark is an example of the leaders produced by the hills to do battle on their behalf. The political position of the aristocrats of the Delta illuminates Stark's rise and fall. Jack Burden is an aristocrat who loses, then finds himself in trying to bridge the gap between the hills and the Delta.

Essential to the understanding of Willie Stark is an understanding of the social construct which produced him. The hill people are a crucial phenomenon in the economic and social structure of middle-western and southern agricultural areas. The geographical dividing line between hills and black belt only serves to draw into sharper focus, in the South more than elsewhere, the economic battle. These hill people are holders of small plots of poor red farmland from which they eke out an existence with the assistance of amazing stubbornness, and an evangelical Protestant code of ethics. They see themselves as the chosen people who do battle with the more prosperous, and evil, Delta planters. They are fiercely individualistic.

They were less inclined to favor the Civil War because they had less interest in Negro slavery. They were more susceptible to Populism with its interest in freeing the small farmer from the control of the bankers, railroads, elevator operators and other more well to do elements of the society. . . . They supported the New Deal and in the election of 1948 they endorsed the Democratic party more than did the Delta, which found the politics of the New and Fair Deals threatening their power position by raising the standards of the Negroes and the rednecks of the hills.

The same Populist sentiment was strong in the Corn Belt and for similar reasons. In the South it was rocky red soil; in Kansas and Nebraska it was rainfall. In the late nineteenth century there was real correlation between the amount of rainfall and the intensity of Populist fervor in western Nebraska. *All the King's Men* is the product of a socio-economic vortex which reduced a proud people to desperate action.

The hill people have a concept of good and evil by which they see themselves as the chosen people who have had their birthright stolen. To the Populist, as to most liberals, good and evil are concentrated. One attribute is found in one group and one in another. Or, the individual is good and governments, or corporations or bankers or what have you, are evil. Thus, reasons the liberal, return the society to its natural owners and there will be peace in the land. (pp. 345-46)

One of the lessons to be learned from *All the King's Men* is that these conditions still exist and this latent evangelical liberalism is always present. In 1948 Henry Wallace (a curious combination of populist and aristocrat) tried to exploit this agrarian liberalism with his "Gideon's Army" and his promises to the "little people." His liberalism had lost its roots, however, and the stronger urban liberalism which dominated the Wallace campaign was not acceptable to rural people. Further, in 1948 Wallace had in Harry S. Truman, an opponent who better fit the picture of the hill people's leader. The conditions—economic, social and religious—which formed the amalgam producing Willie Stark are a significant part of American history. (p. 347)

Willie Stark, the leader produced by the conditions and prejudices of the hill people, is the second of the important social elements in Robert Penn Warren's novel, for while Willie Stark is an individual, he is also an institution. He has all the background and beliefs of the hill people mentioned earlier. As county treasurer he sacrifices his political life in a fight to see that the courthouse gang in Mason City does not make the new schoolhouse a political plum. His opponents tell the people that the company submitting the lowest bid would bring in Negroes from the lowlands and thus deprive the local people of jobs. Incidentally, they tell the people that the Negroes would be the semi-skilled workers and the hill people that were hired would be the common laborers. Essentially this is the point at which the hill people always break with the Negroes. They do not have as many to contend with as in the flat country and so do not fear their political power as the aristocrats do. But when the Negro threatens them economically, race becomes an issue. Willie fights but loses. Other real life Willie Starks are destroyed politically in just such a manner.

The fire escape of the schoolhouse, built of inferior materials, falls during a fire drill and three children are killed. Willie is thus made a political power. He had warned them about what the courthouse gang was trying to do and he was right. With this he advances to the second step in the rise of the redneck leader, what Professor V. O. Key calls the "friends and neighbors" politician. In the hills around Mason City he is a political power. His is the protest for the inarticulate people of the area.

His rise to statewide prominence comes when Willie again sacrifices himself politically. Convinced of his popularity he is induced to enter the race for Governor by Tiny Duffy, the perfect stereotype of the smalltown political boss. During the campaign, Stark discovers that he has been nominated to take votes from MacMurfee, a candidate who is also popular in the hills. Willie goes to the political rally, rather symbolically pushes Tiny Duffy off the platform and reveals his part in the act. He tells the people to vote for MacMurfee and not for him. He tells them to sit in judgment on MacMurfee and remove him if he is wrong. MacMurfee wins the election. Willie, by this sacrifice, becomes a state-wide figure. He fits the standards of honesty that the hill people want and becomes their champion. He was duped as they had been, time and time again.

Probably of interest here is the change in the spoken rhetoric of Willie Stark. Previous to this time Stark talked about issues, about specific problems of taxes, education and roads. His speeches were clearly dull and unemotional. When he speaks at the rally he speaks to the emotional needs of the hill people. One might reflect that this was Willie's awakening, or rebirth if you will, to the realities of political power and the first step to his destruction. (pp. 347-48)

MacMurfee, of course, fails to live up to the promises of the election and the inevitable wave of the future sweeps Willie into the Governor's Mansion. But Willie is different from the rest. He cannot be bought by political machines. Instead he forms his own machine and like too few others who rose in a similar manner, he actually goes about attempting to solve the problems of the hill people. He builds highways, schools and hospitals. He raises the taxes of the rich (the lowland aristocrats) and defends the hill people in the courts.

The greatest fight is the one which Willie goes through in relating his past to the realities of politics. He finds out that there is both good and evil in all men. Byram B. White, as State Auditor, dips his hand into the till and Willie is shaken up. The little man from the hills is just as capable of evil as the folks of the lowlands. Not that putting one's hand into the till is so bad—for Willie had come now to realize that this is an essential part of the machinery of political power, but White does it behind Willie's back. In short, he is disloyal to the cause which Willie represents. And White's willingness to write an undated resignation deepens Stark's realization of his power over men. (p. 348)

Out of his experiences there grows the conclusion that life is not just a clash of good and evil but rather (returning selectively to his fundamentalist Sunday school) all evil. As Willie Stark puts it, "Man is conceived in sin and born in corruption and he passeth from the stink of the didie to the stench of the shroud."

This conviction influences Willie's concept of progress profoundly. His real concern is with the problem of producing that which is good. . . .

Indicative of his change in philosophy, there is a degeneration in Willie Stark's oral rhetoric. The genuine Populist cry for justice is dissipated into demagoguery. (p. 349)

There is further degeneration in Willie. It is exemplified by his infidelity to his wife, Lucy. Lucy, the prime mover in Willie's earlier high moral purpose, is relegated to the position of a publicity piece. She is used for the furtherance of the Governor's political ends. For sexual satisfaction Willie turns to a collection of women who are not the product of the hills. In short, Willie falls into the very pattern of life in his personal affairs which the hill people have hated (or perhaps envied) in the people of the lowlands—heavy drinking and infidelity. In the end it is Anne Stanton's brother Adam who kills Willie when he finds out that his sister had been Willie's mistress. Thus, Willie's failure to do the impossible and fulfill the picture which the redneck has of his leaders caused his downfall. (p. 350)

[In] death, Willie Stark returns to his roots. There is a solution to the evils of the society in which the hill people live and the solution is in the conquest of political power by an articulate spokesman who will act. Whether or not this belief is correct is not an issue. The real point is that the hopes and aspirations of these people are genuine and Willie's attempts to meet these needs are also genuine. It is in the red dirt and man's weaknesses that Willie's failures are rooted. The fallacy of Populism, and perhaps of all liberalism then, is the fallacy of not understanding nature.

The third social element in the novel is the aristocracy of the Delta. Like the geographical division between the hills and the plains, the aristocracy of the deep South is more clearly defined than in other sections of the country. On the plains of the deep South, the plantation owners have built a tradition of aristocratic conservatism. They use political power to protect a social system which is grounded in stability and respect for law. . . . But with all of their respectability they have almost always been lax in their willingness to help the poor farmers of the hills. They are the evil which the hill people see and react to. Because of the code and tradition of these people they do not understand Willie Stark. In *All the King's Men* Judge Irwin of Burden's Landing is the personification of this school of thought. Judge Irwin is the best of his tradition. He, unlike many of the more complacent men and women of the area, sees a need for social improvement. However, the judge is in a dilemma. The society which he represents will not allow change without the overt pressure of Willie Stark. Thus, there is no conservative way to solve problems, it seems. There is only Willie Stark's way and this is unacceptable to the judge.

Robert Penn Warren goes beyond this weakness, however, to show that even the people of the plain, when the hard crust of conservative respectability is removed, are not without corruption. Judge Irwin, while he was Attorney General, was involved in a kickback scheme which eventuated in the suicide of Mortimer L. Littlepaugh, Counsel for the American Electric Power Company. Governor Stanton had known of the action and shielded Irwin. The rectitude which is so lauded in the aristocracy is really only a façade. They are not above corruption when they find it necessary. This element dramatizes the sin of the aristocracy. Their real sin is their failure to recognize and alleviate the economic conditions of the poorer people of the hills. Thus, in the South as well as elsewhere, the aristocracy has a respectable legal conservatism. They contribute greatly by giving powerful and intelligent leadership to the nation. But their conservatism is seldom respectable in dealing with the real socio-economic problems of the area and their legality is constructed to control such socio-economic improvement.

The fourth element in the novel is Jack Burden. From the standpoint of the political nature of the agrarian areas he is significant as a touchstone moving between the hills and the black belt. Jack Burden is a product of the aristocracy. His early association with Judge Irwin makes a great impression on him. His youth is spent with Anne and Adam Stanton. All the elements of his life are linked to the Delta, but his realization that there is something unsatisfactory in this self-satisfied existence sets him adrift. Given the chance to work for Willie Stark, he accepts and quickly falls in with all the activities which characterize Willie. His actions in working to find ammunition for Willie's plans eventually bring him to attack the very roots from which he sprang. Through his revelation of Judge Irwin's and Governor Stanton's actions he destroys the very people who had previously meant the most to him, Adam Stanton, Anne Stanton and Judge Irwin. Anne Stanton becomes Willie Stark's mistress, Adam Stanton kills Willie and is killed himself by Willie's bodyguard and Judge Irwin commits suicide.

Burden seems lost in his conviction that there is no code of ethics or morals but only the "big twitch." Although Willie feels that Jack is the only person who really knows him, Jack realizes that he does not understand Willie at all. Perhaps the products of the aristocracy can never really understand the hill people and their kind of leadership.

As the novel draws to a climax, Jack Burden looks through the cloud of action without purpose in which he has been existing and begins to see clearly. He does, in the end, bridge the gap. There can be, he seems to know, a connection between the hills and the Delta. There can be respect for law and at the same time socio-economic progress. As the novel ends he is telling the reader that he may get back into politics. If so, it will be to help Hugh Miller who resigned as Attorney General when Governor Stark refused to fire Byram B. White. Miller is the symbol of the very leadership which is necessary, a man of respectability who wishes to use the law to help the people.

In surveying the rise and fall of a Populist politician and the people who support and oppose him, *All the King's Men* leaves the reader with the hope of Lucy Stark. Another Willie will come along and he will not fall into the snare of demagoguery, blackmail and thuggery. Contemporary politics would seem to show us that this is possible. George Norris in Nebraska and Bob La Follette in Wisconsin are clear examples of this tradition. And in the South, examples of respectable Populism like John Sparkman and Lister Hill of Alabama prove that agrarian democrats can be law abiding. Further, the enlightened conservatism of such men as Fulbright of Arkansas adds awareness to respectability. It is also true that shortsighted conservatism still exists in the agrarian areas in the personages of Thurmond, Byrnes, Byrd and the like. It is further true that Populism has gone sour of late not only in Huey Long and Theodore Bilbo but most recently in Joseph McCarthy of Wisconsin. But the gap can be bridged either by a Populist who climbs up or an aristocrat who bends down. This is the essential lesson of *All the King's Men* and perhaps of America. (pp. 351-53)

> *Malcolm O. Sillars, "Warren's 'All the King's Men':
> A Study in Populism," in* American Quarterly, *Vol.
> IX, No. 3, Fall, 1957, pp. 345-53.*

JAMES RUOFF

Since the Pulitzer Prize novel *All the King's Men* (1946) is coming to be recognized as the most comprehensive statement of Robert Penn Warren's philosophy and art, it might be worth while to remark upon a very general misconception regarding the title of the novel. Now, ordinarily, of course, a title is not a matter of any great significance, but in this case it is important because it constitutes a symbolic expression of some of the author's basic ideas. It is, in fact, a Pandora's box which opens up to reveal the profoundly spiritual nature of Warren's convictions about the broad themes of man and God. . . . (p. 128)

According to the generally accepted interpretation, "the King" in *All the King's Men* is the protagonist Willie Stark, an interpretation which derives from the fact Willie is governor of the state, a man the other characters in the novel refer to as "the Boss." "The King's Men," on the other hand, are assumed to be all the people who in one way or another serve the Boss—Jack Burden, Willie's research man; Tiny Duffy, the lieutenant governor; Sugar Boy, Willie's bodyguard, etc. Then, too, there are "the King's women," the mistresses of the governor's palace—Sadie Burke, Anne Stanton, Willie's wife Lucy. As tidy as this interpretation undoubtedly is, something more than a casual reading of the story will show Willie Stark was never intended to be "the King" in *All the King's Men*, and that the title of the novel has a meaning more significant than critics have hitherto realized.

There are a number of reasons why Willie Stark cannot be "the King" in *All the King's Men*. There is, first, the nursery rhyme from which the title was derived: Willie is Humpty Dumpty, not "King." Like Humpty Dumpty, Willie "sat on a wall" when he rose to become governor and "had a great fall" when shot down by Adam Stanton. Willie is, like his legendary counterpart, a synthetic creation, a grotesque composite of the abstract needs of the people who have shaped him. As Warren has pointed out, Willie's "power was based on the fact that somehow he could vicariously fulfill the secret needs of the people about him." Hence the principal characters in *All the King's Men*, like Mr. Munn in Warren's *Night Rider* (1939), attempt to find themselves by merging their identities with another person. In Willie Stark the people of the state satisfy their craving for justice . . . while to the narrator, Jack Burden, Willie fulfills Jack's need of a father, his need of the purpose and direction and decisive authority which have been lacking in his aimless life. To Adam Stanton, "the man of idea" who eventually destroys him, Willie represents the concrete power to accomplish the idealistic, humanitarian good which Adam has dedicated his whole life to achieve. In short, it is an obvious truism to say that to Sadie Burke, to Anne Stanton—to virtually every character in the novel—Willie Stark represents the fulfillment of some secret compulsion, some indigenous shortcoming or incompleteness, and in this sense, most of all, Willie is Humpty Dumpty—an artificial composite of the needs inherent in the society which has created him. (pp. 128-29)

But if Willie Stark is Humpty Dumpty, who then is king? In view of the nursery rhyme it is difficult to see how Willie can be Humpty Dumpty and king, too. Part of a solution to our problem is to be found in Warren's introduction to the Modern Library Edition, where he states that in *All the King's Men* he tried to "avoid writing a straight naturalistic novel, the kind of novel the material so readily invited." By the phrase "straight naturalistic novel" Warren apparently intended the bleakly deterministic and materialistic novel which portrays its characters as being merely biological organisms attracted and repelled by hereditary or environmental forces over which they have no control. As we shall see, the "material" of *All the King's Men* "readily invited" a novel of this description, for there is a temptation to think of Willie Stark as an ineluctible demi-urge riding the beast of the people to their moral collapse while the rider himself is pulled to destruction by a gloomy necessity. And yet one of Warren's main problems in writing *All the King's Men* was, I think, to avoid any implications of determinism, to establish a sure balance between the fact of Willie's diabolic attraction for others and the fact of their free wills; for it was essential to Warren's moral purpose, to his whole concept of man, that his characters exercise free will, that Willie Stark remain, after all, only Humpty Dumpty and not king—not Necessity, not God. In Warren's teleology only God is King, and we are all of us "all the King's men."

God is not only King but absolute monarch informing every moment of life with His purposive Will, and this predestination, which under Warren's hand becomes something quite different from determinism of a theological order, is "the material" that "readily invited" what Warren calls "the straight naturalistic novel." . . . This naturalistic tradition is emphati-

cally repudiated in *All the King's Men* when determinism, a chief characteristic of "the straight naturalistic novel," is sardonically labeled "The Big Twitch" by Jack Burden, who abjures it as totally inadequate to explain the events that take place in the story. The philosophy Jack Burden does come to accept, however, is one which has to do with the enigmatic paradox of Christianity—the omnipotence of God and the moral responsibility of man. And if at the end of the novel Jack's acceptance of this view of life is not without some reservations, we must remember that the paradox is baffling, is one that derives not from a spontaneous rational acquiescence but from a hard discipline of faith.

If omnipotent God has power over everything, how can man be said to have responsibility for anything? *All the King's Men* confronts this question cautiously, with a full cognizance of the critical tensions created by Darwin, Marx, Freud, and the holocaust of two world wars. From these spirit-shattering, enervating experiences, we must preserve, Warren tells us, what is most distinctive, significant and compelling about man, his consciousness and spirituality. According to Warren, man has moral choice, lives in an "agony of will," but, paradoxically, he has no choice, no power whatever, in the consequences of his moral life. To put it another way, in Original Sin—which looms darkly in the background of all Warren's novels from *Night Rider* to *Band of Angels*—Adam and Eve devoured a fruit of agony when they ate of the Tree of the Knowledge of Good and Evil, for in that fatal act they took upon themselves the knowledge of what was right and wrong, and consequently the responsibility for their actions; but they were denied the divinity which Satan had promised them, the power to transcend time and perceive, as God perceives, the ultimate consequences of good and evil. (pp. 129-30)

Willie Stark expresses a profound truth when he insists throughout the novel that good must come from evil because "evil is all you have to work with," while Adam Stanton, the more conventionally "noble" of the two, lives a dangerous error when he arbitrarily separates people and events into moral categories. . . . Willie brings about his own destruction when he tries to be like Adam, when, like "the man of idea" that he is not, he sets out to create something which is completely devoid of evil. Inconsistent with his own philosophy that any good there is must come from evil, Willie dreams of building a magnificent hospital that will stand as the purely good achievement of his political administration, and yet, unknown to Willie, the hospital is tainted by evil in the moment of its conception, for the idea of the hospital is really the result of Willie's unconscious effort to compensate for the guilt he feels in protecting from prosecution his corrupt state auditor, Byram B. White. The hospital becomes an instrument of Willie's downfall when he refuses to permit the venal Gummy Larson from having the contract to construct it, when he refuses, in other words, to allow the good he dreams of achieving to be contaminated by evil, and this refusal prompts Tiny Duffy to inform Adam of Willie's affair with Anne. In shooting Willie Stark, Adam becomes himself "the man of fact," acknowledging Willie's dictum that the end justifies the means, but more than that, he proclaims, by his act that he has God's knowledge, a final knowledge of good and evil. In his arrogant effort to usurp divinity, Adam repeats the folly of the Fall.

The fact that Willie's hospital is never built underscores man's tragic limitations. Confined to a tenuous reality of isolated facts, hemmed in by illusory absolutes of good and evil, man cannot perceive the transcendent reality, the ultimate moral purpose and direction of life. Willie, "the man of fact," thinks he knows how things really are, and Adam Stanton, "the man of idea," thinks he knows how things ought to be, but both are incomplete, both presumptuous. So man lives on one moral level of reality, where he suffers an "agony of will," of personal responsibility, and God exists on another, the level of "history" or "direction," a level unknown to man, who yearns toward the fulfillment of some ideal good which in the "moral neutrality of history" has no objective existence. On God's level, good and evil are not as inseparable as man persists in making them. What man conceives as a completed moral action is, in God's omniscient comprehension, merely another phase in man's continuous struggle to create some good in a fallen world he only faintly understands. Warren's concept of man as a fallen, debased, limited, and therefore heroic, creature working out moral decisions in an "agony of will" yet oblivious to the eventual good or evil of those decisions is one which recalls St. Augustine and medieval nominalists like Duns Scotus (the analogues of Warren's Puritanism), who stressed God's awful power and mystery, and man's irrationality and impotence. Like these medieval nominalists who reacted against the liberal rationalism of the Scholastics, Warren has repudiated the optimistic rationalism of the liberal reformers, just as he has repudiated their scientism and materialism—what Jack Burden refers to as "the dream of our age."

In *All the King's Men* man finds solace not in the liberal experience, not in the nineteenth-century dream of power through reason, but in the more ancient Christian experience of humility, repentance and hope; for Warren sees this world as a Dantesque purgatory where man works out his salvation by a process of transgression, acknowledgement of guilt, and contrition. Every character in *All the King's Men* who is worth saving eventually submits to this tortuous ritual of life: Cass Mastern, Judge Irwin, Willie Stark, Jack Burden, Mrs. Burden, Sadie Burke, and Anne Stanton. Tiny Duffy, like his friend Gummy Larson, is a mere shade, an abstraction, while Adam Stanton, paradoxically the "noblest" character in the novel, is, by the fact of his fierce and intransigent pride in virtue, quite beyond all hope of redemption. For the remainder of the characters in *All the King's Men*, however, the epigraph to the novel applies. Appropriately, the epigraph to *All the King's Men* is Manfred's tortured cry of hope in Canto III of Dante's *Purgatorio:* "Mentre che la speranze ha fior del verde." (pp. 131-32)

To assume, then, that Willie Stark is "the King" in *All the King's Men* is to ignore the meaningful symbolism of the title, to lose sight of Warren's basic idea. . . . *All the King's Men* portrays a world which Willie could not have ruled; for in that world of Warren's thoughtful creation there is but one King and we are all of us "all the King's men." From first to last, Willie Stark is but Humpty Dumpty, whose fall is a form of triumph for those who survive him. As Ellis Burden states in another context, "Separateness is identity," and with the death of Willie those who involved their identities in him must find completion within themselves or not at all. As in any great tragedy, there is loss, there is gain: they have lost Willie but have gained the power to find themselves. It may not be a coincidence, therefore, that the conclusion to *All the King's Men* is reminiscent of the ending to another great tragedy as Jack Burden and Anne Stanton, like Adam and Eve departing from the Garden after the Fall, prepare to leave Burden's Landing forever to "go into the convulsion of the world, out of history into history and the awful responsibility of Time." (pp. 133-34)

James Ruoff, "Humpty Dumpty and 'All the King's Men': A Note on Robert Penn Warren's Teleology," in Twentieth Century Literature, *Vol. 3, No. 3, October, 1957, pp. 128-34.*

ROBERT PENN WARREN

When I am asked how much *All the King's Men* owes to the actual politics of Louisiana in the '30's, I can only be sure that if I had never gone to live in Louisiana and if Huey Long had not existed, the novel would never have been written. But this is far from saying that my "state" in *All the King's Men* is Louisiana (or any of the other forty-nine stars in our flag), or that my Willie Stark is the late Senator. What Louisiana and Senator Long gave me was a line of thinking and feeling that did eventuate in the novel.

In the summer of 1934 I was offered a job—a much-needed job—as Assistant Professor at the Louisiana State University, in Baton Rouge. It was "Huey Long's University," and definitely on the make—with a sensational football team and with money to spend even for assistant professors at a time when assistant professors were being fired, not hired—as I knew all too well. It was Huey's University, but he, I was assured, would never mess with my classroom. That was to prove true; he was far too adept in the arts of power to care what an assistant professor might have to say. The only time that his presence was ever felt in my classroom was when, in my Shakespeare course, I gave my little annual lecture on the political background of *Julius Caesar;* and then, for the two weeks we spent on the play, backs grew straighter, eyes grew brighter, notes were taken, and the girls stopped knitting in class, or repairing their faces.

In September 1934 I left Tennessee, where I had been living on a farm near Nashville, drove down across Mississippi, crossed the river by ferry . . . and was in North Louisiana. Along the way I picked up a hitchhiker—a country man, the kind you call a red-neck or a wool-hat, aging, aimless, nondescript, beat up by life and hard times and bad luck. . . . He was, though at the moment I did not sense it, a mythological figure.

He was the god on the battlement, dimly perceived above the darkling tumult and the steaming carnage of the political struggle. He was a voice, a portent, and a natural force like the Mississippi River getting set to bust a levee. Long before the Fascist March on Rome, Norman Douglas, meditating on Naples, had predicted that the fetid slums of Europe would make possible the "inspired idiot." His predictive diagnosis of the origins of fascism—and of communism—may be incomplete, but it is certain that the rutted back roads and slab-side shacks that had spawned my nameless old hitchhiker, with the twine-tied paper parcel in his hand, had, by that fall of 1934, made possible the rise of "Huey." My nameless hitchhiker was, mythologically speaking, Long's *sine qua non.*

So it was appropriate that he should tell me the first episode of the many I had to hear of the myth that was "Huey." The roads, he said, was shore better now. A man could git to market, he said. A man could jist git up and git, if'n a notion come on him. Did'n have to pay no toll at no toll bridge neither. Fer Huey was a free-bridge man. So he went on and told me how, standing on the river bank by a toll bridge (by what river and what bridge was never clear), Huey had made the president of the company that owned the bridge a good, fair cash offer, and the man laughed at him. But, the old hitchhiker said, Huey did'n do nothing but lean over and pick him up a chunk of rock and throwed it off a-ways, and asked did that president-feller see whar the rock hit. The feller said yeah, he seen. Wal, Huey said, the next thing you see is gonna be a big new free bridge right whar that rock hit, and you, you son-of-a-bitch, are goen bankrupt a-ready and doan even know it.

There were a thousand tales, over the years, and some of them were, no doubt, literally and factually true. But they were all true in the world of ''Huey''—that world of myth, folklore, poetry, deprivation, rancor, and dimly envisaged hopes. That world had a strange, shifting, often ironical and sometimes irrelevant relation to the factual world of Senator Huey P. Long and his cold manipulation of the calculus of power. The two worlds, we may hazard, merged only at the moment when in September 1935, in the corridor of the Capitol, the little .32 slug bit meanly into the senatorial vitals.

There was another world—this a factual world—made possible by the factual Long, though not inhabited by him. It was a world that I, as an assistant professor, was to catch fleeting glimpses of, and ponder. It was the world of the parasites of power, a world that Long was, apparently, contemptuous of, but knew how to use, as he knew how to use other things of which he was, perhaps, contemptuous. This was a world of a sick yearning for elegance and the sight of one's name on the society page of a New Orleans paper; it was the world of the electric moon devised, it was alleged, to cast a romantic glow over the garden when the President of the University and his wife entertained their politicos and pseudo-socialites; it was a world of pretentiousness, of bloodcurdling struggles for academic preferment, of drool-jawed grab and arrogant criminality. (pp. 161-63)

For in Louisiana, in the 1930's, you felt somehow that you were living in the great world, or at least in a microcosm with all the forces and fatalities faithfully, if sometimes comically, drawn to scale. And the little Baton Rouge world of campus and Governor's Mansion and Capitol and the gold bathroom fixtures reported to be in the house of the University contractor was, once the weight of Long's contempt and political savvy had been removed by the bullet of the young Brutus in the Capitol, to plunge idiotically rampant to an end almost as dramatic as the scenes in the last bunkers of Berlin or at the filling station on the outskirts of Milan. (pp. 163-64)

But this is getting ahead of the story. Meanwhile, there was, besides the lurid worlds, the world of ordinary life to look at. There were the people who ran stores or sold insurance or had a farm and tried to survive and pay their debts. There were—visible even from the new concrete speedway that Huey had slashed through the cypress swamps toward New Orleans—the palmetto-leaf and sheet-iron hovels of the moss pickers, rising like some fungoid growth from a hummock under the great cypress knees, surrounded by scum-green water that never felt sunlight, back in that Freudianly contorted cypress gloom of cottonmouth moccasins big as the biceps of a prize-fighter, and owl calls, and the murderous metallic grind of insect life, and the smudge fire at the hovel door, that door being nothing but a hole in a hovel wall, with a piece of croker sack hung over it. There were, a few miles off at the University, your colleagues, some as torpid as a gorged alligator in the cold mud of January and some avid to lick the spit of an indifferent or corrupt administration, but many able and gifted and fired by a will to create, out of the seething stew and heaving magma, a distinguished university.

And there were, of course, the students, like students anywhere in the country in the big state universities, except for the ex-traordinary number of pretty girls and the preternatural blankness of the gladiators who were housed beneath the stadium to have their reflexes honed, their diet supervised, and—through the efforts of tutors—their heads crammed with just enough of whatever mash was required (I never found out) to get them past their minimal examinations. Among the students there sometimes appeared, too, that awkward boy from the depth of the 'Cajun country or from some scrabble-farm in North Louisiana, with burning ambition and frightening energy and a thirst for learning; and his presence there, you reminded yourself, with whatever complication of irony seemed necessary at the moment, was due to Huey, and to Huey alone. For the ''better element'' had done next to nothing in fifty years to get that boy out of the grim despair of his ignorance.

Yes, there was the world of the ''good families,'' most of whom hated Huey Long—except, of course, for that percentage who, for one reason or another, had reached an accommodation. They hated him sometimes for good reasons and sometimes for bad, and sometimes for no reason at all, as a mere revulsion of taste; but they never seemed to reflect on what I took to be the obvious fact that if the government of the state had not previously been marked by various combinations of sloth, complacency, incompetence, corruption, and a profound lack of political imagination, there would never have been a Senator Huey P. Long, and my old hitchhiker by the roadside would, in September 1934, have had no tale to tell me.

Conversation in Louisiana always came back to the tales, to the myth, to politics; and to talk politics is to talk about power. So conversation turned, by implication at least, on the question of power and ethics, of power and justification, of means and ends, of ''historical costs.'' The big words were not often used, certainly not by the tellers of tales, but the concepts lurked even behind the most ungrammatical folktale. The tales were shot through with philosophy.

The tales were shot through, too, with folk humor, and the ethical ambiguity of folk humor. And the tales, like the political conversations, were shot through, too, with violence—or rather, with hints of the possibility of violence. There was a hint of revolutionary desperation—often synthetically induced. In Louisiana, in '34 and '35, it took nothing to start a rumor of violence. (pp. 164-65)

Melodrama was the breath of life. There had been melodrama in the life I had known in Tennessee, but with a difference: in Tennessee the melodrama seemed to be different from the stuff of life, something superimposed upon life, but in Louisiana people lived melodrama, seemed to live, in fact, for it, for this strange combination of philosophy, humor, and violence. Life was a tale that you happened to be living—and that ''Huey'' happened to be living before your eyes. And all the while I was reading Elizabethan tragedy, Machiavelli, William James, and American history—and all that I was reading seemed to come alive, in shadowy distortions and sudden clarities, in what I saw around me.

How directly did I try to transpose into fiction Huey P. Long and the tone of that world? The question answers itself in a single fact. The first version of my story was a verse drama; and the actual writing began, in 1938, in the shade of an olive tree by a wheat field near Perugia. In other words, if you are sitting under an olive tree in Umbria and are writing a verse drama, the chances are that you are concerned more with the myth than with the fact, more with the symbolic than with the actual. And so it was. It could not, after all, have been otherwise, for in the strict, literal sense, I had no idea what the now deceased Huey P. Long had been. What I knew was the ''Huey'' of the myth, and that was what I had taken with me to Mussolini's Italy, where the bully boys wore black shirts and gave a funny salute.

I had no way of knowing what went on in the privacy of the heart of Senator Long. Now I could only hope, ambitiously, to know something of the heart of the Governor Talos of my play *Proud Flesh*. For Talos was the first avatar of my Willie Stark, and the fact that I drew that name from the ''iron groom'' who, in murderous blankness, serves Justice in Spenser's *Faerie Queen* should indicate something of the line of thought and feeling that led up to that version and persisted, with modulations, into the novel.

Talos was to become Stark, and *Proud Flesh* was to become *All the King's Men*. Many things, some merely technical, led to this transformation, but one may have some bearing on the question of the ratio of fact and fiction. In 1942 I left Louisiana for good, and when in 1943 I began the version that is more realistic, discursive, and documentary in method . . . than the play, I was doing so after I had definitely left Louisiana and the world in which the story had its roots. By now the literal, factual world was only a memory, and therefore was ready to be absorbed freely into the act of imagination. Even the old man by the roadside—the hitchhiker I had picked up on the way down to take my job—was ready to enter the story: he became, it would seem, the old hitchhiker whom Jack Burden picks up returning from Long Beach, California, the old man with the twitch in the face that gives Jack the idea for the Great Twitch. But my old hitchhiker had had no twitch in his face. Nor had I been Jack Burden.

I had not been Jack Burden except in so far as you have to try to ''be'' whatever you are trying to create. And in that sense I was also Adam Stanton, and Willie Stark, and Sadie Burke, and Sugar Boy, and all the rest. And this brings me to my last notion. However important for my novel was the protracted dialectic between ''Huey'' on the one side, and me on the other, it was far less important, in the end, than that deeper and darker dialectic for which the images and actions of a novel are the only language. And however important was my acquaintance with Louisiana, that was far less important than my acquaintance with another country: for any novel, good or bad, must report, willy-nilly, the history, sociology, and politics of a country even more fantastic than was Louisiana under the consulship of Huey. (pp. 166-67)

> Robert Penn Warren, '' 'All the King's Men': The Matrix of Experience,'' in The Yale Review, Vol. LIII, No. 2, December, 1963, pp. 161-67.

JONATHAN BAUMBACH

Of Warren's eight novels to date, *All the King's Men* (1946) seems to me the most achieved, the most serious and the most enduring—for all its flaws, one of our near-great novels. For some time *All the King's Men* was misread as a disturbingly sympathetic fictionalized account of the demagogic career of Huey Long. Approached as an historical document, the book was condemned by politically liberal critics as a florid, rhetorical justification for a Napoleonic brand of American neofascism. There is no need any longer to point out the irrelevancy of this attack, to explain that Jack Burden is the center of the novel and that Willie Stark, ''the man of fact,'' is not *actually* Huey Long, but a kind of ''Mistah Kurtz.'' . . . Though Warren

intends Jack Burden to be the center of the novel, Willie Stark is by virtue of his energy the more realized and interesting character. Burden, as thinly disguised authorial spokesman, is a literary conception, created from other fiction rather than from life, a combination, if you can imagine it, of Nick Carraway and Sam Spade. Whatever Warren's intention, the character of Willie Stark, a colossus of human and inhuman possibilities, inadvertently dominates the novel. Inevitably, a distortion results, the kind of distortion which would permit *All the King's Men* to be read as the story of Willie Stark's rise and fall (a tragedy of over-reaching pride brought low by retributive justice).

For all that, Jack Burden, acquiescent narrator, at once vicarious Willie and vicarious Adam, is the novel's center, the ultimate synthesizer of its polarities. While Willie and Adam die unfulfilled, Jack completes the spiritual voyage; he moves, an exemplary sleepwalker, from sin to recognition and guilt to redemption and rebirth. Jack's ritual search for a true father, or at least a true absolute, leads him into Willie's employ (on the coat-tails of his political ascension). Ironically, there is a certain amount of narcissism in Jack's discipleship because he has, in part, created Willie the ''Boss,'' catalyzed him from the raw materials of ''Cousin Willie from the country.'' At the outset, Willie is an innocent, a do-gooder whose campaign speeches are scrupulously honest and drearily dull. Jack gives him his first taste of the apple:

> Hell, make 'em cry, make 'em laugh, make 'em think you're God-Almighty. Or make 'em mad. Even mad at you. Just stir 'em up, it doesn't matter how or why, and they'll love you and come back for more. Pinch them in the soft place. They aren't alive, most of 'em haven't been alive in twenty years. Hell, their wives have lost their teeth and their shape, and likker won't set on their stomachs, and they don't believe in God, so it's up to you to give 'em something to stir 'em up and make 'em feel again. . . . But for Sweet Jesus' sake don't try to improve their minds.

This is the first and last time that Jack gives Willie a short course in cynical wisdom. Once having learned the lesson, Willie becomes the teacher, the authority on man's fallen nature. (pp. 17-18)

It is Jack, however, who has initiated Willie's conversion from the man of idea to the man of fact, from romanticism to pragmatism. By demonstrating to him that his start in politics was made possible by political corruption, Jack destroys Willie's sense of innocence, decreates him into manhood. While Jack, who suffers chronically from paralysis of the will, converts Willie through abstract example, Willie converts the uncommitted Jack through practical demonstration. The ''Boss'' Willie is Jack as he would like to be, but only if he could watch himself being it. For all his admiration of action, Jack is essentially a spectator, an historian waiting for history to happen. Willie performs history for him, tests the efficacy of Jack's theories, while Jack with clinical dispassion sits on the sidelines taking notes. (pp. 18-19)

Aside from Willie, Jack has two other fathers: a nominal one who he thinks is real and whom he has rejected (Ellis Burden) and a real one whom he admires and inadvertently kills (Judge Irwin). When Willie assigns him to get ''something on'' Judge Irwin, who has been outspoken in his criticism of Stark's administration, Jack is forced for the first time to choose between the prerogatives of opposing fathers. (Though he doesn't know that Irwin is his natural father, he respects, resents, and feels obligated to Irwin as a son to a father because of Irwin's decency and friendship over the years.) Looking for a way out of his predicament, Jack tells Willie that Irwin is "washed in the blood" and that an investigation of Irwin's past will be a waste of time. Willie knows, however, that man is fallen, that "there is always something." In investigating the facts of Irwin's life, Jack puts to the test the last illusion he has permitted himself to retain, that despite the rank and malodorous corruption which underlies so much of contemporary life, a truly good man like Irwin remains incorruptible. Jack has another naïve notion which justifies the political dirt-digging he does so that Willie can blackmail his opponents: that the truth, regardless of its immediate effects, is always salutary and that unadulterated fact constitutes truth.

In search of the hidden facts of his real father's past, Jack visits Ellis Burden, the Scholarly Attorney turned Religious fanatic, his nominal father. It is here that the divergent influences of his trinity of fathers come into focus and are symbolically defined. Once again, Jack rejects the Scholarly Attorney, the weak saint, whose life of squalor, piety, and undiscriminating compassion seems purposeless to him when contrasted with Willie Stark's vigorous usefulness. This dispossessed nominal father has adopted a substitute son, George, a former circus aerialist who has reverted to childhood. George, redeemed through trauma into helpless innocence, spends his time making angels from masticated bread crusts. He is, in an ironic sense, Jack's brother. George's idiot purity embarrasses Jack and he rejects the image of his opposite (his innocent brother) along with his Scholarly Attorney father, along with the past. But, at the same time, he is again rejected by his father, who refuses to answer his questions about Irwin—who is unable to hear him when Jack calls him "Father." The visit is a failure; Jack learns nothing about Irwin, and he experiences the loss of his father all over again.

The uncovering of Irwin's one dishonorable act has massive, unaccountable ramifications. In consequence of Jack's discovery, Judge Irwin commits suicide, Anne Stanton has a self-destructive affair with Willie Stark, Adam Stanton kills Willie Stark, and Willie Stark's bodyguard kills Adam Stanton. For all his disinterested intentions, Jack must bear the burden of responsibility for this proliferation of tragedy. He has set it in motion as surely and perfectly as if he had consciously planned it. The "facts" that incriminate the Judge also indicate the complicity of Governor Stanton, who deliberately covered up for his friend. This further discovery destroys for both Anne and Adam Stanton the idealized notion of their father that has sustained them in their myth of purity as children of innocence—descendants of innocence. When Anne discovers that the purity of the old governor is tainted, she is able to shed her restrictive moral restraints as a snake sheds its skin. If there is no pure God, a pure Satan is the next best thing—he is at least whole. With the loss of her good father, Anne commits a sort of symbolic incest with the bad father—the new governor—searching for an absolute to replace the one she had lost. The loss of innocence in the novel for Jack, Willie, Anne, and Adam is concomitant with the loss of the good father.

It is Adam, Jack's innocent self, the least convincing of all Warren's characters, who guilelessly gives Jack his first lead in uncovering Irwin's blemished past. Adam answers Jack's cunning, direct question, "Was Judge Irwin ever broke?" because he is too ingenuous not to. However, Adam's innocent volunteering of harmless information about Judge Irwin is, in its effects, irresponsible as only innocence can be. It gives Jack the necessary clue to unearth Irwin's guilty secret, which, in ramification, destroys each of the participants in the central action of the novel. Adam's ingenuousness here anticipates his later, more destructive, act of innocence—his self-righteous assassination of Willie Stark. To say any more about Adam is beside the point. Whereas some of Warren's characters are half-human, half-idea, Adam is pure idea; he is an allegorical personification of *Innocence*. But without life, he is finally nothing, a figment of the author's imagination.

All of Warren's main characters experience at one time or another the loss of innocence and are characterized in terms of their accommodation to their Fall. Judge Irwin, sustained like Adam by the myth of self-purity, has attempted to evade the implications of his one intentionally corrupt act (his Fall) by shutting it out of his memory. Some thirty years later, Jack, the unacknowledged child of his loins, confronts him with the forgotten past. Jack's confrontation has a twofold significance; Jack is the manifestation of Irwin's other sin, his adulterous affair with Jack's mother, so that he becomes for Irwin the symbol of his fallen past, the tale-bearer of one crime and the embodiment of the other. (pp. 19-21)

When Willie loses his innocence, he is transformed almost overnight from the son of his world to its father. Willie's spiritual metamorphosis (which resembles Kurtz's in *Heart of Darkness*), though thematically subordinate to Jack's guilt-and-redemption passage, dominates the action of the novel. Willie's career anticipates and parallels Jack's, as a father's anticipates a son's, though it is enlarged where Jack's is diminished, and Willie never successfully makes the spiritual voyage back from hell. Like Kurtz, the "Boss" has gone too far into darkness ever to return into light.

Willie becomes governor. Ostensibly, his ends have not changed, only his means of achieving them. Gradually, however, the ends become inseparable from their means and Willie yields himself to his most voracious interior devils. The thesis is classic and bromidic: power tends to corrupt; absolute power tends to corrupt absolutely. With a difference, however: Warren inverts the cliché; for all his sins, "Willie is a great man." This is the verdict of his wife Lucy, to whom he has been unfaithful, whose son he has destroyed through vanity, and of Jack Burden, whom he has disillusioned and nearly destroyed. Since the redeemed Jack Burden, who has moved from blindness to whole sight represents, one must believe, the point of view of the novel, this must stand as Warren's judgment of Stark. The question remains: Is it a reasonable judgment borne out by the experience of the novel? Or is it a piece of gratuitous iconoclasm, the cliché-anti-cliché?

Warren enlists sympathy for Willie by indicating that the context in which he is forced to operate (southern politics) is unreclaimably corrupt. Whereas Tiny Duffy and Willie's opponent MacMurfee are interested in petty graft as an end, Willie's ego wants nothing less than recognition by posterity. Willie is a real devil at sup among dwarfed, flabby devils; in that he is more real and more potent than the others, he is to that extent more admirable. Once Willie has fallen, he discovers his true voice, the voice of the rabble rouser, the appeal to primordial violence:

> You asked me what my program is. Here it is, you hicks. And don't you forget it. Nail 'em up! Nail up Joe Harrison. Nail up anybody who stands in your way. Nail up MacMurfee if he don't deliver. You hand me the hammer and I'll do it with my own hand. Nail 'em up on the barn door.

The easier it becomes for Willie to manipulate the crowd, the less respect he has for its common fallen humanity. As he becomes more powerful, he becomes, like Kurtz and like Macbeth, more voracious, more proud, more evil. Willie's palpable moral decline is manifested for us when he covers up for an underling who has taken graft. It is not in the act of covering up but in his justification for it that Willie's inhumanity and presumption are manifested. . . . (pp. 23-4)

Willie's will to power, his lust for omnipotence, is defeated by what might be called a tragic virtue. Despite Willie's professed thesis that "you have to make the good out of the bad because that's all you have to make it out of," that all men are innately corrupt, that "political graft is the grease that keeps the wheels from squeaking," he wants to build a magnificent, immaculate hospital as his gift to the state, untainted by the usual petty corruption and graft. In pursuing this ideal, Willie refuses a deal with Gummy Larson, the power behind his enemy MacMurfee, whose defection to Willie would leave the "Boss" all but unopposed. Having fallen from Paradise into Hell, Willie wishes—his one romantic illusion—to regain his lost purity, to buy back Paradise. (pp. 24-5)

As part of his obsessive desire to transcend his corruption, his dream of greatness, Willie hires Adam Stanton to run his hospital, hoping through connection, through transfusion of spirit, to inform himself with Adam's innocence. Ironically, Willie has, with almost perfect instinct, chosen his redeemer, his redeemer as executioner. Adam and Willie as ideological polarities must inevitably merge or destroy each other. Jack unites them; he is the means of their collaborative self-destruction.

Willie's brief affair with Adam's sister Anne, is another extension of his specious quest for innocence. What Willie pursues is not innocence, really, but seeming innocence—respectability. His holy search for the false grail is the tragic flaw in his otherwise perfect expediency. Willie's lost innocence resides not with Adam and Anne, but with his wife Lucy and his father; his substitution of Anne for Lucy symbolizes his degeneration, his spiritual blindness. In his obsession with purity, Willie makes an enemy of the spiteful Tiny Duffy and puts too much faith in the erratically naïve, the fallen innocent, Adam, thereby predicating his own destruction. Duffy makes an anonymous phone call to Adam, falsifying the implications of Anne's affair with Willie. The inflexibly idealistic Adam, unable to live in an imperfect world, acts as the unwitting tool of vengeful petty corruption and gratuitously murders Willie. Specious innocence and cowardly corruption conspire to destroy the "Boss" at the height of his power and at the threshold of his apparent self-reform.

Willie's deathbed scene is the most potent of the various dramatic climaxes in the novel. In it Warren brings sharply into focus the moral paradox of Willie's ethic—the tragedy of his unachieved, over-reaching ambition; it is rendered as Judge Irwin's death is not, as a profoundly affecting experience. It is the death of Jack's last symbolic father—in extension of all his fathers—leaving him, for a time, alone and uncommitted in the chaos of his ungoverned universe. (pp. 25-6)

In becoming Willie's executioner, Adam, in his blind way, follows the example of Willie's career—he becomes Willie. For the "man of fact" and the "man of idea," as Jack classified them, there has been an alternation of roles. Each incomplete, seeking completeness, has chosen his polar opposite as an exemplary image. In building the hospital without the "grease" of political graft, Willie is operating idealistically—in Adam's

image. In brutally shooting down Willie, Adam is acting as disciple of the man whose power-authority is symbolized by the meat axe. From Jack's standpoint, Willie is superior to Adam: "A man's virtue may be but the defect of his desire, as his crime may be but a function of his virtue." If a man has not faced temptation, or, as in Adam's case, has not admitted its existence, his purity is illusory and beside the point.

Willie's relationship to his son Tom is another variation on the novel's father-son conflict, and it serves as an ironic comment both on Jack's relationship to his real father and to Willie. Jack's search into Irwin's discreditable past is continually juxtaposed to scenes of Willie worshipfully watching Tom perform on the football field: "He's my boy—and there's not any like him—he'll be All-American. . . .'" Tom Stark is the perfect physical extension of Willie's wishful self-image; he is all man of action—with the bottle, on the gridiron, and in bed—one hundred percent performance, no waste. Burden sees him as "one hundred and eighty pounds of split-second, hair trigger, Swiss-watch beautiful mechanism." Inhuman but perfect, he is the embodiment of Willie's crass values. Willie is willing to overlook Tom's personal decay so long as he continues to function as a perfect mechanism on the football field and so sate Willie's rapacious vanity. Willie's attitude toward Tom is symbolic of his attitude toward the governmental machine—proud, permissive, and blind. Corruption is permissible because it "keeps the wheels from squeaking." His failure with Tom is symptomatic of his potential failure as governor; to satisfy his vanity Willie would have all men, even his own son, made into functioning "things." Inadvertently, Willie destroys Tom, who is, outside of personal power, the "thing" he loves most in his world. When Tom has been barred from playing football for breaking college rules (the boy manages, among his heroics, to cripple one girl in an auto crash and to impregnate another), Willie pressures the coach into reinstating him. Almost immediately after Tom comes into the game, as if in direct consequence of Willie's corrupt use of authority, his spine is snapped by a vicious tackle. As a result, the son of the man-of-action is left actionless, without the use of his arms and legs. As the emotional paralysis of Jack catalyzes, in a sense, the action of Willie, Willie's action causes the physical paralysis of Tom. The irony is evident: ultimately a machine stops, even a perfect Swiss-made mechanism breaks down if it is dropped too often. The sins of the father are visited on the son. Similarly, the "breaking" of the son anticipates the destruction of the father; it is an intimation of Willie's mortality.

Whereas in Jack's case the son kills the father, in Willie's the father kills the son. However, Tom is, through the ineluctable chain of cause and effect, also the instrument of Willie's destruction. As a consequence of Tom's impregnating the daughter of one of MacMurfee's men, Willie is forced through blackmail to compromise his principles and give the corrupt Gummy Larson the hospital-construction contract. After Tom's injury, however, the guilt-ridden Willie breaks the contract. Tiny Duffy, who has been intermediary in the deal, exacts his vengeance; he initiates Willie's murder through Adam's pride.

Before Adam shoots him down, Willie accepts Tom's paralysis as a judgment for his sins and seeks expiation through good works: "you got to start somewhere." As Irwin ultimately redeems Jack, Tom almost redeems Willie, but not quite; after his fall, Humpty-Dumpty cannot be put together again. Willie, like Tom's paralyzed body, is denied rebirth. Willie's death does, however, make possible the redemption of Tom's illegitimate son, whom Lucy decides to adopt and name, of all names, Willie Stark. Through his son's son, Willie regains his lost innocence.

With the death of Willie, the effective father, Jack has no one left to whom he can transfer his responsibility. However, before he can achieve manhood, Jack has one other father with whom he has to come to terms—Cass Mastern; the subject of his Ph.D. dissertation is Jack's historic father. . . . . Though it illuminates certain themes in *All the King's Men* and is in itself an exceptionally resonant tale, Cass's tragedy is hardly indispensable to the novel. In any event, at the cost of temporarily stopping the action, it gives added dimension to Burden's odyssey into self-knowledge, his passage from innocence to limbo to guilt to redemption. Though Jack has pieced together all the facts of Cass Mastern's life, he is unable to complete his dissertation. The significance of Cass's story eludes him, though he is aware that it has significance. Neither Jack's early philosophic idealism ("What you don't know won't hurt you") nor his disillusioned belief in the Great Twitch (that man is an involuntary mechanism and no one is responsible for anything) is adequate to a comprehension of Cass's sainthood. Cass, though innocent and virtuous, falls into an affair with Annabelle Trice, his best friend's wife. As a consequence, three lives are destroyed. Thereafter Cass, suffused with guilt, makes his existence a continuous penance for his sin. He finally joins the southern army and gives up his life while refusing to fire a shot in his own defense. Through martyrdom he achieves expiation. (pp. 27-30)

Cass's martyrdom is exemplary; it is not only his own guilt for which he has suffered and died but the guilt of the land, "the common guilt of man." In the mystery of Cass's life and death resides the meaning of Jack's life, which is to say the essential meaning of all our lives. As Cass has written in his journal, and as Jack finally discovers for himself, "'It is a human defect—to try to know oneself by the self of another. One can only know oneself in God and His great eye.'" After the recognition of his guilt, it is in God that Cass does find himself; similarly, after Jack accepts his guilt, it is in himself that he finds Cass and, ultimately, God. (p. 30)

Cass's experience acts as an anticipatory parallel to Jack's own nightmare passage, though the connections are remote and abstract. When Jack discovers that Duffy "had killed Stark as surely as though his own hand had held the revolver," he feels absolved of responsibility, free at last to act, to vindicate the deaths of Willie and Adam. However, Jack's newborn sense of freedom is illusory. It is for him another evasion of responsibility, in a way the least admirable of all. Convincing himself as Willie had, and as Adam had when he squeezed the trigger, that an act is a self-willed moral entity, Jack assumes for himself the role of avenging angel; he wishes to destroy Duffy in order to justify himself. However, after Jack chastises Duffy, "'you are the stinkingest louse God ever let live!'" and threatens him with exposure, he realizes that "'I had tried to make Duffy into a scapegoat for me and to set myself off from Duffy,'" that Duffy is his alter ego, his corrupt brother, and that whatever he had said about Duffy was also true of himself. (p. 31)

Jack, by evading the responsibility for his own sins, had, amid the corruption about him, retained the illusion of innocence. Since he had not acted out of conscious choice, but had merely yielded to the demands of the "Boss," he had been able to slough off the burden of guilt. Once he discovers himself free to act, he becomes aware that the possibility of all acts, the

whole spectrum of good and evil, are in him; that he is, as human being, Oedipus and Duffy and Willie and everyone else. Having discovered the magnitude of his guilt—that he is responsible not only for his own sins but for all sins—Jack begins his return from the interior hell in which he has languished so long. He cannot leave hell, of course, until he has discovered its boundaries.

When Jack runs into "Sugar Boy," Willie's driver and bodyguard (*the* man of action), he is presented with the opportunity of destroying Duffy with no risk to himself. He restrains himself not out of the paralysis ("the defect of desire") which prevented him many years before from making love to Anne when she offered herself to him but because Duffy is his "twin," and if he can sanction Duffy's murder he must sanction his own. . . . Jack's refusal to take easy vengeance on Duffy is not inaction but a decisive moral act.

For a time, as a projection of his self-hate, Jack has a baleful view of all humanity. When he comes to love his mother, whom he has rejected long ago, he is able as a consequence to stop hating himself, which also means no longer hating the rest of the world. The redemption of his mother through the recognition of her love for Irwin (his real father) is Jack's salvation; it re-establishes for him the existential possibility of love. However, as Jack discovers, the process has been circular, for "'by killing my father I have saved my mother's soul.'" This discovery leads Jack into a further revelation (which is Warren's thesis) that "'all knowledge that is worth anything is maybe paid for by blood.'"

For all his belief in the purgative powers of knowledge, Jack lies to his mother when she asks about the motive for Irwin's suicide, telling her that his father killed himself because of failing health. It is, however, a salutary lie, the least he can do for his mother. As his mother's rebirth has resurrected him, Jack's lie resurrects the image of his father for his mother. . . . His reconciliation with his mother begins his reconciliation with the past. For without the past Jack cannot really participate in the world of the present. By rediscovering the past he is able to re-create the present, to be spiritually reborn into a world in which before his destructive self-awareness he had only acquiescently participated. He moves into his father's house, affirming his linear heritage, accepting for himself at last the role of man and father. He marries his boyhood sweetheart Anne Stanton, to whom he had once in love and innocence committed his life irrevocably. In marrying Anne, Jack saves her in much the same way Pip saves Estella at the end of *Great Expectations*. Anne is the symbol to him of his lost innocence, and in redeeming her he at last redeems himself. Having accepted the past with its hate and love, its guilt and pride, its evil and good, Jack can be regenerated into the world of the present, redeemed through suffering and self-knowledge.

When Stark and Adam destroy each other, Jack emerges from the vicarious experience of their deaths as the synthesis of their alternatives, as a whole man. Through the reponsibility his manhood imposes on him, he brings the Scholarly Attorney, old and dying, into his home. Finally, it is the old man, the religious fanatic, the "unreal" father from whom Jack learns the ultimate facts of life, who becomes a "real" father. (pp. 32-3)

Through his "father," Jack is able to understand the significance of Cass Mastern's life in the "eye of God." After Jack's nominal father dies and he has completed his study of Cass Mastern, fulfilling at last all of his obligations to the past, he can leave Judge Irwin's house, the womb of his rebirth, and "go into the convulsion of the world, out of history into history and the awful responsibility of time." While Cass has sacrificed his life to redeem himself, Jack achieves redemption somewhat easily and painlessly. For this reason, Jack's ultimate salvation seems externally imposed (redemption as happy ending), abstract and literary rather than real. Yet to object to Warren's fine novel because it falls short of its potentialities seems finally presumption. To have it better than it is would be at the expense of gambling with what it has already achieved—a fool's risk. *All the King's Men* is a great scarred bear of a book whose faults and virtues determine one another. The greatness of this bear devolves upon the magnificence of its faults and the transcendence into art of its palpable mortality. . . . (p. 34)

> Jonathan Baumbach, "The Metaphysics of Demagoguery: 'All the King's Men' by Robert Penn Warren," in his The Landscape of Nightmare: Studies in the Contemporary Novel, *New York University Press, 1965, pp. 16-34.*

JAMES HALL

While Faulkner dips through light swells toward posterity, the small craft warnings are flying for Warren. His failure to produce a major novel in eighteen years fosters disappointment, common as such cases are in the history of literature. His paperbacks are becoming harder to depend on. They go out, come back in smaller print, go out again. Young people revive the suspicion of academic conspiracy that political opponents raised a generation ago.

Yet none of these flags signals weather as surely as the doubt within. Some of us who cheered Warren as the voice of the age when the good novels came out now find ourselves quick to honor and reluctant to reread. And when we do, uncertainty sets in at points that once seemed exciting. The intricate cross-symbolism [in *All the King's Men*] looks too right. Mother is a thrice-kept woman, the upright judge is the real father, but the Scholarly Attorney is another father and so is Willie, and a complex of murders, suicides, insanities, and cries of "oh, oh" must occur to reconcile Jack and us to them all. The pure girl must take a mud bath to become marriageable, and an ancestor had it worked out the whole time. No one questions the logic of all this—that causes the trouble. As discovery broadens into "wisdom" and mannerism in fiction shifts from management to style, gratitude for the superb diagnostician recedes and the harsh issue becomes what, if anything, Warren does better than others who agree with him.

The current question does not outdate existing answers. From the first, Warren has had good luck in his interpreters. He had helped teach hundreds, and many of the best minds reciprocated by giving him as accurate a reading as we have for any contemporary except Eliot and Faulkner. Skillful critics mapped the conflict between the need to kill father and be reconciled with him, the power of self-recognition, the significance of narrators, the intricacies of structure, the relationship to Faulkner, the meaning of violence, and the reasons for style. Good craftsmen put mortar between these bricks. Less generous interpreters performed their service for truth by naming the vulnerable points—"drug store gothic" and the like.

Yet, though Warren has won a place in history, these concerns may not prove enough to keep him alive. They may help to bury him. For a philosophical novelist benefits immensely at first from the time spirit. Literary historians have explained the effects of the first World War on literature and said much less about the second. . . . The first completed a revolt against simpler souls, vaporized any surviving faith in commercial industrial civilization as a value in itself. The discipline of the second war drove home to rebels that this kind of society remained an ineluctable modality of the visible, but revolt came against an élite committed to sensitivity—not by denying its worth, but by making it seem less satisfying than an earlier generation had hoped.

The short-run literary effect of the second war was thus exactly opposite from that of the first: to parallel rather than fight the imperatives of war. War, after all, gives purpose to the random acts and thoughts of individuals. More than that, it makes naval lieutenants out of automobile salesmen and price control administrators out of academics. The diversity of wartime needs liberated the pent-up energy of the thirties by giving even sensitives a chance to try running the world—or some well marked-off corner of it. The novelists of the forties, formed on the frustrated purposefulness of the preceding decade, transferred their feelings to the new universal need for power and direction. In wartime, communication media drive the idea of organized force into the safest noncombatant consciousness; only an insane detachment could have prevented novelists from taking an interest in self-expression through channeled effort and applied thought.

Moreover, the world suddenly needed its imaginative men. With the depression over and situations everywhere fluid—particularly with the pressure for results making questions public service rather than sedition—novelists as well as scientists found themselves speaking like authorities. In the vacuum of diminished public confidence, imaginative men found their charts, pieced together mostly for fun by their predecessors, more accurate for locating and navigating than popular tradition. After being disregarded for so long, writers naturally turned garrulous and a bit arrogant. Jack Burden's wise-guy voice, an invention not yet obsoleted out of the American novel, speaks for a new man suddenly even prouder of his knowledgeability than of his tender toughness. He can influence events, defy authority with the backing of authority, and intimidate policemen. All by talking. (pp. 81-3)

If Warren is a first-rank novelist, it is not because he is "wise"; he simply brings the most energy and knowledge to bear imaginatively on this point of collision. No other novelist so committed to modernism—with its devotion to truth of the inner life, its alliance with a presumably superior past, its confidence in its vision of something better than commercial industrial society—so powerfully conveys the surprise at being given world enough and time to try translating arrogance into actuality. In all of his best novels, this pent-up anger finds itself freer than it had dreamed possible to press upon living flesh. Where in Faulkner violence counterattacks against unbearable stasis, violence in Warren acts calculatingly in the name of concretely envisaged freedom. Warren is a true shock novelist—not in his plots or his embarrassed sexuality, but in his focus on the tender, murderous imagination of the twentieth century suddenly authorized to practice control upon events. He shows more forcefully than any of his rivals what enthusiasm for control is and where it hurts most. He writes the emerging novel of forces with a more violent drive than Snow or Greene or Sartre or Camus.

My case for Warren thus rests upon his militant imaginative energy warring with his cultural inheritance. The social and self diagnoses are parts of this, though not necessarily the most lasting ones. The clash within the Puritan ethic—maintaining high motives while getting what you want—has diminished. The sense of a locatable crisis has spread out in search of an object. The once central issue of self-knowledge has moved on to, After self-knowledge, what? Acceptance transforms insight into one element in a new equation. And in the hard realities of time, critical emphasis on self-knowledge now threatens Warren's continuance as a live figure. True, the idea of such questing, with its tendency to transform the novels into cautionary tales, can turn into self-recognition forced on a protagonist who can *never* know enough soon enough. But the limits of Warren's explanations appear more starkly now than they did fifteen or twenty years ago. Essentially, he depends upon a commonwealth of guilt grounded in the family romance. Though fewer people now question this chart, more recognize its crudity. Such sophistication can make the wish behind the cross-referencing drama seem too tensely held. Straightening everything into a tight pattern may be impossible and undesirable—may be, as Herzog's psychiatrist says, a dangerous inability to tolerate ambiguous situations. (pp. 84-5)

If Warren is to remain among the major novelists, though, *All the King's Men* must stand as more than a monument to some minor Muse like the American Political Novel. Warren makes this rereading hard to do. Unlike most contemporaries, he does not automatically enlist the reader's collaboration. His drive for definiteness leads him to finish sentences that his fellow novelists like to leave dangling. Above everything else, he is an anxious writer. At the end of *All the King's Men,* his fear of the ferocity within leads him to tie up loose ends in a frenzy of reconciliations—with Jack's mother, Judge Irwin, the Scholarly Attorney, Anne, and Cass Mastern. He has to protect the new life at every point from the threat of emotional kickback. So he returns to that fountain of modern renewal, youthful hopes, and tries to carry them intact across the barrier of adult years.

But up to that point he had been doing better than most novelists. He writes powerful dramatic scenes. He brings together militant energy and a theatrical imagination at a time when the theatricality carried man's hope; and he fixes these upon a double locale admirably suited to testing their range. Even in 1945 no one needed a philosophical fictionist to discover some discrepancy between ends and means; the easier universals get established in the consciousness of the race earlier than that. Warren's theatricality sets up a conflict between subtler ambivalent feelings—a love-fear for the integrity of anger, a love-hatred for slyness, and an impossible yearning for personal force.

Unity of being through anger appears in its pure form in Willie's speech after he finds the city machine has tricked him. Willie is completely himself, the farmers are completely themselves; yet they are all in the betrayal together. The pros, Jack and Sadie, hitherto cut off by their knowledgeability, unite with the One and the Many. Willie taps their animosity toward the process they have devoted their lives to. Though Willie later increases his power to mould the crowd, this unity never reoccurs. Jack and Sadie become themselves again. While the speech lasts, though, it achieves the wanted transcendence: it makes anger and love, public and private, identical. A vindicating unity closes the space between hero and populace, good and mixture, anger and effectiveness. In Warren, as in Elizabeth Bowen, desire for this kind of leap is absolute. Characters come to terms with not getting, but cannot stop wanting.

Yet, for all its satisfying power, spontaneously expressed anger accomplishes little more than the impassive anger of the rednecks. Change and control require mind, applied knowledge, method. The shadow falls between these and pure inspiration. The critical conflict in *All the King's Men* occurs not between ends and means, but between spontaneity and technique. More than anything else, Jack Burden expresses distrust for the use of mind divorced from the integrity of anger. Loss of an exciting, unifying vision determines the opening attitude toward Willie. The means he uses in the drug store speech at Mason City are not immoral in the sense that his coercing Judge Irwin is. They are not even seriously false. They amount to little more than what courses in public speaking inculcate daily in respectable universities—adapting the material to the audience. Willie tells the farm town crowd that he has slopped hogs and got manure on his shoes. He does not need votes just now. He has acted for these people in building highways and schools despite the Establishment's opposition. Everything he says is so.

At the bottom of Jack's resentment lies not untruth but a concept of Nature. He dislikes in Willie what he dislikes in himself—the self-conscious use of mind and knowledge. In so far as the farmers and townspeople represent an untutored self, any intellectualized means of dealing with them becomes by definition unnatural, since it destroys the wanted unity between complex and simple. Willie's skill at reducing distance and getting the rustics to share the glory of the governorship offends Jack because it is technique and not impulse. Jack admires from the heart Willie's ability to impose personal force on other people. He admires Judge Irwin's power to resist. But these are rare gifts. A man of Jack's sensitivity cannot hope to match them. Given a generalized sense of grievance equal to Willie's and the folk's, he must depend upon indirection—talent and acquired skills. So he hates the part of his hero that must also utilize these civilized stratagems. (pp. 87-9)

The traditional case for Warren rests on his "wise" perception of conflicts between means and ends plus his understanding the self in relation to them. But his great claim to endurance rests on his "immoral" impulse, his secret sharing with the enemy. No other contemporary touches Warren's powerful identification with energetic intelligence—his enthusiasm for the efficient producer. In dramatizing the drive that Snow only suggests, he expresses better than anyone else the spirit of the forties. Politics in Warren appeals through its ruthlessness, its ethic of the imposed will, its by-passing the claims of decency and the civilian rules for muffling conflict. It allies with war and hero worship rather than democratic referral to committee. Only because Warren feels this drive in his bones can he raise the serious moral issue for an organizing society—the question of *degrees* of flexibility.

The power of the novel comes from imposing two forms of energy, embodied in Willie and Jack, on the permanent scene of state politics. The driving use of personal force and charisma plus applied intelligence brings on the threat inherent in anger itself, but the chances for men sensitive to suffering as deprivation to take over and hold the machinery of control have become real enough to power a full-scale imaginative test. That the effort could be made at all reflects an enormous shift in the sense of felt life. For Faulkner that collective dream did not die with Sutpen in the nineteenth-century; it never existed.

It is important to be clear on the nature of the action in *All the King's Men.* Vulnerability to the threat of anger within and without makes the structure concentrate on staying power.

Summaries credit Willie with accomplishments—roads, schools, even the hospital contract—but the three main actions after his quick rise to office are all defensive. He defeats the impeachment threat. The purifying hospital plan arises from guilt dramatized by the attack. The last political program fends off MacMurfee's blackmail attempt. (Judge Irwin dies almost accidentally during this episode—a pedestrian who does not get out of the crosswalk fast enough.) Warren has a theatrical mind—loving to elevate forces and bring them to moments of truth—and his political drama poses a single large question: can men sensitive to pain, endowed with anger beyond the pragmatic but clear only on short-run purposes, *retain* any control on the direction life takes? Does enthusiasm have staying power?

So in the over-all action the proponents of directed aggressiveness fight a defensive battle for control and good repute against the reaction of self-interest and earlier styles. The "directed" in their program handicaps the rebels. Both sides use aggressive means, but the new men waver because their use of technique is in its nature "insincere." Keeping in touch with their rural justification forces them into a frantic side-race. Warren records better than anyone else so far the grinding mesh of energy, sensitivity, and applied knowledge. After twenty years the settings, scenes, and language that do this retain their power. And the effect depends upon a plausible but magnificent distortion, inherent in the scene—that government runs mainly by deploying shameful knowledge.

But who is Willie Stark? He is the ideal figure the age had been working toward ever since it had decided to discard the artist's passivity. The New Man, simultaneously effective and sensitive. He embodies the triumph, and strain, of the Energy Principle. His "greatness" means his ability to team hitherto antagonistic forces in the name of righteous anger. As noted before, the novel of forces depends heavily on scene for emotional effects that earlier appeared through fluid consciousness; one of Warren's greatest superiorities to writers who agree with him lies in making a dual scene multiply the vitality of his ideal tragic figure.

For Warren redoubles the energy of his already energetic hero by making him the one and only master of two naturally hostile locales, the soured pastoral of the rednecks and the predictability-loving political machine. These two huge metaphors extend outward from central cores. The pastoral furnishes suppressed anger given, in a state of nature, to sporadic outbreak. Faulkner had already discovered that rhythm. The machine supplies a perfected technique for fighting without being destroyed. The one wants to kill its masters, the other to make them prevail smoothly. Only the Hero can combine these contradictory drives into purposeful force. And only Warren has been able to combine them with theatrical character into the hero that the age demanded and did not like.

Our tolerant present favors mass forgiveness for the Fugitives; their good deeds since have made up for their foolishness about forty acres and a mule. But with Warren we shall be forgiving too much. The same analogical sympathy, along with the same remoteness from the farmers' actual lives and hopes, permeates *All the King's Men*. In other novels the mixture creates the falsest notes in his work. When Warren tries to come close to the folk, he gets corny, but in his masterpiece he holds Mason City and the campaign trail at a photographer's distance that is exactly right for him.

Willie is *of* the soured pastoral world—and he can manage it. Moreover, his discovered talent for dramatizing himself as the

voice of its will not only works, but enables him to live with the discrepancy between *of* and *for* in a comfort that the "sincere" sensitive man, Jack Burden, finds impossible. The protagonists' effort to base the complex upon the simple resembles the impulse that Empson describes for the Elizabethans, but Warren's being the heir to fifty years' increase in range and depth of consciousness expands the gap—quantitatively if not qualitatively. Also, instead of using clownish contentment to contrast with urban whatever, Warren makes clownish frustration and aggressiveness a correlative for a universal sense of being deprived. So the farmers provide the visible moral base—and the only one—for the sophisticates' acts. Even more important, their inexpressible anger steps up the horse-power that drives, enlarges, and justifies the application of mind and technique. (pp. 89-91)

But the rural can no longer serve so unequivocally to represent the counter-ideal of community. The eros of Warren's countryside is individual and not powerful. Lucy Stark does represent love as nurturing and nursing, but she makes her stands for the integrity of anger. Her teaching job, the politicians believe, causes Willie to fight for sound school construction—and get his start. She leaves him when he refuses to fire the corrupt state auditor. Her scene is the porch at the Stark farm, her sister's chicken ranch—and the hospital. She comments on political life chiefly by her absences and serves as the measure of Willie's distance from angry pastoral. (pp. 92-3)

Nevertheless, energized by this soured pastoral, Willie is the man who can heal the Faulknerian fracture. He can harness applied knowledge to the anger arising from deprivation. He has the force and the technique to master the political machine. Warren's keeping this side of his scene omnipresent shows great skill. Some critics complain that Tiny Duffy, its center, is not much of a character. True. The real force is the machinery itself. It does not involve persons in any complex sense, but understandings, chains-of-command, needs, common embarrassments, and agreed-upon rewards. Without the professionals, government will not run; axiomatically, "good people" will not do the daily work or take the daily blows. Though these uncivil servants levy a tax on all transactions, some business does get through. The machinery has no direction, only a will to survive. Tiny Duffy was a power in state politics when Willie was a county treasurer and he succeeds Willie as governor. City or country makes little difference. Professionalism binds courthouse, city hall, and capital. (pp. 94-5)

So Willie ends as a not-quite-successful shepherd king, yoking a double sense of the self as at once simple and complex, basic feeling and sophisticated intellect. Some critics have disliked Warren's failing to show his "corruption" as a straight-line descent, but the genius of Willie's story comes from his waverings. The *eros* of the countryside, Lucy Stark, serves as a gauge of his motion toward and away from his soured pastoral base.

But who is Jack Burden? Several answers are possible. Obviously, the second major energy in the novel. For Willie, the most useful part of the machine. For himself at the end, the grown-up boy from Burden's Landing. For a majority of critics, the passive man caught in a moral muddle, expressing the doubt that attends action. This last view could not have survived so well without having some truth, but it lacks precision. If the active man means solely the leader, then Willie becomes the only candidate in the novel, but few citizens would deny the Secretary of Defense or even the Secretary of State some credit as men of action. And in the progress of the story, as distinct from the retrospective philosophical view, Jack does a good deal. Even as a doubter about the value of activity he falls below almost any average hero of the preceding generation. He is simply the best doubter who is also heavily committed to action.

Actually, during Willie's time in power, Jack is another effective sensitive man. He downgrades himself, of course, for not being an All-American tough guy—envies and hates Tom Stark, the analogue for the purely forceful part of Willie. Lacking this direct strength, he has substituted intelligence and technique. He meets reversals by thinking about them—trying to put them into some acceptable larger perspective—but he has also developed his own method of imposing force. He ambushes potentially stronger opponents by holding the hidden ace. The recurrence of these surprise attacks in Warren suggests how powerful their appeal to him is. In *Night Rider,* Mr. Munn, echoing a legendary Confederate ambush, returns to bushwhack his thwarted pursuers. Slim Sarrett slips in to strangle Sue in *At Heaven's Gate.* Jeremiah Beaumont creeps up in the dark and in stocking feet to stab Colonel Fort in *World Enough and Time.* And in *All the King's Men* itself Adam Stanton appears from behind a pillar to shoot Willie.

Ambush is Warren's figure for the thinking man's mode of attack. And in the modern world this systematic mode of administering shocks can win as many battles as show of force can. Despite disclaimers, Jack likes the game of surprise as much as Willie does. (pp. 98-9)

Willie and Jack like to punish the pride by destroying the dignity of their objects. Enemies who sin by believing themselves more intelligent and knowledgeable bring special pleasure. Judge Irwin has sinned further by thinking himself morally better, but Jack plays at surprise even in their final scene, dramatizing the effect by holding back his evidence until the last moment. . . . And Jack's excitement in quietly accumulating this evidence makes the search one of the best chapters in the novel. Whatever his second thoughts, Jack likes using technique.

And of course he hates it too. As indicated earlier, his hostility to it appears regularly in his disgust with Willie. The same repulsion forms the overt basis for his disgust with himself as executive officer. But Warren uses telling lyric scenes to show the fear of vacancy that makes Jack run. (pp. 101-03)

Politics has a more positive appeal, though, than escape from vacancy. For all the pride of ancestry, the machine is Jack's native habitat—not where he was born, but where he chooses to spend his adulthood. He has lived at its edge for years as reporter and columnist before he meets Willie. It offers some of the sureties of home. There he knows where he is, what everybody will do if somebody else does this or that. There his talent for using knowledge brings the highest price and gains the greatest respect. There, too, he can attach his native disgust to a suitable object. His scorn for legislators and officeholders is, he comes to see, also a form of self-disgust, but he habitually takes pride in his scientific understanding: he can predict exactly how these manlike machines will work. Tiny will cheat within prescribed limits and flatter beyond limit; MacMurfee will back off the impeachment or try to bluff, but hesitate to force a showdown; Gummy Larson will stay bought. By thinking of himself as consciousness and most of his associates as behavior, he satisfyingly simplifies daily life. He has to consider only Willie and Sadie as people.

Over-all, then, Warren shows far more militancy in Jack and more flair for his chosen field than criticism usually admits. Against these qualities the novel sets his saving instinct for seeing all around a problem and avoiding irretrievable outbreak, but Jack does not fit the pattern of the sensitive man leaning totally on the strong one. He and Willie are a team rather than player and pawn, and the combination's formidableness comes in good part from Jack.

Judge Irwin, the third major force, is a masterpiece of dramatic economy. He appears in only three scenes, yet everybody remembers him. The usual view sees him as the upright father who made one mistake—a kind of walking religious ethic secularized into the give-and-take of politics. Much as this view leaves out, he is not even quite so reliable as all that. He refuses the chance to avoid degradation because, he says, he has pledged his word. Still, the impetus for Willie's midnight ride early in the novel comes from Judge Irwin's having gone back on his word—for a reason, of course. Even his final show of reliability leaves him an accessory to MacMurfee's blackmail attempt. (In Snow's *The Masters,* an established scientist acts at once to stop a partisan from threatening a non-tenure fellow; politics in Warren includes no such idea of *noblesse oblige.*) Moreover, though Judge Irwin twice shows the power to make Jack feel guilty, this conscience never inhibits him in day-to-day conflicts. In the capital Jack never thinks of it and even at Burden's Landing finds its disapproval bearable.

The Judge takes his real memorableness from his theatricality—from being the Worthy Antagonist that the Hero must have. He is the counter-personal force. Right or wrong, he cannot be imposed upon. His strength comes from not wanting anything; he is the man of satisfied energies. And as such he is a Hector armored in nostalgia. The one symbol regularly associated with him—his pre-gunpowder artillery model—calls up for Jack memory of boyhood games. The Judge is archaic and likes the archaic. Self-interested individualism has replaced government by a coterie of friends, but Governor Stanton once stopped scandal at a price to anonymous sufferers because Judge Irwin was his friend. Despite his present alliance with the modern rascal MacMurfee, he presumably acts in a class interest, visualized in actual neighbors, rather than an immediately selfish one.

In his greatest appeal, though, he expresses personal force in the *style* of Victorian nobility. Just as his living room draws Willie's scorn for its graciousness, his talk conveys better than Willie's an aspiration to heroism. He can speak tolerantly about new men meeting new demands on state government and he can still believe in grand gesture. Withholding the secret that he is Jack's father just as he is about to commit suicide gives him a theatrical exit, which sums up his aim and Jack's longing for nobility in a self-interested world. (pp. 104-06)

But if the novel retains its power until Willie's death, the ending does not. It may well be plausible for Jack Burden. The divisions between self-consciousness and simplicity, betrayal and just revenge, action and withdrawal fade off into all-passion-spent, awareness-is-all. Sad Cass Mastern does not answer Willie much more than Ike McCaslin answers Sutpen or Ratliff does Mink. Jack is far from being the most distanced character in the history of fiction, and his weariness implicates the author.

Jack and, to a degree, Warren try to restore and reorder the adolescent past without integrating adult life into it. This falling back on the modern literary hope gives the appearance of applying psychoanalytic thought—straightening out the misunderstood family relationships, searching for renewal of interest in abandoned projects. But neither in psychoanalysis or real life can anyone sustain shutting out the intervening experience. As an interim solution, Jack's return may be plausible; as the redemption which some critics take it to be, it looks shaky. For it does not say what will happen when new problems revive Jack's assertive disgust. Warren does not believe that anything so endemic goes away. He simply leaves its recurrence and the acceptance of adult experience to Jeremiah Beaumont and the next novel.

For the time being everything hangs on Anne Stanton. The fiction falters at the point of resurrectng her. She is the objective guarantee of success in Jack's turn to seeking likeness instead of difference, harmony instead of conflict. (pp. 107-08)

The talent and weakness in drawing Anne makes her a metaphor rather than a personality. Possible complexities appear in summary. In youth she amounts to a series of play scenes—beach, roadster, tennis court. Concerning other people's ideal woman, *non disputandum est:* Jack likes the child in the budding girl. (p. 108)

And she proves untouchable—Jack's little sister, perfect playmate, sexually taboo. Too much alike. . . . The return of Jack's mother, his image of woman as shameless sexual object, completes the taboo.

Jack's vision of fingertips touching—excitement and peace yoked perfectly—carries some power as selective memory. Anne's reappearance has logic, if less vitality. Her affair with Willie removes the taboo. And, while maintaining her celebrated "integrity," she reappears passive, receptive, guidable. In the later stages she always materializes in need of help and protection—telephoning, waiting in the hall, asking understanding about Willie or comfort about Adam or aid in finding him. This change from teacher to suppliant removes a barrier. And she has lost her childhood playfulness enough to be the perfect companion in the higher play of comprehending dead Cass Mastern. As with Cass, she is enough like Jack to create harmony and just enough unlike him to assure him that he is not looking at his mirror image.

The final rush of conciliations shows how much author shares character's anxiety to have all the pieces fit together perfectly. Jack's trying to make all events and people mesh asserts a form of control over the uncontrollable parts of experience. If they work into the web, they make sense, become a part of the necessity that anyone can live with. The number and complexity of the conciliations guarantee that they have harmonized *all* the dissonances. The princely father nobly dead, the repentant mother, and the dying saintly father fulfill a lot of wishes quickly. And telling the Cass Mastern story will add a warrior saint to the canon. No matter that Jack seems to have to write the Willie Stark story first. The falling off at the end of the novel does not destroy it. (pp. 109-10)

> James Hall, *"The Poet Turned First-Degree Murderer: Robert Penn Warren,"* in his The Lunatic Giant in the Drawing Room: The British and American Novel since 1930, *Indiana University Press, 1968, pp. 81-110.*

EARL WILCOX

[The essay from which this excerpt is taken was originally published in Four Quarters, *May, 1972.]*

The wide range of critical approaches given to Robert Penn Warren's *All the King's Men* suggests that this novel is his most provocative piece of writing. Between two and three dozen articles is a conservative count of the more important essays. Perhaps, as with all successful artistic endeavors, this novel has prompted comment of such diverse variety because it seems to have a bit of everything for everyone. I think this proliferation of commentary indicates a popularity which stems, in large part, from the reception the book has received in the college and university classroom.

As almost everyone knows, Warren's is a hallowed name in some literary circles because of his co-editing and authoring several anthologies, collections of essays, rhetoric texts, and of course because of his role in expanding New Criticism. But Warren alone of the now unfashionable New Critics has succeeded as a poet, novelist, critic, editor, essayist, and as a teacher. It is fitting, then, to emphasize that one sound reason for the continuing popularity and discussion of *All the King's Men* is that it is eminently teachable. *All The King's Men* has for more than twenty years been the subject of countless discussions in the college and university classrooms and corridors. And I assume that a salient reason for this appeal lies exactly in the complex nature of the novel itself. In particular the novel insists on literary, historical, psychological, sociological, philosophical relevance. Its tone is at once satiric and humorous; its mode is both realism and tragedy. Its style, themes, and characters continue to excite both students and teachers alike. (p. 143)

All the King's Men is most teachable as a piece of fiction primarily because it *is* fiction before it is a tract for dictators or a thinly-veiled biography of Huey Long. (But I do not mean that the novel does not accommodate itself well to all these and other approaches simultaneously: indeed I think that it does accommodate itself to a multiplicity of approaches.) No one has yet claimed that this novel is the mythical "great American novel" which every writer is said to be trying to write; but the novel does have literary excellence on several levels.

There is, for example, the narrator, Jack Burden. Burden is one of our finest literary creations; he is "one of us," as Hemingway's Brett Ashley would say. And, as his name signifies, Burden is a modern Everyman, an Oedipus, a naif for whom things fall apart and who tries to put them back together again. . . . For the student searching for a fictional contemporary that he can dig and who tries to cope, Jack Burden suits well. And in a formal study in the classroom, Burden's counterpart is translatable and recognizable from everywhere. Here once again is Huck Finn or Holden Caulfield or Telemachus in search of a father. Here is the romantic Don Quixote, trying for the longest while to see the world as it ought to be and not as it is. Or Hamlet, who vacillates between being and not-being. The list is long and the spectrum wide in the arena of literary antecedents upon whom the teacher and student calls for useful, insightful comparison. Since some fiction courses seem to organize around comparisons and contrasts, and such courses often proceed chronologically, identifying these literary predecessors is a helpful beginning device.

For the student, Jack Burden-as-fictional-character is, then, a useful literary analogue. But, more importantly, Burden is recognizable as a human being. In the novel, Burden is a youthful, idealistic student who falls in and out of love; gets in and out of bed with his women; tries one job after another; attempts to be a scholar but finds himself being corrupted by a corrupting world; misuses his drive and energy—and so goes his youth. Many students do not know all the literary Eugene Gants, the Hamlets, or even the Hucks and Holdens who have populated the pages of our best drama and fiction. But students have no trouble recognizing Burden as "one of us." Undoubtedly his very human indecisiveness most consistently intrigues students. In Burden's tension between past and present, the present is constantly punctuated by flashbacks into the past. The past is always thoroughly idealistic: the days at Burden's Landing are captured poignantly in passage after passage. (pp. 143-45)

Later, of course, Burden's Landing becomes a nightmare for Jack because Anne Stanton, Adam Stanton, Judge Irwin, Jack, and everyone else changes. The naif becomes a man. His maturation process accounts for the considerable appeal which Burden-as-narrator has. This attraction is produced by the pattern woven into Burden's life: a bifurcated scheme of flight and escape into past (history) toward a belief in a deterministic world ("The Great Twitch") with a concomitant rebound into the present. Burden himself summarizes this rhythm of his life in the closing sentence of the novel: ". . . we shall go out of the house and go into the convulsion of the world, out of history into history and the awful responsibility of Time."

Burden-as-student, aside from his role as the mask of the narrator, deftly captures the spirit and mood of contemporary, evolving man in this flight pattern. His desire for knowledge, coupled with his constant hesitancy in light of the responsibility which that knowledge brings him, reflects the acute dilemma which students themselves express time and again. Numerous passages in the novel show Burden's disquietude. And the various names he gives to his fluctuation interest students, who are themselves great name makers. There is the sense of novelty and nowness in names like the Young Executive, The Scholarly Attorney, The Case of the Upright Judge, The Great Twitch, and The Great Sleeps. But perhaps the richest extended comment which engages students in finding a lot of Jack Burden in themselves is the reflective monologue early in the novel when Burden is listening to Willie Stark make a speech. This speech triggers an emotional awareness in Burden with the full impact of the dilemma he faces. Every man on the road to knowledge faces a similar upheaval. Appropriately, an organic metaphor—the embryo—expresses the trauma well. (p. 145)

I have dwelt this long on Burden-as-human rather than Burden-as-fictive-device because students do not really care about all the literary analogues ultimately, especially not today's students. But whenever the occasion arises, it is useful to exploit Warren's sophistication by pointing out the literary allusions: there is the title (which is not a simple nursery rhyme echo, it turns out, once you start explicating its meaning): or the Dantean epigraph on the title page; and there are other literary devices which shed a good deal of light on the total picture of the complexity of Warren's narrator. For instance, the Dantean motif gives Burden's outlook a rather different cast—an optimistic one—which one sees more precisely by exploring the context of the quotation from *The Divine Comedy*. For despite his escapist attitudes evident in many scenes in the novel, Burden finally does come to grips with his own personality. What he sees is a radically modified determinism, colored by a corrected vision of his own role in shaping his destiny. He does not conclude on a totally optimistic note, but he does more clearly know what effect he can have in shaping his own end. The rebirth and conversion motifs are prominent in the novel, and these leitmotifs are worth bringing to students' attention also in relation to these continuing revelations which

Burden has about himself. As students say, this qualified determinism is about all anyone could ask for. Every teacher now sees that today's student has changed his question from a teleological *why* to a psychological *how*. The question is not *did* Humpty Dumpty fall, or *why* did he fall, or even why do things in general fall apart. But *how* are they to be put back together again. The young soldier returning home from Vietnam, the black student returning to the ghetto from a college education, the WASP grappling with the implications of his history—all of today's children want to know *how* to put it back together again. They all know you can't go home again, but they will keep on trying. And they know Burden's solution is not simple, not even entirely clear. But his formulation, his articulation of a plan holds some promise. Students in today's classrooms are aware of themselves in a historical context, and they are hellbent on finding answers to questions they have about their past, present, and future.

For many readers of **All the King's Men** the more intriguing character is not Jack Burden, but Willie Stark. Such a reading inevitably points toward the Huey Long saga as background for the novel. Warren has told rather fully (and somewhat ambiguously) why the novel is not "about" Long; and, after all, one feels inclined to let the novelist's explanation stand [see Warren's excerpt above]. Yet certain parallels between Willie Stark and Huey Long are obvious, and any study of the novel without a nod toward these parallels is shortsighted. Some recent biographies of Long are especially useful in getting at the Long legend, as historians, political scientists, and others continue to find the Long era an engaging aspect of Americana. Exploiting the Stark-Long analogies is, however, for the short run; in the long run, Stark's role in the novel offers a more extended insight only in its primary relation to Jack Burden. Stark helps Burden reflect, redefine, and rediscover himself.

Willie Stark (as his name also signals) is a man of stark fact. He contrasts sharply with Adam Stanton, the "man of idea," as Burden calls him. These categories are partly ironic, of course, because they are indeed aspects of Burden's own personality. For it is Burden who gives himself fully to his research—the facts—whenever the Boss wants him to do so. And only when the "dirt" rubs off on Burden's own past, his own father and mother, does his idealism become tarnished. The man of fact in the society of the 70's has not as much going for him as he had in the immediate past, even as recently as the 60's. As originally conceived, Warren says that Willie Stark and Stanton were to represent the scientists of our world. Thus the curious blending of the fact-ideal world in the two closest friends of Burden presents a tension which modern students with a science-humanism orientation find themselves grappling with more and more. Burden's own tensions are mirrored in the conflict between his two friends. Perhaps Stark is finally important to us because we recognize him for his Machiavellian demagoguery.

This is not the place to list the Machiavellian demagogues that have traipsed across the stage of our little world, but undoubtedly some of the American Machiavels are recognizable enough to be painful for Americans. For notorious reasons, Southern politicians seem to bear the brunt of comparison when Stark's machinations are analyzed. And the Long dynasty in Louisiana obviously makes a comfortable parallel. Furthermore, Robert Penn Warren is by birth and some training a Southerner; and there is no little interest in this biographical fact since all of his novels have a Southern setting. (This despite the fact that Warren long ago gave up making the mint julep for making mint of the Ft. Knox variety.) Nevertheless, Willie's Machia-vellian roots yield some intriguing revelations for historians and young political scientists in the classroom. What more incisive method of seeing machine politics and the Mafia ori-entation of today's political scene than through the philosophy of Willie Stark. Here rolled up into a neat ball is William James' pragmatism and a set of deep south godfathers long before Talese or Puzo.

Stark's philosophy is best seen in the action of the novel, for he is, after all, a man of action—not idea. (This itself is a provocative concept of the political panorama today.) But suc-cinctly put, Stark's view of the world, God, and man boils down to an aphoristically-sounding doctrine echoing the prag-matic philosophy which guides him for good or for evil: "Man is conceived in sin and born in corruption and he passeth from the stink of the didie to the stench of the shroud. There is always something." The sardonic wit of Burden always filters our impressions of Stark, and one supposes that Stark is really worse than the naive Burden ever sees him, until it is almost too late. But Stark is not only the political manipulator, the Jacobean Machiavel: before the bloody Sunday ending of the novel, the entire political set-up is brought into sharp focus. The "Case of the Upright Judge" is the label Burden puts on his "excursion" into the past. And in that past the taintless Governor Stanton, Judge Irwin, and all the other "pure hearts, clean hands" souls are tarnished through and through. And so that we understand the inevitable link between the past and the present, Burden's ancestors, the Masterns, are shown for their own special brand of manipulation. Wherever he turns, Jack Burden's ultimate education is his understanding that all of life is political. Structurally, the Cass Mastern episode fills a neat intercalary place in Burden's education. Jack accurately links the Masterns' life with the Case of the Upright Judge, and from both cases Jack learns a lesson he tries desperately to avoid. He learns that: ". . . the world is all of one piece . . . that the world is like an enormous spider web and if you touch it, however lightly, at any point, the vibration ripples to the remotest perimeter and the drowsy spider feels the tingle and is drowsy no more. . . . It does not matter whether or not you meant to brush the web of things. Your happy foot or your gay wing may have brushed it ever so lightly, but what happens always happens. . . ." The escape into a deterministic episte-mology no longer works for Burden, though he avoids even this admission until much later. . . . The ultimate significance, then, for the historian or political scientist in a study of *All the King's Men* is not in finding the Machiavellian parallels in the novel, but in showing how these aspects of the novel shed light on the progressive revelations the political events make on the protagonist, Jack Burden. Warren is not, furthermore, satiriz-ing Southern politics; he is not asserting that political action is impossible in an individual with deep personal integrity; and he is not suggesting that a Calvinistic view of man is the most pragmatic approach to understanding how the modern political state operates. Too many people (notably Hugh Miller and Jack Burden himself) contradict these false assumptions which some historians and political scientists have drawn from the novel. Miller and Burden do return to the political arena, and we are left with a far more moral world than we began with in the novel. If the novel shows us anything then from an historical perspective it is that easy generalizations about the nature of man as political animal are likely to be misleading. Burden learns this lesson through much pain and suffering. (pp. 146-50)

Too many claims for greatness have been made for too many works of fiction. A claim of uniqueness for Warren's *All the*

King's Men is not the intention here. Not all readers find the novel as richly humorous, as politically exciting, or as totally pertinent to humanity. . . . In a final analysis, the novel resists categorizing, becoming *sui generis* since it depicts many com-plex matters simultaneously. But above all, the novel does go a long way toward fulfilling William Faulkner's hints about the worthiness of modern authors to fulfill their function in our time. In the Nobel Prize Speech, Faulkner suggested that writers today must continue to write about "the problems of the human heart in conflict with itself which alone can make good writing because only that is worth writing about, worth the agony and the sweat." *All the King's Men* succeeds best in the classroom when one has time enough to explore more precisely how the characters, the plot, structure, tone, sym-bolism—indeed all of these and other elements blend into a pattern. When the multiple themes in the novel are unravelled and made pertinent to modern man, the dimensions of the novel as a work of art begin to unfold.

After all these analyses have been drawn between the novel and life itself, I detect that one important—even overriding aspect of this book often goes unnoted. The novel is finally about the power of love in the universe to change a man. Warren hints at this in the Dantean epigraph, and he develops this theme in several ways throughout the novel. As a love story with far richer impact than the brand offered in Segal's best seller, the novel makes an important comment. Jack Burden serves as the catalyst in the objective correlative: he sees, records, and though trying not to, he reacts to his impressions. All of the "love affairs" (Jack's, Willie's, Anne's, Jack's mother's, and others) eventually amount to far more than all the political affairs. Some critics have urged that the novel ends on a sentimental note, that the essential comic ending is too easy, even weak. Perhaps one should argue that it is difficult for calloused moderns to accept readily that the power of love in the universe does radically alter the lives of those who experience it. Jack Burden learns that he has instinctively loved Judge Irwin, though Burden does not know why until long after he discovers that the Judge is his real father. Burden learns to love his mother, whom he has thoroughly despised previously. Burden finally forgives and accepts Anne with all her blem-ishes, knowing that she too suffers from the deep hurt resulting from her life with Willie and the unmasking of her father's life. Even the Scholarly Attorney takes on a new attraction for Burden, who finally consoles the old man in the face of im-minent death. This newest role for Jack is an entirely different one, a sympathetic, compassionate sensitivity brought about by his Damascus-like conversion foreshadowed throughout the book. Popular lyrics of today's songs suggest that what the world needs now is love, love, love. If the novel ends un-fashionably tame, one must remember that the comedy envi-sioned by Dante was a *divine* comedy. Warren is not depicting a Christian medieval world view, but he is suggesting a thor-oughly moral universe. A world devoid of love, Warren seems to say, is as chaotic, as purposeless, as irreconcilable as it was before man entered it. . . . This is man's world, and man con-trols his destiny, and he can "put it back together again" if it seems to fall apart. The novel is not a program for reform nor an apology for an ethical system to discover precisely how man reassembles Humpty Dumpty. But the novel does assert that so long as Eternal Love exists man can be redeemed. (pp. 151-53)

Earl Wilcox, "Right On! 'All the King's Men' in the Classroom," in Twentieth Century Interpretations of 'All the King's Men': A Collection of Critical Es-says, *edited by Robert H. Chambers, Prentice-Hall, Inc., 1977, pp. 143-53.*

R. GRAY

As soon as anyone begins to discuss *All the King's Men* . . . , he is immediately confronted with a difficulty which is becoming commonplace in the field of American literature. The difficulty is one of saying something fresh about a book which has already been so exhaustively, and even exhaustingly, covered. On the one hand, there have been so many analyses of image and symbol in *All the King's Men,* and its handling of narrative point-of-view, that the reader may begin to suspect Warren of what F. R. Leavis, in another context, once called an excessive amount of 'doing.' On the other, there have been almost as many commentaries which have as their purpose a rebuttal of Warren's apparent reading of history, and more specifically the history of the Louisiana demagogue Huey Long on whom the character of Willie Stark was based. Behind these lies the assumption that Warren has taken the given facts and distorted them almost, but not quite, beyond recognition.

These, I think, have been the two major tendencies in criticism of *All the King's Men* since its first publication, and perhaps the simple mentioning of them suggests the vacuum which still exists and possibilities of approach which remain to be pursued. There have been many, perhaps too many, analyses of the novel which set it in some vast a-historical context in order to pay compliment to Warren's handling of the techniques of fiction. In such cases, the critic assumes that the book is written in a kind of code which it is his task to crack. When he does crack it, or some part of it, he seems so pleased with his success that the value or validity of the message thus communicated hardly engages his interest. To be more exact, the uses to which history and specific social circumstances are put in *All the King's Men,* and the larger meanings Warren extracts from all this, are rarely brought into question. The writer is accepted on the basis of his more obviously symbolic intentions, without reference to some of the rather dubious means by which those intentions are fulfilled. . . . [Such commentary] isolates *All the King's Men* from those powers of history which supply the spine of its narrative and the centre of its interests and, in doing so, it inevitably distorts and impoverishes the meaning of the book. Supposing what is said here to be true, the reader would surely be justified in asking why so much praise has been showered upon Warren; and, more particularly, for what reason Warren should have felt himself impelled to adopt a set of given historical circumstances only to alter them. (pp. 297-98)

This is precisely what other commentators on *All the King's Men* do ask, of course—those constituting the second major stream of criticism. . . . Their questions assume many forms and are presented with different degrees of vehemence but they remain in essentials one question, which asks by what right Robert Penn Warren has transformed Huey Long into Willie Stark. The transformation required an alteration of many of the given facts, and even the suppression of some of the more unsavoury aspects of Long's career, and how can this ever be defended? Their very phrasings of the question suggest their bias, for most of them are firmly convinced that Warren is guilty of irresponsibility or, worse still, of the imaginative equivalent of bad faith. There is an irony to be found here. Most of these commentators see themselves as offering a reply to the formalist school of criticism on *All the King's Men,* raising historical issues which that school prefers to ignore; and yet if to reply can be said to involve the idea of engaging directly with the other side, of achieving some kind of exchange with it, then what they do does not really constitute replying at all. The most that such commentators do is to point out the discrepancies between the facts and the fiction. The possibility

of a justification for these discrepancies is hardly raised because, whereas in the case of the formalists the writer is assumed to be isolated from the processes of history, he is here seen to be so immersed in them as to make his proper status that of their recording instrument. The ideal of the poet without any responsibility to history is replaced by the ideal of the scientific historian who has no responsibilities other than this one. The two ideals can hardly engage, being no more than mirror opposites of one another. And the irony is compounded by the fact that this curious state of affairs is ultimately an example of the 'terrible division' between philosophical ideal and historical reality which *All the King's Men* exists to demonstrate, the division implicit in the contrast between Willie Stark, the political realist, and Adam Stanton, the naïve man of ideas. This in itself suggests that a minimally acceptable interpretation of the book has to bring the two schools of criticism together, to see what made Warren change history in the way he did and whether his motives, as defined by the structure and purpose of the book, are an adequate justification for his changes. If nothing else, it might indicate to what extent the writer has succeeded in implementing his own recommendations, by squaring his inner needs and beliefs with the 'awful responsibility of Time' imposed on him by the outer world of event.

Perhaps one way of understanding what Robert Penn Warren has done in *All the King's Men,* as a preparation for assessing his achievement, is to concentrate in the first place on his raw material; that is, the historical facts with which he was presented in the story of Huey Long. Like most stories, Long's is in detail a complicated one, but its main outlines are clear enough. He was born to a poor family in a poor part of the state. At the time of his birth, Louisiana was run by the wealthy planters of the southern counties and the Catholic families who lived in and around New Orleans. The Long family, on the other hand, came from Anglo-Saxon and Protestant stock and had lived for many years in Winn Parish, a county in northern Louisiana which was at once impoverished and powerless. Deprived of a college education, he went to work quite early as a travelling salesman and in the ordinary course of his business acquired a knowledge of, and acquaintanceship with, local tenant-farmers which later proved invaluable. With his earnings, he managed to buy himself time to study for a law degree and then, armed with it, he began to carve out a political career for himself. The mixture of idealism and opportunism which was to become so characteristic of him is suggested by the fact that his favourite reading at this time consisted of radical political pamphlets, and historical or fictional accounts of magnificent demagogues.

Long rose to power with unusual speed even for a southern populist, which is what in a sense he was. He first took political office at the minimum age of twenty-one, and it was only eleven years later, in 1928, that he was elected Governor of the state. Once in power, it began to seem unlikely that he could ever be removed. He gradually assumed control of the state legislature, with a mixture of bribery and blackmail, and then so redesigned the political structure of Louisiana as to make almost every public official answerable to him. . . . Elections were rigged, the newspapers were carefully watched and punished with heavy taxes if they proved unusually hostile, and it began to seem that to oppose Huey Long openly in Louisiana was to invite self-destruction.

That is not the whole story, though: if it were, Huey Long would be no more than one in a long line of American demagogues, although perhaps more powerful than most. But the fact is that Long did not just want power as an end in itself. He wanted to use power to implement the kind of schemes which had been his ever since he had been able to think about his situation, and the situation of people like him. He wanted to help the 'rednecks' who continued to support him no matter how dictatorial his scheme of government appeared to be. Towards this end, a vast highway system was completed for the state, creating new opportunities for those, usually the poorer classes, trapped until then in the interior. . . . By 1934 he had decided to run for President and, as a preparation for his candidacy, he formulated a 'Share Our Wealth' programme of income redistribution which made the 'New Deal' look positively conservative. It provided, among other things, for the liquidation of all personal fortunes over three million dollars, a generous minimum wages for every American worker white *and* black, a national pension scheme and, in general, close governmental supervision of the economy. Of course, Long's motives in formulating this scheme were practical as well as idealistic: he wanted to appeal to the mass of working-men in the nation just as he had appealed to the poor folk of Louisiana. The scheme cannot be dismissed as simply as that, however, since other American demagogues have proved that there are easier ways of appealing to the popular vote. In the circumstances, to accuse Huey Long of wholesale opportunism would surely be as wrong as to see him as an idealistic man of the people. He was both, in a way, and as such perhaps best defined in terms of the paradox one essentially unsympathetic commentator favoured when he described Huey Long as 'a moral idiot of genius'.

This is surely the point about Huey Long: that, among those who know or have examined him, even those least sympathetic to his cause have tended to call his story tragic rather than iniquitous. It was the story of a man born into a specific set of historical circumstances which demonstrated to his dissatisfaction that the times were out of joint. In every sense, they denied the demands of his innermost being, what Warren calls 'the idea'. What he could do in these circumstances seemed fairly clear to him; and can perhaps be defined in terms of what Arthur Koestler, analyzing a similar and more universal situation, described as the alternative attitudes of the Yogi and the Commissar. He could either retreat into himself, and the kind of self-protective narcissism which rejects the world after acknowledging its irremediable iniquity; or he could commit himself to the desperate manoeuvres and partial fulfilments imposed on him by events. In the one case, he would be tending to deny the power which gives life to values; and, in the other, he would be tending to ignore the values which give meaning to power. Long apparently chose the second course. He tried to use corrupt means, in this case the means made available by the political machinery of his state, to achieve his aims; and in the process he could not help corrupting both those aims and himself.

What was true of Huey Long is also true of Willie Stark, no matter how much Warren may alter or condense specific details to make his point. Stark's story is also a tragic one; as tragic and as poignant as, say, that of Brecht's *Mother Courage*. For Willie Stark and Mother Courage are both placed in situations which demand the worst of them, if they are to survive, even though they may recognize and sometimes wish for the best. In this context, scene III of *Mother Courage and Her Children* in which the protagonist denies her son, a German soldier, in order to avoid the confiscation of her property by the Swedish army, is comparable to the moment in ***All the King's Men*** when

Willie Stark ruefully accepts the resignation of Hugh Miller, his Attorney-General. Miller, a man of genuine principle, resigns because Stark refuses to prosecute one of his underlings for attempting to divert state funds into his own pocket. Stark *will* punish the man privately but to commit himself to any public form of punishment would be, as he recognizes, to invite political death. His enemies, the people removed from power after the election, have already caught the scent of corruption and are eagerly looking for some concrete evidence to use as a means of pulling the Stark empire down. Willie Stark recognizes what he is doing: he is protecting the unprincipled and denying principle in order to survive. The fact that he wants to stay in power so as to implement his principles only adds a further dimension to the irony and Stark recognizes as much when he says to Miller, just before he leaves, 'You're leaving me all alone with the sons-of-bitches. Mine and the other fellow's.' The scene epitomizes the entire novel; or at least Willie Stark's part of it. Stark tries to use the powers offered by his given circumstances to realize an idea, but he eventually becomes so involved in the mired complexitites of the power game that the idea is forgotten or, worse still, prostituted. And part of the tragedy lies in the fact that Willie Stark senses what is happening to him even while it *is* happening.

What Robert Penn Warren has done in the case of Willie Stark, then, as far as his relationship to his historical prototype is concerned, is to take authenticated facts and reproduce them so as to emphasize their tragic pattern. Certain particulars, such as the nature of the powers assumed by Huey Long in Louisiana and the number and scope of the reforms implemented by him, may be changed: but the paradox which informed the character and life of 'the Boss' is not. Perhaps this can be clarified a little more by pointing to one specific example of Warren's treatment of his raw material; and, as in other tragedies, an example more striking than most is supplied by the death of the protagonist. Warren ascribes the death of Willie Stark, with a fine sense of poetic justice, to Dr Adam Stanton; and he accounts for it by suggesting that Adam believed he had been given the dictatorship of the Willie Stark Hospital in return for favours received by the Governor from Anne Stanton, Adam's sister. In fact, Huey Long was shot by one Dr Weiss, who resented the attempts made by the state political machine to deprive his father-in-law, Judge Pavy, of office, and who was even more resentful of remarks made by the Governor to the effect that there was black blood in the Pavy family. The differences here between fact and fiction appear to be radical, but they are only apparently so. . . . [Long's] death was precipitated by a characteristic failure to consider the sensibilities of others; and more particlarly by his apparent inability to remember just how sensitive southerners can be about the racial taboo, which prohibits an overt acknowledgement of miscegenation. The death of Willie Stark is occasioned by a similar and equally characteristic failure that involves him, although indirectly, in a violation of the *sexual* taboo. Stark takes Anne Stanton, a woman from an old and distinguished Louisiana family, as his mistress, and in the course of their relationship gives her financial help with her orphanages and appoints Adam to be director of his hospital. What he does he does not do as a simple means of rewarding Anne for her services: he is never as crass as that. But there can be no doubt that his generosity towards her is related to his affection for her, and that this affection in turn encourages him to make overtures to Adam Stanton. The offence against the Stanton pride, the smear of prostitution, is implied in the situation and Adam, with his acute sensitivity, merely makes the offence explicit. Perhaps it is not necessary to spell out every detail, though. The point is that the deaths of Huey Long and Willie Stark *are* comparable, in terms of their connexion both with previous mistakes and with a general insensitivity to the narcissistic pride of the idealist. In specifics the two stories may differ: but the tragic pattern of blindness occasioning destruction is the same in either case.

To talk about *All the King's Men* in terms only of Willie Stark, however, is to talk about one half of the novel. His story is no more or less important than the story of Jack Burden, the narrator, whose situation throughout most of the narrative is quite the reverse of the protagonist's. Burden is, as he himself acknowledges, an 'Idealist' who has adopted the attitude of the Yogi rather than that of the Commissar. He has retreated from the world and from responsibility into that kind of dismissive cynicism which is perhaps the special prerogative of the disillusioned naïf. His characteristic stance, and the reasons for it, are neatly suggested in a passage like the following:

> . . . I'd be lying there in the hole in the middle of my bed where the springs had given down with the weight of wayfaring humanity . . . watching the cigarette smoke flow up and splash against the ceiling . . . like the pale uncertain spirit rising up out of your mouth on the last exhalation, the way the Egyptians figured it, to leave the horizontal tenement of clay in its ill-fitting pants and vest.

What is important about such a passage, I think, is its violent yoking together of heterogeneous ideas, corporeal and spiritual, so as to emphasize their heterogeneity. As Jack Burden sees it, the word can only become flesh by adopting an outfit so ludicrous that it loses all its original character and value; and in these circumstances the best the idealist can do is stand on the side-lines, mocking the world and its squalor. When this in turn becomes intolerable, and the mask of cynicism begins to slip, there is still 'the Great Sleep', that retreat into vacuous non-being which is always available to the man of ideas when the world is too much with him.

Jack Burden falls into 'the Great Sleep' several times during the course of his life, and the first time is perhaps one of the most significant. This occurs after his abortive attempt at being an historian. Many years ago, Jack explains, he tried to write a dissertation about Cass Mastern, an ancestor who spent most of his life in Kentucky. The facts were compiled over a period of several years and all the details carefully sifted. Burden even went some way towards completing the final draft of the dissertation; and then something happened. . . . What seems to have happened, in effect, was that Burden suddenly found that the dispersed facts in the case of Cass Mastern were assuming shape and significance. The growing coherence of his 'items', and the discovery which that coherence was precipitating, were both inviting him to recognize his involvement in history. It was not just that he was being asked to see that he was as implicated in his times and circumstances as Cass Mastern had been in his. This was a part of the offered vision but not all of it. He was also being asked to acknowledge the existence of a *direct* relationship with Cass Mastern, founded on mutual dependence.

That the dependence is mutual is the important point. It is perhaps not difficult to see that, in the context of the interpretation of history which Cass Mastern offers to Jack Burden, the past can be said to shape the present; it is not difficult to see this, and there would probably be few who would disagree with it. What is at once difficult and more interesting, is something that Robert Penn Warren—and eventually Jack Burden—

takes to be a corollary of this: that, in a sense, the present can be said to shape the past. The meaning of an event, in other words, is not principally in the event itself but in its complicated relationship with events before and after it. One moment in time interacts with other moments in time. So a pattern is created which is greater than the sum of its parts and which gives an added dimension to each of those parts. This is what Jack Burden cannot see when he is placing 'odds and ends' of the past side by side and supposing that, as a result, he is learning the truth about historical experience. He is *not* learning the truth; and he is not simply because he does not realize that what is brought to the past, in terms of the present experience, is at least as important as the separate moment of the past itself.

Such an interpretation of history, which proposes the existence of a dialectical relationship between past and present, is relevant to more of *All the King's Men* than just the story of Jack Burden and Cass Mastern, of course. For it has enormous bearing on the entire structure and meaning of the novel as well. In the first place, it gives the reader a clearer idea of the positive tendencies of the narrative, the alternative to the stances of Yogi and Commissar which is formulated in the course of the action. This alternative is one in which, to quote Warren in another context, values can be said to 'grow out of the act of living' and 'even as they grow . . . modify living'. History, from this standpoint, is neither the set of given and unalterable conditions that Willie Stark takes it to be nor the raw material for the idealistic impulse which Jack Burden would have liked it to be at one time. It is, in a sense, both: a product of the continuing interchange between the human consciousness and his circumstances, past and present. To fail to recognize this is to fall victim to what Burden eventually refers to as 'the terrible division of [the] age': to emphasize one term of the dialectic, that is, at the expense of the other. And that the narrator *has* recognized this as a result of the experiences he is now narrating contributes a lot to the extraordinary richness of the book. For, having learnt the truth about historical experience, Jack Burden can discover the meaning of his own story as well as that of Cass Mastern. In *All the King's Men* he is at once describing the sequence of events which led him to know that 'the world is all of one piece' and, by reformulating his past in the light of his present recognitions, offering the reader a practical demonstration of his knowledge.

Jack Burden is only the narrator of the book, though. The real teller of the tale is Robert Penn Warren; and this brings us back to the original issue of the relationship between the real Huey Long and the fictional Willie Stark, and the possible point of that relationship. It is surely right to say that, in recasting the story of the legendary 'Boss' of Louisiana, Warren is merely doing on a large scale what his narrator does on a slightly smaller one. His revision of history repeats the narrative procedure on another level. For what Warren does is to take the given story, the facts in the case of Huey Long, and set it in the kind of dialectical relationship with an idea that creates a new shape and meaning from both. He does not distort the story, at least in terms of its essential pattern he does not do so. What he does instead is to place it in such a context as will demonstrate its direct and effective relationship with our own experience. The present is changed by the past, in the sense that Warren has found in a specific set of historical circumstances a means of analysing his own predicament and, as he sees it, the predicament of his 'age' as well. And what is more to the point perhaps, the past has been changed by the present since it is only now, in the writing of *All the King's Men,* that the meaning and emphases of the story which Warren recounts become clear. The 'odds and ends' of historical memory have been woven into a pattern which make them 'all of one piece' with each other and with the lives of those remembering. Structure in this context becomes a necessary projection of meaning, with the relationship between the writer and the raw material of his tale offering perhaps the most incisive demonstration of those uses of history with which the narrative is concerned. In a way it is a nicely ironic point, which Jack Burden in one of his more sardonic moods might have appreciated, that the reshaping of fact into fiction which so many critics have questioned in *All the King's Men* is really a part of its meaning and formal achievement. (pp. 299-307)

R. Gray, "The American Novelist and American History: A Revaluation of 'All the King's Men'," in Journal of American Studies, Vol. 6, No. 3, December, 1972, pp. 297-307.

SAUL MALOFF

All the King's Men was published in 1946, was welcomed with glad cries by some serious critics, won the Pulitzer Prize in 1947 and no doubt would have made off with the NBA had there been one at the time. Almost immediately it ascended to the sparsely occupied heights of "important" American novels, indeed an instant "classic" eminently suitable as a required text in college courses. Ordinary human error and bad judgment apart, how can this possibly have occurred? Before looking into this question let me call back to mind some of the novel's properties.

There's a statement in the novel by Governor Willie Stark (the Huey Long character) that calls attention to itself as a "key" to theme and intention. Stark has just been informed that Judge Montague Irwin has announced his support of Stark's political opponent; whereupon he commands his factotum, Jack Burden, the novel's narrator and protagonist, to dig up whatever dirt he can find in Irwin's past as a way of blackmailing him to return to the fold. Irwin is an old family friend of Burden's and his boyhood mentor, a distinguished citizen, an old-school gentleman of absolute integrity and public servant of seemingly untarnished honor. Burden balks feebly saying to Stark: "I don't reckon you will find anything on Irwin." "You find it," Stark repeats. "But suppose," Burden says, "there isn't anything to find?" "There is always something." "Maybe not on the Judge." These terse exchanges have prepared the way for Stark's little sermon on Original Sin: "Man is conceived in sin and born in corruption and he passeth from the stink of the didie to the stench of the shroud"—and adds: "There is always something."

So of course Burden looks to the sources of sin—money and sex; pokes about a bit in old newspapers, and learns that even Irwin was once susceptible. He even cuckolded an old friend and fathered an illegitimate child who became Jack Burden, and when he learns that the child is dredging up the buried truth he kills himself. Burden's filiality is further complicated by his relationship with Stark, which is in some figurative, and certainly intended, sense that of son and father. We must, all of us, kill our father, for "the truth always kills the father." It is all very Greek. (p. 28)

There's enough killing to satisfy the most Jacobean taste for gore: apart from the off-stage deaths, principally Irwin's suicide, there are the almost simultaneous killings of Stark at the hands of Dr. Adam Stanton . . . and of Stanton at the hands of Stark's bodyguard. There is also some saving, though a good

deal less of that, since knowledge mostly kills. Thus the plot combines elements of grand guignol and Southern Gothic with those of sentimental romance, all of it closely stage-managed.

A greater sin than the plot is putting the novel in the mouth of a posturing, prolix, self-dramatizing prig whose whining garrulity never allows us a moment's pause in which to observe characters and events even if we were disposed to want to. The stock of Burden's mind, and the scope of his reading, must resemble Warren's own rather too conveniently. A former newspaperman and political reporter and currently Stark's flunkey, Burden was once a doctoral candidate in American history, was in fact writing a biography of an ancestor killed in the Civil War when, overcome by epistemological anguish or ennui or a sense of futility, he decided that mere accumulation of facts doesn't yield up The Truth and dropped out of graduate school into the "real" world. En route from one to the other he managed as well to assemble an impressive classical, theological, philosophical and literary education: all this, combined with a fatal weakness for metaphoric flourish, a deep compulsion to describe the world to its last hue, shape and texture and a wanton taste for cadenced, purple prose, makes of him a thoroughly effective impediment to the progress of the novel.

Burden vaporizes relentlessly about History, Time, Truth, God, Fate, Chance, the Meaning Of It All; nothing can begin to happen but that it releases torrents of overblown, ornamental creative writing, whether the object—or victim—of his meditations be grand or trivial. Everything is worth describing, and at equal length and great pains: the girl he loves glimpsed by moonlight or a house he will enter for a brief, inconsequential encounter. Warren's high verbal and descriptive powers are Burden's, and our, undoing.

The instances of Burden's verbal excess are endless, but let one stand for all, a cascade of words provoked by the discovery that Stark and Burden's girl Anne are lovers:

> For West is where we all plan to go some day. It is where you go when the land gives out and the old-field pines encroach. It is where you go when you get the letter saying: *Flee, all is discovered*. It is where you go when you look down at the blade in your hand and see the blood on it. It is where you go when you are told that you are a bubble on the tide of empire. It is where you go when you hear that that's gold in them-thar hills. It is where you go to grow up with the country. It is where you go to spend your old age. Or it is just where you go. . . . It is just where I went.

Burden talks that way, all the time, and he won't let up for a breath. And he is the character we are asked to believe, whom knowledge saves, the survivor and hero-of-sorts, the central figure who learns and changes from the wisdom he acquires through pain, loss and suffering.

It's as if there were two quite separate novels held captive within the same binding: one, by far the larger, a huge billowing cumulus cloud, pile on pile of poeticizing and metaphysical effluvium seeded with bravura set-pieces of "colorful" writing; and the other, a family melodrama with Greek overtones in a political setting, tricked out with love "interest" and complicated by a multiple triangle resolved by double killing. If the first of the two had been bodily removed, the remainder would have been not only blessedly lighter but considerably better in the way of a modest entertainment: a kind of thriller involving sex, mayhem, political machinations and finagling. In fact, the prevailing tone, language and conception of the melodrama derives from nowhere if not from the Hammett-Chandler vein of the American Detective Novel. The characters are a gallery of clichés straight out of that tradition: Stark, the "Boss," a hamfisted, hard-drinking, piledriving powerhouse of a benevolent dictator; Sadie Burke, the political brains behind his rise to power, the hard-bitten durable mistress but ultimately the softhearted Irish girl from the other side of the tracks to whom he always returns after his amorous adventures; "Tiny" Duffy, a henchman and sycophant (and naturally, given that name, obscenely fat and diamond beringed); Sugar-Boy O'Sheean, so-named because of his addiction to sugar cubes, a stuttering, spit-spewing runt though a supreme artist behind the wheel of a Cadillac and the barrel of a .38. So it goes down the line; the characters are ciphers all. (pp. 28-9)

The sense of politics in this "political" novel—the political and historical imagination—is of a piece with that of tabloid journalism and the tabloid novel, which is to say it contains that grain of truth hardly worth remarking: it's all a swindle, a deal, corrupt, a fix, every man has a price and everyone's on the take; power resides with those who know where the bodies are buried. It comes down to what the man-on-the-street always tells the inquiring reporter: You can't trust nobody. Stark's populism, and the conclusive evidence that good can come from evil, is the great hospital which is to be his monument; the powerbrokers want the contract, and the pudgy little men want a piece of the action. They'll get theirs by any means necessary; Stark is willing to deal in means, but he'll not compromise the end: that is his heroism, his glory, his saving realism. The only truly virtuous figure is a character scarcely glimpsed: Hugh Miller, Stark's former attorney general, scion of an old landed family, a gentleman of the blood, Harvard-educated, courteous, modest, scrupulous, wise without being sententious, a man who resigns his office because he'll not touch muck, and he does so quietly, gallantly, decorously. He's not in any way associated with ideas, issues, programs; he's just decent and honorable, a matter of breeding and instinct. We never see him performing the work of his office—but that, of course, isn't the point; he's a good man, the best around—that's the point. Miller isn't so much as a shadow of a character; he's a point of reference, the glistening white area on a moral spectrum. When the dust is settled at the end, and Burden is counting the cost and the gain and reckoning a future for himself and Anne that will embody the small human triumph they have managed to wrest from the ruins, he tells us that she has given her ancestral house to the Children's Home which was her philanthropic project and that it will become "a kind of sanatorium." Nothing could be nicer, and that takes care of Anne, and their redeemed life. As for himself, well, he suddenly recalls Hugh Miller, who has been gone for half the book. Miller, he remembers, once said when "they were discussing the theory of the moral neutrality of history: 'History is blind, but man is not.'" That's the kind of man Miller is, and the kind we may now hope Burden will become. "It looks," he goes on, "as though Hugh will get back into politics, and when he does I'll be along to hold his coat. I've had some valuable experience in that line." What kind of politics, and to what end, needn't concern us any more than it does Burden. A patrician, for whatever reason, has decided to "get back into politics"—that is the dazzling prospect, the truly happy ending (though tinged with a certain sweet melancholy) which we are asked to rejoice in.

And so: how did this extraordinarily bad novel become a "classic"? I want briefly to suggest, without elaboration, some elements of a complicated social and academic account. Such an account would have to remark the revulsion against the "proletarian literature" of the preceding decade; uncritical readiness to see a masterpiece in every other passing novel, especially after the literary drought of the war years; the special place of the South in American letters; the industrious search in the academy for an American literature and tradition, at a time when the formal study of the "field" was not yet quite respectable; general cultural anxiety, a kind of lingering colonial mentality, at once clamorous and apologetic. Above all the reception of [*All the King's Men*] should be seen as an episode in the history of taste, and of the higher learning. In a period preoccupied with the "art novel" and equivocal about "fiction," it evidently gratified a taste for highly figurative, metaphoric language, symbolic and mythic overtones—what used to be called, in graduate-school cant, "baroque"—the taste of those who don't quite trust the novel as serious literature, who thought of it an inferior species in its native state which must aspire to the condition of poetry; and it was—at the moment when the New Criticism had won ascendancy, had established itself as orthodoxy without rival, in the schools—a "teachable" novel, that is, a novel that could be taught as a poem, if you didn't much fancy novels. . . . It was regarded and touted as a grave, complex, "serious" poem; and so it was taught—as metaphysics, as myth, as theology, as poetry, though it is none of these; it was taught in other words as everything but a novel.

We taught it badly, I think; I remember with acute embarrassment our solemn fatuities about it; and I think now, as I only suspected then, that had we taught it as a bad novel in a bad time for the American novel we would have done much to clear the mind and improve the taste of a generation. (pp. 29-30)

Saul Maloff, "Reconsideration," in The New Republic, *Vol. 168, No. 9, March 3, 1973, pp. 28-30.*

RICHARD LUCKETT

There are some novels which are not masterpieces, and have never come near to changing the world, which nevertheless deserve to be kept in circulation long after their initial appearance. The more praise, then, to Secker and Warburg, who hav reissued Robert Penn Warren's **All the King's Men** with a long introduction and a chapter originally excised from the English edition restored. When the novel first came out in the United States in 1946 it caused, as Penn Warren recounts in his introduction, a considerable stir. This was principally because the central character of the novel, Willie Stark, was closely modelled on Huey 'Kingfish' Long, the governor of Louisiana, whose assassination in 1935 brought to an abrupt end a career that might possibly have culminated in the White House. Long was, depending on your point of view, a piece of folklore, the embodiment of the old American populist tradition, a combination of cracker-barrel philosopher and Al Capone, a dangerous radical, an enlightened social reformer, a would-be dictator, or a plain crook. The fact that Penn Warren had attempted to write about him in a sympathetic manner caused him to be branded a fascist. But the issue at stake was less the case of Penn Warren than the case of Huey Long; English readers were perhaps better placed than Penn Warren's compatriots to see that what the novel was really about was power, and that matters of detail relating to Long's political and domestic affairs were neither here nor there.

But English readers were also at a disadvantage, since the version that they read was incomplete. It was a period when publishers had strong views on what national audiences would or would not take, and just as Waugh's *A Handful of Dust* was vandalised for American publication, so **All the King's Men** suffered in England. It is written in the first person, the narrator being one Jack Burden, a journalist who had failed in almost everything but his profession. . . . [He] becomes an intimate but disinterested observer of Stark's final years, though in the end his lack of involvement proves to be illusory. Through Burden Penn Warren is enabled to explore Stark's career in every detail, and also to establish it in a historical and social context. But the novel is also the story of Burden, as well as of Stark, and it is to Burden that the chapter absent in the first English edition relates.

The missing chapter gives an account of Burden's [incomplete doctoral] thesis, which was based on family papers, principally the journal of his great uncle Cass Mastern. Mastern, after an affair with a married woman, rejected the slave-owning society of his time, though he continued to live in it. Yet when the civil war came he felt it his duty to join the Confederate army, making a private reservation that he would not take life. He served with conspicuous gallantry and increasing involvement, until he fell wounded outside Atlanta and the infection proved fatal. This tale within a tale is developed in a thoroughly convincing way; it would itself have made an excellent novel. It was conceived, Mr Penn Warren tells us in his introduction, as a means of giving psychological dimension to Burden, and moral depth to the story as a whole. For Cass Mastern believes that "there is always a kind of glory, however stained or obscured, in whatever man's hand does well, and General Johnston does well." Burden's situation, by contrast, is that of the intellectual who has rejected involvement but has not rejected the right to criticise. When he does finally become involved it is at Stark's instigation, and to serve Stark's political ends. . . .

Now that Huey Long is a fading memory the force of **All the King's Men** as a drama of ends and means becomes all the more apparent. In the meantime recent events in the United States have pointed up the significance of Burden's situation. Anyone who has followed the Watergate affair must have been impressed by the strings of qualifications trailed by some of the villains in the piece. . . . There is even a real live novelist involved. And not for nothing do many of the publications on the case resemble dissertations, with whole forests of timber sacrificed to the tissue of inventions with which the accused have sought to cover themselves and further confound confusion. If anyone wants to know why this has come about they will find no comfort in the explanations.

They will find no comfort in his conclusions either. Jack Burden provides much of the fascination of the book, but he is also its weakest link, since the presentation of each incident through his eyes put us too much at the mercy of his defective vision. The obvious influence on **All the King's Men** is *For Whom The Bell Tolls,* which bears both on the subject and the style. It would be unjust to regard Jack Burden's manner as merely derivative of Hemingway; it owes a lot to the circumstantial connections—of employment, temperament and education—which link Burden with Hemingway's heroes. Penn Warren has taken the trouble to return to the social base. But he cannot always control the effect, with the result that there are times when Burden sounds like Robert Jordan, and other moments when he sounds like Philip Marlowe. This is not because Penn Warren has also been reading Chandler, but because they are both using some of the same postulates in the creation of their characters. The difficulty is exacerbated by the ending of the novel. The death of Stark is described with great effectiveness, but it leaves Burden still on stage, and with a great many unresolved problems.

I suspect the unsatisfactoriness of the conclusion encouraged reviewers to label the book fascist. Not only did Penn Warren attempt a sympathetic portrayal of a man ideologically repugnant to many liberals; worse, he implied that some problems were irremediable, stemming from fundamental defects in human nature, and that such problems might afflict a democracy no less severely than other political structures. Even this might have proved palatable, had it not been for the shift of emphasis in the ending. It is at this final but vital juncture that the attempt to interweave two narratives breaks down. The convention of the big narrative novel demands a resolution, and here there are two narratives to resolve. Mr Penn Warren, whose major literary distinction is as a poet, has up to this point managed to write a novel that, one or two brilliant flashes of natural description aside, is determinedly not a 'poet's novel.' But in concluding he introduces a lyrical and private mode, and the suggestion is that this signifies in a way that the Stark saga does not. There is, once again, an unpalatable truth in this, but Penn Warren does not establish his terms strongly enough for this to impinge properly. The consequence is that the conclusion seems a sentimental palliative to the tough world that has been described. It is a pity, since even a good piece is damaged if the final chords are false.

Richard Luckett, "Richard Luckett on a Novelist of Fact," in The Spectator, *Vol. 232, No. 7596, January 26, 1974, p. 106.*

Michael Weller

1942-

American dramatist and scriptwriter.

Weller often depicts changing personal relationships among individuals involved in the American counterculture movement of the late 1960s. His plays, which examine such modern social issues as personal commitment, marriage, and divorce, are praised for skillful, witty dialogue, cohesive structure, and sympathetic characterizations. Reviewing Weller's drama *Loose Ends,* Mel Gussow commented: "Mr. Weller is a perceptive, humane playwright who has something important to say about his contemporaries, a generation that is not lost or silent, but shifting."

Weller attracted critical and popular recognition in London with his first major play, *Cancer* (1970; produced in the United States as *Moonchildren*). This drama, which focuses on the relationships between idealistic and rebellious college students living together in the late 1960s, was praised for Weller's unsentimental yet comic treatment of strict social codes in an avowedly free society. In *Fishing* (1975), Weller follows the wanderings of disillusioned counterculture youths during the 1970s. While several reviewers noted thematic similarities between *Fishing* and *Moonchildren*, others maintained that Weller's portrayal of a generation in transition is strikingly accurate. Weller's next major production, *Loose Ends* (1979), derives from his earlier work, *Split* (1977), which consists of the interrelated one-act plays *At Home* and *Abroad*. *Loose Ends* chronicles a couple's relationship from the beginning of their romance in the late 1960s through their marriage and eventual divorce over conflicts regarding careers and children. While some commentators faulted as superficial the play's approach to the problems of modern life, most considered *Loose Ends* an incisive and sophisticated successor to *Moonchildren* and *Fishing*.

In *The Ballad of Soapy Smith* (1984), Weller portrays a confidence man whose attempts to swindle a turn-of-the-century Klondike gold-rush community by posing as a model citizen are undermined when he begins to believe his own heroic myth. While regarded as predictable by several critics, this play prompted comparisons to the work of Bertolt Brecht and garnered approval for the relevance of its social commentary. In his autobiographical play, *Spoils of War* (1988), Weller returns to contemporary themes to depict a youth's futile attempts to reunite his divorced parents during the 1950s. Frank Rich observed: "Mr. Weller has sifted through familiar themes with exceptional objectivity and, without losing his ironic sense of humor, has written the most intense and affecting work of his admirable career."

(See also *CLC,* Vol. 10 and *Contemporary Authors,* Vols. 85-88.)

MEL GUSSOW

Michael Weller's *Moonchildren* . . . became a pivotal play of its period. It caught, as if for a time capsule, young people of

the 1960's escaping from the demands of their lives by "putting on" their friends and spoofing strangers.

In his new play, *Loose Ends* . . . , the author looks at his moonchildren passing into adulthood in the 1970's, moving from restlessness to rootlessness. Faced with a choice of freedoms, they sample everything and find little sustenance. *Loose Ends* is at the same time a wise and funny play, not only a worthy successor to *Moonchildren,* but also one of the more pertinent plays of this season.

It firmly demonstrates that Mr. Weller is a perceptive, humane playwright who has something important to say about his contemporaries, a generation that is not lost or silent, but shifting. . . .

Just as *Moonchildren* was a play of the 60's, *Loose Ends* speaks about the 70's, and manages to do it without being either topical or political. Although the play reaches from 1970 to 1979, through Vietnam and Watergate, neither event is discussed. The closest that the author comes to politics is a mention of the Peace Corps, which starts the play on a note of regret for failed ideals.

In Mr. Weller's approach, there is a reminder of Chekhov. Offstage there are cataclysmic social upheavals, but the playwright is concerned with the behavior of his representative people, their mutually wounding personal relationships. Mr. Weller speaks with his own, indelibly contemporary voice. He knows the jargon and patter of his peers and has the artist's ability to transform them into revealing theatrical dialogue.

The play begins in Bali, with a young couple [Paul and Susan] falling in love. For a brief moment, Bali is paradise enough, but as the two of them return to civilization, undertake a relationship, and begin to go through changes, we see the widening chasm between them. We grow to like this couple so much that we hope for their happiness even as they head toward their inevitable separation.

For most of the evening, the play is a refreshing exercise in loose ends—with deceptive casualness giving us a complete group portrait of people in flux. However, toward the end of the play, searching for a conclusion, the author grasps the wrong strands, suddenly revealing that what divides his couple is not only a lack of trust, but the husband's obsessive desire to have a child. We are not convinced either by the motivation or the resolution. The scene is damaging, but not fatal.

Then the playwright pulls the strands together with a wistful epilogue as the principals look to their past to find their future. In keeping with its title, *Loose Ends* becomes a play of searching rather than of solutions.

Loose Ends derives from Mr. Weller's one-act *Split*. . . . The far more ambitious full-length play uses the same theme—splitting couples—but not the characters or dialogue. *Split* was like a short story. *Loose Ends* is like a novel, resonant with atmosphere, humor, character and conflict.

To a certain extent, the supporting players are even more evocative than the central couple. Mr. Weller introduces us to a young woman who is as impressionable as clay. One second she is a rapt follower of a complacent guru, another she is the contented wife of a city planner. Dealing with such targets, Mr. Weller has a satiric prowess as sharp as that of Mike Nichols and Elaine May. Similarly, he comments on the source of fraternal and "sisterly" competition—in scenes between [Paul] and his showboating brother and between [Susan] and her own friendly rival [Selina.]

> Mel Gussow, "Adult Moonchildren," in The New York Times, *February 14, 1979, p. C17.*

WALTER KERR

[Mr. Weller's *Loose Ends* has just appeared], and, on almost all counts, it's fascinating. But first we must go back a step. . . .

In a definitive play called *Moonchildren,* playwright Weller pinned down the utter hilarity of total disbelief in the good, the true, the prefabricated beautiful. He also let us hear, underneath the inventive mockery, a melancholy strain. It was almost as though we'd caught one of his youngsters alone for a minute, biting at a hangnail with surprising savagery. For hangnails persist, even when you have no hangups.

Implicit in the ending of *Moonchildren* was the notion that somewhere, around the next corner after college, there was an apparently stupid life to be got through. And if you weren't going to lead it as stupidly as the old rules had wanted you to, you would be faced with a possibly intolerable chore. You were going to have to decide every single move you made freshly, independently, and for 24 hours a day. The ready-made life of the Boy Scout oath was dead. You were going to have to live a life of infinite choice.

Which is not so much the subject matter as the specific dimension of Mr. Weller's engrossing new play. *Loose Ends,* which I commend to you here and now while reserving the right to quibble a bit later on, would scarcely provide material for a play if an earlier structured world, with its gift-wrapped guides to conduct, hadn't been reduced to a shambles. What's it about? A boy and a girl [Paul and Susan] fall in love (romantically, on the sands of Bali). In time they marry and are even happy together (making due allowance for quite customary spats). In greater time they are driven apart by career problems (perhaps a shade of something new there, given feminine liberation, but keep in mind that *A Star Is Born* wasn't born yesterday). What's new? What's worth intensive investigation?

All of it, because the earth's turned turtle. Mr. Weller picks up, in that very first scene, the tone of voice in which *Moonchildren* reveled. Yes, the scene *is* romantic, as the quick attraction between boy and girl is genuinely felt. Yet the skeptical eye of a generation that went to school so profitlessly a few years earlier is still sharply, playfully at work. . . . [Paul] is immensely funny (in his author's god-help-us-all way) as he describes a health program he and a friend have efficiently devised, using the whole of their savings for the necessary medication. When the medicines never arrive, he corners a superior, only to be contemptuously informed that the supplies are not going to arrive. Of *course* he can save local lives, he is told. But is he prepared to support the people he saves for the next 10 years? A calculated obsolescence involving death is at work here, and the irony inside it—the preposterousness of being kept from doing too much good—is as cutting as [Paul's] account of it is cool. Neither he nor the friends he visits at home now and again want to "lose their coolness." . . .

[As Paul and Susan] return to the States, she comes to think marriage might prove practical enough. . . . Not too long after, [Paul], rocking in resolute and self-contained rhythm on a garden swing, admits to his vastly successful, relentlessly jovial elder brother that they have, in fact, married. Asked by the now outraged brother why he hasn't so much as mentioned the fact to their mother, [Paul's] buried angers erupt for once. In a fiercely telling tirade, he makes it plain that "marriage" means only what he permits it to mean, not what it means to a mother who bleeds her husband dry in alimony and pours the loot into a meaningless boutique.

Nor will he have any part of his brother's opulent way of life. He wants neither money nor a career, only what he "can see and touch," a woman, a house, a child. . . . He is, really, a closet idealist, but one who must justify to himself each gesture, each commitment he makes, each aspiration he acknowledges. There is heat in the process, because so much energy is spent; but humor is always scurrying to the rescue. . . .

While little rifts are beginning to scar the relationship, the play bubbles along—for the most part—on interim meetings with old chums. [Doug], a husband and father who has cunningly kept his detachment intact, and [Maraya], pregnant with a third child she admits is a "mistake" (while cautioning the one in her arms that she doesn't mean *it*) make a dandy couple to drop in on. . . . [Selina, an assistant to Paul] in his minor-league filmmaking, fixes a knowing eye on the partners as they begin to indulge in rationalizations and bluntly refuses to play "middle man" in their personal lives. Your decision, your decision, echoes through the play's every inch.

Not every inch is necessary. The evening can easily take some pruning. . . .

The author's most serious miscalculation, though, comes with our return to the loving but liberated private lives of the two principals. [Susan] has stumbled into a successful career as a photographer, in New York; [Paul's] work keeps him in Boston, a city he also happens to prefer. What's affection worth? The surrender of a job, of a congenial environment? It's got to be thought through, as honorably as possible and—if possible—without compromise. "Deals" are distasteful. Love can't be love if it limits either party's options. Thus far Mr. Weller has carried us through his precise reflection of what's going on around us with perception, restrained passion, a lighthearted decency—playing fair with both contenders.

Then, in the process of avoiding the commitments and the rather degrading bargaining of a "deal," the youngsters—no longer quite so young—arrive at a sort of trust-to-chance arrangement. [Paul has] been wanting to have a child; she, at 32 and enjoying her work, resists the notion. [Paul] offers to join her in New York, without stipulation; she offers, spontaneously, to do nothing to interfere with the conception of a child. The relationship survives the threat of separate cities, separate professions. . . .

While [Paul] is away, [Susan] discovers she has become pregnant, and, after a most tentative soul-struggle, has an abortion without telling him anything at all. With this, and much to our shock, we find all sympathy for the girl abruptly washed away. For she's cheated by her own standards. An offer freely made has been furtively withdrawn; the very silence is a lie. In a relationship built on fairness, she hasn't played fair, and the self-betrayal hurts. Oddly, it hurts us: we don't like our own rejection of a girl we've liked so much.

I realize that Mr. Weller may *not* have miscalculated his effect. He may well have wished human nature—unchangeable, irredeemably flawed—to intrude upon the most candid, the most considerate, the most fair-minded of newly minted worlds. . . . Perhaps Mr. Weller's own candor has compelled him to look uncertainty straight in the face again, to take us back to where the **Moonchildren** were before they managed to invent their own demanding code.

In any event, and allowing for our surprise at finding ourselves—in a play of this kind—ultimately aligned with one partner rather than another, *Loose Ends* is the richly entertaining, always provocative work of one of our finest new playwrights.

Walter Kerr, "'Loose Ends' Is Fascinating," in The New York Times, *June 17, 1979, p. 11.*

DEAN VALENTINE

[*Loose Ends*] tries to document, as it were, a typical modern relationship. . . . The result has some merit. Playwright Michael Weller has a fine ear for today's jargon, and his shots at the Bloomingdale's generation are well-aimed. Still, there's a shallowness to his approach that ultimately subverts the drama.

Loose Ends is the story of Paul, an idealistic Peace Corps worker, and Susan, who meet on a beach in Bali in 1970. They fall in love, sort of, but are separated by circumstances. For three years they don't see each other, until Paul runs into Susan on a bus. This time they stay together, indeed, get married and move into a small house in Boston. They are exceptionally happy. He has, he tells his back-slapping brother Ben, everything he wants: Susan, a job that pays enough to live on, a peaceful life missing only children. . . .

By the beginning of the second act, the '70s have set in. Paul and Susan have been separated for three months because she wanted to pursue her career in New York, a place he doesn't much care for. She attempts to convince him to start a new life in the Big Apple. Initially reluctant, he finally gives in—after all, she is all he has; he would rather be miserable with her in New York than without her in Boston. The next time we see them, they are nearly drowning in the Me Decade. Paul has become well-heeled, the owner of a film production company who is constantly checking his watch to make sure he doesn't miss his plane to the coast. Whereas he used to dress in jeans and work shirts, he now wears three piece white suits and tinted horned rimmed glasses. Susan is just as chic. . . .

It would appear that they have everything—but in reality, Weller tells us, they have less than before; they no longer communicate. Pregnant, obsessed by her career and afraid of breaking the news to Paul that she doesn't want the baby, Susan gets an abortion. When he learns of it three months later, he goes on a rampage—everything he's done, he informs her, he's done for the child he's expected; the material goods are worthless without that. Shortly thereafter, they decide to divorce.

Paul and Susan meet for the last time in 1979. . . . They sleep together for one night in an old New Hampshire cabin, and then she leaves to meet her boyfriend, a vegetarian. The play closes with him looking at slides, the poor remnant of their nine years together.

Weller intends, of course, to recount the story of the decade through his two lovers. In his *Weltanschauung*, the energy, beauty, youth and idealism of the '60s and early '70s were displaced within 10 years by middle-aged materialism and self-centeredness. This is not exactly news. Nor is it necessarily true: If there is today pressure on the young to get a good job and make mountains of money, there was in those supposedly halcyon yesteryears an equal pressure to conform in matters of dress [and thought]. . . . Yet, even granting the validity of what Weller says, his argument is preferred at the expense of his characters, who suffer or are glad at Weller's whim, so that he can make his point. Moreover, in his heat to get his message across, the author neglects essential information, such as why Paul and Susan get divorced. They may not be as passionate as they once were, nor communicate as well, but from every indication they continue to love each other; some people have built lasting marriages on less. (p. 24)

Dean Valentine, "Those Were the Days," in The New Leader, *Vol. LXII, No. 13, June 18, 1979, pp. 23-4.*

BRENDAN GILL

[In *Loose Ends*, Weller], keeping abreast of the times (and, indeed, of his own life), undertakes to show how the children of the sixties have been faring through this now nearly extinct decade. The story is told in eight scenes, beginning on a beach in Bali in 1970 and ending in a cabin in New Hampshire in 1979. When Paul and Susan meet on the beach, he is newly out of the Peace Corps, as she is newly out of college; falling in love, they proceed to clamber, not without conflicts, rung by rung up the double ladder of personal and professional life. Susan becomes a successful still photographer, Paul a successful TV and movie producer. But are they happy? For that matter, what is happiness? Material prosperity proves the snare that it has been reputed to be ever since Ecclesiastes long ago started giving it a bad name, and matters are made more difficult for Paul and Susan by the fact that he would like them to have a baby and she wouldn't.

The first four scenes, constituting the first act of the play, are fairly static and without surprises, but the seventh scene, late in the second act, is a stunner, more than sufficient to justify everything that precedes and follows it. A desperate verbal battle between Paul and Susan, in the course of which they terrifyingly lacerate themselves and each other, it is so brilliantly written . . . that it holds the audience spellbound. . . . [Mr. Weller, though,] has found little of interest for anyone except Susan and Paul to say—perhaps getting ahead in the world has not been as fierce a struggle against high odds as it used to be in Horatio Alger's day, and therefore no longer commands the strict attention of those of us who are not subscribers to *Forbes*. (pp. 90, 92)

> Brendan Gill, "Début," in The New Yorker, Vol. LV, No. 18, June 18, 1979, pp. 90, 92.

JACK RICHARDSON

Loose Ends, the new play by Michael Weller, is something of a mystery to me. I found it a sodden effort, a long, drawn-out, meandering chronicle of two lives that had little, dramatic or otherwise, to recommend them. Yet the play was almost universally praised by the daily reviewers, many of whom found it to contain sharply observed characters very much of our time, and a theatrical strategy on the part of the playwright that was fresh and honest. My only explanation for this general enthusiasm is that sometimes a play can be so bad that it simply beguiles criticism.

Loose Ends begins with Paul and Susan, a young couple in their twenties, lolling on a beach in Bali. The year is 1970, and Paul, having just finished two years in the Peace Corps, is on his way back to the States to take up a job and begin his life. . . . [Paul] intends to scale down his idealism to suit the proportions of a personal life. He rejects Susan's offer to go vacationing around the globe, and they part—obviously to meet again.

When they do, it is a year later. They are now lovers, both nervously on the edge of a deeper commitment. Susan wants to move in with Paul, but can't seem to get this through to him. Indeed, they both respect each other's "space" so much that they communicate through intermediaries during most of the play. Finally, they begin to share the same roof, and eventually marry. . . . But trouble arrives when Susan begins to take her work seriously. She comes to New York, gets a taste of the good life, and no longer wants to be a part of Paul's idealistic private world in which money and prestige are viewed as corruptions of hearth and home. After a brief separation, Paul compromises, comes to New York, and, sustained by the vague promise that he will soon be a father, goes about becoming successful.

Have they found happiness? Not a bit of it. Susan becomes pregnant, sees a baby as a threat to her freedom, and, without telling Paul, has an abortion. Of course, he finds out and the final clash occurs. "Let's talk," Paul says, an ominous sentence that is used throughout the play as a prelude to diffuse bursts of dialogue about the direction and meaning of their lives. They argue, shout, entreat, and pity themselves for about ten frantic minutes, then mercifully decide to put their problem in the hands of a lawyer. A final post-divorce scene takes place in a cabin in New Hampshire. They make love, but do not make amends. . . .

It may seem that I have been writing a proposal for a sequence in "As the World Turns," but this is essentially all that happens in *Loose Ends*. Two characters of very dim mind and spirit are dragged through nine years of uneventful life by a playwright who seems not to know how to distill, select, or heighten action in order to give those years any focus or form. As for the other characters in the play, they are all stock figures, predictable generalizations that the author uses in conventional ways. . . .

There are those who see in all this some sort of generational parable. Susan and Paul, children of the high-minded 60's, grow up to find life neither so simple nor so sweet as the songs of Woodstock made it seem. But no matter how hard I try, I simply fail to find anything about this couple that transcends their own self-absorptions and petty, personal details. They talk about nothing but themselves; not a hint of politics or anything else is present to give a broader social context to their lives. There is no *Zeitgeist* tucked away in this play, only a few trendy notions sprinkled through it.

Other enthusiasts of Weller, while admitting that *Loose Ends* is written in a flaccid manner, and that its characters are not very compelling types, nevertheless claim that this dreary effect is achieved because the author does not romanticize his subject. He wants to show us inane, boring people, so he courageously writes an inane, boring play about them. This idea, that treatment and subject should somehow share the same nature, is something only a desperate critic falls back on when he feels obliged to override his honest reaction. A book about child-raising need not be infantile; a theory of acoustics need not be noisy; and a play about stupidity need not be—but I leave it to the reader to tie up the loose ends of this argument. (p. 61)

> Jack Richardson, "How Not to Do Shakespeare & How Not to Write a Play," in Commentary, Vol. 68, No. 2, August, 1979, pp. 59-61.

PAUL RUDNICK

When Michael Weller was still in college, he bought a pamphlet entitled *How to Write a Play:* "It was part of a series, you know, *Learn Swedish, Be a Bartender*. I figured the mechanics could be learned." So, instead of building shelves or becoming a world class, bilingual bartender, Weller became one of America's most popular contemporary playwrights: his best-known work, **Moonchildren,** remains a landmark encapsulation of the sixties, and his most recent play, *Loose Ends,* is currently a Broadway smash. . . . He has also found time to become one of the country's top screenwriters. . . .

Weller is an unashamedly "popular" writer; his major plays form an accessible, jazzy trilogy of comment on American culture from the midsixties till today. **Moonchildren** deals with a squadron of college students embroiled in the various free-love-don't-trust-anyone-over-thirty-stop-the-war manifestoes of the sixties; it is a sharp-witted, affectionate account of a confused, hopeful era. It is not in any sense a political tract, or a documentary . . . ; now, almost ten years after the play was first produced, **Moonchildren** reads more like a drawing room comedy, an astringent tale of a supposedly "free," unshackled time with as many rules and absurd social codes as the Victorians. . . .

[*Fishing*] is the second work in the trilogy, following the lives of the **Moonchildren** set as they drift in the wake of the sixties,

unsure of their politics, morality, and choice of lifestyles. . . .
It is a what-do-we-do-now play; the Moonchildren, once buoyed
by the excitement of revolution, have become dangerously
aimless and withdrawn in the Watergate era, relying on drugs
and aging classmates to make the time pass, to hold decisions
at bay. . . .

[*Loose Ends*] is Weller's look at what finally happened in the
seventies: he follows a central couple from their early, romantic
Peace Corps and macramé days at the beginning of the decade
to the selfish, brutal careerism which eventually destroys their
marriage as 1980 approaches. (p. 36)

Each play of Weller's trilogy concludes on a lonely, desolate
note, with characters unable to deal with the times or each
other. What prevents this pessimism from overwhelming Weller's work are the joy and freshness with which the characters
are created: Weller's people may do terrible things to one
another, or become incapable of facing the day without a toke
or cynical wisecrack, but they are always profoundly nice,
struggling human beings, people the audience enjoys spending
time with. There are no villains in Weller's plays; the chronic
goofballs of *Moonchildren,* the moody, frightened Woodstock
veterans of *Fishing,* and the anxiety-ridden climbers of *Loose
Ends* are all fundamentally decent people, all too aware of their
own failings and the absurdity of American social mores. Humor is important to Weller's people, and so is friendship; the
primary constant in the plays of Weller's trilogy is a sense of
young, over-educated, and alienated Americans grouping
themselves into surrogate families, into "our crowd," for emotional support and good times. (pp. 36, 38)

[An] aura of healthiness, of dealing with the every-day, middle-
class process of life, has led some critics to refer to Weller's
work as shallow, a set of glossy soap operas, mistaking tren-
diness for insight. Weller explains that,

> Anyone dealing with recognizable reality gets dis-
> missed as being merely "popular entertainment." It
> scares writers away from writing about their own
> generation—I'm surprised more people aren't writing
> about today. I tend to follow the British example, of
> observing society in descriptive terms, of simply get-
> ting the portrait right—that's what matters.
>
> You see, there are two branches of theater in America
> right now. The sacred, which deals with symbols and
> big images and confusing mumbo-jumbo, real art
> stuff. . . . Then you have the secular bunch, which
> is the popular theater, and can entertain and also take
> joy in presenting descriptions of real peoples' lives,
> of the things an intelligent audience wants to know
> about.
>
> (pp. 38, 40)

Weller didn't always want to be a secular playwright—his early
love was music. After growing up all over the place . . . he
enrolled at Brandeis University, intent on becoming a composer.

> I wanted to write musicals, but I always had trouble
> getting someone to write a good book. So I finally
> got the *How To Write a Play* guide to try and figure
> out how plays worked—I have a real how-to-do-it
> mind. Then, in my senior year, I had a free course,
> so I took playwrighting. . . .

After graduation Weller moved to England, where he lived for
eight years, studying at Manchester University and "writing
about twenty plays—they were done at little places all over,
fringe colleges, adult education centers." His work eventually

got attention through productions at national festivals, and an
early version of *Moonchildren,* entitled *Cancer,* was done at
the Royal Court in London. "It was a very good production,
but it opened during a newspaper strike and, well, a play called
Cancer naturally got a rather odd response." . . .

Weller's years in England had a lasting influence on his work:

> I developed some of the habits of a British play-
> wright, concentrating on social observation, on de-
> veloping genuine character accuracy—that's the ac-
> complishment. I always try to capture distinct speech
> patterns. . . .
>
> (p. 40)

Weller is still trying to

> loosen up my work. *Loose Ends* began as a Well
> Made Play—it all took place in the final months of
> the main characters' crumbling marriage. It was such
> a constrictive form, so I eventually arrived at some-
> thing more oblique, eight scenes spread out over the
> whole history of the relationship, so you can see how
> the thing actually fell apart, rather than simply being
> presented with a list.

After *Moonchildren,* Weller entered a lengthy "promising"
period—, "everyone kept waiting for me to write the Great
Play." He returned from England to work on *More Than You
Deserve,* a rock musical about Vietnam; "I wanted a sort of
Rodgers and Hammerstein replica, with that misty World War
II romanticism contrasted with the horror of Vietnam. The
composer had an entirely different concept, and it was a real
mishmash; it . . . opened and closed in about a day." . . .

[Weller's next play] was *Fishing,* which was not a critical
success either.

> People said it was a nice try, like *Moonchildren* with-
> out the jokes. Now people look back and call it "val-
> iant, terrifying, his best play." I had to learn to ignore
> all the labeling. I'm still not sure about *Fishing*—I
> was very depressed when I wrote it, and I'm still
> amazed at all the things involving fear and death
> which run through the play. I still have no objectivity,
> it's an extremely personal play. . . .

Weller is now considered one of America's major young playwrights, of a fairly establishment ilk, along with Lanford Wilson, David Mamet, and Thomas Babe. Weller's plays are perhaps the most coherent, solid work of this group; where Wilson
or Babe lapse into mushy, indulgent bouts of pseudo-lyricism,
or Mamet simply becomes grindingly obscure, Weller retains
a core of common sense and tight, involving structure that
delights audiences fed up with chaotic experimentation. Weller's plays may occasionally become a trifle pat, in the "Play-
house 90" vein (some critics feel that the abortion episode in
Loose Ends is merely a gimmick to end the play on an ultra-
seventies, hyped-up note) but his work may well survive as,
at the very least, a sophisticated, appealing record of an age.
(p. 41)

Paul Rudnick, "Recording Our Times," in Horizon:
The Magazine of the Arts, *Vol. XXII, No. 12, December, 1979, pp. 36-41.*

MEL GUSSOW

In his plays Michael Weller has tapped the telephone of contemporary speech. He knows how we can be victimized by our
words, how we lead ourselves into apparent contradictions.

His work is marked by its acuteness and sagacity. As a social commentator, he has a sure feeling for the passage of time, for the quickness with which slang can become outdated and people outmoded. His play **Moonchildren** could be placed in a cornerstone of a building as a capsule of the 60's. In his recent **Loose Ends,** and currently in **Split,** a pair of individual but interrelated short plays . . . , Mr. Weller is working his way into the 80's.

Take the title literally. The subject of **Split** is uncoupling; the first play takes place before, the second, after. In the curtain-raiser, **At Home,** we meet a seemingly happy husband and wife [Paul and Carol]. To their friends, they are The Perfect Couple. In private, they are a mass of imperfections. Waiting for dinner guests to arrive, they alternate between argument and agreement, veering from mockery to mutual affection. Without missing a beat, [Carol] says, "I love you I better put on the rice." The changes of subject and temper are as abrupt as in life. The sketch is a lens-sharp summary of a marriage that is pulling itself apart.

In **Abroad,** the second and more substantial play, The Perfect Couple has split. Friends are amazed at the sundering, and the principals are still a bit stunned themselves. A laugh at a crucial point might have saved the marriage—for a while. Instead, each is thrust into the cold of singleness. He and she shiver and then immediately look for other attachments.

[Paul] chooses a longtime family friend, [Jean]. She is a with-it woman with a crazy-quilt way of summing things up. For example, she says about a bucolic New England hideaway, "The place is total nature city." In order to cajole [Jean] into a romance, [Paul] will use any ploy. Learning that she is embarrassed about sharing a bed formerly occupied by [Carol, Paul] leaps into a lie: "I bought a new mattress this morning."

Simultaneously, [Carol], afflicted with her own wanderlust, is casually letting herself be entrapped by a self-consciously spontaneous television director, whose motto in art as in life is "whatever happens is valid." Wearing an Aunt Jemima kerchief on his head, he coolly pursues [Carol] around his studio with his camera glued to his eyeball. He is an artifact of the 60s; for him 1968 was a vintage year. As the overlapping episodes merrily unravel, we see a cross-section of youthful ardor and mores. **Split,** in two parts, is *La Ronde* for today, a flourishing harvest of insights about the quest for continuity in relationships.

> *Mel Gussow, "A Marriage Unstuck," in* The New York Times, *April 7, 1980, p. C12.*

ROWENA GOLDMAN

[At Home] is a sophisticated piece. . . .

A young, middle-class American couple await the arrival of their dinner guests after a flaming row following some trivial behaviour in the kitchen. In the forty minutes before the doorbell buzzes they alternately pull each other apart and reassert their love for each other, but leave us in no doubt that eventually such pressures will destroy their relationship. He is a history teacher, she does a part-time job but they have, perhaps, become a little complacent with their way of life. Insecurities and doubts as to which of them has been unfaithful begin in the kitchen when Carol pokes a carrot with a pencil. This apparently inexplicable act is, she maintains, the direct result of penis envy. Why should he be adored not only by her but also by his pupils, whilst she does a worthless part-time job

and spends all her time worrying about who he is having an affair with? . . . Michael Weller shows the importance of that well-known stalwart of the American constitution—the family nucleus—and suggests that friends merely serve as a useful device against which one can gauge one's own happiness.

> *Rowena Goldman, in a review of "At Home," in* Drama, *London, No. 140, 2nd Quarter, 1981, p. 40.*

CLIVE BARNES

Michael Weller's new play, **The Ballad of Soapy Smith** . . . , is centered around a subtly contorted con artist who tried to take in a town and ended up by taking in himself.

Soapy Smith, the con man, is a rogue of substance and resource, a gang leader and entrepreneur, a fellow of infinite fancy. Weller's play, however, although centered on Smith, clearly has wider ambitions than a character study.

His scene is the thriving town of Skagway, Alaska, in 1897, the year of the Klondike Gold Rush just across the border in Canada. It was a boom town, lawless and rootless, when Soapy and his boys arrived to clean up.

Weller is seeking to give us a kind of episodic Brechtian overview of the American West, complete with songs, vignettes, and a special Brechtian irony regarding government, property, and justice. And, of course, human avarice and self-esteem.

Soapy starts by trying to dupe the town into accepting his gang as law-enforcers rather than the almost equally dubious vigilante band of merchants. . . .

It is true that Soapy runs a bar that is less than salubrious, but he himself seems a model, law-abiding, public-minded citizen. A benefactor to the community. And Soapy seeks that community's good report, especially that of its moral leader, Frank Reid.

Disaster finally overtakes Soapy, as first he falls victim to his own contrivance, believing himself to be, in actuality, a solid man of good will and charity, and then as he becomes crazily jealous for his bubble reputation, ready to kill his best friend for it.

This gold-nugget saga is narrated by a seedy poetaster, who, almost by chance, becomes entangled in Soapy's gang and Soapy's personal poet laureate, commissioned to compose this commemorative ballad.

The form of the play recalls Brecht's *Resistible Rise of Arturo Ui,* but for many reasons—the obvious one being that Soapy is far less fascinating a character than Brecht's archly devilish Adolf Hitler—Weller falls short of his aspiration. This is a true picture of neither a monster nor a society; nor does it tell anything new about the West (how won or how lost) or the Gold Rush, with its bonanza, avarice, hardship, and that eventual disaster when nothing panned out as it should.

In 1960 the population of Skagway (yes, there is such a town) amounted to 659 souls, according to census. That is the Skagway story I wanted to discover. Soapy Smith himself . . . is a tad too conventional, either as villain or victim, to transfix the imagination. . . .

There are many incidental pleasures here—all of them steadfastly remaining incidental.

> *Clive Barnes, "'Soapy' Sags a Bit in Skagway," in* New York Post, *November 13, 1984.*

FRANK RICH

Now that the dislocations of the 1960's have become mass culture clichés, it's only right that Michael Weller, our most sensitive and knowing dramatist of the big-chill generation, has left the territory behind. In *The Ballad of Soapy Smith* . . . , Mr. Weller has journeyed about as far in period and style from his wounding comedies *Moonchildren* and *Loose Ends* as he could conceivably go.

The only previous Weller project that *Soapy Smith* remotely resembles is his screen adaptation of E. L. Doctorow's *Ragtime*. An epic-size parable about the turn-of-the-century Klondike gold rush, the play is a Brechtian meld of fact, fiction and ideology that requires 31 actors. Mr. Weller's fans, of whom I'm one, will be reassured to discover that his intelligence, as well as his obsessive preoccupation with the meaning of the American experience, are apparent in this adventurous effort. What's disturbing is the play's nearly total lack of humor, feeling and theatrical vigor.

The author may not deserve full blame. Though one wonders whether *The Ballad of Soapy Smith* would sing under the best of circumstances, it has been ill-served by its staging. . . .

Soapy Smith was a real-life frontier con man who, as a program note explains, differed from others of the period by dint of his ''ambition'' and his ''urge to be accepted by polite society.'' Mr. Weller's play shows us how this bunco artist arrives in the primitive boomtown of Skagway, Alaska, and, through stealth and mesmerizing charm, rises to the top of both the settlement's criminal and civic establishments. . . .

To Mr. Weller, this flimflam man is as much hero as villain. If Smith uses patriotic demagoguery and charity as fronts for his illegal activities, at least he is openly cynical about the uses of power and ''makes no excuses about who he is.'' ''Capitalism is the best hustle going,'' Smith explains; he knows that ''a good reputation'' can be bought by any American with money. The town's law-abiding merchants may condemn him, but, in the author's view, they are at best hypocrites—gildedage Babbitts who deny their own ruthlessness and greed by spouting self-righteous pieties.

Passionately held as Mr. Weller's convictions are, they are too familiar to sustain us for nearly three hours. At various times, the play's themes and historical context implicitly or explicitly recall such movies as *Citizen Kane*, Robert Altman's *McCabe and Mrs. Miller* and John Ford's *Man Who Shot Liberty Valance*. Soapy Smith also becomes a retread of Jay Gatsby: A self-invented mystery man who can't fully escape his unsavory past, he finally makes the tragic error of believing his own manufactured legend. The play's other major character—a naïve poet who gets swept up in Smith's rise and fall—narrates Mr. Weller's rueful tale much as Nick Carraway does Fitzgerald's.

A few eloquent speeches notwithstanding, the script is top-heavy with exposition and short on emotional underpinnings. Though the plot is intricate, the drama seems diffuse and predictable—not in the least because the supporting characters are too often archetypes or decorative extras. Some of the dialogue, much of it infected by tortuous, Jack Londonesque diction, is well below the playwright's high standards. The romantic scenes smack of *Oklahoma!*, and there are far too many messengers running in and out to describe calamitous offstage events. . . .

If there's indeed any gold buried in Mr. Weller's mountainous play—as one desperately hopes there might be—it's going to take a lot more dynamite than we find here to bring it out.

Frank Rich, ''Michael Weller's 'Ballad of Soapy Smith','' in The New York Times, *November 13, 1984, p. C15.*

JOHN SIMON

Though *The Ballad of Soapy Smith* is far from a total success, Michael Weller deserves praise for a historical play with contemporary relevance, social satire with serious overtones, and daring to accost a large canvas rather than doing yet another miniature. Best of all, this is a play of ideas, even if they remain somewhat underdeveloped and confused; the questioning of society and politics is earnest enough without being stodgy, ironic but not facile.

''Soapy'' Smith was a celebrated con man who came to Skagway, Alaska, in 1897 to profiteer off the Klondike gold rush. As Weller imagines what happened, Soapy, a gentlemanly sort of rascal, starts a protection racket only slightly more corrupt than the town merchants' cartel and vigilante group, and eventually more lucrative. Soapy gives Skagway a church and an infirmary, and is deeply impressed by the town's incorruptible engineer, to the point of wanting to win him over and beginning to emulate him. The lure of respectability, pride in his newfound virtue, and trust in a young poetaster in his service prove to be Soapy's undoing. Yet his ultimate crime is really a moral act, just as his morality was tainted with criminality. . . .

There are serious inconsistencies in the plotting, and ambiguity is sometimes confused with murkiness. Brechtian echoes may be too strong, and the romantic subplot is sketchy and schematic. But the protagonist . . . is a complex and absorbing creation; there are scenes of true dramatic impact; and the language, though uneven, can sear and even soar. (p. 79)

John Simon, ''All for Nothing,'' in New York Magazine, *Vol. 17, No. 47, November 26, 1984, pp. 76-9.*

JEREMY GERARD

Since 1971, when *Moonchildren* had its premiere . . . in London under the title *Cancer*, Michael Weller has written with a discerning eye and a journalist's detachment about a generation that came of age during the Vietnam War and found its identity in *The Big Chill*. Yet as he concludes his second decade as playwright and screenwriter, Mr. Weller has also shown that his keen vision surveys the personal, not the generic, and that what he maps out, after all, is the landscape of his own heart.

Nowhere is that more evident than in his new play, *Spoils of War*. . . . If Mr. Weller were Neil Simon, *Spoils of War* would be his *Broadway Bound*—a revealing portrait of the child who was father to the artist.

The central character, Martin, is a 16-year-old boy who, just before embarking on a year in Switzerland, orchestrates a meeting between his long-estranged parents, in a wrenching attempt to bring them back together. For Mr. Weller, the play represents a major shift away from the scenes of the 1960's and 70's he observed with so clinical an eye in *Moonchildren, Loose Ends, Split* and *Fishing*.

The rule I used in composing the play was that it was going to be an emotional autobiography—which is to say that all the people would be people toward whom I have a very strong emotional response, but the actual portrait of them would not be the real people. . . . I wanted to write a play that is emotionally riotous; it's about that teen period where you just don't know what the hell is going on and there's an inner and an outer world constantly at conflict. And I wanted to capture that in a strong and vivid way, not a cool way. So the rule I set for myself was that I didn't have to be true to the actual individual but I had to be emotionally true to the people that I've put in that position.

(p. 1)

[*Spoils of War*] is a radical departure for me in more ways than just the territory it covers. . . . The tone and the structure of it are very unusual for my work; I think very few people would even know it was by me if they weren't told. It just fell out that way. The play demanded a much more emotional kind of writing than I'm used to, where the people are much more direct with each other. They live without the protection of wit; they don't defend themselves in the way my characters usually do, with a wisecrack right at the moment of great tension. There were times recently in my writing where I was feeling, "Is that really the character's doing, or is that me being defensive, trying to get a laugh instead of really getting down to the heart of it?"

When Martin's parents are finally brought together, it is not in the loving embrace the boy has envisioned. Indeed, Mr. Weller so dreaded writing about their meeting that in an early draft of *Spoils of War* there was none—"in other words," he admitted, "there was no play. " . . .

"The main character had no immense yearning that would take you on a journey throughout the play," Mr. Weller said. "I thought, what is it you yearn for when you're a teenager? Oh, yeah—it was that they would get together again and you'd be a family. That's what that moment is all about when you're in a broken home." . . .

Even when writing for the movies, Mr. Weller found himself exploring the experiences of his generation. In the late 70's, the playwright Peter Shaffer persuaded him to take on a screenwriting assignment. . . . The project was Milos Forman's film of *Hair*. . . . The movie was a moderate success and has grown in popularity and critical estimation over the years—as has *Ragtime*, in which Mr. Weller imposed a nostalgic, linear sweep on E. L. Doctorow's kaleidoscopic romance of America before World War I. In both films one could detect the playwright's search for more visceral contact with the past than the earlier work had revealed. . . .

In the end, he learned something about himself, as well.

I saw certain patterns that I had followed as a writer that I decided that I'm going to be conscious of from now on and not fall into them without a real calculating reason. You grow to a certain point and things begin to feel old to you. It's not a conscious thing; you just feel a need to go in a new way. I don't know if it's just this one play or some direction I'm going to go off in a little bit more. I've determined not to reach any conclusions about it until I'm at peace after it's over.

(p. 16)

Jeremy Gerard, "Michael Weller's Landscape of the Heart," in The New York Times, May 15, 1988, pp. 1, 16.

FRANK RICH

[In Weller's new play, *The Spoils of War*], a 16-year-old boy named Martin will stop at nothing to mend the pieces of his broken household. The time is the Eisenhower 1950's, and Martin, a precocious only child, is all too keenly aware that the era's promised ideal of the model home has eluded him. His much-married mother, Elise, is a free-living radical who parks him in a progressive boarding school. His father, Andrew, hasn't been heard from in ages. Yet Martin clings to the dream that he can somehow bring his parents back together. . . .

Spoils of War does not end with a happy reunion in Brooklyn, of course. Instead, we watch Martin descend into hysterical rage as he realizes "things can't be different" and settles for impotently kicking the shabby Murphy bed his mother occupies with a one-night stand. Like the 1960's-era idealists in *Moonchildren* and *Loose Ends* . . . , the characters of *Spoils of War* cannot reclaim the old days, whether those of a family's sunnier past or the idealistic birth of a political movement.

But the author isn't Martin; he is the playwright Martin became, a mature writer who *can* retrieve the past and sort it out. By waiting until mid-career to write the sort of autobiographical play that is usually the province of younger writers, Mr. Weller has sifted through familiar themes with exceptional objectivity and, without losing his ironic sense of humor, has written the most intense and affecting work of his admirable career.

This isn't to say that *Spoils of War* . . . would not benefit from its own second stage of artistic refinement. As it swings between concerns as diverse as the two songs that emblemize the action ("That Old Feeling" and "Joe Hill"), the script sows a trail of loose ends. Not only does Mr. Weller chart the destinies of Martin's family but, inveterate social critic that he is, he also delves into the national spoils of World War II—the prosperity that sapped Depression-era radicalism, the rise of McCarthyism, the cold war that becomes the play's metaphor for the chill between the two great powers in Martin's childhood. While *Spoils of War* may not brings its private and public issues together any better than Martin does his parents, one imagines that the play will shake out its principal flaws, among them the overselling of themes and the underwriting of the male characters (Martin included), in another draft.

Right now the play's most remarkable achievement is the mother, Elise. . . . Ravishing, promiscuous, hard-drinking and almost flirtatiously adoring of her son, Elise is someone whom "people don't get over." If she can't be contained by a single man, neither can she be judged by conventional morality. To pay her boy's school bills, Elise labors hard in jobs unworthy of her poetic sensibility, cooks up get-rich-quick pipe dreams and neglects to pay her electric bill. She remains an honorable devotee of political causes. But Elise can also be destructive, betraying her convictions and loved ones alike when stirred by a new man. . . .

It is Mr. Weller's generous point . . . that one must love Elise anyway. . . . [Her] infectious hunger for life and ingenuous hope for the future, however delusionary, make us forgive her almost everything. . . .

The playwright is just as balanced in his presentation of the father, but the character . . . remains sketchy. We're much more fascinated by the father's lover, a sexy, no-nonsense young woman named Penny who works at the zoo. . . . [The] self-protective Penny deflects Martin's efforts to cast her as either a putative stepmother or a sexual fantasy figure, forging instead an independent identity that seems to prefigure the new generation of American women in Mr. Weller's 1960's plays. *Spoils of War* also does splendidly by Emma, the "left-over leftie" who is [Elise's] far less glamorous best friend. . . .

Martin never achieves the introspective gravity of Tennessee Williams's Tom Wingfield [in *The Glass Menagerie*]. As he swivels between vibrant mother and absent father in the harrowing final scenes, once more tangled in the anguishing puzzle of his fractured childhood, the boy remains opaque, a tortured figure without a voice.

That Mr. Weller has deepened his own voice is beyond question. What makes *Spoils of War* so powerful is not a child's mistaken hope that he can resolve the unresolvable lives of his parents but that he can survive their battles into adulthood and find his own resolution, through understanding. The denouement within reach of Mr. Weller's play is indeed that of *The Glass Menagerie*, in which Tom can finally extinguish the candles of his childhood and bid the suffering goodbye. Unfinished as it may be, *Spoils of War* leaves one with the cathartic feeling that the peace so many children dream about is almost at hand.

Frank Rich, "'Spoils of War,' in a Family, Life and the World," in The New York Times, *May 18, 1988, p. 15.*

JOHN SIMON

True, a writer should write from experience; but imagination can't be written off, either. When a playwright is as drastically autobiographical as Michael Weller appears to be, one gets worried. Worse, one gets bored. What has happened to invention? Everything in *Spoils of War,* a fifties story about Martin, a precocious high-school kid with a writing talent, smacks of being the author's story. Back from school, Martin uses every trick to bring together his divorced and recriminatory parents—Andrew, an airline official, and Elise, a poet who works in fashion. Martin is as successful at reuniting them as Michael is here at writing a coherent, original play.

That three actors who are no longer in *Spoils of War* . . . are still listed on the prominently displayed posters does not inspire confidence—any more than that the clumsy confrontational *scène à faire*, in which the ex-spouses have at each other, was, we hear, the director's afterthought. I mention this only to objectify my sense of the disjointedness and aimlessness of the material. Both Andrew and Elise were leftists once, and she and her friend Emma still are; Andrew has swung the other way. But both the nostalgic reminiscences about and the acrid fulminations against the old left have a synthetic ring and do not begin to lift the play out of the tiredly bittersweet myself-when-young slough.

Andrew is currently involved with a very young Central Park Zoo-keeper, Penny; Emma picks up a young Texan would-be builder, Lew, who really covets Elise. . . . As usual, Weller writes good lines, as when Elise explains her disconnected electricity: "Nothing exciting ever entered my life through the icebox, so I chose to pay the phone bill." But why she is so poor remains unexplained. "I guess I strike you as kind of basic," says the apologetic Lew, but why two advanced women should promptly fall for him remains undramatized. There is no compelling evocation of Andrew and Penny's relationship, either.

What is even more important, however, is that such an old-hat topic no longer yields to frontal attack. To be sure, Weller uses the by-now also unstartling device of overlapping scenes. . . . Still and all, *Spoils of War* fills us with enough déjà vu for some two dozen horror movies. . . .

Michael Weller is a proven talent, but he urgently needs to forget about his roots, and maybe about his trunk and branches as well.

John Simon, "Bringing Up Mother," in New York Magazine, *Vol. 21, No. 22, May 30, 1988, p. 88.*

Richard (Purdy) Wilbur

1921-

American poet, translator, critic, nonfiction writer, author of children's books, and editor.

Respected for the craftsmanship and elegance of his verse, Wilbur employs formal poetic structures and smoothly flowing language as a response to disorder and chaos in modern life. He composes subtle and urbane phrasings charged with puns, metaphors, and allusions, creating poetry grounded in concrete detail that reflects his desire for mutuality between reality and imagination. Wendy Salinger commented: "Wilbur mistrusts the imagination that would be a world to itself—it is in this sense that he has described his work as a continuing quarrel with the aesthetics of Edgar Allan Poe, who extolled the transcendent escape into the otherworld of the imagination. Wilbur's deep love of earth things denies him such a flight. Yet his eye beholds a world constantly ramifying outward and upward." Some critics contend that Wilbur's strict adherence to conventional forms occasionally results in awkwardness, and several note a lack of development in his style. Nevertheless, Wilbur is widely praised as a poet of consistency and achievement, and he became the second writer, following Robert Penn Warren, to be named Poet Laureate of the United States, an annual position created in 1986 by an act of Congress. The Poet Laureate is responsible for giving several readings and lectures and also serves as poetry consultant to the Library of Congress.

Wilbur established his reputation with his first volume of verse, *The Beautiful Changes and Other Poems* (1947). The title poem of this collection emphasizes the regenerative qualities in nature and the imagination to represent continual striving for harmony and beauty. Several pieces focus on Wilbur's experiences as a soldier in Europe during World War II and reflect his attempts to instill a sense of order to existence after having witnessed destruction and chaos. Other poems describe natural phenomena and include meditations on spiritual and metaphysical topics. The works in *Ceremony and Other Poems* (1950) also examine the relationship between the material world and the imagination, as Wilbur ponders such topics as mutability and death and celebrates pastoral elements. Several commentators compared Wilbur's verse to that of Marianne Moore for his use of natural imagery to extend the implications of his observations.

Many critics believe that Wilbur's next collection, *Things of This World* (1956), reflects the maturation of his talents. Several of Wilbur's best-known poems appear in this book: "Love Calls Us to the Things of This World," in which an ordinary scene is invested with supernatural images, again emphasizes the need for reciprocity between reality and imagination; "Lamarck Elaborated" includes ironic commentary on the possibilities and limits of imagination; and "A Baroque Wall-Fountain in the Villa Sciarra" offers a lyrical description of its topic to evoke a sense of order, beauty, and dignity. In an examination of this volume, Brad Leithauser identified such distinctive traits in Wilbur's verse as "a breadth of language" and "an elevated grandness of both subject and style." He concluded: "In powerful, fair-spoken lines Wilbur confronts absolutely enormous questions, both timeless (the mediation of body and soul, the

past's claims on the present) and temporal." Wilbur received both the National Book Award and the Pulitzer Prize in poetry for *Things of This World*.

Wilbur's succeeding collection, *Advice to a Prophet and Other Poems* (1961), drew a less enthusiastic critical reception than that accorded *Things of This World*. In a review of this volume, Thom Gunn stated: "The reputation of Richard Wilbur has gone into a slight decline since the time when it stood equal to [Robert] Lowell's. The public prefers a wild and changeable poet to one who has pursued a single end consistently and quietly." Other critics, however, continued to commend both the lyrical qualities of Wilbur's verse and his command of various poetic forms. *Walking to Sleep: New Poems and Translations* (1969), which won the Bollingen Prize, contains pastoral lyrics, an elegy, a Miltonic sonnet, tributes, narratives, and a riddle. In *The Mind-Reader* (1976), Wilbur examines characteristic concerns by employing witty language within tight lyrical structures. Wilbur's previously unpublished pieces contained in *New and Collected Poems* (1987) include a tribute to W. H. Auden, a fable, observations on nature and the imagination, and a cantata on which he collaborated with composer William Schuman to honor the centennial of the Statue of Liberty. Another poem, "Lying," examines ways in which human beings embellish reality by imaginatively exaggerating facts. In a discussion of the phrasings in "Lying," Anthony

Hecht stated: "There is nobility in such utterance that is deeply persuasive, and throughout Wilbur's poetry we are accustomed to finding this rare quality, usually joined to wit, good humor, grace, modesty, and a kind of physical zest or athletic dexterity that is, so far as I know, unrivaled."

Wilbur is also widely acclaimed for his translations. Of these he is perhaps best known for his versions of the Molière plays *The Misanthrope* and *Tartuffe,* having shared the Bollingen Prize for translation for the latter drama. His renderings into English of works by eminent French, Russian, and Spanish authors have been included in several of his poetry collections. Wilbur's other literary endeavors include two books for children, *Loudmouse* (1963) and *Opposites* (1973); *Emily Dickinson: Three Views* (1960), which consists of individual essays by Wilbur, Louise Bogan, and Archibald MacLeish; and *Responses: Prose Pieces, 1953-1976.* He has also edited anthologies of the works of Edgar Allan Poe and William Shakespeare.

(See also *CLC,* Vols. 3, 6, 9, 14; *Contemporary Authors,* Vols. 1-4, rev. ed.; *Contemporary Authors New Revision Series,* Vol. 2; *Contemporary Authors Bibliographical Series,* Vol. 2; *Something about the Author,* Vol. 9; and *Dictionary of Literary Biography,* Vol. 5.)

CLIVE JAMES

[*The essay excerpted below originally appeared in* The Review *in 1971*]

In 1962 a brace of small but influential Penguins waddled into prominence: *Contemporary American Poetry,* selected and edited by Donald Hall, and *The New Poetry,* selected and edited by A. Alvarez. Hall picked on two immediately post-war books as marking the culmination of "past poetries" and the beginning of a new poetry: these were Lowell's *Lord Weary's Castle* and Richard Wilbur's *The Beautiful Changes.* For tremendous power under tremendous pressure, Lowell was your only man. For skilful elegance—but not for passion—Wilbur was likewise nonpareil. As Hall went on to point out, it was Wilbur who had the most plausible imitators, and the typical duff poem of the fifties was the *poème bien fait* that was not *bien fait*—the Wilbur poem not written by Wilbur. By 1962, Wilbur, in addition to *The Beautiful Changes,* had published *Ceremony* (1950) and *Things of This World* (1956) and had brought out a large selection in England, *Poems 1943-1956. Advice to a Prophet* (1961) was also out here by 1962. . . . Wilbur's stock was high on both sides of the pond.

Turning to *The New Poetry,* though, we see that the two American poets Alvarez put forward as exemplary were not Lowell and Wilbur but Lowell and Berryman. Hanging by one well-muscled arm from an ice-axe lodged firmly in the north face of the Future, Alvarez wasn't intrested in grace under pressure so much as in the registration of pressure itself. For the New Seriousness, "gentility, decency and all the other social totems" were not in themselves sufficient for the task of responding to the unique contemporary evils: if skill got in the road of urgency, then skill was out. Not much room for Wilbur there.

Getting on for ten years later, Wilbur has in fact faded right out: it's doubtful if he is now thought of, on either side of the

water, as any kind of force at all. Earlier this year [1971] a further volume came out, *Walking to Sleep.* A disproportionate amount of it consists of translations, and although the original poems retain his customary technical perfection they hold no surprises beyond the usual polite sparkle of his aerated language—it's the same old *aqua minerale* and either it or our liver has lost tone. The book was greeted with muted satisfaction by the squarer critics but otherwise it was correctly thought to be a bit tired. (pp. 34-5)

Wilbur's intricately coherent art is suited to the long allaying of an old mental wound, and not to the sudden coping with a new one. The evidence of his work is that he was able to employ the decade or so after the war as a time of tranquillity in which his experience of wartime Europe could be assimilated and in a way *given back:* his images of order, his virtuosities of symmetry, are particularly orderly and symmetrical when he is dealing with Italy and France, the two countries in which he served. . . . Wilbur's comparative silence in the face of the new (and this time American-inspired) disintegration of the world picture is less likely to be a failure of response than a need for time. There is no doubt, incidentally, about what he thinks of it all—in 1967 he wrote a shattering occasional poem against Johnson's philistinism, comparing him with Jefferson, "Who would have wept to see small nations dread the imposition of our cattle-brand." But otherwise in [the 1960s] he has mainly written mechanically in his own manner, giving the impression that an early challenge to his equilibrium had long been met and that a new one has not yet been faced. For the time being, at any rate, his poetry has lost its relevance. What I want to do now is to indicate what that relevance was when his poetry still had it.

The Beautiful Changes set the level for Wilbur's technical bravura and he has never since dropped very far below it: if the recent products look ordinary, it's worth remembering that they are ordinary in a way that Wilbur himself established. If there were no more going on in his early poems than the dextrous flourishes of the dab hand that put them together, they would still be of permanent interest. Suggestions that Wilbur is fundamentally a punster in his diction are misleading. He is fundamentally a precisionist—he will make a word divert to a parallel, or revert to an antecedent etymological stage, not to pun with it but to refurbish it.

> Easy as cove-water rustles its pebbles and shells
> In the slosh, spread, seethe, and the backsliding
> Wallop and tuck of the wave . . .

The restoration of "backsliding" to pristine condition is characteristic of his handling of language, and the enforced transfer of the reader's eye-line back and down to the next starting-point ("backsliding"—pause—"Wallop and tuck") is an elementary example of his mastery of mimesis. These lines are actually from a poem in *Ceremony:* I choose them because they contain instances of his two main technical preoccupations handily demonstrated in the one spot. But each trick was already everywhere employed in *The Beautiful Changes* and working to perfection. This, for example, is from **"Cicadas"**:

> You know those windless summer evenings, swollen to stasis
> by too-substantial melodies, rich as a
> running-down record, ground round
> to full quiet.

Sound thickens when a disc slows down. Wilbur has noticed the too-muchness of the noise and neatly picked the word "rich" as appropriate: the connotations, partly established by the preceding use of "swollen" and "too-substantial," are of a superabundance of nutrition rather than of pelf. As for the kinetic copy-catting, it's so neatly done he makes it look easy: the two-ton spondee "ground round" slows the line to a crawl, and the enforced pause of the enjambement kills the action stone dead. Sheer class. This point-for-point matching of form to action reached one kind of excellence (I say one kind because I think that elsewhere there is another) in **"My Father Paints the Summer"**:

> They talk by the lobby fire but no one hears
> For the thrum of the rain. In the dim and sounding halls,
> Din at the ears,
> Dark at the eyes well in the head, and the ping-pong balls
> Scatter their hollow knocks
> Like crazy clocks.

Just how it goes: ping/pong: skat! (could be a backhand smash); k/k/k/k/k. Less easily noticed, but still contributory, is the preceding Din/Dark, a duller pair of consonants. What we are given is a kind of Doppler effect as the writer leaves the hotel lobby and walks towards the source of the noises. Copy-cat equivalence has here reached one kind of limit (not that Wilbur didn't go on exploiting it in later volumes), but in his superb poem **"Grace"** it reached another kind—immediately more fruitful and eventually more troublesome. In these two stanzas from the poem, the first shows the first kind, the second the second:

> One is tickled, again, by the dining-car waiter's absurd
> Acrobacy—tipfingered tray like a wind-besting bird
> Plumblines his swinging shoes, the sole things sure
> In the shaken train, but this is all done for food,
> Is habitude, if not pure
>
> Hebetude. It is a graph of a theme that flings
> The dancer kneeling on nothing into the wings,
> And Nijinsky hadn't the words to make the laws
> For learning to loiter in air; he merely said,
> "I merely leap and pause."

The first stanza is Wilbur's customary five or so under par for the course, and one surfaces from the dictionary convinced that the transition from stanza to stanza by way of those two near-homophones is neat and just. What "a graph of a theme" is I don't quite grasp, and can only deduce that it is the opposite of whatever motivates a dining-car waiter. But "The dancer kneeling on nothing into the wings" is a genuinely amazing stroke, probably the best early instance in Wilbur of the mighty, or killer-diller, line. Here the mechanical principles of the mimetic effect are not fully open to inspection as they are in the earlier examples: the feeling, the "art-emotion" that Eliot said could be created out of ordinary emotions, is not reducible to technicalities. Unprogrammed instead of programmed, perhaps even irrational instead of rational, the effect has been snatched out of the air by Wilbur during a temporary holiday from his usual punishing round of meticulous fidelity. When he showed he was capable of effects like this, he showed that the bulk of his poetry—his craftsmanship—was slightly stiff by his own best standards. As a rule of thumb, it can be said that the really glaring moments of falsity throughout Wilbur's poetry are brought about when, in pursuit of such an effect, he snatches and misses. An early example is the last couplet of **"The Peace of Cities,"** which like a good many of his poems has the form of a two-part contention. Cities in peacetime are characterized first, and found to be more dreadful, because more inconsequential, than cities in wartime, which are characterized thus:

> . . . there was a louder and deeper

> Peace in those other cities, when silver fear
> Drove the people to fields, and there they heard
>
> The Luftwaffe waft what let the sunshine in
> And blew the bolt from everybody's door.

This clinching couplet sounds transcendentally silly, like some polished and perfumed banality dropped by Oscar Wilde on an off-night. But the reasons for its emptiness go beyond a mere lapse of taste: they follow from what Wilbur is trying to do with his subject-matter. He is trying to absorb the war's evil into a continuous, self-regulating process—a process in which a subdued Manichaean principle is balanced against an aesthetic Grace. The material resists that absorption. The war is a mental hot spot Wilbur tries to cool out, make sense of, reduce to order: trying to do that, he tends to devalue the experience, and his wealth of language becomes merely expensive-looking. All his poems on wartime subjects are flawed in their handling of language—his best gift goes against him. To take another example from *The Beautiful Changes*, **"First Snow in Alsace"** holds a delicate balance for most of its length as the snowfall softens the deadly starkness:

> The ration stacks are milky domes;
> Across the ammunition pile
> The snow has climbed in sparkling combs.
>
> You think: beyond this town a mile
> Or two, this snowfall fills the eyes
> Of soldiers dead a little while.

But he rounds the poem out with an orgy of consolation, providing the exact verbal equivalent of a Norman Rockwell cover painting:

> The night guard coming from his post,
> Ten first-snows back in thought, walks slow
> And warms him with a boyish boast:
>
> He was the first to see the snow.

With the possible exception of **"Mined Country"** (and even that one is rounded out with a tough-tender metaphysical bromide), the poems in *The Beautiful Changes* that treat the war theme directly are failures in total form as well as in local detail. But they cast light on the poems that treat the war indirectly or leave it out altogether—they demonstrate what kind of pressure it is that makes the successful poems such convincing examples of formal order attained with technical assurance but against great spiritual stress. **"Lightness,"** the best poem in the book and one of the finest things Wilbur ever wrote, is a two-part contention—and equation—about a falling bird's-nest and a dying old American lady. (pp. 36-40)

In all the elements I have so far dealt with, Wilbur's first volume set the course for the subsequent ones—except that the overt treatment of war was for the most part dropped, and any concern for current, well-defined political crises was dropped along with it. He subsumed such things in a general concept of disorderly force, operative throughout history: they were the subjects his poem would redeem, rather than deal with. Each poem was to be a model of limpidity and no disturbance would be admitted which could not be deftly counterbalanced in the quest for equipoise. From *Ceremony* onwards, successes and failures accumulated in about equal number; but what *guaranteed* failure was when the disturbing force, the element of awkwardness, was smoothly denatured before being introduced as a component. It sometimes seemed possible that Wilbur was working in a dream-factory. . . . In poems like [**"A Plain Song for Comadre"**] the images of order came too easily: out-of-the-way hamlets were stiff with peasants who knew their place, and every bucket of slops could be depended upon to house an angel's ailerons. But the successes, when they happened, were of high quality. **"A Baroque Wall-Fountain in the Villa Sciarra"** is the stand-out poem in *Things of This World*. Again a two-part contention, it compares an elaborate fountain with a simple one, and without the slightest sense of strain draws a subtle conclusion that doubles back through its own argument. In describing the plain fountains in front of St. Peter's, Wilbur took his copy-catting to dizzy new heights. . . . Virtuose almost beyond belief, this is *perizia* taken to the limit. The way the vocabulary deflates as the water collapses, the way "patter" and "applause," already connected in the common speech, are separated and exploited mimetically—well, it'll do till something cleverer comes along.

Of the killer-diller line there were a few instances, most notably in **"Loves of the Puppets"** from *Advice to a Prophet*. It's symptomatic, although not necessarily sad, that the lovers in Wilbur's finest love poem should be made of papier mâché. The desperation of the last stanza and the plangency of the tremendous final line are prepared for not only by the rest of the poem but by our knowledge of Wilbur's whole attitude: to ensure order in the real world, the disorder of unbridled passion must be transferred to Toyland.

> Then maladroitly they embraced once more,
> And hollow rang to hollow with a sound
> That tuned the brooks more sweetly than before,
> And made the birds explode for miles around.

But not many attempts at the art-thrill were as startling as that one. As Wilbur solidified his position, the general run of his poetry slipped past limpidity and got close to torpor. By the time of *Advice to a Prophet* self-parody was creeping in. (pp. 40-3)

Ten years have gone by since *Advice to a Prophet* and for most of that time the major American poets have been sweetly engaged in doing all the things Wilbur was intent on avoiding. Instead of ordering disorder, they have revealed the disorder in order; instead of cherishing a personal equilibrium, they have explored their own disintegration; where he clammed up or elegantly hinted, they have clamorously confessed. To be doubtful about the course American poetry (and a lot of British poetry along with it) has taken, you do not have to be in entire agreement with Hannah Arendt's warning that those men are making a mistake who identify their own personalities with the battlefield of history. You need only to be suspicious about artists playing an apocalyptic role. Nevertheless it is true that there is something sadly hermetic about Wilbur's recent who. . . . Apart from the powerful but localized hit at [President Johnson] mentioned earlier, the serenity of previous volumes continues untroubled by any hint of altered circumstances. A solitary war poem, **"The Agent,"** consists entirely of formula situations sketched in flat language: the hardware is World War II surplus and the setting is a back-lot assemblage of instant Europe. It reads like a worn-out answer to a new challenge. The opening lines of the long title poem guilelessly reveal the strain of a metaphysical essay being flogged into existence:

> As a queen sits down, knowing that a chair will be there,
> Or a general raises his hand and is given the field-glasses,
> Step off assuredly into the blank of your mind.
> Something will come to you.

Something does—nearly two hundred lines of wheezing exhortation. ("Avoid the pleasant room/Where someone, smiling to herself, has placed / A bowl of yellow freesias.") Wilbur's judicious retreat from raw experience has turned into mere insularity. It's a relief to get to the collection of translations at the back of the book, and the back goes more than a third of the way towards the front.

Yet with all this taken into account, there is still no reason to think that Wilbur will not eventually come up with something. At present he is off balance, a condition he is constitutionally unfitted to exploit. While he was on balance, though, he wrote a good number of poised, civilized and very beautiful poems. They'll be worth remembering when some of the rough, tough, gloves-off stuff we're lately supposed to admire starts looking thin. The beautiful changes—nobody denies that—but it doesn't change that much. I don't think it changes into *Crow*. (pp. 43-4)

Clive James, "When the Gloves Are Off," in his First Reactions: Critical Essays, 1968-1979, *Alfred A. Knopf, 1980, pp. 34-44.*

FRANK McCONNELL

In his most recent collection, *The Mind-Reader* (1976), Richard Wilbur includes a marvelous and summary poem called **"Children of Darkness."** It is about toadstools, and is certainly the best fungoid lyric in English. In it he invokes with his usual, ostentatious elegance both the real, sometimes obscene creepiness of these non-photosynthetic monsters, and also the folklore of their monstrosity—they are children of darkness indeed, both biologically and mythically. But the last stanza is at once a gentle satire at their diabolic pretensions (at our diabolic pretensions in calling any life, however, alien, "diabolic") and a benediction:

> Gargoyles is what they are at worst, and should
> They preen themselves
> On being demons, ghouls, or elves,
> The holy chiaroscuro of the wood
> Still would embrace them. They are good.

It is a mark of Wilbur's special talent that those last three words force us to remember another poetic occasion on which the universe was pronounced "good": in Genesis, when it was also, as many still believe, made. And it is appropriate for Wilbur that the Hebrew word for "good" is *tov*—as in *mazel tov*—meaning not so much (as with Plato's "good") "pure" or "really real" but rather "just," "well-proportioned," "o.k."

This is literary allusion at its best, which is to say its most serviceable: a recreation of the texts of our common humanity that reminds us not only how textual, how artificial humanity really is, but also how necessary for life, how paradoxically natural the artificial-seeming texts really are. Wilbur has been doing this for 30 years, in six volumes of original verse and assorted children's stories, critical prefaces, and brilliant translations from Molière. But I begin with **"Children of Darkness,"** not only because it incarnates all the qualities that make him our most readable serious poet, but also because it incarnates all the reasons why it is fashionable, these days, to confess no more than an amused, minor enthusiasm for Wilbur. He may be, as Robert Phillips has said, "our national poet of sanity." But sanity, let's face it, is not what we demand most urgently of our poets. "Ho-hum," declared Wilbur in the title poem of *Ceremony* (1950). "I am for wit and wakefulness." Wit and wakefulness, though, have gotten a pretty bad press in the two major directions American poetry has taken since 1950. The scarifying, autovivisectionist confessional verse of Lowell and Berryman (and, with a difference, Allen Ginsberg) is witty like the grin of a skull and wakeful like a nightmare you can't shake off: and that is not what Wilbur meant at all. . . .

The more recent, anti-confessional ''school'' of poetry, represented most splendidly in the ascendancy of John Ashbery (and, with a difference, A. R. Ammons) also fails, by exceeding, Wilbur's humble, quotidian, and challenging standard. (p. 37)

We want our poets, in one way or another, in their lives if not in their verse, to be as troubled as possible: we want the singer of songs to write loonie tunes (one of Ashbery's best poems in *Houseboat Days*, 1977, is ''Daffy Duck in Hollywood''). Saul Bellow in *Humboldt's Gift* suggests that we do this so we can console ourselves on our comparative normality. But Wilbur, at some risk to his reputation, refuses to play that game. The titles of some of his poems are indicative: **''Praise in Summer,'' ''The Beautiful Changes,'' ''A World Without Objects is a Sensible Emptiness''** (that one a quotation from Thomas Traherne), and **''Love Calls Us to the Things of This World.''** Like his contemporary Howard Nemerov he believes, and has argued strenuously for a long time now, that the imagination not only invents the world, but makes that world livable; that intelligence and a sense of form are not just spiritual culs-de-sac but channels of meaningful communication; that language, like the bumblebee, shouldn't work but does. Form unites us in love, tradition opens the future as well as the past to a human use.... It is hard (I've tried) to find among the collected Wilbur any poem articulating the easy assurance, the *self-confident* sanity for which he is sometimes faulted. From toadstools to the end of the world, his chosen subjects are unsettling and disorderly, those moments when chaos erupts into the ordinary, and when it is mastered to ''sanity'' again because, frighteningly, it *needs* to be. As he says in **''C Minor''** (*The Mind-Reader*), listening to Beethoven's thunderous affirmations at breakfast is a bad idea because it claims too much, too early, for the regenerative powers of art:

> There is nothing to do with a day except to live it.
> Let us have music again when the light dies
> (Sullenly, or in glory) and we can give it
>   Something to organize.

''When the light dies'' is the dangerous moment of Wilbur's poetry as it is for all the strong poets of our century. And if his assertions strike a comforting and (to use the word at last) civilized balance between the omnivorous, self-consuming self of the confessional poets and the selfless, dizzyingly convex world of their anti-confessional colleagues, that does not mean that the comfort is not, as all real comfort, all real sanity has to be, earned. To say that love calls us to the things of this world is *not* to say that love is easy, or that the things of this world are incapable of terror. Between the austere plane geometry of Lowell's vision and the topological catastrophe theory of Ashbery's, Wilbur's is indeed a calculus of delight. But a calculus is a way of describing limits you never reach, a science of possibilities intimated, not realized. Children in the park are playing **''Statues''** (*Things of This World*, 1956), with the high seriousness only children and strong poets bring to their games; and the game organizes the park into a momentary culture of charity, and of charity's defeat:

> The soldier breaks his iron pace;
> Linked lovers pause to gaze; and every rôle
> Relents,—until the feet begin to stroll
> Or stride again. But settled in disgrace
>
> Upon his bench, one aging bum,
> Brought by his long evasion and distress
> Into an adamantine shapelessness,
> Stares at the image of his kingdom come.

That bum, I think, frazzled, beaten, and ''shapeless'' in his defeat, staring with Wordsworthian longings at child's play innocent enough to believe in redemptive form, comes close to being Wilbur's Muse. Or at least he is the passive version of that archetypal artist, the **''Juggler''** (*Ceremony*) of whom Wilbur says, ''For him we batter our hands / Who has won for once over the world's weight.'' The bum may be too self-involved to notice anything but his own pain, and the juggler too intent on his elegant performance to notice the audience. But Wilbur manages to mediate between both of these extraordinary characters and us, who notice them.

He is a poet who matters a great deal, and who I think will matter more and more, just because of this mediator's vocation. . . . Wilbur is secondary, the heir of the major romantics as well as of Yeats and Stevens. But his is a poetry of balance over the void, of achieved form curing chaos, that we need. He himself says it best in **''A Hole in the Floor''** (*Advice to a Prophet*) as he looks through a hole his carpenter has made in his parlor, revealing the subterranean jumble of pipes and wiring down there. What is he looking for? What is he looking at? The very souls of things?

> Not these, but the buried strangeness
> Which nourishes the known:
> That spring from which the floor-lamp
> Drinks now a wilder bloom,
> Inflaming the damask love-seat
> And the whole dangerous room.

If his poetry has made a progress, it is in the direction implied by that last line: rendering keener the sense of ''danger'' underlying our serenest assurances of civilization, but maintaining heroically our sense of those assurances as ''rooms,'' habitations that, however dangerously, are still habitable. (pp. 38-39)

Frank McConnell, ''Reconsideration: The Poetry of Richard Wilbur,'' in The New Republic, *Vol. 179, No. 5, July 29, 1978, pp. 37-9.*

BRUCE MICHELSON

One grows used to hearing of Wilbur as the ''mannered'' poet, the ''amiable,'' ''clever,'' ''elegant'' poet, the ''bourgeois citizen'' verse-maker, the ''safe'' artist. People condescend to Wilbur because they misunderstand his taste for rich and echoing language, for that word-play which everyone notices in his poetry and many readers suspect. It is not hard to misread or misvalue Wilbur. It is easy to take his word-play for ornament, for poetic bric-a-brac dressing up an imperfect sensibility, a comfortable optimism, a childish showing-off. It is easy to confuse his puns and spreads of meaning with the familiar game of undermining the validity of language. We are well stocked, after all, with poems which ''prove'' that poems can really say nothing, and poets who indulge in what Roland Barthes calls the *jouissance* of ambiguity which tells us again and again what a hopeless thing language actually is. (p. 97)

Wilbur's poetry is neither charming ornament, nor gimmick, nor fashionable confusion. I believe that Wilbur's use of language—especially his famous word-play—has everything to do with his most urgent reasons for being an artist, that it is as daring an experiment in poetry as we have seen in the past three decades. Wilbur's language is not some handsome machine for carrying messages or dressing up safe little observations. It is an attempt to use words as magical, incantatory, creative forces. His famous word-play is in fact the very essence of his imaginative transcendence of the world, as well as his reconciliation *with* the world. If we cannot understand this, the paramount seriousness of Wilbur's word-play, we cannot appreciate what Wilbur is doing.

To see what Wilbur's word-play is meant to be, we must first understand Wilbur's idea of how the imagination makes sense of the world. As some readers have noted, Wilbur's conception is that the mind reaches cosmic awareness only by an imaginative and intellectual tightrope act. His recurring theme is that our best hope for understanding where in the world we are lies in balancing the dreaming with the waking consciousness, in reconciling dim, momentary intimations of something beyond us with full awareness of the now. Wilbur is sometimes sniffed at as "optimistic," which seems to me another condescending, misleading label. . . . For Wilbur, those moments, when imaginative engagement with the world flashes out at us like a discovery *in* the world, give cause for keeping one's faith alive. Wilbur accepts man as a creature who *may* have a place in other realities—but only by understanding who and where he is now—as a creature of flesh and spirit—can one hope to comprehend anything more of one's place in the universe.

Consequently Wilbur is a nature poet, a superb nature poet, writing about a nature which constantly changes and recreates itself, awakening that wonder in which one seems to transcend, for a moment at least, separation from the general scheme of things. This much every close reader of Wilbur's poetry will grant; and I hold that Wilbur's use of language has everything to do with this intention. His words are meant to be regenerative forces, catching not just diversity, but the unity beyond diversity. A few years ago, when Wilbur spoke of his conception of language in a short essay called **"Poetry and the Landscape,"** he wrote of language as "recreating the creation, giving each creature a relation to himself," and bringing the speaker "a kind of symbolic control over what lay around him." Just as the balanced imagination can see in nature both time and timelessness, the individual word can conjure up the same kind of encounter. The right ambiguous word at the right time provides not proliferation of meaning, but *reconvergence* of meaning, all possibilities drawing towards one.

Like most of the major verse since World War II, Wilbur's verse is the performance of a self-consciously fictive imagination—but it is also an act of hopeful conjuring, done with a wish that the order created in the poem might somehow become an order perceived. Wilbur's word-play, therefore, expresses his conception of our ontological condition, his role as a careful, insightful nature poet, and his idea of the recreative power of language itself. I cannot think of three more serious reasons for a poet to play with words. A look at five poems, spanning the thirty years of Wilbur's career, will indicate how this is so; and they will show that Wilbur's language, far from being a vehicle for themes, changes like nature itself from poem to poem and even from moment to moment *in* the poem, enacting again and again the miracle of transcendence. Further, Wilbur's use of language has undergone a subtle evolution, and lately a radical change, as the poet continues to mature and expand.

"The Regatta" (1947) is a young man's poem—Wilbur was in his mid-twenties when he wrote it—which no one has said much about, perhaps because at first look it may seem too young, too word-dizzy, to be taken seriously. It is a good poem to begin with, however, for although it might seem over-rich, Wilbur's word-play already shows itself not to be preciousness, mechanism, or showing-off. It is not hard to see that **"The Regatta"** is about hope amid hopelessness, evasive intuitions,

and the stubborn duality of human consciousness and the persistent knack of that consciousness for dreaming arrangements beyond the chaotic surface of things. We get all this in a short poem about an elderly couple watching a boat race. It is the multiple meanings of Wilbur's key words, and the fact that all these meanings achieve a common resonance, which make the poem succeed, and which make a punning, puzzling description of the regatta both handsome and right. (pp. 98-100)

There is a great deal of word-play [in **"The Regatta"**], and we must be selective in talking about it. But we are off into bewildering multiplicity already in the opening line. What are we to make of "pushed out?" Billowed, like the sails in the verse after? Or is it pushed away—suggesting either that our pleasant afternoon is gone, or that it is now made grander than it seemed? Or perhaps the wind pushes out the sky the way one pushes out an old-fashioned light switch, leaving everyone in the dark. In line three the sunlight "fails," probably because clouds have swept in, blotting the sun and making those deep "shades" in the sixth stanza. The rest of the quatrain gives us no help, only more possibilities, and no indication of how we ought to feel about this view from the pier. The wind "booms" in the sails of the racing boats, suggesting the deep, ambiguous noise of sheets puffing out, suggesting too the booms on the boats themselves swinging about in response to a freshened mind. If this is becoming a dark afternoon, it still is a fine one for racing. But what does "plummet" suggest, in conjunction with "fails?" We have no trouble with the connotations of light "failing," but if we read "plummet" carefully, we run into more ambiguity. The sunlight has dropped quickly, and the boats flying along the water's surface shine on the darkened seascape. "Plummet" does not, in that reading, seem to suggest trouble any more than does "pushed out." Furthermore, plummet means more than drop; it means to drop a plumb line, to take measure, to sound depths—meanings which also seem to work here. In darkness do we see something more clearly, something besides the darkness itself? Is it possible that light and darkness, order and disorder are reconciled here somehow, much as the pun on "pitch"—suggesting perhaps the dark hulls below the bright sails—denies the "brighten" of the fourth line and makes sense with it too? At this point in the poem, we have nothing but several alleys of ambiguity. But a little patience with **"The Regatta"** takes us someplace worth going.

In the second stanza we get a point of view, an elderly Mrs. Vane on the pier, doing the poet's job of bringing imagination to bear on worldly experience. Perhaps her imaginative involvement befits her name—one way or another; perhaps her "galleons on the Spanish main" are a vain fictionalizing of a dark, pitchy, flying disorder; or perhaps Mrs. Vane is a true "vane"—which by the spelling of her name seems a fair bet— a sensibility which in its fictions is responding rightly to obscure wonders in the landscape, to the winds, if you will, of truth. Mrs. Vane's eyes are "delighted," *de*lighted by the failing of the light, or perhaps by age—and yet "delighted" in the normal sense, able as she is to sit among friends and see things truly, darkness or no. But the endorsement of Mrs. Vane is swift, evasive; it slips by us quickly in the reverberating of a word.

To save time, let us turn to the fifth stanza, in which we begin to look over the shoulder of Mrs. Vane's husband, a man apparently nearer his end and the end of his hope, and in which we hear the voice of the poet more clearly. Mr. Vane is offered the binoculars, but apparently he doesn't take them, out of senility, fatigue, or indifference. The imaginative vantage point is everyone's to take and use as he will, should he choose to pursue that "swift, light" thing which escapes human apprehension. The poem makes the meaning of "light" as elusive and yet as dimly sure as the elusive "thing" it modifies. The passing sailboat is "light" because it gleams on shadowy waters, light because it glides swiftly on the surface of waters, light because it is a mild and gay thing upon the face of "bitter" waters, a disordered and somber world over which, for the moment, it seems to win. Every path we take in chasing the sense of the stanza ends up in the same place, somewhere off in a twilit distance. The poem is swept along by ingenious ambiguities—and yet it is not fair to say either that this is overdone, or even that these are the poem's finest moments. The race after meaning ends with "shades" in line twenty-four, the last mention of the boat race; the word which suggests every sense we customarily attach to it. But the next stanza brings us into the key ambiguity of **"The Regatta."**

What is but a trick? The boat race itself, using nature to defy nature? Or is it the trick of sight, the way these passing sails tease both the naked and the binoculared eye? Both of these tricks might be meant here—or something else. Wilbur also speaks here of the method of the poem itself, of the "trick" of the poet's language, the "trick" of making a regatta on a windy afternoon work as a metaphor for the human condition and the grounds of human hope. Wilbur feels "franchised a little" not simply by what boats do, but by what words do. The artist's own imagination does what Mrs. Vane is doing, looks carefully at the world and makes something greater out of it, which in turn gives the artist hope, however cautious hope has to be. But no sooner has Wilbur recognized his own trick of managed ambiguities than the delicate illusion is gone. For a second, creation has been *re*created, a right blending of intelligence and fancy has made separate worlds seem one again; yet once that second is passed, mere artifice leads nowhere. The poet becomes self-conscious, and his imagination turns as "cold" as his body on this chilly day. In the company of the old couple, he takes his leave from the pier and from the poem. The tone now is colder too, almost mechanical; the word-play is over. For all the skill of the artist as a conjurer, moments of real imaginative engagement come quickly when they will, and pass as quickly away.

"The Regatta" ends with the poet doubting his own magic, having worked it. Perhaps, in this early poem, that cleverness Wilbur is often accused of is too obtrusive for us to feel how serious his intentions really are. There is much beauty in **"The Regatta."** It is not a game, but a rich, many-sided observation, and a compassionate look at people and nature. This **"Regatta"** which the imagination makes so much of is a fine boat race, painted for us in a lean, vigorous, loving way. The poem looks closely at nature as a realm of constant change and mystery, and finds cause to celebrate that mystery. It is easy to find a young man's unsure hand in what we already know is a young man's poem; but anyone who does so should be careful not to miss Wilbur's achievement in language here, and not to write it off as decoration.

Since **"The Regatta,"** Wilbur's use of word-play has grown much less obtrusive; but in the years between *The Beautiful Changes* (1947) and *The Mind Reader* (1976), the word-play continues to resound, and its purposes and its place in Wilbur's style grow ever more clear. **"Year's End"** (1949) and **"Love Calls Us to Things of This World"** (1956) are two poems about flesh and spirit, time and eternity, life and death. One of these poems is elegiac, deliberate, liable to the old charge that Wilbur's thoughtfulness spoils his work. The other is one of the most admired lyrics in the past three decades, a poem full of vigor and spontaneity—yet it is even more astonishing, as far as language is concerned, than **"Year's End."** In both poems, words from which meanings spread wide are used to call separated worlds into a fleeting, miraculous union.

Most of the word-play in **"Year's End"** is outright punning. (pp. 101-03)

This is not a poem like **"The Regatta,"** about something always eluding us in the everyday world. It is about time stopped and held fast in a sudden eternity; and therefore the word-play here has a new task to perform. The object now is to transform "ends of time" into events of both destruction *and* conservation, and to suggest in that duality something of the mystery of eternity. Each pun must convey both temporality and eternity, the world of flesh, time, humanity, and everyday confusion, as well as the patient realities beyond time. "Downs" in the first stanza: the word means "fells" as a hunter fells an animal; or "sets down," as an artist sets down a recognition to deliver it from time and forgetfulness. Or, given the snowy evening, "downs" might mean "packs in down," wraps up snugly for safe keeping. Likewise, "settlement" suggests both a human settlement, a makeshift town made out of snow—and a *final* settlement, a conclusion to worldly turmoil. And "graved" in the stanza after: these falling leaves are both "engraved" and sent to the grave; their death is their transcendence into slow-time, their transformation into a kind of art. And "composedly" in the third stanza, "pause," and "fray," and "wrought" in the last, each make reference both to time and timelessness, to flesh or strife or passion on the one hand, and the creative act, the transcendence of time and flesh, on the other. Further, what is true of the puns in **"Year's End"** is true of "soft" and "shapely." The street is soft because it is snow-covered and quiet, because it is vulnerable and mortal, *and* because it suggests a "soft" untroubled world *beyond* the mortal. And "shapely": the astonished people of Pompeii lose in an instant their chance to give life artistic shape and finish, even as they are frozen by the ash and transformed into their own most perfect monuments. There is a wonderful melding here of diction, theme, and subtle observation of the natural world. The poem is a passionate expression of both intelligent anxiety and guarded affirmation, and an achievement of beauty and remarkable unity which leaves cleverness far behind.

Because **"Love Calls Us to Things of This World"** is Wilbur's most discussed poem, it needs only brief treatment here. . . . People who like little else about Wilbur's work admire this poem for its gusto and its easy, spontaneous air—and I wish to look at the word-play in it for precisely this reason. The poem marks an important development in Wilbur's relationship with words, for here he succeeds as never before in making his word-play look easy. We readily notice the obvious puns on "spirited," "awash," "blessed," "warm," "undone," "dark habits"; but much less attention is paid to "astounded," "simple," "truly," "clear," "changed," and other words which subtly suggest that enduring and ever-changing harmony of matter and spirit which the waking man senses in his hypnagogic state, and which the poet celebrates with wakeful imagination. The sleeper's first look at the morning is giddy, solipsistic—and yet "simple" and foolish as he is in his drowsiness, he is worthy of the affectionate treatment he gets, seeking as he does after a "simple," pure reality beyond the maculate, turmoiled world. The angels on the wash line are "truly" there only to someone whose muddle-headedness has got the better of him—or is it that they *are* "truly" there, in some dimension to which the waking mind cannot find its way? The soul is indeed "astounded" in both senses of the word: it is both stupefied *and* struck with wonder; the dance of the laundry-angels in the sight of heaven is "clear" in all ways: simple and pure they are, as well as transparent to the point of non-existence. The poem is full of affectionate word-jokes, all of which are serious, all of which are one with the theme of the duality of human existence, and the balanced, dual consciousness it takes to see our place in the world. (pp. 104-06)

From *Walking to Sleep,* "In a Churchyard," is a sober rewrite of Gray's "Elegy," yet in the churchyard, too, puns and spreads of meaning have their role. Transformed again from **"Year's End,"** Wilbur's re-echoing language gives his meditation that sober air it needs to avoid both banal gloom and cute artifice. His word-play here is one with his perceptions, his mood, and his place. The key to the poem's success is that the word-games are now more difficult and less obtrusive, the flow of one loaded utterance into the next being not rapid and easy as before, but deliberate, hindered, slow. The meeting of worlds, in both the landscape and the language, is again the theme; but here there are no swift, surprising recognitions. The truth of churchyards has to be found through hard imaginative work. The poem has been busy with the churchyard's suggestions of timeless, speechless realities, a "music innocent of time and sound," when the real world intrudes upon the visitor with even stranger mysteries:

> It shadows all our thought, balked imminence
> Of uncommitted sound,
> And still would tower at the sill of sense
> Were not, as now, its honed abeyance crowned
>
> With a mauled boom of summons far more strange
> Than any stroke unheard,
> Which breaks again with unimagined range
> Through all reverberations of the word,
>
> Pooling the mystery of things that are,
> The buzz of prayer said,
> The scent of grass, the earliest-blooming star,
> These unseen gravestones, and the darker dead.

If there is any sense—much less a manifold sense—to be made of "balked imminence / Of uncommitted sound," it does not lie as close to the surface as the word-play we have looked at before. Of course "shadows" suggests both the shadows in the twilit churchyard and the shadowing of the speaker's thoughts. But what about this "balked imminence," "honed abeyance" and "mauled boom?" "Balked" makes sense if it means thwarted; but it also means heaped up or ridged, like the mound of a grave. That would amount to nothing—except that "honed," besides its modern definition (sharpened) has an interesting archaic one. A hone is a stone marker, like a gravestone; and in a Northumbrian dialect it means hesitate, balk. There is a queer subsurface coherence here to enhance the usual meanings of these words. This meditation takes place in a churchyard, and the landscape of the churchyard enters the language of the meditation. Once more we are met with Wilbur's enduring theme, that the only way we can make sense of our timeless condition is to be intensely aware of the here and the now. The "mauled boom" is both the ambiguous summons of the unknown and the hammering ring of a real churchbell, in a tower itself suggested by the image of eternities towering at the "sill of sense." This is one elegy in a churchyard which does *not* leave the churchyard as the meditation deepens, but rather seeks its answers in the churchyard world. In this meditation, Wilbur's language has changed its sound, its pace, its

strategy, but not its essential object: to be the means by which realms of reality are brought together. It shows the power which distinguishes genius from sheer style, the power both to transform itself and remain the same.

A look at *The Mind-Reader,* Wilbur's latest volume of poetry, demonstrates that the transformation is still going on. The title of the book is drawn from the dramatic monologue which concludes it. . . . While **"The Mind-Reader"** introduces us to a clairvoyant—something of a charlatan—whom Wilbur says he met in Rome many years ago, the poem does not seek to catch anything of the language of its Italian persona. Rather, it is a mind-reading of a mind-reader, an attempt to penetrate to the consciousness pure. The theme is familiar: the true visionary, unlike this failed, unhappy one, must adjust his powers of imagination to a world of waking, rational perception, must reach his mystical awareness *without* forgetting the truth to be had from commonplace realities. The "mind-reader" is a gifted visionary, but because he has no use for temporal experience, his quest for the supernal leads him only into solipsism; and the frustration which results has nearly ended his hope.

Word-play in **"The Mind-Reader"** might therefore have two objects: to convey the duality of the mind-reader's characteristic hypnagogic state; and to underscore the pathetic irony of his condition. The mind-reader reads nothing because he reads himself too closely. The word-play we find in the poem is sparing, to be sure, perhaps because Wilbur must modulate his own familiar voice. But when the reverberating words turn up, as they do at crucial phrases, they serve precisely these purposes. They reveal both the mind itself and its fatal mistake.

The opening line of the poem ought to suggest immediately the difference in outlook between the poet and the persona he now assumes. "Some things are truly lost," the speaker assumes as a way of setting out—but that word "truly" should set us wondering, dangerous word that it is, and one of Wilbur's favorite loaded words. Already we are tempted to doubt all this assurance about what is "truly" lost, and not let this metaphysician off without proof. The sun hat, pipe wrench, and overboard novel he talks about show us that he equates true, absolute loss with removal beyond human senses and recollection, with disappearance into an enormous, unfathomable natural world. (pp. 106-09)

Of course we can never have this hat, wrench, or book back again; but still, they are "truly" lost only if we take reality to be the world we can see into, either with our eyes or our dreams. I am not splitting hairs. For thirty years, Wilbur's self-avowed "quarrel" with Edgar Allan Poe has focused on exactly this point: that the mind which responds solipsistically to the waking world and trusts too much to a world of dreams find only madness when its seeks transcendence.

The rest of the poem shows us that the speaker lacks interest—and faith—in perceived reality, and that this is the cause of his misery. Consider the pun on "printless" which closes the opening stanza. The speaker's joke epitomizes his own dilemma. The sea is "printless" to him in three ways. The fallen book leaves no imprint, no track on the surface; the sea to him is printless, inscrutable; it is also "printless" meaning inexpressible, for no language, no quantity of print, will solve its mysteries. The mind-reader has given up on making sense of the world he lives in. His landscape and seascapes, real and imagined, are disorderly, frightening, perfectly obscure. The play on "printless" is matched shortly thereafter with a similar pun on "groundless," as the mystic takes us on a trek through his own subconscious: we move from the water into the woods, but the effect of the pun, stressing as it does the bewilderment and hopelessness of too much imagination and too little insight, is something we have seen before. The mind-reader is Wilbur's foil, the poet as abject visionary, trapped in a world in which his powerful mind can find no peace. (pp. 109-10)

If **"The Mind-Reader"** shows us nothing else, it suggests that Wilbur knows first-hand about the perils of the imagination, for he haunts us with the very condition of mind he warns us against. The word-play in the poem is meant as homage to a powerful consciousness gone wrong. We should note too that the word-play in the poem is used here not as it is used elsewhere, to celebrate the subtlety and the possibilities of life, but rather to illustrate isolation from life. Only one word in the poem suggests a recognition of underlying order; as one might expect, the word turns up as the speaker almost reaches a larger awareness:

> Sometimes I wonder if the blame is mine,
> If through a sullen fault of the mind's ear
> I miss a resonance in all their fretting.
> Is there some huge attention, do you think,
> Which suffers us and is inviolate,
> To which all hearts are open, which remarks
> The sparrow's weighty fall, and overhears
> In the worst rancor a deflected sweetness?
> I should be glad to know it.

Fretting: misery and music at once, a music born of misfortune, a music one might hear faintly if one listens closely to the real world, and not so fondly to voices in his own dreams. In the world itself resounds that reconciliation which the mind-reader should be glad to comprehend, but which his pathetic consciousness will not allow him to achieve. His monologue is a dignified, credible statement of the tragedy of the contemporary imagination, the tragedy which poetry in this century has been about. Here, then, is Wilbur adopting his word-play to fit voices very different from his own, specifically to the voice of that sensibility with which he has passionately quarreled for thirty years. (pp. 110-11)

> Bruce Michelson, "Wilbur's Words," in The Massachusetts Review, *Vol. XXIII, No. 1, Spring, 1982, pp. 97-111.*

BRAD LEITHAUSER

[*The essay excerpted below was originally published in a slightly different form as "America's Master of Formal Verse—Reconsideration: Richard Wilbur" in* The New Republic, *March 24, 1982.*]

More than a third of a century has elapsed since publication of his broadly praised first book of poems, and now, at sixty, with five more volumes of poetry behind him, Richard Wilbur is almost unanimously acknowledged to be one of the few living American masters of formal verse. Such unanimity is unusual in a world as diffuse and fractional as that of contemporary poetry, and it bespeaks perhaps not only a deserved admiration but also a suspicion that the role is not widely coveted. In a world in which free poetic forms loudly prevail and rhymed, metrical verse is commonly perceived as old-fashioned, Wilbur's eminence as a formalist can be conceded generously and without envy. It is a somewhat singular position, then, that Richard Wilbur occupies—a monarch in a realm which in the last few decades has grown increasingly depopulated.

A great many of Wilbur's rough contemporaries who now work chiefly in free forms—among them, W. S. Merwin, Louis Simpson, Donald Hall—began as formalists and carried their formal training into their freer explorations. This is generally not the case with poets twenty or thirty years younger than Wilbur. Free verse and its various half-disciplined siblings have of course been around a great many years, but only now, for better or worse, are we witnessing the ascendancy of the first generation in the history of English-language verse never to have worked seriously in form. Poets have always rightly resented the way critics can, because they have little first-hand experience with the demands of form, condescendingly dismiss as "mere artifice" or "tour de force" what was achieved only by dint of vast emotional as well as mental labor. This unhappy gap now undergoes a poignant widening when poets themselves may have difficulty grasping how much love and skill has gone into the formalist's craft.

One last singular aspect of Wilbur's position, this one clearly unfortunate, is that because his long fidelity to form makes him something of a rarity, his critics commonly scant the contents for the package, or equate a "conservative" use of old forms with a conservative or narrow outlook. Although Wilbur's use of form is indeed what one first remarks in his poetry, he has, in the vernacular of a plain-speaking poetic age, "something to say" as well. Indeed, however one may ultimately evaluate his work, a careful reader must come away from it convinced that its creator is a man of large, lively and mettlesome intellect. (pp. 282-83)

[It] may be tempting to see in Wilbur a desperation that probably is not there, for in fact Wilbur appears to have kept over the years not only his wits but most of his composure. Yet it is significant that the major tension in his work is the contrary, dissociative tug between the ideal and the actual, and the shuttling role the mind must play between the spirit's hunger for visions and the body's physical hungers.

It is a tension to be found in Wilbur's first book, *The Beautiful Changes* (1947), though not predominant there. Indeed one characteristic of that book is that little—save perhaps an affection for rhymed verse—predominates; it is a wise and expansive young man's miscellany, in which one encounters war poems and nature poems, religious meditations and light verse. The language ranges from a plunging colloquial ("God knows I / Would be the last alive to cry / To Whatzisname, 'I love thy wheels!'") to a formal rhetoric weighted by archaic inversions ("laundry white," "they dream and look not out"). The poems openly display a multiplicity of influences: E. E. Cummings in some of the diction ("Any greenness is deeper than anyone knows") and in the penchant for odd and often neologistic compound words ("herehastening," "fine-shelled," "lightcaped," "muchtouched"); Marianne Moore in the many quirky leapings, linked only by "and," between the general and the concrete ("There's classic and there's quaint, / And then there is that devout intransitive eye / Of Pieter de Hooch"); Frost in some of the apothegmatic, seasonal reflections ("And doubtless it is dangerous to love / This somersault of seasons; / But I am weary of / The winter way of loving things for reasons"). Remarkable in *The Beautiful Changes* is the deft way such debts are acknowledged and paid; by means of a transmuting wit and affection, what might have been mere echoes become tributary extensions of beloved voices. Note, for example, how quietly the choice of "somersault" above, with its homonymous "summer" budded within it, enriches the line. Such delights are often so subtle in Wilbur's work that they could be taken for mere happenstance did they not arise so frequently and so neatly. Few of the poems, I think, in *The Beautiful Changes* are among Wilbur's best, but the work is flush with such bountiful promise as to leave little doubt of his future accomplishment.

It was a promise in large part met with publication of *Ceremony* three years later. A cleaner and more robust line had emerged, with no loss of the technical complexity and intricate music Wilbur had already unveiled in *The Beautiful Changes*. This second book offered new fields of competence—dramatic dialogue, narrative, some fine translations from the French, and an epigrammatic concision whereby large observations are delivered in compact boxes. Take for example this couplet, one of two under the title **"Epistemology"**:

> We milk the cow of the world, and as we do
> We whisper in her ear, "You are not true."

In two lines Wilbur has evoked and wryly commented on that schism with which the philosopher must live—at once insisting that all surrounding objects may be illusions, and yet drawing from these illusory bodies his mundane but essential daily livelihood. (Wilbur may also be taking an offhand slap at men's impossible demands on women.) *Ceremony* also abounds in passages which exhibit a capacious gift for conveying action, as in the opening of **"Part of a Letter"**:

> Easy as cove water rustles its pebbles and shells
> In the slosh, spread, seethe, and the backsliding
> Wallop and tuck of the wave. . . .

With his second book, Wilbur had manifested both so much promise and such achievement that even Randall Jarrell, a critic who found much to censure in Wilbur's early work, granted that "he seems the best of the quite young poets writing in this country." Other critics had fewer reservations; Wilbur was praised warmly by Louise Bogan, M. L. Rosenthal and T. S. Eliot—heady applause for a man who had published both volumes before turning thirty.

In one of his later poems, **"Seed Leaves,"** Wilbur examines the philosophical implications of a plant recently erupted from the soil's "crusty rubble." It has not yet taken on any distinguishing characteristics, any "sure and special signature," and hence serves as a kind of universal vegetation—an everyplant, so to speak. As such, it wields a mystery and potentiality it can never sustain once having identified itself:

> This plant would like to grow
> And yet be embryo;
> Increase, and yet escape
> The doom of taking shape. . . .

In the personification of the plant's dilemma we find a ready analogy to Wilbur's own poetic evolution. A variety of voices and tones sounded in his first two books, leaving his future development, like the plant's, unclear; with the appearance of his third, however (*Things of This World*, 1956), a favored tone, a distinctive voiceprint, had emerged. This is hardly to suggest that Wilbur hasn't altered since the mid-fifties, for he has indeed changed and, in some ways, gotten even better. Nonetheless, the poems of *Things of This World* are far closer kin to his most recent work than to his two earlier books.

What traits, then, can we say are characteristic of Wilbur? Most immediately evident is a breadth of language which comprises many sorts of words regarded suspiciously by most of his contemporaries. He is fond of long words, often latinate, that might be considered "overly poetic" ("quotidian," "in-

vincible," "adamantine," "discarnate"); he employs a number of terms whose range of meaning has all but vanished—another kind of corporate "takeover"—behind their commercial connotations ("franchise," "office," "promotion," "revenue"); he plucks from the litter of advertising slogans a number of wayworn enhancers ("lovely," "gorgeous," "beautiful," "superb"). These salvages are not always successful, but the effect of such "tainted" language when fed into a matrix dense with music and wordplay can be aerating: one feels that a language's musty corridors have been purified.

Characteristic, too, is what might be termed an elevated grandness of both subject and style. In powerful, fair-spoken lines Wilbur confronts absolutely enormous questions, both timeless (the mediation of body and soul, the past's claims on the present) and temporal (nuclear weapons, the Bicentennial, the Vietnam War). His approach is usually direct, or as direct as a complex subject matter will permit (as he said in one of his essays, "If you respect the reality of the world, you know that you can approach that reality only by indirect means"), and he does not flinch from words like "death," "love," "blessed," or "ecstasy." . . . Though Wilbur has often spoken of his inability to write poetry on order for specific occasions, he has managed to bring his elevated style to bear on a range of events, both personal and societal. There are elegies for Auden and Dudley Fitts, a couple of Vietnam War protests, a wedding toast for his son, a birthday poem, a **"Speech for the Repeal of the McCarran Act,"** a Christmas hymn. Just as Wilbur's language is broad, so is the scatter of events on which he has focused his talents; his verse, though elevated, is flexible enough to encompass an impressive sweep of life. (And it should be noted that in Wilbur all is not elevation; no one in America writes finer light verse.)

Implicit in much of this elevated verse is a repudiation of Auden's claim that "poetry makes nothing happen." A poem like **"Advice to a Prophet"** is not merely—though this would itself be ambitious—an attempt to portray something of the horrors of nuclear war; in contriving to set it in the form of advice to a doomsayer, Wilbur with unspoken optimism suggests that it is possible—through prophecy, through poetry—to transform the way people perceive the threat of world destruction. About this poem he has said, "It made it possible for me to feel something beside a kind of abstract horror, a puzzlement, at the thought of nuclear war; and it may so serve other people. I hope so." Wilbur advises the prophet to speak not of mankind's destruction, which we can hardly conceive, but of the destruction of the natural world, which through spoliation of the environment we know all too well. Nature, the poem says, has helped give us our humanity—and hence, indirectly, the poem speaks of mankind's destruction after all. (pp. 284-88)

Formal, elevated utterance is of course a hazardous enterprise that easily balloons into bombast, a danger Wilbur evades by a variety of techniques, perhaps most importantly through a punning lightness and a continual use of the colloquial. Lines dip frequently into bare and simple statement (e.g., "And all we mean or wish to mean"); as Wilbur has put it, "I don't like to stay aloft too long." It is characteristic that a spare image like "A toad the power mower caught / Chewed and clipped of a leg" would cohabit in the same poem with "Toward misted and ebullient seas / And cooling shores, toward lost Amphibia's emperies," or that an "open mouth / Banjo-strung with spittle" would room with "An unseen genius of the middle distance, / Giddy with godhead or with nonexistence."

Wilbur's success with elevated verse also derives from something harder to define and isolate, and which might best be termed a sense of proportionality. Stanzas fit together; asides remain subordinate to the thoughts they spring from. (pp. 288-89)

This control may put off certain readers, in search of a headlong spontaneity rarely present in Wilbur. To return to the image of the plant in **"Seed Leaves,"** one must in fairness ask what losses he incurred in "the doom of taking shape." A reader who turns from later Wilbur to his first two books is apt to feel that a wildness has been tempered, an exuberance curbed; his poetry has lost none of its energy (Anthony Hecht, a poet of prodigious energy himself, has written that Wilbur's is "the most kinetic poetry I know"), but the poet who once placed a full stanza in capital letters, coined neologisms with a counterfeiter's abandon, and wildly prised words out of their fixed parts of speech (creating, for example, the verb "Veniced") has grown more circumspect. And with this circumspection has come, perhaps, some loss in the capacity to surprise.

Linked to this loss is Wilbur's tendency at times to be too articulate about what he confesses is ultimately ineffable. For to analyze a mystery, even in a spirit of humility and praise, is sometimes necessarily to diminish it. Wilbur is fond of excursions to the edge of the knowable ("the pitchy whirl / At the mind's end" in **"The Beacon,"** "the furl / Of waters, blind in muck and shell" in **"Conjuration,"** "the buried strangeness / Which nourishes the known" in **"A Hole in the Floor"**). The reader may be left with a feeling that such attempts finally are, though admirably bold, disappointing—that in *terra incognita* obliquity and implication are the poet's only satisfactory map and compass.

On balance, such reservations must be tentatively muttered, while praise should be sung in full voice, for Wilbur in a glum and occluded poetic age has kept his eyes open to acclaim beauty and the dignity of "the thing done right / From the clay porch / To the white altar" (**"A Plain Song for Comadre"**). And his work—though in recent years it comes with regrettable slowness—shows little sign of depletion; some of his more recent poems (his elegy for Auden, **"The Fourth of July"** and the title poem from *The Mind-Reader*) belong beside his best work. (pp. 289-90)

> *Brad Leithauser, "Richard Wilbur at Sixty," in* Richard Wilbur's Creation, *edited by Wendy Salinger, The University of Michigan Press, 1983, pp. 282-91.*

PETER STITT

[Wilbur] stands apart from his poetic age in a number of ways—he is an optimist among pessimists; he has a classic, objective sensibility in a romantic, subjective time; he is a formalist in the midst of a relentless informality. The underlying worldview that predetermines these characteristics is traditional and religious; admitting the existential primacy of material reality, Wilbur yet believes in a spiritual reality as well, and his goal as a poet—and, one feels, as a man—is to bring these two realms together into a unified whole. There are a few poems scattered throughout the corpus in which Wilbur toys with the idea that dreams may be more substantial than reality, but in general he does not seriously question the actuality of the material world as something that may be objectively perceived and understood. It is concretely there, though observers may interpret it differently from one another. In one of his most recent poems, **"Lying,"** Wilbur addresses this very issue in

the course of considering the function of factual untruth, myth and simile, in mankind's attempts to comprehend the world: "In the strict sense," he says, "of course, / We invent nothing, merely bearing witness".... Wilbur had stated essentially the same idea in prose, in his lecture **"The Bottles Become New, Too"**: "poets can't afford to forget that there is a reality of things which survives all orders great and small. Things *are*. The cow is there. No poetry can have any strength unless it continually bashes itself against the reality of things."

Set against absolute physical reality—the created world—for Wilbur is the world of the Creator, the spiritual realm, which he feels exists just as certainly as does the physical. In his poems, Wilbur is always reaching "Beyond the faint sun, / Toward the hid pulse of things," as he says the fire-bush does in another of his most recent poems, **"Alatus."** (pp. 13-14)

That Wilbur is a Christian, a lifelong Episcopalian, is important information for anyone wanting to understand his poetry fully; a sacramental view of things is at the heart of everything he says. *Advice to a Prophet* may well be his least attractive book, dominated as it is by a wasteland kind of thinking. In its moral attitudes, the volume resembles the "Fire Sermon" section of Eliot's poem [*The Waste Land*], so concerned is Wilbur to point up the ethical and spiritual failings of mankind. (p. 14)

The basic Christian idea on which [**"Christmas Hymn"**] concludes is a crucial one in Wilbur's thinking. Through Christ, the Christian God gave physical manifestation to pure spirituality, thus uniting the two contrasting realms. And this is the way Richard Wilbur would have the two appear in his poetry, as in the universe he inhabits—together, in interaction with one another, neither one alone. He no more desires a pure spirituality, divorced from the physical, than he desires a pure materiality, divorced from the spiritual. The satirical poems in *Advice to a Prophet* are specifically directed against those who would deny the presence of anything sacramental within the concrete world: there we find lust without love (**"Loves of the Puppets"**), work without workmanship (**"Junk"**), ownership without possession (**"A Summer Morning"**), action without life (**"The Undead"**), shame without guilt (**"Shame"**), dream without belief (**"In the Smoking Car"**), acquisition without fulfillment (**"Ballade for the Duke of Orleans"**). Indeed, the entire volume seems almost to be constructed to reaffirm Eliot's point in *The Waste Land*—that all of man's frenzied physical activity only acts to hide his lack of spiritual belief.

Similarly, a complete abstractionism, divorced from contact with all physicality, is also of no value to Wilbur.... In several other poems, Wilbur deals with the cast of mind that prefers to deny the real in favor of the abstract. In *The Poems of Richard Wilbur*, two poems on this topic, both from *Ceremony and Other Poems*, face one another across the page. The second of them, **"Epistemology,"** consists of two epigrams that seem to argue against the solid existence of the real world:

> I
> Kick at the rock, Sam Johnson, break your bones:
> But cloudy, cloudy is the stuff of stones;
> II
> We milk the cow of the world, and as we do
> We whisper in her ear, "You are not true."...

"La Rose des Vents," which faces **"Epistemology,"** is one of Wilbur's dialogue poems; an airy-headed "Poet," who longs for the imperishable, the ideal, speaks first, and is conclusively answered by a "Lady":

> Forsake those roses
> Of the mind
> And tend the true,
> The mortal flower.

Wilbur's most important poem in this regard is another from *Ceremony,* the justly famous **"A World Without Objects Is a Sensible Emptiness"**. The title is taken from Meditation 65 in the *Second Century,* where Thomas Traherne speaks of the necessity of love for the fulfillment and completion of life. The passage concludes: "The whole world ministers to you as the theatre of your Love. It sustains you and all objects that you may continue to love them. Without which it were better for you to have no being. Life without objects is sensible emptiness, and that is a greater misery than Death or Nothing." Wilbur's poem begins by positing the existence of abstractionists, metaphorically identified as "tall camels of the spirit," "connoisseurs of thirst," who

> . . . move with a stilted stride
> To the land of sheer horizon, hunting Traherne's
> *Sensible emptiness,* there where the brain's lantern-slide
> Revels in vast returns.

Most of the poem consists of an apostrophe to these devotees of emptiness, and Wilbur makes his point through light imagery. We note that the light source for the "brain's lantern-slide" is self-generated and abstract, unattracted to corporeal reality. Rather, says Wilbur, "auras, lustres, / And all shinings need to be shaped and borne." He concludes by admonishing the abstractionists to "Turn, O turn"

> Back to the trees arrayed
> In bursts of glare, to the halo-dialing run
> Of the Country creeks, and the hills' bracken tiaras made
> Gold in the sunken sun,
>
> Wisely watch for the sight
> Of the supernova burgeoning over the barn,
> Lampshine blurred in the steam of beasts, the spirit's right
> Oasis, light incarnate.

The words chosen to describe light—"auras, lustres," "halo-dialing," "tiaras"—all suggest the connotations of spirituality that Wilbur wishes carried by the light. And of course he much prefers that this spirituality not be abstract and disembodied, but indissolubly linked with quotidian reality. Thus, the halos hover over creeks, the tiaras crown hills, the supernova glows about the barn, and the lampshine (final answer to the "brain's lantern-slide") is projected through the sweat-steam rising from farm animals—all of these are "the spirit's right / Oasis, light incarnate."

Insisting that these two realms, the physical and the spiritual, be seen as coexisting, commingling, interpenetrating, may be said to be Richard Wilbur's central thematic concern. . . . (pp. 15-17)

In line with Christian thought, Wilbur pictures an unsanctified reality essentially as chaos, in which darkness and death are dominant. Wilbur is consistent in the use and significance of his primary images; one facet of the meaning of light (to suggest spirituality) has already been mentioned, and others will be dealt with later. Water imagery is similarly complex; Wilbur's most consistent image for pure chaos—the threatening nothingness that existed before the creation—is the darkened or untamed ocean. In **"For Dudley,"** a beautiful elegy that appears in *Walking to Sleep,* the ocean is clearly associated with the realm of death that always waits close to mankind. The poem defines civilized human life in this way:

> As if we were perceived
> From a black ship—
> A small knot of island folk,
> The Light-Dwellers, pouring

> A life to the dark sea—
> All that we do
> Is touched with ocean, yet we remain
> On the shore of what we know.

The lines emphasize the tenuous, threatened nature of life itself, and identify chaos, darkness, and death with the ocean. (pp. 17-18)

In Richard Wilbur's dualistic view of the universe, chaos is always an implicit possibility in external, material reality. Pure spirituality—the other extreme—is both unavailable and undesirable for mankind. The best that we can know on this earth is a physical paradise, wherein the material is invested with the spiritual so that neither one is entirely dominant. Wilbur's ideal is a union of the two realms, a mingling of them, so that we deal with a spiritualized reality. The tension that exists in a Wilbur poem is between these two poles; what the poet seeks is a point of balance between them, where neither is slighted or lost. From Wilbur's perspective, the easy thing for twentieth-century man is to see base reality, the tendency toward chaos, darkness, and death. The sacramental view was easy for Traherne, Herbert, Crashaw, Vaughan, but for modern man the spiritual is hard to see. Thus an effort of some kind is always required to keep it in view, and we seem always on the verge of losing it. Wilbur is essentially in agreement with Frost's definition of poetry as "a momentary stay against confusion." His own statement of this principle is fuller:

> One does not use poetry for its major purposes, as a means of organizing oneself and the world, until one's world somehow gets out of hand. A general cataclysm is not required; the disorder must be personal and may be wholly so, but poetry, to be vital, does seem to need a periodic acquaintance with the threat of chaos.

An effort is required; the tension in Wilbur's kind of poetry inheres in the attempt to maintain a sense of order, a sense of spiritual underpinnings, against the ever-present possibility of ultimate chaos.

Wilbur's poetry has a dynamic, kinetic quality to it. His concern, crudely stated, is to discover and use whatever channels, corridors, connectors there may be that will link the physical world that enmeshes us to the spiritual world that hovers so elusively within and beyond. Thus his desire [in **"Regarding Places"**] to reach "Beyond the faint sun, / To the hid pulse of things"; thus too his definition of "the imagination, which when in best health neither slights the world of fact nor stops with it, but seeks the invisible through the visible." It is this desire to reach, seek, connect, balance that gives Wilbur's poetry its dynamic quality. (pp. 18-19)

A tension does exist in Wilbur's work between what we may call the describing process, which reproduces and appreciates the sheer physical beauty of the scene before one, and the poeticizing process, which insists upon comparing that scene with something else imagined within the mind. So great is Wilbur's love for the physical universe, "the world's body," that he sometimes wonders if anything more than accurate description is needed. **"Praise in Summer"**, an ars poetica that appears in Wilbur's first book, *The Beautiful Changes,* begins by recounting figures he had invented to express his sense of praise. . . . This metaphorizing, he realizes, takes attention away from the here and now, the summer scene before his eyes, and since that is so beautiful by itself, he wonders why it isn't enough for the poet simply to describe literal truth:

> To a praiseful eye
> Should it not be enough of fresh and strange
> That trees grow green, and moles can course in clay,
> And sparrows sweep the ceiling of our day?

The answer seems present in the question, the language of which embodies at least two metaphors, the "sparrows *sweep* the *ceiling*," and perhaps a third, the moles "course" through the ground. We must also note that the resemblances dwelt upon in this poem are like that between the bird's wings and tree leaves—both elements in all equations are drawn from the world of materiality. It is only when one of the elements is a concept drawn from the mind that the spiritual may truly be said to enter the poem. (p. 24)

A poem that depicts even more strikingly the effect of art, the process of imagination, upon reality, is **"L'Etoile,"** from *The Beautiful Changes*. The poem describes a ballet dancer at the very end of her practice, as the last note of music hangs still in the air. "Toward her dance's flight," the woman "aspires in loudening shine" while the music plays and she dances, but once silence takes over, she is returned to the realm of an untransformed reality, bordering almost on chaos. . . . It is the dance that animates the dancer, the art that elevates her from bare reality. **"A Plain Song for Comadre,"** from *Things of This World*, makes a similar point, but with an important difference. The poems begins with a rhetorical question:

> Though the unseen may vanish, though insight fails
> And doubter and downcast saint
> Join in the same complaint,
> What holy things were ever frightened off
> By a fly's buzz, or itches, or a cough?

The poem carefully locates the "holy," not as an entity separate from the everyday, but as an intimate and inseparable part of it. Bruna Sandoval, the *comadre* ("cleaning woman") of the title, has worked in "the church / Of San Ysidro" for seventeen years "And seen no visions but the thing done right." The poem ends with this image:

> Sometimes the early sun
> Shines as she flings the scrubwater out, with a crash
> Of grimy rainbows, and the stained suds flash
> Like angel-feathers.

It is once again through the agency of simile that the spiritual is inserted into the mundane. We aren't sure whether the *comadre* sees this or not, but clearly the poet, whose simile it is, has seen the "angel-feathers." It is the richness of his imagination, his creative intelligence, that allows him glimpses of the spiritual within the real.

It is no accident that motion is an important attribute of most of the poems so far cited showing the presence of the spiritual within the material. It is true that chaos, in Wilbur's view, does possess motion—the death-threatening, uncontrollable heaves and surges of the sea. The middle realm in his work—the ordinary, everyday reality of nature especially—which stands between utter chaos and a pure spirituality, may or may not possess motion, however. In fact, a careful reading of several poems shows that Wilbur's injection of motion into a scene is his way of imagistically indicating the presence of the spiritual within the material. This is why Wilbur's most important formulation of the idea of motion is through the concept of "grace." Wilbur means to retain both of the most important senses of this world—using it to refer, that is, to a beautiful, harmonious

(graceful) motion and to "the unmerited love and favor of God toward man" (*Webster's New World Dictionary*, 2d ed.). In some of Wilbur's poems, this kind of motion is specifically human—as with the dancer in **"L'Etoile"** and [the title character in] **"Juggler."** . . . More important in this regard are poems dealing with nature or natural images in motion—reality itself somehow on the move. [Anthony] Hecht was also aware of this dimension [see *CLC*, Vol. 9], and went on to show what in Wilbur's poems resembles the techniques of "cinematic film: the observation of things in motion from a viewpoint that can, if it cares to, move with an equal and astonishing grace. But what these poems can do so magnificently . . . is . . . a dissolving of one realm of reality into another."

Which is precisely what happens in one of the simplest of such poems, **"Fern-Beds in Hampshire County,"** from *Walking to Sleep*. Wilbur is here operating basically at that level of imagination that finds a striking resemblance between two physical realms, but that does not invest either of them with an idea or the concept of spirituality. The poem is organized not in stanzas but in four sentences. The first establishes the relative simplicity of the ferns by comparison to the more complex, highly developed trees that grow above them. In the second sentence, Wilbur allows "a trifling stir / Of air" to pass over the ferns, which then alternatively "dip," "switch," and are "still"— "Sporadic as in guarded bays / The rockweed slaps a bit, or sways." The simile is much less casual than it looks, more studied, for in the third sentence Wilbur proceeds to turn the swaying ferns into a sea. . . . It is the motion caused by the wind upon the ferns that allows for the metaphorical transformation of them from plants into sea. We note too that there is an apocalyptic undercurrent to the poem; as the ferns become the sea, they implicitly take on the destructive function served by ocean as chaos. Thus, in the final sentence:

> These airy plants . . .
> Dwell in the swept recurrence of
> An ancient conquest, shaken by first love
> As when they answered to the boomed command
> That the sea's green rise up and take the land.

The reference, of course, is to the biblical flood, a watery apocalypse that is here presented more in seductive than in destructive terms; what results is, not ruination, but marriage between sea and land. (pp. 25-8)

The spiritualizing effect of motion—and, in this case, of light—upon the everyday is made even more explicit in another poem from *Ceremony*, **"Part of a Letter."** The setting is apparently a French bar, with tables placed outdoors in a grove of trees. In his description of the setting, Wilbur is again speaking primarily of flora—the trees in this instance—and again makes a comparison to water:

> Easy as cove-water rustles its pebbles and shells
> In the slosh, spread, seethe, and the backsliding
> Wallop and tuck of the wave, and just that cheerful,
>   Tables and earth were riding
>
> Back and forth in the minting shades of the trees.

Light and shade are set in motion by the wind, which agitates the leaves on the trees, creating the resemblance to the pebbles and shells moving in the clear water of the wave (and we note how essential, though unexpressed, is the presence of sunlight for this ocean scene to have its effect). Eventually one of the "dazzled" drinkers asks, "Comment s'appelle cet arbre-là?" The answer comes from a girl with "gold on her tongue": "Ça c'est l'acacia." The mythological reference is to Arcadia, a simple, naturalized version of paradise, where the material and the spiritual spontaneously coexist.

The literary device that allows Richard Wilbur's poetry to encompass, in its very texture and imagery, these two different realms is metaphor, here used in the broad sense of the word (the sense, that is, that includes both simile and exact metaphor). Metaphor is the "doubling" device, an effect achieved through comparison, analogy, equivalency. It allows the poet to point out a close physical resemblance (wings and leaves), to transform one thing into another (ferns into ocean waves), or to suggest the presence of the unseen within the seen (Arcadia within an ordinary grove of trees, the Nereids within the sea). It is thus through the use of metaphor that Wilbur's poetry technically accomplishes what he has conceived as true of the world in a philosophical sense. It is at this point that form and content come most profoundly together in his work. (pp. 28-9)

Wilbur's most complex, subtle, and perhaps most successful love poem is **"The Beautiful Changes"**; the first stanza begins with a tranformation of a sort we are by now quite familiar with, and moves to something deeper.

> One wading a Fall meadow finds on all sides
> The Queen Anne's Lace lying like lilies
> On water; it glides
> So from the walker, it turns
> Dry grass to a lake, as the slightest shade of you
> Valleys my mind in fabulous blue Lucernes.

In the last line and a half we are carried from resemblances perceived in external reality into the pure realm of the imagination; or, to put it another way, in the first four and one-half lines, imagination is the agency through which the comparison is achieved and expressed, while in the last line and a half, imagination is both the activating agent and the subject. We also see in this stanza how the title of the poem works in two different ways. That is, in the first complex of images, "the beautiful changes" is used in the sense that one beautiful image (Queen Anne's Lace) turns into another (water lilies). At the end of the stanza, it is the beautiful as essentially an abstract entity that causes something else to change—in this case, a perception is called up in the mind of the speaker.

The final stanza extends these notions even further, in language that is enticingly abstract, allowing Wilbur to suggest many things at once and causing the reader to be fruitfully puzzled over the exact significance of the lines:

> Your hands hold roses always in a way that says
> They are not only yours; the beautiful changes
> In such kind ways,
> Wishing ever to sunder
> Things and things' selves for a second finding, to lose
> For a moment all that it touches back to wonder.

The woman is implicitly identified as "the beautiful"; her way of holding the roses changes them in a conceptual way, apparently separating their strictly physical manifestation from their Platonic essence. Thus, the speaker is enabled to see the relationship between those two things—basically, the material and the spiritual—differently. The spiritual is most directly represented in this poem by the underlying feeling of love that brought the poem into being in the first place. When all that is touched is "lost" "back to wonder," a spiritual intensification is taking place: the inherent loveliness of the woman intensifies and is intensified by the inherent loveliness of the

roses. Such a reading is anticipated in the poem's middle stanza, where:

> . . . a mantis, arranged
> On a green leaf, grows
> Into it, makes the leaf leafier, and proves
> Any greenness is deeper than anyone knows.

There is an alliance established in this poem between various essences that inhere within and give life to outward elements of reality: beauty, love, greenness, wonder, imagination. Thus the poem affords a dense revelation of various forms of spirituality either already existent or potentially so just beneath the veil of external, material reality.

The ordering, harmonizing, unifying power of the imagination is itself specifically the subject of an **"An Event,"** from *Things of This World*. The poem begins with another intricate metaphorical description:

> As if a cast of grain leapt back to the hand,
> A landscapeful of small black birds, intent
> On the far south, convene at some command
> At once in the middle of the air, at once are gone
> With headlong and unanimous consent
> From the pale trees and fields they settled on.

The movement in these lines is remarkable. The action of the birds is described twice, and in reverse chronology, according to the effect that these actions have upon the composition and appearance of reality: first we see them gathering in air, then we see their earlier departure from the trees. Adding to this movement is the metaphorical extension of the first line. The tension established is between the orderliness of grouping, of collective activity, and the relative chaos of a scattered individuality. The eye of the poet sees an example of an orderly gathering-together within nature and matches this by creating a similar (though physically impossible) image in the mind. At this point in the poem, imagination and reality are in a harmonious relationship to one another, and the poet goes on to revel, briefly, in his triumphant vision—until reality dispels it. . . . The collective action of the birds was orderly, a self-justifying outward manifestation of the poet's inward, imaginative vision of harmony. But when the birds break apart, their individual action is a challenge to the poet's ideal conception, and he is left behind by reality—somewhat chagrined, but trying nobly to adjust his inner view of things to the outer evidence provided by his senses.

It is in the concluding stanza of the poem that Wilbur specifically considers the division between reality and the poet's inner vision of things; we discover that the incident, and his attempt to capture it in words, has not left him defeated after all. Instead, he admits the tension and is appreciative of the power each realm possesses:

> Delighted with myself and with the birds,
> I set them down and give them leave to be.
> It is by words and the defeat of words,
> Down sudden vistas of the vain attempt,
> That for a flying moment one may see
> By what cross-purposes the world is dreamt.

Wilbur is no polemicist for the spiritual; he does not preorder the evidence so that a sacramental view of things will always emerge triumphant. Rather, he admits the fertile tension that inevitably is going to exist between reality itself and an ideal view of reality. What results is poetry, for Wilbur the most productive activity possible for the active, engaged imagination.

We are now in a position finally to understand Wilbur's definition of the concept "grace" as it applies to his poetry. We began by asserting that grace for Wilbur encompasses both a sense of graceful motion and God's freely given love. His own definition, which appears in the poem **"Grace"** from his earliest book, ***The Beautiful Changes,*** links these concepts directly with the activity of poetry: "flesh made word / Is grace's revenue". It is the reversal that makes this definition tricky— the standard Christian view is that grace is word made flesh. True—but it is the poet's function, in his attempt to read God's mind, as it were, his attempt to match God's creative intelligence with his own pale version of the same thing, to change that manifest grace back into words. The principle of the beautiful—which in this context is the perceiving, the recording, the altering, the ordering creative imagination of the poet—we may say, changes the raw materials of reality into a version of the ideal, while ever admitting the uncertainty, even the impossibility, of the task. (pp. 30-3)

Peter Stitt, "The Sacramental Vision of Richard Wilbur," in his The World's Hieroglyphic Beauty: Five American Poets, *The University of Georgia Press, 1985, pp. 9-38.*

PAUL GRAY

According to Romantic superstition, poets either flame out young or gutter into unheralded old age. A related notion holds that popularity is intrinsically vulgar and hence earned, always, by inferior poems. The facts largely argue against this mythology, and the accomplishments of Richard Wilbur, 67, make it look silly. For more than 40 years, Wilbur has written poetry that garnered both critical acclaim and public recognition....

This lustrous career is both summed up and continued in *New and Collected Poems,* which gathers together all of Wilbur's six previous volumes and introduces 27 new works. Included among these is **"On Freedom's Ground,"** a cantata written in collaboration with Composer William Schuman that was performed in New York City in 1986 to mark the Statue of Liberty's 100th birthday. That a serious poet would contribute his skill to a national celebration, throwing well-chosen words into the melee of fireworks, bumper stickers and beer, may seem surprising. Yet Wilbur's poetry has never drawn a sharp distinction between public and private occasions. The job of the poet, his work implies, is to be a messenger between outer and inner worlds, to specify and make memorable what everyone already knows or to give narrow personal experience the breadth of shared impressions. This dedication to communal speech is visible throughout *New and Collected Poems,* making the book a singular testament to civility.

Wilbur's **"Leaving,"** for example, moves adroitly from the specific to the universal. A couple depart from a garden party at dusk and stumble slowly into a perception of the pageant of humanity:

> We saw now, loitering there
> Knee-deep in night,
> How even the wheeling children
> Moved in a rite
>
> Or masque, or long charade
> Where we, like these,
> Had blundered into grand
> Identities.

Filling our selves as sculpture
Fills the stone.
We had not played so surely,
Had we known.

At the other extreme, **"On Freedom's Ground"** takes a look at New York harbor as it might have been before it became a beachhead of the New World. The vision is harsh, deterministic, featuring a wind "which blew / Not as it chose, but as it had to do." The invasion of humanity is hardly the despoliation of paradise: "Where was the thought of freedom then? / It came ashore within the minds of men."

This view of nature sounds anthropocentric and hence, by most contemporary creeds, hopelessly old-fashioned. But Wilbur's poems always allow the animal and vegetable kingdoms their tumultuous integrity. Their energy is a cause for celebration, and so, equally, is the power of the human mind to absorb, assimilate and assort all these phenomena. "Odd that a thing is most itself when likened," writes Wilbur, extolling the ability of language, metaphors, similes to capture the spectacle of reality. Even then, abstractions can be unsettled by the tug of the here and now. A bluefish swims beneath the sea:

> He is a type of coolest intellect,
> Or is so to the mind's blue eye until
> He strikes and runs unseen beneath the rip,
> Yanking imagination back and down
> Past recognition to the unlit deep

Yet words prove equal to this primordial plunge. Wilbur's poetry offers, before anything else, the pleasures of craft. (p. 84)

Paul Gray, "A Testament to Civility," in Time, New York, *Vol. 131, No. 19, May 9, 1988, pp. 84-5.*

ANTHONY HECHT

"The work of art is the object seen *sub specie aeternitatis,*" observed Wittgenstein. And since today there are critics who maintain that art and criticism are indistinguishable from one another, it ought to follow that the critical work itself is seen from the same august perspective. Yet our experience of the history of criticism and the morphology of aesthetic theory fails conspicuously to support this view. Nothing is more familiar to us than the changes in the mode of taste that time itself seems to bring round in its course. Bach endured an eclipse of 200 years.... In the comparatively brief course of my lifetime, John Donne's reputation was virtually disinterred, and the Romantics are now enjoying a revival. And I suppose I should add that it must take a very curious and cultivated taste to enjoy reading criticism of Wordsworth as much as reading Wordsworth himself, though I have known such creatures. (p. 23)

These ruminations are brought on by the publication of Richard Wilbur's *New and Collected Poems,* and by a wistful desire to arrive at a large and serene view of his accomplishment, the crowning of a long and distinguished career.... I am already on record as a somewhat defensive admirer of his, having reviewed his last book of poems, *The Mind-Reader* (1976) [see *CLC,* Vol. 9]. And while that review attempted to offer a view of his entire poetic career up to that point (apart from his translations of French drama), I have no desire now to serve up warmed-over views, or to engage again in the parochial and tribal battles that are often waged between rival schools and camps of current poetic taste. Wilbur's distinctions do not need to be set off by the infelicities of others, and his work is by now so well known, and so widely honored, that I can spare the reader a repetition of the formulaic terms of praise that have become the logos and labels of critical approval of his work.

[*New and Collected Poems*] presents all of his previous volumes in reverse order, concluding with his first book, *The Beautiful Changes and Other Poems* (1947)—the same order in which his poems were arranged in the, by now, familiar assemblage, *The Poems of Richard Wilbur,* which brought together everything from the first book to *Advice to a Prophet and Other Poems* (1961). The present volume reprints everything heretofore collected and adds to it the contents of two subsequent volumes, *Walking to Sleep: New Poems and Translations* (1969) and *The Mind-Reader,* and adds to them a volume of new poems with which this rich and impressive collection begins. This new work bears all the hallmarks of excellence that have stamped Wilbur's previous work: a kinetic imagination that is rare among poets, as well as an unusually rich and fertile gift for metaphor. I share with Aristotle a view of the importance of this gift, and cite him accordingly as follows:

> It is a great thing, indeed, to make a proper use of these poetical forms, as also of compound and strange words. But the greatest thing by far is to be a master of metaphor. It is one thing that cannot be learnt from others; and it is also a sign of genius, since a good metaphor implies an intuitive perception of the similarity in dissimilars.

When I try to make a mental list of the major English and American poets from, say, the turn of the century on, I find myself unable to come up with a single one who can match Wilbur in this regard. Each good poet, of course, has his own unique merits, his own vision, style, and idiom. And good poets do not cancel one another out; if we like Blake we are not thereby forbidden to like Marvell as well. But I can think of no other poet who could do what Wilbur does metaphorically in the . . . poem, **"An Event,"** from *Things of This World.* . . . (pp. 23-4)

There is a great deal that might be said about this poem, but I will confine myself to two observations. In its ingenious, philosophic course it plays with the pre-Socratic puzzle of "the One" and "the Many," a playfulness that is carefully carried out in such words as "their image" (which is both singular and plural), "singular vision" (s.), "divergences" (pl.), "alone" (s.), "images" (pl.), and "formation" (both s. and pl.). And then in the course of our progress we come to that matchless simile in answer to the question, "What is an individual thing?" "They roll / Like a drunken fingerprint across the sky!" There isn't a poet I can think of who would not have been overjoyed by a *trouvé* of that sort. It is breathtakingly vivid, accurate, and most astonishingly, *in motion.*

But Wilbur then proceeds to do what virtually no other poet would have the courage to do: he, in effect, throws it away. Or in any case declares that this is only one, and perhaps an imperfect, way to formulate what may in the end defy formulation. He allows the seriousness of his epistemological or metaphysical puzzle to take precedence over any incidental felicities that might be encountered along the way. This *sprezzatura* would be reckless in another poet. But Wilbur's government of his enormous resources is what makes this poem (as well as many others) a triumph over its local details, and an amalgamation that is wonderfully greater than the sum of its parts. The Eleatic auditors of Zeno would have been delighted.

It seems worth adding that the theme of this poem—the delicate and necessarily imperfect attempt at an equation between the exterior world and the human faculties that apprehend and try to "render" it—is one that has preoccupied Wilbur almost from the first. . . . It's a theme that recurs in **"A Fire Truck," "The Mill," "Digging for China," "The Beacon," "A Plain Song for Comadre,"** and **"Altitudes."** In an era when a lot of supremely pompous things have been claimed for the omnipotence of language, it is refreshing in the work of so accomplished a poet to encounter an acknowledgment of "the defeat of words" in the face of the richness and multiplicity of an external reality that will always supersede and evade the limitations of our vocabulary, however well deployed. So there is to such poems a salutary and characteristic humility that is in itself attractive, and in turn points to something else about Wilbur's poetry that is worth remarking on, though I approach it with a certain tentativeness.

It has to do with the character of the man within or behind the poems; with how and to what degree that man gets expressed, if at all. This is a matter both delicate and controversial. There is an impressive body of modern thought that maintains there is no necessary connection between the work of art and the artist's nature, character, or history. Wilde, for one, maintained this view, and it seems implicit in Eliot's theory of the "impersonality" of art. It is a view Auden adopted in the stanzas he later deleted from his elegy to Yeats. . . . The same view is expressed by Shaw in his preface to *The Doctor's Dilemma.* . . . It is quite wonderful to think how widespread is this doctrine among some artists of very doubtful merit; and we are likely to find it so familiar that it will seem a curiously modern attitude, but it isn't. Plutarch reports in his *Life* of Pericles: "Antisthenes . . . when he was told that Ismenias played excellently on the flute, answered very properly, 'Then he is good for nothing else; otherwise he would not have played so well.'"

Yet this view is by no means universally shared, and it is generally felt that though precision in the matter is impossible, the work of art bears some important imprint of the spirit and inmost life of its maker. (pp. 24-5)

[**"Still, Citizen Sparrow"** from *Ceremony and Other Poems* (1950) and **"A Wood,"** from *Walking to Sleep* (1969)] probably were not composed to be matched and mated, and yet they do form a pair by dint of theme and contrast. They are both symbolic poems in which some aspect of nature takes part in a little allegorical pageant, exhibiting human attitudes in a manner that we've become familiar with from poems like Robert Frost's "Spring Pools." And even though there was a long interval between their appearances, it is possible to think of them as a sort of diptych, as poems that face each other and quarrel in a friendly way, as do Milton's "L'Allegro" and "Il Penseroso"; though here we are prompted to wonder if the alternative postures presented by the two Wilbur poems are the consequence of a change of attitude on the part of the poet, or simply an attempt, as in Milton's case, to set up an antiphonal or dialogic relationship.

The question seems worth raising partly because there is something disturbing in the earlier, and in my view, the less successful, of these Wilbur poems. There is, for one thing, a curiously Jacobin flavor to the opening words and the title, suggesting the bloodthirsty resentment of some revolutionary leveler and vengeful egalitarian. The very first word, "Still," invites us to suppose that the speaker is now countering a long and detailed diatribe of condemnation with a word that means,

"In spite of everything you say . . ." The *citoyen* is asked to admire his grotesque and more powerful rival and predator, whose ugliness, at a sufficiently great distance, will not be discernible. This powerful enemy "has heart to make an end" in that he finishes off his rivals, and in this way, it is claimed for him, "keeps nature new." I can't help feeling there is something frightful about this, and the more frightful in that we, and the *citoyen,* are being asked to admire and forgive it. In some way that is to me quite unpersuasive, this creature is identified as "the hero," and further identified with Noah, who, like the vulture, survives the hideous death of everyone else. Nothing is hinted about the merit of Noah and the wickedness of mankind to account for this introduction into the poem of a biblical story.

The poem seems to be about the elect who succeed and survive, in contrast to the masses who perish and are undeserving. Indeed, the biblical citation seems totally unexpected, and by no means easy to assimilate. There is a species of social Darwinism going on here "to which / The ripped mouse, safe in the owl's talon, cries / Concordance," in the words of Wilbur's poem **"Beasts."** I can't believe that this is a skewed or perverse reading of the poem, which seems to invite a sort of class distinction and exclusiveness. In any case, one cannot help feeling that the parable of the trees in **"A Wood"** is a great deal more charitable and generous than the parable of the birds in **"Still, Citizen Sparrow."**

This is the more striking in that, as opposed to the violence, insolence, and outright repulsiveness with which any number of poets now assault us, Wilbur's work has been characterized from the first by an admirable capacity to praise. "Obscurely yet most surely called to praise," begins one of his earliest poems. Long ago there used to be commonplace belief that the end of art was precisely to delight ("Sounds and sweet airs that give delight and hurt not"). This did not mean, of course, that art was therefore purged of any taint of unpleasantness, presenting instead a dilute and sentimental version of existence, any more than Shakespeare's *The Tempest* is free from villainy. But, in Keats's formulation. "The excellency of every art is its intensity, capable of making all disagreeables evaporate"; by which, I assume, he means that even the most terrible matters could be redeemed by their assimilation into art.

Wilbur's poems have exhibited over the years an impressive capacity to confront the shocking, the appalling, the grotesque. Among his finest poems are the powerful dramatic monologues from which his last two books take their titles: *Walking to Sleep* and *The Mind-Reader,* each of which deals with terrors of different sorts. It is an index, in fact, of Wilbur's growth as an artist that his emotional range has become increasingly ample over the years. If there could be said to be any characteristic limitations to his early work, they might be described as a sort of runaway mellifluousness, a Hopkinsian/Swinburnian/Tennysonian drench of language:

> A script of trees before the hill
> Spells cold, with laden serifs; all the walls
> Are battlemented still;
> But winter spring is winnowing the air
> Of chill, and crawls
> Wet-sparkling on the gutters;
> Everywhere
> Walls wince, and there's a steal of waters. . . .

I don't mean that there's anything "wrong" with this, though it is perhaps a little more "mannered" than the later poems, and the calligraphy of the trees is less convincing than the

fingerprint of that flock of birds in flight. Even here there is in "spells" a pun of the sort that will continue to inhabit Wilbur's poems throughout his career. His puns are serious and serviceable, and only occasionally comic; they are a major feature of his work, as are Shakespeare's "quibbles," which are the despair of translators. It was this sort of ambiguity and multivalenced power of words that led Tolstoy to his impatient dismissal of *King Lear* and his assertion that Shakespeare was "only playing with words." But, in a deeply serious way, that is actually what all good poets do: words are their only instruments to convey what is not easily conveyed by words alone. To resort to abusive epithets such as "artifice" or "dandy" is merely to embrace one convention and use it to bludgeon another that is equally valid.

Those who in past years have been stinting in their approval of Wilbur have pointed to his universally admired translations of classic French drama and have gone on to declare that this dated, formalized sensibility perfectly accords with his own tendencies to precision and stateliness. But I remember as an undergraduate reading Molière done, or rather, done in, by Louis Untermeyer in a translation that the veriest lout would recognize as doggerel. And since Wilbur's versions have become available there is no self-respecting production that would resort to another.

The linguistic gifts that have made possible these superb translations from 17th-century French are also at work in the collections of lyric poems, which contain Wilbur's translations from French, Latin, Russian, Spanish, and Italian poems, dating from the fourth or fifth century to the work of his contemporaries. This latitude of sympathy for poets sometimes very idiosyncratic and different from one another (for example, Villon and Voltaire) is itself an expression of Wilbur's reach and suggests that like another American poet, he "contains multitudes."

The new poems that are now added to his six previous collections are as rich, varied, and accomplished as we have come to expect, and in addition he has risked, successfully, an admirable departure from his usual practice. Wilbur has written texts for musical settings before, and with great effect. Two very fine examples that come to mind are **"A Christmas Hymn"** and Pangloss's song about syphilis for the comic opera *Candide.* But now Wilbur has written a more extended text for a full cantata in celebration of the Statue of Liberty. It was written for the composer William Schuman, is divided into five sections, runs to a total of 102 lines, and is called **"On Freedom's Ground."** It seems to me to succeed wonderfully where anyone else I can think of would have failed. And the task was rife with potential pitfalls. There were the twin perils of jingoism and chauvinistic sentimentality on the one hand, and the symmetrical or compensatory danger of leaning over backward to avoid anything that looked suspiciously like "affirmation."

But over and above these was the problem of writing an extensive text for music. . . . Of modern poets Yeats may have been the most intuitive and plausible about writing for music, knowing somehow that he would have to simplify his ways if he wanted his auditors to grasp anything of what he wrote while having to attend to a vocal performance of music with accompaniment.

Wilbur has risked this kind of dangerous simplicity and straightforwardness, and has done so with great success. He has ingeniously made use of the device of the catalog, a genuine relief to a listener's need to follow the thread of an argument or a narrative, and he has cunningly and discreetly worked a famous phrase of Martin Luther King Jr.'s into the fabric of his text, where it is surely but unostentatiously resonant. The cantata stands at the end of this new collection, separated from the rest and intended to be recognized for what it is: something written in a special, ceremonial, accessible idiom that will give the composer room to do some creative work of his own, and command some part of the listener's attention. (pp. 27-9)

The new collection opens with a superb poem called **"The Ride,"** which continues a kind of obsessional theme that Wilbur has made characteristically his own: the poem that plays on the delicate and tenuous relationship between dream and waking. Readers of his work will know how this subject has preoccupied him in such poems as **"Love Calls Us to the Things of This World," "In Limbo," "Walking to Sleep," "For Ellen,"** and **"Marginalia,"** for example. The subtle changes between different states of consciousness are a rich source for poetry, and many of the best modern poets have worked the region with success, but none, I think, as successfully as Wilbur.

He also presents us with a translation of a poem by Joseph Brodsky called "Six Years Later," which Brodsky chose to open his most recent collection, *A Part of Speech.* It is a love poem of great formality, and with an ingenuity of metaphoric structure that is distinctly reminiscent of the poems of Donne. Brodsky was from very early in his career a great admirer of Donne, for whom he wrote an elegy. And it is no small accomplishment on Wilbur's part to have translated a poem from the Russian that allows the influence of the 17th-century poet to exhibit itself in a modern and modulated way.

I should add that Wilbur's translation, also included, of Apollinaire's "Mirabeau Bridge" is as miraculous in its poise and fragility as the original. There is a deftly funny poem called **"A Fable,"** which is a blithe commentary on American foreign policy, and a beautiful elegy for Auden. Again and again these poems take away the breath by the stunning aptness of simile or metaphor, and almost always of something in motion:

> Still, nothing changes as her perfect feet
> Click down the walk that issues in the street,
> Leaving the stations of her body there
> As a whip maps the countries of the air.

And in **"Trolling for Blues"** Wilbur returns to the subject of **"An Event,"** the problem of capturing in words or in the mind some fleeting hint of what is called "reality." This topic is also the focus of one of the very best, wittiest, and most thoughtful poems in the new groups, **"All That Is."** The poem begins with the mootness and growing obscurity of dusk, beautifully described, and with the uncertainty that this blurred hour engenders. As the night darkens the stars come out and we follow "a many-lighted bus" making its way through a city, and a passenger who has turned to the crossword puzzle, as have, at that hour, many others in the kitchens and parlors of their homes.

And somehow, strangely, suddenly, the poet invites us to raise our eyes above these heads bent over their puzzles to behold "a ghostly grille / Through which, as often, we begin to see / The confluence of the Oka and the Aare." We have moved wonderfully into a region of some obscurity, partly because of the approaching night, and partly because the language of crossword puzzles has, as it were, taken over. That grille we have focused upon is partly perhaps the gridwork of a celestial map, but much more surely the checkerboard of squares of a typical crossword puzzle in which we might find that two rivers, the Oka and the Aare, which in prosy geographical fact are located in Russia and Switzerland, can nevertheless form a confluence where their letters intersect. Their very names, perhaps, produce in the poet a kind of crossword reverie of exotic words, in which he giddily proceeds to indulge:

> Is it a vision? Does the eye make out
> A flight of ernes, rising from aits or aeries,
> Whose shadows track across a harsh terrain
> Of esker and arête? At waterside,
> Does the shocked eeler lay his congers by,
> Sighting a Reo driven by an edile?
> And does the edile, from his runningboard,
> Step down to meet a ranee? Does she end
> By reading to him from the works of Elia?

This charming fantasia of unanswered questions, this visionary excursion into the realm of the linguistically obscure, is not, in my view, the sort of text for which notes ought to be supplied or demanded. If it sends you, as it sent me, to the dictionary, and even to the Britannica, that is merely to acknowledge that the poet's mental life has gone off on a delightful toot of its own, and that we should take a puzzler's pleasure in tracking it down, just as he has attempted to trace, "Between the street-lamps and the jotted sky," a grille of crosswords that will resolve everything. There follows a passage I have not yet unravelled, in which the poet presents us with a vision of "A lambent god reposing on the sea, / Full of the knitted light of all that is." (pp. 29-30)

Witty and complex and lovely as this poem may be, I nevertheless feel that another blank verse poem of meditation, titled **"Lying,"** is, at least in my present view of things, the best poem in the collection. It begins with distinct modesty this way:

> To claim, at a dead party, to have spotted a grackle,
> When in fact you haven't of late, can do no harm.
> Your reputation for saying things of interest
> Will not be marred, if you hasten to other topics,
> Nor will the delicate web of human trust
> Be ruptured by that airy fabrication.

The poem then goes on to speculate about what it is that prompts us to these little acts of mendacity. Perhaps, initially, an impatience or boredom with the dailiness, the sheer routine, of things, and even with the more miraculous of things, "the horse's neck / Clothed with its usual thunder," in an echo of the majestic words of God in the 39th chapter of the Book of Job. That biblical catalog of divine wonders is always before us, as are other, still more uncommon, wonders, "And so with that most rare conception, nothing."

Since evil is only the absence of good, and since Satan is the Prince of Lies, he makes his sinuous entrance into the poem with almost unperceived skill, as "the water of a dried-up well / Gone to assail the cliffs of Labrador." He then approaches us, "pretending not to be," and appears, in the words of Milton from the ninth book of *Paradise Lost,* as a *"black mist low creeping,"* which, when it rises, turns to a rainbow. But perhaps because of the invocation of Milton, the poem now finds itself confronting the axiom that art itself is a lie of sorts, and, in the words of Shakespeare's Touchstone, "The truest poetry is the most feigning." All of it is, according to Aristotle, a form of imitation, which is a kind of lie. Wilbur continues:

> Closer to making than the deftest fraud
> Is seeing how the catbird's tail was made

To counterpoise, on the mock-orange spray,
Its light, up-tilted spine; or, lighter still,
How the shucked tunic of an onion, brushed
To one side on a backlit chopping-board
And rocked by trifling currents, prints and prints
Its bright, ribbed shadows like a flapping sail.
Odd that a thing is most itself when likened: . . .

And now we have come to the very heart of metaphor itself. It is metaphor that allows us to contemplate a great deal that might otherwise be intolerable, and, like tragedy, it "Finds pleasure in the cruellest simile." We return to the catbird, which, like a mockingbird, or a poet, is distinguished as a mimic, gifted in the art of imitation. The bird's song is characterized as "a chant / Of the first springs," and as a "tributary / To the great lies told with the eyes half-shut / That have the truth in view: . . ." There follow three such lies, all of them masterpieces of the imagination. The first is the pagan tale of Chiron, who "Instructed brute Achilles in the lyre," another of Wilbur's serious puns. The second is the biblical image of faultless Eden, and the third the concluding sacrifice and valor of Roland:

> who to Charles his king
> And to the dove that hatched the dovetailed world
> Was faithful unto death, and shamed the Devil.

There is nobility in such utterance that is deeply persuasive, and throughout Wilbur's poetry we are accustomed to finding this rare quality, usually joined to wit, good humor, grace, modesty, and a kind of physical zest or athletic dexterity that is, so far as I know, unrivaled. (pp. 30, 32)

Anthony Hecht, "Master of Metaphor," in The New Republic, *Vol. 198, No. 20, May 16, 1988, pp. 23-32.*

ROBERT RICHMAN

The poetry of Richard Wilbur, who has recently become the nation's poet laureate, has long been recognized as being graceful and technically accomplished. The publication of his *New and Collected Poems,* is therefore an occasion to celebrate. . . .

This book reminds us that his verse expresses a very clear and thoughtful view of life. When he writes, in **"Grasse: The Olive Trees,"** about how the landscape of southern France is "full / Of . . . a heavy jammed excess," he could easily be referring to the "heavy jammed excess" of meaning in his verse:

> Here luxury's the common lot. The light
> Lies on the rain-pocked rocks like yellow wool
> And around the rocks the soil is rusty bright
> From too much wealth of water, so that the grass
> Mashes under the foot, and all is full
> Of heat and juice and a heavy jammed excess.

Like the olive, which "teaches the South it is not paradise," Mr. Wilbur's elegant verse reveals it is more than an Eden of beautiful language.

One of Mr. Wilbur's chief interests is the question of the propriety of using the external world to create meaning in poetry. He believes the poet is perfectly justified in altering reality for the sake of the poem. But he is also flexible in his views. Thus, although he will transform the olive into a metaphor for the mind and its "great thirst" for meaning, he is also receptive to those moments when the world defies the "cages of [his] thought." . . .

The distinction Mr. Wilbur makes, in **"A Summer Morning,"** between *possession* and *ownership* of the land, helps clarify his own attitude toward nature: . . .

> A gardener works before the heat of day.
> He straightens for a view
> Of the big house ascending stony-gray
> Out of his beds mosaic with the dew.
>
> His young employers having got in late,
> He and the cook alone
> Receive the morning on their old estate,
> Possessing what the owners can but own.

Unlike the owners, who cannot spiritually possess the land, the cook and gardener are able to "receive the morning" properly.

"Worlds," ones of the new poems here, revolves around the same theme. Mr. Wilbur contrasts Alexander the Great, conqueror of the known world, with Isaac Newton, who is far more content in his benevolent possession of the universe through knowledge. . . .

Mr. Wilbur is preoccupied with the correct "possession" of nature because the transaction holds the possibility of spiritual release. In **"Piazza di Spagna, Early Morning,"** a woman descending the Spanish Steps in Rome lifts the poet out of the world and himself:

> I can't forget
> How she stood at the top of that long marble stair
> Amazed, and then with a sleepy pirouette
> Went dancing slowly down to the fountain-quieted
> square;
>
> Nothing upon her face
> But some impersonal loneliness,—not then a girl,
> But as it were a reverie of the place,
> A called-for falling glide and whirl;
>
> As when a leaf, petal, or thin chip
> Is drawn to the falls of a pool and, circling a moment
> above it,
> Rides on over the lip—
> Perfectly beautiful, perfectly ignorant of it.

Such tranfiguring instants—one also finds them in **"Stop,"** **"A Plain Song for Comadre,"** **"A Glance From the Bridge"** and **"Transit"**—do more than enliven a drab scene. Through these moments Mr. Wilbur registers his disagreement with the prevailing view of what truth is. The poet's desire to, as he puts it, "reach past rain" suggests that truth is more than what is found in the surfaces of reality.

Mr. Wilbur also enriches his verse by showing a willingness to face the dangers entailed in the quest for what Wallace Stevens called the "truth that cannot be arrived at by reason alone." The main peril, of course, is becoming too removed from reality. Mr. Wilbur's awareness of this problem has resulted in an even greater devotion in recent years to the "things of this world" (the phrase was the title of his third book).

Perhaps nothing in Mr. Wilbur's *oeuvre* argues more eloquently for the value of ordinary life than poems such as **"Running,"** **"A Late Aubade,"** **"For Dudley"** and **"The Writer."** These poems focus on incidents requiring no transcendent vision. . . . What poems like **"The Writer"** stress, finally, is how tentative any poetic position must be if the poet wishes to remain truly open to the mystery and wonders of life.

Clearly, Mr. Wilbur's poetry is rich in meaning. But even if there were no intellectual thread in his work, it would demand our attention. There is much to be said for a poet who refuses against all odds to allow his vision of hope (as manifested in the elegance and attractiveness of the verse) to die. If it were not for writers like him, future students might wonder if there were no poets in the late 20th century who championed beauty (as unlikely a cause as it may have been) or who were capable of rising above all the despair and doubt. Fortunately, we do have Richard Wilbur, and I am confident our age will be deemed the better for it.

Robert Richman, "Benevolent Possessions," in The New York Times Book Review, *May 29, 1988, p. 2.*

Judith Wright

1915-

Australian poet, essayist, critic, biographer, editor, nonfiction writer, and author of children's books.

Australia's most celebrated twentieth-century female poet, Wright has garnered critical acclaim for concise, traditional verse in which she demonstrates an intellectual awareness of European and American literary traditions and vividly evokes the landscape and lifestyle of Australia. Vincent Buckley asserted: "Judith Wright surpasses all other Australian poets in the extent to which she mediates the pressure, and reveals the contours, of Australia as a place, an atmosphere, a separate being." Although some critics fault her later poems for lyrical abstraction, vague mysticism, and opinionated political observations, Wright has been widely praised for her attempts to resolve dualistic aspects of existence and her treatment of such themes as humanity's tenuous perception of time and reality, the struggle of the poet to attain permanence and security, and the need to overcome transience through love. For Wright, poetry "is a means of regaining faith in man" as well as "a way of finding a difficult balance" between internal and external reality.

Critics often attribute Wright's interest in Australian landscape to her childhood at her family's sheep station in the New England Tableland area of New South Wales. Wright began her literary career while a clerk at the University of Queensland in Brisbane, where she published poetry during the 1940s in such literary magazines as *Meanjin* and *Southerly*. The title of her first collection of verse, *The Moving Image* (1946; revised, 1953), derives from the Platonic quotation, "Time is a moving image of eternity." This volume balances such concepts as death and decay with birth and renewal while introducing Wright's search for permanence in a chaotic modern world. Using lucid, graceful lyrics to evoke a mythic dimension in her subjects, Wright conveys a vivid sense of the landscape and history of the New England region. In "Bullocky," for example, a poem from *The Moving Image,* an early settler confronted by the impenetrable Australian wilderness imagines himself as Moses and his bullock team as slaves he is leading to the Promised Land. S. Musgrove maintained that Wright's style in *The Moving Image* conveys "the gravity and sincerity that are the marks of inner integrity, so that . . . the most effective passages arise not from contrast with the body of the writing, but from a sudden imaginative deepening of the common idiom itself." Wright's second volume, *Woman to Man* (1949), received critical accolades for its celebration of womanhood, particularly its insights into such topics as conception, pregnancy, childbirth, and parenthood. Often regarded as Wright's most profound work, this collection reflects the influence of Dylan Thomas and W. B. Yeats in its striking imagery and focus on love and chaos. Elizabeth Vassilieff contended that in *Woman to Man* Wright exhibits the "rarest and most precious of poetic powers—the ability to re-create the meanings of common words with every new usage; to refresh, deepen and invigorate the language. . . . And in this power I think she has no equal among Australian poets."

Wright's next collection, *The Gateway* (1953), moves from personal concerns to the external world. This volume reflects the influence of William Blake and T. S. Eliot in its portraits

of landscapes and animals and its transfigurations of love, creation, and eternity. While some critics welcomed Wright's wider thematic scope, most maintained that her abstract and intellectual approach to philosophical and metaphysical problems often results in a loss of immediacy and originality. *The Two Fires* (1955) is frequently regarded as a more clearly defined work than *The Gateway*. This book's title poem refers to antithetical fires, one representing the primordial, Hereclitean concept of love from which humanity originated, and the other referring to the atomic fire created by man through which love may become extinguished. Although Wright's predominant image in this volume is destruction, *The Two Fires* also features descriptive nature pieces and optimistic poems.

Birds (1962) is a collection of Wright's light poems, some of which first appeared in the journal *Australian Letters*. Intended for young adult readers, this volume comments on characteristics of various Australian birds and reflects Wright's activities as cofounder and president of the Wildlife Preservation Society of Queensland. *Five Senses: Selected Poems* (1963; revised, 1972) integrates newly published verse with a selection of her favorite earlier work. Although the new poems center on such metaphysical issues as impermanence, fear, and death, some critics maintained that this book's reassuring, personal tone implies reconciliation and acceptance. In *The Other Half* (1966), Wright continues to widen the scope of her poetry by evoking problems of the external world. *Collected Poems, 1942-1970* (1971), which combines Wright's early work with new verse, contains elegies dedicated to her late husband, Jack McKinney, as well as several pieces in which she attempts to reconcile her private and public roles as poet. Of "Shadow: 1970," a sequence consisting primarily of satirical and sociological poems, K. L. Goodwin commented: "Here [Wright demonstrates] great maturity and assurance, with direct passion and with subtle irony. Some of her earlier poems used metaphysical notions insistently, drily, or irrelevantly; now such notions form part of the natural fabric of her work."

In her next volume, *Alive: Poems, 1971-1972* (1973), Wright contrasts the natural beauty of her home on Tamborine Mountain in Queensland with depictions of urban ruin to comment on the destruction of the Australian wilderness. Val Vallis noted: "The slimness of this book belies its value: the work is a careful distillation of years of criticism and love." In *Fourth Quarter and Other Poems* (1977), Wright interweaves childhood reminiscences with observations on old age and reflects on her move from Queensland to a region outside Canberra. Although some critics faulted her use of free verse as uncontrolled and her protest poems as shrill and difficult, many lauded Wright's personal verse for its more relaxed tone. Wright's previously uncollected newer pieces contained in *The Double Tree: Selected Poems, 1942-1976* (1978) were applauded for their precise language and descriptions of nature.

In addition to her poetry, Wright has earned acclaim for her criticism and fiction. *Preoccupations in Australian Poetry* (1965), a volume of critical essays on Australian writers, amassed widespread praise for its assertive opinions and incisive critiques. *The Nature of Love* (1966) collects autobiographical and anecdotal short stories that John Colmer described as "the characteristic expressions of a deeply sensitive mind." *The Generations of Men* (1959; revised, 1966) is a fictionalized historical memoir relating the attempts of Wright's immigrant grandparents, May and Albert Wright, to clear a farm out of the Australian wilderness during the nineteenth century. This book contrasts the confidence and ruthlessness of May with the introspection of Albert, who seemingly dies of guilt over the settlers' dispossession of native populations and opportunistic exploitation of Australian land. A reviewer for the *Times Literary Supplement* lauded *The Generations of Men* as "a beautiful feat of empathy clearly inspired by [Wright's] devout admiration for her subjects and [her] profound understanding of the ways of the country." In *The Cry for the Dead* (1981), Wright excerpts passages of the diaries that Albert Wright compiled between 1867 and 1890 to further relate the settlement of the Burnett and Dawson river district in central Queensland.

(See also *CLC*, Vol. 11; *Contemporary Authors*, Vols. 13-16, rev. ed.; and *Something about the Author*, Vol. 14.)

S. MUSGROVE

[*The Moving Image*] confirms what we have for some time suspected from Judith Wright's periodical pieces, that she is the only poet among the younger Australians who can challenge the stature of R. D. FitzGerald. Her poetry is the true landscape poetry, in which the physical scene becomes, in Blunden's words, the 'landscape of . . . being' and the movement of cloud

and sky reveals the climate of man's 'spiritual weather.' Her country of the mind, as of the eye, is truly Australian, with its colouring of generous blues and bitter greens, its strong shape. One feels above all a sense of space, of wide air, of a large land; the horizon is the far sweep of Miss Wright's own New England. . . . This is her stage, where the rivers run 'drunken with rain' and, at the edge of the tablelands, 'the eastward spurs tip backwards from the sun': an open arena, drenched with light, which prefigures the exultations and despairs of its lonely combatants. To its slopes she looks for her field of spiritual harvest, and in the tide of night that laps its granite edge she feels the encroaching flood of contemporary history. . . . Her poetry has the touch and feel of [Australia], for she knows that man ('Antaeus-like,' in Yeats's word), must not lose that immediate contact—that the remote and cold eye of abstract flight is distorting:

> Looking from so high the world is evil and small
> like a dried head from the islands with a grin of shell,
> brittle and easy to break. But there is no end to the breaking.

It is especially in this impression of space that Miss Wright's work recalls FitzGerald's best. She is like him, too, in her human confidence. . . . [The] impress of this land and of its best spirit lies on the work of both these poets, perhaps more deeply on Miss Wright's than on FitzGerald's. Here there is native material in plenty—dingoes and Thunderbolt, waddies and the surf—but it is used almost always without that sense of a manufactured determination to be Australian at all costs that makes so much of the work of the Jindyworobaks seem faked. (pp. 249-50)

The same effective naturalness appears in Miss Wright's manner of writing. The modern poetic idiom, with its stopped rhythms and fused imagery, is the voice in which she naturally speaks, but her poems almost never suffer from the fault of straining after effect, of being too clever by half, which that idiom often encourages. Her images and descriptions are no less vivid and original, if less immediately glittering, than those of a poet like Slessor; but they grow naturally out of the poem itself, and are never merely hung upon its branches, like baubles on a Christmas tree. . . . Her style has, in fact, the gravity and sincerity that are the marks of inner integrity, so that (as in the mediaeval *Everyman*) the most effective passages arise not from contrast with the body of the writing, but from a sudden imaginative deepening of the common idiom itself. . . . The general impression left by the tone of the poems is of imaginative richness under the proper control of personal and sincere design.

Because Miss Wright's work is so genuinely Australian, it does not altogether avoid the endemic scourge of this country's poetry, a tendency to wordiness and rhetoric, though she is infinitely less culpable than poets such as Mudie and Hudson. Her favourite line is the near-pentameter of common speech, a steed that is too apt to carry its rider off on a long-winded jog-trot. To my mind, the third part of **"The Moving Image"** comes nearest to the peril of collapsing into preachment. Contrasted with poems like **"The Hawthorn Hedge"** and **"Bullocky"**, in which the inner design emerges clearly from the total poem without overstatement or underlining, its deficiency is obvious. But this tendency—with which goes a very occasional use of the more tiresome specimens of contemporary jargon such as 'synthesis', particularly out of place in Miss Wright's poetry since they are not worthy of it—is only one fault among many virtues. This is living poetry, with no showiness and no spectacular posturing or chromium-plating, with only the spirit to love and the imagination to interpret. . . . (pp. 250-51)

*S. Musgrove, in a review of "The Moving Image,"
in* Meanjin, *Vol. V, No. 3, September, 1946, pp.
249-51.*

ELIZABETH VASSILIEFF

Judith Wright's second collection of poems [*Woman to Man*] established her in my mind at the present time as the most interesting of Australian poets, with no exceptions; and I wish I could speak of her work in language worthy of it. I cannot criticize Miss Wright's poetic world: I can only enter it and acclaim it as an enthralling and convincing one.

A man could not have made such a world. It is not a vast and noisy scene of events and ironies; not a place of violent acts and astonishments: nor of bold jests and fierce gestures. It is the intense and rarefied creation—'half-guesses and half-knowledge'—of one who has stayed still as a tree, and heard 'great images of silence', and 'the river underground': a kind of triumph of persistent quietude which no man born of woman ever achieved! For all their appreciation of certain aspects of her work, none of Miss Wright's earlier reviewers (all males), seem to have recognized that the proprium of her poetry is the feminine quality of her sensibility and skill. I am not suggesting that Judith Wright is a fine poet merely because she is a woman, but that it is necessary, to draw the maximum of meaning from her poetry, to grasp how richly it re-creates a vision which is both a unique one and an essentially feminine one. I think its peculiar value lies, not, as Professor Musgrove has suggested [see excerpt above], in its ability 'to challenge the stature of FitzGerald', or of any other poet, in rendering 'the landscape of being', and not, I must make clear, in any nonsense about 'feminine superiority' but in what it adds to the poetic worlds of men, in its special differences from them. (pp. 69-70)

[Wright's] central theme is the continuity of life eternally swinging between the twin poles of love and chaos—good and evil, joy and pain; life which is at once 'our hunter and our chase', 'the maker and the made,' 'the question and the reply'. The principle of love we meet through the poems in various guises: as the sun, the light, the day, the flame, the burning, the warmth, the knife, the rose; and in some contexts these are related to the growth of consciousness, of personality. We meet frequently the tree of blood, the veins and arteries of physical being; and the eyes, the crystal eyes, suggesting the soul. Birth is given as a resurrection, a rising-again of life, replenished, out of chaos, out of darkness, out of nothing, out of silence, out of night, out of unconsciousness, out of sleep, out of pain, defeat, hate, fear, water, the river, the flood. Chaos and love, not-being and being, unconsciousness and consciousness are indispensable to each other. (p. 70)

[Miss Wright's images] are never fixed in their meanings, as are the intellectual symbols of allegory, and one may not establish a precise interpretation for each image to be forced upon it every time it is met. Each image lives and takes its shade of meaning in its particular context; and the reason why Miss Wright's myth does not grow flat, stale and unprofitable is just this, that she explores the possibilities of subtle and delicate shifts of meaning for her symbols in each new context. She has in high degree this rarest and most precious of poetic powers—the ability to re-create the meanings of common words with every new usage; to refresh, deepen and invigorate the language. Mallarmé's 'Ability to purify the dialect of the tribe'.

And in this power I think she has no equal among Australian poets. (pp. 70-1)

The rhythmic forms of her poems are as closely knit, as richly varied and as sensitively controlled as her language. Their resilience, strong delicacy, amazing combination of toughness with tender refinement speak eloquently of a feminine mode of apprehension. These rhythms are not comparable with those of any male poet; they are of a different order, and for their maker's purpose they are perfect.

When she uses the underlying framework of a traditional metrical line, she counterpoints the 'ideal' stresses of the metre with cunning, quiet, persistent and various stresses of common speech. She very often makes for herself an interesting five-live stanza, whose simple, satisfying-but-not-obtrusive rhyme scheme is happily complicated by the presence of the odd unrhyming line. . . .

Personally, I enjoy most of all the more flexible rhythms of the poems which she casts in irregular accentual verses, with irregular numbers of syllables freely disposed about a few strong stresses. In the intensely concentrated poem **"Winter Kestrel"**, each of whose lines has three stresses and any number of syllables from four to eight, rhythmical interest derives from the presence of triple rising rhythms, bars in light waltz time, as it were, skilfully interspersed among the duple bars; and the poem's several 'imperfect' rhymes . . . accord beautifully with its partial metrical irregularity. . . . (p. 71)

More exciting still is Miss Wright's ordering of totally irregular forms, as in **"Child and Wattle Tree"**, and **"The Child"**. The lines of the latter poem, for instance, have any number of stresses from one to four, and any number of syllables from two to fourteen; the lyrical nature of the theme dictates and is strengthened by a strong predominance of triple rhythms ingeniously varied in their arrangement; the absence of rhyme scheme (which kind of regularity would be out of key) is compensated by the strong end stopping of the lines; and emphasis is brilliantly achieved by the use of short lines having only one or two stresses, where the reader automatically supplies the effective pause. . . .

This power and variety of rhythmical invention gives Miss Wright great freedom in the utterance of more complex statements. I know of no Australian poems which show such mastery of metric as the long poems **"The Blind Man"** and **"The Flood."** They ought to be read as wholes. (p. 72)

I have spoken of the formal aspects of Judith Wright's poetry, rather than about the kinds of thoughts, feelings and sensations expressed by her in specific places, because the *poetry* of her poems, their chief meaning and value, lies in what they *are* as unparaphrasable wholes, as acts of bringing-together, rather than in what is said in isolatable parts of them. To transmute as much as possible of the flowing chaos of experience into an ordered and stable world is the *raison d'etre* of poetry, and a poet's success in this is the measure of his greatness. In the form of her work Miss Wright has found a way of giving us the wealth of her world; to paraphrase is to diminish it. (pp. 72-3)

*Elizabeth Vassilieff, in a review of "Woman to Man,"
in* Meanjin, *Vol. IX, No. 1, March, 1950, pp. 69-73.*

ARTHUR MURPHY

Miss Wright's latest volume [*Woman to Man*] clearly indicates a steady development, a passing from strength to strength. The more subjective poems such as **"Woman to Man"** and **"Woman's Song"** I find less satisfying, however, than other lyrics in the series. They do not exhibit to the same extent the poet's command of vital language, the tension of keenly wrought imagery and thought moving to a perfect whole. But other deeps are sounded in the verse, the primitive cleavage of flesh to flesh in **"Woman to Man"** strongly conveying passion and power. This is not the brutal and pagan world of A.D. Hope's "Necrophile", where love is a physical spasm as final as death, and as remote. Rather does Judith Wright make of the love embrace a supreme attack on the spiritual as well as the physical world of being, a world built up on a foundation of passionate acceptance. . . . In **"Woman's Song"** there is a subtle harmony born of the mother's dreaming urge towards her child, splendid yet fulfilled, lost yet darkly knowing and mournfully prescient of a life that though sprung from spontaneous joy can yet endure deepest travail. A slowness of verse music is evident at the beginning of the poem, but later the lines become charged with love's electricity of feeling, which is sustained until the end of the lyric. (pp. 162-63)

[The poem] **"Conch-shell"** brings in the music and mystery of the sea, its power and the atmosphere that encircles the strange forces given birth in translucent depths where life is something negative and lost, yet having some affinity with human impulse. In **"The Sisters"** many conflicting stages of emotion and experience are outlined, the inevitable passing of youth to age becomes symbolized in the loss of desire, "courting", "dancing", "the smells of leather and wine". Against this background are the nostalgic whisperings of the sisters blending with shadow and sun, there withered heads nodding with the sudden excited frenzy of awakened thought and spent passion as the sun, a life force, "moves on the veranda", illuminating the drabness of the present. **"The Bull"** is remarkable for the unleashed menace of the imagery, the building up of atmosphere with an apparently inconsequent use of fugitive words, but this same structure is impressive when the poem is read as a whole. The first stanza is invested with a dreaminess, a languor born of the sexual content of the bull supreme amongst the sex he has conquered. Power is drawn out of the full recesses of the forests, the green strength of the grasses, and the passive drowsiness of a summer noon. Each of the stanzas perfectly displays the bull in the varying stages of his career. . . . [The] ability of the poet to merge herself with all natural forces, delving deep into the almost inexpressible in verse of highly wrought formation and full content, is again displayed in **"The Cycads"**. Here is the identical music's chant, the passing from time present to time immemorial in one brilliant sweep of thought and image. This world is one doomed and forgotten, chasmed out of the obscure womb of Time.

A different note is struck in **"Metho Drinker"**—a poem terrible in its graphic delineation of human degradation and suffering. The music of the verse contains some of the intense fire of **"Nigger's Leap: New England"**. Both poems are nerved with the immensity of tragic experience and loss of complete salvation with flesh and spirit entrammelled in life's intricate network. The poem **"Metho Drinker"** however, is more powerful in conception and execution, with lines etched deeply on a background of the mind's final dissolution. Phrases such as "his white and burning girl", "his woman of fire", are outstanding examples of keen poetic conception wherein this crazed wisp of humanity is caught up in the white and evil arms of an alluring Circe, whose red lips hold for ever the inmost recesses of tortuous pain and agonized death. . . . (pp. 163-64)

Delicately conceived are the verses **"Stars"** and **"The Old Prison"** with their slender composition of sound and imagery and simplicity of form. These poems are made up of quiet alliterative echoes, especially observed in the verse entitled **"Stars"**. . . . In **"The Bones Speak"** there are darker subtleties of thought and image, and an attempt to pierce the mists of antiquity enveloping the battlements of departed years. This poem has some of the deep philosophic content of **"The Moving Image"** but the roots do not spread as deeply and the thought is somewhat vague. The careful arrangement of words gives the sense of brooding and unvoiced fear that permeates the whole poem, the sense of impending catastrophe brought out by the heap of bones which become a symbol at once of man's triumph and his failure in a mutable world.

This same theme to some extent is brought out in **"The Blind Man"** series which is a chronicle portraying the lives of a family named Delaney. The singer is a blind man and his words seek out the lives of long forgotten generations of Delaneys and their heroic endeavours to carve a living out of virgin scrub. These lines move with fervid assurance and great ease of utterance, and the words conjure out of the past the hates and lusts that are a tradition in the growth of any country. The feud between white and black becomes monumental in realism with the sun and hills and gums as a nostalgic background. Though all are dust, and gone for ever are all aspirations and fears, the singer turns to the child as the promise of a new generation. The poem, as are many of the others, is somewhat fatalistic in tone and theme, and there is no robust affirmation of life's often joy and strength, and the music that moves out into the shadows is the music of subdued defeat. (pp. 164-65)

Judith Wright uses suggestive phrasing as one of her most effective weapons in verse, and her restlessly probing mind can merge at will into all natural manifestations. The final effects of her best work are not just a superficial lushness, a striving after artificial release of emotion, but each poem working as one complete unit stresses in the mind of the reader a more powerful awareness of life's central scene, a penetration to the core of the unexpressed. Perhaps there is room in her work for a more defiant gusto, a more vigorous painting of the world's metaphysical challenge even when her verse medium appears to be shackling adequately her most moving thought. In the longer and the shorter lyrical series, however, we are always made definitely aware that Judith Wright at her most inspired pitch ranks with the best and most highly reflective poets in the land. (p. 165)

> Arthur Murphy, "Poetic Intuition," in Southerly,
> Vol. 11, No. 3, 1950, pp. 162-65.

ELYNE MITCHELL

Vivid imagery, lovely songs of creation and of a creator, poems of a philosophical journey, of the integration of dark and light, of rebirth, characterize Judith Wright's work. When her first poems appeared [in Australian periodicals], one was led to expect something filled with truth born of experience, an imagery that sprang from her own time and from the timeless Australian earth. There were such poems as **"Bora Ring"**, with the subtle haunting rhythm perfectly matched to the rhythm of the dancing nomad feet. . . . There was **"Trapped Dingo"** with its vivid "white shorn mobs of stars on the hill of the sky". These and other poems were collected in ***The Moving Image***.

In the second collection, *Woman to Man,* the biting, vivid imagery is rarer. It appears in "**The Blind Man**", in "**Night After Bushfire**", and superbly, in "**The Bull.**" . . . But the main impression of this book is that it sings most beautifully of the actual process of creating—creating a child or a poem.

In the third collection, *The Gateway,* recently published, there are rather more poems that come from Judith Wright's own country—that live and grow because their existence springs from the roots of the poet's beginnings. Actually their impact in the book is not very noticeable because this book's strength is in the sustained philosophical meaning and direction in a high proportion of the poems; yet there are three which I would particularly mention—"**Train Journey**", "**To a Child**", and "**Eroded Hills**" (which originally had the more suggestive title of "**Inheritor**"). All these have the sudden sharp image that calls up many other pictures.

> These hills my father's father stripped,
> and beggars to the winter wind
> they crouch like shoulders naked and whipped—
> humble, abandoned, out of mind.

It is interesting to note that on this third occasion Judith Wright has used the image of the convict's whipped shoulders it has achieved greater strength, calling up echoes from far back in Australian history, deepening our awareness of the exploitation of the land, making us conscious of greater implications in the poem.

"**Train Journey**" is an earlier poem that missed being included in *Woman to Man.* It draws out many memories of this land that built all our hearts, if we but admitted it. . . . "**To a Child**" I turn to over and over again. Here one enters into . . . the thrilling brightness of frost:

> The sudden sun lit up
> the webs from wire to wire;
> the white webs, the white dew,
> blazed with a holy fire,

and the spiderwebs, threaded with millions of frozen drops of mist, stretched between the fence wires, hung between the thistles—which I have sometimes thought of as the Wheel of Life—burn with the early light and with a new significance. This is experience illuminated—by the sun blazing with the fire of God and "the song of the martyrs out of a bush of fire". This poem has the strength of imagery which was in "**The Moving Image**" but its content is profounder.

To quote only these poems is to ignore the direction of Judith Wright's development—even if I think that these poems and those concerned with the making of life are her most valuable.

In both *Woman to Man* and *The Gateway,* love, not just the love of men and women, but the idea that love is the informing principle of life, seems to me the wellspring of the poems. This is made explicit in "**Song for Easter**", the poem I find the most beautiful in the last collection. . . . Added to this idea of love, in *The Gateway* there are two dominating philosophic themes—the integration of dark and light and the symbolic "journey" and "traveller".

Woman to Man might have given one the idea that Judith Wright leant more towards "the dark gods"—as in . . . the last verse in "**Woman to Child**":

> I wither and you break from me:
> yet though you dance in living light
> I am the earth, I am the root,
> I am the stem that fed the fruit,
> the link that joins you to the night.

In *The Gateway* the philosophy is, I think, more balanced. For instance in the lovely "**Orange-Tree**" dark and light are perfectly integrated, while in the final verse of "**The Lost Man**" the journey through darkness and rebirth into light are described in Jung's symbols of integration. . . . It is in "**Walker in Darkness**", "**The Ancestors**", "**The Forest Path**", "**The Lost Man**", and "**The Gateway**" itself that we get the strongest impact of Judith Wright's philosophical journey, though in *Woman to Man* there is one beautiful poem "**Dream**", in which I think the journey is the Mystic Way, the Mystic's "know thyself." . . . (pp. 33-4)

When the lyrics "**Woman to Man**", "**Woman to Child**", "**Woman's Song**", and "**The Unborn**" were first printed, they came as a complete surprise after the poems in *The Moving Image,* then just published, and yet they, too, were experience made articulate in rhythm and words. They are written with an insight that puts the creation of a child back on the plane of understanding that brought the Madonna image into being

> The eyeless labourer in the night,
> the selfless, shapeless seed I hold,
> builds for its resurrection day—
> silent and swift and deep from sight
> foresees the unimagined light.

In *The Gateway* there are "**Ishtar**", "**The Promised One**", "**A Song to Sing You**", and "**Waiting Ward**", written round the same experience: something truly of life seems to be captured in them all. They are perhaps not as good as the four in *Woman to Man,* but I like them. . . . As I have said, I find [the] poems of creation and the poems with strong imagery the most valuable, perhaps because they more brightly illuminate life.

One would not wish Judith Wright to go on endlessly singing the same songs, but I do feel that her philosophical journey would be more significant if the imagery used was the deeply felt scenery of the part of Australia in which she was born and lived her early impressionable years. Landscape made particular can give great strength to the philosophical content of a poem, because the more intimately the poet knows any part of the world, the nearer he or she is to the creative principle, the Logos, the more the poetry may share its truth. Obviously such poems as "**The Gateway**" require the imagery of chaos and the void, as in Walter de la Mare's "**The Traveller**", but there are other poems in which she could have allowed philosophical experience to fuse with her earlier self and the intimate knowledge of a land that made her whole being. . . . As they stand, the language and the imagery are similar to those recording the spiritual journeys of other poets, and it seems to me that Judith Wright has not, while letting their roots draw on an entirely valid, ancient yet ever new experience, given them what perhaps she alone could have given—a new, satisfying truth for Australians at this time and yet for always. (pp. 34-5)

Elyne Mitchell, "The Vision and the Way," in South-*erly, Vol. 16, No. 1, 1955, pp. 32-5.*

ROBERT D. FITZGERALD

In Judith Wright's *The Two Fires* one finds an innate profundity and a colourful mysticism of the parent earth. (p. 196)

With *The Moving Image* Judith Wright opened up a new vision of the world. A new world of poetry too lay before her in which it seemed she might step out in any direction, complete mistress. Then came *Woman to Man,* with her powers more fully developed, the poetry stronger and surer, and the direction chosen clearer. As the title implied, it was a woman's poetry, yet addressed to man rather than to woman, a poetry from the woman's commanding position within the life-stream of mankind, a poetry of the mystical life of the world. Yet it was a darkening world, becoming self-enclosed; the poet's sight was more turned inward than before. *The Gateway* followed; and it seemed that the cloud was lifting. Love and creation were seen as the moving forces within the universe, therefore woman's central position in the scheme was seen as expanding rather than enclosed. Nevertheless *The Gateway* was a disappointment in some respects. Judith Wright's work, nearly flawless usually, does suffer lapses; and much here appeared to have lapsed, not to any great degree but below what we had come to expect. Perhaps we had come to expect too much; for certainly there were many poems in *The Gateway* as good as any that had gone before; but they were not the sudden discoveries for us that some of the earlier poems had been, so they did not make the same impact. Now, with *The Two Fires,* the direction has changed a little again, and the earlier impressions return of poetry that has almost everything we could ask of it. The work is more compact than *The Gateway,* its purposes more exactly defined.

The new book opens with the namepiece, **"The Two Fires,"** a difficult poem on a first reading, but so clearly poetry of a high order that no poetry-adherent will put it down until after a third or fourth reading. By that time it will be plain enough that:

> In the beginning was the fire;
> out of the death of fire, rock and the waters;
> and out of water and rock, the single spark, the divine truth.

refers to actual fire, the molten mass of the earth preceding geological time, but that 'the bridegroom and the bride' and 'the holy unwearying seed' of elsewhere in the text are the earlier conceptions of love as the mystical meaning within the universe and of life growing, persisting, self-renewing. Man, however, creates another fire—another real fire—in which both that love and that seed could perish. Indeed they are pictured as having already perished. Yet the two fires are linked and in a way are the same: the seed preserves the original fire and so causes the later one. . . . (pp. 201-02)

Interspersed [throughout *The Two Fires*] are poems which could be considered purely personal with little to do with the possible destruction of the world; but the personal problem is in reality only an aspect of the world problem. Life breaks in on the calm of contemplation. . . . (p. 202)

[The] remaining poems generally leave the theme of destruction and accept the earth's persons and things as tangibles rather than as symbols of futility before some final blast. That is just as well. For if the introspective cloud that hung over *Woman to Man* should be succeeded by one of defeatism, that would be regrettable. The defeatist motif can only make one genuine poem (though many sham ones) on its way to its logical conclusion, which is defeat of poetry itself and life as futile and of no avail—conclusion indeed. The devil scribbled that poem long ago; later defeatist poets are but echoists.

Judith Wright does seem to end on a note of despair. . . . [But the] note of despair may be little more than legitimate dramatic effect poised for contrast against the more persistent conception of a universe existing primarily as the force generating life, its symbol being physical love.

The poems which detach themselves from the theme of destruction (and by that detachement oppose it) include the ad-

mirable and now well-known **"Request to a Year,"** and descriptive pieces wherein earth scenes always contain some hint of the living forces of the earth. There are also haunting love lyrics and even some concise animal and nature pieces, though these last suffer a little by inviting direct comparison with similar work by Douglas Stewart. Throughout all this variety one is continuously conscious of a power of vision beyond the ordinary sight of mankind. Judith Wright sees differently and she sees more. (p. 203)

Strangely, though she has that power to imprison a thought in a phrase, she can also be both diffuse and inexact. The poem [**"For Precision"**] recognizes this in a piece of resolute self-criticism far more severe than anyone but herself would consider warranted. . . . Exact or not, whatever she says becomes music, which too conveys meaning and assists interpretation. It is not often a tune that sings in the head; but whether a solemn music or a dancing one, when it dies away the air that carried it is enriched, and the ear that received it. (pp. 203-04)

Robert D. FitzGerald, "Form and Matter in Poetry," in Meanjin, *Vol. XV, No. 2, June, 1956, pp. 196-204.*

JOHN THOMPSON

The best poems in Judith Wright's new collection [*The Two Fires*], **"The Man Beneath the Tree"** and **"Request to a Year"**, are very good poems indeed. They are poems evidently "occasioned" by true flashes of insight. One cannot imagine that they will ever lose their genuineness or their appeal. They are worthy of the Judith Wright who has been praised for several years in terms hardly to be outdone, and the book is worth having for this reason alone.

The other poems are less striking. There were signs of a falling-off in Judith Wright's third book, *The Gateway,* a turning from the concrete towards the abstract and a tendency to "snatch poems out of the air". In her fourth book, *The Two Fires,* there are many poems which lend colour to a suspicion that the author is forcing her art. Leanings to grandiloquence, a vague mysticism and the assumption of a bardic mantle are common indications of forcing; and the name-poem **"The Two Fires"** is a case in point. Obscure and expostulatory, this cry of woe is simply not true, not true to nature, not true to the heart.

The first seven lines of a poem called **"Sanctuary"** could well stand on their own, a charming vignette reminiscent of Robert Frost; but the remaining twenty lines are crowded with irrelevant questions, fancies, parentheses, and the last two lines are vapid. Similarly, in **"For Precision"** the beautiful suggestions of the middle part are blurred and dissipated by solemnity at the beginning and exaggeration at the end of the poem. The first two poems in a group of three, **"Flesh"**, are much more successful, the idea in each instance being developed firmly and consistently. The rough-and-ready verse-form neither helps nor hurts their memorableness, whether or not we are moved by what is said. The same comments apply to **"West Wind"** and **"The Precipice"**.

The conclusion is hard to resist that, if Judith Wright had withheld publication for some time, she would have cancelled or revised many of the poems in this book. Only poetry is poetry, and the vital essence cannot be supplied by philosophizing or phrasemaking, hard work or constancy of purpose. It is not easy, God knows, nor is it given every day to the giants of art, to write a superlative poem. But it is a pity to see Judith Wright, to whom we owe so much, plumping up a book with more or less commonplace verses.

One is tempted to feel that half-baked critics or importunate publishers may have hurried this fine poet into putting out a fourth book before she was ready to do so. It has been her fortune recently . . . to be hailed as "the best Australian poet". The fact is that we have produced a very good crop of minor poets, but the cause of poetry itself and the well-being of individual poets are not served by intemperate boosting. (pp. 99-100)

> John Thompson, "Judith Wright and Nancy Keesing," in Southerly, Vol. 17, No. 2, 1956, pp. 99-100.

V. S. PRITCHETT

Equipped as we are nowadays, we get a shock when we read of the primitive and naked struggle against nature in the new countries in the nineteenth century. It is a grinding, monotonous war, accumulating its casualties, impoverishing some lives, hardening others, operating with all the brutality of a fate. This is the subject of a scrupulous and sensitive Australian family history [*The Generations of Men*] written by [Miss Judith Wright]. From family diaries she has constructed an account of the year-by-year lives of her forebears who were opening up New South Wales and Queensland from 1820 onwards. The book may not enlighten us about the growth of Australian society, but in the intimacy of its account of the daily struggle, it gradually becomes an absorbing document. We are made to see what is done to a man who by temperament and gift was unsuited to the solitude, the natural disasters, the sheer physical claims that were made on him. Born for the study, he had to live on the remote grazing lands, see drought and floods pile up his debts, watch his wife and children sicken with fevers and wilt under malnutrition, travel hundreds of miles every year on horseback, deal with the rough, the tough, the mad in the bush, and spend a large part of his life alone with sheep, horses and cattle.

The first settler in this family out from England in the 1820s was the traditional younger son. He had quarrelled with his father and absorbed the ideas of Godwin and Shelley. Australia was the promised land. But once there his ambition was to reproduce English country life. With convict labour he built a fine stone house. He lived like a squire, became almost a Tory squire. He did well; but as he grew older and richer he was shocked to see that his children were Australians. He returned to England, leaving them to fight the aborigines, rob them of their hunting grounds and speculate in the cattle trades and the new lands. The dreams of Godwin and Shelley had vanished in the successful struggle to maintain tradition and dignity in the face of the economic scramble. Another younger son, from Cornwall, came out and married into the squire's family, was quickly swindled. It is this man's son, Albert Wright, who is the centre of the longest and most vivid part of the book.

The story of Albert Wright must have occurred in varying forms in all the new countries. It is the story of the making of a new man at the expense of his spiritual life, a process of hardening and martyrdom. At the point where he is racked no longer and has triumphed over his own character, he dies. It is a fable of the breaking or numbing of a civilised man. . . . Albert Wright was bookish, brilliant, sensitive, like so many clever men, unsure of himself. But when he was fourteen, the Gold Rush began; shepherds and cattlemen abruptly left their herds and

the boy was taken from school and sent up for six years to work on the half-deserted runs in almost complete solitude. In the saddle all day, at night physically exhausted and utterly lonely and frightened in his hut, he gave up his books—or rather, the ants ate them—saw his youth mangled and stunted. One or two shepherds, half crazed by a life of isolation, or one or two cattlemen with violent, guilt-born ideas about the aborigines they had robbed, were his only occasional acquaintances. He came back hardened, fine to look at, speechless. Marriage healed the wound to some extent but when he set up as a cattleman, buying and driving 'mobs' from one remote pasture to the next, spurred on by the idea of fortune or a sound, settled life, nature met him head-on. Drought and flood, drought and flood, grass fires, disease, cattle and horses dying, debts piling up, sick children, a wife worn out: the struggle with nature is epic, but he met the rankling grind, the sheer sourness of the epic existence. At fifty, his marvellous body gave out. The muscles could stand no more. Awakening again, in his last weeks, his mind rediscovered its early doubts. The white man had stolen; he had crime and blood on his conscience. He had been fortune mad. If there had ever been an Australian dream, it had been betrayed. It is one of the savage jokes of his situation that after he had died, broken, his remarkable wife saved the family fortunes, by character and hard work, but also because the rise in land values had, almost frivolously, wiped out years of debt in a few months. (p. 280)

As a diarist Albert Wright spent more time putting down worry than recording easier times. After all, rain did fall without flooding, the grass was sometimes green, the lambing was good, there were landscapes of rapturous beauty. In time, the aboriginals became comprehensible; through the diaries, one gets the small details that make an empty scene distinct. The twanging of Jews'-harps or some other home-made instrument on the verandahs, when the drovers and shepherds were resting, annoyed Albert Wright. He felt himself under surveillance in the bush and, once or twice, imagined that some black warrior beckoned to him to 'come over' from the fret of the white man's life. Self-absorbed, he was a long time unaware of the new Australians growing up, pitiable but hopeful. When we turn to those passages that come from the records of his remarkable widow, there is more serenity. Albert Wright's one positive achievement, perhaps, was to have informed and supported and equipped someone really stronger than himself. At any rate, she emerges as the clever, confident, bossy, charming and cunning widow who in the end reigns, like a queen.

It is odd and a great relief to read a book of pioneer life which scarcely mentions religion, and which does not push down our throats the conventional colonial optimism or the thick porridge of moral self-commendation. Miss Judith Wright is a sceptical writer, or at any rate, one who is austerely aware that a price has to be paid for new worlds. She is also free of that family complacency which affects so many writers when they are describing their pioneer forbears. She has avoided the patriotic clichés, she has genuinely uncovered the daily life of a century and offers us no moral. A good style and a graceful, independent mind have given a dramatic interest to a subject which is usually overburdened with moral sobriety. (p. 281)

> V. S. Pritchett, "The Bush Fire," in New Statesman, Vol. LVIII, No. 1486, September 5, 1959, pp. 280-81.

LEONIE KRAMER

The arts of history, biography and fiction demand very different, often opposite talents, and to find all three successfully practised in one book is a rare and remarkable experience. In *The Generations of Men* Judith Wright has accomplished a *tour-de-force*. Using the diaries, letters and memoirs of her grandfather and grandmother, who were born in the Hunter Valley in the middle of the last century, she has reconstructed a story of pastoral pioneering into the outback of New South Wales, Queensland and the Gulf country which, for its historical interest alone, must surely remain an important contribution to Australian writing.

Judith Wright is fortunate in that, throughout his life of backbreaking work and continual struggle to build up properties in harsh and fever-ridden country, Albert Wright found time each day to keep a diary. This was not, as might have been expected, merely a record of the daily events of his life, but also a repository for his thoughts and feelings. It was to him a bulwark against loneliness; and, lacking companions with whom he could discuss his ambitions and apprehensions, he told them to his diary. Out of this material Judith Wright has conjured a vivid character—a man of great physical stamina, of courage and endurance, whose determination to fight and conquer the land he acquired was balanced by an often morose and despairing introspectiveness. (pp. 173-74)

In drawing this portrait of her grandfather, Judith Wright has shown herself to be a biographer of rare sensitivity; and at the same time she has employed, in the portrait itself and in the structure of the book, a novelist's feeling for narrative and drama. It seems clear that she herself has a profound sympathy for Albert Wright. Perhaps she would say, as Henry Handel Richardson said of Richard Mahony, that in drawing him she has also drawn herself. In doing so she has gone beyond the truth of biography and given us at times a taste of the more elusive truth of fiction.

This possibly explains what is otherwise a very curious aspect of the book. Until the last few chapters, which deal with the years after Albert's death, his wife May remains a shadowy, almost unreal figure. She is in the forefront of Albert's thoughts, as a source of strength and inspiration, but she is in the background of the book.... [She] never speaks to us or comes alive as Albert does. It may be that Judith Wright had less material to guide her in her portrayal of May, but it seems rather that she gave most of her sympathy and all her imagination to the man who was, for her, the more accessible, perhaps even the more significant character.

Judith Wright's fine sense of discipline has produced a biographical study which has the excitement of a novel. The sources of her narrative are never obtrusive; actual quotations from the diaries and letters are used sparingly and with an eye for their dramatic effect, and the cumbersome and often distracting apparatus of footnotes and appendixes is omitted. Moreover, apart from its biographical interest, the book is a saga of Australia's pastoral development in the last fifty years of the nineteenth century. About the Wrights themselves we feel the presence of those many people who, like them, doggedly drove their herds of cattle and dragged their stores and household goods over miles of lonely country. (p. 174)

The past that is the subject of this book illuminates the present; though it is not possible to believe that others were as sensitive as Albert to the fact that they had made their lives at the expense of the original owners of the land. Albert sees himself as a member of a haunted generation—haunted by the ghosts of murdered and dispossessed blacks. Perhaps one can detect the voice of his granddaughter in his apprehension that these ghosts

will never be laid, but will remain with this country for ever, "making every achievement empty and every struggle vain".

Judith Wright's prose transmits particularly well the atmosphere of the times, and the arid beauty of the country. Sometimes, especially when dealing with Albert's thoughts and moods of gloomy self-analysis, it becomes over-emphatic and cliché-ridden. But it would be captious to labour this point in a book that has so many merits, not the least of which is that, although so much of it concerns the recurring operations of station life, it commands interest and attention from the first page to the last. (pp. 174-75)

Leonie Kramer, "Portrait of a Pioneer," in Southerly, *Vol. 20, No. 3, 1959, pp. 173-75.*

RUSSEL WARD

In *The Generations of Men* Judith Wright tells the story of her ancestors, who were among the first pastoralists in western Queensland and in the New England district of New South Wales in the last century. (p. 211)

In 1830 George Wyndham's convict servants built for him 'Dalwood', a beautiful stone house about twenty miles up the Hunter River valley from Maitland, [Australia].... One of Wyndham's granddaughters married Albert Wright and so became the grandmother of the poet, Judith Wright McKinney.

Though young Albert was said by his masters at the King's School, Parramatta, to be a brilliant scholar, he had to begin work when he was only fourteen.... Such premature shouldering of responsibility was not unusual, here, then. The boy stayed on the distant station until he was twenty. He lived alone in a bark hut. The only light at night was that provided by a slush-lamp. For months on end he often saw no one but a half-mad shepherd. For the first few years he tried to go on studying by himself, but his daylight work was so exacting that it forced him to realize he would never be able to learn much more as long as fate kept him on the inland runs. Fate faithfully did so for the rest of his life. This was not unusual then either. He died in 1890 of pneumonia, which developed from a chill caught on a new run in the Gulf of Carpentaria country. He was still heavily in debt.

Despite the unanimous advice of relatives, friends and creditors, his widow, May, battled on alone to make a better life for their children; and despite doubtless well-meant criticism of her 'un-ladylike' behaviour, and the more considerable obstacle presented by the great depression of the 1890s, she succeeded. When she died in 1929 'Wongwibinda', in the rugged 'falls country' on the coastward edge of the New England tableland, was one of the most prosperous stations in the district. The dead man, who had had to spend his life wrestling with land instead of with ideas, would have been pleased. More comforting still, perhaps, for his shade to have known that within the next thirty years one of his descendants would be one of the leading Australian poets of her generation.... (pp. 213-14)

However, to those who took part in the story only its epilogue seemed reasonably happy. Much of Albert and May Wright's married life was spent on Nunalbin and other Queensland runs inland from Rockhampton. Here they lost one child and were almost chronically ill themselves from overwork, undernourishment and lack of medical care, and in the end they left the district poorer than when they had entered it. Judith Wright has resisted the temptation to romanticise the hard facts of the tale recorded in her grandfather's diaries. The unremitting and disheartening fight with drought, fire, flood, creditors, sickness, distance, flies, mosquitoes and more drought is seen through the eyes of those who fought it—as they saw it from day to day at the time, not as it seemed in the pleasant afterglow of reminiscence. One result is that the reader never has the feeling, so usual when reading an historical novel, that he is watching an artificial period-piece or costume melodrama. Another result was to make it easy for one asinine English reviewer to make fun of the book as a kind of antipodean *Cold Comfort Farm*. With more insight and truth [V. S. Pritchett (see excerpt above)] saw in it a moving assessment of the heavy price paid by human beings who set out to conquer and civilize a savage continent. (p. 214)

> *Russel Ward, "Pastoral Saga," in* Meanjin, *Vol. XIX, No. 2, June, 1960, pp. 211-15.*

H. P. HESELTINE

When Judith Wright's *The Moving Image* first appeared in 1946 it must have derived some of its force and urgency from the contemporary aptness of welding love poetry with wartime imagery. The third re-print by The Meanjin Press sixteen years later reveals that the impact of *The Moving Image* cannot have been solely, or even chiefly, due to its timeliness; it is one of the important books of twentieth century Australian poetry. Some of its poems, such as "Bullocky", "South of My Days", and "The Company of Lovers", have become standard display pieces. But the significance of *The Moving Image* rests in more than a number of individual poems. There is a more than schematic aptness in suggesting that the historical achievement of the book was to bring together the philosophic bent of Baylebridge and the personal passion of Mackenzie within the bounds of a single sensibility.

Judith Wright actually succeeded in making poetry out of her philosophy—most notably, of course, and most single-mindedly in the title poem of the collection, "The Moving Image". Unlike Baylebridge, she realized her ideas in specific, concrete images and gave to her thought a forward drive powered by the metaphoric thrust of her language. However, her philosophic writing does not constitute a separate node of interest in her poetry. Her concern with time is infused into her two other great themes—her relation to the Australian land and its past and the love between man and woman. She does not bring the direct physical ardour of Mackenzie to her love poems, but she matches him in emotional intensity, and betters him in her sense of the value of a formal verse structure.

It is perhaps strange to speak, as it were, historically of the first volume of a still living and productive writer; it is a tribute to Judith Wright's assured achievement that one is able to do so.

> *H. P. Heseltine, in a review of "The Moving Image," in* Meanjin, *Vol. XXI, No. 4, December, 1962, p. 497.*

S. E. LEE

Birds, I'm sure, Judith Wright herself regards as a diversion from the main stream of her serious verse—brilliant and moving as some of the individual poems are. . . .

Judith Wright's slender volume, we're told, developed from the "bird poems" she wrote to entertain her young daughter.

But it is much more than this; though, as one brought up on "Bell Birds" and "My Country", I envy the new generations of school children who'll share the funny "Swamp Pheasant", the kindly old "Pelican", the rude "Apostle Birds" and the simple lyricism of "Magpies" and "Thornbills" with Judith Wright's privileged daughter. Australian children's verse is singularly deficient in poetry, especially poetry of this order. . . . (p. 137)

But *Birds* is scarcely a children's volume—though I do feel teachers are over solicitous in protecting children from adult literature and the realities of living it unfolds. As Miss Wright's poetic imagination and intellect quicken, what may have begun as a simple descriptive piece will suddenly deepen into a contemplation of the relentless and inevitable cruelty of existence—birdlike and human. . . . The silver terns diving for fish and being torn to pieces by bonito have obvious correspondences in modern industrial life; while the "Lory" hunted by butcher-bird and crow symbolizes, to me anyway, the "terrible beauty" Yeats saw in life: the observation that beauty and cruelty so often go together.

The voice of the creator of *The Moving Image* and *Woman to Man* is clearly heard in the poems where a blood relationship almost is sensed with the wounded, the fallen and the defeated "Migrant Swift" and "Rainbow-bird." . . . (pp. 137-38)

There are mystic undertones, too, as now the worship of blue by "Satin Bower-birds" and the symbolic colouring of a "Black-shouldered Kite" are suggested; or the harsh pangs of birth, the mystery of Genesis, is recalled by a childhood memory of the hatching out of "three frail and powdered eggs." . . .

Birds might not tell us a great deal about Judith Wright's poetic development; but the freshness of the vision and the simplicity of statement will delight those whose taste runs more to the direct and simpler lyricism of the volumes before *The Gateway* and *The Two Fires*. All admirers of this fine poet will welcome hearing her voice again, especially as it reveals a lighter facet of the poetic personality not hitherto revealed. (p. 138)

> *S. E. Lee, "Poetry of Distinction," in* Southerly, *Vol. 23, No. 2, 1963, pp. 137-41.*

R. F. BRISSENDEN

The publication of [*Five Senses: Selected Poems*] . . . is a significant event. The volume does not include everything [Miss Wright] has written, but it is remarkably comprehensive nonetheless; and, since the selection has been made by the poet herself, we may assume that in it she has brought together the poems which she regards as most enduring and representative. *Five Senses*, indeed, enables us to see very clearly those qualities in her work which are peculiarly her own: it exhibits the essential form and meaning of her art and the pattern of its development. She has been publishing poetry now for nearly a quarter of a century: to see the best poems of these years assembled in one volume is to realise, with a fresh shock of pleasure and excitement, the weight and substance of her poetic achievement, and also its remarkable unity and coherence. In "The Morning of the Dead", for instance, the penultimate piece in the collection, and one of the most impressive of her late poems, the themes are basically the same as those in "The Moving Image", the title poem of her first volume. Each is a meditation on the problem of how to give meaning to, or discover meaning in, this "flowing and furious world". The earlier poem with its imagery still redolent of "the green world of a child'', has a youthful spontaneity and abundance which are immediately engaging; and it is infused with that sense of personal shock which comes to each of us when ''the clock begins to race'', and we have to acknowledge the uncomfortable realities of time and death. But ''The Moving Image'', when it is placed beside her later work, seems confused and unsure; and it is significant that Miss Wright has omitted one of its three sections from *Five Senses*. ''The Morning of the Dead'' is a much more compact poem than ''The Moving Image'', but it is also much more lucid and meaningful: in it the poet has attained something like that deceptive translucence, that suggestion of ''depth on crystal depth'', which she has taught us to look for in the poetry of John Shaw Neilson.

The production of a poem so impressive as ''**The Morning of the Dead**'' (about which I shall have more to say later) and of the simple, strong, flexible style in which it is written, are evidence of the extent to which Judith Wright has developed as a poet. In bulk, however, her later poetry may seem to some readers curiously disappointing. *Woman to Man*, first published in 1949, in some ways is still the most substantial of the five volumes of verse which she has brought out, and it may well be that the passionate, intensely personal and feminine love poems in that book represent the peak of her achievement. She has not ceased entirely to write poetry of this kind: two of the finest of her recent poems are ''**For my Daughter**'', and ''**Age to Youth**''. Since *Woman to Man,* however, the affairs of individual men and women seem to have interested her less and less: birds, animals, insects, trees and flowers—these things increasingly have formed the subjects of her poetry. The results have not always been happy. *Birds,* the most recent of the individual volumes of her poetry to appear, is also the weakest and least interesting: while it contains some fine pieces, the collection as a whole exhibits a strange uncertainty of tone, betraying at times an unfortunate tendency on the part of the poet to humanise—perhaps even sentimentalise—her subjects. Miss Wright herself may not be completely satisfied with these poems either, for only three of them are included in *Five Senses.*

It would, however, be misleading to suggest that humanity has been excluded from her poetic world. The reverse is true: the majority of her poems are still concerned either with some general aspect of human life or with her own individual response to some general problem. ''General'' is the operative word: the particular incident, the particular moment of ecstasy, grief or illumination, now rarely forms the direct subject of her poetry. Human affairs are now seen *sub specie aeternitatis,* life is regarded not as something self-sufficient, but as part of some universal process. It is because of this, perhaps, that much of what she has written in recent years seems too detached, remote and impersonal. But the strenuous effort to attain such a total comprehension has also resulted in some of her most distinctive and successful poems. Poems such as ''**Return**'', ''**Nameless Flower**'', ''**The Lake**'', ''**Interplay**''—to name but a few—have a spareness and simplicity which is superficial merely: they contain in fact a wealth of dense and complex meaning. (pp. 85-7)

Five Senses demonstrates conclusively that Miss Wright is in every sense of the word a metaphysical poet. Nothing could be closer to the mode and texture of seventeenth century verse, for instance, than ''**Flesh**''—a grave and witty meditation on the contradictions of the human condition reminiscent of Marvell's ''Dialogue between the Soul and Body''. . . . But it is more than her wit and literary affinities which entitle us to describe Judith Wright's poetry as metaphysical. The themes

with which she is preoccupied—the nature of reality and how we apprehend it, the status of values, the problem of meaning and communication—these are metaphysical in the strictest sense: they comprehend the basic ontological and epistemological issues. And it is clear that her concern with them is that of the philosopher as much as it is that of the poet. (p. 87)

[It is clear that Miss Wright] regards cognition as creative in more than a theoretical or analogical sense: the seer and the sight double in their interchange like lovers, and love is meaningless unless it is fruitful. ''Earth'' she writes in ''**A Child's Nightmare**'' is ''Bodied in beast and man and bird'', and it is through them that

> She seeks her vision and her fear,
> old Chaos and the shaping Word.

In so far as the universe is meaningful, its meaning is achieved through the medium of the intelligent beings who inhabit it and give shape to its primal chaos. . . . The growth of meaning, the clarification of man's communal vision of the world, is conceived by the poet to be an evolutionary (or cyclical) process, a process, moreover, which takes on an energy and life of its own. . . . ''Learning,'' she writes, ''desires so to transcend itself that nothing's left to learn.'' As human beings we are inevitably involved in this process, and the involvement is mysterious and paradoxical: we consciously contribute to it, but at the same time it works through us in a way that is quite impersonal. This I take to be the theme of ''**Five Senses**'', the poem which gives the title to the collection. . . . (pp. 88-9)

But although the [learning] process goes on inevitably it imposes, in a religious manner, obligations on us all to participate in it—especially on the poet and the artist. And this obligation makes itself apparent most sharply in the responsibility we owe to the dead: ''What drives us is the dead, their thorned desire'', and what the dead desire is the perfection of their meaning. The task of the artist, of the thinker, then is the perpetual and creative re-interpretation of the past, or of the past in the present. . . . (p. 89)

The poet whose task it is to interpret is an especially gifted person, but he is still a representative human being: the task of reinterpretation is one in which, whether we like it or not, we are all engaged. And this task, Judith Wright insists, is creative—in our expression of what the reality we have apprehended means to us we bring something new into existence: a poem, a philosophical theory, a mathematical theorem. And this in turn modifies the universe: the knower effectually acts upon the known, contributes to that process of change, that Heracleitean fire in which all things are involved. No interpretation, no meaning, therefore can be absolutely correct, for by the mere fact of its coming into existence it alters the situation which the interpreter has been contemplating. (p. 90)

The vision of the world embodied in the poems I have been discussing is individual and hard-won: a vision gained and preserved by that long and lonely wrestle with ideas and words through which every good poet must go. Despite its undoubted originality, however, it seems to me to bear some rather striking affinities with the work of Wallace Stevens. Since Stevens was himself one of the most original and important poets writing in English in this century such affinities are worth noting. Both poets have been fascinated by the problems of the relation of language to reality: like Stevens, Judith Wright is fired with the ''rage for order'', and she shares with him an appreciation, in her case a religious reverence, for the creative power of the word. Stevens, of course, is explicitly nonreligious, and he differs from Judith Wright also in the almost solipsistic rigour with which he emphasises the supremacy of the poetic fiction. But the questions with which she has become increasingly preoccupied are those in the contemplation of which Stevens, throughout his poetic life, found an unfailing source of inspiration. In a piece such as ''The Idea of Order at Key West'' for instance (from which the epigraph to these observations has been taken) he is moving within the same world as that which Judith Wright has been exploring. That her forays into this difficult and perplexing territory have been at once so illuminating and so distinctively her own is a mark of her poetic stature. (pp. 90-1)

> *R. F. Brissenden, in a review of ''Five Senses,'' in* The Australian Quarterly, *Vol. XXXVI, No. 1, March, 1964, pp. 85-91.*

THE TIMES LITERARY SUPPLEMENT

Five Senses is Miss Judith Wright's selection of what she considers to be her finest work to date. These poems, about people, landscapes and animals, are good when she describes her subjects directly. In **''Brother and Sisters''**, for example, a brother and two sisters stay on at the end of a road that had ''turned out to be a cul-de-sac''; the bush gradually encroaches on their loneliness:

> The wrinkled ewes snatch pansies through the fence
> and stare with shallow eyes into the garden. . . .
>   The wall
> groans in the night and settles more awry.

Miss Wright only occasionally attains this simplicity . . . , as much of her work is weakened by conventionality of language, like ''And all my pastures rise as green as spring''. Too often her figurative use of words gets in the way of what she is trying to say. . . . There are too many apostrophes, ''O world, you sly thief''. The metaphors deaden the image instead of bringing it alive, ''The trumpet of the rising sun bursts into sound''. Potentially good poems are ruined throughout this book by unreal trappings of this kind. Miss Wright is a writer who might ponder William Carlos Williams's phrase ''no truth but in things'' and remember that ''direct treatment of the object'' is an essential of good poetry.

> *''Australian Poets,'' in* The Times Literary Supplement, *No. 3263, September 10, 1964, p. 842.*

JOHN COLMER

Some of Judith Wright's stories in *The Nature of Love* have already been published in various periodicals and are therefore familiar. These alone should have been sufficient to remind me that the connection between Judith Wright's poetry and fiction lies chiefly in the themes (childhood, the past, the destruction of old ways of life, the plight of the aboriginal) rather than in the mode of vision or the handling of the language. Of course, there is no reason why there should be any similarity of language, since it is a vulgar error that poets always write ''poetically''. And yet I think it is legitimate to expect that image will play a more important part than character or narrative line. The curious thing about the short stories in *The Nature of Love* is that mere story-telling, whether it is autobiographical reminiscence or invented anecdote, plays so large a part. The best stories are the ones that focus on isolated moments of experience and not those like **''Eighty Acres''** that use a shallow narrator to tell a laudable but not very intensely

imagined story about small-town life and the protection of aboriginals. **''The Lame Duck''** . . . illustrates the disruptive power exercised by a selfish bank manager's widow over a young couple whose love seems so secure until it is put to the test and its shallow basis revealed. In this story and in **''The Vineyard Woman''**, Judith Wright explores the psychology of love with deep insight. She understands the pain of relinquishing familiar patterns of living. She is more at home with the old than the young, those forced by time to recognise the cruelty and selfishness of love and to accept their own frailty and the bitter fruits of self-knowledge.

Although her public conscience often tempts her to deal with social issues, her real strength lies in her Wordsworthian capacity to create simply solitary figures. . . .

Jim in **''The Dugong''** has something of the stoic patience of Wordsworth's Leechgatherer, and the fusion of man and sea-beast into a single image recalls a familiar passage from that poem. All lovers of Judith Wright's other works will enjoy these stories. Uneven as they are, they are the characteristic expressions of a deeply sensitive mind.

> *John Colmer, in a review of ''The Nature of Love,'' in* Australian Book Review, *Vol. 6, No. 4, February, 1967, p. 44.*

D. M. THOMAS

Theme searches for form, and form for theme: 'You are half of some other who may never come,' as the girl tells her image in Judith Wright's **''Naked Girl and Mirror.''** When the match is right, the resulting poem is a constantly surprised act of love, the more beautiful, more poignant, the closer it nears the unattainable—finally *undesirable*—synthesis. . . . [*The Other Half* shows] the crucial nature of the search.

As often as not the iambic (particularly iambic pentameter) is the Cressida whom the English-speaking poet panders into the wrong bed. Such is sometimes the case with Judith Wright. One is a little surprised that a poet with her passionate concern for the mating of halves should let all her themes surrender, apparently, to the same succubus. At a first reading, [*The Other Half*] seems monotonous—a pity, as there is a great variety of subject-matter. Words become enslaved by the metre. . . . (p. 70)

The collection could, I think, have gained from some excising and tightening up. But I don't want to exaggerate that. Growing acquaintance leads one to turn her pages admiringly and (not common these days) affectionately. Her Australian landscape—snakeskin, red rock, creek and jungle-bird—is the setting for her attempt to connect self and not-self, microcosm and macrocosm. Language is the point at which they touch. . . . In **''Camping at Split Rock,''** a characteristically subtle yet unstrained metaphor likens the 'room to live' carved by water out of red rock to the way 'the age-old word / runs on in language and from obstinate dark / hollows us room for seeing'. In the lovely sequence **''New Guinea Legend: The Finding of the Moon,''** Aruako, the lazy, despised village-Endymion, is a poet who, in laying his dark face against the new moon's white, validates both their incomplete existences.

An important, closely related preoccupation is the onset of life's 'other half'; as though, having found herself she must now find the world. In these menopausal poems, she is not afraid of the grand statement. (pp. 70-1)

Whenever [Judith Wright] is most passionately engaged with [her] major themes—and passion there is, in these love-poems between man and the cosmos, behind the deceptively slight-looking feminine body of her work—the basic iambic line moves with an athletic grace to her voice's sincere, gentle resonance; becomes . . . skilfully varied with caesuras and alexandrines. There are at least a dozen poems here where the other half has brilliantly come. She is a very fine poet, still outrageously neglected in [Great Britain]. (p. 71)

D. M. Thomas, in a review of "The Other Half," in London Magazine, *n.s. Vol. 7, No. 2, May, 1967, pp. 70-1.*

S. E. LEE

Miss Wright's poetry does not belong to the ivory tower—her own experiences as housewife, mother and witty observer of the city scene are glimpsed from time to time. At its best her poetry is generated from within, involves the poet in articulate and passionately intelligent attempts to analyse her own complex thoughts and feelings. The poet emerges as a rare combination of metaphysical thinker (after the manner of Baylebridge), intuitive mystic (one thinks of Shaw Neilson here) and down-to-earth realist (the competent mother and housewife). The best poems then integrate the intellect, passion, imagination and commonsense of the thinker-mystic-poet-country wife. In [*The Other Half*], Miss Wright's new concern is to analyse and look for a resolution between those two selves that we know and often fail to reconcile: for example that public *alter ego* that the inside "I" glimpses from time to time with a slight start in the mirror or in a photograph (**"Naked Girl and Mirror"**), or the private subconscious self that defies analysis by the conscious self (**"The Other Half"**), "the self that night undrowns when I'm asleep". Does the poet come to any kind of philosophic and emotional reconciliation of these divided selves? I think she does; and in different ways. First through Art—the truths and insights that come to us with vivid clarity in dream images, but then defy our attempts to pin them down in plain rational words, are the transcendental and elusive truths that artists embody in their creations. . . . The reconciliation is found too in the acceptance of Time and Death as inevitable processes. As we go through life, Time destroys so many selves (first the baby, then the girl, the youth and the young housewife) so that a new and more mature self might be created. . . . Love—ordinary human love, the love of husband for wife, mother for child and so on—is however the great liberating and unifying force. The nature of this love is beautifully illustrated in a short poem called **"The Curtain"**, in which the mother-poet gazes down upon her sleeping daughter now grown up into another person who has forgotten much of her childhood though she lies "in the same unaltered room". **"Clock and Heart"** perhaps brings together all three of the themes I have mentioned. Here Time and Art find their reconciliation in human Love. I think here that not only has the poet reasoned and felt her way to a satisfying intellectual and emotional reconciliation of a complex personal problem but that the resolution is achieved in a beautifully structured and disciplined verse. . . . Poems like [**"Clock and Heart"**] show that Miss Wright's artistic development is not limited to an exploration of new themes or a re-examination of old ones. Increasingly, as she seeks the forms that will best embody her ideas, Miss Wright shows a craftsmanlike mastery of verse technique. Consequently the poetry has more "tension", the tension that James McAuley has written about so illuminatingly

and which results when thought and feeling strain within disciplined verse forms. A poem like **"Clock and Heart"** generates its own energy. (pp. 66-7)

S. E. Lee, "Poetic Fisticuffs," in Southerly, *Vol. 27, No. 1, 1967, pp. 60-71.*

K. L. GOODWIN

Judith Wright's [latest poems] are among the best she has ever written. Her *Collected Poems 1942-1970* concludes with a group written since 1966 under the title **"Shadow: 1970"**. Here she is writing with great maturity and assurance, with direct passion and with subtle irony. Some of her earlier poems used metaphysical notions insistently, drily, or irrelevantly; now such notions form part of the natural fabric of her work. (p. 502)

Some of the recent poems reach out to encompass material fashionable among younger poets. But instead of subverting the material into reflections of her own mind, Judith Wright applies intellectual energy to search for some coherence, order, or meaning in it. **"The City"** draws on images of pollution and high-rise buildings and incorporates them as part of a numbing, Edwin Muir-like apocalyptic vision; **"Christmas Ballad"** presents a horrifying portrait of a 'survivor' of the Vietnam war. (p. 503)

K. L. Goodwin, in a review of "Collected Poems 1942-1970," in Meanjin, *Vol. 31, No. 4, December, 1972, pp. 502-03.*

A. D. HOPE

The young poet of *The Moving Image* was no amateur: [Wright] had at least twenty years of apprenticeship to poetry behind her and unlike most young poets of her generation she had resisted the temptation to publish her prentice work. **"The Moving Image"**, the first poem in the book, is a mature performance. It is an uncompromising prolonged philosophical meditation on the place and task of the poet in the universe, the cracking of the mould of the mind by its effort to take in something beyond its power, so that the poet only becomes capable by becoming mad in the ordinary view of mind. The poem continues to survey the scope of the song that must issue from the mouth of the possessed poet as he becomes the means by which the universe in its wholeness and its minutest parts, by which all history and all civilization gives tongue and renews the song of the world at every instant. This great metaphysical vision of the nature of poetry is what the poet puts before herself as a manifesto and a programme and one could say that the whole of the rest of her poetry develops this theme and issues from it. Nothing could be more unlike the debut, hesitating, probing, trying its wings, of the usual first book of verse. Judith Wright is conscious of herself and her task from the start. The poetry will adventure into new fields, it will develop new methods and discover new resources in the years to follow, but the credo will remain the same and the vision will remain unmoved.

The fundamentals of this credo can be simply expressed more or less as follows. The poet reflecting on her childhood, on that long awakening that is growing up, and on the nature and operation of time, perceives that in her case there was a moment of choice or decision forced upon her. The first effect of this is awareness of Time, which in childhood has some of the characters of eternity. At this point which is both one of choice of a life pattern and realization of the nature of the world 'the clock begins to race', she is fully immersed in time. . . . [The poet] rejects the natural wish to return to the child's almost timeless world: 'the lovelier distance is ahead.' She realizes that she is a maker, the maker not only as poet, but the maker of time and fear which are the material out of which poetry is to be made. . . . (pp. 7-8)

["**The Moving Image**"] moves next to the New England landscape on which there is a new airfield with the dust blowing away and into eyes and mouth—an airfield that stands for the modern technocratic world; from the aeroplane the mystery and beauty of the land shrink to meagre geographical commonplaces, 'the world is evil and small'; there is nothing left to do in our destructive age but wait for the high tide of life to return, 'roar from our depths and send us mad again'. (p. 8)

From the task of life the poem moves on to that of the poet to listen to the inchoate sound of becoming in every part of the world and its life and to give it coherence and form in the word. The poet's task is to help the unpausing birth of the world and to give birth herself to the word that celebrates it. This remarkable metaphysical poem stands as preface to ''Poems 1940-1944'' which makes up the rest of *The Moving Image*.

So universal a programme is for all the poets of all time. It is natural to expect each poet to limit himself, to choose those parts of the human experience to which he feels himself called. *The Moving Image* does indeed fall into poems which group themselves, and the groups are those which define all the chosen paths of Judith Wright's poetry at that time and later. Fundamental to these is the theme of the life of woman, the special metaphysical vision of woman which she has in virtue of being a special kind of human being, and a special kind of living being—for to be female is to be more than a part of the human race. In the past the forms and the vision that constitute poetry have, on the whole, been those determined by the great poets and these have nearly all been men. Women when they entered the field have tended to speak in the forms prescribed. They have not been able to give that 'new word' which makes explicit the peculiar and unique experience of generation, of birth and death, of love and desolation, which can arise from feminine experience alone. This task of speaking the original native word not translated into masculine terms is implicit in the programme outlined for herself by the young poet in "**The Moving Image**" and it is necessary to mention it here because it is fundamental to all her poetry and colours it subtly, influences its forms and its 'tone of voice' in such a way that one could speak of her in a real sense as a *poetess*, without any of the implications of mediocrity, of sentimentalism or of patronage, that the term usually carries with it.

Actually only one or two poems in this first volume specifically devote themselves to this sort of theme. The majority form a celebration of the countryside and people of the world in which Judith Wright grew up, the area rather vaguely indicated by the term 'New England'. . . . New England is an idea in the heart and the mind. Judith Wright may be said to have created it in poetry as her forefathers helped to create it in fact. . . . The poet creates its image, makes it accessible to men as an idea and as a feeling, and it begins to take shape as a fact to form a recognized part of its world. (pp. 8-10)

All the poems of *The Moving Image*, except "**The Company of Lovers**", are set firmly in, and help in turn to set forth, the picture of New England, its landscape, its history, its daily life. "**Bora Ring**", "**Nigger's Leap: New England**", and "**Half-caste Girl**" evoke its pre-history and the tragic fate of the

earliest inhabitants. "**Blue Arab**" and "**Trapped Dingo**" begin that theme which broadens like a river growing from its source through all her poetry: and theme of the animals, the birds, the willing and the involuntary fellow-travellers of mankind in their exploitation of the planet; the theme of the creatures who give her own country a distinctive and beautiful strangeness when set against the rest of the world; the theme in which dumb life finds its 'word' in the poetic imagination. "**Waiting**," "**Remittance Man**", "**Country Town**", "**Sonnet**", "**Bullocky**", and "**For New England**" recreate aspects of the daily life, now and in the past, of the people of this harsh and beautiful countryside. "**The Hawthorn Hedge**", "**South of My Days**", and "**Brothers and Sisters**" form the personal pupil of this eye that surveys the whole, the life of a particular family, rooted in this austere soil and its granite bedrock.

But this tiny first volume, which is so like a litter of puppies, contains two other specimen poems of what have not always proved to be Judith Wright's most successful lines of development: the poems in which she appears in the rôles of prophet and of socio-political commentator. Her war-poem, "**The Trains**", is in fact the more successful of the two, since its comment is not explicit and it avoids the kind of rhetoric into which some of her later political verse is apt to fall. "**To A.H., New Year, 1943**" moves into prophecy only at the end, but it is a personal poem to which the prophetic note is entirely appropriate and convincing as it is not in some later poems which move along this line of country. (pp. 10-11)

[It was initially the] sense of discovering a poet in whom not only the landscape but the whole life of the country was concentrated, that struck me first as I tasted my way round her table of contents [in *The Moving Image*] like Goldilocks breakfasting at the house of the three bears. All the poems seemed to me good, but this one was a bit flat and talkative in parts and that one had a message showing too obviously under the narrative or the meditative medium. And then I came upon "**Bullocky**" and said: 'This is just right'. It is still one of Judith Wright's best and best known poems. It has a finish and a finality that none of the other poems in her first volume quite possesses. Perhaps they were not meant to possess the inevitability of great poetry. . . . But this one poem, "**Bullocky**", has it and stands out from them, because of it. (p. 11)

Woman to Man, [Wright's] next book of poems, is a stronger, more various and more profound book, though it breaks no new ground. Its bias is different; the majority of the poems are now openly metaphysical where before they were mainly so by implication. In particular, many of them are devoted to those experiences of love and love-making from the woman's side on which so few women have commented in poetry. They have written much of love but not much of making love. . . . Where the earlier volume begins with a quotation from Plato, this begins with a quotation from Francis Bacon about love as the basic principle of all the notions of the universe. And it is love in this metaphysical sense, containing and infusing all love in the physical or the spiritual sense, that is largely the theme of *Woman to Man*. (p. 12)

[The] love-poems of *Woman to Man* depart [radically] from the 'masculine' attitudes common to most poetry in the poems of this sort by either sex in the past. In poems like "**Woman to Man**", "**Woman's Song**", "**Woman to Child**", the love of individuals for each other—of woman for man, of mother for child born or yet unborn—is not presented as a relationship which is contained in and penetrated by the continuous epic of generation, in which the personal affection is the core, but becomes also a means of apprehending the world of being and becoming. The centre of this world is not love-making but life-making. . . . And the whole visible sensible world partakes in this mystery of gestation and birth when the poet as woman takes them into her mind, in a poem like **"The Maker"**, as into a womb in which they grow another nature and are finally born into poetry. These opening poems are beautifully sexual but it is the sexuality of the whole mystery of reproduction, felt as one process and directed to one end. And it is presented not notionally or intellectually as by a poet like Lucretius, but as a matter of direct experience, participation and implicit insight. I doubt if any man could have written, even if he could have imagined, the two poems with the title of **"The Unborn"**, where the life that perished without getting past the first stage of pregnancy speaks first through the mother and then, answering, for itself.

The rest of the poems in *Woman to Man* carry on the themes of *The Moving Image* but with more precision of language and a more realized feeling for form. The life of the countryside and the country towns goes on in a series like **"The Blind Man"**, but it comes with a new sense of a past and future that go beyond depiction; these are metaphysical poems in a country setting. Here, too, are experiments like the curious, cadenced and matched prose lines of the long poem 'Letter to a Friend'—not a successful experiment, I think. Away from the guide and map of metrical form it grows diffuse and desultory.

The Gateway, published four years later, seems a straight continuation of the themes and practice of *Woman to Man*. Its opening poem, **"Dark Gift"**, is a companion piece on the same theme as **"Midnight"** in the previous volume. And yet there is a progression between the two, rather like the stages of growth in a plant which is the central image of both poems. . . . The first poem is wholly within the process of time but, in the second, life becomes the key that opens the doors of Eternity. There is indeed, in these earlier volumes, a remarkable sense of a constantly unfolding vision that reminds me of Blake, and it is marked by constantly growing lyric tension. The sensory world remains as vivid as ever and is even more passionately apprehended and presented. What is added is the outlook that Blake had of using the world of the senses not as objects to be examined and questioned but as windows opening on the vistas of a world beyond their own experience.

But there is another process emerging in this volume and, though apparently with the same end in view, actually leading in quite another direction. It begins, I think, with a poem called **"The Journey"**, about a pilot who is sent out alone to find the Blessed Isles from a world dictatorship. And he does just that but, flying his plane over the immaculate archipelago, fails to notice that he is nearing the metaphysical cliff-edge that divides time from eternity; he crashes and is lost. It is an unusual poem for Judith Wright to attempt, and in its way a successful one, yet it strikes a chill because its deliberate and obvious symbolism—indeed its patent allegory—is the very opposite of the metaphysical vision that is characteristic of all her best poetry. The one is a method of exposition of one thing in terms of another, the second a method of revelation of the mystery of one thing actually contained in another. Allegory is nearly always at a lower level of art; it is hortatory, expository, instructional. And Judith Wright sometimes forgets another saying of William Blake's: 'The tygers of wrath are wiser than the horses of instruction'.

In fact, from this point on in her poetry and in one way or another, there are moments when the poet seems to lose her

certainty, her sureness of touch, her instinct for the right phrase—that almost animal nonchalance. . . . It is at times as though her whole attention were not on the poem, as though the constant reworking of the same set of themes which is characteristic of her had led to an occasional unconscious parody of herself. And when she falls into the shapeless coils of free verse as in **"At A Poetry Conference, Expo '67"** (**"Shadow"**), she is helpless and becomes hardly recognizable. (pp. 13-15)

What is the explanation? Poets, as a matter of course, fall below their own standards from time to time. They fluctuate, from natural causes too numerous to make causal enquiry worthwhile. This is so much the case that we naturally judge a poet by his best work and accept or ignore the rest. It is the peaks that matter, not the hollows of the plain. . . . I do not wish to be censorious with Judith Wright because she sometimes writes dull or bad poems and because she sometimes cannot tell the good poems from the bad. But I do wish to say that she seems to me to have been damaged at times by two sterile and destructive poets for whom she has avowed a deep interest: T. S. Eliot and Ezra Pound. Her poems in general are free from obvious literary influences, but in some of those just mentioned, cadences and turns of phrase suggest that she suffered from occasional attacks of 'Eliotismus'.

The Two Fires came out two years after *The Gateway*. It contains some of her most beautiful lyrics: **"Western Star"** **"Searchlight Practice"**, **"Nameless Flower"**, **"Sea-Beach"**, **"In Praise of Marriages"** and **"For a Birthday"**. These lyrics have a different movement and tone from the earlier ones, a more subtle and meditative rhythm—a new singing tone. Another path explored in this volume and to be explored in later poems is the one, too rarely tried, of amused and delighted irony, which appears in such poems as **". . . and Mr Ferritt"**. . . . **"Request to a Year"** is one of my favourite poems in this vein; it purports to record an incident in the life of the poet's great-great-grandmother, 'legendary devotee of the arts', as she sat sketching her second son, who was balanced on a small ice-floe being carried down-stream towards an eighty foot waterfall in Switzerland. . . . (pp. 16-17)

Something of this ease, lightness, and irony runs through her next book, *Birds* (1962), devoted entirely, like a seventeenth century book of Theophrastan 'characters', to portraits of the characters and personalities of individual Australian birds. Judith Wright's poetry is full of these small exquisite sketches of a single flower or beast or bird and they are some of the most characteristic things in it. . . . [These poems], while vivid and accurate in detail, have an element of simple humour since a number of them were apparently written for the entertainment of a child. The volume has as epilogue an adult, serious and curiously moving poem, **"Extinct Birds,"** about birds noted by the poet Charles Harpur in the forests round his home in the early nineteenth century . . . , and the poet reflects on the curious irony of the fact that the records made by Harpur in hope and love were made by a poet who helped to fell the forest and to hasten the destruction of the birds he loved. It is a pity that in her *Collected Poems* she has rearranged the order of these poems so that **"Extinct Birds"** no longer forms the conclusion to this group of poems, a conclusion that casts its prophetic light back over all the rest.

Birds is Judith Wright's only attempt at the *livre composé*, in which all the individual poems are on the one theme and contribute to a common effect. Her next book, *Five Senses*, reverts to the plan of a miscellany like its predecessors. It consists of a selection from her previous work and a collection of poems presumably written after *The Two Fires*, and called **"The Forest."** It includes the poem **"Five Senses"** which gives the title to the whole selection. **"The Forest"** shows a new direction, has a rather different tone from the earlier work. There are fewer of the assured 'singing' lyrics. The rhythms are broken and syncopated; there is a lot of deliberate use of half-rhymes. . . . The poet, who before was able to view the world of experience and look through it to an illumination which seemed a kind of inspired innocence, is now aware of the growth of a new pattern within her, an alien and baffling vision the nature of which she cannot yet grasp. . . . The poem **"Interplay"** is a sufficient indication of this peculiar state of mind. The poet gazing on the world around sees by a light that comes from herself, the light of the mind which mirrors the outside world, yet she becomes aware that she is not the seer nor the world the object of sight (as in the earlier poems). She is merely the voice and focus of an unknown mind, the primal Logos. In several poems of this collection the poet is seen groping for understanding and finding it not in vision or intellect but in love. (pp. 17-18)

Three years elapse before the appearance of [Judith Wright's] next book, *The Other Half* (1966). The two halves are the conscious and the unconscious personalities, the one that 'undrowns' when she is asleep and the other that conducts the business of daily life. These two are partly in conflict yet they meet at midnight 'and by music only', and the daylight self reminds the other that they are really aiming at the same things and may finally be one. Although it is the name-poem of the book, the book is not in any sense a development of this theme. The individual poems exist in their own right and appear to have arisen from their own occasions quite independently. And yet the duality of **"The Other Half"** casts a light over all the other poems. It is a psychological concept which partly replaces the mystical and metaphysical principles that inspired the earlier volumes—and again it seems to be continuous with them. The poems have a more ordinary domestic note, though they are on the same themes as before. (pp. 19-20)

[The] poems of *The Other Half* appear to be formulating a new and uncompromising theory of creation as something willed and controlled from beyond the individual mind. The stance of these poems, if I can so express it, is that of listening for the prompting of a voice from beyond, as that of the earlier poems was one of deliberate looking for some vision of illumination to be supplied by the objective world itself. The mystic's subsumption into the life of nature, his willing abandonment of self in the ecstasy of being part of the all, seems to be eroding and dissolving the conscious practice of poetry as an art. Those who are unwilling to follow the steps of a poet's progress and, having decided what they like best, want the poet to be continually repeating the familiar gestures and the endearing effects, tend to be less than satisfied with *The Other Half*. They rightly prefer a perfect poem in Judith Wright's earlier manner, such as **"Naked Girl and Mirror"**, but they miss the significance of the poems, less expert and more tentative, in which poetry is being encouraged to attempt to open a door into another dimension altogether.

There is, of course, a terrible risk in this. One recalls the similar intransigence of Blake which resulted in the unwieldy and verbose Prophetic Books. The mystic has taken over and the poet is a blind transcriber of visions which come through clumsily and ineptly once the poet as maker has stepped aside. And there is perhaps only Dante to remind us that the mystic vision need not necessarily be destructive of the conscious craft. What will be the outcome with Judith Wright? Her powers appear to be at their zenith but also at a moment of crisis or at least of critical equilibrium. One thing is certain: she will follow the road on which her feet are set to the end.

I have placed the moment of crisis in the period of *The Other Half*. **"Shadow"**, the group of new poems in the next volume, *Collected Poems* (1971), gives very little clue as to what may be the next direction. There are a number of satirical and 'sociological' poems of a rather journalistic kind. There are delightful poems of a half-serious and very profound sort which indicate that the ceaseless adventure into the mystic's realm is still going on. (pp. 21-2)

One thing is certain about Judith Wright: she always means exactly what she says. She is not one of those poets who often write in a spirit of 'As if'. If she has arrived at this point of thinking that silence might be best, something has come to its limit in the development of her poetry as her readers have known it up to now. It may be an end; it may be the silence before a new beginning. I hold my breath and wait.

Alive, Poems 1971-72 leaves the question still in suspense. There are poems here—they form about half of the total— which give the impression of having been jotted down in a hurry in a sort of telegraphese. The song that was richly dressed has not only been made as bare as possible, it has been stripped almost to a verbal skeleton. At first sight one is tempted to put this down to her absorption over recent years in the practical business of politics and propaganda on behalf of conservation. . . . [A poem of deep] despair, **"The Slope"**, is a vision of the whole human race bent on self-destruction like the Gadarene Swine and for much the same reason. The poet, too, might seem to be moving down a slope from pure poetry to applied. Not that she doesn't often do it very well: **"At a Public Dinner"** has the true *saeva indignatio* of great satire, that bitter fire which is tinged with a comprehending sadness. (p. 23)

There is a sharpening of the sense of a crisis in the poetic life which had been growing through the last two or three books. Two poems seem to set the antinomies of choice that constitute the crisis. The first is **"To Mary Gilmore"**. In this poem the poet pictures herself at fifty-six setting out from home for some conference or other and she thinks of Mary Gilmore in her old age still writing copiously and vividly. She too decides for a life of vigour and action, but the contrast between her choice and Mary Gilmore's—the committee-woman and the committed writer—is implicit in the poem.

The other poem is called **"Grace"** and it seems to mark the extreme point of the metaphysical journey which I have traced through these successive volumes of verse. 'Living', she says, 'is dailiness, a simple bread that's worth the eating'. But, from outside living, there are intrusions of illumination which has nothing at all to say, but is something inexplicable, a flash from something beyond experience, contemplation, mystical elevation of the spirit—something that occurs beyond here and now: 'It plunges a sword from a dark star'. For this experience, which is also beyond poetry, she gropes for a word and finds nothing adequate except the old theological term of 'grace'.

It is only a guess, of course. It is simple presumption to predict what may happen next in the case of a poet in whom the unexpected—see the poem **"That Seed"**—is always breaking through the pattern laid down. But surely here is the hint of the end of the trail; a suggestion that, though she will go on writing poems, the quest from which the poems took their *élan* has reached its goal, and it is already a goal beyond what poetry can express.

For this reason it would, I think, be a serious mistake to take the poetry of *Alive* as a sign that the poetic impulse and the poetic means are in any sense drying up or becoming impoverished. What I seem to detect here—and of course I am only guessing—in this rather scrappy, laconic style, this deliberate 'bareness', is in fact a familiar occurrence in some great artists towards the end of their careers, where they begin to divest themselves of mere technical control, to simplify their utterance and to generalize their images in an attempt to go beyond the limitations of the medium. I think of Michelangelo's last carvings, which look forward to Rodin, of Goya's last paintings, of something beginning in the later work of Yeats or of Beethoven. Perhaps it is too early to find such tendencies in the work of Judith Wright, but it would not surprise me if another ten years or so should prove me to have been justified. The last years of a poet are often stranger than anyone could have foreseen, and are not to be anticipated or predicted. The last word is not ours to speak. (pp. 23-4)

A. D. Hope, in his Judith Wright, *Oxford University Press, Melbourne, 1975, 43 p.*

KEITH HARRISON

Judith Wright, one of the finest poets produced by Australia, has given us a handsome new selection [*The Double Tree: Selected Poems, 1942-1976*] . . . from all her books published to this date. . . .

I was brought up on Judith Wright, and some of these poems are in the marrow of my bones. So it was with great delight that I read over many of the poems that had moved me as a student and as an aspiring writer. I remember the pleasure and the envy. She could evoke a sense of being in Australia as few others could. **"Bullocky"** was one of my favorites. . . . [In *The Double Tree*], we begin to see a shape in her still unfinished work—its faults and its strengths stand out in starker outline. The faults have perhaps been plain for a while: an occasional metaphysical vagueness, a lyrical abstraction sometimes too easily gained. But the strengths of her work far outweigh the faults, and here we have them in poem after poem. There is her delight in all created things—in birds and plants and landscapes, all done with the particular precision of first-rate poetry. There is the sense of humility of a poet who inhabits a strange human and non-human world and is glad to be here as a woman, as a person continually finding new things. Finally there is an ease in a use of a language: she is precise without being stuffy. And she has done the thing that is most difficult, and whose results are as fertile as they are unspectacular: she has found the *middle* voice. She found it early, in **"New England"** (the Australian region, not the American). . . . And in [*The Double Tree*] she finds it time and again in poetry that is rooted, urbane, and sometimes very moving. Judith Wright is already known to some extent in this country. I hope the new collection will serve to introduce her to more American readers for hers is a very solid achievement both in the context of Australian letters and in the poetry of the English-speaking world.

Keith Harrison, in a review of "The Double Tree: Selected Poems, 1942-1976," in The Carleton Miscellany, *Vol. XVIII, No. 2, Summer, 1980, p. 227.*

DAVE SMITH

Judith Wright's *The Double Tree: Selected Poems 1942-1976* announces a poet virtually unknown in America. An Austra-

lian, Wright creates poems of the head, heart, and foot in precise but tense cooperation. She celebrates through the roughened line of Yeats; she beats out a private song in public cadences only to catch us up with an unexpected glory, a luminously graven phrase or image. She says of a child lost in the wilderness, aware that is the great human myth, "He has gone climbing the terrible crags of the Sun." I believe that Wright is very nearly a major poet. Her body of work is large, ambitious, substantial, and powerful. Her personal myth encompasses particulate definitions of the civilized and the animal worlds, from nationhood to a shadow of rain; she grounds all in the tragic, fundamental, and local story of wandering in the earth. She believes in the responsibility of man and art to make an "essential music" and her primal conviction is that "the whole plant-history's coded in one seed." Judith Wright's poems range from one seed to entire forests. They cajole, sing, and ritualize as they insist art is consciousness and the rage to live.

If there is a weakness in Wright, it is that her poetry comes so naturally and easily that, combined with a tendency toward socio-philosophical discourse, she allows herself dominations of idea-chatter and habitual verse conventions. Some of her poems pale before the fierce necessity so compelling in her best work. . . . Beside ferocity she manages a liquid compression of description, act, scene, and history in single phrases ("Beneath him slid the furrows of the sea"). Her great and abiding theme, the Lucretian tears of beauty and passing away of all things, is nevertheless so matched in archetypal and locally Australian particulars that she achieves a thorough resonance. We believe that she "joins all, gives all a meaning, makes all whole." A Rounder for certain, her poetry tells us how to be freed to the fullness of human experience, "to celebrate lovelong/life's wholeness, spring's return, the flesh's tune." (p. 32)

Dave Smith, "Trimmers, Rounders, and Myth: Some Recent Poetry from English Speaking Cousins," in The American Poetry Review, *Vol. 9, No. 5, September-October, 1980, pp. 30-3.*

KEN GOODWIN

Although she had had poems published in children's papers from the age of ten, it was not until the early 1940s, when she was living in Brisbane and associated with the magazine *Meanjin Papers* that [Wright] felt she had completed her apprenticeship. Poems such as **"Bullocky"**, **"The Company of Lovers"** and **"South of my Days"** excited interest when they were published in magazines such as *Meanjin*, *Southerly* and the *Bulletin*, and her first volume, *The Moving Image* (1946), was an immediate and continuing success. In these poems she set about her lifelong quest to define Australia as a land, a nation and a metaphysical entity, in language that showed awareness of contemporary overseas writing in English but also recognized the unique environment and society of Australia.

"Bullocky" is a good example of Wright's passage from scene to myth-making, from physicality to metaphysics. The bullocky plodding the 'long solitary tracks' comes to believe that he is Moses and—in some confusion of the biblical details—the bullock team whom he is driving to the Promised Land. This is the kind of sea-change that European mythology commonly makes in Wright's work. This Moses . . . is dead, but his inflamed vision has been transmuted still further into the poet's prayer and assertion that the Promised Land has now covered the countryside where the bullocky used to work. (pp. 126-27)

"The Company of Lovers" is the first of [Wright's] major love poems, relating the poet's love relationship to that of all lovers throughout the world (a 'company' in the collective sense) who think the world well lost for the 'company' (in a more intimate sense) that the grave will soon enough destroy. The same sense of time leaching away both individual and collective accomplishment is to be found in **"Bora Ring,"** one of Wright's many poems about Aborigines. Its opening clause, 'The song is gone', may have suggested the well-known poem "We are Going" to Wright's friend and fellow poet, the Aboriginal writer Kath Walker. Wright herself is well aware of the reason why 'The song is gone' and 'The hunter is gone': it is because of the curse of Cain, the murder and extermination brought by white settlers.

The title poem, **"The Moving Image"**, refers to the Platonic quotation that provides an epigraph for the volume, 'Time is a moving image of eternity'. In it there is the sense of celestial time never suiting the human rhythm of the blood, but also the sense that 'both time and fear' are a creation of the poet, who must resist both her creatures, otherwise she will die. Despite the oppressiveness of time and death, life and desire are to be found in nature, visionary madness, and love. Despite the immensity of the dark and the silence, there is both music and light. . . . (p. 127)

In the mid 1940s Judith Wright met her future husband, Jack McKinney, a philosopher who also wrote at least one well-constructed comic play. Her love for McKinney and her sensations and thought when she was carrying their child form the substance of the opening poems of her next volume, *Woman to Man* (1949). "Woman to Man", "Woman's Song" and "Woman to Child" are solemn, ceremonial lyrics, written in the knowledge of the love poetry of Dylan Thomas and W. B. Yeats but full of Judith Wright's own supple movement of thought. Love and procreation are seen as profound mysteries, shaded by the thought of death. . . . These three poems, celebrating love, fecundity, and the quickening of the child, seemed to most readers thoroughly original poems about subjects rarely touched on. They have been very influential in encouraging other women writers, particularly in the 1970s and later, to write about procreation and childbirth.

Woman to Man also contains some pure lyrics in short lines, notably **"Stars"**, **"The Old Prison"**, and **"Wonga Vine"**. "Stars" and "Wonga Vine" are almost Blake-like in their sense of an infinite world impinging on innocent and beautiful life. The 'swarm of honey-bees' and the flower of the wonga vine are symbols of the childlike quest for eternity. **"The Old Prison"** presents a song of experience to balance the two songs of innocence. The decaying and deserted prison becomes a symbol of man's loneliness enunciated by the hollow fluting of the wind among the ruins. (pp. 127-28)

In her first two volumes, Judith Wright enunciates the three chief concerns of her work. The first is the nature of time, the notion of flux or change, and the resoluteness that the poet must conjure, mostly through love, to defeat her fear of time. The second is the attempt to resolve into a harmony or a creative paradox the basic antinomies of human existence—man and the environment, person and person, past and present, soul and flesh. The third is the Australian landscape and its appropriate expression and sublimation in language. (pp. 128-29)

Wright's third volume, *The Gateway* (1953), disappointed some critics. They found some of the poems too abstract, too philosophical, too factitiously symbolic. Such criticism is perhaps best seen as a belated reaction to the rapturous reception of *The Moving Image* than as a substantive comment on the poems of *The Gateway*. Among them are poems of the poet's response to the magic of landscape, such as **"Train Journey"**. Travelling at night through the New England district she wakes to find the trees transfigured into a symbol of determination, durability and essential life. They imaginatively blossom within and by means of the poem into 'flowers more lovely than the white moon'.

"Our Love is so Natural" is another poem of the transfiguration of the actual into the realm of the ideal, with no loss of the sense of the real. "Our Love" is described in images of a fairy landscape with honey bees, shores on which wild animals become tame, and a star living in a tree. But the human impression is what is asserted: 'Our love is so natural'. (p. 129)

"The Gateway" introduces a new strain to the argument about life and death. It seems to depend on a Jungian sense (perhaps a Buddhist sense) of the dissolution of the self in 'the depth of nothing'. The collective unconscious is the abode of both death and life, for from it emanates 'the bright smoke' that is 'the flowing and furious world'.

The Two Fires (1955) contains a number of poems, including the title poem, written at the time of the Korean War, when the world's destruction by atomic warfare seemed distinctly possible. Images of fire and burning permeate **"The Two Fires"**, the destructive fire being opposed by the resistance of 'rock and the waters'. The original fire (a concept from Heraclitus) yielded to the generation of nature; now, in the apocalyptic fire, 'time has caught on fire'. . . . (pp. 129-30)

In some poems, notably the song lyric **"Nameless Flower"** and **"Gum-trees Stripping"**, Wright privileges nature above language in a manner that was to become increasingly common as she became committed to the conservation and environmental movement. In **"Nameless Flower"** she says that words are incapable of trapping the essence of beauty. They are 'white as a stone is white / carved for a grave', but the flower, symbolizing love, 'blooms in immortal light'. In **"Gum-trees Stripping"** she resists the temptation to engage in the pathetic fallacy when confronted by gum trees shedding their bark; she recognizes instead that 'Words are not meanings for a tree'.

After a lapse of several years, Judith Wright produced a set of poems on the birds of Tamborine Mountain, where she was living. . . . [In her poems in *Birds* (1962)], most of the earlier bardic qualities give way to a personal and intimate delight in the creatures she describes. Sometimes she sees them in anthropomorphic terms (the magpies walk along the road 'with hands in pockets'); sometimes she uses them as reflections of her own mood. . . . (p. 130)

Five Senses (1963) is a retrospective selection, with many new poems. The more relaxed, personal mood continues, though the old images of light, bone and depths continue, and so does the emphasis on time's flux, death and fear. **"For my Daughter"** speaks about the separation of an adolescent daughter from her mother's ways and the mother's need to recognize the change and to retame the lion of her emotions. **"The Other Half"** (1966) continues with the strain of personal poems. It includes **"Turning Fifty"**, in which she reflects on 'having met time and love' and on living in a world where 'we've polluted / even this air I breathe'.

Jack McKinney's death in 1966 is reflected in many of the poems in the final section, **"Shadow"**, of Judith Wright's *Collected Poems: 1942-1970* (1971). Her love continues with resolution and fortitude. Though alone, she overcomes disconsolateness in **"This Time Alone"**, **"Love Song in Absence"**, and **"The Vision"**. In **"The Vision"** she goes close to explaining why some of her earlier metaphysical poems might seem sterile or over-insistent. She admits her envy of her husband's devotion to philosophy, while she lacked his concentration and whole-heartedness.

The first poem of **"Shadow"**, modestly entitled **"Two Sides of a Story"**, is perhaps the best of all the explorer poems of the 1940s, 1950s and 1960s. It concerns Edward Kennedy and his Aboriginal guide, called Jacky-Jacky, who engaged on an expedition to the dense rain forests of Cape York Peninsula in northern Queensland. The poem suggests the complexity and contradictoriness of each man, both in himself and in his relationship to the other. It is particularly understanding of the Aboriginal's confusion of identity: the poet asks whether he was Galmahra, a songman, or the white man's servant, Jacky-Jacky. (pp. 130-31)

Judith Wright's later volumes, *Alive: Poems: 1971-72* (1973) and *Fourth Quarter, and Other Poems* (1976), and her contributions to *Journeys* (1982), edited by Fay Zwicky, continue and extend these interests. *Alive* is one of her best volumes. Its topics are limited to those associated with her home on Tamborine: her house, birds and trees; the contrast with them of city streets and their incidents; . . . and the iniquities of businessmen and politicians. She is grave and gay by turn, righteously indignant and helplessly uncertain, vibrantly alive and almost despairingly half-dead. . . . **"Two Dreamtimes"** addresses Kath Walker as 'My shadow sister', expressing a sense of implication in the wrongs done to the plundered black tribes of Australia.

Fourth Quarter is less successful. Its strident protest poems are often querulous and nagging, shrill and abstract. She borrows images from her earlier poems and inserts them intrusively and distractingly. It is in the more personal poems, about her move from Queensland to near Canberra, about growing old and about memories of childhood, that she writes best, though even these poems are often vitiated by incursion into flabby, undisciplined free verse.

Judith Wright has been a prolific writer apart from her poetry. She has written school plays for the Australian Broadcasting Commission, children's books, short stories, literary criticism,

and history. The best of her literary criticism is to be found in *Preoccupations in Australian Poetry* (1965), a series of perceptive essays on some major Australian poets. . . . *The Cry for the Dead* (1981) tells the story of the settlement of the Burnett and Dawson River district of central Queensland. It is also a story of her family, for her grandfather, Albert Wright, was one of the squatters and she again uses his diaries from 1867-1890 as part of her material. But his book tells less of the official story than of the disastrous neglect of proper land-management procedures and the story of the brutal extermination of Aborigines. It describes too the prickly-pear infestation, when families fled from the land before the advancing 'impenetrable walls of green, taller than a man'.

Judith Wright, in both poetry and prose, presents a wide panorama of the interests of the socially conscious present-day Australian. Unlike Xavier Herbert she does not despair for her country, for the movement of her thought is always inwards to the human resources of fortitude and love and to the sense of eternity that together provide the will to continue. Her constant quest has been, in the words of the early poem **"Waiting"**, that we should be made 'whole in man and time, who build eternity', and that, in the words of another early poem, **"Nigger's Leap, New England"**, 'all men are one man at last'. It is a quest for unity and wholeness analogous to Christopher Brennan's, but conducted through a quite different and [more solid] landscape. (pp. 131-33)

Ken Goodwin, "Major New Voices of the 1930s and 1940s," in his A History of Australian Literature, *St. Martin's Press, 1986, pp. 112-39.*

CLIVE JAMES

Judith Wright's **Collected Poems,** while not to be foregone, is so far from representing the culmination of her achievement that it might with more truth be said to mark the end of her first phase. She has brought out several volumes since, and the fate of the latest one, *Phantom Dwelling,* exemplifies the condition of the major Australian poets in the twentieth century. It was published in Britain in 1985 and sank like a stone, with scarcely a single review, even an unfavourable one. For things to have been otherwise, there would have had to be justice. But as with any other product, there is no innate justice in the marketing and consumption of poetry. (p. 1329)

Clive James, "A Class Apart?" in The Times Literary Supplement, *No. 4417, November 27-December 3, 1987, pp. 1327-29.*

Acknowledgments

The following is a listing of the copyright holders who have granted us permission to reprint material in this volume of *CLC*. Every effort has been made to trace copyright, but if omissions have been made, please let us know.

COPYRIGHTED EXCERPTS IN CLC, VOLUME 53, WERE REPRINTED FROM THE FOLLOWING PERIODICALS:

America, v. 150, March 17, 1984 for a review of "O Albany: An Urban Tapestry" by George W. Hunt; v. 150, May 19, 1984 for "William Kennedy's Albany Trilogy" by George W. Hunt. © 1984. All rights reserved. Both reprinted with permission of the author./ v. 109, October 12, 1963; v. 111, September 19, 1964; v. 114, May 21, 1966; v. 123, October 17, 1970; v. 147, July 31, 1982; v. 148, May 7, 1983. ©1963, 1964, 1966, 1970, 1982, 1983. All rights reserved. All reprinted with permission of America Press, Inc., 106 West 56th Street, New York, NY 10019.

The American Book Review, v. II, May-June, 1980; v. 2, September-October, 1980; v. 3, May-June, 1981; v. 7, May-June, 1985; v. 9, May-August, 1987. © 1980, 1981, 1985, 1987 by *The American Book Review.* All reprinted by permission of the publisher.

The American Poetry Review, v. 9, September-October, 1980 for "Trimmers, Rounders, and Myth: Some Recent Poetry from English Speaking Cousins" by Dave Smith. Copyright © 1980 by World Poetry, Inc. Reprinted by permission of the author.

American Quarterly, v. XX, Summer, 1968 for a review of "The Catacombs" by Edward Margolies. Copyright 1968, American Studies Association. Reprinted by permission of the publisher and the Author's Representative, Gunther Stuhlmann.

The Antioch Review, v. XXX, Fall, 1970 & Winter, 1971. Copyright © 1971 by the Antioch Review Inc. Reprinted by permission of the Editors.

Ariel: A Review of International English Literature, v. 12, July, 1981 for "The Personal and the Political: The Case of Nuruddin Farah" by Kirsten Holst Petersen. Copyright © 1981 The Board of Governors, The University of Calgary. Reprinted by permission of the publisher and the author.

Artworkers News, v. 10, June, 1981. © 1981 by the Foundation for the Community of Artists, Inc. All rights reserved. Reprinted by permission of the publisher.

The Atlantic Bookshelf, a section of *The Atlantic Monthly,* v. 179, January, 1947 for "The Girl and the River" by Edward Weeks; v. 191, June, 1953 for "The Vale of Kashmir" by Edward Weeks. Copyright 1947, renewed 1974; copyright 1953, renewed 1981 by the Atlantic Monthly Company, Boston, MA. Both reprinted by permission of the author./ v. 164, September, 1939. Copyright 1939, renewed 1967 by the Atlantic Monthly Company, Boston, MA. Reprinted by permission of the publisher.

The Atlantic Monthly, v. 261, June, 1988 for "Stalin's Ghost" by Josephine Woll. Copyright 1988 by The Atlantic Monthly Company, Boston, MA. Reprinted by permission of the author.

Australian Book Review, v. 6, February, 1967.

Australian Journal of French Studies, v. V, January-April, 1968 for "Pierre Reverdy and the 'Poeme-Objet' " by Julia Husson. Copyright © 1968 by Australian Journal of French Studies. Reprinted by permission of the publisher and the author.

The Australian Quarterly, v. XXXVI, March, 1964 for a review of "Five Senses" by R. F. Brissenden. Copyright by the author. Reprinted by permission of the publisher and the author.

Book Forum, v. VII, 1984. Copyright © 1984 by The Hudson River Press.

Book Week—New York Herald Tribune, August 2, 1964; June 27, 1965. © 1964, 1965, *The Washington Post.* Both reprinted by permission of the publisher.

Book World—Chicago Tribune, November 23, 1969 for "A Preference for Things Not of This World" by Audrey C. Foote. © 1969 Postrib Corp. Reprinted by permission of *The Washington Post* and the author.

Book World—The Washington Post, September 8, 1968 for "An Echo of Greek Tragedy" by Alfred C. Ames; January 9, 1972 for a review of "The Tiger's Daughter" by J. R. Frakes. © 1968, 1972 Postrib Corp. Both reprinted by permission of *The Washington Post* and the respective authors./ January 31, 1971 for "Fond Memories" by L. J. Davis. © 1971 Postrib Corp. Reprinted by permission of *The Washington Post* and The Sterling Lord Literistic, Inc./ May 18, 1975; January 30, 1977; October 23, 1977; December 24, 1978; June 15, 1980; February 21, 1982; March 7, 1982; August 7, 1983; April 28, 1985; May 15, 1988; July 3, 1988; July 10, 1988. © 1975, 1977, 1978, 1980, 1982, 1983, 1985, 1988, *The Washington Post.* All reprinted by permission of the publisher.

Books and Bookmen, n. 329, February, 1983 for a review of "The Argot Merchant Disaster" by Derek Stanford. © copyright the author 1983. Reprinted by permission of the author./ v. 20, August, 1975 for "MacNeice: Poet of the Passing Show" by Stephen Spender; n. 360, October, 1985 for "Bad Guys" by John Rae. © copyright the respective authors 1985. Both reprinted by permission of the Peters, Fraser & Dunlop Group Ltd.

Books in Canada, v. 9, June-July, 1980 for "Little England Made Him" by Dan Hilts; v. 14, August-September, 1985 for "Flaws in the Mosaic" by Neil Bissoondath; v. 15, October, 1986 for "Hollow Laughter" by Paul Wilson. All reprinted by permission of the respective authors.

Booklist, v. 83, April 1, 1987; v. 83, August, 1987; v. 84, March, 1988. Copyright © 1987, 1988 by the American Library Association. All reprinted by permission of the publisher.

Boston Review, v. X, September, 1985 for a review of "Stars and Bars" by Judith Wynn; v. XIII, June, 1988 for a review of "The New Confessions" by Victor Kantor Burg. Copyright © 1985, 1988 by the Boston Critic, Inc. Both reprinted by permission of the respective authors.

British Book News, May, 1982; January, 1986; May, 1986. © *British Book News,* 1982, 1986. All courtesy of *British Book News.*

The Canadian Forum, August, 1967.

Canadian Literature, n. 107, Winter, 1985 for "Mulberry Bush" by George Woodcock; n. 108, Spring, 1986 for "Cultural Alternatives?" by Diana Brydon; n. 110, Fall, 1986 for "Total Vision" by Peter Nazareth. All reprinted by permission of the respective authors.

The Carleton Miscellany, v. XVIII, Summer, 1980. Copyright 1980 by Carleton College. Reprinted by permission of the publisher.

Carolina Quarterly, v. XXXII, Winter, 1980. © copyright 1980 *Carolina Quarterly.* Reprinted by permission of the publisher.

Chicago Tribune, February 12, 1950; April 6, 1952. Copyrighted 1950, renewed 1978; copyrighted 1952, renewed 1980 Chicago Tribune Company. All rights reserved. Both used with permission.

Chicago Tribune—Books, May 8, 1988 for "The Flip Side of Yuppiedom in All Its Gritty Dimensions" by Catherine Petroski; May 8, 1988 for "The Random Walk: Life in All of Its Haphazard Twists and Turns" by Dan Tucker. © copyrighted 1988, Chicago Tribune Company. All rights reserved. Both reprinted by permission of the respective authors./ February 8, 1987; April 24, 1988. © copyrighted 1987, 1988, Chicago Tribune Company. All rights reserved. Both used with permission.

Choice, v. 25, April, 1988. Copyright © 1988 by American Library Association. Reprinted by permission of the publisher.

The Chowder Review, n. 14, Spring-Summer, 1980. Copyright 1980. Reprinted by permission of the publisher.

The Christian Science Monitor, July 30, 1979. © 1979 The Christian Science Publishing Society. All rights reserved. Reprinted by permission from *The Christian Science Monitor.*

CLA Journal, v. 29, September, 1985. Copyright, 1985 by The College Language Association. Used by permission of The College Language Association.

Commentary, v. 84, October, 1987 for "Beyond Glasnost" by Walter Laqueur. Copyright © 1987 by the American Jewish Committee. All rights reserved. Reprinted by permission of the publisher and the author./ v. 68, August, 1979 for "How Not to Do Shakespeare & How Not to Write a Play" by Jack Richardson. Copyright © 1979 by Jack Richardson. All rights reserved. Reprinted by permission of the publisher and Candida Donadio & Associates.

Commonweal, v. LXXXIX, October 4, 1968; v. XCIII, October 9, 1970; v. XCV, February 4, 1972; v. CV, February 17, 1978; v. CVI, March 2, 1979; v. CIX, October 8, 1982. Copyright © 1968, 1970, 1972, 1978, 1979, 1982 Commonweal Publishing Co., Inc. All reprinted by permission of Commonweal Foundation./ v. CXV, May 20, 1988. Copyright © 1988 Commonweal Foundation. Reprinted by permission of Commonweal Foundation.

The Commonweal, v. LXXII, June 24, 1960. Copyright © 1960 Commonweal Publishing Co., Inc. Reprinted by permission of Commonweal Foundation./ v. XCII, May 4, 1945; v. XLIV, October 4, 1946; v. LVIII, June 12, 1953. Copyright 1945, renewed 1973; copyright 1946, renewed 1974; copyright 1953, renewed 1981 Commonweal Publishing Co., Inc. All reprinted by permission of Commonweal Foundation./ v. LXVIII, May 9, 1958. Copyright © 1958, renewed 1986 Commonweal Publishing Co., Inc. Reprinted by permission of Commonweal Foundation.

Concerning Poetry, v. 18, 1985. Copyright © 1985, Western Washington University. Reprinted by permission of the publisher.

Contemporary Literature, v. 18, Autumn, 1977. © 1977 by the Board of Regents of the University of Wisconsin System. Reprinted by permission of The University of Wisconsin Press.

Contemporary Review, v. 235, October, 1979; v. 251, October, 1987; v. 253, July, 1988. © 1979, 1987, 1988. All reprinted by permission of the publisher.

The Critic, Chicago, v. 27, April-May, 1969. © *The Critic* 1969. Reprinted with the permission of the Thomas More Association, Chicago, IL.

Critique: Studies in Contemporary Fiction, V. XXVII, Fall, 1985; v. XXVII, Spring, 1986; v. XXIX, Winter, 1988. Copyright © 1985, 1986, 1988 Helen Dwight Educational Foundation. Reprinted with permission of the Helen Dwight Reid Educational Foundation, published by Heldref Publications, 4000 Albemarle Street, N. W., Washington, DC 20016.

Critique: Studies in Modern Fiction, v. XXVII, Fall, 1985 for "Fish Traps and Purloined Letters: The Anthropology of Paul Bowles" by Joseph Voelker. Copyright © 1985 Helen Dwight Reid Educational Foundation. Reprinted by permission of the author.

Daily News, New York, March 24, 1987. © 1987 New York News Inc. Reprinted with permission. *The Dalhousie Review,* v. 61, Spring, 1981 for a review of "Growing Up Stupid Under the Union Jack: A Memoir" by Cyril Dabydeen. Reprinted by permission of the publisher and the author.

Drama, London, n. 140, 2nd Quarter, 1981. Reprinted by permission of the British Theatre Association.

Encounter, v. LXVII, June, 1986. © 1986 by Encounter Ltd. Reprinted by permission of the publisher.

Esquire, v. 103, May, 1985 for "A Forgotten Master: Rescuing the Works of Paul Bowles" by Tobias Wolff. Copyright © 1985, Esquire Associates. Reprinted by permission of the author.

fiction international, n. 4/5, 1975; n. 12, 1980. Copyright © 1975, 1980 by the Editors. Both reprinted by permission of the publisher.

Four Quarters, v. 21, May, 1972. Reprinted by permission of La Salle University.

The Georgia Review, v. XXXVII, Fall, 1983. Copyright, 1983, by the University of Georgia. Reprinted by permission of the publisher.

The Hollins Critic, v. XXI, June, 1984. Copyright 1984 by Hollins College. Reprinted by permission of the publisher.

Horizon: The Magazine of the Arts, v. XXII, December, 1979 for "Recording Our Times" by Paul Rudnick. © 1988 by Horizon Publishers, Inc. Reprinted by permission of the publisher.

The Hudson Review, v. XLI, Summer, 1988. Copyright © 1988 by The Hudson Review, Inc. Reprinted by permission of the publisher.

Journal of American Studies, v. 6, December, 1972 for "The American Novelist and American History: A Revaluation of 'All the King's Men'" by R. Gray. © Cambridge University Press 1972. Reprinted with the permission of Cambridge University Press and the author.

Journal of Commonwealth Literature, n. 9, July, 1970 for "The West Indian Novel in North America: A Study of Austin Clarke" by Lloyd W. Brown. Copyright by the author. Reprinted by permission of Hans Zell Publishers, an imprint of the K. G. Saur division of Butterworths.

Journal of Popular Culture, v. 19, Fall, 1985. Copyright © 1985 by Ray B. Brown. Reprinted by permission of the publisher.

Kirkus Reviews, v. XLIX, August 1, 1981; v. LV, August 1, 1987. Copyright © 1981, 1987 The Kirkus Service, Inc. All rights reserved. Both reprinted by permission of the publisher.

Kulchur, v. 5, Winter, 1965-66. Copyright, © 1966, by Kulchur Press, Inc. Reprinted by permission of the publisher.

Landfall, v. 36, December, 1982 for "The New Zealand Stories of Ngaio Marsh" by Bruce Harding. Reprinted by permission of the author.

Library Journal, v. 91, October, 15, 1966 for a review of "White Paper" by Robert F. Cayton; v. 105, June 15, 1980 for a review of "Barn Blind" by Michele M. Leber; v. 106, November 1, 1981 for a review of "At Paradise Gate" by Michele M. Leber; v. 112, May 15, 1987 for a review of "Under the Vulture-Tree" by Bettina Drew. Copyright © 1966, 1981, 1987 by Reed Publishing, USA, Division of Reed Holdings, Inc. All reprinted from *Library Journal,* published by R. R. Bowker, Co., Division of Reed Publishing, USA, by permission of the publisher and the respective authors./ v. 94, September 15, 1969. Copyright © 1969 by Reed Publishing, USA, Division of Reed Holdings, Inc. Reprinted from *Library Journal,* published by R. R. Bowker, Co., Division of Reed Publishing, USA, by permission of the publisher.

The Listener, v. LXXVII, May 25, 1967 for a review of "A State of Change" by Hilary Corke; v. 87, May 11, 1972 for "Perv" by Robert Kee; v. 106, December 31, 1981 for "Beloved Countries" by John Mellors. © British Broadcasting Corp. 1967, 1972, 1981. All reprinted by permission of the respective authors.

The Literary Review, Fairleigh Dickinson University, v. 25, Spring, 1982 for "Vision and Violence in the Fiction of Jerzy Kosinski" by Paul R. Lilly, Jr. Copyright © 1982 by Fairleigh Dickinson University. Reprinted by permission of the publisher and the author.

Lively Arts and Book Review, March 5, 1961. co. 1961 I.H.T. Corporation. Reprinted by permission of the publisher.

London Magazine, n.s. v. 7, May, 1967; n.s. v. 23, February, 1984; n.s. v. 25, December, 1985 & January, 1986. © *London Magazine* 1967, 1984, 1986. All reprinted by permission of the publisher.

London Review of Books, v. 9, April 23, 1987 for "Denis Donoghue Writes About Louis MacNeice, and the Thrusting of Shakespeare into Touch" by Denis Donoghue; v. 10, September 15, 1988 for "Less and More" by Adam Begley. Both appear here by permission of the *London Review of Books* and the respective authors.

Los Angeles Daily News, August 28, 1988 for a review of "The Ark Sakura" by Jascha Kessler. Reprinted by permission of the author.

Los Angeles Times Book Review, January 29, 1984; March 18, 1984; December 28, 1986; July 19, 1987; October 18, 1987. Copyright, 1984, 1986, 1987, *Los Angeles Times.* All reprinted by permission of the publisher.

Maclean's Magazine, v. 95, March 8, 1982. © 1982 by *Maclean's Magazine.* Reprinted by permission of the publisher.

The Massachusetts Review, v. XXIII, Spring, 1982. © 1982. Reprinted from *The Massachusetts Review,* The Massachusetts Review, Inc. by permission.

Meanjin, v. XIX, June, 1960./ v. XXI, December, 1962 for a review of "The Moving Image" by H. P. Heseltine; v. 31, December, 1972 for a review of "Collected Poems 1942-1970" by K. L. Goodwin. Both reprinted by permission of the respective authors.

Mother Jones, v. XIII, June, 1988. Copyright © 1988 by the Foundation for National Progress. Reprinted by permission of the publisher.

The Nation, New York, v. 233, November 21, 1981; v. 237, October 22, 1983. Copyright 1981, 1983 *The Nation* magazine/ The Nation Company, Inc. Both reprinted by permission of the publisher./ v. 170, February 11, 1950. Copyright 1950, renewed 1978 *The Nation* magazine/ The Nation Company, Inc. Reprinted by permission of the publisher.

National Review, New York, v. XXXVII, August 9, 1985; v. XL, August 5, 1988. © 1985, 1988 by National Review, Inc., 150 East 35th Street, New York, NY 10016. Both reprinted with permission of the publisher.

Negro American Literature Forum, v. 10, Fall, 1976 for "William Demby's Fiction: The Pursuit of Muse" by Joseph F. Connelly. © 1976 Indiana State University. Reprinted with the permission of the author and Indiana State University.

Negro Digest, v. XIX, November, 1969. © 1969 Johnson Publishing Company, Inc. Reprinted by permission of *Negro Digest.*

The New Criterion, v. VI, November, 1987 for "No Way Out" by Donna Rifkind. Copyright © 1987 by The Foundation for Cultural Review. Reprinted by permission of the author.

The New Leader, v. XLIII, June 27, 1960; v. LXIII, May 21, 1979; v. LXII, June 18, 1979. © 1960, 1979 by The American Labor Conference on International Affairs, Inc. All reprinted by permission of the publisher.

The New Republic, v. 152, June 19, 1965; v. 168, March 3, 1973; v. 177, July 30, 1977; v. 179, July 29, 1978; v. 180, January 20, 1979; v. 181, November 24, 1979; v. 185, November 11, 1981; v. 186, March 24, 1982; v. 193, July 8, 1985; v. 197, December 14, 1987; v. 198, May 16, 1988; v. 198, May 23, 1988; v. 198, June 13, 1988; v. 198, June 27, 1988. © 1965, 1973, 1977, 1978, 1979, 1981, 1982, 1985, 1987, 1988 The New Republic, Inc. All reprinted by permission of *The New Republic.*

New Statesman, v. LXIX, April 30, 1965; v. LXX, October 8, 1965; v. 75, April 26, 1968; v. 86, July 6, 1973; v. 104, August 20, 1982. © 1965, 1968, 1973, 1982 The Statesman & Nation Publishing Co. Ltd. All reprinted by permission of the publisher.

New Statesman & Society, v. 1, August 19, 1988. © 1988 Statesman & Nation Publishing Company Limited. Reprinted by permission of the publisher.

New York Magazine, v. 20, August 17, 1987 for "Hard-Ball" by Rhoda Koenig; v. 21, May 23, 1988 for "Search and Destroy" by Rhoda Koenig. Copyright © 1987, 1988 by News America Publishing, Inc. All rights reserved. Both reprinted with the permission of *New York* Magazine and the author./ v. 16, April 25, 1983; v. 17, November 26, 1984; v. 20, April 6, 1987; v. 21, May 30, 1988. Copyright © 1983, 1984, 1987, 1988 by News America Publishing, Inc. All rights reserved. All reprinted with the permission of *New York* Magazine.

New York Herald Tribune Book Review, June 12, 1960. © 1960 I.H.T. Corporation. Reprinted by permission of the publisher.

New York Herald Tribune Books, February 3, 1935; March 21, 1937. Copyright 1935, renewed 1963; copyright 1937, renewed 1965 I.H.T. Corporation. Both reprinted by permission of the publisher.

New York Post, April 6, 1983; November 13, 1984; March 24, 1987; September 2, 1987. © 1983, 1984, 1987, *New York Post.* All reprinted by permission of the publisher.

The New York Review of Books, v. IV, February 25, 1965; v. XVI, February 11, 1971; v. XXVI, November 8, 1979; v. XXXIII, May 8, 1986. Copyright © 1965, 1971, 1979, 1986 Nyrev, Inc. All reprinted with permission from *The New York Review of Books.*

The New York Times, January 19, 1958; August 2, 1964; November 11, 1971; February 14, 1979; June 17, 1979; April 7, 1980; December 17, 1980; April 6, 1983; December 23, 1983; November 13, 1984; October 15, 1985; March 27, 1987; July 30, 1987; August 26, 1987; March 23, 1988; May 10, 1988; May 15, 1988; May 16, 1988; May 18, 1988; May 26, 1988. Copyright © 1958, 1964, 1971, 1979, 1980, 1983, 1984, 1985, 1987, 1988 by The New York Times Company. All reprinted by permission of the publisher.

The New York Times Book Review, August 27, 1933; February 3, 1935; March 22, 1936; March 14, 1937; March 6, 1938; July 9, 1939; August 11, 1940; February 8, 1942; November 22, 1942; August 18, 1946; November 3, 1946; August 22, 1948; February 26, 1950; January 28, 1951; March 23, 1952. Copyright 1933, 1935, 1936, 1937, 1938, 1939, 1940, 1942, 1946, 1948, 1950, 1951, 1952 by The New York Times Company. All reprinted by permission of the publisher./ November 27, 1955; March 23, 1958; April 17, 1960; October 23, 1960; March 5, 1961; June 3, 1962; September 29, 1963; July 11, 1965; June 19, 1966; August 18, 1968; August 25, 1968; September 21, 1969; October 31, 1971; January 2, 1972; December 9, 1973; November 9, 1975; December 12, 1976; August 17, 1980; October 18, 1981; November 22, 1981; March 28, 1982; April 11, 1982; February 13, 1983; December 25, 1983; January 1, 1984; April 29, 1984; March 31, 1985; April 14, 1985; October 27, 1985; November 10, 1985; January 12, 1986; March 2, 1986; November 9, 1986; February 15, 1987; June 7, 1987; August 2, 1987; August 23, 1987; September 6, 1987; November 15, 1987; January 3, 1988; April 10, 1988; May 15, 1988; May 22, 1988; May 29, 1988; June 19, 1988; July 3, 1988. Copyright © 1955, 1958, 1960, 1961, 1962, 1963, 1965, 1966, 1968, 1969, 1971, 1972, 1973, 1975, 1976, 1980, 1981, 1982, 1983, 1984, 1985, 1986, 1987, 1988 by The New York Times Company. All reprinted by permission of the publisher.

The New Yorker, v. LIX, April 18, 1983 for "Bellyacher" by Brendan Gill; v. LXIII, August 17, 1987 for "Under the Dryers" by Edith Oliver; v. LXIII, November 16, 1987 for "Seeking Connections in an Insecure Country" by John Updike; v. LXIV, May 9, 1988 for "Severed Futures" by Brad Leithauser; v. LXIV, September 12, 1988 for "Doubt and Difficulty in Leningrad and Moscow" by John Updike. © 1983, 1987, 1988 by the respective authors. All reprinted by permission of the publisher./v. LII, January 10, 1977; v. LV, June 18, 1979; v. LXIII, October 19, 1987. © 1977, 1979, 1987 by The New Yorker Magazine, Inc. All reprinted by permission of the publisher.

Newsweek, v. LXXIX, January 17, 1972. Copyright 1972, by Newsweek, Inc. All rights reserved. Reprinted by permission of the publisher.

The Observer, June 12, 1983; November 6, 1983; April 5, 1987; May 3, 1987; May 1, 1988; August 14, 1988. All reprinted by permission of The Observer Limited, London.

The Paris Review, v. 28, Spring, 1986 for "The Art of Poetry XXXVII: Karl Shapiro" by Robert Phillips. © 1986 The Paris Review, Inc. Reprinted by permission of *The Paris Review* and Robert Phillips.

Parnassus: Poetry in Review, v. 9, 1981; v. 12/13, 1985. Copyright © 1981, 1985 Poetry in Review Foundation, NY. Both reprinted by permission of the publisher.

Partisan Review, v. XXXVI, Winter, 1969 for "The Bourgeois Poet" by Paul Fussell, Jr. Copyright © 1969 by *Partisan Review.* Reprinted by permission of the publisher and the author.

Plays & Players, n. 406, July, 1987. © 1987 Brevet Limited. Reprinted with permission of the publisher.

PN Review 23, v. 8, 1981 for "Between Silences" by Clive Wilmer. © *PN Review* 1981. Reprinted by permission of the author.

Poetry, v. XCVII, February, 1961 for a review of "Bone Thoughts" by James Dickey; v. CVIII, May, 1966 for "Eyes and 'I' " by Richard Duerden; v. CVIII, June, 1966 for a review of "Peace Eye" by A. R. Ammons; v. CXV, February, 1970 for "Poet-Critics and Scholar-Critics" by Laurence Lieberman; v. CXL, April, 1982 for "Laurels" by Charles Berger; v. CXLII, September, 1983 for "The Star of the Disaster" by William Harmon; v. CXLIII, February, 1984 for a review of "In a U-Haul North of Damascus" by Penelope Mesic; v. CXLVI, June, 1985 for a review of "Love & War, Art & God" by David Wojahn; v. CL, July, 1987 for a review of "Ultramarine" by Robert B. Shaw; v. CLII, May, 1988 for a review of "Under the Vulture-Tree" by Vernon Shetley. © 1961, 1966, 1970, 1982, 1983, 1984, 1985, 1987, 1988 by the Modern Poetry Association. All reprinted by permission of the Editor of *Poetry* and the respective authors./ v. LXVIII, April, 1946 for "Mr. Shapiro's Ars Poetica" by Dudley Fitts. Copyright 1946, renewed 1974 by the Modern Poetry Association. Reprinted by permission of the Editor of *Poetry* and the author.

Poetry Review, v. 69, March, 1980 for "The Poetry of Displacement" by Tom Paulin. Copyright © The Poetry Society 1980. Reprinted by permission of the author.

Prairie Schooner, v. 55, Spring & Summer, 1981. © 1981 by University of Nebraska Press. Reprinted from *Prairie Schooner* by permission of the University of Nebraska Press.

Publishers Weekly, v. 230, August 1, 1986; v. 231, March 6, 1987; v. 232, August 14, 1987; v. 232, August 28, 1987; v. 233, February 26, 1988; v. 233, May 6, 1988. Copyright 1986, 1987, 1988 by Reed Publishing USA. All reprinted from *Publishers Weekly,* published by the Bowker Magazine Group of Cahners Publishing Co., a division of Reed Publishing USA.

Punch, v. CCLII, May 17, 1967. © 1967 by Punch Publications Ltd. All rights reserved. May not be reprinted without permission.

Quadrant, v. XXVII, November, 1983 for " 'The Drunkenness of Things': The Poetry of Louis MacNeice" by Donald Moore. Reprinted by permission of *Quadrant,* Sydney, Australia and the author.

Quarterly West, n. 16, Spring-Summer, 1983. © 1983 by *Quarterly West.* Reprinted by permission of the publisher.

Queen's Quarterly, v. 87, Autumn, 1980 for "Prime Minister Unlimited: West Indian Literary Report" by Edward Baugh. Copyright © 1980 by the author. Reprinted by permission of the author.

Quill and Quire, v. 51, July, 1985 for a review of "When Women Rule" by Keith Garebian; v. 51, August, 1985 for "Mukherjee Draws Tales from Fear in the Streets of Toronto" by Patricia Bradbury. Both reprinted by permission of *Quill and Quire* and the respective authors./ v. 43, October 13, 1977. Reprinted by permission of *Quill and Quire.*

Rocky Mountain Review of Language and Literature, v. 35, 1981. Copyright © 1981 by the Rocky Mountain Modern Language Association. All rights reserved. Reprinted by permission of the publisher.

Russian Literature Triquarterly, v. 1, Fall, 1971. © 1971 by Ardis Publishers. Reprinted by permission of the publisher.

The Russian Review, v. 31, January, 1972 for a review of "Fever and Other New Poems" by Richard Gregg. Copyright 1972 by The Russian Review, Inc. Reprinted by permission of the publisher and the author.

Salmagundi, n. 68 & 69, Fall, 1985 & Winter, 1986. Copyright © 1986 by Skidmore College. Reprinted by permission of the publisher.

Saturday Night, v. 80, February, 1965 for "Six Ways to Escape the Canadian Winter" by Philip Stratford; v. 80, November, 1965 for "Caribbean Renaissance" by Kildare Dobbs; v. 90, October, 1975 for "Violence as a Device for Problem-Solving" by Linda Sandler. Copyright © 1965, 1975 by *Saturday Night.* All reprinted by permission of the respective authors.

The Saturday Review of Literature, v. XXXIII, March 4, 1950. Copyright 1950, renewed 1978 *Saturday Review* magazine.

The Sewanee Review, v. LXXIV, July-September, 1966; v. XCII, Winter, 1984. © 1966, 1984 by The University of the South. Both reprinted by permission of the editor of *The Sewanee Review.*

The Small Press Review, v. 17, February, 1985. © 1985 by Dustbooks. Reprinted by permission of the publisher.

Southerly, v. 23, 1963 for "Poetry of Distinction" by S. E. Lee; v. 27, 1967 for "Poetic Fisticuffs" by S. E. Lee. Copyright 1963, 1967 by the author. Both reprinted by permission of the publisher and the author.

The Southern Review, Louisiana State University, v. 20, Summer, 1984 for "Danger and Beauty: David Bottoms' 'In a U-Haul North of Damascus' " by Michael Cass. Copyright 1984, by the author. Reprinted by permission of the author.

Southwest Review, v. XLV, Summer, 1960. Copyright © 1960 by Margaret L. Hartley. Reprinted by permission of the publisher.

Soviet Literature, n. 3, 1977. © *Soviet Literature,* 1977.

The Spectator, v. 258, May 2, 1987 for "Too Much of a Muchness" by Anita Brookner. © 1987 by *The Spectator.* Reprinted by permission of the author./ v. 215, October 8, 1965; v. 218, May 26, 1967; v. 225, October 31, 1970; v. 232, January 26, 1974; v. 253, August 25, 1984. © 1965, 1967, 1970, 1974, 1984 by *The Spectator.* All reprinted by permission of *The Spectator.*

Studies in Black Literature, v. 3, Autumn, 1972. Copyright 1972 by the editor. Reprinted by permission of the publisher.

Sulfur, n. 11, 1984. Copyright © *Sulfur* 1984. Reprinted by permission of the publisher.

Theatre Journal, v. 35, March, 1983; v. 36, March, 1984; v. 40, March, 1988. © 1983, 1984, 1988, University and College Theatre Association of the American Theatre Association. All reprinted by permission of the publisher.

Time, New York, v. 131, May 9, 1988. Copyright 1988 The Time Inc. Magazine Company. All rights reserved. Reprinted by permission of the publisher./ v. LXVII, March 26, 1956. Copyright 1956, renewed 1984 Time Inc. All rights reserved. Reprinted by permission from *Time.*

The Times Literary Supplement, n. 3108, September 22, 1961; n. 3263, September 10, 1964; n. 3296, April 29, 1965; n. 3402, May 11, 1967; n. 3463, July 11, 1968; n. 3582, October 23, 1970; n. 3721, June 29, 1973; n. 3788, October 11, 1974; n. 4050, November 14, 1980; n. 4142, August 20, 1982; n. 4199, September 23, 1983; n. 4211, December 16, 1983; n. 4247, August 24, 1984; n. 4248, August 31, 1984; n. 4252, September 28, 1984; n. 4313, November 29, 1985; n. 4364, November 21, 1986; n. 4387, May 1, 1987; n. 4409, October 2-8, 1987; n. 4414, November 6-12, 1987; n. 4417, November 27-December 3, 1987; n. 4430, February 26-March 3, 1988; n. 4439, April 29-May 5, 1988; n. 4440, May 6-12, 1988; n. 4441, May 13-19, 1988; n. 4454, August 12-18, 1988. © Times Newspapers Ltd. (London) 1961, 1964, 1965, 1967, 1968, 1970, 1973, 1974, 1980, 1982, 1983, 1984, 1985, 1986, 1987, 1988. All reproduced from *The Times Literary Supplements* by permission.

TriQuarterly, n. 15, Spring, 1969 for "William Demby's 'Dance of Life' " by Robert Bone. © 1969 by *TriQuarterly,* Northwestern University. Reprinted by permission of the publisher and the author.

Twentieth Century Literature, v. 32, Fall & Winter, 1986. Copyright 1986, Hofstra University Press. Reprinted by permission of the publisher.

The Village Voice, v. XXIII, July 17, 1978 for "The Chapman Cometh" by Gary L. Fisketjon. Copyright © The Village Voice, Inc., 1978. Reprinted by permission of *The Village Voice* and the author./ v. XXVII, April 20, 1982 for a review of "The Z-D Generation" by Paul Berman; v. XXXII, April 7, 1987 for "Southern Comfort" by Julius Novick. Copyright © News Group Publications, Inc., 1982, 1987. Both reprinted by permission of *The Village Voice* and the respective authors./ v. XXVII, March 16, 1982 for a review of "Pinball" by Lester Bangs. Copyright © News Group Publications, Inc., 1982. Reprinted by permission of *The Village Voice* and the Literary Estate of Lester Bangs.

VLS, n. 44, April, 1986 for "White Light White Heat" by Geoffrey O'Brien; n. 66, June, 1988 for "Home Truths" by Polly Shulman. Copyright © 1986, 1988 News Group Publications, Inc. Both reprinted by permission of *The Village Voice* and the respective authors.

Western American Literature, v. XXII, August, 1987. Copyright, 1987, by the Western Literature Association. Reprinted by permission of the publisher.

The Women's Review of Books, v. V, January, 1988 for "The End of a Dream" by Gayle Greene. Copyright © 1988. All rights reserved. Reprinted by permission of the author.

World Literature Today, v. 57, Winter, 1983; v. 58, Spring, 1984; v. 58, Autumn, 1984; v. 61, Autumn, 1987. Copyright 1983, 1984, 1987 by the University of Oklahoma Press. All reprinted by permission of the publisher.

The Yale Review, v. LIII, December, 1963 for "'All the King's Men': The Matrix of Experience" by Robert Penn Warren. Copyright © 1963 by Robert Penn Warren. Reprinted by permission of the William Morris Agency Inc. on behalf of the author./ v. 73, October, 1983. Copyright 1983, by Yale University. Reprinted by permission of the editors./ v. XXXV, December, 1945; v. XXXVIII, September, 1948. Copyright 1945, renewed 1973; copyright 1948, renewed 1976 by Yale University. Both reprinted by permission of the editors.

Acknowledgments

COPYRIGHTED EXCERPTS IN CLC, VOLUME 53, WERE REPRINTED FROM THE FOLLOWING BOOKS:

Adler, Thomas P. From "The Pirandello in Albee: The Problem of Knowing in 'The Lady from Dubuque'," in *Edward Albee: An Interview and Essays*. Edited by Julian N. Wasserman with Joy L. Linsley and Jerome A. Kramer. University of St. Thomas, 1983. Copyright © 1983 by The University of St. Thomas. All rights reserved. Reprinted by permission of the editor.

Balakian, Anna. From *Surrealism: The Road to the Absolute*. Revised edition. Dutton, 1970. Copyright © 1959, 1970 by Anna Balakian. All rights reserved. Reprinted by permission of the author.

Bargainnier, Earl F. From "Ngaio Marsh," in *10 Women of Mystery*. Edited by Earl F. Bargainnier. Bowling Green State University Popular Press, 1981. Copyright © 1981 by Bowling Green State University Popular Press. Reprinted by permission of the publisher.

Baumbach, Jonathan. From *The Landscape of Nightmare: Studies in the Contemporary American Novel*. New York University Press, 1965. © 1965 by New York University, 1965. Reprinted by permission of the publisher.

Bone, Robert. From *The Negro Novel in America*. Revised edition. Yale University Press, 1965. Copyright © 1965 by Yale University. All rights reserved. Reprinted by permission of the author.

Caws, Mary Ann, and Patricia Terry. From an introduction to *Roof Slates and Other Poems of Pierre Reverdy*. Translated by Mary Ann Caws and Patricia Terry. Northeastern University Press, 1981. Copyright © 1981 by Mary Ann Caws and Patricia Terry. All rights reserved. Reprinted by permission of the publisher.

Cornell, W. Kenneth. From "The Case for Pierre Reverdy," in *Essays in Honor of Albert Feuillerat*. Edited by Henri M. Peyre. Yale University Press, 1943. Copyright, 1943, by Yale University Press. Renewed 1971 by Henri M. Peyre. All rights reserved. Reprinted by permission of the publisher.

Feinstein, Elaine. From "Poetry and Conscience: Russian Women Poets of the Twentieth Century," in *Women Writing and Writing About Women*. Edited by Mary Jacobus. Croom Helm, 1979. © 1979 Elaine Feinstein. Reprinted by permission of the publisher.

George, Diana Hume. From *Oedipus Anne: The Poetry of Anne Sexton*. University of Illinois Press, 1987. © 1987 by the Board of Trustees of the University of Illinois. Reprinted by permission of the publisher and the author.

Goodwin, Ken. From *A History of Australian Literature*. St. Martin's Press, 1986, Macmillan, Basingstoke, 1986. © Kenneth Goodwin, 1986. All rights reserved. Used with permission of St. Martin's Press, Inc. In Canada by Macmillan, London and Basingstoke.

Greene, Robert W. From *The Poetic Theory of Pierre Reverdy*. University of California Press, 1967. Copyright © 1967 by The Regents of the University of California. Reprinted by permission of the publisher.

Hall, James. From *The Lunatic Giant in the Drawing Room: The British and American Novel Since 1930*. Indiana University Press, 1968. Copyright © 1968 by Indiana University Press. All rights reserved. Reprinted by permission of the publisher.

Hannay, John. From *The Intertextuality of Fate: A Study of Margaret Drabble*. University of Missouri Press, 1986. Copyright © 1986 by The Curators of the University of Missouri. All rights reserved. Reprinted by permission of the publisher.

Hicks, Jack. From *In the Singer's Temple: Prose Fictions of Barthelme, Gaines, Brautigan, Piercy, Kesey, and Kosinski*. University of North Carolina Press, 1981. © 1981 The University of North Carolina Press. All rights reserved. Reprinted by permission of the publisher and the author.

Hope, A. D. From *Judith Wright*. Oxford University Press, Melbourne, 1975. Copyright © 1975 by Oxford University Press, Inc. Reprinted by permission of the publisher.

James, Clive. From *First Reactions: Critical Essays, 1968-1979*. Knopf, 1980. Copyright © 1974, 1977, 1979, 1980 by Clive James. Reprinted by permission of Alfred A. Knopf, Inc. In Canada by the author.

Kennelly, Brendan. From "Louis MacNeice: An Irish Outsider," in *Irish Writers and Society at Large*. Edited by Masaru Sekine. Colin Smythe, 1985. Copyright © 1985 by Brendan Kennelly. All rights reserved. Reprinted by permission of the publisher.

Kumin, Maxine. From "How It Was: Maxine Kumin on Anne Sexton," in *The Complete Poems*. By Anne Sexton. Houghton Mifflin Company, 1981. Foreword copyright © 1981 by Maxine Kumin. All rights reserved. Reprinted by permission of Houghton Mifflin Company.

Last, Rex. From "Paul Celan and the Metaphorical Poets," in *Modern Austrian Writing: Literature and Society After 1945*. Edited by Alan Best and Hans Wolfschütz. Wolff, 1980. © 1980 Oswald Wolff (Publishers) Ltd. Reprinted by permission of Berg Publishers Ltd.

Lee, A. Robert. From "Making New: Styles of Innovation in the Contemporary Black American Novel," in *Black Fiction: New Studies in the Afro-American Novel Since 1945*. Edited by A. Robert Lee. Vision, 1980. © 1980 by Vision, Press. All rights reserved. Reprinted by permission of the publisher.

Mann, Jessica. From *Deadlier than the Male: Why Are Respectable English Women So Good at Murder?* Macmillan Publishing Co., Inc., 1981. Copyright © 1981 by Jessica Mann. All rights reserved. Reprinted with permission of Macmillan Publishing Company.

Margolies, Edward. From *Native Sons: A Critical Study of Twentieth-Century Negro American Authors*. J.B. Lippincott Company, 1968. Copyright © 1968 by Edward Margolies. All rights reserved. Reprinted by permission of the Author's Representative, Gunther Stuhlmann.

Rexroth, Kenneth. From an introduction to *Pierre Reverdy: Selected Poems*. Translated by Kenneth Rexroth. New Directions, 1955. Copyright © 1955, 1969 by Kenneth Rexroth. All rights reserved. Reprinted by permission of New Directions Publishing Corporation.

Roudané, Matthew C. From "A Monologue of Cruelty: Edward Albee's 'The Man Who Had Three Arms'," in *Critical Essays on Edward Albee*. Edited by Philip C. Kolin and J. Madison Davis. Hall, 1986. Copyright 1986 by G. K. Hall & Co. All rights reserved. Reprinted with the permission of the publisher.

Schraufnagel, Noel. From *Apology to Protest: The Black American Novel*. Everett/Edwards, Inc., 1973. © 1973 by Noel Schraufnagel. All rights reserved. Reprinted by permission of the publisher.

Smith, Elton Edward. From *The Angry Young Men of the Thirties*. Southern Illinois University Press, 1975. Copyright © 1975 by Southern Illinois University Press. All rights reserved. Reprinted by permission of the publisher.

Stitt, Peter. From *The World's Hieroglyphic Beauty: Five American Poets*. University of Georgia Press, 1985. © 1985 by the University of Georgia Press. All rights reserved. Reprinted by permission of the publisher.

Whittier, Gayle. From "Mistresses and Madonnas in the Novels of Margaret Drabble," in *Gender and Literary Voice*. Edited by Janet Todd. Women and Literature Series, Vol. 1. Holmes & Meier, 1980. Copyright © 1980 by Holmes & Meier Publishers, Inc. All rights reserved. Reprinted by permission of the publisher.

Yevtushenko, Yevgeny. From an introduction to *Fever & Other New Poems*. By Bella Akhmadulina. Translated by Geoffrey Dutton and Igor Mezhakoff-Koriakin. Morrow, 1969. Copyright © 1969 by Geoffrey Dutton. All rights reserved. Reprinted by permission of William Morrow & Company, Inc.

Acknowledgments

PERMISSION TO REPRINT PHOTOGRAPHS APPEARING IN CLC, VOLUME 53, WAS RECEIVED FROM THE FOLLOWING SOURCES:

© Jerry Bauer: pp. 1, 50, 59, 202, 215, 246, 335, 357

Sovfoto/Eastfoto: p. 8

© Alix Jeffry 1984: p. 16

Photograph by Michael Cagle, courtesy of David Bottoms: p. 28

Photograph by Cherie Nutting, courtesy of Paul Bowles: p. 35

© Lütfi Özkök: pp. 68, 131

© John Reeves: p. 84

Courtesy of The College of Staten Island: p. 98

Photograph by Mark Gerson: p. 116

© Nancy Crampton: pp. 142, 295, 395

Courtesy of Rumer Godden: p. 149

© Mario Ruiz: p. 165

Photograph by George Landis, courtesy of Paul Horgan: p. 168

© Layle Silbert 1989: pp. 189, 325

© Rollie McKenna: pp. 230, 311

Jim Wilson/NYT Pictures: p. 261

Photograph by William Mahin, courtesy of Morris Philipson: p. 273

Courtesy of Cultural Service of the French Embassy: p. 278

© Gerard Malanga: p. 303

Photograph by Stephen M. Morteuseu: p. 344

Courtesy of George Starbuck: p. 352

© 1988 Susan Cook: p. 386

Coward of Canberra Photography, reproduced by permission of Judith A. Wright: p. 415

☐ Contemporary
Literary Criticism
Indexes

Literary Criticism Series
    Cumulative Author Index
Cumulative Nationality Index
Title Index, Volume 53

This Index Includes References to Entries in These Gale Series

Contemporary Literary Criticism

Presents excerpts of criticism on the works of novelists, poets, dramatists, short story writers, scriptwriters, and other creative writers who are now living or who have died since 1960. Cumulative indexes to authors and nationalities are included, as well as an index to titles discussed in the individual volume. Volumes 1-53 are in print.

Twentieth-Century Literary Criticism

Contains critical excerpts by the most significant commentators on poets, novelists, short story writers, dramatists, and philosophers who died between 1900 and 1960. Cumulative indexes to authors, nationalities, and titles discussed are included in each new volume. Volumes 1-32 are in print.

Nineteenth-Century Literature Criticism

Offers significant passages from criticism on authors who died between 1800 and 1899. Cumulative indexes to authors, nationalities, and titles discussed are included in each new volume. Volumes 1-22 are in print.

Literature Criticism from 1400 to 1800

Compiles significant passages from the most noteworthy criticism on authors of the fifteenth through eighteenth centuries. Cumulative indexes to authors, nationalities, and titles discussed are included in each new volume. Volumes 1-10 are in print.

Classical and Medieval Literature Criticism

Offers excerpts of criticism on the works of world authors from classical antiquity through the fourteenth century. Cumulative indexes to authors, titles, and critics are included in each volume. Volumes 1-2 are in print.

Short Story Criticism

Compiles excerpts of criticism on short fiction by writers of all eras and nationalities. Cumulative indexes to authors, nationalities, and titles discussed are included in each new volume. Volumes 1-2 are in print.

Children's Literature Review

Includes excerpts from reviews, criticism, and commentary on works of authors and illustrators who create books for children. Cumulative indexes to authors, nationalities, and titles discussed are included in each new volume. Volumes 1-18 are in print.

Contemporary Authors Series

Encompasses five related series. *Contemporary Authors* provides biographical and bibliographical information on more than 92,000 writers of fiction, nonfiction, poetry, journalism, drama, motion pictures, and other fields. Each new volume contains sketches on authors not previously covered in the series. Volumes 1-126 are in print. *Contemporary Authors New Revision Series* provides completely updated information on active authors covered in previously published volumes of *CA*. Only entries requiring significant change are revised for *CA New Revision Series*. Volumes 1-26 are in print. *Contemporary Authors Permanent Series* consists of updated listings for deceased and inactive authors removed from the original volumes 9-36 when these volumes were revised. Volumes 1-2 are in print. *Contemporary Authors Autobiography Series* presents specially commissioned autobiographies by leading contemporary writers. Volumes 1-8 are in print. *Contemporary Authors Bibliographical Series* contains primary and secondary bibliographies as well as analytical bibliographical essays by authorities on major modern authors. Volumes 1-2 are in print.

Dictionary of Literary Biography

Encompasses three related series. *Dictionary of Literary Biography* furnishes illustrated overviews of authors' lives and works and places them in the larger perspective of literary history. Volumes 1-78 are in print. *Dictionary of Literary Biography Documentary Series* illuminates the careers of major figures through a selection of literary documents, including letters, notebook and diary entries, interviews, book reviews, and photographs. Volumes 1-6 are in print. *Dictionary of Literary Biography Yearbook* summarizes the past year's literary activity with articles on genres, major prizes, conferences, and other timely subjects and includes updated and new entries on individual authors. Yearbooks for 1980-1987 are in print. A cumulative index to authors and articles is included in each new volume.

Concise Dictionary of American Literary Biography

A six-volume series that collects revised and updated sketches on major American authors that were originally presented in *Dictionary of Literary Biography*. Volumes 1-3 are in print.

Something about the Author Series

Encompasses two related series. *Something about the Author* contains heavily illustrated biographical sketches on juvenile and young adult authors and illustrators from all eras. Volumes 1-53 are in print. *Something about the Author Autobiography Series* presents specially commissioned autobiographies by prominent authors and illustrators of books for children and young adults. Volumes 1-7 are in print.

Yesterday's Authors of Books for Children

Contains heavily illustrated entries on children's writers who died before 1961. Complete in two volumes. Volumes 1-2 are in print.

Literary Criticism Series
Cumulative Author Index

This index lists all author entries in the Gale Literary Criticism Series and includes cross-references to other Gale sources. For the convenience of the reader, references to the *Yearbook* in the *Contemporary Literary Criticism* series include the page number (in parentheses) after the volume number. References in the index are identified as follows:

AAYA: *Authors & Artists for Young Adults*, Volume 1
CAAS: *Contemporary Authors Autobiography Series*, Volumes 1-8
CA: *Contemporary Authors* (original series), Volumes 1-126
CABS: *Contemporary Authors Bibliographical Series*, Volumes 1-2
CANR: *Contemporary Authors New Revision Series*, Volumes 1-26
CAP: *Contemporary Authors Permanent Series*, Volumes 1-2
CA-R: *Contemporary Authors* (revised editions), Volumes 1-44
CDALB: *Concise Dictionary of American Literary Biography*, Volumes 1-3
CLC: *Contemporary Literary Criticism*, Volumes 1-53
CLR: *Children's Literature Review*, Volumes 1-18
CMLC: *Classical and Medieval Literature Criticism*, Volumes 1-2
DLB: *Dictionary of Literary Biography*, Volumes 1-78
DLB-DS: *Dictionary of Literary Biography Documentary Series*, Volumes 1-6
DLB-Y: *Dictionary of Literary Biography Yearbook*, Volumes 1980-1987
LC: *Literature Criticism from 1400 to 1800*, Volumes 1-10
NCLC: *Nineteenth-Century Literature Criticism*, Volumes 1-22
SAAS: *Something about the Author Autobiography Series*, Volumes 1-7
SATA: *Something about the Author*, Volumes 1-53
SSC: *Short Story Criticism*, Volumes 1-2
TCLC: *Twentieth-Century Literary Criticism*, Volumes 1-32
YABC: *Yesterday's Authors of Books for Children*, Volumes 1-2

Author Index

Author Index

Capote, Truman
1924-1984........CLC 1, 3, 8, 13, 19,
34 (320), 38
.... SSC 2
See also CANR 18
See also CA 5-8R
See also obituary CA 113
See also DLB 2
See also DLB-Y 80, 84
See also CDALB 1941-1968

Capra, Frank 1897-.............CLC 16
See also CA 61-64

Caputo, Philip 1941-.............CLC 32
See also CA 73-76

Card, Orson Scott
1951-...... CLC 44 (163), 47, 50 (142)
See also CA 102

Cardenal, Ernesto 1925-..........CLC 31
See also CANR 2
See also CA 49-52

Carducci, Giosué 1835-1907 ..... TCLC 32

Carey, Ernestine Gilbreth 1908-
See Gilbreth, Frank B(unker), Jr. and
Carey, Ernestine Gilbreth
See also CA 5-8R
See also SATA 2

Carey, Peter 1943-................CLC 40
See also CA 123

Carleton, William 1794-1869...... NCLC 3

Carlisle, Henry (Coffin) 1926-......CLC 33
See also CANR 15
See also CA 13-16R

Carlyle, Thomas 1795-1881 ...... NCLC 22
See also DLB 55

Carman, (William) Bliss
1861-1929..................TCLC 7
See also CA 104

Carpenter, Don(ald Richard)
1931-........................CLC 41
See also CANR 1
See also CA 45-48

Carpentier (y Valmont), Alejo
1904-1980.............CLC 8, 11, 38
See also CANR 11
See also CA 65-68
See also obituary CA 97-100

Carr, Emily 1871-1945......... TCLC 32

Carr, John Dickson 1906-1977......CLC 3
See also CANR 3
See also CA 49-52
See also obituary CA 69-72

Carr, Virginia Spencer
1929-................. CLC 34 (419)
See also CA 61-64

Carrier, Roch 1937- ....CLC 13
See also DLB 53

Carroll, James (P.) 1943-..........CLC 38
See also CA 81-84

Carroll, Jim 1951-................CLC 35
See also CA 45-48

Carroll, Lewis 1832-1898........ NCLC 2
See also Dodgson, Charles Lutwidge
See also CLR 2, 18
See also DLB 18

Carroll, Paul Vincent
1900-1968...................CLC 10
See also CA 9-12R
See also obituary CA 25-28R
See also DLB 10

Carruth, Hayden
1921-................CLC 4, 7, 10, 18
See also CANR 4
See also CA 9-12R
See also SATA 47
See also DLB 5

Carter, Angela (Olive)
1940-..................... CLC 5, 41
See also CANR 12
See also CA 53-56
See also DLB 14

Carver, Raymond
1938-1988...........CLC 22, 36, 53
See also CANR 17
See also CA 33-36R
See also obituary CA 126
See also DLB-Y 84

Cary, (Arthur) Joyce (Lunel)
1888-1957............... TCLC 1, 29
See also CA 104
See also DLB 15

Casares, Adolfo Bioy 1914-
See Bioy Casares, Adolfo

Casely-Hayford, J(oseph) E(phraim)
1866-1930................ TCLC 24
See also CA 123

Casey, John 1880-1964
See O'Casey, Sean

Casey, Michael 1947- ....CLC 2
See also CA 65-68
See also DLB 5

Casey, Warren 1935-
See Jacobs, Jim and Casey, Warren
See also CA 101

Casona, Alejandro 1903-1965 ......CLC 49
See also Alvarez, Alejandro Rodríguez

Cassavetes, John 1929-............CLC 20
See also CA 85-88

Cassill, R(onald) V(erlin)
1919-..................... CLC 4, 23
See also CAAS 1
See also CANR 7
See also CA 9-12R
See also DLB 6

Cassity, (Allen) Turner
1929-..................... CLC 6, 42
See also CAAS 8
See also CANR 11
See also CA 17-20R

Castaneda, Carlos 1935?-..........CLC 12
See also CA 25-28R

Castro, Rosalía de 1837-1885 ..... NCLC 3

Cather, Willa (Sibert)
1873-1947............TCLC 1, 11, 31
.... SSC 2
See also CA 104
See also SATA 30
See also DLB 9, 54, 78
See also DLB-DS 1
See also CDALB 1865-1917

Catton, (Charles) Bruce
1899-1978...................CLC 35
See also CANR 7
See also CA 5-8R
See also obituary CA 81-84
See also SATA 2
See also obituary SATA 24
See also DLB 17

Cauldwell, Frank 1923-
See King, Francis (Henry)

Caunitz, William 1935-...... CLC 34 (35)

Causley, Charles (Stanley)
1917-........................CLC 7
See also CANR 5
See also CA 9-12R
See also SATA 3
See also DLB 27

Caute, (John) David 1936-.........CLC 29
See also CAAS 4
See also CANR 1
See also CA 1-4R
See also DLB 14

Cavafy, C(onstantine) P(eter)
1863-1933................. TCLC 2, 7
See also CA 104

Cavanna, Betty 1909-.............CLC 12
See also CANR 6
See also CA 9-12R
See also SAAS 4
See also SATA 1, 30

Cayrol, Jean 1911- ....CLC 11
See also CA 89-92

Cela, Camilo José 1916-........ CLC 4, 13
See also CANR 21
See also CA 21-24R

Celan, Paul 1920-1970 ..... CLC 10, 19, 53
See also Antschel, Paul
See also DLB 69

Céline, Louis-Ferdinand
1894-1961....... CLC 1, 3, 4, 7, 9, 15,
47
See also Destouches, Louis-Ferdinand-
Auguste
See also DLB 72

Cellini, Benvenuto 1500-1571 .... LC 7

Cendrars, Blaise 1887-1961........CLC 18
See also Sauser-Hall, Frédéric

Cervantes (Saavedra), Miguel de
1547-1616..................... LC 6

Césaire, Aimé (Fernand)
1913-.................... CLC 19, 32
See also CANR 4
See also CA 65-68

Chabrol, Claude 1930- ....CLC 16
See also CA 110

Challans, Mary 1905-1983
See Renault, Mary
See also CA 81-84
See also obituary CA 111
See also SATA 23
See also obituary SATA 36

Chambers, Aidan 1934- ....CLC 35
See also CANR 12
See also CA 25-28R
See also SATA 1

Chambers, James 1948-
See Cliff, Jimmy

Author Index

Author Index

Author Index

Author Index

Author Index

Author Index

Author Index

Author Index

Author Index

Author Index

Author Index

CLC Cumulative Nationality Index

ALBANIAN
Kadare, Ismail **52**

ALGERIAN
Camus, Albert **1, 2, 4, 9, 11, 14, 32**
Cohen-Solal, Annie **50**

ALSATIAN
Arp, Jean **5**

AMERICAN
Abbey, Edward **36**
Abbott, Lee K., Jr. **48**
Abish, Walter **22**
Abrahams, Peter **4**
Abrams, M. H. **24**
Acker, Kathy **45**
Adams, Alice **6, 13, 46**
Addams, Charles **30**
Adler, C. S. **35**
Adler, Renata **8, 31**
Ai **4, 14**
Aiken, Conrad **1, 3, 5, 10, 52**
Albee, Edward **1, 2, 3, 5, 9, 11, 13, 25, 53**
Alexander, Lloyd **35**
Algren, Nelson **4, 10, 33**
Allen, Woody **16, 52**
Alta **19**
Alter, Robert B. **34**
Alther, Lisa **7, 41**
Altman, Robert **16**
Ammons, A. R. **2, 3, 5, 8, 9, 25**
Anaya, Rudolfo A. **23**
Anderson, Jon **9**
Anderson, Poul **15**
Anderson, Robert **23**
Angell, Roger **26**
Angelou, Maya **12, 35**

Anthony Piers **35**
Apple, Max **9, 33**
Appleman, Philip **51**
Archer, Jules **12**
Arnow, Harriette **2, 7, 18**
Arrick, Fran **30**
Ashbery, John **2, 3, 4, 6, 9, 13, 15, 25, 41**
Asimov, Isaac **1, 3, 9, 19, 26**
Auchincloss, Louis **4, 6, 9, 18, 45**
Auden, W. H. **1, 2, 3, 4, 6, 9, 11, 14, 43**
Auel, Jean M. **31**
Auster, Paul **47**
Bach, Richard **14**
Baker, Elliott **8**
Baker, Russell **31**
Bakshi, Ralph **26**
Baldwin, James **1, 2, 3, 4, 5, 8, 13, 15, 17, 42, 50**
Bambara, Toni Cade **19**
Banks, Russell **37**
Baraka, Imamu Amiri **1, 2, 3, 5, 10, 14, 33**
Barbera, Jack **44**
Barnard, Mary **48**
Barnes, Djuna **3, 4, 8, 11, 29**
Barrett, William **27**
Barth, John **1, 2, 3, 5, 7, 9, 10, 14, 27, 51**
Barthelme, Donald **1, 2, 3, 5, 6, 8, 13, 23, 46**
Barthelme, Frederick **36**
Barzun, Jacques **51**
Baumbach, Jonathan **6, 23**
Bausch, Richard **51**
Baxter, Charles **45**
Beagle, Peter S. **7**
Beattie, Ann **8, 13, 18, 40**
Becker, Walter **26**

Beecher, John **6**
Behrman, S. N. **40**
Belitt, Ben **22**
Bell, Madison Smartt **41**
Bell, Marvin **8, 31**
Bellow, Saul **1, 2, 3, 6, 8, 10, 13, 15, 25, 33, 34**
Benary-Isbert, Margot **12**
Benchley, Peter **4, 8**
Benedikt, Michael **4, 14**
Benford, Gregory **52**
Bennett, Hal **5**
Bennett, Jay **35**
Benson, Jackson J. **34**
Benson, Sally **17**
Bentley, Eric **24**
Berger, Melvin **12**
Berger, Thomas **3, 5, 8, 11, 18, 38**
Bergstein, Eleanor **4**
Berrigan, Daniel J. **4**
Berrigan, Ted **37**
Berry, Chuck **17**
Berry, Wendell **4, 6, 8, 27, 46**
Berryman, John **1, 2, 3, 4, 6, 8, 10, 13, 25**
Bessie, Alvah **23**
Betts, Doris **3, 6, 28**
Bidart, Frank **33**
Bishop, Elizabeth **1, 4, 9, 13, 15, 32**
Bishop, John **10**
Blackburn, Paul **9, 43**
Blackmur, R. P. **2, 24**
Blaise, Clark **29**
Blatty, William Peter **2**
Blish, James **14**
Bloch, Robert **33**
Bloom, Harold **24**
Blount, Roy, Jr. **38**
Blume, Judy **12, 30**

Bly, Robert **1, 2, 5, 10, 15, 38**
Bochco, Steven **35**
Bogan, Louise **4, 39, 46**
Bogosian, Eric **45**
Bograd, Larry **35**
Bonham, Frank **12**
Bontemps, Arna **1, 18**
Booth, Philip **23**
Booth, Wayne C. **24**
Bottoms, David **53**
Bourjaily, Vance **8**
Bova, Ben **45**
Bowers, Edgar **9**
Bowles, Jane **3**
Bowles, Paul **1, 2, 19, 53**
Boyle, Kay **1, 5, 19**
Boyle, T. Coraghessan **36**
Bradbury, Ray **1, 3, 10, 15, 42**
Bradley, David, Jr. **23**
Bradley, Marion Zimmer **30**
Brammer, William **31**
Brancato, Robin F. **35**
Brand, Millen **7**
Branden, Barbara **44**
Branley, Franklyn M. **21**
Brautigan, Richard **1, 3, 5, 9, 12, 34, 42**
Brennan, Maeve **5**
Breslin, Jimmy **4, 43**
Bridgers, Sue Ellen **26**
Brin, David **34**
Brodsky, Joseph **4, 6, 13, 36, 50**
Brodsky, Michael **19**
Bromell, Henry **5**
Broner, E. M. **19**
Bronk, William **10**
Brooks, Cleanth **24**
Brooks, Gwendolyn **1, 2, 4, 5, 15, 49**

509

Nationality Index

Nationality Index

CLC-53 Title Index

Title Index